A ROADMAP FOR SELECTING A STATISTICAL METHOD

Type of Analysis	TYPE OF DATA	
	Numerical	Categorical
Describing a Group or Several Groups	Ordered array, stem-and-leaf display, frequency distribution, relative frequency distribution, percentage distribution, cumulative percentage distribution, histogram, polygon, cumulative percentage polygon **(Sections 2.2 and 2.3)** Mean, median, mode, quartiles, range, interquartile range, standard deviation, variance, coefficient of variation, boxplot **(Sections 3.1, 3.2, 3.3, and 3.4)**	Summary table, bar chart, pie chart, Pareto chart **(Section 2.1)**
Inference about One Group	Confidence Interval Estimate for the Mean **(Sections 8.1 and 8.2)** t Test for the Mean **(Section 9.2)**	Confidence Interval Estimate of the Proportion **(Section 8.3)** Z Test for the Proportion **(Section 9.4)**
Comparing Two Groups	Tests for the Difference in the Means of Two Independent Populations **(Section 10.1)** Paired t Test **(Section 10.2)** F Test for the Difference between Two Variances **(Section 10.4)**	Z Test for the Difference between Two Proportions **(Section 10.3)** Chi-Square Test for the Difference between Two Proportions **(Section 11.1)**
Comparing More than Two Groups	One-Way Analysis of Variance **(Section 10.5)**	Chi-Square Test for Differences among More than Two Proportions **(Section 11.2)**
Analyzing the Relationship between Two Variables	Scatter Plot, Time-Series Plot **(Section 2.5)** Covariance, Coefficient of Correlation **(Section 3.5)** Simple Linear Regression **(Chapter 12)** t Test of Correlation **(Section 12.6)**	Contingency Table **(Section 2.4)** Chi-Square Test of Independence **(Section 11.3)**
Analyzing the Relationship between Two or More Variables	Multiple Regression **(Chapter 13)**	

The Cumulative Standardized Normal Distribution

Entry represents area under the cumulative standardized normal distribution from $-\infty$ to Z

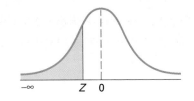

Z	0.00	0.01	0.02	0.03	0.04	0.05	0.06	0.07	0.08	0.09
−6.0	0.000000001									
−5.5	0.000000019									
−5.0	0.000000287									
−4.5	0.000003398									
−4.0	0.000031671									
−3.9	0.00005	0.00005	0.00004	0.00004	0.00004	0.00004	0.00004	0.00004	0.00003	0.00003
−3.8	0.00007	0.00007	0.00007	0.00006	0.00006	0.00006	0.00006	0.00005	0.00005	0.00005
−3.7	0.00011	0.00010	0.00010	0.00010	0.00009	0.00009	0.00008	0.00008	0.00008	0.00008
−3.6	0.00016	0.00015	0.00015	0.00014	0.00014	0.00013	0.00013	0.00012	0.00012	0.00011
−3.5	0.00023	0.00022	0.00022	0.00021	0.00020	0.00019	0.00019	0.00018	0.00017	0.00017
−3.4	0.00034	0.00032	0.00031	0.00030	0.00029	0.00028	0.00027	0.00026	0.00025	0.00024
−3.3	0.00048	0.00047	0.00045	0.00043	0.00042	0.00040	0.00039	0.00038	0.00036	0.00035
−3.2	0.00069	0.00066	0.00064	0.00062	0.00060	0.00058	0.00056	0.00054	0.00052	0.00050
−3.1	0.00097	0.00094	0.00090	0.00087	0.00084	0.00082	0.00079	0.00076	0.00074	0.00071
−3.0	0.00135	0.00131	0.00126	0.00122	0.00118	0.00114	0.00111	0.00107	0.00103	0.00100
−2.9	0.0019	0.0018	0.0018	0.0017	0.0016	0.0016	0.0015	0.0015	0.0014	0.0014
−2.8	0.0026	0.0025	0.0024	0.0023	0.0023	0.0022	0.0021	0.0021	0.0020	0.0019
−2.7	0.0035	0.0034	0.0033	0.0032	0.0031	0.0030	0.0029	0.0028	0.0027	0.0026
−2.6	0.0047	0.0045	0.0044	0.0043	0.0041	0.0040	0.0039	0.0038	0.0037	0.0036
−2.5	0.0062	0.0060	0.0059	0.0057	0.0055	0.0054	0.0052	0.0051	0.0049	0.0048
−2.4	0.0082	0.0080	0.0078	0.0075	0.0073	0.0071	0.0069	0.0068	0.0066	0.0064
−2.3	0.0107	0.0104	0.0102	0.0099	0.0096	0.0094	0.0091	0.0089	0.0087	0.0084
−2.2	0.0139	0.0136	0.0132	0.0129	0.0125	0.0122	0.0119	0.0116	0.0113	0.0110
−2.1	0.0179	0.0174	0.0170	0.0166	0.0162	0.0158	0.0154	0.0150	0.0146	0.0143
−2.0	0.0228	0.0222	0.0217	0.0212	0.0207	0.0202	0.0197	0.0192	0.0188	0.0183
−1.9	0.0287	0.0281	0.0274	0.0268	0.0262	0.0256	0.0250	0.0244	0.0239	0.0233
−1.8	0.0359	0.0351	0.0344	0.0336	0.0329	0.0322	0.0314	0.0307	0.0301	0.0294
−1.7	0.0446	0.0436	0.0427	0.0418	0.0409	0.0401	0.0392	0.0384	0.0375	0.0367
−1.6	0.0548	0.0537	0.0526	0.0516	0.0505	0.0495	0.0485	0.0475	0.0465	0.0455
−1.5	0.0668	0.0655	0.0643	0.0630	0.0618	0.0606	0.0594	0.0582	0.0571	0.0559
−1.4	0.0808	0.0793	0.0778	0.0764	0.0749	0.0735	0.0721	0.0708	0.0694	0.0681
−1.3	0.0968	0.0951	0.0934	0.0918	0.0901	0.0885	0.0869	0.0853	0.0838	0.0823
−1.2	0.1151	0.1131	0.1112	0.1093	0.1075	0.1056	0.1038	0.1020	0.1003	0.0985
−1.1	0.1357	0.1335	0.1314	0.1292	0.1271	0.1251	0.1230	0.1210	0.1190	0.1170
−1.0	0.1587	0.1562	0.1539	0.1515	0.1492	0.1469	0.1446	0.1423	0.1401	0.1379
−0.9	0.1841	0.1814	0.1788	0.1762	0.1736	0.1711	0.1685	0.1660	0.1635	0.1611
−0.8	0.2119	0.2090	0.2061	0.2033	0.2005	0.1977	0.1949	0.1922	0.1894	0.1867
−0.7	0.2420	0.2388	0.2358	0.2327	0.2296	0.2266	0.2236	0.2206	0.2177	0.2148
−0.6	0.2743	0.2709	0.2676	0.2643	0.2611	0.2578	0.2546	0.2514	0.2482	0.2451
−0.5	0.3085	0.3050	0.3015	0.2981	0.2946	0.2912	0.2877	0.2843	0.2810	0.2776
−0.4	0.3446	0.3409	0.3372	0.3336	0.3300	0.3264	0.3228	0.3192	0.3156	0.3121
−0.3	0.3821	0.3783	0.3745	0.3707	0.3669	0.3632	0.3594	0.3557	0.3520	0.3483
−0.2	0.4207	0.4168	0.4129	0.4090	0.4052	0.4013	0.3974	0.3936	0.3897	0.3859
−0.1	0.4602	0.4562	0.4522	0.4483	0.4443	0.4404	0.4364	0.4325	0.4286	0.4247
−0.0	0.5000	0.4960	0.4920	0.4880	0.4840	0.4801	0.4761	0.4721	0.4681	0.4641

continued

Entry represents area under the cumulative standardized normal
distribution from $-\infty$ to Z

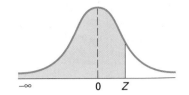

Z	0.00	0.01	0.02	0.03	0.04	0.05	0.06	0.07	0.08	0.09
0.0	0.5000	0.5040	0.5080	0.5120	0.5160	0.5199	0.5239	0.5279	0.5319	0.5359
0.1	0.5398	0.5438	0.5478	0.5517	0.5557	0.5596	0.5636	0.5675	0.5714	0.5753
0.2	0.5793	0.5832	0.5871	0.5910	0.5948	0.5987	0.6026	0.6064	0.6103	0.6141
0.3	0.6179	0.6217	0.6255	0.6293	0.6331	0.6368	0.6406	0.6443	0.6480	0.6517
0.4	0.6554	0.6591	0.6628	0.6664	0.6700	0.6736	0.6772	0.6808	0.6844	0.6879
0.5	0.6915	0.6950	0.6985	0.7019	0.7054	0.7088	0.7123	0.7157	0.7190	0.7224
0.6	0.7257	0.7291	0.7324	0.7357	0.7389	0.7422	0.7454	0.7486	0.7518	0.7549
0.7	0.7580	0.7612	0.7642	0.7673	0.7704	0.7734	0.7764	0.7794	0.7823	0.7852
0.8	0.7881	0.7910	0.7939	0.7967	0.7995	0.8023	0.8051	0.8078	0.8106	0.8133
0.9	0.8159	0.8186	0.8212	0.8238	0.8264	0.8289	0.8315	0.8340	0.8365	0.8389
1.0	0.8413	0.8438	0.8461	0.8485	0.8508	0.8531	0.8554	0.8577	0.8599	0.8621
1.1	0.8643	0.8665	0.8686	0.8708	0.8729	0.8749	0.8770	0.8790	0.8810	0.8830
1.2	0.8849	0.8869	0.8888	0.8907	0.8925	0.8944	0.8962	0.8980	0.8997	0.9015
1.3	0.9032	0.9049	0.9066	0.9082	0.9099	0.9115	0.9131	0.9147	0.9162	0.9177
1.4	0.9192	0.9207	0.9222	0.9236	0.9251	0.9265	0.9279	0.9292	0.9306	0.9319
1.5	0.9332	0.9345	0.9357	0.9370	0.9382	0.9394	0.9406	0.9418	0.9429	0.9441
1.6	0.9452	0.9463	0.9474	0.9484	0.9495	0.9505	0.9515	0.9525	0.9535	0.9545
1.7	0.9554	0.9564	0.9573	0.9582	0.9591	0.9599	0.9608	0.9616	0.9625	0.9633
1.8	0.9641	0.9649	0.9656	0.9664	0.9671	0.9678	0.9686	0.9693	0.9699	0.9706
1.9	0.9713	0.9719	0.9726	0.9732	0.9738	0.9744	0.9750	0.9756	0.9761	0.9767
2.0	0.9772	0.9778	0.9783	0.9788	0.9793	0.9798	0.9803	0.9808	0.9812	0.9817
2.1	0.9821	0.9826	0.9830	0.9834	0.9838	0.9842	0.9846	0.9850	0.9854	0.9857
2.2	0.9861	0.9864	0.9868	0.9871	0.9875	0.9878	0.9881	0.9884	0.9887	0.9890
2.3	0.9893	0.9896	0.9898	0.9901	0.9904	0.9906	0.9909	0.9911	0.9913	0.9916
2.4	0.9918	0.9920	0.9922	0.9925	0.9927	0.9929	0.9931	0.9932	0.9934	0.9936
2.5	0.9938	0.9940	0.9941	0.9943	0.9945	0.9946	0.9948	0.9949	0.9951	0.9952
2.6	0.9953	0.9955	0.9956	0.9957	0.9959	0.9960	0.9961	0.9962	0.9963	0.9964
2.7	0.9965	0.9966	0.9967	0.9968	0.9969	0.9970	0.9971	0.9972	0.9973	0.9974
2.8	0.9974	0.9975	0.9976	0.9977	0.9977	0.9978	0.9979	0.9979	0.9980	0.9981
2.9	0.9981	0.9982	0.9982	0.9983	0.9984	0.9984	0.9985	0.9985	0.9986	0.9986
3.0	0.99865	0.99869	0.99874	0.99878	0.99882	0.99886	0.99889	0.99893	0.99897	0.99900
3.1	0.99903	0.99906	0.99910	0.99913	0.99916	0.99918	0.99921	0.99924	0.99926	0.99929
3.2	0.99931	0.99934	0.99936	0.99938	0.99940	0.99942	0.99944	0.99946	0.99948	0.99950
3.3	0.99952	0.99953	0.99955	0.99957	0.99958	0.99960	0.99961	0.99962	0.99964	0.99965
3.4	0.99966	0.99968	0.99969	0.99970	0.99971	0.99972	0.99973	0.99974	0.99975	0.99976
3.5	0.99977	0.99978	0.99978	0.99979	0.99980	0.99981	0.99981	0.99982	0.99983	0.99983
3.6	0.99984	0.99985	0.99985	0.99986	0.99986	0.99987	0.99987	0.99988	0.99988	0.99989
3.7	0.99989	0.99990	0.99990	0.99990	0.99991	0.99991	0.99992	0.99992	0.99992	0.99992
3.8	0.99993	0.99993	0.99993	0.99994	0.99994	0.99994	0.99994	0.99995	0.99995	0.99995
3.9	0.99995	0.99995	0.99996	0.99996	0.99996	0.99996	0.99996	0.99996	0.99997	0.99997
4.0	0.999968329									
4.5	0.999996602									
5.0	0.999999713									
5.5	0.999999981									
6.0	0.999999999									

Business Statistics

A First Course

FIFTH EDITION

Business Statistics

A First Course

David M. Levine

Department of Statistics and Computer Information Systems

Zicklin School of Business, Baruch College, City University of New York

Timothy C. Krehbiel

Department of Decision Sciences and Management Information Systems

Farmer School of Business, Miami University

Mark L. Berenson

Department of Management and Information Systems

School of Business, Montclair State University

Prentice Hall

Upper Saddle River, New Jersey 07458

Library of Congress Cataloging-in-Publication Data

Levine, David M.
    Business statistics : a first course / David M. Levine, Timothy C. Krehbiel, Mark L.
    Berenson. — 5th ed.
        p. cm.
    Includes bibliographical references and index.
    ISBN-13: 978-0-13-606580-7
    ISBN-10: 0-13-606580-5
    1. Commercial statistics. 2. Industrial management—Statistical methods. I. Krehbiel,
Timothy C. II. Berenson, Mark L. III. Title.
    HF1017.B382 2009
    519.5—dc22   2008046677

AVP/ Executive Editor: Mark Pfaltzgraff
Editorial Director: Sally Yagan
AVP/Editor in Chief: Eric Svendsen
Product Development Manager: Ashley Santora
Editorial Assistant: Valerie Patruno
Editorial Project Manager: Susie Abraham
Marketing Manager: Anne Fahlgren
Marketing Assistant: Susan Osterlitz
Permissions Project Manager: Charles Morris
Senior Managing Editor: Judy Leale
Production Project Manager: Kerri Tomasso
Senior Operations Specialist: Arnold Vila
Operations Specialist: Benjamin Smith
Art Director: Kenny Beck

Designer: Suzanne Behnke
Cover Designer: Suzanne Behnke
Cover Illustration/Photo: Shutterstock/Tomasz Trojanowski
Director, Image Resource Center: Melinda Patelli
Manager, Rights and Permissions: Zina Arabia
Manager, Visual Research: Beth Brenzel
Image Permission Coordinator: Ang'John Ferreri
Manager, Cover Visual Research & Permissions:
    Karen Sanatar
Composition/Full-Service Project Management:
    GGS Higher Education Resources, A Divison of
    Premedia Global, Inc.
Printer/Binder: Courier/Kendallville
Typeface: 10.5/12.5 Times New RomanPS

Photo Credits: Cover, Tomasz Troganowski, Shutterstock; page x, courtesy of Rudy Krehbiel; Chapter 1, pages 2, 3, David Young-Wolff; pages 3, 11, Jeff Zaruba, Getty Images; Chapter 2, pages 24–25, Don Farrall, PhotoDisc/Getty Images; pages 25, 56, Jim Craigmyle, Getty Images, Inc.; Chapter 3, pages 80–81, Don Farrall, PhotoDisc/Getty Images; pages 81, 114, Charles Gupton, Corbis/Bettmann; Chapter 4, pages 124–125, Ljupco Smokovski, Shutterstock; pages 125, 148, Alan Levenson, Corbis-NY, All Rights Reserved; Chapter 5, pages 154–155, Sebastian Kaulitzki, Shutterstock; pages 155, 172, Monkey Business Images, Shutterstock; Chapter 6, pages 180–181, Alexander Kalina, Shutterstock; pages 181, 200, Lee Morris, Shutterstock; Chapter 7, pages 208–209, R. Mackay Photography, Shutterstock; pages 209, 229, Corbis/NY, All Rights Reserved; Chapter 8, pages 238–239, Kristy Pargeter, Shutterstock; pages 239, 263, Marcin Balcerzak, Shutterstock; Chapter 9, page 275, Peter Close, Shutterstock; page 303, Maja Schon, Shutterstock; Chapter 10, page 313, Travis Manley, Shutterstock; pages 313, 356, Michael Bradley, Getty Images; Chapter 11, page 377, KzlKurt, Shutterstock; pages 377, 396, Zastol'skiy' victor Leonidovich, Shutterstock; Chapter 12, page 407, Crystalfoto, Shutterstock; pages 407, 443, Scott Dingman, Getty Images, Inc.—Taxi; Chapter 13, pages 457, 480, George Bailey, Shutterstock; page 457, Courtest of Sharyn Rosenberg; Chapter 14, pages 490–491, Ian Logan, Image Bank/Getty Images; pages 491, 512, Kim Steele, Getty Images, Inc.—Image Bank.

Credits and acknowledgments borrowed from other sources and reproduced, with permission, in this textbook appear on appropriate page within text.

Microsoft® and Windows® are registered trademarks of the Microsoft Corporation in the U.S.A. and other countries. Screen shots and icons reprinted with permission from the Microsoft Corporation. This book is not sponsored or endorsed by or affiliated with the Microsoft Corporation.

MINITAB is a registered trademark of the Minitab, Inc., at
3081 Enterprise Drive
State College, PA 16801 USA
ph: 814.238.3280 fax: 814.238.4383
e-mail: **i n f o @ m i n i t a b . c o m**
URL: **h t t p : / / w w w . m i n i t a b . c o m**

Pearson Education Ltd., London
Pearson Education Singapore, Pte. Ltd
Pearson Education, Canada, Inc.
Pearson Education–Japan
Pearson Education Australia PTY, Limited

Pearson Education North Asia, Ltd., Hong Kong
Pearson Educación de Mexico, S.A. de C.V.
Pearson Education Malaysia, Pte. Ltd
Pearson Education Upper Saddle River,
    New Jersey

Prentice Hall
is an imprint of

www.pearsonhighered.com

10 9 8 7 6 5 4
ISBN-13: 978-0-13-606580-7
ISBN-10: 0-13-606580-5

To our wives,
Marilyn L., Patti K., and Rhoda B.

---

and to our children,
Sharyn, Ed, Rudy, Rhonda, Kathy, and Lori

About the Authors

The textbook authors meet to discuss statistics at Shea Stadium for a Mets v. Phillies game. Shown left to right: David Levine, Mark Berenson, Tim Krehbiel.

David M. Levine is Professor Emeritus of Statistics and Computer Information Systems at Bernard M. Baruch College (City University of New York). He received B.B.A. and M.B.A. degrees in Statistics from City College of New York and a Ph.D. degree from New York University in Industrial Engineering and Operations Research. He is nationally recognized as a leading innovator in statistics education and is the coauthor of 14 books, including such best-selling statistics textbooks as *Statistics for Managers Using Microsoft Excel, Basic Business Statistics: Concepts and Applications, Business Statistics: A First Course*, and *Applied Statistics for Engineers and Scientists using Microsoft Excel and Minitab*.

He is the author of *Even You Can Learn Statistics* and *Statistics for Six Sigma Green Belts* published by Financial Times-Prentice Hall. He is coauthor of *Six Sigma for Green Belts and Champions* and *Design for Six Sigma for Green Belts and Champions*, also published by Financial Times-Prentice Hall, and *Quality Management, Third Ed.*, McGraw-Hill-Irwin (2005). He is also the author of *Video Review of Statistics* and *Video Review of Probability*, both published by Video Aided Instruction. He has published articles in various journals including *Psychometrika, The American Statistician, Communications in Statistics, Multivariate Behavioral Research, Journal of Systems Management, Quality Progress*, and *The American Anthropologist* and given numerous talks at Decision Sciences, American Statistical Association, and Making Statistics More Effective in Schools of Business conferences. Dr. Levine has also received several awards for outstanding teaching and curriculum development from Baruch College.

Timothy C. Krehbiel is Professor of Decision Sciences and Management Information Systems and the Endres Faculty Fellow at the Farmer School of Business at Miami University in Oxford, Ohio. He teaches undergraduate and graduate courses in business statistics. In 1996 he received the prestigious Instructional Innovation Award from the Decision Sciences Institute. He has also received the Farmer School of Business Effective Educator Award and has twice been named MBA professor of the year.

Krehbiel's research interests span many areas of business and applied statistics. His work appears in numerous journals including *Quality Management Journal*, *Ecological Economics*, *International Journal of Production Research*, *Journal of Purchasing and Supply Management*, *Journal of Applied Business Research*, *Journal of Marketing Management*, *Communications in Statistics*, *Decision Sciences Journal of Innovative Education*, *Journal of Education for Business*, *Marketing Education Review*, and *Teaching Statistics*. He is a coauthor of three statistics textbooks published by Prentice Hall: *Business Statistics: A First Course*, *Basic Business Statistics*, and *Statistics for Managers Using Microsoft Excel*. Krehbiel is also a coauthor of the book *Sustainability Perspectives in Business and Resources*.

Krehbiel graduated *summa cum laude* with a B.A. in history from McPherson College, and earned an M.S. and Ph.D. in statistics from the University of Wyoming.

Mark L. Berenson is Professor of Management and Information Systems at Montclair State University (Montclair, New Jersey) and also Professor Emeritus of Statistics and Computer Information Systems at Bernard M. Baruch College (City University of New York). He currently teaches graduate and undergraduate courses in statistics and in operations management in the School of Business and an undergraduate course in international justice and human rights that he codeveloped in the College of Humanities and Social Sciences.

Berenson received a B.A. in economic statistics and an M.B.A. in business statistics from City College of New York and a Ph.D. in business from the City University of New York.

Berenson's research has been published in *Decision Sciences Journal of Innovative Education*, *Review of Business Research*, *The American Statistician*, *Communications in Statistics*, *Psychometrika*, *Educational and Psychological Measurement*, *Journal of Management Sciences and Applied Cybernetics*, *Research Quarterly*, *Stats Magazine*, *The New York Statistician*, *Journal of Health Administration Education*, *Journal of Behavioral Medicine*, and *Journal of Surgical Oncology*. His invited articles have appeared in *The Encyclopedia of Measurement & Statistics* and in *Encyclopedia of Statistical Sciences*. He is coauthor of 11 statistics texts published by Prentice Hall, including *Statistics for Managers using Microsoft Excel*, *Basic Business Statistics: Concepts and Applications*, and *Business Statistics: A First Course*.

Over the years, Berenson has received several awards for teaching and for innovative contributions to statistics education. In 2005 he was the first recipient of The Catherine A. Becker Service for Educational Excellence Award at Montclair State University.

Brief Contents

Contents

10 Two-Sample Tests and One-Way ANOVA 312

11 Chi-Square Tests 376

12 Simple Linear Regression 406

13 Multiple Regression 456

14 Statistical Applications in Quality Management 490

Appendices 527

Preface

Educational Philosophy

In our many years of teaching business statistics, we have continually searched for ways to improve the teaching of these courses. Our active participation in a series of Making Statistics More Effective in Schools and Business (MSMESB), Decision Sciences Institute (DSI), and American Statistical Association (ASA) conferences as well as the reality of serving a diverse group of students at large universities have shaped our vision for teaching these courses. Over the years, our vision has come to include these key principles:

1. **Show students the relevance of statistics.** Students need a frame of reference when learning statistics, especially when statistics is not their major. That frame of reference for business students should be the functional areas of business—that is, accounting, finance, information systems, management, and marketing. Each statistical topic needs to be presented in an applied context related to at least one of these functional areas. The focus in teaching each topic should be on its application in business, the interpretation of results, the presentation of assumptions, the evaluation of the assumptions, and the discussion of what should be done if the assumptions are violated.

2. **Familiarize students with software used in the business world.** Integrating business software into all aspects of an introductory statistics course allows the course to focus on interpretation of results instead of computations. Introductory business statistics courses should recognize that spreadsheet programs and statistical packages are commonly found on a business decision maker's desktop computer, therefore making the *interpretation* of results more important than the tedious hand calculations required to produce them.

3. **Provide guidance to students for using software.** Books should contain clear instructions to help students effectively use the programs that are integrated with the study of statistics, without having those instructions dominating the book or the courses in which they are used.

4. **Give students ample practice in understanding how to apply statistics to business.** Both classroom examples and homework exercises should involve actual or realistic data as much as possible. Students should work with data sets, both small and large, and be encouraged to look beyond the statistical analysis of data to the interpretation of results in a managerial context.

New to This Edition: Enhanced Statistics Coverage

This fifth edition of *Business Statistics: A First Course* enhances the statistical coverage of previous editions in a number of ways:

- *Think About This* essays in selected chapters provide greater insight to what has just been learned as well as raise important issues about the application of statistical knowledge.
- Revised simplified notation for test statistics in hypothesis testing.
- Many new applied examples and exercises with data from *The Wall Street Journal, USA Today*, and other sources have been added to the book.
- Student surveys are included as an integrating theme for exercises across many chapters.
- Even more illustrations of Microsoft Excel and Minitab results are included, all with cross-references to the appropriate software appendix sections.
- Each chapter ends with a Using Statistics Revisited section which reinforces the applications and lessons learned in the chapter.

New to This Edition: Expanded Hands-on Software Appendices

This fifth edition of *Business Statistics: A First Course* now contains separate and expanded appendices for using Microsoft Excel, Minitab, and PHStat2, the Excel add-in that is included on the Student CD-ROM:

- Totally rewritten Excel appendices contain instructions for using all versions of Excel, including Excel 2007. (Some sections contain two sets of instructions, one for using Excel 97 through Excel 2003, the other for using Excel 2007, when appropriate.)
- Minitab appendices feature the use of Minitab 15, the latest Minitab version, but are also fully compatible with Minitab 14.
- PHStat2 appendices at the end of each chapter identify the PHStat2 procedures that can be used for the chapter's statistical methods.
- New PHStat2 version (2.8) that is Excel 2007 compatible and contains new and enhanced procedures including the separate-variance *t* test, and one-way ANOVA.

Chapter-by-Chapter Changes in the Fifth Edition

Each chapter includes a new opening page that displays the chapter sections and subsections. The following changes have been made to this fifth edition:

Chapter 1 has completely new Sections 1.1, 1.2, 1.6, 1.7, and 1.8.

Chapter 2 has new examples throughout the chapter and uses a new mutual fund data set.

Chapter 3 has moved quartiles to the section with boxplots (name changed from box-and-whisker), and has new examples throughout the chapter using a new mutual fund data set.

Chapter 4 has a revised example throughout the chapter, and a *Think About This* essay about Bayes' theorem.

Chapter 5 has changed notation in the binomial and Poisson distributions with p changed to π, and successes changed to items of interest.

Chapter 6 has a revised normal distribution table with additional header lines and a *Think About This* essay about the normal distribution.

Chapter 7 has survey sampling and survey worthiness preceding sampling distributions and a *Think About This* essay on the pros and cons of web-based surveys.

Chapter 8 has a greatly reduced focus on the confidence interval estimate for the mean with sigma known, revised notation that uses a subscript for distributions that indicates the α level (such as $Z_{\alpha/2}$ or $t_{\alpha/2}$), a subsection on sigma known, and revised normal distribution and t distribution tables with additional header lines.

Chapter 9 has combined previous Sections 9.1 and 9.2 to reduce the emphasis on testing the population mean with sigma known, has moved the t test for the mean ahead of the one-tail test, changed notation to use a subscript for distributions to indicate the α level (such as $Z_{\alpha/2}$ or $t_{\alpha/2}$), revised notation that uses subscript *STAT* with the test statistic (such as Z_{STAT} and t_{STAT}), and revised normal distribution and t distribution tables with additional header lines.

Chapter 10 has revised notation that uses a subscript for distributions to indicate the α level (such as $Z_{\alpha/2}$, $t_{\alpha/2}$, or F_{α}), revised notation that uses subscript *STAT* with the test statistic (such as Z_{STAT}, t_{STAT}, and F_{STAT}), revised normal, t, and F distribution tables with additional header lines, revised F test for the difference between variances that consists of the larger variance divided by the smaller variance, and a *Think About This* essay that presents a business application of the differences between two means.

Chapter 11 has revised notation that uses a subscript for distributions to indicate the α level (such as χ^2_{α}), revised notation that uses subscript *STAT* with the test statistic (such as χ^2_{STAT}), and revised χ^2 distribution tables with additional header lines.

Chapter 12 has revised notation that uses the subscript *STAT* with the test statistic such as t_{STAT}, and a *Think About This* essay on using regression in the business world.

Chapter 13 has revised notation that uses the subscript *STAT* with the test statistic such as t_{STAT}.

Chapter 14 has control charts preceding total quality management and Six Sigma and has revised sections on total quality management and Six Sigma including a subsection on the role employees play in a Six Sigma organization (such as green belt or black belt).

Hallmark Features

We have continued many of the traditions of past editions and have highlighted some of those features below:

Using Statistics business scenarios—Each chapter begins with a Using Statistics example that shows how statistics is used in accounting, finance, information systems, management, or marketing. Each scenario is used throughout the chapter to provide an applied context for the concepts.

Emphasis on data analysis and interpretation of software results—We believe that the use of computer software is an integral part of learning statistics. Our focus emphasizes analyzing data by interpreting the results from Microsoft Excel or Minitab while reducing emphasis on doing computations. For example, in the coverage of tables and charts in Chapter 2, the focus is on the interpretation of various charts, not on their construction by hand. In our coverage of hypothesis testing in Chapters 9 through 11, extensive computer results have been included so that the p-value approach can be emphasized.

Pedagogical aides—An active writing style, boxed numbered equations, set-off examples to provide reinforcement for learning concepts, problems divided into "Learning the Basics" and "Applying the Concepts," key equations, and key terms are included.

Answers—Most answers to the even-numbered exercises are provided at the end of the book.

PHStat2—This add-in, included on the Student CD-ROM, extends the statistical capabilities of Microsoft Excel and executes the low-level menu selection and worksheet entry tasks associated with implementing statistical analysis in Excel. When combined with the Analysis ToolPak add-in, virtually all statistical methods taught in an introductory statistics course can be demonstrated using Microsoft Excel.

Web Cases—A chapter-ending Web Case is included for most of the chapters. By visiting Web sites related to the companies and researching the issues raised in the Using Statistics scenarios that start each chapter, students learn to identify misuses of statistical information. The Web Cases require students to sift through claims and assorted information in order to discover the data most relevant to the case. Students then determine whether the conclusions and claims are supported by the data. (Instructional tips for using the Web Cases and solutions to the Web Cases are included in the Instructor's Solutions Manual.)

Case studies and team projects—Detailed case studies are included in numerous chapters. A Managing the *Springville Herald* case is included at the end of most chapters as an integrating theme. A team project relating to mutual funds is included in many chapters as an integrating theme.

Visual Explorations—A Microsoft Excel add-in workbook allows students to interactively explore important statistical concepts in descriptive statistics, the normal distribution, sampling distributions, and regression analysis. For example, in descriptive statistics, students observe the effect of changes in the data on the mean, median, quartiles, and standard deviation. With the normal distribution, students see the effect of changes in the mean and standard deviation on the areas under the normal curve. In sampling distributions, students use simulation to explore the effect of sample size on a sampling distribution. In regression analysis, students have the opportunity of fitting a line and observing how changes in the slope and intercept affect the goodness of fit.

Supplement Package

The supplement package that accompanies this text includes the following:

Instructor's Solutions Manual—This manual includes solutions for end-of-section and end-of-chapter problems, answers to case questions, where applicable, and teaching tips for each chapter. Electronic solutions are provided in PDF and Word formats.

Student Solutions Manual—This manual provides detailed solutions to virtually all the even-numbered exercises and worked-out solutions to the self-test problems.

Test Item File—The Test Item File contains true/false, multiple-choice, fill-in, and problem-solving questions based on the definitions, concepts, and ideas developed in each chapter of the text.

TestGen software—A test bank has been designed for use with the TestGen test-generating software. This computerized package allows instructors to custom design, save, and generate classroom tests. The test program permits instructors to edit, add, or delete questions from the test bank; edit existing graphics and create new graphics; analyze test results; and organize a database of tests and student results. This software allows for flexibility and ease of use. It provides many options for organizing and displaying tests, along with a search-and-sort feature. The program can be found online at the Instructor's Resource Center.

Instructor's Resource Center—The Instructor's Resource Center contains the electronic files for the complete Instructor's Solutions Manual, the Test Item File, and Lecture PowerPoint presentations (**www.pearsonhighered.com**).

Course and Homework Management Tools

MyStatLab—Provides a rich and flexible set of course materials, featuring free-response exercises that are algorithmically generated for unlimited practice and mastery. Students can also use a variety of online tools to independently improve their understanding and performance in the course. Instructors can use MyStatLab's homework and test manager to select and assign their own online exercises and import TestGen tests for added flexibility.

Acknowledgments

We are extremely grateful to the Biometrika Trustees, American Cyanimid Company, the RAND Corporation, the American Society for Testing and Materials for their kind permission to publish various tables in Appendix E, and the American Statistical Association for its permission to publish diagrams from the *American Statistician*.

A Note of Thanks

We would like to thank Luis Borges, Medaille College; Dave Bregenzer, Utah State University; Faruk Guder, Loyola University; Kimberly Killmer Hollister, Montclair State University; John McKenzie, Babson College; Ram Misra, Montclair State University; Susan Pariseau, Merrimack College; Charlie Shi, Diablo Valley College; Erland Sorensen, Bentley College; and Yang Zhang, Depaul University for their comments, which have made this a better book.

We would especially like to thank Mark Pfaltzgraff, Susie Abraham, Kerri Tomasso, Valerie Patruno, Judy Leale, and Anne Fahlgren of the editorial, marketing, and production teams at Prentice Hall. We would like to thank our statistical reader and accuracy checker Annie Puciloski for her diligence in checking our work; Julie Kennedy for her copyediting; Dorothy Pychevicz for her proofreading; and Heidi Allgair of GGS Higher Education Resources, A Division of Premedia Global, Inc., for their work in the production of this text.

Finally, we would like to thank our parents, wives, and children for their patience, understanding, love, and assistance in making this book a reality. It is to them that we dedicate this book.

Concluding Remarks

We have gone to great lengths to make this text both pedagogically sound and error free. If you have any suggestions or require clarification about any of the material, or if you find any errors, please contact us at **davidlevine@davidlevinestatistics.com** or **Krehbitc@muohio.edu**. Include the phrase "BSAFC edition 5" in the subject line of your e-mail. For more information or questions about using PHStat2, review Appendix F and the PHStat2 readme file on the Student CD-ROM. For support issues, visit the PHStat2 Web site, **www.prenhall.com/phstat** and the Pearson Customer Technical Support website, **247.pearsoned.com**.

David M. Levine

Timothy C. Krehbiel

Mark L. Berenson

Business Statistics

A First Course

FIFTH EDITION

1

Introduction and Data Collection

Learning Objectives

In this chapter, you learn:

- How statistics is used in business
- The sources of data used in business
- The types of data used in business
- The basics of Microsoft Excel
- The basics of Minitab

USING STATISTICS

@ Good Tunes

Good Tunes, a growing four-store home entertainment systems retailer, seeks to double their number of stores within the next three years. The managers have decided to approach local area banks for the funding needed to underwrite this expansion. They need to prepare an electronic slide show and a formal prospectus that will argue that Good Tunes is a thriving business and a good candidate for expansion.

You have been asked to assist in the process of preparing the slide show and prospectus. How would you do this job? Learning more about statistics would be a good start.

1.1 Why Learn Statistics

People use numbers every day to describe or analyze the world we live in. For example, consider these recent headlines:

- "Stocks May Fall, But Execs' Pay Doesn't" (G. Farrell and B. Hansen, **usatoday.com**, April 10, 2008)—In 2007, the median compensation for the CEOs of the 50 largest corporations in the S&P 500 was $15.7 million.
- "Americans Gulping More Bottled Water" (*USA Today*, February 28, 2007, p. 1D)—The annual per capita consumption of bottled water has increased from 18.8 gallons in 2001 to 28.3 gallons in 2006.
- "Paying More with Plastic" (*USA Today*, March 6, 2007, p. 1D)—Consumer payment with credit cards increased from 18% in 1995 to 25% in 2005, while payment in cash decreased to 14% from 21%.
- "The Real Most Valuable Players" (R. Adams, *The Wall Street Journal*, April 14, 2007, pp. P1, P4)—Economists have developed models to predict the real value of baseball player performance and have related it to player salary.

You will make better sense of the numbers in the stories behind these headlines if you understand statistics. **Statistics** is the branch of mathematics that transforms numbers into useful information for decision makers. Statistics provides a way of understanding and then reducing—but not eliminating—the variation that is part of any decision-making process, and also can tell you the known risks associated with making a decision.

Statistics does this by providing a set of methods for analyzing the numbers. These methods help you to find patterns in "the numbers" and enable you to determine whether differences in "the numbers" are just due to chance. As you learn these methods, you will also learn the appropriate conditions for using those methods. And because so many statistical methods must be computerized in order to be of practical benefit, as you learn statistics you also need to learn about the programs that help apply statistics in the business world.

1.2 Statistics in the Business World

In the business world, statistics has four important applications:

- To summarize business data
- To draw conclusions from that data
- To make reliable forecasts about business activities
- To improve business processes

The field of statistics consists of two branches, descriptive statistics and inferential statistics.

Descriptive statistics focuses on collecting, summarizing, presenting, and analyzing a set of data. You are probably familiar with presentations such as tables and charts, and statistics such as the mean and median from your previous school experience.

Inferential statistics uses data that have been collected from a small group to draw conclusions about a larger group. These methods are used to make decisions about which investment might lead to a higher return and what marketing strategy might lead to increased sales.

Looking at the first bulleted point above, descriptive statistics allows you to create different tables and charts to summarize your data. It also provides statistical measures such as the mean, median, and standard deviation to describe different characteristics of your data.

Drawing conclusions from your data is the heart of inferential statistics. Using these methods enables you to make decisions based on data rather than just on intuition.

Making reliable forecasts involves developing statistical models for prediction. These models enable you to develop more accurate predictions of future activities.

Improving business processes involves using managerial approaches that focus on quality improvement such as Six Sigma. These approaches are data-driven and use statistical methods as an integral part of the quality improvement approach.

To help you develop the skills for making better decisions, every chapter of *Business Statistics: A First Course* has a Using Statistics scenario. The scenarios describe realistic situations in which you will be asked to make decisions to transform data into statistical information. For example, in one chapter you will be asked to decide the location in a supermarket that best enhances sales of a cola drink; and in another chapter, you will be asked to forecast sales for a clothing store.

In the scenario on page 3, you must ask the following questions. What data should you include that will convince bankers to extend the credit that Good Tunes needs? How should you present that data?

However, presenting the bankers with the thousands of transactions would overwhelm them and not be very useful. You need to transform the transactions data into information by summarizing the details of each transaction in some useful way that would allow the bankers to (perhaps) uncover a favorable pattern about the sales over time.

One piece of information that the bankers would presumably want to see is the yearly dollar sales totals. Tallying and totaling sales is a common process of transforming data into information. When you tally sales—or any other relevant data about Good Tunes you choose to use—you follow normal business practice and tally by a business period such as by month, quarter, or year. When you do so, you end up with multiple values: sales for this year, sales for last year, sales for the year before that, and so on. How to determine the best way to refer to these multiple values requires learning the basic vocabulary of statistics.

1.3 Basic Vocabulary of Statistics

Variables are characteristics of items or individuals and are what you analyze when you use a statistical method. For the Good Tunes scenario, sales, expenses by year, and net profit by year are variables that the bankers would want to analyze.

> VARIABLE
>
> A **variable** is a characteristic of an item or individual.

When used in everyday speech, *variable* suggests that something changes or varies, and you would expect the sales, expenses, and net profit to have different values from year to year. These different values are the **data** associated with a variable, and more simply, the "data" to be analyzed.

Variables can differ for reasons other than time. For example, if you conducted an analysis of the composition of a large lecture class, you would probably want to include the variables class standing, gender, and major field of study. These variables would vary, too, because each student in the class is different. One student might be a sophomore, male, accounting major, while another may be a junior, female, finance major.

You also need to remember that values are meaningless unless their variables have **operational definitions**. These definitions are universally accepted meanings that are clear to all associated with an analysis. Even though the operational definition for sales per year might seem clear, miscommunication could occur if one person was referring to sales per year for the entire chain of stores and another to sales per year per store. Even individual values for variables sometimes need definition—for the class standing variable, for example, what *exactly* is meant by the words *sophomore* and *junior*? (Perhaps the most famous example of vague definitions was the definition of a valid vote in the state of Florida during the 2000 U.S. presidential election. Vagueness about the operational definitions there ultimately required a U.S. Supreme Court ruling.)

Four other basic vocabulary terms are population, sample, parameter, and statistic.

POPULATION

A **population** consists of all the items or individuals about which you want to draw a conclusion.

SAMPLE

A **sample** is the portion of a population selected for analysis.

PARAMETER

A **parameter** is a numerical measure that describes a characteristic of a population.

STATISTIC

A **statistic** is a numerical measure that describes a characteristic of a sample.

All the Good Tunes sales transactions for a specific year, all the customers who shopped at Good Tunes this weekend, all the full-time students enrolled in a college, and all the registered voters in Ohio are examples of populations. Examples of samples from these four populations would be 200 Good Tunes sales transactions randomly selected by an auditor for study, 30 Good Tunes customers asked to complete a customer satisfaction survey, 50 full-time students selected for a marketing study, and 500 registered voters in Ohio contacted via telephone for a political poll. In each sample, the transactions or people in the sample represent a portion of the items or individuals that make up the population.

The mean amount spent by all customers who shopped at Good Tunes this weekend is an example of a parameter because the amount spent in the entire population is needed. In contrast, the mean amount spent by the 30 customers completing the customer satisfaction survey is an example of a statistic because the amount spent by only the sample of 30 people is required.

1.4 How This Textbook Is Organized

If you are someone who likes to skim quickly through a book to learn a book's organization, you should know that we have organized the chapters of this book according to the four business tasks first listed in Section1.2. We use those tasks—summarizing business data, drawing conclusions from that data, making reliable forecasts about business activities, and improving business processes—as a way of organizing our chapters.

Chapters 1 through 3 discuss methods of presenting and describing information. Chapters 4 through 11 discuss drawing conclusions about populations using sample information. Chapters 12 and 13 provide ways of making reliable forecasts and Chapter 14 introduces you to how you can apply statistical methods to improve business processes.

Don't worry if your instructor does not cover all of these chapters—introductory business statistics courses vary in their scope, length, and number of college credits. Traditionally, instructors start with descriptive statistics because some of these methods may already be familiar to you from everyday activities and that's the main reason we've put them in the first three chapters. Chapter 4 discusses probability concepts that are needed in Chapters 5 through 7. Chapters 8 through 11 cover inferential statistics. Chapter 8 introduces the confidence interval approach, while Chapter 9 develops the fundamental hypothesis testing concepts that are expanded on in Chapters 10 and 11. Understanding these concepts will allow you to fully answer questions such as "How can you make decisions about the many based on a few?"—a question business people uneducated in statistics often ask when they challenge the use of statistics. Chapters 12 and 13 cover regression models that are used to make reliable forecasts. Chapter 12 develops the simple regression model, while Chapter 13 expands the simple model to more complex situations. Chapter 14 provides some background into the total quality management and Six Sigma quality improvement approaches and introduces statistical methods used in quality improvement.

Remember that the goal of this book is *not* for you to become a statistician. The goal is to help you understand and apply appropriately the statistical methods commonly used in the area of business in which you are most interested—be it accounting, economics, finance, information systems, marketing, or management.

By the way, if you are the type of person who likes to read the last page of a book first, please don't. Introductory business statistics is somewhat cumulative and if you jump to the back of the book, you may find things a bit puzzling if you are only just beginning to learn statistics. So if you have happened to notice things such as strange-looking tables, don't fret—by the time you get to the point in this book where you need to use such tables, you will know how to use them effectively.

1.5 Data Collection

The managers at Good Tunes believe that they will have a stronger argument for expansion if they can show the bankers that the customers of Good Tunes are highly satisfied with the service they received. How could the managers demonstrate that good service was the typical customer experience at Good Tunes?

In the Good Tunes scenario on page 3, the managers now face the twin challenges to first identify relevant variables for a customer satisfaction study and then devise a method for **data collection**, that is, collecting the values for those variables.

Many different types of circumstances, such as the following, require data collection:

- A marketing research analyst needs to assess the effectiveness of a new television advertisement.
- A pharmaceutical manufacturer needs to determine whether a new drug is more effective than those currently in use.
- An operations manager wants to improve a manufacturing or service process.
- An auditor wants to review the financial transactions of a company in order to determine whether the company is in compliance with generally accepted accounting principles.

In each of these examples, and for the Good Tunes managers as well, collecting data from every item or individual in the population would be too difficult or too time-consuming. Because this is the typical case, data collection almost always involves collecting data from a sample. (Chapter 7 discusses methods of sample selection.)

Data sources are classified as being either **primary sources** or **secondary sources**. When the data collector is the one using the data for analysis, the source is primary. When the person performing the statistical analysis is not the data collector, the source is secondary. Organizations and individuals that collect and publish data typically use that data as a primary source and then let others use it as a secondary source. For example, the United States federal government collects and distributes data in this way for both public and private purposes. The Bureau of Labor Statistics collects data on employment and also distributes the monthly consumer price index. The Census Bureau oversees a variety of ongoing surveys regarding population, housing, and manufacturing and undertakes special studies on topics such as crime, travel, and health care.

Sources of data fall into one of four categories:

- Data distributed by an organization or an individual
- A designed experiment
- A survey
- An observational study

Market research firms and trade associations distribute data pertaining to specific industries or markets. Investment services such as Mergent (see **www.mergent.com**) provide financial data on a company-by-company basis. Syndicated services such as AC Nielsen provide clients with data that enables the comparison of client products with those of their competitors.

Daily newspapers are filled with numerical information regarding stock prices, weather conditions, and sports statistics.

Outcomes of a designed experiment are another data source. These outcomes are the result of an experiment, such as a test of several laundry detergents to compare how well each detergent removes a certain type of stain. Developing proper experimental designs is a subject mostly beyond the scope of this book because such designs often involve sophisticated statistical procedures. However, some of the fundamental experimental design concepts are discussed in Chapter 10.

Conducting a survey is a third type of data source. People being surveyed are asked questions about their beliefs, attitudes, behaviors, and other characteristics. For example, people could be asked their opinion about which laundry detergent best removes a certain type of stain. (This could lead to a result different from a designed experiment seeking the same answer.)

Conducting an observational study is the fourth important data source. A researcher collects data by directly observing a behavior, usually in a natural or neutral setting. Observational studies are a common tool for data collection in business. For example, market researchers use focus groups to elicit unstructured responses to open-ended questions posed by a moderator to a target audience. Observational study techniques are also used to enhance teamwork or improve the quality of products and services.

Identifying the most appropriate source is a critical task because if biases, ambiguities, or other types of errors flaw the data being collected, even the most sophisticated statistical methods will not produce useful information. For the Good Tunes example, variables relevant to the customer experience could take the form of survey questions related to various aspects of the customer experience, examples of which are shown in Figure 1.1. The survey might also ask questions that seek to classify customers into groups for later analysis.

FIGURE 1.1

Questions about the Good Tunes customer experience

1. How many days did it take from the time you ordered your merchandise to the time you received it? _____

2. Did you buy any merchandise that was featured in the Good Tunes Sunday newspaper sales flyer for the week of your purchase?   Yes _____ No_____

3. Was this your first purchase at Good Tunes?   Yes _____ No_____

4. Are you likely to buy additional merchandise from Good Tunes in the next 12 months?   Yes _____ No_____

5. How much money (in U.S. dollars) do you expect to spend on stereo and consumer electronics equipment in the next 12 months? _____

6. How do you rate the overall service provided by Good Tunes with respect to your recent purchase?

Excellent ☐   Very good ☐   Fair ☐   Poor ☐

7. How do you rate the selection of products offered by Good Tunes with respect to other retailers of home entertainment systems?

Excellent ☐   Very good ☐   Fair ☐   Poor ☐

8. How do you rate the quality of the items you recently purchased from Good Tunes?

Excellent ☐   Very good ☐   Fair ☐   Poor ☐

One good way for Good Tunes to avoid data-collection flaws would be to distribute the questionnaire to a random sample of customers (Chapter 7 explains how to collect a random sample). A poor way would be to rely on a business-rating Web site that allows online visitors to rate a merchant. Such Web sites cannot provide assurance that those who do the ratings are representative of the population of customers, or that they even *are* customers.

1.6 Types of Variables

Statisticians classify variables as either being categorical or numerical and further classify numerical variables as having either discrete or continuous values. Figure 1.2 shows the relationships and provides examples of each type of variable.

FIGURE 1.2
Types of variables

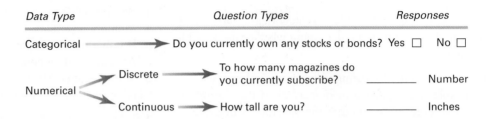

Categorical variables (also known as **qualitative variables**) have values that can only be placed into categories, such as yes and no. "Do you currently own stocks and bonds?" and Questions 2 through 4 in Figure 1.1 are examples of categorical variables, all of which have yes or no as their values. Categorical variables can also have more than two possible responses. For example, you could ask customers to indicate the day of the week on which they made their purchases. In Figure 1.1, there are four possible responses to Questions 6 through 8.

Numerical variables (also known as **quantitative variables**) have values that represent quantities. For example, Questions 1 and 5 in Figure 1.1 are numerical variables. Numerical variables are further subdivided as discrete or continuous variables.

Discrete variables have numerical values that arise from a counting process. "The number of magazines subscribed to" is an example of a discrete numerical variable because the response is one of a finite number of integers. You subscribe to zero, one, two, and so on magazines. The number of items that a customer purchases is also a discrete numerical variable because you are counting the number of items purchased.

Continuous variables produce numerical responses that arise from a measuring process. The time you wait for teller service at a bank is an example of a continuous numerical variable because the response takes on any value within a *continuum*, or interval, depending on the precision of the measuring instrument. For example, your waiting time could be 1 minute, 1.1 minutes, 1.11 minutes, or 1.113 minutes, depending on the precision of the measuring device you use.

Theoretically, with sufficient precision of measurement, no two continuous values are identical. As a practical matter, however, most measuring devices are not precise enough to detect small differences, and tied values for a continuous variable (i.e., two or more items or individuals with the same value) are sometimes present in experimental or survey data.

Problems for Section 1.6

LEARNING THE BASICS

1.1 Three different beverages are sold at a fast-food restaurant—soft drinks, tea, and coffee. Explain why the type of beverage sold is an example of a categorical variable.

1.2 Soft drinks are sold in three sizes at a fast-food restaurant—small, medium, and large. Explain why the size of the soft drink is an example of a categorical variable.

1.3 Suppose that you measure the time it takes to download an MP3 file from the Internet. Explain why the download time is a continuous numerical variable.

APPLYING THE CONCEPTS

✓ SELF Test **1.4** For each of the following variables, determine whether the variable is categorical or numerical. If the variable is numerical, determine whether the variable is discrete or continuous.
a. Number of telephones in a household
b. Length of the longest long-distance call made in a month
c. Whether someone in the household owns a cell phone
d. Whether there is a high-speed Internet connection in the household

1.5 The following information is collected from students upon exiting the campus bookstore during the first week of classes:
a. Amount of time spent shopping in the bookstore
b. Number of textbooks purchased
c. Academic major
d. Gender
Classify each of these variables as categorical or numerical. If the variable is numerical, determine whether the variable is discrete or continuous.

1.6 For each of the following variables, determine whether the variable is categorical or numerical. If the variable is numerical, determine whether the variable is discrete or continuous.
a. Name of Internet provider
b. Amount of time spent surfing the Internet in a week
c. Number of e-mails received in a week
d. Number of online purchases made in a month

1.7 For each of the following variables, determine whether the variable is categorical or numerical. If the variable is numerical, determine whether the variable is discrete or continuous.
a. Amount of money spent on clothing in the past month

b. Favorite department store
c. Most likely time period during which shopping for clothing takes place (weekday, weeknight, or weekend)
d. Number of pairs of shoes owned

1.8 Suppose the following information is collected from Robert Keeler on his application for a home mortgage loan at the Metro County Savings and Loan Association:
a. Monthly payments: $1,427
b. Number of jobs in past 10 years: 1
c. Annual family income: $86,000
d. Marital status: Married
Classify each of the responses by type of data

1.9 The director of market research at a large department store chain wanted to conduct a survey throughout a metropolitan area to determine the amount of time working women spend shopping for clothing in a typical month.
a. Describe both the population and the sample of interest, and indicate the type of data the director might want to collect.
b. Develop a first draft of the questionnaire needed in (a) by writing a series of three categorical questions and three numerical questions that you feel are appropriate for this survey.

1.7 Microsoft Excel and Minitab

In a previous generation, the use of statistical methods in business was limited, often to those few who were fortunate to have access to specialized statistical calculators or large mainframe computers. Today, statistical functionality is so commonplace that many simple statistical tasks, once done exclusively with pencil and paper or simple hand calculators, are now done electronically with the assistance of computers.

Minitab and Microsoft Excel are desktop programs that business people use for statistics. Minitab is an example of a **statistical package**, a program engineered from the ground up to perform statistical analysis as accurately as possible. Microsoft Excel is a general purpose data analysis component of Microsoft Office that is based on electronic spreadsheets that are used in accounting and financial applications. As a general purpose tool, Excel can perform many functions, but none as well as other programs that are more singularly focused (see References 1, 2, 3, and 6). When it comes to teaching introductory business statistics, both programs have their proponents, with those favoring Minitab noting that Minitab as a complete statistical program while those favoring Excel noting that Excel is a program found on many business desktops (and in many business school courses).

Although you are probably more familiar with Microsoft Excel than with Minitab, both programs share many similarities. This is no coincidence as Minitab was inspired by Omnitab, a mainframe computer program from the 1960s that can be considered an ancestor to all electronic spreadsheet programs. Both Minitab and Excel use **worksheets** (their name for spreadsheets) to store the data you have collected for analysis. Worksheets are tabular arrangements of data, in which the intersections of rows and columns form **cells**, boxes into which you make entries. In both Minitab and Excel, the data for each variable are placed in individual columns. (The instructions in this book assume this standard practice.) Both Excel and Minitab allow you to save worksheets, programming information, and results in one file, called **workbooks** in Excel and **projects** in Minitab. Minitab also allows you to save individual worksheets in separate Minitab worksheet (.mtw) files. (The Student CD-ROM packaged with this book contains the data for problems and chapter examples as both Excel workbook files and Minitab worksheet files.)

1.8 Learning To Use Statistical Programs

Because using computer programs to assist in statistical decision making is a common occurrence in the business world, you will probably want to learn to use Minitab, Microsoft Excel, or some other program to help you perform statistical analysis. To learn to use these programs properly, you need to be able to:

- Understand underlying statistical concepts
- Understand how to organize and present information
- Understand how to operate your program's user interface
- Know how to review results for errors
- Make and secure clearly named backups of your work

Understanding the underlying statistical concepts and knowing how to organize and present results are two things that can be overlooked in the rush to "use" a statistical program. If you do not take the time to do these things, you can produce misleading results or, worse, appear as someone ignorant in the necessary foundations of statistics.

Sometimes people wrongly focus on trying to extensively memorize a program's commands or menu choices. You will not need to do that in order to be able to do the other three bulleted abilities. Instead, train yourself to use reference materials to find the instructions that you need when you need them. For example, the Microsoft Excel, PHStat2 (the Excel add-in that simplifies your use of Excel as explained in Section P1.1 on page 20), and Minitab appendices that appear at the end of each chapter will enable you to recreate the in-chapter examples and solve the in-chapter problems. You can also consult Appendix C if you are concerned about your basic computing skills or want to know more about the conventions used in this book to describe computer operations.

Don't worry too much about the program you use. Any choice will help you see how statistical programs are a necessary part of a business decision maker's daily routine.

USING STATISTICS   @ Good Tunes Revisited

In the Using Statistics scenario, you were asked to assist in preparing a slide show and prospectus for the Good Tunes company. The managers had decided to approach banks for funding the expansion of their company, but were not sure what type of data to present and how to present it. A first step was to summarize the details of thousands of transactions into useful information in the form of yearly dollar sales totals. Second, since Good Tunes prides itself in providing its customers with high-quality service, you decided to gather data that would support this aspect of the company.

Of the four sources of data discussed in this chapter (data distributed by an organization or an individual, a designed experiment, a survey, and an observational study), you decided to survey customers on various aspects of their experience with Good Tunes. The survey constructed also contains questions that seek to classify customers into groups for later analyses. Because Good Tunes has so many customers, gathering information from the entire population of customers was deemed impractical. Instead, a random sample of customers will be selected to take the survey.

A survey containing eight questions was constructed (see Figure 1.1 on page 8). The first and fifth questions of the survey will produce numerical data. The responses to the first question (number of days) are discrete, and the responses to the fifth question (amount of money spent) are continuous. Questions 2–4 and 6–8 will produce categorical data. Next, you will need to select the proper types of analyses for the different types of data collected. Chapter 2 presents graphical displays (for example, tables and charts), and Chapter 3 presents descriptive numerical measures (for example, mean, median, and mode).

SUMMARY

In this chapter, you have been introduced to the role of statistics in turning data into information. You learned that businesses use statistics to summarize and draw conclusions from data, to make reliable forecasts, and to improve business processes. In addition, you studied data collection, the various types of data used in business, and the importance of using computer programs such as Microsoft Excel and Minitab. In the next two chapters, tables and charts and a variety of descriptive numerical measures that are useful for data analysis are developed.

KEY TERMS

categorical variables 9	numerical variables 9	sample 6
cell 10	operational definition 5	secondary source 7
continuous variable 9	parameter 6	statistic 6
data 5	population 6	statistical package 10
data collection 7	primary source 7	statistics 4
descriptive statistics 4	projects 10	variable 5
discrete variables 9	qualitative variables 9	workbooks 10
inferential statistics 4	quantitative variables 9	worksheets 10

CHAPTER REVIEW PROBLEMS

CHECKING YOUR UNDERSTANDING

1.10 What is the difference between a sample and a population?

1.11 What is the difference between a statistic and a parameter?

1.12 What is the difference between descriptive statistics and inferential statistics?

1.13 What is the difference between a categorical variable and a numerical variable?

1.14 What is the difference between a discrete variable and a continuous variable?

1.15 What is an operational definition and why is it so important?

APPLYING THE CONCEPTS

1.16 Go to the official Microsoft Excel Web site, **www.microsoft.com/office/excel**, or the official Minitab Web site, **www.minitab.com**. Explain how you think Microsoft Excel or Minitab could be useful in the field of statistics.

1.17 The Gallup organization releases the results of recent polls at its Web site, **www.gallup.com**. Go to this site and read an article of interest.
a. Describe the population of interest.
b. Describe the sample that was collected.
c. Describe a parameter of interest.
d. Describe the statistic used to describe the parameter in (c).

1.18 According to its home page, "Swivel is a place where curious people explore data—all kinds of data." Go to **www. swivel.com** and explore a data set of interest to you.
a. Which of the four sources of data best describes the source of the data set you selected?
b. Describe a variable in the data set you selected.
c. Is the variable categorical or numerical?
d. If the variable in (c) is numerical, is it discrete or continuous?

1.19 At the U.S. Census Bureau site, **www.census.gov**, click **Survey of Business Owners** in the "Business & Industry" section and read about The Survey of Business Owners. Click on **Sample SBO-1 Form** to view a survey form.

a. Give an example of a categorical variable found in this survey.

b. Give an example of a numerical variable found in this survey.

c. Is the variable you selected in (b) discrete or continuous?

1.20 Gallup's 2008 annual Environment Poll indicates that 28% of respondents have made major changes in their shopping and living habits over the last five years to help protect the environment, 55% of respondents have made minor changes, and 17% have made no changes (J. Jones, "In the U.S., 28% Report Major Changes to Live 'Green'," **www.gallup.com**, April 18, 2008). The results are based on telephone interviews with 1,102 people living in the United States, aged 18 and older, conducted March 6–9, 2008.

a. Describe the population of interest.

b. Describe the sample that was collected.

c. Describe a parameter of interest.

d. Describe the statistic used to describe the parameter in (c).

1.21 Three professors at Northern Kentucky University compared two different approaches to teaching courses in the school of business (M. W. Ford, D. W. Kent, and S. Devoto, "Learning from the Pros: Influence of Web-Based Expert Commentary on Vicarious Learning about Financial Markets," *Decision Sciences Journal of Innovative Education*, January 2007, 5(1), 43–63). At the time of the study, there were 2,100 students in the business school and 96 students were involved in the study. Demographic data collected on these 96 students included class (freshman, sophomore, junior, senior), age, gender, and major.

a. Describe the population of interest.

b. Describe the sample that was collected.

c. For each of the four demographic variables mentioned above, indicate if they are categorical or numerical.

1.22 A manufacturer of cat food was planning to survey households in the United States to determine purchasing habits of cat owners. Among the questions to be included are those that relate to

1. where cat food is primarily purchased.
2. whether dry or moist cat food is purchased.
3. the number of cats living in the household.
4. whether the cat is pedigreed.

a. Describe the population.

b. For each of the four items listed, indicate whether the variable is categorical or numerical. If it is numerical, is it discrete or continuous?

c. Develop five categorical questions for the survey.

d. Develop five numerical questions for the survey.

STUDENT SURVEY DATABASE

1.23 A sample of 50 undergraduate students answered the following survey.

1. What is your gender? Female _____ Male _____
2. What is your age (*as of last birthday*)? _____
3. What is your height (*in inches*)? _____
4. What is your current registered class designation?
   Freshman _____ Sophomore _____
   Junior _____ Senior _____
5. What is your major area of study?
   Accounting _____ Economics/Finance _____
   Information Systems _____
   International Business _____ Management _____
   Marketing/Retailing _____ Other _____
   Undecided _____
6. At the present time, do you plan to attend graduate school? Yes _____ No _____ Not sure _____
7. What is your current cumulative grade point average?
   _____
8. What would you expect your starting annual salary (*in $000*) to be if you were to seek employment immediately after obtaining your bachelor's degree? _____
9. What do you anticipate your salary to be (*in $000*) after five years of full-time work experience? _____
10. What is your current employment status?
    Full-time _____ Part-time _____ Unemployed _____
11. How many clubs, groups, organizations, or teams are you currently affiliated with on campus? _____
12. How satisfied are you with the student advisement services on campus? _____
    Extremely   1 2 3 4 5 6 7   Extremely
    unsatisfied   Neutral   satisfied
13. About how much money did you spend this semester for textbooks and supplies? _____
    a. Which variables in the survey are categorical?
    b. Which variables in the survey are numerical?
    c. Which variables are discrete numerical variables?
    The results of the survey are in the file `Undergradsurvey`.

1.24 A sample of 40 MBA students answered the following survey:

1. What is your gender? Female _____ Male _____
2. What is your age (*as of last birthday*)? _____
3. What is your height (*in inches*)? _____
4. What is your current major area of study?
   Accounting _____ Economics/Finance _____
   Information Systems _____
   International Business _____ Management _____
   Marketing/Retailing _____ Other _____
   Undecided _____
5. What is your graduate cumulative grade point average? _____
6. What was your undergraduate major?
   Biological Sciences _____ Business
   Administration _____ Computers or Math _____
   Education _____ Engineering _____
   Humanities _____ Performing Arts _____
   Physical Sciences _____ Social Sciences _____
   Other _____

7. What was your undergraduate cumulative grade point average? _____

8. What was your GMAT score? _____

9. What is your current employment status? _____
   Full-time _____ Part-time _____
   Unemployed _____

10. How many different full-time jobs have you held in the past 10 years? _____

11. What do you expect your annual salary (*in $000*) to be immediately after completion of the MBA program? _____

12. What do you anticipate your salary to be (*in $000*) after five years of full-time work experience following the completion of the MBA program? _____

13. How satisfied are you with the student advisement services on campus?

    Extremely 1 2 3 4 5 6 7 Extremely
    unsatisfied   Neutral   satisfied

14. About how much money did you spend this semester for textbooks and supplies? _____
    a. Which variables in the survey are categorical?
    b. Which variables in the survey are numerical?
    c. Which variables are discrete numerical variables?
    The results of the survey are in the file `Gradsurvey`.

END-OF-CHAPTER CASES

At the end of most chapters, you will find a continuing case study that allows you to apply statistics to problems faced by the management of the *Springville Herald*, a daily newspaper. Complementing this case are a series of Web Cases that extend many of the Using Statistics scenarios that begin each chapter.

LEARNING WITH THE WEB CASES

People use statistical techniques to help communicate and present important information to others both inside and outside their businesses. Every day, as in these examples, people misuse these techniques:

- A sales manager working with an "easy-to-use" charting program chooses an inappropriate chart that obscures data relationships.

- The editor of an annual report presents a chart of revenues with an abridged *Y*-axis that creates the false impression of greatly rising revenues.

- An analyst generates meaningless statistics about a set of categorical data, using analyses designed for numerical data.

Identifying and preventing misuses of statistics, whether intentional or not, is an important responsibility for all managers. The Web Cases help you develop the skills necessary for this important task.

Web Cases send you to Web sites that are related to the Using Statistics scenarios that begin each chapter. You review internal documents as well as publicly stated claims, seeking to identify and correct the misuses of statistics. Unlike a traditional case study, but much like real-world situations, not all of the information you encounter will be relevant to your task, and you may occasionally discover conflicting information that you need to resolve before continuing with the case.

To assist your learning, the Web Case for each chapter begins with the learning objective and a summary of the problem or issue at hand. Each case directs you to one or more Web pages where you can discover information to answer case questions that help guide your exploration. If you prefer, you can view these pages by opening corresponding HTML files that can be found in the **Web Case** folder on the Student CD-ROM. You can find an index of all files/pages by opening the `SpringvilleCC.htm` file in the **Web Case** folder or by visiting the Springville Chamber of Commerce page, at **www.prenhall.com/Springville/ SpringvilleCC.htm**.

WEB CASE EXAMPLE

To illustrate how to learn from a Web Case, open a Web browser and link to **www.prenhall.com/Springville/ Good_Tunes.htm**, or open the `Good_Tunes.htm` file in the Student CD-ROM **Web Case** folder. This Web page represents the home page of Good Tunes, the online retailer mentioned in the Using Statistics scenario in this chapter. Recall that the privately held Good Tunes is seeking financing to expand its business by opening retail locations. Because it is in management's interest to show that Good Tunes is a thriving business, it is not too surprising to discover the "our best sales year ever" claim in the "Good Times at Good Tunes" entry at the top of their home page.

The claim also serves as a hyperlink, so click on **our best sales year ever** to display the page that supports the claim. How would you support such a claim? with a table of numbers? a chart? remarks attributed to a knowledgeable source? Good Tunes has used a chart to present "two years ago" and "latest twelve months" sales data by category. Are there any problems with the choices made on this Web page? *Absolutely*!

First, note that there are no scales for the symbols used, so it is impossible to know what the actual sales volumes are. In fact, as you will learn in Section 2.6, charts that incorporate symbols in this way are considered examples of *chartjunk* and would never be used by people seeking to properly use graphs.

This important point aside, another question that arises is whether the sales data represent the number of units sold or something else. The use of the symbols creates the impression that unit sales data are being presented. If the data are unit sales, does such data best support the claim being made, or would something else, such as dollar volumes, be a better indicator of sales at Good Tunes?

Then there are those curious chart labels. "Latest twelve months" is ambiguous; it could include months from the current year as well as months from one year ago and therefore may not be an equivalent time period to "two years ago." But the business was established in 1997, and the claim being made is "best sales year ever," so why hasn't management included sales figures for *every* year?

Is Good Tunes management hiding something, or are they just unaware of the proper use of statistics? Either way, they have failed to properly communicate a vital aspect of their story.

In subsequent Web Cases, you will be asked to provide this type of analysis, using the open-ended questions of the case as your guide. Not all the cases are as straightforward as this sample, and some cases include perfectly appropriate applications of statistics.

REFERENCES

1. McCullough, B. D., and D. Heiser, "On the Accuracy of Statistical Procedures in Microsoft Excel 2007," *Computational Statistics and Data Analysis*, 52 (2008), 4568–4606.
2. McCullough, B. D., and B. Wilson, "On the Accuracy of Statistical Procedures in Microsoft Excel 97," *Computational Statistics and Data Analysis*, 31 (1999), 27–37.
3. McCullough, B. D., and B. Wilson, "On the Accuracy of Statistical Procedures in Microsoft Excel 2003," *Computational Statistics and Data Analysis*, 49 (2005), 1244–52.
4. *Microsoft Excel 2007* (Redmond, WA: Microsoft Corporation, 2007).
5. *Minitab Release 15* (State College, PA: Minitab, Inc., 2006).
6. Nash, J. C., "Spreadsheets in Statistical Practice—Another Look," *The American Statistician*, 60 (2006), 287–89.

Introduction to Microsoft Excel

E1.1 Opening and Saving Workbooks

As discussed in Section 1.7, Microsoft Excel uses worksheets that are stored in workbooks. You open and save workbooks by selecting the storage folder to use and then specifying the file name of the workbook. You begin the process by selecting **File** from the Excel menu bar in Excel 97–2003 or by clicking the **Office Button** in Excel 2007. You then select either **Open** or **Save As**. These selections display nearly identical Open and Save As dialog boxes that vary only slightly owing to the different Excel versions (Figure E1.1 shows the Excel 2007 Save As dialog box).

Inside these dialog boxes, you select the storage folder using the drop-down list at the top of these dialog boxes. You enter, or select from the list box, a file name for the workbook in the **File name** box. You click **Open** or **Save** to complete the task. Sometimes when saving files, you will want to change the file type before you click **Save**. If you use Excel 2007 and want to save your workbook in the format used by earlier Excel versions, select **Excel 97–2003 Workbook (*.xls)** from the **Save as type** drop-down list before you click **Save** (shown in Figure E1.1). If you use any version of Excel and want to save data in a form that can be opened by programs that cannot open Excel workbooks, you might select either **Text (Tab delimited) (*.txt)** or **CSV (Comma delimited) (*.csv)** as the save type.

When you go to open a file and cannot find its name in the list box, verify that the current **Look in** folder is the correct one. If that fails to help, change the file type to **All Files** (*.*) to see all files in the current folder. (This technique will help you discover inadvertent misspellings or missing file extensions that otherwise prevents the file from being displayed.)

Although all versions of Microsoft Excel include a **Save** command, you should avoid this choice until you gain experience. Using Save makes it too easy for you to inadvertently overwrite your work, and in Excel 2007, it saves your workbook in the new **.xlsx** workbook format that cannot be used by earlier Excel versions. If you open a workbook from a nonmodifiable source, such as the Student CD-ROM, Excel will mark the workbook "read-only," so you must use Save As to save any changes you make to the workbook. (Excel will prevent you from using Save in such situations.)

E1.2 Creating New Workbooks

You create a new workbook through a straightforward process that varies depending on the version of Excel you are using. In Excel 97 or 2000, you select **File → New**. In Excel 2002 (also known as Excel XP) or 2003, you select **File → New** and then click **Blank workbook** in the New Workbook task pane. In Excel 2007, you click **Office Button → New** and in the New Workbook dialog box, you first click **Blank workbook** and then **Create**.

New workbooks are created with a fixed number of worksheets. You can delete extra worksheets or insert more sheets by right-clicking a sheet tab and clicking either **Delete** or **Insert**.

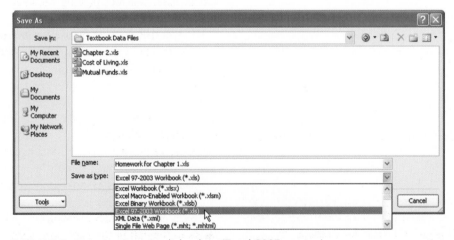

FIGURE E1.1 Save As dialog box (Excel 2007 version)

E1.3 Printing Worksheets

When you want to print the contents of a workbook, you should print one sheet at a time to get the best results. You print sheets by first previewing their printed form onscreen and then making any adjustments to the worksheet and/or to the print setup settings.

To print a specific worksheet, you first click on the sheet tab of that worksheet to make the worksheet the currently active one. Then you display the Print Preview window. If you use a version of Excel other than 2007, select **File → Print Preview**. If you use Excel 2007, click **Office Button**, move the mouse pointer over **Print** (do not click) and select **Print Preview** from the Preview and Print gallery.

The Print Preview windows for all Excel versions are similar to one another. Figure E1.2 shows a partial window for Excel 2003 (top) and Excel 2007 (bottom). If the preview contains errors or displays the worksheet in an undesirable manner, click **Close** (or **Close Print Preview** in Excel 2007), make the changes necessary, and reselect the preview command. You can customize your printout by clicking **Setup** (or **Page Setup**) and making the appropriate entries in the Page Setup dialog box, which is similar for all Excel versions. For example, to print your worksheet with grid lines and numbered row and lettered column headings (similar to the appearance of the worksheet onscreen), you click the **Sheet** tab in the Page Setup dialog box and then click **Gridlines** and **Row and column headings** and click **OK** (see Figure E1.3). (You can find more information about using Page Setup in Section F4 of Appendix F.)

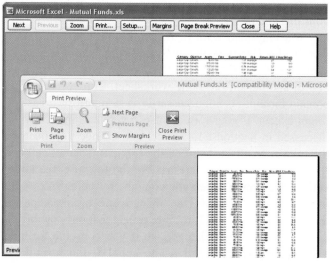

F I G U R E E 1 . 2   Partial Print Preview windows (Excel 2003 and 2007 versions)

When you are ready to print, you can click **Print** in the Print Preview window, but to gain maximum control over your printout, click **Close** (or **Close Print Preview**) and then select **File → Print** (Excel 97–2003) or **Office Button → Print** (Excel 2007). In the Print dialog box that appears, you

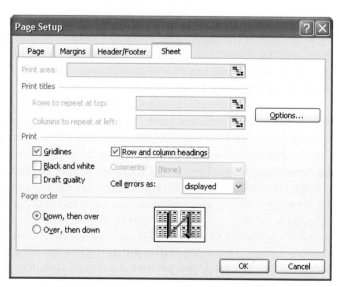

F I G U R E E 1 . 3   Sheet tab of the Page Setup dialog box (Excel 2003 version)

can select the printer to use, make sure you are printing only the currently active worksheet, or print multiple copies at once.

E1.4 Worksheet Entries and References

As first discussed in Section 1.7, worksheets are tabular arrangements of data in which standard practice dictates that you enter the data for each variable in individual columns. You use the cursor keys or your pointing device to move a **cell pointer** through a worksheet and to select a cell for entry. As you type an entry, it appears in the formula bar, and you place that entry into the cell by either pressing the **Tab** or **Enter** keys or clicking the checkmark button in the formula bar.

As you enter the data for a variable in a column, follow the standard practice of using the row 1 cell to store a name or label for the variable. Should you be entering two or more sets of data, consider placing each set of data in a separate worksheet.

In worksheets that you use for intermediate calculations or final results, you might enter **formulas**, instructions to perform a calculation or some other task, in addition to the numeric and text entries you otherwise make into cells. Proper formulas use values found in one or more other cells to produce a new displayed result. The displayed results automatically change; that is, the formula is recalculated, when the values in other cells change. (Such **recalculation** was the original novel feature of spreadsheet programs and led to such programs being widely used in accounting.)

To refer to a cell in a formula, you use a **cell address** in the form *SheetName!ColumnRow*. For example, **Data!A2** refers to the cell in the Data worksheet that is in column A and row 2. You can also use just the *ColumnRow* portion of a full address, for example, **A2**, if you are referring to a cell on the same worksheet as the one into which you are entering a formula. If the sheet name contains spaces or special characters, for example, **City Data** or **Figure-1.2**, you must enclose the sheet name in a pair of single quotes, as in **'City Data'!A2** or **'Figure-1.2'!A2**.

When you want to refer to a group of cells, for example, to the cells of a column that store the data for a particular variable, you use a **cell range**. A cell range names the upper leftmost cell and the lower rightmost cell of the group using the form *SheetName!UpperLeftCell:LowerRightCell*. For example, the cell range **Data!B1:B51** identifies the cells in the UndergradSurvey.xls workbook that store the data for the gender variable (with cell B1 storing the variable label "Gender" as explained earlier). Cell ranges can extend over multiple columns; the cell range **Data!B1:E51** in the same workbook would refer to the data for the gender, age, height, and class variables.

As with a single cell reference, you can skip the *SheetName!* part of the reference if you are referring to a cell range on the current worksheet, and you must use a pair of single quotes if a sheet name contains spaces or special characters. However, in many cases in the Excel instructions in this book, including the sheet name will be necessary in a cell reference in order to get the proper results. Because sheet names are used so frequently, you should change the names that Excel assigns to worksheets (names in the form **Sheet1**, **Sheet2**, and so on) to more meaningful words or phrases. To do so, double-click a sheet tab, type the new name, and press **Enter**.

(Although not a form used in this book, cell references can include a workbook name in the form **'[*Workbook Name*]*SheetName*'!*ColumnRow*** or **'[*WorkbookName*] *SheetName*'!*UpperLeftCell:LowerRightCell***. You may discover such references if you inadvertently copy certain types of worksheets or chart sheets from one workbook to another.)

E1.5 Entering Formulas Into Worksheets

You enter formulas by typing the equal sign symbol (=) and then a combination of mathematical or other data-processing operations. For simple formulas, you use the symbols +, -, *, /, and ∧ for the operations addition, subtraction, multiplication, division, and exponentiation (a number raised to a power), respectively. For example, the formula **=Data!B2 + Data!B3 + Data!B4** adds the contents of the cells B2, B3, and B4 of the Data worksheet and displays the sum as the value in the cell containing the formula. You can also use **worksheet functions** in formulas to simplify formulas.

To use a worksheet function in a formula, either type the function as shown in the instructions in this book or use the Excel Function Wizard feature to insert the function. To use this feature, select **Insert → Function** (Excel 97–2003) or **Formulas → Function Wizard** (Excel 2007) and then make entries and selections in one or more dialog boxes.

E1.6 Verifying Formulas and Worksheets

If you use formulas in your worksheets, you should review and verify formulas before you use their results. To view the formulas in a worksheet, press **Ctrl + `** (grave accent key). To restore the original view, the results of the formulas, press **Ctrl + `** a second time.

As you create and use more complicated worksheets, you may want to visually examine the relationships among a formula and the cells it uses (called the precedents) and the cells that use the results of the formula (the dependents). To display arrows that visually show these relationships, use the formula auditing feature of Excel. Select **Tools → Auditing** (Excel 97 or 2000), or **Tools → Formula Auditing** (Excel 2002 or 2003), or **Formulas** (Excel 2007). Then select one of the choices from the auditing submenu (Excel 97–2003) or from the **Formula Auditing** group (Excel 2007). When you are finished, selecting **Remove All Arrows** restores your display by removing all auditing arrows.

E1.7 Enhancing Workbook Presentation

By formatting the display of individual cells and by rearranging the contents of your workbook, you can enhance the presentation of your workbook.

You can find the most common cell-formatting operations on the Formatting toolbar (Excel 97–2003) or in the Home tab (Excel 2007). Most worksheets shown as illustrations in this book use the **Boldface**, **Fill Color**, **Merge-and-Center**, and **Borders** features to highlight particular cells or cell ranges. Experiment with these features to develop your own style that maximizes the effectiveness of your presentations.

You may also want to rearrange the content of your workbooks. Use the copy-and-paste combination keystroke shortcuts, **Crtl+C** and **Ctrl+V**, to copy content from one cell to another on the same worksheet. Copying cells that contain formulas is not necessarily as straightforward as you might expect. If your formula uses references in the format discussed in Section E1.4, Excel will change to reflect the difference, or offset, between the original (source) cell and the cell into which you are pasting the formula (the target cell). For example, when you copy the formula =A2 + B2 in cell C2 down to cell C3, an offset of one row, Excel pastes the formula =A3 + B3 in C3 to reflect that one-row offset. Cell ranges also get changed, so if you copy the formula =SUM(A1:A4) from cell A5 to cell B5, the formula is changed to =SUM(B1:B4).

You can stop Excel from making such changes by inserting a U.S. dollar symbol ($) before either the column letter or row number (or both) of a cell reference to form an **absolute reference**, for example, A2. Do not confuse the use of the U.S. dollar symbol with the format operation that displays numbers as U.S. currency values. To format cell values for U.S. currency display, you use the **Currency ($)** format button, available on the Formatting toolbar (Excel

97–2003) and in the Number group of **Home** tab (Excel 2007).

Finally, you can also copy entire worksheets for convenience or clarity. To copy a worksheet to a new workbook, you first select the worksheet by clicking its sheet tab. Then you right-click the tab and select **Move or Copy** from the shortcut menu that appears. In the **To book** drop-down list of the Move or Copy dialog box (see Figure E1.4), first select **(new book)** or the name of the preexisting target workbook, and then click **Create a copy** and then click **OK**.

FIGURE E1.4 Move or Copy dialog box (Excel 2007 version)

E1.8 Using Add-Ins

Add-ins can simplify the task of creating something to add to a workbook. Add-ins are programming components not included in the main Excel program and may need to be **installed**, or added, to your computer system separately. Add-ins are not always available for you to use because they can be disabled by other users or system security settings. However, the little extra effort you need to ensure that the right add-ins are installed and enabled is well worth the features that add-ins bring to Excel.

As you use Microsoft Excel with this book, you will use the Excel **Analysis ToolPak** add-in for some statistical tasks. The Analysis ToolPak add-in (which the book simply calls the "ToolPak" from this point forward) adds statistical procedures to Excel, but creates worksheets that do not contain formulas. Should you later change your data, you must repeat the ToolPak procedure to get updated results. Some Excel versions come with the ToolPak preinstalled; others require that you separately install this component from your Microsoft Office or Excel program setup disk. (See Appendix F for additional information about installing the ToolPak.)

As you use Microsoft Excel, you may choose to use **PHStat2**, the Prentice Hall statistics add-in that is included

on the Student CD-ROM. If you plan to use PHStat2, you first need to run its setup program, using the instructions found in Appendix F and in the Student CD-ROM PHStat2 readme file. PHStat2 adds a PHStat menu of procedures to the Excel menu bar in Excel 97–2003 and the Add-ins tab in Excel 2007. Unlike the ToolPak, PHStat2 usually creates worksheets that contain formulas and that will produce new results as the underlying data changes. Sometimes, though, PHStat2 asks the ToolPak to create sheets on its behalf, and the resulting sheets are similar to the no-formulas sheets that the ToolPak creates. In many such cases, PHStat2 enhances the sheets it asks the ToolPak to create, correcting errors the ToolPak makes or adding new formula-based calculations. (If you plan to use PHStat2, be sure to read Appendix P1, which immediately follows this appendix.)

In all Excel versions other than Excel 97, all add-ins that you open will be screened by Microsoft Office security components. If you use Excel 2000, 2002, or 2003, you can review and change the security settings by selecting **Tools →** **Macro → Security** to display a Security dialog box (similar to the one shown in Figure E1.5 for Excel 2003). To use an add-in such as PHStat2 that is "not signed," you would click **Medium** and then click **OK**.

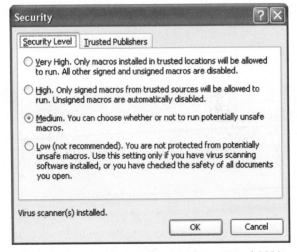

FIGURE E1.5 Security dialog box (Excel 2003 version)

If you use Excel 2007, click the **Office Button**, and then click **Excel Options** in the Office menu. In the Excel Options dialog box (see Figure E1.6) click **Trust Center** in the left pane to display information about security issues. Then click **Trust Center Settings** (obscured in Figure E1.6) to display the Trust Center dialog box. To use an add-in such as PHStat2 that is not signed, click **Add-Ins** in the left pane, and then clear all checkboxes in the right pane (see Figure E1.6). Then click **Macro Settings** in the left pane and click **Disable all macros with notification** in the right pane (see Figure E1.6). On some systems, you may also have to click **Trusted Locations** in the left pane and add the file location of the add-in.

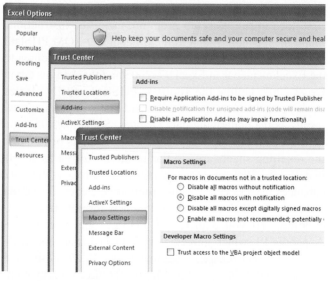

FIGURE E1.6   Excel Options and Trust Center panes (Excel 2007)

With the Security screen set to an appropriate level, you will see a macro virus warning dialog box when you open an add-in such as PHStat2. Figure E1.7 shows the Excel 2003 and Excel 2007 warning boxes. You click the **Enable Macros** button to allow virus-free add-ins, such as PHStat2, to be opened and used.

FIGURE E1.7   Macro warning dialog boxes (Excel 2003 and 2007)

APPENDIX P1

Introduction to PHStat2

P1.1 Overview

PHStat2 is Microsoft Windows software that makes using Microsoft Excel as distraction-free as possible. As a student studying statistics, you can use PHStat2 to maximize your focus on mastering statistics and minimize your worries about learning every little detail about Excel. When combined with the ToolPak add-in, you can use a beginner's knowledge of Microsoft Excel to illustrate nearly all of the statistical methods presented in this book.

PHStat2 was not designed to be used commercially and you should not see it as a replacement for or an equivalent to statistical programs such as Minitab, SPSS, JMP, and SAS. Because PHStat2 emphasizes learning, PHStat2 tries to use the methods of calculation that an introductory statistics student can easily follow, including manual calculation methods presented in this book. In other cases, PHStat2 uses preexisting Microsoft Excel methods to produce results that are too complex to manually calculate or present to the learner. These design choices occasionally produce results

that are not as precise or accurate as those produced by commercial programs, which use methods of calculation that are fine-tuned for precision and accuracy. Even though these differences will not be significant for most sets of data and are *not* significant for all data used in chapter examples and problems, they could be if you used PHStat2 with data that happen to have unusual properties.

P1.2 How PHStat2 Presents Its Results

PHStat2 creates new worksheets and chart sheets inserted into the currently active workbook. Cells containing important values and results are highlighted by a light yellow tint and boldface text. These cells and the cells that hold intermediate calculations are usually only minimally numerically formatted. For some procedures, the values in these cells will have an excessive number of seemingly significant digits and you may want to change the numeric formatting for such cells for presentation purposes.

Worksheets that contain cells tinted in light turquoise are designed to be interactive and you can change the numeric values of those cells to produce different results without reselecting the PHStat2 procedure.

P1.3 Using PHStat2

When properly loaded, PHStat2 adds the PHStat menu entry to the Excel 97–2003 menu bar or the Add-Ins tab of Excel 2007. Selecting **PHStat** for either of these displays the PHStat menu (see Figure P1.1). You make selections from this menu, as discussed in the PHStat2 appendices of later chapters, to select and run a PHStat2 procedure.

In addition to selecting procedures, you can select **About PHStat** to view information about the PHStat2 version that you are using, or select **Help for PHStat** to display the PHStat2 help system inside Microsoft Excel (this feature is not available for Windows Vista users).

To use PHStat2, make sure you have read Section E1.8 "Using Add-Ins," the Student CD-ROM **PHStat2 readme file** and the appropriate sections of Appendix F. If you are inexperienced in the task of installing programs on your computer system, you may additionally want to seek assis-

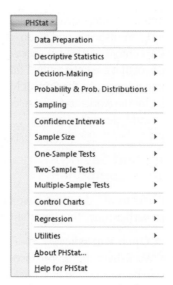

FIGURE P1.1 PHStat Menu

tance from a friend or campus help center if you plan to install PHStat2 on your system. General assistance is also available through the PHStat2 Web site, **www.prenhall. com/phstat**.

APPENDIX M1

Introduction to Minitab

M1.1 Overview

Minitab is a statistical program that initially evolved from efforts at the Pennsylvania State University to improve the teaching of statistics. Over the years, Minitab's accuracy and its availability for many different types of computer systems have attracted such corporate customers as the Ford Motor Company, 3M, and General Electric. This combination of having large-scale commercial acceptance and the legacy of being designed for statistics education makes Minitab an attractive program to use in business statistics courses.

As first discussed in Section 1.7, you create Minitab **projects** to store all of your data and results. A project includes several components: a **session area** that contains all your statistical tables; a **Project Manager** that summarizes the project contents; Minitab worksheets that store your data; and graphs of your data. Project components appear as separate windows *inside* the Minitab window. When you start Minitab, you typically see a new project that contains only the session area and one worksheet window.

(You can view other components by selecting them in the Minitab **Windows** menu.) You can open and save an entire project or, as is done in this book, open and save individual worksheets.

M1.2 Using Worksheets

You enter data for each variable in individual columns of a Minitab worksheet. Minitab worksheets are organized as numbered rows and columns numbered in the form Cn in which C1 is the first column, C2 is the second column, and so forth. You enter variable labels in a special unnumbered row that precedes row 1. You refer to individual variables either using their column number, such as **C1**, or through their variable labels, such as **Risk**. If a variable label is a phrase such as **Return 2006**, you enter the label with a pair of single quotation marks, for example, as **'Return 2006'**. (In this book, variable labels are generally used to refer to variables, a practice that can minimize errors.)

By default, Minitab names open worksheets serially in the form of Worksheet1, Worksheet2, and so on. Better names are ones that reflect the content of the worksheets, such as Mutual Funds for a worksheet that contains mutual funds data. To give a sheet a descriptive name, open the Project Manager window, right-click the icon for the worksheet, and select **Rename** from the shortcut menu and type in the new name.

M1.3 Opening and Saving Worksheets and Other Components

You open worksheets to use data that have been created by you or others at an earlier time. To open a Minitab worksheet:

1. Select **File → Open Worksheet**.
2. In the Open Worksheet dialog box (see Figure M1.1), select the file to be opened and then click **Open**.

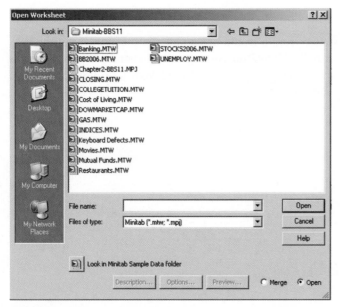

FIGURE M1.1   Open Worksheet dialog box

If you cannot find your file, you may need to do one or more of the following:

- Use the scroll bars or the slider, if present, to scroll through the entire list of files.
- Select the correct folder from the **Look in** drop-down list at the top of the dialog box.
- Change the **Files of type** value from the drop-down list at the bottom of the dialog box. You should select **Text (*.txt)** from the list to see text files, **Excel (*.xls, *.xlsx)** to see Microsoft Excel files, and so forth. To list every file in the folder, select **All Files(*.*)**.

To save a Minitab worksheet:

1. Select **File → Save Current Worksheet As**.
2. In the Save Worksheet As dialog box that appears (similar to the Open Worksheet dialog box), enter the name for your worksheet in the **File name** box and then click **Save**.

If applicable, you can also do the following:

- Change to another folder by selecting that folder from the **Save in** drop-down list.
- Change the **Save as type** value to something other than the default choice, **Minitab. "Minitab Portable"** or an earlier version of **Minitab**, such as **Minitab 13**, are commonly chosen alternatives.

After saving your work, you should consider saving your file a second time, using a different name, in order to create a backup copy of your work. Files opened from non-writable disks, such as the Student CD-ROM, cannot be saved to their original files.

To open an entire Minitab Project, select **File → Open Project**. To save a Minitab Project, select **File → Save Project As**. When you use these commands, the dialog box that appears will contain an **Options** button that you can click to selectively open (or save) parts of your project.

Individual graphs and the session window can also be saved separately by first selecting their windows and then selecting **File → Save Graph As** or **File → Save Session Window As**, as appropriate. Minitab graphs can be saved in either a Minitab graph format or any one of several common graphics formats, and session files can be saved as simple or formatted text files.

M1.4 Printing Worksheets, Graphs, and Sessions

To print a specific worksheet, graph, or session:

1. Select the window that contains the worksheet, graph, or session to be printed.
2. Select **File → Print** *object*, where *object* is either **Worksheet**, **Graph**, or **Session Window**, depending on what you seek to print.

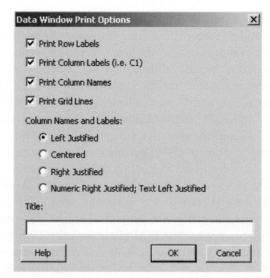

FIGURE M1.2   Data Window Print Options dialog box

If you are printing a graph or a session window, you will then see the Print dialog box. If you are printing a worksheet, you will first see a Data Window Print Options dialog box (Figure M1.2) that allows you to select formatting options for your printout (the default selections should be fine for most of your printouts). Click **OK** in that dialog box to proceed to the Print dialog box.

The Print dialog box contains settings to select the printer to be used, what pages to print, and the number of copies to produce (1 is the default). If you need to change these settings, change them before clicking **OK** to create your printout.

After printing, you should verify the contents of your printout. Most printing failures will trigger the display of onscreen information that you can use to determine the source of the failure. You can change the paper size or paper orientation of your printout by selecting **File → Print Setup** and then making the appropriate entries in the dialog box that appears. (Click **OK** when you are finished making entries.)

2 Presenting Data in Tables and Charts

Learning Objectives

In this chapter, you learn:

- To develop tables and charts for categorical data
- To develop tables and charts for numerical data
- The principles of properly presenting graphs

@ Choice Is Yours, Part I

C hoice Is Yours is a service that helps customers make wise investment choices. You've been hired to assist investors interested in mutual funds, a market basket of securities. According to **investopedia.com**, "A mutual fund is nothing more than a collection of stocks and/or bonds. You can think of a mutual fund as a company that brings together a group of people and invests their money in stocks, bonds, and other securities. Each investor owns shares, which represent a portion of the holdings of the fund." (You can learn more at **investopedia.com/university/mutualfunds**.)

The Choice Is Yours company previously selected a sample of 868 mutual funds that it believes might be of interest to its customers. You have been asked to present data about these funds in a way that will help customers make good investment choices. What facts about each mutual fund would you collect to help customers compare and contrast the many funds?

A good starting point would be to collect data that would help customers classify mutual funds into various categories. You could research such things as the amount of risk involved in a fund's investment strategy and whether the fund focuses on growth securities, those companies that are expected to grow quickly in the next year, or on value securities, those companies whose stock prices are currently considered undervalued. You might also investigate whether a mutual fund specializes in a certain size company and whether the fund charges management fees that would reduce the percentage return earned by an investor.

Of course, you would want to know how well the fund performed in the past. You would also want to supply the customer with several measures of each fund's past performance. Even though past performance is no assurance of future performance, past data could give customers insight into how well each mutual fund has been managed.

As you further think about your task, you realize that all these data for all 868 mutual funds would be a lot for anyone to review. How could you "get your hands around" such data and explore it in a comprehensible manner?

To get your hands around the data described in this chapter's Using Statistics scenario, you need to use methods of descriptive statistics, defined in Chapter 1 as the branch of statistics that collects, summarizes, presents and analyzes data. In this scenario, you need to use descriptive techniques for both categorical variables (to help investors classify the mutual funds) and numerical variables (to help show the return each fund has achieved). Reading this chapter will help you prepare tables and charts that are appropriate for both types of variables. You'll also learn techniques to help answer questions that require two variables, such as "Do growth-oriented mutual funds have lower returns than value mutual funds?" and "Do growth funds tend to be riskier investments than value funds?"

Many examples in this chapter use a sample of 868 mutual funds, the data for which you can find in the Data worksheet of the `Mutual Funds.xls` workbook or in the Minitab worksheet `Mutual Funds.mtw` on the Student CD-ROM.

2.1 Tables and Charts for Categorical Data

When you have categorical data, you tally responses into categories and then present the frequency or percentage in each category in tables and charts.

The Summary Table

A **summary table** indicates the frequency, amount, or percentage of items in a set of categories so that you can see differences between categories. A summary table lists the categories in one column and the frequency, amount, or percentage in a different column or columns. Table 2.1 illustrates a summary table based on a recent survey (see the `Banking` file) that asked people where they prefer to do their banking (K. Chu, "Online Banks Launch Checking Accounts," *USA Today*, January 18, 2007, p. 1B). In Table 2.1, the most common choices are in person at branch and on the Internet, followed by drive-through service at branch and ATM. Very few respondents mentioned automated or live telephone.

TABLE 2.1

Banking Preference

Banking Preference	Percentage (%)
ATM	16
Automated or live telephone	2
Drive-through service at branch	17
In person at branch	41
Internet	24

EXAMPLE 2.1

Summary Table of Levels of Risk of Mutual Funds

The 868 mutual funds that are part of the Using Statistics scenario (see page 25) are classified according to their risk level, categorized as low, average, and high. Construct a summary table of the mutual funds, categorized by risk.

SOLUTION From Table 2.2, you can see that fewer than 25% of the funds are low-risk funds. There are more high-risk funds (355, or 40.90%) than low-risk (202, or 23.27%) or average-risk funds (311, or 35.83%). More than 75% of the funds are average risk or high risk.

TABLE 2.2

Frequency and Percentage Summary Table Pertaining to Risk Level for 868 Mutual Funds

Fund Risk Level	Number of Funds	Percentage of Funds (%)
Low	202	23.27
Average	311	35.83
High	355	40.90
Total	868	100.00

The Bar Chart

In a **bar chart**, a bar shows each category. The length of the bar represents the amount, frequency, or percentage of values falling into a category. Figure 2.1 displays the bar chart for where people prefer to do their banking presented in Table 2.1.

Bar charts allow you to compare percentages in different categories. In Figure 2.1, respondents are most likely to bank in person at a branch and on the Internet, followed by drive-through service at a branch and ATM. Very few respondents mentioned automated or live telephone.

FIGURE 2.1

Microsoft Excel bar chart for where people prefer to do their banking.

See Sections E2.4 or P2.3 to create this. (Minitab users, see Section M2.2 to create an equivalent chart.)

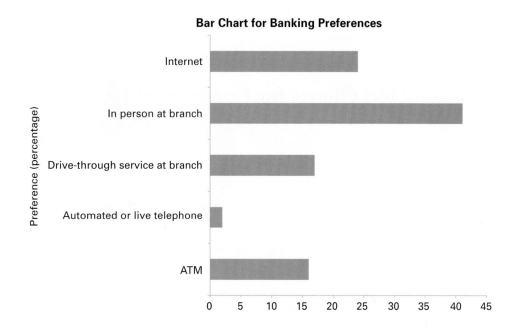

Bar Chart for Banking Preferences

EXAMPLE 2.2

Bar Chart of Levels of Risk of Mutual Funds

Construct a bar chart for the levels of risk of mutual funds (based on the information in Table 2.2 on page 26) and interpret the results.

SOLUTION From Figure 2.2, you can see that approximately 200 of the funds are low risk, whereas more than 650 of the 868 funds are either average risk or high risk. There are more high-risk funds than average-risk or low-risk funds.

FIGURE 2.2

Microsoft Excel bar chart of the levels of risk of mutual funds

See Sections E2.4 or P2.3 to create this. (Minitab users, see Section M2.2 to create an equivalent chart.)

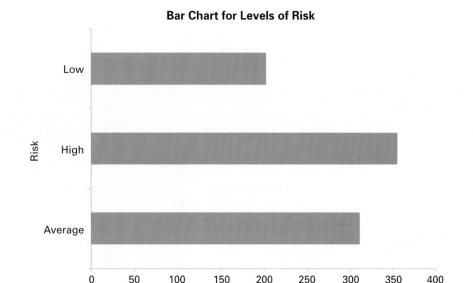

Bar Chart for Levels of Risk

The Pie Chart

The **pie chart** is a circle broken up into slices that represent categories. The size of each slice of the pie varies according to the percentage in each category. In Table 2.1 on page 26, for example, 41% of the respondents stated that they prefer to bank in person at the branch. Thus, in constructing the pie chart, the 360 degrees that makes up a circle is multiplied by 0.41, resulting in a slice of the pie that takes up 147.6 degrees of the 360 degrees of the circle. From Figure 2.3, you can see that the pie chart lets you visualize the portion of the entire pie that is in each category. In this figure, bank in person at the branch takes 41% of the pie and automated or live telephone takes only 2%.

FIGURE 2.3

Microsoft Excel pie chart for where people prefer to do their banking

See Sections E2.4 or P2.3 to create this. (Minitab users, see Section M2.3 to create an equivalent chart.)

Pie Chart for Banking Preferences

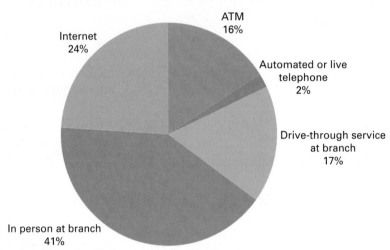

Which chart should you use—a bar chart or a pie chart? The selection of a particular chart often depends on your intention. If a comparison of categories is most important, you should use a bar chart. If observing the portion of the whole that is in a particular category is most important, you should use a pie chart.

EXAMPLE 2.3

Pie Chart of Levels of Risk of Mutual Funds

FIGURE 2.4

Microsoft Excel pie chart of the levels of risk of mutual funds

See Sections E2.4 or P2.3 to create this. (Minitab users, see Section M2.3 to create an equivalent chart.)

Construct a pie chart for the levels of risk of mutual funds (see Table 2.2 on page 26) and interpret the results.

SOLUTION From Figure 2.4, you can see that 41% of the funds are high risk, 36% are average risk, and only 23% are low risk.

Pie Chart for Levels of Risk

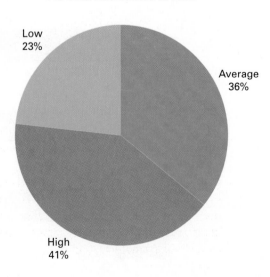

The Pareto Chart

In a **Pareto chart**, the responses in the categories are plotted as vertical bars in descending order, according to their frequencies, and are combined with a cumulative percentage line on the same chart. The Pareto chart can identify situations in which the Pareto principle occurs.

PARETO PRINCIPLE

The **Pareto principle** exists when the majority of items in a set of data occur in a small number of categories and the few remaining items are spread out over a large number of categories. These two groups are often referred to as the "vital few" and the "trivial many."

The Pareto chart has the ability to separate the "vital few" from the "trivial many," enabling you to focus on the important categories. In situations in which the data involved consist of defective or nonconforming items, the Pareto chart is a powerful tool for prioritizing improvement efforts.

Table 2.3 presents data for a large injection-molding company that manufactures plastic components used in computer keyboards, washing machines, automobiles, and television sets (see the Keyboard defects file). The data presented in Table 2.3 consist of all computer keyboards with defects produced during a three-month period.

TABLE 2.3

Summary Table of Causes of Defects in Computer Keyboards in a Three-Month Period

Cause	Frequency	Percentage
Black spot	413	6.53
Damage	1,039	16.43
Jetting	258	4.08
Pin mark	834	13.19
Scratches	442	6.99
Shot mold	275	4.35
Silver streak	413	6.53
Sink mark	371	5.87
Spray mark	292	4.62
Warpage	1,987	31.42
Total	6,324	100.01*

Result differs slightly from 100.00 due to rounding.
Source: *Extracted from U. H. Acharya and C. Mahesh, "Winning Back the Customer's Confidence: A Case Study on the Application of Design of Experiments to an Injection-Molding Process,"* Quality Engineering, *11, 1999, pp. 357–363.*

Table 2.4 on page 30 presents a summary table for the computer keyboard data in which the categories are ordered based on the frequency of defects present (rather than arranged alphabetically). The percentages and cumulative percentages for the ordered categories are also included as part of the table.

In Table 2.4, the first category listed is warpage (with 31.42% of the defects), followed by damage (with 16.43%), followed by pin mark (with 13.19%). The two most frequently occurring categories, warpage and damage, account for 47.85% of the defects; the three most frequently occurring categories—warpage, damage, and pin mark—account for 61.04% of the defects, and so on.

Figure 2.5 is a Pareto chart based on the results displayed in Table 2.4.

TABLE 2.4

Ordered Summary Table of Causes of Defects in Computer Keyboards in a Three-Month Period

Cause	Frequency	Percentage	Cumulative Percentage
Warpage	1,987	31.42	31.42
Damage	1,039	16.43	47.85
Pin mark	834	13.19	61.04
Scratches	442	6.99	68.03
Black spot	413	6.53	74.56
Silver streak	413	6.53	81.09
Sink mark	371	5.87	86.96
Spray mark	292	4.62	91.58
Shot mold	275	4.35	95.93
Jetting	258	4.08	100.01*
Total	6,324	100.01*	

Result differs slightly from 100.00 due to rounding.

FIGURE 2.5

Microsoft Excel Pareto chart for the keyboard defects data

See Sections E2.5 or P2.4 to create this. (Minitab users, see Section M2.4 to create an equivalent chart.)

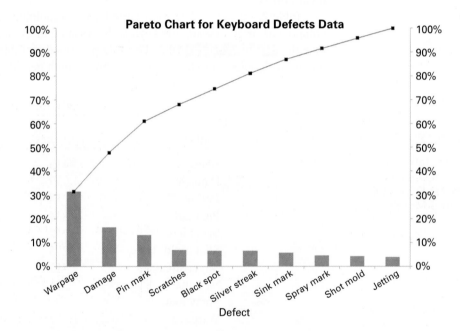

A Pareto chart presents the bars vertically, along with a cumulative percentage line. The cumulative line is plotted at the midpoint of each category, at a height equal to the cumulative percentage. If you follow the line, you see that these first three categories account for about 60% of the defects. Because the categories in the Pareto chart are ordered by the frequency of occurrences, decision makers can see where to concentrate efforts to improve the process. Attempts to reduce defects due to warpage, damage, and pin marks should produce the greatest payoff. Then, efforts can be made to reduce scratches, black spots, and silver streaks.

In order for a Pareto chart to include all categories, even those with few defects, in some situations you need to include a category labeled *Other* or *Miscellaneous*. In these situations, the bar representing these categories should be placed to the right of the other bars.

EXAMPLE 2.4

Pareto Chart of Banking Preference

Construct a Pareto chart of banking preference (see Table 2.1 on page 26).

SOLUTION In Figure 2.6, in person at branch and on the Internet account for 65% of the banking preferences; 98% of the respondents would prefer in person at branch, on the Internet, drive-through at branch, and ATM.

FIGURE 2.6

Microsoft Excel Pareto chart for banking preference

See Sections E2.5 or P2.4 to create this. (Minitab users, see Section M2.4 to create an equivalent chart.)

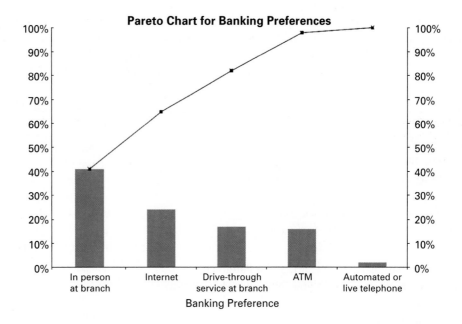

Problems for Section 2.1

LEARNING THE BASICS

2.1 A categorical variable has three categories with the following frequencies of occurrence:

Category	Frequency
A	13
B	28
C	9

a. Compute the percentage of values in each category.
b. Construct a bar chart.
c. Construct a pie chart.
d. Construct a Pareto chart.

2.2 A categorical variable has four categories with the following percentages of occurrence:

Category	Percentage	Category	Percentage
A	12	C	35
B	29	D	24

a. Construct a bar chart.
b. Construct a pie chart.
c. Construct a Pareto chart.

APPLYING THE CONCEPTS

2.3 A survey of 705 workers asked how much they used the Internet at work. The results (*USA Today, Snapshots*, March 21, 2006, p. 1B) were as follows:

Use of the Internet at Work	%
Too much	5
More than I should	4
Within limits	60
Very little	5
Do not use	26

a. Construct a bar chart, a pie chart, and a Pareto chart.
b. Which graphical method do you think is best to portray these data?
c. Based on this survey, what conclusions can you reach about the use of the Internet at work?

✓SELF
Test **2.4** A survey of 1,264 women asked who was their most trusted shopping advisers. The results (*USA Today, Snapshots*, October 19, 2006, p. 1B) were as follows:

Shopping Advisers	%
Advertising	7
Friends/family	45
Manufacturer Web sites	5
News media	11
Online user reviews	13
Retail Web sites	4
Salespeople	1
Other	14

a. Construct a bar chart, a pie chart, and a Pareto chart.
b. Which graphical method do you think is best to portray these data?
c. What conclusions can you reach concerning women's most trusted shopping advisers?

2.5 What changes in their compensation package do workers in the United States want most? A survey by HudsonIndex.com indicated the following:

Perks	%
More money	42
Better health care	20
Better retirement	12
Work/family balance	10
Other	16

Source: *Adapted from Anne R. Carey and Chad Palmer, "What Workers Want," **www.usatoday.com**, April 9, 2007.*

a. Construct a bar chart, a pie chart, and a Pareto chart.
b. Which graphical method do you think is best to portray these data?
c. What conclusions can you reach concerning which perks workers want most?

2.6 The following table represents the North American power generation in 2007:

Source	%
Coal	47
Hydropower	13
Natural gas	19
Nuclear	19
Wind	1
Other	1

Source: *Data extracted from J. Schmit, "Taking on the solar Challenge," USA Today, January 21, 2008, pp. 1B, 2B.*

a. Construct a Pareto chart.
b. What percentage of power is derived from coal, nuclear, or natural gas?
c. Construct a pie chart.
d. For these data, do you prefer the Pareto chart or the pie chart? Why?

2.7 An article (K. Delaney, "How Search Engine Rules Cause Sites to Go Missing," *The Wall Street Journal*, March 13, 2007, pp. B1, B4) discussed the amount of Internet search results that Web surfers typically scan before selecting one. The following table represents the results for a sample of 2,369 people:

Amount of Internet Search Results Scanned	Percentage (%)
A few search results	23
First page of search results	39
First two pages	19
First three pages	9
More than first three pages	10

a. Construct a bar chart and a pie chart.
b. Which graphical method do you think is best to portray these data?
c. What conclusions can you reach concerning how people scan Internet search results?

2.8 U.S. companies spent more than $250 billion in advertising in 2005 (K. Delaney, "In Latest Deal, Google Steps Further into World of Old Media," *The Wall Street Journal*, January 18, 2006, pp. A1, A6). The spending was as follows:

Media	Amount ($billions)	Percentage (%)
Cinema	0.4	0.16
Direct mail	44.5	17.35
Internet	10.0	3.90
Magazines	23.9	9.32
Newspapers	50.2	19.57
Outdoor	5.7	2.22
Radio	20.6	8.03
TV	55.4	21.60
Other	45.8	17.86

a. Construct a bar chart and a pie chart.
b. Which graphical method do you think is best to portray these data?
c. What conclusions can you reach concerning how U.S. companies spend their advertising dollars?

2.2 Organizing Numerical Data

When the number of data values is large, you can organize numerical data into an ordered array or a stem-and-leaf display to help understand the information you have. Suppose you decide to undertake a study that compares the cost of a restaurant meal in an urban area to the cost of a similar meal in the suburbs outside the city. The data file Restaurants contains the data for 50 urban restaurants and 50 suburban restaurants, as shown in Table 2.5. The data are not arranged in order from lowest to highest. This arrangement makes it difficult to arrive at conclusions concerning the price of meals in the two geographical areas.

TABLE 2.5

Cost per Person at 50 Urban Restaurants and 50 Suburban Restaurants

Urban									
65	48	32	27	47	45	36	55	48	33
45	46	39	44	45	63	54	20	55	73
51	34	28	65	44	43	50	29	33	41
41	52	48	48	38	52	33	40	36	51
39	38	22	35	35	16	74	57	52	68
Suburban									
47	43	44	41	44	48	50	48	38	36
28	25	44	55	20	36	30	44	24	32
29	42	53	27	68	34	30	24	61	34
47	29	26	42	54	51	34	39	39	40
42	40	61	27	37	37	40	39	43	36

The Ordered Array

An **ordered array** is a sequence of data, in rank order, from the smallest value to the largest value. Table 2.6 contains ordered arrays for the cost of meals at urban restaurants and suburban restaurants. From Table 2.6 you can see that the cost of a meal at the urban restaurants is between $16 and $74 and the cost of a meal at the suburban restaurants is between $20 and $68.

TABLE 2.6

Ordered Arrays of Cost per Person at 50 Urban Restaurants and 50 Suburban Restaurants

Urban									
16	20	22	27	28	29	32	33	33	33
34	35	35	36	36	38	38	39	39	40
41	41	43	44	44	45	45	45	46	47
48	48	48	48	50	51	51	52	52	52
54	55	55	57	63	65	65	68	73	74
Suburban									
20	24	24	25	26	27	27	28	29	29
30	30	32	34	34	34	36	36	36	37
37	38	39	39	39	40	40	40	41	42
42	42	43	43	44	44	44	44	47	47
48	48	50	51	53	54	55	61	61	68

The Stem-and-Leaf Display

A **stem-and-leaf display** organizes data into groups (called stems) so that the values within each group (the leaves) branch out to the right on each row. The resulting display allows you to see how the data are distributed and where concentrations of data exist. To see how to construct a stem-and-leaf display, suppose that 15 students from your class eat lunch at a fast-food restaurant. The following data are the amounts ($) spent for lunch:

5.40 4.30 4.80 5.50 7.30 8.50 6.10 4.80 4.90 4.90 5.50 3.50 5.90 6.30 6.60

To form the stem-and-leaf display, you use the units as the stems and round the decimals (the leaves) to one decimal place. For example, the first value is 5.40. Its stem (row) is 5, and its leaf is 4. The second value is 4.30. Its stem (row) is 4, and its leaf is 3. You continue with the remainder of the 15 values and then reorder the leaves within each stem as follows:

```
3 | 5
4 | 38899
5 | 4559
6 | 136
7 | 3
8 | 5
```

EXAMPLE 2.5

Stem-and-Leaf Display of the 2006 Return of the Low-Risk Mutual Funds

In this chapter's Using Statistics scenario, you are interested in studying the past performance of low-risk mutual funds. One measure of past performance is the return in 2006. Construct a stem-and-leaf display of the return in 2006 for the low-risk funds.

SOLUTION From Figure 2.7, you can conclude that:

• The lowest return in 2006 was 1.

• The highest return in 2006 was 28.

• The returns in 2006 were concentrated between 18 and 23.

• Only one mutual fund had a 2006 return below 5, and only two low-risk mutual funds had a 2006 return above 25.

Notice that due to the large number of values, Minitab subdivides each stem into five sub-stems containing leaves with 0 and 1, 2 and 3, 4 and 5, 6 and 7, and 8 and 9.

FIGURE 2.7

Minitab Stem-and-Leaf Display of the Returns of Low-Risk Mutual Funds in 2006

See Section M2.5 to create this. (PHStat2 users, see Section P2.5 to create an equivalent display.)

```
Stem-and-leaf of Return 2006-Low Risk  N  = 202
Leaf Unit = 1.0


   1    0  1
   1    0
   2    0  5
   6    0  6667
  13    0  8888899
  26    1  0000001111111
  33    1  2223333
  66    1  444444444444444455555555555555555555
 (40)   1  6666666666666666666666666667777777777777
  96    1  88888888888888888888888888899999999999999999999999999999999
  38    2  0000000000000001111111111
  13    2  2222223333
   3    2  4
   2    2  6
   1    2  8
```

Problems for Section 2.2

LEARNING THE BASICS

2.9 Form an ordered array, given the following data from a sample of $n = 7$ midterm exam scores in accounting:

68 94 63 75 71 88 64

2.10 Form a stem-and-leaf display, given the following data from a sample of $n = 7$ midterm exam scores in finance:

80 54 69 98 93 53 74

2.11 Form an ordered array, given the following data from a sample of $n = 7$ midterm exam scores in marketing:

88 78 78 73 91 78 85

2.12 Form an ordered array, given the following stem-and-leaf display from a sample of $n = 7$ midterm exam scores in information systems:

```
5 | 0
6 |
7 | 446
8 | 19
9 | 2
```

APPLYING THE CONCEPTS

2.13 The following is a stem-and-leaf display representing the amount of gasoline purchased, in gallons (with leaves in tenths of gallons), for a sample of 25 cars that use a particular service station on the New Jersey Turnpike:

```
 9 | 147
10 | 02238
11 | 125566777
12 | 223489
13 | 02
```

a. Place the data into an ordered array.
b. Which of these two displays seems to provide more information? Discuss.
c. What amount of gasoline (in gallons) is most likely to be purchased?
d. Is there a concentration of the purchase amounts in the center of the distribution?

2.14 As player salaries have increased, the cost of attending baseball games has increased dramatically. The following data in the file **BBCost** represent the cost of four tickets, two beers, four soft drinks, four hot dogs, two game programs, two baseball caps, and the parking fee for one car for each of the 30 major league baseball teams in 2007.

166, 321, 215, 192, 190, 151, 140, 166, 260, 207, 191, 137, 148, 230, 165, 157, 252, 167, 160, 164, 215, 229, 142, 251, 200, 146, 217, 202, 184, 196

Source: *Data extracted from* **teammarketing.com** *March 29, 2008.*

a. Place the data into an ordered array.
b. Construct a stem-and-leaf display for these data.
c. Which of these two displays seems to provide more information? Discuss.
d. Around what value, if any, are the costs of attending a baseball game concentrated? Explain.

2.15 The file MoviePrices contains data on the price for two tickets, with online service charges, large popcorn, and two medium soft drinks at a sample of six theater chains:

$36.15 $31.00 $35.05 $40.25 $33.75 $43.00

Source: *Data extracted from K. Kelly, "The Multiplex Under Siege,"* The Wall Street Journal, *December 24–25, 2005, pp. P1, P5.*

a. Place the data into an ordered array.
b. Construct a stem-and-leaf display for these data.
c. Which of these two displays seems to provide more information? Discuss.
d. Around what value, if any, are the movie prices concentrated? Explain.

2.16 The file Chicken contains data on the total fat, in grams per serving, for a sample of 20 chicken sandwiches from fast-food chains. The data are as follows:

7 8 4 5 16 20 20 24 19 30 23 30 25 19 29 29 30 30 40 56

Source: *Data extracted from "Fast Food: Adding Health to the Menu,"* Consumer Reports, *September 2004, pp. 28–31.*

a. Place the data into an ordered array.
b. Construct a stem-and-leaf display.
c. Does the ordered array or the stem-and-leaf display provide more information? Discuss.
d. Around what value, if any, are the total fat amounts concentrated? Explain.

2.17 The data in the file Dark Chocolate represent the cost per ounce ($), for a sample of 14 dark chocolate bars.

0.68 0.72 0.92 1.14 1.42 0.94 0.77
0.57 1.51 0.57 0.55 0.86 1.41 0.90

Source: *Data extracted from "Dark Chocolate: Which Bars are Best?"* Consumer Reports, *September 2007, p. 8.*

a. Place the data into an ordered array.
b. Construct a stem-and-leaf display.
c. Does the ordered array or the stem-and-leaf display provide more information? Discuss.
d. Around what value, if any, is the cost of dark chocolate bars concentrated? Explain.

2.3 Tables and Charts for Numerical Data

When you have a data set that contains a large number of values, reaching conclusions from an ordered array or a stem-and-leaf display can be difficult. In such circumstances, you need to present data in tables and charts such as the frequency and percentage distributions, histogram, polygon, and cumulative percentage polygon (ogive).

The Frequency Distribution

The **frequency distribution** is a summary table in which the data are arranged into numerically ordered **classes**. In constructing a frequency distribution, you must give attention to selecting the appropriate *number* of classes for the table, determining a suitable *width* of a class, and establishing the *boundaries* of each **class grouping** to avoid overlapping.

The number of classes you use depends on the number of values in the data. Larger numbers of values allow for a larger number of classes. In general, the frequency distribution should have at least 5 classes but no more than 15. Having too few or too many classes provides little new information.

When developing a frequency distribution, you define each class by class intervals of equal width. To determine the **width of a class interval**, you divide the **range** (highest value - lowest value) of the data by the number of classes desired.

DETERMINING THE WIDTH OF A CLASS INTERVAL

$$\text{Width of interval} = \frac{\text{Range}}{\text{number of classes}} \qquad (2.1)$$

Because the urban restaurant data consist of a sample of 50 restaurants, about 10 classes are acceptable. From the ordered array in Table 2.6 on page 33, the range of the data is $74 − $16 = $58. Using Equation (2.1), you approximate the width of the class interval as follows:

$$\text{Width of interval} = \frac{58}{10} = 5.8$$

You should choose an interval width that simplifies reading and interpretation. Therefore, instead of using an interval width of $5.80, you should select an interval width of $5.00.

To construct the frequency distribution table, you should establish clearly defined **class boundaries** for each class so that the values can be properly tallied into the classes. You place each value in one and only one class. You must avoid overlapping of classes.

Because you have set the width of each class interval for the restaurant data at $5, you need to establish the boundaries of the various classes so as to include the entire range of values. Whenever possible, you should choose these boundaries to simplify reading and interpretation. Thus, for the urban restaurants, because the cost ranges from $16 to $74, the first class interval ranges from $15 to less than $20, the second from $20 to less than $25, and so on, until they have been tallied into 12 classes. Each class has an interval width of $5, without overlapping. The center of each class, the **class midpoint**, is halfway between the lower boundary of the class and the upper boundary of the class. Thus, the class midpoint for the class from $15 to under $20 is $17.50, the class midpoint for the class from $20 to under $25 is $22.50, and so on. Table 2.7 is a frequency distribution of the cost per meal for the 50 urban restaurants and the 50 suburban restaurants.

TABLE 2.7

Frequency Distributions of the Cost per Meal for 50 Urban Restaurants and 50 Suburban Restaurants

Cost per Meal ($)	Urban Frequency	Suburban Frequency
15 but less than 20	1	0
20 but less than 25	2	3
25 but less than 30	3	7
30 but less than 35	5	6
35 but less than 40	8	9
40 but less than 45	6	13
45 but less than 50	9	4
50 but less than 55	7	4
55 but less than 60	3	1
60 but less than 65	1	2
65 but less than 70	3	1
70 but less than 75	2	0
Total	50	50

The frequency distribution allows you to draw conclusions about the major characteristics of the data. For example, Table 2.7 shows that the cost of meals at urban restaurants is concentrated between $30 and $55, and the cost of meals at suburban restaurants is clustered between $25 and $45.

If the data set does not contain many values, one set of class boundaries may provide a different picture than another set. For example, for the restaurant data, using a class-interval width of 6.0 instead of 5.0 (as was used in Table 2.7) may cause shifts in the way the values distribute among the classes.

You can also get shifts in data concentration when you choose different lower and upper class boundaries. Fortunately, as the sample size increases, alterations in the selection of class boundaries affect the concentration of data less and less.

EXAMPLE 2.6

Frequency Distributions of the 2006 Return for Growth and Value Mutual Funds

TABLE 2.8
Frequency Distributions of the 2006 Return for Growth and Value Mutual Funds

In the Using Statistics scenario, you are interested in comparing the 2006 return of growth and value mutual funds. Construct frequency distributions for the growth funds and the value funds.

SOLUTION The 2006 returns of the growth funds are highly concentrated between 0 and 15, whereas the 2006 returns of the value funds are highly concentrated between 10 and 25 (see Table 2.8). You should not directly compare the frequencies of the growth funds and the value funds because there are 464 growth funds and 404 value funds in the sample. Proportions or relative frequencies and percentages are introduced below.

2006 Return	Growth Frequency	Value Frequency
−10 but less than −5	6	0
−5 but less than 0	21	0
0 but less than 5	75	1
5 but less than 10	189	14
10 but less than 15	121	102
15 but less than 20	39	208
20 but less than 25	12	71
25 but less than 30	1	7
30 but less than 35	0	0
35 but less than 40	0	1
Total	464	404

The Relative Frequency Distribution and the Percentage Distribution

Because you usually want to know the proportion or the percentage of the total that is in each group, the relative frequency distribution or the percentage distribution is preferred to the frequency distribution.

The **proportion** in each group is equal to the number of frequencies in each class divided by the total number of values. The **relative frequency** is another word for the proportion. You then compute the percentage in each group by multiplying the proportion by 100%.

COMPUTING THE PROPORTION OR RELATIVE FREQUENCY

The proportion or relative frequency is the number of frequencies in each class divided by the total number of values.

$$\text{Proportion} = \text{Relative Frequency} = \frac{\text{frequency in each class}}{\text{total number of values}} \quad \text{(2.2)}$$

Thus, if there are 80 values and the frequency in a certain class is 20, the proportion of values in that class is

$$\frac{20}{80} = 0.25$$

and the percentage is

$$0.25 \times 100\% = 25\%$$

When you are comparing two or more groups that have different sample sizes, you must use either a relative frequency distribution or a percentage distribution. You form the **relative frequency distribution** by first determining the frequency (the number of values) in each class and then dividing by the total number of values. See Equation (2.2). For example, in Table 2.7 on page 36, there are 50 urban restaurants and the cost per meal at 3 of these restaurants is between \$25 and \$30. Therefore, as shown in Table 2.9, the proportion (or relative frequency) of meals that cost between \$25 and \$30 at urban restaurants is

$$\frac{3}{50} = 0.06$$

You form the **percentage distribution** by multiplying each proportion (or relative frequency) by 100%. Thus, the proportion of meals at urban restaurants that cost between $50 and $55 is 7 divided by 50, or 0.14, and the percentage is 14%. Table 2.9 presents the relative frequency distribution and percentage distribution of the cost of meals at urban and suburban restaurants.

TABLE 2.9

Relative Frequency Distributions and Percentage Distributions of the Cost of Meals at Urban and Suburban Restaurants

Cost per Meal ($)	Urban		Suburban	
	Relative Frequency	Percentage	Relative Frequency	Percentage
15 but less than 20	0.02	2.0	0.00	0.0
20 but less than 25	0.04	4.0	0.06	6.0
25 but less than 30	0.06	6.0	0.14	14.0
30 but less than 35	0.10	10.0	0.12	12.0
35 but less than 40	0.16	16.0	0.18	18.0
40 but less than 45	0.12	12.0	0.26	26.0
45 but less than 50	0.18	18.0	0.08	8.0
50 but less than 55	0.14	14.0	0.08	8.0
55 but less than 60	0.06	6.0	0.02	2.0
60 but less than 65	0.02	2.0	0.04	4.0
65 but less than 70	0.06	6.0	0.02	2.0
70 but less than 75	0.04	4.0	0.00	0.0
Total	1.00	100.0	1.00	100.0

From Table 2.9, you conclude that meals cost more at urban restaurants than at suburban restaurants. Also 18% of the meals cost between $45 and $50 at urban restaurants as compared to 8% of the meals at suburban restaurants; and only 6% of the meals cost between $25 and $30 at urban restaurants as compared to 14% of the meals at suburban restaurants.

EXAMPLE 2.7

Relative Frequency Distributions and Percentage Distributions of the 2006 Return for Growth and Value Mutual Funds

In the Using Statistics scenario, you are interested in comparing the 2006 return for growth and value mutual funds. Construct relative frequency distributions and percentage distributions for the growth funds and the value funds.

SOLUTION You conclude (see Table 2.10) that the 2006 return for the growth funds is much lower than for the value funds. For example, 5.82% of growth funds have negative returns, while none of the value funds have negative returns. Of the growth funds, 16.16% have returns between 0 and 5 as compared to only 0.25% of the value funds. Also, more of the value funds have higher returns. For example, 51.49% of the value funds have a return between 15 and 20, whereas only 8.41% of the growth funds have a return between 15 and 20.

TABLE 2.10

Relative Frequency Distributions and Percentage Distributions of the 2006 Return for Growth and Value Mutual Funds

2006 Return	Growth		Value	
	Proportion	Percentage	Proportion	Percentage
−10 but less than −5	0.0129	1.29	0.0000	0.00
−5 but less than 0	0.0453	4.53	0.0000	0.00
0 but less than 5	0.1616	16.16	0.0025	0.25
5 but less than 10	0.4073	40.73	0.0347	3.47
10 but less than 15	0.2608	26.08	0.2525	25.25
15 but less than 20	0.0841	8.41	0.5149	51.49
20 but less than 25	0.0259	2.59	0.1757	17.57
25 but less than 30	0.0022	0.22	0.0173	1.73
30 but less than 35	0.0000	0.00	0.0000	0.00
35 but less than 40	0.0000	0.00	0.0025	0.25
Total*	1.0001	100.01	1.0001	100.01

Error due to rounding

The Cumulative Distribution

The **cumulative percentage distribution** provides a way of presenting information about the percentage of items that are less than a certain value. For example, you might want to know what percentage of the urban restaurant meals cost less than $20, less than $30, less than $50, and so on. The percentage distribution is used to form the cumulative percentage distribution. Table 2.11 illustrates how to develop the cumulative percentage distribution for the cost of meals at urban restaurants. This table shows that 0.00% of the meals cost less than $15, 2% cost less than $20, 6% cost less than $25 (because 4% of the meals cost between $20 and $25), and so on, until all 100% of the meals cost less than $75.

Cost per Meal ($)	Percentage	Percentage of Meals Less Than Lower Boundary of Class Interval
15 but less than 20	2	0
20 but less than 25	4	2
25 but less than 30	6	6 = 2 + 4
30 but less than 35	10	12 = 2 + 4 + 6
35 but less than 40	16	22 = 2 + 4 + 6 + 10
40 but less than 45	12	38 = 2 + 4 + 6 + 10 + 16
45 but less than 50	18	50 = 2 + 4 + 6 + 10 + 16 + 12
50 but less than 55	14	68 = 2 + 4 + 6 + 10 + 16 + 12 + 18
55 but less than 60	6	82 = 2 + 4 + 6 + 10 + 16 + 12 + 18 + 14
60 but less than 65	2	88 = 2 + 4 + 6 + 10 + 16 + 12 + 18 + 14 + 6
65 but less than 70	6	90 = 2 + 4 + 6 + 10 + 16 + 12 + 18 + 14 + 6 + 2
70 but less than 75	4	96 = 2 + 4 + 6 + 10 + 16 + 12 + 18 + 14 + 6 + 2 + 6
75 but less than 80	0	100 = 2 + 4 + 6 + 10 + 16 + 12 + 18 + 14 + 6 + 2 + 6 + 4

Table 2.12 summarizes the cumulative percentages of the cost of urban and suburban restaurant meals. The cumulative distribution clearly shows that the cost of meals is lower in suburban restaurants than in urban restaurants. Table 2.12 shows that 20% of the meals at suburban restaurants cost less than $30 as compared to only 12% of the meals at urban restaurants; 32% of the meals at suburban restaurants cost less than $35 as compared to only 22% of the meals at urban restaurants; and 76% of the meals at suburban restaurants cost less than $45 as compared to only 50% of the meals at urban restaurants.

Cost ($)	Urban Percentage of Restaurants with Meals Less Than Indicated Value	Suburban Percentage of Restaurants with Meals Less Than Indicated Value
15	0	0
20	2	0
25	6	6
30	12	20
35	22	32
40	38	50
45	50	76
50	68	84
55	82	92
60	88	94
65	90	98
70	96	100
75	100	100

EXAMPLE 2.8

Cumulative Percentage Distributions of the 2006 Return for Growth and Value Mutual Funds

In the Using Statistics scenario, you are interested in comparing the 2006 return of growth and value mutual funds. Construct cumulative percentage distributions for the growth funds and the value funds.

SOLUTION The cumulative distribution in Table 2.13 indicates that more of the growth funds have lower returns than the value funds. The table shows that 5.82% of the growth funds have negative returns as compared to none of the value funds; 21.98% of the growth funds have returns below 5 as compared to 0.25% of the value funds; and 62.71% of the growth funds have returns below 10 as compared to 3.72% of the value funds.

TABLE 2.13

Cumulative Percentage Distributions of the 2006 Return for Growth and Value Funds

2006 Return	Growth Fund Percentage Less Than Indicated Value	Value Fund Percentage Less Than Indicated Value
−10	0.00	0.00
−5	1.29	0.00
0	5.82	0.00
5	21.98	0.25
10	62.71	3.72
15	88.79	28.97
20	97.20	80.46
25	99.79	98.03
30	100.00	99.76
35	100.00	99.76
40	100.01*	100.01*

Error due to rounding.

The Histogram

A **histogram** is a bar chart for grouped numerical data in which the frequencies or percentages of each group of numerical data are represented as individual vertical bars. In a histogram, there are no gaps between adjacent bars as there is in a bar chart of categorical data. You display the variable of interest along the horizontal (X) axis. The vertical (Y) axis represents either the frequency or the percentage of values per class interval.

Figure 2.8 displays a Microsoft Excel frequency histogram for the cost of meals at urban restaurants and suburban restaurants. The histogram for urban restaurants indicates that the

FIGURE 2.8

Microsoft Excel histograms for the cost of restaurant meals—Urban Restaurants and Suburban Restaurants

See Sections E2.9 or P2.6 to create this. (Minitab users, see Section M2.6 to create an equivalent chart.)

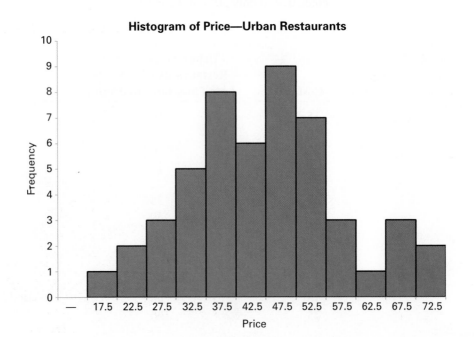

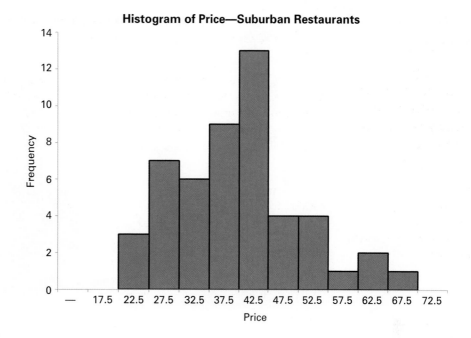

FIGURE 2.8
Continued

Histogram of Price—Suburban Restaurants

cost of meals is concentrated between approximately $30 and $55. Very few meals at urban restaurants cost less than $20 or more than $60. The histogram for suburban restaurants shows that the cost of meals is concentrated between $25 and $45. Very few meals at suburban restaurants cost less than $20 or more than $55.

EXAMPLE 2.9

Histograms of the 2006 Return for Growth and Value Mutual Funds

In the Using Statistics scenario, you are interested in comparing the 2006 return of growth and value mutual funds. Construct histograms for the growth funds and the value funds.

SOLUTION Figure 2.9 shows that the distribution of the growth funds has more low returns as compared to the value funds, which have more high returns. The return for growth funds is concentrated between 0 and 15, whereas the return for value funds is concentrated between 10 and 25.

FIGURE 2.9

Microsoft Excel Histograms of the 2006 return for growth and value funds

See Sections E2.9 or P2.6 to create this. (Minitab users, see Section M2.6 to create an equivalent chart.)

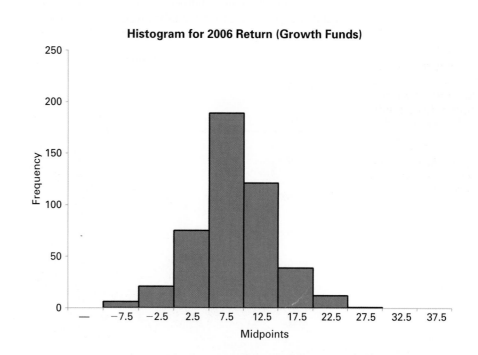

Histogram for 2006 Return (Growth Funds)

FIGURE 2.9
Continued

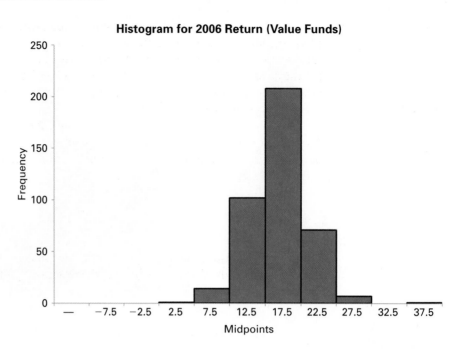

The Polygon

Constructing multiple histograms on the same graph when comparing two or more sets of data is confusing. Superimposing the vertical bars of one histogram on another histogram makes interpretation difficult. When there are two or more groups, you should use a percentage polygon.

> PERCENTAGE POLYGON
>
> A **percentage polygon** is formed by having the midpoint of each class represent the data in that class and then connecting the sequence of midpoints at their respective class percentages.

Figure 2.10 displays percentage polygons for the cost of meals at urban and suburban restaurants. The polygon for the cost of meals at suburban restaurants is concentrated to the left of (corresponding to lower cost) the polygon for the cost of meals at urban restaurants. The highest percentage of meals at the suburban restaurants are for a class midpoint of $42.50, whereas the highest percentage of meals at the urban restaurants are for a class midpoint of $47.50.

FIGURE 2.10

Microsoft Excel percentage polygons of the cost of restaurant meals for urban and suburban restaurants

See Section P2.7 to create this.

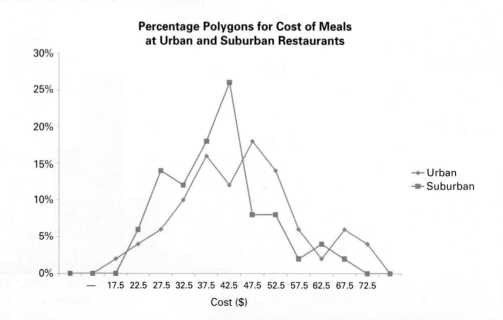

The polygons in Figure 2.10 have points whose values on the X axis represent the midpoint of the class interval. For example, look at the points plotted at $X = 42.5$ ($42.50). The point for the cost of meals at suburban restaurants (the higher one) represents the fact that 26% of the meals at these restaurants cost between $40 and $45. The point for the cost of meals at urban restaurants (the lower one) represents the fact that 12% of meals at these restaurants cost between $40 and $45.

When you construct polygons or histograms, the vertical (Y) axis should show the true zero, or "origin," so as not to distort the character of the data. The horizontal (X) axis does not need to show the zero point for the variable of interest, although the range of the variable should include the major portion of the axis.

EXAMPLE 2.10

Percentage Polygons of the 2006 Return for Growth and Value Mutual Funds

In the Using Statistics scenario, you are interested in comparing the 2006 return of growth and value mutual funds. Construct percentage polygons for the 2006 return for growth funds and value funds.

SOLUTION Figure 2.11 shows that the distribution of the 2006 return of growth funds is lower than the value funds, which has more high returns. The highest percentage of 2006 returns for the growth funds is at 7.5, whereas the highest percentage of 2006 returns for the value funds is at 17.5.

FIGURE 2.11

Microsoft Excel percentage polygons of the 2006 return

See Section P2.7 to create this.

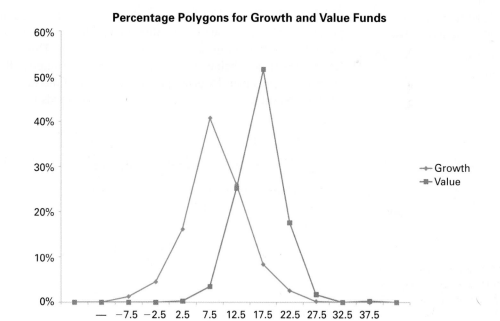

Percentage Polygons for Growth and Value Funds

The Cumulative Percentage Polygon (Ogive)

The **cumulative percentage polygon**, or **ogive**, displays the variable of interest along the X axis and the cumulative percentages along the Y axis.

Figure 2.12 illustrates the Microsoft Excel cumulative percentage polygons of the cost of meals at urban and suburban restaurants. Most of the curve of the cost of meals at the urban restaurants is located to the right of the curve for the suburban restaurants. This indicates that the urban restaurants have fewer meals that cost below a particular value. For example, 38% of the meals at urban restaurants cost less than $40 as compared to 50% of the meals at suburban restaurants.

FIGURE 2.12

Microsoft Excel
cumulative percentage
polygons of the cost of
restaurant meals at urban
and suburban restaurants

*See Section P2.7 to create
this.*

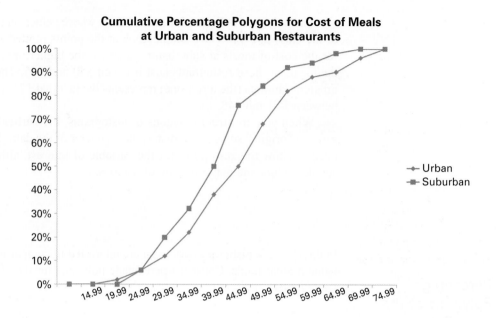

Cumulative Percentage Polygons for Cost of Meals
at Urban and Suburban Restaurants

EXAMPLE 2.11

Cumulative
Percentage
Polygons of the
2006 Return for
Growth and Value
Mutual Funds

In the Using Statistics scenario, you are interested in comparing the 2006 return of growth and value mutual funds. Construct cumulative percentage polygons of the 2006 return for the growth funds and the value funds.

SOLUTION Figure 2.13 illustrates the Microsoft Excel cumulative percentage polygons of the 2006 return for growth and value funds. The curve for the 2006 return of value funds is located to the right of the curve for the growth funds. This indicates that the value funds have fewer 2006 returns below a particular value. For example, 88.79% of the growth funds have 2006 returns less than 15 as compared to 28.97% of the value funds. You can conclude that, in general, the value funds outperformed the growth funds in 2006.

FIGURE 2.13

Microsoft Excel
cumulative percentage
polygons of the 2006
return of growth funds
and value funds

*See Section P2.7 to create
this.*

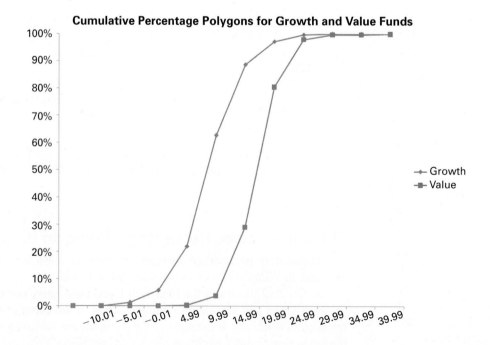

Cumulative Percentage Polygons for Growth and Value Funds

Problems for Section 2.3

LEARNING THE BASICS

2.18 The values for a set of data vary from 11.6 to 97.8.

a. If these values are grouped into nine classes, indicate the class boundaries.

b. What class-interval width did you choose?

c. What are the nine class midpoints?

2.19 The GMAT scores from a sample of 50 applicants to an MBA program indicate that none of the applicants scored below 450. A frequency distribution was formed by choosing class intervals 450 to 499, 500 to 549, and so on, with the last class having an interval from 700 to 749. Two applicants scored in the interval 450 to 499, and 16 applicants scored in the interval 500 to 549.

a. What percentage of applicants scored below 500?

b. What percentage of applicants scored between 500 and 549?

c. What percentage of applicants scored below 550?

d. What percentage of applicants scored below 750?

APPLYING THE CONCEPTS

2.20 The following data (contained in the file **Utility**) represent the cost of electricity during July 2008 for a random sample of 50 one-bedroom apartments in a large city:

Raw Data on Utility Charges ($)									
96	171	202	178	147	102	153	197	127	82
157	185	90	116	172	111	148	213	130	165
141	149	206	175	123	128	144	168	109	167
95	163	150	154	130	143	187	166	139	149
108	119	183	151	114	135	191	137	129	158

a. Form a frequency distribution and a percentage distribution that have class intervals with the upper class boundaries $99, $119, and so on.

b. Construct a histogram and a percentage polygon.

c. Form a cumulative percentage distribution and plot a cumulative percentage polygon.

d. Around what amount does the monthly electricity cost seem to be concentrated?

2.21 As player salaries have increased, the cost of attending baseball games has increased dramatically. The data in the file **BBCost** represent the cost of four tickets, two beers, four soft drinks, four hot dogs, two game programs, two baseball caps, and the parking fee for one car for each of the 30 major league teams 2007. The following is a histogram created for these data.

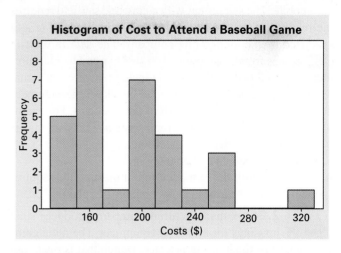

What conclusions can you reach concerning the cost of attending a baseball game at different ballparks?

2.22 The data in the file **PropertyTaxes** contains the property taxes per capita for the fifty states and the District of Columbia. The following is a histogram and cumulative percentage polygon created for these data.

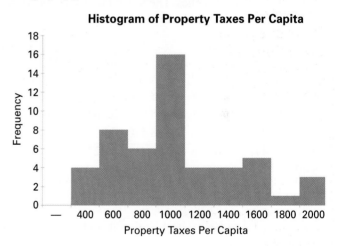

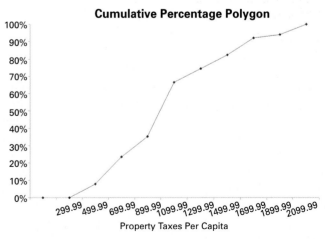

What conclusions can you reach concerning the property taxes per capita?

2.23 One operation of a mill is to cut pieces of steel into parts that will later be used as the frame for front seats in an automobile. The steel is cut with a diamond saw and requires the resulting parts to be within ±0.005 inch of the length specified by the automobile company. The data in the file Steel comes from a sample of 100 steel parts. The measurement reported is the difference in inches between the actual length of the steel part, as measured by a laser measurement device, and the specified length of the steel part. For example, the first value, −0.002, represents a steel part that is 0.002 inch shorter than the specified length.

a. Construct a percentage histogram.

b. Is the steel mill doing a good job in meeting the requirements set by the automobile company? Explain.

✓SELF Test **2.24** A manufacturing company produces steel housings for electrical equipment. The main component part of the housing is a steel trough that is made out of a 14-gauge steel coil. It is produced using a 250-ton progressive punch press with a wipe-down operation that puts two 90-degree forms in the flat steel to make the trough. The distance from one side of the form to the other is critical because of weatherproofing in outdoor applications. The company requires that the width of the trough be between 8.31 inches and 8.61 inches. The following (contained in the file Trough) are the widths of the troughs, in inches, for a sample of 49 troughs.

```
8.312  8.343  8.317  8.383  8.348  8.410  8.351  8.373
8.481  8.422  8.476  8.382  8.484  8.403  8.414  8.419
8.385  8.465  8.498  8.447  8.436  8.413  8.489  8.414
8.481  8.415  8.479  8.429  8.458  8.462  8.460  8.444
8.429  8.460  8.412  8.420  8.410  8.405  8.323  8.420
8.396  8.447  8.405  8.439  8.411  8.427  8.420  8.498
8.409
```

a. Construct a frequency distribution and a percentage distribution.

b. Construct a percentage histogram and a percentage polygon.

c. Plot a cumulative percentage polygon.

d. What can you conclude about the number of troughs that will meet the company's requirements of troughs being between 8.31 and 8.61 inches wide?

2.25 The manufacturing company in Problem 2.24 also produces electric insulators. If the insulators break when in use, a short circuit is likely to occur. To test the strength of the insulators, destructive testing in high-powered labs is carried out to determine how much *force* is required to break the insulators. Force is measured by observing how many pounds must be applied to the insulator before it breaks. The strengths of 30 insulators (contained in the file Force) are as follows:

```
1,870  1,728  1,656  1,610  1,634  1,784  1,522  1,696
1,592  1,662  1,866  1,764  1,734  1,662  1,734  1,774
1,550  1,756  1,762  1,866  1,820  1,744  1,788  1,688
1,810  1,752  1,680  1,810  1,652  1,736
```

a. Construct a frequency distribution and a percentage distribution.

b. Construct a percentage histogram and a percentage polygon.

c. Plot a cumulative percentage polygon.

d. What can you conclude about the strength of the insulators if the company requires a force measurement of at least 1,500 pounds before breaking?

2.26 The ordered arrays in the accompanying table (and contained in the file Bulbs) show the life (in hours) of a sample of forty 100-watt lightbulbs produced by Manufacturer A and a sample of forty 100-watt lightbulbs produced by Manufacturer B.

Manufacturer A					Manufacturer B				
684	697	720	773	821	819	836	888	897	903
831	835	848	852	852	907	912	918	942	943
859	860	868	870	876	952	959	962	986	992
893	899	905	909	911	994	1,004	1,005	1,007	1,015
922	924	926	926	938	1,016	1,018	1,020	1,022	1,034
939	943	946	954	971	1,038	1,072	1,077	1,077	1,082
972	977	984	1,005	1,014	1,096	1,100	1,113	1,113	1,116
1,016	1,041	1,052	1,080	1,093	1,153	1,154	1,174	1,188	1,230

a. Form a frequency distribution and a percentage distribution for each manufacturer, using the following class-interval widths for each distribution:
  1. Manufacturer A: 650 but less than 750, 750 but less than 850, and so on.
  2. Manufacturer B: 750 but less than 850, 850 but less than 950, and so on.

b. Construct percentage histograms on separate graphs and plot the percentage polygons on one graph.

c. Form cumulative percentage distributions and plot cumulative percentage polygons on one graph.

d. Which manufacturer has bulbs with a longer life—Manufacturer A or Manufacturer B? Explain.

2.27 The following data (contained in the file Drink) represent the amount of soft drink in a sample of fifty 2-liter bottles:

```
2.109 2.086 2.066 2.075 2.065 2.057 2.052 2.044 2.036 2.038
2.031 2.029 2.025 2.029 2.023 2.020 2.015 2.014 2.013 2.014
2.012 2.012 2.012 2.010 2.005 2.003 1.999 1.996 1.997 1.992
1.994 1.986 1.984 1.981 1.973 1.975 1.971 1.969 1.966 1.967
1.963 1.957 1.951 1.951 1.947 1.941 1.941 1.938 1.908 1.894
```

a. Construct a frequency distribution and a percentage distribution.

b. Construct a histogram and a percentage polygon.

c. Form a cumulative percentage distribution and plot a cumulative percentage polygon.

d. On the basis of the results of (a) through (c), does the amount of soft drink filled in the bottles concentrate around specific values?

2.4 Cross Tabulations

The study of patterns that may exist between two or more categorical variables is common in business. Often, by cross-tabulating the data, these patterns can be explained.

The Contingency Table

A **contingency table** presents the results of two categorical variables as **cross tabulations**. The joint responses are classified so that the categories of one variable are located in the rows and the categories of the other variable are located in the columns. The values located at the intersections of the rows and columns are called **cells**. Depending on the type of contingency table constructed, the cells for each row-column combination contain the frequency, the percentage of the overall total, the percentage of the row total, or the percentage of the column total.

Suppose that in the Using Statistics scenario, you want to examine whether there is any pattern or relationship between the level of risk and the objective of the mutual fund (growth versus value). Table 2.14 summarizes this information for all 868 mutual funds.

TABLE 2.14

Contingency Table Displaying Fund Objective and Fund Risk

See Sections E2.11, P2.8, or M2.7 to create this.

OBJECTIVE	High	Average	Low	Total
Growth	302	140	22	464
Value	53	171	180	404
Total	355	311	202	868

(RISK LEVEL)

You construct this contingency table by tallying the joint responses for each of the 868 mutual funds with respect to objective and risk into one of the six possible cells in the table. The first fund listed in the Mutual Funds file is classified as a growth fund with a low risk. Thus, you tally this joint response into the cell that is the intersection of the first row and third column. The remaining 867 joint responses are recorded in a similar manner. Each cell contains the frequency for the row-column combination.

In order to further explore any possible pattern or relationship between objective and fund risk, you can construct contingency tables based on percentages. You first convert these results into percentages based on the following three totals:

1. The overall total (i.e., the 868 mutual funds)
2. The row totals (i.e., 464 growth funds and 404 value funds)
3. The column totals (i.e., 355 high, 311 average, and 202 low)

Tables 2.15, 2.16, and 2.17 summarize these percentages.

TABLE 2.15

Contingency Table Displaying Fund Objective and Fund Risk, Based on Percentage of Overall Total

OBJECTIVE	High	Average	Low	Total
Growth	34.79	16.13	2.53	53.46
Value	6.11	19.70	20.74	46.54
Total	40.90	35.83	23.27	100.00

(RISK LEVEL)

TABLE 2.16

Contingency Table Displaying Fund Objective and Fund Risk, Based on Percentage of Row Total

OBJECTIVE	High	Average	Low	Total
Growth	65.09	30.17	4.74	100.00
Value	13.12	42.33	44.55	100.00
Total	40.90	35.83	23.27	100.00

(RISK LEVEL)

TABLE 2.17

Contingency Table Displaying Fund Objective and Fund Risk, Based on Percentage of Column Total

OBJECTIVE	RISK LEVEL			
	High	Average	Low	Total
Growth	85.07	45.02	10.89	53.46
Value	14.93	54.98	89.11	46.54
Total	100.00	100.00	100.00	100.00

Table 2.15 shows that 40.9% of the mutual funds sampled are high risk, 53.46% are growth funds, and 34.79% are high-risk funds that are growth funds. Table 2.16 shows that 65.09% of the growth funds are high risk and 4.74% are low risk. Table 2.17 shows that 85.07% of the high-risk funds and only 10.89% of the low-risk funds are growth funds. The tables reveal that growth funds are more likely to be high risk, whereas value funds are more likely to be low risk.

Problems for Section 2.4

LEARNING THE BASICS

2.28 The following data represent the responses to two questions asked in a survey of 40 college students majoring in business—What is your gender? (male = M; female = F) and What is your major? (accounting = A; computer information systems = C; marketing = M):

Gender:	M	M	M	F	M	F	F	M	F	M	F	M	M	M	M	F	F	M	F	F
Major:	A	C	C	M	A	C	A	A	C	C	A	A	A	M	C	M	A	A	A	C

Gender:	M	M	M	M	F	M	F	F	M	M	F	M	M	M	M	F	M	F	M	M
Major:	C	C	A	A	M	M	C	A	A	A	C	C	A	A	A	A	C	C	A	C

a. Tally the data into a contingency table where the two rows represent the gender categories and the three columns represent the academic-major categories.
b. Construct contingency tables based on percentages of all 40 student responses, based on row percentages and based on column percentages.

APPLYING THE CONCEPTS

2.29 Each day at a large hospital, several hundred laboratory tests are performed. The rate at which these tests are done improperly (and therefore need to be redone) seems steady, at about 4%. In an effort to get to the root cause of these non-conformances (i.e., tests that need to be redone), the director of the lab decided to keep records over a period of one week. The laboratory tests were subdivided by the shift of workers who performed the lab tests. The results are as follows:

LAB TESTS PERFORMED	SHIFT		
	Day	Evening	Total
Nonconforming	16	24	40
Conforming	654	306	960
Total	670	330	1,000

a. Construct contingency tables based on total percentages, row percentages, and column percentages.
b. Which type of percentage—row, column, or total—do you think is most informative for these data? Explain.
c. What conclusions concerning the pattern of nonconforming laboratory tests can the laboratory director reach?

SELF Test **2.30** A sample of 500 shoppers was selected in a large metropolitan area to determine various information concerning consumer behavior. Among the questions asked was "Do you enjoy shopping for clothing?" The results are summarized in the following table:

ENJOY SHOPPING FOR CLOTHING	GENDER		
	Male	Female	Total
Yes	136	224	360
No	104	36	140
Total	240	260	500

a. Construct contingency tables based on total percentages, row percentages, and column percentages.
b. What conclusions do you draw from these analyses?

2.31 As more Americans use cell phones, they question where it is okay to talk on cell phones. The following is a table of results, in percentages, for 2000 and 2006 (extracted from W. Koch, "Businesses Put a Lid on Chatterboxes," *USA Today*, February 7, 2006, p. 3A):

OK TO TALK ON A CELL PHONE IN A RESTAURANT	YEAR	
	2000	2006
Yes	31	21
No	69	79
Total	100	100

Discuss the changes in attitude concerning the use of cell phones in restaurants between 2000 and 2006.

2.32 An experiment was conducted by James Choi, David Laibson, and Brigitte Madrian to study the choices made in fund selection. When presented with four S&P 500 index funds that were identical except for their fees, under-graduate and MBA students chose the funds as follows (in percentages). Note that because the funds are identical, the best choice is the fund with the lowest fee.

	STUDENT GROUP	
FUND	**Undergraduate**	**MBA**
Lowest fee	19	19
Second-lowest fee	37	40
Third-lowest fee	17	23
Highest fee	27	18

Source: *Data extracted from J. Choi, D. Laibson, and B. Madrian, "Why Does the Law of One Practice Fail? An Experiment on Mutual Funds,"* **www.som.yale.edu/faculty/jjc83/fees.pdf.**

What do these results tell you about the differences between undergraduate and MBA students in their ability to choose S&P 500 index funds?

2.33 Where people turn to for news is different for various age groups. A study indicated where different age groups primarily get their news.

	AGE GROUP		
MEDIA	**Under 36**	**36–50**	**50+**
Local TV	107	119	133
National TV	73	102	127
Radio	75	97	109
Local newspaper	52	79	107
Internet	95	83	76

What differences are there in the age groups?

2.5 Scatter Plots and Time-Series Plots

When analyzing a single numerical variable such as the cost of a restaurant meal or the 2006 return, the appropriate charts to use include histograms, polygons, and cumulative percentage polygons, developed in Section 2.3. This section discusses scatter plots and time-series plots, which are used when you have two numerical variables.

The Scatter Plot

You use a **scatter plot** to examine possible relationships between two numerical variables. For each observation, you plot one variable on the horizontal X axis and the other variable on the vertical Y axis. For example, a marketing analyst could study the effectiveness of advertising by comparing weekly sales volumes and weekly advertising expenditures. Or a human resources director interested in the salary structure of the company could compare the employees' years of experience with their current salaries.

To demonstrate a scatter plot, you can examine the relationship between the cost of different items in various cities (extracted from K. Spors, "Keeping Up with . . . Yourself," *The Wall Street Journal*, April 11, 2005, p. R4). Table 2.18 provides the cost of a fast-food hamburger meal and the cost of two movie tickets in 10 cities around the world. The `Cost of Living` file contains the complete data set.

TABLE 2.18

Cost of a Fast-Food Hamburger Meal and Cost of Two Movie Tickets in 10 Cities

City	Hamburger	Movie Tickets
Tokyo	5.99	32.66
London	7.62	28.41
New York	5.75	20.00
Sydney	4.45	20.71
Chicago	4.99	18.00
San Francisco	5.29	19.50
Boston	4.39	18.00
Atlanta	3.70	16.00
Toronto	4.62	18.05
Rio de Janeiro	2.99	9.90

For each city, you plot the cost of a fast-food hamburger meal on the X axis, and the cost of two movie tickets on the Y axis. Figure 2.14 presents a Microsoft Excel scatter plot for these two variables.

FIGURE 2.14

Microsoft Excel scatter plot of the cost of a fast-food hamburger meal and the cost of two movie tickets

See Sections E2.12 or P2.9 to create this. (Minitab users, see Section M2.8 to create an equivalent chart.)

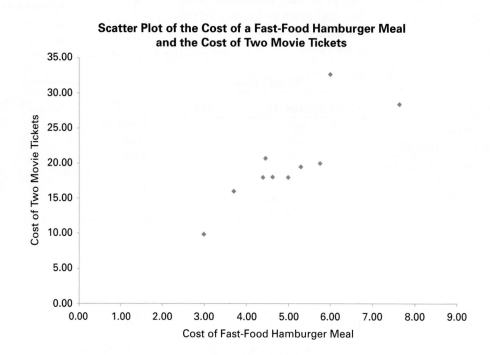

Although there is some variation, there appears to be a clearly increasing (positive) relationship between the cost of a fast-food hamburger meal and the cost of two movie tickets. In other words, cities in which the cost of a fast-food hamburger meal is low seem to also have a low cost of two movie tickets. Other pairs of variables may have a decreasing (negative) relationship in which one variable decreases as the other increases. The scatter plot will be studied again in Chapter 3, when the coefficient of correlation and the covariance are presented, and in Chapter 13, when regression analysis is developed.

The Time-Series Plot

A **time-series plot** is used to study patterns in the values of a numerical variable over time. Each value is plotted as a point in two dimensions with the time period on the horizontal X axis and the variable of interest on the Y axis.

To demonstrate a time-series plot, you can examine the yearly movie attendance, in billions, from 1999 to 2006 (extracted from C. Passy, "Good Night and Good Luck," *Palm Beach Post*, February 5, 2006, p. 1J and S. Bowles, "Box Office Breaks Its Downward Cycle," *USA Today*, March 7, 2007, p. 1D). Table 2.19 presents the data for the yearly movie attendance (see

TABLE 2.19

Movie Attendance, in Billions, from 1999 to 2006

Year	Attendance
1999	1.47
2000	1.42
2001	1.49
2002	1.63
2003	1.57
2004	1.53
2005	1.41
2006	1.45

the file Movies). Figure 2.15 is a time-series plot of the movie attendance (in billions) from 1999 to 2006. You can see that although movie attendance increased from 1999 to 2002, it declined from 2003 to 2005, before increasing slightly in 2006. Attendance in 2005 and 2006 was below attendance in 1999.

FIGURE 2.15

Microsoft Excel time-series plot of movie attendance from 1999 to 2006

See Section E2.13 to create this. (Minitab users, see Section M2.8 to create an equivalent chart.)

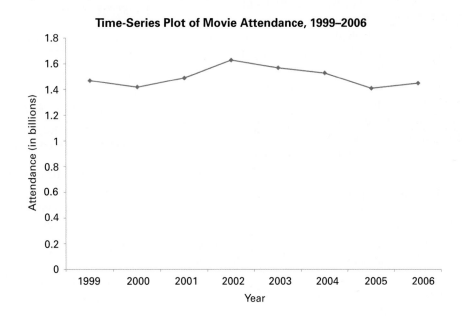

Problems for Section 2.5

LEARNING THE BASICS

2.34 The following is a set of data from a sample of $n = 11$ items:

X	7	5	8	3	6	10	12	4	9	15	18
Y	21	15	24	9	18	30	36	12	27	45	54

a. Construct a scatter plot.
b. Is there a relationship between X and Y? Explain.

2.35 The following is a series of annual sales (in millions of dollars) over an 11-year period (1996 to 2006):

Year	1996	1997	1998	1999	2000	2001	2002	2003	2004	2005	2006
Sales	13.0	17.0	19.0	20.0	20.5	20.5	20.5	20.0	19.0	17.0	13.0

a. Construct a time-series plot.
b. Does there appear to be any change in real annual sales over time? Explain.

APPLYING THE CONCEPTS

✓ SELF Test **2.36** There are several methods for calculating fuel economy. The following table (contained in the file Mileage) indicates the mileage as calculated by owners and by current government standards for nine car models:

Car	Owner	Government
2005 Ford F-150	14.3	16.8
2005 Chevrolet Silverado	15.0	17.8
2002 Honda Accord LX	27.8	26.2
2002 Honda Civic	27.9	34.2
2004 Honda Civic Hybrid	48.8	47.6
2002 Ford Explorer	16.8	18.3
2005 Toyota Camry	23.7	28.5
2003 Toyota Corolla	32.8	33.1
2005 Toyota Prius	37.3	56.0

Source: *Data extracted from J. Healey, "Fuel Economy Calculations to be Altered," USA Today, January 11, 2006, p. 1B.*

a. Construct a scatter plot with owner mileage on the X axis and current government standards mileage on the Y axis.
b. Does there appear to be a relationship between owner and current government standards mileage? If so, is the relationship positive or negative?

2.37 The file Chicken contains data on the calories and total fat (in grams per serving) for a sample of 20 chicken sandwiches from fast-food chains:

Source: *Data extracted from "Fast food: Adding Health to the Menu," Consumer Reports, September 2004, pp. 28–31.*

a. Construct a scatter plot with calories on the X axis and total fat on the Y axis.

b. What conclusions can you reach about the relationship between the calories and total fat in chicken sandwiches?

2.38 College basketball is big business, with coaches' salaries, revenues, and expenses in millions of dollars. The file Colleges-Basketball contains the coaches' salary and revenue for college basketball at selected schools in a recent year (extracted from R. Adams, "Pay for Playoffs," *The Wall Street Journal*, March 11–12, 2006, pp. P1, P8).

a. Do you think schools with higher revenues also have higher coaches' salaries?

b. Construct a scatter plot with revenue on the X axis and coaches' salaries on the Y axis.

c. Does the scatter plot confirm or contradict your answer to (a)?

2.39 College football players trying out for the NFL are given the Wonderlic standardized intelligence test. The file Wonderlic contains the average Wonderlic scores of football players trying out for the NFL and the graduation rate for football players at selected schools (extracted from S. Walker, "The NFL's Smartest Team," *The Wall Street Journal*, September 30, 2005, pp. W1, W10).

a. Construct a scatter plot with average Wonderlic score on the X axis and graduation rate on the Y axis.

b. What conclusions can you reach about the relationship between the average Wonderlic score and graduation rate?

2.40 The U.S. Bureau of Labor Statistics compiles data on a wide variety of workforce issues. The following table (contained in the file Unemployment) gives the monthly seasonally adjusted civilian unemployment rate for the United States from 2000 to 2007:

Month	2000	2001	2002	2003	2004	2005	2006	2007
January	4.0	4.2	5.7	5.8	5.7	5.2	4.7	4.6
February	4.1	4.2	5.7	5.9	5.6	5.4	4.8	4.5
March	4.0	4.3	5.7	5.9	5.7	5.1	4.7	4.4
April	3.8	4.4	5.9	6.0	5.5	5.1	4.7	4.5
May	4.0	4.3	5.8	6.1	5.6	5.1	4.6	4.5
June	4.0	4.5	5.8	6.3	5.6	5.0	4.6	4.6
July	4.0	4.6	5.8	6.2	5.5	5.0	4.8	4.7
August	4.1	4.9	5.7	6.1	5.4	4.9	4.7	4.7
September	3.9	5.0	5.7	6.1	5.4	5.1	4.6	4.7
October	3.9	5.3	5.7	6.0	5.4	4.9	4.4	4.8
November	3.9	5.5	5.9	5.9	5.4	5.0	4.5	4.7
December	3.9	5.7	6.0	5.7	5.4	4.9	4.5	5.0

Source: *"U.S. Bureau of Labour Statistics"* www.bls.gov, *April 22, 2008.*

a. Construct a time-series plot of the U.S. unemployment rate.

b. Does there appear to be any pattern?

2.41 In 2008, Wal-Mart Stores, Inc., operated more than 7,200 Wal-Marts, Supercenters, Sam's Clubs, and Neighborhood Markets, and reported revenues exceeding $373 billion. Sales for Wal-Mart are highly seasonal, and therefore you need to consider quarterly revenue. The fiscal year for the company ends on January 31. Thus, the fourth quarter of 2008 includes November and December of 2007 and January of 2008. The following table lists the quarterly revenues, in billions of dollars, from 2001 to 2008 (see the file Wal-Mart).

Quarter	2001	2002	2003	2004	2005	2006	2007	2008
1 (Feb–Apr)	43.0	48.6	55.0	56.7	64.8	71.6	79.6	85.4
2 (May–July)	46.1	53.3	59.7	62.6	69.7	76.8	84.5	91.2
3 (Aug–Oct)	45.7	51.8	58.8	62.4	68.5	75.4	83.5	90.9
4 (Nov–Jan)	56.6	64.2	71.1	74.5	82.2	88.6	98.1	106.3

Source: *Data extracted from Wal-Mart Stores. Inc.,* **investor.walmartstores.com,** *April 22, 2008.*

a. Construct a time-series plot of Wal-Mart's quarterly revenues.

b. What conclusions can you reach about the seasonal pattern and long-term growth in Wal-Mart's revenues?

2.42 The following table contained in the file Tvchannels (extracted from "At Home With More TV Channels," *USA Today*, April 10, 2007, p. A1) shows the average number of TV channels that the U.S. home received from 1985 to 2005:

Year	Number of TV Channels Received
1985	18.8
1990	33.2
1995	41.1
2000	61.4
2005	96.4

a. Construct a time-series plot for the average number of TV channels that the U.S. home received from 1985 to 2005.

b. What pattern, if any, is present in the data?

c. If you had to make a prediction of the average number of TV channels that the U.S. home will receive in 2010, what would you predict?

2.43 The following data, contained in the file Hotels, provide the average hotel room rate from 1996 to 2006 (data extracted from *USA Today* Snapshots, February 13, 2008, p. 1A):

Year	Rates ($)	Year	Rates ($)
1996	70.63	2002	83.54
1997	75.31	2003	82.52
1998	78.62	2004	86.23
1999	81.33	2005	90.88
2000	85.89	2006	97.78
2001	88.27		

a. Construct a time-series plot.

b. What pattern, if any, is present in the data?

c. If you had to make a prediction of the average room rate in 2007, what would you predict?

2.6 Misusing Graphs and Ethical Issues

Good graphical displays clearly and unambiguously reveal what the data convey. Unfortunately, many graphs presented in the media (broadcast, print, and online) are incorrect, misleading, or so unnecessarily complicated that they should never be used. To illustrate the misuse of graphs, the chart presented in Figure 2.16 is similar to one that was printed in *Time* magazine as part of an article on increasing exports of wine from Australia to the United States.

In Figure 2.16, the wineglass icon representing the 6.77 million gallons for 1997 does not appear to be almost twice the size of the wineglass icon representing the 3.67 million gallons for 1995, nor does the wineglass icon representing the 2.25 million gallons for 1992 appear to be twice the size of the wineglass icon representing the 1.04 million gallons for 1989. Part of the reason for this is that the three-dimensional wineglass icon is used to represent the two dimensions of exports and time. Although the wineglass presentation may catch the eye, the data should instead be presented in a summary table or a time-series plot.

FIGURE 2.16

"Improper" display of Australian wine exports to the United States, in millions of gallons

Source: *Based on S. Watterson, "Liquid Gold—Australians Are Changing the World of Wine. Even the French Seem Grateful,"* Time, November 22, 1999, p. 68.

We're drinking more . . .
Australian wine exports to the U.S. in millions of gallons

1.04   2.25   3.67   6.77

1989   1992   1995   1997

In addition to the type of distortion created by the wineglass icons in the *Time* magazine graph displayed in Figure 2.16, improper use of the vertical and horizontal axes leads to distortions. Figure 2.17 presents another graph used in the same *Time* magazine article.

FIGURE 2.17

"Improper" display of amount of land planted with grapes for the wine industry

Source: *Based on S. Watterson, "Liquid Gold—Australians Are Changing the World of Wine. Even the French Seem Grateful,"* Time, November 22, 1999, pp. 68–69.

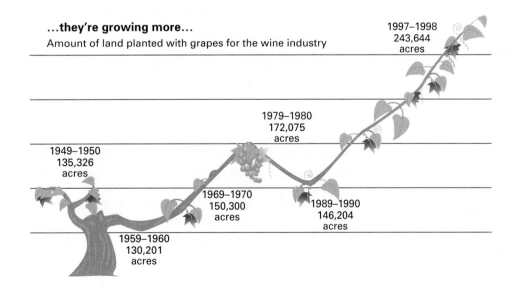

...they're growing more...
Amount of land planted with grapes for the wine industry

1997–1998
243,644
acres

1979–1980
172,075
acres

1949–1950
135,326
acres

1969–1970
150,300
acres

1989–1990
146,204
acres

1959–1960
130,201
acres

There are several problems in this graph. First, there is no zero point on the vertical axis. Second, the acreage of 135,326 for 1949–1950 is plotted above the acreage of 150,300 for 1969–1970. Third, it is not obvious that the difference between 1979–1980 and 1997–1998 (71,569 acres) is approximately 3.5 times the difference between 1979–1980 and 1969–1970 (21,775 acres). Fourth, there are no scale values on the horizontal axis. Years are plotted next to the acreage totals, not on the horizontal axis. Fifth, the values for the time dimension are not properly spaced along the horizontal axis. The value for 1979–1980 is much closer to 1989–1990 than it is to 1969–1970.

Other types of eye-catching displays that you typically see in magazines and newspapers often include information that is not necessary and just adds excessive clutter. Figure 2.18 represents one such display. The graph in Figure 2.18 shows those products with the largest market share for soft drinks. The graph suffers from too much clutter, although it is designed to show the differences in market share among the soft drinks. The display of the fizz for each soft drink takes up too much of the graph relative to the data. The same information could have been conveyed with a bar chart or pie chart.

FIGURE 2.18

"Improper" plot of market share of soft drinks

Source: *Based on Anne B. Carey and Sam Ward, "Coke Still Has Most Fizz," USA Today, May 10, 2000, p. 1B.*

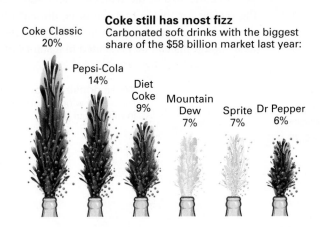

Coke still has most fizz
Carbonated soft drinks with the biggest share of the $58 billion market last year:

Coke Classic 20%
Pepsi-Cola 14%
Diet Coke 9%
Mountain Dew 7%
Sprite 7%
Dr Pepper 6%

Some guidelines for developing good graphs are as follows:

- The graph should not distort the data.
- The graph should not contain **chartjunk**, unnecessary adornments that convey no useful information.
- Any two-dimensional graph should contain a scale for each axis.
- The scale on the vertical axis should begin at zero.
- All axes should be properly labeled.
- The graph should contain a title.
- The simplest possible graph should be used for a given set of data.

Often these guidelines are unknowingly violated by individuals unaware of how to construct appropriate graphs.

Another issue is the temptation to create pretty charts if you use programs such as Microsoft Excel. Excel allows you to easily create fancy charts that may appear pretty, but are unwise choices. Taking a simple pie chart and making it prettier by adding exploded 3D slices is unwise as this can complicate a viewer's interpretation of the data. Uncommon chart choices such as doughnut, radar, surface, bubble, cone, and pyramid charts may look visually striking, but obscure the data in most cases.

To most effectively present information, make sure that the tables and charts you create are simple and clear.

Ethical Concerns

Inappropriate graphs raise ethical concerns. Such graphs can obscure unfavorable information or create false impressions of data, even if the inappropriate chart was developed naively. Consider the following sets of sales trend charts as shown in Figure 2.19. A casual viewer of these charts might think model B had the best sales trend and that models A and D had similar trends. A more careful examination of these line graphs shows that model B has the weakest sales trend and that model C and D actually have the *same* sales trend. A casual viewer gets misled because of the inconsistent scaling of the *Y* axis.

FIGURE 2.19
Four sales trend charts

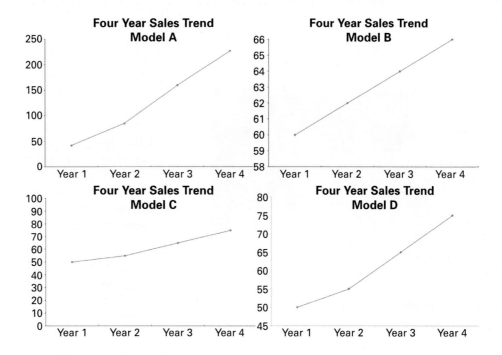

Problems for Section 2.6

APPLYING THE CONCEPTS

2.44 (Student Project) Bring to class a chart from a Web site, newspaper, or magazine that you believe to be a poorly drawn representation of a numerical variable. Be prepared to submit the chart to the instructor with comments as to why you believe it is inappropriate. Do you believe that the intent of the chart is to purposely mislead the reader? Also, be prepared to present and comment on this in class.

2.45 (Student Project) Bring to class a chart from a Web site, newspaper, or magazine that you believe to be a poorly drawn representation of a categorical variable. Be prepared to submit the chart to the instructor with comments as to why you consider it inappropriate. Do you believe that the intent of the chart is to purposely mislead the reader? Also, be prepared to present and comment on this in class.

2.46 (Student Project) According to its home page, Swivel is "a place where curious people explore data—all kinds of data." Go to **www.swivel.com** and explore the various graphical displays.

a. Select a graphical display that you think does a good job revealing what the data convey. Discuss why you think it is a good graphical display.

b. Select a graphical display that you think needs a lot of improvement. Discuss why you think that it is a poorly constructed graphical display.

2.47 The following visual display contains an overembellished chart similar to one that appeared in *USA Today*, dealing with the average consumer's Valentine's Day spending ("USA Today Snapshots: The Price of Romance," *USA Today*, February 14, 2007, p. 1B).

a. Describe at least one good feature of this visual display.
b. Describe at least one bad feature of this visual display.
c. Redraw the graph, using the guidelines given on page 54.

2.48 The following visual display contains an overembellished chart similar to one that appeared in *USA Today*, dealing with the estimated number of hours the typical American will spend using various media ("USA Today Snapshots: Minding Their Media," *USA Today*, March 2, 2007, p. 1B).

Media Usage
Estimated number of hours the typical American will spend using various media this year.

Listening to music 175
Reading newspapers 175
Using Internet 195
Listening to Radio 974
Watching TV 1555

a. Describe at least one good feature of this visual display.
b. Describe at least one bad feature of this visual display.
c. Redraw the graph, using the guidelines given on page 54.

2.49 The following visual display contains an overembellished chart similar to one that appeared in *USA Today*, dealing with which card is safer to use ("USA Today Snapshots: Credit Card vs. Debit Card," *USA Today*, March 14, 2007, p. 1B).

Credit Card vs. Debit Card:
Which one is safer to use?

Don't Mind 49%
Credit Card 32%
Debit Card 19%

a. Describe at least one good feature of this visual display.
b. Describe at least one bad feature of this visual display.
c. Redraw the graph, using the guidelines given on page 54.

2.50 An article in *The New York Times* (D. Rosato, "Worried About the Numbers? How About the Charts?" *The New York Times*, September 15, 2002, p. B7) reported on research done on annual reports of corporations by Professor Deanna Oxender Burgess of Florida Gulf Coast University. Professor Burgess found that even slight distortions in a chart changed readers' perception of the information. The article displayed sales information from the annual report of Zale Corporation and showed how results were exaggerated.

Using Internet or library sources, study the most recent annual report of a selected corporation. Find at least one chart in the report that you think needs improvement and develop an improved version of the chart. Explain why you believe the improved chart is better than the one included in the annual report.

2.51 Figures 2.1, 2.3, and 2.6 consist of a bar chart, a pie chart, and a Pareto chart for where people prefer to do their banking (see pages 27, 28, and 31).
a. Use the chart features of Microsoft Excel to construct an exploded pie chart, a doughnut chart, a cone chart, and a pyramid chart for where people prefer to do their banking.
b. Which graphs do you prefer—the bar chart, pie chart, and Pareto chart or the exploded pie chart, doughnut chart, cone chart, and pyramid chart? Explain.

2.52 Figures 2.2 and 2.4 consist of a bar chart and a pie chart for the risk level for the mutual fund data (see pages 27 and 28).
a. Use the chart features of Microsoft Excel to develop an exploded pie chart, a doughnut chart, a cone chart, and a pyramid chart for the risk level of the mutual funds.
b. Do you prefer the bar chart and pie chart, or the exploded pie chart, doughnut chart, cone chart, and pyramid chart? Explain.

USING STATISTICS @ Choice Is Yours, Part I Revisited

In the Using Statistics scenario, you were hired by the Choice Is Yours Investment company to assist investors interested in mutual funds, a market basket of securities. A sample of 868 mutual funds was selected and information on the funds and past performance history recorded. For each of the 868 funds, data were collected on nine variables. With so much information, summarizing all these numbers required the use of properly selected graphical displays.

From bar charts and pie charts, you were able to illustrate that about 41% of the funds were classified as high risk, about 36% average risk, and only about 23% low risk. Cross tabulations of the funds by risk level and whether the funds main objective was growth or value, revealed that growth funds are more likely to be high risk, whereas value funds are more likely to be low risk. After constructing histograms on the 2006 return, you were able to conclude that both types of funds had returns that were approximately bell-shaped. The growth funds had more low returns as compared to the value funds, which had more high returns. The return for growth funds was concentrated between 0 and 15, whereas the return for vale funds is concentrated between 10 and 25. With these insights, you can inform your clients on how the different funds performed. Of course, past performance history does not guarantee future performance.

Graphical methods such as these are an important first step in summarizing and interpreting data. Although the proper display of data (as discussed in section 2.6) helps to avoid ambiguity, graphical methods always contain a certain degree of subjectivity. Next, you will need to select the proper types of numerical measures to further describe the mutual funds' past performance. Chapter 3 presents descriptive numerical measures (for example, mean, median, and mode).

SUMMARY

As you can see in Table 2.20, this chapter discusses data presentation. You have used various tables and charts to draw conclusions about where people prefer to bank, about the cost of restaurant meals in an urban area and its suburbs, and about the set of mutual funds in the Using Statistics scenario. Now that you have studied tables and charts, in Chapter 3 you will learn about a variety of numerical descriptive measures useful for data analysis and interpretation.

TABLE 2.20

Roadmap for Selecting Tables and Charts

Type of Analysis	Type of Data	
	Numerical	**Categorical**
Tabulating, organizing, and graphically presenting the values of a variable	Ordered array, stem-and-leaf display, frequency distribution, relative frequency distribution, percentage distribution, cumulative percentage distribution, histogram, polygon, cumulative percentage polygon **(Sections 2.2 and 2.3)**	Summary table, bar chart, pie chart, Pareto chart **(Section 2.1)**
Graphically presenting the relationship between two variables	Scatter plot, time-series plot **(Section 2.5)**	Contingency table **(Section 2.4)**

KEY EQUATIONS

WIDTH OF INTERVAL

$$\text{Width of interval} = \frac{\text{Range}}{\text{number of classes}} \qquad (2.1)$$

PROPORTION

$$\text{Proportion} = \text{Relative Frequency} = \frac{\text{frequency in each class}}{\text{total number of values}} \qquad (2.2)$$

KEY TERMS

CHAPTER REVIEW PROBLEMS

CHECKING YOUR UNDERSTANDING

2.53 How do histograms and polygons differ in terms of construction and use?

2.54 Why would you construct a summary table?

2.55 What are the advantages and/or disadvantages of using a bar chart, a pie chart, or a Pareto chart?

2.56 Compare and contrast the bar chart for categorical data with the histogram for numerical data.

2.57 What is the difference between a time-series plot and a scatter plot?

2.58 Why is it said that the main feature of the Pareto chart is its ability to separate the "vital few" from the "trivial many"? Discuss.

2.59 What are the three different ways to break down the percentages in a contingency table?

APPLYING THE CONCEPTS

2.60 The following data represent the breakdown of the price of a new college textbook:

Revenue Categories	Percentage	
Publisher	64.8	
Manufacturing costs		32.3
Marketing and promotion		15.4
Administrative costs and taxes		10.0
After-tax profit		7.1
Bookstore	22.4	
Employee salaries and benefits		11.3
Operations		6.6
Pretax profit		4.5
Author	11.6	
Freight	1.2	

Source: *Data extracted from T. Lewin, "When Books Break the Bank,"* The New York Times, *September 16, 2003, pp. B1, B4.*

a. Using the four categories publisher, bookstore, author, and freight, construct a bar chart, a pie chart, and a Pareto chart.

b. Using the four subcategories of publisher and three subcategories of bookstore along with the author and freight categories, construct a Pareto chart.

c. Based on the results of (a) and (b), what conclusions can you reach concerning who gets the revenue from the sales of new college textbooks? Do any of these results surprise you? Explain.

2.61 The following data represent the payment method used by young adults between 18 and 24 years of age:

Payment Method	Percentage
Cash	37
Check	2
Credit card	16
Debit card	44
Other	1

a. Construct a bar chart, a pie chart, and a Pareto chart.

b. What conclusions can you reach about the payment method used by young adults between 18 and 24 years of age?

2.62 People conduct hundreds of millions of search queries every day. In response, businesses are estimated to spend almost $20 billion annually on online ad spending (K. J. Delaney, "The New Benefits of Web-Search Queries," *The Wall Street Journal*, February 6, 2007, p. B3). The following represents the categories of online ad spending and the results of a Yahoo! keyword tool for searches related to sneakers.

Estimated 2007 U.S. Online Ad Spending

Type	Spending ($billions)
Classified	3.32
Display ads	3.90
Paid search	8.29
Rich media/video	2.15
Other	1.85
Total	19.51

Results of a Yahoo! Keyword Tool for Searches Related to "Sneakers"

Search result	Number of Occurrences
Jordan sneaker	13,240
Nike sneaker	8,139
Puma sneaker	6,768
Sneaker	58,995
Sneaker pimps*	15,357

Sneaker pimps is a British electropop band.

a. For type of online ad spending, construct a bar chart, a pie chart, and a Pareto chart.
b. Which graphical method do you think is best to portray these data?
c. For the results of "sneakers" searches, construct a bar chart, a pie chart, and a Pareto chart.
d. Which graphical method do you think is best to portray these data?
e. What conclusions can you reach concerning online ad spending and the results of "sneakers" searches?

2.63 The owner of a restaurant serving Continental-style entrées is interested in studying patterns of patron demand for the Friday-to-Sunday weekend time period. Records are maintained that indicate the type of entrée ordered. The data are as follows:

Type of Entrée	Number Served
Beef	187
Chicken	103
Duck	25
Fish	122
Pasta	63
Shellfish	74
Veal	26

a. Construct a percentage summary table for the types of entrées ordered.
b. Construct a bar chart, a pie chart, and a Pareto chart for the types of entrées ordered.
c. Do you prefer a Pareto chart or a pie chart for these data? Why?
d. What conclusions can the restaurant owner reach concerning demand for different types of entrées?

2.64 Suppose that the owner of the restaurant in Problem 2.63 is also interested in studying the demand for dessert during the same time period. She decided that two other variables, along with whether a dessert was ordered, are to be studied: the gender of the individual and whether a beef entrée is ordered. The results are as follows:

DESSERT ORDERED	GENDER		
	Male	Female	Total
Yes	96	40	136
No	224	240	464
Total	320	280	600

DESSERT ORDERED	BEEF ENTRÉE		
	Yes	No	Total
Yes	71	65	136
No	116	348	464
Total	187	413	600

a. For each of the two contingency tables, construct a contingency table of row percentages, column percentages, and total percentages.
b. Which type of percentage (row, column, or total) do you think is most informative for each gender? for beef entrée? Explain.
c. What conclusions concerning the pattern of dessert ordering can the owner of the restaurant reach?

2.65 The following data (extracted from R. Wolf, "Paper-Trail Voting Gets Organized Opposition," *USA Today*, April 24, 2007, p. 2A) represent the method for recording votes in the November 2006 election, broken down by percentage of counties in the United States using each method and the number of counties using each method in 2000 and 2006.

Method	Percentage of Counties Using Method in 2006
Electronic	36.6
Hand-counted paper ballots	1.8
Lever	2.0
Mixed	3.0
Optically scanned paper ballots	56.2
Punch card	0.4

Method	Number of Counties	
	2000	2006
Electronic	309	1,142
Hand-counted paper ballots	370	57
Lever	434	62
Mixed	149	92
Optically scanned paper ballots	1,279	1,752
Punch card	572	13

a. Construct a pie chart and a Pareto chart for the percentage of counties using the various methods.

b. What conclusions can you reach concerning the type of voting method used in November 2006?

c. What differences are there in the methods used in 2000 and 2006?

2.66 In summer 2000, a growing number of warranty claims on Firestone tires sold on Ford SUVs prompted Firestone and Ford to issue a major recall. An analysis of warranty-claims data helped identify which models to recall. A breakdown of 2,504 warranty claims based on tire size is given in the following table:

Tire Size	Warranty Claims
23575R15	2,030
311050R15	137
30950R15	82
23570R16	81
331250R15	58
25570R16	54
Others	62

Source: *Data extracted from Robert L. Simison, "Ford Steps Up Recall Without Firestone," The Wall Street Journal, August 14, 2000, p. A3.*

The 2,030 warranty claims for the 23575R15 tires can be categorized into ATX models and Wilderness models. The type of incident leading to a warranty claim, by model type, is summarized in the following table:

Incident	ATX Model Warranty Claims	Wilderness Warranty Claims
Tread separation	1,365	59
Blowout	77	41
Other/unknown	0,422	66
Total	1,864	166

Source: *Data extracted from Robert L. Simison, "Ford Steps Up Recall Without Firestone," The Wall Street Journal, August 14, 2000, p. A3.*

a. Construct a Pareto chart for the number of warranty claims by tire size. What tire size accounts for most of the claims?

b. Construct a pie chart to display the percentage of the total number of warranty claims for the 23575R15 tires that come from the ATX model and Wilderness model. Interpret the chart.

c. Construct a Pareto chart for the type of incident causing the warranty claim for the ATX model. Does a certain type of incident account for most of the claims?

d. Construct a Pareto chart for the type of incident causing the warranty claim for the Wilderness model. Does a certain type of incident account for most of the claims?

2.67 One of the major measures of the quality of service provided by any organization is the speed with which the organization responds to customer complaints. A large family-held department store selling furniture and flooring, including carpet, had undergone a major expansion in the past several years. In particular, the flooring department had expanded from 2 installation crews to an installation supervisor, a measurer, and 15 installation crews. During a recent year, the company got 50 complaints concerning carpet installation. The following data (contained in the file **Furniture**) represent the number of days between the receipt of the complaint and the resolution of the complaint:

```
54   5  35 137  31  27 152   2 123  81  74  27
11  19 126 110 110  29  61  35  94  31  26   5
12   4 165  32  29  28  29  26  25   1  14  13
13  10   5  27   4  52  30  22  36  26  20  23
33  68
```

a. Construct a frequency distribution and a percentage distribution.

b. Construct a histogram and a percentage polygon.

c. Form a cumulative percentage distribution and plot a cumulative percentage polygon (ogive).

d. On the basis of the results of (a) through (c), if you had to tell the president of the company how long a customer should expect to wait to have a complaint resolved, what would you say? Explain.

2.68 Data concerning 71 of the best-selling domestic beers in the United States are located in the file **Domesticbeer** . The values for three variables are included: percentage alcohol, number of calories per 12 ounces, and number of carbohydrates (in grams) per 12 ounces.

Source: *Data extracted from www.Beer100.com, May 1, 2008.*

a. Construct a percentage histogram for each of the three variables.

b. Construct three scatter plots: percentage alcohol versus calories, percentage alcohol versus carbohydrates, and calories versus carbohydrates.

c. Discuss the information you learned from studying the graphs in (a) and (b).

2.69 The data in the file **Spending** are the federal *per capita* spending, in thousands of dollars, for each state in 2004.

a. Develop an ordered array.

b. Plot a percentage histogram.

c. What conclusions can you reach about the differences in federal per-capita spending between the states?

2.70 The data in the file **SavingsRate** are the yields for a money market account, a one-year certificate of deposit (CD), and a five-year CD for 38 banks in south Florida, as of March 28, 2008 (extracted from **www.Bankrate.com**, March 28, 2008).

a. Construct a percentage histogram for each of the three variables.

b. Construct three scatter plots: money market account versus one-year CD, money market account versus five-year CD, and one-year CD versus five-year CD.

c. Discuss the information you learned from studying the graphs in (a) and (b).

2.71 The data in the file **CEO** represent the total compensation (in $millions) of CEOs of the large public companies in 2007 (extracted from "The Boss's Pay" *The Wall Street Journal*, April 14, 2008, pp. R5–R7).

a. Construct a frequency distribution and a percentage distribution.

b. Construct a histogram and a percentage polygon.

c. Construct a cumulative percentage distribution and plot a cumulative percentage polygon (ogive).

d. Based on (a) through (c), what conclusions can you reach concerning CEO compensation in 2007?

e. Are there any companies whose CEO has a total compensation below $500,000? If so, go to the company's Web site and see if you can find out a reason why the CEO has a total compensation below $500,000.

2.72 Studies conducted by a manufacturer of "Boston" and "Vermont" asphalt shingles have shown product weight to be a major factor in customers' perception of quality. Moreover, the weight represents the amount of raw materials being used and is therefore very important to the company from a cost standpoint. The last stage of the assembly line packages the shingles before the packages are placed on wooden pallets. When a pallet is full (a pallet for most brands holds 16 squares of shingles), it is weighed, and the measurement is recorded. The company expects pallets of its "Boston" brand-name shingles to weigh at least 3,050 pounds but less than 3,260 pounds. For the company's "Vermont" brand-name shingles, pallets should weigh at least 3,600 pounds but less than 3,800. The file **Pallet** contains the weights (in pounds) from a sample of 368 pallets of "Boston" shingles and 330 pallets of "Vermont" shingles.

a. For the "Boston" shingles, construct a frequency distribution and a percentage distribution having eight class intervals, using 3,015, 3,050, 3,085, 3,120, 3,155, 3,190, 3,225, 3,260, and 3,295 as the class boundaries.

b. For the "Vermont" shingles, construct a frequency distribution and a percentage distribution having seven class intervals, using 3,550, 3,600, 3,650, 3,700, 3,750, 3,800, 3,850, and 3,900 as the class boundaries.

c. Construct percentage histograms for the "Boston" shingles and for the "Vermont" shingles.

d. Comment on the distribution of pallet weights for the "Boston" and "Vermont" shingles. Be sure to identify the percentage of pallets that are underweight and overweight.

2.73 The data in the file **States** represent the results of the American Community Survey, a sampling of households taken in all states during the 2000 U.S. Census. For each of the variables average travel-to-work time in minutes, percentage of homes with eight or more rooms, median household income, and percentage of mortgage-paying homeowners whose housing costs exceed 30% of income:

a. Construct a frequency distribution and a percentage distribution.

b. Construct a histogram and a percentage polygon.

c. Construct a cumulative percentage distribution and plot a cumulative percentage polygon.

d. What conclusions about these four variables can you make based on the results of (a) through (c)?

2.74 The data in the file **Protein** indicate calorie and cholesterol information concerning popular protein foods (fresh red meats, poultry, and fish).

Source: *U.S. Department of Agriculture.*

a. Construct a percentage histogram for the amount of calories.

b. Construct a percentage histogram for the amount of cholesterol.

c. What conclusions can you reach from your analyses in (a) and (b)?

2.75 In Figure 2.14 on page 50, a scatter plot of the relationship between the cost of a fast-food hamburger meal and the cost of movie tickets in 10 different cities was constructed. The file **Cost of Living** also includes the overall cost index, the monthly rent for a two-bedroom apartment, the cost of a cup of coffee with service, the cost of dry-cleaning a men's blazer, and the cost of toothpaste.

a. Construct six separate scatter plots. For each, use the overall cost index as the Y axis. Use the monthly rent for a two-bedroom apartment, the costs of a cup of coffee with service, a fast-food hamburger meal, dry-cleaning a men's blazer, toothpaste, and movie tickets as the X axis.

b. What conclusions can you reach about the relationship of the overall cost index to these six variables?

2.76 In Problem 2.37 on page 51, using the data in the file **Chicken**, you constructed a scatter plot of calories with the total fat content of chicken sandwiches.

a. Construct a scatter plot of calories on the Y axis and carbohydrates on the X axis.

b. Construct a scatter plot of calories on the Y axis and sodium on the X axis.

c. Which variable (total fat, carbohydrates, or sodium) seems to be most closely related to calories? Explain.

2.77 The file **Gas Prices** contains the monthly average price of gasoline in the United States from January 2003, to April 2008. Prices are in dollars per gallon.

Source: *"U.S. Department of Energy,"* **www.eia.doe.gov,** *May 2, 2008.*

a. Construct a time-series plot.

b. What pattern, if any, is present in the data?

2.78 The data contained in the file Drink represent the amount of soft drink filled in a sample of 50 consecutive 2-liter bottles. The results are listed horizontally in the order of being filled:

2.109 2.086 2.066 2.075 2.065 2.057 2.052 2.044 2.036 2.038

2.031 2.029 2.025 2.029 2.023 2.020 2.015 2.014 2.013 2.014

2.012 2.012 2.012 2.010 2.005 2.003 1.999 1.996 1.997 1.992

1.994 1.986 1.984 1.981 1.973 1.975 1.971 1.969 1.966 1.967

1.963 1.957 1.951 1.951 1.947 1.941 1.941 1.938 1.908 1.894

a. Construct a time-series plot for the amount of soft drink on the *Y* axis and the bottle number (going consecutively from 1 to 50) on the *X* axis.

b. What pattern, if any, is present in these data?

c. If you had to make a prediction of the amount of soft drink filled in the next bottle, what would you predict?

d. Based on the results of (a) through (c), explain why it is important to construct a time-series plot and not just a histogram, as was done in Problem 2.27 on page 46.

2.79 The S&P 500 Index tracks the overall movement of the stock market by considering the stock prices of 500 large corporations. The data file Stocks2008 contains weekly data for this index as well as the daily closing stock price for three companies from January 2, 2008 to May 1, 2008. The variables included are:

WEEK—Week ending on date given
S&P—Weekly closing value for the S&P 500 Index
GE—Weekly closing stock price for General Electric
IBM—Weekly closing stock price for IBM
APPL—Weekly closing stock price for Apple

Source: *Data extracted from* **finance.yahoo.com,** *May 2, 2008.*

a. Construct a time-series plot for the weekly closing values of the S&P 500 Index, General Electric, IBM, and Apple.

b. Explain any patterns present in the plots.

c. Write a short summary of your findings.

2.80 (Class Project) Let each student in the class respond to the question "Which carbonated soft drink do you most prefer?" so that the teacher can tally the results into a summary table.

a. Convert the data to percentages and construct a Pareto chart.

b. Analyze the findings.

2.81 (Class Project) Let each student in the class be cross-classified on the basis of gender (male, female) and current employment status (yes, no) so that the teacher can tally the results.

a. Construct a table with either row or column percentages, depending on which you think is more informative.

b. What would you conclude from this study?

c. What other variables would you want to know regarding employment in order to enhance your findings?

REPORT WRITING EXERCISES

2.82 Referring to the results from Problem 2.72 on page 61 concerning the weight of "Boston" and "Vermont" shingles, write a report that evaluates whether the weight of the pallets of the two types of shingles are what the company expects. Be sure to incorporate tables and charts into the report.

2.83 Referring to the results from Problem 2.66 on page 60 concerning the warranty claims on Firestone tires, write a report that evaluates warranty claims on Firestone tires sold on Ford SUVs. Be sure to incorporate tables and charts into the report.

TEAM PROJECT

The data file Mutual Funds contains information regarding nine variables from a sample of 868 mutual funds. The variables are:

Category—Type of stocks comprising the mutual fund (small cap, mid cap, large cap)
Objective—Objective of stocks comprising the mutual fund (growth or value)
Assets—In millions of dollars
Fees—Sales charges (no or yes)
Expense ratio—Ratio of expenses to net assets in percentage
Return 2006—Twelve-month return in 2006
Three-year return—Annualized return, 2004–2006
Five-year return—Annualized return, 2002–2006
Risk—Risk-of-loss factor of the mutual fund (low, average, or high)

2.84 For the expense ratio:

a. Construct a percentage histogram.

b. Plot percentage polygons of the expense ratio for mutual funds that have fees and mutual funds that do not have fees on the same graph.

c. What conclusions about the expense ratio can you reach based on the results of (a) and (b)?

2.85 For the three-year annualized return from 2004 to 2006:

a. Construct a percentage histogram.

b. Plot percentage polygons of the three-year annualized return from 2004 to 2006 for growth mutual funds and value mutual funds on the same graph.

c. What conclusions about the three-year annualized return from 2004 to 2006 can you reach based on the results of (a) and (b)?

2.86 For the five-year annualized return from 2002 to 2006:

a. Construct a percentage histogram.

b. Plot percentage polygons of the five-year annualized return from 2002 to 2006 for growth mutual funds and value mutual funds on the same graph.

c. What conclusions about the five-year annualized return from 2002 to 2006 can you reach based on the results of (a) and (b)?

STUDENT SURVEY DATABASE

2.87 Problem 1.23 on page 13 describes a survey of 50 undergraduate students (see the file `Undergradsurvey`). For these data, construct all the appropriate tables and charts and write a report summarizing your conclusions.

2.88 Problem 1.23 on page 13 describes a survey of 50 undergraduate students (see the file `Undergradsurvey`).

a. Select a sample of 50 undergraduate students at your school and conduct a similar survey for those students.

b. For the data collected in (a), construct all the appropriate tables and charts and write a report summarizing your conclusions.

c. Compare the results of (b) to those of Problem 2.87.

2.89 Problem 1.24 on page 13 describes a survey of 40 MBA students (see the file `Gradsurvey`). For these data, construct all appropriate tables and charts and write a report summarizing your conclusions.

2.90 Problem 1.24 on page 13 describes a survey of 40 MBA students (see the file `Gradsurvey`).

a. Select a sample of 40 MBA students in your MBA program and conduct a similar survey for those students.

b. For the data collected in (a), construct all the appropriate tables and charts and write a report summarizing your conclusions.

c. Compare the results of (b) to those of Problem 2.89.

MANAGING THE *SPRINGVILLE HERALD*

Advertising fees are an important source of revenue for any newspaper. In an attempt to boost these revenues and to minimize costly errors, the management of the *Herald* has established a task force charged with improving customer service in the advertising department. Open a Web browser and link to **www.prenhall.com/HeraldCase/Ad_Errors.htm** (or open the `Ad_Errors.htm` file in the Student CD-ROM's Herald Case folder) to review the task force's data collection. Identify the data that are important in describing the customer service problems. For each set of data you identify, construct the graphical presentation you think is most appropriate for the data and explain your choice. Also, suggest what other information concerning the different types of errors would be useful to examine. Offer possible courses of action for either the task force or management to take that would support the goal of improving customer service.

WEB CASE

In the Using Statistics scenario, you were asked to gather information to help make wise investment choices. Sources for such information include brokerage firms and investment counselors. Apply your knowledge about the proper use of tables and charts in this Web Case about the claims of foresight and excellence by a Springville financial services firm.

Visit the EndRun Financial Services Web site at **www.prenhall.com/Springville/EndRun.htm** (or open the `EndRun.htm` file in the Student CD-ROM's Web Case folder). Review the company's investment claims and supporting data and then answer the following.

1. How does the presentation of the general information about EndRun on its home page affect your perception of the business?

2. Is EndRun's claim about having more winners than losers a fair and accurate reflection of the quality of its investment service? If you do not think that the claim is a fair and accurate one, provide an alternate presentation that you think is fair and accurate.

3. EndRun's "Big Eight" mutual funds are part of the sample found in the `Mutual Funds` worksheet. Is there any other relevant data from that file that could have been included in the Big Eight table? How would that new data alter your perception of EndRun's claims?

4. EndRun is proud that all Big Eight funds have gained in value over the past five years. Do you agree that EndRun should be proud of its selections? Why or why not?

REFERENCES

1. Huff, D., *How to Lie with Statistics* (New York: Norton, 1954).
2. *Microsoft Excel 2007* (Redmond, WA: Microsoft Corporation, 2007).
3. *Minitab for Windows Version 15* (State College, PA: Minitab, Inc., 2006).
4. Tufte, E. R., *Beautiful Evidence* (Cheshire, CT: Graphics Press, 2006).
5. Tufte, E. R., *Envisioning Information* (Cheshire, CT: Graphics Press, 1990).
6. Tufte, E. R., *The Visual Display of Quantitative Information*, 2nd ed. (Cheshire, CT: Graphics Press, 2002).
7. Tufte, E. R., *Visual Explanations* (Cheshire, CT: Graphics Press, 1997).
8. Wainer, H., *Visual Revelations: Graphical Tales of Fate and Deception from Napoleon Bonaparte to Ross Perot* (New York: Copernicus/Springer-Verlag, 1997).

Using Microsoft Excel for Tables and Charts

E2.1 Introduction

This appendix describes how to use Microsoft Excel to create tables and charts. If you plan to use PHStat2 with Microsoft Excel, read Appendix P2 "Using PHStat2 for Tables and Charts" on page 74. Because Excel 2007 changes many table and chart features, some appendix sections contain paired sets of instructions, such as Sections E2.2A and E2.2B, one for use with Excel 97–2003, the other for use with Excel 2007. Use only the set of instructions that applies to the Excel version that you have.

Before continuing, you should review the material in Appendix E1 on page 16 and Appendix C if you have not done so already.

Occasionally PHStat2 will be the only reasonable way to accomplish a task using Microsoft Excel. In such cases, an Excel appendix section will refer you to the appropriate PHStat2 appendix section.

E2.2 Creating Summary Tables

To create a summary table from unsummarized data, you create a PivotTable. To create a summary table from data already summarized in table form, enter the contents of the table into a blank worksheet, using row 1 cells for column headings.

You create a PivotTable by dragging the variable names of the unsummarized data into a form or template. Because the process differs between Excel 97–2003 and Excel 2007, use the instructions of either Sections E2.2A or E2.2B to complete this task.

E2.2A Creating PivotTables (Excel 97–2003)

To create a PivotTable in Excel 97–2003, open to the worksheet that contains your unsummarized data and select **Data → PivotTable Report** (Excel 97) or **Data → PivotTable and PivotChart Report** (Excel 2000–2003). When you make these selections you start the PivotTable Wizard, a sequence of three dialog boxes (four in Excel 97) that step you through the process of creating a PivotTable. Figure E2.1 shows the dialog boxes for Excel 2003. (Other versions have similar dialog boxes; Excel 97 uses four dialog boxes, breaking the third box into two.)

You step through these dialog boxes by clicking **Next** to advance to the next dialog box or **Back** to move back to a previous one. At any point, you can click **Cancel** to

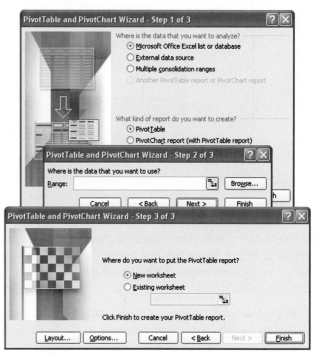

FIGURE E2.1 PivotTable Wizard steps (Excel 2003)

stop creating a PivotTable or click **Finish** to end the wizard and create a PivotTable. To create a summary table, make the following entries in the Wizard Step dialog boxes:

Wizard Step 1 Click **Microsoft Excel list or database** as the source data and **PivotTable** as the report type. (You do not select a report type in Microsoft Excel 97; PivotTable is assumed.)

Wizard Step 2 Enter the cell range of the data to be summarized in the PivotTable. This cell range must contain variable labels (column headings) in the first row of the range because the wizard, in Step 3, will use the cells in the first row as the names for your variables.

Wizard Step 3 First, click the **New worksheet** option as the location for your PivotTable. Then click **Layout** to display the Layout dialog box (see Figure E2.2). Design your table using the instructions in the next paragraph and then click **OK** to return to the Step 3 box. Then, click **Options** to display the PivotTable Options dialog box (see Figure E2.2). Enter **0** as the **For empty cells, show** value and click **OK** to return to the Wizard Step 3 dialog box. Then, click **Finish** to create the PivotTable.

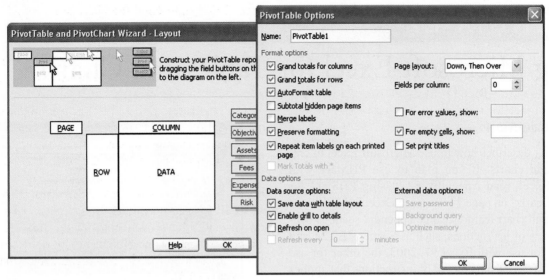

FIGURE E2.2 PivotTable Layout and Options dialog boxes (Excel 2000–2003)

(If you use Excel 97, the Layout dialog box appears as the Step 3 dialog box. When you click **Next** in this box, you then see a Step 4 dialog box that contains location options. There is no Options button in either the Step 3 or Step 4 dialog boxes in Excel 97.)

In the Layout dialog box of Step 3, drag the label of the variable to be summarized and drop it in the ROW area. Drag a second copy of this same label and drop it in the DATA area. This second label changes to **Count of variable** name to indicate that a count, or tally, of the occurrences of each category will be shown in the DATA area.

After Excel creates the PivotTable, close any floating PivotTable toolbar windows. Enter a title in cell A1 of the new worksheet that contains your PivotTable. Also, rename the new worksheet, using a descriptive name. In cell C4, enter **Percentage** and in cell C5, enter the formula in the form **=B5/B$n**, in which **n** is the row that contains the Grand Total. (If you do not understand the significance of the $ symbol, you can review Section E1.7.) For example, if the Grand Total row is row 8, enter **=B5/B$8**. Copy this formula down through all the category rows and format the cell range that contains these formulas for percentage display. Further adjust the table display as is necessary, using Section E1.7 as your guide. (You may also need to adjust the width of columns by dragging the column rules at the top of the worksheet.)

E2.2B Creating Pivottables (Excel 2007)

To create a PivotTable in Excel 2007, open to the worksheet that contains your unsummarized data and select **Insert → PivotTable**. In the Create PivotTable dialog box (see Figure E2.3), leave the **Select a table or range** option selected and change, if necessary, the **Table/Range** cell range. (In Figure E2.3, the cell range is for the mutual funds data found in the Data worksheet of **Mutual Funds.xls**.) Select the **New Worksheet** option and click **OK**.

FIGURE E2.3 Create PivotTable dialog box and PivotTable Field List task pane (Excel 2007)

In the PivotTable Field List task pane, drag the label of the variable to be summarized and drop it in the **Row Labels** box. Drag a second copy of this same label and drop it in the Σ **Values** box. This second label changes to **Count of variable name** to indicate that a count, or tally, of the occurrences of each category will be shown in the DATA area.

Right-click the PivotTable and click **Table Options** in the shortcut menu that appears. In the PivotTable Options dialog box (a reorganized version of the older one shown in Figure E2.2), click the **Layout & Format** tab, check **For empty cells show**, enter **0** as its value, and then click

OK. Close the PivotTable Field List task pane. Enter a title in cell A1 of the new worksheet that contains your PivotTable. Also, rename the new worksheet, using a descriptive name.

In cell C4, enter **Percentage** and in cell C5, enter the formula in the form **=B5/B$*n***, in which ***n*** is the row that contains the Grand Total. (If you do not understand the significance of the $ symbol, you can review Section E1.7.) For example, if the Grand Total row is row 8, enter **=B5/B$8**. Copy this formula down through all the category rows and format the cell range that contains these formulas for percentage display. Further adjust the table display as is necessary, using Section E1.7 as your guide. (You may also need to adjust the width of columns by dragging the column rules at the top of the worksheet.)

E2.3 Creating Charts: Overview

Although Microsoft Excel contains many features that create tables and charts, you can easily get improper results or otherwise get frustrated if you do not properly organize your worksheet data first. In Excel, charts are linked to sets of worksheet data, and the arrangement of that data influences the chart Excel creates. For example, when creating a scatter plot, Excel will always consider the first column of data as the *X* variable data. If you wanted to create the scatter plot of the cost of a fast-food hamburger meal and the cost of two movie tickets (Figure 2.14 on page 50), you would want to place the meal costs in a column to the left of the column containing the ticket costs.

The best way to avoid arrangement errors is to place your data on a separate worksheet using consecutive columns starting with column A. (Data worksheets in the Student CD-ROM Excel workbook files have this arrangement.) If you are using Microsoft Excel 2007, you should also select your data by dragging the mouse over your data, as explained in Appendix C, to prevent Excel 2007 from making a "bad" guess as to the table or chart you seek.

With these simple steps you will eliminate the most common errors that occur when using Excel charting features. However, creating a chart using Excel charting features does not necessarily end your task. Many charts will need minor reformatting to pass the strictest presentation standards. Illustrations in this book reflect such formatting and appendix sections throughout the book include reformatting instructions when appropriate.

Some charts, especially those created in Excel 97–2003, contain colored backgrounds (typically gray) that can interfere with clear printing or displaying of the chart. To remove the background in an Excel 97–2003 chart, right-click the background and click **Format Plot Area** in the shortcut menu. In the dialog box that appears, click the **None** option of the **Area** group and click **OK**. (This was done for all the charts shown in this book.) To remove a background in

Excel 2007, right-click the chart background and select **Layout → Plot Area** and select **None** in the Plot Area gallery.

Occasionally, you may open to a chart sheet and see only part of a (too-large) chart or see a (too-small) chart surrounded by a too-large frame mat. To display an optimally sized chart in Excel 97–2003, open to the chart sheet and press **Esc**. Select **View → Zoom** and then, in the Zoom dialog box, select the **Fit selection** option and click **OK**. To display an optimally sized chart in Excel 2007, use the Zoom slider on the lower right of the Excel window frame or click the chart and then select **Format** and use the items in the Size group. Finally, if the symbols, captions, and/or legends and titles prove too big or too small for you, you can usually change these elements by right-clicking over them and clicking the shortcut menu choice that contains the word **Format**.

If you use PHStat2, the charts created by PHStat2 will generally include these minor reformatting and enhancements discussed above.

E2.3A Creating Charts (Excel 97–2003)

To create a chart in Excel 97–2003, open to the worksheet containing your unsummarized data and select **Insert → Chart** to begin the Chart Wizard, a sequence of four dialog boxes that step you through the process of creating a chart. (Figure E2.4 shows these dialog boxes for Excel 2003. Excel 97, 2000, and 2002 have similar sets of dialog boxes.) To create a chart, make the following entries in the Wizard Step dialog boxes:

Wizard Step 1 Choose the chart type from either the **Standard Types** or **Custom Types** tab. Most of the charts you create in this text are chart types found in the Standard Types tab.

Wizard Step 2 Enter the cell range of the data to be charted in the **Data Range** tab. For some types of charts, you also enter the cell range or ranges that contain chart labeling information in the **Series** tab. Cell ranges in the Series tab must always be entered with their worksheet names as a formula, in the form =*SheetName*!*CellRange*.

Wizard Step 3 Enter titles and select formatting options for your chart in the various tabs of this dialog box. Unless told otherwise in later instructions, make the following entries and selections:

In the **Titles** tab, enter a title and enter axis labels if appropriate. In the **Axes** tab, click both the (X) axis and (Y) axis check boxes and click **Automatic** under the (X) axis check box. In the **Gridlines** tab, clear all the check boxes. In the **Legend** tab, clear the **Show legend** check box. In the **Data Labels** tab, click the **None** option under the **Data labels** heading. In the **Data Table** tab, clear the **Show data table** check box. (Not all tabs are displayed for all chart types. If a tab is not displayed, skip the instructions for the tab.)

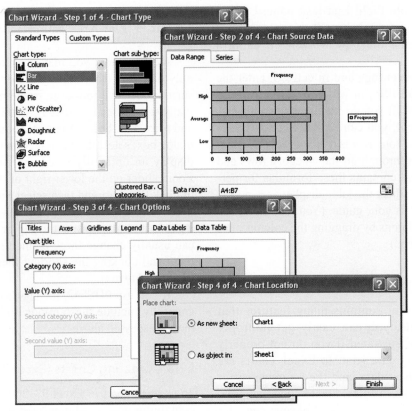

FIGURE E2.4   Chart Wizard dialog boxes (Excel 2003)

Wizard Step 4 Click the **As new sheet** option to place the chart on its own chart sheet. Then click **Finish** to create the chart.

*Because the Wizard Step 4 dialog box instructions never vary, they are not explicitly listed in later instructions. You should always click **As new sheet** and **Finish** in this dialog box when you create a chart.*

If you discover a mistake in your chart after your chart is created, right-click the chart and select **Chart Type, Source Data, Chart Options**, or **Location** to return to versions of the Wizard Step 1, Step 2, Step 3, or Step 4 dialog boxes, respectively.

E2.3B Creating Charts (Excel 2007)

To create a chart in Excel 2007, open to the worksheet that contains your unsummarized data. Select the cell range of the data to be charted. If your cell range contains two nonadjacent areas, hold down the **Ctrl** key as you drag and select each area. Select **Insert** and in the **Charts** group, click the chart type. From the drop-down gallery that appears, click the chart sub-type you want. To help distinguish sub-types, move the mouse pointer over a sub-type and wait for a description to be displayed. In Figure E2.5, the description for the bar chart "clustered bar" sub-type is displayed.

Customize your chart by clicking the chart and selecting the **Layout** tab of the Chart Tools ribbon group (or PivotChart Tools, if the chart is based on a PivotTable).

Review the settings for the members of the **Labels** and **Axes** groups in this tab. Unless told otherwise in later instructions, make the following entries and selections (for a given chart type, some of these items may be disabled and not available):

Click **Chart Title** and choose either **Centered Overlay Title** or **Above Chart**. Click **Axes Titles** ➔ **Primary Horizontal Axis Title** ➔ **Title Below Axis**. Click **Axes Titles** ➔ **Primary Vertical Axis Title** ➔ **Rotated Title**. (For charts with secondary axes, select **Title Below Axis** as the **Secondary Horizontal Axis Title** and **None** as the **Secondary Vertical Axis Title**.) Click **Data Labels** ➔ **None** and click **Data Table** ➔ **None**.

Click **Axes** ➔ **Primary Horizontal Title** ➔ **Show Left to Right Axis**. Click **Axes** ➔ **Primary Vertical Title** ➔ **Show Default Axis**. Some charts have secondary axes; for such charts, select **None** as the **Secondary Horizontal Axis Title** and **Show Default Axis** as the **Secondary Vertical Axis Title**. Click **Gridlines**. Select **None** for both the **Primary Horizontal Gridlines** and **Primary Vertical Gridlines**. Also select **None** for secondary gridlines, if the chart contains those as well.

Excel 2007 creates charts on worksheets. To move a chart to its own chart sheet (recommended), right-click the chart frame and click **Move Chart** in the shortcut menu that appears. In the Move Chart dialog box that appears, select the **New sheet** option and click **OK**.

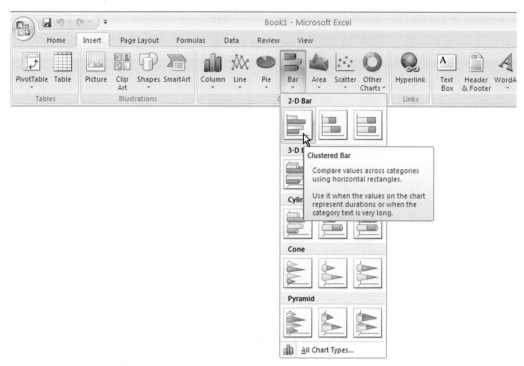

E2.4 Creating Bar and Pie Charts: Overview

You create bar and pie charts from summary tables such as PivotTables using Excel charting features. You cannot create bar and pie charts directly from unsummarized data using Excel unless you use PHStat2.

E2.4A Creating Bar and Pie Charts (Excel 97–2003)

Open to the worksheet that contains your summary table. If your summary table is a PivotTable, click a cell that is outside your PivotTable. Select **Insert → Chart** to begin the Chart Wizard and make the following entries in the Wizard Step dialog boxes:

Wizard Step 1 Click the **Standard Types** tab. For a bar chart, click **Bar** as the **Chart type** and then click the first **Chart sub-type** choice, labeled **Clustered Bar** when selected. For a pie chart, click **Pie** as the **Chart type** and then click the first **Chart sub-type** choice, labeled **Pie** when selected.

Wizard Step 2 Click the **Data Range** tab and enter the cell range of the category labels and the frequency counts as the **Data range**. If you used the instructions in Section E2.2 to create your summary table, this range will always start with cell A4 and end with a cell in column B. (You do not include the column C cells that contain the percentages.) Click the **Columns** option if it is visible. In some Excel versions the model chart shown in the dialog box contains additional boxed labels that you can ignore for now.

Wizard Step 3 Click the **Titles** tab. Enter a title as the **Chart title** and, if you are creating a bar chart, enter appro-

priate values for the **Category (X) axis** and **Value (Y) axis** titles. For a bar chart, click, in turn, the **Axes**, **Gridlines**, **Legend**, **Data Labels**, and **Data Table** tabs and adjust the settings, as discussed in Section E2.3A on page 67. For a pie chart, click the **Legend** tab and clear **Show legend** and then click the **Data Labels** tab. If you are using Excel 97 or Excel 2000, click the **Show label and percent** option; otherwise, click **Category name** and **Percentage**.

If the chart created contains the additional boxed labels, such as "Drop Page Fields Here," that you ignored in the Step 2 dialog box, right-click the category drop-down list on the chart sheet and click **Hide PivotChart Field Buttons**. This eliminates the clutter and makes your chart look more like the ones throughout Chapter 2.

E2.4B Creating Bar and Pie Charts (Excel 2007)

Open to the worksheet that contains your summary table. Click a cell inside your table and then select **Insert**. For a bar chart, click **Column** in the Charts group, and then click **Clustered Column** in the chart gallery. For a pie chart, click **Pie** in the Charts group, and then click **Pie** in the chart gallery. Adjust chart settings as discussed in Section E2.3B on page 68.

E2.5 Creating Pareto Charts: Overview

You create a Pareto chart from a modified summary table by using Excel charting features. You modify your summary table by adding a column for cumulative percentage. If you have used the Section E2.2 instructions to create a PivotTable, enter the heading **Cumulative Pctage** in cell D4 and enter the formula **=C5** in cell D5. In cell D6, enter the formula **=C6+D5** and copy this formula down through all the category rows of the summary table. Format the column D cell range that contains formulas for percentage display. Adjust the number of decimals displayed and the width of column D as necessary.

If you use Excel 2007, click cell B5 (the first frequency) and select **Home → Sort & Filter** (in the Editing group) → **Sort Largest to Smallest**. If you use Excel 97–2003, right-click cell A4 and click **Field Settings** in the shortcut menu (**Field**, if using Microsoft Excel 97). In the PivotTable Field dialog box that appears (see Figure E2.6), click **Advanced**. In the PivotTable Field Advanced Options dialog box that appears (also see Figure E2.4), select the **Descending** option and **Count of** *variable* from the **Using field** drop-down list. Click **OK** to return to the PivotTable Field dialog box and then click **OK** in that dialog box to return to the worksheet. (These last steps reorder the category rows in the table in descending order.)

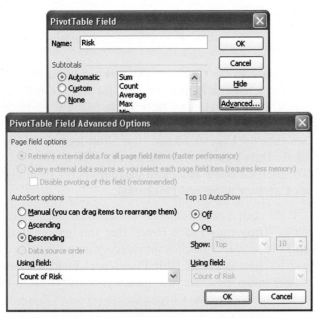

FIGURE E2.6 PivotTable Field and PivotTable Field Advanced Options dialog boxes (Excel 97–2003)

With these changes, you can proceed to creating the actual Pareto chart using the instructions appropriate for the Excel version you use.

E2.5A Creating a Pareto Chart (Excel 97–2003)

With your workbook opened to the worksheet that contains the modified summary table, click a cell that is outside the summary table. Select **Insert → Chart** to begin the Chart Wizard and make the following entries in the Wizard Step dialog boxes:

Wizard Step 1 Click the **Custom Types** tab. Click **Built-in** and then click **Line - Column on 2 Axes** as the **Chart type**.

Wizard Step 2 Click the **Data Range** tab. Enter the cell range of the percentage and cumulative percentage frequencies, without their column headings, in the **Data range** edit box. This range will always start with cell C4 and end with a cell in column D. Click the **Columns** option in the **Series in** group and then click the **Series** tab. Enter as a **formula** the column A cell range that contains the category labels as the **Category (X) axis labels**. Leave the **Second category (X) axis labels** box blank, if it appears.

Wizard Step 3 Click the **Titles** tab. Enter a title as the **Chart title**, the name of the variable in the **Category (X) axis** edit box, and **Percentage** in the **Value (Y) axis** edit box. Leave the other two boxes blank. Click, in turn, the **Gridlines**, **Legend**, **Data Labels**, and **Data Table** tabs and use the settings discussed in Section E2.3A on page 67.

The Pareto chart that the wizard creates contains a secondary (right) *Y*-axis scale that improperly extends past 100%. To correct this error, right-click that axis (you will see the popup message **Secondary Value Axis** when your mouse is properly positioned) and click **Format Axis** in the shortcut menu. In the **Scale** tab of the Format Axis dialog box, change the **Maximum** value to **1** and click **OK**. Right-click the primary (left) axis and repeat these instructions if the left axis needs rescaling too (you will see the popup message **Value Axis** when your mouse is properly positioned).

E2.5B Creating a Pareto Chart (Excel 2007)

Select the cell range of the data to be charted. (This range will begin with cell C4, if you used the Section E2.2B instructions to create a PivotTable.) Select **Insert → Column** (in the Charts group) and select the first sub-type, identified as **Clustered Column** when you move the mouse pointer over that sub-type and pause. Select **Format** and select the cumulative percentage series from the drop-down list in the Current Selection group. Then select **Format Selection** (from the same group) and in the Format Data Series dialog box select the **Secondary Axis** in the **Series Options** panel and click **Close**. With the cumulative percentage series still selected in the Current Selection group, select **Design → Change Chart Type**, and in the **Change Chart Type** gallery, select the line chart identified as **Line with Markers** and click **OK**.

If your chart contains extraneous plots—for example, a plot of percentage frequencies—delete such plots one series at a time by doing the following: Select **Format** and then select an extraneous series from the drop-down list in the Current Selection group. Select **Design → Select Data**. In the Select Data Source dialog box (see Figure E2.7), select the extraneous **Legend Entries** series (**Percentage** in Figure E2.7) and click **Remove** and then **OK**.

Relocate your chart to a chart sheet and customize your chart, using the instructions in Section E.2.3B on page 68. If the secondary (right) *Y*-axis scale improperly extends past 100%, right-click the axis and click **Format Axis** in the shortcut menu. In the **Scale** tab of the Format Axis dialog

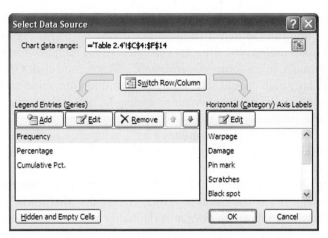

FIGURE E2.7 The Select Data Source dialog box (Excel 2007)

box, change the value in the **Maximum** edit box to **1** and click **Close**. Right-click the primary (left) axis and repeat these instructions if the left axis needs rescaling too.

E2.6 Creating Ordered Arrays

To create an ordered array, first organize your worksheet so that each variable appears in its own column, enter a column heading in row 1, and enter the values for the variable starting in row 2. Select the data to be sorted. If you use Excel 97–2003, select **Data ➜ Sort**. In the Sort dialog box, select the variable to be sorted from the Sort by drop-down list. Click the **Ascending** option button, click **Header row**, and click **OK**. If you use Excel 2007, select **Home ➜ Sort & Filter** (in the Editing group) ➜ **Sort Smallest to Largest**.

E2.7 Creating Stem-and-Leaf Displays

No Microsoft Excel features directly create stem-and-leaf displays. Use PHStat2 Section P2.5 on page 74 to create a stem-and-leaf display in Excel.

E2.8 Creating Bins for Frequency Distributions

To create frequency distributions using Excel features, you must first translate your class groupings into what Excel calls **bins**.

Bins are numbers in an ordered list that define ranges for each row of a frequency distribution or each bar of a histogram. Unlike class groupings, which have well-defined lower and upper boundary values, the boundary values of each bin are implied. For a particular bin number, the range defined is all values that are less than or equal to the bin number and that are greater than the previous bin number, which must be a lower value.

In Chapter 2, Tables 2.7–2.11 on pages 36–39 use class groupings in the form *valueA but less than valueB*. You can

translate class groupings in this form into nearly equivalent bins by creating a list of bin numbers that are slightly less than each *valueB* that appears in the class groupings. For example, the Table 2.7 class groupings on page 36 could be translated into nearly equivalent bins by using this list of bin numbers: 14.99 ("slightly less" than 15.0), 19.99, 24.99, 29.99, 34.99, 39.99, 44.99, 49.99, 54.99, 59.99, 64.99, 69.99, and 74.99).

If you have class groupings in the form "all values from *valueA* to *valueB*," such as the set 0.0 through 4.9, 5.0 through 9.9, 10.0 through 14.9, and 15.0 through 19.9, you can approximate each class grouping by choosing a bin number slightly more than each *valueB*, as in this list of bin numbers: 4.99 (slightly more than 4.9), 9.99, 14.99, and 19.99.

Because the first bin number always represents a range with no explicit lower boundary (other than negative infinity), a first bin can never have a midpoint. (You may have noticed in this chapter that in the charts in which midpoints are used as labels, the first bin is labeled with – and not with a midpoint.) To enter a list of bin numbers, use a blank column in the worksheet that contains your unsummarized data, entering the column heading "Bins" in the row 1 cell.

Unlike the frequency distributions shown in Tables 2.8, 2.10, and 2.13, you typically include frequency, percentage frequency, and cumulative percentage frequencies as columns of one table and not as separate tables. Also, unlike what is done in Chapter 2, in Excel, you create frequency distributions for individual categories, one at a time (e.g., growth funds or value funds) and not frequency distributions that contain two categories (e.g., growth and value funds). To create multiple category tables, such as Tables 2.8, 2.10, and 2.13, you must combine columns from the individual tables using copy-and-paste operations.

E2.9 Creating Frequency Distributions and Histograms

To create frequency distributions and histograms from unsummarized data, use the ToolPak **Histogram** procedure. This procedure requires that you first translate your class groupings into bins, as explained in the previous section.

Open to the worksheet that contains the unsummarized data and verify that bin values have been placed in their own column. Begin the ToolPak add-in and select **Histogram** from the **Analysis Tools** list and then click **OK**. In the Histogram dialog box (see Figure E2.8), enter the cell range of the data to be summarized as the **Input Range**. Enter the cell range of the list of bin numbers (including the column heading "Bins") as the **Bin Range**. (If you leave Bin Range blank, the procedure creates a set of bins for you, but such bins are often not as well chosen as the ones you can specify yourself.) Click **Labels** to indicate that the first cells of the Input Range and Bin Range contain a label. Click **New Worksheet Ply** and **Cumulative Percentage**, and then click **Chart Output** (if you want to create a histogram). Click **OK** to create the frequency distribution (and histogram) on a new worksheet.

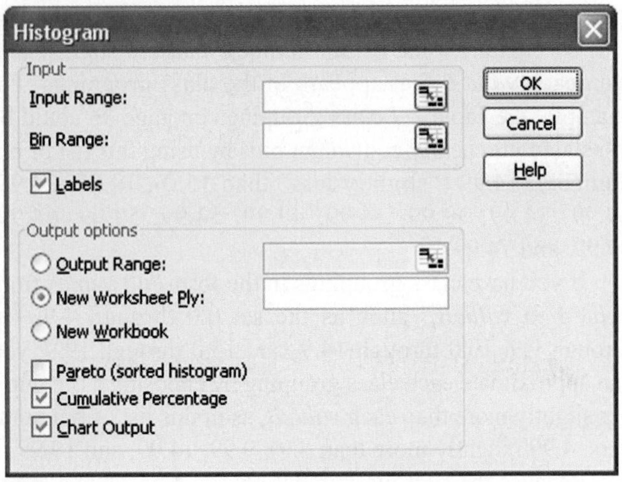

FIGURE E2.8 The Data Analysis Histogram dialog box

The frequency distribution that the ToolPak creates improperly contains an open-ended bin labeled **More**. To eliminate the More class, first manually add the frequency count of the More row to the count of the preceding bin and set the cumulative percentage of the preceding bin to 100%. Then, select the entire row containing the More row. Next, select **Edit → Delete** in Excel 97–2003 or right-click the selected row in Excel 2007. In the Delete dialog box, click **Shift cells up** and then click **OK**.

As you correct your frequency distribution, your histogram also changes, and the bar representing the incorrect More group disappears. However, the histogram will still contain these errors: There are gaps between the bars, the bins are labeled with their maximum bin values and not with their midpoint values, and the secondary Y axis scale exceeds 100%.

To eliminate the gaps between bars, right-click inside one of the histogram bars. (You will see a popup message that begins with **Series 'Frequency'** when your mouse is properly positioned.) Click **Format Data Series** in the shortcut menu to display the Format Data Series dialog box. If you use Excel 97–2003, click the **Options** tab, change the value of **Gap width** to **0**, and click **OK**. If you use Excel 2007, move the **Gap Width** slider to **No Gap** in the **Series Options** panel of this dialog box.

To change the bin labels, enter the list of midpoint values in column D of the worksheet. Cell D2 should contain the heading **Midpoints** and cell D3 should contain ––– (which you should enter as '– to avoid an error). Right-click the tinted background of the chart. (You will see the ToolTip **Plot Area** when your mouse is properly positioned.) Click **Source Data** (Excel 97–2003) or **Select Data** (Excel 2007) in the shortcut menu. If you use Excel 97–2003, select the **Series** tab in the Source Data dialog box and enter the cell range of the midpoints as a formula, in the form =*SheetName!CellRange*, in the **Category (X) axis labels** box. Then delete the entry for the **Second category(X) axis labels** and click **OK**. If you use Excel 2007, click the **Edit**

button under the **Horizontal (Categories) Axis Labels** heading in the Select Data Source dialog box. In the Axis Labels dialog box, enter the cell range of the midpoints as a formula, in the form =*SheetName!CellRange*, and click **OK**. (This range should start with the first midpoint value and not with the midpoint column heading.) Click **OK** a second time (in the original dialog box) to complete the task.

To rescale the secondary Y axis, right-click on the secondary (right) Y axis. (You will see a popup message that includes the words **Secondary** and **Axis** when your mouse is properly positioned.) Click **Format Axis** in the shortcut menu. If you use Excel 97–2003, change the **Maximum** in the **Scale** tab of the Format Axis dialog box to **1** and click **OK**. If you use Excel 2007, select the **Fixed** option for **Maximum** and enter **1** as the maximum value in the **Axis Options** panel of the Format Axis dialog box, and then click **OK**.

If you want to add a percentage frequency column to the frequency distribution, select column C and then select **Insert → Columns**. In the new column C, enter the heading **Percentage** in cell C2. Enter the formula =**B3/SUM(B:B)** in cell C3 and copy the formula down the column through the rest of the frequency distribution. Format column C for percentage display to complete the column.

E2.10 Creating Percentage and Cumulative Percentage Polygons

No Microsoft Excel features directly create percentage or cumulative percentage polygons. Use PHStat2 Section P2.7 on page 75 to create a polygon in Excel.

E2.11 Creating Contingency Tables: Overview

You create a contingency table from unsummarized data by creating a PivotTable using instructions adapted from Section E2.2. To create a contingency table from data already summarized in table form, enter the contents of the table into a blank worksheet, using the column A and row 1 cells for row and column headings.

E2.11A Creating Contingency Tables (Excel 97–2003)

Adapt the instructions of Section E2.2A, "Creating PivotTables (Excel 97–2003)." When you get to the Step 3 instructions, modify them as follows. In the Layout dialog box in Step 3, first drag the label of the first variable to be summarized and drop it in the ROW area. Drag a second copy of this same label and drop it in the DATA area. (The label changes to **Count of variable name**.) Then drag the label of the second variable and drop it in the COLUMN area. In the PivotTable Options dialog box, also in Step 3, verify that both **Grand total for columns** and **Grand totals for rows** are checked (they should be) and that you have entered **0** as the **For empty cells, show** value. (Excel 97 does not contain this options dialog box.)

E2.11B Creating Contingency Tables (Excel 2007)

Adapt the instructions of Section E2.2B, "Creating PivotTables (Excel 2007)." When you get to the instructions for using the PivotTable Field List task pane, modify them as follows. In the PivotTable Field List task pane, drag the label of the variable to be summarized and drop it in the **Row Labels** box. Drag a second copy of this same label and drop it in the Σ **Values** box. (This second label changes to **Count of variable name.**) Then drag the label of the second variable and drop it in the **Column Labels** area. When you later right-click the PivotTable, click **PivotTable Options** in the shortcut menu. In the **Total & Filters** tab of the PivotTable Options dialog box, verify that both **Show grand totals for columns** and **Show grand totals for rows** are checked. Also, as stated in Section E2.2B, click the **Layout & Format** tab, check **For empty cells show**, and enter **0** as its value, and then click **OK**.

E2.12 Creating Scatter Plots: Overview

You use Excel charting features to create scatter plots. To create a scatter plot, the columns to be plotted must be arranged X variable column first, then Y variable column, reading left-to-right. (If your data are arranged Y then X, first cut and paste the Y variable column so it appears to the right of the X variable column before continuing.)

E2.12A Creating Scatter Plots (Excel 97–2003)

Open to the worksheet containing the properly arranged columns. Select **Insert → Chart** (to begin the Chart Wizard) and make the following entries in the Wizard Step dialog boxes:

Wizard Step 1 Click **XY (Scatter)** from the Standard Types Chart type box and click the first Chart sub-type.

Wizard Step 2 Enter the cell range of the two variables in the **Data range** box and select the **Columns** option. If the two variables are in nonadjacent columns, first type or point to the cell range of the first variable, then type a comma, then type or point to the cell range of the second variable, and then press **Enter**. Do not make any entries in the **Series** tab of this dialog box.

Wizard Step 3 Click the **Titles** tab. Enter a title as the **Chart title** and enter appropriate values for the **Value (X) axis** and **Value (Y) axis** titles. Click, in turn, the **Axes, Gridlines, Legend,** and **Data Labels** tabs and use the formatting settings given in Section E2.3A on pages 67–68.

E2.12B Creating Scatter Plots (Excel 2007)

Open to the worksheet containing the properly arranged columns. Select Insert fi Scatter and click the Scatter with only Markers gallery choice. Finish by relocating your chart to a chart sheet and customizing your chart using the instructions in Section E.2.3B on page 68.

E2.13 Creating Time-Series Plots

You create time-series plots by using Excel charting features with a time-series worksheet in which the time periods have been entered into columns. If your data are arranged with the numerical variable before the time variable, first cut and paste the numerical variable column so it appears to the right of the time variable column before continuing.

E2.13A Creating a Time-Series Plot (Excel 97–2003)

Open to the worksheet containing the properly arranged columns. Select **Insert → Chart** to begin the Chart Wizard and make the following entries in the Wizard Step dialog boxes:

Wizard Step 1 Click **Line** from the Standard Types Chart type box and select the first Chart sub-type in the second row, identified as **Line with markers displayed at each data value**.

Wizard Step 2 Enter the cell range of the two variables in the **Data range** box and select the **Columns** option. If the variables are in nonadjacent columns, first type or point to the cell range of the first variable, then type a comma, then type or point to the cell range of the second variable, and then press **Enter**. Do not make any entries in the **Series** tab of this dialog box.

Wizard Step 3 Click the **Titles** tab. Enter a title as the **Chart title** and enter appropriate values for the **Value (X) axis** and **Value (Y) axis** titles. Click, in turn, the **Axes, Gridlines, Legend, Data Labels,** and **Data Table** tabs and use the formatting settings that are given in Section E2.3A on pages 67–68.

E2.13B Creating a Time-Series Plot (Excel 2007)

Open to the worksheet containing the properly arranged columns. In the Select Data Source dialog box, select **Insert → XY (Scatter) → Scatter with Straight Lines and Markers**. Finish by relocating your chart to a chart sheet and customizing your chart using the instructions in Section E.2.3B on page 68.

APPENDIX P2

Using PHStat2 for Tables and Charts

P2.1 Introduction

Before continuing, you should review the material in Appendix P1 on page 20 that presents a general introduction to using PHStat2. You should also review Appendix F and the PHStat2 readme file on the Student CD-ROM if you plan to install PHStat2 on your computer system. Note that for some tasks that are straightforward to do in Excel, there is no equivalent PHStat2 procedure (use the appropriate Excel appendix section for such tasks).

P2.2 Creating Summary Tables

To create summary tables, use **PHStat → Descriptive Statistics → One-Way Tables & Charts**. This procedure accepts either unsummarized data (**Raw Categorical Data**) or data in the form of categories that have already been tallied (**Table of Frequencies**). In both cases, the procedure uses the Excel PivotTable feature to create a summary table.

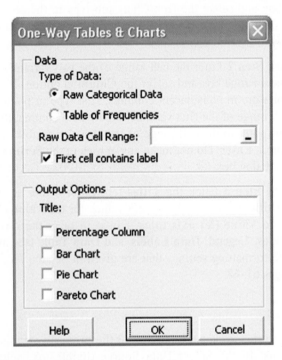

P2.3 Creating Charts

To create summary charts, use various Output Options of the **PHStat → Descriptive Statistics → One-Way Tables & Charts** procedure discussed in the previous section. The options use Excel charting features to create a percentage column, bar, pie, or Pareto chart. (The charts are created with the custom formatting discussed in Sections E2.3 and E2.5.)

P2.4 Creating Pareto Charts

To create summary charts, use the **Pareto Chart** Output Options of the **PHStat → Descriptive Statistics → One-Way Tables & Charts** procedure discussed in Section P2.2.

P2.5 Creating Stem-and-Leaf Displays

To create a stem-and-leaf display, use **PHStat → Descriptive Statistics → Stem-and-Leaf Display**. This procedure creates a stem-and-leaf display from the unsummarized data in the **Variable Cell Range**. The stem-and-leaf display appears as a series of formatted worksheet labels in a new worksheet. If you click **Summary Statistics**, a table of summary statistics is included on that new worksheet.

The **Set stem unit as** option should be used sparingly and, if you use this option, the stem unit you specify must be a power of ten. Only use this option if **Autocalculate stem unit** creates a display that has too few or too many stems.

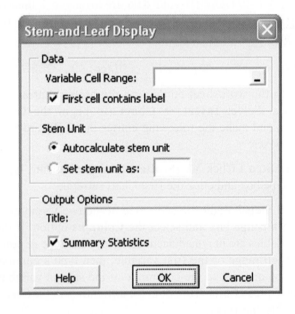

P2.6 Creating Frequency Distributions and Histograms

To create a frequency distribution and histogram from unsummarized data, use **PHStat → Descriptive Statistics → Histogram & Polygons**. This procedure accepts data either for a single group or multiple groups as either unstacked data (column by column) or stacked data (one column). If you use the **Multiple Groups – Stacked** option, you will also need to enter the **Grouping Variable Cell Range**.

This procedure silently uses the ToolPak Histogram procedure but corrects several errors made by the ToolPak procedure. Because the ToolPak is used silently, you must specify a cell range for bins (and not class groupings). Because the first bin will always be open-ended toward negative infinity, this bin will never have a true midpoint. Therefore, the command expects that your **Midpoints Cell Range** will be one cell smaller than your **Bins Cell Range** and will assign the first midpoint to the second class. (Review Section E2.8 "Creating Bins for Frequency Distributions" on page 71 if you are not familiar with the Excel bins concept.)

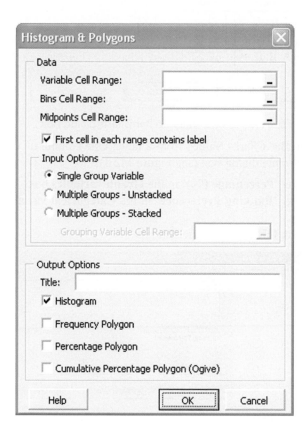

P2.7 Creating Percentage and Cumulative Percentage Polygons

To create percentage and cumulative percentage polygons, use the Output Options of the **PHStat ➔ Descriptive Statistics ➔ Histogram & Polygons** procedure discussed in the previous section. The options use Excel charting features to create a percentage polygon and/or cumulative percentage polygon, as well as a frequency polygon.

P2.8 Creating Contingency Tables

To create a contingency table from unsummarized data, use **PHStat ➔ Descriptive Statistics ➔ Two-Way Tables & Charts**. This procedure uses the Excel PivotTable feature to create a contingency table.

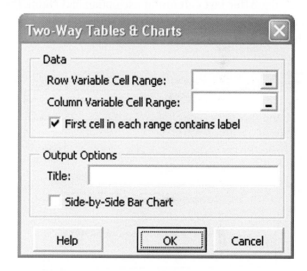

P2.9 Creating Scatter Plots

To create a scatter plot, use the **Scatter Diagram** Output Option of the **PHStat ➔ Regression ➔ Simple Linear Regression** procedure. For full information about using this procedure, see Section P12.2 on page 454.

APPENDIX M2

Using Minitab for Tables and Charts

You can use Minitab to create many of the tables and charts discussed in this chapter. If you are new to Minitab, make sure to review Appendix M1, "Introduction to Minitab," that starts on page 21, before continuing.

M2.1 Unstacking Data

Data are usually arranged so that all of the values of a variable are stacked vertically down a column. In many cases, you need to separately analyze different subgroups in terms of a numerical variable of interest. For example, for the mutual fund data, you may want to analyze the 2006 percentage return for the growth funds separately from the 2006 percentage return for the value funds. This can be accomplished by unstacking the 2006 percentage return variable so that the 2006 percentage returns for the growth funds are located in one column and the 2006 percentage returns for the value funds are located in a different column.

To unstack the growth and value funds data:

1. Open the `Mutual Funds.mtw` worksheet.
2. Select **Data → Unstack Columns**.

In the Unstack Columns dialog box (see Figure M2.1):

3. Enter **'Return 2006'** in the **Unstack the data in** box and **Objective** in the **Using subscripts in** box.
4. Click the **After last column in use** option and **Name the columns containing the unstacked data**.
5. Click **OK**.

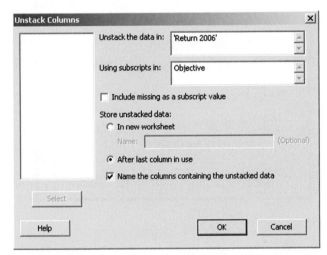

FIGURE M2.1 Minitab Unstack Columns dialog box

The new variables Return2006_Growth and Return2006_Value appear in columns C10 and C11. (You can change these variable names by editing their values in the cell at the top of these columns.)

M2.2 Creating Bar Charts

To create a bar chart similar to Figure 2.1 on page 27:

1. Open the `Banking.mtw` worksheet.
2. Select **Graph → Bar Chart**.

In the Bar Charts dialog box (see Figure M2.2):

3. Select **Values from a table** from the **Bars represent** drop-down list. (Make this selection because the frequencies in each category are provided. If you are using raw data such as is found in the `Mutual Funds.mtw` worksheet, select **Counts of unique values** instead.)
4. In the gallery of choices, click **Simple**.
5. Click **OK**.

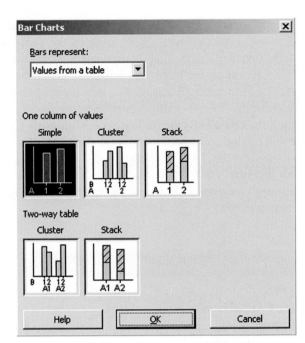

FIGURE M2.2 Minitab Bar Charts dialog box

In the Bar Chart - Values from a table, One column of values, Simple dialog box (see Figure M2.3):

6. Enter **'Percentage (%)'** in the **Graph variables** box.
7. Enter **'Banking Preference'** in the **Categorical variable** box.
8. Click **OK** (to create the chart).

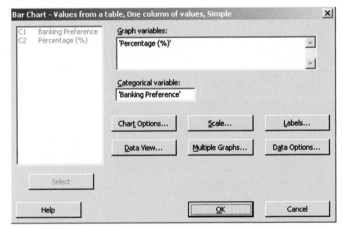

FIGURE M2.3 Minitab Bar Chart - Values from a table, One column of values, Simple dialog box

To modify the bar chart by changing the colors for the bars and borders in the bar chart:

1. Right-click one of the bars of the bar chart.
2. Select **Edit Bars** from the shortcut menu.

In the **Attributes** tab of the Edit Bars dialog box:

3. Click **Custom** under the **Fill Pattern** heading and make selections from the **Type** and **Background color** drop-down lists.
4. Click **Custom** under the **Border and Fill Lines** heading and make selections from the **Type**, **Color**, and **Size** drop-down lists.
5. At the bottom of the dialog box, click **OK**.

M2.3 Creating Pie Charts

To create a pie chart similar to Figure 2.4 on page 28:

1. Open the `Mutual Funds.mtw` worksheet.
2. Select **Graph ➔ Pie Chart**.

In the Pie Chart dialog box (see Figure M2.4):

3. Click **Chart counts of unique values**.

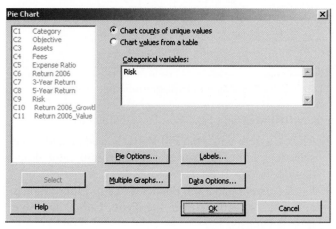

FIGURE M2.4 Minitab Pie Chart dialog box

(If you used a worksheet such as `Banking.mtw` that contained the frequencies in each category, you would click **Chart values from a table** and not **Chart counts of unique values**.)

4. Enter **Risk** in the **Categorical variables** box.
5. Click **Labels**.

In the Pie Chart - Labels dialog box (see Figure M2.5):

6. Click the **Slice Labels** tab.
7. Click **Category name** and **Percent**.
8. Click **OK** (to return to the original Pie Chart dialog box).
9. Back in the original Pie Chart dialog box, click **OK**.

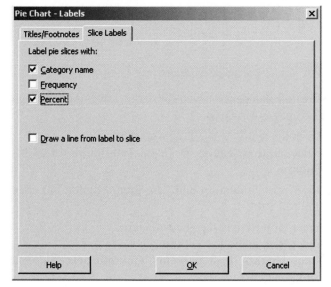

FIGURE M2.5 Minitab Pie Charts - Labels dialog box

M2.4 Creating Pareto Charts

To create a Pareto chart similar to Figure 2.5 on page 30:

1. Open the `Keyboard Defects.mtw` worksheet. (This worksheet contains the causes of the defects in column C1 and the frequency of defects in column C2.)
2. Select **Stat ➔ Quality Tools ➔ Pareto Chart**.

In the Pareto Chart dialog box (see Figure M2.6):

3. Click **Chart defects table**.
4. Enter **Defect** in the **Labels in** box.
5. Enter **Frequency** in the **Frequencies in** box.
6. Click **Do not combine**.
7. Click **OK**.

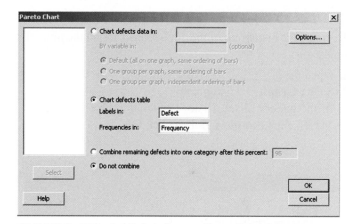

FIGURE M2.6 Minitab Pareto Chart dialog box

If the variable of interest was located in a single column and is in raw form with each row indicating a type of error, you would click **Charts defects data in** and enter the appropriate column number or variable name in the **Chart defects data in** box before doing steps 6 and 7.

M2.5 Creating Stem-and-Leaf Displays

To create the stem-and-leaf display of the 2006 returns for all the mutual funds:

1. Open the `Mutual Funds.mtw` worksheet.
2. Select **Graph ➔ Stem-and-Leaf**.

In the Stem-and-Leaf dialog box (see Figure M2.7):

3. Enter **'Return 2006'** in the **Graph variables** box.
4. Click **OK**.

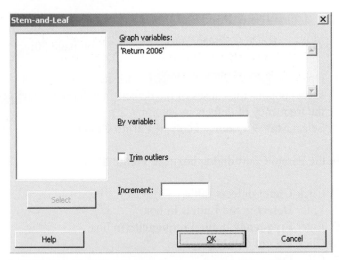

FIGURE M2.7 Minitab Stem-and-Leaf dialog box

M2.6 Creating Histograms

To create the histogram of the 2006 returns for all the mutual funds:

1. Open the **Mutual Funds.mtw** worksheet.
2. Select **Graph → Histogram**.
3. In the gallery of the Histograms dialog box (see Figure M2.8), click **Simple** and then click **OK**.

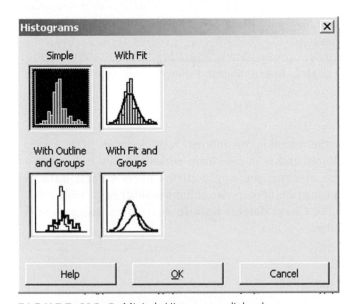

FIGURE M2.8 Minitab Histograms dialog box

4. In the Histogram-Simple dialog box (see Figure M2.9), enter **'Return 2006'** in the **Graph variables** box and then click **OK** (to create the chart).

To modify the histogram by changing the colors for the bars and borders in the histogram:

1. Right-click one of the bars of the histogram.
2. Select **Edit Bars** from the shortcut menu.

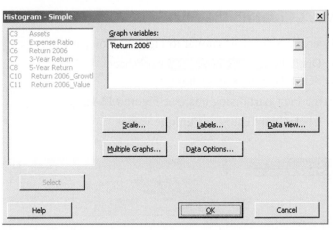

FIGURE M2.9 Minitab Histogram-Simple dialog box

In the **Attributes** tab of the Edit Bars dialog box:

3. Click **Custom** under the **Fill Pattern** heading and make selections from the **Type** and **Background color** drop-down lists.
4. Click **Custom** under the **Border and Fill Lines** heading and make selections from the **Type**, **Color**, and **Size** drop-down lists.
5. In the **Binning** tab of the same dialog box, click **Midpoint** to specify midpoints or click **Cutpoint** to specify class limits. Then click **Midpoint/Cutpoint positions** and enter the set of midpoint or cutpoints values in the box.
6. Click **OK** (to complete the modifications).

If you wish to create separate histograms for the growth and value funds similar to Figure 2.9 on pages 41–42, do the following:

7. Enter **'Return 2006'** in the **Graph variables** box.
8. Select **Multiple Graphs**.
9. Select **On separate graphs** and then select the By Variables tab.
10. Enter **Objective** in the **By variables in groups on separate graphs** box.
11. Click **OK** to return to the Histogram-Simple dialog box, Click **OK**.

M2.7 Creating Contingency Tables

To create contingency tables similar to Tables 2.14 through 2.17 on pages 47–48:

1. Open the **Mutual Funds.mtw** worksheet.
2. Select **Stat → Tables → Cross Tabulation and Chi-Square**.

In the Cross Tabulation and Chi-Square dialog box (see Figure M2.10):

3. Enter **Objective** in the **For rows** box.
4. Enter **Risk** in the **For columns** box.
5. Click **Counts**, **Row percents**, **Column percents**, and **Total percents**.
6. Click **OK**.

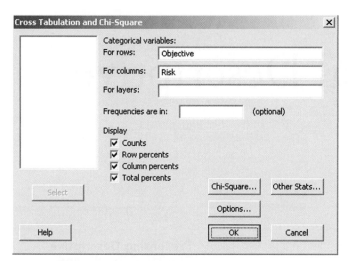

FIGURE M2.10 Minitab Cross Tabulation and Chi-Square dialog box

M2.8 Creating Scatter Plot and Time-Series Plots

To create a scatter plot of the cost of a hamburger and the cost of movie tickets similar to Figure 2.14 on page 50:

1. Open the `Cost of Living.mtw` worksheet.
2. Select **Graph → Scatterplot**.

In the Scatterplots dialog box (see Figure M2.11):

3. In the gallery, click **Simple**.
4. Click **OK**.

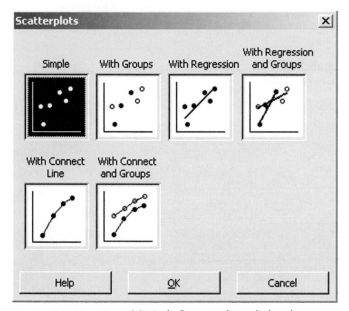

FIGURE M2.11 Minitab Scatterplots dialog box

In the Scatterplot - Simple dialog box (see Figure M2.12):

5. Enter **'Movie Tickets'** in the row **1 Y variables** cell.
6. Enter **Hamburger** in the row **1 X variables** cell.
7. Click **OK** (to create the chart).

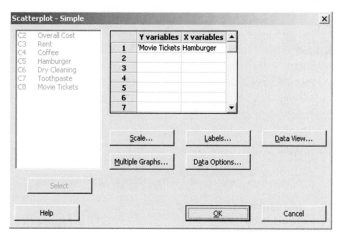

FIGURE M2.12 Minitab Scatterplot - Simple dialog box

To create a time-series plot, use the same eight-step process, entering the variable of interest in step 5 and the time period variable in step 6.

Another approach to constructing a time-series plot is to open the worksheet containing your data and then:

1. Select **Graph → Time Series Plot**.
2. In the gallery of the Time Series Plot dialog box, click **Simple** and then click **OK**.
3. In the Time Series Plot-Simple dialog box, enter the variable name containing your data in the **Series** box and click **OK**.

3

Numerical Descriptive Measures

Learning Objectives

In this chapter, you learn:

- To describe the properties of central tendency, variation, and shape in numerical data
- To compute descriptive summary measures for a population
- To construct and interpret a boxplot
- To describe the covariance and the coefficient of correlation

@ Choice Is Yours, Part II

The tables and charts you prepared for the sample of 868 mutual funds has proved useful to the customers of the Choice Is Yours service. However, customers have become frustrated trying to evaluate mutual fund performance. Although they know how the 2006 returns are distributed, they have no idea what a typical 2006 rate of return would be for a particular category of mutual funds, such as low-risk funds, nor do they know how that typical value compares to the typical values of other categories. They also have no idea of the extent of the variability in the 2006 rate of return. Are all the values relatively similar, or do they include very small and very large values? Are there a lot of small values and a few large ones, or vice versa, or are there a similar number of small and large values?

How could you help the customers get answers to these questions so that they could better evaluate the mutual funds?

The customers in the Using Statistics scenario are asking questions about numerical variables. When summarizing and describing numerical variables, you need to do more than just prepare the tables and charts discussed in Chapter 2. You need to consider the central tendency, variation, and shape of each numerical variable.

> CENTRAL TENDENCY
>
> The **central tendency** is the extent to which all the data values group around a typical or central value.
>
> VARIATION
>
> The **variation** is the amount of dispersion, or scattering, of values away from a central value.
>
> SHAPE
>
> The **shape** is the pattern of the distribution of values from the lowest value to the highest value.

This chapter discusses ways you can measure the central tendency, variation, and shape of a variable. You will also learn about the covariance and the coefficient of correlation, which help measure the strength of the association between two numerical variables. Using these measures would give the customers of the Choice Is Yours service the answers they seek.

3.1 Measures of Central Tendency

Most sets of data show a distinct tendency to group around a central point. When people talk about an "average value" or the "middle value" or the "most frequent value," they are talking informally about the mean, median, and mode—three measures of central tendency.

The Mean

The **arithmetic mean** (typically referred to as the **mean**) is the most common measure of central tendency. The mean is the only common measure in which all the values play an equal role. The mean serves as a "balance point" in a set of data (like the fulcrum on a seesaw). You calculate the mean by adding together all the values in a data set and then dividing that sum by the number of values in the data set.

The symbol $\overline{X}$, called *X-bar*, is used to represent the mean of a sample. For a sample containing n values, the equation for the mean of a sample is written as

$$\overline{X} = \frac{\text{sum of the values}}{\text{number of values}}$$

Using the series $X_1, X_2, \ldots, X_n$ to represent the set of n values and n to represent the number of values in the sample, the equation becomes:

$$\overline{X} = \frac{X_1 + X_2 + \cdots + X_n}{n}$$

By using summation notation (discussed fully in Appendix B), you replace the numerator $X_1 + X_2 + \cdots + X_n$ by the term $\sum_{i=1}^{n} X_i$, which means sum all the X_i values from the first X value, X_1, to the last X value, X_n, to form Equation (3.1), a formal definition of the sample mean.

SAMPLE MEAN

The **sample mean** is the sum of the values divided by the number of values.

$$\overline{X} = \frac{\sum_{i=1}^{n} X_i}{n} \tag{3.1}$$

where

$$\overline{X} = \text{sample mean}$$

$$n = \text{number of values or sample size}$$

$$X_i = i\text{th value of the variable } X$$

$$\sum_{i=1}^{n} X_i = \text{summation of all } X_i \text{ values in the sample}$$

Because all the values play an equal role, a mean is greatly affected by any value that is greatly different from the others in the data set. When you have such extreme values, you should avoid using the mean as a measure of central tendency.

The mean can suggest a typical or central value for a data set. For example, if you knew the typical time it takes you to get ready in the morning, you might be able to better plan your morning and minimize any excessive lateness (or earliness) going to your destination. Suppose you define the time to get ready as the time (rounded to the nearest minute) from when you get out of bed to when you leave your home. You collect the times shown below for 10 consecutive workdays (stored in the file Times):

Day:	1	2	3	4	5	6	7	8	9	10
Time minutes:	39	29	43	52	39	44	40	31	44	35

The mean time is 39.6 minutes, computed as follows:

$$\overline{X} = \frac{\text{sum of the values}}{\text{number of values}}$$

$$\overline{X} = \frac{\sum_{i=1}^{n} X_i}{n}$$

$$\overline{X} = \frac{39 + 29 + 43 + 52 + 39 + 44 + 40 + 31 + 44 + 35}{10}$$

$$= \frac{396}{10} = 39.6$$

Even though no one day in the sample actually had the value 39.6 minutes, allotting about 40 minutes to get ready would be a good rule for planning your mornings. The mean is a good measure of central tendency in this case because the data set does not contain any exceptionally small or large values.

Consider a case in which the value on Day 4 is 102 minutes instead of 52 minutes. This extreme value causes the mean to rise to 44.6 minutes, as follows:

$$\overline{X} = \frac{\text{sum of the values}}{\text{number of values}}$$

$$\overline{X} = \frac{\sum_{i=1}^{n} X_i}{n}$$

$$\overline{X} = \frac{446}{10} = 44.6$$

The one extreme value has increased the mean by more than 10%, from 39.6 to 44.6 minutes. In contrast to the original mean that was in the "middle" (i.e., greater than 5 of the getting-ready times and less than the 5 other times), the new mean is greater than 9 of the 10 getting-ready times. Because of the extreme value, now the mean is not a good measure of central tendency.

EXAMPLE 3.1

The Mean Calories For Coffee Drinks

The data in the file CoffeeDrink represent the calories of 16-ounce iced coffee drinks at Dunkin' Donuts and Starbucks:

Product	Calories
Dunkin' Donuts Iced Mocha Swirl latte (whole milk)	240
Starbucks Coffee Frappuccino blended coffee	260
Dunkin' Donuts Coffee Coolatta (cream)	350
Starbucks Iced Coffee Mocha Expresso (whole milk and whipped cream)	350
Starbucks Mocha Frappuccino blended coffee (whipped cream)	420
Starbucks Chocolate Brownie Frappuccino blended coffee (whipped cream)	510
Starbucks Chocolate Frappuccino Blended Crème (whipped cream)	530

Source: Data extracted from "Coffee as Candy at Dunkin' Donuts and Starbucks," Consumer Reports, June 2004, p. 9.

Compute the mean number of calories for the iced coffee drinks.

SOLUTION The mean number of calories is 380, calculated as follows:

$$\bar{X} = \frac{\text{sum of the values}}{\text{number of values}}$$

$$\bar{X} = \frac{\sum_{i=1}^{n} X_i}{n}$$

$$= \frac{2,660}{7} = 380$$

The Median

The **median** is the middle value in an ordered array of data that has been ranked from smallest to largest. Half the values are smaller than or equal to the median, and half the values are larger than or equal to the median. The median is not affected by extreme values, so you can use the median when extreme values are present.

To calculate the median for a set of data, you first rank the values from smallest to largest and then use Equation (3.2) to compute the rank of the value that is the median.

MEDIAN

$$\text{Median} = \frac{n + 1}{2} \text{ ranked value} \qquad (3.2)$$

You compute the median value by following one of two rules:

- **Rule 1** If there are an *odd* number of values in the data set, the median is the middle-ranked value.
- **Rule 2** If there are an *even* number of values in the data set, then the median is the *average* of the two middle-ranked values.

To compute the median for the sample of 10 times to get ready in the morning, you rank the daily times as follows:

Ranked values:

29 31 35 39 39 40 43 44 44 52

Ranks:

1   2   3   4   5   6   7   8   9   10

↑

Median = 39.5

Because the result of dividing $n + 1$ by 2 is $(10 + 1)/2 = 5.5$ for this sample of 10, you must use Rule 2 and average the fifth and sixth ranked values, 39 and 40. Therefore, the median is 39.5. The median of 39.5 means that for half the days, the time to get ready is less than or equal to 39.5 minutes, and for half the days, the time to get ready is greater than or equal to 39.5 minutes. In this case, the median time to get ready of 39.5 minutes is very close to the mean time to get ready of 39.6 minutes.

EXAMPLE 3.2

Computing the Median From an Odd-Sized Sample

The data in the file **CoffeeDrink** (see Example 3.1 on page 84) represent the calories of 16-ounce iced coffee drinks at Dunkin' Donuts and Starbucks. Compute the median number of calories for the iced coffee drinks at Dunkin' Donuts and Starbucks.

SOLUTION Because the result of dividing $n + 1$ by 2 is $(7 + 1)/2 = 4$ for this sample of seven, using Rule 1, the median is the fourth ranked value. The number of calories of 16-ounce iced coffee drinks at Dunkin' Donuts and Starbucks are ranked from the smallest to the largest:

Ranked values:

240   260   350   350   420   510   530

Ranks:

1   2   3   4   5   6   7

↑

Median = 350

The median number of calories is 350. Half the drinks have equal to or less than 350 calories, and half the drinks have equal to or more than 350 calories.

The Mode

The **mode** is the value in a set of data that appears most frequently. Like the median and unlike the mean, extreme values do not affect the mode. Often, there is no mode or there are several modes in a set of data. For example, consider the time-to-get-ready data shown as follows:

29 31 35 39 39 40 43 44 44 52

There are two modes, 39 minutes and 44 minutes, because each of these values occurs twice.

EXAMPLE 3.3

Determining the Mode

A systems manager in charge of a company's network keeps track of the number of server failures that occur in a day. Determine the mode for the following data, which represents the number of server failures in a day for the past two weeks:

1 3 0 3 26 2 7 4 0 2 3 3 6 3

SOLUTION The ordered array for these data is

0   0   1   2   2   3   3   3   3   3   4   6   7   26

Because 3 appears five times, more times than any other value, the mode is 3. Thus, the systems manager can say that the most common occurrence is having three server failures in a day. For this data set, the median is also equal to 3, and the mean is equal to 4.5. The value 26 is an extreme value. For these data, the median and the mode better measure central tendency than the mean.

A set of data has no mode if none of the values is "most typical." Example 3.4 presents a data set with no mode.

EXAMPLE 3.4
Data with no Mode

The bounced check fees ($) for a sample of 10 banks is

26   28   20   21   22   25   18   23   15   30

Compute the mode.

SOLUTION These data have no mode. None of the values is most typical because each value appears once.

3.2 Variation and Shape

In addition to central tendency, every data set can be characterized by its variation and shape. Variation measures the **spread**, or **dispersion**, of values in a data set. One simple measure of variation is the range, the difference between the largest and smallest values. More commonly used in statistics are the standard deviation and variance, two measures explained later in this section. The shape of a data set represents a pattern of all the values, from the lowest to highest value. As you will learn later in this section, many data sets have a pattern that looks approximately like a bell, with a peak of values somewhere in the middle.

The Range

The **range** is the simplest numerical descriptive measure of variation in a set of data.

> RANGE
> The range is equal to the largest value minus the smallest value.
>
> $$\text{Range} = X_{\text{largest}} - X_{\text{smallest}} \qquad (3.3)$$

To determine the range of the times to get ready in the morning, you rank the data from smallest to largest:

29   31   35   39   39   40   43   44   44   52

Using Equation (3.3), the range is $52 - 29 = 23$ minutes. The range of 23 minutes indicates that the largest difference between any two days in the time to get ready in the morning is 23 minutes.

EXAMPLE 3.5

Computing the Range in the Calories in Iced Coffee Drinks

The data in the file CoffeeDrink (see Example 3.1 on page 84) represent the calories of 16-ounce iced coffee drinks at Dunkin' Donuts and Starbucks. Compute the range in the number of calories for the iced coffee drinks at Dunkin' Donuts and Starbucks.

SOLUTION Ranked from smallest to largest, the number of calories for the seven iced coffee drinks are

240   260   350   350   420   510   530

Therefore, using Equation (3.3), the range $= 530 - 240 = 290$. The largest difference in the number of calories between any two iced coffee drinks is 290.

The range measures the *total spread* in the set of data. Although the range is a simple measure of the total variation in the data, it does not take into account *how* the data are distributed between the smallest and largest values. In other words, the range does not indicate whether the values are evenly distributed throughout the data set, clustered near the middle, or clustered near one or both extremes. Thus, using the range as a measure of variation when at least one value is an extreme value is misleading.

The Variance and the Standard Deviation

Although the range is a simple measure of variation, it does not take into consideration how the values distribute or cluster between the extremes. Two commonly used measures of variation that take into account how all the values in the data are distributed are the **variance** and the **standard deviation**. These statistics measure the "average" scatter around the mean—how larger values fluctuate above it and how smaller values fluctuate below it.

A simple measure of variation around the mean might take the difference between each value and the mean and then sum these differences. However, if you did that, you would find that because the mean is the balance point in a set of data, for *every* set of data, these differences would sum to zero. One measure of variation that differs from data set to data set *squares* the difference between each value and the mean and then sums these squared differences. In statistics, this quantity is called a **sum of squares** (or **SS**). This sum is then divided by the number of values minus 1 (for sample data) to get the sample variance (S^2). The square root of the sample variance is the sample standard deviation (S).

Because the sum of squares is a sum of squared differences that by the rules of arithmetic will always be nonnegative, *neither the variance nor the standard deviation can ever be negative*. For virtually all sets of data, the variance and standard deviation will be a positive value, although both of these statistics will be zero if there is no variation at all in a set of data and each value in the sample is the same.

For a sample containing n values, $X_1, X_2, X_3, \ldots, X_n$, the sample variance (given by the symbol S^2) is

$$S^2 = \frac{(X_1 - \overline{X})^2 + (X_2 - \overline{X})^2 + \cdots + (X_n - \overline{X})^2}{n - 1}$$

Equation (3.4) expresses the sample variance using summation notation, and Equation (3.5) expresses the sample standard deviation.

SAMPLE VARIANCE

The **sample variance** is the sum of the squared differences around the mean divided by the sample size minus one.

$$S^2 = \frac{\sum_{i=1}^{n}(X_i - \overline{X})^2}{n - 1} \qquad (3.4)$$

where

$$\overline{X} = \text{mean}$$

$$n = \text{sample size}$$

$$X_i = \text{ith value of the variable } X$$

$$\sum_{i=1}^{n}(X_i - \overline{X})^2 = \text{summation of all the squared differences between the } X_i \text{ values and } \overline{X}$$

SAMPLE STANDARD DEVIATION

The **sample standard deviation** is the square root of the sum of the squared differences around the mean divided by the sample size minus one.

$$S = \sqrt{S^2} = \sqrt{\frac{\sum_{i=1}^{n}(X_i - \overline{X})^2}{n - 1}} \qquad (3.5)$$

If the denominator were n instead of $n - 1$, Equation (3.4) [and the inner term in Equation (3.5)] would calculate the average of the squared differences around the mean. However, $n - 1$ is used because of certain desirable mathematical properties possessed by the statistic S^2 that make it appropriate for statistical inference (which is discussed in Chapter 7). As the sample size increases, the difference between dividing by n and by $n - 1$ becomes smaller and smaller.

You will most likely use the sample standard deviation as your measure of variation [defined in Equation (3.5)]. Unlike the sample variance, which is a squared quantity, the standard deviation is always a number that is in the same units as the original sample data. The standard deviation helps you to know how a set of data clusters or distributes around its mean. For almost all sets of data, the majority of the observed values lie within an interval of plus and minus one standard deviation above and below the mean. Therefore, knowledge of the mean and the standard deviation usually helps define where at least the majority of the data values are clustering.

To hand-calculate the sample variance, S^2, and the sample standard deviation, S, do the following:

1. Compute the difference between each value and the mean.
2. Square each difference.
3. Add the squared differences.
4. Divide this total by $n - 1$ to get the sample variance.
5. Take the square root of the sample variance to get the sample standard deviation.

Table 3.1 shows the first four steps for calculating the variance and standard deviation for the getting-ready-times data with a mean ($\overline{X}$) equal to 39.6. (See page 83 for the calculation of the mean.) The second column of Table 3.1 shows step 1. The third column of Table 3.1 shows step 2. The sum of the squared differences (step 3) is shown at the bottom of Table 3.1. This total is then divided by $10 - 1 = 9$ to compute the variance (step 4).

TABLE 3.1

Computing the Variance of the Getting-Ready Times

Time (X)	Step 1: $(X_i - \overline{X})$	Step 2: $(X_i - \overline{X})^2$
$\overline{X} = 39.6$		
39	−0.60	0.36
29	−10.60	112.36
43	3.40	11.56
52	12.40	153.76
39	−0.60	0.36
44	4.40	19.36
40	0.40	0.16
31	−8.60	73.96
44	4.40	19.36
35	−4.60	21.16
	Step 3: Sum:	Step 4: Divide by $(n - 1)$:
	412.40	45.82

You can also calculate the variance by substituting values for the terms in Equation (3.4):

$$S^2 = \frac{\sum_{i=1}^{n}(X_i - \overline{X})^2}{n - 1}$$

$$= \frac{(39 - 39.6)^2 + (29 - 39.6)^2 + \cdots + (35 - 39.6)^2}{10 - 1}$$

$$= \frac{412.4}{9}$$

$$= 45.82$$

Because the variance is in squared units (in squared minutes, for these data), to compute the standard deviation, you take the square root of the variance. Using Equation (3.5) on page 88, the sample standard deviation, S, is

$$S = \sqrt{S^2} = \sqrt{\frac{\sum_{i=1}^{n}(X_i - \overline{X})^2}{n - 1}} = \sqrt{45.82} = 6.77$$

This indicates that the getting-ready times in this sample are clustering within 6.77 minutes around the mean of 39.6 minutes (i.e., clustering between $\overline{X} - 1S = 32.83$ and $\overline{X} + 1S = 46.37$). In fact, 7 out of 10 getting-ready times lie within this interval.

Using the second column of Table 3.1, you can also calculate the sum of the differences between each value and the mean to be zero. For any set of data, this sum will always be zero:

$$\sum_{i=1}^{n}(X_i - \overline{X}) = 0 \text{ for all sets of data}$$

This property is one of the reasons that the mean is used as the most common measure of central tendency.

EXAMPLE 3.6

Computing the Variance and Standard Deviation of the Number of Calories in Iced Coffee Drinks

TABLE 3.2

Computing the Variance of the Calories in 16-ounce Iced Coffee Drinks

The data in the file `CoffeeDrink` (see Example 3.1 on page 84) represent the calories of 16-ounce iced coffee drinks at Dunkin' Donuts and Starbucks. Compute the variance and standard deviation of the calories in 16-ounce iced coffee drinks.

SOLUTION Table 3.2 illustrates the computation of the variance and standard deviation for the calories in 16-ounce iced coffee drinks.

$\overline{X} = 380$		
Calories	**Step 1:** $(X_i - \overline{X})$	**Step 2:** $(X_i - \overline{X})^2$
240	−140	19,600
260	−120	14,400
350	−30	900
350	−30	900
420	40	1,600
510	130	16,900
530	150	22,500
	Step 3: Sum:	**Step 4:** Divide by $(n - 1)$:
	76,800	12,800

Using Equation (3.4) on page 88:

$$S^2 = \frac{\sum_{i=1}^{n}(X_i - \overline{X})^2}{n - 1}$$

$$= \frac{(240 - 380)^2 + (260 - 380)^2 + \cdots + (530 - 380)^2}{7 - 1}$$

$$= \frac{76,800}{6}$$

$$= 12,800$$

Using Equation (3.5) on page 88, the sample standard deviation, S, is

$$S = \sqrt{S^2} = \sqrt{\frac{\sum_{i=1}^{n}(X_i - \overline{X})^2}{n - 1}} = \sqrt{12,800} = 113.1371$$

The standard deviation of 113.1371 indicates that the calories in the iced coffee drinks are clustering within 113.1371 around the mean of 380 (i.e., clustering between $\overline{X} - 1S = 266.8629$ and $\overline{X} + 1S = 493.1371$). In fact, 42.9% (3 out of 7) of the calories lie within this interval.

The following summarizes the characteristics of the range, variance, and standard deviation:

- The more the data are spread out or dispersed, the larger the range, variance, and standard deviation.
- The more the data are concentrated or homogeneous, the smaller the range, variance, and standard deviation.
- If the values are all the same (so that there is no variation in the data), the range, variance, and standard deviation will all equal zero.
- None of the measures of variation (the range, standard deviation, and variance) can *ever* be negative.

The Coefficient of Variation

Unlike the previous measures of variation presented, the **coefficient of variation** is a *relative measure* of variation that is always expressed as a percentage rather than in terms of the units of the particular data. The coefficient of variation, denoted by the symbol CV, measures the scatter in the data relative to the mean.

COEFFICIENT OF VARIATION

The coefficient of variation is equal to the standard deviation divided by the mean, multiplied by 100%.

$$CV = \left(\frac{S}{\overline{X}} \right) 100\% \tag{3.6}$$

where

$$S = \text{sample standard deviation}$$
$$\overline{X} = \text{sample mean}$$

For the sample of 10 getting-ready times, because $\overline{X} = 39.6$ and $S = 6.77$, the coefficient of variation is

$$CV = \left(\frac{S}{\overline{X}} \right) 100\% = \left(\frac{6.77}{39.6} \right) 100\% = 17.10\%$$

For the getting-ready times, the standard deviation is 17.1% of the size of the mean.

The coefficient of variation is very useful when comparing two or more sets of data that are measured in different units, as Example 3.7 illustrates.

EXAMPLE 3.7

Comparing Two Coefficients of Variation When Two Variables Have Different Units of Measurement

The operations manager of a package delivery service is deciding whether to purchase a new fleet of trucks. When packages are stored in the trucks in preparation for delivery, you need to consider two major constraints—the weight (in pounds) and the volume (in cubic feet) for each item.

The operations manager samples 200 packages and finds that the mean weight is 26.0 pounds, with a standard deviation of 3.9 pounds, and the mean volume is 8.8 cubic feet, with a standard deviation of 2.2 cubic feet. How can the operations manager compare the variation of the weight and the volume?

SOLUTION Because the measurement units differ for the weight and volume constraints, the operations manager should compare the relative variability in the two types of measurements.

For weight, the coefficient of variation is

$$CV_W = \left(\frac{3.9}{26.0} \right) 100\% = 15\%$$

For volume, the coefficient of variation is

$$CV_V = \left(\frac{2.2}{8.8} \right) 100\% = 25\%$$

Thus, relative to the mean, the package volume is much more variable than the package weight.

Z Scores

An **extreme value** or **outlier** is a value located far away from the mean. Z scores are useful in identifying outliers. The larger the Z score, the greater the distance from the value to the mean. The **Z score** is the difference between the value and the mean, divided by the standard deviation.

Z SCORES

$$Z = \frac{X - \overline{X}}{S} \qquad (3.7)$$

For the time-to-get-ready data (see page 83), the mean is 39.6 minutes, and the standard deviation is 6.77 minutes. The time to get ready on the first day is 39.0 minutes. You compute the Z score for Day 1 by using Equation (3.7):

$$Z = \frac{X - \overline{X}}{S}$$
$$= \frac{39.0 - 39.6}{6.77}$$
$$= -0.09$$

Table 3.3 shows the Z scores for all 10 days. The largest Z score is 1.83 for Day 4, on which the time to get ready was 52 minutes. The lowest Z score was -1.57 for Day 2, on which the time to get ready was 29 minutes. As a general rule, a Z score is considered an outlier if it is less than -3.0 or greater than $+3.0$. None of the times met that criterion to be considered outliers.

TABLE 3.3

Z Scores for the 10 Getting-Ready Times

	Time (X)	Z Score
	39	−0.09
	29	−1.57
	43	0.50
	52	1.83
	39	−0.09
	44	0.65
	40	0.06
	31	−1.27
	44	0.65
	35	−0.68
Mean	39.6	
Standard deviation	6.77	

EXAMPLE 3.8

Computing the Z Scores of the Number of Calories in Iced Coffee Drinks

The data in the file **CoffeeDrink** (see Example 3.1 on page 84) represent the calories of 16-ounce iced coffee drinks at Dunkin' Donuts and Starbucks. Compute the Z scores of the calories of 16-ounce iced coffee drinks.

SOLUTION Table 3.4 illustrates the Z scores of the calories of 16-ounce iced coffee drinks. The largest Z score is 1.33, for an iced coffee drink with 530 calories. The lowest Z score is -1.24, for an iced coffee drink with 240 calories. There are no apparent outliers in these data because none of the Z scores are less than -3.0 or greater than $+3.0$.

TABLE 3.4

Z Scores of the Number of Calories in Iced Coffee Drinks

	Calories	Z Scores
	240	−1.24
	260	−1.06
	350	−0.27
	350	−0.27
	420	0.35
	510	1.15
	530	1.33
Mean	380	
Standard Deviation	113.1371	

Shape

Shape is the pattern of the distribution of data values throughout the entire range of all the values. A distribution is either symmetrical or skewed. In a **symmetrical** distribution, the values below the mean are distributed exactly as the values above the mean. In this case, the low and high values balance each other out. In a **skewed** distribution, the values are not symmetrical around the mean. This skewness results in an imbalance of low values or high values.

Shape influences the relationship of the mean to the median in the following ways:

- Mean < median: negative, or left-skewed
- Mean = median: symmetric, or zero skewness
- Mean > median: positive, or right-skewed

Figure 3.1 depicts three data sets, each with a different shape.

FIGURE 3.1

A comparison of three data sets differing in shape

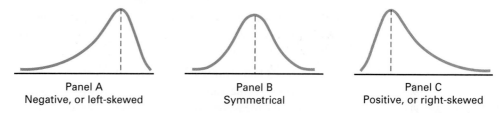

| Panel A | Panel B | Panel C |
| Negative, or left-skewed | Symmetrical | Positive, or right-skewed |

The data in Panel A are negative, or **left-skewed**. In this panel, most of the values are in the upper portion of the distribution. A long tail and distortion to the left is caused by some extremely small values. These extremely small values pull the mean downward so that the mean is less than the median.

The data in Panel B are symmetrical. Each half of the curve is a mirror image of the other half of the curve. The low and high values on the scale balance, and the mean equals the median.

The data in Panel C are positive, or **right-skewed**. In this panel, most of the values are in the lower portion of the distribution. A long tail on the right is caused by some extremely large values. These extremely large values pull the mean upward so that the mean is greater than the median.

Microsoft Excel ToolPak Descriptive Statistics Results

The Microsoft Excel ToolPak Descriptive Statistics procedure (see Appendix E3.1 on page 121) computes the mean, median, mode, standard deviation, variance, range, minimum, maximum, and count (sample size) and displays these statistics on a new worksheet. In addition, the procedure calculates and displays the standard error, the kurtosis, and skewness, three statistics not discussed previously in this section. The standard error, discussed in Chapter 7, is the standard deviation divided by the square root of the sample size. Skewness measures the lack of symmetry in the data. A skewness value of zero indicates a symmetrical distribution. A positive value indicates right-skewness whereas a negative value indicates left-skewness. Kurtosis measures the relative concentration of values in the center of the distribution, as compared with the tails. A kurtosis value of zero indicates a bell-shaped distribution. A negative value indicates a distribution that is flatter than a bell-shaped distribution. A positive value indicates a distribution with a sharper peak than a bell-shaped distribution.

Figure 3.2 shows the results of using the Descriptive Statistics procedure to calculate separate descriptive summary measures for growth and value mutual funds. (The procedure was used twice, and the results that appeared on two separate worksheets were consolidated on one sheet.)

In examining the results, there are large differences in the 2006 return for the growth and value funds. The value funds had a mean 2006 return of 16.8829 and a median return of 16.85. This compares to a mean of 8.7103 and a median of 8.6 for the growth funds. The medians indicate that half of the value funds had returns of 16.85 or better, and half the

FIGURE 3.2

ToolPak descriptive
statistics for growth and
value funds 2006 return

See Section E3.1 to create
this.

	A	B	C
1	*Descriptive Statistics for Return 2006*		
2		Growth	Value
3	Mean	8.7103	16.8829
4	Standard Error	0.2515	0.1968
5	Median	8.6000	16.8500
6	Mode	7.5000	16.6000
7	Standard Deviation	5.4178	3.9553
8	Sample Variance	29.3524	15.6446
9	Kurtosis	0.7390	1.4329
10	Skewness	-0.0118	0.0371
11	Range	37.5	32.2
12	Minimum	-9.0	2.8
13	Maximum	28.5	35.0
14	Sum	4041.6	6820.7
15	Count	464	404

growth funds had returns of only 8.6 or better. The growth funds had a larger standard deviation than the value funds. Neither the growth nor the value funds showed any skewness because their measures of skewness were very close to 0. Both the growth and value funds exhibited positive kurtosis, meaning that the distribution of the returns had a sharper peak than a bell-shaped distribution.

Minitab Descriptive Statistics Results

As shown in Figure 3.3, for descriptive statistics, Minitab computes the sample size (labeled as N), the mean, the standard deviation (labeled as StDev), the coefficient of variation (labeled as CoefVar), first and third quartiles (see Section 3.4), median, maximum, range, and the interquartile range (labeled as IQR—see Section 3.4). In addition, Minitab computes skewness and kurtosis statistics. A skewness value of zero indicates a symmetrical distribution. A positive value indicates right-skewness whereas a negative value indicates left-skewness. Kurtosis measures the relative concentration of values in the center of the distribution, as compared with the tails. A kurtosis value of zero indicates a bell-shaped distribution. A negative value indicates a distribution that is flatter than a bell-shaped distribution. A positive value indicates a distribution with a sharper peak than a bell-shaped distribution.

FIGURE 3.3

Minitab descriptive
statistics of the 2006
returns for growth and
value funds

See Section M3.1 to create
this.

Descriptive Statistics: Return 2006

Variable	Objective	N	Mean	StDev	CoefVar	Minimum	Q1	Median
Return 2006	Growth	464	8.710	5.418	62.20	-9.000	5.325	8.600
	Value	404	16.883	3.955	23.43	2.800	14.500	16.850

Variable	Objective	Q3	Maximum	Range	IQR	Skewness	Kurtosis
Return 2006	Growth	12.400	28.500	37.500	7.075	-0.01	0.74
	Value	19.500	35.000	32.200	5.000	0.04	1.43

In examining the results, there are large differences in the 2006 return for the growth and value funds. The value funds had a mean 2006 return of 16.883 and a median return of 16.85. This compares to a mean of 8.7103 and a median of 8.60 for the growth funds. The medians indicate that half of the value funds had returns of 16.85 or better, and half the growth funds had returns of only 8.60 or better. The growth funds had a larger standard deviation than the value funds. Neither the growth nor the value funds showed any skewness because their skewness statistics were very close to 0. Both the growth and value funds exhibited positive kurtosis, meaning that the distribution of the returns had a sharper peak than a bell-shaped distribution.

VISUAL EXPLORATIONS | Exploring Descriptive Statistics

You can use the Visual Explorations Descriptive Statistics procedure to see the effect of changing data values on measures of central tendency, variation, and shape. Open the **Visual Explorations.xla** add-in workbook (see Appendix D) and select **VisualExplorations → Descriptive Statistics** (Excel 97–2003) or **Add-ins → VisualExplorations → Descriptive Statistics** (Excel 2007) from the Microsoft Excel menu bar. Read the instructions in the pop-up box (see illustration at the right) and click **OK** to examine a dot-scale diagram for the sample of 10 getting-ready times used throughout this chapter. (Review Section E1.8 on page 19 for more information on using add-ins, if necessary.)

Experiment by entering an extreme value such as 10 minutes into one of the tinted cells of column A. Which measures are affected by this change? Which ones are not? You can flip between the "before" and "after" diagrams by repeatedly pressing **Ctrl+Z** (undo) followed by **Ctrl +Y** (redo) to help see the changes the extreme value caused in the diagram.

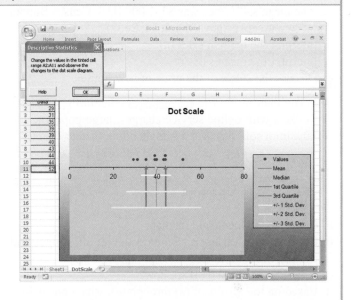

Problems for Sections 3.1 and 3.2

LEARNING THE BASICS

3.1 The following is a set of data from a sample of $n = 5$:

> 7 4 9 8 2

a. Compute the mean, median, and mode.
b. Compute the range, variance, standard deviation, and coefficient of variation.
c. Compute the Z scores. Are there any outliers?
d. Describe the shape of the data set.

3.2 The following is a set of data from a sample of $n = 6$:

> 7 4 9 7 3 12

a. Compute the mean, median, and mode.
b. Compute the range, variance, standard deviation, and coefficient of variation.
c. Compute the Z scores. Are there any outliers?
d. Describe the shape of the data set.

3.3 The following set of data is from a sample of $n = 7$:

> 12 7 4 9 0 7 3

a. Compute the mean, median, and mode.
b. Compute the range, variance, standard deviation, and coefficient of variation.
c. Compute the Z scores. Are there any outliers?
d. Describe the shape of the data set.

3.4 The following is a set of data from a sample of $n = 5$:

> 7 −5 −8 7 9

a. Compute the mean, median, and mode.

b. Compute the range, variance, standard deviation, and coefficient of variation.
c. Compute the Z scores. Are there any outliers?
d. Describe the shape of the data set.

APPLYING THE CONCEPTS

3.5 A business school reported its findings from a study of recent graduates. A sample of $n = 10$ finance majors had a mean starting salary of $45,000, a median starting salary of $45,000, and a standard deviation of $10,000. A sample of $n = 10$ information systems majors had a mean starting salary of $56,000, a median of $45,000, and a standard deviation of $37,000. Discuss the central tendency, variation, and shape of starting salaries for the two majors.

3.6 The operations manager of a plant that manufactures tires wants to compare the actual inner diameters of two grades of tires, each of which is expected to be 575 millimeters. A sample of five tires of each grade was selected, and the results representing the inner diameters of the tires, ranked from smallest to largest, are as follows:

Grade X	Grade Y
568 570 575 578 584	573 574 575 577 578

a. For each of the two grades of tires, compute the mean, median, and standard deviation.
b. Which grade of tire is providing better quality? Explain.
c. What would be the effect on your answers in (a) and (b) if the last value for grade Y were 588 instead of 578? Explain.

3.7 According to the U.S. Census Bureau, in February 2007 the median sales price of new houses was $250,000 and the mean sales price was $331,000 (U.S. Census Bureau News, **www.census.gov**, March 26, 2007).
a. Interpret the median sales price.
b. Interpret the mean sales price.
c. Discuss the shape of the price of new houses.

3.8 The data in the file Movieprices contain the price for two tickets with online service charges, large popcorn, and two medium soft drinks at a sample of six theater chains:

$36.15 $31.00 $35.05 $40.25 $33.75 $43.00

Source: *Data extracted from K. Kelly, "The Multiplex Under Siege," The Wall Street Journal, December 24–25, 2005, pp. P1, P5.*

a. Compute the mean and median.
b. Compute the variance, standard deviation, range, and coefficient of variation.
c. Are the data skewed? If so, how?
d. Based on the results of (a) through (c), what conclusions can you reach concerning the cost of going to the movies?

3.9 The data in the file Sedans represent the overall miles per gallon (MPG) of 2008 sedans priced under $20,000.

31, 27, 27, 28, 28, 28, 25, 25, 26, 25, 33, 23, 24

Source: *Data extracted from "Vehicle Ratings," Consumer Reports, April 2008, p. 32.*

a. Compute the mean, median, and mode.
b. Compute the variance, standard deviation, range, coefficient of variation, and Z scores.
c. Are the data skewed? If so, how?
d. Compare the results of (a) through (c) to those of Problem 3.10 (a) through (c) that refer to the miles per gallon of SUVs priced under $30,000.

3.10 The data in the file SUV represent the overall miles per gallon (MPG) of 2008 SUVs priced under $30,000.

23, 20, 21, 22, 18, 18, 17, 17, 19, 19, 19,
17, 21, 18, 18, 18, 17, 17, 16, 20, 16, 22

Source: *Data extracted from "Vehicle Ratings," Consumer Reports, April 2008, p. 40.*

a. Compute the mean, median, and mode.
b. Compute the variance, standard deviation, range, coefficient of variation, and Z scores.
c. Are the data skewed? If so, how?
d. Compare the results of (a) through (c) to those of Problem 3.9 (a) through (c) that refer to the miles per gallon of sedans priced under $20,000.

3.11 The data in the file Chicken contain the total fat, in grams per serving, for a sample of 20 chicken sandwiches from fast-food chains. The data are as follows:

7 8 4 5 16 20 20 24 19 30 23 30 25 19 29 29 30 30 40 56

Source: *Data extracted from "Fast Food: Adding Health to the Menu," Consumer Reports, September 2004, pp. 28–31.*

a. Compute the mean, median, and mode.
b. Compute the variance, standard deviation, range, coefficient of variation, and Z scores. Are there any outliers? Explain.
c. Are the data skewed? If so, how?
d. Based on the results of (a) through (c), what conclusions can you reach concerning the total fat of chicken sandwiches?

3.12 The data in the file DarkChocolate represent the cost per ounce ($) for a sample of 14 dark chocolate bars.

0.68   0.72   0.92   1.14   1.42   0.94   0.77   0.57   1.51
0.57   0.55   0.86   1.41   0.90

Source: *Data extracted from "Dark Chocolate: Which Bars are Best?" Consumer Reports, September 2007, p. 8.*

a. Compute the mean, median, and mode.
b. Compute the variance, standard deviation, range, coefficient of variation, and Z scores. Are there any outliers? Explain.
c. Are the data skewed? If so, how?
d. Based on the results of (a) through (c), what conclusions can you reach concerning the cost of dark chocolate bars?

3.13 Is there a difference in the variation of the yields of different types of investments between banks? The data in the file Bankyield represent the yields for a sample of money market accounts and five-year CDs as of March 31, 2008:

Money Market	Five-Year CD
3.94	4.21
3.75	4.07
3.74	4.02
3.68	3.93
3.68	3.92

Source: *Data extracted from **www.Bankrate.com**, March 31, 2008.*

a. For money market accounts and five-year CDs, separately compute the variance, standard deviation, range, and coefficient of variation.
b. Based on the results of (a), do money market accounts or five-year CDs have more variation in the highest yields offered? Explain.

3.14 The data in the file Themeparks contain the starting admission price (in $) for one-day tickets to 10 theme parks in the United States:

58   63   41   42   29   50   62   43   40   40

Source: *Data extracted from C. Jackson and E. Gamerman, "Rethinking the Thrill Factor," The Wall Street Journal, April 15–16, 2006, pp. P1, P4.*

a. Compute the mean, median, and mode.
b. Compute the range, variance, and standard deviation.

c. Based on the results of (a) and (b), what conclusions can you reach concerning the starting admission price for one-day tickets.

d. Suppose that the first value was 98 instead of 58. Repeat (a) through (c), using this value. Comment on the difference in the results.

3.15 A bank branch located in a commercial district of a city has developed an improved process for serving customers during the noon-to-1:00 p.m. lunch period. The waiting time, in minutes (defined as the time the customer enters the line to when he or she reaches the teller window), of a sample of 15 customers during this hour is recorded over a period of one week. The results are contained in the data file Bank1 and are listed below:

4.21 5.55 3.02 5.13 4.77 2.34 3.54 3.20 4.50
6.10 0.38 5.12 6.46 6.19 3.79

a. Compute the mean and median.
b. Compute the variance, standard deviation, range, coefficient of variation, and Z scores. Are there any outliers? Explain.
c. Are the data skewed? If so, how?
d. As a customer walks into the branch office during the lunch hour, she asks the branch manager how long she

can expect to wait. The branch manager replies, "Almost certainly less than five minutes." On the basis of the results of (a) through (c), evaluate the accuracy of this statement.

3.16 Suppose that another branch, located in a residential area, is also concerned with the noon-to-1 p.m. lunch hour. The waiting time, in minutes (defined as the time the customer enters the line to when he or she reaches the teller window), of a sample of 15 customers during this hour is recorded over a period of one week. The results are contained in the data file Bank2 and are listed below:

9.66 5.90 8.02 5.79 8.73 3.82 8.01 8.35 10.49
6.68 5.64 4.08 6.17 9.91 5.47

a. Compute the mean and median.
b. Compute the variance, standard deviation, range, coefficient of variation and Z scores. Are there any outliers? Explain.
c. Are the data skewed? If so, how?
d. As a customer walks into the branch office during the lunch hour, he asks the branch manager how long he can expect to wait. The branch manager replies, "Almost certainly less than five minutes." On the basis of the results of (a) through (c), evaluate the accuracy of this statement.

3.3 Numerical Descriptive Measures for a Population

Sections 3.1 and 3.2 present various statistics that described the properties of central tendency and variation for a sample. If your data set represents numerical measurements for an entire population, you need to calculate and interpret parameters, summary measures for a population. In this section, you will learn about three population parameters: the population mean, population variance, and population standard deviation.

To help illustrate these parameters, first review Table 3.5, which contains the one-year return for the five largest bond funds (in terms of total assets) as of May 5, 2008. (The data are contained in the file Largest bonds.)

TABLE 3.5

One-Year Return for the Population Consisting of the Five Largest Bond Funds

Bond Fund	One-Year Return
Pimco: Total Rtn; Inst	11.0
Vanguard Tot Bd; Inv	6.7
American Funds Bond; A	0.8
Dodge & Cox Income	4.4
Vanguard GNMA; Inv	7.3

Source: *Data extracted from* The Wall Street Journal, *May 5, 2008, p. R2.*

The Population Mean

The **population mean** is represented by the symbol μ, the Greek lowercase letter mu. Equation (3.8) defines the population mean.

POPULATION MEAN

The population mean is the sum of the values in the population divided by the population size N.

$$\mu = \frac{\sum_{i=1}^{N} X_i}{N} \tag{3.8}$$

where

$$\mu = \text{population mean}$$

$$X_i = i\text{th value of the variable } X$$

$$\sum_{i=1}^{N} X_i = \text{summation of all } X_i \text{ values in the population}$$

To compute the mean one-year return for the population of bond funds given in Table 3.5, use Equation (3.8):

$$\mu = \frac{\sum_{i=1}^{N} X_i}{N} = \frac{11.0 + 6.7 + 0.8 + 4.4 + 7.3}{5} = \frac{30.2}{5} = 6.04$$

Thus, the mean percentage return for these bond funds is 6.04.

The Population Variance and Standard Deviation

The **population variance** and the **population standard deviation** measure variation in a population. Like the related sample statistics, the population standard deviation is the square root of the population variance. The symbol σ^2, the Greek lowercase letter sigma squared, represents the population variance, and the symbol σ, the Greek lowercase letter sigma, represents the population standard deviation. Equations (3.9) and (3.10) define these parameters. The denominators for the right-side terms in these equations use N and not the $(n-1)$ term that is used in the equations for the sample variance and standard deviation [see Equations (3.4) and (3.5) on page 88].

POPULATION VARIANCE

The population variance is the sum of the squared differences around the population mean divided by the population size N.

$$\sigma^2 = \frac{\sum_{i=1}^{N} (X_i - \mu)^2}{N} \tag{3.9}$$

where

$$\mu = \text{population mean}$$

$$X_i = i\text{th value of the variable } X$$

$$\sum_{i=1}^{N} (X_i - \mu)^2 = \text{summation of all the squared differences between the } X_i \text{ values and } \mu$$

POPULATION STANDARD DEVIATION

$$\sigma = \sqrt{\frac{\sum_{i=1}^{N}(X_i - \mu)^2}{N}}$$ **(3.10)**

To compute the population variance for the data of Table 3.5 on page 97, you use Equation (3.9):

$$\sigma^2 = \frac{\sum_{i=1}^{N}(X_i - \mu)^2}{N}$$

$$= \frac{(11.0 - 6.04)^2 + (6.7 - 6.04)^2 + (0.8 - 6.04)^2 + (4.4 - 6.04)^2 + (7.3 - 6.04)^2}{5}$$

$$= \frac{24.6016 + 0.4356 + 27.4576 + 2.6896 + 1.5876}{5}$$

$$= \frac{56.772}{5} = 11.3544$$

Thus, the variance of the one-year returns is 11.3544 squared percentage return. The squared units make the variance hard to interpret. You should use the standard deviation that is expressed in the original units of the data (percentage return). From Equation (3.10),

$$\sigma = \sqrt{\sigma^2} = \sqrt{\frac{\sum_{i=1}^{N}(X_i - \mu)^2}{N}} = \sqrt{11.3544} = 3.3696$$

Therefore, the typical percentage return differs from the mean of 6.04 by approximately 3.3696. This large amount of variation suggests that these large bond funds produce results that differ greatly.

The Empirical Rule

In most data sets, a large portion of the values tend to cluster somewhere near the median. In right-skewed data sets, this clustering occurs to the left of the mean—that is, at a value less than the mean. In left-skewed data sets, the values tend to cluster to the right of the mean—that is, greater than the mean. In symmetrical data sets, where the median and mean are the same, the values often tend to cluster around the median and mean, producing a bell-shaped distribution. You can use the **empirical rule** to examine the variability in such distributions:

- Approximately 68% of the values are within a distance of ±1 standard deviation from the mean.
- Approximately 95% of the values are within a distance of ±2 standard deviations from the mean.
- Approximately 99.7% of the values are within a distance of ±3 standard deviations from the mean.

The empirical rule helps you measure how the values distribute above and below the mean and can help you identify outliers. The empirical rule implies that for bell-shaped distributions, only about 1 out of 20 values will be beyond two standard deviations from the mean in either direction. As a general rule, you can consider values not found in the interval $\mu \pm 2\sigma$ as potential outliers. The rule also implies that only about 3 in 1,000 will be beyond three standard deviations from the mean. Therefore, values not found in the interval $\mu \pm 3\sigma$ are almost always considered outliers.

EXAMPLE 3.9

Using the Empirical Rule

A population of 12-ounce cans of cola is known to have a mean fill-weight of 12.06 ounces and a standard deviation of 0.02. The population is known to be bell-shaped. Describe the distribution of fill-weights. Is it very likely that a can will contain less than 12 ounces of cola?

SOLUTION
$$\mu \pm \sigma = 12.06 \pm 0.02 = (12.04, 12.08)$$
$$\mu \pm 2\sigma = 12.06 \pm 2(0.02) = (12.02, 12.10)$$
$$\mu \pm 3\sigma = 12.06 \pm 3(0.02) = (12.00, 12.12)$$

Using the empirical rule, approximately 68% of the cans will contain between 12.04 and 12.08 ounces, approximately 95% will contain between 12.02 and 12.10 ounces, and approximately 99.7% will contain between 12.00 and 12.12 ounces. Therefore, it is highly unlikely that a can will contain less than 12 ounces.

For heavily skewed data sets, or those not appearing bell-shaped for any other reason, the Chebyshev rule discussed next should be applied instead of the empirical rule.

The Chebyshev Rule

The **Chebyshev rule** (reference 1) states that for any data set, regardless of shape, the percentage of values that are found within distances of k standard deviations from the mean must be at least

$$(1 - 1/k^2) \times 100\%$$

You can use this rule for any value of k greater than 1. Consider $k = 2$. The Chebyshev rule states that at least $[1 - (1/2)^2] \times 100\% = 75\%$ of the values must be found within ± 2 standard deviations of the mean.

The Chebyshev rule is very general and applies to any type of distribution. The rule indicates *at least* what percentage of the values fall within a given distance from the mean. However, if the data set is approximately bell-shaped, the empirical rule will more accurately reflect the greater concentration of data close to the mean. Table 3.6 compares the Chebyshev and empirical rules.

TABLE 3.6

How Data Vary Around the Mean

	% of Values Found in Intervals Around the Mean	
Interval	Chebyshev (any distribution)	Empirical Rule (bell-shaped distribution)
$(\mu - \sigma, \mu + \sigma)$	At least 0%	Approximately 68%
$(\mu - 2\sigma, \mu + 2\sigma)$	At least 75%	Approximately 95%
$(\mu - 3\sigma, \mu + 3\sigma)$	At least 88.89%	Approximately 99.7%

EXAMPLE 3.10

Using the Chebyshev Rule

As in Example 3.9, a population of 12-ounce cans of cola is known to have a mean fill-weight of 12.06 ounces and a standard deviation of 0.02. However, the shape of the population is unknown, and you cannot assume that it is bell-shaped. Describe the distribution of fill-weights. Is it very likely that a can will contain less than 12 ounces of cola?

SOLUTION
$$\mu \pm \sigma = 12.06 \pm 0.02 = (12.04, 12.08)$$
$$\mu \pm 2\sigma = 12.06 \pm 2(0.02) = (12.02, 12.10)$$
$$\mu \pm 3\sigma = 12.06 \pm 3(0.02) = (12.00, 12.12)$$

Because the distribution may be skewed, you cannot use the empirical rule. Using the Chebyshev rule, you cannot say anything about the percentage of cans containing between 12.04 and 12.08 ounces. You can state that at least 75% of the cans will contain between 12.02 and 12.10 ounces and at least 88.89% will contain between 12.00 and 12.12 ounces. Therefore, between 0 and 11.11% of the cans will contain less than 12 ounces.

You can use these two rules for understanding how data are distributed around the mean when you have sample data. In each case, you use the value you calculated for $\overline{X}$ in place of μ and the value you calculated for S in place of σ. The results you compute using the sample statistics are *approximations* because you used sample statistics $(\overline{X}, S)$ and not population parameters (μ, σ).

Problems for Section 3.3

LEARNING THE BASICS

3.17 The following is a set of data for a population with $N = 10$:

$$7 \quad 5 \quad 11 \quad 8 \quad 3 \quad 6 \quad 2 \quad 1 \quad 9 \quad 8$$

a. Compute the population mean.
b. Compute the population standard deviation.

3.18 The following is a set of data for a population with $N = 10$:

$$7 \quad 5 \quad 6 \quad 6 \quad 6 \quad 4 \quad 8 \quad 6 \quad 9 \quad 3$$

a. Compute the population mean.
b. Compute the population standard deviation.

APPLYING THE CONCEPTS

3.19 The data in the file **Tax** represent the quarterly sales tax receipts (in thousands of dollars) submitted to the comptroller of the Village of Fair Lake for the period ending March 2008 by all 50 business establishments in that locale:

10.3	11.1	9.6	9.0	14.5
13.0	6.7	11.0	8.4	10.3
13.0	11.2	7.3	5.3	12.5
8.0	11.8	8.7	10.6	9.5
11.1	10.2	11.1	9.9	9.8
11.6	15.1	12.5	6.5	7.5
10.0	12.9	9.2	10.0	12.8
12.5	9.3	10.4	12.7	10.5
9.3	11.5	10.7	11.6	7.8
10.5	7.6	10.1	8.9	8.6

a. Compute the mean, variance, and standard deviation for this population.
b. What percentage of these businesses have quarterly sales tax receipts within ± 1, ± 2, or ± 3 standard deviations of the mean?
c. Compare and contrast your findings with what would be expected on the basis of the empirical rule. Are you surprised at the results in (b)?

3.20 Consider a population of 1,024 mutual funds that primarily invest in large companies. You have determined that μ, the mean one-year total percentage return achieved by all the funds, is 8.20 and that σ, the standard deviation, is 2.75. According to the empirical rule, what percentage of these funds is expected to be
a. within ± 1 standard deviation of the mean?
b. within ± 2 standard deviations of the mean?

c. According to the Chebyshev rule, what percentage of these funds are expected to be within ± 1, ± 2, or ± 3 standard deviations of the mean?
d. According to the Chebyshev rule, at least 93.75% of these funds are expected to have one-year total returns between what two amounts?

3.21 The file **Collegetuition** contains the tuition and fees for public four-year colleges in each of the 50 states for the 2006–2007 school year. The amounts do not include room and board. The file also contains the percentage increase in tuition and fees from 2005–2006 to 2006–2007 (extracted from Sandra Block, "Rising Costs Make Climb to Higher Education Steeper," **usatoday.com**, January 12, 2007).
a. Compute the population mean and population standard deviation for tuition and fees.
b. Interpret the parameters in (a).
c. Compute the population mean and population standard deviation for the percentage increase from 2005–2006 to 2006–2007.
d. Interpret the parameters in (c).

3.22 The data in the file **Energy** contains the per-capita energy consumption, in kilowatt hours, for each of the 50 states and the District of Columbia during a recent year.
a. Compute the mean, variance, and standard deviation for the population.
b. What proportion of these states has average per-capita energy consumption within ± 1 standard deviation of the mean, within ± 2 standard deviations of the mean, and within ± 3 standard deviations of the mean?
c. Compare and contrast your findings versus what would be expected based on the empirical rule. Are you surprised at the results in (b)?
d. Repeat (a) through (c) with the District of Columbia removed. How have the results changed?

3.23 Thirty companies comprise the DJIA. Just how big are these companies? One common method to measure the size of a company is to use its market capitalization, which is computed by taking the number of stock shares multiplied by the price of a share of stock. On May 5, 2008, the market capitalization of these companies ranged from General Motors's $12.7 billion to Exxon-Mobil's $477.2 billion. The entire population of market capitalization values is recorded in the file **Dowmarketcap**.
Source: *Data extracted from money.cnn.com, May 5, 2008.*

a. Calculate the mean and standard deviation of the market capitalization for this population of 30 companies.
b. Interpret the parameters calculated in (a).

3.4 Quartiles and the Boxplot

Sections 3.1 through 3.3 discuss measures of central tendency, variation, and shape. Another way of describing numerical data is through an exploratory data analysis that includes the quartiles, the five-number summary, and the boxplot (references 4 and 5).

Quartiles

Quartiles split a set of data into four equal parts—the **first quartile, Q_1,** divides the smallest 25.0% of the values from the other 75.0% that are larger. The **second quartile, Q_2,** is the median—50.0% of the values are smaller than the median and 50.0% are larger. The **third quartile, Q_3,** divides the smallest 75.0% of the values from the largest 25.0%. Equations (3.11) and (3.12) define the first and third quartiles.[1]

[1]The Q_1, median, and Q_3 are also the 25th, 50th, and 75th percentiles, respectively. Equations (3.2), (3.11), and (3.12) can be expressed generally in terms of finding percentiles: $(p \times 100)$th percentile = $p \times (n + 1)$ ranked value.

FIRST QUARTILE, Q_1

25.0% of the values are smaller than or equal to Q_1, the first quartile, and 75.0% are larger than or equal to the first quartile, Q_1.

$$Q_1 = \frac{n + 1}{4} \text{ ranked value} \qquad \text{(3.11)}$$

THIRD QUARTILE, Q_3

75.0% of the values are smaller than or equal to the third quartile, Q_3, and 25.0% are larger than or equal to the third quartile, Q_3.

$$Q_3 = \frac{3(n + 1)}{4} \text{ ranked value} \qquad \text{(3.12)}$$

Use the following rules to calculate the quartiles from a set of ranked values:

- **Rule 1** If the ranked value is a whole number, then the quartile is equal to the measurement that corresponds to that ranked value. For example, if the sample size $n = 7$, the first quartile, Q_1, is equal to the $(7 + 1)/4 =$ second ranked value.
- **Rule 2** If the ranked value is a fractional half (2.5, 4.5, etc.), then the quartile is equal to the measurement that corresponds to the average of the ranked values involved. For example, if the sample size $n = 9$, the first quartile, Q_1, is equal to the $(9 + 1)/4 = 2.5$ ranked value, halfway between the second ranked value and the third ranked value.
- **Rule 3** If the ranked value is neither a whole number nor a fractional half, you round the result to the nearest integer and select that ranked value. For example, if the sample size $n = 10$, the first quartile, Q_1, is equal to the $(10 + 1)/4 = 2.75$ ranked value. Round 2.75 to 3 and use the third ranked value.

To illustrate the computation of the quartiles for the time-to-get-ready data, rank the following data from smallest to largest:

Ranked values:

29	31	35	39	39	40	43	44	44	52

Ranks:

1	2	3	4	5	6	7	8	9	10

The first quartile is the $(n + 1)/4 = (10 + 1)/4 = 2.75$ ranked value. Using Rule 3, you round up to the third ranked value. The third ranked value for the time-to-get-ready data is 35 minutes. You interpret the first quartile of 35 to mean that on 25% of the days, the time to get ready is less than or equal to 35 minutes, and on 75% of the days, the time to get ready is greater than or equal to 35 minutes.

The third quartile is the $3(n + 1)/4 = 3(10 + 1)/4 = 8.25$ ranked value. Using Rule 3 for quartiles, you round this down to the eighth ranked value. The eighth ranked value is 44 minutes. Thus, on 75% of the days, the time to get ready is less than or equal to 44 minutes, and on 25% of the days, the time to get ready is greater than or equal to 44 minutes.

EXAMPLE 3.11

Computing the Quartiles

The data in the file CoffeeDrink (see Example 3.1 on page 84) represent the calories of 16-ounce iced coffee drinks at Dunkin' Donuts and Starbucks. Compute the first quartile (Q_1) and third quartile (Q_3) number of calories for the iced coffee drinks at Dunkin' Donuts and Starbucks.

SOLUTION Ranked from smallest to largest, the number of calories for the seven iced coffee drinks are:

Ranked values:

$$240 \quad 260 \quad 350 \quad 350 \quad 420 \quad 510 \quad 530$$

Ranks:

$$1 \quad 2 \quad 3 \quad 4 \quad 5 \quad 6 \quad 7$$

For these data

$$Q_1 = \frac{(n + 1)}{4} \text{ ranked value}$$

$$= \frac{7 + 1}{4} \text{ ranked value} = \text{2nd ranked value}$$

Therefore, using Rule 1, Q_1 is the second ranked value. Because the second ranked value is 260, the first quartile, Q_1, is 260.

To find the third quartile, Q_3:

$$Q_3 = \frac{3(n + 1)}{4} \text{ ranked value}$$

$$= \frac{3(7 + 1)}{4} \text{ ranked value} = \text{6th ranked value}$$

Therefore, using Rule 1, Q_3 is the sixth ranked value. Because the sixth ranked value is 510, Q_3 is 510.

The first quartile of 260 indicates that 25% of the iced coffee drinks have calories that are below or equal to 260 and 75% are greater than or equal to 260. The third quartile of 510 indicates that 75% of the iced coffee drinks have calories that are below or equal to 510 and 25% are greater than or equal to 510.

The Interquartile Range

The **interquartile range** (also called **midspread**) is the difference between the third and first quartiles in a set of data.

> **INTERQUARTILE RANGE**
>
> The interquartile range is the difference between the third quartile and the first quartile.
>
> $$\text{Interquartile range} = Q_3 - Q_1 \qquad \textbf{(3.13)}$$

The interquartile range measures the spread in the middle 50% of the data. Therefore, it is not influenced by extreme values. To determine the interquartile range of the times to get ready

$$29 \quad 31 \quad 35 \quad 39 \quad 39 \quad 40 \quad 43 \quad 44 \quad 44 \quad 52$$

you use Equation (3.13) and the earlier results on page 102, $Q_1 = 35$ and $Q_3 = 44$:

$$\text{Interquartile range} = 44 - 35 = 9 \text{ minutes}$$

Therefore, the interquartile range in the time to get ready is 9 minutes. The interval 35 to 44 is often referred to as the *middle fifty*.

EXAMPLE 3.12

Computing the Interquartile Range For the Number of Calories in Iced Coffee Drinks

The data in the file **CoffeeDrink** (see Example 3.1 on page 84) represent the calories of 16-ounce iced coffee drinks at Dunkin' Donuts and Starbucks. Compute the interquartile range of the number of calories of 16-ounce iced coffee drinks.

SOLUTION Ranked from smallest to largest, the number of calories for the seven iced coffee drinks are:

$$240 \quad 260 \quad 350 \quad 350 \quad 420 \quad 510 \quad 530$$

Using Equation (3.13) and the earlier results from Example 3.11 on page 103, $Q_1 = 260$ and $Q_3 = 510$:

$$\text{Interquartile range} = 510 - 260 = 250$$

Therefore, the interquartile range of the number of calories of 16-ounce iced coffee drinks is 250 calories.

Because the interquartile range does not consider any value smaller than Q_1 or larger than Q_3, it cannot be affected by extreme values. Summary measures such as the median, Q_1, Q_3, and the interquartile range, which cannot be influenced by extreme values, are called **resistant measures**.

The Five-Number Summary

A **five-number summary** that consists of

$$X_{\text{smallest}} \quad Q_1 \quad \text{Median} \quad Q_3 \quad X_{\text{largest}}$$

provides a way to determine the shape of a distribution. Table 3.7 explains how the relationships among the "five numbers" allows you to recognize the shape of a data set.

For the sample of 10 getting-ready times, the smallest value is 29 minutes and the largest value is 52 minutes (see page 85). Calculations done on pages 85 and 102–103 show that the median = 39.5, $Q_1 = 35$, and $Q_3 = 44$. Therefore, the five-number summary is

$$29 \quad 35 \quad 39.5 \quad 44 \quad 52$$

The distance from X_{smallest} to the median ($39.5 - 29 = 10.5$) is slightly less than the distance from the median to X_{largest} ($52 - 39.5 = 12.5$). The distance from X_{smallest} to Q_1 ($35 - 29 = 6$) is slightly less than the distance from Q_3 to X_{largest} ($52 - 44 = 8$). Therefore, the getting-ready times are slightly right-skewed.

TABLE 3.7

Relationships Among the Five-Number Summary and the Type of Distribution

	Type of Distribution		
Comparison	**Left-Skewed**	**Symmetric**	**Right-Skewed**
The distance from X_{smallest} to the median versus the distance from the median to X_{largest}.	The distance from X_{smallest} to the median is greater than the distance from the median to X_{largest}.	Both distances are the same.	The distance from X_{smallest} to the median is less than the distance from the median to X_{largest}.
The distance from X_{smallest} to Q_1 versus the distance from Q_3 to X_{largest}.	The distance from X_{smallest} to Q_1 is greater than the distance from Q_3 to X_{largest}.	Both distances are the same.	The distance from X_{smallest} to Q_1 is less than the distance from Q_3 to X_{largest}.
The distance from Q_1 to the median versus the distance from the median to Q_3.	The distance from Q_1 to the median is greater than the distance from the median to Q_3.	Both distances are the same.	The distance from Q_1 to the median is less than the distance from the median to Q_3.

EXAMPLE 3.13

Computing the Five-Number Summary of the Number of Calories in Iced Coffee Drinks

The data in the file `CoffeeDrink` (see Example 3.1 on page 84) represent the calories of 16-ounce iced coffee drinks at Dunkin' Donuts and Starbucks. Compute the five-number summary of the number of calories of 16-ounce iced coffee drinks.

SOLUTION From previous computations for the calories of 16-ounce iced coffee drinks (see pages 85 and 103), the median = 350, $Q_1 = 260$, and $Q_3 = 510$. In addition, the smallest value in the data set is 240, and the largest value is 530. Therefore, the five-number summary is

$$240 \quad 260 \quad 350 \quad 510 \quad 530$$

The three comparisons listed in Table 3.7 are used to evaluate skewness. The distance from X_{smallest} to the median ($350 - 240 = 110$) is less than the distance ($530 - 350 = 180$) from the median to X_{largest}. The distance from X_{smallest} to Q_1 ($260 - 240 = 20$) is the same as the distance from Q_3 to X_{largest} ($530 - 510 = 20$). The distance from Q_1 to the median ($350 - 260 = 90$) is less than the distance from the median to Q_3 ($510 - 350 = 160$). Two comparisons indicate a right-skewed distribution whereas the other indicates a symmetric distribution. Therefore, you can conclude that the number of calories in iced coffee drinks is right-skewed.

The Boxplot

A **boxplot** provides a graphical representation of the data based on the five-number summary. Figure 3.4 illustrates the boxplot for the getting-ready times. The vertical line drawn within the box represents the median. The vertical line at the left side of the box represents the location of Q_1, and the vertical line at the right side of the box represents the location of Q_3. Thus, the box contains the middle 50% of the values. The lower 25% of the data are represented by a line connecting the left side of the box to the location of the smallest value, X_{smallest}. Similarly, the upper 25% of the data are represented by a line connecting the right side of the box to X_{largest}.

FIGURE 3.4

Boxplot for the getting ready times

See Appendix E3.3 or P3.1 to create this. (Use Section M3.2 to create the Minitab equivalent.)

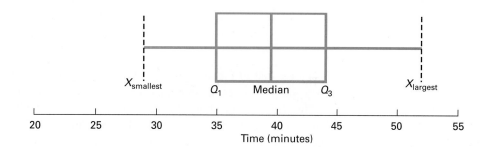

The boxplot of the getting-ready times in Figure 3.4 indicates slight right-skewness because the distance between the median and the highest value is slightly greater than the distance between the lowest value and the median. Also, the right tail is slightly longer than the left tail.

EXAMPLE 3.14

The Boxplots of the 2006 Returns of Growth and Value Mutual Funds

The 868 mutual funds (`Mutual Funds`) that are part of the Using Statistics scenario (see page 81) are classified according to whether the mutual funds are growth or value funds. Construct the boxplot of the 2006 returns for growth and value mutual funds.

SOLUTION Figure 3.5 shows PHStat2 boxplots of the 2006 return for the growth and value mutual funds and Figure 3.6 illustrates Minitab boxplots. The median return, the quartiles, and the minimum and maximum return are much higher for the value funds than for the growth funds. Both the growth and value funds appear to be fairly symmetrical between the quartiles, but the value funds seem to have more extremely high returns.

FIGURE 3.5

PHStat2 boxplots of the 2006 return for growth and value mutual funds

See Appendix E3.3 or P3.1 to create this.

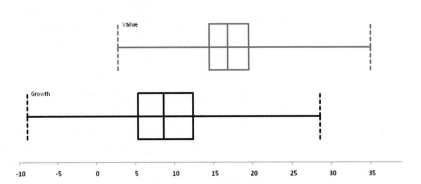

Boxplots for the Growth and Value Funds
2006 Return

FIGURE 3.6

Minitab boxplots of the 2006 return for growth and value mutual funds

See Appendix M3.2 to create this.

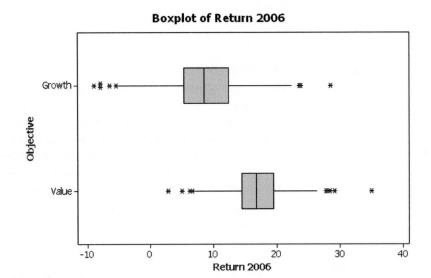

Boxplot of Return 2006

Notice that in Figure 3.6, several * appear in the boxplots. This indicates outliers that are more than 1.5 times the interquartile range beyond the quartiles.

Figure 3.7 demonstrates the relationship between the boxplot and the polygon for four different types of distributions. (*Note:* The area under each polygon is split into quartiles corresponding to the five-number summary for the boxplot.)

FIGURE 3.7

Boxplots and corresponding polygons for four distributions

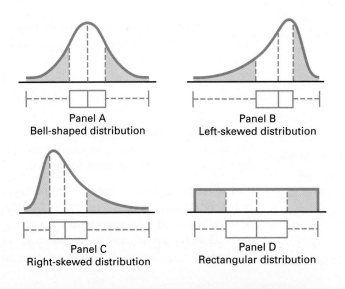

Panel A
Bell-shaped distribution

Panel B
Left-skewed distribution

Panel C
Right-skewed distribution

Panel D
Rectangular distribution

Panels A and D of Figure 3.7 are symmetrical. In these distributions, the mean and median are equal. In addition, the length of the left tail is equal to the length of the right tail, and the median line divides the box in half.

Panel B of Figure 3.7 is left-skewed. The few small values distort the mean toward the left tail. For this left-skewed distribution, there is a heavy clustering of values at the high end of the scale (i.e., the right side); 75% of all values are found between the left edge of the box (Q_1) and the end of the right tail ($X_{largest}$). There is a long left tail that contains the smallest 25% of the values, demonstrating the lack of symmetry in this data set.

Panel C of Figure 3.7 is right-skewed. The concentration of values is on the low end of the scale (i.e., the left side of the boxplot). Here, 75% of all values are found between the beginning of the left tail and the right edge of the box (Q_3) There is a long right tail that contains

Problems for Section 3.4

LEARNING THE BASICS

3.24 The following is a set of data from a sample of $n = 6$:

7 4 9 7 3 12

a. Compute the first quartile (Q_1), the third quartile (Q_3), and the interquartile range.
b. List the five-number summary.
c. Construct a boxplot and describe the shape.
d. Compare your answer in (c) with that from Problem 3.2(d) on page 95. Discuss.

3.25 The following is a set of data from a sample of $n = 7$:

12 7 4 9 0 7 3

a. Compute the first quartile (Q_1), the third quartile (Q_3), and the interquartile range.
b. List the five-number summary.
c. Construct a boxplot and describe the shape.
d. Compare your answer in (c) with that from Problem 3.3(d) on page 95. Discuss.

3.26 The following is a set of data from a sample of $n = 5$:

7 -5 -8 7 9

a. Compute the first quartile (Q_1), the third quartile (Q_3), and the interquartile range.
b. List the five-number summary.
c. Construct a boxplot and describe the shape.
d. Compare your answer in (c) with that from Problem 3.4(d) on page 95. Discuss.

APPLYING THE CONCEPTS

3.27 The data file **Chicken** contains the total fat, in grams per serving, for a sample of 20 chicken sandwiches from fast-food chains. The data are as follows:

7 8 4 5 16 20 20 24 19 30
23 30 25 19 29 29 30 30 40 56

Source: *Data extracted from "Fast Food: Adding Health to the Menu," Consumer Reports, September 2004, pp. 28–31.*

a. Compute the first quartile (Q_1), the third quartile (Q_3), and the interquartile range.

b. List the five-number summary.
c. Construct a boxplot and describe the shape.

3.28 The data in the file **Dark chocolate** represent the cost ($) per ounce for a sample of 14 dark chocolate bars.

0.68 0.72 0.92 1.14 1.42 0.94 0.77 0.57 1.51
0.57 0.55 0.86 1.41 0.90

Source: *Data extracted from "Dark Chocolate Which Bars are Best?" Consumer Reports, September 2007, pp. 1–8.*

a. Compute the first quartile (Q_1), the third quartile (Q_3), and the interquartile range.
b. List the five-number summary.
c. Construct a boxplot and describe the shape.

3.29 The data file **Themeparks** contains data on the starting admission price (in $) for one-day tickets to 10 theme parks in the United States:

58 63 41 42 29 50 62 43 40 40

Source: *Data extracted from C. Jackson and E. Gamerman, "Rethinking the Thrill Factor," The Wall Street Journal, April 15–16, 2006, pp. P1, P4.*

a. Compute the first quartile (Q_1), the third quartile (Q_3), and the interquartile range.
b. List the five-number summary.
c. Construct a boxplot and describe the shape.

3.30 ✓**SELF** **Test** The data in the file **SUV** represent the overall miles per gallon (MPG) of 2008 SUVs priced under $30,000.

23, 20, 21, 22, 18, 18, 17, 17, 19, 19, 19,
17, 21, 18, 18, 18, 17, 17, 16, 20, 16, 22

Source: *Data extracted from "Vehicle Ratings," Consumer Reports, April 2008, p. 40.*

a. Compute the first quartile (Q_1), the third quartile (Q_3), and the interquartile range.
b. List the five-number summary.
c. Construct a boxplot and describe the shape.

3.31 The data in the file `Savings Rate` are the yields for a money market account, a one-year certificate of deposit (CD), and a five-year CD for 38 banks in South Florida as of March 28, 2008 (data extracted from **Bankrate.com**, March 28, 2008).
a. List the five-number summary for the yield of the money market account, one-year CD, and a five-year CD.
b. Construct boxplots for the yield of the money market account, one-year CD, and a five-year CD.
c. What similarities and differences are there in the distributions for the yield of the money market account, one-year CD, and a five-year CD?

3.32 A bank branch located in a commercial district of a city has developed an improved process for serving customers during the noon-to-1:00 p.m. lunch period. The waiting time, in minutes (defined as the time the customer enters the line to when he or she reaches the teller window), of a sample of 15 customers during this hour is recorded over a period of one week. The results are contained in the data file `Bank1` and are listed below:

4.21 5.55 3.02 5.13 4.77 2.34 3.54 3.20
4.50 6.10 0.38 5.12 6.46 6.19 3.79

Another branch, located in a residential area, is also concerned with the noon-to-1 p.m. lunch hour. The waiting time, in minutes (defined as the time the customer enters the line to when he or she reaches the teller window), of a sample of 15 customers during this hour is recorded over a period of one week. The results are contained in the data file `Bank2` and are listed below:

9.66 5.90 8.02 5.79 8.73 3.82 8.01 8.35
10.49 6.68 5.64 4.08 6.17 9.91 5.47

a. List the five-number summaries of the waiting times at the two bank branches.
b. Construct boxplots and describe the shape of the distribution for the two bank branches.
c. What similarities and differences are there in the distributions of the waiting time at the two bank branches?

3.5 The Covariance and the Coefficient of Correlation

In Section 2.5, you used scatter plots to visually examine the relationship between two numerical variables. This section presents two measures of the relationship between two numerical variables: the covariance and the coefficient of correlation.

The Covariance

The **covariance** measures the strength of the linear relationship between two numerical variables (X and Y). Equation (3.14) defines the **sample covariance**, and Example 3.15 illustrates its use.

THE SAMPLE COVARIANCE

$$\text{cov}(X, Y) = \frac{\sum_{i=1}^{n}(X_i - \bar{X})(Y_i - \bar{Y})}{n - 1} \tag{3.14}$$

EXAMPLE 3.15

Computing the Sample Covariance

In Figure 2.14 on page 50, you examined the relationship between the cost of a fast-food hamburger meal and the cost of two movie tickets in 10 cities around the world (extracted from K. Spors, "Keeping Up with . . . Yourself," *The Wall Street Journal*, April 11, 2005, p. R4). The data file `Cost of living` contains the complete data set. Compute the sample covariance.

SOLUTION Table 3.8 provides the cost of a fast-food hamburger meal and the cost of two movie tickets in 10 cities around the world.

TABLE 3.8

Cost of a Fast-Food Hamburger Meal and Cost of Two Movie Tickets in 10 Cities

City	Hamburger	Movie Tickets
Tokyo	5.99	32.66
London	7.62	28.41
New York	5.75	20.00
Sydney	4.45	20.71
Chicago	4.99	18.00
San Francisco	5.29	19.50
Boston	4.39	18.00
Atlanta	3.70	16.00
Toronto	4.62	18.05
Rio de Janeiro	2.99	9.90

Figure 3.8 contains a Microsoft Excel worksheet that calculates the covariance for these data. The Calculations area of Figure 3.8 breaks down Equation (3.14) into a set of smaller calculations. From cell C20, or by using Equation (3.14) directly, you find that the covariance is 6.8378:

$$\text{cov}(X, Y) = \frac{61.5399}{10 - 1}$$

$$= 6.8378$$

FIGURE 3.8

Microsoft Excel worksheet for the covariance between the cost of a fast-food hamburger meal and the cost of two movie tickets in 10 cities

See Appendix E3.4 to create this.

	A	B	C	
1	Covariance Analysis			
2				
3	Hamburger Meal	Movie Ticket	(X-XBar)(Y-YBar)	
4	5.99	32.66	12.6749	=(A4 - C16) * (B4 - C17)
5	7.62	28.41	21.8860	=(A5 - C16) * (B5 - C17)
6	5.75	20.00	-0.0948	=(A6 - C16) * (B6 - C17)
7	4.45	20.71	-0.3105	=(A7 - C16) * (B7 - C17)
8	4.99	18.00	-0.0234	=(A8 - C16) * (B8 - C17)
9	5.29	19.50	-0.1938	=(A9 - C16) * (B9 - C17)
10	4.39	18.00	1.2504	=(A10 - C16) * (B10 - C17)
11	3.70	16.00	5.2733	=(A11 - C16) * (B11 - C17)
12	4.62	18.05	0.7442	=(A12 - C16) * (B12 - C17)
13	2.99	9.90	20.3335	=(A13 - C16) * (B13 - C17)
14				
15		Calculations		
16		XBar	4.9790	=AVERAGE(A4:A13)
17		YBar	20.1230	=AVERAGE(B4:B13)
18		*n*-1	9	=COUNT(A4:A13) - 1
19		Sum	61.5399	=SUM(C4:C13)
20		Covariance	6.8378	=C19 / C18

The covariance has a major flaw as a measure of the linear relationship between two numerical variables. Because the covariance can have any value, you are unable to determine the relative strength of the relationship. In other words, you cannot tell whether the value 6.8378 is an indication of a strong relationship or a weak relationship. To better determine the relative strength of the relationship, you need to compute the coefficient of correlation.

The Coefficient of Correlation

The **coefficient of correlation** measures the relative strength of a linear relationship between two numerical variables. The values of the coefficient of correlation range from -1 for a perfect negative correlation to $+1$ for a perfect positive correlation. Perfect means that if the points were plotted in a scatter plot, all the points could be connected with a straight line. When dealing with population data for two numerical variables, the Greek letter ρ is used as the symbol for the coefficient of correlation. Figure 3.9 illustrates three different types of association between two variables.

FIGURE 3.9

Types of association between variables

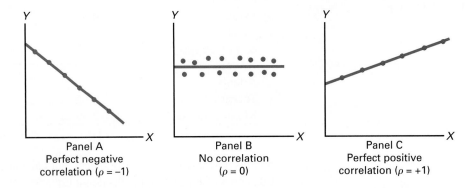

Panel A
Perfect negative
correlation ($\rho = -1$)

Panel B
No correlation
($\rho = 0$)

Panel C
Perfect positive
correlation ($\rho = +1$)

In Panel A of Figure 3.9, there is a perfect negative linear relationship between X and Y. Thus, the coefficient of correlation, ρ, equals -1, and when X increases, Y decreases in a perfectly predictable manner. Panel B shows a situation in which there is no relationship between X and Y. In this case, the coefficient of correlation, ρ, equals 0, and as X increases, there is no tendency for Y to increase or decrease. Panel C illustrates a perfect positive relationship where ρ equals $+1$. In this case, Y increases in a perfectly predictable manner when X increases.

Correlation alone cannot prove that there is a causation effect—that is, that the change in the value of one variable caused the change in the other variable. A strong correlation can be produced simply by chance, by the effect of a third variable not considered in the calculation of the correlation, or by a cause-and-effect relationship. You would need to perform additional analysis to determine which of these three situations actually produced the correlation. Therefore, you can say that causation implies correlation, but correlation alone does not imply causation.

Equation (3.15) defines the **sample coefficient of correlation**, r.

THE SAMPLE COEFFICIENT OF CORRELATION

$$r = \frac{\text{cov}(X, Y)}{S_X S_Y} \qquad (3.15)$$

where

$$\text{cov}(X, Y) = \frac{\sum\limits_{i=1}^{n}(X_i - \overline{X})(Y_i - \overline{Y})}{n - 1}$$

$$S_X = \sqrt{\frac{\sum\limits_{i=1}^{n}(X_i - \overline{X})^2}{n - 1}}$$

$$S_Y = \sqrt{\frac{\sum\limits_{i=1}^{n}(Y_i - \overline{Y})^2}{n - 1}}$$

When you have sample data, you calculate the sample coefficient of correlation, r. When using sample data, you are unlikely to have a sample coefficient of exactly $+1$, 0, or -1. Figure 3.10 presents scatter plots along with their respective sample coefficients of correlation, r, for six data sets, each of which contains 100 values of X and Y.

FIGURE 3.10

Six Minitab scatter plots and their sample coefficients of correlation, r

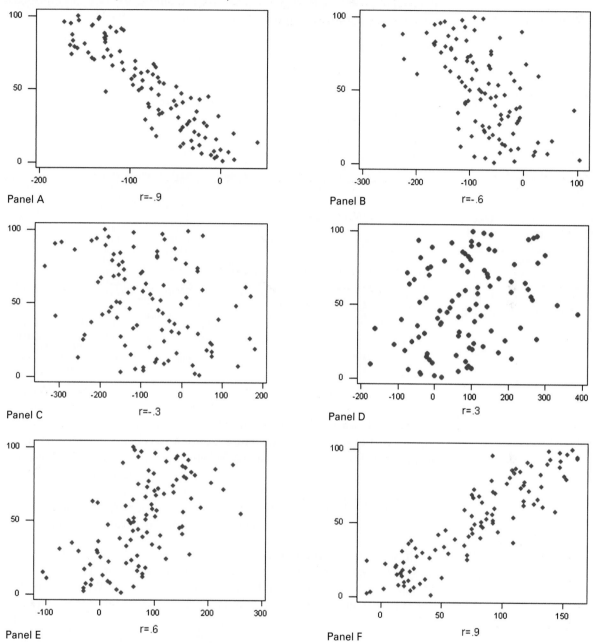

In Panel A, the coefficient of correlation, r, is -0.9. You can see that for small values of X, there is a very strong tendency for Y to be large. Likewise, the large values of X tend to be paired with small values of Y. The data do not all fall on a straight line, so the association between X and Y cannot be described as perfect. The data in Panel B have a coefficient of correlation equal to -0.6, and the small values of X tend to be paired with large values of Y. The linear relationship between X and Y in Panel B is not as strong as that in Panel A. Thus, the coefficient of correlation in Panel B is not as negative as that in Panel A. In Panel C, the linear relationship between X and Y is very weak, $r = -0.3$, and there is only a slight tendency for the small values of X to be paired with the large values of Y. Panels D through F depict data sets that have positive coefficients of correlation because small values of X tend to be paired with small values of Y, and the large values of X tend to be associated with large values of Y.

EXAMPLE 3.16

Computing the
Sample Coefficient
of Correlation

Consider the cost of a fast-food hamburger meal and the cost of two movie tickets in 10 cities around the world (see Table 3.8 on page 109). From Figure 3.11 and Equation (3.15) on page 110, compute the sample coefficient of correlation.

SOLUTION

$$r = \frac{\text{cov}(X, Y)}{S_X S_Y}$$

$$= \frac{6.8378}{(1.2925)(6.337)}$$

$$= 0.8348$$

FIGURE 3.11

Microsoft Excel worksheet for the sample coefficient of correlation, r, between the cost of a fast-food hamburger meal and two movie tickets

See Appendix E3.5 to create this. (Use Section M3.3 to create the Minitab equivalent.)

	A	B	C	D	E
1	Hamburger Meal	Movie Ticket	$(X-\bar{X})^2$	$(Y-\bar{Y})^2$	$(X-\bar{X})(Y-\bar{Y})$
2	5.99	32.66	1.0221	157.1764	12.6749
3	7.62	28.41	6.9749	68.6744	21.8860
4	5.75	20.00	0.5944	0.0151	-0.0948
5	4.45	20.71	0.2798	0.3446	-0.3105
6	4.99	18.00	0.0001	4.5071	-0.0234
7	5.29	19.50	0.0967	0.3881	-0.1938
8	4.39	18.00	0.3469	4.5071	1.2504
9	3.70	16.00	1.6358	16.9991	5.2733
10	4.62	18.05	0.1289	4.2973	0.7442
11	2.99	9.90	3.9561	104.5097	20.3335
12		Sums:	15.03589	361.41901	61.5399
13					
14				Calculations	
15			XBar	4.979	=AVERAGE(A2:A11)
16			YBar	20.123	=AVERAGE(B2:B11)
17			n-1	9	=COUNT(A2:A11)-1
18			Covariance	6.83777	=E12 / E17
19			S_X	1.2925	=SQRT(C12 / E17)
20			S_Y	6.3370	=SQRT(D12 / E17)
21			r	0.8348	=CORREL(A2:A11, B2:B11)

The cost of a fast-food hamburger meal and the cost of two movie tickets are positively correlated. Those cities with the lowest cost of a fast-food hamburger meal tend to be associated with the lowest cost of two movie tickets. Those cities with the highest cost of a fast-food hamburger meal tend to be associated with the highest cost of two movie tickets. This relationship is strong, as indicated by a coefficient of correlation, $r = 0.8348$.

You cannot assume that having a low cost of a fast-food hamburger meal caused the low cost of two movie tickets. You can only say that this is what tended to happen in the sample.

In summary, the coefficient of correlation indicates the linear relationship, or association, between two numerical variables. When the coefficient of correlation gets closer to $+1$ or -1, the linear relationship between the two variables is stronger. When the coefficient of correlation is near 0, little or no linear relationship exists. The sign of the coefficient of correlation indicates whether the data are positively correlated (i.e., the larger values of X are typically paired with the larger values of Y) or negatively correlated (i.e., the larger values of X are typically paired with the smaller values of Y). The existence of a strong correlation does not imply a causation effect. It only indicates the tendencies present in the data.

Problems for Section 3.5

LEARNING THE BASICS

3.33 The following is a set of data from a sample of $n = 11$ items:

X	7	5	8	3	6	10	12	4	9	15	18
Y	21	15	24	9	18	30	36	12	27	45	54

a. Compute the covariance.
b. Compute the coefficient of correlation.
c. How strong is the relationship between X and Y? Explain.

APPLYING THE CONCEPTS

3.34 An article (P. Lim, "An Around-the-World Ticket for Your Portfolio," *The New York Times*, June 3, 2007, p. B5) that discussed investment in foreign stocks (over the last five years) stated that the coefficient of correlation between the return on investment of U.S. stocks (as expressed by the S & P 500) and the German stock market was 0.89, U.S. stocks (as expressed by the S & P 500) and Brazilian stock market was 0.68, and U.S. stocks (as expressed by the S & P

500) and the Japanese stock market was 0.29. What conclusions can you make about the strength of the relationship between the return on investment of U.S. stocks and each of these three other types of investments?

3.35 According to the Mortgage Bankers Association, home mortgage applications were rising as lower loan rates fostered home purchases and refinancings ("Mortgage Applications Creep Up as Rates Fall," **www.usatoday.com**, April 25, 2007).

a. Is the article implying that the number of home mortgages and loan rates are positively correlated, negatively correlated, or independent?

b. If you believe that the article is implying that the number of home mortgages and loan rates are correlated, do you believe that there is a cause-and-effect relationship? Discuss.

3.36 The data in the file `CoffeeDrink` represent the calories and fat, in grams, of 16-ounce iced coffee drinks at Dunkin' Donuts and Starbucks:

Product	Calories	Fat
Dunkin' Donuts Iced Mocha Swirl latte (whole milk)	240	8.0
Starbucks Coffee Frappuccino blended coffee	260	3.5
Dunkin' Donuts Coffee Coolatta (cream)	350	22.0
Starbucks Iced Coffee Mocha Expresso (whole milk and whipped cream)	350	20.0
Starbucks Mocha Frappuccino blended coffee (whipped cream)	420	16.0
Starbucks Chocolate Brownie Frappuccino blended coffee (whipped cream)	510	22.0
Starbucks Chocolate Frappuccino Blended Crème (whipped cream)	530	19.0

Source: *Data extracted from "Coffee as Candy at Dunkin' Donuts and Starbucks," Consumer Reports, June 2004, p. 9.*

a. Compute the covariance.
b. Compute the coefficient of correlation.
c. Which do you think is more valuable in expressing the relationship between calories and fat—the covariance or the coefficient of correlation? Explain.
d. What conclusions can you reach about the relationship between calories and fat?

3.37 There are several methods for calculating fuel economy. The following table (contained in the file `Mileage`) indicates the mileage, as calculated by owners and by current government standards:

Car	Owner	Government
2005 Ford F-150	14.3	16.8
2005 Chevrolet Silverado	15.0	17.8
2002 Honda Accord LX	27.8	26.2
2002 Honda Civic	27.9	34.2
2004 Honda Civic Hybrid	48.8	47.6
2002 Ford Explorer	16.8	18.3
2005 Toyota Camry	23.7	28.5
2003 Toyota Corolla	32.8	33.1
2005 Toyota Prius	37.3	56.0

Source: *Data extracted from J. Healey, "Fuel Economy Calculations to Be Altered," USA Today, January 11, 2006, p. 1B.*

a. Compute the covariance.
b. Compute the coefficient of correlation.
c. Which do you think is more valuable in expressing the relationship between owner and current government standards mileage—the covariance or the coefficient of correlation? Explain.
d. What conclusions can you reach about the relationship between owner and current government standards mileage?

3.38 College basketball is big business, with coaches' salaries, revenues, and expenses in millions of dollars. The data file `Colleges-basketball` contains the coaches' salaries and revenue for college basketball at selected schools in a recent year (data extracted from R. Adams, "Pay for Playoffs," *The Wall Street Journal*, March 11–12, 2006, pp. P1, P8).

a. Compute the covariance.
b. Compute the coefficient of correlation.
c. What conclusions can you reach about the relationship between a coach's salary and revenue?

3.39 College football players trying out for the NFL are given the Wonderlic standardized intelligence test. The data in the file `Wonderlic` contains the average Wonderlic score of football players trying out for the NFL and the graduation rate for football players at selected schools (data extracted from S. Walker, "The NFL's Smartest Team," *The Wall Street Journal*, September 30, 2005, pp. W1, W10).

a. Compute the covariance.
b. Compute the coefficient of correlation.
c. What conclusions can you reach about the relationship between the average Wonderlic score and graduation rate?

3.6 Presenting Descriptive Statistics: Pitfalls and Ethical Issues

This chapter describes how a set of numerical data can be characterized by the statistics that measure the properties of central tendency, variation, and shape. In business, descriptive statistics such as the ones you have learned about are frequently included in summary reports that are prepared periodically.

The volume of information available on the Internet, in newspapers, and in magazines has produced much skepticism about the objectivity of data. When you are reading information that contains descriptive statistics, you should keep in mind the quip often attributed to the famous nineteenth-century British statesman Benjamin Disraeli: "There are three kinds of lies: lies, damned lies, and statistics."

For example, in examining statistics that are provided, you need to compare the mean and the median. Are they similar or are they very different? Or, is only the mean provided? The answers to these questions will enable you to know whether the data are skewed or symmetrical and whether the median might be a better measure of central tendency than the mean. In addition, you should look to see whether the standard deviation has been included in the statistics provided. Without the standard deviation, it is difficult to determine the amount of variation that exists in the data.

Ethical considerations arise when you are deciding what results to include in a report. You should document both good and bad results. In addition, when making oral presentations and presenting written reports, you need to give results in a fair, objective, and neutral manner. Unethical behavior occurs when you selectively fail to report pertinent findings that are detrimental to the support of a particular position.

USING STATISTICS

@ Choice Is Yours, Part II Revisited

In the Using Statistics scenario, you were hired by the Choice Is Yours investment company to assist investors interested in mutual funds. A sample of 868 mutual funds including 464 with a growth objective (i.e., funds holding stock in companies that are expected to grow quickly in the next year) and 404 with a value objective (i.e., funds holding stock in companies whose stock prices are currently considered undervalued). By comparing these two categories, you were able to provide your investors with valuable insights.

The 2006 returns for both the growth funds and the value funds were approximately symmetrical as indicated by the boxplots (see Figure 3.5 or Figure 3.6 on page 106), The descriptive statistics (see Figure 3.2 or 3.3 on page 94) allowed you to compare the central tendency and variability of returns between the growth and value funds. The mean indicated that the growth funds returned an average of 8.71 and the median indicated that half of the funds had returns of 8.60 or more. The value funds' central tendencies were much larger than the growth funds—they had an average of 16.88 and half the funds had returns of 16.85 or more. Moreover, the value funds showed less variability in their returns than the growth funds—they had a range of 32.20 as compared to 37.50; an interquartile range of 5.00 as compared to 7.08; and a standard deviation of 3.96 as compared to 5.42. Thus, not only did a typical value fund have a higher return in 2006 than a typical growth fund, the sample of 404 value funds had returns that were much more closely clustered near the center. An interesting insight is that while 75% of the value funds had returns of 14.50 or higher ($Q_1 = 14.50$), only 25% of the growth funds had returns of 12.40 or higher ($Q_3 = 12.40$). Although past performance is no assurance of future performance, in 2006, the value funds greatly outperformed the growth funds.

SUMMARY

In this and the previous chapter, you studied descriptive statistics—how data are presented in tables and charts, and then summarized, described, analyzed, and interpreted. In Chapter 2, you were able to present useful information through the use of pie charts, histograms, and other graphical methods. In Chapter 3, you learned how numerical descriptive measures such as the mean, median, quartiles, range and standard deviation are used to describe the characteristics of central tendency, variability and shape. You also learned how the coefficient of correlation is used to describe the relationship between two numerical variables. Table 3.9 provides a list of the numerical descriptive measures covered in this chapter.

In the next chapter, the basic principles of probability are presented in order to bridge the gap between the subject of descriptive statistics and the subject of inferential statistics.

TABLE 3.9

Summary of Numerical
Descriptive Measures

Type of Analysis	Numerical Data
Describing central tendency, variation, and shape of a numerical variable	Mean, median, mode, quartiles, range, interquartile range, variance, standard deviation, coefficient of variation, Z scores, boxplot (**Sections 3.1, 3.2, 3.3, 3.4**)
Describing the relationship between two numerical variables	Covariance, coefficient of correlation (**Section 3.5**)

KEY EQUATIONS

Sample Mean

$$\overline{X} = \frac{\sum\limits_{i=1}^{n} X_i}{n} \tag{3.1}$$

Median

$$\text{Median} = \frac{n+1}{2} \text{ ranked value} \tag{3.2}$$

Range

$$\text{Range} = X_{\text{largest}} - X_{\text{smallest}} \tag{3.3}$$

Sample Variance

$$S^2 = \frac{\sum\limits_{i=1}^{n} (X_i - \overline{X})^2}{n-1} \tag{3.4}$$

Sample Standard Deviation

$$S = \sqrt{S^2} = \sqrt{\frac{\sum\limits_{i=1}^{n} (X_i - \overline{X})^2}{n-1}} \tag{3.5}$$

Coefficient of Variation

$$CV = \left(\frac{S}{\overline{X}}\right) 100\% \tag{3.6}$$

Z Scores

$$Z = \frac{X - \overline{X}}{S} \tag{3.7}$$

Population Mean

$$\mu = \frac{\sum\limits_{i=1}^{N} X_i}{N} \tag{3.8}$$

Population Variance

$$\sigma^2 = \frac{\sum\limits_{i=1}^{N} (X_i - \mu)^2}{N} \tag{3.9}$$

Population Standard Deviation

$$\sigma = \sqrt{\frac{\sum\limits_{i=1}^{N} (X_i - \mu)^2}{N}} \tag{3.10}$$

First Quartile Q_1

$$Q_1 = \frac{n+1}{4} \text{ ranked value} \tag{3.11}$$

Third Quartile Q_3

$$Q_3 = \frac{3(n+1)}{4} \text{ ranked value} \tag{3.12}$$

Interquartile Range

$$\text{Interquartile range} = Q_3 - Q_1 \tag{3.13}$$

Sample Covariance

$$\text{cov}(X, Y) = \frac{\sum\limits_{i=1}^{n} (X_i - \overline{X})(Y_i - \overline{Y})}{n-1} \tag{3.14}$$

Sample Coefficient of Correlation

$$r = \frac{\text{cov}(X, Y)}{S_X S_Y} \tag{3.15}$$

KEY TERMS

CHAPTER REVIEW PROBLEMS

CHECKING YOUR UNDERSTANDING

3.40 What are the properties of a set of numerical data?

3.41 What is meant by the property of central tendency?

3.42 What are the differences among the mean, median, and mode, and what are the advantages and disadvantages of each?

3.43 How do you interpret the first quartile, median, and third quartile?

3.44 What is meant by the property of variation?

3.45 What does the Z score measure?

3.46 What are the differences among the various measures of variation, such as the range, interquartile range, variance, standard deviation, and coefficient of variation, and what are the advantages and disadvantages of each?

3.47 How does the empirical rule help explain the ways in which the values in a set of numerical data cluster and distribute?

3.48 How do the empirical rule and the Chebyshev rule differ?

3.49 What is meant by the property of shape?

3.50 How do the covariance and the coefficient of correlation differ?

APPLYING THE CONCEPTS

3.51 The American Society for Quality (ASQ) conducted a salary survey of all its members. ASQ members work in all areas of manufacturing and service-related institutions, with a common theme of an interest in quality. For the U.S. survey, e-mails were sent to 70,645 members, and 10,848 valid responses were received. The two most common job titles were manager and quality engineer. Another title is Master Black Belt, who is a person who takes a leadership role as the keeper of the Six Sigma process (see Section 14.6). Descriptive statistics concerning salaries for these three titles are given below (data extracted from H. Lindborg, "Navigate Your Career Path with QP's Annual Salary Survey," *Quality Progress*, December 2007, pp. 21–50). Compare the salaries of managers, quality engineers, and Master Black Belts.

Title	Sample Size	Minimum	Maximum	Standard Deviation	Mean	Median
Manager	1,848	25,000	184,000	23,179	82,976	80,000
Quality Engineer	1,190	18,000	163,000	17,871	71,093	70,000
Master Black Belt	131	48,000	183,500	21,946	108,879	110,000

3.52 In New York State, savings banks are permitted to sell a form of life insurance called savings bank life insurance (SBLI). The approval process consists of underwriting, which includes a review of the application, a medical information bureau check, possible requests for additional medical information and medical exams, and a policy compilation stage during which the policy pages are generated and sent to the bank for delivery. The ability to deliver approved policies to customers in a timely manner is critical to the profitability of this service to the bank. During a period of one month, a random sample of 27 approved policies was selected, and the following total processing times in days were recorded; the data are contained in the file **Insurance** :

```
73  19  16  64  28  28  31  90  60  56  31  56  22  18
45  48  17  17  17  91  92  63  50  51  69  16  17
```

a. Compute the mean, median, first quartile, and third quartile.
b. Compute the range, interquartile range, variance, standard deviation, and coefficient of variation.
c. Construct a boxplot. Are the data skewed? If so, how?
d. What would you tell a customer who enters the bank to purchase this type of insurance policy and asks how long the approval process takes?

3.53 One of the major measures of the quality of service provided by any organization is the speed with which it responds to customer complaints. A large family-held department store selling furniture and flooring, including carpet, had undergone a major expansion in the past several years. In particular, the flooring department had expanded from 2 installation crews to an installation supervisor, a measurer, and 15 installation crews. A sample of 50 complaints concerning carpet installation was selected during a recent year. The data in the file **Furniture** represent the number of days between the receipt of a complaint and the resolution of the complaint:

54	5	35	137	31	27	152	2	123	81	74	27	11
19	126	110	110	29	61	35	94	31	26	5	12	4
165	32	29	28	29	26	25	1	14	13	13	10	5
27	4	52	30	22	36	26	20	23	33	68		

a. Compute the mean, median, first quartile, and third quartile.
b. Compute the range, interquartile range, variance, standard deviation, and coefficient of variation.
c. Construct a boxplot. Are the data skewed? If so, how?
d. On the basis of the results of (a) through (c), if you had to tell the president of the company how long a customer should expect to wait to have a complaint resolved, what would you say? Explain.

3.54 A manufacturing company produces steel housings for electrical equipment. The main component part of the housing is a steel trough that is made out of a 14-gauge steel coil. It is produced using a 250-ton progressive punch press with a wipe-down operation, putting two 90-degree forms in the flat steel to make the trough. The distance from one side of the form to the other is critical because of weatherproofing in outdoor applications. The company requires that the width of the trough be between 8.31 inches and 8.61 inches. The file **Trough** contains the widths of the troughs, in inches, for a sample of $n = 49$:

8.312 8.343 8.317 8.383 8.348 8.410 8.351 8.373 8.481 8.422

8.476 8.382 8.484 8.403 8.414 8.419 8.385 8.465 8.498 8.447

8.436 8.413 8.489 8.414 8.481 8.415 8.479 8.429 8.458 8.462

8.460 8.444 8.429 8.460 8.412 8.420 8.410 8.405 8.323 8.420

8.396 8.447 8.405 8.439 8.411 8.427 8.420 8.498 8.409

a. Calculate the mean, median, range, and standard deviation for the width. Interpret these measures of central tendency and variability.
b. List the five-number summary.
c. Construct a boxplot and describe its shape.
d. What can you conclude about the number of troughs that will meet the company's requirement of troughs being between 8.31 and 8.61 inches wide?

3.55 The manufacturing company in Problem 3.54 also produces electric insulators. If the insulators break when in use, a short circuit is likely to occur. To test the strength of the insulators, destructive testing is carried out to determine how much force is required to break the insulators. Force is measured by observing how many pounds must be applied to the insulator before it breaks. The data from 30 insulators from this experiment are contained in the file **Force**:

1,870 1,728 1,656 1,610 1,634 1,784 1,522 1,696 1,592 1,662

1,866 1,764 1,734 1,662 1,734 1,774 1,550 1,756 1,762 1,866

1,820 1,744 1,788 1,688 1,810 1,752 1,680 1,810 1,652 1,736

a. Calculate the mean, median, range, and standard deviation for the force needed to break the insulator.
b. Interpret the measures of central tendency and variability in (a).
c. Construct a boxplot and describe its shape.
d. What can you conclude about the strength of the insulators if the company requires a force measurement of at least 1,500 pounds before breakage?

3.56 The data contained in the file **Tuition2006** consist of the in-state tuition and fees and the out-of-state tuition and fees for four-year colleges with the highest percentage of students graduating within six years.

Source: *U.S. Department of Education, 2006.*

For each variable:
a. Compute the mean, median, first quartile, and third quartile.
b. Compute the range, interquartile range, variance, standard deviation, and coefficient of variation.
c. Construct a boxplot. Are the data skewed? If so, how?
d. Compute the coefficient of correlation between the in-state tuition and fees and the out-of-state tuition and fees.
e. What conclusions can you reach concerning the in-state tuition and fees and the out-of-state tuition and fees?

3.57 A quality characteristic of interest for a tea-bag-filling process is the weight of the tea in the individual bags. If the bags are underfilled, two problems arise. First, customers may not be able to brew the tea to be as strong as they wish. Second, the company may be in violation of the truth-in-labeling laws. For this product, the label weight on the package indicates that, on average, there are 5.5 grams of tea in a bag. If the mean amount of tea in a bag exceeds the label weight, the company is giving away product. Getting an exact amount of tea in a bag is problematic because of variation in the temperature and humidity inside the factory, differences in the density of the tea, and the extremely fast filling operation of the machine (approximately 170 bags per minute). The data in the file `Teabags` shown below provide the weight, in grams, of a sample of 50 tea bags produced in one hour by a single machine:

5.65 5.44 5.42 5.40 5.53 5.34 5.54 5.45 5.52 5.41

5.57 5.40 5.53 5.54 5.55 5.62 5.56 5.46 5.44 5.51

5.47 5.40 5.47 5.61 5.53 5.32 5.67 5.29 5.49 5.55

5.77 5.57 5.42 5.58 5.58 5.50 5.32 5.50 5.53 5.58

5.61 5.45 5.44 5.25 5.56 5.63 5.50 5.57 5.67 5.36

a. Compute the mean, median, first quartile, and third quartile.
b. Compute the range, interquartile range, variance, standard deviation, and coefficient of variation.
c. Interpret the measures of central tendency and variation within the context of this problem. Why should the company producing the tea bags be concerned about the central tendency and variation?
d. Construct a boxplot. Are the data skewed? If so, how?
e. Is the company meeting the requirement set forth on the label that, on average, there are 5.5 grams of tea in a bag? If you were in charge of this process, what changes, if any, would you try to make concerning the distribution of weights in the individual bags?

3.58 The manufacturer of Boston and Vermont asphalt shingles provides its customers with a 20-year warranty on most of its products. To determine whether a shingle will last as long as the warranty period, accelerated-life testing is conducted at the manufacturing plant. Accelerated-life testing exposes the shingle to the stresses it would be subject to in a lifetime of normal use via an experiment in a laboratory setting that takes only a few minutes to conduct. In this test, a shingle is repeatedly scraped with a brush for a short period of time, and the shingle granules removed by the brushing are weighed (in grams). Shingles that experience low amounts of granule loss are expected to last longer in normal use than shingles that experience high amounts of granule loss. In this situation, a shingle should experience no more than 0.8 gram of granule loss if it is expected to last the length of the warranty period. The data file `Granule` contains a sample of 170 measurements made on the company's Boston shingles and 140 measurements made on Vermont shingles.

a. List the five-number summary for the Boston shingles and for the Vermont shingles.
b. Construct side-by-side boxplots for the two brands of shingles and describe the shapes of the distributions.
c. Comment on the shingles' ability to achieve a granule loss of 0.8 gram or less.

3.59 A study conducted by Zagat Survey concluded that many first-rate restaurants are located in hotels across the United States. Travelers can find quality food, service, and décor without leaving their hotels. The top-rated hotel restaurant is The French Room, located in The Adolphus Hotel in Dallas, Texas. The estimated price for dinner, including one drink and tip, at The French Room is $80. The highest price reported is $179 at Alain Ducasse, located in the Jumeirah Essex House in New York City (extracted from Gary Stoller, "Top Restaurants Check into Luxury Hotels," *USA Today*, April 11, 2006, p. 5B). The file `Bestrest` contains the top 100 hotel restaurants in the United States and the variables state, city, restaurant, hotel, cost (estimated price of dinner including one drink and tip), and rating (1 to 100, with 1 the top-rated restaurant).

a. Construct the five-number summary of dinner price.
b. Construct a boxplot of dinner price and interpret the distribution of dinner prices.
c. Calculate and interpret the correlation coefficient of the rating and dinner price.

3.60 The data in the file `Chicken` contains the characteristics for a sample of 20 chicken sandwiches from fast-food chains.

a. Compute the correlation coefficient between calories and carbohydrates.
b. Compute the correlation coefficient between calories and sodium.
c. Compute the correlation coefficient between calories and total fat.
d. Which variable (total fat, carbohydrates, or sodium) seems to be most closely related to calories? Explain.

3.61 In Example 3.16 on page 112, the correlation coefficient between the cost of a fast-food hamburger meal and the cost of movie tickets in 10 different cities was computed. The data file `Cost of living` also includes the overall cost index, the monthly rent for a two-bedroom apartment, and the costs of a cup of coffee with service, dry cleaning for a men's blazer, and toothpaste.

a. Compute the correlation coefficient between the overall cost index and the monthly rent for a two-bedroom apartment, the cost of a cup of coffee with service, the cost of a fast-food hamburger meal, the cost of dry-cleaning a men's blazer, the cost of toothpaste, and the cost of movie tickets. (There will be six separate correlation coefficients.)
b. What conclusions can you reach about the relationship of the overall cost index to each of these six variables?

3.62 The data in the file `Spending` is the per-capita spending, in thousands of dollars, for each state in 2004.

a. Compute the mean, median, first quartile, and third quartile.
b. Compute the range, interquartile range, variance, standard deviation, and coefficient of variation.
c. Construct a boxplot. Are the data skewed? If so, how?
d. What conclusions can you reach concerning per-capita spending, in thousands of dollars, for each state in 2004?

3.63 The data in the file CEO represent the total compensation (in $millions) of CEOs of large public companies (data extracted from "The Boss's Pay," *The Wall Street Journal,* April 14, 2008, pp. R5–R7).
a. Compute the mean, median, first quartile, and third quartile.
b. Compute the range, interquartile range, variance, standard deviation, and coefficient of variation.
c. Construct a boxplot. Are the data skewed? If so, how?
d. What conclusions can you draw concerning the total compensation (in $millions) of CEOs?

3.64 You are planning to study for your statistics examination with a group of classmates, one of whom you particularly want to impress. This individual has volunteered to use Microsoft Excel or Minitab to get the needed summary information, tables, and charts for a data set containing several numerical and categorical variables assigned by the instructor for study purposes. This person comes over to you with the printout and exclaims, "I've got it all—the means, the medians, the standard deviations, the boxplots, the pie charts—for all our variables. The problem is, some of the output looks weird—like the boxplots for gender and for major and the pie charts for grade point index and for height. Also, I can't understand why Professor Krehbiel said we can't get the descriptive stats for some of the variables—I got them for everything! See, the mean for height is 68.23, the mean for grade point index is 2.76, the mean for gender is 1.50, the mean for major is 4.33." What is your reply?

REPORT WRITING EXERCISES

3.65 Data concerning 71 of the best-selling domestic beers in the United States are located in the file Domesticbeer. The values for three variables are included: percentage alcohol, number of calories per 12 ounces, and number of carbohydrates (in grams) per 12 ounces.
Source: *Data extracted from* **www.Beer100.com**, *May 6, 2008.*

Your task is to write a report based on a complete descriptive evaluation of each of the numerical variables—percentage alcohol, number of calories per 12 ounces, and number of carbohydrates (in grams) per 12 ounces. Appended to your report should be all appropriate tables, charts, and numerical descriptive measures.

TEAM PROJECTS

The data file Mutual Funds contains information regarding nine variables from a sample of 868 mutual funds:
  Category—Type of stocks comprising the mutual fund (small cap, mid cap, large cap)
  Objective—Objective of stocks comprising the mutual fund (growth or value)
  Assets—In millions of dollars
  Fees—Sales charges (no or yes)
  Expense ratio—Ratio of expenses to net assets in percentage

Return 2006—Twelve-month return in 2006
Three-year return—Annualized return, 2004–2006
Five-year return—Annualized return, 2002–2006
Risk—Risk-of-loss factor of the mutual fund (low, average, high)

3.66 For expense ratio in percentage, three-year return, and five-year return,
a. Compute the mean, median, first quartile, and third quartile.
b. Compute the range, interquartile range, variance, standard deviation, and coefficient of variation.
c. Construct a boxplot. Are the data skewed? If so, how?
d. What conclusions can you reach concerning these variables?

3.67 You wish to compare mutual funds that have fees to those that do not have fees. For each of these two groups, for the variables expense ratio in percentage, Return 2006, three-year return, and five-year return,
a. Compute the mean, median, first quartile, and third quartile.
b. Compute the range, interquartile range, variance, standard deviation, and coefficient of variation.
c. Construct a boxplot. Are the data skewed? If so, how?
d. What conclusions can you reach about differences between mutual funds that have fees and those that do not have fees?

3.68 You wish to compare mutual funds that have a growth objective to those that have a value objective. For each of these two groups, for the variables expense ratio in percentage, three-year return, and five-year return,
a. Compute the mean, median, first quartile, and third quartile.
b. Compute the range, interquartile range, variance, standard deviation, and coefficient of variation.
c. Construct a boxplot. Are the data skewed? If so, how?
d. What conclusions can you reach about differences between mutual funds that have a growth objective and those that have a value objective?

3.69 You wish to compare small cap, mid cap, and large cap mutual funds. For each of these three groups, for the variables expense ratio in percentage, Return 2006, three-year return, and five-year return,
a. Compute the mean, median, first quartile, and third quartile.
b. Compute the range, interquartile range, variance, standard deviation, and coefficient of variation.
c. Construct a boxplot. Are the data skewed? If so, how?
d. What conclusions can you reach about differences between small cap, mid cap, and large cap mutual funds?

STUDENT SURVEY DATA BASE

3.70 Problem 1.23 on page 13 describes a survey of 50 undergraduate students (see the file Undergradsurvey). For these data, for each numerical variable,

a. Compute the mean, median, first quartile, and third quartile.

b. Compute the range, interquartile range, variance, standard deviation, and coefficient of variation.

c. Construct a boxplot. Are the data skewed? If so, how?

d. Write a report summarizing your conclusions.

3.71 Problem 1.23 on page 13 describes a survey of 50 undergraduate students (see the file Undergradsurvey).

a. Select a sample of 50 undergraduate students at your school and conduct a similar survey for those students.

b. For the data collected in (a), repeat (a) through (d) of Problem 3.70.

c. Compare the results of (b) to those of Problem 3.70.

3.72 Problem 1.24 on page 13 describes a survey of 40 MBA students (see the file Gradsurvey). For these data, for each numerical variable,

a. Compute the mean, median, first quartile, and third quartile.

b. Compute the range, interquartile range, variance, standard deviation, and coefficient of variation.

c. Construct a boxplot. Are the data skewed? If so, how?

d. Write a report summarizing your conclusions.

3.73 Problem 1.20 on page 13 describes a survey of 40 MBA students (see the file Gradsurvey).

a. Select a sample of 40 graduate students from your MBA program and conduct a similar survey for those students.

b. For the data collected in (a), repeat (a) through (d) of Problem 3.72.

c. Compare the results of (b) to those of Problem 3.72.

MANAGING THE *SPRINGVILLE HERALD*

For what variable in the Chapter 2 "Managing the *Springville Herald*" case (see page 63) are numerical descriptive measures needed? For the variable you identify:

1. Compute the appropriate numerical descriptive measures, and construct a boxplot.

2. Identify another graphical display that might be useful and construct it. What conclusions can you reach from that plot that cannot be made from the boxplot?

3. Summarize your findings in a report that can be included with the task force's study.

WEB CASE

Apply your knowledge about the proper use of numerical descriptive measures in this continuing Web Case from Chapter 2.

Visit EndRun Financial Services, at **www.prenhall.com/ Springville/EndRun.htm** (or open the EndRun.htm file in the Student CD-ROM Web Case folder) a second time and reexamine their supporting data and then answer the following:

1. Can descriptive measures be computed for any variables? How would such summary statistics support EndRun's claims? How would those summary statistics affect your perception of EndRun's record?

2. Evaluate the methods EndRun used to summarize the results of its customer survey (see **www.prenhall.com/ Springville/ER_Survey.htm** or the ER_Survey.htm file on the Student CD-ROM Web Case folder). Is there anything you would do differently to summarize these results?

3. Note that the last question of the survey has fewer responses than the other questions. What factors may have limited the number of responses to that question?

REFERENCES

1. Kendall, M. G., A. Stuart, and J. K. Ord, *Kendall's Advanced Theory of Statistics, Volume 1: Distribution Theory,* 6th ed. (New York: Oxford University Press, 1994).

2. *Microsoft Excel 2007* (Redmond, WA: Microsoft Corporation, 2007).

3. *Minitab for Windows Version 15* (State College, PA: Minitab, Inc., 2006).

4. Tukey, J., *Exploratory Data Analysis* (Reading, MA: Addison-Wesley, 1977).

5. Velleman, P. F., and D. C. Hoaglin, *Applications, Basics, and Computing of Exploratory Data Analysis* (Boston: Duxbury Press, 1981).

APPENDIX E3

Using Microsoft Excel for Descriptive Statistics

E3.1 Computing Measures of Central Tendency, Variation, and Shape

You compute measures of central tendency, variation, and shape by either using the ToolPak Descriptive Statistics procedure or by using worksheet functions. Use the ToolPak procedure when you want to create a list of summary statistics similar to the one shown in Figure 3.2 on page 94. Use worksheet functions when you want to add one or a few descriptive measures to a worksheet (as is done in Figure 3.8 on page 109).

Using ToolPak Descriptive Statistics

Open to the worksheet containing your data to be summarized. Select **Tools → Data Analysis** (Excel 97–2003) or **Data → Data Analysis** (Excel 2007). In the Data Analysis dialog box, select **Descriptive Statistics** from the **Analysis Tools** list and then click **OK**. In the Descriptive Statistics dialog box (shown in Figure E3.1), enter the cell range of the data as the **Input Range**. Click the **Columns** option and **Labels in first row**. Finish by clicking **New Worksheet Ply**, **Summary statistics**, **Kth Largest**, and **Kth Smallest**, and then **OK**.

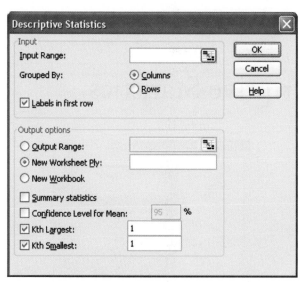

FIGURE E3.1 ToolPak Descriptive Statistics dialog box

To compute descriptive statistics for a variable by subgroups, as was done in Figure 3.2 on page 94 for the growth and value subgroups, first sort your data by the categorical variable to which the subgroups belong. Next, repeat the instructions given at the left for each subgroup using the cell range of the subgroup and the New Worksheet Ply option each time. Then copy and paste the results found in the second and subsequent worksheets to this first sheet to create a multiple column table similar to the one shown in Figure 3.2.

Using Worksheet Functions

You use the worksheet functions SUM, COUNT, AVERAGE (for mean), MEDIAN, MODE, or QUARTILE, to compute measures of central tendency or STDEV, VAR, MIN, MAX, LARGE, or SMALL to compute measures of shape and variation. For all but QUARTILE, enter a formula in the form *=WorksheetFunction(cell range of data to be summarized)*. For QUARTILE enter the formula in the form *=WorksheetFunction(cell range of data to be summarized, quartile number)*. Use 1 as the *quartile number* to compute the first quartile, 2 to compute the second quartile (the median), or 3 to compute the third quartile. In Excel versions earlier than Excel 2003, you may encounter some minor errors in results when using the QUARTILE function.

E3.2 Computing Measures for a Population

To compute the population variance and standard deviation, use the worksheet functions VARP and STDEVP. To use either function, enter a formula into a blank cell in the form *=WorksheetFunction(cell range of data to be summarized)*.

E3.3 Creating Boxplots

You create boxplots by entering a five-number summary into the tinted cell range B2:B6 of the **Plot** worksheet of the `Boxplot.xls` workbook. The workbook uses the contents of this range to create a boxplot on the Plot worksheet.

E3.4 Computing the Covariance

You compute the covariance by making entries in the **Covariance** worksheet of the `Covariance.xls` workbook, shown in Figure 3.8 on page 109. If you want to use this worksheet with other pairs of variables, follow the instructions in the worksheet for modifying the table area. The worksheet gains its flexibility by the cell C18 formula that uses the COUNT function to determine the sample size n. This allows the worksheet to always use the proper value of $n - 1$ for the covariance calculation when you change the size of the table area.

E3.5 Computing the Coefficient of Correlation

You compute the correlation coefficient by making entries in the **Correlation** worksheet of the Correlation.xls workbook, shown in Figure 3.11 on page 112. If you want to use this worksheet with other pairs of variables, follow the instructions in the worksheet for modifying the table area.

This worksheet shares some of the design of the covariance worksheet discussed in the previous section.

This worksheet uses the CORREL function in the formula **=CORREL(A2:A11, B2:B11)** in cell E21 to compute the correlation coefficient. Because the covariance, S_X, and S_Y are computed elsewhere in this worksheet, the formula **=E18/(E19 * E20)** could also be used to compute the correlation coefficient statistic.

APPENDIX P3

Using PHStat2 for Descriptive Statistics

P3.1 Creating Boxplots

To create boxplots, use **PHStat → Descriptive Statistics → Boxplot**. This procedure accepts data for a single group or multiple groups as either unstacked data (column by column) or stacked data (one column). If you use the **Multiple Groups-Stacked** option, you will also need to enter the **Grouping Variable Cell Range**.

The procedure creates a custom worksheet and then uses Excel charting features to create a boxplot from the data of that worksheet. If you click **Five-Number Summary**, a five-number summary appears on a separate worksheet.

APPENDIX M3

Using Minitab for Descriptive Statistics

M3.1 Computing Descriptive Statistics

To create descriptive statistics for the 2006 return for different objectives shown in Figure 3.3 on page 94:

1. Open the Mutual Funds.mtw worksheet.
2. Select **Stat → Basic Statistics → Display Descriptive Statistics**.

In the Display Descriptive Statistics dialog box (see Figure M3.1):

3. Enter **'Return 2006'** in the **Variables** box.
4. Enter **Objective** in the **By variables (optional)** box.
5. Click **Statistics**.
6. In the Display Descriptive Statistics - Statistics dialog box (see Figure M3.2), select **Mean**, **Standard deviation**, **Coefficient of variation**, **First quartile**, **Median**,

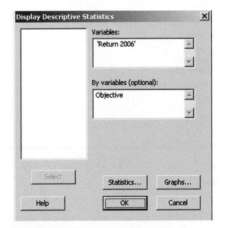

FIGURE M3.1 Minitab Display Descriptive Statistics dialog box

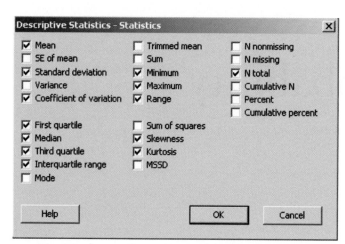

FIGURE M3.2 Minitab Display Descriptive Statistics - Statistics dialog box

Third quartile, **Interquartile range**, **Minimum**, **Maximum**, **Range**, **Skewness**, **Kurtosis**, and **N total** and then click **OK** to return to the Display Descriptive Statistics dialog box.

7. Back in the Display Descriptive Statistics dialog box, click **OK**.

M3.2 Creating Boxplots

To create a boxplot for the 2006 return for different objectives shown in Figure 3.6 on page 106:

1. Open the `Mutual Funds.mtw` worksheet.
2. Select **Graph → Boxplot**.

In the Boxplots dialog box (see Figure M3.3):

3. Click **With Groups** in the **One Y** gallery. (You would click **Simple** in the **One Y** gallery if you were creating a boxplot for one group.)
4. Click **OK**.

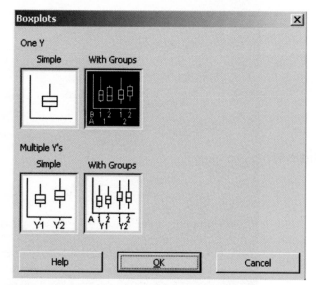

FIGURE M3.3 Minitab Boxplots dialog box

In the Boxplot - One Y, With Groups dialog box (see Figure M3.4):

5. Enter **'Return 2006'** in the **Graph variables** box.
6. Enter **Objective** in the **Categorical variables** box.
7. Click the **Scale** button.
8. Select the **Transpose value and category scales** box.
9. Click **OK**.
10. Click **OK** (to create the boxplot).

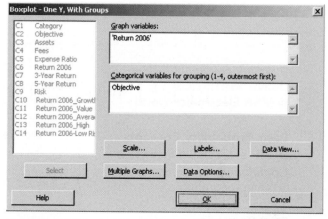

FIGURE M3.4 Minitab Boxplot - One Y, With Groups dialog box

M3.3 Computing the Coefficient of Correlation

To compute the coefficient of correlation for the cost of a fast-food hamburger meal and the cost of two movie tickets in ten cities (see Table 3.8 on page 109):

1. Open the `Cost of Living.mtw` worksheet.
2. Select **Stat → Basic Statistics → Correlation**.

In the Correlation dialog box (see Figure M3.5):

3. Enter **Hamburger** and **'Movie Tickets'** in the **Variables** box.
4. Click **OK**.

FIGURE M3.5 Minitab Correlation dialog box

4

Basic Probability

Learning Objectives

In this chapter, you learn:

- Basic probability concepts
- Conditional probability
- To use Bayes' theorem to revise probabilities

@ M&R Electronics World

As the marketing manager for M&R Electronics World, you are analyzing the survey results of an intent-to-purchase study. This study asked the heads of 1,000 households about their intentions to purchase a big-screen television (defined as 36 inches or larger) sometime during the next 12 months. As a follow-up, you plan to survey the same people 12 months later to see whether such a television was purchased. In addition, for households purchasing big-screen televisions, you would like to know whether the television they purchased was a plasma screen, whether they also purchased a digital video recorder (DVR) in the past 12 months, and whether they were satisfied with their purchase of the big-screen television.

You are expected to use the results of this survey to plan a new marketing strategy that will enhance sales and better target those households likely to purchase multiple or more expensive products. What questions can you ask in this survey? How can you express the relationships among the various intent-to-purchase responses of individual households?

In previous chapters, you learned descriptive methods to summarize categorical and numerical variables. In this chapter, you will learn about probability to answer questions such as the following:

- What is the probability that a household is planning to purchase a big-screen television in the next year?
- What is the probability that a household will actually purchase a big-screen television?
- What is the probability that a household is planning to purchase a big-screen television and actually purchases the television?
- Given that the household is planning to purchase a big-screen television, what is the probability that the purchase is made?
- Does knowledge of whether a household *plans* to purchase the television change the likelihood of predicting whether the household *will* purchase the television?
- What is the probability that a household that purchases a big-screen television will purchase a plasma-screen television?
- What is the probability that a household that purchases a big-screen television with a plasma screen will also purchase a DVR?
- What is the probability that a household that purchases a big-screen television will be satisfied with the purchase?

With answers to questions such as these, you can begin to make decisions about your marketing strategy. Should your strategy for selling more big-screen televisions target those households that have indicated an intent to purchase? Should you concentrate on selling plasma screens? Is it likely that households that purchase big-screen televisions with plasma screens can be easily persuaded to also purchase DVRs?

The principles of probability help bridge the worlds of descriptive statistics and inferential statistics. Reading this chapter will help you learn about different types of probabilities, how to compute probabilities, and how to revise probabilities in light of new information. Probability principles are the foundation for the probability distribution, the concept of mathematical expectation, and the binomial and Poisson distributions, topics that are discussed in Chapter 5.

4.1 Basic Probability Concepts

What is meant by the word *probability*? A **probability** is the numeric value representing the chance, likelihood, or possibility a particular event will occur, such as the price of a stock increasing, a rainy day, a defective product, or the outcome five in a single toss of a die. In all these instances, the probability involved is a proportion or fraction whose value ranges between 0 and 1, inclusive. An event that has no chance of occurring (i.e., the **impossible event**) has a probability of 0. An event that is sure to occur (i.e., the **certain event**) has a probability of 1.

There are three types of probability:

- *A priori*
- Empirical
- Subjective

In *a priori* **probability**, the probability of success is based on prior knowledge of the process involved. In the simplest case, where each outcome is equally likely, the chance of occurrence of the event is defined in Equation (4.1).

PROBABILITY OF OCCURRENCE

$$\text{Probability of occurrence} = \frac{X}{T} \qquad (4.1)$$

where

X = number of ways in which the event occurs

T = total number of possible outcomes

Consider a standard deck of cards that has 26 red cards and 26 black cards. The probability of selecting a black card is $26/52 = 0.50$ because there are $X = 26$ black cards and $T = 52$ total cards. What does this probability mean? If each card is replaced after it is selected, does it mean that 1 out of the next 2 cards selected will be black? No, because you cannot say for certain what will happen on the next several selections. However, you can say that in the long run, if this selection process is continually repeated, the proportion of black cards selected will approach 0.50.

EXAMPLE 4.1

Finding *A Priori* Probabilities

A standard six-sided die has six faces. Each face of the die contains either one, two, three, four, five, or six dots. If you roll a die, what is the probability that you will get a face with five dots?

SOLUTION Each face is equally likely to occur. Because there are six faces, the probability of getting a face with five dots is $\frac{1}{6}$.

The preceding examples use the *a priori* probability approach because the number of ways the event occurs and the total number of possible outcomes are known from the composition of the deck of cards or the faces of the die.

In the **empirical probability** approach, the probabilities are based on observed data, not on prior knowledge of a process. Surveys are often used to generate empirical probabilities. Examples of this type of probability are the proportion of individuals in the Using Statistics scenario who actually purchase a big-screen television, the proportion of registered voters who prefer a certain political candidate, and the proportion of students who have part-time jobs. For example, if you take a survey of students, and 60% state that they have part-time jobs, then there is a 0.60 probability that an individual student has a part-time job.

The third approach to probability, **subjective probability**, differs from the other two approaches because subjective probability differs from person to person. For example, the development team for a new product may assign a probability of 0.6 to the chance of success for the product, even though the president of the company may be less optimistic and assign a probability of 0.3. The assignment of subjective probabilities to various outcomes is usually based on a combination of an individual's past experience, personal opinion, and analysis of a particular situation. Subjective probability is especially useful in making decisions in situations in which you cannot use *a priori* probability or empirical probability.

Events and Sample Spaces

The basic elements of probability theory are the individual outcomes of a variable under study. You need the following definitions to understand probabilities.

> ### EVENT
> Each possible outcome of a variable is referred to as an **event**.
> A **simple event** is described by a single characteristic.

For example, when you toss a coin, the two possible outcomes are heads and tails. Each of these represents a simple event. When you roll a standard six-sided die in which the six faces of the die contain either one, two, three, four, five, or six dots, there are six possible simple events. An event can be any one of these simple events, a set of them, or a subset of all of them. For example, the event of an *even number of dots* consists of three simple events (i.e., two, four, or six dots).

> ### JOINT EVENT
> A **joint event** is an event that has two or more characteristics.

Getting two heads on the toss of two coins is an example of a joint event because it consists of heads on the toss of the first coin and heads on the toss of the second coin.

> ### COMPLEMENT
> The **complement** of event A (represented by the symbol A') includes all events that are not part of A.

The complement of a head is a tail because that is the only event that is not a head. The complement of face five is not getting face five. Not getting face five consists of getting face one, two, three, four, or six.

> **SAMPLE SPACE**
> The collection of all the possible events is called the **sample space**.

The sample space for tossing a coin consists of heads and tails. The sample space when rolling a die consists of one, two, three, four, five, and six dots. Example 4.2 demonstrates events and sample spaces.

EXAMPLE 4.2

Events and Sample Spaces

TABLE 4.1

Purchase Behavior for Big-Screen Televisions

The Using Statistics scenario on page 125 concerns M&R Electronics World. Table 4.1 presents the results of the sample of 1,000 households in terms of purchase behavior for big-screen televisions.

PLANNED TO PURCHASE	ACTUALLY PURCHASED		
	Yes	No	Total
Yes	200	50	250
No	100	650	750
Total	300	700	1,000

What is the sample space? Give examples of simple events and joint events.

SOLUTION The sample space consists of the 1,000 respondents. Simple events are "planned to purchase," "did not plan to purchase," "purchased," and "did not purchase." The complement of the event "planned to purchase" is "did not plan to purchase." The event "planned to purchase and actually purchased" is a joint event because the respondent must plan to purchase the television *and* actually purchase it.

Contingency Tables and Venn Diagrams

There are several ways in which you can view a particular sample space. One way involves assigning the appropriate events to a **contingency table** (see Section 2.4) such as the one displayed in Table 4.1. You get the values in the cells of the table by subdividing the sample space of 1,000 households according to whether someone planned to purchase and actually purchased the big-screen television set. For example, 200 of the respondents planned to purchase a big-screen television set and subsequently did purchase the big-screen television set.

A second way to present the sample space is by using a **Venn diagram**. This diagram graphically represents the various events as "unions" and "intersections" of circles. Figure 4.1 on page 129 presents a typical Venn diagram for a two-variable situation, with each variable having only two events (A and A', B and B'). The circle on the left (the red one) represents all events that are part of A. The circle on the right (the yellow one) represents all events that are part of B. The area contained within circle A and circle B (center area) is the intersection of A and B (written as $A \cap B$), because it is part of A and also part of B. The total area of the two circles is the union of A and B (written as $A \cup B$) and contains all outcomes that are just part of event A, just part of event B, or part of both A and B. The area in the diagram outside of $A \cup B$ contains outcomes that are neither part of A nor part of B.

FIGURE 4.1

Venn diagram for events A and B

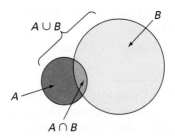

You must define A and B in order to develop a Venn diagram. You can define either event as A or B, as long as you are consistent in evaluating the various events. For the large-screen television example, you can define the events as follows:

A = planned to purchase $\qquad$ B = actually purchased

A' = did not plan to purchase $\qquad$ B' = did not actually purchase

In drawing the Venn diagram in Figure 4.2, you must determine the value of the intersection of A and B so that the sample space can be divided into its parts. $A \cap B$ consists of all 200 households who planned to purchase and actually purchased a big-screen television set. The remainder of event A (planned to purchase) consists of the 50 households who planned to purchase a big-screen television set but did not actually purchase one. The remainder of event B (actually purchased) consists of the 100 households who did not plan to purchase a big-screen television set but actually purchased one. The remaining 650 households represent those who neither planned to purchase nor actually purchased a big-screen television set.

FIGURE 4.2

Venn diagram for the M&R Electronics World example

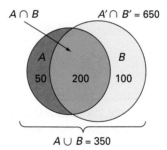

Simple Probability

Now you can answer some of the questions posed in the Using Statistics scenario. Because the results are based on data collected in a survey (refer to Table 4.1), you can use the empirical probability approach.

As stated previously, the most fundamental rule for probabilities is that they range in value from 0 to 1. An impossible event has a probability of 0, and an event that is certain to occur has a probability of 1.

Simple probability refers to the probability of occurrence of a simple event, $P(A)$. A simple probability in the Using Statistics scenario is the probability of planning to purchase a big-screen television. How can you determine the probability of selecting a household that planned to purchase a big-screen television? Using Equation (4.1) on page 126:

$$\text{Probability of occurrence} = \frac{X}{T}$$

$$P(\text{Planned to purchase}) = \frac{\text{Number who planned to purchase}}{\text{Total number of households}}$$

$$= \frac{250}{1,000} = 0.25$$

Thus, there is a 0.25 (or 25%) chance that a household planned to purchase a big-screen television.

Example 4.3 illustrates another application of simple probability.

EXAMPLE 4.3

Computing the Probability that the Big-Screen Television Purchased is a Plasma Screen

TABLE 4.2

Purchase Behavior Regarding Plasma-Screen Televisions and DVR

In the Using Statistics follow-up survey, additional questions were asked of the 300 households that actually purchased big-screen televisions. Table 4.2 indicates the consumers' responses to whether the television purchased was a plasma screen and whether they also purchased a DVR in the past 12 months.

Find the probability that if a household that purchased a big-screen television is randomly selected, the television purchased is a plasma screen.

| | PURCHASED DVR | | |
PURCHASED PLASMA SCREEN	Yes	No	Total
Plasma screen	38	42	80
Not plasma screen	70	150	220
Total	108	192	300

SOLUTION Using the following definitions:

A = purchased a plasma screen B = purchased a DVR

A' = did not purchase a plasma screen B' = did not purchase a DVR

$$P(\text{Plasma screen}) = \frac{\text{Number of plasma-screen televisions}}{\text{Total number of televisions}}$$

$$= \frac{80}{300} = 0.267$$

There is a 26.7% chance that a randomly selected big-screen television purchase is a purchase of a plasma-screen television.

Joint Probability

Whereas simple or marginal probability refers to the probability of occurrence of simple events, **joint probability** refers to the probability of an occurrence involving two or more events. An example of joint probability is the probability that you will get heads on the first toss of a coin and heads on the second toss of a coin.

Referring to Table 4.1 on page 128, those individuals who planned to purchase and actually purchased a big-screen television consist only of the outcomes in the single cell "yes—planned to purchase *and* yes—actually purchased." Because this group consists of 200 households, the probability of picking a household that planned to purchase *and* actually purchased a big-screen television is

$$P(\text{Planned to purchase } and \text{ actually purchased}) = \frac{\text{Planned to purchase } and \text{ actually purchased}}{\text{Total number of respondents}}$$

$$= \frac{200}{1,000} = 0.20$$

Example 4.4 also demonstrates how to determine joint probability.

EXAMPLE 4.4

Determining the Joint Probability that a Big-Screen Television Customer Purchased a Plasma-Screen Television and a DVR

In Table 4.2, the purchases are cross-classified as plasma screen or not plasma screen and whether or not the household purchased a DVR. Find the probability that a randomly selected household that purchased a big-screen television also purchased a plasma-screen television and a DVR.

SOLUTION Using Equation (4.1) on page 126,

$$P(\text{Plasma screen } and \text{ DVR}) = \frac{\text{Number that purchased a plasma screen } and \text{ a DVR}}{\text{Total number of big-screen television purchasers}}$$

$$= \frac{38}{300} = 0.127$$

Therefore, there is a 12.7% chance that a randomly selected household that purchased a big-screen television purchased a plasma-screen television and a DVR.

Marginal Probability

The **marginal probability** of an event consists of a set of joint probabilities. You can determine the marginal probability of a particular event by using the concept of joint probability just discussed. For example, if B consists of two events, B_1 and B_2, then $P(A)$, the probability of event A, consists of the joint probability of event A occurring with event B_1 and the joint probability of event A occurring with event B_2. You use Equation (4.2) to compute marginal probabilities.

> MARGINAL PROBABILITY
> $$P(A) = P(A \text{ and } B_1) + P(A \text{ and } B_2) + \cdots + P(A \text{ and } B_k) \qquad \textbf{(4.2)}$$
>
> where $B_1, B_2, \ldots, B_k$ are k mutually exclusive and collectively exhaustive events, defined as follows:
>
> Two events are **mutually exclusive** if both the events cannot occur simultaneously.
> A set of events is **collectively exhaustive** if one of the events must occur.

Heads and tails in a coin toss are mutually exclusive events. The result of a coin toss cannot simultaneously be a head and a tail. Heads and tails in a coin toss are also collectively exhaustive events. One of them must occur. If heads does not occur, tails must occur. If tails does not occur, heads must occur. Being male and being female are mutually exclusive and collectively exhaustive events. No one is both (the two are mutually exclusive), and everyone is one or the other (the two are collectively exhaustive).

You can use Equation (4.2) to compute the marginal probability of "planned to purchase" a big-screen television:

$$P(\text{Planned to purchase}) = P(\text{Planned to purchase } and \text{ purchased})$$
$$+ \; P(\text{Planned to purchase } and \text{ did not purchase})$$
$$= \frac{200}{1,000} + \frac{50}{1,000}$$
$$= \frac{250}{1,000} = 0.25$$

You get the same result if you add the number of outcomes that make up the simple event "planned to purchase."

General Addition Rule

How do you find the probability of event "*A or B*"? You need to consider the occurrence of either event *A* or event *B* or both *A* and *B*. For example, how can you determine the probability that a household planned to purchase *or* actually purchased a big-screen television? The event "planned to purchase *or* actually purchased" includes all households that planned to purchase and all households that actually purchased the big-screen television. You examine each cell of the contingency table (Table 4.1 on page 128) to determine whether it is part of this event. From Table 4.1, the cell "planned to purchase *and* did not actually purchase" is part of the event because it includes respondents who planned to purchase. The cell "did not plan to purchase *and* actually purchased" is included because it contains respondents who actually purchased. Finally, the cell "planned to purchase *and* actually purchased" has both characteristics of interest. Therefore, one way to calculate the probability of "planned to purchase *or* actually purchased" is:

$$P(\text{Planned to purchase } or \text{ actually purchased}) = P(\text{Planned to purchase } and \text{ did not actually purchase}) + P(\text{Did not plan to purchase } and \text{ actually purchased}) + P(\text{Planned to purchase } and \text{ actually purchased})$$

$$= \frac{50}{1,000} + \frac{100}{1,000} + \frac{200}{1,000} = \frac{350}{1,000} = 0.35$$

Often, it is easier to determine *P(A or B)*, the probability of the event *A or B*, by using the **general addition rule**, defined in Equation (4.3).

GENERAL ADDITION RULE

The probability of *A or B* is equal to the probability of *A* plus the probability of *B* minus the probability of *A and B*.

$$P(A \text{ or } B) = P(A) + P(B) - P(A \text{ and } B) \qquad \textbf{(4.3)}$$

Applying Equation (4.3) to the previous example produces the following result:

$$P(\text{Planned to purchase } or \text{ actually purchased}) = P(\text{Planned to purchase}) + P(\text{Actually purchased}) - P(\text{Planned to purchase } and \text{ actually purchased})$$

$$= \frac{250}{1,000} + \frac{300}{1,000} - \frac{200}{1,000}$$

$$= \frac{350}{1,000} = 0.35$$

The general addition rule consists of taking the probability of *A* and adding it to the probability of *B* and then subtracting the probability of the joint event *A and B* from this total because the joint event has already been included in computing both the probability of *A* and the probability of *B*. Referring to Table 4.1 on page 128, if the outcomes of the event "planned to purchase" are added to those of the event "actually purchased," the joint event "planned to purchase *and* actually purchased" has been included in each of these simple events. Therefore, because this joint event has been double-counted, you must subtract it to provide the correct result. Example 4.5 illustrates another application of the general addition rule.

EXAMPLE 4.5

Using the General Addition Rule for the Households that Purchased Big-Screen Televisions

In Example 4.3 on page 130, the purchases were cross-classified in Table 4.2 as a plasma screen or not a plasma screen and whether or not the household purchased a DVR. Find the probability that among households that purchased a big-screen television, they purchased a plasma-screen television or a DVR.

SOLUTION   Using Equation (4.3),

$$P(\text{Plasma screen } or \text{ DVR}) = P(\text{Plasma screen}) + P(\text{DVR}) - P(\text{Plasma screen } and \text{ DVR})$$

$$= \frac{80}{300} + \frac{108}{300} - \frac{38}{300}$$

$$= \frac{150}{300} = 0.50$$

Therefore, there is a 50.0% chance that a randomly selected household that purchased a big-screen television purchased a plasma-screen television or a DVR.

Problems for Section 4.1

LEARNING THE BASICS

4.1 Two coins are tossed.
a. Give an example of a simple event.
b. Give an example of a joint event.
c. What is the complement of a head on the first toss?

4.2 An urn contains 12 red balls and 8 white balls. One ball is to be selected from the urn.
a. Give an example of a simple event.
b. What is the complement of a red ball?

4.3 Given the following contingency table:

	B	*B'*
A	10	20
A'	20	40

What is the probability of
a. event *A*?
b. event *A'*?
c. event *A and B*?
d. event *A or B*?

4.4 Given the following contingency table:

	B	*B'*
A	10	30
A'	25	35

What is the probability of
a. event *A'*?
b. event *A and B*?
c. event *A' and B'*?
d. event *A' or B'*?

APPLYING THE CONCEPTS

4.5 For each of the following, indicate whether the type of probability involved is an example of *a priori* probability, empirical probability, or subjective probability.
a. The next toss of a fair coin will land on heads.
b. Italy will win soccer's World Cup the next time the competition is held.
c. The sum of the faces of two dice will be seven.
d. The train taking a commuter to work will be more than 10 minutes late.

4.6 For each of the following, state whether the events created are mutually exclusive and collectively exhaustive. If they are not mutually exclusive and collectively exhaustive, either reword the categories to make them mutually exclusive and collectively exhaustive or explain why that would not be useful.
a. Registered voters in the United States were asked whether they registered as Republicans or Democrats.
b. Each respondent was classified by the type of car he or she drives: American, European, Japanese, or none.
c. People were asked, "Do you currently live in (i) an apartment or (ii) a house?"
d. A product was classified as defective or not defective.

4.7 Which of the following events occur with a probability of zero? For eac\h, state why or why not.
a. A voter in the United States who is registered as a Republican and a Democrat
b. A voter in the United States who is female and registered as a Republican
c. An automobile that is a Ford and a Toyota
d. An automobile that is a Toyota and was manufactured in the United States

4.8 According to an Ipsos poll, the perception of unfairness in the U.S. tax code is spread fairly evenly across income groups, age groups, and education levels. In an April 2006 survey of 1,005 adults, Ipsos reported that almost 60% of all people said the code is unfair, whereas slightly more than 60% of those making more than $50,000 viewed the code as unfair ("People Cry Unfairness," *The Cincinnati Enquirer*, April 16, 2006, p. A8). Suppose that the following contingency table represents the specific breakdown of responses:

U.S. TAX CODE	INCOME LEVEL		
	Less Than $50,000	More Than $50,000	Total
Fair	225	180	405
Unfair	280	320	600
Total	505	500	1,005

a. Give an example of a simple event.
b. Give an example of a joint event.
c. What is the complement of "tax code is fair"?
d. Why is "tax code is fair *and* makes less than $50,000" a joint event?

4.9 Referring to the contingency table in Problem 4.8, if a respondent is selected at random, what is the probability that he or she
a. thinks the tax code is unfair?
b. thinks the tax code is unfair *and* makes less than $50,000?
c. thinks the tax code is unfair *or* makes less than $50,000?
d. Explain the difference in the results in (b) and (c).

✓ SELF Test **4.10** A yield improvement study at a semiconductor manufacturing facility provided defect data for a sample of 450 wafers. The following table presents a summary of the responses to two questions: "Was a particle found on the die that produced the wafer?" and "Is the wafer good or bad?"

QUALITY OF WAFER	CONDITION OF DIE		
	No Particles	Particles	Totals
Good	320	14	334
Bad	80	36	116
Totals	400	50	450

Source: *Data extracted from S. W. Hall, "Analysis of Defectivity of Semiconductor Wafers by Contingency Table," Proceedings Institute of Environmental Sciences, Vol. 1, 1994, pp. 177–183.*

a. Give an example of a simple event.
b. Give an example of a joint event.
c. What is the complement of a good wafer?
d. Why is a "good wafer" and a die "with particles" a joint event?

4.11 Referring to the contingency table in Problem 4.10, if a wafer is selected at random, what is the probability that
a. it was produced from a die with no particles?
b. it is a bad wafer *and* was produced from a die with no particles?
c. it is a bad wafer *or* was produced from a die with no particles?
d. Explain the difference in the results in (b) and (c).

4.12 An experiment was conducted to study the choices made in mutual fund selection. Undergraduate and MBA students were presented with different S&P 500 Index funds that were identical except for fees. Suppose 100 undergraduate students and 100 MBA students were selected. Partial results are shown in the following table:

FUND	STUDENT GROUP	
	Undergraduate	MBA
Highest-cost fund	27	18
Not highest-cost fund	73	82

Source: *Data extracted from J. J. Choi, D. Laibson, and B. C. Madrian, Why Does the Law of One Price Fail? www.som.yale.edu/faculty/jjc83/fees.pdf.*

If a student is selected at random, what is the probability that he or she
a. selected the highest-cost fund?
b. selected the highest-cost fund *and* is an undergraduate?
c. selected the highest-cost fund *or* is an undergraduate?
d. Explain the difference in the results in (b) and (c).

4.13 Where people turn to for news is different for various age groups. Suppose that a study conducted on this issue (data extracted from P. Johnson, "Young People Turn to the Web for News," *USA Today*, March 23, 2006, p. 9D) was based on 200 respondents who were between the ages of 36 and 50, and 200 respondents who were over age 50. Of the 200 respondents who were between the ages of 36 and 50, 82 got their news primarily from newspapers. Of the 200 respondents who were over age 50, 104 got their news primarily from newspapers. Construct a contingency table or a Venn diagram to evaluate the probabilities. If a respondent is selected at random, what is the probability that he or she
a. got news primarily from newspapers?
b. got news primarily from newspapers *and* is over 50 years old?
c. got news primarily from newspapers *or* is over 50 years old?
d. Explain the difference in the results in (b) and (c).

4.14 A sample of 500 respondents was selected in a large metropolitan area to study consumer behavior. Among the questions asked was "Do you enjoy shopping for clothing?" Of 240 males, 136 answered yes. Of 260 females, 224 answered yes. Construct a contingency table or a Venn

diagram to evaluate the probabilities. What is the probability that a respondent chosen at random
a. enjoys shopping for clothing?
b. is a female *and* enjoys shopping for clothing?
c. is a female *or* enjoys shopping for clothing?
d. is a male *or* a female?

4.15 Each year, ratings are compiled concerning the performance of new cars during the first 90 days of use. Suppose that the cars have been categorized according to whether the car needs warranty-related repair (yes or no) and the country in which the company manufacturing the car is based (United States or not United States). Based on the data collected, the probability that the new car needs warranty repair is 0.04, the probability that the car was man-

ufactured by a U.S.-based company is 0.60, and the probability that the new car needs a warranty repair *and* was manufactured by a U.S.-based company is 0.025. Construct a contingency table or a Venn diagram to evaluate the probabilities of a warranty-related repair. What is the probability that a new car selected at random
a. needs a warranty repair?
b. needs a warranty repair *and* was manufactured by a U.S.-based company?
c. needs a warranty repair *or* was manufactured by a U.S.-based company?
d. needs a warranty repair *or* was not manufactured by a U.S.-based company?

4.2 Conditional Probability

Each example in Section 4.1 involves finding the probability of an event when sampling from the entire sample space. How do you determine the probability of an event if certain information about the events involved is already known?

Computing Conditional Probabilities

Conditional probability refers to the probability of event A, given information about the occurrence of another event B.

> **CONDITIONAL PROBABILITY**
>
> The probability of A given B is equal to the probability of A *and* B divided by the probability of B.
>
> $$P(A \mid B) = \frac{P(A \text{ and } B)}{P(B)} \qquad (4.4a)$$
>
> The probability of B given A is equal to the probability of A *and* B divided by the probability of A.
>
> $$P(B \mid A) = \frac{P(A \text{ and } B)}{P(A)} \qquad (4.4b)$$
>
> where
>
> $$P(A \text{ and } B) = \text{joint probability of } A \text{ and } B$$
> $$P(A) = \text{marginal probability of } A$$
> $$P(B) = \text{marginal probability of } B$$

Referring to the Using Statistics scenario involving the purchase of big-screen televisions, suppose you were told that a household planned to purchase a big-screen television. Now, what is the probability that the household actually purchased the television? In this example, the objective is to find $P(\text{Actually purchased} \mid \text{Planned to purchase})$. Here you are given the information that the household planned to purchase the big-screen television. Therefore, the sample space does not consist of all 1,000 households in the survey. It consists of only those households that planned to purchase the big-screen television. Of 250 such households, 200 actually purchased the big-screen television. Therefore, based on Table 4.1 on page 128, the probability that a household actually purchased the big-screen television given that he or she planned to purchase is

$$P(\text{Actually purchased} \mid \text{Planned to purchase}) = \frac{\text{Planned to purchase } and \text{ actually purchased}}{\text{Planned to purchase}}$$

$$= \frac{200}{250} = 0.80$$

You can also use Equation (4.4b) to compute this result:

$$P(B \mid A) = \frac{P(A \text{ and } B)}{P(A)}$$

where

$$A = \text{planned to purchase}$$
$$B = \text{actually purchased}$$

then

$$P(\text{Actually purchased} \mid \text{Planned to purchase}) = \frac{200/1{,}000}{250/1{,}000}$$

$$= \frac{200}{250} = 0.80$$

Example 4.6 further illustrates conditional probability.

EXAMPLE 4.6

Finding a Conditional Probability of Purchasing a DVR

Table 4.2 on page 130 is a contingency table for whether the household purchased a plasma-screen television and whether the household purchased a DVR. If a household purchased a plasma-screen television, what is the probability that it also purchased a DVR?

SOLUTION Because you know that the household purchased a plasma-screen television, the sample space is reduced to 80 households. Of these 80 households, 38 also purchased a DVR. Therefore, the probability that a household purchased a DVR, given that the household purchased a plasma-screen television, is:

$$P(\text{Purchased DVR} \mid \text{Purchased plasma screen}) = \frac{\text{Number purchasing plasma screen } and \text{ DVR}}{\text{Number purchasing plasma screen}}$$

$$= \frac{38}{80} = 0.475$$

If you use Equation (4.4b) on page 135:

$$A = \text{Purchased plasma-screen television} \quad B = \text{Purchased DVR}$$

then

$$P(B \mid A) = \frac{P(A \text{ and } B)}{P(A)} = \frac{38/300}{80/300} = 0.475$$

Therefore, given that the household purchased a plasma-screen television, there is a 47.5% chance that the household also purchased a DVR. You can compare this conditional probability to the marginal probability of purchasing a DVR, which is 108/300 = 0.36, or 36%. These results tell you that households that purchased plasma-screen televisions are more likely to purchase DVRs than are households that purchased big-screen televisions that are not plasma-screen televisions.

Decision Trees

In Table 4.1 on page 128, households are classified according to whether they planned to purchase and whether they actually purchased big-screen televisions. A **decision tree** is an alternative to the contingency table. Figure 4.3 represents the decision tree for this example.

FIGURE 4.3

Decision tree for M&R Electronics World example

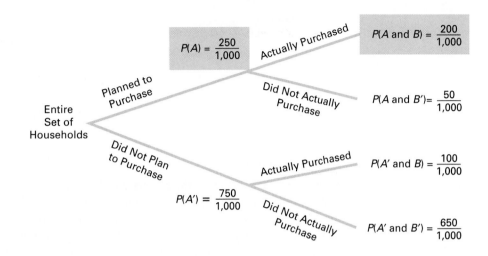

In Figure 4.3, beginning at the left with the entire set of households, there are two "branches" for whether or not the household planned to purchase a big-screen television. Each of these branches has two subbranches, corresponding to whether the household actually purchased or did not actually purchase the big-screen television. The probabilities at the end of the initial branches represent the marginal probabilities of A and A'. The probabilities at the end of each of the four subbranches represent the joint probability for each combination of events A and B. You compute the conditional probability by dividing the joint probability by the appropriate marginal probability.

For example, to compute the probability that the household actually purchased, given that the household planned to purchase the big-screen television, you take P(Planned to purchase *and* actually purchased) and divide by P(Planned to purchase). From Figure 4.3:

$$P(\text{Actually purchased} \mid \text{Planned to purchase}) = \frac{200/1{,}000}{250/1{,}000}$$

$$= \frac{200}{250} = 0.80$$

Example 4.7 illustrates how to construct a decision tree.

EXAMPLE 4.7

Forming the Decision Tree for the Households that Purchased Big-Screen Televisions

Using the cross-classified data in Table 4.2 on page 130, construct the decision tree. Use the decision tree to find the probability that a household purchased a DVR, given that the household purchased a plasma-screen television.

SOLUTION The decision tree for purchased a DVR and a plasma-screen television is displayed in Figure 4.4. Using Equation (4.4b) on page 135 and the following definitions,

$$A = \text{Purchased plasma-screen tlelvision}$$

$$B = \text{Purchased DVR}$$

$$P(B \mid A) = \frac{P(A \text{ and } B)}{P(A)} = \frac{38/300}{80/300} = 0.475$$

FIGURE 4.4

Decision tree for purchased a DVR and a plasma-screen television

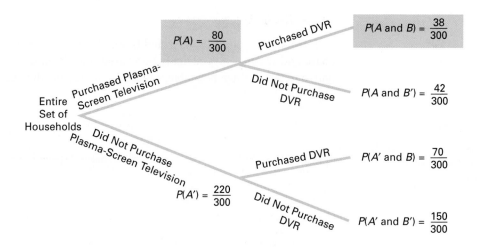

Independence

In the example concerning the purchase of big-screen televisions, the conditional probability is 200/250 = 0.80 that the selected household actually purchased the big-screen television, given that the household planned to purchase. The simple probability of selecting a household that actually purchased is 300/1,000 = 0.30. This result shows that the prior knowledge that the household planned to purchase affected the probability that the household actually purchased the television. In other words, the outcome of one event is *dependent* on the outcome of a second event.

When the outcome of one event does *not* affect the probability of occurrence of another event, the events are said to be independent. **Independence** can be determined by using Equation (4.5).

INDEPENDENCE

Two events, A and B, are independent if and only if

$$P(A \mid B) = P(A) \qquad\qquad (4.5)$$

where

$$P(A \mid B) = \text{conditional probability of } A \text{ given } B$$
$$P(A) = \text{marginal probability of } A$$

Example 4.8 demonstrates the use of Equation (4.5).

EXAMPLE 4.8

Determining Independence

In the follow-up survey of the 300 households that actually purchased big-screen televisions, the households were asked if they were satisfied with their purchases. Table 4.3 cross-classifies the responses to the satisfaction question with the responses to whether the television was a plasma-screen television.

TABLE 4.3

Satisfaction with Purchase of Big-Screen Televisions

TYPE OF TELEVISION	SATISFIED WITH PURCHASE?		
	Yes	No	Total
Plasma screen	64	16	80
Not plasma screen	176	44	220
Total	240	60	300

Determine whether being satisfied with the purchase and type of television purchased are independent.

SOLUTION For these data,

$$P(\text{Satisfied} \mid \text{Plasma screen}) = \frac{64/300}{80/300} = \frac{64}{80} = 0.80$$

which is equal to

$$P(\text{Satisfied}) = \frac{240}{300} = 0.80$$

Thus, being satisfied with the purchase and type of television purchased are independent. Knowledge of one event does not affect the probability of the other event.

Multiplication Rules

The **general multiplication rule** is derived using Equation (4.4a) on page 135:

$$P(A \mid B) = \frac{P(A \text{ and } B)}{P(B)}$$

and solving for the joint probability $P(A \text{ and } B)$.

GENERAL MULTIPLICATION RULE

The probability of A and B is equal to the probability of A given B times the probability of B.

$$P(A \text{ and } B) = P(A \mid B)P(B) \tag{4.6}$$

Example 4.9 demonstrates the use of the general multiplication rule.

EXAMPLE 4.9

Using the Multiplication Rule

Consider the 80 households that purchased plasma-screen televisions. In Table 4.3 on page 138 you see that 64 households are satisfied with their purchase and 16 households are dissatisfied. Suppose two households are randomly selected from the 80 households. Find the probability that both households are satisfied with their purchase.

SOLUTION Here you can use the multiplication rule in the following way. If:

$$A = \text{second household selected is satisfied}$$
$$B = \text{first household selected is satisfied}$$

then, using Equation (4.6),

$$P(A \text{ and } B) = P(A \mid B)P(B)$$

The probability that the first household is satisfied with the purchase is 64/80. However, the probability that the second household is also satisfied with the purchase depends on the result of the first selection. If the first household is not returned to the sample after the satisfaction level is determined (i.e., sampling without replacement), the number of households remaining is 79. If the first household is satisfied, the probability that the second is also satisfied is 63/79 because 63 satisfied households remain in the sample. Therefore,

$$P(A \text{ and } B) = \left(\frac{63}{79}\right)\left(\frac{64}{80}\right) = 0.6380$$

There is a 63.80% chance that both of the households sampled will be satisfied with their purchase.

The **multiplication rule for independent events** is derived by substituting $P(A)$ for $P(A \mid B)$ in Equation (4.6).

MULTIPLICATION RULE FOR INDEPENDENT EVENTS

If A and B are independent, the probability of A and B is equal to the probability of A times the probability of B.

$$P(A \text{ and } B) = P(A)P(B) \tag{4.7}$$

If this rule holds for two events, A and B, then A and B are independent. Therefore, there are two ways to determine independence:

1. Events A and B are independent if, and only if, $P(A \mid B) = P(A)$.
2. Events A and B are independent if, and only if, $P(A \text{ and } B) = P(A)P(B)$.

Marginal Probability Using the General Multiplication Rule

In Section 4.1, marginal probability was defined using Equation (4.2) on page 131. You can state the equation for marginal probability by using the general multiplication rule. If

$$P(A) = P(A \text{ and } B_1) + P(A \text{ and } B_2) + \cdots + P(A \text{ and } B_k)$$

then, using the general multiplication rule, Equation (4.8) defines the marginal probability.

MARGINAL PROBABILITY USING THE GENERAL MULTIPLICATION RULE

$$P(A) = P(A \mid B_1)P(B_1) + P(A \mid B_2)P(B_2) + \cdots + P(A \mid B_k)P(B_k) \tag{4.8}$$

where $B_1, B_2, \ldots, B_k$ are k mutually exclusive and collectively exhaustive events.

To illustrate this equation, refer to Table 4.1 on page 128. Let

$$P(A) = \text{probability of "planned to purchase"}$$

$$P(B_1) = \text{probability of "actually purchased"}$$

$$P(B_2) = \text{probability of "did not actually purchase"}$$

Then, using Equation (4.8), the probability of planned to purchase is:

$$P(A) = P(A \mid B_1)P(B_1) + P(A \mid B_2)P(B_2)$$

$$= \left(\frac{200}{300}\right)\left(\frac{300}{1{,}000}\right) + \left(\frac{50}{700}\right)\left(\frac{700}{1{,}000}\right)$$

$$= \frac{200}{1{,}000} + \frac{50}{1{,}000} = \frac{250}{1{,}000} = 0.25$$

Problems for Section 4.2

LEARNING THE BASICS

4.16 Given the following contingency table:

	B	B'
A	10	20
A'	20	40

What is the probability of
a. $A \mid B$?
b. $A \mid B'$?
c. $A' \mid B'$?
d. Are events A and B independent?

4.17 Given the following contingency table:

	B	B'
A	10	30
A'	25	35

What is the probability of
a. $A \mid B$?
b. $A' \mid B'$?
c. $A \mid B'$?
d. Are events A and B independent?

4.18 If $P(A \text{ and } B) = 0.4$ and $P(B) = 0.8$, find $P(A \mid B)$.

4.19 If $P(A) = 0.7$, $P(B) = 0.6$, and A and B are independent, find $P(A \text{ and } B)$.

4.20 If $P(A) = 0.3$, $P(B) = 0.4$, and $P(A \text{ and } B) = 0.2$, are A and B independent?

APPLYING THE CONCEPTS

4.21 Where people turn to for news is different for various age groups. Suppose that a study conducted on this issue (data extracted from P. Johnson, "Young People Turn to the Web for News," *USA Today*, March 23, 2006, p. 9D) was based on 200 respondents who were between the ages of 36 and 50 and 200 respondents who were over age 50. Of the 200 respondents who were between the ages of 36 and 50, 82 got their news primarily from newspapers. Of the 200 respondents who were over age 50, 104 got their news primarily from newspapers.

a. Given that a respondent is over age 50, what then is the probability that he or she gets news primarily from newspapers?

b. Given that a respondent gets news primarily from newspapers, what is the probability that he or she is over age 50?

c. Explain the difference in the results in (a) and (b).

d. Are the two events, whether the respondent is over age 50 and whether he or she gets news primarily from newspapers, independent?

✓SELF **4.22** A yield improvement study at a semicon-
Test ductor manufacturing facility provided defect data for a sample of 450 wafers. The following table presents a summary of the responses to two questions: "Were particles found on the die that produced the wafer?" and "Is the wafer good or bad?"

QUALITY OF WAFER	CONDITION OF DIE		
	No Particles	Particles	Totals
Good	320	14	334
Bad	80	36	116
Totals	400	50	450

Source: *Data extracted from S. W. Hall, "Analysis of Defectivity of Semiconductor Wafers by Contingency Table,"* Proceedings Institute of Environmental Sciences, Vol. 1, *1994, pp. 177–183.*

a. Suppose you know that a wafer is bad. What is the probability that it was produced from a die that had particles?

b. Suppose you know that a wafer is good. What is the probability that it was produced from a die that had particles?

c. Are the two events, a good wafer and a die with no particles, independent? Explain.

4.23 According to an Ipsos poll, the perception of unfairness in the U.S. tax code is spread fairly evenly across income groups, age groups, and education levels. In an April 2006 survey of 1,005 adults, Ipsos reported that almost 60% of all people said the code is unfair, whereas slightly more than 60% of those making more than $50,000 viewed the code as unfair ("People Cry Unfairness," *The Cincinnati*

Enquirer, April 16, 2006, p. A8). Suppose that the following contingency table represents the specific breakdown of responses:

	INCOME LEVEL		
	Less Than $50,000	More Than $50,000	Total
Fair	225	180	405
Unfair	280	320	600
Total	505	500	1,005

a. Given that a respondent earns less than $50,000, what is the probability that he or she said that the tax code is fair?

b. Given that a respondent earns more than $50,000, what is the probability that he or she said that the tax code is fair?

c. Is income level independent of attitude about whether the tax code is fair? Explain.

4.24 An experiment was conducted to study the choices made in mutual fund selection. Undergraduate and MBA students were presented with different S&P 500 Index funds that were identical except for fees. Suppose 100 undergraduate students and 100 MBA students were selected. Partial results are shown in the following table:

FUND	STUDENT GROUP	
	Undergraduate	MBA
Highest-cost fund	27	18
Not highest-cost fund	73	82

Source: *Data extracted from J. J. Choi, D. Laibson, and B. C. Madrian, Why Does the Law of One Price Fail?* www.som.yale.edu/faculty/jjc83/ fees.pdf.

a. Given that a student is an undergraduate, what is the probability that he or she selected the highest-cost fund?

b. Given that a student selected the highest-cost fund, what is the probability that he or she is an undergraduate?

c. Explain the difference in the results in (a) and (b).

d. Are the two events "student group" and "fund selected" independent? Explain.

4.25 A sample of 500 respondents was selected in a large metropolitan area to study consumer behavior, with the following results:

ENJOYS SHOPPING FOR CLOTHING	GENDER		
	Male	Female	Total
Yes	136	224	360
No	104	36	140
Total	240	260	500

a. Suppose the respondent chosen is a female. What is the probability that she does not enjoy shopping for clothing?

b. Suppose the respondent chosen enjoys shopping for clothing. What is the probability that the individual is a male?

c. Are enjoying shopping for clothing and the gender of the individual independent? Explain.

4.26 Each year, ratings are compiled concerning the performance of new cars during the first 90 days of use. Suppose that the cars have been categorized according to whether the car needs warranty-related repair (yes or no) and the country in which the company manufacturing the car is based (United States or not United States). Based on the data collected, the probability that the new car needs a warranty repair is 0.04, the probability that the car is manufactured by a U.S.-based company is 0.60, and the probability that the new car needs a warranty repair *and* was manufactured by a U.S.-based company is 0.025.

a. Suppose you know that a company based in the United States manufactured a particular car. What is the probability that the car needs warranty repair?

b. Suppose you know that a company based in the United States did not manufacture a particular car. What is the probability that the car needs warranty repair?

c. Are need for warranty repair and location of the company manufacturing the car independent?

4.27 In 37 of the 58 years from 1950 through 2007, the S&P 500 finished higher after the first 5 days of trading. In 32 of those 37 years, the S&P 500 finished higher for the year. Is a good first week a good omen for the upcoming year? The following table gives the first-week and annual performance over this 58-year period:

| FIRST WEEK | S&P 500'S ANNUAL PERFORMANCE | |
	Higher	Lower
Higher	32	5
Lower	11	10

a. If a year is selected at random, what is the probability that the S&P 500 finished higher for the year?

b. Given that the S&P 500 finished higher after the first five days of trading, what is the probability that it finished higher for the year?

c. Are the two events "first-week performance" and "annual performance" independent? Explain.

d. Look up the performance after the first five days of 2008 and the 2008 annual performance of the S&P 500 at **finance.yahoo.com**. Comment on the results.

4.28 A standard deck of cards is being used to play a game. There are four suits (hearts, diamonds, clubs, and spades), each having 13 faces (ace, 2, 3, 4, 5, 6, 7, 8, 9, 10, jack, queen, and king), making a total of 52 cards. This complete deck is thoroughly mixed, and you will receive the first 2 cards from the deck without replacement.

a. What is the probability that both cards are queens?

b. What is the probability that the first card is a 10 and the second card is a 5 or 6?

c. If you were sampling with replacement, what would be the answer in (a)?

d. In the game of blackjack, the picture cards (jack, queen, king) count as 10 points, and the ace counts as either 1 or 11 points. All other cards are counted at their face value. Blackjack is achieved if 2 cards total 21 points. What is the probability of getting blackjack in this problem?

4.29 A box of nine gloves contains two left-handed gloves and seven right-handed gloves.

a. If two gloves are randomly selected from the box without replacement, what is the probability that both gloves selected will be right-handed?

b. If two gloves are randomly selected from the box without replacement, what is the probability there will be one right-handed glove and one left-handed glove selected?

c. If three gloves are selected with replacement, what is the probability that all three will be left-handed?

d. If you were sampling with replacement, what would be the answers to (a) and (b)?

4.3 Bayes' Theorem

Bayes' theorem is used to revise previously calculated probabilities based on new information. Developed by Thomas Bayes in the eighteenth century (see references 1, 2, and 5), Bayes' theorem is an extension of what you previously learned about conditional probability.

You can apply Bayes' theorem to the situation in which M&R Electronics World is considering marketing a new model of television. In the past, 40% of the televisions introduced by the company have been successful, and 60% have been unsuccessful. Before introducing the television to the marketplace, the marketing research department conducts an extensive study and releases a report, either favorable or unfavorable. In the past, 80% of the successful televisions had received favorable market research reports, and 30% of the unsuccessful televisions had received favorable reports. For the new model of television under consideration, the marketing research department has issued a favorable report. What is the probability that the television will be successful?

Bayes' theorem is developed from the definition of conditional probability. To find the conditional probability of B given A, consider Equation (4.4b) [originally presented on page 135 and shown below]:

$$P(B \mid A) = \frac{P(A \text{ and } B)}{P(A)} = \frac{P(A \mid B)P(B)}{P(A)}$$

Bayes' theorem is derived by substituting Equation (4.8) on page 140 for $P(A)$ in the denominator of Equation (4.4b).

BAYES' THEOREM

$$P(B_i \mid A) = \frac{P(A \mid B_i)P(B_i)}{P(A \mid B_1)P(B_1) + P(A \mid B_2)P(B_2) + \cdots + P(A \mid B_k)P(B_k)} \qquad \textbf{(4.9)}$$

where B_i is the ith event out of k mutually exclusive and collectively exhaustive events.

To use Equation (4.9) for the television-marketing example, let

$$\text{event } S = \text{successful television} \qquad \text{event } F = \text{favorable report}$$

$$\text{event } S' = \text{unsuccessful television} \quad \text{event } F' = \text{unfavorable report}$$

and

$$P(S) = 0.40 \quad P(F \mid S) = 0.80$$

$$P(S') = 0.60 \quad P(F \mid S') = 0.30$$

Then, using Equation (4.9),

$$P(S \mid F) = \frac{P(F \mid S)P(S)}{P(F \mid S)P(S) + P(F \mid S')P(S')}$$

$$= \frac{(0.80)(0.40)}{(0.80)(0.40) + (0.30)(0.60)}$$

$$= \frac{0.32}{0.32 + 0.18} = \frac{0.32}{0.50}$$

$$= 0.64$$

The probability of a successful television, given that a favorable report was received, is 0.64. Thus, the probability of an unsuccessful television, given that a favorable report was received, is $1 - 0.64 = 0.36$. Table 4.4 summarizes the computation of the probabilities, and Figure 4.5 presents the decision tree.

TABLE 4.4

Bayes' Theorem Calculations for the Television-Marketing Example

Event S_i	Prior Probability $P(S_i)$	Conditional Probability $P(F \mid S_i)$	Joint Probability $P(F \mid S_i)P(S_i)$	Revised Probability $P(S_i \mid F)$
S = successful television	0.40	0.80	0.32	$P(S \mid F) = 0.32/0.50$ $= 0.64$
S' = unsuccessful television	0.60	0.30	$\dfrac{0.18}{0.50}$	$P(S' \mid F) = 0.18/0.50$ $= 0.36$

FIGURE 4.5
Decision tree for marketing a new television

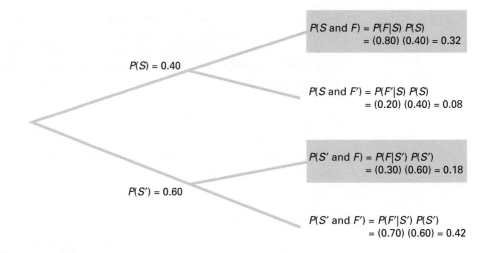

Example 4.10 applies Bayes' theorem to a medical diagnosis problem.

EXAMPLE 4.10

Using Bayes' Theorem in a Medical Diagnosis Problem

The probability that a person has a certain disease is 0.03. Medical diagnostic tests are available to determine whether the person actually has the disease. If the disease is actually present, the probability that the medical diagnostic test will give a positive result (indicating that the disease is present) is 0.90. If the disease is not actually present, the probability of a positive test result (indicating that the disease is present) is 0.02. Suppose that the medical diagnostic test has given a positive result (indicating that the disease is present). What is the probability that the disease is actually present? What is the probability of a positive test result?

SOLUTION Let

$$\text{event } D = \text{has disease} \qquad \text{event } T = \text{test is positive}$$
$$\text{event } D' = \text{does not have disease} \quad \text{event } T' = \text{test is negative}$$

and

$$P(D) = 0.03 \quad P(T\,|\,D) = 0.90$$
$$P(D') = 0.97 \quad P(T\,|\,D') = 0.02$$

Using Equation (4.9) on page 143,

$$P(D\,|\,T) = \frac{P(T\,|\,D)P(D)}{P(T\,|\,D)P(D) + P(T\,|\,D')P(D')}$$
$$= \frac{(0.90)(0.03)}{(0.90)(0.03) + (0.02)(0.97)}$$
$$= \frac{0.0270}{0.0270 + 0.0194} = \frac{0.0270}{0.0464}$$
$$= 0.582$$

The probability that the disease is actually present, given that a positive result has occurred (indicating that the disease is present), is 0.582. Table 4.5 summarizes the computation of the probabilities, and Figure 4.6 presents the decision tree.

TABLE 4.5

Bayes' Theorem Calculations for the Medical Diagnosis Problem

Event D_i	Prior Probability $P(D_i)$	Conditional Probability $P(T \mid D_i)$	Joint Probability $P(T \mid D_i)P(D_i)$	Revised Probability $P(D_i \mid T)$
D = has disease	0.03	0.90	0.0270	$P(D \mid T) = 0.0270/0.0464$ $= 0.582$
D′ = does not have disease	0.97	0.02	$\dfrac{0.0194}{0.0464}$	$P(D' \mid T) = 0.0194/0.0464$ $= 0.418$

FIGURE 4.6

Decision tree for the medical diagnosis problem

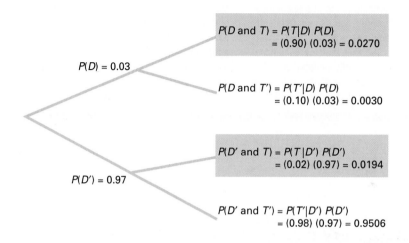

$P(D) = 0.03$

$P(D \text{ and } T) = P(T|D)\ P(D)$
$= (0.90)\ (0.03) = 0.0270$

$P(D \text{ and } T') = P(T'|D)\ P(D)$
$= (0.10)\ (0.03) = 0.0030$

$P(D') = 0.97$

$P(D' \text{ and } T) = P(T|D')\ P(D')$
$= (0.02)\ (0.97) = 0.0194$

$P(D' \text{ and } T') = P(T'|D')\ P(D')$
$= (0.98)\ (0.97) = 0.9506$

The denominator in Bayes' theorem represents $P(T)$, the probability of a positive test result, which in this case is 0.0464, or 4.64%.

THINK ABOUT THIS   Divine Providence and Spam

If asked, you probably would not guess that the essays *Divine Benevolence: Or, An Attempt to Prove That the Principal End of the Divine Providence and Government Is the Happiness of His Creatures* and *An Essay Towards Solving a Problem in the Doctrine of Chances* were written by the same person. But they were! Don't feel bad if you would not have said they were as your thinking illustrates a modern-day application of Bayesian statistics—spam, or junk mail, filters.

In not guessing that the two essays just named were written by the same person, you probably looked at the words in the titles of the essays and concluded that they were talking about two different things. An implicit rule you used was that word frequencies vary by subject matter. A statistics essay would very likely contain the word *statistics* as well as words such as *chance, problem*, and *solving*. An eighteenth-century essay about theology and religion would be more likely to contain the uppercase forms of *Divine* and *Providence*.

Likewise, there are words you would guess to be very unlikely to appear in either book, such

as technical terms from finance and words that are most likely to appear in both—common words such as *a, and*, and *the*. That words would either be likely and unlikely suggests an application of probability theory. Of course, likely and unlikely are fuzzy concepts and we might occasionally misclassify an essay if we kept things too simple, such as relying solely on the occurrence of the words *Divine* and *Providence*.

For example, a profile of the late Harris Milstead, better known as *Divine,* the star of *Hairspray* and other films, visiting Providence (Rhode Island), would most certainly not be an essay about theology. But if we widened the number of words we examined and found such words as *movie* or the name John Waters (Divine's director in many films), we probably would quickly realize the essay had something to do with twentieth-century cinema and little to do directly with theology and religion.

We can use a similar process to try to classify a new e-mail message in your in-box as either spam or a legitimate message (called "ham" in this context). We would first need to

add a "spam filter" to your e-mail program that has the ability to track word frequencies associated with spam and ham messages as you identify them on a day-to-day basis. This would allow the filter to constantly update the prior probabilities necessary to use Bayes' theorem. With these probabilities, the filter can ask, "What is the probability that an e-mail is spam, given the presence of a certain word?"

Applying the terms of Equation (4.9) on page 143, such a Bayesian spam filter would multiply the probability of finding the word in a spam e-mail, $P(A|B)$, by the probability that the e-mail is spam, $P(B)$, and then divide by the probability of finding the word in an e-mail, the denominator in Equation (4.9). Bayesian spam filters also use shortcuts by focusing on a small set of words that have a high probability of being found in a spam message as well as on a small set of other words that have a low probability of being found in a spam message.

As spammers (people who send junk e-mail) learned of these new filters, they tried to outfox them. Having learned that Bayesian filters might be assigning a high $P(A|B)$ value to words such as Viagra commonly found in spam, spammers thought they could fool the filter by misspelling the word as Vi@gr@ or V1agra. What they overlooked was that the misspelled variants were even *more likely* to be found in a spam message than the original word. Thus, the misspelled variants made the job of spotting spam *easier* for the Bayesian filters.

Other spammers tried to fool the filters by adding "good" words, words that would have a low probability of being found in a spam message, or "rare" words, words not frequently encountered in any message. But these spammers overlooked the fact that the conditional probabilities are constantly updated and that words once considered "good" would be soon discarded from the good list by the filter as their

$P(A|B)$ value increased. Likewise as "rare" words grew more common in spam and yet stayed rare in ham, such words acted like the misspelled variants that others had tried earlier.

Even then, and perhaps after reading about Bayesian statistics, spammers thought that they could "break" Bayesian filters by inserting random words in their messages. Those random words would affect the filter by causing it to see many words whose $P(A|B)$ value would be low. The Bayesian filter would begin to label many spam messages as ham and end up being of no practical use. Because the Internet still contains some Web pages and posts that triumph this approach, we will leave it to you to figure out why this method of attack cannot succeed in the long run and why this method is not as initially successful as some would claim.

Today, spammers are still trying to outwit Bayesian filters. Some spammers have decided to eliminate all or most of the words in their messages and replace them with graphics so that Bayesian filters will have very few words to work with. But this approach will fail too, as Bayesian filters are rewritten to consider things other than words in a message. After all, Bayes' theorem concerns *events,* and "graphics present with no text" is as valid an event as "some word *X* present in a message." Other future tricks will ultimately fail for the same reason. (By the way, spam filters use non-Bayestan techniques as well, which make spammers' lives that much more difficult.)

Bayesian spam filters are an example of the unexpected way that applications of statistics can show up in your daily life. You will discover more examples as you read the rest of this book.

Problems for Section 4.3

LEARNING THE BASICS

4.30 If $P(B) = 0.05$, $P(A \mid B) = 0.80$, $P(B') = 0.95$, and $P(A \mid B') = 0.40$, find $P(B \mid A)$.

4.31 If $P(B) = 0.30$, $P(A \mid B) = 0.60$, $P(B') = 0.70$, and $P(A \mid B') = 0.50$, find $P(B \mid A)$.

APPLYING THE CONCEPTS

4.32 In Example 4.10 on page 144, suppose that the probability that a medical diagnostic test will give a positive result if the disease is not present is reduced from 0.02 to 0.01. Given this information,

a. if the medical diagnostic test has given a positive result (indicating that the disease is present), what is the probability that the disease is actually present?

b. if the medical diagnostic test has given a negative result (indicating that the disease is not present), what is the probability that the disease is not present?

4.33 An advertising executive is studying television viewing habits of married men and women during prime-time hours. Based on past viewing records, the executive has determined that during prime time, husbands are watching television 60% of the time. When the husband is watching television, 40% of the time the wife is also watching. When the husband is not watching television, 30% of the time the wife is watching television. Find the probability that

a. if the wife is watching television, the husband is also watching television.

b. the wife is watching television in prime time.

4.34 Olive Construction Company is determining whether it should submit a bid for a new shopping center. In the past, Olive's main competitor, Base Construction Company, has submitted bids 70% of the time. If Base Construction Company does not bid on a job, the probability that Olive Construction Company will get the job is 0.50. If Base Construction Company bids on a job, the probability that Olive Construction Company will get the job is 0.25.

a. If Olive Construction Company gets the job, what is the probability that Base Construction Company did not bid?

b. What is the probability that Olive Construction Company will get the job?

4.35 Laid-off workers who become entrepreneurs because they cannot find meaningful employment with another company are known as *entrepreneurs by necessity. The Wall Street Journal* reports that these entrepreneurs by necessity are less likely to grow into large businesses than are *entrepreneurs by choice* (J. Bailey, "Desire—More Than Need—Builds a Business," *The Wall Street Journal*, May 21, 2001, p. B4). This article states that 89% of the entrepreneurs in the United States are entrepreneurs by choice and 11% are entrepreneurs by necessity. Only 2% of entrepreneurs by necessity expect their new business to employ 20 or more people within five years, whereas 14% of entrepreneurs by choice expect to employ at least 20 people within five years.

a. If an entrepreneur is selected at random, and that individual expects that his or her new business will employ 20 or more people within five years, what is the probability that this individual is an entrepreneur by choice?

b. Discuss several possible reasons why entrepreneurs by choice are more likely to believe that they will grow their businesses.

4.36 The editor of a textbook publishing company is trying to decide whether to publish a proposed business statistics textbook. Information on previous textbooks published indicates that 10% are huge successes, 20% are modest successes, 40% break even, and 30% are losers. However, before a publishing decision is made, the book will be reviewed. In the past, 99% of the huge successes received favorable reviews, 70% of the moderate successes received favorable reviews, 40% of the break-even books received favorable reviews, and 20% of the losers received favorable reviews.

a. If the proposed textbook receives a favorable review, how should the editor revise the probabilities of the various outcomes to take this information into account?

b. What proportion of textbooks receives favorable reviews?

4.37 A municipal bond service has three rating categories (*A, B,* and *C*). Suppose that in the past year, of the municipal bonds issued throughout the United States, 70% were rated *A*, 20% were rated *B*, and 10% were rated *C*. Of the municipal bonds rated *A*, 50% were issued by cities, 40% by suburbs, and 10% by rural areas. Of the municipal bonds rated *B*, 60% were issued by cities, 20% by suburbs, and 20% by rural areas. Of the municipal bonds rated *C*, 90% were issued by cities, 5% by suburbs, and 5% by rural areas.

a. If a new municipal bond is to be issued by a city, what is the probability that it will receive an *A* rating?

b. What proportion of municipal bonds are issued by cities?

c. What proportion of municipal bonds are issued by suburbs?

4.4 Ethical Issues and Probability

Ethical issues can arise when any statements related to probability are presented to the public, particularly when these statements are part of an advertising campaign for a product or service. Unfortunately, many people are not comfortable with numerical concepts (see reference 4) and tend to misinterpret the meaning of the probability. In some instances, the misinterpretation is not intentional, but in other cases, advertisements may unethically try to mislead potential customers.

One example of a potentially unethical application of probability relates to advertisements for state lotteries. When purchasing a lottery ticket, the customer selects a set of numbers (such as 6) from a larger list of numbers (such as 54). Although virtually all participants know that they are unlikely to win the lottery, they also have very little idea of how unlikely it is for them to select all 6 winning numbers from the list of 54 numbers. They have even less idea of the probability of winning a consolation prize by selecting either 4 or 5 winning numbers.

Given this background, you might consider a recent commercial for a state lottery that stated, "We won't stop until we have made everyone a millionaire" to be deceptive and possibly unethical. Do you think the state has any intention of ever stopping the lottery, given the fact that the state relies on it to bring millions of dollars into the treasury? Is it possible that the lottery can make everyone a millionaire? Is it ethical to suggest that the purpose of the lottery is to make everyone a millionaire?

Another example of a potentially unethical application of probability relates to an investment newsletter promising a 90% probability of a 20% annual return on investment. To make the claim in the newsletter an ethical one, the investment service needs to (a) explain the basis on which this probability estimate rests, (b) provide the probability statement in another format, such as 9 chances in 10, and (c) explain what happens to the investment in the 10% of the cases in which a 20% return is not achieved (e.g., is the entire investment lost?).

These are serious ethical issues. If you were going to write an advertisement for the state lottery that ethically describes the probablity of winning a certain prize, what would you say? If you were gong to write an advertisement for the investment newsletter that ethically states the probability of a 20% return on an investment, what would you say?

USING STATISTICS @ M&R Electronics World Revisited

As the marketing manager for M&R Electronics World, you analyzed the survey results of an intent-to-purchase study. This study asked the heads of 1,000 households about their intentions to purchase a big-screen television sometime during the next 12 months, and as a follow-up, M&R surveyed the same people 12 months later to see whether such a television was purchased. In addition, for households purchasing big-screen televisions, the survey asked whether the television they purchased was a plasma screen, whether they also purchased a digital video recorder (DVR) in the past 12 months, and whether they were satisfied with their purchase of the big-screen television.

By analyzing the results of these surveys, you were able to uncover many pieces of valuable information that will help you plan a marketing strategy that will enhance sales and better target those households likely to purchase multiple or more expensive products. Whereas only 30% of the households actually purchased a big-screen television, if a household indicated that they planned to purchase a big-screen television in the next 12 months there was an 80% chance that the household actually made the purchase. Thus the marketing strategy should target those households that have indicated an intention to purchase.

You determined that for households which purchased a plasma-screen television, there was a 47.5% chance that the household also purchased a DVR. You then compared this conditional probability to the marginal probability of purchasing a DVR, which was 36%. Thus, households that purchased plasma-screen televisions are more likely to purchase DVRs than are households that purchased big-screen televisions that are not plasma-screen televisions.

You were also able to apply Bayes' theorem to M&R Electronics World's market research reports. The reports investigate a potential new television model prior to its scheduled release. If a favorable report was received, then there was a 64% chance that the new television model would be successful. However, if an unfavorable report was issued, there was only a 16% chance that it would be successful. Therefore, the marketing strategy of M&R needs to pay close attention to whether a report's conclusion is favorable or unfavorable.

SUMMARY

This chapter began by developing the basic concepts of probability. You learned that probability is a numeric value from zero to one that represents the chance, likelihood, or possibility a particular event will occur. In addition to simple probability, you learned about conditional probabilities and independent events. Bayes' theorem was used to revise previously calculated probabilities based on new information. Throughout the chapter, contingency tables, Venn diagrams, and decision trees were used to display information. In the next chapter, important discrete probability distributions such as the binomial and Poisson distributions are developed.

KEY EQUATIONS

Probability of Occurrence

$$\text{Probability of occurrence} = \frac{X}{T} \qquad (4.1)$$

Marginal Probability

$$P(A) = P(A \text{ and } B_1) + P(A \text{ and } B_2) \\ + \cdots + P(A \text{ and } B_k) \qquad (4.2)$$

General Addition Rule

$$P(A \text{ or } B) = P(A) + P(B) - P(A \text{ and } B) \qquad (4.3)$$

Conditional Probability

$$P(A \,|\, B) = \frac{P(A \text{ and } B)}{P(B)} \qquad (4.4a)$$

$$P(B \,|\, A) = \frac{P(A \text{ and } B)}{P(A)} \qquad (4.4b)$$

Independence

$$P(A \mid B) = P(A) \quad\quad (4.5)$$

General Multiplication Rule

$$P(A \text{ and } B) = P(A \mid B)P(B) \quad\quad (4.6)$$

Multiplication Rule for Independent Events

$$P(A \text{ and } B) = P(A)P(B) \quad\quad (4.7)$$

Marginal Probability Using the General Multiplication Rule

$$P(A) = P(A \mid B_1)P(B_1) + P(A \mid B_2)P(B_2) \\ + \cdots + P(A \mid B_k)P(B_k) \quad\quad (4.8)$$

Bayes' Theorem

$$P(B_i \mid A) = \\ \frac{P(A \mid B_i)P(B_i)}{P(A \mid B_1)P(B_1) + P(A \mid B_2)P(B_2) + \cdots + P(A \mid B_k)P(B_k)} \quad (4.9)$$

KEY TERMS

CHAPTER REVIEW PROBLEMS

CHECKING YOUR UNDERSTANDING

4.38 What are the differences between *a priori* probability, empirical probability, and subjective probability?

4.39 What is the difference between a simple event and a joint event?

4.40 How can you use the general addition rule to find the probability of occurrence of event *A* or *B*?

4.41 What is the difference between mutually exclusive events and collectively exhaustive events?

4.42 How does conditional probability relate to the concept of independence?

4.43 How does the multiplication rule differ for events that are and are not independent?

4.44 How can you use Bayes' theorem to revise probabilities in light of new information?

4.45 In Bayes' theorem, how does the prior probability differ from the revised probability?

APPLYING THE CONCEPTS

4.46 A survey by the Pew Research Center ("Snapshots: Goals of 'Gen next' vs. 'Gen X'," *USA Today*, March 27, 2007, p. 1A) indicated that 81% of 18- to 25-year-olds had getting rich as a goal as compared to 62% of 26- to 40-year-

olds. Suppose that the survey was based on 500 respondents from each of the two groups.
a. Form a contingency table or a Venn diagram.
b. Give an example of a simple event and a joint event.
c. What is the probability that a randomly selected respondent has a goal of getting rich?
d. What is the probability that a randomly selected respondent has a goal of getting rich *and* is in the 26- to 40-year-old group?
e. Are the events "age group" and "has getting rich as a goal" independent? Explain.

4.47 The owner of a restaurant serving Continental-style entrées was interested in studying ordering patterns of patrons for the Friday-to-Sunday weekend time period. Records were maintained that indicated the demand for dessert during the same time period. The owner decided to study two other variables, along with whether a dessert was ordered: the gender of the individual and whether a beef entrée was ordered. The results are as follows:

DESSERT ORDERED	GENDER		
	Male	**Female**	**Total**
Yes	96	40	136
No	224	240	464
Total	320	280	600

DESSERT ORDERED	BEEF ENTRÉE		
	Yes	**No**	**Total**
Yes	71	65	136
No	116	348	464
Total	187	413	600

A waiter approaches a table to take an order. What is the probability that the first customer to order at the table

a. orders a dessert?

b. orders a dessert *or* a beef entrée?

c. is a female *and* does not order a dessert?

d. is a female *or* does not order a dessert?

e. Suppose the first person that the waiter takes the dessert order from is a female. What is the probability that she does not order dessert?

f. Are gender and ordering dessert independent?

g. Is ordering a beef entrée independent of whether the person orders dessert?

4.48 Unsolicited commercial e-mail messages containing product advertisements, commonly referred to as spam, are routinely deleted before being read by more than 80% of all e-mail users. Furthermore, a small percentage of those reading the spam actually follow through and purchase items. Yet many companies use these unsolicited e-mail advertisements because of the extremely low cost involved. Movies Unlimited, a mail-order video and DVD business in Philadelphia, is one of the more successful companies in terms of generating sales through this form of e-marketing. Ed Weiss, general manager of Movies Unlimited, estimates that somewhere from 15% to 20% of the company's e-mail recipients read the advertisements. Moreover, approximately 15% of those who read the advertisements place orders (S. Forster, "E-Marketers Look to Polish Spam's Rusty Image," *The Wall Street Journal*, May 20, 2002, p. D2).

a. Using Mr. Weiss's lower estimate that the probability a recipient will read the advertisement is 0.15, what is the probability that a recipient will read the advertisement *and* place an order?

b. Movies Unlimited uses a 175,000-customer database to send e-mail advertisements. If an e-mail advertisement is sent to everyone in its customer database, how many customers do you expect will read the advertisement and place an order?

c. If the probability a recipient will read the advertisement is 0.20, what is the probability that a recipient will read the advertisement *and* place an order?

d. What is your answer to (b) if the probability that a recipient will read the advertisement is 0.20?

4.49 An experiment was conducted by James Choi, David Laibson, and Brigitte Madrian to study the choices made in fund selection. Suppose 100 undergraduate students and 100 MBA students were selected. When presented with four

S&P 500 Index funds that were identical except for their fees, undergraduate and MBA students chose the funds as follows:

FUND	STUDENT GROUP	
	Undergraduate	**MBA**
Lowest-cost fund	19	19
Second-lowest-cost fund	37	40
Third-lowest-cost fund	17	23
Highest-cost fund	27	18

Source: *Data extracted from J. J. Choi, D. Laibson, and B. C. Madrian, Why Does the Law of One Price Fail?* **www.som.yale.edu/faculty/jjc83/fees.pdf.**

If a student is selected at random, what is the probability that he or she

a. selected the lowest- *or* second-lowest cost fund?

b. selected the lowest-cost fund *and* is an undergraduate?

c. selected the lowest-cost fund *or* is an undergraduate?

d. Given that the student is an undergraduate, what is the probability that he or she selected the highest-cost fund?

e. Do you think undergraduate students and graduate students differ in their fund selection? Explain.

4.50 Sport utility vehicles (SUVs), vans, and pickups are generally considered to be more prone to roll over than cars. In 1997, 24.0% of all highway fatalities involved rollovers; 15.8% of all fatalities in 1997 involved SUVs, vans, and pickups, given that the fatality involved a rollover. Given that a rollover was not involved, 5.6% of all fatalities involved SUVs, vans, and pickups (A. Wilde Mathews, "Ford Ranger, Chevy Tracker Tilt in Test," *The Wall Street Journal*, July 14, 1999, p. A2). Consider the following definitions:

$$A = \text{fatality involved an SUV, van, or pickup}$$

$$B = \text{fatality involved a rollover}$$

a. Use Bayes' theorem to find the probability that a fatality involved a rollover, given that the fatality involved an SUV, a van, or a pickup.

b. Compare the result in (a) to the probability that a fatality involved a rollover and comment on whether SUVs, vans, and pickups are generally more prone to rollover accidents than other vehicles.

4.51 Enzyme-linked immunosorbent assay (ELISA) is the most common type of screening test for detecting the HIV virus. A positive result from an ELISA indicates that the HIV virus is present. For most populations, ELISA has a high degree of sensitivity (to detect infection) and specificity (to detect noninfection). (See HIVInsite, at **HIVInsite.ucsf.edu**.) Suppose that the probability a person is infected with the HIV virus for a certain population is 0.015. If the HIV virus is actually present, the probability that the ELISA test will give a positive result is 0.995. If the HIV virus is not actually present, the probability of a positive result from an ELISA is 0.01. If the ELISA has given a positive result, use Bayes' theorem to find the probability that the HIV virus is actually present.

TEAM PROJECT

The data file Mutual Funds contains information regarding four categorical variables from a sample of 868 mutual funds. The variables are:

Category—Type of stocks comprising the mutual fund (small cap, mid cap, large cap)

Objective—Objective of stocks comprising the mutual fund (growth or value)

Fees—Sales charges (no or yes)

Risk—Risk-of-loss factor of the mutual fund (low, average, high)

4.52 Construct contingency tables of category and objective, category and fees, category and risk, objective and fees, and fees and risk.

a. For each of these contingency tables, compute all the conditional and marginal probabilities.

b. Based on (a), what conclusions can you reach about whether these variables are independent?

STUDENT SURVEY DATA BASE

4.53 Problem 1.23 on page 13 describes a survey of 50 undergraduate students (see the file Undergradsurvey). For these data, construct contingency tables of gender and major, gender and graduate school intention, gender and employment status, class and graduate school intention, class and employment status, major and graduate school intention, and major and employment status.

a. For each of these contingency tables, compute all the conditional and marginal probabilities.

b. Based on (a), what conclusions can you reach about whether these variables are independent?

4.54 Problem 1.23 on page 13 describes a survey of 50 undergraduate students (see the file Undergradsurvey).

a. Select a sample of 50 undergraduate students at your school and conduct a similar survey for those students.

b. For these data, construct contingency tables of gender and major, gender and graduate school intention, gender and employment status, class and graduate school intention, class and employment status, major and graduate school intention, and major and employment status. For each of these contingency tables, compute all the conditional and marginal probabilities.

c. Based on (b), what conclusions can you reach about whether these variables are independent?

d. Compare the results of (c) to those of Problem 4.53(b).

4.55 Problem 1.24 on page 13 describes a survey of 40 MBA students (see the file Gradsurvey). For these data, construct contingency tables of gender and graduate major, gender and undergraduate major, gender and employment status, graduate major and undergraduate major, and graduate major and employment status.

a. For each of these contingency tables, compute all the conditional and marginal probabilities.

b. Based on (b), what conclusions can you reach about whether these variables are independent?

4.56 Problem 1.24 on page 13 describes a survey of 40 MBA students (see the file Gradsurvey).

a. Select a sample of 40 MBA students from your MBA program and conduct a similar survey for those students.

b. For these data, construct contingency tables of gender and graduate major, gender and undergraduate major, gender and employment status, graduate major and undergraduate major, and graduate major and employment status. For each of these contingency tables, compute all the conditional and marginal probabilities.

c. Based on (b), what conclusions can you reach about whether these variables are independent?

d. Compare the results of (c) to those of Problem 4.55(b).

WEB CASE

Apply your knowledge about contingency tables and the proper application of simple and joint probabilities in this continuing Web Case from Chapter 3.

Visit the EndRun Guaranteed Investment Package (GIP) Web page, at **www.prenhall.com/Springville/ER_Guaranteed.htm** or open this Web page file from the Student CD-ROM Web Case folder. Read the claims and examine the supporting data. Then answer the following:

1. How accurate is the claim of the probability of success for EndRun's GIP? In what ways is the claim misleading?

How would you calculate and state the probability of having an annual rate of return not less than 15%?

2. What mistake was made in reporting the 7% probability claim? Using the table found on the "Winning Probabilities" Web page, ER_Guaranteed3.htm, compute the proper probabilities for the group of investors.

3. Are there any probability calculations that would be appropriate for rating an investment service? Why or why not?

REFERENCES

1. Bellhouse, D. R., "The Reverend Thomas Bayes, FRS: A Biography to Celebrate the Tercentenary of His Birth," *Statistical Science* 19 (2004), 3–43.

2. Lowd, D., and C. Meek, "Good Word Attacks on Statistical Spam Filters," presented at the Second Conference on Email and Anti-Spam, CEAS 2005.

3. *Microsoft Excel 2007* (Redmond, WA: Microsoft Corp., 2007).

4. Paulos, J. A., *Innumeracy* (New York: Hill and Wang, 1988).

5. Silberman, S., "The Quest for Meaning," *Wired 8.02*, February 2000.

6. T. Zeller, "The Fight Against V1@gra (and Other Spam)," *The New York Times*, May 21, 2006, pp. B1, B6.

APPENDIX E4

Using Microsoft Excel for Basic Probability

E4.1 Computing Basic Probabilities (all Excel versions)

To compute basic probabilities, open to the **Probabilities** worksheet of the **Probabilities.xls** workbook. Enter event labels and counts in the tinted cells in rows 3 through 6. Figure E4.1 shows a completed worksheet for the "Purchase Behavior for Big-Screen Television" data of Table 4.1 on page 128. Also shown offset in Figure E4.1 are the formulas this worksheet uses to compute the various probabilities.

	A	B	C	D	E
1	Probabilities for Purchase Behavior for Big-Screen Televisions				
2					
3	Sample Space		Actually Purchased		
4			Yes	No	Totals
5	Planned to Purchase	Yes	200	50	250
6		No	100	650	750
7		Totals	300	700	1000
8					
9	Simple Probabilities				
10	P(Yes)	0.25			
11	P(No)	0.75			
12	P(Yes)	0.30			
13	P(No)	0.70			
14					
15	Joint Probabilities				
16	P(Yes and Yes)	0.20			
17	P(Yes and No)	0.05			
18	P(No and Yes)	0.10			
19	P(No and No)	0.65			
20					
21	Addition Rule				
22	P(Yes or Yes)	0.35			
23	P(Yes or No)	0.90			
24	P(No or Yes)	0.95			
25	P(No or No)	0.80			

Simple Probabilities	
="P(" & B5 & ")"	=E5 / E7
="P(" & B6 & ")"	=E6 / E7
="P(" & C4 & ")"	=C7 / E7
="P(" & D4 & ")"	=D7 / E7
Joint Probabilities	
="P(" & B5 & " and " & C4 & ")"	=C5 / E7
="P(" & B5 & " and " & D4 & ")"	=D5 / E7
="P(" & B6 & " and " & C4 & ")"	=C6 / E7
="P(" & B6 & " and " & D4 & ")"	=D6 / E7
Addition Rule	
="P(" & B5 & " or " & C4 & ")"	=B10 + B12 - B16
="P(" & B5 & " or " & D4 & ")"	=B10 + B13 - B17
="P(" & B6 & " or " & C4 & ")"	=B11 + B12 - B18
="P(" & B6 & " or " & D4 & ")"	=B11 + B13 - B19

FIGURE E4.1 Probabilities worksheet

The worksheet also "computes" the *labels* for the probabilities table with formulas that use the ampersand (**&**) operator to combine parts of a label. For example, the cell A10 formula **="P(" & B5 & ")"** asks Excel to combine the contents of B5 (**Yes**) to the label **"P("** to get **"P(Yes"** and then to "add" **")"** to get **"P(Yes)"** and form the formula **="P(Yes)"**–a novel, but acceptable, way of entering the label value **P(Yes)** in a cell.

E4.2 Using Bayes' Theorem (all Excel versions)

You calculate probabilities using Bayes' theorem by making entries in the cell range B5:C6 of the **Bayes** worksheet of the **Bayes.xls** workbook. Figure E4.2 shows a completed worksheet for the television-marketing example shown in Table 4.4 on page 143.

	A	B	C	D	E
1	Bayes Theorem Calculations				
2					
3		Probabilities			
4	Event	Prior	Conditional	Joint	Revised
5	S	0.4	0.8	0.32	0.64
6	S'	0.6	0.3	0.18	0.36
7			Total:	0.5	

Joint	Revised
=B5 * C5	=D5 / D7
=B6 * C6	=D6 / D7
=D5 + D6	

FIGURE E4.2 Bayes' theorem worksheet

APPENDIX P4

Using PHStat2 for Basic Probability

P4.1 Computing Basic Probabilities

To compute basic probabilities, use **PHStat → Probability & Prob. Distributions → Simple & Joint Probabilities**.

This procedure inserts a **Basic Probabilities** worksheet similar to Figure E4.1 on this page into the current workbook. To use the worksheet, fill in the Sample Space area with your data. (Unlike most PHStat2 procedures, this procedure does *not* display a dialog box.)

5 Discrete Probability Distributions

Learning Objectives

In this chapter, you learn:

- The properties of a probability distribution
- To compute the expected value and variance of a probability distribution
- To compute probabilities from the binomial and Poisson distributions
- How to use the binomial and Poisson distributions to solve business problems

@ Saxon Home Improvement

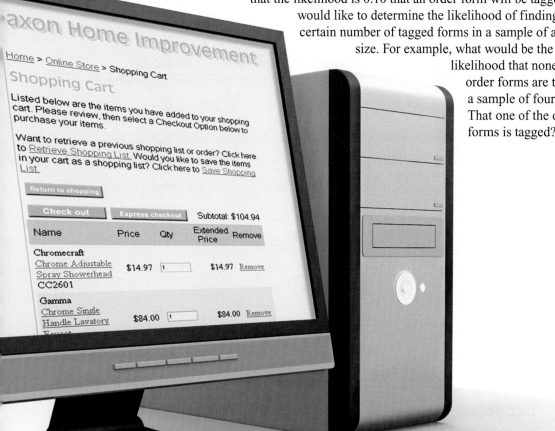

Y ou are an accountant for the Saxon Home Improvement Company which uses a state-of-the-art accounting information system to manage its accounting and financial operations.

Accounting information systems collect, process, store, transform, and distribute financial information to decision makers both internal and external to a business organization (see reference 7). These systems continuously audit accounting information, looking for errors or incomplete or improbable information. For example, when customers of the Saxon Home Improvement Company submit online orders, the company's accounting information system reviews the order forms for possible mistakes. Any questionable invoices are *tagged* and included in a daily *exceptions report*. Recent data collected by the company show that the likelihood is 0.10 that an order form will be tagged. Saxon would like to determine the likelihood of finding a certain number of tagged forms in a sample of a specific size. For example, what would be the likelihood that none of the order forms are tagged in a sample of four forms? That one of the order forms is tagged?

How could the Saxon Home Improvement Company determine the solution to this type of probability problem? One way is to use a model, or small-scale representation, that approximates the process. By using such an approximation, Saxon managers could make inferences about the actual order process. In this case, the Saxon managers can use *probability distributions*, mathematical models suited for solving the type of probability problems the managers are facing. Reading this chapter will help you learn about characteristics of a probability distribution and how to specifically apply the binomial and Poisson distributions to business problems.

5.1 The Probability Distribution for a Discrete Random Variable

In Section 1.6, a *numerical variable* was defined as a variable that yielded numerical responses, such as the number of magazines you subscribe to or your height. Numerical variables are classified as *discrete* or *continuous*. Continuous numerical variables produce outcomes that come from a measuring process (e.g., your height). Discrete numerical variables produce outcomes that come from a counting process (e.g., the number of magazines you subscribe to). This chapter deals with probability distributions that represent discrete numerical variables.

> PROBABILITY DISTRIBUTION FOR A DISCRETE RANDOM VARIABLE
>
> A **probability distribution for a discrete random variable** is a mutually exclusive listing of all the possible numerical outcomes along with the probability of occurrence of each outcome.

For example, Table 5.1 gives the distribution of the number of mortgages approved per week at the local branch office of a bank. The listing in Table 5.1 is collectively exhaustive because all possible outcomes are included. Thus, the probabilities sum to 1. Figure 5.1 is a graphical representation of Table 5.1.

TABLE 5.1

Probability Distribution of the Number of Home Mortgages Approved per Week

Home Mortgages Approved per Week	Probability
0	0.10
1	0.10
2	0.20
3	0.30
4	0.15
5	0.10
6	0.05

FIGURE 5.1

Probability distribution of the number of home mortgages approved per week

Expected Value of a Discrete Random Variable

The mean, μ, of a probability distribution is the **expected value** of its random variable. To calculate the expected value, you multiply each possible outcome, X, by its corresponding probability, $P(X)$, and then sum these products.

EXPECTED VALUE, μ, OF A DISCRETE RANDOM VARIABLE

$$\mu = E(X) = \sum_{i=1}^{N} X_i P(X_i) \tag{5.1}$$

where

$$X_i = \text{the } i\text{th outcome of the discrete random variable } X$$

$$P(X_i) = \text{probability of occurrence of the } i\text{th outcome of } X$$

For the probability distribution of the number of home mortgages approved per week (Table 5.1), the expected value is computed below using Equation (5.1) and is also shown in Table 5.2.

$$\mu = E(X) = \sum_{i=1}^{N} X_i P(X_i)$$

$$= (0)(0.1) + (1)(0.1) + (2)(0.2) + (3)(0.3) + (4)(0.15) + (5)(0.1) + (6)(0.05)$$

$$= 0 + 0.1 + 0.4 + 0.9 + 0.6 + 0.5 + 0.3$$

$$= 2.8$$

TABLE 5.2

Computing the Expected Value of the Number of Home Mortgages Approved per Week

Home Mortgages Approved per Week (X_i)	$P(X_i)$	$X_iP(X_i)$
0	0.10	$(0)(0.10) = 0.0$
1	0.10	$(1)(0.10) = 0.1$
2	0.20	$(2)(0.20) = 0.4$
3	0.30	$(3)(0.30) = 0.9$
4	0.15	$(4)(0.15) = 0.6$
5	0.10	$(5)(0.10) = 0.5$
6	0.05	$(6)(0.05) = 0.3$
	1.00	$\mu = E(X) = 2.8$

The expected value is 2.8. The expected value of 2.8 for the number of mortgages approved is not a possible outcome because the actual number of mortgages approved in a given week must be an integer value. The expected value represents the *mean* number of mortgages approved per week.

Variance and Standard Deviation of a Discrete Random Variable

You compute the variance of a probability distribution by multiplying each possible squared difference $[X_i - E(X)]^2$ by its corresponding probability, $P(X_i)$, and then summing the resulting products. Equation (5.2) defines the **variance of a discrete random variable**.

VARIANCE OF A DISCRETE RANDOM VARIABLE

$$\sigma^2 = \sum_{i=1}^{N} [X_i - E(X)]^2 P(X_i) \tag{5.2}$$

where

$$X_i = \text{the } i\text{th outcome of the discrete random variable } X$$

$$P(X_i) = \text{probability of occurrence of the } i\text{th outcome of } X$$

Equation (5.3) defines the **standard deviation of a discrete random variable**.

> STANDARD DEVIATION OF A DISCRETE RANDOM VARIABLE
>
> $$\sigma = \sqrt{\sigma^2} = \sqrt{\sum_{i=1}^{N}[X_i - E(X)]^2 P(X_i)} \qquad (5.3)$$

The variance and the standard deviation of the number of home mortgages approved per week are computed below and in Table 5.3, using Equations (5.2) and (5.3):

$$\sigma^2 = \sum_{i=1}^{N}[X_i - E(X)]^2 P(X_i)$$

$$= (0 - 2.8)^2(0.10) + (1 - 2.8)^2(0.10) + (2 - 2.8)^2(0.20) + (3 - 2.8)^2(0.30)$$

$$+ (4 - 2.8)^2(0.15) + (5 - 2.8)^2(0.10) + (6 - 2.8)^2(0.05)$$

$$= 0.784 + 0.324 + 0.128 + 0.012 + 0.216 + 0.484 + 0.512$$

$$= 2.46$$

TABLE 5.3

Computing the Variance and Standard Deviation of the Number of Home Mortgages Approved per Week

Home Mortgages Approved per Week (X_i)	$P(X_i)$	$X_i P(X_i)$	$[X_i - E(X)]^2 P(X_i)$
0	0.10	$(0)(0.10) = 0.0$	$(0 - 2.8)^2(0.10) = 0.784$
1	0.10	$(1)(0.10) = 0.1$	$(1 - 2.8)^2(0.10) = 0.324$
2	0.20	$(2)(0.20) = 0.4$	$(2 - 2.8)^2(0.20) = 0.128$
3	0.30	$(3)(0.30) = 0.9$	$(3 - 2.8)^2(0.30) = 0.012$
4	0.15	$(4)(0.15) = 0.6$	$(4 - 2.8)^2(0.15) = 0.216$
5	0.10	$(5)(0.10) = 0.5$	$(5 - 2.8)^2(0.10) = 0.484$
6	0.05	$(6)(0.05) = 0.3$	$(6 - 2.8)^2(0.05) = 0.512$
	1.00	$\mu = E(X) = 2.8$	$\sigma^2 = 2.46$

and

$$\sigma = \sqrt{\sigma^2} = \sqrt{2.46} = 1.57$$

Thus, the mean number of mortgages approved per week is 2.8, the variance is 2.46, and the standard deviation is 1.57.

Problems for Section 5.1

LEARNING THE BASICS

5.1 Given the following probability distributions:

Distribution *A*		Distribution *B*	
X	**P(X)**	**X**	**P(X)**
0	0.50	0	0.05
1	0.20	1	0.10
2	0.15	2	0.15
3	0.10	3	0.20
4	0.05	4	0.50

a. Compute the expected value for each distribution.
b. Compute the standard deviation for each distribution.
c. Compare the results of distributions *A* and *B*.

APPLYING THE CONCEPTS

✓ SELF Test **5.2** The following table contains the probability distribution for the number of traffic accidents daily in a small city:

Number of Accidents Daily (*X*)	**P(X)**
0	0.10
1	0.20
2	0.45
3	0.15
4	0.05
5	0.05

a. Compute the mean number of accidents per day.
b. Compute the standard deviation.

5.3 The manager of a large computer network has developed the following probability distribution of the number of interruptions per day:

Interruptions (X)	$P(X)$
0	0.32
1	0.35
2	0.18
3	0.08
4	0.04
5	0.02
6	0.01

a. Compute the expected number of interruptions per day.
b. Compute the standard deviation.

5.4 In the carnival game Under-or-Over-Seven, a pair of fair dice is rolled once, and the resulting sum determines whether the player wins or loses his or her bet. For example, the player can bet $1 that the sum will be under 7—that is, 2, 3, 4, 5, or 6. For this bet, the player wins $1 if the result is under 7 and loses $1 if the outcome equals or is greater than 7. Similarly, the player can bet $1 that the sum will be over 7—that is, 8, 9, 10, 11, or 12. Here, the player wins $1 if the result is over 7 but loses $1 if the result is 7 or under. A third method of play is to bet $1 on the outcome 7. For this bet, the player wins $4 if the result of the roll is 7 and loses $1 otherwise.

a. Construct the probability distribution representing the different outcomes that are possible for a $1 bet on under 7.
b. Construct the probability distribution representing the different outcomes that are possible for a $1 bet on over 7.
c. Construct the probability distribution representing the different outcomes that are possible for a $1 bet on 7.
d. Show that the expected long-run profit (or loss) to the player is the same, no matter which method of play is used.

5.5 The number of arrivals per minute at a bank located in the central business district of a large city was recorded over a period of 200 minutes with the following results:

Arrivals	Frequency
0	14
1	31
2	47
3	41
4	29
5	21
6	10
7	5
8	2

a. Compute the expected number of arrivals per minute.
b. Compute the standard deviation.

5.6 The manager of a commercial mortgage department of a large bank has collected data during the past two years concerning the number of commercial mortgages approved per week. The results from these two years (104 weeks) indicated the following:

Number of Commercial Mortgages Approved	Frequency
0	13
1	25
2	32
3	17
4	9
5	6
6	1
7	1

a. Compute the expected number of mortgages approved per week.
b. Compute the standard deviation.

5.2 Binomial Distribution

The next two sections use mathematical models to solve business problems.

> MATHEMATICAL MODEL
>
> A **mathematical model** is a mathematical expression that represents a variable of interest.

When a mathematical expression is available, you can compute the exact probability of occurrence of any particular outcome of the variable.

The **binomial distribution** is one of the most useful mathematical models. You use the binomial distribution when the discrete random variable is the number of events of interest in a sample of n observations. The binomial distribution has four basic properties:

- The sample consists of a fixed number of observations, n.
- Each observation is classified into one of two mutually exclusive and collectively exhaustive categories.

- The probability of an observation being classified as the event of interest, π, is constant from observation to observation. Thus, the probability of an observation being classified as not being the event of interest, $1 - \pi$, is constant over all observations.
- The outcome of any observation is independent of the outcome of any other observation. To ensure independence, the observations can be randomly selected either from an *infinite population with or without replacement* or from a *finite population with replacement*.

Returning to the Using Statistics scenario presented on page 155 concerning the accounting information system, suppose the event of interest is defined as a tagged order form. You are interested in the number of tagged order forms in a given sample of orders.

What results can occur? If the sample contains four orders, there could be none, one, two, three, or four tagged order forms. The binomial random variable, the number of tagged order forms, cannot take on any other value because the number of tagged order forms cannot be more than the sample size, n, and cannot be less than zero. Therefore, the binomial random variable has a range from 0 to n.

Suppose that you observe the following result in a sample of four orders:

First Order	Second Order	Third Order	Fourth Order
Tagged	Tagged	Not tagged	Tagged

What is the probability of having three tagged order forms in a sample of four orders in this particular sequence? Because the historical probability of a tagged order is 0.10, the probability that each order occurs in the sequence is

First Order	Second Order	Third Order	Fourth Order
$\pi = 0.10$	$\pi = 0.10$	$1 - \pi = 0.90$	$\pi = 0.10$

Each outcome is independent of the others because the order forms were selected from an extremely large or practically infinite population without replacement. Therefore, the probability of having this particular sequence is

$$\pi\pi(1 - \pi)\pi = \pi^3(1 - \pi)^1$$
$$= (0.10)^3(0.90)^1$$
$$= (0.10)(0.10)(0.10)(0.90)$$
$$= 0.0009$$

This result indicates only the probability of three tagged order forms (events of interest) from a sample of four order forms in a *specific sequence*. To find the number of ways of selecting X objects from n objects, *irrespective of sequence*, you use the **rule of combinations** given in Equation (5.4) below.

COMBINATIONS

[1]On many scientific calculators, there is a button labeled $_nC_r$ that allows you to compute the number of combinations. The symbol r is used instead of X.

The number of combinations[1] of selecting X objects out of n objects is given by

$$_nC_X = \frac{n!}{X!(n - X)!} \tag{5.4}$$

where

$n! = (n)(n - 1)\cdots(1)$ is called n factorial. By definition, $0! = 1$.

With $n = 4$ and $X = 3$, there are

$$_nC_X = \frac{n!}{X!(n - X)!} = \frac{4!}{3!(4 - 3)!} = \frac{4 \times 3 \times 2 \times 1}{(3 \times 2 \times 1)(1)} = 4$$

such sequences. The four possible sequences are:

Sequence 1 = *tagged, tagged, tagged, not tagged*, with probability
$$\pi\pi\pi(1 - \pi) = \pi^3(1 - \pi)^1 = 0.0009$$

Sequence 2 = *tagged, tagged, not tagged, tagged*, with probability
$$\pi\pi(1 - \pi)\pi = \pi^3(1 - \pi)^1 = 0.0009$$

Sequence 3 = *tagged, not tagged, tagged, tagged*, with probability
$$\pi(1 - \pi)\pi\pi = \pi^3(1 - \pi)^1 = 0.0009$$

Sequence 4 = *not tagged, tagged, tagged, tagged*, with probability
$$(1 - \pi)\pi\pi\pi = \pi^3(1 - \pi)^1 = 0.0009$$

Therefore, the probability of three tagged order forms is equal to

$$(\text{Number of possible sequences}) \times (\text{Probability of a particular sequence})$$
$$= (4) \times (0.0009) = 0.0036$$

You can make a similar, intuitive derivation for the other possible outcomes of the random variable—zero, one, two, and four tagged order forms. However, as n, the sample size, gets large, the computations involved in using this intuitive approach become time-consuming. Equation (5.5) is the mathematical model that provides a general formula for computing any probability from the binomial distribution with the number of events of interest, X, given the values of n and π.

BINOMIAL DISTRIBUTION

$$P(X) = \frac{n!}{X!(n - X)!} \pi^X(1 - \pi)^{n-X} \qquad (5.5)$$

where

$P(X)$ = probability of X events of interest, given n and π

n = number of observations

π = probability of an event of interest

$1 - \pi$ = probability of not having an event of interest

X = number of events of interest in the sample ($X = 0, 1, 2, \ldots, n$)

Equation (5.5) restates what you had intuitively derived. The binomial variable X can have any integer value X from 0 through n. In Equation (5.5), the product

$$\pi^X(1 - \pi)^{n-X}$$

represents the probability of exactly X events of interest from n observations in a *particular sequence*.

The term

$$\frac{n!}{X!(n - X)!}$$

represents the number of *combinations* of the X events of interest from the n observations that are possible. Hence, given the number of observations, n, and the probability of an event of interest, π, the probability of X events of interest is:

$$P(X) = (\text{Number of possible sequences}) \times (\text{Probability of a particular sequence})$$

$$= \frac{n!}{X!(n-X)!}\ \pi^X(1-\pi)^{n-X}$$

Example 5.1 illustrates the use of Equation (5.5).

EXAMPLE 5.1

Determining $P(X = 3)$, Given $n = 4$ and $\pi = 0.1$

If the likelihood of a tagged order form is 0.1, what is the probability that there are three tagged order forms in the sample of four?

SOLUTION Using Equation (5.5) on page 161, the probability of three tagged orders from a sample of four is

$$P(X = 3) = \frac{4!}{3!(4-3)!}\ (0.1)^3(1-0.1)^{4-3}$$

$$= \frac{4!}{3!(1)!}\ (0.1)^3(0.9)^1$$

$$= 4(0.1)(0.1)(0.1)(0.9) = 0.0036$$

Examples 5.2 and 5.3 show the computations for other values of X.

EXAMPLE 5.2

Determining $P(X \geq 3)$, Given $n = 4$ and $\pi = 0.1$

If the likelihood of a tagged order form is 0.1, what is the probability that there are three or more (i.e., at least three) tagged order forms in the sample of four?

SOLUTION In Example 5.1, you found that the probability of *exactly* three tagged order forms from a sample of four is 0.0036. To compute the probability of *at least* three tagged order forms, you need to add the probability of three tagged order forms to the probability of four tagged order forms. The probability of four tagged order forms is

$$P(X = 4) = \frac{4!}{4!(4-4)!}\ (0.1)^4(1-0.1)^{4-4}$$

$$= \frac{4!}{4!(0)!}\ (0.1)^4(0.9)^0$$

$$= 1(0.1)(0.1)(0.1)(0.1) = 0.0001$$

Thus, the probability of at least three tagged order forms is

$$P(X \geq 3) = P(X = 3) + P(X = 4)$$

$$= 0.0036 + 0.0001$$

$$= 0.0037$$

There is a 0.37% chance that there will be at least three tagged order forms in a sample of four.

EXAMPLE 5.3

Determining
$P(X < 3)$, Given
$n = 4$ and $\pi = 0.1$

If the likelihood of a tagged order form is 0.1, what is the probability that there are less than three tagged order forms in the sample of four?

SOLUTION The probability that there are less than three tagged order forms is

$$P(X < 3) = P(X = 0) + P(X = 1) + P(X = 2)$$

Using Equation (5.5) on page 161, these probabilities are

$$P(X = 0) = \frac{4!}{0!(4-0)!}(0.1)^0(1-0.1)^{4-0} = 0.6561$$

$$P(X = 1) = \frac{4!}{1!(4-1)!}(0.1)^1(1-0.1)^{4-1} = 0.2916$$

$$P(X = 2) = \frac{4!}{2!(4-2)!}(0.1)^2(1-0.1)^{4-2} = 0.0486$$

Therefore, $P(X < 3) = 0.6561 + 0.2916 + 0.0486 = 0.9963$. $P(X < 3)$ could also be calculated from its complement, $P(X \geq 3)$, as follows:

$$P(X < 3) = 1 - P(X \geq 3)$$
$$= 1 - 0.0037 = 0.9963$$

Computations such as those in Example 5.3 can become tedious, especially as n gets large. To avoid computational drudgery, you can find many binomial probabilities directly from Table E.6 (in Appendix E), a portion of which is reproduced in Table 5.4. Table E.6 provides binomial probabilities for $X = 0, 1, 2, \ldots, n$ for various selected combinations of n and π. For example, to find the probability of exactly two events of interest in a sample of four when the probability of an event is 0.1, you first find $n = 4$ and then look in the row $X = 2$ and column $\pi = 0.10$. The result is 0.0486.

TABLE 5.4

Finding a Binomial
Probability for
$n = 4$, $X = 2$, and
$\pi = 0.1$

				π	
n	X	0.01	0.02	....	0.10
4	0	0.9606	0.9224	....	0.6561
	1	0.0388	0.0753	....	0.2916
	2	0.0006	0.0023	....	0.0486
	3	0.0000	0.0000	....	0.0036
	4	0.0000	0.0000	....	0.0001

Source: *Table E.6.*

You can also compute the binomial probabilities given in Table E.6 by using Microsoft Excel or Minitab as shown in Figures 5.2 and 5.3 (note that Minitab uses the letter p instead of π to denote the probability of an event of interest).

FIGURE 5.2

Microsoft Excel worksheet for computing binomial probabilities

See Section E5.2 or P5.1 to create this.

	A	B	
1	Tagged Orders		
2			
3	Data		
4	Sample size	4	
5	Probability of an event of interest	0.1	
6			
7	Statistics		
8	Mean	0.4	=B4 * B5
9	Variance	0.36	=B8 * (1 - B5)
10	Standard deviation	0.6	=SQRT(B9)
11			
12	Binomial Probabilities Table		
13	X	P(X)	
14	0	0.6561	=BINOMDIST(A14, B4, B5, FALSE)
15	1	0.2916	=BINOMDIST(A15, B4, B5, FALSE)
16	2	0.0486	=BINOMDIST(A16, B4, B5, FALSE)
17	3	0.0036	=BINOMDIST(A17, B4, B5, FALSE)
18	4	0.0001	=BINOMDIST(A18, B4, B5, FALSE)

FIGURE 5.3

Minitab results for computing binomial probabilities

See Section M5.1 to create this.

```
Binomial with n = 4 and p = 0.1

x    P( X = x )
0       0.6561
1       0.2916
2       0.0486
3       0.0036
4       0.0001
```

The shape of a binomial probability distribution depends on the values of n and π. Whenever $\pi = 0.5$, the binomial distribution is symmetrical, regardless of how large or small the value of n. When $\pi \neq 0.5$, the distribution is skewed. The closer π is to 0.5 and the larger the number of observations, n, the less skewed the distribution becomes. For example, the distribution of the number of tagged order forms is highly skewed to the right because $\pi = 0.1$ and $n = 4$ (see Figure 5.4).

FIGURE 5.4

Microsoft Excel histogram of the binomial probability distribution with $n = 4$ and $\pi = 0.1$

See Section E5.2 and E2.9 or P5.1 to create this.

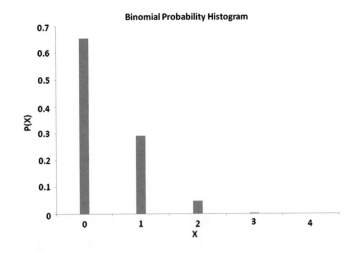

Binomial Probability Histogram

The mean (or expected value) of the binomial distribution is equal to the product of n and π. Instead of using Equation (5.1) on page 157 to compute the mean of the probability distribution, you use Equation (5.6) to compute the mean for variables that follow the binomial distribution.

MEAN OF THE BINOMIAL DISTRIBUTION

The mean, μ, of the binomial distribution is equal to the sample size, n, multiplied by the probability of an event of interest, π.

$$\mu = E(X) = n\pi \tag{5.6}$$

On the average, over the long run, you theoretically expect $\mu = E(X) = n\pi = (4)(0.1) = 0.4$ tagged order form in a sample of four orders.

The standard deviation of the binomial distribution is calculated using Equation (5.7).

STANDARD DEVIATION OF THE BINOMIAL DISTRIBUTION

$$\sigma = \sqrt{\sigma^2} = \sqrt{Var(X)} = \sqrt{n\pi(1 - \pi)} \qquad (5.7)$$

The standard deviation of the number of tagged order forms is

$$\sigma = \sqrt{4(0.1)(0.9)} = 0.60$$

You get the same result if you use Equation (5.3) on page 158.

Example 5.4 applies the binomial distribution to service at a fast-food restaurant.

EXAMPLE 5.4

Computing
Binomial
Probabilities

Accuracy in taking orders at a drive-through window is important for fast-food chains. Each month, *QSR Magazine*, **www.qsrmagazine.com**, publishes the results of its surveys. Accuracy is measured as the percentage of orders that are filled correctly. In a recent month, the percentage of orders filled correctly at McDonald's was approximately 91%. If a sample of three orders is taken, what are the mean and standard deviation of the binomial distribution for the number of orders filled correctly? Suppose that you go to the drive-through window at McDonald's and place an order. Two friends of yours independently place orders at the drive-through window at the same McDonald's. What are the probabilities that all three, that none of the three, and that at least two of the three orders will be filled correctly?

SOLUTION Because there are three orders and the probability of a correct order is 0.91, $n = 3$ and $\pi = 0.91$. Using Equations (5.6) and (5.7),

$$\mu = E(X) = n\pi = 3(0.91) = 2.73$$
$$\sigma = \sqrt{\sigma^2} = \sqrt{Var(X)} = \sqrt{n\pi(1 - \pi)}$$
$$= \sqrt{3(0.91)(0.09)}$$
$$= \sqrt{0.2457} = 0.4957$$

Using Equation (5.5) on page 161,

$$P(X = 3) = \frac{3!}{3!(3-3)!}(0.91)^3(1 - 0.91)^{3-3}$$

$$= \frac{3!}{3!(3-3)!}(0.91)^3(0.09)^0$$

$$= 1(0.91)(0.91)(0.91)(1) = 0.7536$$

$$P(X = 0) = \frac{3!}{0!(3-0)!}(0.91)^0(1 - 0.91)^{3-0}$$

$$= \frac{3!}{0!(3-0)!}(0.91)^0(0.09)^3$$

$$= 1(1)(0.09)(0.09)(0.09) = 0.0007$$

$$P(X = 2) = \frac{3!}{2!(3-2)!}(0.91)^2(1 - 0.91)^{3-2}$$

$$= \frac{3!}{2!(3-2)!}(0.91)^2(0.09)^1$$

$$= 3(0.91)(0.91)(0.09) = 0.2236$$

$$P(X \geq 2) = P(X = 2) + P(X = 3)$$

$$= 0.2236 + 0.7536$$

$$= 0.9772$$

The mean number of orders filled correctly in a sample of three orders is 2.73, and the standard deviation is 0.4957. The probability that all three orders are filled correctly is 0.7536, or 75.36%. The probability that none of the orders are filled correctly is 0.0007, or 0.07%. The probability that at least two orders are filled correctly is 0.9772, or 97.72%.

In this section, you have been introduced to the binomial distribution. The binomial distribution is an important mathematical model in many business situations.

Problems for Section 5.2

LEARNING THE BASICS

5.7 If $n = 5$ and $\pi = 0.40$, what is the probability that
a. $X = 4$?
b. $X \leq 3$?
c. $X < 2$?
d. $X > 1$?

5.8 Determine the following:
a. For $n = 4$ and $\pi = 0.12$, what is $P(X = 0)$?
b. For $n = 10$ and $\pi = 0.40$, what is $P(X = 9)$?
c. For $n = 10$ and $\pi = 0.50$, what is $P(X = 8)$?
d. For $n = 6$ and $\pi = 0.83$, what is $P(X = 5)$?

APPLYING THE CONCEPTS

5.9 The increase or decrease in the price of a stock between the beginning and the end of a trading day is assumed to be an equally likely random event. What is the probability that a stock will show an increase in its closing price on five consecutive days?

5.10 A recent article in *Quality Progress* (Dennis R. Owens, "The Probability of Reoccurrence: P(r)," April 2007, 40, p. 88) discusses a manufacturing company assessing the chance that its product will fail. The article identifies six independent events that can cause a failure. The probability of each of these events failing is quite low, 0.05, but for a product to ultimately be a success, it must not experience a failure in any of the six events.
a. Use the binomial probability distribution to calculate the probability that a product will ultimately be successful (i.e., that it will not fail).
b. If the probabilities of the six events are not all equal, how could you calculate the probability in (a)?

5.11 A student is taking a multiple-choice exam in which each question has four choices. Assuming that she has no knowledge of the correct answers to any of the questions, she has decided on a strategy in which she will place four

balls (marked *A*, *B*, *C*, and *D*) into a box. She randomly selects one ball for each question and replaces the ball in the box. The marking on the ball will determine her answer to the question. There are five multiple-choice questions on the exam. What is the probability that she will get
a. five questions correct?
b. at least four questions correct?
c. no questions correct?
d. no more than two questions correct?

 5.12 In Example 5.4 on page 165, you and two friends decided to go to McDonald's. Instead, suppose that you went to KFC, which last month filled 86.1% of the orders correctly. What is the probability that
a. all three orders will be filled correctly?
b. none of the three will be filled correctly?
c. at least two of the three will be filled correctly?
d. What are the mean and standard deviation of the binomial distribution used in (a) through (c)? Interpret these values.

5.13 When a customer places an order with Rudy's On-Line Office Supplies, a computerized accounting information system (AIS) automatically checks to see if the customer has exceeded his or her credit limit. Past records indicate that the probability of customers exceeding their credit limit is 0.05. Suppose that, on a given day, 20 customers place orders. Assume that the number of customers that the AIS detects as having exceeded their credit limit is distributed as a binomial random variable.
a. What are the mean and standard deviation of the number of customers exceeding their credit limits?
b. What is the probability that 0 customers will exceed their limits?
c. What is the probability that 1 customer will exceed his or her limit?
d. What is the probability that 2 or more customers will exceed their limits?

5.14 In a survey conducted by the Society for Human Resource Management, 68% of workers said that employers have the right to monitor their telephone use ("Snapshots," **usatoday.com**, April 18, 2006). Suppose that a random sample of 20 workers is selected, and they are asked if employers have the right to monitor telephone use. What is the probability that
a. 5 or less of the workers agree?
b. 10 or less of the workers agree?
c. 15 or less of the workers agree?

5.15 Referring to Problem 5.14, when the same workers were asked if employers have the right to monitor their cellphone use, the percentage dropped to 52%. Suppose that the 20 workers are asked if employers have the right to monitor cellphone use. What is the probability that
a. 5 or less of the workers agree?
b. 10 or less of the workers agree?
c. 15 or less of the workers agree?
d. Compare the results of (a) through (c) to those for Problem 5.14.

5.3 Poisson Distribution

Many studies are based on counts of the times a particular event occurs in a given *area of opportunity*. An **area of opportunity** is a continuous unit or interval of time, volume, or any physical area in which there can be more than one occurrence of an event. Examples are the surface defects on a new refrigerator, the number of network failures in a day, the number of people arriving at a bank, and the number of fleas on the body of a dog. You can use the **Poisson distribution** to calculate probabilities in situations such as these if the following properties hold:

- You are interested in counting the number of times a particular event occurs in a given area of opportunity. The area of opportunity is defined by time, length, surface area, and so forth.
- The probability that an event occurs in a given area of opportunity is the same for all the areas of opportunity.
- The number of events that occur in one area of opportunity is independent of the number of events that occur in any other area of opportunity.
- The probability that two or more events will occur in an area of opportunity approaches zero as the area of opportunity becomes smaller.

Consider the number of customers arriving during the lunch hour at a bank located in the central business district in a large city. You are interested in the number of customers that arrive each minute. Does this situation match the four properties of the Poisson distribution given above? First, the *event* of interest is a customer arriving, and the *given area of opportunity* is defined as a 1-minute interval. Will zero customers arrive, one customer arrive, two customers arrive, and so on? Second, it is reasonable to assume that the probability that a customer arrives during a particular 1-minute interval is the same as the probability for all the other 1-minute intervals. Third, the arrival of one customer in any 1-minute interval has no effect on (i.e., is independent of) the arrival of any other customer in any other 1-minute interval. Finally, the probability that two or more customers will arrive in a given time period approaches zero as the time interval becomes small. For example, the probability is virtually zero that two customers will arrive in a time interval of 0.01 second. Thus, you can use the Poisson distribution to determine probabilities involving the number of customers arriving at the bank in a 1-minute time interval during the lunch hour.

The Poisson distribution has one parameter, called λ (the Greek lowercase letter *lambda*), which is the mean or expected number of events per unit. The variance of a Poisson distribution is also equal to λ, and the standard deviation is equal to $\sqrt{\lambda}$. The number of events, X, of the Poisson random variable ranges from 0 to infinity (∞).

Equation (5.8) presents the mathematical expression for the Poisson distribution for computing the probability of X events, given that λ events are expected.

POISSON DISTRIBUTION

$$P(X) = \frac{e^{-\lambda}\lambda^X}{X!} \qquad \textbf{(5.8)}$$

where

$P(X)$ = the probability of X events in an area of opportunity

λ = expected number of events

e = mathematical constant approximated by 2.71828

X = number of events ($X = 0, 1, 2, \ldots, \infty$)

To demonstrate the Poisson distribution, suppose that the mean number of customers who arrive per minute at the bank during the noon-to-1 p.m. hour is equal to 3.0. What is the probability that in a given minute, exactly two customers will arrive? And what is the probability that more than two customers will arrive in a given minute?

Using Equation (5.8) and $\lambda = 3$, the probability that in a given minute exactly two customers will arrive is

$$P(X = 2) = \frac{e^{-3.0}(3.0)^2}{2!} = \frac{9}{(2.71828)^3(2)} = 0.2240$$

To determine the probability that in any given minute more than two customers will arrive,

$$P(X > 2) = P(X = 3) + P(X = 4) + \cdots + P(X = \infty)$$

Because in a probability distribution, all the probabilities must sum to 1, the terms on the right side of the equation $P(X > 2)$ also represent the complement of the probability that X is less than or equal to 2 [i.e., $1 - P(X \leq 2)$]. Thus,

$$P(X > 2) = 1 - P(X \leq 2) = 1 - [P(X = 0) + P(X = 1) + P(X = 2)]$$

Now, using Equation (5.8),

$$P(X > 2) = 1 - \left[\frac{e^{-3.0}(3.0)^0}{0!} + \frac{e^{-3.0}(3.0)^1}{1!} + \frac{e^{-3.0}(3.0)^2}{2!} \right]$$

$$= 1 - [0.0498 + 0.1494 + 0.2240]$$

$$= 1 - 0.4232 = 0.5768$$

Thus, there is a 57.68% chance that more than two customers will arrive in the same minute.

To avoid drudgery involved in these computations, you can find Poisson probabilities directly from Table E.7 (in Appendix E), a portion of which is reproduced in Table 5.5. Table E.7 provides the probabilities that the Poisson random variable takes on values of $X = 0, 1, 2, \ldots$, for selected values of the parameter λ. To find the probability that exactly two customers will arrive in a given minute when the mean number of customers arriving is 3.0 per minute, you can read the probability corresponding to the row $X = 2$ and column $\lambda = 3.0$ from the table. The result is 0.2240, as demonstrated in Table 5.5.

TABLE 5.5

Finding a Poisson Probability for $\lambda = 3$

X	2.1	2.2	$\lambda \ldots$	3.0
0	.1225	.1108	....	.0498
1	.2572	.2438	....	.1494
2	.2700	.2681	....	.2240
3	.1890	.1966	....	.2240
4	.0992	.1082	....	.1680
5	.0417	.0476	....	.1008
6	.0146	.0174	....	.0504
7	.0044	.0055	....	.0216
8	.0011	.0015	....	.0081
9	.0003	.0004	....	.0027
10	.0001	.0001	....	.0008
11	.0000	.0000	....	.0002
12	.0000	.0000	....	.0001

Source: *Table E.7.*

You can also compute the Poisson probabilities given in Table E.7 by using Microsoft Excel or Minitab, as illustrated in Figures 5.5 and 5.6.

FIGURE 5.5

Microsoft Excel worksheet for computing Poisson probabilities with $\lambda = 3$

See Section E5.3 or P5.2 to create this.

	A	B	C	D	E
1	**Customer Arrivals Analysis**				
2					
3	**Data**				
4	**Mean/Expected number of events of interest:**				3
5					
6	**Poisson Probabilities Table**				
7	**X**	**P(X)**			
8	0	0.049787	=POISSON(A8, E4, FALSE)		
9	1	0.149361	=POISSON(A9, E4, FALSE)		
10	2	0.224042	=POISSON(A10, E4, FALSE)		
11	3	0.224042	=POISSON(A11, E4, FALSE)		
12	4	0.168031	=POISSON(A12, E4, FALSE)		
13	5	0.100819	=POISSON(A13, E4, FALSE)		
14	6	0.050409	=POISSON(A14, E4, FALSE)		
15	7	0.021604	=POISSON(A15, E4, FALSE)		
16	8	0.008102	=POISSON(A16, E4, FALSE)		
17	9	0.002701	=POISSON(A17, E4, FALSE)		
18	10	0.000810	=POISSON(A18, E4, FALSE)		
19	11	0.000221	=POISSON(A19, E4, FALSE)		
20	12	0.000055	=POISSON(A20, E4, FALSE)		
21	13	0.000013	=POISSON(A21, E4, FALSE)		
22	14	0.000003	=POISSON(A22, E4, FALSE)		
23	15	0.000001	=POISSON(A23, E4, FALSE)		
24	16	0.000000	=POISSON(A24, E4, FALSE)		
25	17	0.000000	=POISSON(A25, E4, FALSE)		
26	18	0.000000	=POISSON(A26, E4, FALSE)		
27	19	0.000000	=POISSON(A27, E4, FALSE)		
28	20	0.000000	=POISSON(A28, E4, FALSE)		

FIGURE 5.6

Minitab results for computing Poisson probabilities with $\lambda = 3$

See Section M5.2 to create this.

```
Poisson with mean = 3

 x   P( X = x )
 0     0.049787
 1     0.149361
 2     0.224042
 3     0.224042
 4     0.168031
 5     0.100819
 6     0.050409
 7     0.021604
 8     0.008102
 9     0.002701
10     0.000810
11     0.000221
12     0.000055
13     0.000013
14     0.000003
15     0.000001
```

EXAMPLE 5.5

Computing Poisson Probabilities

The number of work-related injuries per month in a manufacturing plant is known to follow a Poisson distribution with a mean of 2.5 work-related injuries a month. What is the probability that in a given month no work-related injuries occur? That at least one work-related injury occurs?

SOLUTION Using Equation (5.8) on page 168 with $\lambda = 2.5$ (or using Table E.7 or Microsoft Excel or Minitab), the probability that in a given month no work-related injuries occur is

$$P(X = 0) = \frac{e^{-2.5}(2.5)^0}{0!} = \frac{1}{(2.71828)^{2.5}(1)} = 0.0821$$

The probability that there will be no work-related injuries in a given month is 0.0821 or 8.21%. Thus,

$$P(X \geq 1) = 1 - P(X = 0)$$

$$= 1 - 0.0821$$

$$= 0.9179$$

The probability that there will be at least one work-related injury is 0.9179 or 91.79%.

Problems for Section 5.3

LEARNING THE BASICS

5.16 Assume a Poisson distribution.
a. If $\lambda = 2.5$, find $P(X = 2)$.
b. If $\lambda = 8.0$, find $P(X = 8)$.
c. If $\lambda = 0.5$, find $P(X = 1)$.
d. If $\lambda = 3.7$, find $P(X = 0)$.

5.17 Assume a Poisson distribution.
a. If $\lambda = 2.0$, find $P(X \geq 2)$.
b. If $\lambda = 8.0$, find $P(X \geq 3)$.

c. If $\lambda = 0.5$, find $P(X \leq 1)$.
d. If $\lambda = 4.0$, find $P(X \geq 1)$.
e. If $\lambda = 5.0$, find $P(X \leq 3)$.

5.18 Assume a Poisson distribution with $\lambda = 5.0$. What is the probability that
a. $X = 1$?
b. $X < 1$?
c. $X > 1$?
d. $X \leq 1$?

APPLYING THE CONCEPTS

5.19 Assume that the number of network errors experienced in a day on a local area network (LAN) is distributed as a Poisson random variable. The mean number of network errors experienced in a day is 2.4. What is the probability that in any given day

a. zero network errors will occur?

b. exactly one network error will occur?

c. two or more network errors will occur?

d. less than three network errors will occur?

SELF Test **5.20** The quality control manager of Marilyn's Cookies is inspecting a batch of chocolate-chip cookies that has just been baked. If the production process is in control, the mean number of chip parts per cookie is 6.0. What is the probability that in any particular cookie being inspected

a. less than five chip parts will be found?

b. exactly five chip parts will be found?

c. five or more chip parts will be found?

d. either four or five chip parts will be found?

5.21 Refer to Problem 5.20. How many cookies in a batch of 100 should the manager expect to discard if company policy requires that all chocolate-chip cookies sold have at least four chocolate-chip parts?

5.22 The U.S. Department of Transportation maintains statistics for mishandled bags per 1,000 airline passengers. In 2007, airlines had mishandled 7 bags per 1,000 passengers (data extracted from R. Yu, "Airline Performance Nears 20 Year Low," *USA Today*, April 8, 2008, p. B1). What is the probability that in the next 1,000 passengers, airlines will have

a. no mishandled bags?

b. at least one mishandled bag?

c. at least two mishandled bags?

5.23 The U.S. Department of Transportation also maintains statistics for consumer complaints per 100,000 airline passengers. In 2007, consumer complaints were 1.42 per 100,000 passengers (data extracted from R. Yu, "Airline Performance Nears 20 Year Low," *USA Today*, April 8, 2008, p. B1). What is the probability that in the next 100,000 passengers, there will be

a. no complants?

b. at least one complaint?

c. at least two complaints?

5.24 Based on past experience, it is assumed that the number of flaws per foot in rolls of grade 2 paper follows a Poisson distribution with a mean of 1 flaw per 5 feet of paper (0.2 flaw per foot). What is the probability that in a

a. 1-foot roll, there will be at least 2 flaws?

b. 12-foot roll, there will be at least 1 flaw?

c. 50-foot roll, there will be greater than or equal to 5 flaws and less than or equal to 15 flaws?

5.25 J.D. Power and Associates calculates and publishes various statistics concerning car quality. The initial quality score measures the number of problems per new car sold. For 2008 model cars, Ford had 1.12 problems per car. Dodge had 1.41 problems per car (S. Carty, "Ford Moves Up in Quality Survey," *USA Today*, June 5, 2008, p. 3B). Let the random variable X be equal to the number of problems with a newly purchased 2008 Ford.

a. What assumptions must be made in order for X to be distributed as a Poisson random variable? Are these assumptions reasonable?

Making the assumptions as in (a), if you purchased a 2008 Ford, what is the probability that the new car will have

b. zero problems?

c. two or less problems?

d. Give an operational definition for *problem*. Why is the operational definition important in interpreting the initial quality score?

5.26 Refer to Problem 5.25. If you purchased a 2008 Dodge, what is the probability that the new car will have

a. zero problems?

b. two or less problems?

c. Compare your answers in (a) and (b) to those for the Ford in Problem 5.25(b) and (c).

5.27 Refer to Problem 5.25. The same article reported that in 2007, Ford had 1.27 problems per car, and Dodge had 1.32 problems per car. If you purchased a 2007 Ford, what is the probability that the new car will have

a. zero problems?

b. two or less problems?

c. Compare your answers in (a) and (b) to those for the 2008 Ford in Problem 5.25(b) and (c).

5.28 Refer to Problem 5.27. If you purchased a 2007 Dodge, what is the probability that the new car will have

a. zero problems?

b. two or less problems?

c. Compare your answers in (a) and (b) to those for the 2008 Dodge in Problem 5.26(a) and (b).

5.29 A toll-free phone number is available from 9 a.m. to 9 p.m. for your customers to register complaints about a product purchased from your company. Past history indicates that an average of 0.4 calls are received per minute.

a. What properties must be true about the situation described here in order to use the Poisson distribution to calculate probabilities concerning the number of phone calls received in a 1-minute period?

Assuming that this situation matches the properties discussed in (a), what is the probability that during a 1-minute period

b. zero phone calls will be received?

c. three or more phone calls will be received?

d. What is the maximum number of phone calls that will be received in a 1-minute period 99.99% of the time?

USING STATISTICS @ Saxon Home Improvement Revisited

I n the Using Statistics scenario, you were an accountant for the Saxon Home Improvement Company. The company's accounting information system automatically reviews order forms from online customers for possible mistakes. Any questionable invoices are tagged and included in a daily exceptions report. Knowing that the probability that an order will be tagged is 0.10, you were able to use the binomial distribution to determine the chance of finding a certain number of tagged forms in a sample of size 4. There was a 65.6% chance that none of the forms would be tagged, a 29.2% chance that one would be tagged, and a 5.2% chance that two or more would be tagged. You were also able to determine that on average, you would expect 0.4 forms to be tagged and the standard deviation of the number of tagged order forms would be 0.6. Now that you have learned the mechanics of using the binomial distribution for a known probability of 0.10 and a sample size of four, you will be able to apply the same approach to any given probability and sample size. Thus, you will be able to make inferences about the online ordering process and, more importantly, evaluate any changes or proposed changes to the process.

SUMMARY

In this chapter, you have studied mathematical expectation and two important discrete probability distributions, the binomial and Poisson distributions. In the following chapter, you will study the most important continuous distribution, the normal distribution.

To help decide what probability distribution to use for a particular situation, you need to ask the following question:

• Is there a fixed number of observations, n, each of which is classified as an event of interest or not an event of interest, or is there an area of opportunity? If there is a fixed number of observations, n, each of which is classified as an event of interest or not an event of interest, you use the binomial distribution. If there is an area of opportunity, you use the Poisson distribution.

KEY EQUATIONS

Expected Value, μ, of a Discrete Random Variable

$$\mu = E(X) = \sum_{i=1}^{N} X_i P(X_i) \qquad (5.1)$$

Variance of a Discrete Random Variable

$$\sigma^2 = \sum_{i=1}^{N} [X_i - E(X)]^2 P(X_i) \qquad (5.2)$$

Standard Deviation of a Discrete Random Variable

$$\sigma = \sqrt{\sigma^2} = \sqrt{\sum_{i=1}^{N} [X_i - E(X)]^2 P(X_i)} \qquad (5.3)$$

Combinations

$$_nC_X = \frac{n!}{X!(n-X)!} \qquad (5.4)$$

Binomial Distribution

$$P(X) = \frac{n!}{X!(n-X)!} \pi^X (1-\pi)^{n-X} \qquad (5.5)$$

Mean of the Binomial Distribution

$$\mu = E(X) = n\pi \qquad (5.6)$$

Standard Deviation of the Binomial Distribution

$$\sigma = \sqrt{\sigma^2} = \sqrt{Var(X)} = \sqrt{n\pi(1-\pi)} \qquad (5.7)$$

Poisson Distribution

$$P(X) = \frac{e^{-\lambda}\lambda^X}{X!} \qquad (5.8)$$

KEY TERMS

area of opportunity 167
binomial distribution 159
expected value 156
mathematical model 159

Poisson distribution 167
probability distribution for a discrete
    random variable 156
rule of combinations 160

standard deviation of a discrete ran-
    dom variable 158
variance of a discrete random variable
    157

CHAPTER REVIEW PROBLEMS

CHECKING YOUR UNDERSTANDING

5.30 What is the meaning of the expected value of a probability distribution?

5.31 What are the four properties that must be present in order to use the binomial distribution?

5.32 What are the four properties that must be present in order to use the Poisson distribution?

APPLYING THE CONCEPTS

5.33 Darwin Head, a 35-year-old sawmill worker, won $1 million and a Chevrolet Malibu Hybrid by scoring 15 goals within 24 seconds at the Vancouver Canucks National Hockey League game (B. Ziemer, "Darwin Evolves into an Instant Millionaire," *Vancouver Sun*, February 28, 2008, p.1). Head said he would use the money to pay off his mortgage and provide for his children and had no plans to quit his job. The contest was part of the Chevrolet Malibu Million Dollar Shootout, sponsored by General Motors Canadian Division. Did GM-Canada risk the $1 million? No! GM-Canada purchased event insurance from a company specializing in promotions at sporting events like a half-court basketball shot or a hole-in-one giveaway at the local charity golf outing. The event insurance company estimates the probability of a contestant winning the contest, and for a modest charge, insures the event. The promoters pay the insurance premium but take on no added risk as the insurance company will make the large payout in the unlikely event that a contestant wins. To see how it works, suppose that the insurance company estimates that the probability a contestant would win a million dollar shootout is 0.001 and that the insurance company charges $4,000.
a. Calculate the expected value of the profit made by the insurance company.
b. Many call this kind of situation a win-win opportunity for the insurance company and the promoter. Do you agree? Explain.

5.34 Between 1872 and 2000, stock prices rose in 74% of the years (M. Hulbert, "The Stock Market Must Rise in

2002? Think Again," *The New York Times*, December 6, 2001, Business, p. 6). Based on this information, and assuming a binomial distribution, what do you think the probability is that the stock market will rise
a. next year?
b. the year after next?
c. in four of the next five years?
d. in none of the next five years?
e. For this situation, what assumption of the binomial distribution might not be valid?

5.35 The mean cost of a phone call handled by an automated customer-service system is $0.45. The mean cost of a phone call passed on to a "live" operator is $5.50. However, as more and more companies have implemented automated systems, customer annoyance with such systems has grown. Many customers are quick to leave the automated system when given an option such as "Press zero to talk to a customer-service representative." According to the Center for Client Retention, 40% of all callers to automated customer-service systems automatically opt to go to a live operator when given the chance (J. Spencer, "In Search of the Operator," *The Wall Street Journal*, May 8, 2002, p. D1).
    If 10 independent callers contact an automated customer-service system, what is the probability that
a. 0 will automatically opt to talk to a live operator?
b. exactly 1 will automatically opt to talk to a live operator?
c. 2 or less will automatically opt to talk to a live operator?
d. all 10 will automatically opt to talk to a live operator?
e. If all 10 automatically opt to talk to a live operator, do you think that the 40% value given in the article applies to this particular system? Explain.

5.36 One theory concerning the Dow Jones Industrial Average is that it is likely to increase during U.S. presidential election years. From 1964 through 2004, the Dow Jones Industrial Average increased in 9 of the 11 U.S. presidential election years. Assuming that this indicator is a random event with no predictive value, you would expect that the indicator would be correct 50% of the time.
a. What is the probability of the Dow Jones Industrial Average increasing in 9 or more of the 11 U.S. presiden-

tial election years if the true probability of an increase in the Dow Jones Industrial Average is 0.50?

b. From 1964 to 2004, the Dow Jones Industrial Average increased in 74% of the years. What is the probability that the Dow Jones Industrial Average will increase in 9 or more of the 11 U.S. presidential election years if the probability of an increase in the Dow Jones Industrial Average in any year is 0.74?

5.37 Errors in a billing process often lead to customer dissatisfaction and ultimately hurt bottom line profits. An article in *Quality Progress* (L. Tatikonda, "A Less Costly Billing Process," January, 2008, pp. 30–38) discussed a company where 40% of the bills prepared contained an error. If 10 bills are processed, what is the probability that:

a. 0 bills will contain an error?

b. exactly 1 bill will contain an error?

c. 2 or more bills will contain an error?

d. What are the mean and the standard deviation of the probability distribution?

5.38 Refer to Problem 5.37. Suppose that a quality improvement initiative has reduced the percentage of bills containing an error to 20%. If 10 bills are processed, what is the probability that:

a. 0 bills will contain an error?

b. exactly 1 bill will contain an error?

c. 2 or more bills will contain an error?

d. What are the mean and the standard deviation of the probability distribution?

e. Compare the results of (a) through (c) to those of Problem 5.37 (a) through (c).

5.39 A study by the Center for Financial Services Innovation showed that only 64% of U.S. income earners aged 15 and older had a bank account (A. Carrns, "Banks Court a New Client," *The Wall Street Journal*, March 16, 2007, p. D1).

If a random sample of 20 U.S. income earners aged 15 and older is selected, what is the probability that

a. all 20 have a bank account?

b. no more than 15 have a bank account?

c. more than 10 have a bank account?

d. What assumptions did you have to make to answer (a) through (c)?

5.40 One of the retail industry's biggest frustrations is customers who abuse the return and exchange policies (S. Kang, "New Return Policy: Retailers Say 'No' to Serial Exchangers," *The Wall Street Journal*, November 29, 2004, pp. B1, B3). In a recent year, returns were 13% of sales in department stores. Consider a sample of 20 customers who make a purchase at a department store. Use the binomial model to answer the following questions:

a. What is the expected value, or mean, of the binomial distribution?

b. What is the standard deviation of the binomial distribution?

c. What is the probability that none of the 20 customers will make a return?

d. What is the probability that no more than 2 of the customers will make a return?

e. What is the probability that 3 or more of the customers will make a return?

5.41 Refer to Problem 5.40. In the same year, returns were 1% of sales in grocery stores.

a. What is the expected value, or mean, of the binomial distribution?

b. What is the standard deviation of the binomial distribution?

c. What is the probability that none of the 20 customers will make a return?

d. What is the probability that no more than 2 of the customers will make a return?

e. What is the probability that 3 or more of the customers will make a return?

f. Compare the results of (a) through (e) to those of Problem 5.40 (a) through (e).

5.42 One theory concerning the S&P 500 index is that if it increases during the first five trading days of the year, it is likely to increase during the entire year. From 1950 through 2007, the S&P 500 index had these early gains in 38 years. In 32 of these 38 years, the S&P 500 index increased for the entire year. Assuming that this indicator is a random event with no predictive value, you would expect that the indicator would be correct 50% of the time. What is the probability of the S&P 500 index increasing in 32 or more years if the true probability of an increase in the S&P 500 index is

a. 0.50?

b. 0.70?

c. 0.90?

d. Based on the results of (a) through (c), what do you think is the probability that the S&P 500 index will increase if there is an early gain in the first five trading days of the year? Explain.

5.43 *Spurious correlation* refers to the apparent relationship between variables that either have no true relationship or are related to other variables that have not been measured. One widely publicized stock market indicator in the United States that is an example of spurious correlation is the relationship between the winner of the National Football League Super Bowl and the performance of the Dow Jones Industrial Average in that year. The indicator states that when a team representing the National Football Conference wins the Super Bowl, the Dow Jones Industrial Average will increase in that year. When a team representing the American Football Conference wins the Super Bowl, the Dow Jones Industrial Average will decline in that year. Since the first Super Bowl was held in 1967 through 2007, the indicator has been correct 32 out of 41 times. Assuming that this indicator is a random event with no predictive value, you would expect that the indicator would be correct 50% of the time.

a. What is the probability that the indicator would be correct 32 or more times in 41 years?

b. What does this tell you about the usefulness of this indicator?

5.44 Worldwide golf ball sales total more than $1 billion annually. One reason for such a large number of golf ball purchases is that golfers lose them at a rate of 4.5 per 18-hole round ("Snapshots," **www.usatoday.com**, January 29, 2004). Assume that the number of golf balls lost in an 18-hole round is distributed as a Poisson random variable.

a. What assumptions need to be made so that the number of golf balls lost in an 18-hole round is distributed as a Poisson random variable?

Making the assumptions given in (a), what is the probability that

b. 0 balls will be lost in an 18-hole round?

c. 5 or less balls will be lost in an 18-hole round?

d. 6 or more balls will be lost in an 18-hole round?

5.45 According to a Virginia Tech survey, college students make an average of 11 calls per day on their cellphone. Moreover, 80% of the students surveyed indicated that their parents pay their cellphone expenses (Jean Elliot, "Professor Researches Cell Phone Usage among Students," **www.physorg.com**, February 26, 2007).

a. What distribution can you use to model the number of calls a student makes in a day?

b. If you select a student at random, what is the probability that he or she makes more than 10 calls in a day? More than 15? More than 20?

c. If you select a random sample of 10 students, what distribution can you use to model the proportion of students who have parents that pay their cellphone expenses?

d. Using the distribution selected in (c), what is the probability that all 10 have parents that pay their cellphone expenses? At least 9? At least 8?

MANAGING THE *SPRINGVILLE HERALD*

The *Herald* marketing department is seeking to increase home-delivery sales through an aggressive direct-marketing campaign that includes mailings, discount coupons, and telephone solicitations. Feedback from these efforts indicates that getting their newspapers delivered early in the morning is a very important factor for both prospective as well as existing subscribers. After several brainstorming sessions, a team consisting of members from the marketing and circulation departments decided that guaranteeing newspaper delivery by a specific time could be an important selling point in retaining and getting new subscribers. The team concluded that the *Herald* should offer a guarantee that customers will receive their newspapers by a certain time or else that day's issue is free.

To assist the team in setting a guaranteed delivery time, Al Leslie, the research director, determined that the circulation department had data that showed the percentage of newspapers yet undelivered every quarter hour from 6 A.M. to 8 A.M. Jan Shapiro remembered that customers were asked on their subscription forms at what time they would be looking for their copy of the *Herald* to be delivered. These data were subsequently combined and posted on an internal *Herald* Web page. (See `Circulation_Data.htm` in the Herald Case folder on the Student CD-ROM or go to **www.prenhall.com/HeraldCase/Circulation_Data.htm**).

EXERCISES

Review the internal data and propose a reasonable time (to the nearest quarter hour) to guarantee delivery. To help explore the effects of your choice, calculate the following probabilities:

SH5.1 If a sample of 50 customers is selected on a given day, what is the probability, given your selected delivery time, that

a. less than 3 customers will receive a free newspaper?

b. 2, 3, or 4 customers will receive a free newspaper?

c. more than 5 customers will receive a free newspaper?

SH5.2 Consider the effects of improving the newspaper delivery process so that the percentage of newspapers that go undelivered by your guaranteed delivery time decreases by 2%. If a sample of 50 customers is selected on a given day, what is the probability, given your selected delivery time (and the delivery improvement), that

a. less than 3 customers will receive a free newspaper?

b. 2, 3, or 4 customers will receive a free newspaper?

c. more than 5 customers will receive a free newspaper?

REFERENCES

1. Bernstein, P. L., *Against the Gods: The Remarkable Story of Risk* (New York: Wiley, 1996).
2. Emery, D. R., J. D. Finnerty, and J. D. Stowe, *Corporate Financial Management*, 3rd ed. (Upper Saddle River, NJ: Prentice Hall, 2007).
3. Kirk, R. L., ed., *Statistical Issues: A Reader for the Behavioral Sciences* (Belmont, CA: Wadsworth, 1972).
4. Levine, D. M., P. Ramsey, and R. Smidt, *Applied Statistics for Engineers and Scientists Using Microsoft Excel and Minitab* (Upper Saddle River, NJ: Prentice Hall, 2001).
5. *Microsoft Excel 2007* (Redmond, WA: Microsoft Corp., 2007).
6. *Minitab Version 15* (State College, PA: Minitab, Inc., 2006).
7. Moscove, S. A., M. G. Simkin, and N. A. Bagranoff, *Core Concepts of Accounting Information Systems*, 10th ed. (New York: Wiley, 2007).

Using Microsoft Excel for Discrete Probability Distributions

E5.1 Computing the Expected Value of a Discrete Random Variable

You compute the expected value of a discrete random variable by making entries in the **Discrete** worksheet of the **Expected Value.xls** workbook. This worksheet uses the SUM and SQRT (square root) functions to calculate its statistics.

Figure E5.1 shows a completed worksheet using the mortgage probability distribution of Table 5.1 on page 156. To adapt this worksheet to other problems that have more or less than seven outcomes, first select the cell range **A5:E5**. To add table rows, right-click and click **Insert**. (If a box of options appears, click **Shift cells down** and then click **OK**.) Then, copy the formulas in cell range C4:E4 down through the new table rows and enter the new X and P(X) values in columns A and B.

To delete table rows, right-click and click **Delete**. (If a box of options appears, click **Shift cells up** and then click **OK**.) Enter a corrected list of X values starting with **1** in cell A5 in column A and enter the new P(X) values in column B.

E5.2 Computing Binomial Probabilities

You compute binomial probabilities by making entries in the **Binomial** worksheet of the **Binomial.xls** workbook. This worksheet (shown in Figure 5.2 on page 164) already contains the entries for the tagged orders example of Section 5.2. To adapt this worksheet to other problems, change the **Sample size** and **Probability of an event of interest** values in cells B4 and B5. If your problem has a sample size other than 4, first select **row 15** and then add or delete rows one at a time by right-clicking row 15 and clicking either **Insert** or **Delete** and adjusting the X values in column A. (If you inserted rows, you will also have to copy formulas down to those new rows.)

The worksheet features the **BINOMDIST(X, n, π, cumulative)** function in which X is the number of events of interest, n is the sample size, π is the probability of an event of interest, and cumulative is a True or False value. When cumulative is **True**, the function computes the probability of X or fewer events of interest; when cumulative is **False**, the function computes the probability of exactly X events of interest.

E5.3 Computing Poisson Probabilities

You compute Poisson probabilities by making entries in the **Poisson** worksheet of the **Poisson.xls** workbook. This worksheet (shown in Figure 5.5 on page 169) already contains the entries for the bank customer arrivals problem of Section 5.3. To adapt this worksheet to other problems, change the **Mean/Expected number of events of interest value** in cell **E4**.

The worksheet features the **POISSON(X, lambda, cumulative)** function in which X is the number of events of interest, lambda is the average or expected number of events of interest, and cumulative is a True or False value. When cumulative is **True**, the function computes the probability of X or fewer events of interest; when cumulative is **False**, the function computes the probability of exactly X events of interest.

	A	B	C	D	E	F	G	H
1	**Discrete Random Variable Probability Distribution**							
2							**Statistics**	
3	X	P(X)	X*P(X)	[X-E(X)]^2	[X-E(X)]^2*P(X)		Expected value	2.8	=SUM(C:C)
4	0	0.10	0	7.84	0.784		Variance	2.46	=SUM(E:E)
5	1	0.10	0.1	3.24	0.324		Standard deviation	1.57	=SQRT(H4)
6	2	0.20	0.4	0.64	0.128				
7	3	0.30	0.9	0.04	0.012		X*P(X)	[X - E(X)]^2	[X - E(X)]^2*P(X)
8	4	0.15	0.6	1.44	0.216		=A4 * B4	=(A4 - H3)^2	=D4 * B4
9	5	0.10	0.5	4.84	0.484		=A5 * B5	=(A5 - H3)^2	=D5 * B5
10	6	0.05	0.3	10.24	0.512		=A6 * B6	=(A6 - H3)^2	=D6 * B6
							=A7 * B7	=(A7 - H3)^2	=D7 * B7
							=A8 * B8	=(A8 - H3)^2	=D8 * B8
							=A9 * B9	=(A9 - H3)^2	=D9 * B9
							=A10 * B10	=(A10 - H3)^2	=D10 * B10

FIGURE E5.1 Discrete worksheet

177

APPENDIX P5

Using PHStat2 for Discrete Probability Distributions

P5.1 Computing Binomial Probabilities

To compute binomial probabilities, use **PHStat → Probability & Prob. Distributions → Binomial**. This procedure creates a worksheet similar to Figure 5.2 on page 164 using the sample size, probability of an event of interest, and an outcomes range that you specify. If you click **Cumulative Probabilities**, the binomial table will include additional columns for $P(< = X)$, $P(<X)$, $P(>X)$, and $P(> = X)$. If you click **Histogram**, the procedure uses Excel charting features to create a histogram on a separate sheet.

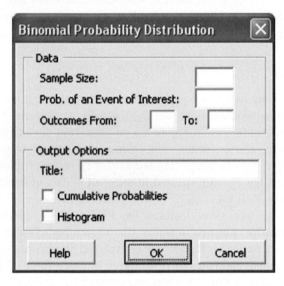

P5.2 Computing Poisson Probabilities

To compute Poisson probabilities, use **PHStat → Probability & Prob. Distributions → Poisson**. This procedure creates a worksheet similar to Figure 5.5 on page 169 using the mean or expected number of events of interest that you specify. If you select the **Cumulative Probabilities** check box, the Poisson table will include additional columns for $P(< = X)$, $P(<X)$, $P(>X)$, and $P(> = X)$. If you click **Histogram**, the procedure uses Excel charting features to create a histogram on a separate sheet.

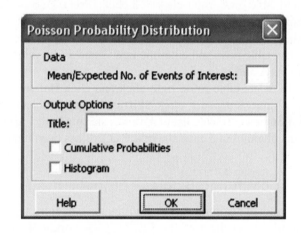

APPENDIX M5

Using Minitab for Discrete Probability Distributions

M5.1 Computing Binomial Probabilities

To compute binomial probabilities for the Section 5.2 accounting information system example, shown in Figure 5.3 on page 164:

1. Open to a new, blank worksheet.
2. Enter the values **0, 1, 2, 3**, and **4** in rows 1 to 5 of column C1, leaving the unnumbered variable label cell at the top of the column empty.
3. Select **Calc → Probability Distributions → Binomial**.

In the Binomial Distribution dialog box (see Figure M5.1):

4. Click **Probability** (to compute the probabilities of exactly *X* events of interest for all values of *X*).
5. Enter **4** (the sample size) in the **Number of trials** box.
6. Enter **.1** in the **Event probability** box.
7. Click **Input column** and enter **C1** in its box.
8. Click **OK**.

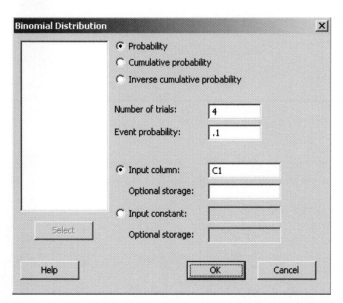

FIGURE M5.1 Minitab Binomial Distribution dialog box

M5.2 Computing Poisson Probabilities

To compute Poisson probabilities for the Section 5.3 bank customer arrival example, shown in Figure 5.6 on page 170:

1. Open to a new, blank worksheet.
2. Enter the values **0** through **15** in rows 1 to 16 of column C1, leaving the unnumbered variable label cell at the top of the column empty.
3. Select **Calc → Probability Distributions → Poisson**.

In the Poisson Distribution dialog box (see Figure M5.2 below):

4. Click **Probability** (to compute the probabilities of exactly *X* events for all values of *X*).
5. Enter **3** (the λ value) in the **Mean** box.
6. Click **Input column** and enter **C1** in its box.
7. Click **OK**.

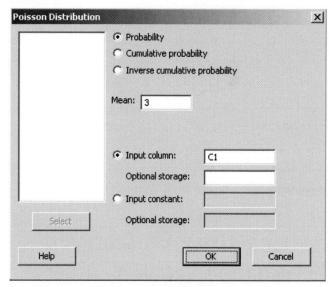

FIGURE M5.2 Minitab Poisson Distribution dialog box

6

The Normal Distribution

Learning Objectives

In this chapter, you learn:

- To compute probabilities from the normal distribution
- How to use the normal distribution to solve business problems
- To use the normal probability plot to determine whether a set of data is approximately normally distributed

USING STATISTICS

@ OurCampus!

You are a designer for the OurCampus! Web site, which targets college students. To attract and retain customers, you need to make sure that the home page downloads quickly. Both the design of the home page and the load on the company's Web servers affect the download time. To check how fast the home page loads, you open a Web browser on a PC at the corporate offices of OurCampus! and measure the download time—the amount of time in seconds that pass from first linking to the Web site until the home page is fully displayed.

Past data indicate that the mean download time is 7 seconds and that the standard deviation is 2 seconds. Approximately two-thirds of the download times are between 5 and 9 seconds, and about 95% of the download times are between 3 and 11 seconds. In other words, the download times are distributed as a bell-shaped curve, with a clustering around the mean of 7 seconds. How could you use this information to answer questions about the download times of the current home page?

I n Chapter 5, Saxon Home Improvement Company managers wanted to be able to solve problems about the number of tagged items in a given sample size. As an OurCampus! Web designer, you face a different task, one that involves a continuous measurement because a download time could be any value and not just a whole number. How can you answer questions about this *continuous numerical variable*, such as:

- What proportion of the home page downloads take more than 10 seconds?
- How many seconds elapse before 10% of the downloads are complete?
- How many seconds elapse before 99% of the downloads are complete?
- How would redesigning the home page to download faster affect the answers to these questions?

As in Chapter 5, you can use a probability distribution as a model. Reading this chapter will help you learn about characteristics of continuous probability distributions and how to use the normal distribution to solve business problems.

6.1 Continuous Probability Distributions

A **continuous probability density function** is the mathematical expression that defines the distribution of the values for a continuous random variable. Figure 6.1 graphically displays three continuous probability density functions.

FIGURE 6.1

Three continuous distributions

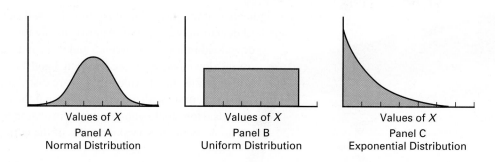

Values of X	Values of X	Values of X
Panel A	Panel B	Panel C
Normal Distribution	Uniform Distribution	Exponential Distribution

Panel A depicts a normal distribution. The normal distribution is symmetrical and bell shaped, implying that most values tend to cluster around the mean, which, due to the distribution's symmetrical shape, is equal to the median. Although the values in a normal distribution can range from negative infinity to positive infinity, the shape of the distribution makes it very unlikely that extremely large or extremely small values will occur.

Panel B depicts a **uniform distribution** where each value has an equal probability of occurrence anywhere in the range between the smallest value, *a*, and the largest value, *b*. Sometimes referred to as the **rectangular distribution**, the uniform distribution is symmetrical and therefore the mean equals the median.

Panel C illustrates an **exponential distribution**. This distribution is skewed to the right, making the mean larger than the median. The range for an exponential distribution is zero to positive infinity, but the distribution's shape makes the occurrence of extremely large values unlikely.

6.2 The Normal Distribution

The **normal distribution** (sometimes referred to as the *Gaussian distribution*) is the most common continuous distribution used in statistics. The normal distribution is vitally important in statistics for three main reasons:

- Numerous continuous variables common in business have distributions that closely resemble the normal distribution.

- The normal distribution can be used to approximate various discrete probability distributions.
- The normal distribution provides the basis for *classical statistical inference* because of its relationship to the *Central Limit Theorem* (which is discussed in Section 7.4).

The normal distribution is represented by the classic bell shape shown in Panel A of Figure 6.1. In the normal distribution, you can calculate the probability that various values occur within certain ranges or intervals. However, the *exact* probability of a *particular value* from a continuous distribution such as the normal distribution is zero. This property distinguishes continuous variables, which are measured, from discrete variables, which are counted. As an example, time (in seconds) is measured and not counted. Therefore, you can determine the probability that the download time for a home page on a Web browser is between 7 and 10 seconds, or the probability that the download time is between 8 and 9 seconds, or the probability that the download time is between 7.99 and 8.01 seconds. However, the probability that the download time is *exactly* 8 seconds is zero.

The normal distribution has several important theoretical properties:

- It is symmetrical and thus its mean and median are equal.
- It is bell shaped in its appearance.
- Its interquartile range is equal to 1.33 standard deviations. Thus, the middle 50% of the values are contained within an interval of two-thirds of a standard deviation below the mean and two-thirds of a standard deviation above the mean.
- It has an infinite range $(-\infty < X < \infty)$.

In practice, many variables have distributions that closely resemble the theoretical properties of the normal distribution. The data in Table 6.1 represent the thickness (in inches) of 10,000 brass washers manufactured by a large company. The continuous variable of interest, thickness, can be approximated by the normal distribution. The measurements of the thickness of the 10,000 brass washers cluster in the interval 0.0190 to 0.0192 inch and distribute symmetrically around that grouping, forming a bell-shaped pattern.

TABLE 6.1

Thickness of 10,000 Brass Washers

Thickness (inches)	Relative Frequency
< 0.0180	48/10,000 = 0.0048
0.0180 < 0.0182	122/10,000 = 0.0122
0.0182 < 0.0184	325/10,000 = 0.0325
0.0184 < 0.0186	695/10,000 = 0.0695
0.0186 < 0.0188	1,198/10,000 = 0.1198
0.0188 < 0.0190	1,664/10,000 = 0.1664
0.0190 < 0.0192	1,896/10,000 = 0.1896
0.0192 < 0.0194	1,664/10,000 = 0.1664
0.0194 < 0.0196	1,198/10,000 = 0.1198
0.0196 < 0.0198	695/10,000 = 0.0695
0.0198 < 0.0200	325/10,000 = 0.0325
0.0200 < 0.0202	122/10,000 = 0.0122
0.0202 or above	48/10,000 = 0.0048
Total	1.0000

Figure 6.2 shows the relative frequency histogram and polygon for the distribution of the thickness of 10,000 brass washers. For these data, the first three theoretical properties of the normal distribution are approximately satisfied. However, the fourth one, having an infinite range, does not hold. The thickness of the washer cannot possibly be zero or below, nor can a washer be so thick that it becomes unusable. From Table 6.1, you see that only 48 out of every 10,000 brass washers manufactured are expected to have a thickness of 0.0202 inch or more, whereas an equal number are expected to have a thickness under 0.0180 inch. Thus, the chance of randomly getting a washer so thin or so thick is 0.0048 + 0.0048 = 0.0096, less than 1 in 100.

FIGURE 6.2

Relative frequency histogram and polygon of the thickness of 10,000 brass washers

Source: Data are taken from Table 6.1.

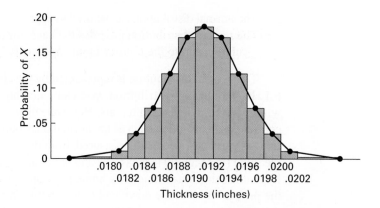

The mathematical expression representing a continuous probability density function is denoted by the symbol $f(X)$. For the normal distribution, the **normal probability density function** is given in Equation (6.1).

NORMAL PROBABILITY DENSITY FUNCTION

$$f(X) = \frac{1}{\sqrt{2\pi}\sigma} e^{-(1/2)[(X-\mu)/\sigma]^2} \tag{6.1}$$

where

e = the mathematical constant approximated by 2.71828

π = the mathematical constant approximated by 3.14159

μ = the mean

σ = the standard deviation

X = any value of the continuous variable, where $-\infty < X < \infty$

Because e and π are mathematical constants, the probabilities of the random variable X are dependent only on the two parameters of the normal distribution—the mean, μ, and the standard deviation, σ. Every time you specify a *particular combination* of μ and σ, a *different* normal probability distribution is generated. Figure 6.3 illustrates three different normal distributions.

FIGURE 6.3

Three normal distributions

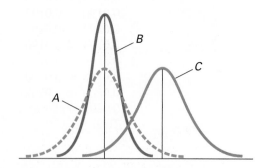

Distributions A and B have the same mean (μ) but have different standard deviations. Distributions A and C have the same standard deviation (σ) but have different means. Distributions B and C differ with respect to both μ and σ.

The mathematical expression in Equation (6.1) is computationally tedious and requires integral calculus. Fortunately, normal probability tables are available, and you *never* need to use Equation (6.1) to make computations of normal distribution probabilities. The first step in finding normal probabilities is to use the **transformation formula**, given in Equation (6.2), to convert any normal random variable, X, to a **standardized normal random variable**, Z.

TRANSFORMATION FORMULA

The Z value is equal to the difference between X and the mean, μ, divided by the standard deviation, σ.

$$Z = \frac{X - \mu}{\sigma}$$ (6.2)

Although the original data for the random variable X had mean μ and standard deviation σ, the standardized random variable, Z, will always have mean $\mu = 0$ and standard deviation $\sigma = 1$.

Any set of normally distributed values can be converted to its standardized form. Then you can determine the desired probabilities by using Table E.2, the **cumulative standardized normal distribution**. To see how the transformation formula is applied and the results are used to find probabilities from Table E.2, recall from the Using Statistics scenario on page 181 that past data indicate that the time to download the Web page is normally distributed, with a mean, $\mu = 7$ seconds and a standard deviation, $\sigma = 2$ seconds. From Figure 6.4, you see that every measurement, X, has a corresponding standardized measurement, Z, computed from the transformation formula [Equation (6.2)]. Therefore, a download time of 9 seconds is equivalent to 1 standardized unit (i.e., 1 standard deviation above the mean) because

$$Z = \frac{9 - 7}{2} = +1$$

FIGURE 6.4

Transformation of scales

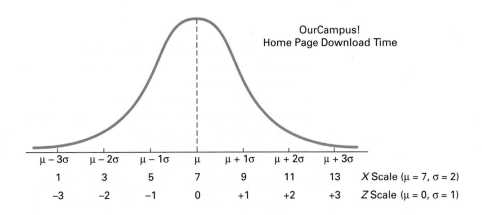

A download time of 1 second is equivalent to 3 standardized units (3 standard deviations) below the mean because

$$Z = \frac{1 - 7}{2} = -3$$

Thus, the standard deviation is the unit of measurement. In other words, a time of 9 seconds is 2 seconds (i.e., 1 standard deviation) higher, or *slower*, than the mean time of 7 seconds. Similarly, a time of 1 second is 6 seconds (i.e., 3 standard deviations) lower, or *faster*, than the mean time.

To further illustrate the transformation formula, suppose that the home page of another Web site has a download time that is normally distributed, with a mean, $\mu = 4$ seconds, and a standard deviation, $\sigma = 1$ second. This distribution is illustrated in Figure 6.5.

Comparing these results with those of the OurCampus! Web site, you see that a download time of 5 seconds is 1 standard deviation above the mean download time because

$$Z = \frac{5 - 4}{1} = +1$$

FIGURE 6.5

A different transformation of scales

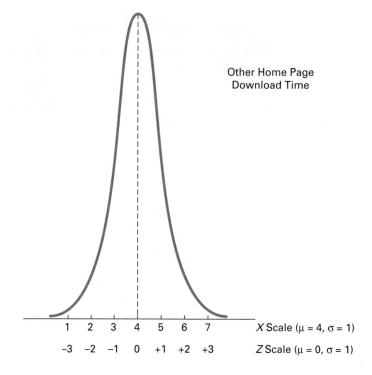

A time of 1 second is 3 standard deviations below the mean download time because

$$Z = \frac{1 - 4}{1} = -3$$

Suppose you wanted to find the probability that the download time for the OurCampus! site is less than 9 seconds. First, you use Equation (6.2) on page 185 to transform $X = 9$ to standardized Z units. Because $X = 9$ is one standard deviation above the mean, $Z = +1.00$. Next, you use Table E.2, a portion of which is shown below in Table 6.2, to find the cumulative area under the normal curve less than (i.e., to the left of) $Z = +1.00$. To read the probability or area under the curve less than $Z = +1.00$, you scan down the Z column from Table E.2 until you locate the Z value of interest (in 10ths) in the Z row for 1.0. Next, you read across this row until you intersect the column that contains the 100ths place of the Z value. Therefore, in the body of the table, the tabulated probability for $Z = 1.00$ corresponds to the intersection of the row $Z = 1.0$ with the column $Z = .00$, as shown in Table 6.2. This probability is 0.8413. As illustrated in Figure 6.6, there is an 84.13% chance that the download time will be less than 9 seconds.

TABLE 6.2

Finding a Cumulative Area Under the Normal Curve

					Cumulative Probabilities					
Z	**.00**	**.01**	**.02**	**.03**	**.04**	**.05**	**.06**	**.07**	**.08**	**.09**
0.0	.5000	.5040	.5080	.5120	.5160	.5199	.5239	.5279	.5319	.5359
0.1	.5398	.5438	.5478	.5517	.5557	.5596	.5636	.5675	.5714	.5753
0.2	.5793	.5832	.5871	.5910	.5948	.5987	.6026	.6064	.6103	.6141
0.3	.6179	.6217	.6255	.6293	.6331	.6368	.6406	.6443	.6480	.6517
0.4	.6554	.6591	.6628	.6664	.6700	.6736	.6772	.6808	.6844	.6879
0.5	.6915	.6950	.6985	.7019	.7054	.7088	.7123	.7157	.7190	.7224
0.6	.7257	.7291	.7324	.7357	.7389	.7422	.7454	.7486	.7518	.7549
0.7	.7580	.7612	.7642	.7673	.7704	.7734	.7764	.7794	.7823	.7852
0.8	.7881	.7910	.7939	.7967	.7995	.8023	.8051	.8078	.8106	.8133
0.9	.8159	.8186	.8212	.8238	.8264	.8289	.8315	.8340	.8365	.8389
1.0	.8413	.8438	.8461	.8485	.8508	.8531	.8554	.8577	.8599	.8621

Source: *Extracted from Table E.2.*

FIGURE 6.6

Determining the area less than Z from a cumulative standardized normal distribution

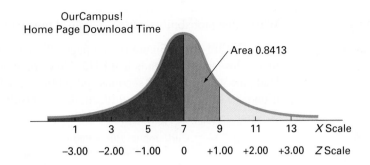

However, for the other home page, you see that a time of 5 seconds is 1 standardized unit above the mean time of 4 seconds. Thus, the probability that the download time will be less than 5 seconds is also 0.8413. Figure 6.7 shows that regardless of the value of the mean, μ, and standard deviation, σ, of a normally distributed variable, Equation (6.2) can transform the problem to Z values.

FIGURE 6.7

Demonstrating a transformation of scales for corresponding cumulative portions under two normal curves

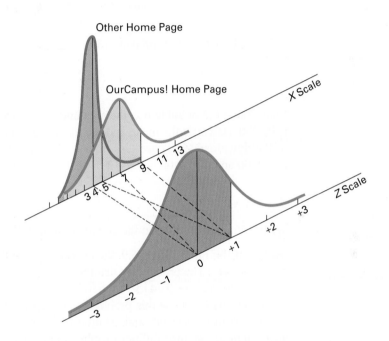

Now that you have learned to use Table E.2 with Equation (6.2), you can answer many questions related to the OurCampus! home page, using the normal distribution.

EXAMPLE 6.1

Finding $P(X > 9)$

What is the probability that the download time will be more than 9 seconds?

SOLUTION The probability that the download time will be less than 9 seconds is 0.8413 (see Figure 6.6 above). Thus, the probability that the download time will be more than 9 seconds is the *complement* of less than 9 seconds, $1 - 0.8413 = 0.1587$. Figure 6.8 illustrates this result.

FIGURE 6.8

Finding $P(X > 9)$

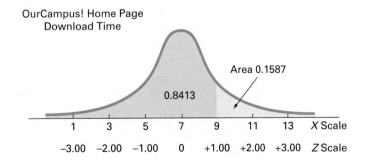

EXAMPLE 6.2

Finding $P(7 < X < 9)$

What is the probability that the download time will be between 7 and 9 seconds?

SOLUTION From Figure 6.6 on page 187, you can see that the probability that a download time is less than 9 seconds is 0.8413. Now you must determine the probability that the download time will be under 7 seconds and subtract this from the probability that the download time is under 9 seconds. Figure 6.9 illustrates this result.

FIGURE 6.9
Finding $P(7 < X < 9)$

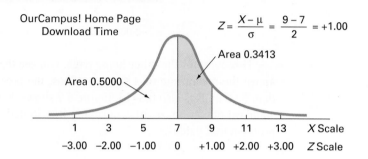

Using Equation (6.2) on page 185,

$$Z = \frac{7 - 7}{2} = 0.00$$

Using Table E.2 or Table 6.2, the area under the normal curve less than the mean of $Z = 0.00$ is 0.5000. (Because the mean and the median are the same for normally distributed data, 50% of the download times are less than 7 seconds.) Hence, the area under the curve between $Z = 0.00$ and $Z = 1.00$ is $0.8413 - 0.5000 = 0.3413$.

EXAMPLE 6.3

Finding $P(X < 7 \text{ or } X > 9)$

What is the probability that the download time will be under 7 seconds or over 9 seconds?

SOLUTION From Figure 6.9, the probability that the download time is between 7 and 9 seconds is 0.3413. The probability that the download time is under 7 seconds or over 9 seconds is its complement, $1 - 0.3413 = 0.6587$.

Another way to view this problem, is to separately calculate the probability of a download time of less than 7 seconds and the probability of a download time of greater than 9 seconds and then add these two probabilities together. Figure 6.10 illustrates this result. Because the mean is seven seconds, 50% of download times are under 7 seconds. From Example 6.1, the probability that the download time is greater than 9 seconds is 0.1587. Hence, the probability that a download time is under 7 or over 9 seconds, $P(X < 7 \text{ or } X > 9)$, is $0.5000 + 0.1587 = 0.6587$.

FIGURE 6.10
Finding $P(X < 7 \text{ or } X > 9)$

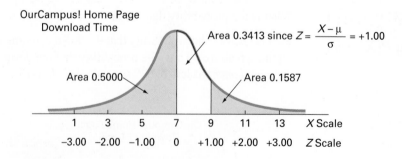

EXAMPLE 6.4

Finding $P(5 < X < 9)$

What is the probability that the download time will be between 5 and 9 seconds—that is, $P(5 < X < 9)$?

SOLUTION In Figure 6.11, you can see that the area of interest is located between two values, 5 and 9.

FIGURE 6.11
Finding $P(5 < X < 9)$

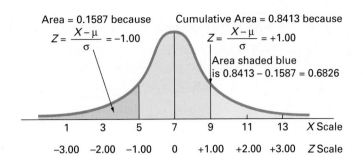

In Example 6.1 on page 187, you already found that the area under the normal curve less than 9 seconds is 0.8413. To find the area under the normal curve less than 5 seconds,

$$Z = \frac{5 - 7}{2} = -1.00$$

Using Table E.2, you look up $Z = -1.00$ and find 0.1587. Thus, the probability that the download time will be between 5 and 9 seconds is $0.8413 - 0.1587 = 0.6826$, as displayed in Figure 6.11.

The result of Example 6.4 enables you to state that for any normal distribution, 68.26% of the values will fall within ± 1 standard deviation of the mean. From Figure 6.12, 95.44% of the values will fall within ± 2 standard deviations of the mean. Thus, 95.44% of the download times are between 3 and 11 seconds. From Figure 6.13, 99.73% of the values are within ± 3 standard deviations above or below the mean. Thus, 99.73% of the download times are between 1 and 13 seconds. Therefore, it is unlikely (0.0027, or only 27 in 10,000) that a download time will be so fast or so slow that it will take under 1 second or more than 13 seconds. In general, you can use 6σ (that is, 3 standard deviations below the mean to 3 standard deviations above the mean) as a practical approximation of the range for normally distributed data.

FIGURE 6.12
Finding $P(3 < X < 11)$

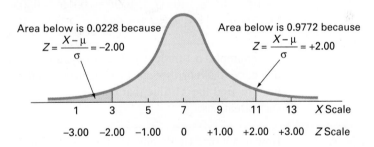

FIGURE 6.13
Finding $P(1 < X < 13)$

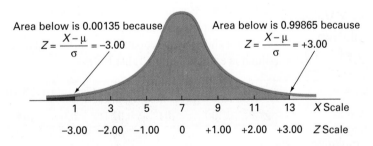

Figures 6.11, 6.12, and 6.13 illustrate how the values of a normal distribution cluster near the mean. For any normal distribution:

- Approximately 68.26% of the values fall within ± 1 standard deviation of the mean.
- Approximately 95.44% of the values fall within ± 2 standard deviations of the mean.
- Approximately 99.73% of the values fall within ± 3 standard deviations of the mean.

This result is the justification for the empirical rule presented on page 99. The accuracy of the empirical rule improves as a data set follows the normal distribution more closely.

EXAMPLE 6.5

Finding $P(X < 3.5)$

FIGURE 6.14

Finding $P(X < 3.5)$

What is the probability that a download time will be under 3.5 seconds?

SOLUTION To calculate the probability that a download time will be under 3.5 seconds, you need to examine the shaded lower-left tail region of Figure 6.14.

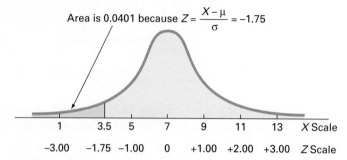

Area is 0.0401 because $Z = \dfrac{X - \mu}{\sigma} = -1.75$

| | 1 | 3.5 | 5 | 7 | 9 | 11 | 13 | X Scale |
| | -3.00 | -1.75 | -1.00 | 0 | +1.00 | +2.00 | +3.00 | Z Scale |

To determine the area under the curve below 3.5 seconds, you first calculate

$$Z = \frac{X - \mu}{\sigma} = \frac{3.5 - 7}{2} = -1.75$$

You then look up the Z value of -1.75 by matching the appropriate Z row (-1.7) with the appropriate Z column $(.05)$, as shown in Table 6.3 (which is extracted from Table E.2). The resulting probability or area under the curve less than -1.75 standard deviations below the mean is 0.0401.

TABLE 6.3

Finding a Cumulative Area Under the Normal Curve

					Cumulative Probabilities				
Z	**.00**	**.01**	**.02**	**.03**	**.04**	**.05**	**.06**	**.07**	**.08**	**.09**
.	.	.	.	.	.	.	.	.	.
.	.	.	.	.	.	.	.	.	.
-1.7	.0446	.0436	.0427	.0418	.0409	.0401	.0392	.0384	.0375	.0367
-1.6	.0548	.0537	.0526	.0516	.0505	.0495	.0485	.0475	.0465	.0455

Source: *Extracted from Table E.2.*

Examples 6.1 through 6.5 require you to use the normal table to find an area under the normal curve that corresponds to a specific X value. There are many circumstances in which you want to find the X value that corresponds to a specific area. Examples 6.6 and 6.7 illustrate such situations.

EXAMPLE 6.6

Finding the X Value for a Cumulative Probability of 0.10

How much time (in seconds) will elapse before 10% of the downloads are complete?

SOLUTION Because 10% of the home pages are expected to download in under X seconds, the area under the normal curve less than this value is 0.1000. Using the body of Table E.2, you search for the area or probability of 0.1000. The closest result is 0.1003, as shown in Table 6.4 (which is extracted from Table E.2).

TABLE 6.4

Finding a Z Value Corresponding to a Particular Cumulative Area (0.10) Under the Normal Curve

					Cumulative Probabilities				
Z	**.00**	**.01**	**.02**	**.03**	**.04**	**.05**	**.06**	**.07**	**.08**	**.09**
.	.	.	.	.	.	.	.	.	.
.	.	.	.	.	.	.	.	.	.
.	.	.	.	.	.	.	.	.	.
.	.	.	.	.	.	.	.	.	.
-1.5	.0668	.0655	.0643	.0630	.0618	.0606	.0594	.0582	.0571	.0559
-1.4	.0808	.0793	.0778	.0764	.0749	.0735	.0721	.0708	.0694	.0681
-1.3	.0968	.0951	.0934	.0918	.0901	.0885	.0869	.0853	.0838	.0823
-1.2	.1151	.1131	.1112	.1093	.1075	.0156	.0138	.1020	.1003	.0985

Source: *Extracted from Table E.2.*

Working from this area to the margins of the table, the Z value corresponding to the particular Z row (-1.2) and Z column $(.08)$ is -1.28 (see Figure 6.15).

FIGURE 6.15
Finding Z to
determine X

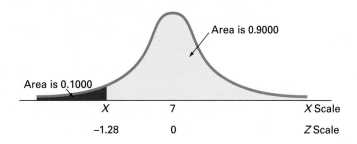

Once you find Z, you use the transformation formula Equation (6.2) on page 185 to determine the X value, as follows. Let

$$Z = \frac{X - \mu}{\sigma}$$

then

$$X = \mu + Z\sigma$$

Substituting $\mu = 7$, $\sigma = 2$, and $Z = -1.28$,

$$X = 7 + (-1.28)(2) = 4.44 \text{ seconds}$$

Thus, 10% of the download times are 4.44 seconds or less.

In general, you use Equation (6.3) for finding an X value.

FINDING AN X VALUE ASSOCIATED WITH KNOWN PROBABILITY

The X value is equal to the mean μ plus the product of the Z value and the standard deviation σ.

$$X = \mu + Z\sigma \tag{6.3}$$

To find a *particular* value associated with a known probability, follow these steps:

1. Sketch the normal curve and then place the values for the mean and X on the X and Z scales.
2. Find the cumulative area less than X.
3. Shade the area of interest.
4. Using Table E.2, determine the Z value corresponding to the area under the normal curve less than X.
5. Using Equation (6.3), solve for X:

$$X = \mu + Z\sigma$$

EXAMPLE 6.7

Finding the X
Values that Include
95% of the
Download Times

What are the lower and upper values of X, symmetrically distributed around the mean, that include 95% of the download times?

SOLUTION First, you need to find the lower value of X (called X_L). Then you find the upper value of X (called X_U). Because 95% of the values are between X_L and X_U, and because X_L and X_U are equally distant from the mean, 2.5% of the values are below X_L (see Figure 6.16).

FIGURE 6.16

Finding Z to
determine X_L

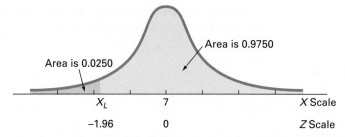

Although X_L is not known, you can find the corresponding Z value because the area under the normal curve less than this Z is 0.0250. Using the body of Table 6.5, you search for the probability 0.0250.

TABLE 6.5

Finding a Z Value
Corresponding to a
Cumulative Area of
0.025 Under the
Normal Curve

					Cumulative Area					
Z	.00	.01	.02	.03	.04	.05	.06	.07	.08	.09
.	.	.	.	.	.	.	.	.	.	.
.	.	.	.	.	.	.	.	.	.	.
.	.	.	.	.	.	.	.	.	.	.
−2.0	.0228	.0222	.0217	.0212	.0207	.0202	.0197	.0192	.0188	.0183
−1.9	.0287	.0281	.0274	.0268	.0262	.0256	.0250	.0244	.0239	.0233
−1.8	.0359	.0351	.0344	.0336	.0329	.0232	.0314	.0307	.0301	.0294

Source: *Extracted from Table E.2.*

Working from the body of the table to the margins of the table, you see that the Z value corresponding to the particular Z row (-1.9) and Z column $(.06)$ is -1.96.

Once you find Z, the final step is to use Equation (6.3) on page 191 as follows:

$$X = \mu + Z\sigma$$
$$= 7 + (-1.96)(2)$$
$$= 7 - 3.92$$
$$= 3.08 \text{ seconds}$$

You use a similar process to find X_U. Because only 2.5% of the home page downloads take longer than X_U seconds, 97.5% of the home page downloads take less than X_U seconds. From the symmetry of the normal distribution, the desired Z value, as shown in Figure 6.17, is $+1.96$ (because Z lies to the right of the standardized mean of 0). You can also extract this Z value from Table 6.6. You can see that 0.975 is the area under the normal curve less than the Z value of $+1.96$.

FIGURE 6.17

Finding Z to
determine X_U

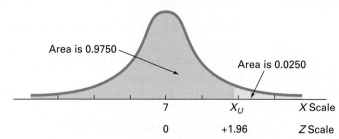

TABLE 6.6

Finding a Z Value
Corresponding to a
Cumulative Area of
0.975 Under the
Normal Curve

					Cumulative Area					
Z	.00	.01	.02	.03	.04	.05	.06	.07	.08	.09
.	.	.	.	.	.	.	.	.	.	.
.	.	.	.	.	.	.	.	.	.	.
.	.	.	.	.	.	.	.	.	.	.
+1.8	.9641	.9649	.9656	.9664	.9671	.9678	.9686	.9693	.9699	.9706
+1.9	.9713	.9719	.9726	.9732	.9738	.9744	.9750	.9756	.9761	.9767
+2.0	.9772	.9778	.9783	.9788	.9793	.9798	.9803	.9808	.9812	.9817

Source: *Extracted from Table E.2.*

Using Equation (6.3) on page 191,

$$X = \mu + Z\sigma$$
$$= 7 + (+1.96)(2)$$
$$= 7 + 3.92$$
$$= 10.92 \text{ seconds}$$

Therefore, 95% of the download times are between 3.08 and 10.92 seconds.

You can also use Microsoft Excel or Minitab to compute normal probabilities. Figure 6.18 below illustrates a Microsoft Excel worksheet for Examples 6.5 and 6.6 and Figure 6.19 on page 194 illustrates Minitab results for Examples 6.1 and 6.6.

FIGURE 6.18

Microsoft Excel worksheet for computing normal probabilities

See Section E6.1 or P6.1 to create this.

	A	B	
1	**Normal Probabilities**		
2			
3	**Common Data**		
4	**Mean**	7	
5	**Standard Deviation**	2	
6			
7	**Probability for X <=**		
8	**X Value**	3.5	
9	**Z Value**	-1.75	=STANDARDIZE(B8, B4, B5)
10	**P(X<=3.5)**	0.0401	=NORMDIST(B8, B4, B5, TRUE)
11			
12	**Find X and Z Given Cum. Pctage.**		
13	**Cumulative Percentage**	10.00%	
14	**Z Value**	-1.2816	=NORMSINV(B13)
15	**X Value**	4.4369	=NORMINV(B13, B4, B5)

VISUAL EXPLORATIONS   Exploring the Normal Distribution

You can use the Visual Explorations Normal Distribution procedure to see the effects of changes in the mean and standard deviation on the area under a normal distribution curve.

Open the `Visual Explorations.xla` add-in workbook and select **VisualExplorations → Normal Distribution** (Excel 97–2003) or **Add-Ins → VisualExplorations → Normal Distribution** (Excel 2007). You will see a normal curve for the Using Statistics home page download example and a floating control panel that allows you to adjust the shape of the curve and the shaded area under the curve (see illustration at right). Use the control panel spinner buttons to change the values for the mean, standard deviation, and *X* value, while noting their effects on the probability of *X* <= value and the corresponding shaded area under the curve (see illustration at right). If you prefer, you can select the **Z Values** option button to see the normal curve labeled with *Z* values.

Click the **Reset** button to reset the control panel values or click **Help** for additional information about the prob-

lem. Click **Finish** when you are done exploring. (Review Section E1.8 on page 19 for more information on using add-ins, if necessary.)

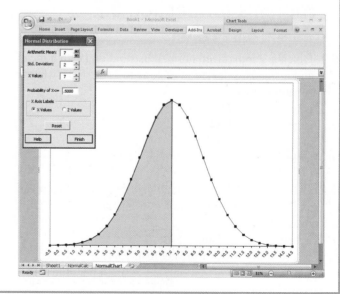

FIGURE 6.19
Minitab results for normal probabilities

See Section M6.1 to create this.

Cumulative Distribution Function

Normal with mean = 7 and standard deviation = 2

```
x   P( X <= x )
9      0.841345
```

Inverse Cumulative Distribution Function

Normal with mean = 7 and standard deviation = 2

```
P( X <= x )          x
           0.1   4.43690
```

THINK ABOUT THIS   What Is Normal?

Ironically the statistician who popularized the use of "normal" to describe the distribution discussed in Section 6.2 was someone who saw the distribution as anything but the everyday, anticipated occurrence that the adjective normal usually suggests.

Starting with an 1894 paper, Karl Pearson argued that measurements of phenomena do not naturally or "normally" conform to the classic bell shape. Pearson believed that individuals in populations could show true variability, and that variability in the measurement of individuals in populations reflected true variability and not errors made in measurement. While this principle underlies statistics today, Pearson's point of view was radical to contemporaries who saw the world as standardized and normal. Pearson changed minds by showing that some populations are naturally skewed (coining that word in

passing) and he helped put to rest the notion that the normal distribution underlies all phenomena.

Today, unfortunately, people still make the type of mistake that Pearson refuted. One of us recalls the story about a small college class of three students in which the professor announced one student would get an A, one would get a B, and one would get a C "because grades need to be normally distributed." (That the professor was describing a uniform distribution was a double irony.) As a student, you have probably heard many discussions about grade inflation (undoubtedly a phenomena at many schools). But, have you ever realized that an argument offered as "proof" of this inflation—that there are "too few" low grades because grades are skewed towards A's and B's—wrongly implies that grades should be "normally" distributed. By the time you finish reading this book, you may

realize that because college students represent small nonrandom samples, there are plenty of reasons to suspect that the distribution of grades would not be "normal."

Misunderstandings about the normal distribution can be found both in business and in the public sector through the years. These misunderstandings have caused a number of business blunders as well as sparked some famous public policy debates. As you continue to study this chapter, make sure you understand the "normal" distribution and the assumptions that must hold for its proper use. Not verifying whether these assumptions hold is another common error made by decision makers using this distribution. And most importantly, always remember that the name *normal* distribution does not mean to suggest normal in the everyday (*dare we say "normal"*) sense of the word!

Problems for Section 6.2

LEARNING THE BASICS

6.1 Given a standardized normal distribution (with a mean of 0 and a standard deviation of 1, as in Table E.2), what is the probability that
a. Z is less than 1.57?
b. Z is greater than 1.84?
c. Z is between 1.57 and 1.84?
d. Z is less than 1.57 or greater than 1.84?

6.2 Given a standardized normal distribution (with a mean of 0 and a standard deviation of 1, as in Table E.2), what is the probability that
a. Z is between −1.57 and 1.84?
b. Z is less than −1.57 or greater than 1.84?
c. What is the value of Z if only 2.5% of all possible Z values are larger?

d. Between what two values of Z (symmetrically distributed around the mean) will 68.26% of all possible Z values be contained?

6.3 Given a standardized normal distribution (with a mean of 0 and a standard deviation of 1, as in Table E.2), what is the probability that
a. Z is less than 1.08?
b. Z is greater than −0.21?
c. Z is less than −0.21 or greater than the mean?
d. Z is less than −0.21 or greater than 1.08?

6.4 Given a standardized normal distribution (with a mean of 0 and a standard deviation of 1, as in Table E.2), determine the following probabilities:
a. $P(Z > 1.08)$
b. $P(Z < -0.21)$

c. $P(-1.96 < Z < -0.21)$

d. What is the value of Z if only 15.87% of all possible Z values are larger?

6.5 Given a normal distribution with $\mu = 100$ and $\sigma = 10$, what is the probability that

a. $X > 75$?

b. $X < 70$?

c. $X < 80$ or $X > 110$?

d. 80% of the values are between what two X values (symmetrically distributed around the mean)?

6.6 Given a normal distribution with $\mu = 50$ and $\sigma = 4$, what is the probability that

a. $X > 43$?

b. $X < 42$?

c. 5% of the values are less than what X value?

d. 60% of the values are between what two X values (symmetrically distributed around the mean)?

APPLYING THE CONCEPTS

6.7 In a recent year, about two-thirds of U.S. households purchased ground coffee. Consider the annual ground coffee expenditures for households purchasing ground coffee, assuming that these expenditures are approximately distributed as a normal random variable with a mean of $45.16 and a standard deviation of $10.00.

a. Find the probability that a household spent less than $25.00.

b. Find the probability that a household spent more than $50.00.

c. What proportion of the households spent between $30.00 and $40.00?

d. 99% of the households spent less than what amount?

 6.8 Toby's Trucking Company determined that the distance traveled per truck per year is normally distributed, with a mean of 50.0 thousand miles and a standard deviation of 12.0 thousand miles.

a. What proportion of trucks can be expected to travel between 34.0 and 50.0 thousand miles in the year?

b. What percentage of trucks can be expected to travel either below 30.0 or above 60.0 thousand miles in the year?

c. How many miles will be traveled by at least 80% of the trucks?

d. What are your answers to (a) through (c) if the standard deviation is 10.0 thousand miles?

6.9 The breaking strength of plastic bags used for packaging produce is normally distributed, with a mean of 5 pounds per square inch and a standard deviation of 1.5 pounds per square inch. What proportion of the bags have a breaking strength of

a. less than 3.17 pounds per square inch?

b. at least 3.6 pounds per square inch?

c. between 5 and 5.5 pounds per square inch?

d. 95% of the breaking strengths will be contained between what two values symmetrically distributed around the mean?

6.10 A set of final examination grades in an introductory statistics course is normally distributed, with a mean of 73 and a standard deviation of 8.

a. What is the probability of getting a grade below 91 on this exam?

b. What is the probability that a student scored between 65 and 89?

c. The probability is 5% that a student taking the test scores higher than what grade?

d. If the professor grades on a curve (i.e., gives A's to the top 10% of the class, regardless of the score), are you better off with a grade of 81 on this exam or a grade of 68 on a different exam, where the mean is 62 and the standard deviation is 3? Show your answer statistically and explain.

6.11 A statistical analysis of 1,000 long-distance telephone calls made from the headquarters of the Bricks and Clicks Computer Corporation indicates that the length of these calls is normally distributed, with $\mu = 240$ seconds and $\sigma = 40$ seconds.

a. What is the probability that a call lasted less than 180 seconds?

b. What is the probability that a call lasted between 180 and 300 seconds?

c. What is the probability that a call lasted between 110 and 180 seconds?

d. What is the length of a call if only 1% of all calls are shorter?

6.12 According to the American Society for Quality, a certified quality engineer (CQE) is a professional who understands the principles of product and service quality evaluation and control. In a 2007 survey, the mean salary of 1,190 CQEs was $71,093, with a standard deviation of $17,871 (H. Lindborg, "Navigate Your Career Path With QP's Annual Salary Survey," *Quality Progress*, December, 2007, pp. 21–50). Assume that the salaries of CQEs is approximately normally distributed. For a randomly selected CQE, what is the probability that he or she has a salary

a. below $50,000?

b. above $75,000?

c. above $100,000?

6.13 Many manufacturing problems involve the matching of machine parts, such as shafts that fit into a valve hole. A particular design requires a shaft with a diameter of 22.000 mm, but shafts with diameters between 21.900 mm and 22.010 mm are acceptable. Suppose that the manufacturing process yields shafts with diameters normally distributed, with a mean of 22.002 mm and a standard deviation of 0.005 mm. For this process, what is

a. the proportion of shafts with a diameter between 21.90 mm and 22.00 mm?

b. the probability that a shaft is acceptable?

c. the diameter that will be exceeded by only 2% of the shafts?

d. What would be your answers in (a) through (c) if the standard deviation of the shaft diameters was 0.004 mm?

6.3 Evaluating Normality

As discussed in Section 6.2, many continuous variables used in business closely follow a normal distribution. This section presents two approaches for determining whether a set of data can be approximated by the normal distribution:

1. Compare the characteristics of the data with the theoretical properties of the normal distribution.
2. Construct a normal probability plot.

Comparing Data Characteristics to Theoretical Properties

The normal distribution has several important theoretical properties:

- It is symmetrical; thus, the mean and median are equal.
- It is bell shaped; thus, the empirical rule applies.
- The interquartile range equals 1.33 standard deviations.
- The range is approximately equal to 6 standard deviations.

In actual practice, a continuous variable may have characteristics that approximate these theoretical properties. However, many continuous variables are neither normally distributed nor approximately normally distributed. For such variables, the descriptive characteristics of the data do not match well with the properties of a normal distribution. One approach to determining whether a data set follows a normal distribution is to compare the characteristics of the data with the corresponding properties from an underlying normal distribution, as follows:

- Construct charts and observe their appearance. For small- or moderate-sized data sets, construct a stem-and-leaf display or a boxplot. For large data sets, plot a histogram or polygon.
- Compute descriptive numerical measures and compare the characteristics of the data with the theoretical properties of the normal distribution. Compare the mean and median. Is the interquartile range approximately 1.33 times the standard deviation? Is the range approximately 6 times the standard deviation?
- Evaluate how the values in the data are distributed. Determine whether approximately two-thirds of the values lie between the mean and ±1 standard deviation. Determine whether approximately four-fifths of the values lie between the mean and ±1.28 standard deviations. Determine whether approximately 19 out of every 20 values lie between the mean and ±2 standard deviations.

Do the returns in 2006 discussed in Chapters 2 and 3 (see the Mutual Funds file) have the properties of the normal distribution? Figure 6.20 displays descriptive statistics for these data, and Figure 6.21 presents a boxplot.

FIGURE 6.20

Microsoft Excel descriptive statistics for the 2006 returns

See Section E3.1 to create this. (Use Section M3.1 to create the Minitab equivalent.)

	A	B
1	*Return 2006*	
2		
3	Mean	12.5142
4	Standard Error	0.2136
5	Median	13.1000
6	Mode	16.6000
7	Standard Deviation	6.2916
8	Sample Variance	39.5840
9	Kurtosis	0.0200
10	Skewness	-0.2982
11	Range	44.0000
12	Minimum	-9.0000
13	Maximum	35.0000
14	Sum	10862.3000
15	Count	868.0000
16	Largest(1)	35.0000
17	Smallest(1)	-9.0000

FIGURE 6.21

Minitab boxplot for the
2006 returns

*See Section M3.2 to create
this. (Use Section P3.1 to
create the PHStat2
equivalent.)*

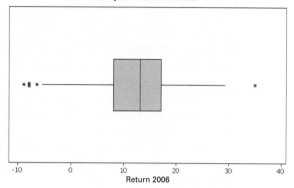

From Figures 6.20 and 6.21 and from an ordered array of the 2006 returns (not shown here), you can make the following statements:

1. The mean of 12.5142 is slightly lower than the median of 13.1. (In a normal distribution, the mean and median are equal.)
2. The boxplot appears symmetrical, with four lower outliers at -9.0, -8.0, -8.0, and -6.5 and one upper outlier at 35.0. (The normal distribution is symmetrical.)
3. The interquartile range of 9.2 is approximately 1.46 standard deviations. (In a normal distribution, the interquartile range is 1.33 standard deviations.)
4. The range of 44 is equal to 6.99 standard deviations. (In a normal distribution, the range is approximately six standard deviations.)
5. 72.2% of the returns are within ± 1 standard deviation of the mean. (In a normal distribution, 68.26% of the values lie between the mean ± 1 standard deviation.)
6. 87.0% of the returns are within ± 1.28 standard deviations of the mean. (In a normal distribution, 80% of the values lie between the mean ± 1.28 standard deviations.)

Based on these statements and the criteria given on page 196, the 2006 returns are slightly left-skewed and contain more values closer to the mean than expected. The range is higher than would be expected in a normal distribution, but this is mostly due to the single outlier at 35.0. You can conclude that the data characteristics of the 2006 returns do not greatly differ from the theoretical properties of a normal distribution.

Constructing the Normal Probability Plot

A **normal probability plot** is a graphical approach for evaluating whether data are normally distributed. One common approach is called the **quantile-quantile plot**. In this method, you first transform each ordered value to a Z value. For example, if you have a sample of $n = 19$, the

Z value for the smallest value corresponds to a cumulative area of $\dfrac{1}{n+1} = \dfrac{1}{19+1} = \dfrac{1}{20} = 0.05$.

The Z value for a cumulative area of 0.05 (from Table E.2) is -1.65. Table 6.7 illustrates the entire set of Z values for a sample of $n = 19$.

TABLE 6.7

Ordered Values and
Corresponding Z Values
for a Sample of $n = 19$

Ordered Value	Z Value	Ordered Value	Z Value
1	−1.65	11	0.13
2	−1.28	12	0.25
3	−1.04	13	0.39
4	−0.84	14	0.52
5	−0.67	15	0.67
6	−0.52	16	0.84
7	−0.39	17	1.04
8	−0.25	18	1.28
9	−0.13	19	1.65
10	0.00		

To construct the quantile-quantile plot, the Z values are plotted on the X axis, and the corresponding values of the variable are plotted on the Y axis. If the data are normally distributed, the values will plot along an approximately straight line. (Minitab uses a different approach that plots the original values on the X axis and a theoretical percentage score based on the normal distribution on the Y axis. Once again, if the data are normally distributed, the values will plot along an approximately straight line.)

Figure 6.22 illustrates the typical shape of normal probability plots for a left-skewed distribution (Panel A), a normal distribution (Panel B), and a right-skewed distribution (Panel C). If the data are left-skewed, the curve will rise more rapidly at first and then level off. If the data are normally distributed, the points will plot along an approximately straight line. If the data are right-skewed, the data will rise more slowly at first and then rise at a faster rate for higher values of the variable being plotted.

FIGURE 6.22

Normal probability plots for a left-skewed distribution, a normal distribution, and a right-skewed distribution

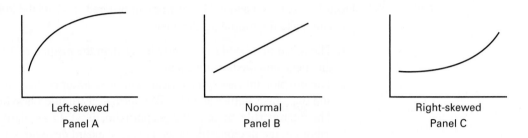

| Left-skewed | Normal | Right-skewed |
| Panel A | Panel B | Panel C |

Figure 6.23 shows a Microsoft Excel quantile-quantile normal probability plot and Figure 6.24 displays a Minitab normal probability plot for the 2006 returns.

FIGURE 6.23

Microsoft Excel normal probability plot for 2006 returns

See Section P6.2 to create this.

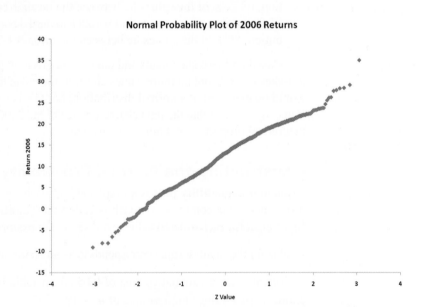

FIGURE 6.24

Minitab normal probability plot for 2006 returns

See Section M6.2 to create this.

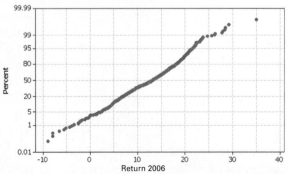

Figures 6.23 and 6.24 show that the 2006 returns approximate a straight line with the exception of a few outliers at the lower and upper ends of the distribution. Thus, it is reasonable for you to conclude that the 2006 returns do not depart greatly from a normal distribution.

Problems for Section 6.3

LEARNING THE BASICS

6.14 Show that for a sample of $n = 39$, the smallest and largest Z values are -1.96 and $+1.96$, and the middle (i.e., 20th) Z value is 0.00.

6.15 For a sample of $n = 6$, list the six Z values.

APPLYING THE CONCEPTS

✓ SELF Test **6.16** The data in the file **Chicken** contains the total fat, in grams per serving, for a sample of 20 chicken sandwiches from fast-food chains. The data are as follows:

7 8 4 5 16 20 20 24 19 30 23 30 25 19 29 29 30 30 40 56

Source: *Data extracted from "Fast Food: Adding Health to the Menu,"* Consumer Reports, *September 2004, pp. 28–31.*

Decide whether the data appear to be approximately normally distributed by
a. comparing data characteristics to theoretical properties.
b. constructing a normal probability plot.

6.17 As player salaries have increased, the cost of attending games has increased dramatically. The data in the file **BBCost** (data extracted from **teammarketing.com**, March 29, 2008) represent the cost of four tickets, two beers, four soft drinks, four hot dogs, two game programs, two baseball caps, and the parking fee for one car for each of the 30 major league teams. Decide whether the data appear to be approximately normally distributed by
a. comparing data characteristics to theoretical properties.
b. constructing a normal probability plot.

6.18 The data in the file **Property Taxes** contain the property taxes per capita for the fifty states and the District of Columbia. Decide whether the data appear to be approximately normally distributed by
a. comparing data characteristics to theoretical properties.
b. constructing a normal probability plot.

6.19 The number of shares traded daily on the New York Stock Exchange (NYSE) is referred to as the *volume* of trading. During the first three months of 2008, daily volume ranged from 1.976 billion to 4.312 billion. The daily value of the stocks traded ranged from $70.688 billion to $153.062 billion (NYSE Group, **www.nyse.com**, April 2, 2008). The file **NYSE** contains the date, volume (in billions), and value (in billions of U.S. dollars) for the first three months of 2008. Decide whether the volume of trades appear to be approximately normally distributed by
a. comparing data characteristics to theoretical properties.
b. constructing a normal probability plot.
c. constructing a histogram.
d. Repeat (a) through (c) using the value data.

6.20 One operation of a mill is to cut pieces of steel into parts that will later be used as the frame for front seats in an automotive plant. The steel is cut with a diamond saw and requires the resulting parts to be within ± 0.005 inch of the length specified by the automobile company. The data come from a sample of 100 steel parts and are stored in the file **Steel**. The measurement reported is the difference, in inches, between the actual length of the steel part, as measured by a laser measurement device, and the specified length of the steel part. Decide whether the data appear to be approximately normally distributed by
a. comparing data characteristics to theoretical properties.
b. constructing a normal probability plot.

6.21 The data in the file **Savings Rate** are the yields for a money market account, a one-year certificate of deposit (CD), and a five-year CD for 38 banks in south Florida, as of March 28, 2008 (data extracted from **Bankrate.com**, March 28, 2008). For each of the three types of investments, decide whether the data appear to be approximately normally distributed by
a. comparing data characteristics to theoretical properties.
b. constructing a normal probability plot.

6.22 The following data, stored in the file **Utility**, represent the electricity costs in dollars during July 2008 for a random sample of 50 two-bedroom apartments in a large city:

96	171	202	178	147	102	153	197	127	82
157	185	90	116	172	111	148	213	130	165
141	149	206	175	123	128	144	168	109	167
95	163	150	154	130	143	187	166	139	149
108	119	183	151	114	135	191	137	129	158

Decide whether the data appear to be approximately normally distributed by
a. comparing data characteristics to theoretical properties.
b. constructing a normal probability plot.

USING STATISTICS   @ OurCampus! Revisited

I n the Using Statistics scenario, you were a Web-page designer for OurCampus! The home page must download quickly but still be flashy enough to attract and retain the college student customers using OurCampus! By running experiments in the corporate offices, you determined that the amount of time in seconds that pass from first linking to the Web site until the home page is fully displayed was a bell-shaped distribution with a mean download time of 7 seconds and standard deviation of 2 seconds. Using the normal distribution, you were able to calculate that approximately 84% of the download times are 9 seconds or less, and 95% of the download times are between 3.08 and 10.92 seconds.

Now that you understand how to calculate probabilities from the normal distribution, you can evaluate download times of home pages with different designs. For example, if the standard deviation remained at 2 seconds, lowering the mean to 6 seconds would shift the entire distribution lower by one second. Thus, approximately 84% of the download times would be 8 seconds or less, and 95% of the download times would be between 2.08 and 9.92 seconds. Another change that could reduce long download times would be lowering the variation. For example, consider the case where the mean remained at the original 7 seconds but the standard deviation was reduced to 1 second. Again, approximately 84% of the download times would be 8 seconds or less, and 95% of the download times would be between 5.04 and 8.96 seconds.

SUMMARY

In this and the previous chapter, you have learned about mathematical models called probability distributions and how they can be used to solve business problems. In Chapter 5, you used discrete probability distributions in situations where the outcomes come from a counting process (e.g., the number of courses you are enrolled in, or the number of tagged order forms in a report generated by an accounting information system). In this chapter, you learned about continuous probability distributions where the outcomes come from a measuring process (e.g., your height, or the download time of a Web page). Continuous probability distributions come in all kinds of shapes, but the most common and most important in business is the normal distribution. The normal distribution is symmetrical thus its mean

and median are equal. It is also bell-shaped and approximately 68.26% of its observations are within one standard deviation of the mean, approximately 95.44% of its observations are within two standard deviations of the mean, and approximately 99.73% of its observations are within three standard deviations of the mean. Although many data sets in business are closely approximated by the normal distribution, do not think that all data can be approximated using the normal distribution. In Section 6.3, you learned various methods used to evaluate normality in order to determine whether or not the normal distribution is a reasonable mathematical model to use in specific situations. In Chapter 7, the normal distribution is used in developing the subject of statistical inference.

KEY EQUATIONS

Normal Probability Density Function

$$f(X) = \frac{1}{\sqrt{2\pi}\sigma} e^{-(1/2)[(X-\mu)/\sigma]^2} \tag{6.1}$$

Transformation Formula

$$Z = \frac{X - \mu}{\sigma} \tag{6.2}$$

Finding an X Value Associated with Known Probability

$$X = \mu + Z\sigma \tag{6.3}$$

KEY TERMS

CHAPTER REVIEW PROBLEMS

CHECKING YOUR UNDERSTANDING

6.23 Why is it that only one normal distribution table such as Table E.2 is needed to find any probability under the normal curve?

6.24 How do you find the area between two values under the normal curve?

6.25 How do you find the X value that corresponds to a given percentile of the normal distribution?

6.26 What are some of the distinguishing properties of a normal distribution?

6.27 How does the shape of the normal distribution differ from those of the uniform and exponential distributions?

6.28 How can you use the normal probability plot to evaluate whether a set of data is normally distributed?

APPLYING THE CONCEPTS

6.29 An industrial sewing machine uses ball bearings that are targeted to have a diameter of 0.75 inch. The lower and upper specification limits under which the ball bearings can operate are 0.74 inch and 0.76 inch, respectively. Past experience has indicated that the actual diameter of the ball bearings is approximately normally distributed, with a mean of 0.753 inch and a standard deviation of 0.004 inch. What is the probability that a ball bearing is
a. between the target and the actual mean?
b. between the lower specification limit and the target?
c. above the upper specification limit?
d. below the lower specification limit?
e. 93% of the diameters are greater than what value?

6.30 The fill amount of soft drink bottles is normally distributed, with a mean of 2.0 liters and a standard deviation of 0.05 liter. If bottles contain less than 95% of the listed net content (1.90 liters, in this case), the manufacturer may be subject to penalty by the state office of consumer affairs. Bottles that have a net content above 2.10 liters may cause excess spillage upon opening. What proportion of the bottles will contain
a. between 1.90 and 2.0 liters?
b. between 1.90 and 2.10 liters?
c. below 1.90 liters or above 2.10 liters?

d. 99% of the bottles contain at least how much soft drink?
e. 99% of the bottles contain an amount that is between which two values (symmetrically distributed) around the mean?

6.31 In an effort to reduce the number of bottles that contain less than 1.90 liters, the bottler in Problem 6.30 sets the filling machine so that the mean is 2.02 liters. Under these circumstances, what are your answers in (a) through (e)?

6.32 An orange juice producer buys all his oranges from a large orange grove. The amount of juice squeezed from each of these oranges is approximately normally distributed, with a mean of 4.70 ounces and a standard deviation of 0.40 ounce.
a. What is the probability that a randomly selected orange will contain between 4.70 and 5.00 ounces of juice?
b. What is the probability that a randomly selected orange will contain between 5.00 and 5.50 ounces of juice?
c. 77% of the oranges will contain at least how many ounces of juice?
d. 80% of the oranges contain between what two values (in ounces of juice), symmetrically distributed around the population mean?

6.33 Data concerning 71 of the best-selling domestic beer in the United States are located in the file **Domesticbeer**. The values for three variables are included: percentage alcohol, number of calories per 12 ounces, and number of carbohydrates (in grams) per 12 ounces. For each of the three variables, decide whether the data appear to be approximately normally distributed. Support your decision through the use of appropriate statistics and graphs.
Source: *Data extracted from* **www.Beer100.com**, *May 4, 2007.*

6.34 The evening manager of a restaurant was very concerned about the length of time some customers were waiting in line to be seated. She also had some concern about the seating times—that is, the length of time between when a customer is seated and the time he or she leaves the restaurant. Over the course of one week, 100 customers (no more than 1 per party) were randomly selected, and their waiting and seating times (in minutes) were recorded in the file **Wait**.
a. Think about your favorite restaurant. Do you think waiting times more closely resemble a uniform, exponential, or normal distribution?

b. Again, think about your favorite restaurant. Do you think seating times more closely resemble a uniform, exponential, or normal distribution?

c. Construct a histogram and a normal probability plot of the waiting times. Do you think these waiting times more closely resemble a uniform, exponential, or normal distribution?

d. Construct a histogram and a normal probability plot of the seating times. Do you think these seating times more closely resemble a uniform, exponential, or normal distribution?

6.35 At the end of 2007, all the major stock market indexes had posted gains in the previous 12 months. The mean one-year return for stocks in the S&P 500, a group of 500 very large companies, was 3.5%. The mean one-year return for the Nasdaq, a group of 3,200 small and medium-sized companies, was 9.8%. Historically, the one-year returns are approximately normal, the standard deviation in the S&P 500 is approximately 20%, and the standard deviation in the Nasdaq is approximately 30%.

a. What is the probability that a stock in the S&P 500 gained 25% or more in 2007? gained 50% or more?

b. What is the probability that a stock in the S&P 500 lost money in 2007? lost 25% or more? lost 50% or more?

c. Repeat (a) and (b) for a stock in the Nasdaq.

d. Write a short summary on your findings. Be sure to include a discussion of the risks associated with a large standard deviation.

6.36 *The New York Times* reported (L. J. Flynn, "Tax Surfing," March 25, 2002, p. C10) that the mean time to download the home page for the Internal Revenue Service, **www.irs.gov**, is 0.8 second. Suppose that the download time is normally distributed with a standard deviation of 0.2 second. What is the probability that a download time is

a. less than 1 second?

b. between 0.5 and 1.5 seconds?

c. above 0.5 second?

d. 99% of the download times are above how many seconds?

e. 95% of the download times are between what two values, symmetrically distributed around the mean?

6.37 The same article mentioned in Problem 6.36 also reported that the mean download time for the H&R Block Web site, **www.hrblock.com**, is 2.5 seconds. Suppose that the download time is normally distributed with a standard deviation of 0.5 second. What is the probability that a download time is

a. less than 1 second?

b. between 0.5 and 1.5 seconds?

c. above 0.5 second?

d. 99% of the download times are above how many seconds?

e. Compare the results for the IRS site computed in Problem 6.36 to those of the H&R Block site.

6.38 When obtaining a mortgage, the borrower will pay closing costs to the lender. These costs vary from bank to bank, and from state to state. **Bankrate.com** conducted a survey in all fifty states to identify average closing costs on a $200,000 loan, assuming a 20-percent down payment and good credit. The file Closing includes the average rate for all fifty states and the District of Columbia for 2006, along with the state rank.

Source: *Data extracted from "Closing Cost Survey,"* **www.bankrate.com**, *May 15, 2007.*

a. Is the distribution of state closing costs approximately distributed as a normal random variable?

b. The variable "RANK 2006" includes 51 numbers, 1, 2, 3, . . . , 51. What type of distribution does this column of numbers resemble? Construct a graphical display that supports your answer.

6.39 **(Class Project)** According to Burton G. Malkiel, the daily changes in the closing price of stock follow a *random walk*—that is, these daily events are independent of each other and move upward or downward in a random manner—and can be approximated by a normal distribution. To test this theory, use either a newspaper or the Internet to select one company traded on the NYSE, one company traded on the American Stock Exchange, and one company traded on the Nasdaq and then do the following:

1. Record the daily closing stock price of each of these companies for six consecutive weeks (so that you have 30 values per company).

2. Record the daily changes in the closing stock price of each of these companies for six consecutive weeks (so that you have 30 values per company).

For each of your six data sets, decide whether the data are approximately normally distributed by

a. examining the stem-and-leaf display, histogram or polygon, and boxplot.

b. comparing data characteristics to theoretical properties.

c. constructing a normal probability plot.

d. Discuss the results of (a) through (c). What can you say about your three stocks with respect to daily closing prices and daily changes in closing prices? Which, if any, of the data sets are approximately normally distributed?

Note: *The random-walk theory pertains to the daily changes in the closing stock price, not the daily closing stock price.*

TEAM PROJECTS

The data file Mutual Funds contains information regarding nine variables from a sample of 868 mutual funds. The variables are:

Category—Type of stocks comprising the mutual fund (small cap, mid cap, large cap)

Objective—Objective of stocks comprising the mutual fund (growth or value)

Assets—In millions of dollars

Fees—Sales charges (no or yes)

Expense ratio—Ratio of expenses to net assets, in percentage

Return 2006—Twelve-month return in 2006

Three-year return—Annualized return, 2004–2006
Five-year return—Annualized return, 2002–2006
Risk—Risk-of-loss factor of the mutual fund (low, average, high)

6.40 For the expense ratio, three-year return, and five-year return, decide whether the data are approximately normally distributed by
a. comparing data characteristics to theoretical properties.
b. constructing a normal probability plot.

STUDENT SURVEY DATA BASE

6.41 Problem 1.23 on page 13 describes a survey of 50 undergraduate students (see the file Undergradsurvey). For these data, for each numerical variable, decide whether the data are approximately normally distributed by
a. comparing data characteristics to theoretical properties.
b. constructing a normal probability plot.

6.42 Problem 1.23 on page 13 describes a survey of 50 undergraduate students (see the file Undergradsurvey).

a. Select a sample of 50 undergraduate students and conduct a similar survey for those students.
b. For the data collected in (a), repeat (a) and (b) of Problem 6.41.
c. Compare the results of (b) to those of Problem 6.41.

6.43 Problem 1.24 on page 13 describes a survey of 40 MBA students (see the file Gradsurvey). For these data, for each numerical variable, decide whether the data are approximately normally distributed by
a. comparing data characteristics to theoretical properties.
b. constructing a normal probability plot.

6.44 Problem 1.24 on page 13 describes a survey of 40 MBA students (see the file Gradsurvey).
a. Select a sample of 40 graduate students and conduct a similar survey for those students.
b. For the data collected in (a), repeat (a) and (b) of Problem 6.43.
c. Compare the results of (b) to those of Problem 6.43.

MANAGING THE *SPRINGVILLE HERALD*

The production department of the newspaper has embarked on a quality improvement effort. Its first project relates to the blackness of the newspaper print. Each day, a determination needs to be made concerning how black the newspaper is printed. Blackness is measured on a standard scale in which the target value is 1.0. Data collected over the past year indicate that the blackness is approximately normally distributed, with a mean of 1.005 and a standard deviation of 0.10. Each day, one spot on the first newspaper printed is chosen, and the blackness of the spot is measured. The blackness of the newspaper is considered acceptable if the blackness of a spot is between 0.95 and 1.05.

EXERCISES

SH6.1 Assuming that the distribution has not changed from what it was in the past year, what is the probability that the blackness of the spot is

a. less than 1.0?
b. between 0.95 and 1.0?
c. between 1.0 and 1.05?
d. less than 0.95 or greater than 1.05?

SH6.2 The objective of the production team is to reduce the probability that the blackness is below 0.95 or above 1.05. Should the team focus on process improvement that lowers the mean to the target value of 1.0 or on process improvement that reduces the standard deviation to 0.075? Explain.

WEB CASE

Apply your knowledge about the normal distribution in this Web Case, which extends the Using Statistics scenario from this chapter.

To satisfy concerns of potential advertisers, the management of OurCampus! has undertaken a research project to learn the amount of time it takes users to download a complex video features page. The marketing department has collected data and has made some claims based on the assertion that the data follow a normal distribution. These data and conclusions can be found in a report located on the internal Web page www.prenhall.com/Springville/

Our_DownloadResearch.htm (or in the file with the same name in the Student CD-ROM Web Case folder).

Read this marketing report and then answer the following:

1. Can the collected data be approximated by the normal distribution?

2. Review and evaluate the conclusions made by the OurCampus! marketing department. Which conclusions are correct? Which ones are incorrect?

3. If OurCampus! could improve the mean time by five minutes, how would the probabilities change?

REFERENCES

1. Gunter, B., "Q-Q Plots," *Quality Progress* (February 1994), 81–86.

2. Levine, D. M., P. Ramsey, and R. Smidt, *Applied Statistics for Engineers and Scientists Using Microsoft Excel and Minitab* (Upper Saddle River, NJ: Prentice Hall, 2001).

3. *Microsoft Excel 2007* (Redmond, WA: Microsoft Corp., 2007).

4. Miller, J., "Earliest Known Uses of Some of the Words of Mathematics," **http://members.aol.com/jeff570/n.html**.

5. *Minitab for Windows Version 15* (State College, PA: Minitab, Inc., 2006).

6. Pearl, R., "Karl Pearson, 1857–1936," *Journal of the American Statistical Association*, 31 (1936), 653–664.

7. Pearson, E. S., "Some Incidents in the Early History of Biometry and Statistics, 1890–94," *Biometrika*, 52 (1965), 3–18.

8. Walker, H., "The Contributions of Karl Pearson," *Journal of the American Statistical Association*, 53 (1958), 11–22.

Using Microsoft Excel to Compute Probabilities from the Normal Distribution

E6.1 Computing Normal Probabilities

You compute normal probabilities by using either the **Normal** or **Normal Expanded** worksheets of the `Normal.xls` workbook. The **Normal** worksheet, shown in Figure 6.18 on page 193, contains the entries to solve the Example 6.5 and 6.6 problems on page 190. Change the **Mean, Standard Deviation, X Value**, and/or **Cumulative Percentage** to solve similar problems. Use the **Normal Expanded** worksheet (part of which is shown in Figure E6.1) to compute all types of normal probabilities. In these worksheets, the STANDARDIZE function returns the Z value for a specific X value, mean, and standard deviation; the NORMDIST function returns the area or probability of less than a given X value for a specific mean and standard deviation; the NORMSINV function returns the Z value for a given probability of less than a given X, and the NORMINV function returns the X value for a given probability, mean, and standard deviation.

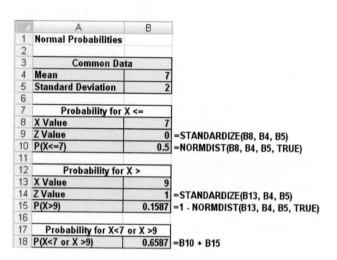

FIGURE E6.1 Normal Expanded worksheet (columns A and B)

E6.2 Creating Normal Probability Plots

There are no Microsoft Excel features that directly create normal probability plots. Use PHStat2 (see Section P6.2) to create a normal probability plot in Excel.

APPENDIX P6

Using PHStat2 to Compute Probabilities from the Normal Distribution

P6.1 Computing Normal Probabilities

To compute normal probabilities, use **PHStat → Probability & Prob. Distributions → Normal.** The procedure creates a normal probabilities worksheet, similar to Figure 6.18 on page 193, that solves one or more types of normal probability problems based on the Input Options you select.

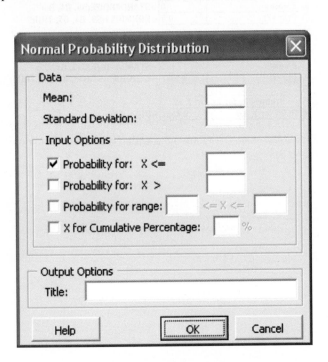

P6.2 Creating Normal Probability Plots

To create a normal probability plot, use **PHStat2 → Probability & Prob. Distributions → Normal Probability Plot.** This procedure uses Excel charting features to create a normal probability plot for data from a custom worksheet that the procedure also creates.

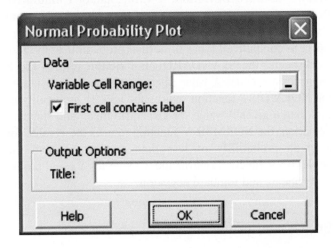

The procedure creates a **Plot** worksheet on which the Z values to be plotted are calculated using the NORMSINV function. The procedure then uses Excel charting features to create a normal probability plot from the calculated Z values and the data in the **Variable Cell Range**.

APPENDIX M6

Using Minitab to Compute Probabilities from the Normal Distribution

M6.1 Computing Normal Probabilities

To illustrate computing normal probabilities, to find the probability that a download time is less than 9 seconds with $\mu = 7$ and $\sigma = 2$:

1. Open to a new, blank worksheet.
2. Enter **9** in the row 1 cell of column C1, leaving the unnumbered variable label cell at the top of the column empty.
3. Select **Calc → Probability Distributions → Normal**.

In the Normal Distribution dialog box (see Figure M6.1):

4. Click **Cumulative probability**.
5. Enter **7** in the **Mean** box.
6. Enter **2** in the **Standard deviation** box.
7. Click **Input column** and enter **C1** in its box.
8. Click **OK** (to create the results shown in the top portion of Figure 6.19 on page 194).

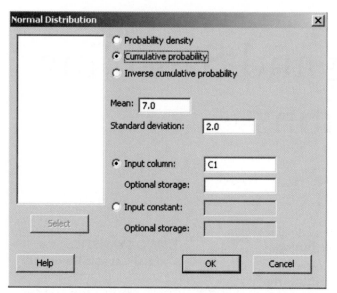

FIGURE M6.1   Minitab Normal Distribution dialog box

To find the *Z* value corresponding to a cumulative area of 0.10:

1. Continue with the same worksheet and enter **.10** in the row 1 cell of column C2.
2. Select **Calc → Probability Distributions → Normal**.

In the Normal Distribution dialog box (see Figure M6.1):

3. Click **Inverse cumulative probability**.
4. Enter **7** in the **Mean** box
5. Enter **2** in the **Standard deviation** box.
6. Click **Input Column** and enter **C2** in its box.
7. Click **OK** (to create the results displayed in the bottom portion of Figure 6.19 on page 194).

M6.2 Creating Normal Probability Plots

To create a normal probability plot for the 2006 returns of mutual funds:

1. Open the **Mutual Funds.mtw** worksheet.
2. Select **Graph → Probability Plot**.
3. In the Probability Plots dialog box gallery, click **Single** and then click **OK**.

In the Probability Plot - Single dialog box (see Figure M6.2):

4. Enter **'Return 2006'** in the **Graph variables** box.
5. Click **Distribution**.

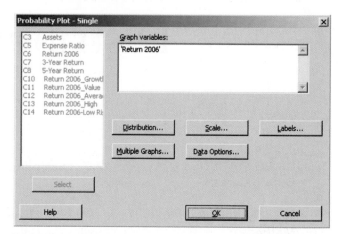

FIGURE M6.2   Minitab Probability Plot - Single dialog box

6. In the Probability Plot - Distribution dialog box (see Figure M6.3), select **Normal** from the **Distribution** drop-down list and then click **OK** to return to the Probability Plot - Single dialog box.
7. Back in the Probability Plot - Single dialog box, click **OK** (to create the plot).

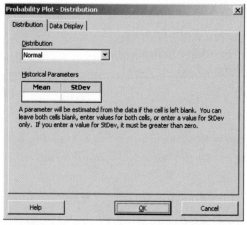

FIGURE M6.3   Minitab Probability Plot - Distribution

7

Sampling and Sampling Distributions

Learning Objectives

In this chapter, you learn:

- To distinguish between different sampling methods
- The concept of the sampling distribution
- To compute probabilities related to the sample mean and the sample proportion
- The importance of the Central Limit Theorem

@ Oxford Cereals

O xford Cereals fills thousands of boxes of cereal during an eight-hour shift. As the plant operations manager, you are responsible for monitoring the amount of cereal placed in each box. To be consistent with package labeling, boxes should contain a mean of 368 grams of cereal. Because of the speed of the process, the cereal weight varies from box to box, causing some boxes to be underfilled and others overfilled. If the process is not working properly, the mean weight in the boxes could vary too much from the label weight of 368 grams to be acceptable.

Because weighing every single box is too time-consuming, costly, and inefficient, you must take a sample of boxes. For each sample you select, you plan to weigh the individual boxes and calculate a sample mean. You need to determine the probability that such a sample mean could have been randomly selected from a population whose mean is 368 grams. Based on your analysis, you will have to decide whether to maintain, alter, or shut down the cereal-filling process.

I n Chapter 6, you used the normal distribution to study the distribution of download times for the OurCampus! Web site. In this chapter, you need to make a decision about the cereal-filling process, based on the weights of a sample of cereal boxes packaged at Oxford Cereals. You will learn different methods of sampling and about sampling distributions and how to use them to solve business problems.

7.1 Types of Sampling Methods

In Section 1.3, a sample was defined as the portion of a population that has been selected for analysis. Rather than selecting every item in the population, statistical sampling procedures focus on collecting a small representative group of the larger population. The results of the sample are then used to estimate characteristics of the entire population. There are three main reasons for selecting a sample:

- Selecting a sample is less time-consuming than selecting every item in the population.
- Selecting a sample is less costly than selecting every item in the population.
- An analysis of a sample is less cumbersome and more practical than an analysis of the entire population.

The sampling process begins by defining the **frame**. The frame is a listing of items that make up the population. Frames are data sources such as population lists, directories, or maps. Samples are drawn from frames. Inaccurate or biased results can occur if a frame excludes certain portions of the population. Using different frames to generate data can lead to dissimilar conclusions.

After you select a frame, you draw a sample from the frame. As illustrated in Figure 7.1, there are two kinds of samples: nonprobability samples and probability samples.

FIGURE 7.1

Types of samples

See Sections P7.1 or M7.1 to select a random sample without replacement.

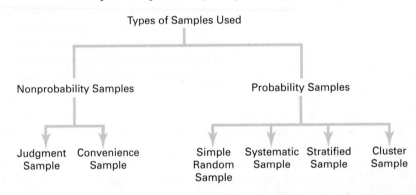

In a **nonprobability sample**, you select the items or individuals without knowing their probabilities of selection. Thus, the theory of statistical inference that has been developed for probability sampling cannot be applied to nonprobability samples. A common type of nonprobability sampling is **convenience sampling**. In convenience sampling, items selected are easy, inexpensive, or convenient to sample. For example, if you were sampling tires stacked in a warehouse, it would be much more convenient to sample tires that were at the top of a stack than tires that were at the bottom of a stack. In many cases, participants in the sample select themselves. For example, many companies conduct surveys by giving visitors to their Web site the opportunity to complete survey forms and submit them electronically. The responses to these surveys can provide large amounts of data quickly and inexpensively, but the sample consists of self-selected Web users. For many studies, only a nonprobability sample such as a judgment sample is available. In a **judgment sample**, you get the opinions of preselected experts in the subject matter. Although the experts may be well informed, you cannot generalize their results to the general public.

Nonprobability samples can have certain advantages, such as convenience, speed, and low cost. However, their lack of accuracy due to selection bias and the fact that the results cannot be used for statistical inference more than offset these advantages.

In a **probability sample**, you select the items based on known probabilities. Whenever possible, you should use probability sampling methods. Probability samples allow you to make unbiased inferences about the population of interest. The four types of probability samples most commonly used are simple random, systematic, stratified, and cluster samples. These sampling methods vary in their cost, accuracy, and complexity.

Simple Random Samples

In a **simple random sample**, every item from a frame has the same chance of selection as every other item. In addition, every sample of a fixed size has the same chance of selection as every other sample of that size. Simple random sampling is the most elementary random sampling technique. It forms the basis for the other random sampling techniques.

With simple random sampling, you use n to represent the sample size and N to represent the frame size. You number every item in the frame from 1 to N. The chance that you will select any particular member of the frame on the first selection is $1/N$.

You select samples with replacement or without replacement. **Sampling with replacement** means that after you select an item, you return it to the frame, where it has the same probability of being selected again. Imagine that you have a fishbowl containing N business cards. On the first selection, you select the card for Judy Craven. You record pertinent information and replace the business card in the bowl. You then mix up the cards in the bowl and select the second card. On the second selection, Judy Craven has the same probability of being selected again, $1/N$. You repeat this process until you have selected the desired sample size, n. However, usually you do not want the same item to be selected again.

Sampling without replacement means that once you select an item, you cannot select it again. The chance that you will select any particular item in the frame—for example, the business card for Judy Craven—on the first draw is $1/N$. The chance that you will select any card not previously selected on the second draw is now 1 out of $N - 1$. This process continues until you have selected the desired sample of size n.

Regardless of whether you have sampled with or without replacement, "fishbowl" methods of sample selection have a major drawback—the ability to thoroughly mix the cards and randomly select the sample. As a result, fishbowl methods are not very useful. You need to use less cumbersome and more scientific methods of selection.

One such method uses a **table of random numbers** (see Table E.1 in Appendix E) for selecting the sample. A table of random numbers consists of a series of digits listed in a randomly generated sequence (see reference 7). Because the numeric system uses 10 digits (0, 1, 2, . . . , 9), the chance that you will randomly generate any particular digit is equal to the probability of generating any other digit. This probability is 1 out of 10. Hence, if you generate a sequence of 800 digits, you would expect about 80 to be the digit 0, 80 to be the digit 1, and so on. Because every digit or sequence of digits in the table is random, the table can be read either horizontally or vertically. The margins of the table designate row numbers and column numbers. The digits themselves are grouped into sequences of five in order to make reading the table easier.

To use Table E.1 instead of a fishbowl for selecting the sample, you first need to assign code numbers to the individual items of the frame. Then you generate the random sample by reading the table of random numbers and selecting those individuals from the frame whose assigned code numbers match the digits found in the table. You can better understand the process of sample selection by studying Example 7.1.

EXAMPLE 7.1 Selecting a Simple Random Sample by Using a Table of Random Numbers	A company wants to select a sample of 32 full-time workers from a population of 800 full-time employees in order to collect information on expenditures concerning a company-sponsored dental plan. How do you select a simple random sample? **SOLUTION** The company decides to conduct an e-mail survey. Assuming that not everyone will respond to the survey, you need to send more than 32 surveys to get the necessary 32 responses. Assuming that 8 out of 10 full-time workers will respond to such a survey (i.e., a response rate of 80%), you decide to send 40 surveys. Because you want to send the 40 surveys to 40 different individuals, you should sample without replacement. The frame consists of a listing of the names and e-mail addresses of all $N = 800$ full-time employees taken from the company personnel files. Thus, the frame is a complete listing of the

population. To select the random sample of 40 employees from this frame, you use a table of random numbers. Because the frame size (800) is a three-digit number, each assigned code number must also be three digits so that every full-time worker has an equal chance of selection. You assign a code of 001 to the first full-time employee in the population listing, a code of 002 to the second full-time employee in the population listing, and so on, until a code of 800 is assigned to the Nth full-time worker in the listing. Because $N = 800$ is the largest possible coded value, you discard all three-digit code sequences greater than 800 (i.e., 801 through 999 and 000).

To select the simple random sample, you choose an arbitrary starting point from the table of random numbers. One method you can use is to close your eyes and strike the table of random numbers with a pencil. Suppose you used this procedure and you selected row 06, column 05, of Table 7.1 (which is extracted from Table E.1) as the starting point. Although you can go in any direction, in this example you read the table from left to right, in sequences of three digits, without skipping.

TABLE 7.1

Using a Table of Random Numbers

		Column							
	Row	00000 12345	00001 67890	11111 12345	11112 67890	22222 12345	22223 67890	33333 12345	33334 67890
	01	49280	88924	35779	00283	81163	07275	89863	02348
	02	61870	41657	07468	08612	98083	97349	20775	45091
	03	43898	65923	25078	86129	78496	97653	91550	08078
	04	62993	93912	30454	84598	56095	20664	12872	64647
	05	33850	58555	51438	85507	71865	79488	76783	31708
Begin	06	97340	03364	88472	04334	63919	36394	11095	92470
selection	07	70543	29776	10087	10072	55980	64688	68239	20461
(row 06,	08	89382	93809	00796	95945	34101	81277	66090	88872
column 05)	09	37818	72142	67140	50785	22380	16703	53362	44940
	10	60430	22834	14130	96593	23298	56203	92671	15925
	11	82975	66158	84731	19436	55790	69229	28661	13675
	12	39087	71938	40355	54324	08401	26299	49420	59208
	13	55700	24586	93247	32596	11865	63397	44251	43189
	14	14756	23997	78643	75912	83832	32768	18928	57070
	15	32166	53251	70654	92827	63491	04233	33825	69662
	16	23236	73751	31888	81718	06546	83246	47651	04877
	17	45794	26926	15130	82455	78305	55058	52551	47182
	18	09893	20505	14225	68514	46427	56788	96297	78822
	19	54382	74598	91499	14523	68479	27686	46162	83554
	20	94750	89923	37089	20048	80336	94598	26940	36858
	21	70297	34135	53140	33340	42050	82341	44104	82949
	22	85157	47954	32979	26575	57600	40881	12250	73742
	23	11100	02340	12860	74697	96644	89439	28707	25815
	24	36871	50775	30592	57143	17381	68856	25853	35041
	25	23913	48357	63308	16090	51690	54607	72407	55538

Source: Data extracted from The Rand Corporation, A Million Random Digits with 100,000 Normal Deviates (Glencoe, IL: The Free Press, 1955) and displayed in Table E.1 in Appendix E.

The individual with code number 003 is the first full-time employee in the sample (row 06 and columns 05–07), the second individual has code number 364 (row 06 and columns 08–10), and the third individual has code number 884. Because the highest code for any employee is 800, you discard the number 884. Individuals with code numbers 720, 433, 463, 363, 109, 592, 470, and 705 are selected third through tenth, respectively.

You continue the selection process until you get the required sample size of 40 full-time employees. If any three-digit sequence repeats during the selection process, you discard the repeating sequence because you are sampling without replacement.

Systematic Samples

In a **systematic sample**, you partition the N items in the frame into n groups of k items, where

$$k = \frac{N}{n}$$

You round k to the nearest integer. To select a systematic sample, you choose the first item to be selected at random from the first k items in the frame. Then, you select the remaining $n - 1$ items by taking every kth item thereafter from the entire frame.

If the frame consists of a listing of prenumbered checks, sales receipts, or invoices, a systematic sample is faster and easier to take than a simple random sample. A systematic sample is also a convenient mechanism for collecting data from telephone books, class rosters, and consecutive items coming off an assembly line.

To take a systematic sample of $n = 40$ from the population of $N = 800$ full-time employees, you partition the frame of 800 into 40 groups, each of which contains 20 employees. You then select a random number from the first 20 individuals and include every twentieth individual after the first selection in the sample. For example, if the first random number you select is 008, your subsequent selections are 028, 048, 068, 088, 108, . . . , 768, and 788.

Although they are simpler to use, simple random sampling and systematic sampling are generally less efficient than other, more sophisticated, probability sampling methods. Even greater possibilities for selection bias and lack of representation of the population characteristics occur when using systematic samples than with simple random samples. If there is a pattern in the frame, you could have severe selection biases. To overcome the potential problem of disproportionate representation of specific groups in a sample, you can use either stratified sampling methods or cluster sampling methods.

Stratified Samples

In a **stratified sample**, you first subdivide the N items in the frame into separate subpopulations, or **strata**. A stratum is defined by some common characteristic, such as gender or year in school. You select a simple random sample within each of the strata and combine the results from the separate simple random samples. Stratified sampling is more efficient than either simple random sampling or systematic sampling because you are ensured of the representation of items across the entire population. The homogeneity of items within each stratum provides greater precision in the estimates of underlying population parameters.

EXAMPLE 7.2

Selecting a Stratified Sample

A company wants to select a sample of 32 full-time workers from a population of 800 full-time employees in order to estimate expenditures from a company-sponsored dental plan. Of the full-time employees, 25% are managers and 75% are nonmanagerial workers. How do you select the stratified sample in order for the sample to represent the correct percentage of managers and nonmanagerial workers?

SOLUTION If you assume an 80% response rate, you need to send 40 surveys to get the necessary 32 responses. The frame consists of a listing of the names and e-mail addresses of all $N = 800$ full-time employees included in the company personnel files. Because 25% of the full-time employees are managers, you first separate the frame into two strata: a subpopulation listing of all 200 managerial-level personnel and a separate subpopulation listing of all 600 full-time nonmanagerial workers. Because the first stratum consists of a listing of 200 managers, you assign three-digit code numbers from 001 to 200. Because the second stratum contains a listing of 600 nonmanagerial workers, you assign three-digit code numbers from 001 to 600.

To collect a stratified sample proportional to the sizes of the strata, you select 25% of the overall sample from the first stratum and 75% of the overall sample from the second stratum. You take two separate simple random samples, each of which is based on a distinct random starting point from a table of random numbers (Table E.1). In the first sample, you select 10 managers from the listing of 200 in the first stratum, and in the second sample, you select 30 nonmanagerial workers from the listing of 600 in the second stratum. You then combine the results to reflect the composition of the entire company.

Cluster Samples

In a **cluster sample**, you divide the N items in the frame into several clusters so that each cluster is representative of the entire population. **Clusters** are naturally occurring designations, such as counties, election districts, city blocks, households, or sales territories. You then take a random sample of one or more clusters and study all items in each selected cluster. If clusters are large, a probability-based sample taken from a single cluster is all that is needed.

Cluster sampling is often more cost-effective than simple random sampling, particularly if the population is spread over a wide geographic region. However, cluster sampling often requires a larger sample size to produce results as precise as those from simple random sampling or stratified sampling. A detailed discussion of systematic sampling, stratified sampling, and cluster sampling procedures can be found in reference 1.

Problems for Section 7.1

LEARNING THE BASICS

7.1 For a population containing $N = 902$ individuals, what code number would you assign for
a. the first person on the list?
b. the fortieth person on the list?
c. the last person on the list?

7.2 For a population of $N = 902$, verify that by starting in row 05, column 01 of the table of random numbers (Table E.1), you need only six rows to select a sample of $n = 60$ *without* replacement.

7.3 Given a population of $N = 93$, starting in row 29, column 01 of the table of random numbers (Table E.1), and reading across the row, select a sample of $n = 15$
a. *without* replacement.
b. *with* replacement.

APPLYING THE CONCEPTS

7.4 For a study that consists of personal interviews with participants (rather than mail or phone surveys), explain why simple random sampling might be less practical than some other sampling methods.

7.5 You want to select a random sample of $n = 1$ from a population of three items (which are called A, B, and C). The rule for selecting the sample is: Flip a coin; if it is heads, pick item A; if it is tails, flip the coin again; this time, if it is heads, choose B; if it is tails, choose C. Explain why this is a probability sample but not a simple random sample.

7.6 A population has four members (called A, B, C, and D). You would like to select a random sample of $n = 2$, which you decide to do in the following way: Flip a coin; if it is heads, the sample will be items A and B; if it is tails, the sample will be items C and D. Although this is a random sample, it is not a simple random sample. Explain why. (If you did Problem 7.5, compare the procedure described there with the procedure described in this problem.)

7.7 The registrar of a college with a population of $N = 4,000$ full-time students is asked by the president to conduct a survey to measure satisfaction with the quality of life on campus. The following table contains a breakdown of the 4,000 registered full-time students, by gender and class designation:

Gender	Class Designation				
	Fr.	So.	Jr.	Sr.	Total
Female	700	520	500	480	2,200
Male	560	460	400	380	1,800
Total	1,260	980	900	860	4,000

The registrar intends to take a probability sample of $n = 200$ students and project the results from the sample to the entire population of full-time students.
a. If the frame available from the registrar's files is an alphabetical listing of the names of all $N = 4,000$ registered full-time students, what type of sample could you take? Discuss.
b. What is the advantage of selecting a simple random sample in (a)?
c. What is the advantage of selecting a systematic sample in (a)?
d. If the frame available from the registrar's files is a listing of the names of all $N = 4,000$ registered full-time students compiled from eight separate alphabetical lists, based on the gender and class designation breakdowns shown in the class designation table, what type of sample should you take? Discuss.
e. Suppose that each of the $N = 4,000$ registered full-time students lived in one of the 10 campus dormitories. Each dormitory accommodates 400 students. It is college policy to fully integrate students by gender and class designation in each dormitory. If the registrar is able to compile a listing of all students by dormitory, explain how you could take a cluster sample.

7.8 Prenumbered sales invoices are kept in a sales journal. The invoices are numbered from 0001 to 5000.
a. Beginning in row 16, column 01, and proceeding horizontally in Table E.1, select a simple random sample of 50 invoice numbers.
b. Select a systematic sample of 50 invoice numbers. Use the random numbers in row 20, columns 05–07, as the starting point for your selection.
c. Are the invoices selected in (a) the same as those selected in (b)? Why or why not?

7.9 Suppose that 5,000 sales invoices are separated into four strata. Stratum 1 contains 50 invoices, stratum 2 contains 500 invoices, stratum 3 contains 1,000 invoices, and stratum 4 contains 3,450 invoices. A sample of 500 sales invoices is needed.
a. What type of sampling should you do? Why?
b. Explain how you would carry out the sampling according to the method stated in (a).
c. Why is the sampling in (a) not simple random sampling?

7.2 Evaluating Survey Worthiness

Surveys are used to collect data. Nearly every day, you read or hear about survey or opinion poll results in newspapers, on the Internet, or on radio or television. To identify surveys that lack objectivity or credibility, you must critically evaluate what you read and hear by examining the worthiness of the survey. First, you must evaluate the purpose of the survey, why it was conducted, and for whom it was conducted.

The second step in evaluating the worthiness of a survey is to determine whether it was based on a probability or nonprobability sample (as discussed in Section 7.1). You need to remember that the only way to make valid statistical inferences from a sample to a population is through the use of a probability sample. Surveys that use nonprobability sampling methods are subject to serious, perhaps unintentional, biases that may make the results meaningless.

Survey Error

Even when surveys use random probability sampling methods, they are subject to potential errors. There are four types of survey errors:

- Coverage error
- Nonresponse error
- Sampling error
- Measurement error

Well-designed surveys reduce or minimize these four types of errors, often at considerable cost.

Coverage Error The key to proper sample selection is an adequate frame. Remember, a frame is an up-to-date list of all the items from which you will select the sample. **Coverage error** occurs if certain groups of items are excluded from this frame so that they have no chance of being selected in the sample. Coverage error results in a **selection bias.** If the frame is inadequate because certain groups of items in the population were not properly included, any random probability sample selected will only provide an estimate of the characteristics of the frame, not the *actual* population.

Nonresponse Error Not everyone is willing to respond to a survey. In fact, research has shown that individuals in the upper and lower economic classes tend to respond less frequently to surveys than do people in the middle class. **Nonresponse error** arises from the failure to collect data on all items in the sample and results in a **nonresponse bias.** Because you cannot always assume that persons who do not respond to surveys are similar to those who do, you need to follow up on the nonresponses after a specified period of time. You should make several attempts to convince such individuals to complete the survey. The follow-up responses are then compared to the initial responses in order to make valid inferences from the survey (reference 1). The mode of response you use affects the rate of response. The personal interview and the telephone interview usually produce a higher response rate than does the mail survey—but at a higher cost.

Sampling Error   A sample is selected because it is simpler, less costly, and more efficient. However, chance dictates which individuals or items will or will not be included in the sample. **Sampling error** reflects the variation, or "chance differences," from sample to sample, based on the probability of particular individuals or items being selected in the particular samples.

When you read about the results of surveys or polls in newspapers or magazines, there is often a statement regarding a margin of error, such as "the results of this poll are expected to be within ±4 percentage points of the actual value." This **margin of error** is the sampling error. You can reduce sampling error by taking larger sample sizes, although this also increases the cost of conducting the survey.

Measurement Error   In the practice of good survey research, you design a questionnaire with the intention of gathering meaningful information. But you have a dilemma here: Getting meaningful measurements is often easier said than done. Consider the following proverb:

A person with one watch always knows what time it is;

A person with two watches always searches to identify the correct one;

A person with ten watches is always reminded of the difficulty in measuring time.

Unfortunately, the process of measurement is often governed by what is convenient, not what is needed. The measurements you get are often only a proxy for the ones you really desire. Much attention has been given to measurement error that occurs because of a weakness in question wording (reference 2). A question should be clear, not ambiguous. Furthermore, in order to avoid *leading questions*, you need to present them in a neutral manner.

Three sources of **measurement error** are ambiguous wording of questions, the Hawthorne effect, and respondent error. As an example of ambiguous wording, in November 1993, the U.S. Department of Labor reported that the unemployment rate in the United States had been underestimated for more than a decade because of poor questionnaire wording in the Current Population Survey. In particular, the wording had led to a significant undercount of women in the labor force. Because unemployment rates are tied to benefit programs such as state unemployment compensation, survey researchers had to rectify the situation by adjusting the questionnaire wording.

The "Hawthorne effect" occurs when the respondent feels obligated to please the interviewer. Proper interviewer training can minimize the Hawthorne effect.

Respondent error occurs as a result of an overzealous or underzealous effort by the respondent. You can minimize this error in two ways: (1) by carefully scrutinizing the data and then recontacting those individuals whose responses seem unusual and (2) by establishing a program of recontacting a small number of randomly chosen individuals in order to determine the reliability of the responses.

Ethical Issues

Ethical considerations arise with respect to the four types of potential errors that can occur when designing surveys: coverage error, nonresponse error, sampling error, and measurement error. Coverage error can result in selection bias and becomes an ethical issue if particular groups or individuals are *purposely* excluded from the frame so that the survey results are more favorable to the survey's sponsor. Nonresponse error can lead to nonresponse bias and becomes an ethical issue if the sponsor knowingly designs the survey so that particular groups or individuals are less likely than others to respond. Sampling error becomes an ethical issue if the findings are purposely presented without reference to sample size and margin of error so that the sponsor can promote a viewpoint that might otherwise be truly insignificant. Measurement error becomes an ethical issue in one of three ways: (1) a survey sponsor chooses leading questions that guide the responses in a particular direction; (2) an interviewer, through mannerisms and tone, purposely creates a Hawthorne effect or otherwise guides the responses in a particular direction; or (3) a respondent willfully provides false information.

Ethical issues also arise when the results of nonprobability samples are used to form conclusions about the entire population. When you use a nonprobability sampling method, you need to explain the sampling procedures and state that the results cannot be generalized beyond the sample.

THINK ABOUT THIS | Probability Sampling vs. Web-Based Surveys

In Sections 7.1 and 7.2, you learned that statistical inferences about populations can only be made by analyzing data collected from probability samples. This type of sampling has been the "gold standard" in survey research for more than fifty years. Companies using surveys based on probability sampling typically make a great effort (and spend large sums) to deal with coverage error, nonresponse error, sampling error, and measurement error.

A recent article (T. Crampton, "About Online Surveys, Traditional Pollsters Are Somewhat Disappointed," **http://www.nytimes.com/2007/05/31/business media**), reported that some survey companies are offering an Internet alternative to traditional surveys based on random sampling. YouGov, a British company, is planning to introduce Internet-based polling in the United States for the 2008 presidential election.

YouGov uses a large panel of respondents who answer questions online. These panelists

supposedly come from a diverse group with special efforts made to include people who are less likely to use the Internet. In addition, panelists are paid to participate. This method of sampling (and the fact that respondents are paid and are not volunteers) makes Web-based sampling scientifically unacceptable to traditional pollsters.

Despite these concerns, YouGov has partnered with Polimetrix, an online company based in Palo Alto, California, to conduct surveys in the United States. The founder of Polimetrix, Professor Douglas Rivers of Stanford University, claims that the margin of error of Polimetrix polls is similar to telephone polls. YouGov's chief executive, Nadhim Zahawi, points out that modern technology, such as cell phones, has made old-fashioned polls more unreliable due to the increased difficulty of contacting people at home. In fact, a recent article (M. Thee, "Cellphones Challenge Poll Sampling," *The New York Times*, December 7, 2007, p. A27) indicated that cell-

phone-only households make up 16% of the households in the United States.

However, Leendert de Voogd, managing director of TSN Opinion in Brussels, believes that "Internet polling is like the Wild West, with no rules, no sheriff, and no reference points." He believes that only polling with probability sampling will deliver valid results. On the other hand, Professor Anthony King of the University of Essex does not believe that Internet polling fails to reflect a nation's population. According to Professor King, "There is no evidence to suggest that people who use the Internet are fundamentally different from those without it. One mad, awful lady living in a poor neighborhood without Internet does not differ much from her mad, awful friend next door who goes online." Perhaps only time will tell who is right.

Problems for Section 7.2

APPLYING THE CONCEPTS

7.10 "A survey indicates that the vast majority of college students own their own personal computers." What information would you want to know before you accepted the results of this survey?

7.11 A simple random sample of $n = 300$ full-time employees is selected from a company list containing the names of all $N = 5,000$ full-time employees in order to evaluate job satisfaction.
a. Give an example of possible coverage error.
b. Give an example of possible nonresponse error.
c. Give an example of possible sampling error.
d. Give an example of possible measurement error.

7.12 Business professor Thomas Callarman traveled to China more than a dozen times from 2000 to 2005. He warns people about believing everything they read about surveys conducted in China and gives two specific reasons. Callarman stated, "First, things are changing so rapidly that what you hear today may not be true tomorrow. Second, the people who answer the surveys may tell you what they think you want to hear, rather than what they really believe" (T. E. Callarman, "Some Thoughts on China," *Decision Line*, March, 2006, pp. 1, 43–44).

a. List the four types of survey error discussed in this section.
b. Which of the types of survey errors in (a) are the basis for Professor Callarman's two reasons to question the surveys being conducted in China?

7.13 A recent survey of college freshmen investigated the amount of involvement their parents have with decisions concerning their education. When asked about the decision to go to college, 84% said their parents' involvement was about right, 10.3% said too much, and 5.7% said too little. When it came to selecting individual courses, 72.5% said their parents' involvement was about right, 3.5% said too much, and 24.0% said too little (M. B. Marklein, "Study: Colleges Shouldn't Fret Over Hands-On Parents," **usatoday.com**, January 23, 2008). What additional information would you want to know about the survey before you accepted the results of the study?

7.14 Seventy-three percent of Americans say now is a bad time to find a quality job, according to a Gallup Poll taken May 16, 2008. ("Americans' Job Market Worries," *The Gallup Poll*, **galluppoll.com**, May 16, 2008.) What additional information would you want to know before you accepted the results of the survey?

7.3 Sampling Distributions

In many applications, you want to make inferences that are based on statistics calculated from samples to estimate the values of population parameters. In the next two sections, you will learn about how the sample mean (a statistic) is used to estimate the population mean (a parameter) and how the sample proportion (a statistic) is used to estimate the population proportion (a parameter). Your main concern when making a statistical inference is drawing conclusions about a population, *not* about a sample. For example, a political pollster is interested in the sample results only as a way of estimating the actual proportion of the votes that each candidate will receive from the population of voters. Likewise, as plant operations manager for Oxford Cereals, you are only interested in using the sample mean weight calculated from a sample of cereal boxes for estimating the mean weight contained in a population of boxes.

In practice, you select a single random sample of a predetermined size from the population. Hypothetically, to use the sample statistic to estimate the population parameter, you could examine *every* possible sample of a given size that could occur. A **sampling distribution** is the distribution of the results if you actually selected all possible samples. The single result you obtain in practice is just one of the results in the sampling distribution.

7.4 Sampling Distribution of the Mean

In Chapter 3, several measures of central tendency, including the mean, median, and mode, were discussed. Undoubtedly, the mean is the most widely used measure of central tendency. The sample mean is often used to estimate the population mean. The **sampling distribution of the mean** is the distribution of all possible sample means if you select all possible samples of a given size.

The Unbiased Property of the Sample Mean

The sample mean is **unbiased** because the mean of all the possible sample means (of a given sample size, n) is equal to the population mean, μ. A simple example concerning a population of four administrative assistants demonstrates this property. Each assistant is asked to type the same page of a manuscript. Table 7.2 presents the number of errors. This population distribution is shown in Figure 7.2.

TABLE 7.2

Number of Errors Made by Each of Four Administrative Assistants

Administrative Assistant	Number of Errors
Ann	$X_1 = 3$
Bob	$X_2 = 2$
Carla	$X_3 = 1$
Dave	$X_4 = 4$

FIGURE 7.2

Number of errors made by a population of four administrative assistants

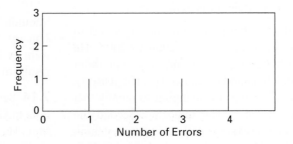

When you have the data from a population, you compute the mean by using Equation (7.1).

POPULATION MEAN

The population mean is the sum of the values in the population divided by the population size, N.

$$\mu = \frac{\sum_{i=1}^{N} X_i}{N} \tag{7.1}$$

You compute the population standard deviation, σ, using Equation (7.2):

POPULATION STANDARD DEVIATION

$$\sigma = \sqrt{\frac{\sum_{i=1}^{N} (X_i - \mu)^2}{N}} \tag{7.2}$$

Thus, for the data of Table 7.2,

$$\mu = \frac{3 + 2 + 1 + 4}{4} = 2.5 \text{ errors}$$

and

$$\sigma = \sqrt{\frac{(3 - 2.5)^2 + (2 - 2.5)^2 + (1 - 2.5)^2 + (4 - 2.5)^2}{4}} = 1.12 \text{ errors}$$

If you select samples of two administrative assistants *with* replacement from this population, there are 16 possible samples ($N^n = 4^2 = 16$). Table 7.3 lists the 16 possible sample outcomes. If you average all 16 of these sample means, the mean of these values, $\mu_{\bar{X}}$, is equal to 2.5, which is also the mean of the population μ.

TABLE 7.3

All 16 Samples of $n = 2$ Administrative Assistants from a Population of $N = 4$ Administrative Assistants When Sampling with Replacement

Sample	Administrative Assistants	Sample Outcomes	Sample Means
1	Ann, Ann	3, 3	$\bar{X}_1 = 3$
2	Ann, Bob	3, 2	$\bar{X}_2 = 2.5$
3	Ann, Carla	3, 1	$\bar{X}_3 = 2$
4	Ann, Dave	3, 4	$\bar{X}_4 = 3.5$
5	Bob, Ann	2, 3	$\bar{X}_5 = 2.5$
6	Bob, Bob	2, 2	$\bar{X}_6 = 2$
7	Bob, Carla	2, 1	$\bar{X}_7 = 1.5$
8	Bob, Dave	2, 4	$\bar{X}_8 = 3$
9	Carla, Ann	1, 3	$\bar{X}_9 = 2$
10	Carla, Bob	1, 2	$\bar{X}_{10} = 1.5$
11	Carla, Carla	1, 1	$\bar{X}_{11} = 1$
12	Carla, Dave	1, 4	$\bar{X}_{12} = 2.5$
13	Dave, Ann	4, 3	$\bar{X}_{13} = 3.5$
14	Dave, Bob	4, 2	$\bar{X}_{14} = 3$
15	Dave, Carla	4, 1	$\bar{X}_{15} = 2.5$
16	Dave, Dave	4, 4	$\bar{X}_{16} = 4$
			$\mu_{\bar{X}} = 2.5$

Because the mean of the 16 sample means is equal to the population mean, the sample mean is an unbiased estimator of the population mean. Therefore, although you do not know how close the sample mean of any particular sample selected comes to the population mean, you are at least assured that the mean of all the possible sample means that could have been selected is equal to the population mean.

Standard Error of the Mean

Figure 7.3 illustrates the variation in the sample means when selecting all 16 possible samples. In this small example, although the sample means vary from sample to sample, depending on which two administrative assistants are selected, the sample means do not vary as much as the individual values in the population. That the sample means are less variable than the individual values in the population follows directly from the fact that each sample mean averages together all the values in the sample. A population consists of individual outcomes that can take on a wide range of values, from extremely small to extremely large. However, if a sample contains an extreme value, although this value will have an effect on the sample mean, the effect is reduced because the value is averaged with all the other values in the sample. As the sample size increases, the effect of a single extreme value becomes smaller because it is averaged with more values.

FIGURE 7.3

Sampling distribution of the mean, based on all possible samples containing two administrative assistants

Source: Data are from Table 7.3

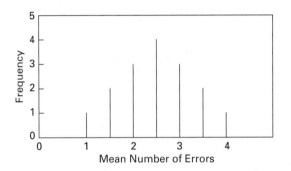

The value of the standard deviation of all possible sample means, called the **standard error of the mean**, expresses how the sample means vary from sample to sample. Equation (7.3) defines the standard error of the mean when sampling *with* replacement or *without* replacement from large or infinite populations.

STANDARD ERROR OF THE MEAN

The standard error of the mean, $\sigma_{\bar{X}}$, is equal to the standard deviation in the population, σ, divided by the square root of the sample size, n.

$$\sigma_{\bar{X}} = \frac{\sigma}{\sqrt{n}} \qquad (7.3)$$

Therefore, as the sample size increases, the standard error of the mean decreases by a factor equal to the square root of the sample size.

You can also use Equation (7.3) as an approximation of the standard error of the mean when the sample is selected without replacement if the sample contains less than 5% of the entire population. Example 7.3 computes the standard error of the mean for such a situation.

EXAMPLE 7.3

Computing the Standard Error of the Mean

Returning to the cereal-filling process described in the Using Statistics scenario on page 209, if you randomly select a sample of 25 boxes without replacement from the thousands of boxes filled during a shift, the sample contains far less than 5% of the population. Given that the standard deviation of the cereal-filling process is 15 grams, compute the standard error of the mean.

SOLUTION Using Equation (7.3) with $n = 25$ and $\sigma = 15$, the standard error of the mean is

$$\sigma_{\bar{X}} = \frac{\sigma}{\sqrt{n}} = \frac{15}{\sqrt{25}} = \frac{15}{5} = 3$$

The variation in the sample means for samples of $n = 25$ is much less than the variation in the individual boxes of cereal (i.e., $\sigma_{\bar{X}} = 3$ while $\sigma = 15$).

Sampling from Normally Distributed Populations

Now that the concept of a sampling distribution has been introduced and the standard error of the mean has been defined, what distribution will the sample mean, $\overline{X}$, follow? If you are sampling from a population that is normally distributed with mean, μ, and standard deviation, σ, then regardless of the sample size, n, the sampling distribution of the mean is normally distributed, with mean, $\mu_{\overline{X}} = \mu$, and standard error of the mean, $\sigma_{\overline{X}} = \sigma/\sqrt{n}$.

In the simplest case, if you take samples of size $n = 1$, each possible sample mean is a single value from the population because

$$\overline{X} = \frac{\sum_{i=1}^{n} X_i}{n} = \frac{X_1}{1} = X_1$$

Therefore, if the population is normally distributed, with mean, μ, and standard deviation, σ, the sampling distribution of $\overline{X}$ for samples of $n = 1$ must also follow the normal distribution, with mean $\mu_{\overline{X}} = \mu$ and standard error of the mean $\sigma_{\overline{X}} = \sigma/\sqrt{1} = \sigma$. In addition, as the sample size increases, the sampling distribution of the mean still follows a normal distribution, with $\mu_{\overline{X}} = \mu$, but the standard error of the mean decreases, so that a larger proportion of sample means are closer to the population mean. Figure 7.4 below illustrates this reduction in variability. Note that 500 samples of 1, 2, 4, 8, 16, and 32 were randomly selected from a normally distributed population. From the polygons in Figure 7.4, you can see that, although the sampling distribution of the mean is approximately[1] normal for each sample size, the sample means are distributed more tightly around the population mean as the sample size increases.

[1]Remember that "only" 500 samples out of an infinite number of samples have been selected, so that the sampling distributions shown are only approximations of the true population distributions.

FIGURE 7.4

Sampling distributions of the mean from 500 samples of sizes $n = 1, 2, 4, 8, 16,$ and 32 selected from a normal population

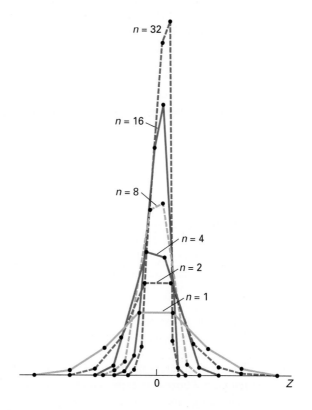

To further examine the concept of the sampling distribution of the mean, consider the Using Statistics scenario described on page 209. The packaging equipment that is filling 368-gram boxes of cereal is set so that the amount of cereal in a box is normally distributed, with a mean of 368 grams. From past experience, you know the population standard deviation for this filling process is 15 grams.

If you randomly select a sample of 25 boxes from the many thousands that are filled in a day and the mean weight is computed for this sample, what type of result could you expect? For example, do you think that the sample mean could be 368 grams? 200 grams? 365 grams?

The sample acts as a miniature representation of the population, so if the values in the population are normally distributed, the values in the sample should be approximately normally distributed. Thus, if the population mean is 368 grams, the sample mean has a good chance of being close to 368 grams.

How can you determine the probability that the sample of 25 boxes will have a mean below 365 grams? From the normal distribution (Section 6.2), you know that you can find the area below any value X by converting to standardized Z values:

$$Z = \frac{X - \mu}{\sigma}$$

In the examples in Section 6.2, you studied how any single value, X, differs from the population mean. Now, in this example, you want to study how a sample mean, $\overline{X}$ differs from the population mean. Substituting $\overline{X}$ for X, $\mu_{\overline{X}}$ for μ, and $\sigma_{\overline{X}}$ for σ in the equation above results in Equation (7.4).

FINDING Z FOR THE SAMPLING DISTRIBUTION OF THE MEAN

The Z value is equal to the difference between the sample mean, $\overline{X}$, and the population mean, μ, divided by the standard error of the mean, $\sigma_{\overline{X}}$.

$$Z = \frac{\overline{X} - \mu_{\overline{X}}}{\sigma_{\overline{X}}} = \frac{\overline{X} - \mu}{\dfrac{\sigma}{\sqrt{n}}} \tag{7.4}$$

To find the area below 365 grams, from Equation (7.4),

$$Z = \frac{\overline{X} - \mu_{\overline{X}}}{\sigma_{\overline{X}}} = \frac{365 - 368}{\dfrac{15}{\sqrt{25}}} = \frac{-3}{3} = -1.00$$

The area corresponding to $Z = -1.00$ in Table E.2 is 0.1587. Therefore, 15.87% of all the possible samples of 25 boxes have a sample mean below 365 grams.

The preceding statement is not the same as saying that a certain percentage of *individual* boxes will have less than 365 grams of cereal. You compute that percentage as follows:

$$Z = \frac{X - \mu}{\sigma} = \frac{365 - 368}{15} = \frac{-3}{15} = -0.20$$

The area corresponding to $Z = -0.20$ in Table E.2 is 0.4207. Therefore, 42.07% of the *individual* boxes are expected to contain less than 365 grams. Comparing these results, you see that many more *individual boxes* than *sample means* are below 365 grams. This result is explained by the fact that each sample consists of 25 different values, some small and some large. The averaging process dilutes the importance of any individual value, particularly when the sample size is large. Thus, the chance that the sample mean of 25 boxes is far away from the population mean is less than the chance that a *single* box is far away.

Examples 7.4 and 7.5 show how these results are affected by using different sample sizes.

EXAMPLE 7.4

The Effect of Sample Size *n* on the Computation of $\sigma_{\overline{X}}$

How is the standard error of the mean affected by increasing the sample size from 25 to 100 boxes?

SOLUTION If $n = 100$ boxes, then using Equation (7.3) on page 220:

$$\sigma_{\overline{X}} = \frac{\sigma}{\sqrt{n}} = \frac{15}{\sqrt{100}} = \frac{15}{10} = 1.5$$

The fourfold increase in the sample size from 25 to 100 reduces the standard error of the mean by half—from 3 grams to 1.5 grams. This demonstrates that taking a larger sample results in less variability in the sample means from sample to sample.

EXAMPLE 7.5

The Effect of Sample Size *n* on the Clustering of Means in the Sampling Distribution

If you select a sample of 100 boxes, what is the probability that the sample mean is below 365 grams?

SOLUTION Using Equation (7.4) on page 222,

$$Z = \frac{\overline{X} - \mu_{\overline{X}}}{\sigma_{\overline{X}}} = \frac{365 - 368}{\dfrac{15}{\sqrt{100}}} = \frac{-3}{1.5} = -2.00$$

From Table E.2, the area less than $Z = -2.00$ is 0.0228. Therefore, 2.28% of the samples of 100 boxes have means below 365 grams, as compared with 15.87% for samples of 25 boxes.

Sometimes you need to find the interval that contains a fixed proportion of the sample means. You need to determine a distance below and above the population mean containing a specific area of the normal curve. From Equation (7.4) on page 222,

$$Z = \frac{\overline{X} - \mu}{\dfrac{\sigma}{\sqrt{n}}}$$

Solving for $\overline{X}$ results in Equation (7.5).

FINDING $\overline{X}$ FOR THE SAMPLING DISTRIBUTION OF THE MEAN

$$\overline{X} = \mu + Z\frac{\sigma}{\sqrt{n}} \tag{7.5}$$

Example 7.6 illustrates the use of Equation (7.5).

EXAMPLE 7.6

Determining the Interval That Includes a Fixed Proportion of the Sample Means

In the cereal-fill example, find an interval symmetrically distributed around the population mean that will include 95% of the sample means based on samples of 25 boxes.

SOLUTION If 95% of the sample means are in the interval, then 5% are outside the interval. Divide the 5% into two equal parts of 2.5%. The value of Z in Table E.2 corresponding to an area of 0.0250 in the lower tail of the normal curve is -1.96, and the value of Z corresponding to a cumulative area of 0.9750 (i.e., 0.0250 in the upper tail of the normal curve) is $+1.96$. The lower value of $\overline{X}$ (called $\overline{X}_L$) and the upper value of $\overline{X}$ (called $\overline{X}_U$) are found by using Equation (7.5):

$$\overline{X}_L = 368 + (-1.96)\frac{15}{\sqrt{25}} = 368 - 5.88 = 362.12$$

$$\overline{X}_U = 368 + (1.96)\frac{15}{\sqrt{25}} = 368 + 5.88 = 373.88$$

Therefore, 95% of all sample means based on samples of 25 boxes are between 362.12 and 373.88 grams.

Sampling from Non-Normally Distributed Populations—The Central Limit Theorem

Thus far in this section, only the sampling distribution of the mean for a normally distributed population has been considered. However, in many instances, either you know that the population is not normally distributed or it is unrealistic to assume that the population is normally distributed. An important theorem in statistics, the Central Limit Theorem, deals with this situation.

THE CENTRAL LIMIT THEOREM

The **Central Limit Theorem** states that as the sample size (i.e., the number of values in each sample) gets *large enough*, the sampling distribution of the mean is approximately normally distributed. This is true regardless of the shape of the distribution of the individual values in the population.

What sample size is large enough? A great deal of statistical research has gone into this issue. As a general rule, statisticians have found that for many population distributions, when the sample size is at least 30, the sampling distribution of the mean is approximately normal. However, you can apply the Central Limit Theorem for even smaller sample sizes if the population distribution is approximately bell shaped. In the uncommon case in which the distribution is extremely skewed or has more than one mode, you may need sample sizes larger than 30 to ensure normality.

Figure 7.5 illustrates the application of the Central Limit Theorem to different populations. The sampling distributions from three different continuous distributions (normal, uniform, and exponential) for varying sample sizes ($n = 2, 5, 30$) are displayed.

FIGURE 7.5

Sampling distribution of the mean for different populations for samples of $n = 2$, 5, and 30

See Section E7.2, P7.2, or M7.2 to create a simulated sampling distribution.

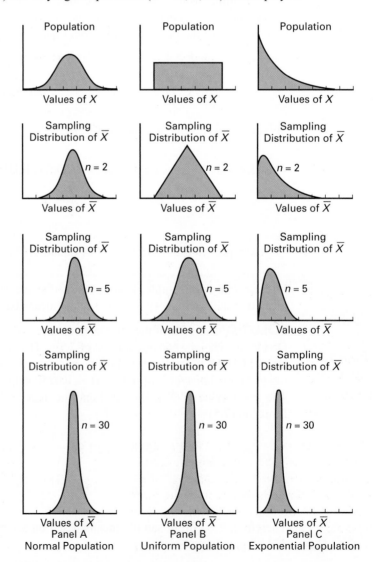

Panel A
Normal Population

Panel B
Uniform Population

Panel C
Exponential Population

In each of the panels, because the sample mean has the property of being unbiased, the mean of any sampling distribution is always equal to the mean of the population.

Panel A of Figure 7.5 shows the sampling distribution of the mean selected from a normal population. As mentioned earlier in this section, when the population is normally distributed, the sampling distribution of the mean is normally distributed for any sample size. [You can measure the variability by using the standard error of the mean, Equation (7.3), on page 220.]

Panel B of Figure 7.5 depicts the sampling distribution from a population with a uniform (or rectangular) distribution (see Section 6.1). When samples of size $n = 2$ are selected, there is a peaking, or *central limiting*, effect already working. For $n = 5$, the sampling distribution is bell shaped and approximately normal. When $n = 30$, the sampling distribution looks very similar to a normal distribution. In general, the larger the sample size, the more closely the sampling distribution will follow a normal distribution. As with all cases, the mean of each sampling distribution is equal to the mean of the population, and the variability decreases as the sample size increases.

Panel C of Figure 7.5 presents an exponential distribution (see Section 6.1). This population is extremely right-skewed. When $n = 2$, the sampling distribution is still highly right-skewed but less so than the distribution of the population. For $n = 5$, the sampling distribution is slightly right-skewed. When $n = 30$, the sampling distribution looks approximately normal. Again, the mean of each sampling distribution is equal to the mean of the population, and the variability decreases as the sample size increases.

Using the results from the normal, uniform, and exponential distributions, you can reach the following conclusions regarding the Central Limit Theorem:

- For most population distributions, regardless of shape, the sampling distribution of the mean is approximately normally distributed if samples of at least size 30 are selected.
- If the population distribution is fairly symmetric, the sampling distribution of the mean is approximately normal for samples as small as size 5.
- If the population is normally distributed, the sampling distribution of the mean is normally distributed, regardless of the sample size.

The Central Limit Theorem is of crucial importance in using statistical inference to draw conclusions about a population. It allows you to make inferences about the population mean without having to know the specific shape of the population distribution.

VISUAL EXPLORATIONS   Exploring Sampling Distributions

Use the Visual Explorations **Two Dice Probability** procedure to observe the effects of simulated throws on the frequency distribution of the sum of the two dice. Open the `Visual Explorations.xla` add-in workbook and select **VisualExplorations → Two Dice Probability** (Excel 97-2003) or **Add-Ins → VisualExplorations → Two Dice Probability** (Excel 2007). The procedure produces a worksheet that contains an empty frequency distribution table and histogram and a floating control panel (see right).

Click the **Tally** button to tally a set of throws in the frequency distribution table and histogram. Optionally, use the spinner buttons to adjust the number of throws per tally (round). Click the **Help** button for more information about this simulation. Click **Finish** when you are done with this exploration.

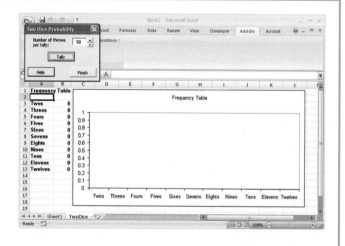

Problems for Section 7.4

LEARNING THE BASICS

7.15 Given a normal distribution with $\mu = 100$ and $\sigma = 10$, if you select a sample of $n = 25$, what is the probability that $\overline{X}$ is
a. less than 95?
b. between 95 and 97.5?
c. above 102.2?
d. There is a 65% chance that $\overline{X}$ is above what value?

7.16 Given a normal distribution with $\mu = 50$ and $\sigma = 5$, if you select a sample of $n = 100$, what is the probability that $\overline{X}$ is
a. less than 47?
b. between 47 and 49.5?
c. above 51.1?
d. There is a 35% chance that $\overline{X}$ is above what value?

APPLYING THE CONCEPTS

7.17 For each of the following three populations, indicate what the sampling distribution for samples of 25 would consist of:
a. Travel expense vouchers for a university in an academic year
b. Absentee records (days absent per year) in 2007 for employees of a large manufacturing company
c. Yearly sales (in gallons) of unleaded gasoline at service stations located in a particular state

7.18 The following data represent the number of days absent per year in a population of six employees of a small company:

$$1 \quad 3 \quad 6 \quad 7 \quad 9 \quad 10$$

a. Assuming that you sample without replacement, select all possible samples of $n = 2$ and construct the sampling distribution of the mean. Compute the mean of all the sample means and also compute the population mean. Are they equal? What is this property called?
b. Repeat (a) for all possible samples of $n = 3$.
c. Compare the shape of the sampling distribution of the mean in (a) and (b). Which sampling distribution has less variability? Why?
d. Assuming that you sample with replacement, repeat (a) through (c) and compare the results. Which sampling distributions have the least variability—those in (a) or (b)? Why?

7.19 The diameter of a brand of Ping-Pong balls is approximately normally distributed, with a mean of 1.30 inches and a standard deviation of 0.04 inch. If you select a random sample of 16 Ping-Pong balls,
a. what is the sampling distribution of the mean?

b. what is the probability that the sample mean is less than 1.28 inches?
c. what is the probability that the sample mean is between 1.31 and 1.33 inches?
d. The probability is 60% that the sample mean will be between what two values, symmetrically distributed around the population mean?

7.20 The U.S. Census Bureau announced that the median sales price of new houses sold in February 2008 was $244,100, whereas the mean sales price was $296,400 (**www.census.gov/newhomesales**, March 28, 2008). Assume that the standard deviation of the prices is $90,000.
a. If you select samples of $n = 2$, describe the shape of the sampling distribution of $\overline{X}$.
b. If you select samples of $n = 100$, describe the shape of the sampling distribution of $\overline{X}$.
c. If you select a random sample of $n = 100$, what is the probability that the sample mean will be less than $300,000?
d. If you select a random sample of $n = 100$, what is the probability that the sample mean will be between $275,000 and $290,000?

7.21 Time spent using e-mail per session is normally distributed, with $\mu = 8$ minutes and $\sigma = 2$ minutes. If you select a random sample of 25 sessions,
a. what is the probability that the sample mean is between 7.8 and 8.2 minutes?
b. what is the probability that the sample mean is between 7.5 and 8 minutes?
c. If you select a random sample of 100 sessions, what is the probability that the sample mean is between 7.8 and 8.2 minutes?
d. Explain the difference in the results of (a) and (c).

✓ SELF Test **7.22** The amount of time a bank teller spends with each customer has a population mean, μ, of 3.10 minutes and standard deviation, σ, of 0.40 minute. If you select a random sample of 16 customers,
a. what is the probability that the mean time spent per customer is at least 3 minutes?
b. there is an 85% chance that the sample mean is less than how many minutes?
c. What assumption must you make in order to solve (a) and (b)?
d. If you select a random sample of 64 customers, there is an 85% chance that the sample mean is less than how many minutes?

7.5 Sampling Distribution of the Proportion

Consider a categorical variable that has only two categories, such as the customer prefers your brand or the customer prefers the competitor's brand. Of interest is the proportion of items belonging to one of the categories—for example, the proportion of customers that prefers your brand. The population proportion, represented by π, is the proportion of items in the entire population with the characteristic of interest. The sample proportion, represented by p, is the proportion of items in the sample with the characteristic of interest. The sample proportion, a statistic, is used to estimate the population proportion, a parameter. To calculate the sample proportion, you assign the two possible outcomes scores of 1 or 0 to represent the presence or absence of the characteristic. You then sum all the 1 and 0 scores and divide by n, the sample size. For example, if, in a sample of five customers, three preferred your brand and two did not, you have three 1s and two 0s. Summing the three 1s and two 0s and dividing by the sample size of 5 gives you a sample proportion of 0.60.

SAMPLE PROPORTION

$$p = \frac{X}{n} = \frac{\text{Number of items having the characteristic of interest}}{\text{Sample size}} \qquad (7.6)$$

The sample proportion, p, takes on values between 0 and 1. If all items have the characteristic, you assign each a score of 1, and p is equal to 1. If half the items have the characteristic, you assign half a score of 1 and assign the other half a score of 0, and p is equal to 0.5. If none of the items have the characteristic, you assign each a score of 0, and p is equal to 0.

In Section 7.4, you learned that the sample mean, $\overline{X}$, is an unbiased estimator of the population mean, μ. Similarly, the statistic p is an unbiased estimator of the population proportion, π.

By analogy to the sampling distribution of the mean whose standard error is $\sigma_{\overline{X}} = \dfrac{\sigma}{\sqrt{n}}$, the **standard error of the proportion**, σ_p, is given in Equation (7.7).

STANDARD ERROR OF THE PROPORTION

$$\sigma_p = \sqrt{\frac{\pi(1 - \pi)}{n}} \qquad (7.7)$$

The **sampling distribution of the proportion** follows the binomial distribution, as discussed in Section 5.2. However, you can use the normal distribution to approximate the binomial distribution when $n\pi$ and $n(1 - \pi)$ are each at least 5. In most cases in which inferences are made about the proportion, the sample size is substantial enough to meet the conditions for using the normal approximation (see reference 1). Therefore, in many instances, you can use the normal distribution to estimate the sampling distribution of the proportion.

Substituting p for $\overline{X}$, π for μ, and $\sqrt{\dfrac{\pi(1 - \pi)}{n}}$ for $\dfrac{\sigma}{\sqrt{n}}$ in Equation (7.4) on page 222 results in Equation (7.8).

FINDING Z FOR THE SAMPLING DISTRIBUTION OF THE PROPORTION

$$Z = \frac{p - \pi}{\sqrt{\dfrac{\pi(1 - \pi)}{n}}} \qquad (7.8)$$

To illustrate the sampling distribution of the proportion, suppose that the manager of the local branch of a bank determines that 40% of all depositors have multiple accounts at the bank. If you select a random sample of 200 depositors, the probability that the sample proportion of depositors with multiple accounts is less than 0.30 is calculated as follows: Because

$n\pi = 200(0.40) = 80 \geq 5$ and $n(1 - \pi) = 200(0.60) = 120 \geq 5$, the sample size is large enough to assume that the sampling distribution of the proportion is approximately normally distributed. Using Equation (7.8),

$$Z = \frac{p - \pi}{\sqrt{\dfrac{\pi(1 - \pi)}{n}}}$$

$$= \frac{0.30 - 0.40}{\sqrt{\dfrac{(0.40)(0.60)}{200}}} = \frac{-0.10}{\sqrt{\dfrac{0.24}{200}}} = \frac{-0.10}{0.0346}$$

$$= -2.89$$

Using Table E.2, the area under the normal curve less than -2.89 is 0.0019. Therefore, if the true proportion of items of interest in the population is 0.40, then only 0.19% of the samples of $n = 200$ would be expected to have sample proportions less than 0.30.

Problems for Section 7.5

LEARNING THE BASICS

7.23 In a random sample of 64 people, 48 are classified as "successful."
a. Determine the sample proportion, p, of "successful" people.
b. If the population proportion is 0.70, determine the standard error of the proportion.

7.24 A random sample of 50 households was selected for a telephone survey. The key question asked was, "Do you or any member of your household own a cellular telephone with a built-in camera?" Of the 50 respondents, 15 said yes and 35 said no.
a. Determine the sample proportion, p, of households with cellular telephones with built-in cameras.
b. If the population proportion is 0.40, determine the standard error of the proportion.

7.25 The following data represent the responses (Y for yes and N for no) from a sample of 40 college students to the question "Do you currently own shares in any stocks?"

```
N N Y N N Y N Y N Y N N Y N Y Y N N N Y
N Y N N N N Y N N Y Y N N N Y N N Y N N
```

a. Determine the sample proportion, p, of college students who own shares of stock.
b. If the population proportion is 0.30, determine the standard error of the proportion.

APPLYING THE CONCEPTS

✓ SELF Test **7.26** A political pollster is conducting an analysis of sample results in order to make predictions on election night. Assuming a two-candidate election, if a spe-cific candidate receives at least 55% of the vote in the sam-ple, then that candidate will be forecast as the winner of the election. If you select a random sample of 100 voters, what is the probability that a candidate will be forecast as the winner when
a. the true percentage of her vote is 50.1%?
b. the true percentage of her vote is 60%?
c. the true percentage of her vote is 49% (and she will actu-ally lose the election)?
d. If the sample size is increased to 400, what are your answers to (a) through (c)? Discuss.

7.27 You plan to conduct a marketing experiment in which students are to taste one of two different brands of soft drink. Their task is to correctly identify the brand tasted. You select a random sample of 200 students and assume that the stu-dents have no ability to distinguish between the two brands. (Hint: If an individual has no ability to distinguish between the two soft drinks, then each brand is equally likely to be selected.)
a. What is the probability that the sample will have between 50% and 60% of the identifications correct?
b. The probability is 90% that the sample percentage is con-tained within what symmetrical limits of the population percentage?
c. What is the probability that the sample percentage of cor-rect identifications is greater than 65%?
d. Which is more likely to occur—more than 60% correct identifications in the sample of 200 or more than 55% correct identifications in a sample of 1,000? Explain.

7.28 An online quiz available at **www.pewinternet.org/ quiz** divides up people according to their usage of the com-puter. In a survey of 4,001 respondents, 8% were classified as productivity enhancers who are comfortable with technology and use the Internet for its practical value (M. Himowitz, "How to Tell What Kind of Tech User You Are," *Newsday*, May 27, 2007, p. F6). Suppose you select a sample of 400 students at your school, and the population proportion of productivity enhancers is 0.08.

a. What is the probability that in the sample, less than 10% of the students will be productivity enhancers?

b. What is the probability that in the sample, between 6% and 10% of the students will be productivity enhancers?

c. What is the probability that in the sample, more than 5% of the students will be productivity enhancers?

d. If a sample of 100 is taken, how does this change your answers to (a) through (c)?

7.29 Companies often make flextime scheduling available to help recruit and keep women employees who have children at home. Other workers sometimes view these flextime schedules as unfair. An article in *USA Today* indicates that 25% of male employees state that they have to pick up the slack for moms working flextime schedules (D. Jones, "Poll Finds Resentment of Flextime," **usatoday.com**, May 11, 2007). Suppose you select a random sample of 100 male employees working for companies offering flextime.

a. What is the probability that 25% or fewer male employees will indicate that they have to pick up the slack for moms working flextime?

b. What is the probability that 20% or fewer will indicate that they have to pick up the slack for moms working flextime?

c. If a random sample of 500 is taken, how does this change your answers to (a) and (b)?

7.30 According to Gallup's poll on personal finances, 46% of U.S. workers say they feel they will have enough money to live comfortably when they retire. (*The Gallup Poll*, **galluppoll.com**, May 6, 2008.) If you select a random sample of 200 U.S. workers,

a. what is the probability that the sample will have between 45% and 55% who say they have enough money to live comfortably now and expect to do so in the future?

b. the probability is 90% that the sample percentage will be contained within what symmetrical limits of the population percentage?

c. the probability is 95% that the sample percentage will be contained within what symmetrical limits of the population percentage?

7.31 New research shows (J. O'Donnell, "Gen Y Sits on Top of Consumer Food Chain," *USA Today*, October 11, 2006, p. 3B) that members of generation Y (people born from 1982 to 2000) have a great say in household purchases. Specifically, 68% of Gen Y people have a say in computer purchases. Suppose you select a sample of 100 Gen Y respondents.

a. What is the probability that the sample percentage will be contained between 65% and 75%?

b. The probability is 90% that the sample percentage will be contained within what symmetrical limits of the population percentage?

c. The probability is 95% that the sample percentage will be contained within what symmetrical limits of the population percentage?

d. Suppose you selected a sample of 400 respondents. How does this change your answers in (a) through (c)?

7.32 Yahoo HotJobs reported that 56% of full-time office workers believe that dressing-down can affect jobs, salaries, or promotions (J. Yang and K. Carter, "Dress Can Affect Size of Paycheck," **usatoday.com**, May 9, 2007).

a. Suppose that you take a sample of 100 full-time workers. If the true population proportion of workers who believe that dressing-down can affect jobs, salaries, or promotions is 0.56, what is the probability that less than half in your sample hold that same belief?

b. Suppose that you take a sample of 500 full-time workers. If the true population proportion of workers who believe that dressing-down can affect jobs, salaries, or promotions is 0.56, what is the probability that less than half in your sample hold that same belief?

c. Discuss the effect of sample size on the sampling distribution of the proportion in general, and the effect on the probabilities in (a) and (b).

USING STATISTICS @ Oxford Cereals Revisited

As the plant operations manager for Oxfords Cereals, you were responsible for monitoring the amount of cereal placed in each box. To be consistent with package labeling, boxes should contain a mean of 368 grams of cereal. Thousands of boxes are produced during a shift, and thus weighing every single box was determined to be too time-consuming, costly, and inefficient. Instead a sample of boxes was selected. Based on your analysis of the sample, you had to decide whether to maintain, alter, or shut down the process.

Using the concept of the sampling distribution of the mean, you were able to determine probabilities that such a sample mean could have been randomly selected from a population with a mean of 368 grams. Specifically, if a sample of size $n = 25$ is selected from a population with a mean of 368 and standard deviation of 15, you calculated that the probability of selecting a sample with a mean of 365 grams or less to be 15.87%. If a larger sample size is selected, the sample mean should be closer to the population mean. This result was illustrated when you calculated the probability if the sample size were increased to $n = 100$. Using the larger sample size, you determined that the probability of selecting a sample with a mean of 365 grams or less to be 2.28%.

SUMMARY

You have learned that in many business situations the population is so large that you cannot gather information on every item. Instead, statistical sampling procedures focus on collecting a small representative group of the larger population. The results of the sample are then used to estimate characteristics of the entire population. Selecting a sample is less time-consuming, less costly, and more practical than an analysis of the entire population.

In this chapter, you studied four common sampling methods—simple random, systematic, stratified, and clus-

ter. You also studied the sampling distribution of the sample mean, the Central Limit Theorem, and the sampling distribution of the sample proportion. You learned that the sample mean is an unbiased estimator of the population mean, and the sample proportion is an unbiased estimator of the population proportion. In the next four chapters, the techniques of confidence intervals and tests of hypotheses commonly used for statistical inference are discussed.

KEY EQUATIONS

Population Mean

$$\mu = \frac{\sum_{i=1}^{N} X_i}{N} \tag{7.1}$$

Population Standard Deviation

$$\sigma = \sqrt{\frac{\sum_{i=1}^{N} (X_i - \mu)^2}{N}} \tag{7.2}$$

Standard Error of the Mean

$$\sigma_{\bar{X}} = \frac{\sigma}{\sqrt{n}} \tag{7.3}$$

Finding Z for the Sampling Distribution of the Mean

$$Z = \frac{\bar{X} - \mu_{\bar{X}}}{\sigma_{\bar{X}}} = \frac{\bar{X} - \mu}{\frac{\sigma}{\sqrt{n}}} \tag{7.4}$$

Finding $\bar{X}$ for the Sampling Distribution of the Mean

$$\bar{X} = \mu + Z \frac{\sigma}{\sqrt{n}} \tag{7.5}$$

Sample Proportion

$$p = \frac{X}{n} \tag{7.6}$$

Standard Error of the Proportion

$$\sigma_p = \sqrt{\frac{\pi(1 - \pi)}{n}} \tag{7.7}$$

Finding Z for the Sampling Distribution of the Proportion

$$Z = \frac{p - \pi}{\sqrt{\frac{\pi(1 - \pi)}{n}}} \tag{7.8}$$

KEY TERMS

CHAPTER REVIEW PROBLEMS

CHECKING YOUR UNDERSTANDING

7.33 Why is the sample mean an unbiased estimator of the population mean?

7.34 Why does the standard error of the mean decrease as the sample size, n, increases?

7.35 Why does the sampling distribution of the mean follow a normal distribution for a large enough sample size, even though the population may not be normally distributed?

7.36 What is the difference between a population and a sampling distribution?

7.37 Under what circumstances does the sampling distribution of the proportion approximately follow the normal distribution?

7.38 What is the difference between probability and nonprobability sampling?

7.39 What are some potential problems with using "fishbowl" methods to select a simple random sample?

7.40 What is the difference between sampling *with* replacement versus *without* replacement?

7.41 What is the difference between a simple random sample and a systematic sample?

7.42 What is the difference between a simple random sample and a stratified sample?

7.43 What is the difference between a stratified sample and a cluster sample?

APPLYING THE CONCEPTS

7.44 An industrial sewing machine uses ball bearings that are targeted to have a diameter of 0.75 inch. The lower and upper specification limits under which the ball bearing can operate are 0.74 inch (lower) and 0.76 inch (upper). Past experience has indicated that the actual diameter of the ball bearings is approximately normally distributed, with a mean of 0.753 inch and a standard deviation of 0.004 inch. If you select a random sample of 25 ball bearings, what is the probability that the sample mean is

a. between the target and the population mean of 0.753?
b. between the lower specification limit and the target?
c. greater than the upper specification limit?
d. less than the lower specification limit?
e. The probability is 93% that the sample mean diameter will be greater than what value?

7.45 The fill amount of bottles of a soft drink is normally distributed, with a mean of 2.0 liters and a standard deviation of 0.05 liter. If you select a random sample of 25 bottles, what is the probability that the sample mean will be

a. between 1.99 and 2.0 liters?
b. below 1.98 liters?
c. greater than 2.01 liters?
d. The probability is 99% that the sample mean amount of soft drink will be at least how much?
e. The probability is 99% that the sample mean amount of soft drink will be between which two values (symmetrically distributed around the mean)?

7.46 An orange juice producer buys all his oranges from a large orange grove that has one variety of orange. The amount of juice squeezed from these oranges is approximately normally distributed, with a mean of 4.70 ounces and a standard deviation of 0.40 ounce. Suppose that you select a sample of 25 oranges.

a. What is the probability that the sample mean amount of juice will be at least 4.60 ounces?
b. The probability is 70% that the sample mean amount of juice will be contained between what two values symmetrically distributed around the population mean?
c. The probability is 77% that the sample mean amount of juice will be greater than what value?

7.47 In his management information systems textbook, Professor David Kroenke raises an interesting point: "If 98% of our market has Internet access, do we have a responsibility to provide non-Internet materials to that other 2%?" (D. M. Kroenke, *Using MIS*, Upper Saddle River, NJ: Prentice Hall, 2007, p. 29a). Suppose that 98% of the customers in your market have Internet access and you select a random sample of 500 customers. What is the probability that the sample has

a. greater than 99% with Internet access?

b. between 97% and 99% with Internet access?

c. less than 97% with Internet access?

7.48 International mutual funds reported strong earnings in 2007. The population of international mutual funds earned a mean return of 14.52% in 2007 (*The Wall Street Journal*, January 2, 2008, p. R8). Assume that the returns for international mutual funds were distributed as a normal random variable, with a mean of 14.57 and a standard deviation of 20. If you selected a random sample of 10 funds from this population, what is the probability that the sample would have a mean return

a. less than 0—that is, a loss?

b. between 0 and 20?

c. greater than 10?

7.49 The same article as in Problem 7.48 reported that long-term treasury bonds had a mean return of 7.81% during this time. Assume that the returns for the long-term treasury bonds were distributed as a normal random variable, with a mean of 7.81 and a standard deviation of 10. If you select an individual treasury bond from this population, what is the probability that it would have a return

a. less than 0—that is, a loss?

b. between 0 and 20?

c. greater than 10?

If you selected a random sample of 10 treasury bonds from this population, what is the probability that the sample would have a mean return

d. less than 0—that is, a loss?

e. between 0 and 20?

f. greater than 10?

g. Compare your results in parts (d) through (f) to (a) through (c).

h. Compare your results in parts (d) through (f) to Problem 7.48 (a) through (c).

7.50 Telephone interviews have traditionally been the number one tool in political polling. Recently, many have argued that Internet polling is faster and less expensive and produces a higher response rate. Dr. Doug Usher, a leading authority on political polling, agrees that the telephone poll is still the gold standard in political polls due to its superior statistical reliability even though it is getting harder to reach people via the telephone with the growing use of caller ID and the fact that many younger people no longer have landlines (D. Usher, "The Internet's Unfulfilled Promise for Political Polling," **www.mysterypollster.com**, June 30, 2005). What concerns, if any, do you have on Internet polling?

7.51 A survey sponsored by The American Dietetic Association and the agribusiness giant ConAgra found that 53% of office workers take 30 minutes or less for lunch each day. Approximately 37% take 30 to 60 minutes, and 10% take more than an hour ("Snapshots," **usatoday.com**, April 26, 2006).

a. What additional information would you want to know before you accepted the results of the survey?

b. Discuss the four types of survey errors in the context of this survey.

c. One of the types of survey errors discussed in part (b) should have been measurement error. Explain how the root cause of measurement error in this survey could be the Hawthorne effect.

7.52 In a survey conducted by AOL and the Associated Press, less than 25% of adults use instant messaging (IM), and almost 75% of adults who use IM use e-mail more often than IM. The survey also showed that almost 50% of teens use IM, and almost 75% of teens who use IM use IM more often than e-mail (M. Levitt, "Bridging the Collaboration Age Gap with Unified Communications and Web 2.0," *KM World*, June 2007, p. 10).

a. What other information would you want to know before you used the results of this survey?

b. Suppose you work for AOL and wanted to investigate IM and e-mail usage by AOL users. Define the population, frame, and sampling method you would use.

7.53 (Class Project) The table of random numbers is an example of a uniform distribution because each digit is equally likely to occur. Starting in the row corresponding to the day of the month in which you were born, use the table of random numbers (Table E.1) to take one digit at a time.

Select five different samples each of $n = 2$, $n = 5$, and $n = 10$. Compute the sample mean of each sample. Develop a frequency distribution of the sample means for the results of the entire class, based on samples of sizes $n = 2$, $n = 5$, and $n = 10$.

What can be said about the shape of the sampling distribution for each of these sample sizes?

7.54 (Class Project) Toss a coin 10 times and record the number of heads. If each student performs this experiment five times, a frequency distribution of the number of heads can be developed from the results of the entire class. Does this distribution seem to approximate the normal distribution?

7.55 (Class Project) The number of cars waiting in line at a car wash is distributed as follows:

Number of Cars	Probability
0	0.25
1	0.40
2	0.20
3	0.10
4	0.04
5	0.01

You can use the table of random numbers (Table E.1) to select samples from this distribution by assigning numbers as follows:

1. Start in the row corresponding to the day of the month in which you were born.
2. Select a two-digit random number.
3. If you select a random number from 00 to 24, record a length of 0; if from 25 to 64, record a length of 1; if from 65 to 84, record a length of 2; if from 85 to 94, record a length of 3; if from 95 to 98, record a length of 4; if 99, record a length of 5.

   Select samples of $n = 2, n = 5$, and $n = 10$. Compute the mean for each sample. For example, if a sample of size 2 results in the random numbers 18 and 46, these would correspond to lengths of 0 and 1, respectively, producing a sample mean of 0.5. If each student selects five different samples for each sample size, a frequency distribution of the sample means (for each sample size) can be developed from the results of the entire class. What conclusions can you reach concerning the sampling distribution of the mean as the sample size is increased?

7.56 (Class Project) Using Table E.1, simulate the selection of different-colored balls from a bowl as follows:

1. Start in the row corresponding to the day of the month in which you were born.
2. Select one-digit numbers.
3. If a random digit between 0 and 6 is selected, consider the ball white; if a random digit is a 7, 8, or 9, consider the ball red.

   Select samples of $n = 10, n = 25$, and $n = 50$ digits. In each sample, count the number of white balls and compute the proportion of white balls in the sample. If each student in the class selects five different samples for each sample size, a frequency distribution of the proportion of white balls (for each sample size) can be developed from the results of the entire class. What conclusions can you reach about the sampling distribution of the proportion as the sample size is increased?

7.57 (Class Project) Suppose that step 3 of Problem 7.56 uses the following rule: "If a random digit between 0 and 8 is selected, consider the ball to be white; if a random digit of 9 is selected, consider the ball to be red." Compare and contrast the results in this problem and those in Problem 7.56.

MANAGING THE *SPRINGVILLE HERALD*

Continuing its quality improvement effort first described in the Chapter 6 "Managing the *Springville Herald*" case, the production department of the newspaper has been monitoring the blackness of the newspaper print. As before, blackness is measured on a standard scale in which the target value is 1.0. Data collected over the past year indicate that the blackness is approximately normally distributed, with a mean of 1.005 and a standard deviation of 0.10.

EXERCISE

SH7.1 Each day, 25 spots on the first newspaper printed are chosen, and the blackness of the spots is measured. Assuming that the distribution has not changed from what it was in the past year, what is the probability that the mean blackness of the spots is

a. less than 1.0?
b. between 0.95 and 1.0?
c. between 1.0 and 1.05?
d. less than 0.95 or greater than 1.05?
e. Suppose that the mean blackness of today's sample of 25 spots is 0.952. What conclusion can you reach about the blackness of today's newspaper based on this result? Explain.

WEB CASE

Apply your knowledge about sampling distributions in this Web Case, which reconsiders the Oxford Cereals Using Statistics scenario.

The advocacy group Consumers Concerned About Cereal Cheaters (CCACC) suspects that cereal companies, including Oxford Cereals, are cheating consumers by packaging cereals at less than labeled weights. Visit the organization's home page at **www.prenhall.com/Springville/ConsumersConcerned.**

htm (or open the `ConsumersConcerned.htm` file in the Student CD-ROM Web Case folder), examine their claims and supporting data, and then answer the following:

1. Are the data collection procedures that the CCACC uses to form its conclusions flawed? What procedures could the group follow to make their analysis more rigorous?
2. Assume that the two samples of five cereal boxes (one sample for each of two cereal varieties) listed on the

CCACC Web site were collected randomly by organization members. For each sample, do the following:

a. Calculate the sample mean.

b. Assume that the standard deviation of the process is 15 grams and a population mean is 368 grams. Calculate the percentage of all samples for each process that have a sample mean less than the value you calculated in (a).

c. Again, assuming that the standard deviation is 15 grams, calculate the percentage of individual boxes of cereal that have a weight less than the value you calculated in (a).

3. What, if any, conclusions can you form by using your calculations about the filling processes of the two different cereals?

4. A representative from Oxford Cereals has asked that the CCACC take down its page discussing shortages in Oxford Cereals boxes. Is that request reasonable? Why or why not?

5. Can the techniques discussed in this chapter be used to prove cheating in the manner alleged by the CCACC? Why or why not?

REFERENCES

1. Cochran, W. G., *Sampling Techniques*, 3rd ed. (New York: Wiley, 1977).

2. Gallup, G. H., *The Sophisticated Poll-Watcher's Guide* (Princeton, NJ: Princeton Opinion Press, 1972).

3. Goleman, D., "Pollsters Enlist Psychologists in Quest for Unbiased Results," *The New York Times*, September 7, 1993, pp. C1, C11.

4. Hahn, G., and W. Meeker, *Statistical Intervals, A Guide for Practioners* (New York: John Wiley and Sons, Inc., 1991).

5. *Microsoft Excel 2007* (Redmond, WA: Microsoft Corp., 2007).

6. *Minitab for Windows Version 15* (State College, PA: Minitab, Inc., 2006).

7. Rand Corporation, *A Million Random Digits with 100,000 Normal Deviates* (New York: The Free Press, 1955).

Using Microsoft Excel for Sampling and Sampling Distributions

E7.1 Creating Simple Random Samples Without Replacement

No Microsoft Excel features directly create simple random samples. Use PHStat2 Section P7.1 to create such samples.

E7.2 Creating Simulated Sampling Distributions

You create simulated sampling distributions by first using the ToolPak Random Number Generation procedure to create a worksheet of multiple random samples and then adding formulas to that worksheet to compute the sample means and other appropriate measures.

To start, select **Tools → Data Analysis** and in the Data Analysis dialog box, click **Random Number Generation** and then click **OK**. In the Random Number Generation dialog box (shown at right), enter the number of samples as the **Number of Variables** and enter the sample size of each sample as the **Number of Random Numbers**. Select the type of distribution from the **Distribution** drop-down list and make entries in the Parameters area, the contents of which vary according to the distribution selected. (If you select the

Discrete option, you will need to be opened to a worksheet that contains a table of X and $P(X)$ values and enter the range of the table as the **Value and Probability Input Range**.) To finish, click **New Worksheet Ply** and then **OK**.

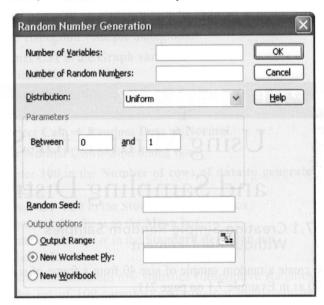

Using PHStat2 for Sampling and Sampling Distributions

P7.1 Creating Simple Random Samples Without Replacement

To create a random sample without replacement use **PHStat → Sampling → Random Sample Generation**. In the Random Sample Generation dialog box, click **Select values from range** to have the procedure create the random sample for the values in the **Values Cell Range**. The created random sample appears on a new worksheet.

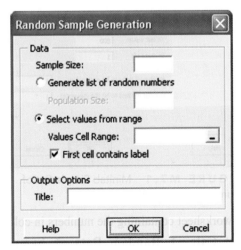

In Section 7.4, you used the Central Limit Theorem and knowledge of the population distribution to determine the percentage of sample means that are within certain distances of the population mean. For instance, in the cereal-fill example used throughout Chapter 7 (see Example 7.6 on page 223), you can conclude that 95% of all sample means are between 362.12 and 373.88 grams. This is an example of *deductive* reasoning because the conclusion is based on taking something that is true in general (for the population) and applying it to something specific (the sample means).

To get the results that Saxon Home Improvement needs requires *inductive* reasoning. Inductive reasoning lets you use some specifics to make broader generalizations. You cannot guarantee that the broader generalizations are absolutely correct, but with a careful choosing of the specifics and a rigorous methodology, you can get useful conclusions. As a Saxon accountant, you need to use inferential statistics, the process of using sample results (the "some specifics") to *estimate* ("the making of the broader generalization") unknown population parameters such as a population mean or a population proportion. Note that statisticians use the word *estimate* in the same sense of the everyday usage, something you are reasonably certain about, but cannot flatly say is absolutely correct.

You estimate population parameters using either point estimates or interval estimates. A **point estimate** is the value of a single sample statistic. A **confidence interval estimate** is a range of numbers, called an interval, constructed around the point estimate. The confidence interval is constructed such that the probability that the population parameter is located somewhere within the interval is known.

Suppose you want to estimate the mean GPA of all the students at your university. The mean GPA for all the students is an unknown population mean, denoted by μ. You select a sample of students and find that the sample mean is 2.80. The sample mean, $\overline{X} = 2.80$, is a point estimate of the population mean, μ. How accurate is 2.80? To answer this question, you must construct a confidence interval estimate.

Recall that the sample mean, $\overline{X}$, is a point estimate of the population mean, μ. However, the sample mean varies from sample to sample because it depends on the items selected in the sample. By taking into account the known variability from sample to sample (see Section 7.4 on the sampling distribution of the mean), you can develop the interval estimate for the population mean. The interval constructed should have a specified confidence of correctly estimating the value of the population parameter, μ. In other words, there is a specified confidence that μ is somewhere in the range of numbers defined by the interval.

Suppose that after studying this chapter, you find that a 95% confidence interval for the mean GPA at your university is $(2.75 \leq \mu \leq 2.85)$. You can interpret this interval estimate by stating that you are 95% confident that the mean GPA at your university is between 2.75 and 2.85. There is a 5% chance that the mean GPA is below 2.75 or above 2.85.

After learning about the confidence interval for the mean, you will learn how to develop an interval estimate for the population proportion. Then you will learn how large a sample to select when constructing confidence intervals.

8.1 Confidence Interval Estimation for the Mean (σ Known)

In Section 7.4, you used the Central Limit Theorem and knowledge of the population distribution to determine the percentage of sample means that are within certain distances of the population mean. Suppose that in the cereal-fill example, you wished to estimate the population mean using the information from a single sample. Thus, rather than taking $\mu \pm (1.96)(\sigma/\sqrt{n})$ to find the upper and lower limits around μ, as in Section 7.4, you substitute the sample mean, $\overline{X}$, for the unknown μ and use $\overline{X} \pm (1.96)(\sigma/\sqrt{n})$ as an interval to estimate the unknown μ. Although in practice you select a single sample of n values and compute the mean, $\overline{X}$, in order to understand the full meaning of the interval estimate, you need to examine a hypothetical set of all possible samples of n values.

Suppose that a sample of $n = 25$ boxes has a mean of 362.3 grams. The interval developed to estimate μ is $362.3 \pm (1.96)(15)/(\sqrt{25})$ or 362.3 ± 5.88. The estimate of μ is

$$356.42 \leq \mu \leq 368.18$$

Because the population mean, μ (equal to 368), is included within the interval, this sample results in a correct statement about μ (see Figure 8.1).

FIGURE 8.1

Confidence interval estimates for five different samples of $n = 25$ taken from a population where $\mu = 368$ and $\sigma = 15$

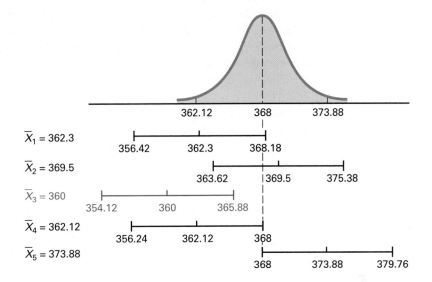

To continue this hypothetical example, suppose that for a different sample of $n = 25$ boxes, the mean is 369.5. The interval developed from this sample is

$$369.5 \pm (1.96)(15)/(\sqrt{25})$$

or 369.5 ± 5.88. The estimate is

$$363.62 \leq \mu \leq 375.38$$

Because the population mean, μ (equal to 368), is also included within this interval, this statement about μ is correct.

Now, before you begin to think that correct statements about μ are always made by developing a confidence interval estimate, suppose a third hypothetical sample of $n = 25$ boxes is selected and the sample mean is equal to 360 grams. The interval developed here is $360 \pm (1.96)(15)/(\sqrt{25})$, or 360 ± 5.88. In this case, the estimate of μ is

$$354.12 \leq \mu \leq 365.88$$

This estimate is *not* a correct statement because the population mean, μ, is not included in the interval developed from this sample (see Figure 8.1). Thus, for some samples, the interval estimate of μ is correct, but for others it is incorrect. In practice, only one sample is selected, and because the population mean is unknown, you cannot determine whether the interval estimate is correct. To resolve this dilemma of sometimes having an interval that provides a correct estimate and sometimes having an interval that provides an incorrect estimate, you need to determine the proportion of samples producing intervals that result in correct statements about the population mean, μ. To do this, consider two other hypothetical samples: the case in which $\overline{X} = 362.12$ grams and the case in which $\overline{X} = 373.88$ grams. If $\overline{X} = 362.12$, the interval is $362.12 \pm (1.96)(15)/(\sqrt{25})$, or 362.12 ± 5.88. This leads to the following interval:

$$356.24 \leq \mu \leq 368.00$$

Because the population mean of 368 is at the upper limit of the interval, the statement is a correct one (see Figure 8.1).

When $\overline{X} = 373.88$, the interval is $373.88 \pm (1.96)(15)/(\sqrt{25})$, or 373.88 ± 5.88. The interval estimate for the mean is

$$368.00 \leq \mu \leq 379.76$$

In this case, because the population mean of 368 is included at the lower limit of the interval, the statement is correct.

In Figure 8.1, you see that when the sample mean falls anywhere between 362.12 and 373.88 grams, the population mean is included *somewhere* within the interval. In Example 7.6 on page 223 you found that 95% of the sample means fall between 362.12 and 373.88 grams. Therefore, 95% of all samples of $n = 25$ boxes have sample means that will result in intervals that include the population mean.

Because, in practice, you select only one sample of size n, and μ is unknown, you never know for sure whether your specific interval includes the population mean. However, if you take all possible samples of n and compute their 95% confidence intervals, 95% of the intervals will include the population mean, and only 5% of them will not. In other words, you have 95% confidence that the population mean is somewhere in your interval.

Consider once again the first sample discussed in this section. A sample of $n = 25$ boxes had a sample mean of 362.3 grams. The interval constructed to estimate μ is:

$$362.3 \pm (1.96)(15)/(\sqrt{25})$$

$$362.3 \pm 5.88$$

$$356.42 \leq \mu \leq 368.18$$

The interval from 356.42 to 368.18 is referred to as a 95% confidence interval. The following contains an interpretation of the interval that most business professionals will understand. (For a technical discussion of different ways to interpret confidence intervals, see Reference 3.)

"I am 95% confident that the mean amount of cereal in the population of boxes is somewhere between 356.42 and 368.18 grams."

To assist in your understanding of the meaning of the confidence interval, the following example concerns the order-filling process at a Web site. Filling orders consists of several steps including receiving an order, picking the parts of the order, checking the order, packing, and shipping the order. The data in the file **Order** consists of the time in minutes to fill orders for a population of 200 on a recent day. Although in practice, the population characteristics are rarely known, for this population of orders, the mean μ is known to be equal to 69.637 minutes and the standard deviation σ is known to be equal to 10.411 minutes. To illustrate how the sample mean and sample standard deviation can vary from one sample to another, 20 different samples of $n = 10$ were selected from the population of 200 orders and the sample mean and sample standard deviation (and other statistics) were calculated for each sample using Minitab. Figure 8.2 shows these results.

FIGURE 8.2

Minitab sample statistics and 95% confidence intervals for 20 samples of $n = 10$ selected from the population of 200 orders

Variable	Count	Mean	StDev	Minimum	Median	Maximum	Range	95% CI
Sample 1	10	74.15	13.39	56.10	76.85	97.70	41.60	(67.6973, 80.6027)
Sample 2	10	61.10	10.60	46.80	61.35	79.50	32.70	(54.6473, 67.5527)
Sample 3	10	74.36	6.50	62.50	74.50	84.00	21.50	(67.9073, 80.8127)
Sample 4	10	70.40	12.80	47.20	70.95	84.00	36.80	(63.9473, 76.8527)
Sample 5	10	62.18	10.85	47.10	59.70	84.00	36.90	(55.7273, 68.6327)
Sample 6	10	67.03	9.68	51.10	69.60	83.30	32.20	(60.5773, 73.4827)
Sample 7	10	69.03	8.81	56.60	68.85	83.70	27.10	(62.5773, 75.4827)
Sample 8	10	72.30	11.52	54.20	71.35	87.00	32.80	(65.8473, 78.7527)
Sample 9	10	68.18	14.10	50.10	69.95	86.20	36.10	(61.7273, 74.6327)
Sample 10	10	66.67	9.08	57.10	64.65	86.10	29.00	(60.2173, 73.1227)
Sample 11	10	72.42	9.76	59.60	74.65	86.10	26.50	(65.9673, 78.8727)
Sample 12	10	76.26	11.69	50.10	80.60	87.00	36.90	(69.8073, 82.7127)
Sample 13	10	65.74	12.11	47.10	62.15	86.10	39.00	(59.2873, 72.1927)
Sample 14	10	69.99	10.97	51.00	73.40	84.60	33.60	(63.5373, 76.4427)
Sample 15	10	75.76	8.60	61.10	75.05	87.80	26.70	(69.3073, 82.2127)
Sample 16	10	67.94	9.19	56.70	67.70	87.80	31.10	(61.4873, 74.3927)
Sample 17	10	71.05	10.48	50.10	71.15	86.20	36.10	(64.5973, 77.5027)
Sample 18	10	71.68	7.96	55.60	72.35	82.60	27.00	(65.2273, 78.1327)
Sample 19	10	70.97	9.83	54.40	70.05	84.60	30.20	(64.5173, 77.4227)
Sample 20	10	74.48	8.80	62.00	76.25	85.70	23.70	(68.0273, 80.9327)

From Figure 8.2, you can see the following:

1. The sample statistics differ from sample to sample. The sample means vary from 61.10 to 76.26 minutes, the sample standard deviations vary from 6.50 to 14.10 minutes, the sample medians vary from 59.70 to 80.60 minutes, and the sample ranges vary from 21.50 to 41.60 minutes.
2. Some of the sample means are greater than the population mean of 69.637 minutes, and some of the sample means are less than the population mean.
3. Some of the sample standard deviations are greater than the population standard deviation of 10.411 minutes, and some of the sample standard deviations are less than the population standard deviation.
4. The variation in the sample range from sample to sample is much more than the variation in the sample standard deviation.

The fact that sample statistics vary from sample to sample is called sampling error. Sampling error is the variation that occurs due to selecting a single sample from the population. The size of the sampling error is primarily based on the amount of variation in the population and on the sample size. Larger samples have less sampling error than small samples, but will cost more.

The last column of Figure 8.2 contains 95% confidence interval estimates of the population mean order-filling time based on the results of those 20 samples of $n = 10$. Begin by examining the first sample selected. The sample mean is 74.15 minutes, and the interval estimate for the population mean is 67.6973 to 80.6027 minutes. In a typical study, you would not know for sure whether this interval estimate is correct because you rarely know the value of the population mean. However, for this example *concerning the order-filling times*, the population mean is known to be 69.637 minutes. If you examine the interval 67.6973 to 80.6027 minutes, you see that the population mean of 69.637 minutes is located *between* these lower and upper limits. Thus, the first sample provides a correct estimate of the population mean in the form of an interval estimate. Looking over the other 19 samples, you see that similar results occur for all the other samples *except* for samples 2, 5, and 12. For each of the intervals generated (other than samples 2, 5, and 12), the population mean of 69.637 minutes is located *somewhere* within the interval.

For sample 2, the sample mean is 61.10 minutes, and the interval is 54.6473 to 67.5527 minutes; for sample 5, the sample mean is 62.18, and the interval is between 55.7273 and 68.6327; whereas for sample 12, the sample mean is 76.26, and the interval is between 69.8073 and 82.7127 minutes. The population mean of 69.637 minutes is *not* located within any of these intervals, and the estimate of the population mean made using these intervals is incorrect.

In some situations, you might want a higher degree of confidence (such as 99%) of including the population mean within the interval. In other cases, you might accept less confidence (such as 90%) of correctly estimating the population mean. In general, the **level of confidence** is symbolized by $(1 - \alpha) \times 100\%$, where α is the proportion in the tails of the distribution that is outside the confidence interval. The proportion in the upper tail of the distribution is $\alpha/2$, and the proportion in the lower tail of the distribution is $\alpha/2$. You use Equation (8.1) to construct a $(1 - \alpha) \times 100\%$ confidence interval estimate of the mean with σ known.

CONFIDENCE INTERVAL FOR THE MEAN (σ KNOWN)

$$\overline{X} \pm Z_{\alpha/2} \frac{\sigma}{\sqrt{n}}$$

or

$$\overline{X} - Z_{\alpha/2} \frac{\sigma}{\sqrt{n}} \leq \mu \leq \overline{X} + Z_{\alpha/2} \frac{\sigma}{\sqrt{n}} \tag{8.1}$$

where $Z_{\alpha/2}$ is the value corresponding to an upper-tail probability of $\alpha/2$ from the standardized normal distribution (i.e., a cumulative area of $1 - \alpha/2$).

The value of $Z_{\alpha/2}$ needed for constructing a confidence interval is called the **critical value** for the distribution. 95% confidence corresponds to an α value of 0.05. The critical Z value corresponding to a cumulative area of 0.975 is 1.96 because there is 0.025 in the upper tail of the distribution and the cumulative area less than $Z = 1.96$ is 0.975.

There is a different critical value for each level of confidence, $1 - \alpha$. A level of confidence of 95% leads to a Z value of 1.96 (see Figure 8.3). 99% confidence corresponds to an α value of 0.01. The Z value is approximately 2.58 because the upper-tail area is 0.005 and the cumulative area less than $Z = 2.58$ is 0.995 (see Figure 8.4).

FIGURE 8.3

Normal curve for determining the Z value needed for 95% confidence

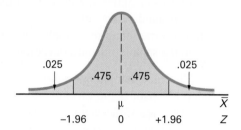

FIGURE 8.4

Normal curve for determining the Z value needed for 99% confidence

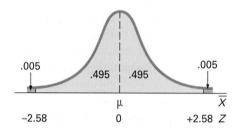

Now that various levels of confidence have been considered, why not make the confidence level as close to 100% as possible? Before doing so, you need to realize that any increase in the level of confidence is achieved only by widening (and making less precise) the confidence interval. There is no "free lunch" here. You would have more confidence that the population mean is within a broader range of values; however, this might make the interpretation of the confidence interval less useful. The trade-off between the width of the confidence interval and the level of confidence is discussed in greater depth in the context of determining the sample size in Section 8.4. Example 8.1 illustrates the application of the confidence interval estimate.

EXAMPLE 8.1

Estimating the Mean Paper Length With 95% Confidence

A paper manufacturer has a production process that operates continuously throughout an entire production shift. The paper is expected to have a mean length of 11 inches, and the standard deviation of the length is 0.02 inch. At periodic intervals, a sample is selected to determine whether the mean paper length is still equal to 11 inches or whether something has gone wrong in the production process to change the length of the paper produced. You select a random sample of 100 sheets, and the mean paper length is 10.998 inches. Construct a 95% confidence interval estimate for the population mean paper length.

SOLUTION Using Equation (8.1) on page 243, with $Z_{\alpha/2} = 1.96$ for 95% confidence,

$$\bar{X} \pm Z_{\alpha/2} \frac{\sigma}{\sqrt{n}} = 10.998 \pm (1.96) \frac{0.02}{\sqrt{100}}$$

$$= 10.998 \pm 0.00392$$

$$10.99408 \le \mu \le 11.00192$$

Thus, with 95% confidence, you conclude that the population mean is between 10.99408 and 11.00192 inches. Because the interval includes 11, the value indicating that the production process is working properly, you have no reason to believe that anything is wrong with the production process.

To see the effect of using a 99% confidence interval, examine Example 8.2.

EXAMPLE 8.2

Estimating the Mean
Paper Length with
99% Confidence

Construct a 99% confidence interval estimate for the population mean paper length.

SOLUTION Using Equation (8.1) on page 243, with $Z_{\alpha/2} = 2.58$ for 99% confidence,

$$\overline{X} \pm Z_{\alpha/2} \frac{\sigma}{\sqrt{n}} = 10.998 \pm (2.58)\frac{0.02}{\sqrt{100}}$$

$$= 10.998 \pm 0.00516$$

$$10.99284 \le \mu \le 11.00316$$

Once again, because 11 is included within this wider interval, you have no reason to believe that anything is wrong with the production process.

As discussed in Section 7.4, the sampling distribution of the sample mean $\overline{X}$ is normally distributed if the population for your characteristic of interest X is a normal distribution. And, if the population of X is not a normal distribution, the Central Limit Theorem almost always ensures that $\overline{X}$ is normally distributed when n is large. However, when dealing with a small sample size and a population of X that is not a normal distribution, the sampling distribution of $\overline{X}$ is not normally distributed and therefore the confidence interval discussed in this section is inappropriate. In practice, however, as long as the sample size is large enough and the population is not very skewed, you can use the confidence interval defined in Equation (8.1) to estimate the population mean when σ is known. To assess the assumption of normality, you can evaluate the shape of the sample data by using a histogram, stem-and-leaf display, boxplot, or normal probability plot.

Can You Ever *Really* Know Sigma?

This section discusses the concept of the confidence interval estimate, how to develop it, and how to interpret it. The discussion limited itself to the case where the population standard deviation, sigma, is known. But, can you ever *really* know sigma? Probably not, but it is much easier to explain the confidence interval estimate using an example where the population standard deviation, sigma, is known. If sigma is known, then you can use the normal distribution, which you are already familiar with from Chapters 6 and 7. In Section 8.2, you will learn how to construct confidence interval estimates when sigma is not known, and you will use the t distribution instead of the normal distribution.

In virtually all real-world business applications, you do not know the standard deviation of the population. If, for a particular case, you knew the population standard deviation, you would also already know (or could compute) the population mean. Why is that so? You could only know the population standard deviation if you have access to all of the population data. And if you knew all of the population data, you could compute the population mean. There would be no need to employ the *inductive* reasoning of inferential statistics to estimate the population mean.

So why study the confidence interval estimate of the mean when sigma is known? Because it is a good way to understand the confidence interval concept—a very important concept to know when studying the rest of this book.

Problems for Section 8.1

LEARNING THE BASICS

8.1 If $\overline{X} = 85, \sigma = 8$, and $n = 64$, construct a 95% confidence interval estimate of the population mean, μ.

8.2 If $\overline{X} = 125, \sigma = 24$ and $n = 36$, construct a 99% confidence interval estimate of the population mean, μ.

APPLYING THE CONCEPTS

8.3 A market researcher selects a simple random sample of $n = 100$ customers from its population of two million customers. After analyzing the sample, she states that she has 95% confidence that the mean annual income of its two million customers is between $70,000 and $85,000. Explain the meaning of this statement.

8.4 If you were to collect a set of data, either from an entire population or from a random sample taken from that population:
a. Which statistical measure would you compute first: the mean or the standard deviation? Explain.
b. What does your answer to (a) tell you about the "practicality" of using the confidence interval estimate formula given in Equation (8.1)?

8.5 Consider the confidence interval estimate discussed in Problem 8.3. Suppose that the population mean annual income is $71,000. Is the confidence interval estimate stated in Problem 8.3 correct? Explain.

8.6 You are working as an assistant to the dean of institutional research at your university. She wants to survey members of the alumni association who obtained their baccalaureate degrees 5 years ago to learn what their starting salaries were in their first full-time job after receiving their degrees. A sample of 100 alumni is to be randomly selected from the list of 2,500 graduates in that class. If her goal is to construct a 95% confidence interval estimate of the population mean starting salary, why is it unlikely that you will be able to use Equation (8.1) on page 243 for this purpose? Explain.

8.2 Confidence Interval Estimation for the Mean (σ Unknown)

Just as the mean of the population, μ, is usually unknown, you virtually never know the standard deviation of the population, σ. Therefore, you need to construct a confidence interval estimate of μ, using the sample statistic S as an estimate of the population parameter σ.

Student's *t* Distribution

At the beginning of the twentieth century, William S. Gosset, a statistician for Guinness Breweries in Ireland (see reference 4), wanted to make inferences about the mean when σ was unknown. Because Guinness employees were not permitted to publish research work under their own names, Gosset adopted the pseudonym "Student." The distribution that he developed is known as **Student's *t* distribution** and is commonly referred to as the *t* distribution.

If the random variable X is normally distributed, then the following statistic has a *t* distribution with $n - 1$ **degrees of freedom**:

$$t = \frac{\bar{X} - \mu}{\frac{S}{\sqrt{n}}}$$

This expression has the same form as the Z statistic in Equation (7.4) on page 222, except that S is used to estimate the unknown σ.

Properties of the *t* Distribution

The *t* distribution looks very similar to the standardized normal distribution. Both distributions are symmetrical and bell shaped with means and medians equal to zero. However, the *t* distribution has more area in the tails and less in the center than does the standardized normal distribution (see Figure 8.5). Because S is used to estimate the unknown σ, the values of *t* are more variable than those for Z.

FIGURE 8.5

Standardized normal distribution and *t* distribution for 5 degrees of freedom

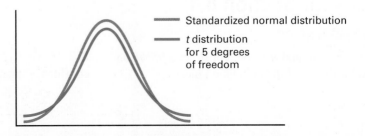

— Standardized normal distribution

— *t* distribution for 5 degrees of freedom

The degrees of freedom, $n - 1$, are directly related to the sample size, n. The concept of *degrees of freedom* is discussed further on page 248. As the sample size and degrees of freedom increase, S becomes a better estimate of σ, and the t distribution gradually approaches the standardized normal distribution, until the two are virtually identical. With a sample size of about 120 or more, S estimates σ precisely enough so that there is little difference between the t and Z distributions.

As stated earlier, the t distribution assumes that the random variable X is normally distributed. In practice, however, when the sample size is large enough and the population is not very skewed, in most cases you can use the t distribution to estimate the population mean when σ is unknown. When dealing with a small sample size and a skewed population distribution, the confidence interval estimate may not provide a valid estimate of the population mean. To assess the assumption of normality, you can evaluate the shape of the sample data by using a histogram, stem-and-leaf display, boxplot, or normal probability plot. However, the usefulness of any of these graphs to evaluate normality is limited when you have a small sample size.

You find the critical values of t for the appropriate degrees of freedom from the table of the t distribution (see Table E.3). The columns of the table present the most commonly needed cumulative probabilities and corresponding upper-tail areas. The rows of the table represent the degrees of freedom. The critical t values are found in the cells of the table. For example, with 99 degrees of freedom, if you want 95% confidence, you find the appropriate value of t, as shown in Table 8.1. The 95% confidence level means that 2.5% of the values (an area of 0.025) are in each tail of the distribution. Looking in the column for a cumulative probability of 0.975 and an upper-tail area of 0.025 in the row corresponding to 99 degrees of freedom gives you a critical value for t of 1.9842 (see Figure 8.6). Because t is a symmetrical distribution with a mean of 0, if the upper-tail value is $+1.9842$, the value for the lower-tail area (lower 0.025) is -1.9842. A t value of -1.9842 means that the probability that t is less than -1.9842 is 0.025, or 2.5%.

TABLE 8.1

Determining the Critical Value from the t Table for an Area of 0.025 in Each Tail with 99 Degrees of Freedom

	Cumulative Probabilities					
	.75	.90	.95	.975	.99	.995
	Upper Tail Areas					
Degrees of Freedom	.25	.10	.05	.025	.01	.005
1	1.0000	3.0777	6.3138	12.7062	31.8207	63.6574
2	0.8165	1.8856	2.9200	4.3027	6.9646	9.9248
3	0.7649	1.6377	2.3534	3.1824	4.5407	5.8409
4	0.7407	1.5332	2.1318	2.7764	3.7469	4.6041
5	0.7267	1.4759	2.0150	2.5706	3.3649	4.0322
⋅	⋅	⋅	⋅	⋅	⋅	⋅
⋅	⋅	⋅	⋅	⋅	⋅	⋅
⋅	⋅	⋅	⋅	⋅	⋅	⋅
96	0.6771	1.2904	1.6609	1.9850	2.3658	2.6280
97	0.6770	1.2903	1.6607	1.9847	2.3654	2.6275
98	0.6770	1.2902	1.6606	1.9845	2.3650	2.6269
99	0.6770	1.2902	1.6604	1.9842	2.3646	2.6264
100	0.6770	1.2901	1.6602	1.9840	2.3642	2.6259

Source: *Extracted from Table E.3.*

FIGURE 8.6

t distribution with 99 degrees of freedom

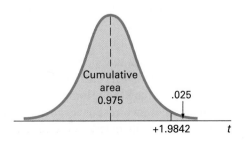

Cumulative area 0.975

.025

+1.9842 t

Note that for a 95% confidence interval, you will always use a cumulative probability of 0.975 and an upper-tail area of 0.025. Similarly, for a 99% confidence interval, use 0.995 and 0.005, and for a 90% confidence interval use 0.95 and 0.05.

The Concept of Degrees of Freedom

In Chapter 3, you learned that the numerator of the sample variance, S^2 [see Equation (3.4) on page 88], requires the computation of

$$\sum_{i=1}^{n}(X_i - \overline{X})^2$$

In order to compute S^2, you first need to know $\overline{X}$. Therefore, only $n - 1$ of the sample values are free to vary. This means that you have $n - 1$ degrees of freedom. For example, suppose a sample of five values has a mean of 20. How many values do you need to know before you can determine the remainder of the values? The fact that $n = 5$ and $\overline{X} = 20$ also tells you that

$$\sum_{i=1}^{n}X_i = 100$$

because

$$\frac{\sum_{i=1}^{n}X_i}{n} = \overline{X}$$

Thus, when you know four of the values, the fifth one is *not* free to vary because the sum must add to 100. For example, if four of the values are 18, 24, 19, and 16, the fifth value must be 23 so that the sum equals 100.

The Confidence Interval Statement

Equation (8.2) defines the $(1 - \alpha) \times 100\%$ confidence interval estimate for the mean with σ unknown.

CONFIDENCE INTERVAL FOR THE MEAN (σ UNKNOWN)

$$\overline{X} \pm t_{\alpha/2}\frac{S}{\sqrt{n}}$$

or

$$\overline{X} - t_{\alpha/2}\frac{S}{\sqrt{n}} \leq \mu \leq \overline{X} + t_{\alpha/2}\frac{S}{\sqrt{n}} \qquad (8.2)$$

where $t_{\alpha/2}$ is the critical value corresponding to an upper-tail probability of $\alpha/2$ from the t distribution with $n - 1$ degrees of freedom (i.e., a cumulative area of $1 - \alpha/2$).

To illustrate the application of the confidence interval estimate for the mean when the standard deviation, σ, is unknown, recall the Using Statistics scenario presented on page 239. As an accountant for Saxon Home Improvement, you want to estimate the mean dollar amount listed on the sales invoices for the month. You select a sample of 100 sales invoices from the population of sales invoices during the month, and the sample mean of the 100 sales invoices is

$110.27, with a sample standard deviation of $28.95. For 95% confidence, the critical value from the t distribution (as shown in Table 8.1 on page 247) is 1.9842. Using Equation (8.2),

$$\overline{X} \pm t_{\alpha/2}\frac{S}{\sqrt{n}}$$

$$= 110.27 \pm (1.9842)\frac{28.95}{\sqrt{100}}$$

$$= 110.27 \pm 5.74$$

$$\$104.53 \leq \mu \leq \$116.01$$

A Microsoft Excel worksheet for these data is presented in Figure 8.7.

FIGURE 8.7

Microsoft Excel worksheet to compute a confidence interval estimate for the mean sales invoice amount for the Saxon Home Improvement Company

See Section E8.2 or P8.2 to create this. (Minitab users, see Section M8.2 to create the equivalent results.)

	A	B
1	**Estimate for the Mean Sales Invoice Amount**	
2		
3	**Data**	
4	Sample Standard Deviation	28.95
5	Sample Mean	110.27
6	Sample Size	100
7	Confidence Level	95%
8		
9	**Intermediate Calculations**	
10	Standard Error of the Mean	2.8950 =B4/SQRT(B6)
11	Degrees of Freedom	99 =B6 - 1
12	*t* Value	1.9842 =TINV(1 - B7, B11)
13	Interval Half Width	5.7443 =B12 * B10
14		
15	**Confidence Interval**	
16	Interval Lower Limit	104.53 =B5 - B13
17	Interval Upper Limit	116.01 =B5 + B13

Thus, with 95% confidence, you conclude that the mean amount of all the sales invoices is between $104.53 and $116.01. The 95% confidence level indicates that if you selected all possible samples of 100 (something that is never done in practice), 95% of the intervals developed would include the population mean somewhere within the interval. The validity of this confidence interval estimate depends on the assumption of normality for the distribution of the amount of the sales invoices. With a sample of 100, the normality assumption is not overly restrictive (see the Central Limit Theorem on page 224), and the use of the t distribution is likely appropriate. Example 8.3 further illustrates how you construct the confidence interval for a mean when the population standard deviation is unknown.

EXAMPLE 8.3

Estimating the Mean Force Required to Break Electric Insulators

A manufacturing company produces electric insulators. If the insulators break when in use, a short circuit is likely. To test the strength of the insulators, you carry out destructive testing to determine how much *force* is required to break the insulators. You measure force by observing how many pounds are applied to the insulator before it breaks. Table 8.2 lists 30 values from this experiment, which are located in the file **Force**. Construct a 95% confidence interval estimate for the population mean force required to break the insulator.

TABLE 8.2

Force (in Pounds) Required to Break the Insulator

1,870	1,728	1,656	1,610	1,634	1,784	1,522	1,696	1,592	1,662
1,866	1,764	1,734	1,662	1,734	1,774	1,550	1,756	1,762	1,866
1,820	1,744	1,788	1,688	1,810	1,752	1,680	1,810	1,652	1,736

SOLUTION Figure 8.8 shows that the sample mean is $\overline{X} = 1,723.4$ pounds and the sample standard deviation is $S = 89.55$ pounds. Using Equation (8.2) on page 248 to construct the confidence interval, you need to determine the critical value from the t table using the row for 29 degrees of freedom. For 95% confidence, you use the column corresponding to an upper-tail area of 0.025 and a cumulative probability of 0.975. From Table E.3, you see that $t_{\alpha/2} = 2.0452$. Thus, using $\overline{X} = 1,723, S = 89.55, n = 30$, and $t_{\alpha/2} = 2.0452$,

$$\overline{X} \pm t_{\alpha/2} \frac{S}{\sqrt{n}}$$

$$= 1,723.4 \pm (2.0452)\frac{89.55}{\sqrt{30}}$$

$$= 1,723.4 \pm 33.44$$

$$1,690.0 \le \mu \le 1,756.8$$

FIGURE 8.8

Minitab confidence interval estimate for the mean amount of force required to break electric insulators

See Section M8.2 to create this. (Use Section E8.2 or P8.2 to create the Excel equivalent.)

One-Sample T: Force

Variable	N	Mean	StDev	SE Mean	95% CI
Force	30	1723.4	89.6	16.3	(1690.0, 1756.8)

You conclude with 95% confidence that the mean breaking force required for the population of insulators is between 1,690.0 and 1,756.8 pounds. The validity of this confidence interval estimate depends on the assumption that the force required is normally distributed. Remember, however, that you can slightly relax this assumption for large sample sizes. Thus, with a sample of 30, you can use the *t* distribution even if the amount of force required is only slightly left-skewed. From the normal probability plot displayed in Figure 8.9 or the boxplot displayed in Figure 8.10, the amount of force required appears only slightly left-skewed. Thus, the *t* distribution is appropriate for these data.

FIGURE 8.9

Minitab normal probability plot for the amount of force required to break electric insulators

See Section M6.2 to create this. (PHStat2 users, see Section P6.2 to create an equivalent chart.)

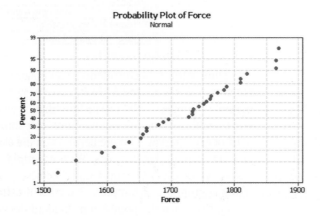

FIGURE 8.10

Minitab boxplot for the amount of force required to break electric insulators

See Section M3.2 to create this. (Microsoft Excel users, see Section E3.3 or P3.1 to create an equivalent chart.)

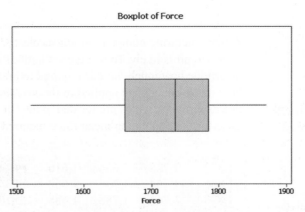

The interpretation of the confidence interval when σ is unknown is the same as when σ is known. To illustrate the fact that the confidence interval for the mean varies more when σ is unknown, return to the example concerning the order-filling times discussed in Section 8.1 on pages 242–243. Suppose that, in this case, you do not know the population standard deviation. Figure 8.11 shows the results for each of 20 samples of $n = 10$ orders.

FIGURE 8.11

Minitab confidence interval estimates of the mean for 20 samples of $n = 10$ selected from the population of 200 orders with σ unknown

See Section M8.2 to create this. (Microsoft Excel users, see Section E8.2 or P8.2 to create equivalent results.)

```
Variable    N   Mean   StDev  SE Mean      95% CI
Sample 1   10  71.64   7.58     2.40    (66.22, 77.06)
Sample 2   10  67.22  10.95     3.46    (59.39, 75.05)
Sample 3   10  67.97  14.83     4.69    (57.36, 78.58)
Sample 4   10  73.90  10.59     3.35    (66.33, 81.47)
Sample 5   10  67.11  11.12     3.52    (59.15, 75.07)
Sample 6   10  68.12  10.83     3.43    (60.37, 75.87)
Sample 7   10  65.80  10.85     3.43    (58.03, 73.57)
Sample 8   10  77.58  11.04     3.49    (69.68, 85.48)
Sample 9   10  66.69  11.45     3.62    (58.50, 74.88)
Sample 10  10  62.55   8.58     2.71    (56.41, 68.69)
Sample 11  10  71.12  12.82     4.05    (61.95, 80.29)
Sample 12  10  70.55  10.52     3.33    (63.02, 78.08)
Sample 13  10  65.51   8.16     2.58    (59.67, 71.35)
Sample 14  10  64.90   7.55     2.39    (59.50, 70.30)
Sample 15  10  66.22  11.21     3.54    (58.20, 74.24)
Sample 16  10  70.43  10.21     3.23    (63.12, 77.74)
Sample 17  10  72.04   6.25     1.98    (67.57, 76.51)
Sample 18  10  73.91  11.29     3.57    (65.83, 81.99)
Sample 19  10  71.49   9.76     3.09    (64.51, 78.47)
Sample 20  10  70.15  10.84     3.43    (62.39, 77.91)
```

From Figure 8.11, observe that the standard deviation of the samples varies from 6.25 (sample 17) to 14.83 (sample 3). Thus, the width of the confidence interval developed varies from 8.94 in sample 17 to 21.22 in sample 3. Because you know that the population mean order time $\mu = 69.637$ minutes, you can see that the interval for sample 8 $(69.68 - 85.48)$ and the interval for sample 10 $(56.41 - 68.69)$ do not correctly estimate the population mean. All the other intervals correctly estimate the population mean. Once again, remember that in practice you select only one sample and you have no way of knowing for sure whether this one sample provides a confidence interval that includes the population mean.

Problems for Section 8.2

LEARNING THE BASICS

8.7 If $\overline{X} = 75, S = 24$, and $n = 36$, and assuming that the population is normally distributed, construct a 95% confidence interval estimate of the population mean, μ.

8.8 Determine the critical value of t in each of the following circumstances:
a. $1 - \alpha = 0.95, n = 10$
b. $1 - \alpha = 0.99, n = 10$
c. $1 - \alpha = 0.95, n = 32$
d. $1 - \alpha = 0.95, n = 65$
e. $1 - \alpha = 0.90, n = 16$

8.9 Assuming that the population is normally distributed, construct a 95% confidence interval estimate for the population mean for each of the following samples:

Sample A: 1, 1, 1, 1, 8, 8, 8, 8
Sample B: 1, 2, 3, 4, 5, 6, 7, 8
Explain why these two samples produce different confidence intervals even though they have the same mean and range.

8.10 Assuming that the population is normally distributed, construct a 95% confidence interval for the population mean, based on the following sample of size $n = 7$:

1, 2, 3, 4, 5, 6, and 20. Change the number 20 to 7 and recalculate the confidence interval. Using these results, describe the effect of an outlier (i.e., an extreme value) on the confidence interval.

APPLYING THE CONCEPTS

8.11 A stationery store wants to estimate the mean retail value of greeting cards that it has in its inventory. A random sample of 100 greeting cards indicates a mean value of $2.55 and a standard deviation of $0.44.
a. Assuming a normal distribution, construct a 95% confidence interval estimate of the mean value of all greeting cards in the store's inventory.
b. Suppose there were 2,500 greeting cards in the store's inventory. How are the results in (a) useful in assisting the store owner to estimate the total value of her inventory?

SELF Test **8.12** Southside Hospital in Bay Shore, New York, commonly conducts stress tests to study the heart muscle after a person has a heart attack. Members of the diagnostic imaging department conducted a quality improvement project to try to reduce the turnaround time for stress tests. Turnaround time is defined as the time from when the test is ordered to when the radiologist signs off on the test results. Initially, the mean turnaround time for a stress test was 68 hours. After incorporating changes into the stress-test process, the quality improvement team collected a sample of 50 turnaround times. In this sample, the mean turnaround time was 32 hours, with a standard deviation of 9 hours (data extracted from E. Godin, D. Raven, C. Sweetapple, and F. R. Del Guidice, "Faster Test Results," *Quality Progress*, January 2004, 37(1), pp. 33–39).

a. Construct a 95% confidence interval estimate for the population mean turnaround time.
b. Interpret the interval constructed in (a).
c. Do you think the quality improvement project was a success?

8.13 The U.S. Department of Transportation requires tire manufacturers to provide tire performance information on the sidewall of the tire to better inform prospective customers when making purchasing decisions. One very important measure of tire performance is the tread wear index, which indicates the tire's resistance to tread wear compared with a tire graded with a base of 100. This means that a tire with a grade of 200 should last twice as long, on average, as a tire graded with a base of 100. A consumer organization wants to estimate the actual tread wear index of a brand name of tires that claims "graded 200" on the sidewall of the tire. A random sample of $n = 18$ indicates a sample mean tread wear index of 195.3 and a sample standard deviation of 21.4.

a. Assuming that the population of tread wear indexes is normally distributed, construct a 95% confidence interval estimate of the population mean tread wear index for tires produced by this manufacturer under this brand name.
b. Do you think that the consumer organization should accuse the manufacturer of producing tires that do not meet the performance information provided on the sidewall of the tire? Explain.
c. Explain why an observed tread wear index of 210 for a particular tire is not unusual, even though it is outside the confidence interval developed in (a).

8.14 The data in the file **Movieprices** contain the price for two tickets with online service charges, large popcorn, and two medium soft drinks at a sample of six theater chains:

$36.15 $31.00 $35.05 $40.25 $33.75 $43.00

Source: *Data extracted from K. Kelly, "The Multiplex Under Siege," The Wall Street Journal, December 24–25, 2005, pp. P1, P5.*

a. Construct a 95% confidence interval estimate for the population mean price for two tickets with online service charges, large popcorn, and two medium soft drinks, assuming a normal distribution.
b. Interpret the interval constructed in (a).

8.15 The data in the file **Sedans** represents the overall miles per gallon (MPG) of 2008 sedans priced under $20,000.

31, 27, 27, 28, 28, 28, 25, 25, 26, 25, 33, 23, 24

Source: *Data extracted from "Vehicle Ratings," Consumer Reports, April 2008, p. 32.*

a. Construct a 95% confidence interval estimate for the population mean miles per gallon of 2008 sedans (4 cylinder) priced under $20,000 assuming a normal distribution.
b. Interpret the interval constructed in (a).
c. Compare the results in (a) to those in Problem 8.16(a).

8.16 The data in the file **SUV** represents the overall miles per gallon (MPG) of 2008 SUVs priced under $30,000.

23, 20, 21, 22, 18, 18, 17, 17, 19, 19, 19,
17, 21, 18, 18, 18, 17, 17, 16, 20, 16, 22

Source: *Extracted from "Vehicle Ratings," Consumer Reports, April 2008, p. 40.*

a. Construct a 95% confidence interval estimate for the population mean miles per gallon of 2008 SUVs priced under $30,000 assuming a normal distribution.
b. Interpret the interval constructed in (a).
c. Compare the results in (a) to those in Problem 8.15(a).

8.17 The data in the file **Chicken** represent the total fat, in grams per serving, for a sample of 20 chicken sandwiches from fast-food chains. The data are as follows:

7	8	4	5	16	20	20	24	19	30
23	30	25	19	29	29	30	30	40	56

Source: *Data extracted from "Fast Food: Adding Health to the Menu," Consumer Reports, September 2004, pp. 28–31.*

a. Construct a 95% confidence interval for the population mean total fat, in grams per serving.
b. Interpret the interval constructed in (a).
c. What assumption must you make about the population distribution in order to construct the confidence interval estimate in (a)?
d. Do you think that the assumption needed in order to construct the confidence interval estimate in (a) is valid? Explain.

8.18 One of the major measures of the quality of service provided by any organization is the speed with which it responds to customer complaints. A large family-held department store selling furniture and flooring, including carpet, had undergone a major expansion in the past several years. In particular, the flooring department had expanded from 2 installation crews to an installation supervisor, a measurer, and 15 installation crews. Last year, there were 50 complaints concerning carpet installation. The following data, also in the file **Furniture**, represent the number of days between the receipt of a complaint and the resolution of the complaint:

54	5	35	137	31	27	152	2	123	81	74	27
11	19	126	110	110	29	61	35	94	31	26	5
12	4	165	32	29	28	29	26	25	1	14	13
13	10	5	27	4	52	30	22	36	26	20	23
33	68										

a. Construct a 95% confidence interval estimate of the population mean number of days between the receipt of a complaint and the resolution of the complaint.

b. What assumption must you make about the population distribution in order to construct the confidence interval estimate in (a)?

c. Do you think that the assumption needed in order to construct the confidence interval estimate in (a) is valid? Explain.

d. What effect might your conclusion in (c) have on the validity of the results in (a)?

8.19 In New York State, savings banks are permitted to sell a form of life insurance called savings bank life insurance (SBLI). The approval process consists of underwriting, which includes a review of the application, a medical information bureau check, possible requests for additional medical information and medical exams, and a policy compilation stage in which the policy pages are generated and sent to the bank for delivery. The ability to deliver approved policies to customers in a timely manner is critical to the profitability of this service to the bank. During a period of one month, a random sample of 27 approved policies was selected, and the total processing time, in days, was as shown below and stored in the file **Insurance**:

```
73  19  16  64  28  28  31  90  60  56  31  56  22  18
45  48  17  17  17  91  92  63  50  51  69  16  17
```

a. Construct a 95% confidence interval estimate of the population mean processing time.

b. What assumption must you make about the population distribution in order to construct the confidence interval estimate in (a)?

c. Do you think that the assumption needed in order to construct the confidence interval estimate in (a) is valid? Explain.

8.20 The data in the file **Dark Chocolate** represent the cost per ounce ($) for a sample of fourteen dark chocolate bars.

```
0.68  0.72  0.92  1.14  1.42  0.94  0.77
0.57  1.51  0.57  0.55  0.86  1.41  0.90
```

Source: *Data extracted from "Dark Chocolate: Which Bars Are Best?" Consumer Reports, September 2007, p. 8.*

a. Construct a 95% confidence interval estimate for the population cost per ounce ($) of dark chocolate bars.

b. What assumption do you need to make about the population distribution to construct the interval in (a)?

c. Given the data presented, do you think the assumption needed in (a) is valid? Explain.

8.21 One operation of a mill is to cut pieces of steel into parts that are used later in the frame for front seats in an automobile. The steel is cut with a diamond saw and requires the resulting parts to be within ± 0.005 inch of the length specified by the automobile company. The measurement reported from a sample of 100 steel parts (and stored in the file **Steel**) is the difference, in inches, between the actual length of the steel part, as measured by a laser measurement device, and the specified length of the steel part. For example, the first observation, -0.002, represents a steel part that is 0.002 inch shorter than the specified length.

a. Construct a 95% confidence interval estimate of the population mean difference between the actual length of the steel part and the specified length of the steel part.

b. What assumption must you make about the population distribution in order to construct the confidence interval estimate in (a)?

c. Do you think that the assumption needed in order to construct the confidence interval estimate in (a) is valid? Explain.

d. Compare the conclusions reached in (a) with those of Problem 2.23 on page 46.

8.3 Confidence Interval Estimation for the Proportion

This section extends the concept of the confidence interval to categorical data. Here you are concerned with estimating the proportion of items in a population having a certain characteristic of interest. The unknown population proportion is represented by the Greek letter π. The point estimate for π is the sample proportion, $p = X/n$, where n is the sample size and X is the number of items in the sample having the characteristic of interest. Equation (8.3) defines the confidence interval estimate for the population proportion.

> CONFIDENCE INTERVAL ESTIMATE FOR THE PROPORTION
>
> $$p \pm Z_{\alpha/2} \sqrt{\frac{p(1-p)}{n}}$$
>
> or
>
> $$p - Z_{\alpha/2} \sqrt{\frac{p(1-p)}{n}} \le \pi \le p + Z_{\alpha/2} \sqrt{\frac{p(1-p)}{n}} \qquad \textbf{(8.3)}$$

where

$$p = \text{sample proportion} = \frac{X}{n} = \frac{\text{Number of items having the characteristic}}{\text{Sample size}}$$

π = population proportion

$Z_{\alpha/2}$ = critical value from the standardized normal distribution

n = sample size

Note: To use this interval, the sample size n must be large enough to ensure that both X and $n - X$ are greater than 5.

You can use the confidence interval estimate of the proportion defined in Equation (8.3) to estimate the proportion of sales invoices that contain errors (see the Using Statistics scenario on page 239). Suppose that in a sample of 100 sales invoices, 10 contain errors. Thus, for these data, $p = X/n = 10/100 = 0.10$. Using Equation (8.3) and $Z_{\alpha/2} = 1.96$ for 95% confidence,

$$p \pm Z_{\alpha/2}\sqrt{\frac{p(1 - p)}{n}}$$

$$= 0.10 \pm (1.96)\sqrt{\frac{(0.10)(0.90)}{100}}$$

$$= 0.10 \pm (1.96)(0.03)$$

$$= 0.10 \pm 0.0588$$

$$0.0412 \le \pi \le 0.1588$$

Therefore, you have 95% confidence that between 4.12% and 15.88% of all the sales invoices contain errors. Figure 8.12 shows a Microsoft Excel worksheet for these data and Figure 8.13 shows Minitab results.

FIGURE 8.12

Microsoft Excel worksheet to construct a confidence interval estimate for the proportion of sales invoices that contain errors

See Section E8.3 or P8.3 to create this.

	A	B	
1	**Proportion of In-Error Sales Invoices**		
2			
3	**Data**		
4	**Sample Size**	100	
5	**Number of Successes**	10	
6	**Confidence Level**	95%	
7			
8	**Intermediate Calculations**		
9	Sample Proportion	0.1	=B5/B4
10	Z Value	-1.9600	=NORMSINV((1 - B6)/2)
11	Standard Error of the Proportion	0.03	=SQRT(B9 * (1 - B9)/B4)
12	Interval Half Width	0.0588	=ABS(B10 * B11)
13			
14	**Confidence Interval**		
15	**Interval Lower Limit**	0.0412	=B9 - B12
16	**Interval Upper Limit**	0.1588	=B9 + B12

FIGURE 8.13

Minitab confidence interval estimate for the proportion of sales invoices that contain errors

See Section M8.3 to create this.

```
Sample   X    N   Sample p          95% CI
1       10  100   0.100000   (0.041201, 0.158799)

Using the normal approximation.
```

Example 8.4 illustrates another application of a confidence interval estimate for the proportion.

EXAMPLE 8.4

Estimating the Proportion of Nonconforming Newspapers Printed

The operations manager at a large newspaper wants to estimate the proportion of newspapers printed that have a nonconforming attribute, such as excessive ruboff, improper page setup, missing pages, or duplicate pages. A random sample of $n = 200$ newspapers is selected from all the newspapers printed during a single day. In this sample, 35 contain some type of nonconformance. Construct and interpret a 90% confidence interval for the proportion of newspapers printed during the day that have a nonconforming attribute.

SOLUTION Using Equation (8.3),

$$p = \frac{X}{n} = \frac{35}{200} = 0.175, \text{ and with a 90\% level of confidence } Z_{\alpha/2} = 1.645$$

$$p \pm Z_{\alpha/2}\sqrt{\frac{p(1-p)}{n}}$$

$$= 0.175 \pm (1.645)\sqrt{\frac{(0.175)(0.825)}{200}}$$

$$= 0.175 \pm (1.645)(0.0269)$$

$$= 0.175 \pm 0.0442$$

$$0.1308 \le \pi \le 0.2192$$

You conclude with 90% confidence that between 13.08% and 21.92% of the newspapers printed on that day have some type of nonconformance.

Equation (8.3) contains a Z statistic because you can use the normal distribution to approximate the binomial distribution when the sample size is sufficiently large. In Example 8.4, the confidence interval using Z provides an excellent approximation for the population proportion because both X and $n - X$ are greater than 5. However, if you do not have a sufficiently large sample size, you should use the binomial distribution rather than Equation (8.3) (see references 1, 2, and 7). The exact confidence intervals for various sample sizes and proportions of successes have been tabulated by Fisher and Yates (reference 2) and can be computed using Minitab.

Problems for Section 8.3

LEARNING THE BASICS

8.22 If $n = 200$ and $X = 50$, construct a 95% confidence interval estimate of the population proportion.

8.23 If $n = 400$ and $X = 25$, construct a 99% confidence interval estimate of the population proportion.

APPLYING THE CONCEPTS

✓ SELF Test **8.24** The telephone company wants to estimate the proportion of households that would purchase an additional telephone line if it were made available at a substantially reduced installation cost. A random sample of 500 households is selected. The results indicate that 135 of the households would purchase the additional telephone line at a reduced installation cost.

a. Construct a 99% confidence interval estimate of the population proportion of households that would purchase the additional telephone line.

b. How would the manager in charge of promotional programs concerning residential customers use the results in (a)?

8.25 CareerBuilder.com surveyed 1,124 moms who were currently employed full-time. Of the women surveyed, 281 said that they were dissatisfied with their work-life balance, and 495 said that they would take a pay cut to spend more time with their kids (data extracted from D. Jones, "Poll Finds Resentment of Flextime," **usatoday.com** May 11, 2007).

a. Construct a 95% confidence interval estimate for the population proportion of moms employed full-time who are dissatisfied with their work-life balance.

b. Construct a 95% confidence interval estimate for the population proportion of moms employed full-time who would take a pay cut to spend more time with their kids.

c. Write a short summary of the information derived from (a) and (b).

8.26 In a survey conducted for American Express, 27% of small business owners indicated that they never check in with the office when on vacation (data extracted from "Snapshots," **usatoday.com**, April 18, 2006). The article did not disclose the sample size used in the study.

a. Suppose that the survey was based on 500 small business owners. Construct a 95% confidence interval estimate for the population proportion of small business owners who never check in with the office when on vacation.

b. Suppose that the survey was based on 1,000 small business owners. Construct a 95% confidence interval estimate for the population proportion of small business owners who never check in with the office when on vacation.

c. Discuss the effect of sample size on the confidence interval estimate.

8.27 The start of the twenty-first century saw many corporate scandals and many individuals lost faith in business. In a 2007 poll conducted by the New York City-based Edelman Public Relations firm, 57% of respondents say they trust business to "do what is right." This percentage was the highest in the annual survey since 2001 (data extracted from G. Colvin, "Business is Back!" *Fortune*, May 14, 2007, pp. 40–48).

a. Construct a 95% confidence interval estimate of the population proportion of individuals who trust business to "do what is right" assuming that the poll surveyed:
  1. 100 individuals.
  2. 200 individuals.
  3. 300 individuals.

b. Discuss the effect that sample size has on the width of confidence intervals.

c. Interpret the intervals in (a).

8.28 A survey of 705 workers (data extracted from "Snapshots," *USA Today*, March 21, 2006, p. 1B) were asked how much they used the Internet at work. 423 said they used it within limits, and 183 said that they did not use the Internet at work.

a. Construct a 95% confidence interval estimate for the proportion of all workers who use the Internet within limits.

b. Construct a 95% confidence interval estimate for the proportion of all workers who did not use the Internet at work.

8.29 The utility of mobile devices raises new questions about the intrusion of work into personal life. In a recent survey by **CareerJournal.com** (data extracted from P. Kitchen, "Can't Turn It Off," *Newsday*, October 20, 2006, pp. F4–F5), 158 of 473 employees responded that they typically took work with them on vacation and 85 responded that there are unwritten and unspoken expectations that they stay connected.

a. Construct a 95% confidence interval estimate for the population proportion of employees who typically take work with them on vacation.

b. Construct a 95% confidence interval estimate for the population proportion of employees who said that there are unwritten and unspoken expectations that they stay connected.

c. Interpret the intervals in (a) and (b).

d. Explain the difference in the results in (a) and (b).

8.4 Determining Sample Size

In each confidence interval developed so far in this chapter, the sample size was reported along with the results with little discussion of the width of the resulting confidence interval. In the business world, sample sizes are determined prior to data collection to ensure that the confidence interval is narrow enough to be useful in making decisions. Determining the proper sample size is a complicated procedure, subject to the constraints of budget, time, and the amount of acceptable sampling error. In the Saxon Home Improvement example, if you want to estimate the mean dollar amount of the sales invoices, you must determine in advance how large a sampling error to allow in estimating the population mean. You must also determine, in advance, the level of confidence (i.e., 90%, 95%, or 99%) to use in estimating the population parameter.

Sample Size Determination for the Mean

To develop an equation for determining the appropriate sample size needed when constructing a confidence interval estimate of the mean, recall Equation (8.1) on page 243:

$$\bar{X} \pm Z_{\alpha/2} \frac{\sigma}{\sqrt{n}}$$

The amount added to or subtracted from $\overline{X}$ is equal to half the width of the interval. This quantity represents the amount of imprecision in the estimate that results from sampling error. The **sampling error**[1], e, is defined as

[1]In this context, some statisticians refer to e as the "**margin of error**."

$$e = Z_{\alpha/2}\frac{\sigma}{\sqrt{n}}$$

Solving for n gives the sample size needed to construct the appropriate confidence interval estimate for the mean. "Appropriate" means that the resulting interval will have an acceptable amount of sampling error.

SAMPLE SIZE DETERMINATION FOR THE MEAN

The sample size, n, is equal to the product of the $Z_{\alpha/2}$ value squared and the standard deviation, σ, squared, divided by the square of the sampling error, e.

$$n = \frac{Z_{\alpha/2}^2 \sigma^2}{e^2} \tag{8.4}$$

To compute the sample size, you must know three factors:

1. The desired confidence level, which determines the value of $Z_{\alpha/2}$, the critical value from the standardized normal distribution[2]

2. The acceptable sampling error, e

3. The standard deviation, σ

[2]You use Z instead of t because, to determine the critical value of t, you need to know the sample size, but you do not know it yet. For most studies, the sample size needed is large enough that the standardized normal distribution is a good approximation of the t distribution.

In some business-to-business relationships that require estimation of important parameters, legal contracts specify acceptable levels of sampling error and the confidence level required. For companies in the food or drug sectors, government regulations often specify sampling errors and confidence levels. In general, however, it is usually not easy to specify the three factors needed to determine the sample size. How can you determine the level of confidence and sampling error? Typically, these questions are answered only by the subject matter expert (i.e., the individual most familiar with the variables under study). Although 95% is the most common confidence level used, if more confidence is desired, then 99% might be more appropriate; if less confidence is deemed acceptable, then 90% might be used. For the sampling error, you should think not of how much sampling error you would like to have (you really do not want any error) but of how much you can tolerate when reaching conclusions from the confidence interval.

In addition to specifying the confidence level and the sampling error, you need an estimate of the standard deviation. Unfortunately, you rarely know the population standard deviation, σ. In some instances, you can estimate the standard deviation from past data. In other situations, you can make an educated guess by taking into account the range and distribution of the variable. For example, if you assume a normal distribution, the range is approximately equal to 6σ (i.e., $\pm 3\sigma$ around the mean) so that you estimate σ as the range divided by 6. If you cannot estimate σ in this way, you can conduct a small-scale study and estimate the standard deviation from the resulting data.

To explore how to determine the sample size needed for estimating the population mean, consider again the audit at Saxon Home Improvement. In Section 8.2, you selected a sample of 100 sales invoices and constructed a 95% confidence interval estimate of the population mean sales invoice amount. How was this sample size determined? Should you have selected a different sample size?

Suppose that, after consultation with company officials, you determine that a sampling error of no more than ±$5 is desired, along with 95% confidence. Past data indicate that the standard deviation of the sales amount is approximately $25. Thus, $e = \$5, \sigma = \$25$, and $Z_{\alpha/2} = 1.96$ (for 95% confidence). Using Equation (8.4),

$$n = \frac{Z_{\alpha/2}^2 \sigma^2}{e^2} = \frac{(1.96)^2 (25)^2}{(5)^2}$$

$$= 96.04$$

Because the general rule is to slightly oversatisfy the criteria by rounding the sample size up to the next whole integer, you should select a sample of size 97. Thus, the sample of size $n = 100$ used on page 248 is close to what is necessary to satisfy the needs of the company, based on the estimated standard deviation, desired confidence level, and sampling error. Because the calculated sample standard deviation is slightly higher than expected, $28.95 compared to $25.00, the confidence interval is slightly wider than desired. Figure 8.14 shows a Microsoft Excel worksheet to determine the sample size.

FIGURE 8.14

Microsoft Excel worksheet for determining sample size for estimating the mean sales invoice amount for the Saxon Home Improvement Company

See Section E8.4 or P8.4 to create this.

	A	B	
1	**For Mean Sales Invoice Amount**		
2			
3	**Data**		
4	**Population Standard Deviation**	25	
5	**Sampling Error**	5	
6	**Confidence Level**	95%	
7			
8	**Intermediate Calculations**		
9	Z Value	-1.9600	=NORMSINV((1 - B6)/2)
10	Calculated Sample Size	96.0365	=((B9 * B4)/B5)^2
11			
12	**Result**		
13	**Sample Size Needed**	97	=ROUNDUP(B10, 0)

Example 8.5 illustrates another application of determining the sample size needed to develop a confidence interval estimate for the mean.

EXAMPLE 8.5

Determining the Sample Size for the Mean

Returning to Example 8.3 on page 249, suppose you want to estimate the population mean force required to break the insulator to within ±25 pounds with 95% confidence. On the basis of a study taken the previous year, you believe that the standard deviation is 100 pounds. Find the sample size needed.

SOLUTION Using Equation (8.4) on page 257 and $e = 25, \sigma = 100$, and $Z_{\alpha/2} = 1.96$ for 95% confidence,

$$n = \frac{Z_{\alpha/2}^2 \sigma^2}{e^2} = \frac{(1.96)^2 (100)^2}{(25)^2}$$

$$= 61.47$$

Therefore, you should select a sample size of 62 insulators because the general rule for determining sample size is to always round up to the next integer value in order to slightly oversatisfy the criteria desired. An actual sampling error slightly larger than 25 will result if the sample standard deviation calculated in this sample of 62 is greater than 100 and slightly smaller if the sample standard deviation is less than 100.

Sample Size Determination for the Proportion

So far in this section, you have learned how to determine the sample size needed for estimating the population mean. Now suppose that you want to determine the sample size necessary for estimating a population proportion.

To determine the sample size needed to estimate a population proportion, π, you use a method similar to the method for a population mean. Recall that in developing the sample size for a confidence interval for the mean, the sampling error is defined by

$$e = Z_{\alpha/2} \frac{\sigma}{\sqrt{n}}$$

When estimating a proportion, you replace σ with $\sqrt{\pi(1 - \pi)}$. Thus, the sampling error is

$$e = Z_{\alpha/2} \sqrt{\frac{\pi(1 - \pi)}{n}}$$

Solving for n, you have the sample size necessary to develop a confidence interval estimate for a proportion.

SAMPLE SIZE DETERMINATION FOR THE PROPORTION

The sample size n is equal to the product of $Z_{\alpha/2}$ squared, the population proportion, π, and 1 minus the population proportion, π, divided by the square of the sampling error, e.

$$n = \frac{Z_{\alpha/2}^2 \pi(1 - \pi)}{e^2} \tag{8.5}$$

To determine the sample size, you must know three factors:

1. The desired confidence level, which determines the value of $Z_{\alpha/2}$, the critical value from the standardized normal distribution
2. The acceptable sampling error (or margin of error), e
3. The population proportion, π

In practice, selecting these quantities requires some planning. Once you determine the desired level of confidence, you can find the appropriate $Z_{\alpha/2}$ value from the standardized normal distribution. The sampling error, e, indicates the amount of error that you are willing to tolerate in estimating the population proportion. The third quantity, π, is actually the population parameter that you want to estimate! Thus, how do you state a value for what you are trying to determine?

Here you have two alternatives. In many situations, you may have past information or relevant experience that provide an educated estimate of π. Or, if you do not have past information or relevant experience, you can try to provide a value for π that would never *underestimate* the sample size needed. Referring to Equation (8.5), you can see that the quantity $\pi(1 - \pi)$ appears in the numerator. Thus, you need to determine the value of π that will make the quantity $\pi(1 - \pi)$ as large as possible. When $\pi = 0.5$, the product $\pi(1 - \pi)$ achieves its maximum value. To show this result, consider the following values of π, along with the accompanying products of $\pi(1 - \pi)$:

When $\pi = 0.9$, then $\pi(1 - \pi) = (0.9)(0.1) = 0.09$

When $\pi = 0.7$, then $\pi(1 - \pi) = (0.7)(0.3) = 0.21$

When $\pi = 0.5$, then $\pi(1 - \pi) = (0.5)(0.5) = 0.25$

When $\pi = 0.3$, then $\pi(1 - \pi) = (0.3)(0.7) = 0.21$

When $\pi = 0.1$, then $\pi(1 - \pi) = (0.1)(0.9) = 0.09$

Therefore, when you have no prior knowledge or estimate of the population proportion, π, you should use $\pi = 0.5$ for determining the sample size. Using $\pi = 0.5$ produces the largest possible sample size and results in the narrowest and most precise confidence interval. This increased precision comes at the cost of spending more time and money for an increased sample size. Also, note that if you use $\pi = 0.5$ and the proportion is different from 0.5, you will overestimate the sample size needed, because you will get a confidence interval narrower than originally intended.

Returning to the Saxon Home Improvement Using Statistics scenario on page 239, suppose that the auditing procedures require you to have 95% confidence in estimating the population proportion of sales invoices with errors to within ±0.07. The results from past months indicate that the largest proportion has been no more than 0.15. Thus, using Equation (8.5) on page 259 and $e = 0.07$, $\pi = 0.15$, and $Z_{\alpha/2} = 1.96$ for 95% confidence,

$$n = \frac{Z_{\alpha/2}^2 \pi (1 - \pi)}{e^2}$$

$$= \frac{(1.96)^2 (0.15)(0.85)}{(0.07)^2}$$

$$= 99.96$$

Because the general rule is to round the sample size up to the next whole integer to slightly oversatisfy the criteria, a sample size of 100 is needed. Thus, the sample size needed to satisfy the requirements of the company, based on the estimated proportion, desired confidence level, and sampling error, is equal to the sample size taken on page 254. The actual confidence interval is narrower than required because the sample proportion is 0.10, whereas 0.15 was used for π in Equation (8.5). Figure 8.15 shows a Microsoft Excel worksheet for determining sample size.

FIGURE 8.15

Microsoft Excel worksheet for determining sample size for estimating the proportion of sales invoices with errors for the Saxon Home Improvement Company

See Section E8.5 or P8.5 to create this.

	A	B	
1	**For Proportion of In-Error Sales Invoices**		
2			
3	**Data**		
4	**Estimate of True Proportion**	0.15	
5	**Sampling Error**	0.07	
6	**Confidence Level**	95%	
7			
8	Intermediate Calculations		
9	Z Value	-1.9600	=NORMSINV((1 - B6)/2)
10	Calculated Sample Size	99.9563	=(B9^2 * B4 * (1 - B4))/B5^2
11			
12	**Result**		
13	**Sample Size Needed**	100	=ROUNDUP(B10, 0)

Example 8.6 provides another application of determining the sample size for estimating the population proportion.

EXAMPLE 8.6

Determining the Sample Size for the Population Proportion

You want to have 90% confidence of estimating the proportion of office workers who respond to e-mail within an hour to within ±0.05. Because you have not previously undertaken such a study, there is no information available from past data. Determine the sample size needed.

SOLUTION Because no information is available from past data, assume that $\pi = 0.50$. Using Equation (8.5) on page 259 and $e = 0.05$, $\pi = 0.50$, and $Z_{a/2} = 1.645$ for 90% confidence,

$$n = \frac{Z_{\alpha/2}^2 \pi (1 - \pi)}{e^2}$$

$$= \frac{(1.645)^2 (0.50)(0.50)}{(0.05)^2}$$

$$= 270.6$$

Therefore, you need a sample of 271 office workers to estimate the population proportion to within ±0.05 with 90% confidence.

Problems for Section 8.4

LEARNING THE BASICS

8.30 If you want to be 95% confident of estimating the population mean to within a sampling error of ±5 and the standard deviation is assumed to be 15, what sample size is required?

8.31 If you want to be 99% confident of estimating the population mean to within a sampling error of ±20 and the standard deviation is assumed to be 100, what sample size is required?

8.32 If you want to be 99% confident of estimating the population proportion to within a sampling error of ±0.04, what sample size is needed?

8.33 If you want to be 95% confident of estimating the population proportion to within a sampling error of ±0.02 and there is historical evidence that the population proportion is approximately 0.40, what sample size is needed?

APPLYING THE CONCEPTS

✓SELF Test **8.34** A survey is planned to determine the mean annual family medical expenses of employees of a large company. The management of the company wishes to be 95% confident that the sample mean is correct to within ±$50 of the population mean annual family medical expenses. A previous study indicates that the standard deviation is approximately $400.
a. How large a sample size is necessary?
b. If management wants to be correct to within ±$25, how many employees need to be selected?

8.35 If the manager of a paint supply store wants to estimate the mean amount of paint in a 1-gallon can to within ±0.004 gallon with 95% confidence and also assumes that the standard deviation is 0.02 gallon, what sample size is needed?

8.36 If a quality control manager wants to estimate the mean life of lightbulbs to within ±20 hours with 95% confidence and also assumes that the population standard deviation is 100 hours, how many lightbulbs need to be selected?

8.37 If the inspection division of a county weights and measures department wants to estimate the mean amount of soft-drink fill in 2-liter bottles to within ±0.01 liter with 95% confidence and also assumes that the standard deviation is 0.05 liter, what sample size is needed?

8.38 A consumer group wants to estimate the mean electric bill for the month of July for single-family homes in a large city. Based on studies conducted in other cities, the standard deviation is assumed to be $25. The group wants to estimate the mean bill for July to within ±$5 with 99% confidence.

a. What sample size is needed?
b. If 95% confidence is desired, how many homes need to be selected?

8.39 An advertising agency that serves a major radio station wants to estimate the mean amount of time that the station's audience spends listening to the radio daily. From past studies, the standard deviation is estimated as 45 minutes.
a. What sample size is needed if the agency wants to be 90% confident of being correct to within ±5 minutes?
b. If 99% confidence is desired, how many listeners need to be selected?

8.40 A growing niche in the restaurant business is gourmet-casual breakfast, lunch, and brunch. Chains in this group include Le Peep, Good Egg, Eggs & I, First Watch, and Eggs Up Grill. The mean per-person check for First Watch is approximately $7, and the mean per-person check for Eggs Up Grill is $6.50 (data extracted from J. Hayes, "Competition Heats Up as Breakfast Concepts Eye Growth," *Nation's Restaurant News*, April 24, 2006, pp. 8, 66).
a. Assuming a standard deviation of $2.00, what sample size is needed to estimate the mean per-person check for Good Egg to within ±$0.25 with 95% confidence?
b. Assuming a standard deviation of $2.50, what sample size is needed to estimate the mean per-person check for Good Egg to within ±$0.25 with 95% confidence?
c. Assuming a standard deviation of $3.00, what sample size is needed to estimate the mean per-person check for Good Egg to within ±$0.25 with 95% confidence?
d. Discuss the effect of variation on selecting the sample size needed.

8.41 What proportion of people hit snags with online transactions? According to a poll conducted by Harris Interactive, 89% hit snags with online transactions (data extracted from "Snapshots: Top Online Transaction Trouble," *USA Today*, April 4, 2006, p. 1D).
a. To conduct a follow-up study that would provide 95% confidence that the point estimate is correct to within ±0.04 of the population proportion, how large a sample size is required?
b. To conduct a follow-up study that would provide 99% confidence that the point estimate is correct to within ±0.04 of the population proportion, how many people need to be sampled?
c. To conduct a follow-up study that would provide 95% confidence that the point estimate is correct to within ±0.02 of the population proportion, how large a sample size is required?
d. To conduct a follow-up study that would provide 99% confidence that the point estimate is correct to within ±0.02 of the population proportion, how many people need to be sampled?

e. Discuss the effects of changing the desired confidence level and the acceptable sampling error on sample size requirements.

8.42 A poll of 1,286 young adult cellphone users was conducted in March 2006. These cellphone users, aged 18 to 29, were actively engaged in multiple uses of their cellphones. The data suggest that 707 took still pictures with their phones, 604 played games, and 360 used the Internet (data extracted from "Poll: Cellphones Are Annoying but Invaluable," **usatoday.com**, April 3, 2006). Construct a 95% confidence interval estimate of the population proportion of young adults that used their cellphone to
a. take still pictures.
b. play games.
c. use the Internet.
d. You have been asked to update the results of this study. Determine the sample size necessary to estimate the population proportions in (a) through (c) to within ±0.02 with 95% confidence.

8.43 A study of 658 CEOs conducted by the Conference Board reported that 250 stated that their company's greatest concern was sustained and steady top-line growth (data extracted from "Snapshots: CEOs' Greatest Concerns," *USA Today*, May 8, 2006, p. 1D).
a. Construct a 95% confidence interval for the proportion of CEOs whose greatest concern was sustained and steady top-line growth.
b. Interpret the interval constructed in (a).
c. To conduct a follow-up study to estimate the population proportion of CEOs whose greatest concern was sustained and steady top-line growth to within ±0.01 with 95% confidence, how many CEOs would you survey?

8.44 In 2007, oil companies posted huge profits and consumers paid record high prices at the gas pump. The president of Shell Oil stated that "we know for a fact that the favorability rating of oil companies today ranges from 10–15%" (data extracted from D. J. Lynch, "Shell Oil Tries Different Path to Engage Public Opinion," **usatoday.com**, May 14, 2007).
a. If you conduct a follow-up study to estimate the population proportion of individuals who view oil companies favorably, would you use a π of 0.10, 0.15, or 0.50 in the sample size formula? Discuss.
b. Using your answer to (a), find the sample size necessary to estimate the population proportion to within ±0.03 with 95% certainty.

8.45 The Department of Commerce announced that the national rental vacancy rate during the first quarter of 2007 was 10.1%. The report noted that the proportion of rentals vacant was 0.101 and with 95% confidence a margin of error of 0.004 (data extracted from R. R. Callis and L. B. Cavanaugh, "Census Bureau Reports on Residential Vacancies and Homeownership," *United States Department of Commerce News*, April 27, 2007, p.1).
a. Construct a 95% confidence interval estimate for the national rental vacancy rate.
b. Interpret the interval found in (a).
c. If the estimate reported was constructed using the methods in this section, what sample size was used?

8.5 Confidence Interval Estimation and Ethical Issues

Ethical issues relating to the selection of samples and the inferences that accompany them can occur in several ways. The major ethical issue relates to whether confidence interval estimates are provided along with the point estimates. To provide a point estimate without also including the confidence interval limits (typically set at 95%), the sample size used, and an interpretation of the meaning of the confidence interval in terms that a person untrained in statistics can understand raises ethical issues. Failure to include a confidence interval estimate might mislead the user of the results into thinking that the point estimate is all that is needed to predict the population characteristic with certainty. Thus, it is important that you indicate the interval estimate in a prominent place in any written communication, along with a simple explanation of the meaning of the confidence interval. In addition, you should highlight the sample size and sampling error.

One of the most common areas where ethical issues concerning confidence intervals occurs is in the publication of the results of political polls. Often, the results of the polls are highlighted on the front page of the newspaper, and the sampling error involved along with the methodology used is printed on the page where the article is continued, often in the middle of the newspaper. To ensure an ethical presentation of statistical results, the confidence levels, sample size, sampling error, and confidence limits should be made available for all surveys and other statistical studies.

USING STATISTICS @ Saxon Home Improvement Revisited

I n the Using Statistics scenario, you were an accountant for Saxon Home Improvement, a distributor of home improvement supplies in the northeastern United States. You were responsible for the accuracy of the integrated inventory management and sales information system. You used confidence interval estimation techniques to draw conclusions about the population of all records from a relatively small sample collected during an audit.

At the end of the month, you collected a random sample of 100 sales invoices and made the following inferences:

- With 95% confidence, you concluded that the mean amount of all the sales invoices is between $104.53 and $116.01.
- With 95% confidence, you concluded that between 4.12% and 15.88% of all the sales invoices contain errors.

These estimates provide an interval of values that you believe contain the true population parameters. If these intervals are too wide (i.e., the sampling error is too large) for the types of decisions Saxon Home Improvement needs to make, you will need to take a larger sample. You can use the sample size formulas in Section 8.4 to determine the number of sales invoices to sample to ensure that the size of the sampling error is acceptable.

SUMMARY

This chapter discusses confidence intervals for estimating the characteristics of a population, along with how you can determine the necessary sample size. You learned how to apply these methods to numerical and categorical data. Table 8.3 provides a list of topics covered in this chapter.

To determine what equation to use for a particular situation, you need to answer two questions:

- Are you developing a confidence interval or are you determining sample size?
- Do you have a numerical variable or do you have a categorical variable?

The next three chapters develop a hypothesis-testing approach to making decisions about population parameters.

TABLE 8.3

Summary of Topics in Chapter 8

| | Type of Data | |
Type of Analysis	Numerical	Categorical
Confidence interval for a population parameter	Confidence interval estimate for the mean (Sections 8.1 and 8.2)	Confidence interval estimate for the proportion (Section 8.3)
Determining sample size	Sample size determination for the mean (Section 8.4)	Sample size determination for the proportion (Section 8.4)

KEY EQUATIONS

Confidence Interval for the Mean (σ Known)

$$\bar{X} \pm Z_{\alpha/2} \frac{\sigma}{\sqrt{n}}$$

or

$$\bar{X} - Z_{\alpha/2} \frac{\sigma}{\sqrt{n}} \le \mu \le \bar{X} + Z_{\alpha/2} \frac{\sigma}{\sqrt{n}} \qquad \textbf{(8.1)}$$

Confidence Interval for the Mean (σ Unknown)

$$\bar{X} \pm t_{\alpha/2} \frac{S}{\sqrt{n}}$$

or

$$\bar{X} - t_{\alpha/2} \frac{S}{\sqrt{n}} \le \mu \le \bar{X} + t_{\alpha/2} \frac{S}{\sqrt{n}} \qquad \textbf{(8.2)}$$

Confidence Interval Estimate for the Proportion

$$p \pm Z_{\alpha/2}\sqrt{\frac{p(1-p)}{n}}$$

or

$$p - Z_{\alpha/2}\sqrt{\frac{p(1-p)}{n}} \leq \pi \leq p + Z_{\alpha/2}\sqrt{\frac{p(1-p)}{n}} \quad \textbf{(8.3)}$$

Sample Size Determination for the Mean

$$n = \frac{Z_{\alpha/2}^2\sigma^2}{e^2} \quad \textbf{(8.4)}$$

Sample Size Determination for the Proportion

$$n = \frac{Z_{\alpha/2}^2\pi(1-\pi)}{e^2} \quad \textbf{(8.5)}$$

KEY TERMS

confidence interval estimate 240	level of confidence 243	sampling error 257
critical value 244	margin of error 257	Student's t distribution 246
degrees of freedom 246	point estimate 240	

CHAPTER REVIEW PROBLEMS

CHECKING YOUR UNDERSTANDING

8.46 Why can you never really have 100% confidence of correctly estimating the population characteristic of interest?

8.47 When are you able to use the t distribution to develop the confidence interval estimate for the mean?

8.48 Why is it true that for a given sample size, n, an increase in confidence is achieved by widening (and making less precise) the confidence interval?

8.49 Why is the sample size needed to determine the proportion smaller when the population proportion is 0.20 than when the population proportion is 0.50?

APPLYING THE CONCEPTS

8.50 You work in the corporate office for a nationwide convenience store franchise that operates nearly 10,000 stores. The per-store daily customer count has been steady at 900 for some time (i.e., the mean number of customers in a store in one day is 900). To increase the customer count, the franchise is considering cutting coffee prices by approximately half. The 12-ounce size will now be $.59 instead of $.99, and the 16-ounce size will be $.69 instead of $1.19. Even with this reduction in price, the franchise will have a 40% gross margin on coffee. To test the new initiative, the franchise has reduced coffee prices in a sample of 34 stores, where customer counts have been running almost exactly at the national average of 900. After four weeks, the sample stores stabilize at a mean customer count of 974 and a standard deviation of 96. This increase seems like a substantial amount to you, but it also seems like a pretty small sample. Is there some way to get a feel for what the mean per-store count in all the stores will be if you cut coffee prices nationwide? Do you think reducing coffee prices is a good strategy for increasing the mean customer count?

8.51 Companies are spending more time screening applicants than in the past. A study of 102 recruiters conducted by ExecuNet found that 77 did Internet research on candidates (data extracted from P. Kitchen, "Don't Let Any 'Digital Dirt' Bury Your Job Prospects," *Newsday*, August 21, 2005, p. A59).

a. Construct a 95% confidence interval estimate of the population proportion of recruiters who do Internet research on candidates.
b. Based on (a), is it correct to conclude that more than 70% of recruiters do Internet research on candidates?
c. Suppose that the study uses a sample size of 400 recruiters and 302 did Internet research on candidates. Construct a 95% confidence interval estimate of the population proportion of recruiters who do Internet research on candidates.
d. Based on (c), is it correct to conclude that more than 70% of recruiters do Internet research on candidates?
e. Discuss the effect of sample size on your answers to (a) through (d).

8.52 A market researcher for a consumer electronics company wants to study the television viewing habits of residents of a particular area. A random sample of 40 respondents is selected, and each respondent is instructed to keep a detailed record of all television viewing in a particular week. The results are as follows:
- Viewing time per week: $\overline{X}$ = 15.3 hours, S = 3.8 hours.
- 27 respondents watch the evening news on at least 3 weeknights.

a. Construct a 95% confidence interval estimate for the mean amount of television watched per week in this city.
b. Construct a 95% confidence interval estimate for the population proportion who watch the evening news on at least 3 weeknights per week.

Suppose that the market researcher wants to take another survey in a different city. Answer these questions:

c. What sample size is required to be 95% confident of estimating the population mean to within ±2 hours and assumes that the population standard deviation is equal to 5 hours?

d. How many respondents need to be selected to be 95% confident of being within ±0.035 of the population proportion who watch the evening news on at least 3 weeknights if no previous estimate is available?

e. Based on (c) and (d), how many respondents should the market researcher select if a single survey is being conducted?

8.53 The real estate assessor for a county government wants to study various characteristics of single-family houses in the county. A random sample of 70 houses reveals the following:

- Heated area of the houses (in square feet): $\overline{X} = 1,759$, $S = 380$.
- 42 houses have central air-conditioning.

a. Construct a 99% confidence interval estimate of the population mean heated area of the houses.

b. Construct a 95% confidence interval estimate of the population proportion of houses that have central air-conditioning.

8.54 The personnel director of a large corporation wishes to study absenteeism among clerical workers at the corporation's central office during the year. A random sample of 25 clerical workers reveals the following:

- Absenteeism: $\overline{X} = 9.7$ days, $S = 4.0$ days.
- 12 clerical workers were absent more than 10 days.

a. Construct a 95% confidence interval estimate of the mean number of absences for clerical workers during the year.

b. Construct a 95% confidence interval estimate of the population proportion of clerical workers absent more than 10 days during the year.

Suppose that the personnel director also wishes to take a survey in a branch office. Answer these questions:

c. What sample size is needed to have 95% confidence in estimating the population mean absenteeism to within ±1.5 days if the population standard deviation is estimated to be 4.5 days?

d. How many clerical workers need to be selected to have 90% confidence in estimating the population proportion to within ±0.075 if no previous estimate is available?

e. Based on (c) and (d), what sample size is needed if a single survey is being conducted?

8.55 The market research director for Dotty's Department Store wants to study women's spending on cosmetics. A survey of the store's credit card holders is designed in order to estimate the proportion of women who purchase their cosmetics primarily from Dotty's Department Store and the mean yearly amount that women spend on cosmetics. A pre-

vious survey found that the standard deviation of the amount women spend on cosmetics in a year is approximately $18.

a. What sample size is needed to have 99% confidence of estimating the population mean to within ±$5?

b. How many of the store's credit card holders need to be selected to have 90% confidence of estimating the population proportion to within ±0.045?

8.56 The owner of a restaurant that serves continental food wants to study characteristics of his customers. He decides to focus on two variables: the amount of money spent by customers and whether customers order dessert. The results from a sample of 60 customers are as follows:

- Amount spent: $\overline{X} = \$38.54, S = \$7.26$.
- 18 customers purchased dessert.

a. Construct a 95% confidence interval estimate of the population mean amount spent per customer in the restaurant.

b. Construct a 90% confidence interval estimate of the population proportion of customers who purchase dessert.

The owner of a competing restaurant wants to conduct a similar survey in her restaurant. This owner does not have access to the information of the owner of the first restaurant. Answer the following questions:

c. What sample size is needed to have 95% confidence of estimating the population mean amount spent in her restaurant to within ±$1.50, assuming that the standard deviation is estimated to be $8?

d. How many customers need to be selected to have 90% confidence of estimating the population proportion of customers who purchase dessert to within ±0.04?

e. Based on your answers to (c) and (d), how large a sample should the owner take?

8.57 The manufacturer of "Ice Melt" claims its product will melt snow and ice at temperatures as low as 0° Fahrenheit. A representative for a large chain of hardware stores is interested in testing this claim. The chain purchases a large shipment of 5-pound bags for distribution. The representative wants to know with 95% confidence, within ±0.05, what proportion of bags of Ice Melt perform the job as claimed by the manufacturer.

a. How many bags does the representative need to test? What assumption should be made concerning the population proportion? (This is called *destructive testing*; that is, the product being tested is destroyed by the test and is then unavailable to be sold.)

b. The representative tests 50 bags, and 42 of them do the job as claimed. Construct a 95% confidence interval estimate for the population proportion that will do the job as claimed.

c. How can the representative use the results of (b) to determine whether to sell the Ice Melt product?

8.58 A manufacturing company produces steel housings for electrical equipment. The main component part of the housing is a steel trough that is made out of a 14-gauge steel coil. It is produced using a 250-ton progressive punch press with a wipe-down operation that puts two 90-degree forms in the flat steel to make the trough. The distance from one side of the form to the other is critical because of weatherproofing in outdoor applications. The widths (in inches) and stored in the file **Trough** from a sample of 49 troughs follows:

8.312 8.343 8.317 8.383 8.348 8.410 8.351 8.373 8.481 8.422

8.476 8.382 8.484 8.403 8.414 8.419 8.385 8.465 8.498 8.447

8.436 8.413 8.489 8.414 8.481 8.415 8.479 8.429 8.458 8.462

8.460 8.444 8.429 8.460 8.412 8.420 8.410 8.405 8.323 8.420

8.396 8.447 8.405 8.439 8.411 8.427 8.420 8.498 8.409

a. Construct a 95% confidence interval estimate of the mean width of the troughs.
b. Interpret the interval developed in (a).
c. Do you think the assumption needed to construct the confidence interval estimate in (a) in valid?

8.59 A quality characteristic of interest for a tea-bag-filling process is the weight of the tea in the individual bags. In this example, the label weight on the package indicates that the mean amount is 5.5 grams of tea in a bag. If the bags are underfilled, two problems arise. First, customers may not be able to brew the tea to be as strong as they wish. Second, the company may be in violation of the truth-in-labeling laws. On the other hand, if the mean amount of tea in a bag exceeds the label weight, the company is giving away product. Getting an exact amount of tea in a bag is problematic because of variation in the temperature and humidity inside the factory, differences in the density of the tea, and the extremely fast filling operation of the machine (approximately 170 bags per minute). The following data (stored in the file **Teabags**) are the weights, in grams, of a sample of 50 tea bags produced in one hour by a single machine:

5.65 5.44 5.42 5.40 5.53 5.34 5.54 5.45 5.52 5.41

5.57 5.40 5.53 5.54 5.55 5.62 5.56 5.46 5.44 5.51

5.47 5.40 5.47 5.61 5.53 5.32 5.67 5.29 5.49 5.55

5.77 5.57 5.42 5.58 5.58 5.50 5.32 5.50 5.53 5.58

5.61 5.45 5.44 5.25 5.56 5.63 5.50 5.57 5.67 5.36

a. Construct a 99% confidence interval estimate of the population mean weight of the tea bags.
b. Is the company meeting the requirement set forth on the label that the mean amount of tea in a bag is 5.5 grams?
c. Do you think the assumption needed to construct the confidence interval estimate in (a) is valid?

8.60 The manufacturer of Boston and Vermont asphalt shingles provides its customers with a 20-year warranty on most of its products. To determine whether a shingle will last as long as the warranty period, accelerated-life testing is conducted at the manufacturing plant. Accelerated-life testing exposes the shingle to the stresses it would be subject to in a lifetime of normal use via a laboratory experiment that takes only a few minutes to conduct. In this test, a shingle is repeatedly scraped with a brush for a short period of time,

and the shingle granules removed by the brushing are weighed (in grams). Shingles that experience low amounts of granule loss are expected to last longer in normal use than shingles that experience high amounts of granule loss. In this situation, a shingle should experience no more than 0.8 grams of granule loss if it is expected to last the length of the warranty period. The file **Granule** contains a sample of 170 measurements made on the company's Boston shingles and 140 measurements made on Vermont shingles.

a. For the Boston shingles, construct a 95% confidence interval estimate of the mean granule loss.
b. For the Vermont shingles, construct a 95% confidence interval estimate of the mean granule loss.
c. Do you think the assumption needed to construct the confidence interval estimates in (a) and (b) is valid?
d. Based on the results of (a) and (b), what conclusions can you reach concerning the mean granule loss of the Boston and Vermont shingles?

8.61 The manufacturer of Boston and Vermont asphalt shingles knows that product weight is a major factor in the customer's perception of quality. The last stage of the assembly line packages the shingles before they are placed on wooden pallets. Once a pallet is full (a pallet for most brands holds 16 squares of shingles), it is weighed, and the measurement is recorded. The file **Pallet** contains the weight (in pounds) from a sample of 368 pallets of Boston shingles and 330 pallets of Vermont shingles.

a. For the Boston shingles, construct a 95% confidence interval estimate of the mean weight.
b. For the Vermont shingles, construct a 95% confidence interval estimate of the mean weight.
c. Do you think the assumption needed to construct the confidence interval estimates in (a) and (b) is valid?
d. Based on the results of (a) and (b), what conclusions can you reach concerning the mean weight of the Boston and Vermont shingles?

REPORT WRITING EXERCISES

8.62 Referring to the results in Problem 8.58 concerning the width of a steel trough, write a report that summarizes your conclusions.

TEAM PROJECT

8.63 Refer to the team project on page 62. Construct all appropriate confidence interval estimates of the population characteristics of low-risk, average-risk, and high-risk mutual funds. Include these estimates in a report to the vice president for research at the financial investment service (The data are stored in the **Mutual Funds** file).

STUDENT SURVEY DATABASE

8.64 Problem 1.23 on page 13 describes a survey of 50 undergraduate students (see the file **Undergradsurvey**).

a. For these data, for each variable, construct a 95% confidence interval estimate of the population characteristic.
b. Write a report that summarizes your conclusions.

8.65 Problem 1.23 on page 13 describes a survey of 50 undergraduate students (see the file Undergradsurvey).
a. Select a sample of 50 undergraduate students at your school and conduct a similar survey for those students.
b. For the data collected in (a), repeat (a) and (b) of Problem 8.64.
c. Compare the results of (b) to those of Problem 8.64.

8.66 Problem 1.24 on page 13 describes a survey of 40 MBA students (see the file Gradsurvey).

a. For these data, for each variable, construct a 95% confidence interval estimate of the population characteristic.
b. Write a report that summarizes your conclusions.

8.67 Problem 1.24 on page 13 describes a survey of 40 MBA students (see the file Gradsurvey).
a. Select a sample of 40 graduate students in your MBA program and conduct a similar survey for those students.
b. For the data collected in (a), repeat (a) and (b) of Problem 8.66.
c. Compare the results of (b) to those of Problem 8.66.

MANAGING THE *SPRINGVILLE HERALD*

The marketing department has been considering ways to increase the number of new subscriptions and increase the rate of retention among customers who agreed to a trial subscription. Following the suggestion of Assistant Manager Lauren Adler, the department staff designed a survey to help determine various characteristics of readers of the newspaper who were not home-delivery subscribers. The survey consists of the following 10 questions:

1. Do you or a member of your household ever purchase the *Springville Herald*?
   (1) Yes   (2) No
   [If the respondent answers no, the interview is terminated.]

2. Do you receive the *Springville Herald* via home delivery?
   (1) Yes   (2) No
   [If no, skip to question 4.]

3. Do you receive the *Springville Herald*:
   (1) Monday–Saturday (2) Sunday only (3) Every day
   [If every day, skip to question 9.]

4. How often during the Monday–Saturday period do you purchase the *Springville Herald*?
   (1) Every day
   (2) Most days
   (3) Occasionally or never

5. How often do you purchase the *Springville Herald* on Sundays?
   (1) Every Sunday
   (2) 2–3 Sundays per month
   (3) No more than once a month

6. Where are you most likely to purchase the *Springville Herald*?
   (1) Convenience store
   (2) Newsstand/candy store
   (3) Vending machine
   (4) Supermarket
   (5) Other

7. Would you consider subscribing to the *Springville Herald* for a trial period if a discount were offered?
   (1) Yes   (2) No
   [If no, skip to question 9.]

8. The *Springville Herald* currently costs $0.50 Monday–Saturday and $1.50 on Sunday, for a total of $4.50 per week. How much would you be willing to pay per week to get home delivery for a 90-day trial period?

9. Do you read a daily newspaper other than the *Springville Herald*?
   (1) Yes   (2) No

10. As an incentive for long-term subscribers, the newspaper is considering the possibility of offering a card that would provide discounts at certain restaurants in the Springville area to all subscribers who pay in advance for six months of home delivery. Would you want to get such a card under the terms of this offer?
    (1) Yes   (2) No

The group agreed to use a random-digit dialing method to poll 500 local households by telephone. Using this approach, the last four digits of a telephone number are randomly selected to go with an area code and exchange (the first 6 digits of a 10-digit telephone number). Only those pairs of area codes and exchanges that were for the Springville city area were used for this survey.

Of the 500 households selected, 94 households either refused to participate, could not be contacted after repeated attempts, or represented telephone numbers that were not in service. The summary results are as follows:

Households That Purchase the *Springville Herald*	Frequency
Yes	352
No	54

Households with Home Delivery	Frequency
Yes	136
No	216

Type of Home Delivery Subscription	Frequency
Monday–Saturday	18
Sunday only	25
7 days a week	93

Purchase Behavior of Nonsubscribers for Monday–Saturday Editions	Frequency
Every day	78
Most days	95
Occasionally or never	43

Purchase Behavior of Nonsubscribers for Sunday Editions	Frequency
Every Sunday	138
2–3 Sundays a month	54
No more than once a month	24

Nonsubscribers' Purchase Location	Frequency
Convenience store	74
Newsstand/candy store	95
Vending machine	21
Supermarket	13
Other locations	13

Would Consider Trial Subscription If Offered a Discount	Frequency
Yes	46
No	170

Rate ($) Willing to Pay per Week (data file SH8) for a 90-Day Home-Delivery Trial Subscription

4.15	3.60	4.10	3.60	3.60	3.60	4.40	3.15	4.00	3.75	4.00
3.25	3.75	3.30	3.75	3.65	4.00	4.10	3.90	3.50	3.75	3.00
3.40	4.00	3.80	3.50	4.10	4.25	3.50	3.90	3.95	4.30	4.20
3.50	3.75	3.30	3.85	3.20	4.40	3.80	3.40	3.50	2.85	3.75
3.80	3.90									

Read a Daily Newspaper Other Than the *Springville Herald*	Frequency
Yes	138
No	214

Would Prepay Six Months to Receive a Restaurant Discount Card	Frequency
Yes	66
No	286

EXERCISES

SH8.1 Some members of the marketing department are concerned about the random-digit dialing method used to collect survey responses. Prepare a memorandum that examines the following issues:
- The advantages and disadvantages of using the random-digit dialing method.
- Possible alternative approaches for conducting the survey and their advantages and disadvantages.

SH8.2 Analyze the results of the survey of Springville households. Write a report that discusses the marketing implications of the survey results for the *Springville Herald*.

WEB CASE

Apply your knowledge about confidence interval estimation in this Web Case, which extends the OurCampus! Web Case from Chapter 6.

Among its other features, the OurCampus! Web site allows customers to purchase OurCampus! LifeStyles merchandise online. To handle payment processing, the management of OurCampus! has contracted with the following firms:

- PayAFriend (PAF): an online payment system with which customers and businesses such as OurCampus! register in order to exchange payments in a secure and convenient manner without the need for a credit card.
- Continental Banking Company (Conbanco): a processing services provider that allows OurCampus! customers to pay for merchandise using nationally recognized credit cards issued by a financial institution.

To reduce costs, the management is considering eliminating one of these two payment systems. However, Virginia Duffy of the sales department suspects that customers use the two forms of payment in unequal numbers and that customers display different buying behaviors when using the two forms of payment. Therefore, she would like to first determine:

a. The proportion of customers using PAF and the proportion of customers using a credit card to pay for their purchases.

b. The mean purchase amount when using PAF and the mean purchase amount when using a credit card.

Assist Ms. Duffy by preparing an appropriate analysis based on a random sample of 50 transactions that she has prepared and placed in an internal file on the OurCampus! Web site, **www.prenhall.com/Springville/OurCampus_PymtSample. htm** or open **OurCampus_PymtSample.htm** from the Student CD-ROM Web Case folder. Summarize your findings and determine whether Ms. Duffy's conjectures about OurCampus! customer purchasing behaviors are correct. If you want the sampling error to be no more than $3 when estimating the mean purchase amount, is Ms. Duffy's sample large enough to perform a valid analysis?

REFERENCES

1. Cochran, W. G., *Sampling Techniques*, 3rd ed. (New York: Wiley, 1977).
2. Fisher, R. A., and F. Yates, *Statistical Tables for Biological, Agricultural and Medical Research*, 5th ed. (Edinburgh: Oliver & Boyd, 1957).
3. Hahn, G., and W. Meeker, *Statistical Intervals, A Guide for Practioners* (New York: John Wiley and Sons, Inc., 1991).
4. Kirk, R. E., ed., *Statistical Issues: A Reader for the Behavioral Sciences* (Belmont, CA: Wadsworth, 1972).
5. Larsen, R. L., and M. L. Marx, *An Introduction to Mathematical Statistics and Its Applications*, 4th ed. (Upper Saddle River, NJ: Prentice Hall, 2006).
6. *Microsoft Excel 2007* (Redmond, WA: Microsoft Corp., 2007).
7. *Minitab for Windows Version 15* (State College, PA: Minitab, Inc., 2006).
8. Snedecor, G. W., and W. G. Cochran, *Statistical Methods*, 7th ed. (Ames, IA: Iowa State University Press, 1980).

Using Microsoft Excel for Confidence Interval Estimation

E8.1 Computing the Confidence Interval Estimate for the Mean (σ Known)

You compute the confidence interval estimate for the mean (σ known) by making entries in the **CIE_SK** worksheet of the `CIE sigma known.xls` workbook. This worksheet uses the **NORMSINV($P < X$)** and **CONFIDENCE(1-*confidence level, population standard deviation, sample size*)** functions to compute the Z value and interval half width for the Example 8.1 mean paper length problem on page 244. To adapt this worksheet to other problems, change the population standard deviation, sample mean, sample size, and confidence level values in the tinted cells B4 through B7, and enter a new title in cell A1.

E8.2 Computing the Confidence Interval Estimate for the Mean (σ Unknown)

You compute the confidence interval estimate for the mean (σ unknown) by making entries in the **CIE_SU** worksheet of the `CIE sigma unknown.xls` workbook. The worksheet (see Figure 8.7 on page 249) uses the **TINV(1-*confidence level, degrees of freedom*)** function to determine the critical value from the t distribution and compute the interval half width for the Section 8.2 Saxon Home Improvement Company example. To adapt this worksheet to other problems, change the sample statistics and confidence level values in the tinted cells B4 through B7, and enter a new title in cell A1.

E8.3 Computing the Confidence Interval Estimate for the Proportion

You compute the confidence interval estimate for the proportion by making entries in the **CIE_P** worksheet of the `CIE Proportion.xls` workbook. The worksheet (see Figure 8.12 on page 254) uses the **NORMSINV($P < X$)** function

to determine the Z value and uses the square root function to compute the standard error of the proportion for the Section 8.3 Saxon Home Improvement Company example. To adapt this worksheet to other problems, change the sample size, number of successes, and confidence level values in the tinted cells B4, B5, and B6, and enter a new title in cell A1.

E8.4 Computing the Sample Size Needed for Estimating the Mean

You compute the sample size needed for estimating the mean by making entries in the **SampleSize_M** worksheet of the `Sample Size Mean.xls` workbook. The worksheet (see Figure 8.14 on page 258) uses the **NORMSINV($P < X$)** function to compute the Z value and uses the **ROUNDUP(*value*)** function to round up the sample size needed to the next higher integer for the Section 8.4 Saxon Home Improvement Company example. To adapt this worksheet to other problems, change the population standard deviation, sampling error, and confidence level values in the tinted cells B4, B5, and B6, and enter a new title in cell A1.

E8.5 Computing the Sample Size Needed for Estimating the Proportion

You compute the sample size needed for estimating the proportion by making entries in the **SampleSize_P** worksheet of the `Sample Size Proportion.xls` workbook. The worksheet (see Figure 8.15 on page 260) uses the **ROUNDUP(*value*)** function to round up the sample size needed to the next higher integer for the Section 8.4 Saxon Home Improvement Company example. To adapt this worksheet to other problems, change the estimate of true proportion, sampling error, and confidence level values in the tinted cells B4 through B6, and enter a new title in cell A1.

APPENDIX P8

Using PHStat2 for Confidence Interval Estimation

P8.1 Computing the Confidence Interval Estimate for the Mean (σ Known)

To compute the confidence interval estimate for the mean (σ known), use **PHStat → Confidence Intervals → Estimate for the Mean, sigma known.** This procedure creates a worksheet (similar to the **CIE_SK** worksheet of the `CIE sigma known.xls` workbook) using the population standard deviation, sample mean, sample size, and confidence level values that you specify. If you have unsummarized data, click **Sample Statistics Unknown** and the procedure will calculate the sample statistics for you.

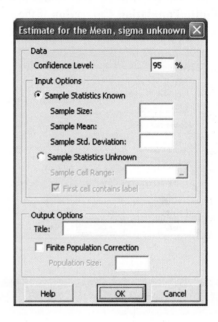

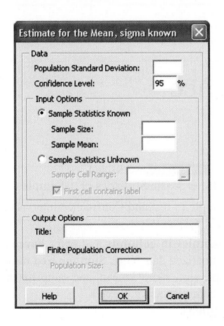

P8.3 Computing the Confidence Interval Estimate for the Proportion

To compute the confidence interval estimate for the proportion, use **PHStat → Confidence Intervals → Estimate for the Proportion.** This procedure creates a worksheet similar to Figure 8.12 on page 254 using the sample size, number of successes, and confidence level values that you specify. Click **Finite Population Correction** if the sampling is done without replacement from a finite population.

P8.2 Computing the Confidence Interval Estimate for the Mean (σ Unknown)

To compute the confidence interval estimate for the mean (σ unknown), use **PHStat → Confidence Intervals → Estimate for the Mean, sigma unknown.** This procedure creates a worksheet similar to Figure 8.7 on page 249 using the sample statistics and a confidence level value that you specify. If you have unsummarized data, click **Sample Statistics Unknown** and the procedure will calculate the sample statistics for you.

P8.4 Computing the Sample Size Needed for Estimating the Mean

To compute the sample size needed for estimating the mean, use **PHStat → Sample Size → Determination for the Mean**. This procedure creates a worksheet similar to Figure 8.14 on page 258 using the population standard deviation, sampling error, and confidence level values that you specify. Click **Finite Population Correction** if the sampling is done without replacement from a finite population.

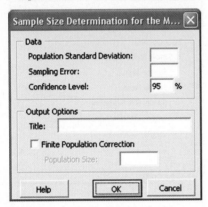

P8.5 Computing the Sample Size Needed for Estimating the Proportion

To compute the sample size needed for estimating the proportion, use **PHStat → Sample Size → Determination for the Proportion**. This procedure creates a worksheet similar to Figure 8.15 on page 260 using the estimate of true proportion, sampling error, and confidence level values that you specify. Click **Finite Population Correction** if the sampling is done without replacement from a finite population.

APPENDIX M8

Using Minitab for Confidence Interval Estimation

M8.1 Computing the Confidence Interval Estimation for the Mean (σ Known)

To compute a confidence interval estimate for the mean when ∧ is known

1. Select **Stat → Basic Statistics → 1-Sample Z**.

In the 1-Sample Z (Test and Confidence Interval) dialog box

2. Click **Samples in columns**.
3. Enter the variable name in the **Samples in columns** box.
4. Enter the value for σ in the **Standard deviation** box.
5. Click **Options**.

In the 1-Sample Z - Options dialog box:

6. Enter the level of confidence in the **Confidence level** box.
7. Click **OK** (to return to the previous dialog box).
8. Back in the first dialog box, click **OK** (to compute the confidence interval estimate).

M8.2 Computing the Confidence Interval Estimation for the Mean (σ Unknown)

To compute the confidence interval estimate for the population mean force required to break the insulators presented in Figure 8.8 on page 250:

1. Open the **Force.mtw** worksheet.
2. Select **Stat → Basic Statistics → 1-Sample t**.

In the 1-Sample t (Test and Confidence Interval) dialog box (see Figure M8.1):

3. Click **Samples in columns** and enter **Force** in its box. (For summarized data, click **Summarized data** and enter the sample size, sample mean, and sample standard deviation in their respective boxes.)
4. Click **Options**.

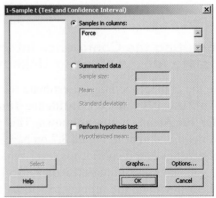

FIGURE M8.1   Minitab 1-Sample t (Test and Confidence Interval) dialog box

In the 1-Sample t - Options dialog box (see Figure M8.2):

5. Enter **95.0** in the **Confidence level** box.
6. Click **OK**.
7. Back in the first dialog box, click **OK**.

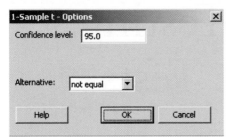

FIGURE M8.2   Minitab 1-Sample t - Options dialog box

M8.3 Computing the Confidence Interval Estimation for the Proportion

To compute the confidence interval estimate for the population proportion for the Saxon Home Improvement Company problem of Section 8.3 on page 254:

1. Select **Stat → Basic Statistics → 1 Proportion**.

In the 1 Proportion (Test and Confidence Interval) dialog box (see Figure M8.3):

2. Click **Summarized data**.
3. Enter **10** in the **Number of events** box.
4. Enter **100** in the **Number of trials** box.
5. Click **Options**.

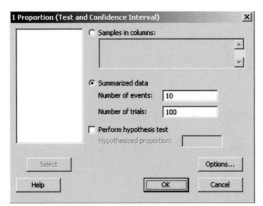

FIGURE M8.3   Minitab 1 Proportion (Test and Confidence Interval) dialog box

In the 1 Proportion - Options dialog box (see Figure M8.4):

6. Enter **95** in the **Confidence level** box.
7. Select **not equal** from the **Alternative** drop-down list.
8. Click **Use test and interval based on normal distribution**.
9. Click **OK**.
10. Back in the first dialog box, click **OK**.

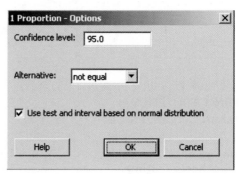

FIGURE M8.4   Minitab 1 Proportion - Options dialog box

9 Fundamentals of Hypothesis Testing: One-Sample Tests

Learning Objectives

In this chapter, you learn:

- The basic principles of hypothesis testing
- How to use hypothesis testing to test a mean or proportion
- The assumptions of each hypothesis-testing procedure, how to evaluate them, and the consequences if they are seriously violated
- How to avoid the pitfalls involved in hypothesis testing
- Ethical issues involved in hypothesis testing

@ Oxford Cereals, Part II

As in Chapter 7, you again find yourself as plant operations manager for Oxford Cereals. You are responsible for monitoring the amount in each cereal box filled. Company specifications require a mean weight of 368 grams per box. It is your responsibility to adjust the process when the mean fill weight in the population of boxes differs from 368 grams. How can you rationally make the decision whether or not to adjust the process when it is impossible to weigh every single box as it is being filled? You begin by selecting and weighing a random sample of 25 cereal boxes. After computing a sample mean, how do you proceed?

In Chapter 7, you learned methods to determine whether a sample mean is consistent with a known population mean. In this Oxford Cereals scenario, you seek to use a sample mean to validate a claim about the population mean, a somewhat different problem. For this type of problem, you use an inferential method called **hypothesis testing**. Hypothesis testing requires that you state a claim unambiguously. In this scenario, the claim is that the population mean is 368 grams. You examine a sample statistic to see if it better supports the stated claim, called the *null hypothesis*, or the mutually exclusive alternative (for this scenario, that the population mean is not 368 grams).

In this chapter, you will learn several applications of hypothesis testing. You will learn how to make inferences about a population parameter by *analyzing differences* between the results observed, the sample statistic, and the results you would expect to get if an underlying hypothesis were actually true. For the Oxford Cereals scenario, hypothesis testing would allow you to infer one of the following:

- The mean weight of the cereal boxes in the sample is a value consistent with what you would expect if the mean of the entire population of cereal boxes is 368 grams.
- The population mean is not equal to 368 grams because the sample mean is significantly different from 368 grams.

9.1 Fundamentals of Hypothesis-Testing Methodology

Hypothesis testing typically begins with some theory, claim, or assertion about a particular parameter of a population. For example, your initial hypothesis about the cereal example is that the process is working properly, so the mean fill is 368 grams, and no corrective action is needed.

The Null and Alternative Hypotheses

The hypothesis that the population parameter is equal to the company specification is referred to as the null hypothesis. A **null hypothesis** is always one of status quo and is identified by the symbol H_0. Here the null hypothesis is that the filling process is working properly, and therefore the mean fill is the 368-gram specification provided by Oxford Cereals. This is stated as

$$H_0: \mu = 368$$

Even though information is available only from the sample, the null hypothesis is written in terms of the population. Remember, your focus is on the population of all cereal boxes. The sample statistic is used to make inferences about the entire filling process. One inference may be that the results observed from the sample data indicate that the null hypothesis is false. If the null hypothesis is considered false, something else must be true.

Whenever a null hypothesis is specified, an alternative hypothesis is also specified, and it must be true if the null hypothesis is false. The **alternative hypothesis**, H_1, is the opposite of the null hypothesis, H_0. This is stated in the cereal example as

$$H_1: \mu \neq 368$$

The alternative hypothesis represents the conclusion reached by rejecting the null hypothesis. The null hypothesis is rejected when there is sufficient evidence from the sample information that the null hypothesis is false. In the cereal example, if the weights of the sampled boxes are sufficiently above or below the expected 368-gram mean specified by Oxford Cereals, you reject the null hypothesis in favor of the alternative hypothesis that the mean fill is different from 368 grams. You stop production and take whatever action is necessary to correct the problem. If the null hypothesis is not rejected, you should continue to believe in the status quo, that the process is working correctly and therefore no corrective action is necessary. In this second circumstance, you have not proven that the process is working correctly. Rather, you have failed to prove that it is working incorrectly, and therefore you continue your belief (although unproven) in the null hypothesis.

In hypothesis testing, you reject the null hypothesis when the sample evidence suggests that it is far more likely that the alternative hypothesis is true. However, failure to reject the null hypothesis is not proof that it is true. You can never prove that the null hypothesis is correct because the decision is based only on the sample information, not on the entire population. Therefore, if you fail to reject the null hypothesis, you can only conclude that there is insufficient evidence to warrant its rejection. The following key points summarize the null and alternative hypotheses:

- The null hypothesis, H_0, represents the status quo or the current belief in a situation.
- The alternative hypothesis, H_1, is the opposite of the null hypothesis and represents a research claim or specific inference you would like to prove.
- If you reject the null hypothesis, you have statistical proof that the alternative hypothesis is correct.
- If you do not reject the null hypothesis, you have failed to prove the alternative hypothesis. The failure to prove the alternative hypothesis, however, does not mean that you have proven the null hypothesis.
- The null hypothesis, H_0, always refers to a specified value of the population parameter (such as μ), not a sample statistic (such as $\overline{X}$).
- The statement of the null hypothesis always contains an equal sign regarding the specified value of the population parameter (e.g., H_0: $\mu = 368$ grams).
- The statement of the alternative hypothesis never contains an equal sign regarding the specified value of the population parameter (e.g., H_1: $\mu \neq 368$ grams).

EXAMPLE 9.1

The Null and Alternative Hypotheses

You are the manager of a fast-food restaurant. You want to determine whether the waiting time to place an order has changed in the past month from its previous population mean value of 4.5 minutes. State the null and alternative hypotheses.

SOLUTION The null hypothesis is that the population mean has not changed from its previous value of 4.5 minutes. This is stated as

$$H_0: \mu = 4.5$$

The alternative hypothesis is the opposite of the null hypothesis. Because the null hypothesis is that the population mean is 4.5 minutes, the alternative hypothesis is that the population mean is not 4.5 minutes. This is stated as

$$H_1: \mu \neq 4.5$$

The Critical Value of the Test Statistic

The logic of hypothesis testing involves determining how likely the null hypothesis is to be true by considering the information gathered in a sample. In the Oxford Cereal Company scenario, the null hypothesis is that the mean amount of cereal per box in the entire filling process is 368 grams (the population parameter specified by the company). You select a sample of boxes from the filling process, weigh each box, and compute the sample mean. This statistic is an estimate of the corresponding parameter (the population mean, μ). Even if the null hypothesis is true, the statistic (the sample mean, $\overline{X}$) is likely to differ from the value of the parameter (the population mean, μ) because of variation due to sampling. However, you expect the sample statistic to be close to the population parameter if the null hypothesis is true. If the sample statistic is close to the population parameter, you have insufficient evidence to reject the null hypothesis. For example, if the sample mean is 367.9, you conclude that the population mean has not changed (i.e., $\mu = 368$) because a sample mean of 367.9 is very close to the hypothesized value of 368. Intuitively, you think that it is likely that you could get a sample mean of 367.9 from a population whose mean is 368.

However, if there is a large difference between the value of the statistic and the hypothesized value of the population parameter, you conclude that the null hypothesis is false. For example, if the sample mean is 320, you conclude that the population mean is not 368 (i.e., $\mu \neq 368$), because the sample mean is very far from the hypothesized value of 368. In such a case, you conclude that it is very unlikely to get a sample mean of 320 if the population mean is really 368. Therefore, it is more logical to conclude that the population mean is not equal to 368. Here you reject the null hypothesis.

Unfortunately, the decision-making process is not always so clear-cut. Determining what is "very close" and what is "very different" is arbitrary without clear definitions. Hypothesis-testing methodology provides clear definitions for evaluating differences. Furthermore, it enables you to quantify the decision-making process by computing the probability of getting a given sample result if the null hypothesis is true. You calculate this probability by determining the sampling distribution for the sample statistic of interest (e.g., the sample mean) and then computing the particular **test statistic** based on the given sample result. Because the sampling distribution for the test statistic often follows a well-known statistical distribution, such as the standardized normal distribution or t distribution, you can use these distributions to help determine whether the null hypothesis is true.

Regions of Rejection and Nonrejection

The sampling distribution of the test statistic is divided into two regions, a **region of rejection** (sometimes called the critical region) and a **region of nonrejection** (see Figure 9.1). If the test statistic falls into the region of nonrejection, you do not reject the null hypothesis. In the Oxford Cereals scenario, you conclude that there is insufficient evidence that the population mean fill is different from 368 grams. If the test statistic falls into the rejection region, you reject the null hypothesis. In this case, you conclude that the population mean is not 368 grams.

FIGURE 9.1

Regions of rejection and nonrejection in hypothesis testing

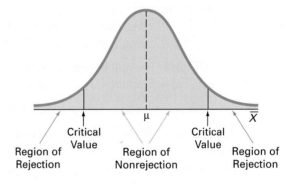

The region of rejection consists of the values of the test statistic that are unlikely to occur if the null hypothesis is true. These values are much more likely to occur if the null hypothesis is false. Therefore, if a value of the test statistic falls into this *rejection region*, you reject the null hypothesis because that value is unlikely if the null hypothesis is true.

To make a decision concerning the null hypothesis, you first determine the **critical value** of the test statistic. The critical value divides the nonrejection region from the rejection region. Determining this critical value depends on the size of the rejection region. The size of the rejection region is directly related to the risks involved in using only sample evidence to make decisions about a population parameter.

Risks in Decision Making Using Hypothesis Testing

When using a sample statistic to make decisions about a population parameter, there is a risk that you will reach an incorrect conclusion. You can make two different types of errors when applying hypothesis testing, Type I and Type II errors.

A **Type I error** occurs if you reject the null hypothesis, H_0, when it is true and should not be rejected. The probability of a Type I error occurring is α.

A **Type II error** occurs if you do not reject the null hypothesis, H_0, when it is false and should be rejected. The probability of a Type II error occurring is β.

In the Oxford Cereals scenario, you make a Type I error if you conclude that the population mean fill is *not* 368 when it *is* 368. This error causes you to adjust the filling process even though the process is working properly. Thus, a Type I error is a "false alarm." You make a Type II error if you conclude that the population mean fill *is* 368 when it is *not* 368. Here, you would allow the process to continue without adjustment even though adjustments are needed. Thus, a Type II error represents a "missed opportunity."

The Level of Significance (α) The probability of committing a Type I error, denoted by α (the lowercase Greek letter *alpha*), is referred to as the **level of significance** of the statistical test. Traditionally, you control the Type I error by deciding the risk level, α, that you are willing to have of rejecting the null hypothesis when it is true. Because you specify the level of significance before the hypothesis test is performed, the risk of committing a Type I error, α, is directly under your control. Traditionally, you select levels of 0.01, 0.05, or 0.10. The choice of a particular risk level for making a Type I error depends on the cost of making a Type I error. After you specify the value for α, you can then determine the critical values that divide the rejection and nonrejection regions. You know the size of the rejection region because α is the probability of rejection when the null hypothesis is true. From this, you can then determine the critical value or values that divide the rejection and nonrejection regions.

The Confidence Coefficient The complement of the probability of a Type I error, $(1 - \alpha)$, is called the confidence coefficient. When multiplied by 100%, the confidence coefficient yields the confidence level that was studied when constructing confidence intervals (see Section 8.1).

> The **confidence coefficient**, $(1 - \alpha)$, is the probability that you will not reject the null hypothesis, H_0, when it is true and should not be rejected. The **confidence level** of a hypothesis test is $(1 - \alpha) \times 100\%$.

In terms of hypothesis testing, the confidence coefficient represents the probability of concluding that the value of the parameter as specified in the null hypothesis is plausible when it is true. In the Oxford Cereals scenario, the confidence coefficient measures the probability of concluding that the population mean fill is 368 grams when it is actually 368 grams.

The β Risk The probability of committing a Type II error is denoted by β (the lowercase Greek letter *beta*). Unlike a Type I error, which you control by the selection of α, the probability of making a Type II error depends on the difference between the hypothesized and actual values of the population parameter. Because large differences are easier to find than small ones, if the difference between the hypothesized and actual value of the population parameter is large, β is small. For example, if the population mean is 330 grams, there is a small chance (β) that you will conclude that the mean has not changed from 368. However, if the difference between the hypothesized and actual values of the parameter is small, β is large. For example, if the population mean is actually 367 grams, there is a large chance (β) that you will conclude that the mean is still 368 grams.

The Power of a Test The complement of the probability of a Type II error, $(1 - \beta)$, is called the power of a statistical test.

> The **power of a statistical test**, $(1 - \beta)$, is the probability that you will reject the null hypothesis when it is false and should be rejected.

In the Oxford Cereals scenario, the power of the test is the probability that you will correctly conclude that the mean fill amount is not 368 grams when it actually is not 368 grams.

Risks in Decision Making: A Delicate Balance Table 9.1 illustrates the results of the two possible decisions (do not reject H_0 or reject H_0) that you can make in any hypothesis test. You can make a correct decision or make one of two types of errors.

	Actual Situation	
Statistical Decision	H_0 **True**	H_0 **False**
Do not reject H_0	Correct decision Confidence $= (1 - \alpha)$	Type II error $P(\text{Type II error}) = \beta$
Reject H_0	Type I error $P(\text{Type I error}) = \alpha$	Correct decision Power $= (1 - \beta)$

One way to reduce the probability of making a Type II error is by increasing the sample size. Large samples generally permit you to detect even very small differences between the hypothesized values and the actual population parameters. For a given level of α, increasing the sample size decreases β and therefore increases the power of the test to detect that the null hypothesis, H_0, is false. However, there is always a limit to your resources, and this affects the decision as to how large a sample you can take. Thus, for a given sample size, you must consider the trade-offs between the two possible types of errors. Because you can directly control the risk of Type I error, you can reduce this risk by selecting a smaller value for α. For example, if the negative consequences associated with making a Type I error are substantial, you could select $\alpha = 0.01$ instead of 0.05. However, when you decrease α, you increase β, so reducing the risk of a Type I error results in an increased risk of a Type II error. However, if you wish to reduce β, you could select a larger value for α. Therefore, if it is important to try to avoid a Type II error, you can select α of 0.05 or 0.10 instead of 0.01.

In the Oxford Cereals scenario, the risk of a Type I error involves concluding that the mean fill amount has changed from the hypothesized 368 grams when it actually has not changed. The risk of a Type II error involves concluding that the mean fill amount has not changed from the hypothesized 368 grams when it actually has changed. The choice of reasonable values for α and β depends on the costs inherent in each type of error. For example, if it is very costly to change the cereal-fill process, you would want to be very confident that a change is needed before making any changes. In this case, the risk of a Type I error is more important, and you would choose a small α. However, if you want to be very certain of detecting changes from a mean of 368 grams, the risk of a Type II error is more important, and you would choose a higher level of α.

Now that you have been introduced to hypothesis testing, recall that in the Using Statistics scenario on page 275, Oxford Cereals wants to determine whether the cereal-fill process is working properly (i.e., whether the mean fill throughout the entire packaging process remains at the specified 368 grams, and no corrective action is needed). To evaluate the 368-gram requirement, you take a random sample of 25 boxes, weigh each box, and then evaluate the difference between the sample statistic and the hypothesized population parameter by comparing the mean weight (in grams) from the sample to the expected mean of 368 grams specified by the company. The null and alternative hypotheses are

$$H_0\colon \mu = 368$$

$$H_1\colon \mu \neq 368$$

When the standard deviation, σ, is known (which rarely occurs), you use the **Z test for the mean** if the population is normally distributed. If the population is not normally distributed, you can still use the Z test if the sample size is large enough for the Central Limit Theorem to take effect (see Section 7.4). Equation (9.1) defines the Z_{STAT} test statistic for determining the difference between the sample mean, $\overline{X}$, and the population mean, μ, when the standard deviation, σ, is known.

Z TEST FOR THE MEAN (σ KNOWN)

$$Z_{STAT} = \frac{\overline{X} - \mu}{\dfrac{\sigma}{\sqrt{n}}} \tag{9.1}$$

In Equation (9.1), the numerator measures the difference between the observed sample mean, $\overline{X}$, and the hypothesized mean, μ. The denominator is the standard error of the mean, so Z_{STAT} represents the difference between $\overline{X}$ and μ in standard error units.

The Critical Value Approach to Hypothesis Testing

In the critical value approach to hypothesis testing, the observed value of the Z_{STAT} test statistic from Equation (9.1) is compared to critical values. The critical values are expressed as standardized Z values (i.e., in standard error units). For example, if you use a level of significance of 0.05, the size of the rejection region is 0.05. Because the rejection region is divided into the two tails of the distribution (this is called a **two-tail test**), you divide the 0.05 into two equal parts of 0.025 each. A rejection region of 0.025 in each tail of the normal distribution results in a cumulative area of 0.025 below the lower critical value and a cumulative area of 0.975 below the upper critical value (i.e., an area of 0.025 in the upper tail). According to the cumulative standardized normal distribution table (Table E.2), the critical values that divide the rejection and nonrejection regions are -1.96 and $+1.96$. Figure 9.2 illustrates that if the mean is actually 368 grams, as H_0 claims, the values of the Z_{STAT} test statistic have a standardized normal distribution centered at $Z = 0$ (which corresponds to an $\overline{X}$ value of 368 grams). Values of Z_{STAT} greater than $+1.96$ or less than -1.96 indicate that $\overline{X}$ is sufficiently different from the hypothesized $\mu = 368$ that it is unlikely that such an $\overline{X}$ value would occur if H_0 were true.

FIGURE 9.2

Testing a hypothesis about the mean (σ known) at the 0.05 level of significance

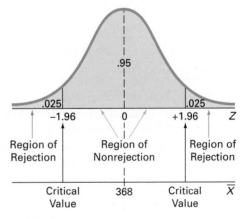

Therefore, the decision rule is

$$\text{Reject } H_0 \text{ if } Z_{STAT} > +1.96$$
$$\text{or if } Z_{STAT} < -1.96;$$
$$\text{otherwise, do not reject } H_0.$$

Suppose that the sample of 25 cereal boxes indicates a sample mean, $\overline{X}$, of 372.5 grams, and the population standard deviation, σ, is 15 grams. Using Equation (9.1) on page 280,

$$Z_{STAT} = \frac{\overline{X} - \mu}{\dfrac{\sigma}{\sqrt{n}}} = \frac{372.5 - 368}{\dfrac{15}{\sqrt{25}}} = +1.50$$

Because $Z_{STAT} = +1.50$ is between -1.96 and $+1.96$, you do not reject H_0 (see Figure 9.3). You continue to believe that the mean fill amount is 368 grams. To take into account the

FIGURE 9.3

Testing a hypothesis about the mean cereal weight (σ known) at the 0.05 level of significance

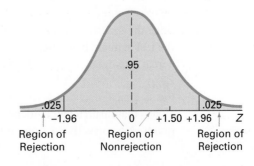

possibility of a Type II error, you state the conclusion as "there is insufficient evidence that the mean fill is different from 368 grams."

Exhibit 9.1 provides a summary of the critical value approach to hypothesis testing.

EXHIBIT 9.1 THE SIX-STEP METHOD OF HYPOTHESIS TESTING

1. State the null hypothesis, H_0, and the alternative hypothesis, H_1.
2. Choose the level of significance, α, and the sample size, n. The level of significance is based on the relative importance of the risks of committing Type I and Type II errors in the problem.
3. Determine the appropriate test statistic and sampling distribution.
4. Determine the critical values that divide the rejection and nonrejection regions.
5. Collect the sample data and compute the value of the test statistic.
6. Make the statistical decision and state the managerial conclusion. If the test statistic falls into the nonrejection region, you do not reject the null hypothesis. If the test statistic falls into the rejection region, you reject the null hypothesis. The managerial conclusion is written in the context of the real-world problem.

EXAMPLE 9.2

Applying the Six-Step Method of Hypothesis Testing at Oxford Cereals

State the six-step method of hypothesis testing at Oxford Cereals.

SOLUTION

Step 1: State the null and alternative hypotheses. The null hypothesis, H_0, is always stated as a mathematical expression using population parameters. In testing whether the mean fill is 368 grams, the null hypothesis states that μ equals 368. The alternative hypothesis, H_1, is also stated as a mathematical expression using population parameters. Therefore, the alternative hypothesis states that μ is not equal to 368 grams.

Step 2: Choose the level of significance and the sample size. You choose the level of significance, α, according to the relative importance of the risks of committing Type I and Type II errors in the problem. The smaller the value of α, the less risk there is of making a Type I error. In this example, making a Type I error means that you conclude that the population mean is not 368 grams when it is 368 grams. Thus, you will take corrective action on the filling process even though the process is working properly. Here, $\alpha = 0.05$ is selected. The sample size, n, is 25.

Step 3: Select the appropriate test statistic. Because σ is known from information about the filling process, you use the normal distribution and the Z_{STAT} test statistic.

Step 4: Determine the rejection region. Critical values for the appropriate test statistic are selected so that the rejection region contains a total area of α when H_0 is true and the nonrejection region contains a total area of $1 - \alpha$ when H_0 is true. Because $\alpha = 0.05$ in the cereal example, the critical values of the Z_{STAT} test statistic are -1.96 and $+1.96$. The rejection region is therefore $Z_{STAT} < -1.96$ or $Z_{STAT} > +1.96$. The nonrejection region is $-1.96 \leq Z_{STAT} \leq +1.96$.

Step 5: Collect the sample data and compute the value of the test statistic. In the cereal example, $\overline{X} = 372.5$, and the value of the test statistic is $Z_{STAT} = +1.50$.

Step 6: State the statistical decision and the managerial conclusion. First, determine whether the test statistic has fallen into the rejection region or the nonrejection region. For the cereal example, $Z_{STAT} = +1.50$ is in the region of nonrejection because $-1.96 \leq Z_{STAT} = +1.50 \leq +1.96$. Because the test statistic falls into the nonrejection region, the statistical decision is to not reject the null hypothesis, H_0. The managerial conclusion is that insufficient evidence exists to prove that the mean fill is different from 368 grams. No corrective action on the filling process is needed.

EXAMPLE 9.3

Testing and Rejecting a Null Hypothesis

You are the manager of a fast-food restaurant. You want to determine whether the population mean waiting time to place an order has changed in the past month from its previous population mean value of 4.5 minutes. From past experience, you can assume that the population is normally distributed with a population standard deviation of 1.2 minutes. You select a sample of 25 orders during a one-hour period. The sample mean is 5.1 minutes. Use the six-step approach listed in Exhibit 9.1 on page 282 to determine whether there is evidence at the 0.05 level of significance that the population mean waiting time to place an order has changed in the past month from its previous population mean value of 4.5 minutes.

SOLUTION

Step 1: The null hypothesis is that the population mean has not changed from its previous value of 4.5 minutes:

$$H_0: \mu = 4.5$$

The alternative hypothesis is the opposite of the null hypothesis. Because the null hypothesis is that the population mean is 4.5 minutes, the alternative hypothesis is that the population mean is not 4.5 minutes:

$$H_1: \mu \neq 4.5$$

Step 2: You have selected a sample of $n = 25$. The level of significance is 0.05 (i.e., $\alpha = 0.05$).

Step 3: Because σ is assumed known, you use the normal distribution and the Z_{STAT} test statistic.

Step 4: Because $\alpha = 0.05$, the critical values of the Z_{STAT} test statistic are -1.96 and $+1.96$. The rejection region is $Z_{STAT} < -1.96$ or $Z_{STAT} > +1.96$. The nonrejection region is $-1.96 \leq Z_{STAT} \leq +1.96$

Step 5: You collect the sample data and compute $\overline{X} = 5.1$. Using Equation (9.1) on page 280, you compute the test statistic:

$$Z_{STAT} = \frac{\overline{X} - \mu}{\dfrac{\sigma}{\sqrt{n}}} = \frac{5.1 - 4.5}{\dfrac{1.2}{\sqrt{25}}} = +2.50$$

Step 6: Because $Z_{STAT} = +2.50 > +1.96$, you reject the null hypothesis. You conclude that there is evidence that the population mean waiting time to place an order has changed from its previous value of 4.5 minutes. The mean waiting time for customers is longer now than it was last month.

The p-Value Approach to Hypothesis Testing

Most software packages, including Microsoft Excel and Minitab, compute the p-value when performing a test of hypothesis.

> The **p-value** is the probability of getting a test statistic equal to or more extreme than the sample result, given that the null hypothesis, H_0, is true. The p-value is often referred to as the *observed level of significance*.

The decision rules for rejecting H_0 in the p-value approach are

- If the p-value is greater than or equal to α, do not reject the null hypothesis.
- If the p-value is less than α, reject the null hypothesis.

Many people confuse these rules, mistakenly believing that a high p-value is grounds for rejection. You can avoid this confusion by remembering the following mantra:

If the p-value is low, then H_0 must go.

To understand the p-value approach, consider the Oxford Cereals scenario. You tested whether the mean fill was equal to 368 grams. The test statistic resulted in a Z_{STAT} value of $+1.50$, and you did not reject the null hypothesis because $+1.50$ was less than the upper critical value of $+1.96$ and more than the lower critical value of -1.96.

To use the p-value approach for the *two-tail test*, you find the probability of getting a test statistic Z_{STAT} that is equal to or *more extreme than* 1.50 standard error units from the center of a standardized normal distribution. In other words, you need to compute the probability of a Z_{STAT} value greater than $+1.50$, along with the probability of a Z_{STAT} value less than -1.50. Table E.2 shows that the probability of a Z_{STAT} value below -1.50 is 0.0668. The probability of a value below $+1.50$ is 0.9332, and the probability of a value above $+1.50$ is $1 - 0.9332 = 0.0668$. Therefore, the p-value for this two-tail test is $0.0668 + 0.0668 = 0.1336$ (see Figure 9.4). Thus, the probability of a test statistic equal to or more extreme than the sample result is 0.1336. Because 0.1336 is greater than $\alpha = 0.05$, you do not reject the null hypothesis.

FIGURE 9.4

Finding a p-value for a two-tail test

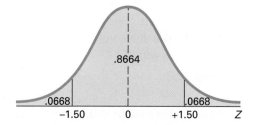

In this example, the observed sample mean is 372.5 grams, 4.5 grams above the hypothesized value, and the p-value is 0.1336. Thus, if the population mean is 368 grams, there is a 13.36% chance that the sample mean differs from 368 grams by at least 4.5 grams (i.e., is $\geq$ 372.5 grams or $\leq$ 363.5 grams). Therefore, even though 372.5 is above the hypothesized value of 368, a result as extreme as or more extreme than 372.5 is not highly unlikely when the population mean is 368.

Unless you are dealing with a test statistic that follows the normal distribution, you will only be able to approximate the p-value from the tables of the distribution. However, Microsoft Excel and Minitab routinely compute the p-values in each hypothesis-testing procedure. Once you understand the p-value approach, and assuming that you are using software such as Microsoft Excel or Minitab, you can just use the p-value approach instead of the critical value approach.

Figure 9.5 shows a Microsoft Excel worksheet for the cereal-filling example discussed in this section.

FIGURE 9.5

Microsoft Excel Z-test results for the cereal-fill example

See Section E9.1 or P9.1 to create this. (Minitab users, see Section M9.1 to create the equivalent results.)

	A	B	
1	**Cereal-Filling Process Hypothesis Test**		
2			
3	**Data**		
4	**Null Hypothesis** $\mu=$	368	
5	**Level of Significance**	0.05	
6	**Population Standard Deviation**	15	
7	**Sample Size**	25	
8	**Sample Mean**	372.5	
9			
10	Intermediate Calculations		
11	Standard Error of the Mean	3	=B6/SQRT(B7)
12	Z Test Statistic	1.5	=(B8 - B4)/B11
13			
14	**Two-Tail Test**		
15	Lower Critical Value	-1.9600	=NORMSINV(B5/2)
16	Upper Critical Value	1.9600	=NORMSINV(1 - B5/2)
17	p-Value	0.1336	=2 * (1 - NORMSDIST(ABS(B12)))
18	Do not reject the null hypothesis		=IF(B17 < B5, "Reject the null hypothesis", "Do not reject the null hypothesis")

Exhibit 9.2 provides a summary of the *p*-value approach for hypothesis testing.

EXHIBIT 9.2 THE FIVE-STEP *p*-VALUE APPROACH TO HYPOTHESIS TESTING

1. State the null hypothesis, H_0, and the alternative hypothesis, H_1.
2. Choose the level of significance, α, and the sample size, n. The level of significance is based on the relative importance of the risks of committing Type I and Type II errors in the problem.
3. Determine the appropriate test statistic and the sampling distribution.
4. Collect the sample data, compute the value of the test statistic, and compute the *p*-value.
5. Make the statistical decision and state the managerial conclusion. If the *p*-value is greater than or equal to α, you do not reject the null hypothesis. If the *p*-value is less than α, you reject the null hypothesis. Remember the mantra: If the *p*-value is low, then H_0 must go. The managerial conclusion is written in the context of the real-world problem.

EXAMPLE 9.4

Testing and Rejecting a Null Hypothesis, Using the *p*-Value Approach

You are the manager of a fast-food restaurant. You want to determine whether the population mean waiting time to place an order has changed in the past month from its previous value of 4.5 minutes. From past experience, you can assume that the population standard deviation is 1.2 minutes. You select a sample of 25 orders during a one-hour period. The sample mean is 5.1 minutes. Use the five-step *p*-value approach of Exhibit 9.2 to determine whether there is evidence that the population mean waiting time to place an order has changed in the past month from its previous population mean value of 4.5 minutes.

SOLUTION

Step 1: The null hypothesis is that the population mean has not changed from its previous value of 4.5 minutes:

$$H_0: \mu = 4.5$$

The alternative hypothesis is the opposite of the null hypothesis. Because the null hypothesis is that the population mean is 4.5 minutes, the alternative hypothesis is that the population mean is not 4.5 minutes:

$$H_1: \mu \neq 4.5$$

Step 2: You have selected a sample of $n = 25$ and you have chosen a 0.05 level of significance (i.e., $\alpha = 0.05$).

Step 3: Select the appropriate test statistic. Because σ is assumed known, you use the normal distribution and the Z_{STAT} test statistic.

Step 4: You collect the data and compute $\overline{X} = 5.1$. Using Equation (9.1) on page 280, you compute the test statistic as follows:

$$Z_{STAT} = \frac{\overline{X} - \mu}{\dfrac{\sigma}{\sqrt{n}}} = \frac{5.1 - 4.5}{\dfrac{1.2}{\sqrt{25}}} = +2.50$$

To find the probability of getting a Z_{STAT} test statistic that is equal to or more extreme than 2.50 standard error units from the center of a standardized normal distribution, you compute the probability of a Z_{STAT} value greater than $+2.50$ along with the probability of a Z_{STAT} value less than -2.50. From Table E.2, the probability of a Z_{STAT} value below -2.50 is 0.0062. The probability of a value below $+2.50$ is 0.9938. Therefore, the probability of a value above $+2.50$ is $1 - 0.9938 = 0.0062$. Thus, the *p*-value for this two-tail test is $0.0062 + 0.0062 = 0.0124$.

Step 5: Because the *p*-value $= 0.0124 < \alpha = 0.05$, you reject the null hypothesis. You conclude that there is evidence that the population mean waiting time to place an order has changed from its previous population mean value of 4.5 minutes. The mean waiting time for customers is longer now than it was last month.

A Connection Between Confidence Interval Estimation and Hypothesis Testing

This chapter and Chapter 8 discuss the two major components of statistical inference: confidence interval estimation and hypothesis testing. Although they are based on the same set of concepts, they are used for different purposes. In Chapter 8, confidence intervals were used to estimate parameters. In this chapter, hypothesis testing is used for making decisions about specified values of population parameters. Hypothesis tests are used when trying to prove that a parameter is less than, more than, or not equal to a specified value. Proper interpretation of a confidence interval, however, can also indicate whether a parameter is less than, more than, or not equal to a specified value. For example, in this section, you tested whether the population mean fill amount was different from 368 grams by using Equation (9.1) on page 280:

$$Z_{STAT} = \frac{\bar{X} - \mu}{\dfrac{\sigma}{\sqrt{n}}}$$

Instead of testing the null hypothesis that $\mu = 368$ grams, you can reach the same conclusion by constructing a confidence interval estimate of μ. If the hypothesized value of $\mu = 368$ is contained within the interval, you do not reject the null hypothesis because 368 would not be considered an unusual value. However, if the hypothesized value does not fall into the interval, you reject the null hypothesis because "$\mu = 368$ grams" is then considered an unusual value. Using Equation (8.1) on page 243 and the following data:

$$n = 25, \bar{X} = 372.5 \text{ grams}, \sigma = 15 \text{ grams}$$

for a confidence level of 95% (i.e., $\alpha = 0.05$),

$$\bar{X} \pm Z_{\alpha/2} \frac{\sigma}{\sqrt{n}}$$

$$372.5 \pm (1.96) \frac{15}{\sqrt{25}}$$

$$372.5 \pm 5.88$$

so that

$$366.62 \le \mu \le 378.38$$

Because the interval includes the hypothesized value of 368 grams, you do not reject the null hypothesis. There is insufficient evidence that the mean fill amount over the entire filling process is not 368 grams. You reached the same decision by using two-tail hypothesis testing.

Can You Ever *Really* Know Sigma? Part II

This section discussed the fundamentals of hypothesis testing. Just as in Chapter 8 when confidence intervals were developed, using an example in which the population standard deviation σ is known makes it much easier to explain the fundamentals of hypothesis testing. With a known population standard deviation, you can use the normal distribution and compute p-values from the tables of the normal distribution.

In virtually all situations, you do not know the standard deviation of the population. If you did, you would also know the population mean and therefore would not need to test a hypothesis about it. So, use this section to understand the fundamentals of hypothesis testing, but don't think that, in practice, you will ever know the population standard deviation σ.

Problems for Section 9.1

LEARNING THE BASICS

9.1 For $H_0: \mu = 100$, $H_1: \mu \neq 100$, and for a sample of size n, why is β larger if the actual value of μ is 90 than if the actual value of μ is 75?

9.2 If you use a 0.05 level of significance in a (two-tail) hypothesis test, what will you decide if $Z_{STAT} = +2.21$?

9.3 If you use a 0.10 level of significance in a (two-tail) hypothesis test, what is your decision rule for rejecting a null hypothesis that the population mean is 500 if you use the Z test?

9.4 If you use a 0.01 level of significance in a (two-tail) hypothesis test, what is your decision rule for rejecting $H_0: \mu = 12.5$ if you use the Z test?

9.5 What is your decision in Problem 9.4 if $Z_{STAT} = -2.61$?

9.6 What is the *p*-value if, in a two-tail hypothesis test, $Z_{STAT} = +2.00$?

9.7 In Problem 9.6, what is your statistical decision if you test the null hypothesis at the 0.10 level of significance?

9.8 What is the *p*-value if, in a two-tail hypothesis test, $Z_{STAT} = -1.38$?

APPLYING THE CONCEPTS

9.9 In the U.S. legal system, a defendant is presumed innocent until proven guilty. Consider a null hypothesis, H_0, that the defendant is innocent, and an alternative hypothesis, H_1, that the defendant is guilty. A jury has two possible decisions: Convict the defendant (i.e., reject the null hypothesis) or do not convict the defendant (i.e., do not reject the null hypothesis). Explain the meaning of the risks of committing either a Type I or Type II error in this example.

9.10 Suppose the defendant in Problem 9.9 is presumed guilty until proven innocent, as in some other judicial systems. How do the null and alternative hypotheses differ from those in Problem 9.9? What are the meanings of the risks of committing either a Type I or Type II error here?

9.11 The U.S. Food and Drug Administration (FDA) is responsible for approving new drugs. Many consumer groups feel that the approval process is too easy and, therefore, too many drugs are approved that are later found to be unsafe. On the other hand, a number of industry lobbyists are pushing for a more lenient approval process so that pharmaceutical companies can get new drugs approved more easily and quickly (data extracted from R. Sharpe, "FDA Tries to Find Right Balance on Drug Approvals," *The Wall Street Journal*, April 20, 1999, p. A24). Consider a null hypothesis that a new, unapproved drug is unsafe and an alternative hypothesis that a new, unapproved drug is safe.
a. Explain the risks of committing a Type I or Type II error.
b. Which type of error are the consumer groups trying to avoid? Explain.
c. Which type of error are the industry lobbyists trying to avoid? Explain.
d. How would it be possible to lower the chances of both Type I and Type II errors?

 9.12 As a result of complaints from both students and faculty about lateness, the registrar at a large university wants to adjust the scheduled class times to allow for adequate travel time between classes and is ready to undertake a study. Until now, the registrar has believed that there should be 20 minutes between scheduled classes. State the null hypothesis, H_0, and the alternative hypothesis, H_1.

9.13 Do students at your school study more, less, or about the same as at other business schools? *Business Week* reported that at the top 50 business schools, students studied an average of 14.6 hours (data extracted from "Cracking the Books," SPECIAL REPORT/Online Extra, **www.businessweek.com**, March 19, 2007). Set up a hypothesis test to try to prove that the mean number of hours studied at your school is different from the 14.6 hour benchmark reported by *Business Week*.
a. State the null and alternative hypotheses.
b. What is a Type I error for your test?
c. What is a Type II error for your test?

9.14 The manager of a paint supply store wants to determine whether the amount of paint contained in 1-gallon cans purchased from a nationally known manufacturer actually averages 1 gallon. State the null and alternative hypotheses.

9.15 The quality control manager at a lightbulb factory needs to determine whether the mean life of a large shipment of lightbulbs is equal to the specified value of 375 hours. State the null and alternative hypotheses.

9.2 *t* Test of Hypothesis for the Mean (σ Unknown)

In virtually all hypothesis-testing situations concerning the population mean, μ, you do not know the population standard deviation, σ. Instead, you use the sample standard deviation, S. If you assume that the population is normally distributed, then the sampling distribution of the mean follows a *t* distribution with $n - 1$ degrees of freedom and you use the ***t* test for the**

mean. If the population is not normally distributed, you can still use the t test if the sample size is large enough for the Central Limit Theorem to take effect (see Section 7.4). Equation (9.2) defines the test statistic for determining the difference between the sample mean, $\overline{X}$, and the population mean, μ, when using the sample standard deviation, S.

---

t TEST OF HYPOTHESIS FOR THE MEAN (σ UNKNOWN)

$$t_{STAT} = \frac{\overline{X} - \mu}{\dfrac{S}{\sqrt{n}}} \tag{9.2}$$

where the t_{STAT} test statistic follows a t distribution having $n - 1$ degrees of freedom.

To illustrate the use of this t test, return to the Using Statistics scenario concerning the Saxon Home Improvement company on page 249. Over the past five years, the mean amount per sales invoice is $120. As an accountant for the company, you need to inform the finance department if this amount changes. In other words, the hypothesis test is used to try to prove that the mean amount per sales invoice is increasing or decreasing.

The Critical Value Approach

To perform this two-tail hypothesis test, you use the six-step method listed in Exhibit 9.1 on page 282.

Step 1: H_0: $\mu = \$120$

H_1: $\mu \neq \$120$

The alternative hypothesis contains the statement you are trying to prove. If the null hypothesis is rejected, then there is statistical proof that the population mean amount per sales invoice is no longer $120. If the statistical conclusion is "do not reject H_0," then you will conclude that there is insufficient evidence to prove that the mean amount differs from the long-term mean of $120.

Step 2: You have selected a sample of $n = 12$. You decide to use $\alpha = 0.05$.

Step 3: Because σ is unknown, you use the t distribution and the t_{STAT} test statistic. You must assume that the population of sales invoices is normally distributed. This assumption is discussed on page 290.

Step 4: For a given sample size, n, the test statistic t_{STAT} follows a t distribution with $n - 1$ degrees of freedom. The critical values of the t distribution with $12 - 1 = 11$ degrees of freedom are found in Table E.3, as illustrated in Table 9.2 and Figure 9.6. The alternative hypothesis, H_1: $\mu \neq \$120$ is two-tail. Thus, the area in the rejection region of the t distribution's left (lower) tail is 0.025, and the area in the rejection region of the t distribution's right (upper) tail is also 0.025.

From the t table as given in Table E.3, a portion of which is shown in Table 9.2, the critical values are ± 2.2010. The decision rule is

$$\text{Reject } H_0 \text{ if } t_{STAT} < -t_{\alpha/2} = -2.2010$$

$$\text{or if } t_{STAT} > t_{\alpha/2} = +2.2010;$$

$$\text{otherwise, do not reject } H_0.$$

Step 5: A random sample of 12 sales invoices is selected. The dollar amounts for the 12 invoices are given below (and in the file **Invoices**):

108.98	152.22	111.45	110.59	127.46	107.26
93.32	91.97	111.56	75.71	128.58	135.11

TABLE 9.2

Determining the Critical Value from the *t* Table for an Area of 0.025 in Each Tail with 11 Degrees of Freedom

	Cumulative Probabilities					
	.75	.90	.95	.975	.99	.995
	Upper-Tail Areas					
Degrees of Freedom	.25	.10	.05	.025	.01	.005
1	1.0000	3.0777	6.3138	12.7062	31.8207	63.6574
2	0.8165	1.8856	2.9200	4.3027	6.9646	9.9248
3	0.7649	1.6377	2.3534	3.1824	4.5407	5.8409
4	0.7407	1.5332	2.1318	2.7764	3.7469	4.6041
5	0.7267	1.4759	2.0150	2.5706	3.3649	4.0322
6	0.7176	1.4398	1.9432	2.4469	3.1427	3.7074
7	0.7111	1.4149	1.8946	2.3646	2.9980	3.4995
8	0.7064	1.3968	1.8595	2.3060	2.8965	3.3554
9	0.7027	1.3830	1.8331	2.2622	2.8214	3.2498
10	0.6998	1.3722	1.8125	2.2281	2.7638	3.1693
11	0.6974	1.3634	1.7959	2.2010	2.7181	3.1058

Source: *Extracted from Table E.3.*

FIGURE 9.6

Testing a hypothesis about the mean (σ unknown) at the 0.05 level of significance with 11 degrees of freedom

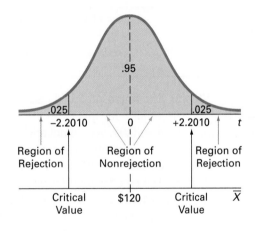

Using Equations (3.1) and (3.5) on pages 83 and 88, or Microsoft Excel or Minitab as shown in Figures 9.7 and 9.8 on page 290,

$$\bar{X} = \frac{\sum_{i=1}^{n} X_i}{n} = \$112.85 \quad \text{and} \quad S = \sqrt{\frac{\sum_{i=1}^{n} (X_i - \bar{X})^2}{n - 1}} = \$20.80$$

From Equation (9.2) on page 288,

$$t_{STAT} = \frac{\bar{X} - \mu}{\dfrac{S}{\sqrt{n}}} = \frac{112.85 - 120}{\dfrac{20.80}{\sqrt{12}}} = -1.1908$$

Step 6: Because $-2.2010 < t_{STAT} = -1.1908 < 2.2010$, you do not reject H_0. You have insufficient evidence to conclude that the mean amount per sales invoice differs from $120. You should inform the finance department that the audit suggests that the mean amount per invoice has not changed.

The *p*-Value Approach

Step 1–3: These steps are the same as in the critical value approach on page 288.

Step 4: From the Microsoft Excel worksheet of Figure 9.7 or from the Minitab results of Figure 9.8, $t_{STAT} = -1.19$ and the *p*-value = 0.259.

FIGURE 9.7

Microsoft Excel results for the *t* test of sales invoices

See Section E9.2 or P9.2 to create this.

	A	B	
1	t Test for the Hypothesis of the Mean		
2			
3	Data		
4	Null Hypothesis μ=	120	
5	Level of Significance	0.05	
6	Sample Size	12	
7	Sample Mean	112.85	
8	Sample Standard Deviation	20.8	
9			
10	Intermediate Calculations		
11	Standard Error of the Mean	6.0044	=B8/SQRT(B6)
12	Degrees of Freedom	11	=B6 - 1
13	t Test Statistic	-1.1908	=(B7 - B4)/B11
14			
15	Two-Tail Test		
16	Lower Critical Value	-2.2010	=-(TINV(B5, B12))
17	Upper Critical Value	2.2010	=TINV(B5, B12)
18	p-Value	0.2588	=TDIST(ABS(B13), B12, 2)
19	Do not reject the null hypothesis		=IF(B18 < B5, "Reject the null hypothesis", "Do not reject the null hypothesis")

FIGURE 9.8

Minitab results for the *t* test of sales invoices

See Section M9.2 to create this.

```
Test of mu = 120 vs not = 120


Variable    N    Mean   StDev   SE Mean      95% CI        T      P
Amount     12   112.85  20.80     6.00   (99.64, 126.07)  -1.19  0.259
```

Step 5: The Microsoft Excel results in Figure 9.7 and the Minitab results in Figure 9.8 give the *p*-value for this two-tail test as 0.259. Because the *p*-value of 0.259 is greater than $\alpha = 0.05$, you do not reject H_0. The data provide insufficient evidence to conclude that the mean amount per sales invoice differs from $120. You should inform the finance department that the audit suggests that the mean amount per invoice has not changed. The *p*-value indicates that if the null hypothesis is true, the probability that a sample of 12 invoices could have a sample mean that differs by $7.15 or more from the stated $120 is 0.259. In other words, if the mean amount per sales invoice is truly $120, then there is a 25.9% chance of observing a sample mean below $112.85 or above $127.15.

In the preceding example, it is incorrect to state that there is a 25.9% chance that the null hypothesis is true. This misinterpretation of the *p*-value is sometimes used by those not properly trained in statistics. Remember that the *p*-value is a conditional probability, calculated by *assuming* that the null hypothesis is true. In general, it is proper to state the following:

If the null hypothesis is true, there is a (*p*-value)*100% chance of observing a test statistic at least as contradictory to the null hypothesis as the sample result.

Checking the Normality Assumption

You use the *t* test when the population standard deviation, σ, is not known and is estimated using the sample standard deviation, *S*. To use the *t* test, you assume that the data represent a random sample from a population that is normally distributed. In practice, as long as the sample size is not very small and the population is not very skewed, the *t* distribution provides a good approximation to the sampling distribution of the mean when σ is unknown.

There are several ways to evaluate the normality assumption necessary for using the *t* test. You can observe how closely the sample statistics match the normal distribution's theoretical properties. You can also use a histogram, stem-and-leaf display, boxplot, or normal probability plot. For details on evaluating normality, see Section 6.3 on pages 196–199.

Figure 9.9 presents descriptive statistics generated by Microsoft Excel. Figure 9.10 is a Microsoft Excel boxplot. Figure 9.11 is a Microsoft Excel normal probability plot.

FIGURE 9.9

Microsoft Excel descriptive statistics for the sales invoice data

See Section E3.1 to create this. (Minitab users, see Section M3.1 to create the equivalent results.)

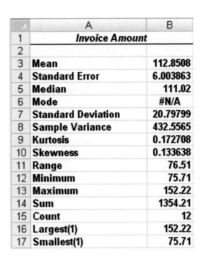

	A	B
1	*Invoice Amount*	
2		
3	Mean	112.8508
4	Standard Error	6.003863
5	Median	111.02
6	Mode	#N/A
7	Standard Deviation	20.79799
8	Sample Variance	432.5565
9	Kurtosis	0.172708
10	Skewness	0.133638
11	Range	76.51
12	Minimum	75.71
13	Maximum	152.22
14	Sum	1354.21
15	Count	12
16	Largest(1)	152.22
17	Smallest(1)	75.71

FIGURE 9.10

Microsoft Excel boxplot for the sales invoice data

See Section E3.3 or P3.1 to create this. (Minitab users, see Section M3.2 to create the equivalent chart.)

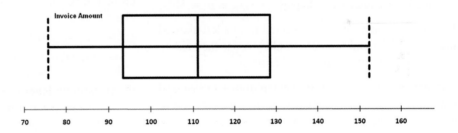

Boxplot of Invoice Amount

FIGURE 9.11

Microsoft Excel normal probability plot for the sales invoice data

See Section P6.2 to create this. (Minitab users, see Section M6.2 to create the equivalent chart.)

Normal Probability Plot of Invoice Amount

The mean is very close to the median and the points on the normal probability plot appear to be increasing approximately in a straight line. The boxplot appears approximately symmetrical. Thus, you can assume that the population of sales invoices is approximately normally distributed. The normality assumption is valid, and therefore the auditor's results are valid.

The t test is a **robust** test. It does not lose power if the shape of the population departs somewhat from a normal distribution, particularly when the sample size is large enough to enable the test statistic t to be influenced by the Central Limit Theorem (see Section 7.4). However, you can reach erroneous conclusions and can lose statistical power if you use the t test incorrectly. If the sample size, n, is small (i.e., less than 30) and you cannot easily make the assumption that the underlying population is at least approximately normally distributed, then *nonparametric* testing procedures are more appropriate (see references 1 and 2).

Problems for Section 9.2

LEARNING THE BASICS

9.16 If, in a sample of $n = 16$ selected from a normal population, $\overline{X} = 56$ and $S = 12$, what is the value of t_{STAT} if you are testing the null hypothesis $H_0: \mu = 50$?

9.17 In Problem 9.16, how many degrees of freedom are there in the t test?

9.18 In Problems 9.16 and 9.17, what are the critical values of t if the level of significance, α, is 0.05 and the alternative hypothesis, H_1, is $\mu \neq 50$?

9.19 In Problems 9.16, 9.17, and 9.18, what is your statistical decision if the alternative hypothesis, H_1, is $\mu \neq 50$?

9.20 If, in a sample of $n = 16$ selected from a left-skewed population, $\overline{X} = 65$ and $S = 21$, would you use the t test to test the null hypothesis $H_0: \mu = 60$? Discuss.

9.21 If, in a sample of $n = 160$ selected from a left-skewed population, $\overline{X} = 65$ and $S = 21$, would you use the t test to test the null hypothesis $H_0: \mu = 60$? Discuss.

APPLYING THE CONCEPTS

✓SELF **9.22** You are the manager of a restaurant for a **Test** fast-food franchise. Last month, the mean waiting time at the drive-through window for branches in your geographical region, as measured from the time a customer places an order until the time the customer receives the order, was 3.7 minutes. You select a random sample of 64 orders. The sample mean waiting time is 3.57 minutes, with a sample standard deviation of 0.8 minute.
a. At the 0.05 level of significance, is there evidence that the population mean waiting time is different from 3.7 minutes?
b. Because the sample size is 64, do you need to be concerned about the shape of the population distribution when conducting the t test in (a)? Explain.

9.23 A manufacturer of chocolate candies uses machines to package candies as they move along a filling line. Although the packages are labeled as 8 ounces, the company wants the packages to contain a mean of 8.17 ounces so that virtually none of the packages contain less than 8

ounces. A sample of 50 packages is selected periodically, and the packaging process is stopped if there is evidence that the mean amount packaged is different from 8.17 ounces. Suppose that in a particular sample of 50 packages, the mean amount dispensed is 8.159 ounces, with a sample standard deviation of 0.051 ounce.
a. Is there evidence that the population mean amount is different from 8.17 ounces? (Use a 0.05 level of significance.)
b. Determine the p-value and interpret its meaning.

9.24 The data in the file **MoviePrices** contain prices (in dollars) for two tickets, with online service charges, large popcorn, and two medium soft drinks at a sample of six theater chains:

> 36.15   31.00   35.05   40.25   33.75   43.00

Source: *Data extracted from K. Kelly, "The Multiplex Under Siege,"* The Wall Street Journal, *December 24–25, 2005, pp. P1, P5.*

a. At the 0.05 level of significance, is there evidence that the mean price for two tickets, with online service charges, large popcorn, and two medium soft drinks, is different from $35?
b. Determine the p-value in (a) and interpret its meaning.
c. What assumption must you make about the population distribution in order to conduct the t test in (a) and (b)?
d. Because the sample size is 6, do you need to be concerned about the shape of the population distribution when conducting the t test in (a)? Explain.

9.25 In New York State, savings banks are permitted to sell a form of life insurance called savings bank life insurance (SBLI). The approval process consists of underwriting, which includes a review of the application, a medical information bureau check, possible requests for additional medical information and medical exams, and a policy compilation stage in which the policy pages are generated and sent to the bank for delivery. The ability to deliver approved policies to customers in a timely manner is critical to the profitability of this service. During a period of one month, a random sample of 27 approved policies is selected, and the total processing time, in days, is recorded (as stored in the **Insurance** file):
73 19 16 64 28 28 31 90 60 56 31 56 22 18
45 48 17 17 17 91 92 63 50 51 69 16 17

a. In the past, the mean processing time was 45 days. At the 0.05 level of significance, is there evidence that the mean processing time has changed from 45 days?

b. What assumption about the population distribution is needed in order to conduct the *t* test in (a)?

c. Use a boxplot or a normal probability plot to evaluate the assumption made in (b).

d. Do you think that the assumption needed in order to conduct the *t* test in (a) is valid? Explain.

9.26 The following data (see the `Drink` file) represent the amount of soft-drink filled in a sample of 50 consecutive 2-liter bottles. The results, listed horizontally in the order of being filled, were:

2.109 2.086 2.066 2.075 2.065 2.057 2.052 2.044 2.036 2.038

2.031 2.029 2.025 2.029 2.023 2.020 2.015 2.014 2.013 2.014

2.012 2.012 2.012 2.010 2.005 2.003 1.999 1.996 1.997 1.992

1.994 1.986 1.984 1.981 1.973 1.975 1.971 1.969 1.966 1.967

1.963 1.957 1.951 1.951 1.947 1.941 1.941 1.938 1.908 1.894

a. At the 0.05 level of significance, is there evidence that the mean amount of soft drink filled is different from 2.0 liters?

b. Determine the *p*-value in (a) and interpret its meaning.

c. In (a), you assumed that the distribution of the amount of soft drink filled was normally distributed. Evaluate this assumption using a boxplot or a normal probability plot.

d. Do you think that the assumption needed in order to conduct the *t* test in (a) is valid? Explain.

e. Examine the values of the 50 bottles in their sequential order, as given in the problem. Is there a pattern to the results? If so, what impact might this pattern have on the validity of the results in (a)?

9.27 One of the major measures of the quality of service provided by any organization is the speed with which it responds to customer complaints. A large family-held department store selling furniture and flooring, including carpet, had undergone a major expansion in the past several years. In particular, the flooring department had expanded from 2 installation crews to an installation supervisor, a measurer, and 15 installation crews. Last year there were 50 complaints concerning carpet installation. The following data (stored in the `Furniture` file) represent the number of days between the receipt of a complaint and the resolution of the complaint:

54	5	35	137	31	27	152	2	123	81	74	27
11	19	126	110	110	29	61	35	94	31	26	5
12	4	165	32	29	28	29	26	25	1	14	13
13	10	5	27	4	52	30	22	36	26	20	23
33	68										

a. The installation supervisor claims that the mean number of days between the receipt of a complaint and the resolution of the complaint is 20 days. At the 0.05 level of significance, is there evidence that the claim is not true (i.e., that the mean number of days is different from 20)?

b. What assumption about the population distribution is needed in order to conduct the *t* test in (a)?

c. Use a boxplot or a normal probability plot to evaluate the assumption made in (b).

d. Do you think that the assumption needed in order to conduct the *t* test in (a) is valid? Explain.

9.28 A manufacturing company produces steel housings for electrical equipment. The main component part of the housing is a steel trough that is made out of a 14-gauge steel coil. It is produced using a 250-ton progressive punch press with a wipe-down operation that puts two 90-degree forms in the flat steel to make the trough. The distance from one side of the form to the other is critical because of weatherproofing in outdoor applications. The company requires that the width of the trough be between 8.31 inches and 8.61 inches. The file `Trough` contains the widths of the troughs, in inches, for a sample of *n* = 49.

8.312 8.343 8.317 8.383 8.348 8.410 8.351 8.373 8.481 8.422

8.476 8.382 8.484 8.403 8.414 8.419 8.385 8.465 8.498 8.447

8.436 8.413 8.489 8.414 8.481 8.415 8.479 8.429 8.458 8.462

8.460 8.444 8.429 8.460 8.412 8.420 8.410 8.405 8.323 8.420

8.396 8.447 8.405 8.439 8.411 8.427 8.420 8.498 8.409

a. At the 0.05 level of significance, is there evidence that the mean width of the troughs is different from 8.46 inches?

b. What assumption about the population distribution is needed in order to conduct the *t* test in (a)?

c. Evaluate the assumption made in (b).

d. Do you think that the assumption needed in order to conduct the *t* test in (a) is valid? Explain.

9.29 One operation of a steel mill is to cut pieces of steel into parts that are used in the frame for front seats in an automobile. The steel is cut with a diamond saw and requires the resulting parts to be within ±0.005 inch of the length specified by the automobile company. The data in the file `Steel` come from a sample of 100 steel parts. The measurement reported is the difference, in inches, between the actual length of the steel part, as measured by a laser measurement device, and the specified length of the steel part. For example, a value of −0.002 represents a steel part that is 0.002 inch shorter than the specified length.

a. At the 0.05 level of significance, is there evidence that the mean difference is not equal to 0.0 inches?

b. Construct a 95% confidence interval estimate of the population mean. Interpret this interval.

c. Compare the conclusions reached in (a) and (b).

d. Because *n* = 100, do you have to worry about the normality assumption needed for the *t* test and *t* interval?

9.30 In Problem 3.57 on page 117, you were introduced to a tea-bag-filling operation. An important quality characteristic of interest for this process is the weight of the tea in the individual bags. The data in the file `Teabags` are provided in an ordered array of the weight, in grams, of a sample of 50 tea bags produced during an eight-hour shift.

a. Is there evidence that the mean amount of tea per bag is different from 5.5 grams (use $\alpha = 0.01$)?
b. Construct a 99% confidence interval estimate of the population mean amount of tea per bag. Interpret this interval.
c. Compare the conclusions reached in (a) and (b).

9.31 Although many people think they can put a meal on the table in a short period of time, a recent article reported that they end up spending about 40 minutes doing so (data extracted from N. Hellmich, "Americans Go for the Quick Fix for Dinner," *USA Today*, February 14, 2006). Suppose another study is conducted to test the validity of this statement. A sample of 25 people is selected, and the length of time to prepare and cook dinner (in minutes) is recorded, with the following results (stored in the file **Dinner**).

44.0 51.9 49.7 40.0 55.5 33.0 43.4 41.3 45.2 40.7 41.1 49.1 30.9
45.2 55.3 52.1 55.1 38.8 43.1 39.2 58.6 49.8 43.2 47.9 46.6

a. Is there evidence that the population mean time to prepare and cook dinner is different from 40 minutes? Use the *p*-value approach and a level of significance of 0.05.
b. What assumption about the population distribution is needed in order to conduct the *t* test in (a)?
c. Make a list of the various ways you could evaluate the assumption noted in (b).
d. Evaluate the assumption noted in (b) and determine whether the *t* test in (a) is valid.

9.3 One-Tail Tests

In Section 9.1, hypothesis testing was used to examine the question of whether the population mean amount of cereal filled is 368 grams. The alternative hypothesis (H_1: $\mu \neq 368$) contains two possibilities: Either the mean is less than 368 grams, or the mean is more than 368 grams. For this reason, the rejection region is divided into the two tails of the sampling distribution of the mean. In Section 9.2, once again a two-tail test was used to determine whether the mean amount per invoice had changed from $120.

In contrast to these two examples, many situations require an alternative hypothesis that focuses on a *particular direction*. For example, the population mean is *less than* a specified value. One such situation involves the service time at the drive-through window of a fast-food restaurant. The speed with which customers are served is of critical importance to the success of the service (see **www.qsrmagazine.com/reports/drive-thru_time_study**). In a recent study, McDonald's had a mean service time of 163.9 seconds, which was the fourth best in the industry. Suppose that McDonald's has embarked on a quality improvement effort to reduce the service time and has developed improvements to the service process at the drive-through. The new process will be tested in a sample of 25 stores. Because McDonald's would only want to institute the new process in all of its stores if it resulted in *decreased* drive-through time, the entire rejection region is located in the lower tail of the distribution.

The Critical Value Approach

You wish to determine whether the new drive-through process has a mean that is less than 163.9 seconds. To perform this one-tail hypothesis test, you use the six-step method listed in Exhibit 9.1 on page 282.

Step 1:
$$H_0: \mu \geq 163.9$$
$$H_1: \mu < 163.9$$

The alternative hypothesis contains the statement you are trying to prove. If the conclusion of the test is "reject H_0," there is statistical proof that the mean drive-through time is less than the drive-through time in the old process. This would be reason to change the drive-through process for the entire population of stores. If the conclusion of the test is "do not reject H_0," then there is insufficient evidence to prove that the mean drive-through time in the new process is significantly less than the drive-through time in the old process. If this occurs, there would be insufficient reason to institute the new drive-through process in the population of stores.

Step 2: You have selected a sample size of $n = 25$ stores. You decide to use $\alpha = 0.05$.

Step 3: Because σ is unknown, you use the *t* distribution and the t_{STAT} test statistic. You must assume that the service time is normally distributed.

Step 4: The rejection region is entirely contained in the lower tail of the sampling distribution of the mean because you want to reject H_0 only when the sample mean is significantly less than 163.9 seconds. When the entire rejection region is contained in one tail of the sampling distribution of the test statistic, the test is called a **one-tail** or **directional test**. If the alternative hypothesis includes the *less than* sign, the critical value of t is negative. As shown in Table 9.3 and Figure 9.12, because the entire rejection region is in the lower tail of the t distribution and contains an area of 0.05, owing to the symmetry of the t distribution, the critical value of the t test statistic with $25 - 1 = 24$ degrees of freedom is -1.7109.

The decision rule is

$$\text{Reject } H_0 \text{ if } t_{STAT} < -1.7109;$$

$$\text{otherwise, do not reject } H_0.$$

TABLE 9.3

Determining the Critical Value from the t Table for an Area of 0.05 in the Lower Tail with 24 Degrees of Freedom

	Cumulative Probabilities					
	.75	.90	.95	.975	.99	.995
	Upper-Tail Areas					
Degrees of Freedom	.25	.10	.05	.025	.01	.005
1	1.0000	3.0777	6.3138	12.7062	31.8207	63.6574
2	0.8165	1.8856	2.9200	4.3027	6.9646	9.9248
3	0.7649	1.6377	2.3534	3.1824	4.5407	5.8409
.	.	.	.	.	.	.
.	.	.	.	.	.	.
23	0.6853	1.3195	1.7139	2.0687	2.4999	2.8073
24	0.6848	1.3178	1.7109	2.0639	2.4922	2.7969
25	0.6844	1.3163	1.7081	2.0595	2.4851	2.7874

Source: *Extracted from Table E.3.*

FIGURE 9.12

One-tail test of hypothesis for a mean (σ unknown) at the 0.05 level of significance

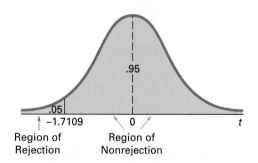

Region of Rejection Region of Nonrejection

Step 5: You select a sample of 25 stores and find that the sample mean service time at the drive-through equals 152.7 seconds and the sample standard deviation equals 20 seconds. Using $n = 25, \overline{X} = 152.7, S = 20$, and Equation (9.2) on page 288,

$$t_{STAT} = \frac{\overline{X} - \mu}{\dfrac{S}{\sqrt{n}}} = \frac{152.7 - 163.9}{\dfrac{20}{\sqrt{25}}} = -2.80$$

Step 6: Because $t_{STAT} = -2.80 < -1.7109$, you reject the null hypothesis (see Figure 9.12). You conclude that the mean service time at the drive-through is below 163.9 seconds. There is sufficient evidence to change the drive-through process for the entire population of stores.

The *p*-Value Approach

Use the five steps listed in Exhibit 9.2 on page 285 to illustrate the *t* test for the drive-through time study using the *p*-value approach.

Step 1–3: These steps are the same as in the critical value approach on pages 294–295.

Step 4: $t_{STAT} = -2.80$ (see step 5 of the critical value approach). Because the alternative hypothesis indicates a rejection region entirely in the *lower* tail of the sampling distribution, to compute the *p*-value you need to find the probability that the *t*-value will be *less than* the t_{STAT} test statistic of -2.80. From Figure 9.13, the *p*-value is 0.0050.

FIGURE 9.13

Microsoft Excel *t* test results for the drive-through time study

See Section E9.2 or P9.2 to create this. (Minitab users, see Section M9.2 to create the equivalent results.)

	A	B	
1	**Service Time at Drive-Through Study**		
2			
3	**Data**		
4	**Null Hypothesis** μ=	163.9	
5	**Level of Significance**	0.05	
6	**Sample Size**	25	
7	**Sample Mean**	152.7	
8	**Sample Standard Deviation**	20	
9			
10	**Intermediate Calculations**		
11	Standard Error of the Mean	4	=B8/SQRT(B6)
12	Degrees of Freedom	24	=B6 - 1
13	*t* Test Statistic	-2.8	=(B7 - B4)/B11
14			
15	**Lower-Tail Test**		
16	Lower Critical Value	-1.7109	=-(TINV(2 * B5, B12))
17	*p*-Value	0.0050	=IF(B13 < 0, E17, E18)
18	**Reject the null hypothesis**		=IF(B17 < B5, "Reject the null hypothesis", "Do not reject the null hypothesis")

Not shown
Cell E17: =TDIST(ABS(B13), B12, 1)
Cell E18: =1 - E17

Step 5: The *p*-value of 0.0050 is less than $\alpha = 0.05$ (see Figure 9.14). You reject H_0, and conclude that the mean service time at the drive-through is less than 163.9 seconds. There is sufficient evidence to change the drive-through process for the entire population of stores.

FIGURE 9.14

Determining the *p*-value for a one-tail test

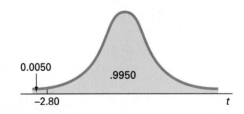

0.0050   .9950

−2.80   *t*

EXAMPLE 9.5

A One-Tail Test for the Mean

A company that manufactures chocolate bars is particularly concerned that the mean weight of a chocolate bar is not greater than 6.03 ounces. A sample of 50 chocolate bars is selected, and the sample mean is 6.034 ounces and the sample standard deviation is 0.02 ounces. Using the $\alpha = 0.01$ level of significance, is there evidence that the population mean weight of the chocolate bars is greater than 6.03 ounces?

SOLUTION Using the critical value approach,

Step 1: $H_0: \mu \leq 6.03$

$H_1: \mu > 6.03$

Step 2: You have selected a sample size of $n = 50$. You decide to use $\alpha = 0.01$.

Step 3: Because σ is unknown, you use the *t* distribution and the t_{STAT} test statistic.

Step 4: The rejection region is entirely contained in the upper tail of the sampling distribution of the mean because you want to reject H_0 only when the sample mean is significantly greater than 6.03 ounces. Because the entire rejection region is in the upper tail of the

t distribution and contains an area of 0.01, the critical value of the t distribution with $50 - 1 = 49$ degrees of freedom is 2.4049 (see Table E.3).

The decision rule is

$$\text{Reject } H_0 \text{ if } t_{STAT} > 2.4049;$$

$$\text{otherwise, do not reject } H_0.$$

Step 5: You select a sample of 50 chocolate bars, and the sample mean weight is 6.034 ounces. Using $n = 50, \overline{X} = 6.034, S = 0.02$, and Equation (9.2) on page 288,

$$t_{STAT} = \frac{\overline{X} - \mu}{\dfrac{S}{\sqrt{n}}} = \frac{6.034 - 6.03}{\dfrac{0.02}{\sqrt{50}}} = 1.414$$

Step 6: Because $t_{STAT} = 1.414 < 2.4049$, or using Microsoft Excel or Minitab, the p-value is $0.0818 > 0.01$, you do not reject the null hypothesis. There is insufficient evidence to conclude that the population mean weight is greater than 6.03 ounces.

To perform one-tail tests of hypotheses, you must properly formulate H_0 and H_1. A summary of the null and alternative hypotheses for one-tail tests is as follows:

- The null hypothesis, H_0, represents the status quo or the current belief in a situation.
- The alternative hypothesis, H_1, is the opposite of the null hypothesis and represents a research claim or specific inference you would like to prove.
- If you reject the null hypothesis, you have statistical proof that the alternative hypothesis is correct.
- If you do not reject the null hypothesis, then you have failed to prove the alternative hypothesis. The failure to prove the alternative hypothesis, however, does not mean that you have proven the null hypothesis.
- The null hypothesis always refers to a specified value of the *population parameter* (such as μ), not to a *sample statistic* (such as $\overline{X}$).
- The statement of the null hypothesis *always* contains an equal sign regarding the specified value of the parameter (e.g., $H_0: \mu \geq 163.9$).
- The statement of the alternative hypothesis *never* contains an equal sign regarding the specified value of the parameter (e.g., $H_1: \mu < 163.9$).

Problems for Section 9.3

LEARNING THE BASICS

9.32 In a one-tail hypothesis test where you reject H_0 only in the *upper* tail, what is the p-value if $Z_{STAT} = +2.00$?

9.33 In Problem 9.32, what is your statistical decision if you test the null hypothesis at the 0.05 level of significance?

9.34 In a one-tail hypothesis test where you reject H_0 only in the *lower* tail, what is the p-value if $Z_{STAT} = -1.38$?

9.35 In Problem 9.34, what is your statistical decision if you test the null hypothesis at the 0.01 level of significance?

9.36 In a one-tail hypothesis test where you reject H_0 only in the *lower* tail, what is the p-value if $Z_{STAT} = +1.38$?

9.37 In Problem 9.36, what is the statistical decision if you test the null hypothesis at the 0.01 level of significance?

9.38 In a one-tail hypothesis test where you reject H_0 only in the *upper* tail, what is the critical value of the t-test statistic with 10 degrees of freedom at the 0.01 level of significance?

9.39 In Problem 9.38, what is your statistical decision if $t_{STAT} = +2.39$?

9.40 In a one-tail hypothesis test where you reject H_0 only in the *lower* tail, what is the critical value of the t_{STAT} test statistic with 20 degrees of freedom at the 0.01 level of significance?

9.41 In Problem 9.40, what is your statistical decision if $t_{STAT} = -1.15$?

APPLYING THE CONCEPTS

✓SELF **9.42** The Glen Valley Steel Company manufac-
Test tures steel bars. If the production process is working properly, it turns out steel bars that are normally distributed with mean length of *at least* 2.8 feet. Longer steel bars
can be used or altered, but shorter bars must be scrapped.
You select a sample of 25 bars, and the mean length is 2.73
feet and the sample standard deviation is 0.20 foot. Do you
need to adjust the production equipment?
a. If you test the null hypothesis at the 0.05 level of significance, what decision do you make using the critical value
   approach to hypothesis testing?
b. If you test the null hypothesis at the 0.05 level of significance, what decision do you make using the *p*-value
   approach to hypothesis testing?
c. Interpret the meaning of the *p*-value in this problem.
d. Compare your conclusions in (a) and (b).

9.43 You are the manager of a restaurant that delivers pizza
to college dormitory rooms. You have just changed your
delivery process in an effort to reduce the mean time
between the order and completion of delivery from the current 25 minutes. A sample of 36 orders using the new delivery process yields a sample mean of 22.4 minutes and a
sample standard deviation of 6 minutes.
a. Using the six-step critical value approach, at the 0.05
   level of significance, is there evidence that the population mean delivery time has been reduced below the previous population mean value of 25 minutes?
b. At the 0.05 level of significance, use the five-step *p*-value
   approach.
c. Interpret the meaning of the *p*-value in (b).
d. Compare your conclusions in (a) and (b).

9.44 Children in the United States account directly for
$36 billion in sales annually. When their indirect influence
over product decisions from stereos to vacations is considered, the total economic spending affected by children in
the United States is $290 billion. It is estimated that by

age 10, a child makes an average of more than five trips a
week to a store (data extracted from M. E. Goldberg,
G. J. Gorn, L. A. Peracchio, and G. Bamossy, "Understanding Materialism Among Youth," *Journal of Consumer
Psychology*, 2003, 13(3), pp. 278–288). Suppose that you
want to prove that children in your city average more than
five trips a week to a store. Let μ represent the population
mean number of times children in your city make trips to
a store.
a. State the null and alternative hypotheses.
b. Explain the meaning of the Type I and Type II errors in
   the context of this scenario.
c. Suppose that you carry out a similar study in the city in
   which you live. You take a sample of 100 children and
   find that the mean number of trips to the store is 5.47 and
   the sample standard deviation of the number of trips to
   the store is 1.6. At the 0.01 level of significance, is there
   evidence that the population mean number of trips to the
   store is greater than 5 per week?
d. Interpret the meaning of the *p*-value in (c).

9.45 The waiting time to check out of a supermarket has
had a population mean of 10.73 minutes. Recently, in an
effort to reduce the waiting time, the supermarket has
experimented with a system in which there is a single waiting line with multiple checkout servers. A sample of 100
customers was selected, and their mean waiting time to
check out was 9.52 minutes with a sample standard deviation of 5.8 minutes.
a. At the 0.05 level of significance, using the critical value
   approach to hypothesis testing, is there evidence that the
   population mean waiting time to check out is less than
   10.73 minutes?
b. At the 0.05 level of significance, using the *p*-value
   approach to hypothesis testing, is there evidence that the
   population mean waiting time to check out is less than
   10.73 minutes?
c. Interpret the meaning of the *p*-value in this problem.
d. Compare your conclusions in (a) and (b).

9.4 *Z* Test of Hypothesis for the Proportion

In some situations, you want to test a hypothesis about the proportion of events of interest in
the population, π, rather than testing the population mean. To begin, you select a random sample and compute the **sample proportion**, $p = X/n$. You then compare the value of this statistic to the hypothesized value of the parameter, π, in order to decide whether to reject the null
hypothesis. If the number of events of interest (X) and the number of events that are not of
interest ($n - X$) are each at least five, the sampling distribution of a proportion approximately
follows a normal distribution. You use the **Z test for the proportion** given in Equation (9.3) to
perform the hypothesis test for the difference between the sample proportion, p, and the
hypothesized population proportion, π.

Z TEST FOR THE PROPORTION

$$Z_{STAT} = \frac{p - \pi}{\sqrt{\dfrac{\pi(1 - \pi)}{n}}} \qquad (9.3)$$

where

$$p = \text{sample proportion} = \frac{X}{n} = \frac{\text{Number of events of interest in the sample}}{\text{Sample size}}$$

$\pi = $ hypothesized proportion of events of interest in the population

The Z_{STAT} test statistic approximately follows a standardized normal distribution when X and $(n - X)$ are each at least 5.

Alternatively, by multiplying the numerator and denominator by n, you can write the Z_{STAT} test statistic in terms of the number of events of interest, X, as shown in Equation (9.4).

Z TEST FOR THE PROPORTION IN TERMS OF THE NUMBER OF EVENTS OF INTEREST

$$Z_{STAT} = \frac{X - n\pi}{\sqrt{n\pi(1 - \pi)}} \qquad (9.4)$$

The Critical Value Approach

To illustrate the *Z* test for a proportion, consider a survey that sought to determine whether customer service is better or worse at e-commerce sites than it is at physical stores (data extracted from "Consumers Happier With E-Commerce," *USA Today Snapshots*, March 13, 2007, p. 1B). Of 1,100 respondents, 561 stated that customer service was better at e-commerce sites than at physical stores. For this survey, the null and alternative hypotheses are stated as follows:

H_0: $\pi = 0.50$ (i.e., half of all consumers believe that customer service is better at e-commerce sites than at physical stores)

H_1: $\pi \neq 0.50$ (i.e., either less than half or more than half of all consumers believe that customer service is better at e-commerce sites than at physical stores)

Because you are interested in determining whether the population proportion of consumers who believe that customer service is better at e-commerce sites than at physical stores is less than or more than 0.50, you use a two-tail test. If you select the $\alpha = 0.05$ level of significance, the rejection and nonrejection regions are set up as in Figure 9.15, and the decision rule is

Reject H_0 if $Z_{STAT} < -1.96$ or if $Z_{STAT} > +1.96$;

otherwise, do not reject H_0.

FIGURE 9.15

Two-tail test of hypothesis for the proportion at the 0.05 level of significance

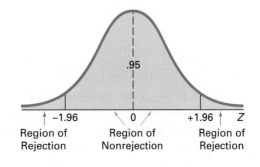

Because 561 of the 1,100 respondents stated that customer service was better at e-commerce sites than at physical stores,

$$p = \frac{561}{1,100} = 0.51$$

Using Equation (9.3),

$$Z_{STAT} = \frac{p - \pi}{\sqrt{\dfrac{\pi(1 - \pi)}{n}}} = \frac{0.51 - 0.50}{\sqrt{\dfrac{0.50(1 - 0.50)}{1,100}}} = \frac{0.01}{0.0151} = 0.6633$$

or, using Equation (9.4),

$$Z_{STAT} = \frac{X - n\pi}{\sqrt{n\pi(1 - \pi)}} = \frac{561 - (1,100)(0.50)}{\sqrt{1,100(0.50)(0.50)}} = \frac{11}{16.5831} = 0.6633$$

Because $-1.96 < Z_{STAT} = 0.6633 < 1.96$, you do not reject H_0. There is insufficient evidence to prove that the population proportion of all consumers who believe that customer service is better at e-commerce sites than at physical stores is not 0.50. Figure 9.16 presents a Microsoft Excel worksheet and Figure 9.17 presents Minitab results for these data.

FIGURE 9.16

Microsoft Excel results for the survey of whether customer service is better or worse at e-commerce sites than it is at physical stores

See Section E9.3 or P9.3 to create this.

	A	B	
1	Z Test of Hypothesis for the Proportion		
2			
3	**Data**		
4	Null Hypothesis p=	0.5	
5	Level of Significance	0.05	
6	Number of Items of Interest	561	
7	Sample Size	1100	
8			
9	Intermediate Calculations		
10	Sample Proportion	0.5100	=B6/B7
11	Standard Error	0.0151	=SQRT(B4*(1 - B4)/B7)
12	Z Test Statistic	0.6633	=(B10 - B4)/B11
13			
14	Two-Tail Test		
15	Lower Critical Value	-1.9600	=NORMSINV(B5/2)
16	Upper Critical Value	1.9600	=NORMSINV(1 - B5/2)
17	p-Value	0.5071	=2 * (1 - NORMSDIST(ABS(B12)))
18	Do not reject the null hypothesis		=IF(B17 < B5, "Reject the null hypothesis", "Do not reject the null hypothesis")

FIGURE 9.17

Minitab results for the survey of whether customer service is better or worse at e-commerce sites than it is at physical stores

See Section M9.3 to create this.

```
Sample    X    N   Sample p        95% CI          Z-Value  P-Value
1        561  1100  0.510000  (0.480458, 0.539542)    0.66    0.507

Using the normal approximation.
```

The *p*-Value Approach

As an alternative to the critical value approach, you can compute the *p*-value. For this two-tail test in which the rejection region is located in the lower tail and the upper tail, you need to find the area below a Z value of -0.66 and above a Z value of $+0.66$. Figures 9.16 and 9.17 report a *p*-value of 0.507. Because this value is greater than the selected level of significance ($\alpha = 0.05$), you do not reject the null hypothesis.

EXAMPLE 9.6

Testing a Hypothesis for a Proportion

A fast-food chain has developed a new process to ensure that orders at the drive-through are filled correctly. The previous process filled orders correctly 85% of the time. Based on a sample of 100 orders using the new process, 94 were filled correctly. At the 0.01 level of significance, can you conclude that the new process has increased the proportion of orders filled correctly?

SOLUTION The null and alternative hypotheses are

H_0: $\pi \leq 0.85$ (i.e., the population proportion of orders filled correctly using the new process is less than or equal to 0.85)

H_1: $\pi > 0.85$ (i.e., the population proportion of orders filled correctly using the new process is greater than 0.85)

Using Equation (9.3) on page 299,

$$p = \frac{X}{n} = \frac{94}{100} = 0.94$$

$$Z_{STAT} = \frac{p - \pi}{\sqrt{\dfrac{\pi(1 - \pi)}{n}}} = \frac{0.94 - 0.85}{\sqrt{\dfrac{0.85(1 - 0.85)}{100}}} = \frac{0.09}{0.0357} = 2.52$$

The *p*-value for $Z_{STAT} > 2.52$ is 0.0059.

Using the critical value approach, you reject H_0 if $Z_{STAT} > 2.33$. Using the *p*-value approach, you reject H_0 if the *p*-value < 0.01. Because $Z_{STAT} = 2.52 > 2.33$ or the *p*-value = 0.0059 < 0.01, you reject H_0. You have evidence that the new process has increased the proportion of correct orders above 0.85.

Problems for Section 9.4

LEARNING THE BASICS

9.46 If, in a random sample of 400 items, 88 are defective, what is the sample proportion of defective items?

9.47 In Problem 9.46, if the null hypothesis is that 20% of the items in the population are defective, what is the value of Z_{STAT}?

9.48 In Problems 9.46 and 9.47, suppose you are testing the null hypothesis H_0: $\pi = 0.20$ against the two-tail alternative hypothesis H_1: $\pi \neq 0.20$ and you choose the level of significance $\alpha = 0.05$. What is your statistical decision?

APPLYING THE CONCEPTS

9.49 Late payment of medical claims can add to the cost of health care. An article (M. Freudenheim, "The Check Is Not in the Mail," *The New York Times*, May 25, 2006, pp. C1, C6) reported that for one insurance company, 85.1% of the claims were paid in full when first submitted. Suppose that the insurance company developed a new payment system in an effort to increase this percentage. A sample of 200 claims processed under this system revealed that 180 of the claims were paid in full when first submitted.
a. At the 0.05 level of significance, is there evidence that the population proportion of claims processed under this new system is higher than the article reported for the previous system?
b. Compute the *p*-value and interpret its meaning.

9.50 Online magazines make it easy for readers to link to an advertiser's Web site directly from an advertisement placed in the digital magazine. A recent survey indicated that 56% of online magazine readers have clicked on an advertisement and linked directly to the advertiser's Web site. The survey was based on a sample size of $n = 6,403$ (data extracted from "Metrics," *EContent*, January/February, 2007, p. 20).
a. Use the five-step *p*-value approach to try to determine whether there is evidence that more than half of all the readers of online magazines have linked to an advertiser's Web site. (Use the 0.05 level of significance.)
b. Suppose that the sample size was only $n = 100$, and as before, 56% of the online magazine readers indicated that they had clicked on an advertisement to link directly to the advertiser's Web site. Use the five-step *p*-value approach to try to determine whether there is evidence that more than half of all the readers of online magazines have linked to an advertiser's Web site. (Use the 0.05 level of significance.)
c. Discuss the effect that sample size has on hypothesis testing.
d. What do you think your chances are of rejecting any null hypothesis concerning a population proportion if a sample size of $n = 20$ is used?

9.51 One of the issues facing organizations is increasing diversity throughout the organization. One of the ways to evaluate an organization's success at increasing diversity is to compare the percentage of employees in the organization in a particular position with a specific background to the percentage in a particular position with that specific background in the general workforce. Recently, a large academic medical center determined that 9 of 17 employees in a particular position were female whereas 55% of the employees for this position in the general workforce were female. At the 0.05 level of significance, is there evidence that the proportion of females in this position at this medical center is different from what would be expected in the general workforce?

9.52 Sixty-five percent of 1,000 respondents aged 24 to 35 reported that they preferred to "look for a job in a place where I would like to live" rather than "look for the best job I can find, the place where I live is secondary" (data extracted from L. Belkin, "What Do Young Jobseekers Want? (Something Other Than a Job)," *The New York Times*, September 6, 2007, p. G2). At the 0.05 level of significance, is there evidence that the proportion of all young jobseekers aged 24 to 35 who preferred to "look for a job in a place where I would like to live" rather than "look for the best job I can find, the place where I live is secondary" is different from 60%?

9.53 One of the biggest issues facing e-retailers is the ability to reduce the proportion of customers who cancel their transactions after they have selected their products. It has been estimated that about half of prospective customers cancel their transactions after they have selected their products (data extracted from B. Tedeschi, "E-Commerce, a Cure for Abandoned Shopping Carts: A Web Checkout System That Eliminates the Need for Multiple Screens," *The New York Times*, February 14, 2005, p. C3). Suppose that a company changed its Web site so that customers could use a single-page checkout process rather than multiple pages. A sample of 500 customers who had selected their products were provided with the new checkout system. Of these 500 customers, 210 cancelled their transactions after they had selected their products.

a. At the 0.01 level of significance, is there evidence that the population proportion of customers who select products and then cancel their transaction is less than 0.50 with the new system?

b. Suppose that a sample of $n = 100$ customers (instead of $n = 500$ customers) were provided with the new checkout system and that 42 of those customers cancelled their transactions after they had selected their products. At the 0.01 level of significance, is there evidence that the population proportion of customers who select products and then cancel their transaction is less than 0.50 with the new system?

c. Compare the results of (a) and (b) and discuss the effect that sample size has on the outcome, and, in general, in hypothesis testing.

9.54 A recent study by the Pew Internet and American Life Project (**pewinternet.org**) found that Americans had a complex and ambivalent attitude toward technology (data extracted from M. Himowitz, "How to Tell What Kind of Tech User You Are," *Newsday*, May 27, 2007, p. F6). The study reported that 8% of the respondents were "Omnivores" who are gadget lovers, text messengers, and online gamers who often had their own blogs, Web pages, video makers, and YouTube posters. You believe that the percentage of students at your school who are Omnivores is greater than 8% and you plan to carry out a study to prove that this is so.

a. State the null and alternative hypothesis.

You select a sample of 200 students at your school and find that 30 students can be classified as Omnivores.

b. Use either the six-step critical value hypothesis-testing approach or the five-step *p*-value approach to determine at the 0.05 level of significance whether there is evidence that the percentage of Omnivores at your school is greater than 8%.

9.5 Potential Hypothesis-Testing Pitfalls and Ethical Issues

To this point, you have studied the fundamental concepts of hypothesis testing. You have used hypothesis testing to analyze differences between sample statistics and hypothesized population parameters in order to make business decisions concerning the underlying population characteristics. You have also learned how to evaluate the risks involved in making these decisions.

When planning to carry out a hypothesis test based on a survey, research study, or designed experiment, you must ask several questions to ensure that you use proper methodology. You need to raise and answer questions such as the following in the planning stage:

1. What is the goal of the survey, study, or experiment? How can you translate the goal into a null hypothesis and an alternative hypothesis?
2. Is the hypothesis test a two-tail test or one-tail test?
3. Can you select a random sample from the underlying population of interest?
4. What types of data will you collect in the sample? Are the variables numerical or categorical?
5. At what level of significance should you conduct the hypothesis test?

6. Is the intended sample size large enough to achieve the desired power of the test for the level of significance chosen?

7. What statistical test procedure should you use and why?

8. What conclusions and interpretations can you reach from the results of the hypothesis test?

Failing to consider these questions early in the planning process can lead to biased or incomplete results. Proper planning can help ensure that the statistical study will provide objective information needed to make good business decisions.

Statistical Significance versus Practical Significance You need to make the distinction between the existence of a statistically significant result and its practical significance in the context within a field of application. Sometimes, due to a very large sample size, you may get a result that is statistically significant but has little practical significance. For example, suppose that prior to a national marketing campaign focusing on a series of expensive television commercials, you believe that the proportion of people who recognize your brand is 0.30. At the completion of the campaign, a survey of 20,000 people indicates that 6,168 recognized your brand. A one-tail test trying to prove that the proportion is now greater than 0.30 results in a p-value of 0.0047 and the correct statistical conclusion is that the proportion of consumers recognizing your brand name has now increased. Was the campaign successful? The result of the hypothesis test indicates a statistically significant increase in brand awareness, but is this increase practically important? The population proportion is now estimated at $6,168/20,000 = 0.3084$, or 30.84%. This increase is less than 1% more than the hypothesized value of 30%. Did the large expenses associated with the marketing campaign produce a result with a meaningful increase in brand awareness? Because of the minimal real-world impact an increase of less than 1% has on the overall marketing strategy and the huge expenses associated with the marketing campaign, you should conclude that the campaign was not successful. On the other hand, if the campaign increased brand awareness by 20%, you could conclude that the campaign was successful.

Reporting of Findings In conducting research, you should document both good and bad results. You should not just report the results of hypothesis tests that show statistical significance but omit those for which there is insufficient evidence in the findings. In instances in which there is insufficient evidence to reject H_0, you must make it clear that this does not prove that the null hypothesis is true. What the result does indicate is that with the sample size used, there is not enough information to *disprove* the null hypothesis.

Ethical Issues You also need to distinguish between poor research methodology and unethical behavior. Ethical considerations arise when the hypothesis-testing process is manipulated. Some of the areas where ethical issues can arise include the use of human subjects in experiments, data collection method, the type of test (one-tail or two-tail test), the choice of the level of significance, the cleansing and discarding of data, and the failure to report pertinent findings.

USING STATISTICS # @ Oxford Cereals, Part II Revisited

As the plant operations manager for Oxford Cereals, you were responsible for the cereal-filling process. It was your responsibility to adjust the process when the mean fill weight in the population of boxes deviated from the company specifications of 368 grams. Since weighing all the cereal boxes would be too time-consuming and impractical, you needed to select and weigh a sample of boxes and conduct a hypothesis test.

You determined that the null hypothesis should be that the population mean fill was 368 grams. If the weights of the sampled boxes were sufficiently above or below the expected 368-gram mean specified by Oxford Cereals, you would reject the null hypothesis in favor of the alternative hypothesis that the mean fill was different from 368 grams. If this happened, you would stop production and take whatever action is necessary to correct the problem. If the null hypothesis was not rejected, you would continue to believe in the status quo, that the process was working correctly, and therefore take no corrective action.

Before proceeding, you considered the risks involved with hypothesis tests known as Type I and Type II errors. If you rejected a true null hypothesis, then you would make a Type I error and conclude that the population mean fill was not 368 when it actually was 368. This error would result in adjusting the filling process even though the process was working properly. If you did not reject a false null hypothesis, then you would make a Type II error and conclude that the population mean fill was 368 when it actually was not 368. Here, you would allow the process to continue without adjustment even though the process was not working properly.

After collecting a random sample of 25 cereal boxes, you used the six-step critical value approach to hypothesis testing. Because the test statistic fell into the nonrejection region, you did not reject the null hypothesis. You concluded that there was insufficient evidence to prove that the mean fill differed from 368 grams. No corrective action on the filling process was needed.

SUMMARY

This chapter presented the foundation of hypothesis testing. You learned how to perform tests on the population mean and on the population proportion. The chapter developed both the critical value approach and the p-value approach to hypothesis testing.

In deciding which test to use, you should ask the following question:

Does the test involve a numerical variable or a categorical variable? If the test involves a categorical variable, use the Z test for the proportion. If the test involves a numerical variable, use the t test for the mean.

TABLE 9.4

Summary of Topics in Chapter 9

Type of Analysis	Type of Data	
	Numerical	Categorical
Hypothesis test concerning a single parameter	t test of hypothesis for the mean (Section 9.2)	Z test of hypothesis for the proportion (Section 9.4)

KEY EQUATIONS

Z Test for the Mean (σ Known)

$$Z_{STAT} = \frac{\overline{X} - \mu}{\frac{\sigma}{\sqrt{n}}} \qquad (9.1)$$

t Test for the Mean (σ Unknown)

$$t_{STAT} = \frac{\overline{X} - \mu}{\frac{S}{\sqrt{n}}} \qquad (9.2)$$

Z Test for the Proportion

$$Z_{STAT} = \frac{p - \pi}{\sqrt{\frac{\pi(1 - \pi)}{n}}} \qquad (9.3)$$

Z Test for the Proportion in Terms of the Number of Events of Interest

$$Z_{STAT} = \frac{X - n\pi}{\sqrt{n\pi(1 - \pi)}} \qquad (9.4)$$

KEY TERMS

α (level of significance) 279
alternative hypothesis (H_1) 276
β risk 279
confidence coefficient 279
confidence level 279
critical value 278
directional test 295
hypothesis testing 276

level of significance (α) 279
null hypothesis (H_0) 276
one-tail test 295
p-value 283
power of a statistical test 279
region of nonrejection 278
region of rejection 278
robust 292

sample proportion 298
t test for the mean 287
test statistic 278
two-tail test 281
Type I error 278
Type II error 278
Z test for the mean 280
Z test for the proportion 298

CHAPTER REVIEW PROBLEMS

CHECKING YOUR UNDERSTANDING

9.55 What is the difference between a null hypothesis, H_0, and an alternative hypothesis, H_1?

9.56 What is the difference between a Type I error and a Type II error?

9.57 What is meant by the power of a test?

9.58 What is the difference between a one-tail test and a two-tail test?

9.59 What is meant by a p-value?

9.60 How can a confidence interval estimate for the population mean provide conclusions to the corresponding two-tail hypothesis test for the population mean?

9.61 What is the six-step critical value approach to hypothesis testing?

9.62 What is the five-step p-value approach to hypothesis testing?

APPLYING THE CONCEPTS

9.63 An article in *Marketing News* (T. T. Semon, "Consider a Statistical Insignificance Test," *Marketing News*, February 1, 1999) argued that the level of significance used when comparing two products is often too low—that is, sometimes you should be using an α value greater than 0.05. Specifically, the article recounted testing the proportion of potential customers with a preference for product 1 over product 2. The null hypothesis was that the population proportion of potential customers preferring product 1 was 0.50, and the alternative hypothesis was that it was not equal to 0.50. The p-value for the test was 0.22. The article suggested that, in some cases, this should be enough evidence to reject the null hypothesis.
a. State the null and alternative hypotheses for this example in statistical terms.
b. Explain the risks associated with Type I and Type II errors in this case.

c. What would be the consequences if you rejected the null hypothesis for a p-value of 0.22?
d. Why do you think the article suggested raising the value of α?
e. What would you do in this situation?
f. What is your answer in (e) if the p-value equals 0.12? What if it equals 0.06?

9.64 La Quinta Motor Inns developed a computer model to help predict the profitability of sites that are being considered as locations for new hotels. If the computer model predicts large profits, La Quinta buys the proposed site and builds a new hotel. If the computer model predicts small or moderate profits, La Quinta chooses not to proceed with that site (data extracted from S. E. Kimes and J. A. Fitzsimmons, "Selecting Profitable Hotel Sites at La Quinta Motor Inns," *Interfaces*, Vol. 20, March–April 1990, pp. 12–20). This decision-making procedure can be expressed in the hypothesis-testing framework. The null hypothesis is that the site is not a profitable location. The alternative hypothesis is that the site is a profitable location.
a. Explain the risks associated with committing a Type I error in this case.
b. Explain the risks associated with committing a Type II error in this case.
c. Which type of error do you think the executives at La Quinta Motor Inns are trying hard to avoid? Explain.
d. How do changes in the rejection criterion affect the probabilities of committing Type I and Type II errors?

9.65 In 2006, Visa wanted to move away from its long-running television advertising theme of "Visa, it's every-where you want to be." During the Winter Olympics, Visa featured Olympians in commercials with a broader message, including security, check cards, and payment technologies such as contactless processing. One of the first commercials featured snowboarder Lindsey Jacobellis being coached to calm down before a big race by imagining that her Visa Check Card got stolen. A key metric for the success of television advertisements is the proportion of viewers who "like

10 Two-Sample Tests and One-Way ANOVA

Learning Objectives

In this chapter, you learn how to use hypothesis testing for comparing the difference between:

- The means of two independent populations
- The means of two related populations
- The proportions of two independent populations
- The variances of two independent populations
- The means of more than two populations

@ BLK Foods

Does the type of display used in a supermarket affect the sales of products? As the regional sales manager for BLK Foods, you want to compare the sales volume of BLK Cola when the product is placed in the normal shelf location to the sales volume when the product is featured in a special end-aisle display. To test the effectiveness of the end-aisle displays, you select 20 stores from the BLK supermarket chain that all experience similar storewide sales volumes. You then randomly assign 10 of the 20 stores to sample 1 and 10 to sample 2. The managers of the 10 stores in sample 1 place the BLK Cola in the normal shelf location alongside the other cola products. The 10 stores in sample 2 use the special end-aisle promotional display. At the end of one week, the sales of BLK Cola are recorded. How can you determine whether sales of BLK Cola using the end-aisle displays are the same as those when the cola is placed in the normal shelf location? How can you decide if the variability in BLK cola sales from store to store is the same for the two types of displays? How could you use the answers to these questions to improve sales of BLK Cola?

Hypothesis testing provides a *confirmatory* approach to data analysis. In Chapter 9, you learned a variety of commonly used hypothesis-testing procedures that relate to a single sample of data selected from a single population. In this chapter, you learn how to extend hypothesis testing to procedures that compare statistics from samples of data selected from two or more populations. One such extension would be asking the question, "Are the mean weekly sales of BLK Cola when using the normal shelf location equal to the mean weekly sales of BLK Cola when placed in an end-aisle display?"

10.1 Comparing the Means of Two Independent Populations

Pooled-Variance t Test for the Difference Between Two Means

Suppose that you take a random sample of n_1 from the first population and a random sample of n_2 from the second population. The data collected in each sample are from a numerical variable. In the first population, the mean is represented by the symbol μ_1 and the standard deviation is represented by the symbol σ_1. In the second population, the mean is represented by the symbol μ_2 and the standard deviation is represented by the symbol σ_2.

In almost all cases, the variances of the two populations are not known. The only information you usually have are the sample means and the sample variances. If you assume that the samples are randomly and independently selected from populations that are normally distributed and that the population variances are equal (i.e., $\sigma_1^2 = \sigma_2^2$), you can use a **pooled-variance t test** to determine whether there is a significant difference between the means of the two populations. If the populations are not normally distributed, the pooled-variance t test is still appropriate if the sample sizes are large enough (typically n_1 and $n_2 \geq 30$; see the Central Limit Theorem in Section 7.4 on page 224).

To test the null hypothesis of no difference in the means of two independent populations:

$$H_0: \mu_1 = \mu_2 \quad \text{or} \quad \mu_1 - \mu_2 = 0$$

against the alternative that the means are not the same

$$H_1: \mu_1 \neq \mu_2 \quad \text{or} \quad \mu_1 - \mu_2 \neq 0$$

you use the pooled-variance t-test statistic t_{STAT} shown in Equation (10.1). The pooled-variance t test gets its name from the fact that the test statistic pools or combines the two sample variances S_1^2 and S_2^2 to compute S_p^2, the best estimate of the variance common to both populations under the assumption that the two population variances are equal.[1]

[1] When the two sample sizes are equal (i.e., $n_1 = n_2$), the equation for the pooled variance can be simplified to

$$S_p^2 = \frac{S_1^2 + S_2^2}{2}$$

POOLED-VARIANCE t TEST FOR THE DIFFERENCE BETWEEN TWO MEANS

$$t_{STAT} = \frac{(\overline{X}_1 - \overline{X}_2) - (\mu_1 - \mu_2)}{\sqrt{S_p^2 \left(\dfrac{1}{n_1} + \dfrac{1}{n_2} \right)}}$$

where

$$S_p^2 = \frac{(n_1 - 1)S_1^2 + (n_2 - 1)S_2^2}{(n_1 - 1) + (n_2 - 1)}$$

(10.1)

and

S_p^2 = pooled variance

$\overline{X}_1$ = mean of the sample taken from population 1

S_1^2 = variance of the sample taken from population 1

$$n_1 = \text{size of the sample taken from population 1}$$
$$\overline{X}_2 = \text{mean of the sample taken from population 2}$$
$$S_2^2 = \text{variance of the sample taken from population 2}$$
$$n_2 = \text{size of the sample taken from population 2}$$

The t_{STAT} test statistic follows a t distribution with $n_1 + n_2 - 2$ degrees of freedom.

For a given level of significance α, in a two-tail test, you reject the null hypothesis if the computed t_{STAT} test statistic is greater than the upper-tail critical value from the t distribution or if the computed t_{STAT} test statistic is less than the lower-tail critical value from the t distribution. Figure 10.1 displays the regions of rejection.

FIGURE 10.1

Regions of rejection and nonrejection for the pooled-variance t test for the difference between the means (two-tail test)

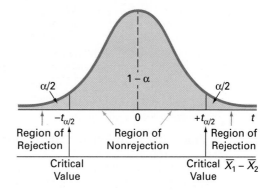

In a one-tail test in which the rejection region is in the lower tail, you reject the null hypothesis if the computed t_{STAT} test statistic is less than the lower-tail critical value from the t distribution. In a one-tail test in which the rejection region is in the upper tail, you reject the null hypothesis if the computed t_{STAT} test statistic is greater than the upper-tail critical value from the t distribution.

To demonstrate the use of the pooled-variance t test, return to the Using Statistics scenario on page 313. You want to determine whether the mean weekly sales of BLK Cola are the same when using a normal shelf location and when using an end-aisle display. There are two populations of interest. The first population is the set of all possible weekly sales of BLK Cola *if* all the BLK supermarkets used the normal shelf location. The second population is the set of all possible weekly sales of BLK Cola *if* all the BLK supermarkets used the end-aisle displays. The first sample contains the weekly sales of BLK Cola from the 10 stores selected to use the normal shelf location, and the second sample contains the weekly sales of BLK Cola from the 10 stores selected to use the end-aisle display. Table 10.1 contains the cola sales (in number of cases) for the two samples (see the `Cola` file).

TABLE 10.1

Comparing BLK Cola Weekly Sales from Two Different Display Locations (in Number of Cases)

Display Location									
Normal					**End-Aisle**				
22	34	52	62	30	52	71	76	54	67
40	64	84	56	59	83	66	90	77	84

The null and alternative hypotheses are

$$H_0: \mu_1 = \mu_2 \quad \text{or} \quad \mu_1 - \mu_2 = 0$$
$$H_1: \mu_1 \neq \mu_2 \quad \text{or} \quad \mu_1 - \mu_2 \neq 0$$

Assuming that the samples are from normal populations having equal variances, you can use the pooled-variance t test. The t_{STAT} test statistic follows a t distribution with

$10 + 10 - 2 = 18$ degrees of freedom. Using $\alpha = 0.05$ level of significance, you divide the rejection region into the two tails for this two-tail test (i.e., two equal parts of 0.025 each). Table E.3 shows that the critical values for this two-tail test are $+2.1009$ and -2.1009. As shown in Figure 10.2, the decision rule is:

$$\text{Reject } H_0 \text{ if } t_{STAT} > +2.1009$$

$$\text{or if } t_{STAT} < -2.1009;$$

$$\text{otherwise do not reject } H_0.$$

FIGURE 10.2

Two-tail test of hypothesis for the difference between the means at the 0.05 level of significance with 18 degrees of freedom

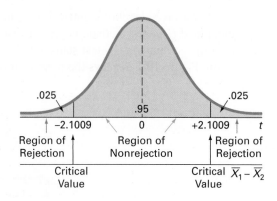

From Figures 10.3 or 10.4, the computed t_{STAT} test statistic for this test is -3.0446 and the p-value is 0.0070.

FIGURE 10.3

Microsoft Excel *t*-test results for the two display locations

See Section E10.2 to create this.

	A	B	C
1	**t-Test: Two-Sample Assuming Equal Variances**		
2			
3		***Normal***	***End-Aisle***
4	**Mean**	50.3	72
5	**Variance**	350.6778	157.3333
6	**Observations**	10	10
7	**Pooled Variance**	254.0056	
8	**Hypothesized Mean Difference**	0	
9	**df**	18	
10	**t Stat**	-3.0446	
11	**P(T<=t) one-tail**	0.0035	
12	**t Critical one-tail**	1.7341	
13	**P(T<=t) two-tail**	0.0070	
14	**t Critical two-tail**	2.1009	

FIGURE 10.4

Minitab *t*-test results for the two display locations

See Section M10.2 to create this.

```
Two-sample T for Sales_Normal vs Sales_EndAisle

              N   Mean   StDev   SE Mean
Sales_Normal   10   50.3   18.7     5.9
Sales_EndAisle 10   72.0   12.5     4.0


Difference = mu (Sales_Normal) - mu (Sales_EndAisle)
Estimate for difference:  -21.70
95% CI for difference:   (-36.67, -6.73)

T-Test of difference = 0 (vs not =): T-Value = -3.04   P-Value = 0.007   DF = 18
Both use Pooled StDev = 15.9376
```

Using Equation (10.1) on page 314 and the descriptive statistics provided in Figures 10.3 and 10.4,

$$t_{STAT} = \frac{(\bar{X}_1 - \bar{X}_2) - (\mu_1 - \mu_2)}{\sqrt{S_p^2\left(\frac{1}{n_1} + \frac{1}{n_2}\right)}}$$

where

$$S_p^2 = \frac{(n_1 - 1)S_1^2 + (n_2 - 1)S_2^2}{(n_1 - 1) + (n_2 - 1)}$$

$$= \frac{9(350.6778) + 9(157.3333)}{9 + 9} = 254.0056$$

Therefore,

$$t_{STAT} = \frac{(50.3 - 72.0) - 0.0}{\sqrt{254.0056\left(\frac{1}{10} + \frac{1}{10}\right)}} = \frac{-21.7}{\sqrt{50.801}} = -3.0446$$

You reject the null hypothesis because $t_{STAT} = -3.0446 < -2.1009$. The p-value (as computed from Microsoft Excel or Minitab) is 0.0070. In other words, the probability that $t_{STAT} > 3.0446$ or $t_{STAT} < -3.0446$ is equal to 0.0070. This p-value indicates that if the population means are equal, the probability of observing a difference this large or larger in the two sample means is only 0.0070. Because the p-value is less than $\alpha = 0.05$, there is sufficient evidence to reject the null hypothesis. You can conclude that the mean sales are different for the normal shelf location and the end-aisle location. Based on these results, the sales are lower for the normal location (i.e., higher for the end-aisle location). Example 10.1 provides another application of the pooled-variance t test.

EXAMPLE 10.1

Testing for the Difference in the Mean Delivery Times

A local pizza restaurant and a local branch of a national chain are located across the street from a college campus. The local pizza restaurant advertises that they deliver to the dormitories faster than the national chain. In order to determine whether this advertisement is valid, you and some friends have decided to order 10 pizzas from the local pizza restaurant and 10 pizzas from the national chain, all at different times. The delivery times in minutes (see the Pizzatime file) are shown in Table 10.2:

TABLE 10.2

Delivery Times (in minutes) for Local Pizza Restaurant and National Pizza Chain

Local		Chain	
16.8	18.1	22.0	19.5
11.7	14.1	15.2	17.0
15.6	21.8	18.7	19.5
16.7	13.9	15.6	16.5
17.5	20.8	20.8	24.0

At the 0.05 level of significance, is there evidence that the mean delivery time for the local pizza restaurant is less than the mean delivery time for the national pizza chain?

SOLUTION Because you want to know whether the mean is *lower* for the local pizza restaurant than for the national pizza chain, you have a one-tail test with the following null and alternative hypotheses:

H_0: $\mu_1 \geq \mu_2$ (The mean delivery time for the local pizza restaurant is equal to or greater than the mean delivery time for the national pizza chain.)

H_1: $\mu_1 < \mu_2$ (The mean delivery time for the local pizza restaurant is less than the mean delivery time for the national pizza chain.)

Figure 10.5 displays Microsoft Excel results of the pooled t test for these data.

FIGURE 10.5

Microsoft Excel results of the pooled t test for the pizza delivery time data

See Section E10.2 to create this. (Minitab users, see Section M10.2 to create equivalent results.)

	A	B	C
1	t-Test: Two-Sample Assuming Equal Variances		
2			
3		Local	Chain
4	Mean	16.7	18.88
5	Variance	9.5822	8.2151
6	Observations	10	10
7	Pooled Variance	8.8987	
8	Hypothesized Mean Difference	0	
9	df	18	
10	t Stat	-1.6341	
11	P(T<=t) one-tail	0.0598	
12	t Critical one-tail	1.7341	
13	P(T<=t) two-tail	0.1196	
14	t Critical two-tail	2.1009	

Using Equation (10.1) on page 314,

$$t_{STAT} = \frac{(\bar{X}_1 - \bar{X}_2) - (\mu_1 - \mu_2)}{\sqrt{S_p^2\left(\dfrac{1}{n_1} + \dfrac{1}{n_2}\right)}}$$

where

$$S_p^2 = \frac{(n_1 - 1)S_1^2 + (n_2 - 1)S_2^2}{(n_1 - 1) + (n_2 - 1)}$$

$$= \frac{9(9.5822) + 9(8.2151)}{9 + 9} = 8.8987$$

Therefore,

$$t_{STAT} = \frac{(16.7 - 18.88) - 0.0}{\sqrt{8.8987\left(\dfrac{1}{10} + \dfrac{1}{10}\right)}} = \frac{-2.18}{\sqrt{1.7797}} = -1.6341$$

You do not reject the null hypothesis because $t_{STAT} = -1.6341 > -1.7341$. The p-value (as computed from Microsoft Excel) is 0.0598. This p-value indicates that the probability that $t_{STAT} < -1.6341$ is equal to 0.0598. In other words, if the population means are equal, the probability that the sample mean delivery time for the local pizza restaurant is at least 2.18 minutes faster than the national chain is 0.0598. Because the p-value is greater than $\alpha = 0.05$, there is insufficient evidence to reject the null hypothesis. Based on these results, there is insufficient evidence for the local pizza restaurant to make the advertising claim that they have a faster delivery time.

In testing for the difference between the means, you assume that the populations are normally distributed with equal variances. For situations in which the two populations have equal variances, the pooled-variance t test is **robust** (or not sensitive) to moderate departures from the assumption of normality, provided that the sample sizes are large. In such situations, you can use the pooled-variance t test without serious effects on its power. However, if you cannot assume that both populations are normally distributed, you have two choices. You can use a nonparametric procedure, such as the Wilcoxon rank sum test (see references 1 and 2), that does not depend on the assumption of normality for the two populations, or you can use a normalizing transformation (see reference 9) on each of the outcomes and then use the pooled-variance t test.

To check the assumption of normality in each of the two populations, observe the boxplot of the sales for the two display locations in Figure 10.6 on page 319. For these two small samples, there appears to be only moderate departure from normality, so the assumption of normality needed for the t test is not seriously violated.

FIGURE 10.6

Minitab boxplot for the sales for two display locations

See Section M3.2 to create this. (Microsoft Excel users, see Section E3.3. PHStat2 users, see Section P3.1 to create an equivalent chart.)

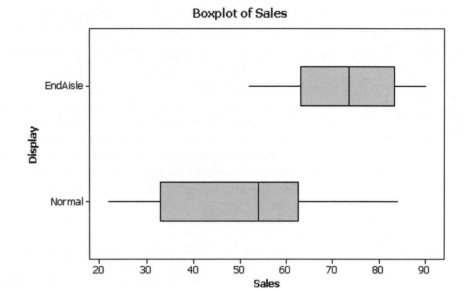

Confidence Interval Estimate for the Difference Between Two Means

Instead of, or in addition to, testing for the difference in the means of two independent populations, you can use Equation (10.2) to develop a confidence interval estimate of the difference in the means.

CONFIDENCE INTERVAL ESTIMATE OF THE DIFFERENCE IN THE MEANS OF TWO INDEPENDENT POPULATIONS

$$(\overline{X}_1 - \overline{X}_2) \pm t_{\alpha/2}\sqrt{S_p^2\left(\frac{1}{n_1} + \frac{1}{n_2}\right)} \qquad (10.2)$$

or

$$(\overline{X}_1 - \overline{X}_2) - t_{\alpha/2}\sqrt{S_p^2\left(\frac{1}{n_1} + \frac{1}{n_2}\right)} \le \mu_1 - \mu_2 \le (\overline{X}_1 - \overline{X}_2) + t_{\alpha/2}\sqrt{S_p^2\left(\frac{1}{n_1} + \frac{1}{n_2}\right)}$$

where $t_{\alpha/2}$ is the critical value of the t distribution with $n_1 + n_2 - 2$ degrees of freedom for an area of $\alpha/2$ in the upper tail.

For the sample statistics pertaining to the two aisle locations reported in Figures 10.3 or 10.4 on page 316, using 95% confidence, and Equation (10.2),

$$\overline{X}_1 = 50.3, n_1 = 10, \overline{X}_2 = 72, n_2 = 10, S_p^2 = 254.0056, \text{ and with } 10 + 10 - 2$$

$$= 18 \text{ degrees of freedom, } t_{0.025} = 2.1009$$

$$(50.3 - 72) \pm (2.1009)\sqrt{254.0056\left(\frac{1}{10} + \frac{1}{10}\right)}$$

$$-21.7 \pm (2.1009)(7.1275)$$

$$-21.7 \pm 14.97$$

$$-36.67 \le \mu_1 - \mu_2 \le -6.73$$

Therefore, you are 95% confident that the difference in mean sales between the normal aisle location and the end-aisle location is between -36.67 cases of cola and -6.73 cases of cola. In other words, the end-aisle location sells, on average, 6.73 to 36.67 cases more than the normal aisle location. From a hypothesis-testing perspective, because the interval does not include zero, you reject the null hypothesis of no difference between the means of the two populations.

Separate-Variance *t* Test for the Difference Between Two Means

In testing for the difference between the means of two independent populations when the population variances are assumed to be equal, the sample variances are pooled together into a common estimate S_p^2. However, if you cannot make this assumption, then the pooled-variance *t* test is inappropriate. In this case, you should use the **separate-variance *t* test** developed by Satterthwaite (see reference 8). This test procedure includes the two separate sample variances in the computation of the *t*-test statistic. Although the computations for the separate-variance *t* test are complicated, you can use Microsoft Excel or Minitab to perform the test.

Figure 10.7 illustrates Microsoft Excel results for this separate-variance *t* test, and Figure 10.8 illustrates Minitab output. Note that Excel rounds the degrees of freedom while Minitab uses the integer portion.

FIGURE 10.7

Microsoft Excel results of the separate-variance *t* test for the display location data

See Section E10.4 to create this.

	A	B	C
1	t-Test: Two-Sample Assuming Unequal Variances		
2			
3		*Normal*	*End-Aisle*
4	**Mean**	50.3	72
5	**Variance**	350.6778	157.3333
6	**Observations**	10	10
7	**Hypothesized Mean Difference**	0	
8	**df**	16	
9	**t Stat**	-3.0446	
10	**P(T<=t) one-tail**	0.0039	
11	**t Critical one-tail**	1.7459	
12	**P(T<=t) two-tail**	0.0077	
13	**t Critical two-tail**	2.1199	

FIGURE 10.8

Minitab results of the separate-variance *t* test for the display location data

See Section M10.2 to create this.

```
Two-sample T for Sales_Normal vs Sales_EndAisle

                N   Mean   StDev   SE Mean
Sales_Normal    10  50.3   18.7    5.9
Sales_EndAisle  10  72.0   12.5    4.0


Difference = mu (Sales_Normal) - mu (Sales_EndAisle)
Estimate for difference:  -21.70
95% CI for difference:  (-36.89, -6.51)
T-Test of difference = 0 (vs not =): T-Value = -3.04  P-Value = 0.008  DF = 15
```

In Figures 10.7 and 10.8 the test statistic $t_{STAT} = -3.0446$ and the *p*-value is $0.0077 < 0.05$. Thus, the results for the separate-variance *t* test are almost exactly the same as those of the pooled-variance *t* test. The assumption of equality of population variances had no real effect on the results. Sometimes, however, the results from the pooled-variance and separate-variance *t* tests conflict because the assumption of equal variances is violated. Therefore, it is important that you evaluate the assumptions and use those results as a guide in appropriately selecting a test procedure. In Section 10.4, the *F* test is used to determine whether there is evidence of a difference in the two population variances. The results of that test can help you determine which of the *t* tests—pooled-variance or separate-variance—is more appropriate.

THINK ABOUT THIS   "This Call May Be Monitored . . ."

If you have ever used a telephone to seek customer service, you've probably heard at least once a message that begins "this call may be monitored . . ." Most of the time the message explains the monitoring is for "quality assurance purposes," but do companies really monitor your calls to improve quality?

From one of our previous students, we've learned that a certain large financial corporation really does monitor calls for quality purposes. This student was asked to develop an improved training program for a call center that was hiring people to answer phone calls customers make about outstanding loans. For feedback and evaluation, she planned to randomly select phone calls received by each new employee and rate the employee on ten aspects of the call including did the employee maintain a pleasant tone with the customer?

Who You Gonna Call?

She presented her plan to her boss for approval, but her boss, remembering the words of a famous statistician, said, "In God we trust, all others must bring data." That is, her boss wanted proof that her new training program would improve customer service. Faced with such a request, who would you call? She called one of us. "Hey professor, you'll never believe why I called. I work for a large company and in the project I am currently working on, I have to put some of the statistics you taught us to work! Can you help?" The answer was "Yes" and together they formulated this test:

- Randomly assign the 60 most recent hires into two training programs. Half would go through the preexisting training program, and half would be trained using the new program.

- At the end of the first month, compare the mean score for the 30 employees in the new training program against the mean score for the 30 employees in the preexisting training program.

She listened as her professor explained, "What you are trying to prove is that the mean score from the new training program is higher than the mean score from the current program. You can make the null hypothesis that the means are equal, and see if you can reject it in favor of the alternative that the mean score from the new program is higher."

"Or, as you used to say, 'if the p-value is low, H_0 must go!'—yes, I do remember!" she replied. Her professor chuckled and said, "Yes, that's correct. And if you can reject H_0, you will have the proof to present to your boss." She thanked him for his help and got back to work with the newfound confidence that she would be able to successfully apply the t test that compares the means of two independent populations.

Problems for Section 10.1

LEARNING THE BASICS

10.1 If you have samples of $n_1 = 12$ and $n_2 = 15$, in performing the pooled-variance t test, how many degrees of freedom do you have?

10.2 Assume that you have a sample of $n_1 = 8$, with the sample mean $\overline{X}_1 = 42$, and a sample standard deviation of $S_1 = 4$, and you have an independent sample of $n_2 = 15$ from another population with a sample mean of $\overline{X}_2 = 34$ and the sample standard deviation $S_2 = 5$.
a. What is the value of the pooled-variance t_{STAT} test statistic for testing H_0: $\mu_1 = \mu_2$?
b. In finding the critical value $t_{\alpha/2}$, how many degrees of freedom are there?
c. Using the level of significance $\alpha = 0.01$, what is the critical value for a one-tail test of the hypothesis H_0: $\mu_1 \leq \mu_2$ against the alternative H_1: $\mu_1 > \mu_2$?
d. What is your statistical decision?

10.3 What assumptions about the two populations are necessary in Problem 10.2?

10.4 Referring to Problem 10.2, construct a 95% confidence interval estimate of the population mean difference between μ_1 and μ_2.

10.5 Referring to Problem 10.2, if $n_1 = 5$ and $n_2 = 4$, how many degrees of freedom do you have?

10.6 Referring to Problem 10.2, if $n_1 = 5$ and $n_2 = 4$, at the 0.01 level of significance, is there evidence that $\mu_1 > \mu_2$?

APPLYING THE CONCEPTS

10.7 According to a recent study, when shopping online for luxury goods, men spend a mean of $2,401 as compared to women who spend a mean of $1,527 (data extracted from R. A. Smith, "Fashion Online: Retailers Tackle the Gender Gap," *The Wall Street Journal*, March 13, 2008, pp. D1, D10). Suppose that the study was based on a sample of 600 men and 700 females and the standard deviation of the amount spent was $1,200 for men and $1,000 for women.
a. State the null and alternative hypothesis if you want to determine whether the mean amount spent is higher for men than for women.
b. In the context of this study, what is the meaning of the Type I error?
c. In the context of this study, what is the meaning of the Type II error?
d. At the 0.01 level of significance, is there evidence that the mean amount spent is higher for men than for women?

10.8 The American Society for Quality recently conducted a salary survey of its members. The following table includes summary statistics concerning annual salary for reliability/safety engineers and software quality engineers for respondents working in the United States.

Title	n	Mean	Standard Deviation
Reliability/safety engineer	85	87,239	21,094
Software quality engineer	142	84,795	19,344

Source: *Data extracted from H. Lindborg, "Navigate Your Career Path with QP's Annual Salary Survey,"* Quality Progress, *December 2007, pp. 21–50.*

a. Assuming that the population variances are equal and $\alpha = 0.05$, can you prove that the mean salary of reliability/safety engineers differs from the mean salary of software quality engineers?
b. Assuming that the population variances are equal, construct a 95% confidence interval on the difference between the mean salary of reliability/safety engineers and the mean salary of software quality engineers.
c. Compare the results of (a) and (b) and discuss.

10.9 A problem with a telephone line that prevents a customer from receiving or making calls is disconcerting to both the customer and the telephone company. The data in the file **PHONE** represent samples of 20 problems reported to two different offices of a telephone company and the time to clear these problems (in minutes) from the customers' lines:

Central Office I Time to Clear Problems (minutes)
1.48 1.75 0.78 2.85 0.52 1.60 4.15 3.97 1.48 3.10
1.02 0.53 0.93 1.60 0.80 1.05 6.32 3.93 5.45 0.97

Central Office II Time to Clear Problems (minutes)
7.55 3.75 0.10 1.10 0.60 0.52 3.30 2.10 0.58 4.02
3.75 0.65 1.92 0.60 1.53 4.23 0.08 1.48 1.65 0.72

a. Assuming that the population variances from both offices are equal, is there evidence of a difference in the mean waiting time between the two offices? (Use $\alpha = 0.05$.)
b. Find the p-value in (a) and interpret its meaning.
c. What other assumption is necessary in (a)?
d. Assuming that the population variances from both offices are equal, construct and interpret a 95% confidence interval estimate of the difference between the population means in the two offices.

✓SELF Test **10.10** The Computer Anxiety Rating Scale (CARS) measures an individual's level of computer anxiety, on a scale from 20 (no anxiety) to 100 (highest level of anxiety). Researchers at Miami University administered CARS to 172 business students. One of the objectives of the study was to determine whether there is a difference in the level of computer anxiety experienced by female and male business students. They found the following:

	Males	Females
$\overline{X}$	40.26	36.85
S	13.35	9.42
n	100	72

Source: *Data extracted from T. Broome and D. Havelka, "Determinants of Computer Anxiety in Business Students,"* The Review of Business Information Systems, *Spring 2002, 6(2), pp. 9–16.*

a. At the 0.05 level of significance, is there evidence of a difference in the mean computer anxiety experienced by female and male business students?
b. Determine the p-value and interpret its meaning.
c. What assumptions do you have to make about the two populations in order to justify the use of the t test?

10.11 Digital cameras have taken over the majority of the point-and-shoot camera market. One of the important features of a camera is the battery life as measured by the number of shots taken until the battery needs to be recharged. The data in the file **Digitalcameras** contain the battery life of 31 subcompact cameras and 15 compact cameras (data extracted from "Cameras," *Consumer Reports*, November 2006, pp. 20–21).

a. Assuming that the population variances from both types of digital cameras are equal, is there evidence of a difference in the mean battery life between the two types of digital cameras ($\alpha = 0.05$)?
b. Determine the p-value in (a) and interpret its meaning.
c. Assuming that the population variances from both types of digital cameras are equal, construct and interpret a 95% confidence interval estimate of the difference between the population mean battery life of the two types of digital cameras.

10.12 A bank with a branch located in a commercial district of a city has developed an improved process for serving customers during the noon-to-1 P.M. lunch period. The waiting time (operationally defined as the time elapsed from when the customer enters the line until he or she reaches the teller window) needs to be shortened to increase customer satisfaction. A random sample of 15 customers is selected (and stored in the file **Bank1**), and the results (in minutes) are as follows:

4.21 5.55 3.02 5.13 4.77 2.34 3.54 3.20
4.50 6.10 0.38 5.12 6.46 6.19 3.79

Suppose that another branch, located in a residential area, is also concerned with the noon-to-1 P.M. lunch period. A random sample of 15 customers is selected (and stored in the file **Bank2**), and the results are as follows:

9.66 5.90 8.02 5.79 8.73 3.82 8.01 8.35
10.49 6.68 5.64 4.08 6.17 9.91 5.47

a. Assuming that the population variances from both banks are equal, is there evidence of a difference in the mean waiting time between the two branches? (Use $\alpha = 0.05$.)
b. Determine the p-value in (a) and interpret its meaning.
c. In addition to equal variances, what other assumption is necessary in (a)?
d. Construct and interpret a 95% confidence interval estimate of the difference between the population means in the two branches.

10.13 Repeat Problem 10.12(a), assuming that the population variances in the two branches are not equal. Compare the results with those of Problem 10.12(a).

10.14 In intaglio printing, a design or figure is carved beneath the surface of hard metal or stone. Suppose that an experiment is designed to compare differences in mean surface hardness of steel plates used in intaglio printing (measured in indentation numbers), based on two different surface conditions—untreated and treated by lightly polishing with emery paper. In the experiment, 40 steel plates are randomly assigned—20 that are untreated, and 20 that are treated. The data are shown here and stored in the file **Intaglio**:

Untreated		Treated	
164.368	177.135	158.239	150.226
159.018	163.903	138.216	155.620
153.871	167.802	168.006	151.233
165.096	160.818	149.654	158.653
157.184	167.433	145.456	151.204
154.496	163.538	168.178	150.869
160.920	164.525	154.321	161.657
164.917	171.230	162.763	157.016
169.091	174.964	161.020	156.670
175.276	166.311	167.706	147.920

a. Assuming that the population variances from both conditions are equal, is there evidence of a difference in the mean surface hardness between untreated and treated steel plates? (Use $\alpha = 0.05$.)
b. Determine the *p*-value in (a) and interpret its meaning.
c. In addition to equal variances, what other assumption is necessary in (a)?
d. Construct and interpret a 95% confidence interval estimate of the difference between the population means from treated and untreated steel plates.

10.15 Repeat Problem 10.14(a), assuming that the population variances from untreated and treated steel plates are not equal. Compare the results with those of Problem 10.14(a).

10.16 The director of training for an electronic equipment manufacturer is interested in determining whether different training methods have an effect on the productivity of assembly-line employees. She randomly assigns 42 recently hired employees into two groups of 21. The first group receives a computer-assisted, individual-based training program, and the other receives a team-based training program. Upon completion of the training, the employees are evaluated on the time (in seconds) it takes to assemble a part. The results are in the data file Training .

a. Assuming that the variances in the populations of training methods are equal, is there evidence of a difference between the mean assembly times (in seconds) of employees trained in a computer-assisted, individual-based program and those trained in a team-based program? (Use a 0.05 level of significance.)
b. In addition to equal variances, what other assumption is necessary in (a)?
c. Repeat (a), assuming that the population variances are not equal.
d. Compare the results of (a) and (c).
e. Assuming normality and equal variances, construct and interpret a 95% confidence interval estimate of the difference between the population means of the two training methods.

10.17 Nondestructive evaluation is a method that is used to describe the properties of components or materials without causing any permanent physical change to the units. It includes the determination of properties of materials and the classification of flaws by size, shape, type, and location. This method is most effective for detecting surface flaws and characterizing surface properties of electrically conductive materials. Recently, data were collected that classified each component as having a flaw or not based on manual inspection and operator judgment and also reported the size of the crack in the material. Do the components classified as unflawed have a smaller mean crack size than components classified as flawed? The results in terms of crack size (in inches) are in the data file Crack (data extracted from B. D. Olin and W. Q. Meeker, "Applications of Statistical Methods to Nondestructive Evaluation," *Technometrics*, 38, 1996, p. 101).

a. Assuming that the population variances are equal, is there evidence that the mean crack size is smaller for the unflawed specimens than for the flawed specimens? (Use $\alpha = 0.05$.)
b. Repeat (a), assuming that the population variances are not equal.
c. Compare the results of (a) and (b).

10.2 Comparing the Means of Two Related Populations

The hypothesis-testing procedures examined in Section 10.1 enable you to make comparisons and examine differences in the means of two *independent* populations. In this section, you will learn about a procedure for analyzing the difference between the means of two populations when you collect sample data from populations that are related—that is, when results of the first population are *not* independent of the results of the second population.

There are two situations that involve related data between populations. Either you take repeated measurements from the same set of items or individuals or you match items or individuals according to some characteristic. In either situation, you are interested in the *difference between the two related values* rather than the *individual values* themselves.

When you take **repeated measurements** on the same items or individuals, you assume that the same items or individuals will behave alike if treated alike. Your objective is to show that any differences between two measurements of the same items or individuals are due to different treatment conditions. For example, when performing a taste-testing experiment comparing two beverages, you can use each person in the sample as his or her own control so that you can have *repeated measurements* on the same individual.

The second situation that involves related data between populations is when you have **matched samples**. Here items or individuals are paired together according to some characteristic of interest. For example, in test marketing a product under two different advertising campaigns, a sample of test markets can be *matched* on the basis of the test market population size and/or demographic variables. By accounting for the differences in test market population size and/or demographic variables, you are better able to measure the effects of the two different advertising campaigns.

Regardless of whether you have matched samples or repeated measurements, the objective is to study the difference between two measurements by reducing the effect of the variability that is due to the items or individuals themselves. Table 10.3 shows the differences in the individual values for two related populations. To read this table, let $X_{11}, X_{12}, \ldots, X_{1n}$ represent the n values from a sample. And let $X_{21}, X_{22}, \ldots, X_{2n}$ represent either the corresponding n matched values from a second sample or the corresponding n repeated measurements from the initial sample. Then, $D_1, D_2, \ldots, D_n$ will represent the corresponding set of n difference *scores* such that

$$D_1 = X_{11} - X_{21}, D_2 = X_{12} - X_{22}, \ldots, \text{and } D_n = X_{1n} - X_{2n}.$$

To test for the mean difference between two related populations, you treat the difference scores, each D_i, as values from a single sample.

TABLE 10.3

Determining the Difference Between Two Related Samples

Value	Sample 1	Sample 2	Difference
1	X_{11}	X_{21}	$D_1 = X_{11} - X_{21}$
2	X_{12}	X_{22}	$D_2 = X_{12} - X_{22}$
.	.	.	.
.	.	.	.
.	.	.	.
i	X_{1i}	X_{2i}	$D_i = X_{1i} - X_{2i}$
.	.	.	.
.	.	.	.
.	.	.	.
n	X_{1n}	X_{2n}	$D_n = X_{1n} - X_{2n}$

Paired *t* Test

If you assume that the difference scores are randomly and independently selected from a population that is normally distributed, you can use the **paired *t* test for the mean difference** in related populations to determine whether there is a significant population mean difference. Like the one-sample t test developed in Section 9.2 [see Equation (9.2) on page 288], the t-test statistic developed here follows the t distribution, with $n - 1$ degrees of freedom. Although you must assume that the population is normally distributed, as long as the sample size is not very small and the population is not highly skewed, you can use the paired t test.

To test the null hypothesis that there is no difference in the means of two related populations:

$$H_0: \mu_D = 0 \text{ (where } \mu_D = \mu_1 - \mu_2)$$

against the alternative that the means are not the same:

$$H_1: \mu_D \neq 0$$

you compute the t_{STAT} test statistic using Equation (10.3).

PAIRED t TEST FOR THE MEAN DIFFERENCE

$$t_{STAT} = \frac{\overline{D} - \mu_D}{\dfrac{S_D}{\sqrt{n}}} \tag{10.3}$$

where

$$\mu_D = \text{hypothesized mean difference}$$

$$\overline{D} = \frac{\displaystyle\sum_{i=1}^{n} D_i}{n}$$

$$S_D = \sqrt{\frac{\displaystyle\sum_{i=1}^{n}(D_i - \overline{D})^2}{n - 1}}$$

The t_{STAT} test statistic follows a t distribution with $n - 1$ degrees of freedom.

For a two-tail test with a given level of significance, α, you reject the null hypothesis if the computed t_{STAT} test statistic is greater than the upper-tail critical value $t_{\alpha/2}$ from the t distribution, or if the computed t_{STAT} test statistic is less than the lower-tail critical value $-t_{\alpha/2}$ from the t distribution. The decision rule is

$$\text{Reject } H_0 \text{ if } t_{STAT} > t_{\alpha/2}$$

$$\text{or if } t_{STAT} < -t_{\alpha/2};$$

$$\text{otherwise, do not reject } H_0.$$

The following example illustrates the use of the t test for the mean difference. The Automobile Association of America (AAA) conducted a mileage test to compare the gasoline mileage from real-life driving done by AAA members and results of driving done according to government standards (J. Healey, "Fuel Economy Calculations to Be Altered," *USA Today*, January 11, 2006, p. 1B).

What is the best way to design an experiment to compare the gasoline mileage from real-life driving done by AAA members and results of driving done according to government standards? One approach is to take two independent samples and then use the hypothesis tests discussed in Section 10.1. In this approach, you would use one set of automobiles to test the real-life driving done by AAA members. Then you would use a second set of different automobiles to test the results of driving done according to government standards.

However, because the first set of automobiles to test the real-life driving done by AAA members may get lower or higher gasoline mileage than the second set of automobiles, this is not a good approach. A better approach is to use a repeated-measurements experiment. In this experiment, you use one set of automobiles. For each automobile, you conduct a test of real-life driving done by an AAA member and a test of driving done according to government standards. Measuring the two gasoline mileages for the same automobiles serves to reduce the variability in the gasoline mileages compared with what would occur if you used two independent sets of automobiles. This approach focuses on the differences between the real-life driving done by an AAA member and the driving done according to government standards.

Table 10.4 displays results (stored in the file **AAAMileage**) from a sample of $n = 9$ automobiles from such an experiment.

You want to determine whether there is any difference in the mean gasoline mileage between the real-life driving done by an AAA member and the driving done according to

TABLE 10.4

Repeated Measurements of Gasoline Mileage for Real-Life Driving by AAA Members and Driving Done According to Government Standards

Model	Members	Government	Difference (D_i)
2005 Ford F-150	14.3	16.8	−2.5
2005 Chevrolet Silverado	15.0	17.8	−2.8
2002 Honda Accord LX	27.8	26.2	+1.6
2002 Honda Civic	27.9	33.2	−5.3
2004 Honda Civic Hybrid	48.8	47.6	+1.2
2002 Ford Explorer	16.8	18.3	−1.5
2005 Toyota Camry	23.7	28.5	−4.8
2003 Toyota Corolla	32.8	33.1	−0.3
2005 Toyota Prius	37.3	44.0	−6.7

government standards. In other words, is there evidence that the mean gasoline mileage is different between the two types of driving? Thus, the null and alternative hypotheses are

H_0: $\mu_D = 0$ (There is no difference in mean gasoline mileage between the real-life driving done by an AAA member and the driving done according to government standards.)

H_1: $\mu_D \neq 0$ (There is a difference in mean gasoline mileage between the real-life driving done by an AAA member and the driving done according to government standards.)

Choosing the level of significance of $\alpha = 0.05$ and assuming that the differences are normally distributed, you use the paired t test [Equation (10.3)]. For a sample of $n = 9$ automobiles, there are $n - 1 = 8$ degrees of freedom. Using Table E.3, the decision rule is

$$\text{Reject } H_0 \text{ if } t_{STAT} > t_{0.025} = 2.3060$$

$$\text{or if } t_{STAT} < -t_{0.025} = -2.3060;$$

$$\text{otherwise, do not reject } H_0.$$

For the $n = 9$ differences (see Table 10.4), the sample mean difference is

$$\overline{D} = \frac{\sum_{i=1}^{n} D_i}{n} = \frac{-21.1}{9} = -2.3444$$

and

$$S_D = \sqrt{\frac{\sum_{i=1}^{n}(D_i - \overline{D})^2}{n - 1}} = 2.893575$$

From Equation (10.3) on page 325,

$$t_{STAT} = \frac{\overline{D} - \mu_D}{\dfrac{S_D}{\sqrt{n}}} = \frac{-2.3444 - 0}{\dfrac{2.893575}{\sqrt{9}}} = -2.4307$$

Because $t_{STAT} = -2.4307$ is less than −2.3060, you reject the null hypothesis, H_0 (see Figure 10.9). There is evidence of a difference in mean gasoline mileage between the real-life driving

FIGURE 10.9

Two-tail paired t test at the 0.05 level of significance with 8 degrees of freedom

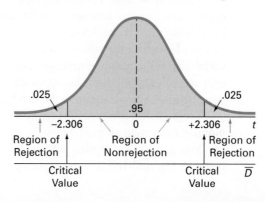

done by an AAA member and the driving done according to government standards. Real-life driving results in a lower mean gasoline mileage.

You can compute this test statistic along with the p-value by using Microsoft Excel or Minitab (see Figures 10.10 and 10.11). Because the p-value $= 0.0412 < \alpha = 0.05$, you reject H_0. The p-value indicates that if the two types of driving have the same population mean gasoline mileage, the probability that one type of driving would have a sample mean that was 2.3444 miles per gallon less than the other type is 0.0412. Because this probability is less than $\alpha = 0.05$, you conclude that the alternative hypothesis is true.

FIGURE 10.10

Microsoft Excel results of paired t test for the car mileage data

See Section E10.6 to create this worksheet.

	A	B	C
1	t-Test: Paired Two Sample for Means		
2			
3		*Members*	*Government*
4	**Mean**	27.1556	29.5
5	**Variance**	129.5528	125.0025
6	**Observations**	9	9
7	**Pearson Correlation**	0.9673	
8	**Hypothesized Mean Difference**	0	
9	**df**	8	
10	**t Stat**	-2.4307	
11	**P(T<=t) one-tail**	0.0206	
12	**t Critical one-tail**	1.8595	
13	**P(T<=t) two-tail**	0.0412	
14	**t Critical two-tail**	2.3060	

FIGURE 10.11

Minitab results of paired t test for the car mileage data

See Section M10.3 to create this.

```
Paired T-Test and CI: Owner, Government

Paired T for Owner - Government

               N    Mean   StDev   SE Mean
Owner          9   27.16   11.38      3.79
Government     9   29.50   11.18      3.73
Difference     9  -2.344   2.894     0.965


95% CI for mean difference: (-4.569, -0.120)
T-Test of mean difference = 0 (vs not = 0): T-Value = -2.43  P-Value = 0.041
```

From Figure 10.12, observe that the boxplot shows approximate symmetry. Thus, the data do not greatly contradict the underlying assumption of normality. If a boxplot, histogram, or normal probability plot reveals that the assumption of underlying normality in the population is severely violated, then the t test is inappropriate. If this occurs, you can use either a *nonparametric* procedure that does not make the assumption of underlying normality (see references 1 and 2) or make a data transformation (see reference 9), and then recheck the assumptions to determine whether you should use the t test.

FIGURE 10.12

Minitab results of boxplot for the car mileage data

See Section M3.2 to create this. (Microsoft Excel users, see Section E3.3. PHStat2 users, see Section P3.1 to create an equivalent chart.)

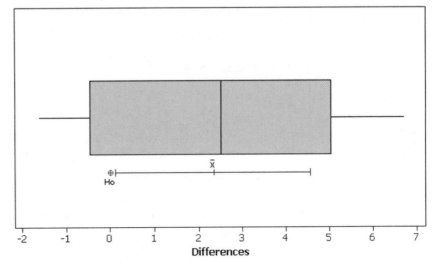

Boxplot of Differences
(with Ho and 95% t-confidence interval for the mean)

EXAMPLE 10.2

Paired *t* Test of Pizza Delivery Times

Recall from Example 10.1 on page 317 that a local pizza restaurant situated across the street from a college campus advertises that it delivers to the dormitories faster than the local branch of a national pizza chain. In order to determine whether this advertisement is valid, you and some friends have decided to order 10 pizzas from the local pizza restaurant and 10 pizzas from the national chain. In fact, each time you ordered a pizza from the local pizza restaurant, your friends ordered a pizza from the national pizza chain. Thus, you have matched samples. For each of the ten times that pizzas were ordered, you have one measurement from the local pizza restaurant and one from the national chain. At the 0.05 level of significance, is the mean delivery time for the local pizza restaurant less than the mean delivery time for the national pizza chain?

SOLUTION Use the paired *t* test to analyze the data in Table 10.5 (see the file `Pizzatime`). Figure 10.13 illustrates Microsoft Excel paired *t*-test results for the pizza delivery data and Figure 10.14 shows Minitab results.

TABLE 10.5

Delivery Times for Local Pizza Restaurant and National Pizza Chain

Time	Local	Chain	Difference
1	16.8	22.0	−5.2
2	11.7	15.2	−3.5
3	15.6	18.7	−3.1
4	16.7	15.6	1.1
5	17.5	20.8	−3.3
6	18.1	19.5	−1.4
7	14.1	17.0	−2.9
8	21.8	19.5	2.3
9	13.9	16.5	−2.6
10	20.8	24.0	−3.2
			−21.8

FIGURE 10.13

Microsoft Excel paired *t*-test results for the pizza delivery data

See Section E10.6 to create this.

	A	B	C
1	t-Test: Paired Two Sample for Means		
2			
3		Local	Chain
4	Mean	16.7	18.88
5	Variance	9.5822	8.2151
6	Observations	10	10
7	Pearson Correlation	0.7141	
8	Hypothesized Mean Difference	0	
9	df	9	
10	t Stat	-3.0448	
11	P(T<=t) one-tail	0.0070	
12	t Critical one-tail	1.8331	
13	P(T<=t) two-tail	0.0139	
14	t Critical two-tail	2.2622	

FIGURE 10.14

Minitab paired *t*-test results for the pizza delivery data

See Section M10.3 to create this.

```
Paired T-Test and CI: Local, Chain

Paired T for Local - Chain

                N    Mean   StDev   SE Mean
Local          10  16.700  3.096    0.979
Chain          10  18.880  2.866    0.906
Difference     10  -2.180  2.264    0.716


95% upper bound for mean difference: -0.868
T-Test of mean difference = 0 (vs < 0): T-Value = -3.04   P-Value = 0.007
```

The null and alternative hypotheses are

H_0: $\mu_D \geq 0$ (Mean delivery time for the local pizza restaurant is greater than or equal to the mean delivery time for the national pizza chain.)

H_1: $\mu_D < 0$ (Mean delivery time for the local pizza restaurant is less than the mean delivery time for the national pizza chain.)

To test the null hypothesis that there is no difference between the proportions of two independent populations:

$$H_0: \pi_1 = \pi_2$$

against the alternative that the two population proportions are not the same:

$$H_1: \pi_1 \neq \pi_2$$

use the Z_{STAT} test statistic, given by Equation (10.5). For a given level of significance α, reject the null hypothesis if the computed Z_{STAT} test statistic is greater than the upper-tail critical value from the standardized normal distribution, or if the computed Z_{STAT} test statistic is less than the lower-tail critical value from the standardized normal distribution.

To illustrate the use of the Z test for the equality of two proportions, suppose that you are the manager of T.C. Resort Properties, a collection of five upscale resort hotels located on two tropical islands. On one of the islands, T.C. Resort Properties has two hotels, the Beachcomber and the Windsurfer. In tabulating the responses to the single question, "Are you likely to choose this hotel again?" 163 of 227 guests at the Beachcomber responded yes, and 154 of 262 guests at the Windsurfer responded yes. At the 0.05 level of significance, is there evidence of a significant difference in guest satisfaction (as measured by the likelihood to return to the hotel) between the two hotels?

The null and alternative hypotheses are

$$H_0: \pi_1 = \pi_2 \quad \text{or} \quad \pi_1 - \pi_2 = 0$$

$$H_1: \pi_1 \neq \pi_2 \quad \text{or} \quad \pi_1 - \pi_2 \neq 0$$

Using the 0.05 level of significance, the critical values are -1.96 and $+1.96$ (see Figure 10.15), and the decision rule is

$$\text{Reject } H_0 \text{ if } Z_{STAT} < -1.96$$

$$\text{or if } Z_{STAT} > +1.96;$$

$$\text{otherwise, do not reject } H_0.$$

FIGURE 10.15

Regions of rejection and nonrejection when testing a hypothesis for the difference between two proportions at the 0.05 level of significance

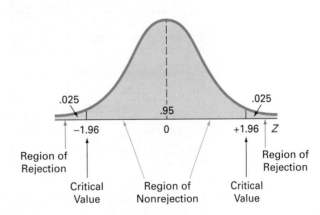

Using Equation (10.5) on page 332,

$$Z_{STAT} = \frac{(p_1 - p_2) - (\pi_1 - \pi_2)}{\sqrt{\bar{p}(1 - \bar{p})\left(\dfrac{1}{n_1} + \dfrac{1}{n_2}\right)}}$$

where

$$p_1 = \frac{X_1}{n_1} = \frac{163}{227} = 0.7181 \quad p_2 = \frac{X_2}{n_2} = \frac{154}{262} = 0.5878$$

and

$$\bar{p} = \frac{X_1 + X_2}{n_1 + n_2} = \frac{163 + 154}{227 + 262} = \frac{317}{489} = 0.6483$$

so that

$$Z_{STAT} = \frac{(0.7181 - 0.5878) - (0)}{\sqrt{0.6483(1 - 0.6483)\left(\frac{1}{227} + \frac{1}{262}\right)}}$$

$$= \frac{0.1303}{\sqrt{(0.228)(0.0082)}}$$

$$= \frac{0.1303}{\sqrt{0.00187}}$$

$$= \frac{0.1303}{0.0432} = +3.0088$$

Using the 0.05 level of significance, reject the null hypothesis because $Z_{STAT} = +3.0088 > +1.96$. The p-value is 0.0026 (calculated from Table E.2 or from the Microsoft Excel results of Figure 10.16 or the Minitab results of Figure 10.17), and indicates that if the null hypothesis is true, the probability that a Z_{STAT} test statistic is less than -3.0088 is 0.0013, and, similarly, the probability that a Z_{STAT} test statistic is greater than $+3.0088$ is 0.0013. Thus, for this two-tail test, the p-value is $0.0013 + 0.0013 = 0.0026$. Because $0.0026 < \alpha = 0.05$, you reject the null hypothesis. There is evidence to conclude that the two hotels are significantly different with respect to guest satisfaction; a greater proportion of guests are willing to return to the Beachcomber than to the Windsurfer.

FIGURE 10.16

Microsoft Excel results for the Z test for the difference between two proportions for the hotel guest satisfaction problem

See Section E10.7 or P10.4 to create this.

	A	B	
1	**Z Test for Differences in Two Proportions**		
2			
3	**Data**		
4	**Hypothesized Difference**	0	
5	**Level of Significance**	0.05	
6	**Group 1**		
7	**Number of Items of Interest**	163	
8	**Sample Size**	227	
9	**Group 2**		
10	**Number of Items of Interest**	154	
11	**Sample Size**	262	
12			
13	Intermediate Calculations		
14	Group 1 Proportion	0.7181	=B7/B8
15	Group 2 Proportion	0.5878	=B10/B11
16	Difference in Two Proportions	0.1303	=B14 - B15
17	Average Proportion	0.6483	=(B7 + B10)/(B8 + B11)
18	Z Test Statistic	3.0088	=(B16 - B4)/SQRT(B17 * (1 - B17) * (1/B8 + 1/B11))
19			
20	Two-Tail Test		
21	Lower Critical Value	-1.9600	=NORMSINV(B5/2)
22	Upper Critical Value	1.9600	=NORMSINV(1 - B5/2)
23	p-Value	0.0026	=2 * (1 - NORMSDIST(ABS(B18)))
24	**Reject the null hypothesis**		=IF(B23 < B5, "Reject the null hypothesis", "Do not reject the null hypothesis")

FIGURE 10.17

Minitab results for the Z test for the difference between two proportions for the hotel guest satisfaction problem

See Section M10.4 to create this.

```
Test and CI for Two Proportions

Sample   X    N   Sample p
1       163  227  0.718062
2       154  262  0.587786


Difference = p (1) - p (2)
Estimate for difference:  0.130275
95% CI for difference:  (0.0467379, 0.213813)
Test for difference = 0 (vs not = 0):  Z = 3.01  P-Value = 0.003
```

EXAMPLE 10.3

Testing for the Difference in Two Proportions

Technology has led to the rise of extreme workers who are on the job 60 hours a week or more. One of the reasons cited by employees about why they worked long hours was that they loved their job because it is stimulating/challenging/provides an adrenaline rush (data extracted from S. Armour, "Hi, I'm Joan and I'm a Workaholic," *USA Today*, May 23, 2007, pp. 1B, 2B). Suppose that the survey of 1,564 workaholics included 786 men and 778 women, and that 707 men and 638 women loved their job because it is stimulating/challenging/provides an adrenaline rush. At the 0.05 level of significance, you would like to determine whether the proportion of workaholic men who love their job because it is stimulating/challenging/provides an adrenaline rush is greater than the proportion of women.

SOLUTION Because you want to know whether there is evidence that the proportion of workaholic men who love their job because it is stimulating/challenging/provides an adrenaline rush is *greater* than the proportion of women, you have a one-tail test. The null and alternative hypotheses are

$H_0: \pi_1 \leq \pi_2$ (Proportion of workaholic men who love their job because it is stimulating/challenging/provides an adrenaline rush is less than or equal to the proportion of women.)

$H_1: \pi_1 > \pi_2$ (Proportion of workaholic men who love their job because it is stimulating/challenging/provides an adrenaline rush is greater than the proportion of women.)

Using the 0.05 level of significance, for the one-tail test in the upper tail, the critical value is $+1.645$. The decision rule is

$$\text{Reject } H_0 \text{ if } Z_{STAT} > +1.645;$$

$$\text{otherwise, do not reject } H_0.$$

Using Equation (10.5) on page 332,

$$Z_{STAT} = \frac{(p_1 - p_2) - (\pi_1 - \pi_2)}{\sqrt{\bar{p}(1 - \bar{p})\left(\dfrac{1}{n_1} + \dfrac{1}{n_2}\right)}}$$

where

$$p_1 = \frac{X_1}{n_1} = \frac{707}{786} = 0.8995 \quad p_2 = \frac{X_2}{n_2} = \frac{638}{778} = 0.8201$$

and

$$\bar{p} = \frac{X_1 + X_2}{n_1 + n_2} = \frac{707 + 638}{786 + 778} = \frac{1,345}{1,564} = 0.8600$$

so that

$$Z_{STAT} = \frac{(0.8995 - 0.8201) - (0)}{\sqrt{0.86(1 - 0.86)\left(\dfrac{1}{786} + \dfrac{1}{778}\right)}}$$

$$= \frac{0.0794}{\sqrt{(0.1204)(0.0025575)}}$$

$$= \frac{0.0794}{\sqrt{0.0003079}}$$

$$= \frac{0.0794}{0.017547} = +4.5266$$

Using the 0.05 level of significance, you reject the null hypothesis because $Z_{STAT} = +4.5266 > +1.645$. The p-value is approximately 0.0000. Therefore, if the null hypothesis is true, the probability that a Z_{STAT} test statistic is greater than $+4.5266$ is approximately 0.0000 (which is less than $\alpha = 0.05$). You conclude that there is evidence that the proportion of workaholic men who love their job because it is stimulating/challenging/provides an adrenaline rush is greater than the proportion of women.

Confidence Interval Estimate for the Difference Between Two Proportions

Instead of, or in addition to, testing for the difference between the proportions of two independent populations, you can construct a confidence interval estimate of the difference between the two proportions using Equation (10.6).

CONFIDENCE INTERVAL ESTIMATE FOR THE DIFFERENCE BETWEEN TWO PROPORTIONS

$$(p_1 - p_2) \pm Z_{\alpha/2}\sqrt{\frac{p_1(1 - p_1)}{n_1} + \frac{p_2(1 - p_2)}{n_2}} \tag{10.6}$$

or

$$(p_1 - p_2) - Z_{\alpha/2}\sqrt{\frac{p_1(1 - p_1)}{n_1} + \frac{p_2(1 - p_2)}{n_2}} \leq (\pi_1 - \pi_2)$$

$$\leq (p_1 - p_2) + Z_{\alpha/2}\sqrt{\frac{p_1(1 - p_1)}{n_1} + \frac{p_2(1 - p_2)}{n_2}}$$

To construct a 95% confidence interval estimate of the population difference between the proportion of guests who would return to the Beachcomber and who would return to the Windsurfer, you use the results on page 333 or from Figures 10.16 or 10.17 on page 334:

$$p_1 = \frac{X_1}{n_1} = \frac{163}{227} = 0.7181 \quad p_2 = \frac{X_2}{n_2} = \frac{154}{262} = 0.5878$$

Using Equation (10.6),

$$(0.7181 - 0.5878) \pm (1.96)\sqrt{\frac{0.7181(1 - 0.7181)}{227} + \frac{0.5878(1 - 0.5878)}{262}}$$

$$0.1303 \pm (1.96)(0.0426)$$

$$0.1303 \pm 0.0835$$

$$0.0468 \leq (\pi_1 - \pi_2) \leq 0.2138$$

Thus, you have 95% confidence that the difference between the population proportion of guests who would return again to the Beachcomber and the Windsurfer is between 0.0468 and 0.2138. In percentages, the difference is between 4.68% and 21.38%. Guest satisfaction is higher at the Beachcomber than at the Windsurfer.

Problems for Section 10.3

LEARNING THE BASICS

10.27 Let $n_1 = 100, X_1 = 50, n_2 = 100$, and $X_2 = 30$.
a. At the 0.05 level of significance, is there evidence of a significant difference between the two population proportions?
b. Construct a 95% confidence interval estimate of the difference between the two population proportions.

10.28 Let $n_1 = 100, X_1 = 45, n_2 = 50$, and $X_2 = 25$.
a. At the 0.01 level of significance, is there evidence of a significant difference between the two population proportions?
b. Construct a 99% confidence interval estimate of the difference between the two population proportions.

APPLYING THE CONCEPTS

10.29 A sample of 500 shoppers was selected in a large metropolitan area to determine various information concerning consumer behavior. Among the questions asked was, "Do you enjoy shopping for clothing?" Of 240 males, 136 answered yes. Of 260 females, 224 answered yes.
a. Is there evidence of a significant difference between males and females in the proportion that enjoy shopping for clothing at the 0.01 level of significance?
b. Find the p-value in (a) and interpret its meaning.
c. Construct and interpret a 99% confidence interval estimate of the difference between the proportion of males and females who enjoy shopping for clothing.
d. What are your answers to (a) through (c) if 206 males enjoyed shopping for clothing?

10.30 A study funded by the Massachusetts Institute of Technology tested the notion that even when it comes to sugar pills, some people think a costly one works better than a cheap one. Researchers randomly divided 82 healthy paid volunteers into two groups. All the volunteers thought they would be testing a new pain reliever. One group was told the pain reliever they would be using cost $2.50 a pill, and the other group was told it cost only 10 cents a pill. In reality, the pills they were all about to take were simply sugar pills. The volunteers were given a light electric shock on the wrist. Then the volunteers were given a sugar pill, and a short time later shocked again. Of the volunteers who took the expensive pill, 35 of the 41 said they felt less pain afterward. Of the volunteers who took the cheap pill, 25 of the 41 said they felt less pain afterward (R. Rubin, "Placebo Study Tests 'Costlier is Better' Notion," *usatoday.com*, March 5, 2008).

a. Set up the null and alternative hypotheses to try to prove that people think an expensive pill works better than a cheap pill.

b. Conduct the hypotheses defined in (a), using the 0.05 level of significance.

c. Does the result of your test in (b) make it appropriate to claim that people think an expensive pill works better than a cheap pill?

10.31 The results of a study conducted as part of a yield-improvement effort at a semiconductor manufacturing facility provided defect data for a sample of 450 wafers. The following contingency table presents a summary of the responses to two questions: "Was a particle found on the die that produced the wafer?" and "Is the wafer good or bad?"

PARTICLES	QUALITY OF WAFER		
	Good	Bad	Totals
Yes	14	36	50
No	320	80	400
Totals	334	116	450

Source: *Data extracted from S.W. Hall, "Analysis of Defectivity of Semiconductor Wafers by Contingency Table,"* Proceedings Institute of Environmental Sciences, Vol. 1, *1994, pp. 177–183.*

a. At the 0.05 level of significance, is there evidence of a significant difference between the proportion of good and bad wafers that have particles?

b. Determine the *p*-value in (a) and interpret its meaning.

c. Construct and interpret a 95% confidence interval estimate of the difference between the population proportion of good and bad wafers that contain particles.

d. What conclusions can you reach from this analysis?

10.32 According to an Ipsos poll, the perception of unfairness in the U.S. tax code is spread fairly evenly across income groups, age groups, and edu-

cation levels. In an April 2006 survey of 1,005 adults, Ipsos reported that almost 60% of all people said the code is unfair, whereas slightly more that 60% of those making more than $50,000 viewed the code as unfair (data extracted from "People Cry Unfairness," *The Cincinnati Enquirer*, April 16, 2006, p. A8). Suppose that the following contingency table represents the specific breakdown of responses:

U.S. TAX CODE	INCOME LEVEL		
	Less Than $50,000	More Than $50,000	Total
Fair	225	180	405
Unfair	280	320	600
Total	505	500	1,005

a. At the 0.05 level of significance, is there evidence of a difference in the proportion of adults who think the U.S. tax code is unfair between the two income groups?

b. Find the *p*-value in (a) and interpret its meaning.

10.33 Are women more risk averse in the stock market? A sample of men and women were asked the following question: "If both the stock market and a stock you owned dropped 25% in three months, would you buy more shares while the price is low?" (data extracted from "Snapshots: Women Are More Risk Averse in the Stock Market," *USA Today*, September 25, 2006, p. 1C). Of 965 women, 338 said yes. Of 1,066 men, 554 said yes.

a. At the 0.05 level of significance, is there evidence that the proportion of women who would buy more shares while the price is low is less than the proportion of men?

b. Find the *p*-value in (a) and interpret its meaning.

10.34 An experiment was conducted to study the choices made in mutual fund selection. Undergraduate and MBA students were presented with different S&P 500 index funds that were identical except for fees. Suppose 100 undergraduate students and 100 MBA students were selected. Partial results are shown in the following table:

FUND	STUDENT GROUP	
	Undergraduate	MBA
Highest-cost fund	27	18
Not-highest-cost fund	73	82

Source: *Data extracted from J. Choi, D. Laibson, and B. Madrian, "Why Does the Law of One Practice Fail? An Experiment on Mutual Funds,"* www.som.yale.edu/faculty/jjc83/fees.pdf.

a. At the 0.05 level of significance, is there evidence of a difference between undergraduate and MBA students in the proportion who selected the highest-cost fund?

b. Find the *p*-value in (a) and interpret its meaning.

10.35 Where people turn for news is different for various age groups (data extracted from P. Johnson, "Young People

Turn to the Web for News," *USA Today*, March 23, 2006, p. 9D). Suppose that a study conducted on this issue was based on 200 respondents who were between the ages of 36 and 50, and 200 respondents who were above age 50. Of the 200 respondents who were between the ages of 36 and 50, 82 got their news primarily from newspapers. Of the 200 respondents who were above age 50, 104 got their news primarily from newspapers.

a. Is there evidence of a significant difference in the proportion that get their news primarily from newspapers between those respondents 36 to 50 years old and those above 50 years old? (Use $\alpha = 0.05$.)

b. Determine the *p*-value in (a) and interpret its meaning.

c. Construct and interpret a 95% confidence interval estimate of the difference between the population proportion of respondents who get their news primarily from newspapers between those respondents 36 to 50 years old and those above 50 years old.

10.4 *F* Test for the Difference Between Two Variances

Often you need to determine whether two independent populations have the same amount of variability. By testing variances, you can detect differences in the amount of variability. One important reason to test for the difference between the variances of two populations is to determine whether to use the pooled-variance *t* test (which assumes equal variances) or the separate-variance *t* test (which does not assume equal variances) while comparing two means.

The test for the difference between the variances of two independent populations is based on the ratio of the two sample variances. If you assume that each population is normally distributed, then the ratio S_1^2/S_2^2 follows the *F* distribution (see Table E.5). The critical values of the **F distribution** in Table E.5 depend on the degrees of freedom in the two samples. The degrees of freedom in the numerator of the ratio are for the first sample, and the degrees of freedom in the denominator are for the second sample. The first sample taken from the first population is defined as the sample that has the *larger* sample variance. The second sample taken from the second population is the sample with the *smaller* sample variance. Equation (10.7) defines the **F test for the equality of two variances**.

F-TEST STATISTIC FOR TESTING THE EQUALITY OF TWO VARIANCES

The F_{STAT} test statistic is equal to the variance of sample 1 (the larger sample variance) divided by the variance of sample 2 (the smaller sample variance).

$$F_{STAT} = \frac{S_1^2}{S_2^2} \tag{10.7}$$

where

$S_1^2 =$ variance of sample 1 (the larger sample variance)

$S_2^2 =$ variance of sample 2 (the smaller sample variance)

$n_1 =$ size of sample 1

$n_2 =$ size of sample 2

$n_1 - 1 =$ degrees of freedom from sample 1 (i.e., the numerator degrees of freedom)

$n_2 - 1 =$ degrees of freedom from sample 2 (i.e., the denominator degrees of freedom)

The F_{STAT} test statistic follows an *F* distribution with $n_1 - 1$ and $n_2 - 1$ degrees of freedom.

For a given level of significance, α, to test the null hypothesis of equality of population variances:

$$H_0: \sigma_1^2 = \sigma_2^2$$

against the alternative hypothesis that the two population variances are not equal:

$$H_1: \sigma_1^2 \neq \sigma_2^2$$

you reject the null hypothesis if the computed F_{STAT} test statistic is greater than the upper-tail critical value, $F_{\alpha/2}$, from the F distribution with $n_1 - 1$ degrees of freedom in the numerator and $n_2 - 1$ degrees of freedom in the denominator. Thus, the decision rule is

$$\text{Reject } H_0 \text{ if } F_{STAT} > F_{\alpha/2};$$

otherwise, do not reject H_0.

To illustrate how to use the F test to determine whether the two variances are equal, return to the Using Statistics scenario on page 313 concerning the sales of BLK Cola in two different aisle locations. To determine whether to use the pooled-variance t test or the separate-variance t test in Section 10.1, you can test the equality of the two population variances. The null and alternative hypotheses are

$$H_0: \sigma_1^2 = \sigma_2^2$$
$$H_1: \sigma_1^2 \neq \sigma_2^2$$

Because you are defining sample 1 as having the larger sample variance, the rejection region in the upper tail of the F distribution contains $\alpha/2$. Using the level of significance $\alpha = 0.05$, the rejection region in the upper tail contains 0.025 of the distribution.

Because there are samples of 10 stores for each of the two display locations, there are $10 - 1 = 9$ degrees of freedom in the numerator (the sample with the larger variance) and also in the denominator (the sample with the smaller variance). $F_{\alpha/2}$, the upper-tail critical value of the F distribution, is found directly from Table E.5, a portion of which is presented in Table 10.6. Because there are 9 degrees of freedom in the numerator and 9 degrees of freedom in the denominator, you find the upper-tail critical value, $F_{\alpha/2}$, by looking in the column labeled 9 and the row labeled 9. Thus, the upper-tail critical value of this F distribution is 4.03. Therefore the decision rule is

$$\text{Reject } H_0 \text{ if } F_{STAT} > F_{0.025} = 4.03;$$

otherwise, do not reject H_0.

TABLE 10.6

Finding the Upper-Tail Critical Value of *F* with 9 and 9 Degrees of Freedom for Upper-Tail Area of 0.025

| | Cumulative Probabilities = 0.975 Upper-Tail Area = 0.025 Numerator df_1 | | | | | | |
Denominator df_2	1	2	3	...	7	8	9
1	647.80	799.50	864.20	...	948.20	956.70	963.30
2	38.51	39.00	39.17	...	39.36	39.37	39.39
3	17.44	16.04	15.44	...	14.62	14.54	14.47
.	.	.	.	.	.	.	
.	.	.	.	.	.	.	
.	.	.	.	.	.	.	
7	8.07	6.54	5.89	...	4.99	4.90	4.82
8	7.57	6.06	5.42	...	4.53	4.43	4.36
9	7.21	5.71	5.08	...	4.20	4.10	4.03

Source: *Extracted from Table E.5.*

Using Equation (10.7) on page 338 and the cola sales data (see Table 10.1 on page 315),

$$F_{STAT} = \frac{S_1^2}{S_2^2}$$
$$= \frac{350.6778}{157.3333} = 2.2289$$

Because $F_{STAT} = 2.2289 < 4.03$, you do not reject H_0. The *p*-value is 0.2482 for a two-tail test (twice the *p*-value for the one-tail test shown in the Microsoft Excel results in Figure 10.18). Because $0.2482 > 0.05$, you conclude that there is no significant difference in the variability of the sales of cola for the two display locations. Notice that in Figure 10.19, Minitab reports the F statistic as 0.45, the reciprocal of 2.2289. This occurs because Minitab assigns samples in alphabetical order, so EndAisle is assigned to the numerator (sample 1) and Normal is assigned to the denominator (sample 2).

FIGURE 10.18

Microsoft Excel *F* test results for the BLK Cola sales data

See Section E10.9 or P10.5 to create this.

	A	B	C
1	**F-Test Two-Sample for Variances**		
2			
3		*Normal*	*End-Aisle*
4	Mean	50.3	72
5	Variance	350.6778	157.3333
6	Observations	10	10
7	df	9	9
8	F	2.2289	
9	P(F<=f) one-tail	0.1241	
10	F Critical one-tail	3.1789	

FIGURE 10.19

Minitab *F* test results for the BLK Cola sales data

See Section M10.5 to create this.

```
Display   N   Lower    StDev    Upper
EndAisle  10  8.2048   12.5433  25.2578
Normal    10  12.2494  18.7264  37.7085


F-Test (Normal Distribution)
Test statistic = 0.45, p-value = 0.248
```

In testing for a difference between two variances using the F test described in this section, you assume that each of the two populations is normally distributed. The F test is very sensitive to the normality assumption. If boxplots or normal probability plots suggest even a mild departure from normality for either of the two populations, you should not use the F test. If this happens, you should use the Levene test (see Section 10.5) or a nonparametric approach (see references 1 and 2).

In testing for the equality of variances as part of assessing the validity of the pooled-variance t test procedure, the F test is a two-tail test with $\alpha/2$ in the upper tail. However, when you are interested in examining the variability in situations other than the pooled-variance t test, the F test is often a one-tail test. Example 10.4 illustrates a one-tail test.

EXAMPLE 10.4

A One-Tail Test for the Difference Between Two Variances

Shipments of meat, meat by-products, and other ingredients are mixed together in several filling lines at a pet food canning factory. Operations managers suspect that, although the mean amount filled per can of pet food is usually the same, the variability of the cans filled in line A is greater than that of line B. The following data from a sample of eight-ounce cans is as follows:

	Line A	Line B
$\overline{X}$	8.005	7.997
S	0.012	0.005
n	11	16

At the 0.05 level of significance, is there evidence that the variance in line A is greater than the variance in line B? Assume that the population amounts filled are normally distributed.

SOLUTION The null and alternative hypotheses are

$$H_0: \sigma_A^2 \leq \sigma_B^2$$

$$H_1: \sigma_A^2 > \sigma_B^2$$

The F_{STAT} test statistic is given by Equation (10.7) on page 338:

$$F_{STAT} = \frac{S_1^2}{S_2^2}$$

You use Table E.5 to find the upper critical value of the F distribution. With $n_1 - 1 = 11 - 1 = 10$ degrees of freedom in the numerator, $n_2 - 1 = 16 - 1 = 15$ degrees of freedom in the denominator, and $\alpha = 0.05$, the upper critical value, $F_{0.05}$, is 2.54.

The decision rule is

Reject H_0 if $F_{STAT} > 2.54$;

otherwise, do not reject H_0.

From Equation (10.7) on page 338,

$$F_{STAT} = \frac{S_1^2}{S_2^2}$$
$$= \frac{(0.012)^2}{(0.005)^2} = 5.76$$

Because $F_{STAT} = 5.76 > 2.54$, you reject H_0. Using a 0.05 level of significance, you conclude that there is evidence that the variance of line A is greater than the variance of line B. In other words, the amount of pet food in the cans filled by line A is more variable than the amount of pet food in cans filled by line B.

Problems for Section 10.4

LEARNING THE BASICS

10.36 Determine the upper-tail critical values of F, in each of the following two-tail tests:
a. $\alpha = 0.10, n_1 = 16, n_2 = 21$
b. $\alpha = 0.05, n_1 = 16, n_2 = 21$
c. $\alpha = 0.01, n_1 = 16, n_2 = 21$

10.37 Determine the upper-tail critical value of F in each of the following one-tail tests:
a. $\alpha = 0.05, n_1 = 16, n_2 = 21$
b. $\alpha = 0.01, n_1 = 16, n_2 = 21$

10.38 The following information is available for two samples drawn from independent normally distributed populations:

Population A: $n = 25$ $S^2 = 16$
Population B: $n = 25$ $S^2 = 25$

a. Which sample variance do you place in the numerator of F_{STAT}?
b. What is the value of F_{STAT}?

10.39 The following information is available for two samples drawn from independent normally distributed populations:

Population A: $n = 25$ $S^2 = 161.9$
Population B: $n = 25$ $S^2 = 133.7$

What is the value of F_{STAT} if you are testing the null hypothesis $H_0: \sigma_1^2 = \sigma_2^2$?

10.40 In Problem 10.39, how many degrees of freedom are there in the numerator and denominator of the F test?

10.41 In Problems 10.39 and 10.40, what is the upper critical value for F if the level of significance, α, is 0.05 and the alternative hypothesis is $H_1: \sigma_1^2 \neq \sigma_2^2$?

10.42 In Problems 10.39 through 10.40, what is your statistical decision?

10.43 The following information is available for two samples selected from independent but very right-skewed populations:

Population A: $n = 16$ $S^2 = 47.3$
Population B: $n = 13$ $S^2 = 36.4$

Should you use the F test to test the null hypothesis of equality of variances? Discuss.

10.44 In Problem 10.43, assume that two samples are selected from independent normally distributed populations.
a. At the 0.05 level of significance, is there evidence of a difference between σ_1^2 and σ_2^2?
b. Suppose that you want to perform a one-tail test. At the 0.05 level of significance, what is the upper-tail critical value of F to determine whether there is evidence that $\sigma_1^2 > \sigma_2^2$? What is your statistical decision?

APPLYING THE CONCEPTS

10.45 A professor in the accounting department of a business school claims that there is much more variability in the final exam scores of students taking the introductory accounting course who are not majoring in accounting than for students taking the course who are majoring in accounting. Random samples of 13 non-accounting majors and 10 accounting majors are taken from the professor's class roster in his large lecture, and the following results are computed based on the final exam scores:

$$\text{Non-Accounting:} \quad n = 13 \quad S^2 = 210.2$$
$$\text{Accounting:} \quad n = 10 \quad S^2 = 36.5$$

a. At the 0.05 level of significance, is there evidence to support the professor's claim?
b. Interpret the p-value.
c. What assumption do you need to make in (a) about the two populations in order to justify your use of the F test?

✓ SELF **✓ Test** **10.46** The Computer Anxiety Rating Scale (CARS) measures an individual's level of computer anxiety, on a scale from 20 (no anxiety) to 100 (highest level of anxiety). Researchers at Miami University administered CARS to 172 business students. One of the objectives of the study was to determine whether there is a difference between the level of computer anxiety experienced by female students and male students. They found the following:

	Males	Females
$\overline{X}$	40.26	36.85
S	13.35	9.42
n	100	72

Source: *Data extracted from T. Broome and D. Havelka, "Determinants of Computer Anxiety in Business Students," The Review of Business Information Systems, Spring 2002, 6(2), pp. 9–16.*

a. At the 0.05 level of significance, is there evidence of a difference in the variability of the computer anxiety experienced by males and females?
b. Interpret the p-value.
c. What assumption do you need to make about the two populations in order to justify the use of the F test?
d. Based on (a) and (b), which t test defined in Section 10.1 should you use to test whether there is a significant difference in mean computer anxiety for female and male students?

10.47 A bank with a branch located in a commercial district of a city has developed an improved process for serving customers during the noon-to-1 P.M. lunch period. The waiting time (defined as the time elapsed from when the customer enters the line until he or she reaches the teller window) needs to be shortened to increase customer satisfaction. A random sample of 15 customers is selected (and stored in the file **Bank1**), and the results (in minutes) are as follows:

4.21	5.55	3.02	5.13	4.77	2.34	3.54	3.20
4.50	6.10	0.38	5.12	6.46	6.19	3.79	

Suppose that another branch, located in a residential area, is also concerned with the noon-to-1 P.M. lunch period. A random sample of 15 customers is selected (and stored in the file **Bank2**), and the results (in minutes) are as follows:

9.66	5.90	8.02	5.79	8.73	3.82	8.01	8.35
10.49	6.68	5.64	4.08	6.17	9.91	5.47	

a. Is there evidence of a difference in the variability of the waiting time between the two branches? (Use $\alpha = 0.05$.)
b. Determine the p-value in (a) and interpret its meaning.
c. What assumption about the population distribution of the two banks is necessary in (a)? Is the assumption valid for these data?
d. Based on the results of (a), is it appropriate to use the pooled-variance t test to compare the means of the two branches?

10.48 Digital cameras have taken over the majority of the point-and-shoot camera market. One of the important features of a camera is the battery life as measured by the number of shots taken until the battery needs to be recharged. The data in the file **Digitalcameras** contains the battery life of 31 subcompact cameras and 15 compact cameras (data extracted from "Cameras," *Consumer Reports*, November 2006, pp. 20–21).

a. Is there evidence of a difference in the variability of the battery life between the two types of digital cameras? (Use $\alpha = 0.05$.)
b. Determine the p-value in (a) and interpret its meaning.
c. What assumption about the population distribution of the two types of cameras is necessary in (a)? Is the assumption valid for these data?
d. Based on the results of (a), which t test defined in Section 10.1 should you use to compare the mean battery life of the two types of cameras?

10.49 The director of training for a company that manufactures electronic equipment is interested in determining whether different training methods have an effect on the productivity of assembly-line employees. She randomly assigns 21 of the 42 recently hired employees to a computer-assisted, individual-based training program. The other 21 are assigned to a team-based training program. Upon completion of the training, the employees are evaluated on the time (in seconds) it takes to assemble a part. The results are in the data file **Training**.

a. Using a 0.05 level of significance, is there evidence of a difference between the variances in assembly times (in seconds) of employees trained in a computer-assisted, individual-based program and those trained in a team-based program?
b. On the basis of the results in (a), which t test defined in Section 10.1 should you use to compare the means of the two training programs? Discuss.

10.50 Is there a difference in the variation of the yield of different types of investment between banks? The following data, from the file **Bankyield**, represent the yields for a sample of money market accounts and five-year CDs as of March 31, 2008:

Money Market Accounts	Five-Year CD
3.94 3.75 3.74 3.68 3.68	4.21 4.07 4.02 3.93 3.92

Source: *Data extracted from Bankrate.com, March 31, 2008.*

At the 0.05 level of significance, is there evidence of a difference in the variance of the yield between money market accounts and five-year CDs? Assume that the population yields are normally distributed.

10.5 One-Way Analysis of Variance

In Sections 10.1 through 10.4, you used hypothesis testing to reach conclusions about possible differences between two populations. In many situations you need to examine differences among *more than two* populations. In theses situations, populations are referred to as *groups*. The groups involved can be classified according to **levels** of a **factor** of interest. For example, a factor such as baking temperature may have several groups defined by *numerical levels* such as 300°, 350°, 400°, 450°, and a factor such as preferred supplier for a parachute manufacturer may have several groups defined by *categorical levels* such as Supplier 1, Supplier 2, Supplier 3, and Supplier 4.

F Test for Differences Among More Than Two Means

When you are analyzing a numerical variable and certain assumptions are met, you use the **analysis of variance (ANOVA)** to compare the means of the groups. The ANOVA procedure used when there is one factor of interest is referred to as the **one-way ANOVA**, and it is an extension of the *t* test for the difference between two means discussed in Section 10.1. Although ANOVA is an acronym for *analysis of variance*, the term is misleading because the objective is to analyze differences among the group means, *not* the variances. However, by analyzing the variation among and within the groups, you can reach conclusions about possible differences in group means. In ANOVA, the total variation is subdivided into variation that is due to differences *among* the groups and variation that is due to differences *within* the groups (see Figure 10.20). **Within-group variation** measures random variation. **Among-group variation** is due to differences from group to group. The symbol *c* is used to indicate the number of groups.

FIGURE 10.20

Partitioning the total variation in a completely randomized design

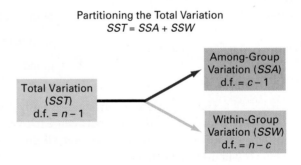

Partitioning the Total Variation
$SST = SSA + SSW$

Assuming that the *c* groups represent samples whose values are randomly and independently selected, from normal populations that have equal variances, the null hypothesis of no differences in the population means:

$$H_0: \mu_1 = \mu_2 = \cdots = \mu_c$$

is tested against the alternative that not all the *c* population means are equal:

$$H_1: \text{Not all } \mu_j \text{ are equal (where } j = 1, 2, \ldots, c).$$

To perform an ANOVA test of equality of population means, you subdivide the total variation in the values into two parts—that which is due to variation among the groups and that which is due to variation within the groups. The **total variation** is represented by the **sum of squares total (SST)**. Because the population means of the c groups are assumed to be equal under the null hypothesis, you compute the total variation among all the values by summing the squared differences between each individual value and the **grand mean**, $\overline{\overline{X}}$. The grand mean is the mean of all the values in all the groups combined. Equation (10.8) shows the computation of the total variation.

TOTAL VARIATION IN ONE-WAY ANOVA

$$SST = \sum_{j=1}^{c} \sum_{i=1}^{n_j} (X_{ij} - \overline{\overline{X}})^2 \tag{10.8}$$

where

$$\overline{\overline{X}} = \frac{\sum_{j=1}^{c} \sum_{i=1}^{n_j} X_{ij}}{n} = \text{Grand mean}$$

X_{ij} = ith value in group j

n_j = number of values in group j

n = total number of values in all groups combined (that is, $n = n_1 + n_2 + \cdots + n_c$)

c = number of groups

You compute the among-group variation, usually called the **sum of squares among groups (SSA)**, by summing the squared differences between the sample mean of each group, $\overline{X}_j$, and the grand mean, $\overline{\overline{X}}$, weighted by the sample size, n_j, in each group. Equation (10.9) shows the computation of the among-group variation.

AMONG-GROUP VARIATION IN ONE-WAY ANOVA

$$SSA = \sum_{j=1}^{c} n_j (\overline{X}_j - \overline{\overline{X}})^2 \tag{10.9}$$

where

c = number of groups

n_j = number of values in group j

$\overline{X}_j$ = sample mean of group j

$\overline{\overline{X}}$ = grand mean

The within-group variation, usually called the **sum of squares within groups (SSW)**, measures the difference between each value and the mean of its own group and sums the squares of these differences over all groups. Equation (10.10) shows the computation of the within-group variation.

WITHIN-GROUP VARIATION IN ONE-WAY ANOVA

$$SSW = \sum_{j=1}^{c} \sum_{i=1}^{n_j} (X_{ij} - \overline{X}_j)^2 \tag{10.10}$$

where

X_{ij} = ith value in group j

$\overline{X}_j$ = sample mean of group j

Because you are comparing c groups, there are $c - 1$ degrees of freedom associated with the sum of squares among groups. Because each of the c groups contributes $n_j - 1$ degrees of freedom, there are $n - c$ degrees of freedom associated with the sum of squares within groups. In addition, there are $n - 1$ degrees of freedom associated with the sum of squares total because you are comparing each value, X_{ij}, to the grand mean, $\overline{\overline{X}}$, based on all n values.

If you divide each of these sums of squares by its associated degrees of freedom, you have three variances or **mean square** terms—*MSA* (mean square among), *MSW* (mean square within), and *MST* (mean square total).

MEAN SQUARES IN ONE-WAY ANOVA

$$MSA = \frac{SSA}{c - 1} \qquad \textbf{(10.11a)}$$

$$MSW = \frac{SSW}{n - c} \qquad \textbf{(10.11b)}$$

$$MST = \frac{SST}{n - 1} \qquad \textbf{(10.11c)}$$

Although you want to compare the means of the c groups to determine whether a difference exists among them, the name ANOVA comes from the fact that you are comparing variances. If the null hypothesis is true and there are no differences in the c group means, all three mean squares (or *variances*)—*MSA, MSW,* and *MST*—provide estimates of the overall variance in the data. Thus, to test the null hypothesis:

$$H_0: \mu_1 = \mu_2 = \cdots = \mu_c$$

against the alternative:

$$H_1: \text{Not all } \mu_j \text{ are equal } (\text{where } j = 1, 2, \ldots, c)$$

you compute the one-way ANOVA F_{STAT} test statistic as the ratio of *MSA* to *MSW*, as in Equation (10.12).

ONE-WAY ANOVA F_{STAT} TEST STATISTIC

$$F_{STAT} = \frac{MSA}{MSW} \qquad \textbf{(10.12)}$$

The F_{STAT} test statistic follows an F distribution, with $c - 1$ degrees of freedom in the numerator and $n - c$ degrees of freedom in the denominator. For a given level of significance, α, you reject the null hypothesis if the F_{STAT} test statistic computed in Equation (10.12), is greater than the upper-tail critical value, F_α, from the F distribution having $c - 1$ degrees of freedom in the numerator and $n - c$ in the denominator (see Table E.5). Thus, as shown in Figure 10.21, the decision rule is

Reject H_0 if $F_{STAT} > F_\alpha$;

otherwise, do not reject H_0.

FIGURE 10.21

Regions of rejection and nonrejection when using ANOVA

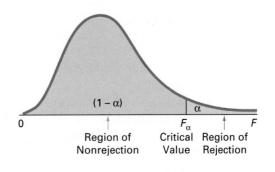

(1 − α)	α
0	F_α ⟶ F
Region of Nonrejection	Critical Value	Region of Rejection

If the null hypothesis is true, the computed F_{STAT} test statistic is expected to be approximately equal to 1 because both the numerator and denominator mean square terms are estimating the overall variance in the data. If H_0 is false (and there are differences in the group means), the computed F_{STAT} test statistic is expected to be larger than 1 because the numerator, MSA, is estimating the differences among groups in addition to the overall variability in the values, whereas the denominator, MSW, is measuring only the overall variability. Thus, the ANOVA procedure provides an F test in which you reject the null hypothesis at a selected level of significance, α, only if the computed F_{STAT} test statistic is greater than F_{α}, the upper-tail critical value of the F distribution having $c - 1$ and $n - c$ degrees of freedom, as illustrated in Figure 10.21 on page 345.

The results of an analysis of variance are usually displayed in an **ANOVA summary table**, as shown in Table 10.7. The entries in this table include the sources of variation (i.e., among-groups, within-groups, and total), the degrees of freedom, the sums of squares, the mean squares (i.e., the variances), and the computed F_{STAT} test statistic. In addition, Microsoft Excel and Minitab include the p-value (i.e., the probability of having an F_{STAT} as large as or larger than the one computed, given that the null hypothesis is true) in the ANOVA summary table. The p-value allows you to make direct conclusions about the null hypothesis without referring to a table of critical values of the F distribution. If the p-value is less than the chosen level of significance, α, you reject the null hypothesis.

TABLE 10.7

Analysis-of-Variance Summary Table

Source	Degrees of Freedom	Sum of Squares	Mean Square (Variance)	F
Among groups	$c - 1$	SSA	$MSA = \dfrac{SSA}{c - 1}$	$F_{STAT} = \dfrac{MSA}{MSW}$
Within groups	$n - c$	SSW	$MSW = \dfrac{SSW}{n - c}$	
Total	$n - 1$	SST		

To illustrate the one-way ANOVA F test, you can consider a company that weaves parachutes using synthetic fibers purchased from one of four different suppliers. The strength of the fibers is an important characteristic and you need to decide whether the synthetic fibers from each of the four suppliers result in parachutes of equal strength. The results of an experiment (in terms of tensile strength) are contained in the Parachute file and are displayed in Figure 10.22, along with the sample mean and the sample standard deviation for each group.

FIGURE 10.22

Microsoft Excel worksheet of the tensile strength for parachutes woven with synthetic fibers from four different suppliers along with the sample mean and sample standard deviation

	A	B	C	D	E
1		Supplier 1	Supplier 2	Supplier 3	Supplier 4
2		18.5	26.3	20.6	25.4
3		24.0	25.3	25.2	19.9
4		17.2	24.0	20.8	22.6
5		19.9	21.2	24.7	17.5
6		18.0	24.5	22.9	20.4
7					
8	Sample Mean	19.52	24.26	22.84	21.16
9	Sample Standard Deviation	2.69	1.92	2.13	2.98

In Figure 10.22, observe that there are differences in the sample means for the four suppliers. For Supplier 1, the mean tensile strength is 19.52. For Supplier 2, the mean tensile strength is 24.26. For Supplier 3, the mean tensile strength is 22.84, and for Supplier 4, the mean tensile strength is 21.16. What you need to determine is whether these sample results are sufficiently different to conclude that the *population* means are not all equal.

In the scatter plot shown in Figure 10.23, you can visually inspect the data and see how the measurements of tensile strength distribute. You can also observe differences among the groups as well as within groups. If the sample sizes in each group were larger, you could develop stem-and-leaf displays, boxplots, and normal probability plots to evaluate the assumption of normality in each group.

FIGURE 10.23

Microsoft Excel scatter plot of tensile strengths for four different suppliers

See Section E2.12 or P2.9 to create this. (Minitab users, see Section M2.8 to create an equivalent chart.)

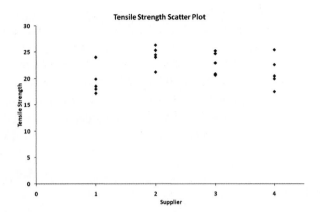

The null hypothesis states that there is no difference in mean tensile strength among the four suppliers:

$$H_0: \mu_1 = \mu_2 = \mu_3 = \mu_4$$

The alternative hypothesis states that at least one of the suppliers differs with respect to the mean tensile strength:

$$H_1: \text{Not all the means are equal.}$$

To construct the ANOVA summary table, you first compute the sample means in each group (see Figure 10.22 on page 346). Then you compute the grand mean by summing all 20 values and dividing by the total number of values:

$$\overline{\overline{X}} = \frac{\sum_{j=1}^{c} \sum_{i=1}^{n_j} X_{ij}}{n} = \frac{438.9}{20} = 21.945$$

Then, using Equations (10.8) through (10.10) on page 344, you compute the sum of squares:

$$SSA = \sum_{j=1}^{c} n_j(\overline{X}_j - \overline{\overline{X}})^2 = (5)(19.52 - 21.945)^2 + (5)(24.26 - 21.945)^2$$

$$+ (5)(22.84 - 21.945)^2 + (5)(21.16 - 21.945)^2$$

$$= 63.2855$$

$$SSW = \sum_{j=1}^{c} \sum_{i=1}^{n_j} (X_{ij} - \overline{X}_j)^2$$

$$= (18.5 - 19.52)^2 + \cdots + (18 - 19.52)^2 + (26.3 - 24.26)^2 + \cdots + (24.5 - 24.26)^2$$

$$+ (20.6 - 22.84)^2 + \cdots + (22.9 - 22.84)^2 + (25.4 - 21.16)^2 + \cdots + (20.4 - 21.16)^2$$

$$= 97.5040$$

$$SST = \sum_{j=1}^{c} \sum_{i=1}^{n_j} (X_{ij} - \overline{\overline{X}})^2$$

$$= (18.5 - 21.945)^2 + (24 - 21.945)^2 + \cdots + (20.4 - 21.945)^2$$

$$= 160.7895$$

You compute the mean square terms by dividing the sum of squares by the corresponding degrees of freedom [see Equation (10.11) on page 345]. Because $c = 4$ and $n = 20$,

$$MSA = \frac{SSA}{c - 1} = \frac{63.2855}{4 - 1} = 21.0952$$

$$MSW = \frac{SSW}{n - c} = \frac{97.5040}{20 - 4} = 6.0940$$

so that using Equation (10.12) on page 345,

$$F_{STAT} = \frac{MSA}{MSW} = \frac{21.0952}{6.0940} = 3.4616$$

For a selected level of significance, α, you find the upper-tail critical value, F_{α}, from the F distribution using Table E.5. A portion of Table E.5 is presented in Table 10.8. In the parachute supplier example, there are 3 degrees of freedom in the numerator and 16 degrees of freedom in the denominator. F_{α}, the upper-tail critical value at the 0.05 level of significance, is 3.24.

TABLE 10.8

Finding the Critical Value of F with 3 and 16 Degrees of Freedom at the 0.05 Level of Significance

	Cumulative Probabilities = 0.95 Upper-Tail Area = 0.05 Numerator df_1								
Denominator df_2	**1**	**2**	**3**	**4**	**5**	**6**	**7**	**8**	**9**
.	.	.	.	.	.	.	.	.	.
.	.	.	.	.	.	.	.	.	.
.	.	.	.	.	.	.	.	.	.
11	4.84	3.98	3.59	3.36	3.20	3.09	3.01	2.95	2.90
12	4.75	3.89	3.49	3.26	3.11	3.00	2.91	2.85	2.80
13	4.67	3.81	3.41	3.18	3.03	2.92	2.83	2.77	2.71
14	4.60	3.74	3.34	3.11	2.96	2.85	2.76	2.70	2.65
15	4.54	3.68	3.29	3.06	2.90	2.79	2.71	2.64	2.59
16	4.49	3.63	3.24	3.01	2.85	2.74	2.66	2.59	2.54

Source: *Extracted from Table E.5.*

Because $F_{STAT} = 3.4616$ is greater than $F_{\alpha} = 3.24$, you reject the null hypothesis (see Figure 10.24). You conclude that there is a significant difference in the mean tensile strength among the four suppliers.

FIGURE 10.24

Regions of rejection and nonrejection for the one-way ANOVA at the 0.05 level of significance, with 3 and 16 degrees of freedom

Figure 10.25 shows the Microsoft Excel ANOVA summary table and p-value. Figure 10.26 shows Minitab results.

FIGURE 10.25

Microsoft Excel ANOVA results for the parachute example

See Section E10.10 to create this.

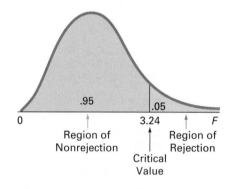

	A	B	C	D	E	F	G
1	**Anova: Single Factor**						
2							
3	**SUMMARY**						
4	*Groups*	*Count*	*Sum*	*Average*	*Variance*		
5	Supplier 1	5	97.6	19.52	7.237		
6	Supplier 2	5	121.3	24.26	3.683		
7	Supplier 3	5	114.2	22.84	4.553		
8	Supplier 4	5	105.8	21.16	8.903		
9							
10							
11	**ANOVA**						
12	*Source of Variation*	*SS*	*df*	*MS*	*F*	*P-value*	*F crit*
13	**Between Groups**	63.2855	3	21.0952	3.4616	0.0414	3.2389
14	**Within Groups**	97.5040	16	6.094			
15							
16	Total	160.7895	19				

```
Source   DF     SS      MS     F      P
Factor    3   63.29   21.10  3.46  0.041
Error    16   97.50    6.09
Total    19  160.79

S = 2.469   R-Sq = 39.36%   R-Sq(adj) = 27.99%


                                  Individual 95% CIs For Mean Based on Pooled StDev
Level  N   Mean   StDev      -+---------+---------+---------+--------
1      5  19.520  2.690      (--------*--------)
2      5  24.260  1.919                         (--------*--------)
3      5  22.840  2.134                      (--------*---------)
4      5  21.160  2.984          (---------*-------)
                              -+---------+---------+---------+--------
                            17.5      20.0      22.5      25.0

Pooled StDev = 2.469
```

The *p*-value, or probability of getting a computed F_{STAT} statistic of 3.4616 or larger when the null hypothesis is true, is 0.0414. Because this *p*-value is less than the specified α of 0.05, you reject the null hypothesis. The *p*-value of 0.0414 indicates that there is a 4.14% chance of observing differences this large or larger if the population means for the four suppliers are all equal.

After performing the one-way ANOVA and finding a significant difference among the suppliers, you still do not know *which* suppliers differ. All that you know is that there is sufficient evidence to state that the population means are not all the same. In other words, at least one or more population means are significantly different.

Multiple Comparisons: The Tukey-Kramer Procedure

In the parachute company example, you used the one-way ANOVA *F* test to determine that there was a difference among the suppliers. The next step is to construct **multiple comparisons** to determine which suppliers are different.

Although many procedures are available (see references 5–7), this text uses the **Tukey-Kramer multiple comparisons procedure for one-way ANOVA** to determine which of the *c* means are significantly different. The Tukey-Kramer procedure enables you to simultaneously make comparisons between all pairs of groups. You use the following four steps to construct the comparisons.

1. Compute the absolute mean differences, $|\overline{X}_j - \overline{X}_{j'}|$ (where $j \neq j'$), among all $c(c - 1)/2$ pairs of sample means.
2. Compute the **critical range** for the Tukey-Kramer procedure using Equation (10.13). If the sample sizes differ, you compute a critical range for each pairwise comparison of sample means.

CRITICAL RANGE FOR THE TUKEY-KRAMER PROCEDURE

$$\text{Critical range} = Q_\alpha \sqrt{\frac{MSW}{2}\left(\frac{1}{n_j} + \frac{1}{n_{j'}}\right)} \qquad (10.13)$$

where Q_α is the upper-tail critical value from a **Studentized range distribution** having *c* degrees of freedom in the numerator and $n - c$ degrees of freedom in the denominator. (Values for the Studentized range distribution are found in Table E.8.)

3. Compare each of the $c(c - 1)/2$ pairs of means against its corresponding critical range. You declare a specific pair significantly different if the absolute difference in the sample means $|\overline{X}_j - \overline{X}_{j'}|$ is greater than the critical range.
4. Interpret the results.

In the parachute example, there are four suppliers. Thus, there are $4(4-1)/2 = 6$ pairwise comparisons. To apply the Tukey-Kramer multiple comparison procedure, you first compute the absolute mean differences for all six pairwise comparisons. *Multiple comparison* refers to the fact that you are going to simultaneously make an inference about all six of these comparisons:

1. $|\bar{X}_1 - \bar{X}_2| = |19.52 - 24.26| = 4.74$
2. $|\bar{X}_1 - \bar{X}_3| = |19.52 - 22.84| = 3.32$
3. $|\bar{X}_1 - \bar{X}_4| = |19.52 - 21.16| = 1.64$
4. $|\bar{X}_2 - \bar{X}_3| = |24.26 - 22.84| = 1.42$
5. $|\bar{X}_2 - \bar{X}_4| = |24.26 - 21.16| = 3.10$
6. $|\bar{X}_3 - \bar{X}_4| = |22.84 - 21.16| = 1.68$

You need to compute only one critical range because the sample sizes in the four groups are equal. From the ANOVA summary table (Figure 10.25 on page 348 or 10.26 on page 349), $MSW = 6.094$ and $n_j = n_{j'} = 5$. From Table E.8, for $\alpha = 0.05, c = 4$, and $n - c = 20 - 4 = 16, Q_\alpha$, the upper-tail critical value of the test statistic, is 4.05 (see Table 10.9).

TABLE 10.9

Finding the Studentized Range Q_α Statistic for $\alpha = 0.05$, with 4 and 16 Degrees of Freedom

	Cumulative Probabilities = 0.95							
	Upper-Tail Area = 0.05							
	Numerator df_1							
Denominator df_2	**2**	**3**	**4**	**5**	**6**	**7**	**8**	**9**
.		.	.			.	.	.
.		.	.			.	.	.
.		.	.	.	.	.	.	.
11	3.11	3.82	4.26	4.57	4.82	5.03	5.20	5.35
12	3.08	3.77	4.20	4.51	4.75	4.95	5.12	5.27
13	3.06	3.73	4.15	4.45	4.69	4.88	5.05	5.19
14	3.03	3.70	4.11	4.41	4.64	4.83	4.99	5.13
15	3.01	3.67	4.08	4.37	4.60	4.78	4.94	5.08
16	3.00	3.65	4.05	4.33	4.56	4.74	4.90	5.03

Source: Extracted from Table E.8.

From Equation (10.13),

$$\text{Critical range} = 4.05\sqrt{\left(\frac{6.094}{2}\right)\left(\frac{1}{5} + \frac{1}{5}\right)} = 4.4712$$

Because $4.74 > 4.4712$, there is a significant difference between the means of Suppliers 1 and 2. All other pairwise differences are small enough that they may be due to chance. With 95% confidence, you can conclude that parachutes woven using fiber from Supplier 1 have a lower mean tensile strength than those from Supplier 2, but there are no statistically significant differences between Suppliers 1 and 3, Suppliers 1 and 4, Suppliers 2 and 3, Suppliers 2 and 4, and Suppliers 3 and 4. Note that by using $\alpha = 0.05$, you are able to make all six of the comparisons with an overall error rate of only 5%.

These results are shown in Figures 10.27 and 10.28 on page 351. Figure 10.27 follows the steps used on page 349 for evaluating the comparisons. Each mean is computed and the absolute differences are determined, the critical range is computed, and then each comparison is declared significant or not significant. In Figure 10.28, the comparisons are made using interval estimates. Each interval is computed. Any interval that does not include 0 is considered significant. Thus, in Figure 10.28, the only significant comparison is Supplier 1 versus Supplier 2 because its interval 0.269 to 9.211 does not include 0.

FIGURE 10.27

Microsoft Excel Tukey-Kramer procedure worksheet for the parachute example

See Section E10.10 or P10.6 to create this.

	A	B	C	D	E	F	G	H	I
1	Parachute Tensile-Strength Analysis								
2									
3		Sample	Sample			Absolute	Std. Error	Critical	
4	Group	Mean	Size		Comparison	Difference	of Difference	Range	Results
5	1	19.52	5		Group 1 to Group 2	4.74	1.10399275	4.4712	Means are different
6	2	24.26	5		Group 1 to Group 3	3.32	1.10399275	4.4712	Means are not different
7	3	22.84	5		Group 1 to Group 4	1.64	1.10399275	4.4712	Means are not different
8	4	21.16	5		Group 2 to Group 3	1.42	1.10399275	4.4712	Means are not different
9					Group 2 to Group 4	3.1	1.10399275	4.4712	Means are not different
10	Other Data				Group 3 to Group 4	1.68	1.10399275	4.4712	Means are not different
11	Level of significance	0.05							
12	Numerator d.f.	4							
13	Denominator d.f.	16							
14	MSW	6.094							
15	Q Statistic	4.05							

FIGURE 10.28

Minitab Tukey-Kramer results for the parachute example

See Section M10.6 to create this.

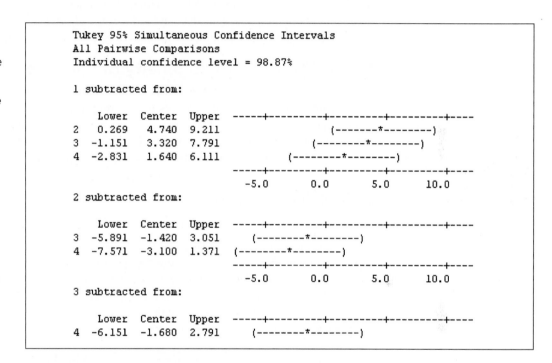

```
Tukey 95% Simultaneous Confidence Intervals
All Pairwise Comparisons
Individual confidence level = 98.87%

1 subtracted from:

     Lower  Center  Upper   -----+---------+---------+---------+----
2    0.269   4.740  9.211                    (--------*--------)
3   -1.151   3.320  7.791                 (--------*--------)
4   -2.831   1.640  6.111            (--------*--------)
                             -----+---------+---------+---------+----
                                -5.0       0.0       5.0      10.0

2 subtracted from:

     Lower  Center  Upper   -----+---------+---------+---------+----
3   -5.891  -1.420  3.051       (--------*--------)
4   -7.571  -3.100  1.371    (--------*--------)
                             -----+---------+---------+---------+----
                                -5.0       0.0       5.0      10.0

3 subtracted from:

     Lower  Center  Upper   -----+---------+---------+---------+----
4   -6.151  -1.680  2.791       (--------*--------)
```

ANOVA Assumptions

In Chapter 9 and Sections 10.1–10.4, you learned about the assumptions required in order to use each hypothesis-testing procedure and the consequences of departures from these assumptions. To use the one-way ANOVA F test, you must also make certain assumptions about the populations. These assumptions are

- Randomness and independence
- Normality
- Homogeneity of variance

The first assumption, **randomness and independence**, is critically important. The validity of any experiment depends on random sampling and/or a randomization process. To avoid biases in the outcomes, you need to select random samples from the c groups or randomly assign the items to the c levels of the factor. Selecting a random sample, or randomly assigning the levels, ensures that a value from one group is independent of any other value in the experiment. Departures from this assumption can seriously affect inferences from the ANOVA. These problems are discussed more thoroughly in references 5–7.

The second assumption, **normality**, states that the sample values in each group are from a normally distributed population. Just as in the case of the t test, the one-way ANOVA F test is fairly robust against departures from the normal distribution. As long as the distributions are not extremely different from a normal distribution, the level of significance of the ANOVA F test is usually not greatly affected, particularly for large samples. You can assess the normality of each of the c samples by constructing a normal probability plot or a boxplot.

The third assumption, **homogeneity of variance**, states that the variances of the c groups are equal (that is, $\sigma_1^2 = \sigma_2^2 = \cdots = \sigma_c^2$). If you have equal sample sizes in each group, inferences based on the F distribution are not seriously affected by unequal variances. However, if you have unequal sample sizes, unequal variances can have a serious effect on inferences developed from the ANOVA procedure. Thus, when possible, you should have equal sample sizes in all groups. The modified Levene test for homogeneity of variance presented below is one method used to test whether the variances of the c groups are equal.

When only the normality assumption is violated, the Kruskal-Wallis rank test, a nonparametric procedure (See references 1 and 2), is appropriate. When only the homogeneity-of-variance assumption is violated, procedures similar to those used in the separate-variance t test of Section 10.1 are available (see references 1 and 2). When both the normality and homogeneity-of-variance assumptions have been violated, you need to use an appropriate data transformation that both normalizes the data and reduces the differences in variances (see reference 9) or use a more general nonparametric procedure (see references 1 and 2).

Levene Test for Homogeneity of Variance

Although the one-way ANOVA F test is relatively robust with respect to the assumption of equal group variances, large differences in the group variances can seriously affect the level of significance and the power of the F test. One procedure for testing the equality of the variances with high statistical power is the modified **Levene test** (see references 1 and 6). To test for the homogeneity of variance, you use the following null hypothesis:

$$H_0: \sigma_1^2 = \sigma_2^2 = \cdots = \sigma_c^2$$

against the alternative hypothesis:

$$H_1: \text{Not all } \sigma_j^2 \text{ are equal } (j = 1, 2, 3, \ldots, c).$$

To test the null hypothesis of equal variances, you first compute the absolute value of the difference between each value and the median of the group. Then you perform a one-way ANOVA on these *absolute differences*. Most statisticians suggest using a level of significance of $\alpha = 0.05$ when performing the ANOVA. To illustrate the modified Levene test, return to the example concerning the tensile strength of parachutes. Table 10.10 summarizes the absolute differences from the median of each supplier.

TABLE 10.10

Absolute Differences from the Median Tensile Strength for Four Suppliers

Supplier 1 (Median = 18.5)	Supplier 2 (Median = 24.5)	Supplier 3 (Median = 22.9)	Supplier 4 (Median = 20.4)
$\lvert 18.5 - 18.5 \rvert = 0.0$	$\lvert 26.3 - 24.5 \rvert = 1.8$	$\lvert 20.6 - 22.9 \rvert = 2.3$	$\lvert 25.4 - 20.4 \rvert = 5.0$
$\lvert 24.0 - 18.5 \rvert = 5.5$	$\lvert 25.3 - 24.5 \rvert = 0.8$	$\lvert 25.2 - 22.9 \rvert = 2.3$	$\lvert 19.9 - 20.4 \rvert = 0.5$
$\lvert 17.2 - 18.5 \rvert = 1.3$	$\lvert 24.0 - 24.5 \rvert = 0.5$	$\lvert 20.8 - 22.9 \rvert = 2.1$	$\lvert 22.6 - 20.4 \rvert = 2.2$
$\lvert 19.9 - 18.5 \rvert = 1.4$	$\lvert 21.2 - 24.5 \rvert = 3.3$	$\lvert 24.7 - 22.9 \rvert = 1.8$	$\lvert 17.5 - 20.4 \rvert = 2.9$
$\lvert 18.0 - 18.5 \rvert = 0.5$	$\lvert 24.5 - 24.5 \rvert = 0.0$	$\lvert 22.9 - 22.9 \rvert = 0.0$	$\lvert 20.4 - 20.4 \rvert = 0.0$

Using the absolute differences given in Table 10.10, you perform a one-way ANOVA (see Figures 10.29 and 10.30).

FIGURE 10.29

Microsoft Excel ANOVA results for the absolute differences for the parachute data

See Section E10.11 or P10.7 to create this.

	A	B	C	D	E	F	G
1	**Parachute Tensile-Strength Analysis**						
2							
3	**SUMMARY**						
4	*Groups*	*Count*	*Sum*	*Average*	*Variance*		
5	**Supplier 1**	5	8.7	1.74	4.753		
6	**Supplier 2**	5	6.4	1.28	1.707		
7	**Supplier 3**	5	8.5	1.7	0.945		
8	**Supplier 4**	5	10.6	2.12	4.007		
9							
10							
11	**ANOVA**						
12	*Source of Variation*	*SS*	*df*	*MS*	*F*	*P-value*	*F crit*
13	**Between Groups**	1.77	3	0.59	0.2068	0.8902	3.2389
14	**Within Groups**	45.648	16	2.853			
15							
16	**Total**	47.418	19				

FIGURE 10.30
Minitab Levene test results for the absolute differences for the parachute data

See Section M10.8 to create this.

```
Levene's Test (Any Continuous Distribution)
Test statistic = 0.21, p-value = 0.890
```

From Figure 10.29 or 10.30, observe that $F_{STAT} = 0.2068$ (Excel labels this value "F" and Minitab calls it the "Test statistic.") Because $F_{STAT} = 0.2068 < 3.2389$ (or the p-value $= 0.8902 > 0.05$), you do not reject H_0. There is no evidence of a significant difference among the four variances. In other words, it is reasonable to assume that the materials from the four suppliers produce parachutes with an equal amount of variability. Therefore, the homogeneity-of-variance assumption for the ANOVA procedure is justified.

EXAMPLE 10.5

ANOVA of the Speed of Drive-Through Service at Fast-Food Chains

For fast-food restaurants, the drive-through window is an increasing source of revenue. The chain that offers the fastest service is likely to attract additional customers. Each month QSR Magazine, **www.qsrmagazine.com**, publishes its results of drive-through service times (from menu board to departure) at fast-food chains. In a recent month, the mean time was 135.1 seconds for Wendy's, 156.2 seconds for Taco Bell, 163.9 seconds for McDonald's, 166 seconds for Burger King, and 173.2 seconds for KFC. Suppose the study was based on 20 customers for each fast-food chain and the ANOVA table given in Table 10.11 was developed.

TABLE 10.11

ANOVA Summary Table of Drive-Through Service Times at Fast-Food Chains

Source	Degrees of Freedom	Sum of Squares	Mean Squares	F	p-Value
Among chains	4	17,072.56	4,268.14	32.68	0.0000
Within chains	95	12,407.00	130.60		

At the 0.05 level of significance, is there evidence of a difference in the mean drive-through service times of the five chains?

SOLUTION

H_0: $\mu_1 = \mu_2 = \mu_3 = \mu_4 = \mu_5$ where 1 = Wendy's, 2 = Taco Bell, 3 = McDonald's, 4 = Burger King, 5 = KFC

H_1: Not all μ_j are equal   where $j = 1, 2, 3, 4, 5$

Decision rule: If p-value < 0.05, reject H_0. Because the p-value is virtually 0, which is less than $\alpha = 0.05$, reject H_0. You have sufficient evidence to conclude that the mean drive-through times of the five chains are not all equal.

To determine which of the means are significantly different from one another, use the Tukey-Kramer procedure [Equation (10.13) on page 349] to establish the critical range:

Critical value of Q with 5 and 95 degrees of freedom ≈ 3.92

$$\text{Critical range} = Q_\alpha \sqrt{\left(\frac{MSW}{2}\right)\left(\frac{1}{n_j} + \frac{1}{n_{j'}}\right)} = (3.92)\sqrt{\left(\frac{130.6}{2}\right)\left(\frac{1}{20} + \frac{1}{20}\right)}$$

$$= 10.02$$

Any observed difference greater than 10.02 is considered significant. The mean drive-through service times are different between Wendy's (mean of 135.1 seconds) and each of the other four chains. Also, the mean drive-through service time for Taco Bell is statistically different from KFC. Thus, with 95% confidence, you can conclude that the mean drive-through service time for Wendy's is faster than Taco Bell, McDonald's, Burger King, and KFC; Taco Bell is faster than KFC; and the other five differences between the mean drive-through service times are not statistically different.

Problems for Section 10.5

LEARNING THE BASICS

10.51 An experiment has five groups and seven values in each group.
a. How many degrees of freedom are there in determining the among-group variation?
b. How many degrees of freedom are there in determining the within-group variation?
c. How many degrees of freedom are there in determining the total variation?

10.52 You are working with the same experiment as in Problem 10.51.
a. If $SSA = 60$ and $SST = 210$, what is SSW?
b. What is MSA?
c. What is MSW?
d. What is the value of F_{STAT}?

10.53 You are working with the same experiment as in Problems 10.51 and 10.52.
a. Construct the ANOVA summary table and fill in all values in the table.
b. At the 0.05 level of significance, what is the upper-tail critical value from the F distribution?
c. State the decision rule for testing the null hypothesis that all five groups have equal population means.
d. What is your statistical decision?

10.54 Consider an experiment with three groups, with seven values in each.
a. How many degrees of freedom are there in determining the among-group variation?
b. How many degrees of freedom are there in determining the within-group variation?
c. How many degrees of freedom are there in determining the total variation?

10.55 Consider an experiment with four groups, with eight values in each. For the ANOVA summary table below, fill in all the missing results:

Source	Degrees of Freedom	Sum of Squares	Mean Square (Variance)	F
Among groups	$c - 1 = ?$	$SSA = ?$	$MSA = 80$	$F_{STAT} = ?$
Within groups	$n - c = ?$	$SSW = 560$	$MSW = ?$	
Total	$n - 1 = ?$	$SST = ?$		

10.56 You are working with the same experiment as in Problem 10.55.
a. At the 0.05 level of significance, state the decision rule for testing the null hypothesis that all four groups have equal population means.

b. What is your statistical decision?
c. At the 0.05 level of significance, what is the upper-tail critical value from the Studentized range distribution?
d. To perform the Tukey-Kramer procedure, what is the critical range?

APPLYING THE CONCEPTS

10.57 The Computer Anxiety Rating Scale (CARS) measures an individual's level of computer anxiety, on a scale from 20 (no anxiety) to 100 (highest level of anxiety). Researchers at Miami University administered CARS to 172 business students. One of the objectives of the study was to determine whether there are differences in the amount of computer anxiety experienced by students with different majors. They found the following:

Source	Degrees of Freedom	Sum of Squares	Mean Squares	F
Among majors	5	3,172		
Within majors	166	21,246		
Total	171	24,418		

Major	n	Mean
Marketing	19	44.37
Management	11	43.18
Other	14	42.21
Finance	45	41.80
Accountancy	36	37.56
MIS	47	32.21

Source: *Data extracted from T. Broome and D. Havelka, "Determinants of Computer Anxiety in Business Students,"* The Review of Business Information Systems, *Spring 2002, 6(2), pp. 9–16.*

a. Complete the ANOVA summary table.
b. At the 0.05 level of significance, is there evidence of a difference in the mean computer anxiety experienced by different majors?
c. If the results in (b) indicate that it is appropriate, use the Tukey-Kramer procedure to determine which majors differ in mean computer anxiety. Discuss your findings.

✓ SELF Test **10.58** Students in a business statistics course performed an experiment to test the strength of four brands of trash bags. One-pound weights were placed into a bag, one at a time, until the bag broke. A total of 40 bags, 10 for each brand, were used. The data in the file **Trashbags** give the weight (in pounds) required to break the trash bags.
a. At the 0.05 level of significance, is there evidence of a difference in the mean strength of the four brands of trash bags?

b. If appropriate, determine which brands differ in mean strength.

c. At the 0.05 level of significance, is there evidence of a difference in the variation in strength among the four brands of trash bags?

d. Which brand(s) should you buy and which brand(s) should you avoid? Explain.

10.59 A hospital conducted a study of the waiting time in its emergency room. The hospital has a main campus and three satellite locations. Management had a business objective of reducing waiting time for emergency room cases that did not require immediate attention. To study this, a random sample of 15 emergency room cases at each location were selected on a particular day, and the waiting time (measured from check-in to when the patient was called into the clinic area) was measured. The results are stored in the file **ERwaiting** .

a. At the 0.05 level of significance, is there evidence of a difference in the mean waiting times in the four locations?

b. If appropriate, determine which locations differ in mean waiting time.

c. At the 0.05 level of significance, is there evidence of a difference in the variation in waiting time among the four locations?

10.60 An advertising agency has been hired by a manufacturer of pens to develop an advertising campaign for the upcoming holiday season. To prepare for this project, the research director decides to initiate a study of the effect of advertising on product perception. An experiment is designed to compare five different advertisements. Advertisement *A* greatly undersells the pen's characteristics. Advertisement *B* slightly undersells the pen's characteristics. Advertisement *C* slightly oversells the pen's characteristics. Advertisement *D* greatly oversells the pen's characteristics. Advertisement *E* attempts to correctly state the pen's characteristics. A sample of 30 adult respondents, taken from a larger focus group, is randomly assigned to the five advertisements (so that there are six respondents to each). After reading the advertisement and developing a sense of "product expectation," all respondents unknowingly receive the same pen to evaluate. The respondents are permitted to test the pen and the plausibility of the advertising copy. The respondents are then asked to rate the pen from 1 to 7 (lowest to highest) on the product characteristic scales of appearance, durability, and writing performance. The *combined* scores of three ratings (appearance, durability, and writing performance) for the 30 respondents (stored in the file **Pen**) are as follows:

A	B	C	D	E
15	16	8	5	12
18	17	7	6	19
17	21	10	13	18
19	16	15	11	12
19	19	14	9	17
20	17	14	10	14

a. At the 0.05 level of significance, is there evidence of a difference in the mean rating of the five advertisements?

b. If appropriate, determine which advertisements differ in mean ratings.

c. At the 0.05 level of significance, is there evidence of a difference in the variation in ratings among the five advertisements?

d. Which advertisement(s) should you use and which advertisement(s) should you avoid? Explain.

10.61 The following data (stored in the file **CDyield**) represent the nationwide highest yield of different types of accounts (extracted from **Bankrate.com**, March 31, 2008):

Money Market	Six-Month CD	One-Year CD	2.5-Year CD	Five-Year CD
4.00	3.85	4.05	3.80	4.30
3.82	3.60	3.61	3.70	4.15
3.80	3.60	3.60	3.51	4.10
3.75	3.45	3.60	3.35	4.00
3.75	3.43	3.50	3.35	4.00

a. At the 0.05 level of significance, is there evidence of a difference in the mean yields of the different accounts?

b. If appropriate, determine which accounts differ in mean yields.

c. At the 0.05 level of significance, is there evidence of a difference in the variation in yields among the different accounts?

d. What effect does your result in (c) have on the validity of the results in (a) and (b)?

10.62 A sporting goods manufacturing company wanted to compare the distance traveled by golf balls produced using each of four different designs. Ten balls were manufactured with each design and were brought to the local golf course for the club professional to test. The order in which the balls were hit with the same club from the first tee was randomized so that the pro did not know which type of ball was being hit. All 40 balls were hit in a short period of time, during which the environmental conditions were essentially the same. The results (distance traveled in yards) for the four designs were as follows (and are stored in the file **Golfball**):

Design			
1	2	3	4
206.32	217.08	226.77	230.55
207.94	221.43	224.79	227.95
206.19	218.04	229.75	231.84
204.45	224.13	228.51	224.87
209.65	211.82	221.44	229.49
203.81	213.90	223.85	231.10
206.75	221.28	223.97	221.53
205.68	229.43	234.30	235.45
204.49	213.54	219.50	228.35
210.86	214.51	233.00	225.09

a. At the 0.05 level of significance, is there evidence of a difference in the mean distances traveled by the golf balls with different designs?

b. If the results in (a) indicate that it is appropriate, use the Tukey-Kramer procedure to determine which designs differ in mean distances.

c. What assumptions are necessary in (a)?

d. At the 0.05 level of significance, is there evidence of a difference in the variation of the distances traveled by the golf balls with different designs?

e. What golf ball design should the manufacturing manager choose? Explain.

USING STATISTICS   @ BLK Foods Revisited

In the Using Statistics scenario, you were the regional sales manager for BLK Foods. You compared the sales volume of the BLK cola when the product is placed in the normal shelf location to the sales volume when the product is featured in a special end-aisle display. An experiment was performed where 10 stores used the normal shelf location and 10 stores used the end-aisle displays. Using a *t* test for the difference between two means, you were able to conclude that the mean sales using end-aisle location are higher than the mean sales for the normal shelf location. A confidence interval allowed you to infer with 95% confidence that the end-aisle location sells, on average, 6.73 to 36.67 cases more than the normal shelf location. You also performed the *F* test for the difference between two variances to see if the store-to-store variability in sales in stores using the end-aisle location differed from the store-to-store variability in sales in stores using the normal shelf location. You concluded that there was no significant difference in the variability of the sales of cola for the two display locations. As regional sales manager, your next step in increasing sales is to convince more stores to use the special end-aisle display.

SUMMARY

In this chapter, you were introduced to a variety of tests for two or more samples. For situations in which the samples are independent, you learned statistical test procedures for analyzing possible differences between means, variances, and proportions. In addition, you learned a test procedure that is frequently used when analyzing differences between the means of two related samples. Remember that you need to select the test that is most appropriate for a given set of conditions and to critically investigate the validity of the assumptions underlying each of the hypothesis-testing procedures.

The roadmap in Figure 10.31 illustrates the steps needed in determining which test of hypothesis to use. The following are the questions you need to consider.

1. What type of data do you have? If you are dealing with categorical variables, use the *Z* test for the difference between two proportions. (This test assumes independent samples.)

2. If you have a numerical variable, determine whether you have independent samples or related samples. If you have related samples, use the paired *t* test.

3. If you have independent samples, is your focus on variability or central tendency? If the focus is variability, use the *F* test.

4. If your focus is central tendency, determine whether you can assume that the variances of the two populations are equal. (This assumption can be tested using the *F* test.)

5. If you can assume that the two populations have equal variances, use the pooled-variance *t* test. If you cannot assume that the two populations have equal variances, use the separate-variance *t* test.

6. If you have more than two independent samples, you can use the one-way ANOVA.

Table 10.12 provides a list of topics covered in this chapter.

FIGURE 10.31

Roadmap for selecting a test of hypothesis for two or more samples

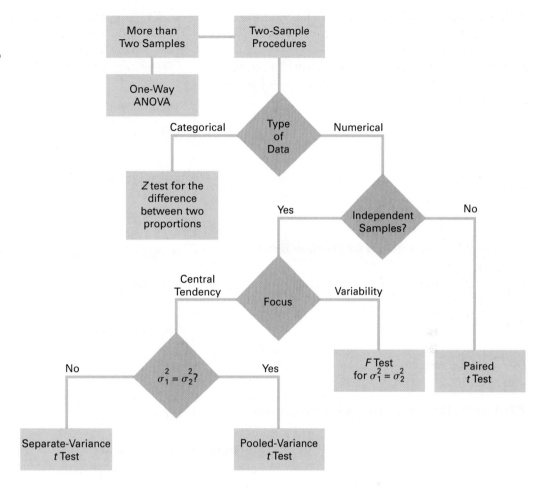

TABLE 10.12

Summary of Topics in Chapter 10

Type of Analysis	Types of Data	
	Numerical	**Categorical**
Comparing two populations	t tests for the difference in the means of two independent populations (Section 10.1)	Z test for the difference between two proportions (Section 10.3)
	Paired t test (Section 10.2)	
	F test for the difference between two variances (Section 10.4)	
Comparing more than two populations	One-way ANOVA (Section 10.5)	

KEY EQUATIONS

Pooled-Variance t Test for the Difference Between Two Means

$$t_{STAT} = \frac{(\overline{X}_1 - \overline{X}_2) - (\mu_1 - \mu_2)}{\sqrt{S_p^2\left(\frac{1}{n_1} + \frac{1}{n_2}\right)}} \qquad (10.1)$$

Confidence Interval Estimate of the Difference in the Means of Two Independent Populations

$$(\overline{X}_1 - \overline{X}_2) \pm t_{\alpha/2}\sqrt{S_p^2\left(\frac{1}{n_1} + \frac{1}{n_2}\right)} \qquad (10.2)$$

or

$$(\bar{X}_1 - \bar{X}_2) - t_{\alpha/2}\sqrt{S_p^2\left(\frac{1}{n_1} + \frac{1}{n_2}\right)} \leq \mu_1 - \mu_2$$

$$\leq (\bar{X}_1 - \bar{X}_2) + t_{\alpha/2}\sqrt{S_p^2\left(\frac{1}{n_1} + \frac{1}{n_2}\right)}$$

Paired t Test for the Mean Difference

$$t_{STAT} = \frac{\bar{D} - \mu_D}{\dfrac{S_D}{\sqrt{n}}} \tag{10.3}$$

Confidence Interval Estimate for the Mean Difference

$$\bar{D} \pm t_{\alpha/2}\frac{S_D}{\sqrt{n}} \tag{10.4}$$

or

$$\bar{D} - t_{\alpha/2}\frac{S_D}{\sqrt{n}} \leq \mu_D \leq \bar{D} + t_{\alpha/2}\frac{S_D}{\sqrt{n}}$$

Z Test for the Difference Between Two Proportions

$$Z_{STAT} = \frac{(p_1 - p_2) - (\pi_1 - \pi_2)}{\sqrt{\bar{p}(1 - \bar{p})\left(\dfrac{1}{n_1} + \dfrac{1}{n_2}\right)}} \tag{10.5}$$

Confidence Interval Estimate for the Difference Between Two Proportions

$$(p_1 - p_2) \pm Z_{\alpha/2}\sqrt{\left(\frac{p_1(1 - p_1)}{n_1} + \frac{p_2(1 - p_2)}{n_2}\right)} \tag{10.6}$$

or

$$(p_1 - p_2) - Z_{\alpha/2}\sqrt{\frac{p_1(1 - p_1)}{n_1} + \frac{p_2(1 - p_2)}{n_1}} \leq (\pi_1 - \pi_2)$$

$$\leq (p_1 - p_2) + Z_{\alpha/2}\sqrt{\frac{p_1(1 - p_1)}{n_1} + \frac{p_2(1 - p_2)}{n_1}}$$

F Test for the Equality of Two Variances

$$F_{STAT} = \frac{S_1^2}{S_2^2} \tag{10.7}$$

Total Variation in One-Way ANOVA

$$SST = \sum_{j=1}^{c}\sum_{i=1}^{n_j}(X_{ij} - \bar{\bar{X}})^2 \tag{10.8}$$

Among-Group Variation in One-Way ANOVA

$$SSA = \sum_{j=1}^{c}n_j(\bar{X}_j - \bar{\bar{X}})^2 \tag{10.9}$$

Within-Group Variation in One-Way ANOVA

$$SSW = \sum_{j=1}^{c}\sum_{i=1}^{n_j}(X_{ij} - \bar{X}_j)^2 \tag{10.10}$$

Mean Squares in One-Way ANOVA

$$MSA = \frac{SSA}{c - 1} \tag{10.11a}$$

$$MSW = \frac{SSW}{n - c} \tag{10.11b}$$

$$MST = \frac{SST}{n - 1} \tag{10.11c}$$

One-Way ANOVA F_{STAT} Test Statistic

$$F_{STAT} = \frac{MSA}{MSW} \tag{10.12}$$

Critical Range for the Tukey-Kramer Procedure

$$\text{Critical range} = Q_\alpha\sqrt{\frac{MSW}{2}\left(\frac{1}{n_j} + \frac{1}{n_{j'}}\right)} \tag{10.13}$$

KEY TERMS

CHAPTER REVIEW PROBLEMS

CHECKING YOUR UNDERSTANDING

10.63 What are some of the criteria used in the selection of a particular hypothesis-testing procedure?

10.64 Under what conditions should you use the pooled-variance *t* test to examine possible differences in the means of two independent populations?

10.65 Under what conditions should you use the *F* test to examine possible differences in the variances of two independent populations?

10.66 What is the distinction between two independent populations and two related populations?

10.67 What is the distinction between repeated measurements and matched items?

10.68 When you have two independent populations, explain the similarities and differences between the test of hypothesis for the difference between the means and the confidence interval estimate of the difference between the means.

10.69 What are the assumptions of ANOVA?

10.70 Under what conditions should you select the one-way ANOVA *F* test to examine possible differences among the means of *c* independent populations?

10.71 When and how should you use multiple comparison procedures for evaluating pairwise combinations of the group means?

APPLYING THE CONCEPTS

10.72 A study compared music compact disc prices for Internet-based retailers and traditional brick-and-mortar retailers [extracted from L. Zoonky and S. Gosain, "A Longitudinal Price Comparison for Music CDs in Electronic and Brick-and-Mortar Markets: Pricing Strategies in Emergent Electronic Commerce," *Journal of Business Strategies*, Spring 2002, 19(1), pp. 55–72]. Before collecting the data, the researchers carefully defined several research hypotheses, including:
1. The price dispersion on the Internet is lower than the price dispersion in the brick-and-mortar market.

2. Prices in electronic markets are lower than prices in physical markets.
   a. Consider research hypothesis 1. Write the null and alternative hypotheses in terms of population parameters. Carefully define the population parameters used.
   b. Define a Type I and Type II error for the hypotheses in (a).
   c. What type of statistical test should you use?
   d. What assumptions are needed to perform the test you selected?
   e. Repeat (a) through (d) for research hypothesis 2.

10.73 The pet-drug market is growing very rapidly. Before new pet drugs can be introduced into the marketplace, they must be approved by the U.S. Food and Drug Administration (FDA). In 1999, the Novartis company was trying to get Anafranil, a drug to reduce dog anxiety, approved. According to an article (E. Tanouye, "The Ow in Bowwow: With Growing Market in Pet Drugs, Makers Revamp Clinical Trials," *The Wall Street Journal*, April 13, 1999), Novartis had to find a way to translate a dog's anxiety symptoms into numbers that could be used to prove to the FDA that the drug had a statistically significant effect on the condition.
a. What is meant by the phrase *statistically significant effect*?
b. Consider an experiment in which dogs suffering from anxiety are divided into two groups. One group will be given Anafranil, and the other will be given a placebo (i.e., a drug without active ingredients). How can you translate a dog's anxiety symptoms into numbers? In other words, define a continuous variable, X_1, that measures the effectiveness of the drug Anafranil, and X_2, that measures the effectiveness of the placebo.
c. Building on your answer to part (b), define the null and alternative hypotheses for this study.

10.74 In response to lawsuits filed against the tobacco industry, many companies, such as Philip Morris, are running television advertisements that are supposed to educate teenagers about the dangers of smoking. Are these tobacco industry antismoking campaigns successful? Are state-sponsored antismoking commercials more effective? An article (G. Fairclough, "Philip Morris's Antismoking Campaign Draws Fire," *The Wall Street Journal*, April 6, 1999, p. B1) discussed a study in California that compared commercials made by the state of California and commercials produced by Philip Morris. Researchers showed the state ads and the Philip Morris ads to a group of California teenagers and measured the effectiveness of both. The researchers concluded that the state ads were more effective in relaying the dangers of smoking than the Philip Morris ads. The article suggests, however, that the study is not *statistically reliable* because the sample size was too small and because the study specifically selected participants who are considered more likely to start smoking than others.

a. How do you think the researchers measured effectiveness?
b. Define the null and alternative hypotheses for this study.
c. Explain the risks associated with Type I and Type II errors in this study.
d. What type of test is most appropriate in this situation?
e. What do you think is meant by the phrase *statistically reliable*?

10.75 Do male and female students study the same amount per week? In 2007, 58 sophomore business students were surveyed at a large university, which has over 1,000 sophomore business students each year. The file Studytime contains the gender and the number of hours spent studying in a typical week for the sampled students.

a. At the 0.05 level of significance, is there a difference in the variance of the study time for male students and female students?
b. Using the results of (a), which *t* test is appropriate to compare the mean study time for male and female students?
c. At the 0.05 level of significance, conduct the test selected in (b).
d. Write a short summary of your findings.

10.76 Two professors wanted to study how students from their two universities compared in their capabilities of using Excel spreadsheets in undergraduate information systems courses (data extracted from H. Howe and M. G. Simkin, "Factors Affecting the Ability to Detect Spreadsheet Errors," *Decision Sciences Journal of Innovative Education*, January 2006, pp. 101–122). A comparison of the student demographics was also performed. One school is a state university in the Western United States, and the other school is a state university in the Eastern United States. The following table contains information regarding the ages of the students:

School	Sample Size	Mean Age	Standard Deviation
Western	93	23.28	6.29
Eastern	135	21.16	1.32

a. Using a 0.01 level of significance, is there evidence of a difference between the variances in age of students at the Western school and at the Eastern school?
b. Discuss the practical implications of the test performed in (a). Address, specifically, the impact equal (or unequal) variances in age has on teaching an undergraduate information systems course.
c. To test for a difference in the mean age of students, is it most appropriate to use the pooled-variance *t* test or the separate-variance *t* test?

The following table contains information regarding the years of spreadsheet usage of the students:

School	Sample Size	Mean Years	Standard Deviation
Western	93	2.6	2.4
Eastern	135	4.0	2.1

d. Using a 0.01 level of significance, is there evidence of a difference between the variances in years of spreadsheet usage of students at the Western school and at the Eastern school?
e. Based on the results of (d), use the most appropriate test to determine, at the 0.01 level of significance, whether there is evidence of a difference in the mean years of spreadsheet usage of students at the Western school and at the Eastern school.

10.77 The data file Restaurants contains the ratings for food, decor, service, and the price per person for a sample of 50 restaurants located in an urban area and 50 restaurants located in a suburban area. Completely analyze the differences between urban and suburban restaurants for the variables food rating, decor rating, service rating, and price per person, using $\alpha = 0.05$.

Source: *Data extracted from* Zagat Survey 2006: New York City Restaurants *and* Zagat Survey 2005–2006: Long Island Restaurants.

10.78 A computer information systems professor is interested in studying the amount of time it takes students enrolled in the introduction to computers course to write and run a program in Visual Basic. The professor hires you to analyze the following results (in minutes) from a random sample of nine students (the data are stored in the VB file):

10   13   9   15   12   13   11   13   12

a. At the 0.05 level of significance, is there evidence that the population mean amount is greater than 10 minutes? What will you tell the professor?
b. Suppose the computer professor, when checking her results, realizes that the fourth student needed 51 minutes rather than the recorded 15 minutes to write and run the Visual Basic program. At the 0.05 level of significance,

reanalyze the question posed in (a), using the revised data. What will you tell the professor now?

c. The professor is perplexed by these paradoxical results and requests an explanation from you regarding the justification for the difference in your findings in (a) and (b). Discuss.

d. A few days later, the professor calls to tell you that the dilemma is completely resolved. The original number 15 (the fourth data value) was correct, and therefore your findings in (a) are being used in the article she is writing for a computer journal. Now she wants to hire you to compare the results from that group of introduction to computers students against those from a sample of 11 computer majors in order to determine whether there is evidence that computer majors can write a Visual Basic program in less time than introductory students. For the computer majors, the sample mean is 8.5 minutes, and the sample standard deviation is 2.0 minutes. At the 0.05 level of significance, completely analyze these data. What will you tell the professor?

e. A few days later, the professor calls again to tell you that a reviewer of her article wants her to include the *p*-value for the "correct" result in (a). In addition, the professor inquires about an unequal-variances problem, which the reviewer wants her to discuss in her article. In your own words, discuss the concept of *p*-value and also describe the unequal-variances problem. Then, determine the *p*-value in (a) and discuss whether the unequal-variances problem had any meaning in the professor's study.

10.79 An article in *The New York Times* (A. Jennings, "What's Good for a Business Can be Hard on Friends," *The New York Times*, August 4, 2007, pp. C1–C2) reported that according to a poll, the mean number of cellphone calls per month was 290 for 18- to 24-year-olds and 194 for 45- to 54-year-olds, whereas the mean number of text messages per month was 290 for 18- to 24-year-olds and 57 for 45- to 54-year-olds. Suppose that the poll was based on a sample of 100 18- to 24-year-olds and 100 45- to 54-year-olds, and that the standard deviation of the number of cellphone calls per month was 100 for 18- to 24-year-olds and 90 for 45- to 54-year-olds, whereas the standard deviation of the number of text messages per month was 90 for 18- to 24-year-olds and 77 for 45- to 54-year-olds.

Use a level of significance of 0.05.

a. Is there evidence of a difference in the variances of the number of cellphone calls per month for 18- to 24-year-olds and 45- to 54-year-olds?

b. Is there evidence of a difference in the mean number of cellphone calls per month for 18- to 24-year-olds and 45- to 54-year-olds?

c. Construct and interpret a 95% confidence interval estimate of the difference in the mean number of cellphone calls per month for 18- to 24-year-olds and 45- to 54-year-olds.

d. Is there evidence of a difference in the variances of the number of text messages per month for 18- to 24-year-olds and 45- to 54-year-olds?

e. Is there evidence of a difference in the mean number of text messages per month for 18- to 24-year-olds and 45- to 54-year-olds?

f. Construct and interpret a 95% confidence interval estimate of the difference in the mean number of text messages per month for 18- to 24-year-olds and 45- to 54-year-olds.

g. Based on the results of (a) through (f), what conclusions can you make concerning cellphone and text message usage between 18- to 24-year-olds and 45- to 54-year-olds?

10.80 The lengths of life (in hours) of a sample of 40 100-watt lightbulbs produced by manufacturer A and a sample of 40 100-watt lightbulbs produced by manufacturer B are in the file **Bulbs**. Completely analyze the differences between the lengths of life of the bulbs produced by the two manufacturers (use $\alpha = 0.05$).

10.81 A hotel manager is concerned with increasing the return rate for hotel guests. One aspect of first impressions by guests relates to the time it takes to deliver the guest's luggage to the room after check-in to the hotel. A random sample of 20 deliveries on a particular day were selected in Wing A of the hotel, and a random sample of 20 deliveries were selected in Wing B. The results are stored in the file **Luggage**. Analyze the data and determine whether there is a difference in the mean delivery time in the two wings of the hotel. (Use $\alpha = 0.05$.)

10.82 Many companies are finding that customers are using various types of online content before purchasing products (data extracted from K. Spors, "How Are We Doing?" *The Wall Street Journal*, November 13, 2006, p. R9). The following results are the percentages of adults and youths who use various sources of online content. Suppose the survey was based on 100 adults and 100 youths.

TYPE OF ONLINE CONTENT	USE ONLINE CONTENT	
	Adult	Youth
Customer product ratings/reviews	71	81
For sale listings with seller ratings	69	77
For sale listings without seller ratings	58	65
Online classified ads	57	66
Message-board posts	57	71
Web blogs	55	67
Dating site profiles/personals	49	59
Peer-generated and peer-reference information	49	68
Peer-posted event listings	46	71

For *each type of online content*, determine whether there is a difference between adults and youths in the proportion who use the type of online content at the 0.05 level of significance.

10.83 The manufacturer of Boston and Vermont asphalt shingles knows that product weight is a major factor in the customer's perception of quality. Moreover, the weight represents the amount of raw materials being used and is therefore very important to the company from a cost standpoint. The last stage of the assembly line packages the shingles before they are placed on wooden pallets. Once a pallet is full (a pallet for most brands holds 16 squares of shingles), it is weighed, and the measurement is recorded. The data file Pallet contains the weight (in pounds) from a sample of 368 pallets of Boston shingles and 330 pallets of Vermont shingles. Completely analyze the differences in the weights of the Boston and Vermont shingles, using $\alpha = 0.05$.

10.84 The manufacturer of Boston and Vermont asphalt shingles provides its customers with a 20-year warranty on most of its products. To determine whether a shingle will last as long as the warranty period, accelerated-life testing is conducted at the manufacturing plant. Accelerated-life testing exposes the shingle to the stresses it would be subject to in a lifetime of normal use in a laboratory setting via an experiment that takes only a few minutes to conduct. In this test, a shingle is repeatedly scraped with a brush for a short period of time, and the shingle granules removed by the brushing are weighed (in grams). Shingles that experience low amounts of granule loss are expected to last longer in normal use than shingles that experience high amounts of granule loss. In this situation, a shingle should experience no more than 0.8 grams of granule loss if it is expected to last the length of the warranty period. The data file Granule contains a sample of 170 measurements made on the company's Boston shingles and 140 measurements made on Vermont shingles. Completely analyze the differences in the granule loss of the Boston and Vermont shingles, using $\alpha = 0.05$.

10.85 The quality control director for a clothing manufacturer wants to study the effect of machines on the breaking strength (in pounds) of wool serge material. A batch of the material is cut into square-yard pieces, and these are randomly assigned, 12 each, to the three machines chosen specifically for the experiment. The results (stored in the file Breakstw) are shown at the top of the next column:

At the 0.05 level of significance,
a. is there an effect due to machine?
b. Plot the mean breaking strength for each machine.
c. If appropriate, use the Tukey-Kramer procedure to examine differences among machines.
d. What can you conclude about the effects of machines on breaking strength? Explain.

MACHINE		
I	**II**	**III**
115	111	109
115	108	110
119	114	107
117	105	110
114	102	113
114	106	114
109	100	103
110	103	102
106	101	105
112	105	108
115	107	111
111	107	110

10.86 An operations manager wants to examine the effect of air-jet pressure (in psi) on the breaking strength of yarn. Three different levels of air-jet pressure are to be considered: 30 psi, 40 psi, and 50 psi. A random sample of 18 homogeneous filling yarns are selected from the same batch, and the yarns are randomly assigned, 6 each, to the 3 levels of air-jet pressure. The breaking strength scores are in the file Yarn.
a. Is there evidence of a significant difference in the variances of the breaking strengths for the three air-jet pressures? (Use $\alpha = 0.05$).
b. At the 0.05 level of significance, is there evidence of a difference among mean breaking strengths for the three air-jet pressures?
c. If appropriate, use the Tukey-Kramer procedure to determine which air-jet pressures significantly differ with respect to mean breaking strength. (Use $\alpha = 0.05$.)
d. What should the operations manager conclude?

REPORT WRITING EXERCISE

10.87 Referring to the results of Problems 10.83 and 10.84 concerning the weight and granule loss of Boston and Vermont shingles, write a report that summarizes your conclusions.

TEAM PROJECT

The data file Mutual Funds contains information regarding nine variables from a sample of 868 mutual funds. The variables are
   Category—Type of stocks comprising the mutual fund (small cap, mid cap, or large cap)
   Objective—Objective of stocks comprising the mutual fund (growth or value)
   Assets—In millions of dollars
   Fees—Sales charges (no or yes)
   Expense ratio—Ratio of expenses to net assets, in percentage

Return 2006—Twelve-month return in 2006
Three-year return—Annualized return, 2004–2006
Five-year return—Annualized return, 2002–2006
Risk—Risk-of-loss factor of the mutual fund (low, average, or high)

10.88 Completely analyze the difference between mutual funds without fees and mutual funds with fees in terms of 2006 return, three-year return, five-year return, and expense ratio. Write a report summarizing your findings.

10.89 Completely analyze the difference between mutual funds that have a growth objective and mutual funds that have a value objective in terms of 2006 return, three-year return, five-year return, and expense ratio. Write a report summarizing your findings.

10.90 Completely analyze the difference between small cap, mid cap, and large cap mutual funds in terms of 2006 return, three-year return, five-year return, and expense ratio. Write a report summarizing your findings.

10.91 Completely analyze the difference between low-risk, average-risk, and high-risk mutual funds in terms of 2006 return, three-year return, five-year return, and expense ratio. Write a report summarizing your findings.

STUDENT SURVEY DATA BASE

10.92 Problem 1.23 on page 13 describes a survey of 50 undergraduate students (see the file Undergradsurvey). For these data,
a. at the 0.05 level of significance, is there evidence of a difference between males and females in grade point average, expected starting salary, salary expected in five years, age, and spending on textbooks and supplies?
b. at the 0.05 level of significance, is there evidence of a difference between those students who plan to go to graduate school and those who do not plan to go to graduate school in grade point average, expected starting salary, salary expected in five years, age, and spending on textbooks and supplies?

10.93 Problem 1.23 on page 13 describes a survey of 50 undergraduate students (see the file Undergradsurvey).
a. Select a sample of 50 undergraduate students at your school and conduct a similar survey for them.
b. For the data collected in (a), repeat (a) and (b) of Problem 10.92.
c. Compare the results of (b) to those of Problem 10.92.

10.94 Problem 1.24 on page 13 describes a survey of 40 MBA students (see the file Gradsurvey). For these data, at the 0.05 level of significance, is there evidence of a difference between males and females in age, undergraduate grade point average, graduate grade point average, GMAT score, expected salary upon graduation, salary expected in five years, and spending on textbooks and supplies?

10.95 Problem 1.24 on page 13 describes a survey of 40 MBA students (see the file Gradsurvey).
a. Select a sample of 40 graduate students in your MBA program and conduct a similar survey for those students.
b. For the data collected in (a), repeat Problem 10.94.
c. Compare the results of (b) to those of Problem 10.94.

10.96 Problem 1.23 on page 13 describes a survey of 50 undergraduate students (see the file). For these data,
a. at the 0.05 level of significance, is there evidence of a difference based on academic major in grade point average, expected starting salary, salary expected in five years, age, and spending on textbooks and supplies?
b. at the 0.05 level of significance, is there evidence of a difference based on graduate school intention in grade point average, expected starting salary, salary expected in five years, age, and spending on textbooks and supplies?
c. at the 0.05 level of significance, is there evidence of a difference based on employment status in grade point average, expected starting salary, salary expected in five years, age, and spending on textbooks and supplies?

10.97 Problem 1.23 on page 13 describes a survey of 50 undergraduate students (see the file Undergradsurvey).
a. Select a sample of 50 undergraduate students at your school and conduct a similar survey for those students.
b. For the data collected in (a), repeat (a) through (c) of Problem 10.96.
c. Compare the results of (b) to those of Problem 10.96.

10.98 Problem 1.24 on page 13 describes a survey of 40 MBA students (see the file Gradsurvey). For these data, at the 0.05 level of significance,
a. is there evidence of a difference, based on undergraduate major, in age, undergraduate grade point average, graduate grade point average, GMAT score, expected salary upon graduation, salary expected in five years, and spending on textbooks and supplies?
b. is there evidence of a difference, based on graduate major, in age, undergraduate grade point average, graduate grade point average, GMAT score, expected salary upon graduation, salary expected in five years, and spending on textbooks and supplies?
c. is there evidence of a difference, based on employment status, in age, undergraduate grade point average, graduate grade point average, GMAT score, expected salary upon graduation, salary expected in five years, and spending on textbooks and supplies?

10.99 Problem 1.24 on page 13 describes a survey of 40 MBA students (see the file Gradsurvey).
a. Select a sample of 40 graduate students in your MBA program and conduct a similar survey for those students.
b. For the data collected in (a), repeat (a) through (c) of Problem 10.98.
c. Compare the results of (b) to those of Problem 10.98.

MANAGING THE *SPRINGVILLE HERALD*

Phase 1

A marketing department team is charged with improving the telemarketing process in order to increase the number of home-delivery subscriptions sold. After several brainstorming sessions, it was clear that the longer a caller speaks to a respondent, the greater the chance that the caller will sell a home-delivery subscription. Therefore, the team decided to find ways to increase the length of the phone calls.

Initially, the team investigated the impact that the time of a call might have on the length of the call. Under current arrangements, calls were made in the evening hours, between 5:00 P.M. and 9:00 P.M., Monday through Friday. The team wanted to compare the length of calls made early in the evening (before 7:00 P.M.) with those made later in the evening (after 7:00 P.M.) to determine whether one of these time periods leads to longer calls and, correspondingly, to increased subscription sales. The team selected a sample of 30 female callers who staff the telephone bank on Wednesday evenings and randomly assigned 15 of them to the "early" time period and 15 to the "later" time period. The callers knew that the team was observing their efforts that evening but didn't know which calls were monitored. The callers had been trained to make their telephone presentations in a structured manner. They were to read from a script, and their greeting was personal but informal ("Hi, this is Leigh Richardson from the *Springville Herald*. May I speak to Stuart Knoll?").

Measurements were taken on the length of the call (defined as the difference, in seconds, between the time the person answered the phone and the time he or she hung up). The results (stored in the file SH10-1) are presented in Table SH10.1.

TABLE SH10.1

Length of Calls, in Seconds, Based on Time of Call—Early Versus Late in the Evening

Time of Call		Time of Call	
Early	**Late**	**Early**	**Late**
41.3	37.1	40.6	40.7
37.5	38.9	33.3	38.0
39.3	42.2	39.6	43.6
37.4	45.7	35.7	43.8
33.6	42.4	31.3	34.9
38.5	39.0	36.8	35.7
32.6	40.9	36.3	47.4
37.3	40.5		

EXERCISES

SH10.1 Analyze the data in Table SH10.1 and write a report to the marketing department team that indicates your findings. Include an attached appendix in which you discuss the reason you selected a particular statistical test to compare the two independent groups of callers.

SH10.2 Suppose that instead of the research design described here, there were only 15 callers sampled, and each caller was to be monitored twice in the evening—once in the early time period and once in the later time period. Thus, in Table SH10.1, each pair of values represents a particular caller's two measurements. Reanalyze these data and write a report for presentation to the team that indicates your findings.

SH10.3 What other variables should be investigated next? Why?

DO NOT CONTINUE UNTIL THE PHASE 1 EXERCISES HAVE BEEN COMPLETED

Phase 2

In studying the home delivery solicitation process, the marketing department team determined that the so-called "later" calls made between 7:00 P.M. and 9:00 P.M. led to significantly longer calls than those made earlier in the evening (between 5:00 P.M. and 7:00 P.M.).

Knowing that the 7:00 P.M. to 9:00 P.M. time period is superior, the team sought to investigate the effect of the type of presentation on the length of the call. A group of 24 female callers was randomly assigned, 8 each, to one of three presentation plans—structured, semistructured, and unstructured and trained to make the telephone presentation. All calls were made between 7:00 P.M. and 9:00 P.M., the later time period, and the callers were to provide an introductory greeting that was personal but informal ("Hi, this is Leigh Richardson from the *Springville Herald*. May I speak to Stuart Knoll?"). The callers knew that the team was observing their efforts that evening but didn't know which particular calls were monitored. Measurements were taken on the length of call (defined as the difference, in seconds, between the time the person answers the phone and the time he or she hangs up). Table SH10.2 presents the results (which are stored in the file SH10-2).

TABLE SH10.2

Length of Calls (in Seconds) Based on Presentation Plan

PRESENTATION PLAN		
Structured	**Semistructured**	**Unstructured**
38.8	41.8	32.9
42.1	36.4	36.1
45.2	39.1	39.2
34.8	28.7	29.3
48.3	36.4	41.9
37.8	36.1	31.7
41.1	35.8	35.2
43.6	33.7	38.1

EXERCISE

SH10.4 Analyze the data in Table SH10.2 and write a report to the team that indicates your findings. Be sure to include your recommendations based on your findings.

WEB CASE

Apply your knowledge about hypothesis testing and ANOVA in this Web Case, which continues the cereal-fill packaging dispute Web Case from Chapters 7 and 9.

Even after the recent public experiment about cereal box weights, the Consumers Concerned About Cereal Cheaters (CCACC) remains convinced that Oxford Cereals has misled the public. The group has created and posted a document in which it claims that cereal boxes produced at Plant Number 2 in Springville weigh less than the claimed mean of 368 grams. Visit the CCACC More Cheating page at **www.prenhall.com/Springville/MoreCheating.htm** (or open this Web page file from the Student CD-ROM Web Case folder) and then answer the following:

1. Do the CCACC's results prove that there is a statistically significant difference in the mean weights of cereal boxes produced at Plant Numbers 1 and 2?

2. Perform the appropriate analysis to test the CCACC's hypothesis. What conclusions can you reach based on the data?

After reviewing CCACC's latest posting, Oxford Cereals is complaining that CCACC is guilty of using selective data. Visit Oxford Cereals' response page at **www.prenhall. com/Springville/OC_DataSelective.htm**, or open the `OC_DataSelective.htm` file from the Student CD-ROM Web Case folder and then answer the following:

3. Does Oxford Cereals have a legitimate argument? Why or why not?

4. Assuming that the samples Oxford Cereals has posted were randomly selected, perform the appropriate analysis to resolve the ongoing weight dispute.

5. What conclusions can you reach from your results? If you were called as an expert witness, would you support the claims of the CCACC or the claims of Oxford Cereals? Explain.

REFERENCES

1. Conover, W. J., *Practical Nonparametric Statistics*, 3rd ed. (New York: Wiley, 2000).
2. Daniel, W., *Applied Nonparametric Statistics*, 2nd ed. (Boston: Houghton Mifflin, 1990).
3. *Microsoft Excel 2007* (Redmond, WA: Microsoft Corp., 2007).
4. *Minitab for Windows Version 15* (State College, PA: Minitab, Inc., 2006).
5. Hicks, C. R., and K. V. Turner, *Fundamental Concepts in the Design of Experiments*, 5th ed. (New York: Oxford University Press, 1999).
6. Montgomery, D. M., *Design and Analysis of Experiments*, 6th ed. (New York: Wiley, 2005).
7. Neter, J., M. H. Kutner, C. Nachtsheim, and W. Wasserman, *Applied Linear Statistical Models*, 5th ed. (New York: McGraw-Hill-Irwin, 2005).
8. Satterthwaite, F. E., "An Approximate Distribution of Estimates of Variance Components," *Biometrics Bulletin*, 2(1946): 110–114.
9. Snedecor, G. W., and W. G. Cochran, *Statistical Methods*, 8th ed. (Ames, IA: Iowa State University Press, 1989).
10. Winer, B. J., D. R. Brown, and K. M. Michels, *Statistical Principles in Experimental Design*, 3rd ed. (New York: McGraw-Hill, 1989).

Using Microsoft Excel for Two-Sample Tests and One-Way ANOVA

E10.1 Stacking and Unstacking Data

Unsummarized data for two (or more) samples can be entered as **stacked** or **unstacked** worksheet data. In a stacked arrangement, all the variable values appear in a single column next to a column that identifies the sample to which individual values belong. In an unstacked arrangement, the values for each sample appear in separate columns.

Specific ToolPak procedures or Excel worksheets for analyses involving two or more samples will require that your data be arranged either as stacked or unstacked data. If you need to change stacked data into its unstacked equivalent, you can sort your data by sample and then cut and paste the data of the second sample (now in contiguous rows) to a new column. (Use row 1 in that column to identify the second sample.) Likewise, to stack unstacked data, you can copy the data of the second sample to below the first sample and then add a column that identifies the sample. The `StackedAndUnstacked.xls` workbook illustrates both the stacked and unstacked arrangement of the BLK Cola weekly sales data of Table 10.1 on page 315.

E10.2 Using the Pooled-Variance t test (unsummarized data)

For unsummarized data, you perform the pooled-variance *t* test by using the ToolPak t-Test: Two-Sample Assuming Equal Variances procedure.

Open to the worksheet containing the unsummarized data for the two samples. Select **Tools → Data Analysis** (Excel 97–2003) or **Data → Data Analysis** (Excel 2007). Then select **t-Test: Two-Sample Assuming Equal Variances** from the **Analysis Tools** list and then click **OK**. In the procedure's dialog box (shown at the top of the next column), enter the cell range of one sample as the **Variable 1 Range** and the cell range of the other sample as the **Variable 2 Range**. Enter the **Hypothesized Mean Difference**, click **Labels**, and click **OK**. Results appear on a new worksheet. Figure 10.3 on page 316 shows the results for the Table 10.1 BLK Cola sales data.

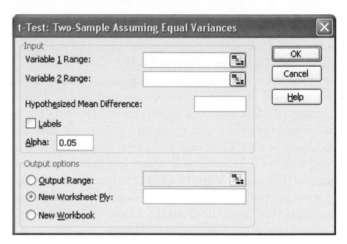

E10.3 Using the Pooled-Variance t test (summarized data)

For summarized data, you perform the pooled-variance *t* test by making entries in the **PVt** worksheet of the `Pooled-Variance T.xls` workbook. This worksheet (see Figure E10.1 and E10.2) uses the **TINV(1-*confidence level, degrees***

	A	B
1	**Pooled-Variance t Test for Differences in Two Means**	
2	(assumes equal population variances)	
3	**Data**	
4	**Hypothesized Difference**	0
5	**Level of Significance**	0.05
6	**Population 1 Sample**	
7	**Sample Size**	10
8	**Sample Mean**	50.3
9	**Sample Standard Deviation**	18.7
10	**Population 2 Sample**	
11	**Sample Size**	10
12	**Sample Mean**	72
13	**Sample Standard Deviation**	12.5
14		
15	**Intermediate Calculations**	
16	Population 1 Sample Degrees of Freedom	9 =B7 - 1
17	Population 2 Sample Degrees of Freedom	9 =B11 - 1
18	Total Degrees of Freedom	18 =B16 + B17
19	Pooled Variance	252.97 =((B16 * B9^2) + (B17 * B13^2))/B18
20	Difference in Sample Means	-21.7 =B8 - B12
21	*t* Test Statistic	-3.0508 =(B20 - B4)/SQRT(B19 * (1/B7 + 1/B11))
22		
23	**Two-Tail Test**	
24	**Lower Critical Value**	-2.1009 =-(TINV(B5, B18))
25	**Upper Critical Value**	2.1009 =TINV(B5, B18)
26	*p*-Value	0.0069 =TDIST(ABS(B21), B18, 2)
27	**Reject the null hypothesis**	=IF(B26 < B5, "Reject the null hypothesis", "Do not reject the null hypothesis")
28		
29	**Lower-Tail Test**	
30	**Lower Critical Value**	-1.7341 =-TINV(2 * B5, B18))
31	*p*-Value	0.0034 =IF(B21 < 0, E32, E33)
32	**Reject the null hypothesis**	=IF(B31 < B5, "Reject the null hypothesis", "Do not reject the null hypothesis")
33		
34	**Upper-Tail Test**	
35	**Upper Critical Value**	1.7341 =(TINV(2 * B5, B18))
36	*p*-Value	0.9966 =IF(B21 < 0, E33, E32)
37	Do not reject the null hypothesis	=IF(B36 < B5, "Reject the null hypothesis", "Do not reject the null hypothesis")

Not shown
Cell E32: =TDIST(ABS(B21), B18, 1)
Cell E33: =1 - E32

FIGURE E10.1 PVt worksheet

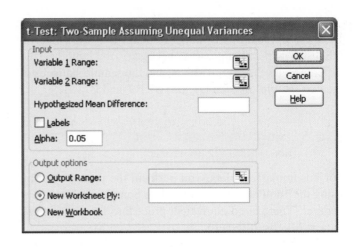

	D	E	
1			
2			
3	**Confidence Interval Estimate**		
4	**of the Difference Between Two Means**		
5			
6	**Data**		
7	Confidence Level	95%	
8			
9	**Intermediate Calculations**		
10	Degrees of Freedom	18	=B16 + B17
11	*t* Value	2.1009	=TINV(1 - E7, E10)
12	Interval Half Width	14.9437	=(E11 * SQRT(B19 * (1/B7 + 1/B11)))
13			
14	**Confidence Interval**		
15	Interval Lower Limit	-36.6437	=B20 - E12
16	Interval Upper Limit	-6.7563	=B20 + E12

FIGURE E10.2 Confidence interval estimate area of PVt worksheet

of freedom) function to determine the lower and upper critical values. The worksheet also uses the **TDIST(ABS(*t*), degrees of freedom, tails)** function, in which **ABS(*t*)** is the absolute value of the *t*-test statistic, and *tails* is either 1, for a one-tail test, or 2, for a two-tail test, to help compute the *p*-values. IF functions in cells B31 and B36 select which one of two values computed in a calculations area (not shown in Figure E10.3) to use. IF functions in cells A27, A32, and A37 determine which one of two phrases will be displayed in those cells.

The worksheet contains entries based on the Table 10.1 BLK Cola weekly sales data. To adapt this worksheet to other problems, change, as is necessary, the hypothesized difference, level of significance, and the sample statistics of the two samples in cells B4, B5, B7:B9, and B11:B13. If you do not want to include a confidence interval estimate in your worksheet (see Figure E10.2), select and delete the cell range D3:E16.

E10.4 Using the Separate-Variance *t* test (unsummarized data)

For unsummarized data, you perform the separate-variance *t* test by using the ToolPak t-Test: Two-Sample Assuming Unequal Variances procedure. (There is no equivalent procedure for summarized data in Microsoft Excel.)

Open to the worksheet containing the unsummarized data for the two samples. Select **Tools → Data Analysis** (Excel 97–2003) or **Data → Data Analysis** (Excel 2007). Then select **t-Test: Two-Sample Assuming Unequal Variances** from the **Data Analysis** list and click **OK**. In the procedure's dialog box (shown at the top of the next column), enter the cell range of one sample as the **Variable 1 Range** and the cell range of the other sample as the **Variable 2 Range**. Enter the **Hypothesized Mean Difference**, click **Labels**, and click **OK**. Figure 10.7 on page 320 shows the results of applying this procedure to the Table 10.1 BLK Cola weekly sales data.

E10.5 Using the Separate-Variance *t* test (summarized data)

For summarized data, you perform the separate-variance *t* test by making entries in the SVt worksheet of the Separate-Variance T.xls workbook. This worksheet (see Figure E10.3) uses the TINV and TDIST functions in ways similar to their use in the pooled-variance worksheet (see Section E10.3). IF functions in cells B32 and B37 select which one of two values computed in a calculations area (not shown in Figure E10.3) to use. IF functions in cells A28, A33, and A38 determine which one of two phrases will be displayed in those cells.

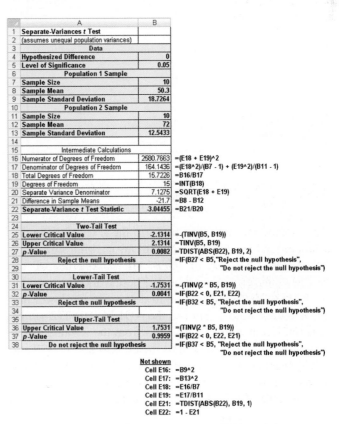

	A	B	
1	**Separate-Variances *t* Test**		
2	(assumes unequal population variances)		
3	**Data**		
4	**Hypothesized Difference**	0	
5	**Level of Significance**	0.05	
6	**Population 1 Sample**		
7	**Sample Size**	10	
8	**Sample Mean**	50.3	
9	**Sample Standard Deviation**	18.7264	
10	**Population 2 Sample**		
11	**Sample Size**	10	
12	**Sample Mean**	72	
13	**Sample Standard Deviation**	12.5433	
14			
15	**Intermediate Calculations**		
16	Numerator of Degrees of Freedom	2580.7663	=(E18 + E19)^2
17	Denominator of Degrees of Freedom	164.1436	=(E18^2)/(B7 - 1) + (E19^2)/(B11 - 1)
18	Total Degrees of Freedom	15.7226	=B16/B17
19	Degrees of Freedom	15	=INT(B18)
20	Separate Variance Denominator	7.1275	=SQRT(E18 + E19)
21	Difference in Sample Means	-21.7	=B8 - B12
22	**Separate-Variance *t* Test Statistic**	-3.04455	=B21/B20
23			
24	**Two-Tail Test**		
25	**Lower Critical Value**	-2.1314	=-(TINV(B5, B19))
26	**Upper Critical Value**	2.1314	=TINV(B5, B19)
27	***p*-Value**	0.0082	=TDIST(ABS(B22), B19, 2)
28	**Reject the null hypothesis**		=IF(B27 < B5, "Reject the null hypothesis",
29			"Do not reject the null hypothesis")
30	**Lower-Tail Test**		
31	**Lower Critical Value**	-1.7531	=-(TINV(2 * B5, B19))
32	***p*-Value**	0.0041	=IF(B22 < 0, E21, E22)
33	**Reject the null hypothesis**		=IF(B32 < B5, "Reject the null hypothesis",
34			"Do not reject the null hypothesis")
35	**Upper-Tail Test**		
36	**Upper Critical Value**	1.7531	=TINV(2 * B5, B19)
37	***p*-Value**	0.9959	=IF(B22 < 0, E22, E21)
38	**Do not reject the null hypothesis**		=IF(B37 < B5, "Reject the null hypothesis",
			"Do not reject the null hypothesis")

Not shown
Cell E16: =B9^2
Cell E17: =B13^2
Cell E18: =E16/B7
Cell E19: =E17/B11
Cell E21: =TDIST(ABS(B22), B19, 1)
Cell E22: =1 - E21

FIGURE E10.3 Separate-variance (SVt) worksheet

The worksheet contains entries based on the Table 10.1 BLK Cola weekly sales data. To adapt this worksheet to other problems, change, as is necessary, the hypothesized difference, level of significance, and the sample statistics of the two samples in cells B4, B5, B7:B9, and B11:B13.

E10.6 Using the Paired t Test (unsummarized data)

For unsummarized data, you perform the paired t test by using the ToolPak t-Test: Paired Two Sample for Mean procedure. (There is no equivalent procedure for summarized data in Microsoft Excel.)

Open to the worksheet containing the unsummarized data for the two samples. Select **Tools → Data Analysis** (Excel 97–2003) or **Data → Data Analysis** (Excel 2007). Then select **t-Test: Paired Two Sample for Means** from the **Data Analysis** list and click **OK**. In the procedure's dialog box (shown below), enter the cell range of one sample as the **Variable 1 Range** and the cell range of the other sample as the **Variable 2 Range**. Enter the **Hypothesized Mean Difference**, click **Labels**, and click **OK**. Figure 10.10 on page 327 shows the results for the Table 10.4 car mileage data.

E10.7 Using the Z Test for the Difference Between Two Proportions

For summarized data, you perform the Z test for the difference between two proportions by making entries in either the **ZTP_TT** or **ZTP_All** worksheets of the **Z Two Proportions.xls** workbook. These worksheets use the **NORMSINV($P<X$)** function to determine the lower and upper critical values and use the **NORMSDIST(Z value)** function to compute the p-values from the Z value calculated in cell B12. IF functions in cell A24 and in A29 and A34 determine which one of two phrases will be displayed in those cells.

The **ZTP_TT** worksheet (see Figure 10.16 on page 334) applies the two-tail Z test to the Section 10.3 guest satisfaction example. The **ZTP_All** worksheet includes the two-tail test, the upper one-tail test, and the lower one-tail test on

one worksheet and contains a confidence interval estimate of the difference between the two proportions. To adapt these worksheets to other problems, enter the hypothesized difference, level of significance, and the number of items of interest and sample size for each sample in cells B4, B5, B7, B8, B10, and B11, as is necessary.

E10.8 Using the F Test for the Difference Between Two Variances (unsummarized data)

For unsummarized data, you use the F test for the difference between two variances by using the ToolPak F Test Two-Sample for Variances procedure.

Open to the worksheet containing the unsummarized data for the two samples. Select **Tools → Data Analysis** (Excel 97–2003) or **Data → Data Analysis** (Excel 2007). Then select **F Test Two-Sample for Variances** from the **Data Analysis** list and click **OK**. In the procedure's dialog box, enter the cell range of one sample as the **Variable 1 Range** and the cell range of the other sample as the **Variable 2 Range**. Click **Labels** and click **OK**. Results appear on a new worksheet. Figure 10.18 on page 340 shows results for the Table 10.1 BLK Cola weekly sales data.

E10.9 Using the F Test for the Difference Between Two Variances (summarized data)

For summarized data, you perform the F test for the difference between two variances by making entries in the **F Two Variances** worksheet of the **F Two Variances.xls** workbook.

The worksheet uses the **FINV(*upper-tailed* p-*value*, *numerator degrees of freedom*, *denominator degrees of freedom*)** function, in which **upper-tailed p-value** is the probability that F will be greater than the value, to compute the upper and lower critical values and **FDIST(F-*test statistic*, *numerator degrees of freedom*, *denominator degrees of freedom*)** function to compute the p-values.

The worksheet (shown in Figure E10.4) applies the F test to the Section 10.4 BLK Cola weekly sales example. Because sample 1 has been defined as the sample with the

	A	B	
1	F Test for Differences in Two Variances		
2			
3	Data		
4	Level of Significance	0.05	
5	Larger-Variance Sample		
6	Sample Size	10	
7	Sample Standard Deviation	18.7264	
8	Smaller-Variance Sample		
9	Sample Size	10	
10	Sample Standard Deviation	12.543	
11			
12	Intermediate Calculations		
13	F Test Statistic	2.2290	=B7^2/B10^2
14	Population 1 Sample Degrees of Freedom	9	=B6 - 1
15	Population 2 Sample Degrees of Freedom	9	=B9 - 1
16			
17	Two-Tail Test		
18	Upper Critical Value	4.0260	=FINV(B4/2, B14, B15)
19	p-Value	0.2482	=2 * E17
20	Do not reject the null hypothesis		=IF(B20 < B4, "Reject the null hypothesis",
21			"Do not reject the null hypothesis")
22	Upper-Tail Test		
23	Upper Critical Value	3.1789	=FINV(B4, B14, B15)
24	p-Value	0.1241	=E17
25	Do not reject the null hypothesis		=IF(B24 < B4, "Reject the null hypothesis",
			"Do not reject the null hypothesis")

Not shown
Cell E17: =FDIST(B13, B14, B15)

FIGURE E10.4 *F* Two Variances worksheet

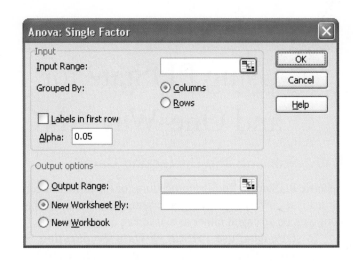

larger variance, a lower-tail test section is unnecessary in this worksheet.

To adapt this worksheet to other problems, change the level of significance and the sample statistics for the two population samples in the tinted cells B4, B6, B7, B9, and B10. Should you inadvertently enter the data of the sample with the largest standard deviation as the "smaller-variance sample," IF functions in cells A28 and A29 (not shown in Figure E10.4) will display messages asking you to review your entries.

E10.10 Using One-Way ANOVA with Multiple Comparisons

You perform a one-way ANOVA with multiple comparisons by first using the ToolPak Anova: Single Factor procedure and then making entries in a worksheet in the Tukey-Kramer.xls workbook.

Open to the worksheet containing unstacked data for the three or more independent groups. Select **Tools → Data Analysis** (Excel 97–2003) or **Data → Data Analysis** (Excel 2007). Then select **Anova: Single Factor** from the **Data Analysis** list and click **OK**. In the procedure's dialog box (shown at the top of the next column), enter the cell range of the data as the **Input Range**, click **Columns** (if necessary), click **Labels in first row**, and click **OK**. Results appear on a new worksheet. Record the sample size and sample mean of each group (found in the Count and Average columns, respectively). Also record the *MSW* value, found in the cell that is the intersection of the **MS** column and **Within Groups** row, and the denominator degrees of freedom, found in the cell that is the intersection of the **df** column and **Within Groups** row.

Next, open the **Tukey-Kramer.xls** workbook and select the worksheet for your number of groups. If you have three groups, select the **TukeyKramer3** worksheet. If you have four groups, select the **TukeyKramer4** worksheet. (There are also worksheets for five, six, and seven groups.) Enter the sample size, sample mean, *MSW* value, and the denominator degrees of freedom you recorded earlier. Then look up the Studentized Range *Q* statistic from Table E.8 on page 564 for the level of significance of 0.05 and the numerator and denominator degrees of freedom values displayed in the worksheet.

To learn about the formulas used in the worksheets, open to the **TukeyKramer4Formulas** worksheet that displays the formulas that are used to compute the results shown in Figure 10.27 on page 351.

E10.11 Using the Levene Test

You perform the Levene test by using the instructions of Section E10.10 with data from an Excel worksheet. Open to the worksheet that contains your unstacked multiple group data. The procedure must contain groups with equal sample sizes.

Add a row of formulas that use the **MEDIAN(*cell range*)** function to compute the median for each group. Then add a new set of columns that compute the absolute differences of each measurement and its corresponding median. Use the worksheets of the Absolute Differences.xls workbook as guides for creating these formulas. Once you create your new columns, follow the instructions of Section E10.10, using the cell range of the set of new absolute difference columns as the **Input Range** cell range. For example, if you were using the **Model** worksheet of the Absolute Differences workbook, you would enter **F1:I6** as the **Input Range**.

APPENDIX P10

Using PHStat2 for Two-Sample Tests and One-Way ANOVA

P10.1 Stacking and Unstacking Data

Specific PHStat2 or ToolPak procedures or Excel worksheets for analyses involving two or more samples will require that your data be arranged either as stacked or unstacked data.

To stack data, use **PHStat → Data Preparation → Stack Data**. This procedure places the data of the **Unstacked Data Cell Range** into a new worksheet containing two columns, one for the sample labels, the other for the data. The **Unstacked Data Cell Range** must be a contiguous multiple-column cell range in which each column contains the data of a sample.

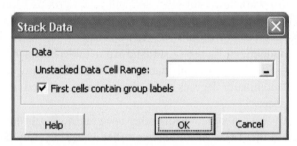

To unstack data, use **PHStat → Data Preparation → Unstack Data**. This procedure places data into a new worksheet in which each column contains the data for one of the samples. The **Grouping Variable Cell Range** must be a single-column cell range containing the sample labels and the **Stacked Data Cell Range** must be a single-column cell range containing the data.

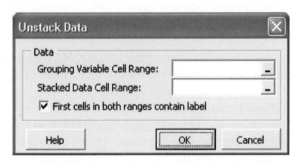

P10.2 Using the Pooled-Variance t Test

To perform the pooled-variance *t* test, use **PHStat → Two-Sample Tests → Pooled-Variance t Test**. This procedure creates a worksheet similar to Figure E10.1 on page 366, based on the test option and the hypothesized difference, level of significance, and the sample statistics values that you specify. If you click **Confidence Interval Estimate**, the worksheet will also include a confidence interval estimate in columns D and E (shown in Figure E10.2 on page 367).

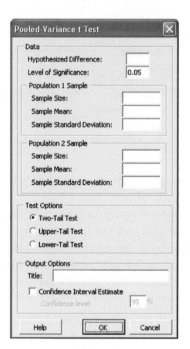

P10.3 Using the Separate-Variance t Test

To perform the separate-variance *t* test, use **PHStat → Two-Sample Tests → Separate-Variance t Test**. This procedure creates a worksheet similar to Figure E10.3 on page 367, based on the test option and the hypothesized difference, level of significance, and the sample statistics values that you specify.

P10.4 Using the *Z* Test for the Difference Between Two Proportions

To perform the *Z* test for the differences in two proportions, use **PHStat → Two-Sample Tests → Z Test for the Differences in Two Proportions**. This procedure creates a worksheet similar to Figure 10.16 on page 334, based on the test option and the null hypothesis, level of significance, number of items of interest, and sample size values that you specify.

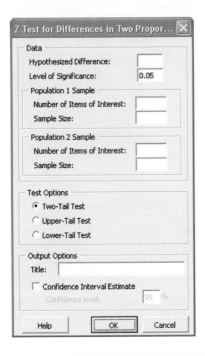

P10.5 Using the *F* Test for the Difference Between Two Variances

To perform the *F* test for the difference between two variances, use **PHStat → Two-Sample Tests → F Test for the Differences in Two Variances**. This procedure creates a worksheet similar to Figure E10.3 on page 367, based on the level of significance, sample statistics values, and the test option that you specify.

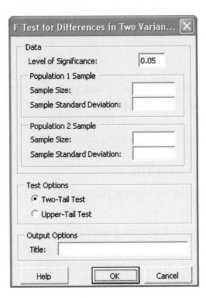

P10.6 Using One-Way ANOVA with Multiple Comparisons

To perform a one-way ANOVA with multiple comparisons, use **PHStat → Multiple-Sample Tests → One-Way ANOVA**. This procedure uses the ToolPak ANOVA: Single Factor procedure to create a worksheet of ANOVA results and then creates a Tukey-Kramer worksheet similar to the ones described in Section E10.10 based on the unstacked data found in the **Group Data Cell Range**.

To complete the analysis, you will need to look up the Studentized Range *Q* statistic from Table E.8 on page 564 for the level of significance (α) equal to 0.05 and the numerator and denominator degrees of freedom displayed in the worksheet.

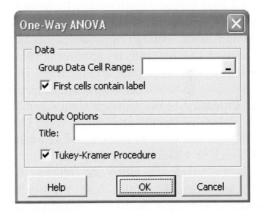

P10.7 Using the Levene Test

To perform the Levene test, use **PHStat → Multiple-Sample Tests → Levene Test**. This procedure runs the ToolPak ANOVA: Single Factor procedure using a worksheet of absolute differences from the median that the procedure creates using the unstacked data from the **Sample Data Cell Range** that you specify. The procedure must contain groups with equal sample sizes.

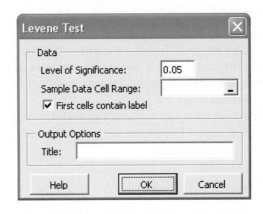

APPENDIX M10

Using Minitab for Two-Sample Tests and One-Way ANOVA

M10.1 Stacking and Unstacking Data

Unsummarized data for two (or more) samples can be entered as **stacked** or **unstacked** worksheet data. As first mentioned in Section M2.1 on pages 75–76, in a stacked arrangement, all the values for a variable appear in a single column next to a column that identifies the sample to which individual values belong. In an unstacked arrangement, the values for each sample appear in separate columns.

Although most Minitab procedures accept either stacked or unstacked data, you may discover situations when you need to change your data arrangement. To change stacked data into its unstacked equivalent, select **Data → Unstack Columns**. In the Unstack Columns dialog box enter the column that identifies the sample in the **Using subscripts in** box. Likewise, to stack unstacked data, select **Data → Stack → Columns** and enter the columns to be stacked in the **Stack the following columns** box. The `Cola.mtw` worksheet illustrates both the stacked and unstacked arrangement of the BLK Cola weekly sales data of Table 10.1 on page 315.

M10.2 Using the *t* Test for the Difference Between Two Means

To illustrate the *t* test of the difference in two means:

1. Open the `Cola.mtw` worksheet.
2. Select **Stat → Basic Statistics → 2-Sample t**.

In the 2-Sample t (Test and Confidence Interval) dialog box (see Figure M10.1):

3. Click **Samples in one column** and enter **Sales** in the **Samples** box and **Display** in the **Subscripts** box. (If you had unstacked data, you would click **Samples in different columns** and enter the column names in the **First** and **Second** boxes.)
4. Click **Assume equal variances** to perform the pooled-variance *t* test. (To perform the separate-variance *t* test, leave this unchecked.)
5. Click **Options**.

In the 2-Sample t - Options dialog box (see Figure M10.2):

6. Leave the **Confidence level** and **Test difference** values unchanged.

7. Select **not equal** from the **Alternative** drop-down list to perform the two-tail test. (To perform a one-tail test, select **less than** or **greater than**.)

8. Click **OK**.

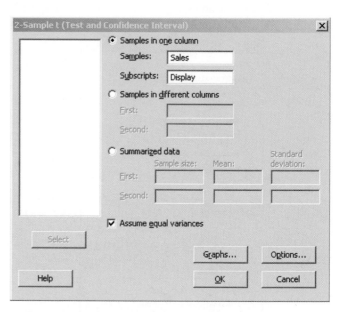

FIGURE M10.1 Minitab 2-Sample t (Test and Confidence Interval) dialog box

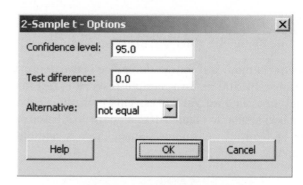

FIGURE M10.2 Minitab 2-Sample t - Options dialog box

9. Back in the 2-Sample t (Test and Confidence Interval) dialog box, click **Graphs**.
10. In the 2-Sample t - Graphs dialog box (not shown), click **Boxplots of data** and then click **OK**.
11. Back in the 2-Sample t (Test and Confidence Interval) dialog box, click **OK**.

To get the results in Figure 10.4 on page 316, you need to unstack the data.

1. Select **Data → Unstack Columns**.
2. Enter **Sales** in the **Unstack the data in** box.
3. Enter **Display** in the **Using subscripts in** box.
4. Click **After last column in use**.

5. Click **OK**.
6. Rename the **Sales_Normal** column as **Normal** and rename the **Sales_End_Aisle** column as **EndAisle**. (This will simplify entering their names.)

Then repeat the 11-step instructions, changing step 3 as follows: Click **Samples in different columns**. Enter **Normal** in the **First** box and enter **EndAisle** in the **Second** box.

M10.3 Using the Paired *t* Test

To illustrate the paired *t* test shown in Figure 10.11 on page 327,

1. Open the AAAMileage.mtw worksheet.
2. Select **Stat → Basic Statistics → Paired t**.

In the Paired t (Test and Confidence Interval) dialog box (see Figure M10.3):

3. Click **Samples in columns**.
4. Enter **Owner** in the **First sample** box.
5. Enter **Government** in the **Second sample** box.
6. Click **Options**.

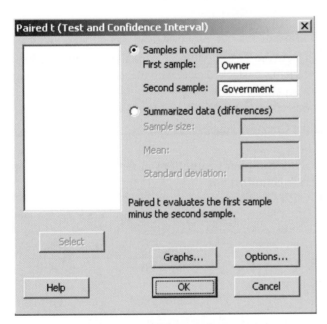

FIGURE M10.3 Minitab Paired t (Test and Confidence Interval) dialog box

In the Paired t - Options dialog box (see Figure M10.4),

7. Leave the **Confidence level** and **Test mean** values unchanged.
8. Select **not equal** from the **Alternative** drop-down list to perform the two-tail test shown in Figure 10.11 on page 327.
9. Click **OK**.
10. Back in the Paired t (Test and Confidence Interval) dialog box, click **Graphs**.

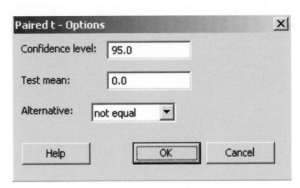

FIGURE M10.4 Minitab Paired t - Options dialog box

In the Paired t - Graphs dialog box (see Figure M10.5),

11. Click **Boxplot of differences**.
12. Click **OK**.
13. Back in the Paired t (Test and Confidence Interval) dialog box, click **OK**.

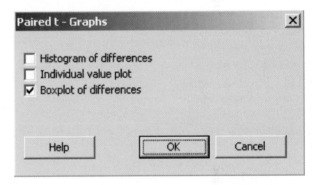

FIGURE M10.5 Minitab Paired t - Graphs dialog box

M10.4 Using the *Z* Test for the Difference Between Two Proportions

To illustrate the test for the difference between two proportions, using the example shown in Figure 10.17 on page 334.

1. Select **Stat → Basic Statistics → 2 Proportions**.

In the 2 Proportions (Test and Confidence Interval) dialog box (see Figure M10.6 on page 374),

2. Click **Summarized data**.
3. In the **First** row, enter **163** in the **Events** box and **227** in the **Trials** box.
4. In the **Second** row, enter **154** in the **Events** box and **262** in the **Trials** box.
5. Click **Options**.

In the 2 Proportions - Options dialog box (see Figure M10.7 on page 374),

6. Leave the **Confidence level** and **Test difference** values unchanged.
7. Select **not equal** from the **Alternative** drop-down list to perform the two-tail test presented in Figure 10.17 on page 334.
8. Click **Use pooled estimate of p for test**.

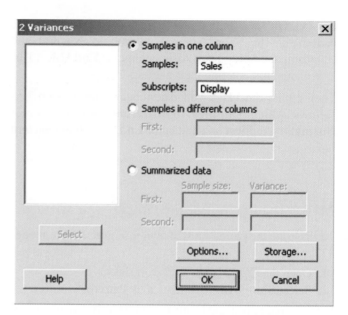

FIGURE M10.6 Minitab 2 Proportions (Test and Confidence Interval) dialog box

FIGURE M10.7 Minitab 2 Proportions - Options dialog box

9. Click **OK**.
10. Back in the 2-Proportions (Test and Confidence Interval) dialog box click **OK**.

M10.5 Using the *F* Test for the Difference Between Two Variances

To illustrate the *F* test of the difference in two variances as shown in Figure 10.19 on page 340,

1. Open the Cola.mtw worksheet.
2. Select **Stat → Basic Statistics → 2 Variances**.

In the 2 Variances dialog box (see Figure M10.8),

3. Click **Samples in one column**.
4. Enter **Sales** in the **Samples** box, and enter **Display** in the **Subscripts** box. (If you have unstacked data, click **Samples in different columns** and enter the names of the two columns in the **First** and **Second** boxes. If you have summarized data instead of the actual data, click

FIGURE M10.8 Minitab 2 Variances dialog box

Summarized data and enter the sample size and variance for each sample.)
5. Click **OK**.

M10.6 Using One-Way ANOVA with Multiple Comparisons

To illustrate the one-way ANOVA:

1. Open the Parachute.mtw worksheet. (This worksheet contains unstacked data, with the data from each group in a separate column.)
2. Select **Stat → ANOVA → One-Way (Unstacked)**.

In the One-Way Analysis of Variance dialog box (see Figure M10.9):

3. Enter **Supplier1-Supplier4** in the **Responses (in separate columns)** box.
4. Click **Comparisons**.

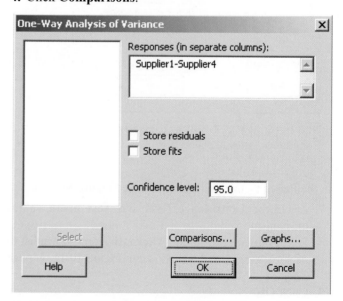

FIGURE M10.9 Minitab One-Way Analysis of Variance dialog box

In the One-Way Multiple Comparisons dialog box (see Figure M10.10):

5. Click **Tukey's, family error rate** and enter **5** in its box. (A family error rate of 5 produces confidence intervals with an overall confidence level of 95%.)

6. Click **OK**.

7. Back in the original dialog box, click **Graphs**.

8. In the One-Way Analysis of Variance - Graphs dialog box (not shown), click **Boxplots of data** and then click **OK**.

9. Back in the original dialog box, click **OK**.

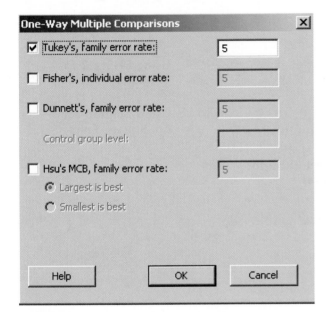

FIGURE M10.10   Minitab One-Way Multiple Comparisons dialog box

For stacked data, replace steps 2 and 3 with these instructions:

2. Select **Stat → ANOVA → Oneway**.

In the One-Way Analysis of Variance dialog box (not shown):

3. Enter the column containing the response variable (**Strength** for the `Parachute.mtw` worksheet) in the **Response** box and enter the column in containing the factor (**Suppliers** for the `Parachute.mtw` worksheet) in the **Factor** box.

M10.7 Creating Main Effects Plots

To illustrate creating a main effects plot:

1. Open the `Parachute.mtw` worksheet.

2. Select **Stat → ANOVA → Main Effects Plot**.

In the Main Effects Plot dialog box (see Figure M10.11):

3. Enter **Strength** in the **Responses** box.

4. Enter **Suppliers** in the **Factors** box.

5. Click **OK**.

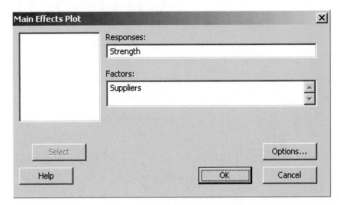

FIGURE M10.11   Minitab Main Effects Plot dialog box

M10.8 Using the Levene Test

To illustrate the Levene test:

1. Open the `Parachute.mtw` worksheet.

2. Select **Stat → ANOVA → Test for Equal Variances**.

In the Test for Equal Variances dialog box (see Figure M10.12):

3. Enter **Strength** in the **Response** box

4. Enter **Suppliers** in the **Factor** box.

5. Enter **95.0** in the **Confidence level** box.

6. Click **OK**.

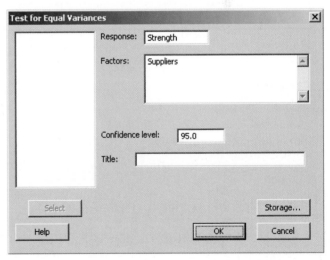

FIGURE M10.12   Minitab Test for Equal Variances dialog box

11

Chi-Square Tests

Learning Objective

In this chapter, you learn:

• How and when to use the chi-square test for contingency tables

@ T.C. Resort Properties

You are the manager of T.C. Resort Properties, a collection of five upscale hotels located on two tropical islands. Guests who are satisfied with the quality of services during their stay are more likely to return on a future vacation and to recommend the hotel to friends and relatives. To assess the quality of services being provided by your hotels, guests are encouraged to complete a satisfaction survey when they check out. You need to analyze the data from these surveys to determine the overall satisfaction with the services provided, the likelihood that the guests will return to the hotel, and the reasons some guests indicate that they will not return. For example, on one island, T.C. Resort Properties operates the Beachcomber and Windsurfer hotels. Is the perceived quality at the Beachcomber Hotel the same as at the Windsurfer Hotel? If a difference is present, how can you use this information to improve the overall quality of service at T.C. Resort Properties? Furthermore, if guests indicate that they are not planning to return, what are the most common reasons given for this decision? Are the reasons given unique to a certain hotel or common to all hotels operated by T.C. Resort Properties?

I n the preceding two chapters, you used hypothesis-testing procedures to analyze both numerical and categorical data. Chapter 9 presented some one-sample tests, and Chapter 10 developed several two-sample tests and the one-way analysis of variance (ANOVA). This chapter extends hypothesis testing to analyze differences between population proportions based on two or more samples, as well as the hypothesis of *independence* in the joint responses to two categorical variables.

11.1 Chi-Square Test for the Difference Between Two Proportions

In Section 10.3, you studied the Z test for the difference between two proportions. In this section, the data are examined from a different perspective. The hypothesis-testing procedure uses a test statistic that is approximated by a chi-square (χ^2) distribution. The results of this χ^2 test are equivalent to those of the Z test described in Section 10.3.

If you are interested in comparing the counts of categorical responses between two independent groups, you can develop a two-way **contingency table** (see Section 2.4) to display the frequency of occurrence of items of interest and items not of interest for each group. In Chapter 4, contingency tables were used to define and study probability.

To illustrate the contingency table, return to the Using Statistics scenario concerning T.C. Resort Properties. On one of the islands, T.C. Resort Properties has two hotels (the Beachcomber and the Windsurfer). In tabulating the responses to the single question "Are you likely to choose this hotel again?" 163 of 227 guests at the Beachcomber responded yes, and 154 of 262 guests at the Windsurfer responded yes. At the 0.05 level of significance, is there evidence of a significant difference in guest satisfaction (as measured by likelihood to return to the hotel) between the two hotels?

The contingency table displayed in Table 11.1 has two rows and two columns and is called a **2 × 2 contingency table**. The cells in the table indicate the frequency for each row and column combination.

TABLE 11.1

Layout of a 2 × 2 Contingency Table

ROW VARIABLE	COLUMN VARIABLE (GROUP)		
	1	2	Totals
Items of interest	X_1	X_2	X
Items not of interest	$n_1 - X_1$	$n_2 - X_2$	$n - X$
Totals	n_1	n_2	n

where

X_1 = number of items of interest in group 1

X_2 = number of items of interest in group 2

$n_1 - X_1$ = number of items that are not of interest in group 1

$n_2 - X_2$ = number of items that are not of interest in group 2

$X = X_1 + X_2$, the total number of items of interest

$n - X = (n_1 - X_1) + (n_2 - X_2)$, the total number of items that are not of interest

n_1 = sample size in group 1

n_2 = sample size in group 2

$n = n_1 + n_2$ = total sample size

Table 11.2 contains the contingency table for the hotel guest satisfaction study. The contingency table has two rows, indicating whether the guests would return to the hotel or would not return to the hotel, and two columns, one for each hotel. The cells in the table indicate the frequency of each row and column combination. The row totals indicate the number of guests who would return to the hotel and those who would not return to the hotel. The column totals are the sample sizes for each hotel location.

TABLE 11.2

2 × 2 Contingency Table for the Hotel Guest Satisfaction Survey

	HOTEL		
CHOOSE HOTEL AGAIN?	**Beachcomber**	**Windsurfer**	**Total**
Yes	163	154	317
No	64	108	172
Total	227	262	489

To test whether the population proportion of guests who would return to the Beachcomber, π_1, is equal to the population proportion of guests who would return to the Windsurfer, π_2, you can use the **χ^2 test for the difference between two proportions**. To test the null hypothesis that there is no difference between the two population proportions:

$$H_0: \pi_1 = \pi_2$$

against the alternative that the two population proportions are not the same:

$$H_1: \pi_1 \neq \pi_2$$

you use the χ^2_{STAT} test statistic, shown in Equation (11.1).

χ^2 TEST FOR THE DIFFERENCE BETWEEN TWO PROPORTIONS

The χ^2_{STAT} test statistic is equal to the squared difference between the observed and expected frequencies, divided by the expected frequency in each cell of the table, summed over all cells of the table.

$$\chi^2_{STAT} = \sum_{\text{all cells}} \frac{(f_o - f_e)^2}{f_e} \qquad \textbf{(11.1)}$$

where

    f_o = **observed frequency** in a particular cell of a contingency table

    f_e = **expected frequency** in a particular cell if the null hypothesis is true

The χ^2_{STAT} test statistic approximately follows a chi-square distribution with 1 degree of freedom.[1]

---

[1] In general, the degrees of freedom in a contingency table are equal to the (number of rows − 1) multiplied by the (number of columns − 1).

To compute the expected frequency, f_e, in any cell, you need to understand that if the null hypothesis is true, the proportion of items of interest in the two populations will be equal. Then the sample proportions you compute from each of the two groups would differ from each other only by chance. Each would provide an estimate of the common population parameter, π. A statistic that combines these two separate estimates together into one overall estimate of the population parameter provides more information than either of the two separate estimates could provide by itself. This statistic, given by the symbol $\bar{p}$, represents the estimated overall proportion of items of interest for the two groups combined (i.e., the total number of items of interest divided by the total sample size). The complement of $\bar{p}$, $1 - \bar{p}$, represents the estimated overall proportion of items that are not of interest in the two groups. Using the notation presented in Table 11.1 on page 378, Equation (11.2) defines $\bar{p}$.

COMPUTING THE ESTIMATED OVERALL PROPORTION FOR 2 GROUPS

$$\bar{p} = \frac{X_1 + X_2}{n_1 + n_2} = \frac{X}{n} \qquad (11.2)$$

To compute the expected frequency, f_e, for each cell pertaining to items of interest (i.e., the cells in the first row in the contingency table), you multiply the sample size (or column total) for a group by $\bar{p}$. To compute the expected frequency, f_e, for each cell pertaining to items that are not of interest (i.e., the cells in the second row in the contingency table), you multiply the sample size (or column total) for a group by $1 - \bar{p}$.

The χ^2_{STAT} test statistic shown in Equation (11.1) on page 379 approximately follows a **chi-square (χ^2) distribution** (see Table E.4) with 1 degree of freedom. Using a level of significance α, you reject the null hypothesis if the computed χ^2_{STAT} test statistic is greater than χ^2_α, the upper-tail critical value from the χ^2 distribution having 1 degree of freedom. Thus, the decision rule is

$$\text{Reject } H_0 \text{ if } \chi^2_{STAT} > \chi^2_\alpha;$$

$$\text{otherwise do not reject } H_0.$$

Figure 11.1 illustrates the decision rule.

FIGURE 11.1

Regions of rejection and nonrejection when using the chi-square test for the difference between two proportions, with level of significance α

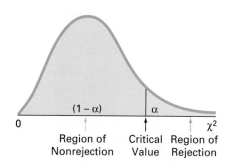

If the null hypothesis is true, the computed χ^2_{STAT} test statistic should be close to zero because the squared difference between what is actually observed in each cell, f_o, and what is theoretically expected, f_e, should be very small. If H_0 is false, then there are differences in the population proportions and the computed χ^2_{STAT} test statistic is expected to be large. However, what is a large difference in a cell is relative. The same actual difference between f_o and f_e from a cell with a small number of expected frequencies contributes more to the χ^2_{STAT} test statistic than a cell with a large number of expected frequencies.

To illustrate the use of the chi-square test for the difference between two proportions, return to the Using Statistics scenario concerning T.C. Resort Properties on page 377 and the corresponding contingency table displayed in Table 11.2 on page 379. The null hypothesis $(H_0: \pi_1 = \pi_2)$ states that there is no difference between the proportion of guests who are likely to choose either of these hotels again. To begin,

$$\bar{p} = \frac{X_1 + X_2}{n_1 + n_2} = \frac{163 + 154}{227 + 262} = \frac{317}{489} = 0.6483$$

$\bar{p}$ is the estimate of the common parameter π, the population proportion of guests who are likely to choose either of these hotels again if the null hypothesis is true. The estimated proportion of guests who are *not* likely to choose these hotels again is the complement of $\bar{p}$, $1 - 0.6483 = 0.3517$. Multiplying these two proportions by the sample size for the Beachcomber Hotel gives the number of guests expected to choose the Beachcomber again and the number not expected to choose this hotel again. In a similar manner, multiplying the two proportions by the Windsurfer Hotel's sample size yields the corresponding expected frequencies for that group.

EXAMPLE 11.1

Computing the Expected Frequencies

Compute the expected frequencies for each of the four cells of Table 11.2 on page 379.

SOLUTION

Yes—Beachcomber: $\bar{p} = 0.6483$ and $n_1 = 227$, so $f_e = 147.16$

Yes—Windsurfer: $\bar{p} = 0.6483$ and $n_2 = 262$, so $f_e = 169.84$

No—Beachcomber: $1 - \bar{p} = 0.3517$ and $n_1 = 227$, so $f_e = 79.84$

No—Windsurfer: $1 - \bar{p} = 0.3517$ and $n_2 = 262$, so $f_e = 92.16$

Table 11.3 presents these expected frequencies next to the corresponding observed frequencies.

TABLE 11.3

Comparing the Observed (f_o) and Expected (f_e) Frequencies

	HOTEL				
	BEACHCOMBER		**WINDSURFER**		
CHOOSE HOTEL AGAIN?	**Observed**	**Expected**	**Observed**	**Expected**	**Total**
Yes	163	147.16	154	169.84	317
No	64	79.84	108	92.16	172
Total	227	227.00	262	262.00	489

To test the null hypothesis that the population proportions are equal:

$$H_0: \pi_1 = \pi_2$$

against the alternative that the population proportions are not equal:

$$H_1: \pi_1 \neq \pi_2$$

you use the observed and expected frequencies from Table 11.3 to compute the χ^2_{STAT} test statistic given by Equation (11.1) on page 379. Table 11.4 presents the calculations.

TABLE 11.4

Computing the χ^2_{STAT} Test Statistic for the Hotel Guest Satisfaction Survey

f_o	f_e	$(f_o - f_e)$	$(f_o - f_e)^2$	$(f_o - f_e)^2/f_e$
163	147.16	15.84	250.91	1.71
154	169.84	−15.84	250.91	1.48
64	79.84	−15.84	250.91	3.14
108	92.16	15.84	250.91	2.72
				9.05

The chi-square (χ^2) distribution is a right-skewed distribution whose shape depends solely on the number of degrees of freedom. You find the critical value for the χ^2 test from Table E.4, a portion of which is presented as Table 11.5.

TABLE 11.5

Finding the Critical Value from the Chi-Square Distribution with 1 Degree of Freedom, Using the 0.05 Level of Significance

	Cumulative Probabilities						
	.005	.01	...	.95	.975	.99	.995
				Upper-Tail Area			
Degrees of Freedom	.995	.99	...	.05	.025	.01	.005
1			...	3.841	5.024	6.635	7.879
2	0.010	0.020	...	5.991	7.378	9.210	10.597
3	0.072	0.115	...	7.815	9.348	11.345	12.838
4	0.207	0.297	...	9.488	11.143	13.277	14.860
5	0.412	0.554	...	11.071	12.833	15.086	16.750

The values in Table 11.5 refer to selected upper-tail areas of the χ^2 distribution. A 2×2 contingency table has $(2 - 1)(2 - 1) = 1$ degree of freedom. Using $\alpha = 0.05$, with 1 degree of freedom, the critical value of χ^2 from Table 11.5 is 3.841. You reject H_0 if the computed χ^2_{STAT} test statistic is greater than 3.841 (see Figure 11.2). Because $\chi^2_{STAT} = 9.05 > 3.841$, you reject H_0. You conclude that the proportion of guests who would return to the Beachcomber is different from the proportion of guests who would return to the Windsurfer.

FIGURE 11.2

Regions of rejection and nonrejection when finding the χ^2 critical value with 1 degree of freedom, at the 0.05 level of significance

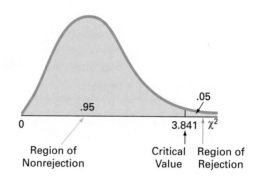

Figure 11.3 represents a Microsoft Excel worksheet for the guest satisfaction contingency table (Table 11.2 on page 379) and Figure 11.4 illustrates Minitab results.

FIGURE 11.3

Microsoft Excel worksheet for the hotel guest satisfaction data

See Section E11.1 or P11.1 to create this.

1	**Guest Satisfaction Analysis**				
2					
3	**Observed Frequencies**				
4		**Hotel**			
5	**Choose Again?**	**Beachcomber**	**Windsurfer**	**Total**	
6	Yes	163	154	317	=SUM(B6:C6)
7	No	64	108	172	=SUM(B7:C7)
8	Total	227	262	489	=SUM(B8:C8)
9					
10	Expected Frequencies				
11		Hotel			
12	Choose Again?	Beachcomber	Windsurfer	Total	
13	Yes	147.1554	169.8446	317	=SUM(B13:C13)
14	No	79.8446	92.1554	172	=SUM(B14:C14)
15	Total	227	262	489	=SUM(B15:C15)
16					
17	**Data**				
18	**Level of Significance**	0.05			
19	Number of Rows	2			
20	Number of Columns	2			
21	Degrees of Freedom	1			
22					
23	**Results**				
24	**Critical Value**	3.8415	=CHIINV(B18, B21)		
25	**Chi-Square Test Statistic**	9.0526	=SUM(F13:G14)		
26	**p-Value**	0.0026	=CHIDIST(B25, B21)		
27	**Reject the null hypothesis**		=IF(B26 < B18, "Reject the null hypothesis",		
28			"Do not reject the null hypothesis")		
29	*Expected frequency assumption*				
30	*is met.*		=IF(OR(B13 < 5, C13 < 5, B14 < 5, C14 < 5),		
			" is violated.", " is met.")		

```
            Expected counts are printed below observed counts
            Chi-Square contributions are printed below expected counts


               Beachcomber  Windsurfer   Total
         1            163          154     317
                   147.16       169.84
                    1.706        1.478

         2             64          108     172
                    79.84        92.16
                    3.144        2.724

      Total           227          262     489

      Chi-Sq = 9.053, DF = 1, P-Value = 0.003
```

These results include the expected frequencies, χ^2_{STAT}, degrees of freedom, and *p*-value. The computed χ^2_{STAT} test statistic is 9.0526, which is greater than the critical value of 3.8415 (or the *p*-value $= 0.0026 < 0.05$), so you reject the null hypothesis that there is no difference in guest satisfaction between the two hotels. The *p*-value of 0.0026 is the probability of observing sample proportions as different as or more different than the actual difference $(0.718 - 0.588 = 0.13)$ observed in the sample data, if the population proportions for the Beachcomber and Windsurfer hotels are equal. Thus, there is strong evidence to conclude that the two hotels are significantly different with respect to guest satisfaction, as measured by whether a guest is likely to return to the hotel again. An examination of Table 11.3 on page 381 indicates that a greater proportion of guests are likely to return to the Beachcomber than to the Windsurfer.

For the χ^2 test to give accurate results for a 2×2 table, you must assume that each expected frequency is at least 5. If this assumption is not satisfied, you can use alternative procedures such as Fisher's exact test (see references 1, 2, and 4).

In the hotel guest satisfaction survey, both the *Z* test based on the standardized normal distribution (see Section 10.3) and the χ^2 test based on the chi-square distribution provide the same conclusion. You can explain this result by the interrelationship between the standardized normal distribution and a chi-square distribution with 1 degree of freedom. For such situations, the χ^2_{STAT} test statistic is the square of the Z_{STAT} test statistic. For instance, in the guest satisfaction study, the computed Z_{STAT} test statistic is $+3.0088$ and the computed χ^2_{STAT} test statistic is 9.0526. Except for rounding error, this latter value is the square of $+3.0088$ [i.e., $(+3.0088)^2 \cong 9.0526$]. Also, if you compare the critical values of the test statistics from the two distributions, at the 0.05 level of significance, the χ^2 value of 3.841 with one degree of freedom is the square of the *Z* value of ± 1.96. Furthermore, the *p*-values for both tests are equal. Therefore, when testing the null hypothesis of equality of proportions:

$$H_0: \pi_1 = \pi_2$$

against the alternative that the population proportions are not equal:

$$H_1: \pi_1 \neq \pi_2$$

the *Z* test and the χ^2 test are equivalent. If you are interested in determining whether there is evidence of a *directional* difference, such as $\pi_1 > \pi_2$, then you must use the *Z* test, with the entire rejection region located in one tail of the standardized normal distribution. In Section 11.2, the χ^2 test is extended to make comparisons and evaluate differences between the proportions among more than two groups. However, you cannot use the *Z* test if there are more than two groups.

Problems for Section 11.1

LEARNING THE BASICS

11.1 Determine the critical value of χ^2 with 1 degree of freedom in each of the following circumstances:
a. $\alpha = 0.01$
b. $\alpha = 0.005$
c. $\alpha = 0.10$

11.2 Determine the critical value of χ^2 with 1 degree of freedom in each of the following circumstances:
a. $\alpha = 0.05$
b. $\alpha = 0.025$
c. $\alpha = 0.01$

11.3 Use the following contingency table:

	A	B	Total
1	20	30	50
2	30	45	75
Total	50	75	125

a. Find the expected frequency for each cell.
b. Compare the observed and expected frequencies for each cell.
c. Compute χ^2_{STAT}. Is it significant at $\alpha = 0.05$?

11.4 Use the following contingency table:

	A	B	Total
1	20	30	50
2	30	20	50
Total	50	50	100

a. Find the expected frequency for each cell.
b. Compute χ^2_{STAT}. Is it significant at $\alpha = 0.05$?

APPLYING THE CONCEPTS

11.5 A sample of 500 shoppers was selected in a large metropolitan area to determine various information concerning consumer behavior. Among the questions asked was, "Do you enjoy shopping for clothing?" The results are summarized in the following contingency table:

ENJOY SHOPPING	GENDER		
FOR CLOTHING	Male	Female	Total
Yes	136	224	360
No	104	36	140
Total	240	260	500

a. Is there evidence of a significant difference between the proportion of males and females who enjoy shopping for clothing at the 0.01 level of significance?

b. Determine the p-value in (a) and interpret its meaning.
c. What are your answers to (a) and (b) if 206 males enjoyed shopping for clothing and 34 did not?
d. Compare the results of (a) through (c) to those of Problem 10.29(a), (b), and (d) on page 336.

11.6 A study funded by the Massachusetts Institute of Technology tested the notion that even when it comes to sugar pills, some people think a costly one works better than a cheap one. Researchers randomly divided 82 healthy paid volunteers into two groups. All the volunteers thought they would be testing a new pain reliever. One group was told the pain reliever they would be using cost $2.50 a pill, and the other group was told it cost only 10 cents a pill. In reality, the pills they were all about to take were simply sugar pills. The volunteers were given a light electric shock on the wrist. Then the volunteers were given a sugar pill, and a short time later shocked again. Of the volunteers who took the expensive pill, 35 of the 41 said they felt less pain afterward. Of the volunteers who took the cheap pill, 25 of the 41 said they felt less pain afterward (R. Rubin, "Placebo Study Tests 'Costlier is Better' Notion," *usatoday.com*, March 5, 2008).
a. Is there evidence of a difference in the proportion of people who think an expensive pill works to reduce pain and the proportion of people who think a cheap pill works to reduce pain at the 0.05 level of significance?
b. Determine the p-value in (a) and interpret its meaning.
c. Why shouldn't you compare the results in (a) to those of Problem 10.30 (b) on p. 337?

11.7 Some people enjoy the *anticipation* of an upcoming product or event and prefer to pay in advance and delay the actual consumption/delivery date. In other cases, people do not want a delay. An article in the *Journal of Marketing Research* reported on an experiment where 50 individuals were told that they had just purchased a ticket to a concert and 50 were told that they had just purchased a personal digital assistant (PDA). The participants were then asked to indicate their preferences for attending the concert or receiving the PDA. Did they prefer tonight or tomorrow, or would they prefer to wait two to four weeks? The individuals were told to ignore their schedule constraints in order to better measure their willingness to delay the consumption/delivery of their purchase. The following table gives partial results of the study.

	Concert	PDA
Tonight or Tomorrow	28	47
Two to Four Weeks	22	3
Total	50	50

Source: *Data adapted from O. Amir and D. Ariely, "Decisions by Rules: The Case of Unwillingness to Pay for Beneficial Delays,"* Journal of Marketing Research, *February 2007, Vol. XLIV, pp. 142–152.*

a. What proportion of the participants would prefer delaying the date of the concert?

b. What proportion of the participants would prefer delaying receipt of a new PDA?

c. Using the 0.05 level of significance, is there evidence of a significant difference in the proportion willing to delay the date of the concert and the proportion willing to delay receipt of a new PDA?

SELF Test **11.8** According to an Ipsos poll, the perception of unfairness in the U.S. tax code is spread fairly evenly across income groups, age groups, and education levels. In an April 2006 survey of 1,005 adults, Ipsos reported that almost 60% of all people said the code is unfair, whereas slightly more than 60% of those making more than $50,000 viewed the code as unfair (data extracted from "People Cry Unfairness," *The Cincinnati Enquirer*, April 16, 2006, p. A8). Suppose that the following contingency table represents the specific breakdown of responses:

U.S. TAX CODE	INCOME LEVEL		
	Less Than $50,000	**More Than $50,000**	**Total**
Fair	225	180	405
Unfair	280	320	600
Total	505	500	1,005

a. At the 0.05 level of significance, is there evidence of a difference in the proportion of adults who think the U.S. tax code is unfair between the two income groups?

b. Determine the *p*-value in (a) and interpret its meaning.

c. Compare the results of (a) and (b) to those of Problem 10.32 on page 337.

11.9 Where people turn to for news is different for various age groups. Suppose that a study conducted on this issue (data extracted from P. Johnson, "Young People Turn to the Web for News," *USA Today*, March 23, 2006, p. 9D) was based on 200 respondents who were between the ages of 36 and 50 and 200 respondents who were above age 50. Of the 200 respondents who were between the ages of 36 and 50, 82 got their news primarily from newspapers. Of the 200 respondents who were above age 50, 104 got their news primarily from newspapers.

a. Construct a 2 × 2 contingency table.

b. Is there evidence of a significant difference in the proportion who get their news primarily from newspapers between those 36 to 50 years old and those above 50 years old? (Use $\alpha = 0.05$.)

c. Determine the *p*-value in (b) and interpret its meaning.

d. Compare the results of (b) and (c) to those of Problem 10.35(a) and (b) on page 338.

11.10 An experiment was conducted to study the choices made in mutual fund selection. Undergraduate and MBA students were presented with different S&P 500 index funds that were identical except for fees. Suppose 100 undergraduate students and 100 MBA students were selected. Partial results are shown as follows:

FUND	STUDENT GROUP	
	Undergraduate	**MBA**
Highest-cost fund	27	18
Not highest-cost fund	73	82

Source: *Data extracted from J. Choi, D. Laibson, and B. Madrian, "Why Does the Law of One Practice Fail? An Experiment on Mutual Funds," www.som.yale.edu/faculty/jjc83/fees.pdf.*

a. At the 0.05 level of significance, is there evidence of a difference between undergraduate and MBA students in the proportion who selected the highest-cost fund?

b. Determine the *p*-value in (a) and interpret its meaning.

c. Compare the results of (a) and (b) to those of Problem 10.34 on page 337.

11.2 Chi-Square Test for Differences Among More Than Two Proportions

In this section, the χ^2 test is extended to compare more than two independent populations. The letter c is used to represent the number of independent populations under consideration. Thus, the contingency table now has two rows and c columns. To test the null hypothesis that there are no differences among the c population proportions:

$$H_0: \pi_1 = \pi_2 = \cdots = \pi_c$$

against the alternative that not all the c population proportions are equal:

$$H_1: \text{Not all } \pi_j \text{ are equal (where } j = 1, 2, \ldots, c)$$

you use Equation (11.1) on page 379:

$$\chi^2_{STAT} = \sum_{all\ cells} \frac{(f_o - f_e)^2}{f_e}$$

where

f_o = observed frequency in a particular cell of a $2 \times c$ contingency table

f_e = expected frequency in a particular cell if the null hypothesis is true

If the null hypothesis is true and the proportions are equal across all c populations, the c sample proportions should differ only by chance. In such a situation, a statistic that combines these c separate estimates into one overall estimate of the population proportion, π, provides more information than any one of the c separate estimates alone. To expand on Equation (11.2) on page 380, the statistic $\bar{p}$ in Equation (11.3) represents the estimated overall proportion for all c groups combined.

COMPUTING THE ESTIMATED OVERALL PROPORTION FOR c GROUPS

$$\bar{p} = \frac{X_1 + X_2 + \cdots + X_c}{n_1 + n_2 + \cdots + n_c} = \frac{X}{n} \qquad \textbf{(11.3)}$$

To compute the expected frequency, f_e, for each cell in the first row in the contingency table, multiply each sample size (or column total) by $\bar{p}$. To compute the expected frequency, f_e, for each cell in the second row in the contingency table, multiply each sample size (or column total) by $(1 - \bar{p})$. The test statistic shown in Equation (11.1) on page 379 approximately follows a chi-square distribution, with degrees of freedom equal to the number of rows in the contingency table minus 1, times the number of columns in the table minus 1. For a **$2 \times c$ contingency table**, there are $c - 1$ degrees of freedom:

$$\text{Degrees of freedom} = (2 - 1)(c - 1) = c - 1$$

Using the level of significance α, you reject the null hypothesis if the computed χ^2_{STAT} test statistic is greater than χ^2_α, the upper-tail critical value from a chi-square distribution with $c - 1$ degrees of freedom. Therefore, the decision rule is

$$\text{Reject } H_0 \text{ if } \chi^2_{STAT} > \chi^2_\alpha;$$

otherwise do not reject H_0.

Figure 11.5 illustrates the decision rule.

FIGURE 11.5

Regions of rejection and nonrejection when testing for differences among c proportions using the χ^2 test

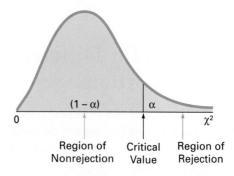

To illustrate the χ^2 test for equality of proportions when there are more than two groups, return to the Using Statistics scenario on page 377 concerning T.C. Resort Properties. A similar survey was recently conducted on a different island on which T.C. Resort Properties has three different hotels. Table 11.6 presents the responses to a question concerning whether guests would be likely to choose this hotel again.

TABLE 11.6

2 × 3 Contingency Table for Guest Satisfaction Survey

	HOTEL			
CHOOSE HOTEL AGAIN?	**Golden Palm**	**Palm Royale**	**Palm Princess**	**Total**
Yes	128	199	186	513
No	88	33	66	187
Total	216	232	252	700

Because the null hypothesis states that there are no differences among the three hotels in the proportion of guests who would likely return again, you use Equation (11.3) to calculate an estimate of π, the population proportion of guests who would likely return again:

$$\bar{p} = \frac{X_1 + X_2 + \cdots + X_c}{n_1 + n_2 + \cdots + n_c} = \frac{X}{n}$$

$$= \frac{(128 + 199 + 186)}{(216 + 232 + 252)} = \frac{513}{700}$$

$$= 0.733$$

The estimated overall proportion of guests who would *not* be likely to return again is the complement, $(1 - \bar{p})$, or 0.267. Multiplying these two proportions by the sample size taken at each hotel yields the expected number of guests who would and would not likely return.

EXAMPLE 11.2

Computing the Expected Frequencies

Compute the expected frequencies for each of the six cells in Table 11.6.

SOLUTION

Yes—Golden Palm: $\bar{p} = 0.733$ and $n_1 = 216$, so $f_e = 158.30$
Yes—Palm Royale: $\bar{p} = 0.733$ and $n_2 = 232$, so $f_e = 170.02$
Yes—Palm Princess: $\bar{p} = 0.733$ and $n_3 = 252$, so $f_e = 184.68$
No—Golden Palm: $1 - \bar{p} = 0.267$ and $n_1 = 216$, so $f_e = 57.70$
No—Palm Royale: $1 - \bar{p} = 0.267$ and $n_2 = 232$, so $f_e = 61.98$
No—Palm Princess: $1 - \bar{p} = 0.267$ and $n_3 = 252$, so $f_e = 67.32$

Table 11.7 presents these expected frequencies.

TABLE 11.7

Contingency Table of Expected Frequencies from a Guest Satisfaction Survey of Three Hotels

	HOTEL			
CHOOSE HOTEL AGAIN?	**Golden Palm**	**Palm Royale**	**Palm Princess**	**Total**
Yes	158.30	170.02	184.68	513
No	57.70	61.98	67.32	187
Total	216.00	232.00	252.00	700

To test the null hypothesis that the proportions are equal:

$$H_0: \pi_1 = \pi_2 = \pi_3$$

against the alternative that not all three proportions are equal:

$$H_1: \text{Not all } \pi_j \text{ are equal (where } j = 1, 2, 3)$$

you use the observed frequencies from Table 11.6 above and the expected frequencies from Table 11.7 to compute the χ^2_{STAT} test statistic [given by Equation (11.1) on page 379]. Table 11.8 presents the calculations.

TABLE 11.8

Computing the χ^2_{STAT} Test Statistic for the Guest Satisfaction Survey of Three Hotels

f_o	f_e	$(f_o - f_e)$	$(f_o - f_e)^2$	$(f_o - f_e)^2/f_e$
128	158.30	−30.30	918.09	5.80
199	170.02	28.98	839.84	4.94
186	184.68	1.32	1.74	0.01
88	57.70	30.30	918.09	15.91
33	61.98	−28.98	839.84	13.55
66	67.32	−1.32	1.74	0.02
				40.23

You use Table E.4 to find the critical value of the χ^2 test statistic. In the guest satisfaction survey, because three hotels are evaluated, there are $(2 - 1)(3 - 1) = 2$ degrees of freedom. Using $\alpha = 0.05$, the χ^2 critical value with 2 degrees of freedom is 5.991. Because the computed χ^2_{STAT} test statistic is 40.23 which is greater than this critical value, you reject the null hypothesis (see Figure 11.6). Microsoft Excel and Minitab (see Figures 11.7 below and 11.8 on page 389) also report the *p*-

FIGURE 11.6

Regions of rejection and nonrejection when testing for differences in three proportions at the 0.05 level of significance, with 2 degrees of freedom

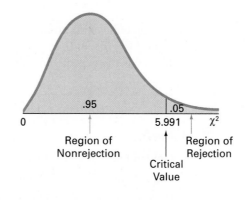

FIGURE 11.7

Microsoft Excel worksheet for the guest satisfaction data of Table 11.6

See Section E11.2 or P11.2 to create this.

	A	B	C	D	E
1	**Guest Satisfaction (3-Hotels) Analysis**				
2					
3		**Observed Frequencies**			
4			**Hotel**		
5	**Choose Again?**	**Golden Palm**	**Palm Royale**	**Palm Princess**	**Total**
6	Yes	128	199	186	513
7	No	88	33	66	187
8	Total	216	232	252	700
9					
10		Expected Frequencies			
11			Hotel		
12	Choose Again?	Golden Palm	Palm Royale	Palm Princess	Total
13	Yes	158.2971	170.0229	184.68	513
14	No	57.7029	61.9771	67.32	187
15	Total	216	232	252	700
16					
17	**Data**				
18	**Level of Significance**	0.05			
19	Number of Rows	2			
20	Number of Columns	3			
21	Degrees of Freedom	2	=(B19 - 1) * (B20 - 1)		
22					
23	**Results**				
24	**Critical Value**	5.9915	=CHIINV(B18, B21)		
25	**Chi-Square Test Statistic**	40.2284	=SUM(G13:I14)		
26	**p-Value**	0.0000	=CHIDIST(B25, B21)		
27	**Reject the null hypothesis**		=IF(B26 < B18, "Reject the null hypothesis",		
28			"Do not reject the null hypothesis")		
29	**Expected frequency assumption**				
30	**is met.**		=IF(OR(B13 < 1, C13 < 1, D13 < 1, B14 < 1, C14 < 1, D14 < 1),		
			" is violated.", " is met.")		

FIGURE 11.8

Minitab results for the guest satisfaction data of Table 11.6

See Section M11.2 to create this.

```
Chi-Square Test: C3, C4, C5

Expected counts are printed below observed counts
Chi-Square contributions are printed below expected counts

              C3       C4       C5    Total
     1       128      199      186      513
          158.30   170.02   184.68
           5.799    4.939    0.009

     2        88       33       66      187
           57.70    61.98    67.32
          15.908   13.548    0.026

  Total      216      232      252      700

  Chi-Sq = 40.228, DF = 2, P-Value = 0.000
```

value. Likewise, because the *p*-value is approximately 0.0000, which is less than $\alpha = 0.05$, you reject the null hypothesis. Further, this *p*-value indicates that there is virtually no chance to see differences this large or larger among the three sample proportions, if the population proportions for the three hotels are equal. Thus, there is sufficient evidence to conclude that the hotel properties are different with respect to the proportion of guests who are likely to return.

For the χ^2 test to give accurate results when dealing with $2 \times c$ contingency tables, all expected frequencies must be large. There is much debate among statisticians about the definition of *large*. Some statisticians (see reference 5) have found that the test gives accurate results as long as all expected frequencies are at least 0.5. Other statisticians, more conservative in their approach, require that no more than 20% of the cells contain expected frequencies less than 5 and no cells have expected frequencies less than 1 (see reference 3). A reasonable compromise between these points of view is to make sure that each expected frequency is at least 1. To ensure that the expected frequencies are sufficiently large to conduct the χ^2 test accurately, you may need to collapse two or more low-expected-frequency categories into one category in the contingency table before performing the test. If combining categories is undesirable, alternative procedures are available (see references 1, 2, and 7).

Problems for Section 11.2

LEARNING THE BASICS

11.11 Consider a contingency table with two rows and five columns.
a. Find the degrees of freedom.
b. Find the critical value for $\alpha = 0.05$.
c. Find the critical value for $\alpha = 0.01$.

11.12 Use the following contingency table:

	A	B	C	Total
1	10	30	50	90
2	40	45	50	135
Total	50	75	100	225

a. Compute the expected frequencies for each cell.
b. Compute χ^2_{STAT}. Is it significant at $\alpha = 0.05$?

11.13 Use the following contingency table:
a. Compute the expected frequencies for each cell.
b. Compute χ^2_{STAT}. Is it significant at $\alpha = 0.05$?

	A	B	C	Total
1	20	30	25	75
2	30	20	25	75
Total	50	50	50	150

APPLYING THE CONCEPTS

11.14 A survey was conducted in five countries. The percentages of respondents who said that they eat out once a week or more are as follows:

Germany	10%
France	12%
United Kindom	28%
Greece	39%
United States	57%

Source: *Data adapted from M. Kissel, "Americans Are Keen on Cocooning," The Wall Street Journal, July 22, 2003, p. D3.*

Suppose that the survey was based on 1,000 respondents in each country.

a. At the 0.05 level of significance, determine whether there is a significant difference in the proportion of people who eat out at least once a week in the various countries.
b. Find the p-value in (a) and interpret its meaning.

11.15 The health-care industry and consumer advocacy groups are at odds over the sharing of a patient's medical records without the patient's consent. The health-care industry believes that no consent should be necessary to openly share data among doctors, hospitals, pharmacies, and insurance companies.

Suppose a study is conducted in which 600 patients are randomly assigned, 200 each, to three "organizational groupings"—insurance companies, pharmacies, and medical researchers. Each patient is given material to read about the advantages and disadvantages concerning the sharing of medical records within the assigned "organizational grouping." Each patient is then asked "would you object to the sharing of your medical records with . . ." and the results are recorded in the cross-classification table below.

OBJECT TO SHARING INFORMATION	ORGANIZATIONAL GROUPING		
	Insurance	Pharmacies	Research
Yes	40	80	90
No	160	120	110

a. Is there evidence of a difference in objection to sharing information among the organizational groupings? (Use $\alpha = 0.05$.)
b. Compute the p-value and interpret its meaning.

✓SELF Test **11.16** More shoppers do the majority of their grocery shopping on Saturday than any other day of the week. However, is there a difference in the various age groups in the proportion of people who do the majority of their grocery shopping on Saturday? A study showed the results for the different age groups (data extracted from "Major Shopping by Day,"

Progressive Grocer Annual Report, April 30, 2002). The data were reported as percentages, and no sample sizes were given:

MAJOR SHOPPING DAY	AGE		
	Under 35	35–54	Over 54
Saturday	24%	28%	12%
A day other than Saturday	76%	72%	88%

Assume that 200 shoppers for each age category were surveyed.

a. Is there evidence of a significant difference among the age groups with respect to major grocery shopping day? (Use $\alpha = 0.05$.)
b. Determine the p-value in (a) and interpret its meaning.
c. Discuss the managerial implications of (a) and (b). How can grocery stores use this information to improve marketing and sales? Be specific.

11.17 Repeat (a) through (b) of Problem 11.16, assuming that only 50 shoppers for each age category were surveyed. Discuss the implications of sample size on the χ^2 test for differences among more than two populations.

11.18 More and more people are finding that they need to delay retirement for financial reasons (data extracted from T. Luhby, "When Retirement Is a Luxury You Can't Afford," *Newsday*, September 30, 2006, pp. B4, B5, B8). A study reported that 52% of men age 62–64 were still working, 41% of women age 62–64 were still working, 31% men age 65–69 were still working, and 23% of women age 65–69 were still working. Suppose that the study was based on a sample size of 100 in each group.

a. Is there evidence of a significant difference among the groups with respect to the proportion who are still working? (Use $\alpha = 0.05$.)
b. Determine the p-value in (a) and interpret its meaning.

11.19 More and more people are paying with plastic (extracted from *USA Today Snapshots*, March 6, 2007, p. 1B). A study taken in 1995 reported that 18% of the respondents paid for a specific type of purchase with plastic, whereas a similar study in 2005 indicated that 25% paid for a specific type of purchase with plastic. (No sample sizes were reported for either study.) Suppose that a new survey taken in 2007 indicated that 31% paid for a specific type of purchase with plastic. Suppose that all three studies used a sample size of 500.

a. Is there evidence of a significant difference among the three years in the proportion of respondents who paid for a specific type of purchase with plastic? (Use $\alpha = 0.05$.)
b. Determine the p-value in (a) and interpret its meaning.

11.3 Chi-Square Test of Independence

In Sections 11.1 and 11.2, you used the χ^2 test to evaluate potential differences among population proportions. For a contingency table that has r rows and c columns, you can generalize the χ^2 test as a *test of independence* for two categorical variables.

For a test of independence, the null and alternative hypotheses follow:

H_0: The two categorical variables are independent (i.e., there is no relationship between them).

H_1: The two categorical variables are dependent (i.e., there is a relationship between them).

Once again, you use Equation (11.1) on page 379 to compute the test statistic:

$$\chi^2_{STAT} = \sum_{all\,cells} \frac{(f_o - f_e)^2}{f_e}$$

You reject the null hypothesis at the α level of significance if the computed value of the χ^2_{STAT} test statistic is greater than χ^2_α, the upper-tail critical value from a chi-square distribution with $(r - 1)(c - 1)$ degrees of freedom (see Figure 11.9). Thus, the decision rule is

Reject H_0 if $\chi^2_{STAT} > \chi^2_\alpha$;

otherwise do not reject H_0.

FIGURE 11.9

Regions of rejection and nonrejection when testing for independence in an $r \times c$ contingency table, using the χ^2 test

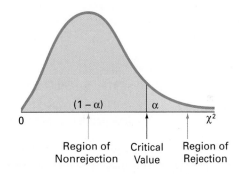

The χ^2 **test of independence** is similar to the χ^2 test for equality of proportions. The test statistics and the decision rules are the same, but the stated hypotheses and conclusions are different. For example, in the guest satisfaction survey of Sections 11.1 and 11.2, there is evidence of a significant difference between the hotels with respect to the proportion of guests who would return. From a different viewpoint, you could conclude that there is a significant relationship between the hotels and the likelihood that a guest would return. Nevertheless, there is a fundamental difference between the two types of tests. The major difference is in how the samples are selected.

In a test for equality of proportions, there is one factor of interest, with two or more levels. These levels represent samples drawn from independent populations. The categorical responses in each sample group or level are classified into two categories, such as *item of interest* and *not an item of interest*. The objective is to make comparisons and evaluate differences between the proportions of *the items of interest* among the various levels. However, in a test for independence, there are two factors of interest, each of which has two or more levels. You select one sample and tally the joint responses to the two categorical variables into the cells of a contingency table.

To illustrate the χ^2 test for independence, suppose that, in the survey on hotel guest satisfaction, a second question was asked of all respondents who indicated that they were not likely to return. These guests were asked to indicate the primary reason for their response. Table 11.9 presents the resulting 4 × 3 contingency table.

In Table 11.9, observe that of the primary reasons for not planning to return to the hotel, 67 were due to price, 60 were due to location, 31 were due to room accommodation, and 29 were

PRIMARY REASON FOR NOT RETURNING	HOTEL			
	Golden Palm	**Palm Royale**	**Palm Princess**	**Total**
Price	23	7	37	67
Location	39	13	8	60
Room accommodation	13	5	13	31
Other	13	8	8	29
Total	88	33	66	187

due to other reasons. As in Table 11.6 on page 387, there were 88 guests in the Golden Palm, 33 guests in the Palm Royale, and 66 guests in the Palm Princess who were not planning to return. The observed frequencies in the cells of the 4×3 contingency table represent the joint tallies of the sampled guests with respect to primary reason for not returning and the hotel.

The null and alternative hypotheses are:

H_0: There is no relationship between the primary reason for not returning and the hotel.

H_1: There is a relationship between the primary reason for not returning and the hotel.

To test this null hypothesis of independence against the alternative that there is a relationship between the two categorical variables, you use Equation (11.1) on page 379 to compute the test statistic:

$$\chi^2_{STAT} = \sum_{all\ cells} \frac{(f_o - f_e)^2}{f_e}$$

where

f_o = observed frequency in a particular cell of the $r \times c$ contingency table

f_e = expected frequency in a particular cell if the null hypothesis of independence were true

To compute the expected frequency, f_e, in any cell, you use the multiplication rule for independent events discussed on page 140 [see Equation (4.7)]. For example, under the null hypothesis of independence, the probability of responses expected in the upper-left-corner cell representing primary reason of price for the Golden Palm is the product of the two separate probabilities: $P(Price)$ and $P(Golden\ Palm)$. Here, the proportion of reasons that are due to price, $P(Price)$, is $67/187 = 0.3583$, and the proportion of all responses from the Golden Palm, $P(Golden\ Palm)$, is $88/187 = 0.4706$. If the null hypothesis is true, then the primary reason for not returning and the hotel are independent:

$$P(Price\ and\ Golden\ Palm) = P(Price) \times P(Golden\ Palm)$$
$$= (0.3583) \times (0.4706)$$
$$= 0.1686$$

The expected frequency is the product of the overall sample size, n, and this probability, $187 \times 0.1686 = 31.53$. The f_e values for the remaining cells are calculated in a similar manner (see Table 11.10).

Equation (11.4) presents a simpler way to compute the expected frequency.

COMPUTING THE EXPECTED FREQUENCY

The expected frequency in a cell is the product of its Row total and Column total, divided by the overall sample size.

$$f_e = \frac{Row\ total \times Column\ total}{n} \qquad (11.4)$$

where

$$\text{row total} = \text{sum of all the frequencies in the row}$$

$$\text{column total} = \text{sum of all the frequencies in the column}$$

$$n = \text{overall sample size}$$

For example, using Equation (11.4) for the upper-left-corner cell (price for the Golden Palm),

$$f_e = \frac{\text{Row total} \times \text{Column total}}{n} = \frac{(67)(88)}{187} = 31.53$$

and for the lower-right-corner cell (other reason for the Palm Princess),

$$f_e = \frac{\text{Row total} \times \text{Column total}}{n} = \frac{(29)(66)}{187} = 10.24$$

Table 11.10 lists the entire set of f_e values.

TABLE 11.10

Contingency Table of Expected Frequencies of Primary Reason for Not Returning with Hotel

PRIMARY REASON FOR NOT RETURNING	HOTEL			
	Golden Palm	Palm Royale	Palm Princess	Total
Price	31.53	11.82	23.65	67
Location	28.24	10.59	21.18	60
Room accommodation	14.59	5.47	10.94	31
Other	13.65	5.12	10.24	29
Total	88.00	33.00	66.00	187

To perform the test of independence, you use the χ^2_{STAT} test statistic shown in Equation (11.1) on page 379. The χ^2_{STAT} test statistic approximately follows a chi-square distribution, with degrees of freedom equal to the number of rows in the contingency table minus 1, times the number of columns in the table minus 1:

$$\text{Degrees of freedom} = (r - 1)(c - 1)$$
$$= (4 - 1)(3 - 1) = 6$$

Table 11.11 illustrates the computations for the χ^2_{STAT} test statistic.

TABLE 11.11

Computing the χ^2_{STAT} Test Statistic for the Test of Independence

Cell	f_o	f_e	$(f_o - f_e)$	$(f_o - f_e)^2$	$(f_o - f_e)^2/f_e$
Price/Golden Palm	23	31.53	−8.53	72.76	2.31
Price/Palm Royale	7	11.82	−4.82	23.23	1.97
Price/Palm Princess	37	23.65	13.35	178.22	7.54
Location/Golden Palm	39	28.24	10.76	115.78	4.10
Location/Palm Royale	13	10.59	2.41	5.81	0.55
Location/Palm Princess	8	21.18	−13.18	173.71	8.20
Room/Golden Palm	13	14.59	−1.59	2.53	0.17
Room/Palm Royale	5	5.47	−0.47	0.22	0.04
Room/Palm Princess	13	10.94	2.06	4.24	0.39
Other/Golden Palm	13	13.65	−0.65	0.42	0.03
Other/Palm Royale	8	5.12	2.88	8.29	1.62
Other/Palm Princess	8	10.24	−2.24	5.02	0.49
					27.41

Using the level of significance $\alpha = 0.05$, the upper-tail critical value from the chi-square distribution with 6 degrees of freedom is 12.592 (see Table E.4). Because $\chi^2_{STAT} = 27.41 > 12.592$, you reject the null hypothesis of independence (see Figure 11.10).

FIGURE 11.10

Regions of rejection and nonrejection when testing for independence in the hotel guest satisfaction survey example at the 0.05 level of significance, with 6 degrees of freedom

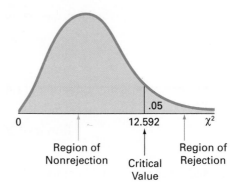

You can use the Microsoft Excel worksheet in Figure 11.11 or the Minitab results of Figure 11.12 on page 395 to conduct the test of independence using the p-value approach. Because the p-value $= 0.0001 < 0.05$, you reject the null hypothesis of independence. The p-value indicates that there is virtually no chance of having a relationship this strong or stronger between hotels and primary reasons for not returning in a sample, if the primary reasons for not returning are independent of the specific hotels in the entire population. Thus, there is strong evidence of a relationship between primary reason for not returning and the hotel.

Examination of the observed and expected frequencies (see Table 11.11) reveals that price is underrepresented as a reason for not returning to the Golden Palm (i.e., $f_o = 23$ and $f_e = 31.53$) but is overrepresented at the Palm Princess. Guests are more satisfied with the price at the Golden

FIGURE 11.11

Microsoft Excel worksheet for the 4 × 3 contingency table for primary reason for not returning and hotel

See Section E11.3 or P11.3 to create this.

	A	B	C	D	E
1	**Cross-Classification Hotel Analysis**				
2					
3			**Observed Frequencies**		
4			**Hotel**		
5	**Reason for Not Returning**	**Golden Palm**	**Palm Royale**	**Palm Princess**	**Total**
6	Price	23	7	37	67
7	Location	39	13	8	60
8	Room accommodation	13	5	13	31
9	Other	13	8	8	29
10	Total	88	33	66	187
11					
12			Expected Frequencies		
13			Hotel		
14	Reason for Not Returning	Golden Palm	Palm Royale	Palm Princess	Total
15	Price	31.5294	11.8235	23.6471	67
16	Location	28.2353	10.5882	21.1765	60
17	Room accommodation	14.5882	5.4706	10.9412	31
18	Other	13.6471	5.1176	10.2353	29
19	Total	88	33	66	187
20					
21	**Data**				
22	**Level of Significance**	0.05			
23	Number of Rows	4			
24	Number of Columns	3			
25	Degrees of Freedom	6	=(B23 - 1) * (B24 - 1)		
26					
27	**Results**				
28	**Critical Value**	12.5916	=CHIINV(B22, B25)		
29	**Chi-Square Test Statistic**	27.4104	=SUM(G15:I18)		
30	**p-Value**	0.0001	=CHIDIST(B29, B25)		
31	**Reject the null hypothesis**		=IF(B30 < B22, "Reject the null hypothesis",		
32			"Do not reject the null hypothesis')		
33	**Expected frequency assumption**				
34	***is met.***		=IF(OR(B15 < 1, C15 < 1, D15 < 1, B16 < 1, C16 < 1 ,D16 < 1,		
			B17 < 1, C17 < 1, D17 < 1, B18 < 1, C18 < 1, D18 < 1)		
			" is violated."," is met.")		

FIGURE 11.12

Minitab results for the 4 × 3 contingency table for primary reason for not returning and hotel

See Section M11.2 to create this.

```
Expected counts are printed below observed counts
Chi-Square contributions are printed below expected counts

          C6      C7      C8   Total
   1      23       7      37      67
        31.53   11.82   23.65
        2.307   1.968   7.540

   2      39      13       8      60
        28.24   10.59   21.18
        4.104   0.549   8.199

   3      13       5      13      31
        14.59    5.47   10.94
        0.173   0.040   0.387

   4      13       8       8      29
        13.65    5.12   10.24
        0.031   1.623   0.488

Total     88      33      66     187

Chi-Sq = 27.410, DF = 6, P-Value = 0.000
```

Palm compared to the Palm Princess. Location is overrepresented as a reason for not returning to the Golden Palm but greatly underrepresented at the Palm Princess. Thus, guests are much more satisfied with the location of the Palm Princess than that of the Golden Palm.

To ensure accurate results, all expected frequencies need to be large in order to use the χ^2 test when dealing with $r \times c$ contingency tables. As in the case of $2 \times c$ contingency tables in Section 11.2, all expected frequencies should be at least 1. For cases in which one or more expected frequencies are less than 1, you can use the test after collapsing two or more low-frequency rows into one row (or collapsing two or more low-frequency columns into one column). Merging of rows or columns usually results in expected frequencies sufficiently large to conduct the χ^2 test accurately.

Problems for Section 11.3

LEARNING THE BASICS

11.20 If a contingency table has three rows and four columns, how many degrees of freedom are there for the χ^2 test for independence?

11.21 When performing a χ^2 test for independence in a contingency table with r rows and c columns, determine the upper-tail critical value of the test statistic in each of the following circumstances:
a. $\alpha = 0.05$, $r = 4$ rows, $c = 5$ columns
b. $\alpha = 0.01$, $r = 4$ rows, $c = 5$ columns
c. $\alpha = 0.01$, $r = 4$ rows, $c = 6$ columns
d. $\alpha = 0.01$, $r = 3$ rows, $c = 6$ columns
e. $\alpha = 0.01$, $r = 6$ rows, $c = 3$ columns

APPLYING THE CONCEPTS

11.22 The Committee of 200 is an international not-for-profit association comprised of preeminent business-women who collectively control over $100 billion annually in revenue. According to the association's Web site, **www.c200.org**, the purpose of the Committee of 200 "is to meet the needs of our membership in areas of business synergies, leadership advancement, education, mentoring, and recognition. Additionally, as an agent of change, we want to improve opportunities for women business leaders, be a source for governmental representation, and a source for research on issues relevant to women in business." The association sponsored a survey where MBAs from top business schools were asked if executives were paid too much. The responses (in percentages, but without sample sizes) are in the following table and were published in "Snapshots: Are Execs Paid Too Much?" *USA Today*, **www.usatoday.com**, January 15, 2007.

	Yes	No	Neutral
Women	61%	11%	28%
Men	49%	27%	24%

a. Do you think executives are paid too much?
b. Suppose that the survey was based on 100 males and 100 females. Using the 0.01 level of significance, perform a hypothesis test to see if you can prove that men and women feel differently about executive pay.
c. Suppose that the survey was based on 200 males and 200 females. Using the 0.01 level of significance, perform a hypothesis test to see if you can prove that men and women feel differently about executive pay.
d. Discuss the importance of sample size on reporting survey results.

11.23 *USA Today* reported on preferred types of office communication by different age groups ("Talking Face to Face vs. Group Meetings," *USA Today*, October 13, 2003, p. A1). Suppose the results were based on a survey of 500 respondents in each age group. The results are cross-classified in the following table:

	TYPE OF COMMUNICATION PREFERRED				
		Face-to-Face Meetings			
	Group	with			
AGE GROUP	Meetings	Individuals	E-mails	Other	Total
Generation Y	180	260	50	10	500
Generation X	210	190	65	35	500
Boomer	205	195	65	35	500
Mature	200	195	50	55	500
Total	795	840	230	135	2,000

Source: *Data extracted from "Talking Face to Face vs. Group Meetings,"* USA Today, *October 13, 2003, p. A1.*

At the 0.05 level of significance, is there evidence of a relationship between age group and type of communication preferred?

SELF Test **11.24** A large corporation is interested in determining whether a relationship exists between the commuting time of its employees and the level of stress-related problems observed on the job. A study of 116 assembly-line workers reveals the following:

	STRESS LEVEL			
COMMUTING TIME	High	Moderate	Low	Total
Under 15 min.	9	5	18	32
15–45 min.	17	8	28	53
Over 45 min.	18	6	7	31
Total	44	19	53	116

a. At the 0.01 level of significance, is there evidence of a significant relationship between commuting time and stress level?
b. What is your answer to (a) if you use the 0.05 level of significance?

11.25 Where people turn to for news is different for various age groups. A study indicated where different age groups primarily get their news:

	AGE GROUP		
MEDIA	Under 36	36–50	50 +
Local TV	107	119	133
National TV	73	102	127
Radio	75	97	109
Local newspaper	52	79	107
Internet	95	83	76

At the 0.05 level of significance, is there evidence of a significant relationship between the age group and where people primarily get their news? If so, explain the relationship.

11.26 *USA Today* reported on when the decision of what to have for dinner is made. Suppose the results were based on a survey of 1,000 respondents and considered whether the household included any children under 18 years old. The results were cross-classified in the following table:

	TYPE OF HOUSEHOLD		
WHEN DECISION MADE	One Adult/ No Children	Two or More Adults/ Children	Two or More Adults/ No Children
Just before eating	162	54	154
In the afternoon	73	38	69
In the morning	59	58	53
A few days before	21	64	45
The night before	15	50	45
Always eat the same thing on this night	2	16	2
Not sure	7	6	7

Source: *Data extracted from "What's for Dinner,"* USA Today, *January 10, 2000.*

At the 0.05 level of significance, is there evidence of a significant relationship between when the decision is made of what to have for dinner and the type of household?

USING STATISTICS @ T.C. Resort Properties Revisited

I n the Using Statistics scenario, you were the manager of T.C. Resort Properties, a collection of five upscale hotels located on two tropical islands. To assess the quality of services being provided by your hotels, guests are encouraged to complete a satisfaction survey when they check out. You analyzed the data from these surveys to determine the overall satisfaction with the services provided, the likelihood that the guests will return to the hotel, and the reasons given by some guests for not wanting to return.

On one island, T.C. Resort Properties operates the Beachcomber and Windsurfer hotels. You performed a chi-square test for the difference in two proportions and concluded that a greater proportion of guests are willing to return to the Beachcomber Hotel than to the Windsurfer. On the other island, T.C. Resort Properties operates the Golden Palm, Palm Royale, and Palm Princess hotels. To see if guest satisfaction was the same among the three hotels, you performed a chi-square test for the differences among more than two proportions. The test confirmed that the three proportions are not equal, and guests are most likely to return to the Palm Royale, and least likely to return to the Golden Palm.

In addition, you investigated whether the reasons given for not returning to the Golden Palm, Palm Royale, and Palm Princess were unique to a certain hotel or common to all three hotels. By performing a chi-square test of independence, you determined that the reasons given for wanting to return or not depended on which hotel they had been staying in. By examining the observed and expected frequencies, you concluded that guests are more satisfied with the price at the Golden Palm, and were much more satisfied with the location of the Palm Princess. Guest satisfaction with room accommodations was not significantly different among the three hotels.

SUMMARY

Figure 11.13 presents a roadmap for this chapter. For analyzing categorical response data from two samples, a chi-square test was presented. This chi-square test is equivalent to the Z test based on the standardized normal distribution in Section 10.3. Then, the chi-square test was generalized for use in analyzing categorical response data from three or more samples. In addition, the rules of probability from Section 4.2 were extended to the hypothesis of independence in the joint responses to two categorical variables.

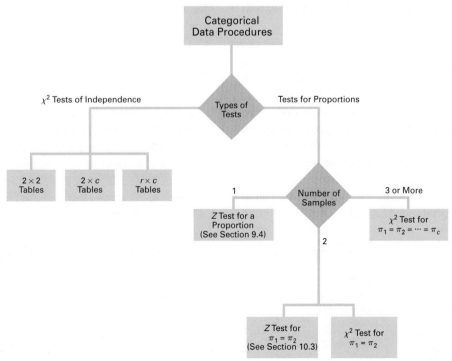

FIGURE 11.13 Roadmap of Chapter 11

KEY EQUATIONS

χ^2 Test for the Difference Between Two Proportions

$$\chi^2_{STAT} = \sum_{all\ cells} \frac{(f_0 - f_e)^2}{f_e} \qquad \textbf{(11.1)}$$

Computing the Estimated Overall Proportion for 2 Groups

$$\bar{p} = \frac{X_1 + X_2}{n_1 + n_2} = \frac{X}{n} \qquad \textbf{(11.2)}$$

Computing the Estimated Overall Proportion for c Groups

$$\bar{p} = \frac{X_1 + X_2 + \cdots + X_c}{n_1 + n_2 + \cdots + n_c} = \frac{X}{n} \qquad \textbf{(11.3)}$$

Computing the Expected Frequencies

$$f_e = \frac{\text{Row total} \times \text{Column total}}{n} \qquad \textbf{(11.4)}$$

KEY TERMS

chi-square (χ^2) distribution   380
chi-square (χ^2) test of independence   391
chi-square (χ^2) test for the difference between two proportions   379

contingency table   378
expected frequency (f_e) 379
observed frequency (f_o) 379

$2 \times c$ contingency table   386
2×2 contingency table   378

CHAPTER REVIEW PROBLEMS

CHECKING YOUR UNDERSTANDING

11.27 Under what conditions should you use the χ^2 test to determine whether there is a difference between the proportions of two independent populations?

11.28 Under what conditions should you use the χ^2 test to determine whether there is a difference between the proportions of more than two independent populations?

11.29 Under what conditions should you use the χ^2 test of independence?

APPLYING THE CONCEPTS

11.30 Undergraduate students at Miami University in Oxford, Ohio, were surveyed in order to evaluate the effect of gender and price on purchasing a pizza from Pizza Hut. Students were told to suppose that they were planning on having a large two-topping pizza delivered to their residence that evening. The students had to decide between ordering from Pizza Hut at a reduced price of $8.49 (the regular price for a large two-topping pizza from the Oxford Pizza Hut at this time was $11.49) and ordering a pizza from a different pizzeria. The results from this question are summarized in the following contingency table:

	PIZZERIA		
GENDER	**Pizza Hut**	**Other**	**Total**
Female	4	13	17
Male	6	12	18
Total	10	25	35

The survey also evaluated purchase decisions at other prices. These results are summarized in the following contingency table:

	PRICE			
PIZZERIA	**$8.49**	**$11.49**	**$14.49**	**Total**
Pizza Hut	10	5	2	17
Other	25	23	27	75
Total	35	28	29	92

a. Using a 0.05 level of significance and using the data in the first contingency table, is there evidence of a significant relationship between a student's gender and his or her pizzeria selection?

b. What is your answer to (a) if nine of the male students selected Pizza Hut and nine selected other?

c. Using a 0.05 level of significance and using the data in the second contingency table, is there evidence of a difference in pizzeria selection based on price?

d. Determine the p-value in (c) and interpret its meaning.

11.31 Many companies are finding that customers are using various types of online content before purchasing products (data extracted from K. Spors, "How Are We Doing?" *The Wall Street Journal*, November 13, 2006, p. R9). The following results are the percentages of older adults (over age 45), younger adults (21–45), and youths (below 21) who use various sources of online content. Suppose the survey was based on 100 older adults, 100 younger adults, and 100 youths.

TYPE OF ONLINE CONTENT	USE ONLINE CONTENT		
	Older Adults	Younger Adults	Youth
Customer product ratings/ reviews	71	78	81
For sale listings with seller ratings	69	72	77
For sale listings without seller ratings	58	60	65
Online classified ads	57	59	66
Message-board posts	57	65	71
Webblogs	55	61	67
Dating site profiles/personals	49	52	59
Peer-generated and peer-reference information	49	55	68
Peer-posted event listings	46	53	71

For *each type of online content*, is there a significant difference among the age groups in the proportion who use the type of online content? (Use $\alpha = 0.05$.)

11.32 A company is considering an organizational change by adopting the use of self-managed work teams. To assess the attitudes of employees of the company toward this change, a sample of 400 employees is selected and asked whether they favor the institution of self-managed work teams in the organization. Three responses are permitted: favor, neutral, or oppose. The results of the survey, cross-classified by type of job and attitude toward self-managed work teams, are summarized as follows:

TYPE OF JOB	SELF-MANAGED WORK TEAMS			
	Favor	Neutral	Oppose	Total
Hourly worker	108	46	71	225
Supervisor	18	12	30	60
Middle management	35	14	26	75
Upper management	24	7	9	40
Total	185	79	136	400

a. At the 0.05 level of significance, is there evidence of a relationship between attitude toward self-managed work teams and type of job?

The survey also asked respondents about their attitudes toward instituting a policy whereby an employee could take one additional vacation day per month without pay. The results, cross-classified by type of job, are as follows:

TYPE OF JOB	VACATION TIME WITHOUT PAY			
	Favor	Neutral	Oppose	Total
Hourly worker	135	23	67	225
Supervisor	39	7	14	60
Middle management	47	6	22	75
Upper management	26	6	8	40
Total	247	42	111	400

b. At the 0.05 level of significance, is there evidence of a relationship between attitude toward vacation time without pay and type of job?

11.33 A company that produces and markets recorded DVDs continuing education programs for the financial industry has traditionally mailed sample DVDs that contain previews of the programs to prospective customers. Customers then agree to purchase the DVDs or return the sample DVDs. A group of sales representatives studied how to increase sales and found that many prospective customers believed it was difficult to tell from a sample DVD alone whether the educational programs would meet their needs. The sales representatives performed an experiment to test whether sending the complete DVDs for review by customers would increase sales. They selected 80 customers from the mailing list and randomly assigned 40 to receive the sample DVDs and 40 to receive the full-program DVDs for review. They then determined the number of DVDs that were purchased and returned in each group. The results of the experiment are as follows:

ACTION	TYPE OF DVD RECEIVED		
	Sample	Full	Total
Purchased	6	14	20
Returned	34	26	60
Total	40	40	80

a. At the 0.05 level of significance, is there evidence of a difference in the proportion of DVDs purchased on the basis of the type of DVD sent to the customer?
b. On the basis of the results of (a), which type do you think a representative should send in the future? Explain the rationale for your decision.

The sales representatives also wanted to determine which of three initial sales approaches result in the most sales: (1) a sales-information DVD mailed to prospective customers, (2) a personal sales call to prospective customers, and (3) a telephone call to prospective customers. A random sample of 300 prospective customers was selected, and 100 were randomly assigned to each of the three sales approaches.

The results, in terms of purchases of the full-program DVD, are as follows:

ACTION	SALES APPROACH			
	DVD	Personal Sales Call	Telephone	Total
Purchase	19	27	14	60
Don't purchase	81	73	86	240
Total	100	100	100	300

c. At the 0.05 level of significance, is there evidence of a difference in the proportion of DVDs purchased on the basis of the sales strategy used?

d. On the basis of the results of (c), which sales approach do you think a representative should use in the future? Explain the rationale for your decision.

11.34 Researchers studied the goals and outcomes of 349 work teams from various manufacturing companies in Ohio. In the first table, teams are categorized as to whether they had specified environmental improvements as a goal and also according to one of four types of manufacturing processes that best described their workplace. The following three tables indicate different outcomes the teams accomplished, based on whether the team had specified cost cutting as one of the team goals.

TYPE OF MANUFACTURING PROCESS	ENVIRONMENTAL GOAL		
	Yes	No	Total
Job shop or batch	2	42	44
Repetitive batch	4	57	61
Discrete process	15	147	162
Continuous process	17	65	82
Total	38	311	349

OUTCOME	COST-CUTTING GOAL		
	Yes	No	Total
Improved environmental performance	77	52	129
Environmental performance not improved	91	129	220
Total	168	181	349

OUTCOME	COST-CUTTING GOAL		
	Yes	No	Total
Improved profitability	70	68	138
Profitability not improved	98	113	211
Total	168	181	349

OUTCOME	COST-CUTTING GOAL		
	Yes	No	Total
Improved morale	67	55	122
Morale not improved	101	126	227
Total	168	181	349

Source: *Data extracted from M. Hanna, W. Newman, and P. Johnson, "Linking Operational and Environmental Improvement Thru Employee Involvement,"* International Journal of Operations and Production Management, *2000, 20, pp. 148–165.*

a. At the 0.05 level of significance, determine whether there is evidence of a significant relationship between the presence of environmental goals and the type of manufacturing process.

b. Determine the p-value in (a) and interpret its meaning.

c. At the 0.05 level of significance, is there evidence of a difference in improved environmental performance for teams with and without a specified goal of cutting costs?

d. Determine the p-value in (c) and interpret its meaning.

e. At the 0.05 level of significance, is there evidence of a difference in improved profitability for teams with a specified goal of cutting costs?

f. Determine the p-value in (e) and interpret its meaning.

g. At the 0.05 level of significance, is there evidence of a difference in improved morale for teams with and without a specified goal of cutting costs?

h. Determine the p-value in (g) and interpret its meaning.

TEAM PROJECT

The data file **Mutual Funds** contains information regarding nine variables from a sample of 868 mutual funds. The variables are:

Category—Type of stocks comprising the mutual fund (small cap, mid cap, or large cap)

Objective—Objective of stocks comprising the mutual fund (growth or value)

Assets—In millions of dollars

Fees—Sales charges (no or yes)

Expense ratio—Ratio of expenses to net assets in percentage

Return 2006—Twelve-month return in 2006

Three-year return—Annualized return, 2004–2006

Five-year return—Annualized return, 2002–2006

Risk—Risk-of-loss factor of the mutual fund (low, average, or high)

11.35 a. Construct a 2 × 2 contingency table, using fees as the row variable and objective as the column variable.

b. At the 0.05 level of significance, is there evidence of a significant relationship between the objective of a mutual fund and whether there is a fee?

11.36 a. Construct a 2 × 3 contingency table, using fees as the row variable and risk as the column variable.

b. At the 0.05 level of significance, is there evidence of a significant relationship between the perceived risk of a mutual fund and whether there is a fee?

11.37 a. Construct a 3 × 2 contingency table, using risk as the row variable and objective as the column variable.

b. At the 0.05 level of significance, is there evidence of a significant relationship between the objective of a mutual fund and its perceived risk?

11.38 a. Construct a 3 × 3 contingency table, using risk as the row variable and category as the column variable.

b. At the 0.05 level of significance, is there evidence of a significant relationship between the category of a mutual fund and its perceived risk?

STUDENT SURVEY DATA BASE

11.39 Problem 1.23 on page 13 describes a survey of 50 undergraduate students (see the file Undergradsurvey). For these data, construct contingency tables, using gender, major, plans to go to graduate school, and employment status. (You need to construct six tables, taking two variables at a time.) Analyze the data at the 0.05 level of significance to determine whether any significant relationships exist among these variables.

11.40 Problem 1.23 on page 13 describes a survey of 50 undergraduate students (see the file Undergradsurvey).

a. Select a sample of 50 undergraduate students at your school and conduct a similar survey for those students.

b. For the data collected in (a), repeat Problem 11.39.

c. Compare the results of (b) to those of Problem 11.39.

11.41 Problem 1.24 on page 13 describes a survey of 40 MBA students (see the file Gradsurvey). For these data, construct contingency tables, using gender, undergraduate major, graduate major, and employment status. (You need to construct six tables, taking two variables at a time.) Analyze the data at the 0.05 level of significance to determine whether any significant relationships exist among these variables.

11.42 Problem 1.24 on page 13 describes a survey of 40 MBA students (see the file Gradsurvey).

a. Select a sample of 40 graduate students in your MBA program and conduct a similar survey for those students.

b. For the data collected in (a), repeat Problem 11.41.

c. Compare the results of (b) to those of Problem 11.41.

MANAGING THE *SPRINGVILLE HERALD*

PHASE 1

Reviewing the results of its research, the marketing department team concluded that a segment of Springville households might be interested in a discounted trial home subscription to the *Herald*. The team decided to test various discounts before determining the type of discount to offer during the trial period. It decided to conduct an experiment using three types of discounts plus a plan that offered no discount during the trial period:

1. No discount for the newspaper. Subscribers would pay $4.50 per week for the newspaper during the 90-day trial period.

2. Moderate discount for the newspaper. Subscribers would pay $4.00 per week for the newspaper during the 90-day trial period.

3. Substantial discount for the newspaper. Subscribers would pay $3.00 per week for the newspaper during the 90-day trial period.

4. Discount restaurant card. Subscribers would be given a card providing a discount of 15% at selected restaurants in Springville during the trial period.

Each participant in the experiment was randomly assigned to a discount plan. A random sample of 100 subscribers to each plan during the trial period was tracked to determine how many would continue to subscribe to the *Herald* after the trial period. Table SH11.1 summarizes the results.

TABLE SH11.1

Number of Subscribers Who Continue Subscriptions After Trial Period with Four Discount Plans

CONTINUE SUBSCRIPTIONS AFTER TRIAL PERIOD	DISCOUNT PLANS				
	No Discount	Moderate Discount	Substantial Discount	Restaurant Card	Total
Yes	34	37	38	61	170
No	66	63	62	39	230
Total	100	100	100	100	400

EXERCISE

SH11.1 Analyze the results of the experiment. Write a report to the team that includes your recommendation for which discount plan to use. Be prepared to discuss the limitations and assumptions of the experiment.

DO NOT CONTINUE UNTIL THE PHASE 1 EXERCISE HAS BEEN COMPLETED.

PHASE 2

The marketing department team discussed the results of the survey presented in Chapter 8, on pages 267–268. The team realized that the evaluation of individual questions was providing only limited information. In order to further understand the market for home-delivery subscriptions, the data were organized in the following contingency tables:

	READ OTHER NEWSPAPER		
HOME DELIVERY	Yes	No	Total
Yes	61	75	136
No	77	139	216
Total	138	214	352

	RESTAURANT CARD		
HOME DELIVERY	Yes	No	Total
Yes	26	110	136
No	40	176	216
Total	66	286	352

	MONDAY–SATURDAY PURCHASE BEHAVIOR			
INTEREST IN TRIAL SUBSCRIPTION	Every Day	Most Days	Occasionally or Never	Total
Yes	29	14	3	46
No	49	81	40	170
Total	78	95	43	216

	SUNDAY PURCHASE BEHAVIOR			
INTEREST IN TRIAL SUBSCRIPTION	Every Sunday	2–3 Times a Month	No More Than Once a Month	Total
Yes	35	10	1	46
No	103	44	23	170
Total	138	54	24	216

	INTEREST IN TRIAL SUBSCRIPTION		
WHERE PURCHASED	Yes	No	Total
Convenience store	12	62	74
Newsstand/candy store	15	80	95
Vending machine	10	11	21
Supermarket	5	8	13
Other locations	4	9	13
Total	46	170	216

	MONDAY–SATURDAY PURCHASE BEHAVIOR			
SUNDAY PURCHASE BEHAVIOR	Every Day	Most Days	Occasionally or Never	Total
Every Sunday	55	65	18	138
2–3 times/month	19	23	12	54
Once/month	4	7	13	24
Total	78	95	43	216

EXERCISE

SH11.2 Analyze the results of the contingency tables. Write a report for the marketing department team and discuss the marketing implications of the results for the *Springville Herald*.

WEB CASE

Apply your knowledge of testing for the difference between two proportions in this Web Case, which extends the T.C. Resort Properties Using Statistics scenario of this chapter.

As T.C. Resort Properties seeks to improve its customer service, the company faces new competition from SunLow Resorts. SunLow has recently opened resort hotels on the islands where T.C. Resort Properties has its five hotels. SunLow is currently advertising that a random survey of 300 customers revealed that about 60% percent of the customers preferred its "Concierge Class" travel reward program over the T.C. Resorts "TCPass Plus" program. Visit the SunLow Web site, **www.prenhall.com/Springville/**

SunLowHome.htm (or open the `SunLowHome.htm` file in the Student CD-ROM Web Case folder), and examine the survey data. Then answer the following:

1. Are the claims made by SunLow valid?

2. What analyses of the survey data would lead to a more favorable impression about T.C. Resort Properties?

3. Perform one of the analyses identified in your answer to step 2.

4. Review the data about the T.C. Resorts Properties customers presented in this chapter. Are there any other questions that you might include in a future survey of travel reward programs? Explain.

REFERENCES

1. Conover, W. J., *Practical Nonparametric Statistics*, 3rd ed. (New York: Wiley, 2000).
2. Daniel, W. W., *Applied Nonparametric Statistics*, 2nd ed. (Boston: PWS Kent, 1990).
3. Dixon, W. J., and F. J. Massey, Jr., *Introduction to Statistical Analysis*, 4th ed. (New York: McGraw-Hill, 1983).
4. Hollander, M., and D. A. Wolfe, *Nonparametric Statistical Methods*, 2nd ed. (New York: Wiley, 1999).
5. Lewontin, R. C., and J. Felsenstein, "Robustness of Homogeneity Tests in $2 \times n$ Tables," *Biometrics* 21 (March 1965): pp. 19–33.
6. Marascuilo, L. A., "Large-Sample Multiple Comparisons," *Psychological Bulletin* 65 (1966): pp. 280–290.
7. Marascuilo, L. A., and M. McSweeney, *Nonparametric and Distribution-Free Methods for the Social Sciences* (Monterey, CA: Brooks/Cole, 1977).
8. *Microsoft Excel 2007* (Redmond, WA: Microsoft Corp., 2007).
9. *Minitab for Windows Version 15* (State College, PA: Minitab, Inc., 2006).

APPENDIX E11

Using Microsoft Excel for Chi-Square Tests

E11.1 Using the Chi-Square Test for the Difference Between Two Proportions

You perform the chi-square test for the difference between two proportions by making entries in the **ChiSquare2P** worksheet of the Chi-Square.xls workbook. This worksheet (see Figure 11.3 on page 382) uses the **CHIINV(***level of significance, degrees of freedom***)** and **CHIDIST(**χ^2 ***test statistic, degrees of freedom***)** functions to compute the critical value and *p*-value, respectively, for the Section 11.1 guest satisfaction example. To adapt this worksheet to other problems, enter the problem's contingency table data into the rows 4 through 7 Observed Frequencies area, the level of significance in cell B18, and enter a new title in cell A1. To examine all formulas in this worksheet, including the ones not shown in Figure 11.3, open to the **ChiSquare2PFormulas** worksheet in the same workbook.

E11.2 Using the Chi-Square Test for the Difference Among More Than Two Proportions

You perform the chi-square test for the difference among more than two proportions by making entries in one of the worksheets in the Chi-Square Worksheets.xls workbook.

Open the workbook to the worksheet that contains the appropriate $2 \times c$ observed frequency table for your problem. For example, for the Section 11.2 guest satisfaction example that requires a 2×3 table, open to the **ChiSquare2×3** worksheet. Worksheets with empty observed frequencies table will display the message #DIV/0! in many cells. This is not an error and these messages will disappear once you enter your contingency table data.

All $2 \times c$ worksheets contain formulas similar to those in the ChiSquare2P worksheet discussed in Section E11.1. To examine all formulas in the ChiSquare2×3 worksheet, including those not shown in Figure 11.7 on page 388, open to the **ChiSquare2x3Formulas** worksheet.

E11.3 Using the Chi-Square Test of Independence

You perform the chi-square test of independence by making entries in one of the worksheets in the Chi-Square Worksheets.xls workbook. The workbook contains worksheets for 3×4, 4×3, 7×3, and 8×3 tables, in addition to the $2 \times c$ worksheets discussed in Section E11.2. Figure 11.11 on page 394 uses the ChiSquare4×3 worksheet.

APPENDIX P11

Using PHStat2 for Chi-Square Tests

P11.1 Using the Chi-Square Test for the Difference Between Two Proportions

To perform the chi-square test for the difference between two proportions, use **PHStat → Two-Sample Tests → Chi-Square Test for Differences in Two Proportions**. This procedure creates a new worksheet similar to Figure 11.3 on page 382 into which you enter observed frequency table data. Before you enter your data, many worksheet cells will display the message #DIV/0!. This is not an error.

P11.2 Using the Chi-Square Test for the Difference Among More Than Two Proportions

To perform the chi-square test for the difference among more than two proportions, use **PHStat → Multiple-Sample Tests → Chi-Square Test**. This procedure creates a worksheet based on the number of rows and number of columns that you specify, similar in design to Figure 11.7 on page 388, into which you enter observed frequency table data. Before you enter your data, many worksheet cells will display the message #DIV/0!. This is not an error.

P11.3 Using the Chi-Square Test of Independence

To perform the chi-square test of independence, use **PHStat → Multiple-Sample Tests → Chi-Square Test**. For more information about this procedure, see Section P11.2.

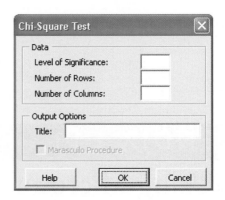

APPENDIX M11

Using Minitab for Chi-Square Tests

M11.1 Using Chi-Square Tests (unsummarized data)

To create a two-way contingency table from unsummarized data:

1. Open the worksheet of interest.
2. Select **Stat → Tables → Cross Tabulation and Chi-Square**.

In the Cross Tabulation and Chi-Square dialog box (see Figure M11.1):

3. Enter the row variable in the **For rows** box and the column variable in the **For columns** box.
4. Click **Counts, Row percents, Column percents**, and **Total percents**.
5. Click **Chi-Square**.

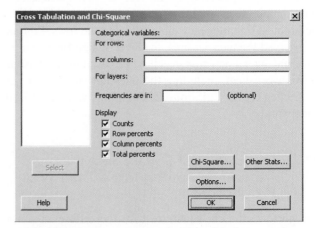

FIGURE M11.1 Minitab Cross Tabulation and Chi-Square dialog box

In the Cross Tabulation - Chi-Square dialog box (see Figure M11.2),

6. Click **Chi-Square analysis, Expected cell counts**, and **Each cell's contribution to the Chi-Square statistic**.

7. Click **OK**.

8. Back in the original dialog box, click **OK** again.

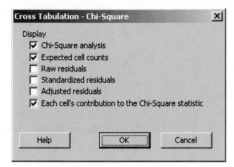

FIGURE M11.2   Minitab Cross Tabulation - Chi-Square dialog box

M11.2 Using Chi-Square Tests (summarized data)

To create a $2 \times c$ contingency table from summarized data, enter the set of cell frequencies that summarize the data into a new worksheet. For example, to enter Table 11.2 on page 379 (the 2×2 Contingency Table for the Hotel Guest Satisfaction Survey):

1. Open a new worksheet. (If necessary, select **File → New** and in the New dialog box, click **Minitab Worksheet** and then click **OK**.)

2. Enter **163** and **64** in column C1 rows 1 and 2

3. Enter **154** and **108** in column C2, rows 1 and 2.

4. Enter **Beachcomber** as the name of column C1 and **Windsurfer** as the name of column C2.

5. Select **Stat → Tables → Chi-Square Test (Two-Way Table in Worksheet)**.

In the Chi-Square Test (Table in Worksheet) dialog box (see Figure M11.3):

6. Enter **Beachcomber** and **Windsurfer** in the **Columns containing the table** box.

7. Click **OK**.

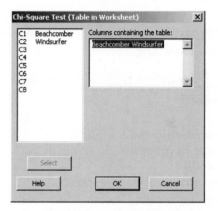

FIGURE M11.3   Minitab Chi-Square Test (Table in Worksheet) dialog box

12 Simple Linear Regression

Learning Objectives

In this chapter, you learn:

- To use regression analysis to predict the value of a dependent variable based on an independent variable
- The meaning of the regression coefficients b_0 and b_1
- To evaluate the assumptions of regression analysis and know what to do if the assumptions are violated
- To make inferences about the slope and correlation coefficient
- To estimate mean values and predict individual values

@ Sunflowers Apparel

The sales for Sunflowers Apparel, a chain of upscale clothing stores for women, have increased during the past 12 years as the chain has expanded the number of stores. Until now, Sunflowers managers selected sites based on subjective factors, such as the availability of a good lease or the perception that a location seemed ideal for an apparel store. As the new director of planning, you need to develop a systematic approach that will lead to making better decisions during the site selection process. As a starting point, you believe that the size of the store significantly contributes to store sales, and you want to use this relationship in the decision-making process. How can you use statistics so that you can forecast the annual sales of a proposed store based on the size of that store?

In this chapter and the next chapter, you learn how **regression analysis** enables you to develop a model to predict the values of a numerical variable, based on the value of other variables. In regression analysis, the variable you wish to predict is called the **dependent variable**. The variables used to make the prediction are called **independent variables**. In addition to predicting values of the dependent variable, regression analysis also allows you to identify the type of mathematical relationship that exists between a dependent and an independent variable, to quantify the effect that changes in the independent variable have on the dependent variable, and to identify unusual observations. For example, as the director of planning, you may wish to predict sales for a Sunflowers store, based on the size of the store. Other examples include predicting the monthly rent of an apartment, based on its size, and predicting the monthly sales of a product in a supermarket, based on the amount of shelf space devoted to the product.

This chapter discusses **simple linear regression**, in which a *single* numerical independent variable, X, is used to predict the numerical dependent variable Y, such as using the size of a store to predict the annual sales of the store. Chapter 13 discusses *multiple regression models*, which use *several* independent variables to predict a numerical dependent variable, Y. For example, you could use the amount of advertising expenditures, price, and the amount of shelf space devoted to a product to predict its monthly sales.

12.1 Types of Regression Models

In Section 2.5, you used a **scatter plot** (also known as a **scatter diagram**) to examine the relationship between an X variable on the horizontal axis and a Y variable on the vertical axis. The nature of the relationship between two variables can take many forms, ranging from simple to extremely complicated mathematical functions. The simplest relationship consists of a straight-line or **linear relationship**. Figure 12.1 illustrates a straight-line relationship.

FIGURE 12.1

A straight-line relationship

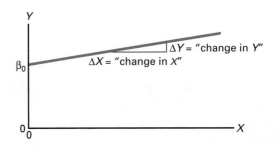

Equation (12.1) represents the straight-line (linear) model.

> **SIMPLE LINEAR REGRESSION MODEL**
>
> $$Y_i = \beta_0 + \beta_1 X_i + \varepsilon_i \qquad \textbf{(12.1)}$$
>
> where
>
> $\beta_0 = Y$ intercept for the population
>
> $\beta_1 = $ slope for the population
>
> $\varepsilon_i = $ random error in Y for observation i
>
> $Y_i = $ dependent variable (sometimes referred to as the **response variable**) for observation i
>
> $X_i = $ independent variable (sometimes referred to as the **explanatory variable**) for observation i

The portion $Y_i = \beta_0 + \beta_1 X_i$ of the simple linear regression model expressed in Equation (12.1) is a straight line. The **slope** of the line, β_1, represents the expected change in Y per unit change in X. It represents the mean amount that Y changes (either positively or negatively) for a one-unit change in X. The **Y intercept**, β_0, represents the mean value of Y when X equals 0. The last component of the model, ε_i, represents the random error in Y for each observation, i. In other words, ε_i is the vertical distance of the actual value of Y_i above or below the expected value of Y_i on the line.

The selection of the proper mathematical model depends on the distribution of the X and Y values on the scatter plot. In Panel A of Figure 12.2, the values of Y are generally increasing linearly as X increases. This panel is similar to Figure 12.3 on page 410, which illustrates the positive relationship between the square footage of the store and the annual sales at branches of the Sunflowers Apparel women's clothing store chain.

FIGURE 12.2

Six types of relationships found in scatter plots

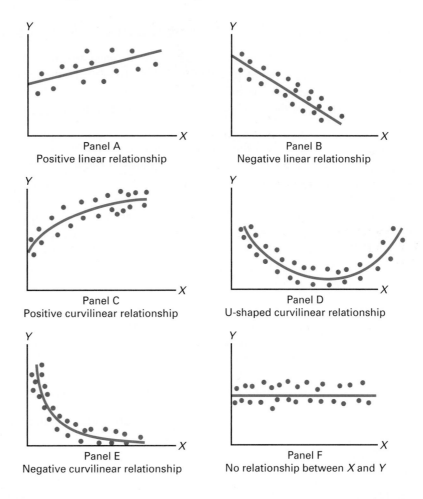

The data in Panel B is an example of a negative linear relationship. As X increases, the values of Y are generally decreasing. An example of this type of relationship might be the price of a particular product and the amount of sales.

The data in Panel C show a positive curvilinear relationship between X and Y. The values of Y increase as X increases, but this increase tapers off beyond certain values of X. An example of a positive curvilinear relationship might be the age and maintenance cost of a machine. As a machine gets older, the maintenance cost may rise rapidly at first, but then level off beyond a certain number of years.

Panel D shows a U-shaped relationship between X and Y. As X increases, at first Y generally decreases; but as X continues to increase, Y not only stops decreasing but actually increases above its minimum value. An example of this type of relationship might be the number of errors per hour at a task and the number of hours worked. The number of errors per hour decreases as the individual becomes more proficient at the task, but then it increases beyond a certain point because of factors such as fatigue and boredom.

Panel E indicates an exponential relationship between X and Y. In this case, Y decreases very rapidly as X first increases, but then it decreases much less rapidly as X increases further.

An example of an exponential relationship could be the resale value of an automobile and its age. The resale value drops drastically from its original price in the first year, but decreases much less rapidly in subsequent years.

Finally, Panel F shows a set of data in which there is very little or no relationship between X and Y. High and low values of Y appear at each value of X.

In this section, a variety of different models that represent the relationship between two variables were briefly examined. Although scatter plots are useful in visually displaying the mathematical form of a relationship, more sophisticated statistical procedures are available to determine the most appropriate model for a set of variables. The rest of this chapter discusses the model used when there is a *linear* relationship between variables.

12.2 Determining the Simple Linear Regression Equation

In the Using Statistics scenario on page 407, the stated goal is to forecast annual sales for all new stores, based on store size. To examine the relationship between the store size in square feet and its annual sales, a sample of 14 stores was selected. Table 12.1 summarizes the results for these 14 stores, which are stored in the file **Site**.

TABLE 12.1

Square Footage (in Thousands of Square Feet) and Annual Sales (in Millions of Dollars) for a Sample of 14 Branches of Sunflowers Apparel

Store	Square Feet (Thousands)	Annual Sales (in Millions of Dollars)	Store	Square Feet (Thousands)	Annual Sales (in Millions of Dollars)
1	1.7	3.7	8	1.1	2.7
2	1.6	3.9	9	3.2	5.5
3	2.8	6.7	10	1.5	2.9
4	5.6	9.5	11	5.2	10.7
5	1.3	3.4	12	4.6	7.6
6	2.2	5.6	13	5.8	11.8
7	1.3	3.7	14	3.0	4.1

Figure 12.3 displays the scatter plot for the data in Table 12.1. Observe the increasing relationship between square feet (X) and annual sales (Y). As the size of the store increases, annual sales increase approximately as a straight line. Thus, you can assume that a straight line provides a useful mathematical model of this relationship. Now you need to determine the specific straight line that is the *best* fit to these data.

FIGURE 12.3

Microsoft Excel scatter plot for the Sunflowers Apparel data

See Section E2.12 or P2.9 to create this. (Minitab users, see Section M2.8 to create an equivalent chart.)

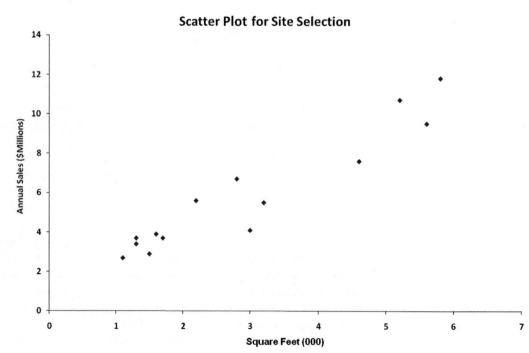

The Least-Squares Method

In the preceding section, a statistical model is hypothesized to represent the relationship between two variables, square footage and sales, in the entire population of Sunflowers Apparel stores. However, as shown in Table 12.1, the data are from only a random sample of stores. If certain assumptions are valid (see Section 12.4), you can use the sample Y intercept, b_0, and the sample slope, b_1, as estimates of the respective population parameters, β_0 and β_1. Equation (12.2) uses these estimates to form the **simple linear regression equation**. This straight line is often referred to as the **prediction line**.

SIMPLE LINEAR REGRESSION EQUATION: THE PREDICTION LINE

The predicted value of Y equals the Y intercept plus the slope multiplied by the value of X.

$$\hat{Y}_i = b_0 + b_1 X_i \qquad\qquad \textbf{(12.2)}$$

where

$\hat{Y}_i$ = predicted value of Y for observation i

X_i = value of X for observation i

b_0 = sample Y intercept

b_1 = sample slope

Equation (12.2) requires the determination of two **regression coefficients**—b_0 (the sample Y intercept) and b_1 (the sample slope). The most common approach to finding b_0 and b_1 is the method of least squares. This method minimizes the sum of the squared differences between the actual values (Y_i) and the predicted values ($\hat{Y}_i$) using the simple linear regression equation [i.e., the prediction line; see Equation (12.2)]. This sum of squared differences is equal to

$$\sum_{i=1}^{n}(Y_i - \hat{Y}_i)^2$$

Because $\hat{Y}_i = b_0 + b_1 X_i$,

$$\sum_{i=1}^{n}(Y_i - \hat{Y}_i)^2 = \sum_{i=1}^{n}[Y_i - (b_0 + b_1 X_i)]^2$$

Because this equation has two unknowns, b_0 and b_1, the sum of squared differences depends on the sample Y intercept, b_0, and the sample slope, b_1. The **least-squares method** determines the values of b_0 and b_1 that minimize the sum of squared differences around the prediction line. Any values for b_0 and b_1 other than those determined by the least-squares method result in a greater

sum of squared differences between the actual values (Y_i) and the predicted values ($\hat{Y}_i$). In this book, Microsoft Excel and Minitab are used to perform the computations involved in the least-squares method. For the data of Table 12.1, Figure 12.4 presents results from Microsoft Excel and Figure 12.5 shows Minitab results.

To understand how the results are computed, many of the computations involved are illustrated in Examples 12.3 and 12.4 on page 415 and 422–423. In Figure 12.4 or 12.5, observe that $b_0 = 0.9645$ and $b_1 = 1.6699$. Thus, the prediction line [see Equation (12.2) above] for these data is

$$\hat{Y}_i = 0.9645 + 1.6699 X_i$$

FIGURE 12.4

Microsoft Excel results worksheet for the Sunflowers Apparel data

See Section E12.1 or P12.1 to create this.

	A	B	C	D	E	F	G
1	Site Selection Analysis						
2							
3	*Regression Statistics*						
4	Multiple R	0.9509					
5	R Square	0.9042					
6	Adjusted R Square	0.8962					
7	Standard Error	0.9664					
8	Observations	14					
9							
10	ANOVA						
11		*df*	*SS*	*MS*	*F*	*Significance F*	
12	Regression	1	105.7476	105.7476	113.2335	0.0000	
13	Residual	12	11.2067	0.9339			
14	Total	13	116.9543				
15							
16		*Coefficients*	*Standard Error*	*t Stat*	*P-value*	*Lower 95%*	*Upper 95%*
17	Intercept	0.9645	0.5262	1.8329	0.0917	-0.1820	2.1110
18	Square Feet	1.6699	0.1569	10.6411	0.0000	1.3280	2.0118

FIGURE 12.5

Minitab results for the Sunflowers Apparel data

See Section M12.1 to create this.

```
The regression equation is
Annual Sales = 0.964 + 1.67 Square Feet


Predictor      Coef   SE Coef       T      P
Constant     0.9645    0.5262    1.83  0.092
Square Feet  1.6699    0.1569   10.64  0.000



S = 0.966380   R-Sq = 90.4%   R-Sq(adj) = 89.6%

Analysis of Variance

Source           DF      SS      MS       F      P
Regression        1  105.75  105.75  113.23  0.000
Residual Error   12   11.21    0.93
Total            13  116.95


Predicted Values for New Observations

New
Obs    Fit  SE Fit      95% CI           95% PI
  1  7.644   0.309  (6.971, 8.317)  (5.433, 9.854)
```

The slope, b_1, is $+1.6699$. This means that for each increase of 1 unit in X, the mean value of Y is estimated to increase by 1.6699 units. In other words, for each increase of 1.0 thousand square feet in the size of the store, the mean annual sales are estimated to increase by 1.6699 millions of dollars. Thus, the slope represents the portion of the annual sales that are estimated to vary according to the size of the store.

The Y intercept, b_0, is $+0.9645$. The Y intercept represents the mean value of Y when X equals 0. Because the square footage of the store cannot be 0, this Y intercept has little or no practical interpretation. Also, the Y intercept for this example is outside the range of the observed values of the X variable, and therefore interpretations of the value of b_0 should be made cautiously. Figure 12.6 displays the actual observations and the prediction line. To illustrate a situation in which there is a direct interpretation for the Y intercept, b_0, see Example 12.1.

FIGURE 12.6

Microsoft Excel scatter plot and prediction line for Sunflowers Apparel data

See Section E12.2 or P12.2 to create this. (Minitab users, see Section M12.2 to create an equivalent chart.)

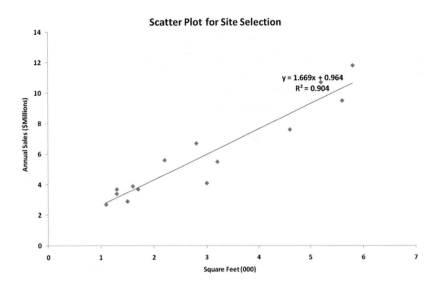

Scatter Plot for Site Selection

$y = 1.669x + 0.964$
$R^2 = 0.904$

EXAMPLE 12.1

Interpreting the *Y* Intercept, b_0, and the Slope, b_1

A statistics professor wants to use the number of hours a student studies for a statistics final exam (*X*) to predict the final exam score (*Y*). A regression model was fit based on data collected for a class during the previous semester, with the following results:

$$\hat{Y}_i = 35.0 + 3X_i$$

What is the interpretation of the *Y* intercept, b_0, and the slope, b_1?

SOLUTION The *Y* intercept $b_0 = 35.0$ indicates that when the student does not study for the final exam, the predicted final exam score is 35.0. The slope $b_1 = 3$ indicates that for each increase of one hour in studying time, the mean change in the final exam score is predicted to be +3.0. In other words, the final exam score is predicted to increase by 3 points for each one-hour increase in studying time.

Return to the Using Statistics scenario on page 407 concerning the Sunflowers Apparel stores. Example 12.2 illustrates how you use the prediction equation to predict the mean annual sales.

EXAMPLE 12.2

Predicting Annual Sales, Based on Square Footage

Use the prediction line to predict the annual sales for a store with 4,000 square feet.

SOLUTION You can determine the predicted value by substituting $X = 4$ (thousands of square feet) into the simple linear regression equation:

$$\hat{Y}_i = 0.9645 + 1.6699X_i$$
$$\hat{Y}_i = 0.9645 + 1.6699(4) = 7.644 \text{ or } \$7,644,000$$

Thus, the predicted annual sales of a store with 4,000 square feet is $7,644,000.

Predictions in Regression Analysis: Interpolation versus Extrapolation

When using a regression model for prediction purposes, you need to consider only the **relevant range** of the independent variable in making predictions. This relevant range includes all values from the smallest to the largest *X* used in developing the regression model. Hence, when predicting *Y* for a given value of *X*, you can interpolate within this relevant range of the *X* values, but you should not extrapolate beyond the range of *X* values.

When you use the square footage to predict annual sales, the square footage (in thousands of square feet) varies from 1.1 to 5.8 (see Table 12.1 on page 410). Therefore, you should predict annual sales *only* for stores whose size is between 1.1 and 5.8 thousands of square feet. Any prediction of annual sales for stores outside this range assumes that the observed relationship between sales and store size for store sizes from 1.1 to 5.8 thousand square feet is the same as for stores outside this range. For example, you cannot extrapolate the linear relationship beyond 5,800 square feet in Example 12.2. It would be improper to use the prediction line to forecast the sales for a new store containing 8,000 square feet because it is quite possible that store size has a point of diminishing returns. If that is true, as square footage increases beyond 5,800 square feet, the effect on sales becomes smaller and smaller.

Computing the *Y* Intercept, b_0, and the Slope, b_1

For small data sets, you can use a hand calculator to compute the least-squares regression coefficients. Equations (12.3) and (12.4) give the values of b_0 and b_1, which minimize

$$\sum_{i=1}^{n}(Y_i - \hat{Y}_i)^2 = \sum_{i=1}^{n}[Y_i - (b_0 + b_1 X_i)]^2$$

COMPUTATIONAL FORMULA FOR THE SLOPE, b_1

$$b_1 = \frac{SSXY}{SSX} \tag{12.3}$$

where

$$SSXY = \sum_{i=1}^{n}(X_i - \overline{X})(Y_i - \overline{Y}) = \sum_{i=1}^{n}X_iY_i - \frac{\left(\sum_{i=1}^{n}X_i\right)\left(\sum_{i=1}^{n}Y_i\right)}{n}$$

$$SSX = \sum_{i=1}^{n}(X_i - \overline{X})^2 = \sum_{i=1}^{n}X_i^2 - \frac{\left(\sum_{i=1}^{n}X_i\right)^2}{n}$$

COMPUTATIONAL FORMULA FOR THE *Y* INTERCEPT, b_0

$$b_0 = \overline{Y} - b_1\overline{X} \tag{12.4}$$

where

$$\overline{Y} = \frac{\sum_{i=1}^{n}Y_i}{n}$$

$$\overline{X} = \frac{\sum_{i=1}^{n}X_i}{n}$$

EXAMPLE 12.3

Computing the Y Intercept, b_0, and the Slope, b_1

Compute the Y intercept, b_0, and the slope, b_1, for the Sunflowers Apparel data.

SOLUTION Examining Equations (12.3) and (12.4), you see that five quantities are needed to determine b_1 and b_0. These are n, the sample size; $\sum_{i=1}^{n} X_i$, the sum of the X values; $\sum_{i=1}^{n} Y_i$, the sum of the Y values; $\sum_{i=1}^{n} X_i^2$, the sum of the squared X values; and $\sum_{i=1}^{n} X_i Y_i$, the sum of the product of X and Y. For the Sunflowers Apparel data, the number of square feet is used to predict the annual sales in a store. Table 12.2 presents the computations of the various sums needed for the site selection problem. The table also includes $\sum_{i=1}^{n} Y_i^2$, the sum of the squared Y values that will be used to compute SST in Section 12.3.

TABLE 12.2

Computations for the Sunflowers Apparel Data

Store	Square Feet (X)	Annual Sales (Y)	X^2	Y^2	XY
1	1.7	3.7	2.89	13.69	6.29
2	1.6	3.9	2.56	15.21	6.24
3	2.8	6.7	7.84	44.89	18.76
4	5.6	9.5	31.36	90.25	53.20
5	1.3	3.4	1.69	11.56	4.42
6	2.2	5.6	4.84	31.36	12.32
7	1.3	3.7	1.69	13.69	4.81
8	1.1	2.7	1.21	7.29	2.97
9	3.2	5.5	10.24	30.25	17.60
10	1.5	2.9	2.25	8.41	4.35
11	5.2	10.7	27.04	114.49	55.64
12	4.6	7.6	21.16	57.76	34.96
13	5.8	11.8	33.64	139.24	68.44
14	3.0	4.1	9.00	16.81	12.30
Totals	40.9	81.8	157.41	594.90	302.30

Using Equations (12.3) and (12.4), you can compute the values of b_0 and b_1:

$$SSXY = \sum_{i=1}^{n}(X_i - \bar{X})(Y_i - \bar{Y}) = \sum_{i=1}^{n} X_i Y_i - \frac{\left(\sum_{i=1}^{n} X_i\right)\left(\sum_{i=1}^{n} Y_i\right)}{n}$$

$$SSXY = 302.3 - \frac{(40.9)(81.8)}{14}$$

$$= 302.3 - 238.97285$$

$$= 63.32715$$

$$SSX = \sum_{i=1}^{n}(X_i - \bar{X})^2 = \sum_{i=1}^{n} X_i^2 - \frac{\left(\sum_{i=1}^{n} X_i\right)^2}{n}$$

$$= 157.41 - \frac{(40.9)^2}{14}$$

$$= 157.41 - 119.48642$$

$$= 37.92358$$

Therefore,

$$b_1 = \frac{SSXY}{SSX}$$

$$= \frac{63.32715}{37.92358}$$

$$= 1.6699$$

And,

$$\overline{Y} = \frac{\sum_{i=1}^{n} Y_i}{n} = \frac{81.8}{14} = 5.842857$$

$$\overline{X} = \frac{\sum_{i=1}^{n} X_i}{n} = \frac{40.9}{14} = 2.92143$$

Therefore,

$$b_0 = \overline{Y} - b_1\overline{X}$$

$$= 5.842857 - (1.6699)(2.92143)$$

$$= 0.9645$$

VISUAL EXPLORATIONS   Exploring Simple Linear Regression Coefficients

Use the Visual Explorations Simple Linear Regression procedure to create a prediction line that is as close as possible to the prediction line defined by the least-squares solution. Open the Visual Explorations.xla add-in workbook and select **VisualExplorations → Simple Linear Regression** (Excel 97–2003) or **Add-ins → VisualExplorations → Simple Linear Regression** (Excel 2007).

The procedure displays a scatter plot of the Sunflowers Apparel data of Table 12.1 on page 410, along with an initial prediction line (see illustration on page 417). In the Simple Linear Regression dialog box, click the spinner buttons to change the values for b_1, the slope of the prediction line, and b_0, the Y intercept of the prediction line to change the prediction line.

Using the chart display as visual feedback, try to create a prediction line that is as close as possible to the prediction line defined by the least-squares estimates and thus make the Difference from Target SSE value as small as possible (see page 420 for an explanation of SSE). At any time, click **Reset** to reset the b_1 and b_0 values or **Solution** to reveal the prediction line defined by the least-squares method. Click **Finish** when you are finished with this exercise.

Using Your Own Regression Data

To use Visual Explorations to find a prediction line for your own data, select **VisualExplorations → Simple**

Linear Regression with your worksheet data (Excel 97–2003) or **Add-ins → VisualExplorations → Simple Linear Regression with your worksheet data** (Excel 2007). In the procedure's dialog box (shown below), enter your Y variable cell range as the **Y Variable Cell Range** and your X variable cell range as the **X Variable Cell Range**. Click **First cells in both ranges contain a label**, enter a title as the **Title**, and click **OK**. When the scatter plot with an initial prediction line appears, use the instructions in the first part of this section to try to produce the prediction line defined by the least-squares plot.

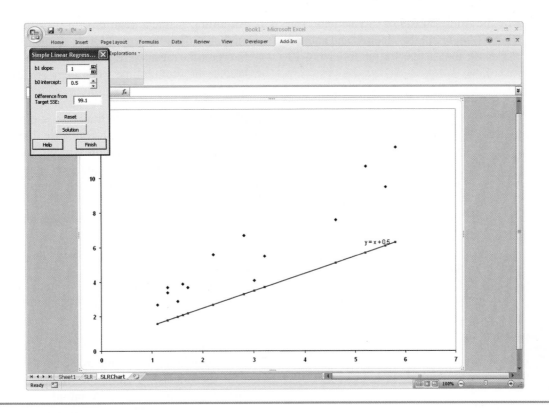

Problems for Section 12.2

LEARNING THE BASICS

12.1 Fitting a straight line to a set of data yields the following prediction line:

$$\hat{Y}_i = 2 + 5X_i$$

a. Interpret the meaning of the Y intercept, b_0.
b. Interpret the meaning of the slope, b_1.
c. Predict the value of Y for $X = 3$.

12.2 If the values of X in Problem 12.1 range from 2 to 25, should you use this model to predict the mean value of Y when X equals

a. 3?
b. −3?
c. 0?
d. 24?

12.3 Fitting a straight line to a set of data yields the following prediction line:

$$\hat{Y}_i = 16 - 0.5X_i$$

a. Interpret the meaning of the Y intercept, b_0.
b. Interpret the meaning of the slope, b_1.
c. Predict the value of Y for $X = 6$.

APPLYING THE CONCEPTS

✓SELF Test **12.4** The marketing manager of a large supermarket chain would like to use shelf space to predict the sales of pet food. A random sample of 12 equal-sized stores is selected, with the following results (stored in the file **Petfood**):

Store	Shelf Space (X) (Feet)	Weekly Sales (Y) ($)
1	5	160
2	5	220
3	5	140
4	10	190
5	10	240
6	10	260
7	15	230
8	15	270
9	15	280
10	20	260
11	20	290
12	20	310

a. Construct a scatter plot.
For these data, $b_0 = 145$ and $b_1 = 7.4$.
b. Interpret the meaning of the slope, b_1, in this problem.
c. Predict the weekly sales of pet food for stores with 8 feet of shelf space for pet food.

12.5 Circulation is the lifeblood of the publishing business. The larger the sales of a magazine, the more it can charge advertisers. Recently, a circulation gap has appeared between the publishers' reports of magazines' newsstand sales and subsequent audits by the Audit Bureau of Circulations. The data in the file **Circulation** represent the reported and audited newsstand yearly sales (in thousands) for the following 10 magazines:

Magazine	Reported (X)	Audited (Y)
YM	621.0	299.6
CosmoGirl	359.7	207.7
Rosie	530.0	325.0
Playboy	492.1	336.3
Esquire	70.5	48.6
TeenPeople	567.0	400.3
More	125.5	91.2
Spin	50.6	39.1
Vogue	353.3	268.6
Elle	263.6	214.3

Source: *Data extracted from M. Rose, "In Fight for Ads, Publishers Often Overstate Their Sales," The Wall Street Journal, August 6, 2003, pp. A1, A10.*

a. Construct a scatter plot.
For these data, $b_0 = 26.724$ and $b_1 = 0.5719$.
b. Interpret the meaning of the slope, b_1, in this problem.
c. Predict the audited newsstand sales for a magazine that reports newsstand sales of 400,000.

12.6 The owner of a moving company typically has his most experienced manager predict the total number of labor hours that will be required to complete an upcoming move. This approach has proved useful in the past, but he would like to be able to develop a more accurate method of predicting labor hours by using the number of cubic feet moved. In a preliminary effort to provide a more accurate method, he has collected data for 36 moves in which the origin and destination were within the borough of Manhattan in New York City and in which the travel time was an insignificant portion of the hours worked. The data are stored in the file **Moving**.
a. Construct a scatter plot.
b. Assuming a linear relationship, use the least-squares method to find the regression coefficients b_0 and b_1.
c. Interpret the meaning of the slope, b_1, in this problem.
d. Predict the labor hours for moving 500 cubic feet.

12.7 A critically important aspect of customer service in a supermarket is the waiting time at the checkout (defined as the time the customer enters the line until he or she is served). Data were collected during time periods where there were a constant number of checkout counters open. The total number of customers in the store and the waiting times (in minutes) were recorded. The results are stored in the **Supermarket** file.
a. Construct a scatter plot.

b. Assuming a linear relationship, use the least-squares method to find the regression coefficients b_0 and b_1.
c. Interpret the meaning of the slope, b_1, in this problem.
d. Predict the waiting time when there are 20 customers in the store.

12.8 The value of a sports franchise is directly related to the amount of revenue that a franchise can generate. The data in the file **BBrevenue** represent the value in 2005 (in millions of dollars) and the annual revenue (in millions of dollars) for 30 baseball franchises. Suppose you want to develop a simple linear regression model to predict franchise value based on annual revenue generated.
a. Construct a scatter plot.
b. Use the least-squares method to find the regression coefficients b_0 and b_1.
c. Interpret the meaning of b_0 and b_1 in this problem.
d. Predict the value of a baseball franchise that generates $150 million of annual revenue.

12.9 An agent for a residential real estate company in a large city would like to be able to predict the monthly rental cost for apartments, based on the size of the apartment, as defined by square footage. A sample of 25 apartments (stored in the file **Rent**) in a particular residential neighborhood was selected, and the information gathered revealed the following:
a. Construct a scatter plot.
b. Use the least-squares method to find the regression coefficients b_0 and b_1.
c. Interpret the meaning of b_0 and b_1 in this problem.
d. Predict the monthly rent for an apartment that has 1,000 square feet.
e. Why would it not be appropriate to use the model to predict the monthly rent for apartments that have 500 square feet?
f. Your friends Jim and Jennifer are considering signing a lease for an apartment in this residential neighborhood. They are trying to decide between two apartments, one with 1,000 square feet for a monthly rent of $1,275 and the other with 1,200 square feet for a monthly rent of $1,425. Based on (a) through (d), which apartment do you think is a better deal?

12.10 A company that holds the DVD distribution rights to movies previously released only in theaters wants to estimate sales of DVDs based on box office success. Data are available in the file **Movie** that indicate the box office gross (in $millions) for each of 30 movies and the number of DVDs sold (in thousands). For these data:
a. Construct a scatter plot.
b. Assuming a linear relationship, use the least-squares method to find the regression coefficients b_0 and b_1.
c. Interpret the meaning of the slope, b_1, in this problem.
d. Predict the sales for a movie that had a box office gross of $75 million.

12.3 Measures of Variation

When using the least-squares method to determine the regression coefficients for a set of data, you need to compute three important measures of variation. The first measure, the **total sum of squares (SST)**, is a measure of variation of the Y_i values around their mean, $\overline{Y}$. The **total variation** or total sum of squares is subdivided into **explained variation** and **unexplained variation**. The explained variation or **regression sum of squares (SSR)** is due to the relationship between X and Y, and the unexplained variation, or **error sum of squares (SSE)**, is due to factors other than the relationship between X and Y. Figure 12.7 shows these different measures of variation.

FIGURE 12.7

Measures of variation

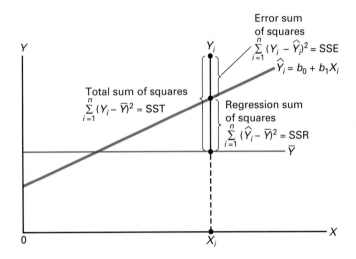

Computing the Sum of Squares

The regression sum of squares (SSR) is based on the difference between $\hat{Y}_i$ (the predicted value of Y from the prediction line) and $\overline{Y}$ (the mean value of Y). The error sum of squares (SSE) represents the part of the variation in Y that is not explained by the regression. It is based on the difference between Y_i and $\hat{Y}_i$. Equations (12.5), (12.6), (12.7), and (12.8) define these measures of variation.

MEASURES OF VARIATION IN REGRESSION

The total sum of squares is equal to the regression sum of squares plus the error sum of squares.

$$SST = SSR + SSE \tag{12.5}$$

TOTAL SUM OF SQUARES (SST)

The total sum of squares (SST) is equal to the sum of the squared differences between each observed value of Y and the mean value of Y.

$$SST = \text{Total sum of squares}$$

$$= \sum_{i=1}^{n}(Y_i - \overline{Y})^2 \tag{12.6}$$

REGRESSION SUM OF SQUARES (*SSR*)

The regression sum of squares (*SSR*) is equal to the sum of the squared differences between each predicted value of Y and the mean value of Y.

$$SSR = \text{Explained variation or regression sum of squares}$$

$$= \sum_{i=1}^{n} (\hat{Y}_i - \overline{Y})^2 \tag{12.7}$$

ERROR SUM OF SQUARES (*SSE*)

The error sum of squares (*SSE*) is equal to the sum of the squared differences between each observed value of Y and the predicted value of Y.

$$SSE = \text{Unexplained variation or error sum of squares}$$

$$= \sum_{i=1}^{n} (Y_i - \hat{Y}_i)^2 \tag{12.8}$$

Figure 12.8 shows the sum of squares portion of the worksheet containing the Microsoft Excel results for the Sunflowers Apparel data, and Figure 12.9 shows Minitab results. The total variation, *SST*, is equal to 116.9543. This amount is subdivided into the sum of squares explained by the regression (*SSR*), equal to 105.7476, and the sum of squares unexplained by the regression (*SSE*), equal to 11.2067. From Equation (12.5) on page 419:

$$SST = SSR + SSE$$

$$116.9543 = 105.7476 + 11.2067$$

FIGURE 12.8

Microsoft Excel sum of squares for the Sunflowers Apparel data

See Section E12.1 or P12.1 to create the worksheet that contains this area.

	A	B	C	D	E	F	G
10	ANOVA						
11		*df*	*SS*	*MS*	*F*	*Significance F*	
12	Regression	1	105.7476	105.7476	113.2335	0.0000	
13	Residual	12	11.2067	0.9339			
14	Total	13	116.9543				
15							
16		Coefficients	Standard Error	t Stat	P-value	Lower 95%	Upper 95%
17	Intercept	0.9645	0.5262	1.8329	0.0917	-0.1820	2.1110
18	Square Feet	1.6699	0.1569	10.6411	0.0000	1.3280	2.0118

FIGURE 12.9

Minitab sum of squares for the Sunflowers Apparel data

See Section M12.1 to create this.

```
Analysis of Variance

Source           DF     SS      MS      F      P
Regression        1  105.75  105.75  113.23  0.000
Residual Error   12   11.21    0.93
Total            13  116.95
```

In a data set that has a large number of significant digits, the results of a regression analysis are sometimes displayed using a numerical format known as *scientific notation*. This type of format is used to display very small or very large values. The number after the letter E represents the number of digits that the decimal point needs to be moved to the left (for a negative number) or to the right (for a positive number). For example, the number 3.7431E+02 means that the decimal point should be moved two places to the right, producing the number 374.31. The number 3.7431E−02 means that the decimal point should be moved two places to the left, producing the number 0.037431. When scientific notation is used, fewer significant digits are usually displayed, and the numbers may appear to be rounded.

The Coefficient of Determination

By themselves, *SSR, SSE,* and *SST* provide little information. However, the ratio of the regression sum of squares (*SSR*) to the total sum of squares (*SST*) measures the proportion of variation in *Y* that is explained by the independent variable *X* in the regression model. This ratio is called the coefficient of determination, r^2, and is defined in Equation (12.9).

COEFFICIENT OF DETERMINATION

The coefficient of determination is equal to the regression sum of squares (i.e., explained variation) divided by the total sum of squares (i.e., total variation).

$$r^2 = \frac{\text{Regression sum of squares}}{\text{Total sum of squares}} = \frac{SSR}{SST} \qquad \textbf{(12.9)}$$

The **coefficient of determination** measures the proportion of variation in *Y* that is explained by the independent variable *X* in the regression model.

For the Sunflowers Apparel data, with *SSR* = 105.7476, *SSE* = 11.2067, and *SST* = 116.9543,

$$r^2 = \frac{105.7476}{116.9543} = 0.9042$$

Therefore, 90.42% of the variation in annual sales is explained by the variability in the size of the store as measured by the square footage. This large r^2 indicates a strong linear relationship between these two variables because the use of a regression model has reduced the variability in predicting annual sales by 90.42%. Only 9.58% of the sample variability in annual sales is due to factors other than what is accounted for by the linear regression model that uses square footage.

Figure 12.10 presents the coefficient of determination portion of the Microsoft Excel results for the Sunflowers Apparel data, and Figure 12.11 shows Minitab results.

FIGURE 12.10

Partial Microsoft Excel regression results for the Sunflowers Apparel data

See Section E12.1 or P12.1 to create the worksheet that contains this.

	A	B
3	*Regression Statistics*	
4	Multiple R	0.9509
5	R Square	0.9042
6	Adjusted R Square	0.8962
7	Standard Error	0.9664
8	Observations	14

FIGURE 12.11

Partial Minitab regression results for the Sunflowers Apparel data

See Section M12.1 to create this.

```
Predictor      Coef   SE Coef     T      P
Constant     0.9645   0.5262   1.83   0.092
Square Feet  1.6699   0.1569  10.64   0.000


S = 0.966380   R-Sq = 90.4%   R-Sq(adj) = 89.6%
```

EXAMPLE 12.4

Computing the
Coefficient of
Determination

Compute the coefficient of determination, r^2, for the Sunflowers Apparel data.

SOLUTION You can compute SST, SSR, and SSE, that are defined in Equations (12.6), (12.7), and (12.8) on pages 419 and 420, by using Equations (12.10), (12.11), and (12.12).

COMPUTATIONAL FORMULA FOR SST

$$SST = \sum_{i=1}^{n}(Y_i - \bar{Y})^2 = \sum_{i=1}^{n}Y_i^2 - \frac{\left(\sum_{i=1}^{n}Y_i\right)^2}{n} \qquad (12.10)$$

COMPUTATIONAL FORMULA FOR SSR

$$SSR = \sum_{i=1}^{n}(\hat{Y}_i - \bar{Y})^2$$

$$= b_0\sum_{i=1}^{n}Y_i + b_1\sum_{i=1}^{n}X_iY_i - \frac{\left(\sum_{i=1}^{n}Y_i\right)^2}{n} \qquad (12.11)$$

COMPUTATIONAL FORMULA FOR SSE

$$SSE = \sum_{i=1}^{n}(Y_i - \hat{Y}_i)^2 = \sum_{i=1}^{n}Y_i^2 - b_0\sum_{i=1}^{n}Y_i - b_1\sum_{i=1}^{n}X_iY_i \qquad (12.12)$$

Using the summary results from Table 12.2 on page 415,

$$SST = \sum_{i=1}^{n}(Y_i - \bar{Y})^2 = \sum_{i=1}^{n}Y_i^2 - \frac{\left(\sum_{i=1}^{n}Y_i\right)^2}{n}$$

$$= 594.9 - \frac{(81.8)^2}{14}$$

$$= 594.9 - 477.94571$$

$$= 116.95429$$

$$SSR = \sum_{i=1}^{n}(\hat{Y}_i - \bar{Y})^2$$

$$= b_0\sum_{i=1}^{n}Y_i + b_1\sum_{i=1}^{n}X_iY_i - \frac{\left(\sum_{i=1}^{n}Y_i\right)^2}{n}$$

$$= (0.9645)(81.8) + (1.6699)(302.3) - \frac{(81.8)^2}{14}$$

$$= 105.74726$$

$$SSE = \sum_{i=1}^{n}(Y_i - \hat{Y}_i)^2$$

$$= \sum_{i=1}^{n} Y_i^2 - b_0 \sum_{i=1}^{n} Y_i - b_1 \sum_{i=1}^{n} X_i Y_i$$

$$= 594.9 - (0.9645)(81.8) - (1.6699)(302.3)$$

$$= 11.2067$$

Therefore,

$$r^2 = \frac{105.74726}{116.95429} = 0.9042$$

Standard Error of the Estimate

Although the least-squares method results in the line that fits the data with the minimum amount of error, unless all the observed data points fall on a straight line, the prediction line is not a perfect predictor. Just as all data values cannot be expected to be exactly equal to their mean, neither can all the values in a regression analysis be expected to fall exactly on the prediction line. Figure 12.6 on page 413 illustrates the variability around the prediction line for the Sunflowers Apparel data. Observe that, although many of the actual values of Y fall near the prediction line, none of the values are exactly on the line.

The **standard error of the estimate** measures the variability of the actual Y values from the predicted Y values in the same way that the standard deviation in Chapter 3 measures the variability of each value around the sample mean. In other words, the standard error of the estimate is the standard deviation *around* the prediction line, whereas the standard deviation in Chapter 3 is the standard deviation *around* the sample mean. Equation (12.13) defines the standard error of the estimate, represented by the symbol S_{YX}.

STANDARD ERROR OF THE ESTIMATE

$$S_{YX} = \sqrt{\frac{SSE}{n-2}} = \sqrt{\frac{\sum_{i=1}^{n}(Y_i - \hat{Y}_i)^2}{n-2}} \qquad \textbf{(12.13)}$$

where

$$Y_i = \text{actual value of } Y \text{ for a given } X_i$$

$$\hat{Y}_i = \text{predicted value of } Y \text{ for a given } X_i$$

$$SSE = \text{error sum of squares}$$

From Equation (12.8) and Figure 12.8 or Figure 12.9 on pages 420–421, $SSE = 11.2067$. Thus,

$$S_{YX} = \sqrt{\frac{11.2067}{14-2}} = 0.9664$$

This standard error of the estimate, equal to 0.9664 millions of dollars (i.e., \$966,400), is labeled Standard Error in the Microsoft Excel results shown in Figure 12.10 and S in the Minitab results in Figure 12.11 on page 421. The standard error of the estimate represents a measure of the variation around the prediction line. It is measured in the same units as the dependent variable Y. The interpretation of the standard error of the estimate is similar to that of the standard deviation. Just as the standard deviation measures variability around the mean, the standard error of the estimate measures variability around the prediction line. For Sunflowers Apparel, the typical difference between actual annual sales at a store and the predicted annual sales using the regression equation is approximately \$966,400.

Problems for Section 12.3

LEARNING THE BASICS

12.11 How do you interpret a coefficient of determination, r^2, equal to 0.80?

12.12 If $SSR = 36$ and $SSE = 4$, determine SST and then compute the coefficient of determination, r^2, and interpret its meaning.

12.13 If $SSR = 66$ and $SST = 88$, compute the coefficient of determination, r^2, and interpret its meaning.

12.14 If $SSE = 10$ and $SSR = 30$, compute the coefficient of determination, r^2, and interpret its meaning.

12.15 If $SSR = 120$, why is it impossible for SST to equal 110?

APPLYING THE CONCEPTS

12.16 In Problem 12.4 on page 417, the marketing manager used shelf space for pet food to predict weekly sales (stored in the file **Petfood**). For that data, $SSR = 20,535$ and $SST = 30,025$.
a. Determine the coefficient of determination, r^2, and interpret its meaning.
b. Determine the standard error of the estimate.
c. How useful do you think this regression model is for predicting sales?

12.17 In Problem 12.5 on page 417, you used reported magazine newsstand sales to predict audited sales (stored in the file **Circulation**). For that data, $SSR = 130,301.41$ and $SST = 144,538.64$.
a. Determine the coefficient of determination, r^2, and interpret its meaning.
b. Determine the standard error of the estimate.
c. How useful do you think this regression model is for predicting audited sales?

12.18 In Problem 12.6 on page 418, an owner of a moving company wanted to predict labor hours, based on the cubic feet moved (stored in the file **Moving**). Using the results of that problem,
a. determine the coefficient of determination, r^2, and interpret its meaning.
b. determine the standard error of the estimate.
c. How useful do you think this regression model is for predicting labor hours?

12.19 In Problem 12.7 on page 418, you used the number of customers to predict the waiting time at the checkout line in a supermarket (stored in the file **Supermarket**). Using the results of that problem,
a. determine the coefficient of determination, r^2, and interpret its meaning.
b. determine the standard error of the estimate.
c. How useful do you think this regression model is for predicting the waiting time at the checkout line in a supermarket?

12.20 In Problem 12.8 on page 418, you used annual revenues to predict the value of a baseball franchise (stored in the file **BBrevenue**). Using the results of that problem,
a. determine the coefficient of determination, r^2, and interpret its meaning.
b. determine the standard error of the estimate.
c. How useful do you think this regression model is for predicting the value of a baseball franchise?

12.21 In Problem 12.9 on page 418, an agent for a real estate company wanted to predict the monthly rent for apartments, based on the size of the apartment (stored in the file **Rent**). Using the results of that problem,
a. determine the coefficient of determination, r^2, and interpret its meaning.
b. determine the standard error of the estimate, and interpret its meaning.
c. How useful do you think this regression model is for predicting the monthly rent?
d. Can you think of other variables that might explain the variation in monthly rent?

12.22 In Problem 12.10 on page 418, you used box office gross to predict sales of DVDs (stored in the file **Movie**). Using the results of that problem,
a. determine the coefficient of determination, r^2, and interpret its meaning.
b. determine the standard error of the estimate, and interpret its meaning.
c. How useful do you think this regression model is for predicting sales of DVDs?
d. Can you think of other variables that might explain the variation in DVD sales?

12.4 Assumptions

The discussion of hypothesis testing and the analysis of variance emphasized the importance of the assumptions to the validity of any conclusions reached. The assumptions necessary for regression are similar to those of the analysis of variance because both topics fall in the general category of *linear models* (reference 4).

The four **assumptions of regression** (known by the acronym LINE) are as follows:

- **L**inearity
- **I**ndependence of errors
- **N**ormality of error
- **E**qual variance

The first assumption, **linearity**, states that the relationship between variables is linear. Relationships between variables that are not linear are discussed in Reference 4.

The second assumption, **independence of errors**, requires that the errors (ε_i) are independent of one another. This assumption is particularly important when data are collected over a period of time. In such situations, the errors for a specific time period are sometimes correlated with those of the previous time period.

The third assumption, **normality**, requires that the errors (ε_i) are normally distributed at each value of X. Like the t test and the ANOVA F test, regression analysis is fairly robust against departures from the normality assumption. As long as the distribution of the errors at each level of X is not extremely different from a normal distribution, inferences about β_0 and β_1 are not seriously affected.

The fourth assumption, **equal variance** or **homoscedasticity**, requires that the variance of the errors (ε_i) are constant for all values of X. In other words, the variability of Y values is the same when X is a low value as when X is a high value. The equal variance assumption is important when making inferences about β_0 and β_1. If there are serious departures from this assumption, you can use either data transformations or weighted least-squares methods (see reference 4).

12.5 Residual Analysis

In Section 12.1, regression analysis was introduced. In Sections 12.2 and 12.3, a regression model was developed using the least-squares approach for the Sunflowers Apparel data. Is this the correct model for these data? Are the assumptions introduced in Section 12.4 valid? In this section, a graphical approach called **residual analysis** is used to evaluate the assumptions and determine whether the regression model selected is an appropriate model.

The **residual** or estimated error value, e_i, is the difference between the observed (Y_i) and predicted ($\hat{Y}_i$) values of the dependent variable for a given value of X_i. Graphically, a residual appears on a scatter plot as the vertical distance between an observed value of Y and the prediction line. Equation (12.14) defines the residual.

> RESIDUAL
>
> The residual is equal to the difference between the observed value of Y and the predicted value of Y.
>
> $$e_i = Y_i - \hat{Y}_i \qquad \textbf{(12.14)}$$

Evaluating the Assumptions

Recall from Section 12.4 that the four assumptions of regression (known by the acronym LINE) are linearity, independence, normality, and equal variance.

Linearity To evaluate linearity, you plot the residuals on the vertical axis against the corresponding X_i values of the independent variable on the horizontal axis. If the linear model is appropriate for the data, there is no apparent pattern in this plot. However, if the linear model is not appropriate, there is a relationship between the X_i values and the residuals, e_i. You can see such a pattern in Figure 12.12. Panel A shows a situation in which, although there is an increasing trend in Y as X increases, the relationship seems curvilinear because the upward trend decreases for increasing values of X. This quadratic effect is highlighted in Panel B, where there is a clear relationship between X_i and e_i. By plotting the residuals, the linear trend of X with Y has been removed, thereby exposing the lack of fit in the simple linear model. Thus, a quadratic model is a better fit and should be used in place of the simple linear model. (See Reference 4 for further discussion of fitting curvilinear models.)

FIGURE 12.12

Studying the appropriateness of the simple linear regression model

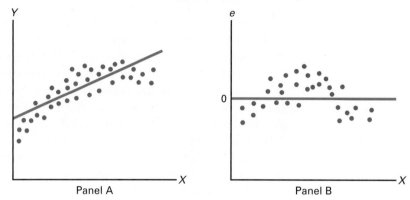

Panel A   Panel B

To determine whether the simple linear regression model is appropriate, return to the evaluation of the Sunflowers Apparel data. Figure 12.13 provides the predicted values and residuals computed by Microsoft Excel. To assess linearity, the residuals are plotted against the independent variable (store size, in thousands of square feet) in Figure 12.14. Although there is widespread scatter in the residual plot, there is no apparent pattern or relationship between the residuals and X_i. The residuals appear to be evenly spread above and below 0 for the differing values of X. You can conclude that the linear model is appropriate for the Sunflowers Apparel data.

FIGURE 12.13

Microsoft Excel residual output area for the Sunflowers Apparel data

See Sections E12.3 or P12.3 to create the worksheet that contains this. (Minitab users, see Section M12.1 to create equivalent results.)

	A	B	C
22	**RESIDUAL OUTPUT**		
23			
24	**Observation**	**Predicted Annual Sales**	**Residuals**
25	1	3.803239598	-0.103239598
26	2	3.636253367	0.263746633
27	3	5.640088147	1.059911853
28	4	10.31570263	-0.815702635
29	5	3.135294672	0.264705328
30	6	4.638170757	0.961829243
31	7	3.135294672	0.564705328
32	8	2.801322208	-0.101322208
33	9	6.308033074	-0.808033074
34	10	3.469267135	-0.569267135
35	11	9.647757708	1.052242292
36	12	8.645840318	-1.045840318
37	13	10.6496751	1.150324902
38	14	5.974060611	-1.874060611

FIGURE 12.14

Microsoft Excel plot of residuals against the square footage of a store for the Sunflowers Apparel data

See Sections E2.12 and E12.1 or P12.1 and P12.3 to create this. (Minitab users, see Section M12.1 to create an equivalent plot.)

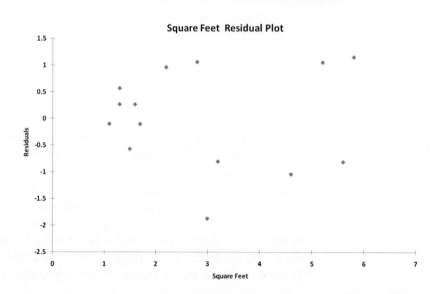

Independence You can evaluate the assumption of independence of the errors by plotting the residuals in the order or sequence in which the data were collected. If the values of Y are part of a time series (see Section 2.5), a value of Y is sometimes related to the previous value of Y, and thus there is a relationship between consecutive residuals. If this relationship exists (which violates the assumption of independence), there is a cyclical pattern in the plot of the residuals versus the time in which the data were collected. Because the Sunflowers Apparel data were collected during the same time period, you do not need to evaluate the independence assumption.

Normality You can evaluate the assumption of normality in the errors by tallying the residuals into a frequency distribution and displaying the results in a histogram (see Section 2.3). For the Sunflowers Apparel data, the residuals have been tallied into a frequency distribution in Table 12.3. (There is an insufficient number of values, however, to construct a histogram.) You can also evaluate the normality assumption by comparing the actual versus theoretical values of the residuals or by constructing a boxplot (see Section 3.4) or normal probability plot (see Section 6.3) of the residuals. Figure 12.15 is a normal probability plot of the residuals for the Sunflower Apparel data.

TABLE 12.3

Frequency Distribution of 14 Residual Values for the Sunflowers Apparel Data

Residuals	Frequency
-2.25 but less than -1.75	1
-1.75 but less than -1.25	0
-1.25 but less than -0.75	3
-0.75 but less than -0.25	1
-0.25 but less than $+0.25$	2
$+0.25$ but less than $+0.75$	3
$+0.75$ but less than $+1.25$	4
	14

FIGURE 12.15

Microsoft Excel normal probability plot of the residuals for the Sunflowers Apparel data

See Section E6.2 or P6.2 to create this. (Minitab users, see Section M6.2 to create an equivalent chart.)

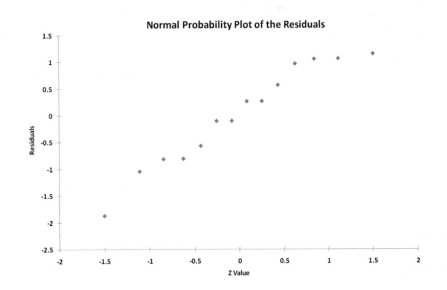

It is difficult to evaluate the normality assumption for a sample of only 14 values, regardless of whether you use a histogram, stem-and-leaf display, boxplot, or normal probability plot. You can see from Figure 12.15 that the data do not appear to depart substantially from a normal distribution. The robustness of regression analysis with modest departures from normality enables you to conclude that you should not be overly concerned about departures from this normality assumption in the Sunflowers Apparel data.

Equal Variance You can evaluate the assumption of equal variance from a plot of the residuals with X_i. For the Sunflowers Apparel data of Figure 12.14 on page 426, there do not appear to be major differences in the variability of the residuals for different X_i values. Thus, you can conclude that there is no apparent violation in the assumption of equal variance at each level of X.

To examine a case in which the equal variance assumption is violated, observe Figure 12.16, which is a plot of the residuals with X_i for a hypothetical set of data. In this plot, the variability of the residuals increases dramatically as X increases, demonstrating the lack of homogeneity in the variances of Y_i at each level of X. For these data, the equal variance assumption is invalid.

FIGURE 12.16
Violation of equal variance

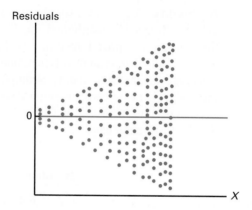

Problems for Section 12.5

LEARNING THE BASICS

12.23 The results below provide the X values, residuals, and a residual plot from a regression analysis:

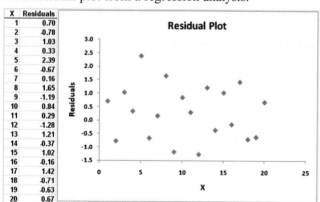

Is there any evidence of a pattern in the residuals? Explain.

12.24 The results below show the X values, residuals, and a residual plot from a regression analysis:

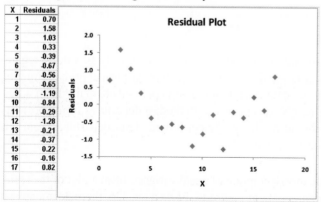

Is there any evidence of a pattern in the residuals? Explain.

APPLYING THE CONCEPTS

12.25 In Problem 12.5 on page 417, you used reported magazine newsstand sales to predict audited sales. The data are stored in the file **Circulation**. Perform a residual analysis for these data. Evaluate whether the assumptions of regression have been seriously violated.

SELF Test **12.26** In Problem 12.4 on page 417, the marketing manager used shelf space for pet food to predict weekly sales. The data are stored in the file **Petfood**. Perform a residual analysis for these data. Evaluate whether the assumptions of regression have been seriously violated.

12.27 In Problem 12.7 on page 418, you used the number of customers to predict the waiting time at a supermarket checkout. The data are stored in the file **Supermarket**. Perform a residual analysis for these data. Based on these results, evaluate whether the assumptions of regression have been seriously violated.

12.28 In Problem 12.6 on page 418, the owner of a moving company wanted to predict labor hours based on the cubic feet moved. The data are stored in the file **Moving**. Perform a residual analysis for these data. Based on these results, evaluate whether the assumptions of regression have been seriously violated.

12.29 In Problem 12.9 on page 418, an agent for a real estate company wanted to predict the monthly rent for apartments, based on the size of the apartments. The data are stored in the file **Rent**. Perform a residual analysis for these data. Based on these results, evaluate whether the assumptions of regression have been seriously violated.

12.30 In Problem 12.8 on page 418, you used annual revenues to predict the value of a baseball franchise. The data are stored in the file BBrevenue. Perform a residual analysis for these data. Based on these results, evaluate whether the assumptions of regression have been seriously violated.

12.31 In Problem 12.10 on page 418, you used box office gross to predict the sales of DVDs. The data are stored in the file Movie. Perform a residual analysis for these data. Based on these results, evaluate whether the assumptions of regression have been seriously violated.

12.6 Inferences About the Slope and Correlation Coefficient

In Sections 12.1 through 12.3, regression was used solely for descriptive purposes. You learned how the least-squares method determines the regression coefficients and how to predict Y for a given value of X. In addition, you learned how to compute and interpret the standard error of the estimate and the coefficient of determination.

When residual analysis, as discussed in Section 12.5, indicates that the assumptions of a least-squares regression model are not seriously violated and that the straight-line model is appropriate, you can make inferences about the linear relationship between the variables in the population.

t Test for the Slope

To determine the existence of a significant linear relationship between the X and Y variables, you test whether β_1 (the population slope) is equal to 0. The null and alternative hypotheses are as follows:

H_0: $\beta_1 = 0$ [There is no linear relationship (the slope is zero).]

H_1: $\beta_1 \neq 0$ [There is a linear relationship (the slope is not zero).]

If you reject the null hypothesis, you conclude that there is evidence of a linear relationship. Equation (12.15) defines the test statistic.

TESTING A HYPOTHESIS FOR A POPULATION SLOPE, β_1, USING THE t TEST

The t_{STAT} test statistic equals the difference between the sample slope and hypothesized value of the population slope divided by the standard error of the slope.

$$t_{STAT} = \frac{b_1 - \beta_1}{S_{b_1}} \tag{12.15}$$

where

$$S_{b_1} = \frac{S_{YX}}{\sqrt{SSX}}$$

$$SSX = \sum_{i=1}^{n} (X_i - \bar{X})^2$$

The t_{STAT} test statistic follows a t distribution with $n - 2$ degrees of freedom.

Return to the Using Statistics scenario on page 407 concerning Sunflowers Apparel. To test whether there is a significant linear relationship between the size of the store and the annual sales at the 0.05 level of significance, refer to the Microsoft Excel worksheet for the t test results presented in Figure 12.17 or the Minitab results shown in Figure 12.18.

FIGURE 12.17
Microsoft Excel t-test results of the slope for the Sunflowers Apparel data

See Section E12.1 or P12.1 to create the worksheet that contains this area.

	A	B	C	D	E	F	G
16		Coefficients	Standard Error	t Stat	P-value	Lower 95%	Upper 95%
17	Intercept	0.9645	0.5262	1.8329	0.0917	-0.1820	2.1110
18	Square Feet	1.6699	0.1569	10.6411	0.0000	1.3280	2.0118

FIGURE 12.18
Minitab *t*-test results
of the slope for the
Sunflowers Apparel data

```
Predictor      Coef   SE Coef     T      P
Constant     0.9645   0.5262   1.83   0.092
Square Feet  1.6699   0.1569  10.64   0.000
```

*See Section M12.1 to create
this worksheet.*

From Figure 12.17 or Figure 12.18,

$$b_1 = +1.6699 \quad n = 14 \quad S_{b_1} = 0.1569$$

and

$$t_{STAT} = \frac{b_1 - \beta_1}{S_{b_1}}$$

$$= \frac{1.6699 - 0}{0.1569} = 10.64$$

Microsoft Excel labels this t_{STAT} test statistic *t* Stat (see Figure 12.17) whereas Minitab labels it T (see Figure 12.18). Using the 0.05 level of significance, the critical value of *t* with $n - 2 = 12$ degrees of freedom is 2.1788. Because $t_{STAT} = 10.6411 > 2.1788$, you reject H_0 (see Figure 12.19). Using the *p*-value, you reject H_0 because the *p*-value is approximately 0, which is less than $\alpha = 0.05$. Hence, you can conclude that there is a significant linear relationship between mean annual sales and the size of the store.

FIGURE 12.19

Testing a hypothesis
about the population
slope at the 0.05 level
of significance, with 12
degrees of freedom

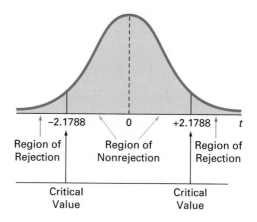

F Test for the Slope

As an alternative to the *t* test, you can use an *F* test to determine whether the slope in simple linear regression is statistically significant. In Section 10.4, you used the *F* distribution to test the ratio of two variances. Equation (12.16) defines the *F* test for the slope as the ratio of the variance that is due to the regression (*MSR*) divided by the error variance ($MSE = S_{YX}^2$).

TESTING A HYPOTHESIS FOR A POPULATION SLOPE, β_1, USING THE *F* TEST

The F_{STAT} test statistic is equal to the regression mean square (*MSR*) divided by the error mean square (*MSE*).

$$F_{STAT} = \frac{MSR}{MSE} \tag{12.16}$$

where

$$MSR = \frac{SSR}{1} = SSR$$

$$MSE = \frac{SSE}{n - 2}$$

The F_{STAT} test statistic follows an *F* distribution with 1 and $n - 2$ degrees of freedom.

Using a level of significance α, the decision rule is

$$\text{Reject } H_0 \text{ if } F_{STAT} > F_\alpha;$$

$$\text{otherwise, do not reject } H_0.$$

Table 12.4 organizes the complete set of results into an Analysis of Variance (ANOVA) table.

TABLE 12.4

ANOVA Table for Testing the Significance of a Regression Coefficient

Source	df	Sum of Squares	Mean Square (Variance)	F
Regression	1	SSR	$MSR = \dfrac{SSR}{1} = SSR$	$F_{STAT} = \dfrac{MSR}{MSE}$
Error	$n - 2$	SSE	$MSE = \dfrac{SSE}{n - 2}$	
Total	$n - 1$	SST		

The completed ANOVA table is also part of the Microsoft Excel results shown in Figure 12.20 or the Minitab results shown in Figure 12.21. These results show that the computed F_{STAT} test statistic is 113.2335 and the p-value is approximately 0.

FIGURE 12.20

Microsoft Excel F-test results for the Sunflowers Apparel data

See Section E12.1 or P12.1 to create the worksheet that contains this.

	A	B	C	D	E	F	G
10	**ANOVA**						
11		*df*	*SS*	*MS*	*F*	*Significance F*	
12	**Regression**	1	105.7476	105.7476	113.2335	0.0000	
13	**Residual**	12	11.2067	0.9339			
14	**Total**	13	116.9543				
15							
16		*Coefficients*	*Standard Error*	*t Stat*	*P-value*	*Lower 95%*	*Upper 95%*
17	**Intercept**	0.9645	0.5262	1.8329	0.0917	-0.1820	2.1110
18	**Square Feet**	1.6699	0.1569	10.6411	0.0000	1.3280	2.0118

FIGURE 12.21

Minitab F-test results for the Sunflowers Apparel data

See Section M12.1 to create this.

```
Analysis of Variance

Source          DF    SS       MS              F      P
Regression       1  105.75  105.75 MSR      113.23  0.000
Residual Error  12   11.21    0.93 MSE
Total           13  116.95
```

Using a level of significance of 0.05, from Table E.5, the critical value of the F distribution, with 1 and 12 degrees of freedom, is 4.75 (see Figure 12.22). Because $F_{STAT} = 113.2335 > 4.75$ or because the p-value $= 0.0000 < 0.05$, you reject H_0 and conclude that the size of the store is significantly related to annual sales. Because the F test in Equation (12.16) on page 430 is equivalent to the t test in Equation (12.15) on page 429, you reach the same conclusion.

FIGURE 12.22

Regions of rejection and nonrejection when testing for the significance of the slope at the 0.05 level of significance, with 1 and 12 degrees of freedom

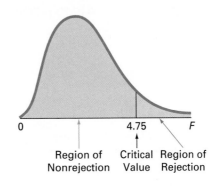

Confidence Interval Estimate for the Slope

In testing for the existence of a linear relationship between the variables, you can construct a confidence interval estimate of β_1 using Equation (12.17).

CONFIDENCE INTERVAL ESTIMATE OF THE SLOPE, β_1

The confidence interval estimate for the population slope can be constructed by taking the sample slope, b_1, and adding and subtracting the critical t value multiplied by the standard error of the slope.

$$b_1 \pm t_{\alpha/2}S_{b_1} \tag{12.17}$$

where $t_{\alpha/2}$ is the critical value corresponding to an upper-tail probability of $\alpha/2$ from the t distribution with $n - 2$ degrees of freedom (i.e., a cumulative area of $1 - \alpha/2$).

From the Microsoft Excel results of Figure 12.17 on page 429 or the Minitab results of Figure 12.18 on page 430,

$$b_1 = 1.6699 \quad n = 14 \quad S_{b_1} = 0.1569$$

To construct a 95% confidence interval estimate, $\alpha/2 = 0.025$, and from Table E.3, $t_{\alpha/2} = 2.1788$. Thus,

$$b_1 \pm t_{\alpha/2}S_{b_1} = 1.6699 \pm (2.1788)(0.1569)$$

$$= 1.6699 \pm 0.3419$$

$$1.3280 \leq \beta_1 \leq 2.0118$$

Therefore, you estimate with 95% confidence that the population slope is between 1.3280 and 2.0118. Because these values are both above 0, you conclude that there is a significant linear relationship between annual sales and the size of the store. Had the interval included 0, you would have concluded that no significant relationship exists between the variables. The confidence interval indicates that for each increase of 1,000 square feet, mean annual sales are estimated to increase by at least \$1,328,000 but no more than \$2,011,800.

t Test for the Correlation Coefficient

In Section 3.5 on page 110, the strength of the relationship between two numerical variables was measured, using the **correlation coefficient**, r. The values of the coefficient of correlation range from -1 for a perfect negative correlation to $+1$ for a perfect positive correlation. You can use the correlation coefficient to determine whether there is a statistically significant linear relationship between X and Y. To do so, you hypothesize that the population correlation coefficient, ρ, is 0. Thus, the null and alternative hypotheses are

$$H_0: \rho = 0 \text{ (no correlation)}$$

$$H_1: \rho \neq 0 \text{ (correlation)}$$

Equation (12.18) defines the test statistic for determining the existence of a significant correlation.

TESTING FOR THE EXISTENCE OF CORRELATION

$$t_{STAT} = \frac{r - \rho}{\sqrt{\dfrac{1 - r^2}{n - 2}}} \tag{12.18a}$$

where

$$r = +\sqrt{r^2} \text{ if } b_1 > 0$$

$$r = -\sqrt{r^2} \text{ if } b_1 < 0$$

The t_{STAT} test statistic follows a t distribution with $n - 2$ degrees of freedom.

An alternative method to calculate r is as follows:

$$r = \frac{\text{cov}(X,Y)}{S_X S_Y} \tag{12.18b}$$

where

$$\text{cov}(X,Y) = \frac{\displaystyle\sum_{i=1}^{n}(X_i - \bar{X})(Y_i - \bar{Y})}{n - 1}$$

$$S_X = \sqrt{\frac{\displaystyle\sum_{i=1}^{n}(X_i - \bar{X})^2}{n - 1}}$$

$$S_Y = \sqrt{\frac{\displaystyle\sum_{i=1}^{n}(Y_i - \bar{Y})^2}{n - 1}}$$

In the Sunflowers Apparel problem, $r^2 = 0.9042$ and $b_1 = +1.6699$ (see Figure 12.4 or 12.5 on page 412). Because $b_1 > 0$, the correlation coefficient for annual sales and store size is the positive square root of r^2, that is, $r = +\sqrt{0.9042} = +0.9509$. Using Equation (12.18a) to test the null hypothesis that there is no correlation between these two variables results in the following observed t statistic:

$$t_{STAT} = \frac{r - 0}{\sqrt{\dfrac{1 - r^2}{n - 2}}}$$

$$= \frac{0.9509 - 0}{\sqrt{\dfrac{1 - (0.9509)^2}{14 - 2}}} = 10.6411$$

Using the 0.05 level of significance, because $t_{STAT} = 10.6411 > 2.1788$, you reject the null hypothesis. You conclude that there is a significant association between annual sales and store size. This t_{STAT} test statistic is equivalent to the t_{STAT} test statistic found when testing whether the population slope, β_1, is equal to zero.

Problems for Section 12.6

LEARNING THE BASICS

12.32 You are testing the null hypothesis that there is no linear relationship between two variables, X and Y. From your sample of $n = 18$, you determine that $b_1 = +4.5$ and $S_{b_1} = 1.5$.
a. What is the value of t_{STAT}?
b. At the $\alpha = 0.05$ level of significance, what are the critical values?
c. Based on your answers to (a) and (b), what statistical decision should you make?
d. Construct a 95% confidence interval estimate of the population slope, β_1.

12.33 You are testing the null hypothesis that there is no linear relationship between two variables, X and Y. From your sample of $n = 20$, you determine that $SSR = 60$ and $SSE = 40$.
a. What is the value of F_{STAT}?
b. At the $\alpha = 0.05$ level of significance, what is the critical value?
c. Based on your answers to (a) and (b), what statistical decision should you make?
d. Compute the correlation coefficient by first computing r^2 and assuming that b_1 is negative.
e. At the 0.05 level of significance, is there a significant correlation between X and Y?

APPLYING THE CONCEPTS

✓ SELF Test **12.34** In Problem 12.4 on page 417, the marketing manager used shelf space for pet food to predict weekly sales. The data are stored in the file **Petfood**. From the results of that problem, $b_1 = 7.4$ and $S_{b_1} = 1.59$.
a. At the 0.05 level of significance, is there evidence of a linear relationship between shelf space and sales?
b. Construct a 95% confidence interval estimate of the population slope, β_1.

12.35 In Problem 12.5 on page 417, you used reported magazine newsstand sales to predict audited sales. The data are stored in the file **Circulation**. Using the results of that problem, $b_1 = 0.5719$ and $S_{b_1} = 0.0668$.
a. At the 0.05 level of significance, is there evidence of a linear relationship between reported sales and audited sales?
b. Construct a 95% confidence interval estimate of the population slope, β_1.

12.36 In Problem 12.6 on page 418, the owner of a moving company wanted to predict labor hours, based on the number of cubic feet moved. The data are stored in the file **Moving**. Using the results of that problem,
a. at the 0.05 level of significance, is there evidence of a linear relationship between the number of cubic feet moved and labor hours?
b. construct a 95% confidence interval estimate of the population slope, β_1.

12.37 In Problem 12.7 on page 418, you used the number of customers to predict the waiting time on the checkout line. The data are stored in the file **Supermarket**. Using the results of that problem,
a. at the 0.05 level of significance, is there evidence of a linear relationship between the number of customers and the waiting time on the checkout line?
b. construct a 95% confidence interval estimate of the population slope, β_1.

12.38 In Problem 12.8 on page 418, you used annual revenues to predict the value of a baseball franchise. The data are stored in the file **BBrevenue**. Using the results of that problem,
a. at the 0.05 level of significance, is there evidence of a linear relationship between annual revenue and franchise value?
b. construct a 95% confidence interval estimate of the population slope, β_1.

12.39 In Problem 12.9 on page 418, an agent for a real estate company wanted to predict the monthly rent for apartments, based on the size of the apartment. The data are stored in the file **Rent**. Using the results of that problem,
a. at the 0.05 level of significance, is there evidence of a linear relationship between the size of the apartment and the monthly rent?
b. construct a 95% confidence interval estimate of the population slope, β_1.

12.40 In Problem 12.10 on page 418, you used box office gross to predict the sales of DVDs. The data are stored in the file **Movie**. Using the results of that problem,
a. at the 0.05 level of significance, is there evidence of a linear relationship between box office gross and sales of DVDs?
b. construct a 95% confidence interval estimate of the population slope, β_1.

12.41 The volatility of a stock is often measured by its beta value. You can estimate the beta value of a stock by developing a simple linear regression model, using the percentage weekly change in the stock as the dependent variable and the percentage weekly change in a market index as the independent variable. The S&P 500 Index is a common index to use. For example, if you wanted to estimate the beta for Disney, you could use the following model, which is sometimes referred to as a *market model*:

$$(\% \text{ weekly change in Disney}) = \beta_0$$
$$+ \beta_1(\% \text{ weekly change in S\&P 500 index}) + \varepsilon$$

The least-squares regression estimate of the slope b_1 is the estimate of the beta value for Disney. A stock with a beta value of 1.0 tends to move the same as the overall market. A stock with a beta value of 1.5 tends to move 50% more than the overall market, and a stock with a beta value of 0.6 tends to move only 60% as much as the overall market. Stocks with negative beta values tend to move in a direction opposite that of the overall market. The following table gives some beta values for some widely held stocks:

Company	Ticker Symbol	Beta
AT&T	T	1.07
Disney Company	DIS	0.64
Alcoa	AA	1.26
LSI Logic	LSI	1.81
Wave Systems	WAVX	2.72

Source: *Data extracted from* **finance.yahoo.com**, *April 29, 2008.*

a. For each of the five companies, interpret the beta value.
b. How can investors use the beta value as a guide for investing?

12.42 Index funds are mutual funds that try to mimic the movement of leading indexes, such as the S&P 500 Index, the NASDAQ 100 Index, or the Russell 2000 Index. The beta values (as described in Problem 12.41) for these funds are therefore approximately 1.0. The estimated market models for these funds are approximately

$$(\% \text{ weekly change in index fund}) = 0.0$$
$$+ 1.0(\% \text{ weekly change in the index})$$

Leveraged index funds are designed to magnify the movement of major indexes. An article in *Mutual Funds* (L. O'Shaughnessy, "Reach for Higher Returns," *Mutual Funds*, July 1999, pp. 44–49) described some of the risks and rewards associated with these funds and gave details on some of the most popular leveraged funds, including those in the following table:

Name (Ticker Symbol)	Fund Description
Potomac Small Cap Plus (POSCX)	125% of Russell 2000 Index
Rydex "Inv" Nova (RYNVX)	150% of the S&P 500 Index
ProFund UltraOTC "Inv" (UOPIX)	Double (200%) the NASDAQ 100 Index

The estimated market models for these funds are approximately

(% weekly change in POSCX) = 0.0
  + 1.25 (% weekly change in the Russell 2000 Index)

(% weekly change in RYNVX) = 0.0
  + 1.50 (% weekly change in the S&P 500 Index)

(% weekly change in UOPIX fund) = 0.0
  + 2.0 (% weekly change in the NASDAQ 100 Index)

Thus, if the Russell 2000 Index gains 10% over a period of time, the leveraged mutual fund POSCX gains approximately 12.5%. On the downside, if the same index loses 20%, POSCX loses approximately 25%.

a. Consider the leveraged mutual fund ProFund UltraOTC "Inv" (UOPIX), whose description is 200% of the performance of the NASDAQ 100 Index. What is its approximate market model?

b. If the NASDAQ gains 30% in a year, what return do you expect UOPIX to have?

c. If the NASDAQ loses 35% in a year, what return do you expect UOPIX to have?

d. What type of investors should be attracted to leveraged funds? What type of investors should stay away from these funds?

12.43 The data in the file Coffeedrink represent the calories and fat (in grams) of 16-ounce iced coffee drinks at Dunkin' Donuts and Starbucks:

Product	Calories	Fat
Dunkin' Donuts Iced Mocha Swirl latte (whole milk)	240	8.0
Starbucks Coffee Frappuccino blended coffee	260	3.5
Dunkin' Donuts Coffee Coolatta (cream)	350	22.0
Starbucks Iced Coffee Mocha Espresso (whole milk and whipped cream)	350	20.0
Starbucks Mocha Frappuccino blended coffee (whipped cream)	420	16.0
Starbucks Chocolate Brownie Frappuccino blended coffee (whipped cream)	510	22.0
Starbucks Chocolate Frappuccino Blended Crème (whipped cream)	530	19.0

Source: *Data extracted from "Coffee as Candy at Dunkin' Donuts and Starbucks,"* Consumer Reports, *June 2004, p. 9.*

a. Compute and interpret the coefficient of correlation, r.

b. At the 0.05 level of significance, is there a significant linear relationship between calories and fat?

12.44 There are several methods for calculating fuel economy. The following table (contained in the file Mileage) indicates the mileage as calculated by owners and by current government standards:

Vehicle	Owner	Government Standards
2005 Ford F-150	14.3	16.8
2005 Chevrolet Silverado	15.0	17.8
2002 Honda Accord LX	27.8	26.2
2002 Honda Civic	27.9	34.2
2004 Honda Civic Hybrid	48.8	47.6
2002 Ford Explorer	16.8	18.3
2005 Toyota Camry	23.7	28.5
2003 Toyota Corolla	32.8	33.1
2005 Toyota Prius	37.3	56.0

a. Compute and interpret the coefficient of correlation, r.

b. At the 0.05 level of significance, is there a significant linear relationship between the mileage as calculated by owners and by current government standards?

12.45 College basketball is big business, with coaches' salaries, revenues, and expenses in millions of dollars. The data in the file Colleges-basketball represent the coaches' salaries and revenues for college basketball at selected schools in a recent year (data extracted from R. Adams, "Pay for Playoffs," *The Wall Street Journal*, March 11–12, 2006, pp. P1, P8).

a. Compute and interpret the coefficient of correlation, r.

b. At the 0.05 level of significance, is there a significant linear relationship between a coach's salary and revenue?

12.46 College football players trying out for the NFL are given the Wonderlic standardized intelligence test. The data in the file Wonderlic represent the average Wonderlic scores of football players trying out for the NFL and the graduation rates for football players at the schools they attended (data extracted from S. Walker, "The NFL's Smartest Team," *The Wall Street Journal*, September 30, 2005, pp. W1, W10).

a. Compute and interpret the coefficient of correlation, r.

b. At the 0.05 level of significance, is there a significant linear relationship between the average Wonderlic score of football players trying out for the NFL and the graduation rates for football players at selected schools?

c. What conclusions can you reach about the relationship between the average Wonderlic score of football players trying out for the NFL and the graduation rates for football players at selected schools?

12.7 Estimation of Mean Values and Prediction of Individual Values

This section presents methods of making inferences about the mean of Y and predicting individual values of Y.

The Confidence Interval Estimate

In Example 12.2 on page 413, you used the prediction line to predict the value of Y for a given X. The mean annual sales for stores with 4,000 square feet was predicted to be 7.644 millions of dollars ($7,644,000). This estimate, however, is a *point estimate* of the population mean. In Chapter 8, you studied the concept of the confidence interval estimate of the population mean. In a similar fashion, Equation (12.19) defines the **confidence interval estimate for the mean response** for a given X.

CONFIDENCE INTERVAL ESTIMATE FOR THE MEAN OF Y

$$\hat{Y}_i \pm t_{\alpha/2} S_{YX} \sqrt{h_i}$$

$$\hat{Y}_i - t_{\alpha/2} S_{YX} \sqrt{h_i} \leq \mu_{Y|X=X_i} \leq \hat{Y}_i + t_{\alpha/2} S_{YX} \sqrt{h_i} \tag{12.19}$$

where

$$h_i = \frac{1}{n} + \frac{(X_i - \overline{X})^2}{SSX}$$

$\hat{Y}_i$ = predicted value of Y; $\hat{Y}_i = b_0 + b_1 X_i$

S_{YX} = standard error of the estimate

n = sample size

X_i = given value of X

$\mu_{Y|X=X_i}$ = mean value of Y when $X = X_i$

$$SSX = \sum_{i=1}^{n} (X_i - \overline{X})^2$$

$t_{\alpha/2}$ is the critical value corresponding to an upper-tail probability of $\alpha/2$ from the t distribution with $n - 2$ degrees of freedom (i.e., a cumulative area of $1 - \alpha/2$).

The width of the confidence interval in Equation (12.19) depends on several factors. Increased variation around the prediction line, as measured by the standard error of the estimate, results in a wider interval. However, as you would expect, increased sample size reduces the width of the interval. In addition, the width of the interval also varies at different values of X. When you predict Y for values of X close to $\overline{X}$, the interval is narrower than for predictions for X values more distant from $\overline{X}$.

In the Sunflowers Apparel example, suppose you want to construct a 95% confidence interval estimate of the mean annual sales for the entire population of stores that contain 4,000 square feet ($X = 4$). Using the simple linear regression equation,

$$\hat{Y}_i = 0.9645 + 1.6699 X_i$$

$$= 0.9645 + 1.6699(4) = 7.6439 \text{ (millions of dollars)}$$

Also, given the following:

$$\overline{X} = 2.9214 \quad S_{YX} = 0.9664$$

$$SSX = \sum_{i=1}^{n} (X_i - \overline{X})^2 = 37.9236$$

From Table E.3, $t_{\alpha/2} = 2.1788$. Thus,

$$\hat{Y}_i \pm t_{\alpha/2} S_{YX} \sqrt{h_i}$$

where

$$h_i = \frac{1}{n} + \frac{(X_i - \overline{X})^2}{SSX}$$

so that

$$\hat{Y}_i \pm t_{\alpha/2} S_{YX} \sqrt{\frac{1}{n} + \frac{(X_i - \overline{X})^2}{SSX}}$$

$$= 7.6439 \pm (2.1788)(0.9664) \sqrt{\frac{1}{14} + \frac{(4 - 2.9214)^2}{37.9236}}$$

$$= 7.6439 \pm 0.6728$$

so

$$6.9711 \leq \mu_{Y|X=4} \leq 8.3167$$

Therefore, the 95% confidence interval estimate is that the mean annual sales are between $6,971,100 and $8,316,700 for the population of stores with 4,000 square feet.

The Prediction Interval

Often, it is important to predict the response for an individual value. In addition to calculating the predicted value $\hat{Y}$, you can construct a prediction interval. Although the form of the prediction interval is similar to that of the confidence interval estimate of Equation (12.19), the prediction interval is predicting an individual value, not estimating a parameter. Equation (12.20) defines the **prediction interval for an individual response, Y,** at a particular value, X_i, denoted by $Y_{X=X_i}$.

PREDICTION INTERVAL FOR AN INDIVIDUAL RESPONSE, Y

$$\hat{Y}_i \pm t_{\alpha/2} S_{YX} \sqrt{1 + h_i} \qquad \textbf{(12.20)}$$

$$\hat{Y}_i - t_{\alpha/2} S_{YX} \sqrt{1 + h_i} \leq Y_{X=X_i} \leq \hat{Y}_i + t_{\alpha/2} S_{YX} \sqrt{1 + h_i}$$

where h_i, $\hat{Y}_i$, S_{YX}, n, and X_i are defined as in Equation (12.19) on page 436 and $Y_{X=X_i}$ is a future value of Y when $X = X_i$.

$t_{\alpha/2}$ is the critical value corresponding to an upper-tail probability of $\alpha/2$ from the t distribution with $n - 2$ degrees of freedom (i.e., a cumulative area of $1 - \alpha/2$).

To construct a 95% prediction interval of the annual sales for an individual store that contains 4,000 square feet ($X = 4$), you first compute $\hat{Y}_i$. Using the prediction line:

$$\hat{Y}_i = 0.9645 + 1.6699 X_i$$

$$= 0.9645 + 1.6699(4)$$

$$= 7.6439 \text{ (millions of dollars)}$$

Also, given the following:

$$\bar{X} = 2.9214 \quad S_{YX} = 0.9664$$

$$SSX = \sum_{i=1}^{n}(X_i - \bar{X})^2 = 37.9236$$

From Table E.3, $t_{\alpha/2} = 2.1788$. Thus,

$$\hat{Y}_i \pm t_{\alpha/2}S_{YX}\sqrt{1 + h_i}$$

where

$$h_i = \frac{1}{n} + \frac{(X_i - \bar{X})^2}{\sum_{i=1}^{n}(X_i - \bar{X})^2}$$

so that

$$\hat{Y}_i \pm t_{\alpha/2}S_{YX}\sqrt{1 + \frac{1}{n} + \frac{(X_i - \bar{X})^2}{SSX}}$$

$$= 7.6439 \pm (2.1788)(0.9664)\sqrt{1 + \frac{1}{14} + \frac{(4 - 2.9214)^2}{37.9236}}$$

$$= 7.6439 \pm 2.2104$$

so

$$5.4335 \le Y_{X=4} \le 9.8543$$

Therefore, with 95% confidence, you predict that the annual sales for an individual store with 4,000 square feet is between $5,433,500 and $9,854,300.

Figure 12.23 is a Microsoft Excel worksheet that illustrates the confidence interval estimate and the prediction interval for the Sunflowers Apparel problem and Figure 12.24 contains Minitab results. If you compare the results of the confidence interval estimate and the prediction interval, you see that the width of the prediction interval for an individual store is much wider than the confidence interval estimate for the mean. Remember that there is much more variation in predicting an individual value than in estimating a mean value.

FIGURE 12.23

Microsoft Excel confidence interval estimate and prediction interval worksheet for the Sunflowers Apparel data

See Section E12.4 or P12.4 to create this.

	A	B	
1	**Site Selection Analysis**		
2			
3	**Data**		
4	**X Value**	**4**	
5	**Confidence Level**	**95%**	
6			
7	Intermediate Calculations		
8	Sample Size	14	=DataCopy!F2
9	Degrees of Freedom	12	=B8 - 2
10	t Value	2.1788	=TINV(1 - B5, B9)
11	Sample Mean	2.9214	=DataCopy!F3
12	Sum of Squared Difference	37.9236	=DataCopy!F4
13	Standard Error of the Estimate	0.9664	**from regression worksheet cell B7**
14	h Statistic	0.1021	=1/B8 + (B4 - B11)^2/B12
15	Predicted Y (YHat)	7.6439	=DataCopy!F5
16			
17	**For Average Y**		
18	Interval Half Width	0.6728	=B10 * B13 * SQRT(B14)
19	**Confidence Interval Lower Limit**	**6.9711**	=B15 - B18
20	**Confidence Interval Upper Limit**	**8.3167**	=B15 + B18
21			
22	**For Individual Response Y**		
23	Interval Half Width	2.2104	=B10 * B13 * SQRT(1 + B14)
24	**Prediction Interval Lower Limit**	**5.4335**	=B15 - B23
25	**Prediction Interval Upper Limit**	**9.8544**	=B15 + B23

FIGURE 12.24

Minitab confidence interval estimate and prediction interval for the Sunflowers Apparel data

See Section M12.1 to create this.

```
Predicted Values for New Observations

New
Obs    Fit  SE Fit      95% CI          95% PI
  1  7.644   0.309  (6.971, 8.317)  (5.433, 9.854)


Values of Predictors for New Observations

New   Square
Obs    Feet
  1    4.00
```

Problems for Section 12.7

LEARNING THE BASICS

12.47 Based on a sample of $n = 20$, the least-squares method was used to develop the following prediction line: $\hat{Y}_i = 5 + 3X_i$. In addition,

$$S_{YX} = 1.0 \quad \bar{X} = 2 \quad \sum_{i=1}^{n}(X_i - \bar{X})^2 = 20$$

a. Construct a 95% confidence interval estimate of the population mean response for $X = 2$.
b. Construct a 95% prediction interval of an individual response for $X = 2$.

12.48 Based on a sample of $n = 20$, the least-squares method was used to develop the following prediction line: $\hat{Y}_i = 5 + 3X_i$. In addition,

$$S_{YX} = 1.0 \quad \bar{X} = 2 \quad \sum_{i=1}^{n}(X_i - \bar{X})^2 = 20$$

a. Construct a 95% confidence interval estimate of the population mean response for $X = 4$.
b. Construct a 95% prediction interval of an individual response for $X = 4$.
c. Compare the results of (a) and (b) with those of Problem 12.47(a) and (b). Which interval is wider? Why?

APPLYING THE CONCEPTS

12.49 In Problem 12.5 on page 417, you used reported sales to predict audited sales of magazines. The data are stored in the file **Circulation**. For these data $S_{YX} = 42.186$ and $h_i = 0.108$ when $X = 400$.
a. Construct a 95% confidence interval estimate of the mean audited sales for magazines that report newsstand sales of 400,000.
b. Construct a 95% prediction interval of the audited sales for an individual magazine that reports newsstand sales of 400,000.
c. Explain the difference in the results in (a) and (b).

 SELF Test **12.50** In Problem 12.4 on page 417, the marketing manager used shelf space for pet food to pre-

dict weekly sales. The data are stored in the file **Petfood**. For these data $S_{YX} = 30.81$ and $h_i = 0.1373$ when $X = 8$.
a. Construct a 95% confidence interval estimate of the mean weekly sales for all stores that have 8 feet of shelf space for pet food.
b. Construct a 95% prediction interval of the weekly sales of an individual store that has 8 feet of shelf space for pet food.
c. Explain the difference in the results in (a) and (b).

12.51 In Problem 12.7 on page 418, you used the total number of customers in the store to predict the waiting time at the checkout counter. The data are stored in the file **Supermarket**.
a. Construct a 95% confidence interval estimate of the mean waiting time for all customers when there are 20 customers in the store.
b. Construct a 95% prediction interval of the waiting time for an individual customer when there are 20 customers in the store.
c. Why is the interval in (a) narrower than the interval in (b)?

12.52 In Problem 12.6 on page 418, the owner of a moving company wanted to predict labor hours based on the number of cubic feet moved. The data are stored in the file **Moving**.
a. Construct a 95% confidence interval estimate of the mean labor hours for all moves of 500 cubic feet.
b. Construct a 95% prediction interval of the labor hours of an individual move that has 500 cubic feet.
c. Why is the interval in (a) narrower than the interval in (b)?

12.53 In Problem 12.9 on page 418, an agent for a real estate company wanted to predict the monthly rent for apartments, based on the size of the apartment. The data are stored in the file **Rent**.
a. Construct a 95% confidence interval estimate of the mean monthly rental for all apartments that are 1,000 square feet in size.
b. Construct a 95% prediction interval of the monthly rental of an individual apartment that is 1,000 square feet in size.
c. Explain the difference in the results in (a) and (b).

12.54 In Problem 12.8 on page 418, you predicted the value of a baseball franchise, based on current revenue. The data are stored in the file BBrevenue.
a. Construct a 95% confidence interval estimate of the mean value of all baseball franchises that generate $150 million of annual revenue.
b. Construct a 95% prediction interval of the value of an individual baseball franchise that generates $150 million of annual revenue.
c. Explain the difference in the results in (a) and (b).

12.55 In Problem 12.10 on page 418, you used box office gross to predict the number of DVDs sold. The data are stored in the file Movie. The company is about to release a movie on DVD that had a box office gross of $30 million.
a. What is the predicted number of DVDs that the company will sell?
b. Which interval is more useful here, the confidence interval estimate of the mean or the predicted interval for an individual response? Explain.
c. Construct and interpret the interval you selected in (b).

12.8 Pitfalls in Regression

Some of the pitfalls involved in using regression analysis are as follows:

- Lacking an awareness of the assumptions of least-squares regression
- Not knowing how to evaluate the assumptions of least-squares regression
- Not knowing what the alternatives are to least-squares regression if a particular assumption is violated
- Using a regression model without knowledge of the subject matter
- Extrapolating outside the relevant range
- Concluding that a significant relationship identified in an observational study is due to a cause-and-effect relationship

The widespread availability of spreadsheet and statistical software has made regression analysis much more feasible. However, for many users, this enhanced availability of software has not been accompanied by an understanding of how to use regression analysis properly. Someone who is not familiar with either the assumptions of regression or how to evaluate the assumptions cannot be expected to know what the alternatives to least-squares regression are if a particular assumption is violated.

The data in Table 12.5 (stored in the file Anscombe) illustrate the importance of using scatter plots and residual analysis to go beyond the basic number crunching of computing the Y intercept, the slope, and r^2.

TABLE 12.5

Four Sets of Artificial Data

Data Set A		Data Set B		Data Set C		Data Set D	
X_i	Y_i	X_i	Y_i	X_i	Y_i	X_i	Y_i
10	8.04	10	9.14	10	7.46	8	6.58
14	9.96	14	8.10	14	8.84	8	5.76
5	5.68	5	4.74	5	5.73	8	7.71
8	6.95	8	8.14	8	6.77	8	8.84
9	8.81	9	8.77	9	7.11	8	8.47
12	10.84	12	9.13	12	8.15	8	7.04
4	4.26	4	3.10	4	5.39	8	5.25
7	4.82	7	7.26	7	6.42	19	12.50
11	8.33	11	9.26	11	7.81	8	5.56
13	7.58	13	8.74	13	12.74	8	7.91
6	7.24	6	6.13	6	6.08	8	6.89

Source: *Data extracted from F. J. Anscombe, "Graphs in Statistical Analysis,"* American Statistician, *vol. 27 (1973), pp. 17–21.*

Anscombe (reference 1) showed that all four data sets given in Table 12.5 have the following identical results:

$$\hat{Y}_i = 3.0 + 0.5X_i$$

$$S_{YX} = 1.237$$

$$S_{b_1} = 0.118$$

$$r^2 = 0.667$$

$$SSR = \text{Explained variation} = \sum_{i=1}^{n}(\hat{Y}_i - \overline{Y})^2 = 27.51$$

$$SSE = \text{unexplained variation} = \sum_{i=1}^{n}(Y_i - \hat{Y}_i)^2 = 13.76$$

$$SST = \text{Total variation} = \sum_{i=1}^{n}(Y_i - \overline{Y})^2 = 41.27$$

Thus, with respect to these statistics associated with a simple linear regression analysis, the four data sets are identical. Were you to stop the analysis at this point, you would fail to observe the important differences among the four data sets.

From the scatter plots of Figure 12.25 and the residual plots of Figure 12.26 on page 442, you see how different the data sets are. Each has a different relationship between X and Y. The only data set that seems to approximately follow a straight line is data set A. The residual plot for data set A does not show any obvious patterns or outlying residuals. This is certainly not true for data sets B, C, and D. The scatter plot for data set B shows that a curvilinear regression model is more appropriate. This conclusion is reinforced by the residual plot for data set B. The scatter plot and the residual plot for data set C clearly show an outlying observation. If this is the case, you may want to remove the outlier and reestimate the regression model (see reference 4). Similarly, the scatter plot for data set D represents the situation in which the model is heavily dependent on the outcome of a single response ($X_8 = 19$ and $Y_8 = 12.50$). You would have to cautiously evaluate any regression model because its regression coefficients are heavily dependent on a single observation.

FIGURE 12.25

Scatter plots for four data sets

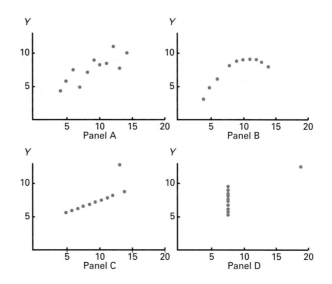

FIGURE 12.26
Residual plots for four
data sets

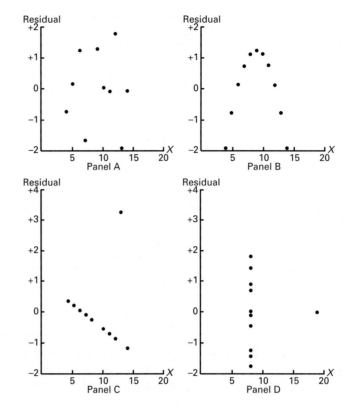

In summary, scatter plots and residual plots are of vital importance to a complete regression analysis. The information they provide is so basic to a credible analysis that you should always include these graphical methods as part of a regression analysis. Thus, a strategy that you can use to help avoid the pitfalls of regression is as follows:

1. Start with a scatter plot to observe the possible relationship between X and Y.
2. Check the assumptions of regression (**L**inearity, **I**ndependence, **N**ormality, **E**qual variance) by performing a residual analysis that includes:
   a. Plotting the residuals versus the independent variable to determine whether the linear model is appropriate and to check for equal variance.
   b. Constructing a histogram, stem-and-leaf display, boxplot, or normal probability plot of the residuals to check for normality.
   c. Plotting the residuals versus time to check for independence (this step is necessary only if the data are collected over time).
3. If there are violations of the assumptions, use alternative methods to least-squares regression or alternative least-squares models (see Reference 4).
4. If there are no violations of the assumptions, carry out tests for the significance of the regression coefficients and develop confidence and prediction intervals.
5. Avoid making predictions and forecasts outside the relevant range of the independent variable.
6. Keep in mind that the relationships identified in observational studies may or may not be due to cause-and-effect relationships. Remember that, although causation implies correlation, correlation does not imply causation.

America's Top Models

Perhaps you are familiar with the TV competition produced by Tyra Banks to find "America's top model." You may be less familiar with another set of top models that are emerging from the business world.

In a *Business Week* article from its January 23, 2006, edition (S. Baker, "Why Math Will Rock Your World: More Math Geeks Are Calling the Shots in Business. Is Your Industry Next?" *Business Week*, pp. 54–62), Stephen Baker talks about how "quants" turned finance upside down and are moving on to other business fields. The name *quants* derives from the "quantitative methods" that "math geeks" use to develop models and forecasts. These methods are built on the principles of regression analysis discussed in this chapter, although the actual models are much more complicated than the simple linear models discussed in this chapter.

Regression-based models have become the top models for many types of business analyses. Some examples include:

- **Advertising and marketing** Managers use econometric models (in other words, regression models) to determine the effect of an advertisement on sales, based on a set of

factors. Also, managers use data mining to predict patterns of behavior of what customers will buy in the future, based on historic information about the consumer.

- **Finance** Any time you read about a financial "model," you should understand that some type of regression model is being used. For example, a *New York Times* article on June 18, 2006, titled "An Old Formula That Points to New Worry" by Mark Hulbert (p. BU8) discusses a market timing model that predicts the return of stocks in the next three to five years, based on the dividend yield of the stock market and the interest rate of 90-day Treasury bills.
- **Food and beverage** Believe it or not, Enologix, a California consulting company, has developed a "formula" (a regression model) that predicts a wine's quality index, based on a set of chemical compounds found in the wine (see D. Darlington, "The Chemistry of a 90+ Wine," *The New York Times Magazine*, August 7, 2005, pp. 36–39).
- **Publishing** A study of the effect of price changes on sales at Amazon.com and

BN.com (again, regression analysis) found that a 1% price increase at BN.com pushed sales down 4%, but the same price increase at Amazon.com pushed sales down only 0.5%.

- **Transportation** Farecast.com uses data mining and predictive technologies to objectively predict airfare pricing (see D. Darlin, "Airfares Made Easy (Or Easier)," *The New York Times*, July 1, 2006, pp. C1, C6).
- **Real estate** Zillow.com uses information about the features contained in a home and its location to develop estimates about the market value of the home, using a "formula" built with a proprietary model.

In the *Business Week* article, Baker stated that statistics and probability will become core skills for businesspeople and consumers. Those who are successful will know how to use statistics, whether they are building financial models or making marketing plans. He also strongly endorsed the need for people in business to know how to use Microsoft Excel to perform statistical analysis and create reports.

USING STATISTICS @ Sunflowers Apparel Revisited

In the Using Statistics scenario, you were the director of planning for Sunflowers Apparel, a chain of upscale clothing stores for women. Until now, Sunflowers managers selected sites based on factors such as the availability of a good lease or a subjective opinion that a location seemed like a good place for a store. To make more objective decisions, you developed a regression model to analyze the relationship between the size of a store and its annual sales. The model indicated that about 90.4% of the variation in sales was explained by the size of the store. Furthermore, for each increase of one thousand square feet, mean annual sales were estimated to increase by $1.67 million. You can now use your model to help make better decisions when selecting new sites for stores as well as to forecast sales for existing stores.

SUMMARY

As you can see from the chapter roadmap in Figure 12.27, this chapter develops the simple linear regression model and discusses the assumptions and how to evaluate them. Once you are assured that the model is appropriate, you can predict values by using the prediction line and test for the significance of the slope. In Chapter 13, regression analysis is extended to situations in which more than one independent variable is used to predict the value of a dependent variable.

FIGURE 12.27
Roadmap for simple
linear regression

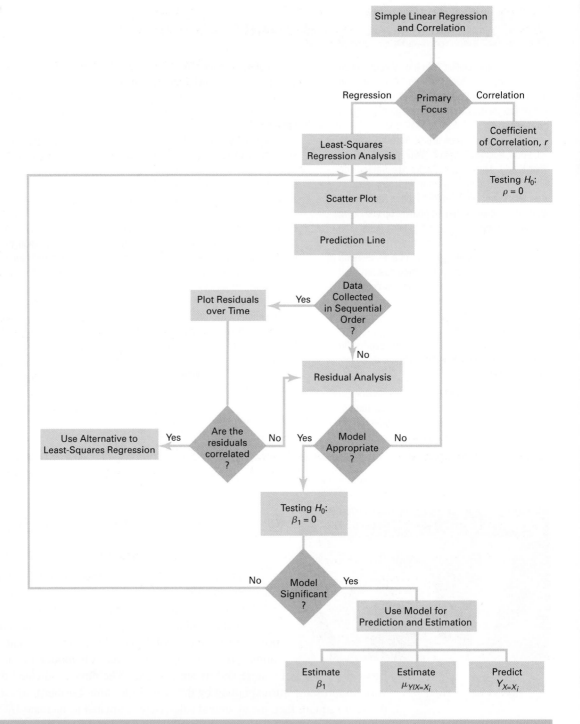

KEY EQUATIONS

Simple Linear Regression Model

$$Y_i = \beta_0 + \beta_1 X_i + \varepsilon_i \qquad \textbf{(12.1)}$$

Simple Linear Regression Equation: The Prediction Line

$$\hat{Y}_i = b_0 + b_1 X_i \qquad \textbf{(12.2)}$$

Computational Formula for the Slope, b_1

$$b_1 = \frac{SSXY}{SSX} \qquad \textbf{(12.3)}$$

Computational Formula for the Y Intercept, b_0

$$b_0 = \overline{Y} - b_1\overline{X} \qquad \textbf{(12.4)}$$

Measures of Variation in Regression

$$SST = SSR + SSE \qquad \textbf{(12.5)}$$

Total Sum of Squares (SST)

$$SST = \text{Total sum of squares} = \sum_{i=1}^{n}(Y_i - \overline{Y})^2 \qquad \textbf{(12.6)}$$

Regression Sum of Squares (*SSR*)

SSR = Explained variation or regression sum of squares

$$= \sum_{i=1}^{n} (\hat{Y}_i - \bar{Y})^2 \qquad (12.7)$$

Error Sum of Squares (*SSE*)

SSE = Unexplained variation or error sum of squares

$$= \sum_{i=1}^{n} (Y_i - \hat{Y}_i)^2 \qquad (12.8)$$

Coefficient of Determination

$$r^2 = \frac{\text{Regression sum of squares}}{\text{Total sum of squares}} = \frac{SSR}{SST} \qquad (12.9)$$

Computational Formula for *SST*

$$SST = \sum_{i=1}^{n} (Y_i - \bar{Y})^2 = \sum_{i=1}^{n} Y_i^2 - \frac{\left(\sum_{i=1}^{n} Y_i\right)^2}{n} \qquad (12.10)$$

Computational Formula for *SSR*

$$SSR = \sum_{i=1}^{n} (\hat{Y}_i - \bar{Y})^2$$

$$= b_0 \sum_{i=1}^{n} Y_i + b_1 \sum_{i=1}^{n} X_i Y_i - \frac{\left(\sum_{i=1}^{n} Y_i\right)^2}{n} \qquad (12.11)$$

Computational Formula for *SSE*

$$SSE = \sum_{i=1}^{n} (Y_i - \hat{Y}_i)^2 = \sum_{i=1}^{n} Y_i^2 - b_0 \sum_{i=1}^{n} Y_i - b_1 \sum_{i=1}^{n} X_i Y_i \qquad (12.12)$$

Standard Error of the Estimate

$$S_{YX} = \sqrt{\frac{SSE}{n-2}} = \sqrt{\frac{\sum_{i=1}^{n} (Y_i - \hat{Y}_i)^2}{n-2}} \qquad (12.13)$$

Residual

$$e_i = Y_i - \hat{Y}_i \qquad (12.14)$$

Testing a Hypothesis for a Population Slope β_1, Using the *t* Test

$$t_{STAT} = \frac{b_1 - \beta_1}{S_{b_1}} \qquad (12.15)$$

Testing a Hypothesis for a Population Slope, β_1, Using the *F* Test

$$F_{STAT} = \frac{MSR}{MSE} \qquad (12.16)$$

Confidence Interval Estimate of the Slope, β_1

$$b_1 \pm t_{\alpha/2} S_{b_1}$$

$$b_1 - t_{\alpha/2} S_{b_1} \leq \beta_1 \leq b_1 + t_{\alpha/2} S_{b_1} \qquad (12.17)$$

Testing for the Existence of Correlation

$$t_{STAT} = \frac{r - \rho}{\sqrt{\dfrac{1 - r^2}{n - 2}}} \qquad (12.18a)$$

$$r = \frac{cov(X,Y)}{S_X S_Y} \qquad (12.18b)$$

Confidence Interval Estimate for the Mean of *Y*

$$\hat{Y}_i \pm t_{\alpha/2} S_{YX} \sqrt{h_i}$$

$$\hat{Y}_i - t_{\alpha/2} S_{YX} \sqrt{h_i} \leq \mu_{Y|X=X_i} \leq \hat{Y}_i + t_{\alpha/2} S_{YX} \sqrt{h_i} \qquad (12.19)$$

Prediction Interval for an Individual Response, *Y*

$$\hat{Y}_i \pm t_{\alpha/2} S_{YX} \sqrt{1 + h_i}$$

$$\hat{Y}_i - t_{\alpha/2} S_{YX} \sqrt{1 + h_i} \leq Y_{X=X_i} \leq \hat{Y}_i + t_{\alpha/2} S_{YX} \sqrt{1 + h_i} \qquad (12.20)$$

KEY TERMS

CHAPTER REVIEW PROBLEMS

CHECKING YOUR UNDERSTANDING

12.56 What is the interpretation of the Y intercept and the slope in the simple linear regression equation?

12.57 What is the interpretation of the coefficient of determination?

12.58 When is the unexplained variation (i.e., error sum of squares) equal to 0?

12.59 When is the explained variation (i.e., regression sum of squares) equal to 0?

12.60 Why should you always carry out a residual analysis as part of a regression model?

12.61 What are the assumptions of regression analysis and how do you evaluate them?

12.62 What is the difference between a confidence interval estimate of the mean response, $\mu_{Y|X=X_i}$, and a prediction interval of $Y_{X=X_i}$?

APPLYING THE CONCEPTS

12.63 Researchers from the Lubin School of Business at Pace University in New York City conducted a study on Internet-supported courses. In one part of the study, four numerical variables were collected on 108 students in an introductory management course that met once a week for an entire semester. One variable collected was *hit consistency*. To measure hit consistency, the researchers did the following: If a student did not visit the Internet site between classes, the student was given a 0 for that time period. If a student visited the Internet site one or more times between classes, the student was given a 1 for that time period. Because there were 13 time periods, a student's score on hit consistency could range from 0 to 13.

The other three variables included the student's course average, the student's cumulative grade point average (GPA), and the total number of hits the student had on the Internet site supporting the course. The following table gives the correlation coefficient for all pairs of variables. Note that correlations marked with an * are statistically significant, using $\alpha = 0.001$:

Variable	Correlation
Course Average, Cumulative GPA	0.72*
Course Average, Total Hits	0.08
Course Average, Hit Consistency	0.37*
Cumulative GPA, Total Hits	0.12
Cumulative GPA, Hit Consistency	0.32*
Total Hits, Hit Consistency	0.64*

Source: *Data extracted from D. Baugher, A. Varanelli, and E. Weisbord, "Student Hits in an Internet-Supported Course: How Can Instructors Use Them and What Do They Mean?" Decision Sciences Journal of Innovative Education, Fall 2003, 1(2), pp. 159–179.*

a. What conclusions can you reach from this correlation analysis?

b. Are you surprised by the results, or are they consistent with your own observations and experiences?

12.64 Management of a soft-drink bottling company wants to develop a method for allocating delivery costs to customers. Although one cost clearly relates to travel time within a particular route, another variable cost reflects the time required to unload the cases of soft drink at the delivery point. A sample of 20 deliveries within a territory was selected. The delivery times and the number of cases delivered were recorded in the Delivery file:

Customer	Number of Cases	Delivery Time (Minutes)	Customer	Number of Cases	Delivery Time (Minutes)
1	52	32.1	11	161	43.0
2	64	34.8	12	184	49.4
3	73	36.2	13	202	57.2
4	85	37.8	14	218	56.8
5	95	37.8	15	243	60.6
6	103	39.7	16	254	61.2
7	116	38.5	17	267	58.2
8	121	41.9	18	275	63.1
9	143	44.2	19	287	65.6
10	157	47.1	20	298	67.3

Develop a regression model to predict delivery time, based on the number of cases delivered.

a. Use the least-squares method to compute the regression coefficients b_0 and b_1.

b. Interpret the meaning of b_0 and b_1 in this problem.

c. Predict the delivery time for 150 cases of soft drink.

d. Should you use the model to predict the delivery time for a customer who is receiving 500 cases of soft drink? Why or why not?

e. Determine the coefficient of determination, r^2, and explain its meaning in this problem.

f. Perform a residual analysis. Is there any evidence of a pattern in the residuals? Explain.

g. At the 0.05 level of significance, is there evidence of a linear relationship between delivery time and the number of cases delivered?

h. Construct a 95% confidence interval estimate of the mean delivery time for 150 cases of soft drink and a 95% prediction interval of the delivery time for a single delivery of 150 cases of soft drink.

12.65 Mixed costs are very common in business and consist of a fixed cost element and a variable cost element. Fixed costs are a recurring, constant cost that does not vary when business activity varies. Variable costs are added costs associated with each unit of business activity the organiza-

Interpreting the Regression Coefficients

When there are several independent variables, you can extend the simple linear regression model of Equation (12.1) on page 408 by assuming a linear relationship between each independent variable and the dependent variable. For example, with k independent variables, the multiple regression model is expressed in Equation (13.1).

MULTIPLE REGRESSION MODEL WITH k INDEPENDENT VARIABLES

$$Y_i = \beta_0 + \beta_1 X_{1i} + \beta_2 X_{2i} + \beta_3 X_{3i} + \cdots + \beta_k X_{ki} + \varepsilon_i \qquad \textbf{(13.1)}$$

where

$\beta_0 = Y$ intercept

$\beta_1 = $ slope of Y with variable X_1, holding variables $X_2, X_3, \ldots, X_k$ constant

$\beta_2 = $ slope of Y with variable X_2, holding variables $X_1, X_3, \ldots, X_k$ constant

$\beta_3 = $ slope of Y with variable X_3, holding variables $X_1, X_2, X_4, \ldots, X_k$ constant

.

.

.

$\beta_k = $ slope of Y with variable X_k, holding variables $X_1, X_2, X_3, \ldots, X_{k-1}$ constant

$\varepsilon_i = $ random error in Y for observation i

Equation (13.2) defines the multiple regression model with two independent variables.

MULTIPLE REGRESSION MODEL WITH TWO INDEPENDENT VARIABLES

$$Y_i = \beta_0 + \beta_1 X_{1i} + \beta_2 X_{2i} + \varepsilon_i \qquad \textbf{(13.2)}$$

where

$\beta_0 = Y$ intercept

$\beta_1 = $ slope of Y with variable X_1, holding variable X_2 constant

$\beta_2 = $ slope of Y with variable X_2, holding variable X_1 constant

$\varepsilon_i = $ random error in Y for observation i

Compare the multiple regression model to the simple linear regression model [Equation (12.1) on page 408]:

$$Y_i = \beta_0 + \beta_1 X_i + \varepsilon_i$$

In the simple linear regression model, the slope, β_1, represents the change in the mean of Y per unit change in X and does not take into account any other variables. In the multiple regression model with two independent variables [Equation (13.2)], the slope, β_1, represents the change in the mean of Y per unit change in X_1, taking into account the effect of X_2.

As in the case of simple linear regression, you use the sample regression coefficients (b_0, b_1, and b_2) as estimates of the population parameters (β_0, β_1, and β_2). Equation (13.3) defines the regression equation for a multiple regression model with two independent variables.

MULTIPLE REGRESSION EQUATION WITH TWO INDEPENDENT VARIABLES

$$\hat{Y}_i = b_0 + b_1 X_{1i} + b_2 X_{2i} \qquad \textbf{(13.3)}$$

You can use Microsoft Excel or Minitab to compute the values of the three regression coefficients for the OmniPower sales data (see Figure 13.2 or 13.3).

FIGURE 13.2

Partial Microsoft Excel regression results worksheet for OmniPower sales data

See Section E13.1 or P13.1 to create this.

	A	B	C	D	E	F	G
1	**OmniPower Sales Analysis**						
2							
3	*Regression Statistics*						
4	**Multiple R**	0.8705					
5	**R Square**	0.7577					
6	**Adjusted R Square**	0.7421					
7	**Standard Error**	638.0653					
8	**Observations**	34					
9							
10	**ANOVA**						
11		*df*	*SS*	*MS*	*F*	*Significance F*	
12	**Regression**	2	39472730.77	19736365.387	48.4771	2.86258E-10	
13	**Residual**	31	12620946.67	407127.312			
14	**Total**	33	52093677.44				
15							
16		*Coefficients*	*Standard Error*	*t Stat*	*P-value*	*Lower 95%*	*Upper 95%*
17	**Intercept**	5837.5208	628.1502	9.2932	1.791E-10	4556.3992	7118.6423
18	**Price**	-53.2173	6.8522	-7.7664	9.200E-09	-67.1925	-39.2421
19	**Promotion**	3.6131	0.6852	5.2728	9.822E-06	2.2155	5.0106

FIGURE 13.3

Partial Minitab results for OmniPower sales data

See Section M13.2 to create this.

```
The regression equation is
sales = 5838 - 53.2 price + 3.61 promotion

Predictor      Coef   SE Coef      T      P
Constant     5837.5     628.2   9.29  0.000
price       -53.217     6.852  -7.77  0.000
promotion    3.6131    0.6852   5.27  0.000

S = 638.065   R-Sq = 75.8%   R-Sq(adj) = 74.2%

Analysis of Variance

Source           DF        SS        MS      F      P
Regression        2  39472731  19736365  48.48  0.000
Residual Error   31  12620947    407127
Total            33  52093677

Predicted Values for New Observations
New
Obs    Fit  SE Fit      95% CI          95% PI
  1   3079     110  (2854, 3303)   (1758, 4399)
```

From Figure 13.2 or 13.3, the computed values of the regression coefficients are

$$b_0 = 5,837.5208 \quad b_1 = -53.2173 \quad b_2 = 3.6131$$

Therefore, the multiple regression equation is

$$\hat{Y}_i = 5,837.5208 - 53.2173X_{1i} + 3.6131X_{2i}$$

where

$\hat{Y}_i$ = predicted monthly sales of OmniPower bars for store i

X_{1i} = price of OmniPower bar (in cents) for store i

X_{2i} = monthly in-store promotional expenditures (in dollars) for store i

The sample Y intercept ($b_0 = 5,837.5208$) estimates the number of OmniPower bars sold in a month if the price is $0.00 and the total amount spent on promotional expenditures is also $0.00. Because these values of price and promotion are outside the range of price and promotion used in the test-market study, and are nonsensical, the value of b_0 has little or no practical interpretation.

The slope of price with OmniPower sales ($b_1 = -53.2173$) indicates that, for a given amount of monthly promotional expenditures, the mean sales of OmniPower are estimated to decrease by 53.2173 bars per month for each 1-cent increase in the price. The slope of monthly promotional expenditures with OmniPower sales ($b_2 = 3.6131$) indicates that, for a given price, the mean sales of OmniPower are estimated to increase by 3.6131 bars for each additional $1 spent on promotions. These estimates allow you to better understand the likely effect that price and promotion decisions will have in the marketplace. For example, a 10-cent decrease in price is estimated to increase mean sales by 532.173 bars, with a fixed amount of monthly promotional expenditures. A $100 increase in promotional expenditures is estimated to increase mean sales by 361.31 bars, for a given price.

Regression coefficients in multiple regression are called **net regression coefficients**; they estimate the mean change in Y per unit change in a particular X, *holding constant the effect of the other X variables*. For example, in the study of OmniPower bar sales, for a store with a given amount of promotional expenditures, the mean sales are estimated to decrease by 53.2173 bars per month for each 1-cent increase in the price of an OmniPower bar. Another way to interpret this "net effect" is to think of two stores with an equal amount of promotional expenditures. If the first store charges 1 cent more than the other store, the net effect of this difference is that the first store is predicted to sell 53.2173 fewer bars per month than the second store. To interpret the net effect of promotional expenditures, you can consider two stores that are charging the same price. If the first store spends $1 more on promotional expenditures, the net effect of this difference is that the first store is predicted to sell 3.6131 more bars per month than the second store.

Predicting the Dependent Variable Y

You can use the multiple regression equation computed by Microsoft Excel or Minitab to predict values of the dependent variable. For example, what are the predicted sales for a store charging 79 cents during a month in which promotional expenditures are $400? Using the multiple regression equation,

$$\hat{Y}_i = 5,837.5208 - 53.2173X_{1i} + 3.6131X_{2i}$$

with $X_{1i} = 79$ and $X_{2i} = 400$,

$$\hat{Y}_i = 5,837.5208 - 53.2173(79) + 3.6131(400)$$

$$= 3,078.57$$

Thus, your sales prediction for stores charging 79 cents and spending $400 in promotional expenditures is 3,078.57 OmniPower bars per month.

After you have developed the regression equation, done a residual analysis (see Section 13.3), and determined the significance of the overall fitted model (see Section 13.2), the next step often involves a confidence interval estimate of the mean value and a prediction interval for an individual value. The computation of these intervals is too complex to do by hand, and you should use Microsoft Excel or Minitab to perform the calculations. Figure 13.3 on page 460 presents a confidence interval and a prediction interval computed by Minitab. Figure 13.4 on page 462 illustrates Microsoft Excel results.

The 95% confidence interval estimate of the mean OmniPower sales for all stores charging 79 cents and spending $400 in promotional expenditures is 2,854.07 to 3,303.08 bars. The prediction interval for an individual store is 1,758.01 to 4,399.14 bars.

FIGURE 13.4

Microsoft Excel confidence interval estimate and prediction interval worksheet for the OmniPower sales data

See Section E13.3 or P13.3 to create this.

	A	B	C	D
1	Confidence Interval Estimate and Prediction Interval			
2				
3	Data			
4	Confidence Level	95%		
5		1		
6	Price given value	79		
7	Promotion given value	400		
8				
9	X'X	34	2646	13200
10		2646	214674	1018800
11		13200	1018800	6000000
12				
13	Inverse of X'X	0.969163	-0.00941	-0.00053
14		-0.009408	0.000115	1.12E-06
15		-0.000535	1.12E-06	1.15E-06
16				
17	X'G times Inverse of X'X	0.012054	0.000149	1.49E-05
18				
19	[X'G times Inverse of X'X] times XG	0.029762	=MMULT(B17:D17, B5:B7)	
20	t Statistic	2.0395	=TINV(1 - B4, MR!B13)	
21	Predicted Y (YHat)	3078.57	{=MMULT(TRANSPOSE(B5:B7), MR!B17:B19)}	
22				
23	For Average Predicted Y (YHat)			
24	Interval Half Width	224.50	=B20 * SQRT(B19) * MR!B7	
25	Confidence Interval Lower Limit	2854.07	=B21 - B24	
26	Confidence Interval Upper Limit	3303.08	=B21 + B24	
27				
28	For Individual Response Y			
29	Interval Half Width	1320.57	=B20 * SQRT(1 + B19) * MR!B7	
30	Prediction Interval Lower Limit	1758.01	=B21 - B29	
31	Prediction Interval Upper Limit	4399.14	=B21 + B29	

Problems for Section 13.1

LEARNING THE BASICS

13.1 For this problem, use the following multiple regression equation:

$$\hat{Y}_i = 10 + 5X_{1i} + 3X_{2i}$$

a. Interpret the meaning of the slopes.
b. Interpret the meaning of the Y intercept.

13.2 For this problem, use the following multiple regression equation:

$$\hat{Y}_i = 50 - 2X_{1i} + 7X_{2i}$$

a. Interpret the meaning of the slopes.
b. Interpret the meaning of the Y intercept.

APPLYING THE CONCEPTS

13.3 A marketing analyst for a shoe manufacturer is considering the development of a new brand of running shoes. The marketing analyst wants to determine which variables to use in predicting durability (i.e., the effect of long-term impact). Two independent variables under consideration are X_1 (FOREIMP), a measurement of the forefoot shock-absorbing capability, and X_2 (MIDSOLE), a measurement of the change in impact properties over time. The dependent variable Y is LTIMP, a measure of the shoe's durability after a repeated impact test. A random sample of 15 types of currently manufactured running shoes was selected for testing, with the following results:

Variable	Coefficients	Standard Error	t Statistic	p-Value
INTERCEPT	-0.02686	0.06905	-0.39	0.7034
FOREIMP	0.79116	0.06295	12.57	0.0000
MIDSOLE	0.60484	0.07174	8.43	0.0000

a. State the multiple regression equation.
b. Interpret the meaning of the slopes, b_1 and b_2, in this problem.

✓ SELF Test **13.4** A mail-order catalog business selling personal computer supplies, software, and hardware maintains a centralized warehouse. Management is currently examining the process of distribution from the warehouse and wants to study the factors that affect warehouse distribution costs. Currently, a small handling fee is added to each order, regardless of the amount of the order. Data collected over the past 24 months (stored in the file **Warecost**) indicate the warehouse distribution costs (in thousands of dollars), the sales (in thousands of dollars), and the number of orders received.

a. State the multiple regression equation.
b. Interpret the meaning of the slopes, b_1 and b_2, in this problem.
c. Explain why the regression coefficient, b_0, has no practical meaning in the context of this problem.
d. Predict the monthly warehouse distribution cost when sales are $400,000 and the number of orders is 4,500.
e. Construct a 95% confidence interval estimate for the mean monthly warehouse distribution cost when sales are $400,000 and the number of orders is 4,500.
f. Construct a 95% prediction interval for the monthly warehouse distribution cost for a particular month when sales are $400,000 and the number of orders is 4,500.
g. Explain why the interval in (e) is narrower than the interval in (f).

13.5 A consumer organization wants to develop a regression model to predict gasoline mileage (as measured by miles per gallon) based on the horsepower of the car's engine and the weight of the car (in pounds). A sample of 50 recent car models was selected, with the results recorded in the file **Auto**.

a. State the multiple regression equation.
b. Interpret the meaning of the slopes, b_1 and b_2, in this problem.
c. Explain why the regression coefficient, b_0, has no practical meaning in the context of this problem.
d. Predict the miles per gallon for a car that has 60 horsepower and weigh 2,000 pounds.
e. Construct a 95% confidence interval estimate for the mean miles per gallon for cars that have 60 horsepower and weigh 2,000 pounds.
f. Construct a 95% prediction interval for the miles per gallon for an individual car that has 60 horsepower and weighs 2,000 pounds.

13.6 A consumer products company wants to measure the effectiveness of different types of advertising media in the promotion of its products. Specifically, the company is interested in the effectiveness of radio advertising and newspaper advertising (including the cost of discount coupons). A sample of 22 cities with approximately equal populations is selected for study during a test period of one month. Each city is allocated a specific expenditure level both for radio advertising and for newspaper advertising. The sales of the product (in thousands of dollars) and also the levels of media expenditure (in thousands of dollars) during the test month are recorded, with the results stored in the file **Advertise**:

a. State the multiple regression equation.
b. Interpret the meaning of the slopes, b_1 and b_2, in this problem.
c. Interpret the meaning of the regression coefficient, b_0.
d. Which type of advertising is more effective? Explain.

13.7 The director of broadcasting operations for a television station wants to study the issue of standby hours (i.e., hours in which unionized graphic artists at the station are paid but are not actually involved in any activity). The variables in the study include:

Standby hours (Y)—Total number of standby hours in a week
Total staff present (X_1)—Weekly total of people-days
Remote hours (X_2)—Total number of hours worked by employees at locations away from the central plant

The results for a period of 26 weeks are in the data file **Standby**.

a. State the multiple regression equation.
b. Interpret the meaning of the slopes, b_1 and b_2, in this problem.
c. Explain why the regression coefficient, b_0, has no practical meaning in the context of this problem.
d. Predict the standby hours for a week in which the total staff present have 310 people-days and the remote hours are 400.
e. Construct a 95% confidence interval estimate for the mean standby hours for weeks in which the total staff present have 310 people-days and the remote hours are 400.
f. Construct a 95% prediction interval for the standby hours for a single week in which the total staff present have 310 people-days and the remote hours are 400.

13.8 Nassau County is located approximately 25 miles east of New York City. Data in the file **GlenCove** include the appraised value, land area of the property in acres, and age, in years, for a sample of 30 single-family homes located in Glen Cove, a small city in Nassau County. Develop a multiple linear regression model to predict appraised value based on land area of the property and age, in years.

a. State the multiple regression equation.
b. Interpret the meaning of the slopes, b_1 and b_2, in this problem.
c. Explain why the regression coefficient, b_0, has no practical meaning in the context of this problem.
d. Predict the appraised value for a house that has a land area of 0.25 acres and is 45 years old.
e. Construct a 95% confidence interval estimate for the mean appraised value for houses that have a land area of 0.25 acres and are 45 years old.
f. Construct a 95% prediction interval for the appraised value for an individual house that has a land area of 0.25 acres and is 45 years old.

13.2 r^2, Adjusted r^2, and the Overall F Test

This section discusses three methods you can use to evaluate the overall multiple regression model: the coefficient of multiple determination r^2, the adjusted r^2, and the overall F test.

Coefficient of Multiple Determination

Recall from Section 12.3 that the coefficient of determination, r^2, measures the proportion of the variation in Y that is explained by the independent variable X in the simple linear regression model. In multiple regression, the **coefficient of multiple determination** represents the proportion of the variation in Y that is explained by the set of independent variables. Equation (13.4) defines the coefficient of multiple determination for a multiple regression model with two or more independent variables.

> COEFFICIENT OF MULTIPLE DETERMINATION
>
> The coefficient of multiple determination is equal to the regression sum of squares (SSR) divided by the total sum of squares (SST).
>
> $$r^2 = \frac{\text{Regression sum of squares}}{\text{Total sum of squares}} = \frac{SSR}{SST} \qquad (13.4)$$
>
> where
>
> $$SSR = \text{Regression sum of squares}$$
> $$SST = \text{Total sum of squares}$$

In the OmniPower example, from Figure 13.2 or 13.3 on page 460, $SSR = 39{,}472{,}730.77$ and $SST = 52{,}093{,}677.44$. Thus,

$$r^2 = \frac{SSR}{SST} = \frac{39{,}472{,}730.77}{52{,}093{,}677.44} = 0.7577$$

The coefficient of multiple determination ($r^2 = 0.7577$) indicates that 75.77% of the variation in sales is explained by the variation in the price and in the promotional expenditures. You can also find the coefficient of multiple determination directly from the Microsoft Excel results in Figure 13.2, labeled "R Square"; or from the Minitab results in Figure 13.3, labeled "R-Sq."

Adjusted r^2

When considering multiple regression models, some statisticians suggest that you should use the **adjusted r^2** to reflect both the number of independent variables in the model and the sample size. Reporting the adjusted r^2 is extremely important when you are comparing two or more regression models that predict the same dependent variable but have a different number of independent variables. Equation (13.5) defines the adjusted r^2.

> ADJUSTED r^2
>
> $$r^2_{\text{adj}} = 1 - \left[(1 - r^2) \frac{n - 1}{n - k - 1} \right] \qquad (13.5)$$
>
> where k is the number of independent variables in the regression equation.

Thus, for the OmniPower data, because $r^2 = 0.7577$, $n = 34$, and $k = 2$,

$$r_{adj}^2 = 1 - \left[(1 - 0.7577)\frac{34 - 1}{34 - 2 - 1} \right]$$

$$= 1 - \left[(0.2423)\frac{33}{31} \right]$$

$$= 1 - 0.2579$$

$$= 0.7421$$

Hence, 74.21% of the variation in sales is explained by the multiple regression model after adjusting for the number of independent variables and the sample size. You can also find the adjusted r^2 directly from the Microsoft Excel results in Figure 13.2 on page 460, labeled "Adjusted R Square"; or from the Minitab results in Figure 13.3 on page 460, labeled "R-Sq(adj)."

Test for the Significance of the Overall Multiple Regression Model

You use the **overall F test** to test whether there is a significant relationship between the dependent variable and the entire set of independent variables (the overall multiple regression model). Because there is more than one independent variable, you use the following null and alternative hypotheses:

H_0: $\beta_1 = \beta_2 = \cdots = \beta_k = 0$ (There is no linear relationship between the dependent variable and the independent variables.)

H_1: At least one $\beta_j \neq 0$, $j = 1, 2, \ldots, k$ (There is a linear relationship between the dependent variable and at least one of the independent variables.)

Equation (13.6) defines the statistic for the overall F test. Table 13.2 presents the associated ANOVA summary table.

OVERALL F TEST

The F_{STAT} test statistic is equal to the regression mean square (*MSR*) divided by the mean square error (*MSE*).

$$F_{STAT} = \frac{MSR}{MSE} \tag{13.6}$$

where

F_{STAT} = test statistic from an F distribution with k and $n - k - 1$ degrees of freedom

k = number of independent variables in the regression model

TABLE 13.2

ANOVA Summary Table for the Overall F Test

Source	Degrees of Freedom	Sum of Squares	Mean Square (Variance)	F
Regression	k	SSR	$MSR = \dfrac{SSR}{k}$	$F_{STAT} = \dfrac{MSR}{MSE}$
Error	$n - k - 1$	SSE	$MSE = \dfrac{SSE}{n - k - 1}$	
Total	$n - 1$	SST		

The decision rule is

Reject H_0 at the α level of significance if $F_{STAT} > F_\alpha$;

otherwise, do not reject H_0.

Using a 0.05 level of significance, the critical value of the F distribution with 2 and 31 degrees of freedom found from Table E.5 is approximately 3.32 (see Figure 13.5 below). From Figure 13.2 or 13.3 on page 460, the F_{STAT} test statistic given in the ANOVA summary table is 48.4771. Because $48.4771 > 3.32$, or because the p-value $= 0.000 < 0.05$, you reject H_0 and conclude that at least one of the independent variables (price and/or promotional expenditures) is related to sales.

FIGURE 13.5

Testing for the significance of a set of regression coefficients at the 0.05 level of significance, with 2 and 31 degrees of freedom

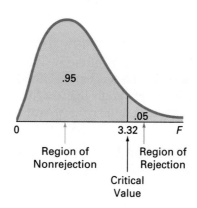

Region of Nonrejection	Region of Rejection
	Critical Value

Problems for Section 13.2

LEARNING THE BASICS

13.9 The following ANOVA summary table is for a multiple regression model with two independent variables:

Source	Degrees of Freedom	Sum of Squares	Mean Squares	F
Regression	2	60		
Error	18	120		
Total	20	180		

a. Determine the regression mean square (MSR) and the mean square error (MSE).
b. Compute the overall F_{STAT} test statistic.
c. Determine whether there is a significant relationship between Y and the two independent variables at the 0.05 level of significance.
d. Compute the coefficient of multiple determination, r^2, and interpret its meaning.
e. Compute the adjusted r^2.

13.10 The following ANOVA summary table is for a multiple regression model with two independent variables:

Source	Degrees of Freedom	Sum of Squares	Mean Squares	F
Regression	2	30		
Error	10	120		
Total	12	150		

a. Determine the regression mean square (MSR) and the mean square error (MSE).
b. Compute the overall F_{STAT} test statistic.

c. Determine whether there is a significant relationship between Y and the two independent variables at the 0.05 level of significance.
d. Compute the coefficient of multiple determination, r^2, and interpret its meaning.
e. Compute the adjusted r^2.

APPLYING THE CONCEPTS

13.11 Eileen M. Van Aken and Brian M. Kleiner, professors at Virginia Polytechnic Institute and State University, investigated the factors that contribute to the effectiveness of teams (data extracted from "Determinants of Effectiveness for Cross-Functional Organizational Design Teams," *Quality Management Journal*, 1997, 4, pp. 51–79). The researchers studied 34 independent variables, such as team skills, diversity, meeting frequency, and clarity in expectations. For each of the teams studied, each of the variables was given a value of 1 through 100, based on the results of interviews and survey data, where 100 represents the highest rating. The dependent variable, team performance, was also given a value of 1 through 100, with 100 representing the highest rating. Many different regression models were explored, including the following:

Model 1

Team performance $= \beta_0 + \beta_1(\text{Team skill}) + \varepsilon,$

$$r_{adj}^2 = 0.68$$

Model 2

Team performance $= \beta_0 + \beta_1(\text{Clarity in expectations}) + \varepsilon,$

$$r_{adj}^2 = 0.78$$

Model 3

$$\text{Team performance} = \beta_0 + \beta_1(\text{Team skills}) +$$
$$\beta_2(\text{Clarity in expectations}) + \varepsilon$$
$$r_{adj}^2 = 0.97$$

a. Interpret the adjusted r^2 for each of the three models.
b. Which of these three models do you think is the best predictor of team performance?

13.12 In Problem 13.3 on page 462, you predicted the durability of a brand of running shoe, based on the forefoot shock-absorbing capability and the change in impact properties over time. The regression analysis resulted in the following ANOVA summary table:

Source	Degrees of Freedom	Sum of Squares	Mean Squares	F	p-value
Regression	2	12.61020	6.30510	97.69	0.0001
Error	12	0.77453	0.06454		
Total	14	13.38473			

a. Determine whether there is a significant relationship between durability and the two independent variables at the 0.05 level of significance.
b. Interpret the meaning of the p-value.
c. Compute the coefficient of multiple determination, r^2, and interpret its meaning.
d. Compute the adjusted r^2.

13.13 In Problem 13.5 on page 463, you used horsepower and weight to predict gasoline mileage (see the **Auto** file). Using the results from that problem,
a. determine whether there is a significant relationship between gasoline mileage and the two independent variables (horsepower and weight) at the 0.05 level of significance.
b. interpret the meaning of the p-value.
c. compute the coefficient of multiple determination, r^2, and interpret its meaning.
d. compute the adjusted r^2.

13.14 In Problem 13.4 on page 462, you used sales and number of orders to predict distribution costs at a mail-order catalog business (see the **Warecost** file). Using the results from that problem,

a. determine whether there is a significant relationship between distribution costs and the two independent variables (sales and number of orders) at the 0.05 level of significance.
b. interpret the meaning of the p-value.
c. compute the coefficient of multiple determination, r^2, and interpret its meaning.
d. compute the adjusted r^2.

13.15 In Problem 13.7 on page 463, you used the total staff present and remote hours to predict standby hours (see the file **Standby**). Using the results from that problem,
a. determine whether there is a significant relationship between standby hours and the two independent variables (total staff present and remote hours) at the 0.05 level of significance.
b. interpret the meaning of the p-value.
c. compute the coefficient of multiple determination, r^2, and interpret its meaning.
d. compute the adjusted r^2.

13.16 In Problem 13.6 on page 463, you used radio advertising and newspaper advertising to predict sales (see the **Advertise** file). Using the results from that problem,
a. determine whether there is a significant relationship between sales and the two independent variables (radio advertising and newspaper advertising) at the 0.05 level of significance.
b. interpret the meaning of the p-value.
c. compute the coefficient of multiple determination, r^2, and interpret its meaning.
d. compute the adjusted r^2.

13.17 In Problem 13.8 on page 463, you used the land area of a property and the age of a house to predict appraised value (see the **GlenCove** file). Using the results from that problem,
a. determine whether there is a significant relationship between appraised value and the two independent variables (land area of a property and age of a house) at the 0.05 level of significance.
b. interpret the meaning of the p-value.
c. compute the coefficient of multiple determination, r^2, and interpret its meaning.
d. compute the adjusted r^2.

13.3 Residual Analysis for the Multiple Regression Model

In Section 12.5, you used residual analysis to evaluate the adequacy of the simple linear regression model. For the multiple regression model with two independent variables, you need to construct and analyze the following residual plots:

1. Residuals versus $\hat{Y}_i$
2. Residuals versus X_{1i}
3. Residuals versus X_{2i}
4. Residuals versus time

FIGURE 13.6

Microsoft Excel residual plots for the OmniPower sales data: Panel *A*, residuals versus predicted *Y*; Panel *B*, residuals versus price; Panel *C*, residuals versus promotional expenditures

See Section E13.2 or P13.2 to create this. Minitab users, see Section M13.2 to create equivalent plots.

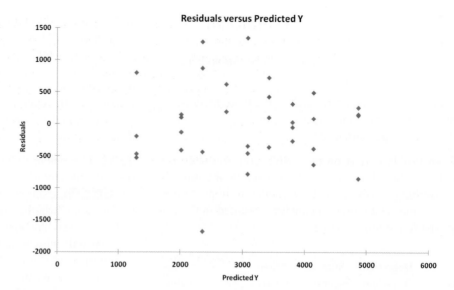

Panel A

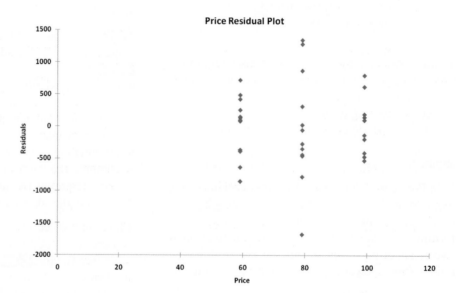

Panel B

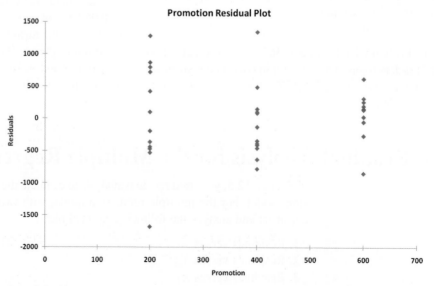

Panel C

The first residual plot examines the pattern of residuals versus the predicted values of Y. If the residuals show a pattern for different predicted values of Y, then there is a curvilinear effect in at least one independent variable, a possible violation of the assumption of equal variance (see Figure 12.16 on page 428), and/or the need to transform the Y variable.

The second and third residual plots involve the independent variables. Patterns in the plot of the residuals versus an independent variable may indicate the existence of a curvilinear effect and, therefore, the need to add a curvilinear independent variable to the multiple regression model. The fourth plot is used to investigate patterns in the residuals in order to validate the independence assumption when the data are collected in time order. A cyclical pattern with this residual plot indicates that the residuals are correlated, not independent.

Figure 13.6 illustrates the Microsoft Excel residual plots for the OmniPower sales example. There is very little or no pattern in the relationship between the residuals and the predicted value of Y, the value of X_1 (price), or the value of X_2 (promotional expenditures). Thus, you can conclude that the multiple regression model is appropriate for predicting sales. There is no need to plot the residuals versus time since the data were not collected in time order.

Problems for Section 13.3

APPLYING THE CONCEPTS

13.18 In Problem 13.4 on page 462, you used sales and number of orders to predict distribution costs at a mail-order catalog business (see the **Warecost** file).
a. Plot the residuals versus $\hat{Y}_i$.
b. Plot the residuals versus X_{1i}.
c. Plot the residuals versus X_{2i}.
d. Plot the residuals versus time.
e. In the residuals plots created in (a) through (d), is there any evidence of a violation to the regression assumptions? Explain.

13.19 In Problem 13.5 on page 463, you used horsepower and weight to predict gasoline mileage (see the **Auto** file).
a. Plot the residuals versus $\hat{Y}_i$.
b. Plot the residuals versus X_{1i}.
c. Plot the residuals versus X_{2i}.
d. In the residuals plots created in (a) through (c), is there any evidence of a violation to the regression assumptions? Explain.

13.20 In Problem 13.6 on page 463, you used radio advertising and newspaper advertising to predict sales (see the **Advertise** file).
a. Perform a residual analysis on your results.
b. Are the regression assumptions valid for these data?

13.21 In Problem 13.7 on page 463, you used the total staff present and remote hours to predict standby hours (see the **Standby** file).
a. Perform a residual analysis on your results.
b. Are the regression assumptions valid for these data?

13.22 In Problem 13.8 on page 463, you used the land area of a property and the age of a house to predict appraised value (see the **GlenCove** file).
a. Perform a residual analysis on your results.
b. Are the regression assumptions valid for these data?

13.4 Inferences Concerning the Population Regression Coefficients

In Section 12.6, you tested the slope in a simple linear regression model to determine the significance of the relationship between X and Y. In addition, you constructed a confidence interval estimate of the population slope. This section extends those procedures to multiple regression.

Tests of Hypothesis

In a simple linear regression model, to test a hypothesis concerning the population slope, β_1, you used Equation (12.15) on page 429:

$$t_{STAT} = \frac{b_1 - \beta_1}{S_{b_1}}$$

Equation (13.7) generalizes this equation for multiple regression.

TESTING FOR THE SLOPE IN MULTIPLE REGRESSION

$$t_{STAT} = \frac{b_j - \beta_j}{S_{b_j}}$$

(13.7)

where

b_j = slope of variable j with Y, holding constant the effects of all other independent variables

S_{b_j} = standard error of the regression coefficient b_j

t_{STAT} = test statistic for a t distribution with $n - k - 1$ degrees of freedom

k = number of independent variables in the regression equation

β_j = hypothesized value of the population slope for variable j, holding constant the effects of all other independent variables

---

To determine whether variable X_2 (amount of promotional expenditures) has a significant effect on sales, taking into account the price of OmniPower bars, the null and alternative hypotheses are

$$H_0: \beta_2 = 0$$

$$H_1: \beta_2 \neq 0$$

From Equation (13.7) and Figures 13.2 or 13.3 on page 460.

$$t_{STAT} = \frac{b_2 - \beta_2}{S_{b_2}}$$

$$= \frac{3.6131 - 0}{0.6852} = 5.2728$$

If you select a level of significance of 0.05, the critical values of t for 31 degrees of freedom from Table E.3 are -2.0395 and $+2.0395$ (see Figure 13.7).

FIGURE 13.7

Testing for significance of a regression coefficient at the 0.05 level of significance, with 31 degrees of freedom

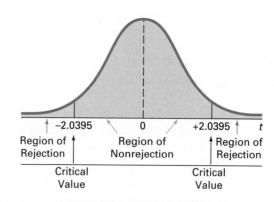

From Figure 13.2 or 13.3 on page 460, observe that the computed t_{STAT} test statistic is 5.2728. Because $t_{STAT} = 5.2728 > 2.0395$, you reject H_0 and conclude that there is a significant relationship between the variable X_2 (promotional expenditures) and sales, taking into

account the price, X_1. Using the p-value approach, note that the p-value is approximately zero. This extremely small p-value allows you to strongly reject the null hypothesis that there is no linear relationship between sales and promotional expenditures. Example 13.1 presents the test for the significance of β_1, the slope of sales with price.

EXAMPLE 13.1 Testing for the Significance of the Slope of Sales with Price

At the 0.05 level of significance, is there evidence that the slope of sales with price is different from zero?

SOLUTION From Figure 13.2 or 13.3 on page 460, $t_{STAT} = -7.7664 < -2.0395$ (the critical value for $\alpha = 0.05$) or the p-value $= 0.0000000092 < 0.05$. Thus, there is a significant relationship between price, X_1, and sales, taking into account the promotional expenditures, X_2.

As seen with each of the two X variables, the test of significance for a specific regression coefficient is actually a test for the significance of adding that variable into a regression model, given that the other variable is included. Therefore, the t test for the regression coefficient is equivalent to testing for the contribution of each independent variable.

Confidence Interval Estimation

Instead of testing the significance of a population slope, you may want to estimate the value of a population slope. Equation (13.8) defines the confidence interval estimate for a population slope in multiple regression.

> CONFIDENCE INTERVAL ESTIMATE FOR THE SLOPE
>
> $$b_j \pm t_{\alpha/2}S_{b_j} \qquad\qquad (13.8)$$
>
> where $t_{\alpha/2}$ is the critical value corresponding to an upper-tail probability of $\alpha/2$ from the t distribution with $n - k - 1$ degrees of freedom (i.e., a cumulative area of $1 - \alpha/2$), and k is the number of independent variables.

To construct a 95% confidence interval estimate of the population slope, β_1 (the effect of price, X_1, on sales, Y, holding constant the effect of promotional expenditures, X_2), the critical value of t at the 95% confidence level with 31 degrees of freedom is 2.0395 (see Table E.3). Then, using Equation (13.8) and Figure 13.2 or 13.3 on page 460,

$$b_1 \pm t_{\alpha/2}S_{b_1}$$

$$-53.2173 \pm (2.0395)(6.8522)$$

$$-53.2173 \pm 13.9752$$

$$-67.1925 \le \beta_1 \le -39.2421$$

Taking into account the effect of promotional expenditures, the estimated effect of a 1-cent increase in price is to reduce mean sales by approximately 39.2 to 67.2 bars. You have 95% confidence that this interval correctly estimates the relationship between these variables. From a hypothesis-testing viewpoint, because this confidence interval does not include 0, you conclude that the regression coefficient, β_1, has a significant effect.

Example 13.2 constructs and interprets a confidence interval estimate for the slope of sales with promotional expenditures.

EXAMPLE 13.2

Constructing a
Confidence Interval
Estimate for the
Slope of Sales
with Promotional
Expenditures

Construct a 95% confidence interval estimate of the population slope of sales with promotional expenditures.

SOLUTION The critical value of t at the 95% confidence level, with 31 degrees of freedom, is 2.0395 (see Table E.3). Using Equation (13.8) and Figure 13.2 or 13.3 on page 460,

$$b_2 \pm t_{\alpha/2} S_{b_2}$$

$$3.6131 \pm (2.0395)(0.6852)$$

$$3.6131 \pm 1.3975$$

$$2.2156 \le \beta_2 \le 5.0106$$

Thus, taking into account the effect of price, the estimated effect of each additional dollar of promotional expenditures is to increase mean sales by approximately 2.2 to 5.0 bars. You have 95% confidence that this interval correctly estimates the relationship between these variables. From a hypothesis-testing viewpoint, because this confidence interval does not include 0, you can conclude that the regression coefficient, β_2, has a significant effect.

Problems for Section 13.4

LEARNING THE BASICS

13.23 Given the following information from a multiple regression analysis:

$$n = 25 \quad b_1 = 5 \quad b_2 = 10 \quad S_{b_1} = 2 \quad S_{b_2} = 8$$

a. Which variable has the largest slope, in units of a t statistic?
b. Construct a 95% confidence interval estimate of the population slope, β_1.
c. At the 0.05 level of significance, determine whether each independent variable makes a significant contribution to the regression model. On the basis of these results, indicate the independent variables to include in this model.

13.24 Given the following information from a multiple regression analysis:

$$n = 20 \quad b_1 = 4 \quad b_2 = 3 \quad S_{b_1} = 1.2 \quad S_{b_2} = 0.8$$

a. Which variable has the largest slope, in units of a t statistic?
b. Construct a 95% confidence interval estimate of the population slope, β_1.
c. At the 0.05 level of significance, determine whether each independent variable makes a significant contribution to the regression model. On the basis of these results, indicate the independent variables to include in this model.

APPLYING THE CONCEPTS

13.25 In Problem 13.3 on page 462, you predicted the durability of a brand of running shoe, based on the forefoot shock-absorbing capability (FOREIMP) and the change in

impact properties over time (MIDSOLE) for a sample of 15 pairs of shoes. Use the following results:

Variable	Coefficient	Standard Error	t Statistic	p-Value
INTERCEPT	−0.02686	0.06905	−0.39	0.7034
FOREIMP	0.79116	0.06295	12.57	0.0000
MIDSOLE	0.60484	0.07174	8.43	0.0000

a. Construct a 95% confidence interval estimate of the population slope between durability and forefoot shock-absorbing capability.
b. At the 0.05 level of significance, determine whether each independent variable makes a significant contribution to the regression model. On the basis of these results, indicate the independent variables to include in this model.

✓SELF **13.26** In Problem 13.4 on page 462, you used
Test sales and number of orders to predict distribution costs at a mail-order catalog business (see the **Warecost** file). Using the results from that problem,
a. construct a 95% confidence interval estimate of the population slope between distribution cost and sales.
b. at the 0.05 level of significance, determine whether each independent variable makes a significant contribution to the regression model. On the basis of these results, indicate the independent variables to include in this model.

13.27 In Problem 13.5 on page 463, you used horsepower and weight to predict gasoline mileage (see the **Auto** file). Using the results from that problem,

a. construct a 95% confidence interval estimate of the population slope between gasoline mileage and horsepower.

b. at the 0.05 level of significance, determine whether each independent variable makes a significant contribution to the regression model. On the basis of these results, indicate the independent variables to include in this model.

13.28 In Problem 13.6 on page 463, you used radio advertising and newspaper advertising to predict sales (see the Advertise file). Using the results from that problem,

a. construct a 95% confidence interval estimate of the population slope between sales and radio advertising.

b. at the 0.05 level of significance, determine whether each independent variable makes a significant contribution to the regression model. On the basis of these results, indicate the independent variables to include in this model.

13.29 In Problem 13.7 on page 463, you used the total number of staff present and remote hours to predict standby hours (see the Standby file). Using the results from that problem,

a. construct a 95% confidence interval estimate of the population slope between standby hours and total number of staff present.

b. at the 0.05 level of significance, determine whether each independent variable makes a significant contribution to the regression model. On the basis of these results, indicate the independent variables to include in this model.

13.30 In Problem 13.8 on page 463, you used land area of a property and age of a house to predict appraised value (see the GlenCove file). Using the results from that problem,

a. construct a 95% confidence interval estimate of the population slope between appraised value and land area of a property.

b. at the 0.05 level of significance, determine whether each independent variable makes a significant contribution to the regression model. On the basis of these results, indicate the independent variables to include in this model.

13.5 Using Dummy Variables and Interaction Terms in Regression Models

The multiple regression models discussed in Sections 13.1 through 13.4 assumed that each independent variable is numerical. However, in some situations, you might need to include categorical independent variables in the regression model. For example, in Section 13.1, you used price and promotional expenditures to predict the monthly sales of OmniPower high-energy bars. In addition to these numerical independent variables, you may need to include the effect of the shelf location in the store (e.g., end-aisle display or no end-aisle display) when developing a model to predict OmniPower sales.

The use of **dummy variables** allows you to include categorical independent variables in the regression model. If a given categorical independent variable has two categories, then you need only one dummy variable to represent the two categories. A dummy variable, X_d, is defined as

$$X_d = 0 \text{ if the observation is in category 1}$$

$$X_d = 1 \text{ if the observation is in category 2}$$

To illustrate the application of dummy variables in regression, consider a model for predicting the assessed value from a sample of 15 houses, based on the size of the house (in thousands of square feet) and whether the house has a fireplace. To include the categorical variable concerning the presence of a fireplace, the dummy variable X_2 is defined as

$$X_2 = 0 \text{ if the house does not have a fireplace}$$

$$X_2 = 1 \text{ if the house has a fireplace}$$

Table 13.3 presents the data, which are also stored in the file House3. In the last column of Table 13.3, you can see how the categorical variable is converted to a dummy variable with numerical values.

TABLE 13.3

Predicting Assessed
Value, Based on Size of
the House and Presence
of a Fireplace

Assessed Value	Size	Fireplace	Fireplace Coded
234.4	2.00	Yes	1
227.4	1.71	No	0
225.7	1.45	No	0
235.9	1.76	Yes	1
229.1	1.93	No	0
220.4	1.20	Yes	1
225.8	1.55	Yes	1
235.9	1.93	Yes	1
228.5	1.59	Yes	1
229.2	1.50	Yes	1
236.7	1.90	Yes	1
229.3	1.39	Yes	1
224.5	1.54	No	0
233.8	1.89	Yes	1
226.8	1.59	No	0

Assuming that the slope of assessed value with the size of the house is the same for houses that have and do not have a fireplace, the multiple regression model is

$$Y_i = \beta_0 + \beta_1 X_{1i} + \beta_2 X_{2i} + \varepsilon_i$$

where

Y_i = assessed value in thousands of dollars for house i

β_0 = Y intercept

X_{1i} = size of the house, in thousands of square feet, for house i

β_1 = slope of assessed value with size of the house, holding constant the presence or absence of a fireplace

X_{2i} = dummy variable representing the presence or absence of a fireplace for house i

β_2 = net effect of the presence of a fireplace on assessed value, holding constant the size of the house

ε_i = random error in Y for house i

Figure 13.8 illustrates the Microsoft Excel results for this model. Figure 13.9 shows Minitab results.

FIGURE 13.8

Microsoft Excel
regression results
worksheet for the
regression model that
includes size of the
house and presence
of fireplace

*See Section E13.4 and either
E13.1 or P13.1 to create this.*

	A	B	C	D	E	F	G
1	**Assessed Value Analysis**						
2							
3	*Regression Statistics*						
4	**Multiple R**	0.9006					
5	**R Square**	0.8111					
6	**Adjusted R Square**	0.7796					
7	**Standard Error**	2.2626					
8	**Observations**	15					
9							
10	**ANOVA**						
11		*df*	*SS*	*MS*	*F*	*Significance F*	
12	**Regression**	2	263.7039	131.8520	25.7557	0.0000	
13	**Residual**	12	61.4321	5.1193			
14	**Total**	14	325.1360				
15							
16		*Coefficients*	*Standard Error*	*t Stat*	*P-value*	*Lower 95%*	*Upper 95%*
17	**Intercept**	200.0905	4.3517	45.9803	0.0000	190.6090	209.5719
18	**Size**	16.1858	2.5744	6.2871	0.0000	10.5766	21.7951
19	**FireplaceCoded**	3.8530	1.2412	3.1042	0.0091	1.1486	6.5574

FIGURE 13.9

Minitab results for the regression model that includes size of the house and presence of fireplace

See Sections M13.3 and M13.2 to create this.

```
The regression equation is
Value = 200 + 16.2 Size + 3.85 Fireplace Coded


Predictor          Coef  SE Coef      T      P
Constant        200.090    4.352  45.98  0.000
Size             16.186    2.574   6.29  0.000
Fireplace Coded   3.853    1.241   3.10  0.009


S = 2.26260   R-Sq = 81.1%   R-Sq(adj) = 78.0%


Analysis of Variance

Source          DF      SS      MS      F      P
Regression       2  263.70  131.85  25.76  0.000
Residual Error  12   61.43    5.12
Total           14  325.14
```

From Figure 13.8 or 13.9, the regression equation is

$$\hat{Y}_i = 200.0905 + 16.1858 X_{1i} + 3.8530 X_{2i}$$

For houses without a fireplace, you substitute $X_2 = 0$ into the regression equation:

$$\hat{Y}_i = 200.0905 + 16.1858 X_{1i} + 3.8530 X_{2i}$$

$$= 200.0905 + 16.1858 X_{1i} + 3.8530(0)$$

$$= 200.0905 + 16.1858 X_{1i}$$

For houses with a fireplace, you substitute $X_2 = 1$ into the regression equation:

$$\hat{Y}_i = 200.0905 + 16.1858 X_{1i} + 3.8530 X_{2i}$$

$$= 200.0905 + 16.1858 X_{1i} + 3.8530(1)$$

$$= 203.9435 + 16.1858 X_{1i}$$

In this model, the regression coefficients are interpreted as follows:

1. Holding constant whether a house has a fireplace, for each increase of 1.0 thousand square feet in the size of the house, the mean assessed value is estimated to increase by 16.1858 thousand dollars (i.e., $16,185.80).
2. Holding constant the size of the house, the presence of a fireplace is estimated to increase the mean assessed value of the house by 3.8530 thousand dollars (i.e. $3,853).

In Figure 13.8 or 13.9, the t_{STAT} test statistic for the slope of the size of the house with assessed value is 6.2871, and the *p*-value is approximately 0.000; the t_{STAT} test statistic for presence of a fireplace is 3.1042, and the *p*-value is 0.0091. Thus, each of the two variables makes a significant contribution to the model at a level of significance of 0.01. In addition, the coefficient of multiple determination indicates that 81.11% of the variation in assessed value is explained by variation in the size of the house and whether the house has a fireplace.

Interactions

In all the regression models discussed so far, the *effect* an independent variable has on the dependent variable was assumed to be statistically independent of the other independent variables in the model. An **interaction** occurs if the effect of an independent variable on the dependent variable is affected by the *value* of a second independent variable. For example, it is possible for advertising to have a large effect on the sales of a product when the price of a product is low. However, if the price of the product is too high, increases in advertising will not dramatically change sales. In this case, price and advertising are said to interact. In other words, you cannot make general statements about the effect of advertising on sales. The effect that advertising has on sales is *dependent* on the price. You use an **interaction term** (sometimes referred to as a **cross-product term**) to model an interaction effect in a regression model.

To illustrate the concept of interaction and use of an interaction term, return to the example concerning the assessed values of homes discussed on pages 473–475. In the regression model, you assumed that the effect the size of the house has on the assessed value is independent of whether the house has a fireplace. In other words, you assumed that the slope of assessed value with size is the same for houses with fireplaces as it is for houses without fireplaces. If these two slopes are different, then an interaction exists between the size of the house and the presence of a fireplace.

To evaluate the possibility of an interaction, you first define an interaction term that equals the product of the independent variable X_1 (size of house) and the dummy variable X_2 (fireplace). You then test whether this interaction variable makes a significant contribution to the regression model. If the interaction is significant, you cannot use the original model for prediction. For the data of Table 13.3 on page 474, let

$$X_3 = X_1 \times X_2$$

Figure 13.10 illustrates Microsoft Excel results for this regression model (and Figure 13.11 displays Minitab results), which includes the size of the house, X_1, the presence of a fireplace, X_2, and the interaction of X_1 and X_2 (which is defined as X_3).

FIGURE 13.10

Microsoft Excel regression results worksheet for a regression model that includes size, presence of fireplace, and interaction of size and fireplace

See Sections E13.4 and E13.5 and either E13.1 or P13.1 to create this.

	A	B	C	D	E	F	G
1	**Assessed Value Analysis**						
2							
3	*Regression Statistics*						
4	**Multiple R**	0.9179					
5	**R Square**	0.8426					
6	**Adjusted R Square**	0.7996					
7	**Standard Error**	2.1573					
8	**Observations**	15					
9							
10	**ANOVA**						
11		*df*	*SS*	*MS*	*F*	*Significance F*	
12	**Regression**	3	273.9441	91.3147	19.6215	0.0001	
13	**Residual**	11	51.1919	4.6538			
14	**Total**	14	325.1360				
15							
16		*Coefficients*	*Standard Error*	*t Stat*	*P-value*	*Lower 95%*	*Upper 95%*
17	**Intercept**	212.9522	9.6122	22.1544	0.0000	191.7959	234.1084
18	**Size**	8.3624	5.8173	1.4375	0.1784	-4.4414	21.1662
19	**FireplaceCoded**	-11.8404	10.6455	-1.1122	0.2898	-35.2710	11.5902
20	**Size * FireplaceCoded**	9.5180	6.4165	1.4834	0.1661	-4.6046	23.6406

FIGURE 13.11

Minitab results for a regression model that includes size, presence of fireplace, and interaction of size and fireplace

See Sections M13.2–M13.4 to create this.

```
The regression equation is
Value = 213 + 8.36 Size - 11.8 Fireplace Coded + 9.52 Size*Fireplace


Predictor          Coef   SE Coef      T      P
Constant        212.952     9.612  22.15  0.000
Size              8.362     5.817   1.44  0.178
Fireplace Coded -11.84     10.65   -1.11  0.290
Size*Fireplace    9.518     6.416   1.48  0.166


S = 2.15727   R-Sq = 84.3%   R-Sq(adj) = 80.0%


Analysis of Variance

Source          DF      SS      MS      F      P
Regression       3  273.944  91.315  19.62  0.000
Residual Error  11   51.192   4.654
Total           14  325.136
```

To test for the existence of an interaction, you use the null hypothesis

$$H_0: \beta_3 = 0$$

versus the alternative hypothesis

$$H_1: \beta_3 \neq 0.$$

In Figure 13.10 or 13.11, the t_{STAT} test statistic for the interaction of size and fireplace is 1.4834. Because $t_{STAT} = 1.4834 < 2.201$ or the p-value $= 0.1661 > 0.05$, you do not reject the null hypothesis. Therefore, the interaction does not make a significant contribution to the model, given that size and presence of a fireplace are already included. You can conclude that the slope of assessed value with size is the same for houses with fireplaces and without fireplaces.

Problems for Section 13.5

LEARNING THE BASICS

13.31 Suppose X_1 is a numerical variable and X_2 is a dummy variable and the regression equation for a sample of $n = 20$ is

$$\hat{Y}_i = 6 + 4X_{1i} + 2X_{2i}$$

a. Interpret the regression coefficient associated with variable X_1.
b. Interpret the regression coefficient associated with variable X_2.

13.32 Suppose that in Problem 13.31, the t_{STAT} test statistic for testing the contribution of variable X_2 is 3.27. At the 0.05 level of significance, is there evidence that variable X_2 makes a significant contribution to the model?

APPLYING THE CONCEPTS

13.33 The chair of the accounting department wants to develop a regression model to predict the grade point average in accounting for graduating accounting majors, based on the student's SAT score and whether the student received a grade of B or higher in the introductory statistics course (0 = no and 1 = yes).
a. Explain the steps involved in developing a regression model for these data. Be sure to indicate the particular models you need to evaluate and compare.
b. Suppose the regression coefficient for the variable of whether the student received a grade of B or higher in the introductory statistics course is +0.30. How do you interpret this result?

13.34 A real estate association in a suburban community would like to study the relationship between the size of a single-family house (as measured by the number of rooms) and the selling price of the house (in thousands of dollars). Two different neighborhoods are included in the study, one on the east side of the community (=0) and the other on the west side (=1). A random sample of 20 houses was selected, with the results given in the file Neighbor . For (a) through (j) do not include an interaction term.
a. State the multiple regression equation that predicts the selling price based on the number of rooms and the neighborhood.
b. Interpret the regression coefficients in (a).
c. Predict the selling price for a house with nine rooms that is located in an east-side neighborhood. Construct a 95% confidence interval estimate and a 95% prediction interval.
d. Perform a residual analysis on the results and determine if the regression assumptions are valid.
e. Is there a significant relationship between selling price and the two independent variables (rooms and neighborhood) at the 0.05 level of significance?
f. At the 0.05 level of significance, determine whether each independent variable makes a contribution to the regression model. Indicate the most appropriate regression model for this set of data.
g. Construct and interpret a 95% confidence interval estimate for the relationship between selling price and number of rooms.
h. Construct and interpret a 95% confidence interval estimate for the relationship between selling price and neighborhood.
i. Compute and interpret the adjusted r^2.
j. What assumption do you need to make about the slope of selling price with number of rooms?

k. Add an interaction term to the model and, at the 0.05 level of significance, determine whether it makes a significant contribution to the model.

l. On the basis of the results of (f) and (k), which model is most appropriate? Explain.

13.35 The marketing manager of a large supermarket chain would like to determine the effect of shelf space and whether the product was placed at the front (=1) or back (=0) of the aisle on the sales of pet food. A random sample of 12 equal-sized stores is selected, with the results stored in the file **Petfood**.

For (a) through (l), do not include an interaction term.

a. State the multiple regression equation that predicts sales based on shelf space and location.

b. Interpret the regression coefficients in (a).

c. Predict the weekly sales of pet food for a store with 8 feet of shelf space situated at the back of the aisle. Construct a 95% confidence interval estimate and a 95% prediction interval.

d. Perform a residual analysis on the results and determine if the regression assumptions are valid.

e. Is there a significant relationship between sales and the two independent variables (shelf space and aisle position) at the 0.05 level of significance?

f. At the 0.05 level of significance, determine whether each independent variable makes a contribution to the regression model. Indicate the most appropriate regression model for this set of data.

g. Construct and interpret a 95% confidence interval estimates for the relationship between sales and shelf space and between sales and aisle location.

h. Compare the slope in (b) with the slope for the simple linear regression model of Problem 12.4 on page 417. Explain the difference in the results.

i. Computer and interpret the meaning of the coefficient of multiple determination, r^2.

j. Compute and interpret the adjusted r^2.

k. Compare r^2 with the r^2 value computed in Problem 12.16(a) on page 424.

l. What assumption about the slope of shelf space with sales do you need to make in this problem?

m. Add an interaction term to the model and, at the 0.05 level of significance, determine whether it makes a significant contribution to the model.

n. On the basis of the results of (f) and (m), which model is most appropriate? Explain.

13.36 In mining engineering, holes are often drilled through rock, using drill bits. As the drill hole gets deeper, additional rods are added to the drill bit to enable additional drilling to take place. It is expected that drilling time increases with depth. This increased drilling time could be caused by several factors, including the mass of the drill rods that are strung together. A key question relates to whether drilling is faster using dry drilling holes or wet drilling holes. Using dry drilling holes involves forcing compressed air down the drill rods to flush the cuttings and drive the hammer. Using wet drilling holes involves forcing water rather than air down the hole. The data file **Drill** contains measurements for a sample of 50 drill holes of the time to drill each additional 5 feet (in minutes), the depth (in feet), and whether the hole was a dry drilling hole or a wet drilling hole. Develop a model to predict additional drilling time, based on depth and type of drilling hole (dry or wet). For (a) through (j) do not include an interaction term.

Source: *Data extracted from R. Penner and D. G. Watts, "Mining Information," The American Statistician, 45, 1991, pp. 4–9.*

a. State the multiple regression equation.

b. Interpret the regression coefficients in (a).

c. Predict the additional drilling time for a dry drilling hole at a depth of 100 feet. Construct a 95% confidence interval estimate and a 95% prediction interval.

d. Perform a residual analysis on the results and determine if the regression assumptions are valid.

e. Is there a significant relationship between additional drilling time and the two independent variables (depth and type of drilling hole) at the 0.05 level of significance?

f. At the 0.05 level of significance, determine whether each independent variable makes a contribution to the regression model. Indicate the most appropriate regression model for this set of data.

g. Construct a 95% confidence interval estimate for the relationship between additional drilling time and depth.

h. Construct a 95% confidence interval estimate for the relationship between additional drilling time and the type of hole drilled.

i. Compute and interpret the adjusted r^2.

j. What assumption do you need to make about the slope of additional drilling time with depth?

k. Add an interaction term to the model and, at the 0.05 level of significance, determine whether it makes a significant contribution to the model.

l. On the basis of the results of (f) and (k), which model is most appropriate? Explain.

13.37 The owner of a moving company typically has his most experienced manager predict the total number of labor hours that will be required to complete an upcoming move. This approach has proved useful in the past, but the owner would like to be able to develop a more accurate method of predicting the labor hours by using the number of cubic feet moved and whether there is an elevator in the apartment building. In a preliminary effort to provide a more accurate method, he has collected data for 36 moves in which the origin and destination were within the borough of Manhattan in New York City and the travel time was an insignificant portion of the hours worked. The data are stored in the file **Moving**. For (a) through (j) do not include an interaction term.

a. State the multiple regression equation for predicting labor hours using the number of cubic feet moved and whether there is an elevator.

b. Interpret the regression coefficients in (a).

c. Predict the labor hours for moving 500 cubic feet in an apartment building that has an elevator, and construct a 95% confidence interval estimate and a 95% prediction interval.

d. Perform a residual analysis on the results and determine if the regression assumptions are valid.

e. Is there a significant relationship between labor hours and the two independent variables (cubic feet moved and whether there is an elevator in the apartment building) at the 0.05 level of significance?

f. At the 0.05 level of significance, determine whether each independent variable makes a contribution to the regression model. Indicate the most appropriate regression model for this set of data.

g. Construct a 95% confidence interval estimate for the relationship between labor hours and cubic feet moved.

h. Construct a 95% confidence interval estimate for the relationship between labor hours and the presence of an elevator.

i. Compute and interpret the adjusted r^2.

j. What assumption about the slope of labor hours with cubic feet moved do you need to make?

k. Add an interaction term to the model and, at the 0.05 level of significance, determine whether it makes a significant contribution to the model.

l. On the basis of the results of (f) and (k), which model is most appropriate? Explain.

SELF Test **13.38** In Problem 13.4 on page 462, you used sales and orders to predict distribution cost (see the file **Warecost**). Develop a regression model to predict distribution cost that includes the sales, orders, and the interaction of sales and orders.

a. At the 0.05 level of significance, is there evidence that the interaction term makes a significant contribution to the model?

b. Which regression model is more appropriate, the one used in (a) or the one used in Problem 13.4? Explain.

13.39 Zagat's publishes restaurant ratings for various locations in the United States. The data file **Restaurants** contains the Zagat rating for food, décor, service, and the price per person for a sample of 50 restaurants located in an urban area and 50 restaurants located in a suburban area. Develop a regression model to predict the price per person based on a variable that represents the sum of the ratings for food, décor, and service and a dummy variable concerning location (urban versus suburban). For (a) through (l) do not include an interaction term.

Source: *Data extracted from* Zagat Survey 2006 New York City Restaurants *and* Zagat Survey 2005–2006 Long Island Restaurants.

a. State the multiple regression equation.

b. Interpret the regression coefficients in (a).

c. Predict the price for a restaurant with a summated rating of 60 that is located in an urban area and construct a 95% confidence interval estimate and a 95% prediction interval.

d. Perform a residual analysis on the results and determine if the regression assumptions are satisfied.

e. Is there a significant relationship between price and the two independent variables (summated rating and location) at the 0.05 level of significance?

f. At the 0.05 level of significance, determine whether each independent variable makes a contribution to the regression model. Indicate the most appropriate regression model for this set of data.

g. Construct a 95% confidence interval estimate for the relationship between price and summated rating.

h. Compare the slope in (b) with the slope for the simple linear regression model of Problem 12.80 on page 450. Explain the difference in the results.

i. Compute and interpret the meaning of the coefficient of multiple determination.

j. Compute and interpret the adjusted r^2.

k. Compare r^2 with the r^2 value computed in Problem 12.80(d) on page 450.

l. What assumption about the slope of price with summated rating do you need to make in this problem?

m. Add an interaction term to the model and, at the 0.05 level of significance, determine whether it makes a significant contribution to the model.

n. On the basis of the results of (f) and (m), which model is most appropriate? Explain.

13.40 In Problem 13.6 on page 463, you used radio advertising and newspaper advertising to predict sales (see the file **Advertise**). Develop a regression model to predict sales that includes radio advertising, newspaper advertising, and the interaction of radio advertising and newspaper advertising.

a. At the 0.05 level of significance, is there evidence that the interaction term makes a significant contribution to the model?

b. Which regression model is more appropriate, the one used in this problem or the one used in Problem 13.6? Explain.

13.41 In Problem 13.5 on page 463, horsepower and weight were used to predict miles per gallon (see the file **Auto**). Develop a regression model that includes horsepower, weight, and the interaction of horsepower and weight to predict miles per gallon.

a. At the 0.05 level of significance, is there evidence that the interaction term makes a significant contribution to the model?

b. Which regression model is more appropriate, the one used in this problem or the one used in Problem 13.5? Explain.

13.42 In Problem 13.7 on page 463, you used total staff present and remote hours to predict standby hours (see the file **Standby**). Develop a regression model to predict standby hours that includes total staff present, remote hours, and the interaction of total staff present and remote hours.

a. At the 0.05 level of significance, is there evidence that the interaction term makes a significant contribution to the model?

b. Which regression model is more appropriate, the one used in this problem or the one used in Problem 13.7? Explain.

USING STATISTICS @ OmniFoods Revisited

In the Using Statistics scenario, you were the marketing manager for OmniFoods, a large food products company planning a nationwide introduction of a new high-energy bar, OmniPower. You needed to determine the effect that price and in-store promotions would have on the sales of OmniPower in order to develop an effective marketing strategy. A sample of 34 stores in a supermarket chain was selected for a test-market study. The stores charged between 59 and 99 cents per bar, and were given an in-store promotion budget between $200 and $600.

At the end of the one month test-market study, you performed a multiple regression analysis on the data. Two independent variables were considered, the price of an OmniPower bar and the monthly budget for in-store promotional expenditures. The dependent variable was the number of OmniPower bars sold in a month. The coefficient of determination indicated that 75.8% of the variation in sales was explained by knowing the price charged and the amount spent on in-store promotions. The model indicated that the mean sales of OmniPower are estimated to decrease by 532 bars per month for each 10-cent increase in the price, and estimated to increase by 361 bars for each additional $100 spent on promotions.

After studying the relative effects of price and promotion, OmniFoods needs to set price and promotion standards for a nationwide introduction (obviously lower prices and higher promotion budgets lead to more sales, but do so at a lower profit margin). You determined that if stores spend $400 a month in in-store promotions and charge 79 cents, the 95% confidence interval estimate of the mean monthly sales was 2,854 to 3,303 bars. OmniFoods can multiply the lower and upper bounds of this confidence interval by the number of stores included in the nationwide introduction to estimate total monthly sales. For example, if 1,000 stores are in the nationwide introduction, then total monthly sales should be between 2.854 million and 3.308 million bars.

SUMMARY

In this chapter, you learned how multiple regression models allow you to use two or more independent variables to predict the value of a dependent variable. You also learned how to include categorical independent variables and interaction terms in regression models. Figure 13.12 presents a road map of the chapter.

KEY EQUATIONS

Multiple Regression Model with k Independent Variables

$$Y_i = \beta_0 + \beta_1 X_{1i} + \beta_2 X_{2i} + \beta_3 X_{3i} + \cdots + \beta_k X_{ki} + \varepsilon_i \tag{13.1}$$

Multiple Regression Model with Two Independent Variables

$$Y_i = \beta_0 + \beta_1 X_{1i} + \beta_2 X_{2i} + \varepsilon_i \tag{13.2}$$

Multiple Regression Equation with Two Independent Variables

$$\hat{Y}_i = b_0 + b_1 X_{1i} + b_2 X_{2i} \tag{13.3}$$

Coefficient of Multiple Determination

$$r^2 = \frac{\text{Regression sum of squares}}{\text{Total sum of squares}} = \frac{SSR}{SST} \tag{13.4}$$

FIGURE 13.12
Roadmap for multiple regression

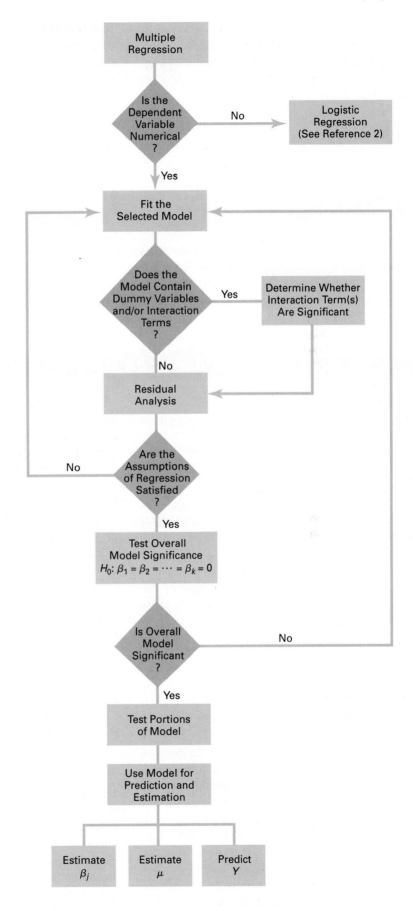

Adjusted r^2

$$r_{adj}^2 = 1 - \left[(1 - r^2)\frac{n-1}{n-k-1}\right] \quad (13.5)$$

Testing for the Slope in Multiple Regression

$$t_{STAT} = \frac{b_j - \beta_j}{S_{b_j}} \quad (13.7)$$

Overall F Test

$$F_{STAT} = \frac{MSR}{MSE} \quad (13.6)$$

Confidence Interval Estimate for the Slope

$$b_j \pm t_{\alpha/2}S_{b_j} \quad (13.8)$$

KEY TERMS

CHAPTER REVIEW PROBLEMS

CHECKING YOUR UNDERSTANDING

13.43 What is the difference between r^2 and the adjusted r^2?

13.44 How does the interpretation of the regression coefficients differ in multiple regression and simple linear regression?

13.45 How does testing the significance of the entire multiple regression model differ from testing the contribution of each independent variable?

13.46 Why and how do you use dummy variables?

13.47 How can you evaluate whether the slope of the dependent variable with an independent variable is the same for each level of the dummy variable?

13.48 Under what circumstances do you include an interaction term in a regression model?

APPLYING THE CONCEPTS

13.49 Increasing customer satisfaction typically results in increased purchase behavior. For many products, there is more than one measure of customer satisfaction. In many of these instances, purchase behavior can increase dramatically with an increase in any one of the customer satisfaction measures, not necessarily all of them at the same time. Gunst and Barry ("One Way to Moderate Ceiling Effects," *Quality Progress*, October 2003, pp. 83–85) consider a product with two satisfaction measures, X_1 and X_2, that range from the lowest level of satisfaction, 1, to the highest level of satisfaction, 7. The dependent variable, Y, is a measure of purchase behavior, with the highest value generating the most sales. The following regression equation is presented:

$$\hat{Y}_i = -3.888 + 1.449X_{1i} + 1.462X_{2i} - 0.190X_{1i}X_{2i}$$

Suppose that X_1 is the perceived quality of the product and X_2 is the perceived value of the product. (*Note:* If the product is overpriced in the view of the customer, he or she perceives it to be of low value and vice versa.)

a. What is the predicted purchase behavior when $X_1 = 2$ and $X_2 = 2$?

b. What is the predicted purchase behavior when $X_1 = 2$ and $X_2 = 7$?

c. What is the predicted purchase behavior when $X_1 = 7$ and $X_2 = 2$?

d. What is the predicted purchase behavior when $X_1 = 7$ and $X_2 = 7$?

e. What is the regression equation when $X_2 = 2$? What is the slope for X_1 now?

f. What is the regression equation when $X_2 = 7$? What is the slope for X_1 now?

g. What is the regression equation when $X_1 = 2$? What is the slope for X_2 now?

h. What is the regression equation when $X_1 = 7$? What is the slope for X_2 now?

i. Discuss the implications of (a) through (h) within the context of increasing sales for this product with two customer satisfaction measures.

13.50 The owner of a moving company typically has his most experienced manager predict the total number of labor hours that will be required to complete an upcoming move. This approach has proved useful in the past, but the owner would like to be able to develop a more accurate method of predicting the labor hours by using the number of cubic feet moved and the number of pieces of large furniture. In a preliminary effort to provide a more accurate method, he has collected data for 36 moves in which the origin and destination were within the borough of Manhattan in New York

City and the travel time was an insignificant portion of the hours worked. The data are stored in the file **Moving**.
a. State the multiple regression equation.
b. Interpret the meaning of the slopes in this equation.
c. Predict the labor hours for moving 500 cubic feet with two large pieces of furniture.
d. Perform a residual analysis on your results and determine if the regression assumptions are valid.
e. Determine whether there is a significant relationship between labor hours and the two independent variables (the amount of cubic feet moved and the number of pieces of large furniture) at the 0.05 level of significance.
f. Determine the *p*-value in (e) and interpret its meaning.
g. Interpret the meaning of the coefficient of multiple determination in this problem.
h. Determine the adjusted r^2.
i. At the 0.05 level of significance, determine whether each independent variable makes a significant contribution to the regression model. Indicate the most appropriate regression model for this set of data.
j. Determine the *p*-values in (i) and interpret their meaning.
k. Construct a 95% confidence interval estimate of the population slope between labor hours and the number of cubic feet moved. How does the interpretation of the slope here differ from that in Problem 12.36 on page 434?

13.51 Professional basketball has truly become a sport that generates interest among fans around the world. More and more players come from outside the United States to play in the National Basketball Association (NBA). You want to develop a regression model to predict the number of wins achieved by each NBA team, based on field goal (shots made) percentage for the team and for the opponent. The data are stored in the file **NBA2008**.
a. State the multiple regression equation.
b. Interpret the meaning of the slopes in this equation.
c. Predict the number of wins for a team that has a field goal percentage of 45% and an opponent field goal percentage of 44%.
d. Perform a residual analysis on your results and determine if the regression assumptions are valid.
e. Is there a significant relationship between number of wins and the two independent variables (field goal percentage for the team and for the opponent) at the 0.05 level of significance?
f. Determine the *p*-value in (e) and interpret its meaning.
g. Interpret the meaning of the coefficient of multiple determination in this problem.
h. Determine the adjusted r^2.
i. At the 0.05 level of significance, determine whether each independent variable makes a significant contribution to the regression model. Indicate the most appropriate regression model for this set of data.
j. Determine the *p*-values in (i) and interpret their meaning.

13.52 A sample of 30 recently sold single-family houses in a small city is selected. Develop a model to predict the selling price (in thousands of dollars), using the assessed value (in thousands of dollars) as well as time period when sold (in months since reassessment). The houses in the city had been reassessed at full value one year prior to the study. The results are contained in the file **House1**.
a. State the multiple regression equation.
b. Interpret the meaning of the slopes in this equation.
c. Predict the selling price for a house that has an assessed value of $170,000 and was sold in time period 12.
d. Perform a residual analysis on your results and determine if the regression assumptions are valid.
e. Determine whether there is a significant relationship between selling price and the two independent variables (assessed value and time period) at the 0.05 level of significance.
f. Determine the *p*-value in (e) and interpret its meaning.
g. Interpret the meaning of the coefficient of multiple determination in this problem.
h. Determine the adjusted r^2.
i. At the 0.05 level of significance, determine whether each independent variable makes a significant contribution to the regression model. Indicate the most appropriate regression model for this set of data.
j. Determine the *p*-values in (i) and interpret their meaning.
k. Construct a 95% confidence interval estimate of the population slope between selling price and assessed value. How does the interpretation of the slope here differ from that in Problem 12.66 on page 447?

13.53 Measuring the height of a California redwood tree is very difficult because these trees grow to heights of over 300 feet. People familiar with these trees understand that the height of a California redwood tree is related to other characteristics of the tree, including the diameter of the tree at the breast height of a person and the thickness of the bark of the tree. The data in the file **Redwood** represent the height, diameter at breast height of a person, and bark thickness for a sample of 21 California redwood trees.
a. State the multiple regression equation that predicts the height of a tree based on the tree's diameter at breast height and the thickness of the bark.
b. Interpret the meaning of the slopes in this equation.
c. Predict the height for a tree that has a breast height diameter of 25 inches and a bark thickness of 2 inches.
d. Interpret the meaning of the coefficient of multiple determination in this problem.
e. Perform a residual analysis on the results and determine if the regression assumptions are valid.
f. Determine whether there is a significant relationship between the height of redwood trees and the two independent variables (breast-height diameter and the bark thickness) at the 0.05 level of significance.
g. Construct a 95% confidence interval estimate of the population slope between the height of redwood trees and breast-height diameter and between the height of redwood trees and the bark thickness.

h. At the 0.05 level of significance, determine whether each independent variable makes a significant contribution to the regression model. Indicate the independent variables to include in this model.

i. Construct a 95% confidence interval estimate of the mean height for trees that have a breast-height diameter of 25 inches and a bark thickness of 2 inches along with a prediction interval for an individual tree.

13.54 Develop a model to predict the assessed value (in thousands of dollars), using the size of the houses (in thousands of square feet) and the age of the houses (in years) from the data stored in the file **House2** .

a. State the multiple regression equation.

b. Interpret the meaning of the slopes in this equation.

c. Predict the assessed value for a house that has a size of 1,750 square feet and is 10 years old.

d. Perform a residual analysis on the results and determine if the regression assumptions are valid.

e. Determine whether there is a significant relationship between assessed value and the two independent variables (size and age) at the 0.05 level of significance.

f. Determine the p-value in (e) and interpret its meaning.

g. Interpret the meaning of the coefficient of multiple determination in this problem.

h. Determine the adjusted r^2.

i. At the 0.05 level of significance, determine whether each independent variable makes a significant contribution to the regression model. Indicate the most appropriate regression model for this set of data.

j. Determine the p-values in (i) and interpret their meaning.

k. Construct a 95% confidence interval estimate of the population slope between assessed value and size. How does the interpretation of the slope here differ from that of Problem 12.67 on page 447?

l. The real estate assessor's office has been publicly quoted as saying that the age of a house has no bearing on its assessed value. Based on your answers to (a) through (k), do you agree with this statement? Explain.

13.55 Crazy Dave, a well-known baseball analyst, wants to determine which variables are important in predicting a team's wins in a given season. He has collected data related to wins, earned run average (ERA), and runs scored for the 2007 season (stored in the file **BB2007**). Develop a model to predict the number of wins based on ERA and runs scored.

a. State the multiple regression equation.

b. Interpret the meaning of the slopes in this equation.

c. Predict the number of wins for a team that has an ERA of 4.50 and has scored 750 runs.

d. Perform a residual analysis on the results and determine if the regression assumptions are valid.

e. Is there a significant relationship between number of wins and the two independent variables (ERA and runs scored) at the 0.05 level of significance?

f. Determine the p-value in (e) and interpret its meaning.

g. Interpret the meaning of the coefficient of multiple determination in this problem.

h. Determine the adjusted r^2.

i. At the 0.05 level of significance, determine whether each independent variable makes a significant contribution to the regression model. Indicate the most appropriate regression model for this set of data.

j. Determine the p-values in (i) and interpret their meaning.

k. Which is more important in predicting wins—pitching, as measured by ERA, or offense, as measured by runs scored? Explain.

13.56 Referring to Problem 13.55, suppose that in addition to using ERA to predict the number of wins, Crazy Dave wants to include the league (American vs. National) as an independent variable. Develop a model to predict wins based on ERA and league. For (a)–(h), do not include an interaction term.

a. State the multiple regression equation.

b. Interpret the regression coefficients in (a).

c. Predict the number of wins for a team with an ERA of 4.50 in the American League. Construct a 95% confidence interval estimate for all teams and a 95% prediction interval for an individual team.

d. Perform a residual analysis on the results and determine if the regression assumptions are valid.

e. Is there a significant relationship between wins and the two independent variables (ERA and league) at the 0.05 level of significance?

f. At the 0.05 level of significance, determine whether each independent variable makes a contribution to the regression model. Indicate the most appropriate regression model for this set of data.

g. Compute and interpret the adjusted r^2.

h. What assumption do you have to make about the slope of wins with ERA?

i. Add an interaction term to the model and, at the 0.05 level of significance, determine whether it makes a significant contribution to the model.

j. On the basis of the results of (f) and (i), which model is most appropriate? Explain.

13.57 You are a real estate broker who wants to compare property values in Glen Cove and Roslyn (which are located approximately 8 miles apart). In order to do so, you will analyze the data in the **GCRoslyn** file that includes samples of houses from Glen Cove and Roslyn. Making sure to include the dummy variable for location (Glen Cove or Roslyn), develop a regression model to predict appraised value, based on the land area of a property, the age of a house, and location. Be sure to determine whether any interaction terms need to be included in the model.

13.58 Many factors determine the attendance at Major League Baseball games. These factors can include when the game is played, the weather, the opponent, and whether the team is having a good season. In an effort to increase ticket sales, ball clubs run promotions such as free concerts after the game, or giveaways of team hats or bobbleheads of star players (T. C. Boyd and T. C. Krehbiel, "An Analysis of the Effects of Specific Promotion Types on Attendance at Major League Baseball Games," *American Journal of Business*, 2006, 21, pp. 21–32). The data file `Phillies` includes the following variables for a recent season:

Attendance—Paid attendance for each Philadelphia Phillies home game

Temp—High temperature for the day

Win—Team's winning percentage at the time of the game

OpWin—Opponent team's winning percentage at the time of the game

Weekend—Dummy variable, 1 if game played on Friday, Saturday, or Sunday; 0 otherwise

Promotion—Dummy variable, 1 if a promotion was held; 0 if no promotion was held

a. Perform a regression analysis using attendance as the dependent variable and the other five variables as independent variables.

b. Interpret the coefficient of determination.

c. Determine which factors significantly influenced attendance (use $\alpha = 0.05$).

d. Interpret the regression coefficient associated with the variable Promotion. Do you think the promotions run by the Phillies were effective? Explain.

MANAGING THE *SPRINGVILLE HERALD*

In its continuing study of the home-delivery subscription solicitation process, a marketing department team wants to test the effects of two types of structured sales presentations (personal formal and personal informal) and the number of hours spent on telemarketing on the number of new subscriptions. The staff has recorded these data in the file `SH13` for the past 24 weeks. You can find this data set at **www.prenhall.com/HeraldCase/EffectsData.htm** and in

the `EffectsData.htm` file in the **Herald Case** folder on the Student CD-ROM that accompanies this book.

Analyze these data and develop a multiple regression model to predict the number of new subscriptions for a week, based on the number of hours spent on telemarketing and the sales presentation type. Write a report, giving detailed findings concerning the regression model used.

WEB CASE

Apply your knowledge of multiple regression models in this Web Case, which extends the Using Statistics OmniFoods scenario from this chapter.

To ensure a successful test marketing of its OmniPower energy bars, the OmniFoods marketing department has contracted with In-Store Placements Group (ISPG), a merchandising consultancy. ISPG will work with the grocery store chain that is conducting the test-market study. Using the same 34-store sample used in the test-market study, ISPG claims that the choice of shelf location and the presence of in-store OmniPower coupon dispensers each increase sale of the energy bars.

Review the ISPG claims and supporting data at the OmniFoods internal Web page, **www.prenhall.com/Springville/Omni_ISPGMemo.htm** (or open the

`Omni_ISPGMemo.htm` file from the Student CD-ROM Web Case folder) and then answer the following:

1. Are the supporting data consistent with ISPG's claims? Perform an appropriate statistical analysis to confirm (or discredit) the stated relationship between sales and the two independent variables of product shelf location and the presence of in-store OmniPower coupon dispensers.

2. If you were advising OmniFoods, would you recommend using a specific shelf location and in-store coupon dispensers to sell OmniPower bars?

3. What additional data would you advise collecting in order to determine the effectiveness of the sales promotion techniques used by ISPG?

REFERENCES

1. Davenport, T., and J. Harris, *Competing on Analytics: The New Science of Winning* (Boston, MA: Harvard Business School Press, 2007).
2. Hosmer, D. W., and S. Lemeshow, *Applied Logistic Regression*, 2nd ed. (New York: Wiley, 2001).
3. Kutner, M., C. Nachtsheim, J. Neter, and W. Li, *Applied Linear Statistical Models*, 5th ed. (New York: McGraw-Hill/Irwin, 2005).
4. *Microsoft Excel 2007* (Redmond, WA: Microsoft Corp., 2007).
5. *Minitab for Windows Version 15* (State College, PA: Minitab, Inc., 2006).

Using Microsoft Excel for Multiple Regression Models

E13.1 Performing Multiple Regression Analyses

You perform a multiple regression analysis by using the ToolPak Regression procedure.

Open to the worksheet that contains data for the Y variable and the X variables. Data for the X variables must be placed in contiguous columns. (Use cut-and-paste to rearrange the data, if necessary.) Select **Tools → Data Analysis** (Excel 97–2003) or **Data → Data Analysis** (Excel 2007). Then select **Regression** from the Data Analysis list, and click **OK**. In the procedure's dialog box (see below), enter the cell range of the Y variable data as the **Input Y Range**, the cell range of the X variables data as the **Input X Range**, and click **Labels**. Click **Confidence Level**, enter a value in its box, and then click **OK**. Results appear on a new worksheet similar to Figure 13.2 on page 460.

E13.2 Performing Multiple Regression Residual Analysis

You perform multiple regression residual analysis using a two-step process. You first modify the instructions of Section E13.1, clicking **Residuals** in the Regression dialog box before you click **OK**. This option adds a residual table. You then use Excel charting features to do a residual analysis of a multiple regression model. (Although the Regression dialog box contains a **Residuals Plots** option, this option will create only the residual plots for each independent variable.)

The residuals table allows you to create the residual plot of the residuals versus $\hat{Y}_i$, the predicted values of Y. Apply the instructions of Section E2.12 on page 73 to create this residual plot, using the cell range of the residuals as

the Y variable and the cell range of the predicted Y as the X variable.

Residual plots of residuals versus X_{1i}, X_{2i}, or *Observation* require more work as initially data for these plots will not be in proper order (X variable first, then Y variable) or will not appear together on one worksheet, as required when creating scatter plots.

For these plots, first copy the Residuals cell range column to column A of a new worksheet and then copy the $X_{1i}X_{2i}$ or *Observation* values to column B. The X_{1i} and X_{2i} values appear on your original data worksheet and the *Observation* values appear on the regression results worksheet. Then apply the instructions of Section E2.12 to create a residual plot, using the column A (residuals) cell range as the Y variable and the column B cell range as the X variable.

E13.3 Computing the Confidence Interval Estimate of the Mean Response and the Prediction Interval

You compute the confidence interval estimate of the mean response and the prediction interval using Excel techniques that are beyond the scope of this book. If you are an advanced Excel user, you can use the **CIEandPI** worksheet of the **CIEandPIforMR.xls** workbook (shown in Figure 13.4 on page 462) as a model for your own solutions. This worksheet uses the **TINV(1-*confidence level, degrees of freedom*)** function to compute the t statistic in cell B20 and uses the **TRANSPOSE(*cell range*)**, **MMULT(*cell range 1, cell range 2*)**, and **MINVERSE(*cell range*)** array functions to perform advanced matrix mathematics. Some worksheet formulas reference a regression results worksheet named **MR**, whereas others, not shown in Figure 13.4, refer to a **DC** worksheet that contains a copy of the regression data and a column of all 1's. (Review the **CIEandPIFormulas** worksheet to see all of the formulas in the **CIEandPI** worksheet.)

E13.4 Creating Dummy Variables

You create dummy variables by using the Excel find-and-replace command to "find" each categorical value and "replace" it with a number.

Open the worksheet that contains your data. Copy all of the values of the categorical variable for which you are creating a dummy variable and paste the values into the first empty column of your worksheet.

Select all of the newly pasted values and press **Crtl+H**, the keyboard shortcut that displays the Find and Replace dialog box (shown below). For each unique categorical value in the column:

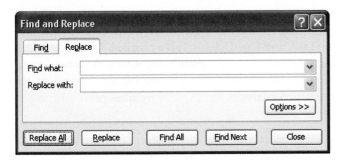

1. Enter the categorical value in the **Find what** box.
2. Enter the number that will represent that categorical value in the **Replace with** box.
3. Click **Replace All**. If a message box to confirm the replacement appears, click **OK** to continue.

Click **Close** when you are finished making all replacements. If you inadvertently click the worksheet while using this dialog box, reselect all of the newly pasted values before continuing to replace. When you finish, verify your work by comparing the original column of categorical values to your new column of numeric values.

E13.5 Defining Interaction Terms

You define the interaction term of an independent variable X_1 and a second independent variable X_2 by creating a column of formulas that multiply the X_1 variable by the X_2 variable. For example, if the first independent variable appeared in column B and the second independent variable appeared in column C, you would enter the formula **=B2*C2** in the row 2 cell of an empty column and then copy the formula down through all rows of data.

APPENDIX P13

Using PHStat2 for Multiple Regression Models

P13.1 Performing Multiple Regression Analyses

To perform a multiple regression analysis, use **PHStat → Regression → Multiple Regression**. This procedure creates a regression results worksheet based on sample data and a confidence level that you specify. The procedure uses the ToolPak Regression procedure to perform the regression

analysis and creates a worksheet similar to Figure 13.2 on page 460 if you leave **Regression Statistics Table** and **ANOVA and Coefficients Table** checked. Other sections of this PHStat2 appendix explain the use of the other Output Options to create charts and worksheets related to the regression analysis.

P13.2 Performing Multiple Regression Residual Analyses

To perform a multiple regression residual analysis, use the Section P13.1 instructions but click **Residuals Table** and **Residual Plots** before you click **OK** in the Multiple Regression dialog box.

P13.3 Computing the Confidence Interval Estimate of the Mean and the Prediction Interval

To compute the confidence interval estimate of the mean and the prediction interval, use the Section P13.1 instructions, but click **Confidence Interval Estimate & Prediction Interval** and enter a value for the **Confidence level for interval estimates** before you click **OK** in the Multiple Regression dialog box. PHStat2 will compute the confidence interval estimate and prediction interval on a separate, second worksheet that will be similar to Figure 13.4 on page 462.

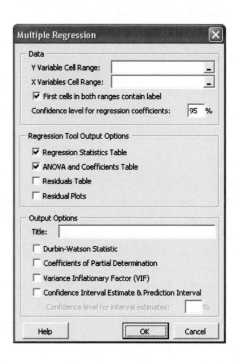

APPENDIX M13

Using Minitab for Multiple Regression Models

M13.1 Creating Three-Dimensional Plots

To illustrate creating a three-dimensional plot (for use only when there are two independent variables in the regression model):

1. Open the `OmniPower.mtw` worksheet.
2. Select **Graph → 3D Scatterplot**.
3. In the 3D Scatterplots dialog box (see Figure M13.1), click **Simple** and then **OK** (to proceed to the next dialog box).

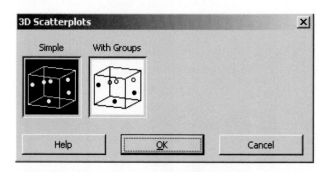

FIGURE M13.1 Minitab 3D Scatterplots dialog box

In the 3D Scatterplot - Simple dialog box (see Figure M13.2):

4. Enter **Sales** in the **Z variable** box.
5. Enter **Price** in the **Y variable** box.
6. Enter **Promotion** in the **X variable** box.
7. Click **OK**.

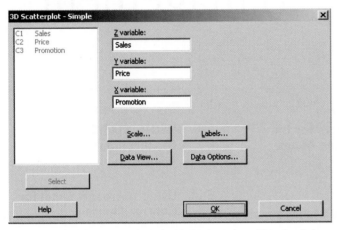

FIGURE M13.2 Minitab 3D Scatterplot - Simple dialog box

M13.2 Performing Multiple Regression Analyses

In Minitab, performing a multiple regression analysis is similar to performing a simple linear regression (see Section M12.1 on pages 454–455). To illustrate performing a multiple regression analysis:

1. Open the **OmniPower.mtw** worksheet.
2. Select **Stat → Regression → Regression**.

In the Regression dialog box (see Figure M12.1 on page 454):

3. Enter **Sales** in the **Response** box.
4. Enter **Price** and **Promotion** in the **Predictors** box.
5. Click **Graphs**.

In the Regression - Graphs dialog box (see Figure M12.2 on page 454):

6. Click **Regular**.
7. Click **Individual plots** and then click **Residuals versus fits** (to check for equal variance) and **Histogram of residuals** (to check for normality). Leave the other check boxes cleared.
8. Enter **Price** and **Promotion** in the **Residuals versus the variables** box.
9. Click **OK**.
10. Back in the Regression dialog box, click **Results**.

In the Regression - Results dialog box (see Figure M12.3 on page 455):

11. Click **In addition, the full table of fits and residuals**.
12. Click **OK**.
13. Back in the Regression dialog box, click **Options**.

In the Regression - Options dialog box (see Figure M12.4 on page 455):

14. Leave all of the **Display** check boxes unchecked because the OmniPower data was not collected over time.
15. Enter **79 400** in the **Prediction intervals for new observations** box.
16. Enter **95** in the **Confidence level** box.
17. Click **OK**.
18. Back in the Regression dialog box, click **OK**.

M13.3 Creating Dummy Variables

To illustrate creating a dummy variable using the data of Table 13.3 on page 474:

1. Open the **House3.mtw** worksheet. (The fireplace variable in column C3 of this worksheet is entered as Yes and No values.)
2. Enter **FireplaceCoded** as the name of the blank column C4.
3. Select **Data → Code → Text to Numeric**.

In the Code - Text to Numeric dialog box:

4. Enter **Fireplace** in the **Code data from columns** box.
5. Enter **FireplaceCoded** in the **Store coded data in columns** box.
6. In the first **Original values** box, enter **Yes**.
7. In the first **New** box, enter **1**.
8. In the second **Original values** box, enter **No**.
9. In the second **New** box, enter **0**.
10. Click **OK**.

M13.4 Defining Interaction Terms

To illustrate defining an interaction term using the data of Table 13.3 on page 474:

1. Use the instructions for Section M13.3 to create the **FireplaceCoded** column in the **House3.mtw** worksheet.
2. Select **Calc → Calculator**.
3. Enter **C5** in the **Store result in variable** box.
4. Enter **Size * FireplaceCoded** in the **Expression** box.
5. Click **OK**.
6. Enter **Size * FireplaceCoded** as the name for column C5.

14

Statistical Applications in Quality Management

Learning Objectives

In this chapter, you learn:

- How to construct various control charts
- Which control chart to use for a particular type of data
- The basic themes of total quality management and Deming's 14 points
- The basic aspects of Six Sigma

@ Beachcomber Hotel

You find yourself managing the Beachcomber Hotel, one of the resorts owned by T.C. Resort Properties (see Chapter 11). You want to continually improve the quality of service that your guests receive so that overall guest satisfaction increases. To help you achieve this improvement, T.C. Resort Properties has provided its managers with training in Six Sigma. In order to meet the business objective of increasing the return rate of guests at your hotel, you have decided to focus on the critical first impressions of the service that your hotel provides. Is the assigned hotel room ready when a guest checks in? Are all expected amenities, such as extra towels and a complimentary guest basket, in the room when the guest first walks in? Are the video-entertainment center and high-speed Internet access working properly? And do guests receive their luggage in a reasonable amount of time?

To study these guest satisfaction issues, you have embarked on an improvement project that focuses on the readiness of the room and the time it takes to deliver luggage. You would like to learn the following:

- Are the proportion of rooms ready and the time required to deliver luggage to the rooms acceptable?
- Are the proportion of rooms ready and the luggage delivery time consistent from day to day, or are they increasing or decreasing?
- On the days when the proportion of rooms that are not ready or the time to deliver luggage is greater than normal, are these due to a chance occurrence, or are there fundamental flaws in the processes used to make rooms ready and to deliver luggage?

ompanies manufacturing products, as well as those providing services, such as the Beachcomber Hotel in the "Using Statistics" scenario, realize that quality is essential for survival in the global economy. Among the areas in which quality has an impact on our everyday work and personal lives are the design, production, and reliability of our automobiles; the services provided by hotels, banks, schools, retailing operations, and mail-order companies; the continuous improvement in computer chips that makes for faster and more powerful computers; and the availability of new technology and equipment that has led to improved diagnosis of illnesses and the improved delivery of health care services.

In this chapter you will learn how to develop and analyze control charts, a statistical tool that is widely used for quality improvement. You will then learn how business and organizations around the world are using control charts as part of two important quality improvement approaches, total quality management (TQM) and Six Sigma.

14.1 The Theory of Control Charts

A **process** is the value-added transformation of inputs to outputs. Control charts, developed by Walter Shewhart in the 1920s (see reference 16), are commonly used statistical tools for monitoring and improving processes. The inputs and outputs of a process can involve machines, materials, methods, measurement, people, and the environment. Each of the inputs is a source of variability. Variability in the output can result in poor service and poor product quality, both of which often decrease customer satisfaction.

The **control chart** is used to analyze a process in which data are collected sequentially over time. You can use a control chart to study past performance, to evaluate present conditions, or to predict future outcomes. Control charts are used at the beginning of quality improvement efforts to study an existing process (called Phase 1 control charts). Information gained from analyzing Phase I control charts forms the basis for process improvement. After improvements to the process are implemented, control charts are then used to monitor the processes to ensure that the improvements continue (called Phase 2 control charts).

Different types of control charts allow you to analyze different types of critical-to-quality (CTQ in Six Sigma lingo—see Section 14.6) variables—for categorical variables, such as the proportion of hotel rooms that are nonconforming in terms of the availability of amenities and the working order of all appliances in the room; and for continuous variables, such as the length of time required for delivering luggage to the room.

In addition to providing a visual display of data representing a process, a principal focus of a control chart is the attempt to separate special causes of variation from common causes of variation.

> **Special causes of variation** represent large fluctuations or patterns in the data that are not part of a process. These fluctuations are often caused by unusual events and represent either problems to correct or opportunities to exploit. Some organizations refer to special causes of variation as **assignable causes of variation**.
>
> **Common causes of variation** represent the inherent variability that exists in a process. These fluctuations consist of the numerous small causes of variability that operate randomly or by chance. Some organizations refer to common causes of variation as **chance causes of variation**.

One experiment that is useful to help you appreciate the distinction between common and special causes of variation was developed by Walter Shewhart (see reference 16) more than 80 years ago. The experiment requires that you repeatedly write the letter A over and over again in a horizontal line across a piece of paper:

AAAAAAAAAAAAAAAAA

When you do this, you immediately notice that the A's are all similar but not exactly the same. In addition, you may notice some difference in the size of the A's from letter to letter. This difference is due to common cause variation. Nothing special happened that caused the differences in the size of the A's. You probably would have a hard time trying to explain why the largest A is bigger than the smallest A. These types of differences almost certainly represent common cause variation.

However, if you did the experiment over again, but wrote half of the A's with your right hand and the other half of the A's with your left hand, you would almost certainly see a very big difference in the A's written with each hand. In this case, which hand was used to write the A's is the source of the special cause variation.

The distinction between the two causes of variation is crucial because special causes of variation are not part of a process and are correctable or exploitable without changing the process. Common causes of variation, however, can be reduced only by changing the process. Such systemic changes are the responsibility of management.

Control charts allow you to monitor a process and identify the presence or absence of special causes. By doing so, control charts help prevent two types of errors. The first type of error involves the belief that an observed value represents special cause variation when it is due to the common cause variation of the process. Treating common cause variation as special cause variation often results in overadjusting a process. This overadjustment, known as **tampering**, increases the variation in the process. The second type of error involves treating special cause variation as common cause variation. This error results in not taking immediate corrective action when necessary. Although both of these types of errors can occur even when using a control chart, they are far less likely.

To construct a control chart, you collect samples from the output of a process over time. The samples used for constructing control charts are known as **subgroups**. For each subgroup (i.e., sample), you calculate a sample statistic. Commonly used statistics include the sample proportion for a categorical variable (see Section 14.2), and the mean and range of a numerical variable (see Section 14.4). You then plot the values over time and add control limits to the chart. The most typical form of a control chart sets control limits that are within ± 3 standard deviations[1] of the statistical measure of interest. Equation (14.1) defines, in general, the upper and lower control limits for control charts.

[1]Recall from Section 6.2 that in the normal distribution, $\mu \pm 3\sigma$ includes almost all (99.73%) of the values in the population.

CONSTRUCTING CONTROL LIMITS

$$\text{Process mean} \pm 3 \text{ standard deviations} \qquad (14.1)$$

so that

Upper control limit (UCL) = process mean $+3$ standard deviations

Lower control limit (LCL) = process mean -3 standard deviations

---

When these control limits are set, you evaluate the control chart by trying to find any pattern that might exist in the values over time and by determining whether any points fall outside the control limits. Figure 14.1 illustrates three different patterns.

FIGURE 14.1

Three control chart patterns

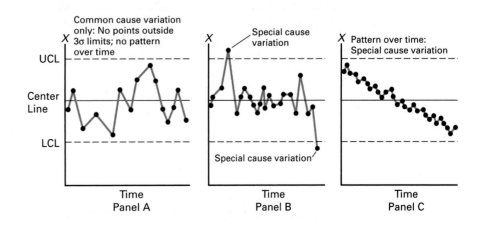

In Panel A of Figure 14.1, there is no apparent pattern in the values over time, and there are no points that fall outside the 3 standard deviation control limits. The process appears stable and contains only common cause variation. Panel B, on the contrary, contains two points that fall outside the 3 standard deviation control limits. You should investigate these points to try to determine the special causes that led to their occurrence. Although Panel C does not have any points outside the control limits, it has a series of consecutive points above the mean value (the center line) as well as a series of consecutive points below the mean value. In addition, a long-term overall downward trend is clearly visible. You should investigate the situation to try to determine what may have caused this pattern.

Detecting a pattern is not always so easy. The following simple rule (see references 9, 13, and 18) can help you to detect a trend or a shift in the mean level of a process:

- Eight or more *consecutive* points that lie above the center line or eight or more *consecutive* points that lie below the center line[2]

[2]This rule is often referred to as the runs rule. A similar rule used by some companies is called the trend rule: Eight or more consecutive points that increase in value or eight or more consecutive points that decrease in value. Some statisticians (see reference 5) have criticized the trend rule. It should only be used with extreme caution.

A process whose control chart indicates an out-of-control condition (i.e., a point outside the control limits or a series of points that exhibits a pattern) is said to be out of control. An **out-of-control process** contains both common causes of variation and special causes of variation. Because special causes of variation are not part of the process design, an out-of-control process is unpredictable. When you determine that a process is out of control, you must identify the special causes of variation that are producing the out-of-control conditions. If the special causes are detrimental to the quality of the product or service, you need to implement plans to eliminate this source of variation. When a special cause increases quality, you should change the process so that the special cause is incorporated into the process design. Thus, this beneficial special cause now becomes a common cause source of variation, and the process is improved.

A process whose control chart does not indicate any out-of-control conditions is said to be in control. An **in-control process** contains only common causes of variation. Because these sources of variation are inherent to the process itself, an in-control process is predictable. In-control processes are sometimes said to be in a **state of statistical control**. When a process is in control, you must determine whether the amount of common cause variation in the process is small enough to satisfy the customers of the products or services. If the common cause variation is small enough to consistently satisfy the customer, you then use control charts to monitor the process on a continuing basis to make sure the process remains in control. If the common cause variation is too large, you need to alter the process itself.

14.2 Control Chart for the Proportion: The *p* Chart

Various types of control charts are used to monitor processes and determine whether special cause variation is present in a process. **Attribute control charts** are used for categorical or discrete variables. This section introduces the *p* **chart**, which is used for categorical variables. The *p* chart gets its name from the fact that you plot the *proportion* of items in a sample that are in a category of interest. For example, sampled items are often classified according to whether they conform or do not conform to operationally defined requirements. Thus, the *p* chart is frequently used to monitor and analyze the proportion of nonconforming items in repeated samples (i.e., subgroups) selected from a process.

To begin the discussion of *p* charts, recall that you studied proportions and the binomial distribution in Section 5.2. Then, in Section 7.5 on page 227, the sample proportion is defined as $p = X/n$, and the standard deviation of the sample proportion is defined as

$$\sigma_p = \sqrt{\frac{\pi(1-\pi)}{n}}$$

[3]In this chapter, and in quality management, the phrase "proportion of nonconforming items" is often used, although the *p* chart can be used to monitor any proportion of interest. Recall that in the earlier discussions of the binomial distribution, the phrase "proportion of items of interest" was used.

Using Equation (14.1) on page 493, control limits for the proportion of nonconforming[3] items from the sample data are established in Equation (14.2).

CONTROL LIMITS FOR THE *p* CHART

$$\bar{p} \pm 3\sqrt{\frac{\bar{p}(1 - \bar{p})}{\bar{n}}}$$

$$\text{UCL} = \bar{p} + 3\sqrt{\frac{\bar{p}(1 - \bar{p})}{\bar{n}}}$$

$$\text{LCL} = \bar{p} - 3\sqrt{\frac{\bar{p}(1 - \bar{p})}{\bar{n}}}$$

(14.2)

For equal n_i,

$$\bar{n} = n_i \text{ and } \bar{p} = \frac{\sum_{i=1}^{k} p_i}{k}$$

or in general,

$$\bar{n} = \frac{\sum_{i=1}^{k} n_i}{k} \text{ and } \bar{p} = \frac{\sum_{i=1}^{k} X_i}{\sum_{i=1}^{k} n_i}$$

where

X_i = number of nonconforming items in subgroup i

n_i = sample (or subgroup) size for subgroup i

$p_i = \dfrac{X_i}{n_i}$ = proportion of nonconforming items in subgroup i

k = number of subgroups selected

$\bar{n}$ = mean subgroup size

$\bar{p}$ = proportion of nonconforming items in the k subgroups combined

Any negative value for the LCL means that the LCL does not exist.

To show the application of the *p* chart, return to the Using Statistics scenario on page 491 concerning the Beachcomber Hotel. During the process improvement effort in the *Measure* phase of Six Sigma (see Section 14.6), a nonconforming room was operationally defined as the absence of an amenity or an appliance not in working order upon check-in. During the *Analyze* phase of Six Sigma, data on the nonconformances were collected daily from a sample of 200 rooms (see the file **Hotel1**). Table 14.1 lists the number and proportion of nonconforming rooms for each day in the four-week period.

For these data, $k = 28$, $\sum_{i=1}^{k} p_i = 2.315$ and, because the n_i are equal, $n_i = \bar{n} = 200$. Thus,

$$\bar{p} = \frac{\sum_{i=1}^{k} p_i}{k} = \frac{2.315}{28} = 0.0827$$

TABLE 14.1

Nonconforming Hotel Rooms at Check-in over a 28-Day Period

Day (i)	Rooms Studied (n_i)	Rooms Not Ready (X_i)	Proportion (p_i)	Day (i)	Rooms Studied (n_i)	Rooms Not Ready (X_i)	Proportion (p_i)
1	200	16	0.080	15	200	18	0.090
2	200	7	0.035	16	200	13	0.065
3	200	21	0.105	17	200	15	0.075
4	200	17	0.085	18	200	10	0.050
5	200	25	0.125	19	200	14	0.070
6	200	19	0.095	20	200	25	0.125
7	200	16	0.080	21	200	19	0.095
8	200	15	0.075	22	200	12	0.060
9	200	11	0.055	23	200	6	0.030
10	200	12	0.060	24	200	12	0.060
11	200	22	0.110	25	200	18	0.090
12	200	20	0.100	26	200	15	0.075
13	200	17	0.085	27	200	20	0.100
14	200	26	0.130	28	200	22	0.110

Using Equation (14.2),

$$0.0827 \pm 3\sqrt{\frac{(0.0827)(0.9173)}{200}}$$

so that

$$UCL = 0.0827 + 0.0584 = 0.1411$$

and

$$LCL = 0.0827 - 0.0584 = 0.0243$$

Figure 14.2 displays the Microsoft Excel p chart for the data of Table 14.1. Figure 14.3 on page 497 illustrates Minitab results. Figure 14.2 and Figure 14.3 show a process in a state of statistical control, with the individual points distributed around $\bar{p}$ without any pattern and all the points within the control limits. Thus, any improvement in the process of making rooms ready for guests must come from the reduction of common cause variation. Such reductions require changes in the process. These changes are the responsibility of management. Remember that improvements in quality cannot occur until changes to the process itself are successfully implemented.

FIGURE 14.2

Microsoft Excel p chart for the nonconforming hotel rooms

See Sections E14.1 and E14.2 or Section P14.1 to create this.

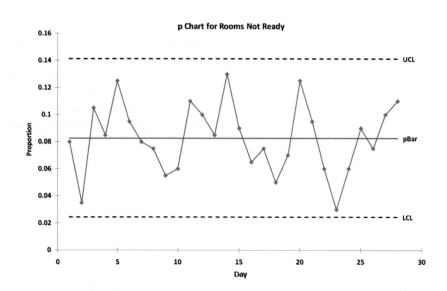

FIGURE 14.3

Minitab *p* chart for the nonconforming hotel rooms

See Section M14.1 to create this.

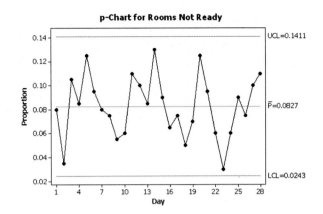

This example illustrates a situation in which the subgroup size does not vary. As a general rule, as long as none of the subgroup sizes, n_i, differ from the mean subgroup size, $\bar{n}$, by more than $\pm 25\%$ of $\bar{n}$ (see reference 9), you can use Equation (14.2) on page 495 to compute the control limits for the *p* chart. If any subgroup size differs by more than $\pm 25\%$ of $\bar{n}$, you use alternative formulas for calculating the control limits (see references 9 and 13). To illustrate the use of the *p* chart when the subgroup sizes are unequal, Example 14.1 studies the production of medical sponges.

EXAMPLE 14.1

Using the *p* Chart for Unequal Subgroup Sizes

TABLE 14.2

Medical Sponges Produced and Number Nonconforming over a 32-Day Period

Table 14.2 indicates the number of medical sponges produced daily and the number that are nonconforming for a period of 32 days (see the file **Sponge**). Construct a control chart for these data.

Day (i)	Sponges Produced (n_i)	Nonconforming Sponges (X_i)	Proportion (p_i)	Day (i)	Sponges Produced (n_i)	Nonconforming Sponges (X_i)	Proportion (p_i)
1	690	21	0.030	17	575	20	0.035
2	580	22	0.038	18	610	16	0.026
3	685	20	0.029	19	596	15	0.025
4	595	21	0.035	20	630	24	0.038
5	665	23	0.035	21	625	25	0.040
6	596	19	0.032	22	615	21	0.034
7	600	18	0.030	23	575	23	0.040
8	620	24	0.039	24	572	20	0.035
9	610	20	0.033	25	645	24	0.037
10	595	22	0.037	26	651	39	0.060
11	645	19	0.029	27	660	21	0.032
12	675	23	0.034	28	685	19	0.028
13	670	22	0.033	29	671	17	0.025
14	590	26	0.044	30	660	22	0.033
15	585	17	0.029	31	595	24	0.040
16	560	16	0.029	32	600	16	0.027

SOLUTION For these data,

$$k = 32, \sum_{i=1}^{k} n_i = 19,926$$

$$\sum_{i=1}^{k} X_i = 679$$

Thus, using Equation (14.2) on page 495,

$$\bar{n} = \frac{19{,}926}{32} = 622.69$$

$$\bar{p} = \frac{679}{19{,}926} = 0.034$$

so that

$$0.034 \pm 3\sqrt{\frac{(0.034)(1 - 0.034)}{622.69}}$$

$$= 0.034 \pm 0.022$$

Thus,

$$UCL = 0.034 + 0.022 = 0.056$$

$$LCL = 0.034 - 0.022 = 0.012$$

Figure 14.4 displays the Microsoft Excel control chart for the sponge data. In Figure 14.5, Minitab calculates separate control limits for each day, depending on the subgroup size for that day and therefore the UCL and LCL are represented by jagged lines. From Figure 14.4 or Figure 14.5, you can see that day 26, on which there were 39 nonconforming sponges produced out of 651 sampled, is above the UCL. Management needs to determine the reason (i.e., root cause) for this special cause variation and take corrective action. Once actions are taken, you can remove the data from day 26 and then construct and analyze a new control chart.

FIGURE 14.4

Microsoft Excel *p* chart for the proportion of nonconforming medical sponges

See Sections E14.1 and E14.2 or Section P14.1 to create this.

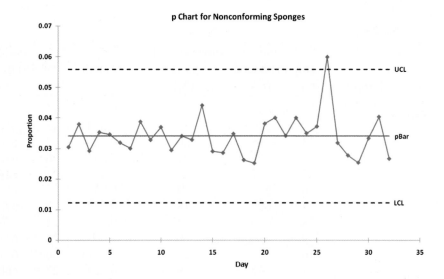

FIGURE 14.5

Minitab *p* chart for the proportion of nonconforming medical sponges

See Section M14.1 to create this.

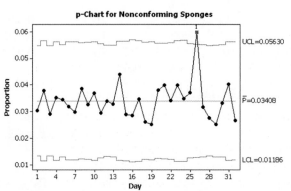

Problems for Section 14.2

LEARNING THE BASICS

14.1 The following data were collected on nonconformances for a period of 10 days:

Day	Sample Size	Nonconformances
1	100	12
2	100	14
3	100	10
4	100	18
5	100	22
6	100	14
7	100	15
8	100	13
9	100	14
10	100	16

a. On what day is the proportion of nonconformances largest? smallest?
b. What are the LCL and UCL?
c. Are there any special causes of variation?

14.2 The following data were collected on nonconformances for a period of 10 days:

Day	Sample Size	Nonconformances
1	111	12
2	93	14
3	105	10
4	92	18
5	117	22
6	88	14
7	117	15
8	87	13
9	119	14
10	107	16

a. On what day is the proportion of nonconformances largest? smallest?
b. What are the LCL and UCL?
c. Are there any special causes of variation?

APPLYING THE CONCEPTS

14.3 A medical transcription service enters medical data on patient files for hospitals. The service studied ways to improve the turnaround time (defined as the time between sending data and the time the client receives completed files). After studying the process, it was determined that turnaround time was increased by transmission errors. A transmission error was defined as data transmitted that did not go through as planned and needed to be retransmitted. For a period of 31 days, a sample of 125 transmissions were randomly selected and evaluated for errors (see the file **Transmit**). The following table presents the number and proportion of transmissions with errors:

Day (i)	Number of Errors (X_i)	Proportion of Errors (p_i)	Day (i)	Number of Errors (X_i)	Proportion of Errors (p_i)
1	6	0.048	17	4	0.032
2	3	0.024	18	6	0.048
3	4	0.032	19	3	0.024
4	4	0.032	20	5	0.040
5	9	0.072	21	1	0.008
6	0	0.000	22	3	0.024
7	0	0.000	23	14	0.112
8	8	0.064	24	6	0.048
9	4	0.032	25	7	0.056
10	3	0.024	26	3	0.024
11	4	0.032	27	10	0.080
12	1	0.008	28	7	0.056
13	10	0.080	29	5	0.040
14	9	0.072	30	0	0.000
15	3	0.024	31	3	0.024
16	1	0.008			

a. Construct a *p* chart.
b. Is the process in a state of statistical control? Why?

✓ SELF Test **14.4** The following data represent the findings from a study conducted at a factory that manufactures film canisters. For 32 days, 500 film canisters were sampled and inspected (see the file **Canister**). The following table lists the number of defective film canisters (i.e., nonconforming items) for each day (i.e., subgroup):

Day	Number Nonconforming	Day	Number Nonconforming
1	26	17	23
2	25	18	19
3	23	19	18
4	24	20	27
5	26	21	28
6	20	22	24
7	21	23	26
8	27	24	23
9	23	25	27
10	25	26	28
11	22	27	24
12	26	28	22
13	25	29	20
14	29	30	25
15	20	31	27
16	19	32	19

a. Construct a *p* chart.
b. Is the process in a state of statistical control? Why?

14.5 A hospital administrator is concerned with the time to process patients' medical records after discharge. She determined that all records should be processed within 5 days of discharge. Thus, any record not processed within 5 days of a patient's discharge is nonconforming. The administrator recorded the number of patients discharged and the number of records not processed within the 5-day standard for a 30-day period in the file Medrec.

a. Construct a *p* chart for these data.

b. Does the process give an out-of-control signal? Explain.

c. If the process is out of control, assume that special causes were subsequently identified and corrective action was taken to keep them from happening again. Then eliminate the data causing the out-of-control signals and recalculate the control limits.

14.6 The bottling division of Sweet Suzy's Sugarless Cola maintains daily records of the occurrences of unacceptable cans flowing from the filling and sealing machine. The data stored in the file Colaspc, lists the number of cans filled and the number of nonconforming cans for one month (based on a 5-day workweek).

a. Construct a *p* chart for the proportion of unacceptable cans for the month. Does the process give an out-of-control signal?

b. If you want to develop a process for reducing the proportion of unacceptable cans, how should you proceed?

14.7 The manager of the accounting office of a large hospital is studying the problem of entering incorrect account numbers into the computer system. A subgroup of 200 account numbers is selected from each day's output, and each account number is inspected to determine whether it is a nonconforming item. The results for a period of 39 days are in the file Errorspc.

a. Construct a *p* chart for the proportion of nonconforming items. Does the process give an out-of-control signal?

b. Based on your answer to (a), if you were the manager of the accounting office, what would you do to improve the process of account number entry?

14.8 A regional manager of a telephone company is responsible for processing requests concerning additions, changes, or deletions of telephone service. She forms a service improvement team to look at the corrections in terms of central office equipment and facilities required to process the orders that are issued to service requests. Data collected over a period of 30 days are in the file Telespc.

a. Construct a *p* chart for the proportion of corrections. Does the process give an out-of-control signal?

b. What should the regional manager do to improve the processing of requests for changes in telephone service?

14.3 The Red Bead Experiment: Understanding Process Variability

This chapter began with a discussion of common cause variation and special cause variation. Now that you have studied the *p* chart, this section presents a famous parable, the **red bead experiment**, to enhance your understanding of common cause and special cause variation. The red bead experiment involves the selection of beads from a bowl that contains 4,000 beads.[4] Unknown to the participants in the experiment, 3,200 (80%) of the beads are white and 800 (20%) are red. You can use several different scenarios for conducting the experiment. The one used here begins with a facilitator (who will play the role of company supervisor) asking members of the audience to volunteer for the jobs of workers (at least four are needed), inspectors (two are needed), chief inspector (one is needed), and recorder (one is needed). A worker's job consists of using a paddle that has five rows of 10 bead-size holes to select 50 beads from the bowl of beads.

When the participants have been selected, the supervisor explains the jobs to them. The job of the workers is to produce white beads because red beads are unacceptable to the customers. Strict procedures are to be followed. Work standards call for the daily production of exactly 50 beads by each worker (a strict quota system). Management has established a standard that no more than 2 red beads (4%) per worker are to be produced on any given day.

Each worker dips the paddle into the box of beads so that when it is removed, each of the 50 holes contains a bead. The worker carries the paddle to the two inspectors, who independently record the count of red beads. The chief inspector compares their counts and announces the results to the audience. The recorder writes down the number and percentage of red beads next to the name of the worker.

[4]For information on how to purchase such a bowl, contact Lightning Calculator at **www.qualityting.com** or call 248-641-7030.

When all the people know their jobs, "production" can begin. Suppose that on the first "day," the number of red beads "produced" by the four workers (call them Alyson, David, Peter, and Sharyn) was 9, 12, 13, and 7, respectively. How should management react to the day's production when the standard says that no more than 2 red beads per worker should be produced? Should all the workers be reprimanded, or should only David and Peter be warned that they will be fired if they don't improve?

Suppose that production continues for an additional two days. Table 14.3 summarizes the results for all three days.

TABLE 14.3

Red Bead Experiment Results for Four Workers over Three Days

NAME	DAY 1	DAY 2	DAY 3	All Three Days
Alyson	9 (18%)	11 (22%)	6 (12%)	26 (17.33%)
David	12 (24%)	12 (24%)	8 (16%)	32 (21.33%)
Peter	13 (26%)	6 (12%)	12 (24%)	31 (20.67%)
Sharyn	7 (14%)	9 (18%)	8 (16%)	24 (16.0%)
All four workers	41	38	34	113
Mean	10.25	9.5	8.5	9.42
Percentage	20.5%	19%	17%	18.83%

From Table 14.3, on each day, some of the workers were above the mean and some below the mean. On day 1, Sharyn did best, but on day 2, Peter (who had the worst record on day 1) was best, and on day 3, Alyson was best. How can you explain all this variation? Using Equation (14.2) on page 495 to develop a p chart for these data,

$$k = 4 \text{ workers} \times 3 \text{ days} = 12, n = 50, \sum_{i=1}^{k} X_i = 113, \text{ and } \sum_{i=1}^{k} n_i = 600$$

Thus,

$$\bar{p} = \frac{113}{600} = 0.1883$$

so that

$$\bar{p} \pm 3\sqrt{\frac{\bar{p}(1 - \bar{p})}{n}}$$

$$= 0.1883 \pm 3\sqrt{\frac{0.1883(1 - 0.1883)}{50}}$$

$$= 0.1883 \pm 0.1659$$

Thus,

$$\text{UCL} = 0.1883 + 0.1659 = 0.3542$$

$$\text{LCL} = 0.1883 - 0.1659 = 0.0224$$

Figure 14.6 represents the p chart for the data of Table 14.3. In Figure 14.6, all the points are within the control limits, and there are no patterns in the results. The differences between the workers merely represent common cause variation inherent in an in-control process.

Four morals to the parable of the red beads are

- Variation is an inherent part of any process.
- Workers work within a process over which they have little control. It is the process that primarily determines their performance.
- Only management can change the process.
- There will always be some workers above the mean and some workers below the mean.

FIGURE 14.6

p Chart for the Red Bead
Experiment

See Sections E14.1 and
E14.2, or Sections P14.1
or M14.1, to create an
equivalent chart.

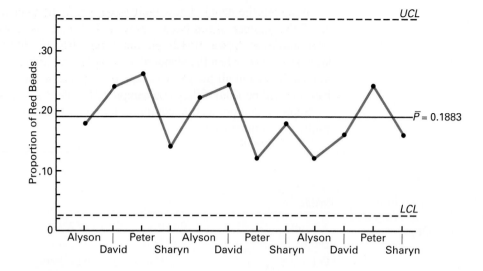

Problems for Section 14.3

APPLYING THE CONCEPTS

14.9 In the red bead experiment, how do you think many managers would have reacted after day 1? day 2? day 3?

14.10 (Class Project) Obtain a version of the red bead experiment for your class.

a. Conduct the experiment in the same way as described in this section.

b. Remove 400 red beads from the bead bowl before beginning the experiment. How do your results differ from those in (a)? What does this tell you about the effect of the process on the workers?

14.4 Control Charts for the Range and the Mean

You use **variables control charts** to monitor and analyze a process when you have numerically measured data. Common numerical variables include time, money, and weight. Because numerical variables provide more information than categorical data, such as the proportion of nonconforming items, variables control charts are more sensitive in detecting special cause variation than the p chart. Variables charts are typically used in pairs. One chart monitors the variability in a process, and the other monitors the process mean. You must examine the chart that monitors variability first because if it indicates the presence of out-of-control conditions, the interpretation of the chart for the mean will be misleading. Although businesses currently use several alternative pairs of charts (see references 9, 13, and 18), this book considers only the control charts for the range and the mean.

The R Chart

You can use several different types of control charts to monitor the variability in a numerically measured characteristic of interest. The simplest and most common is the control chart for the range, the **R chart**. You use the range chart only when the sample size or subgroup is 10 or less. If the sample size is greater than 10, a standard deviation chart is preferable (see references 9, 13, and 18). Because sample sizes of five or less are typically used in many applications, the standard deviation chart is not illustrated in this book. The R chart enables you to determine whether the variability in a process is in control or whether changes in the amount of variability are occurring over time. If the process range is in control, then the amount of variation in the process is consistent over time, and you can use the results of the R chart to develop the control limits for the mean.

To develop control limits for the range, you need an estimate of the mean range and the standard deviation of the range. As shown in Equation (14.3), these control limits depend on two constants, the **d_2 factor**, which represents the relationship between the standard deviation and the range for varying sample sizes, and the **d_3 factor**, which represents the relationship between the standard deviation and the standard error of the range for varying sample sizes. Table E.9 contains values for these factors. Equation (14.3) defines the control limits for the R chart.

CONTROL LIMITS FOR THE RANGE

$$\bar{R} \pm 3\bar{R}\frac{d_3}{d_2}$$

$$\text{UCL} = \bar{R} + 3\bar{R}\frac{d_3}{d_2}$$

$$\text{LCL} = \bar{R} - 3\bar{R}\frac{d_3}{d_2} \tag{14.3}$$

where

$$\bar{R} = \frac{\sum\limits_{i=1}^{k} R_i}{k}$$

You can simplify the calculations in Equation (14.3) by using the **D_3 factor**, equal to $1 - 3(d_3/d_2)$, and the **D_4 factor**, equal to $1 + 3(d_3/d_2)$, to express the control limits (see Table E.9), as shown in Equations (14.4a) and (14.4b).

CALCULATING CONTROL LIMITS FOR THE RANGE

$$\text{UCL} = D_4\bar{R} \tag{14.4a}$$

$$\text{LCL} = D_3\bar{R} \tag{14.4b}$$

To illustrate the R chart, return to the Using Statistics scenario concerning hotel service quality on page 491. As part of the *Measure* phase of a Six Sigma project (see Section 14.6), the amount of time to deliver luggage was operationally defined as the time from when the guest completes check-in procedures to the time the luggage arrives in the guest's room. During the *Analyze* phase of the Six Sigma project, data were recorded over a four-week period (see the file Hotel2). Subgroups of five deliveries were selected from the evening shift on each day. Table 14.4 on page 504 summarizes the results for all 28 days.

For the data in Table 14.4,

$$k = 28, \ \sum\limits_{i=1}^{k} R_i = 97.5, \ \bar{R} = \frac{\sum\limits_{i=1}^{k} R_i}{k} = \frac{97.5}{28} = 3.482$$

For $n = 5$, from Table E.9, $D_3 = 0$ and $D_4 = 2.114$. Then, using Equation (14.4),

$$\text{UCL} = D_4\bar{R} = (2.114)(3.482) = 7.36$$

and the LCL does not exist.

Figure 14.7 displays the Microsoft Excel R chart for the luggage delivery times. Figure 14.7 does not indicate any individual ranges outside the control limits or any obvious patterns.

TABLE 14.4

Luggage Delivery Times and Subgroup Mean and Range for 28 Days

Day	Luggage Delivery Times (in minutes)					Mean	Range
1	6.7	11.7	9.7	7.5	7.8	8.68	5.0
2	7.6	11.4	9.0	8.4	9.2	9.12	3.8
3	9.5	8.9	9.9	8.7	10.7	9.54	2.0
4	9.8	13.2	6.9	9.3	9.4	9.72	6.3
5	11.0	9.9	11.3	11.6	8.5	10.46	3.1
6	8.3	8.4	9.7	9.8	7.1	8.66	2.7
7	9.4	9.3	8.2	7.1	6.1	8.02	3.3
8	11.2	9.8	10.5	9.0	9.7	10.04	2.2
9	10.0	10.7	9.0	8.2	11.0	9.78	2.8
10	8.6	5.8	8.7	9.5	11.4	8.80	5.6
11	10.7	8.6	9.1	10.9	8.6	9.58	2.3
12	10.8	8.3	10.6	10.3	10.0	10.00	2.5
13	9.5	10.5	7.0	8.6	10.1	9.14	3.5
14	12.9	8.9	8.1	9.0	7.6	9.30	5.3
15	7.8	9.0	12.2	9.1	11.7	9.96	4.4
16	11.1	9.9	8.8	5.5	9.5	8.96	5.6
17	9.2	9.7	12.3	8.1	8.5	9.56	4.2
18	9.0	8.1	10.2	9.7	8.4	9.08	2.1
19	9.9	10.1	8.9	9.6	7.1	9.12	3.0
20	10.7	9.8	10.2	8.0	10.2	9.78	2.7
21	9.0	10.0	9.6	10.6	9.0	9.64	1.6
22	10.7	9.8	9.4	7.0	8.9	9.16	3.7
23	10.2	10.5	9.5	12.2	9.1	10.30	3.1
24	10.0	11.1	9.5	8.8	9.9	9.86	2.3
25	9.6	8.8	11.4	12.2	9.3	10.26	3.4
26	8.2	7.9	8.4	9.5	9.2	8.64	1.6
27	7.1	11.1	10.8	11.0	10.2	10.04	4.0
28	11.1	6.6	12.0	11.5	9.7	10.18	5.4
					Sums:	265.38	97.5

FIGURE 14.7

Microsoft Excel *R* chart for the luggage delivery times

See Sections E14.3 and E14.4 or Section P14.2 to create this. (Minitab users, see Section M14.2 to create an equivalent chart.)

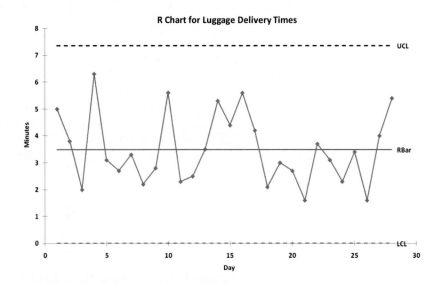

The $\overline{X}$ Chart

Now that you have determined from the control chart that the range is in control, you continue by examining the control chart for the process mean, the $\overline{X}$ **chart**.

The control chart for $\overline{X}$ uses k subgroups collected in k consecutive periods of time. Each subgroup contains n items. You calculate an $\overline{X}$ for each subgroup and plot these $\overline{X}$ values on the control chart. To compute control limits for the mean, you need to compute the mean of the subgroup means (called X double bar, and denoted $\bar{\bar{X}}$) and the estimate of the standard error of the mean (denoted $\bar{R}/(d_2 \sqrt{n})$). The estimate of the standard error of the mean is a function of the d_2 factor, which represents the relationship between the standard deviation and the range for varying sample sizes.[5] Equations (14.5) and (14.6) define the control limits for the $\bar{X}$ chart.

[5]R/d_2 is used to estimate the standard deviation of the individual items in the population, and $\bar{R}/d_2 \sqrt{n}$ is used to estimate the standard error of the mean.

CONTROL LIMITS FOR THE $\bar{X}$ CHART

$$\bar{\bar{X}} \pm 3 \frac{\bar{R}}{d_2 \sqrt{n}}$$

$$UCL = \bar{\bar{X}} + 3 \frac{\bar{R}}{d_2 \sqrt{n}} \tag{14.5}$$

$$LCL = \bar{\bar{X}} - 3 \frac{\bar{R}}{d_2 \sqrt{n}}$$

where

$$\bar{\bar{X}} = \frac{\sum_{i=1}^{k} \bar{X}_i}{k}, \quad \bar{R} = \frac{\sum_{i=1}^{k} R_i}{k}$$

$\bar{X}_i$ = sample mean of n observations at time i

R_i = range of n observations at time i

k = number of subgroups

You can simplify the calculations in Equation (14.5) by utilizing the **A_2 factor** given in Table E.9, equal to $3/d_2 \sqrt{n}$. Equations (14.6a) and (14.6b) show the simplified control limits.

CALCULATING CONTROL LIMITS FOR THE MEAN, USING THE A_2 FACTOR

$$UCL = \bar{\bar{X}} + A_2 \bar{R} \tag{14.6a}$$

$$LCL = \bar{\bar{X}} - A_2 \bar{R} \tag{14.6b}$$

From Table 14.4 on page 504,

$$k = 28, \quad \sum_{i=1}^{k} \bar{X}_i = 265.38, \quad \sum_{i=1}^{k} R_i = 97.5$$

so that

$$\bar{\bar{X}} = \frac{\sum_{i=1}^{k} \bar{X}_i}{k} = \frac{265.38}{28} = 9.478$$

$$\bar{R} = \frac{\sum_{i=1}^{k} R_i}{k} = \frac{97.5}{28} = 3.482$$

Using Equations (14.6a) and (14.6b), since $n = 5$, from Table E.9, $A_2 = 0.577$, so that

$$UCL = 9.478 + (0.577)(3.482) = 9.478 + 2.009 = 11.487$$

$$LCL = 9.478 - (0.577)(3.482) = 9.478 - 2.009 = 7.469$$

Figure 14.8 displays the Microsoft Excel $\bar{X}$ chart for the luggage delivery time data. Figure 14.9 presents Minitab R and $\bar{X}$ charts.

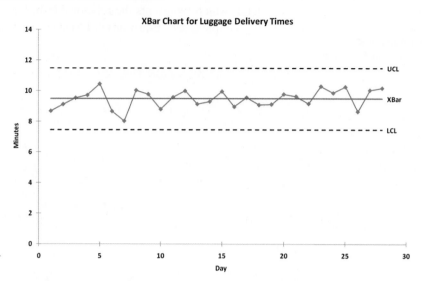

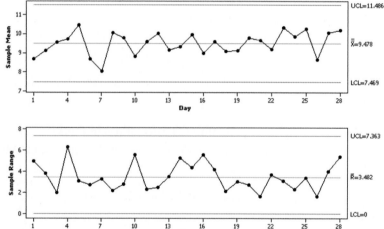

Figures 14.8 or 14.9 do not reveal any points outside the control limits, and there are no obvious patterns in either chart. Although there is a considerable amount of variability among the 28 subgroup means, because both the R chart and the $\bar{X}$ chart are in control, the luggage delivery process is in a state of statistical control. If you want to reduce the variation or lower the mean delivery time, you need to change the process.

Problems for Section 14.4

LEARNING THE BASICS

14.11 For subgroups of $n = 3$, what is the value of
a. the d_2 factor?
b. the d_3 factor?
c. the D_3 factor?
d. the D_4 factor?
e. the A_2 factor?

14.12 For subgroups of $n = 4$, what is the value of
a. the d_2 factor?
b. the d_3 factor?
c. the D_3 factor?
d. the D_4 factor?
e. the A_2 factor?

14.13 The following summary of data is for subgroups of $n = 3$ for a 10-day period:

Day	Mean	Range	Day	Mean	Range
1	48.03	0.29	6	48.07	0.22
2	48.08	0.43	7	47.99	0.16
3	47.90	0.16	8	48.04	0.15
4	48.03	0.13	9	47.99	0.46
5	47.81	0.32	10	48.04	0.15

a. Compute control limits for the range.
b. Is there evidence of special cause variation in (a)?
c. Compute control limits for the mean.
d. Is there evidence of special cause variation in (c)?

APPLYING THE CONCEPTS

✓ **SELF** **Test** **14.14** The manager of a branch of a local bank wants to study waiting times of customers for teller service during the 12:00 noon-to-1:00 P.M. lunch hour. A subgroup of four customers is selected (one at each 15-minute interval during the hour), and the time, in minutes, is measured from the point each customer enters the line to when he or she reaches the teller window. The results over a four-week period are in the data file **Banktime** and are as follows:

Day	Time in Minutes			
1	7.2	8.4	7.9	4.9
2	5.6	8.7	3.3	4.2
3	5.5	7.3	3.2	6.0
4	4.4	8.0	5.4	7.4
5	9.7	4.6	4.8	5.8
6	8.3	8.9	9.1	6.2
7	4.7	6.6	5.3	5.8
8	8.8	5.5	8.4	6.9
9	5.7	4.7	4.1	4.6
10	3.7	4.0	3.0	5.2
11	2.6	3.9	5.2	4.8
12	4.6	2.7	6.3	3.4
13	4.9	6.2	7.8	8.7
14	7.1	6.3	8.2	5.5
15	7.1	5.8	6.9	7.0
16	6.7	6.9	7.0	9.4
17	5.5	6.3	3.2	4.9
18	4.9	5.1	3.2	7.6
19	7.2	8.0	4.1	5.9
20	6.1	3.4	7.2	5.9

a. Construct control charts for the range and the mean.
b. Is the process in control?

14.15 The manager of a warehouse for a telephone company is involved in a process that receives expensive circuit boards and returns them to central stock so that they can be reused at a later date. Speedy processing of these circuit boards is critical in providing good service to customers and reducing capital expenditures. The data in the file **Warehse** represent the number of circuit boards processed per day by a subgroup of five employees over a 30-day period.
a. Construct control charts for the range and the mean.
b. Is the process in control?

14.16 An article in the *Mid-American Journal of Business* presents an analysis for a spring water bottling operation. One of the characteristics of interest is the amount of magnesium, measured in parts per million (ppm), in the water. The data in the following table (stored in the file **SPwater**)

represent the magnesium levels from 30 subgroups of four bottles collected over a 30-hour period:

Hour	1	2	3	4
1	19.91	19.62	19.15	19.85
2	20.46	20.44	20.34	19.61
3	20.25	19.73	19.98	20.32
4	20.39	19.43	20.36	19.85
5	20.02	20.02	20.13	20.34
6	19.89	19.77	20.92	20.09
7	19.89	20.45	19.44	19.95
8	20.08	20.13	20.11	19.32
9	20.30	20.42	20.68	19.60
10	20.19	20.00	20.23	20.59
11	19.66	21.24	20.35	20.34
12	20.30	20.11	19.64	20.29
13	19.83	19.75	20.62	20.60
14	20.27	20.88	20.62	20.40
15	19.98	19.02	20.34	20.34
16	20.46	19.97	20.32	20.83
17	19.74	21.02	19.62	19.90
18	19.85	19.26	19.88	20.20
19	20.77	20.58	19.73	19.48
20	20.21	20.82	20.01	19.93
21	20.30	20.09	20.03	20.13
22	20.48	21.06	20.13	20.42
23	20.60	19.74	20.52	19.42
24	20.20	20.08	20.32	19.51
25	19.66	19.67	20.26	20.41
26	20.72	20.58	20.71	19.99
27	19.77	19.40	20.49	19.83
28	19.99	19.65	19.41	19.58
29	19.44	20.15	20.14	20.76
30	20.03	19.96	19.86	19.91

Source: *Data extracted from Susan K. Humphrey and Timothy C. Krehbiel, "Managing Process Capability,"* The Mid-American Journal of Business, *14, Fall 1999, pp. 7–12.*

a. Construct a control chart for the range.
b. Construct a control chart for the mean.
c. Is the process in control?

14.17 The data in the file **Tensile** are the tensile strengths of bolts of cloth. The data were collected in subgroups of three bolts of cloth over a 25-hour period:
a. Construct a control chart for the range.
b. Construct a control chart for the mean.
c. Is the process in control?

14.18 The director of radiology at a large metropolitan hospital is concerned about scheduling in the radiology facilities. On a typical day, 250 patients are transported to the radiology department for treatment or diagnostic procedures. If patients do not reach the radiology unit at their scheduled times, backups occur, and other patients experience delays. The time it takes to transport patients to the

radiology unit is operationally defined as the time between when the transporter is assigned to the patient and when the patient arrives at the radiology unit. A sample of $n = 4$ patients was selected each day for 20 days, and the time to transport each patient (in minutes) was determined, with the results in the data file Transport .
a. Construct control charts for the range and the mean.
b. Is the process in control?

14.19 A filling machine for a tea bag manufacturer produces approximately 170 tea bags per minute. The process manager monitors the weight of the tea placed in individual bags. A subgroup of $n = 4$ tea bags is taken every 15 minutes for 25 consecutive time periods. The results are stored in the file Tea3 :

a. What are some of the sources of common cause variation that might be present in this process?
b. What problems might occur that would result in special causes of variation?
c. Construct control charts for the range and the mean.
d. Is the process in control?

14.20 A manufacturing company makes brackets for bookshelves. The brackets provide critical structural support and must have a 90-degree bend ±1 degree. Measurements of the bend of the brackets were taken at 18 different times. Five brackets were sampled at each time. The data are in the file Angle .
a. Construct control charts for the range and the mean.
b. Is the process in control?

14.5 Total Quality Management

An increased interest in improving the quality of products and services in the United States occurred as a reaction to improvements of Japanese industry that began as early as 1950. Individuals such as W. Edwards Deming, Joseph Juran, and Kaoru Ishikawa developed an approach that focuses on continuous improvement of products and services through an increased emphasis on statistics, process improvement, and optimization of the total system. This approach, widely known as **total quality management (TQM)**, is characterized by these themes:

- The primary focus is on process improvement.
- Most of the variation in a process is due to the system and not the individual.
- Teamwork is an integral part of a quality management organization.
- Customer satisfaction is a primary organizational goal.
- Organizational transformation must occur in order to implement quality management.
- Fear must be removed from organizations.
- Higher quality costs less, not more, but requires an investment in training.

In the 1980s, the federal government of the United States increased its efforts to encourage the improvement of quality in American business. Congress passed the Malcolm Baldrige National Improvement Act of 1987 and began awarding the Malcolm Baldrige Award to companies making the greatest strides in improving quality and customer satisfaction. Deming became a prominent consultant to many Fortune 500 companies, including Ford, General Motors, and Procter & Gamble. Many companies adopted some or all the basic themes of TQM.

Today, many quality improvement systems are in place in organizations worldwide. Although most organizations no longer use the name TQM, the underlying philosophy and statistical methods used in today's quality improvement systems are consistent with TQM and the work of Deming. This holistic approach to quality is captured in **Deming's 14 points for management** listed here:

1. Create constancy of purpose for improvement of product and service.
2. Adopt the new philosophy.
3. Cease dependence on inspection to achieve quality.
4. End the practice of awarding business on the basis of price tag alone. Instead, minimize total cost by working with a single supplier.
5. Improve constantly and forever every process for planning, production, and service.
6. Institute training on the job.
7. Adopt and institute leadership.
8. Drive out fear.

9. Break down barriers between staff areas.
10. Eliminate slogans, exhortations, and targets for the workforce.
11. Eliminate numerical quotas for the workforce and numerical goals for management.
12. Remove barriers that rob people of pride of workmanship. Eliminate the annual rating or merit system.
13. Institute a vigorous program of education and self-improvement for everyone.
14. Put everyone in the company to work to accomplish the transformation.

Points 1, 2, 5, 7, and 14 focus on the need for organizational transformation and the responsibility of top management to assert leadership in committing to the transformation. Without this commitment, any improvements obtained will be limited.

One aspect of the improvement process is illustrated by the **Shewhart-Deming cycle**, shown in Figure 14.10. The Shewhart-Deming cycle represents a continuous cycle of "plan, do, study, and act." The first step, planning, represents the initial design phase for planning a change in a manufacturing or service process. This step involves teamwork among individuals from different areas within an organization. The second step, doing, involves implementing the change, preferably on a small scale. The third step, studying, involves analyzing the results, using statistical methods to determine what was learned. The fourth step, acting, involves the acceptance of the change, its abandonment, or further study of the change under different conditions.

FIGURE 14.10
Shewhart-Deming cycle

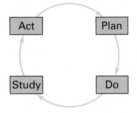

Point 3, cease dependence on inspection to achieve quality, implies that any inspection whose purpose is to improve quality is too late because the quality is already built into the product. It is better to focus on making it right the first time. Among the difficulties involved in inspection (besides high costs) are the failure of inspectors to agree on the operational definitions for nonconforming items and the problem of separating good and bad items. The following example illustrates the difficulties inspectors face.

Suppose your job involves proofreading the sentence in Figure 14.11, with the objective of counting the number of occurrences of the letter F. Perform this task and record the number of occurrences of the letter F that you discover.

FIGURE 14.11

An example of a proofreading process

Source: *Adapted from W. W. Scherkenbach,* The Deming Route to Quality and Productivity: Road Maps and Roadblocks *(Washington, DC: CEEP Press, 1986).*

FINISHED FILES ARE THE RESULT OF YEARS OF SCIENTIFIC STUDY COMBINED WITH THE EXPERIENCE OF MANY YEARS

People usually see either three F's or six F's. The correct number is six F's. The number you see depends on the method you use to examine the sentence. You are likely to find three F's if you read the sentence phonetically and six F's if you count the number of F's carefully. The point of the exercise is to show that, if such a simple process as counting F's leads to inconsistency of inspectors' results, what will happen when a much more complicated process fails to provide clear operational definitions?

Point 4, end the practice of awarding business on the basis of price tag alone, focuses on the idea that there is no real long-term meaning to price without knowledge of the quality of the product. In addition, minimizing the number of entities in the supply chain will reduce the variation involved.

Points 6 and 13 refer to training and reflect the needs of all employees. Continuous learning is critical for quality improvement within an organization. In particular, management needs to understand the differences between special causes and common causes of variation so that proper action is taken in each circumstance.

Points 8 through 12 relate to the evaluation of employee performance. Deming believed that an emphasis on targets and exhortations places an improper burden on the workforce. Workers cannot produce beyond what the system allows (as illustrated in the red bead experiment in Section 14.3). It is management's job to *improve* the system, not to raise the expectations on workers beyond the system's capability.

Although Deming's points are thought provoking, some have criticized his approach for lacking a formal, objective accountability (see reference 12). Many managers of large organizations, used to seeing financial analyses of policy changes, need a more prescriptive approach.

14.6 Six Sigma

Six Sigma is a quality improvement system originally developed by Motorola in the mid-1980s. After seeing the huge financial successes at Motorola, GE, and other early adopters of Six Sigma, many companies worldwide have now instituted Six Sigma to improve efficiency, cut costs, eliminate defects, and reduce product variation (see references 1, 4, 11, and 17). Six Sigma offers a more prescriptive and systematic approach to process improvement than TQM. It is also distinguished from other quality improvement systems by its clear focus on achieving bottom-line results in a relatively short three- to six-month period of time.

The name Six Sigma comes from the fact that it is a managerial approach designed to create processes that result in no more than 3.4 defects per million. The Six Sigma approach assumes that processes are designed so that the upper and lower specification limits are six standard deviations away from the mean. Then, if the processes are monitored correctly with control charts, the worst possible scenario is for the mean to shift to within 4.5 standard deviations from the nearest specification limit. The area under the normal curve less than 4.5 standard deviations below the mean is approximately 3.4 out of a million. (Table E.2 reports this probability as 0.000003398.)

The DMAIC Model

To guide managers in their task of improving short- and long-term results, Six Sigma uses a five-step process known as the **DMAIC model**—named for the five steps in the process:

- *Define* The problem is defined, along with the costs, the benefits, and the impact on the customer.
- *Measure* Important characteristics relating to the quality of the service or product are identified and discussed. Variables measuring these characteristics are defined and called **critical-to-quality (CTQ)** variables. Operational definitions for all the CTQ variables are then developed. In addition, the measurement procedure is verified so that it is consistent over repeated measurements.
- *Analyze* The root causes of *why* defects occur are determined, and variables in the process causing the defects are identified. Data are collected to determine benchmark values for each process variable. This analysis often uses control charts (discussed in Sections 14.2–14.4).
- *Improve* The importance of each process variable on the CTQ variable is studied using designed experiments (see references 9, 10, and 13). The objective is to determine the best level for each variable.
- *Control* The objective is to maintain the benefits for the long term by avoiding potential problems that can occur when a process is changed.

The Define phase of a Six Sigma project consists of the development of a project charter, performing a SIPOC analysis, and identifying the customers for the output of the process. The development of a project charter involves forming a table of business objectives and indicators for all potential Six Sigma projects. Importance ratings are assigned by top management, projects are prioritized, and the most important project is selected. A **SIPOC analysis** is used to identify the **S**uppliers to the process, list the **I**nputs provided by the suppliers, flowchart the **P**rocess, list the process **O**utputs, and identify the **C**ustomers of the process. This is followed by a Voice of the Customer analysis that involves market segmentation in which different types of users of the process are identified and the circumstances of their use of the process are identified. Statistical methods used in the *Define* phase include tables and charts, descriptive statistics, and control charts.

In the *Measure* phase of a Six Sigma project, members of a team identify the CTQ variables that measure important quality characteristics. Next, operational definitions (see Section 1.3) of each CTQ variable are developed so that everyone will have a firm understanding of the CTQ. Then studies are undertaken to ensure that there is a valid measurement system for the CTQ that is consistent across measurements. Finally, baseline data are collected to determine the capability and stability of the current process. Statistical methods used in the *Measure* phase include tables and charts, descriptive statistics, the normal distribution, the Analysis of Variance, and control charts.

The *Analyze* phase of a Six Sigma project focuses on the factors that affect the central tendency, variation, and shape of each CTQ variable. Factors are identified, and the relationships between the factors and the CTQs are analyzed. Statistical methods used in the *Analyze* phase include tables and charts, descriptive statistics, the Analysis of Variance, regression analysis, and control charts.

In the *Improve* phase of a Six Sigma project, team members carry out designed experiments to actively intervene in a process. The objective of the experiments is to determine the settings of the factors that will optimize the central tendency, variation, and shape of each CTQ variable. Statistical methods used in the *Improve* phase include tables and charts, descriptive statistics, regression analysis, hypothesis testing, the Analysis of Variance, and designed experiments.

The *Control* phase of a Six Sigma project focuses on the maintenance of improvements that have been made in the Improve phase. A risk abatement plan is developed to identify elements that can cause damage to a process. Statistical methods used in the *Control* phase include tables and charts, descriptive statistics, and control charts.

Roles in a Six Sigma Organization

Six Sigma requires that the employees of an organization have well-defined roles. The roles of senior executive (C.E.O. or president), executive committee, champion, process owner, master black belt, black belt, and green belt are critical to Six Sigma. More importantly, everyone must be properly trained in order to successfully fulfill their roles' tasks and responsibilities.

The role of the **senior executive** is critical for Six Sigma's ultimate success. The most successful, highly publicized Six Sigma efforts have all had unwavering, clear, and committed leadership from top management. Although Six Sigma concepts and processes can be initiated at lower levels, high-level success cannot be achieved without the leadership of the senior executive.

The members of the **executive committee** consist of the top management of an organization. They need to operate at the same level of commitment to Six Sigma as the senior executive.

Champions take a strong sponsorship and leadership role in conducting and implementing Six Sigma projects. They work closely with the executive committee, the black belt assigned to their project, and the master black belt overseeing their project. A champion should be a member of the executive committee, or at least someone who reports directly to a member of the executive committee. He or she should have enough influence to remove obstacles or provide resources without having to go higher in the organization.

A **process owner** is the manager of a process. He or she has responsibility for the process and has the authority to change the process on her or his signature. The process owner should be identified and involved immediately in all Six Sigma projects relating to his or her own area.

A **master black belt** takes on a leadership role in the implementation of the Six Sigma process and as an advisor to senior executives. The master black belt must use his or her skills while working on projects that are led by black belts and green belts. A master black belt has successfully led many teams through complex Six Sigma projects. He or she is a proven change agent, leader, facilitator, and technical expert in Six Sigma.

A **black belt** works full-time on Six Sigma projects. A black belt is mentored by a master black belt, but may report to a manager for his or her tour of duty as a black belt. Ideally, a black belt works well in a team format, can manage meetings, is familiar with statistics and systems theory, and has a focus on the customer.

A **green belt** is an individual who works on Six Sigma projects part-time (approximately 25%), either as a team member for complex projects or as a project leader for simpler projects. Most managers in a mature Six Sigma organization are green belts. Green belt certification is a critical prerequisite for advancement into upper management in a Six Sigma organization.

Recent research (see reference 4) indicates that more than 80% of the top 100 publicly traded companies in the United States use Six Sigma. So, you do need to be aware of the distinction between master black belt, black belt, and green belt if you are to function effectively in a Six Sigma organization.

In a Six Sigma organization, 25% to 50% of the organization will be green belts, only 6% to 12% of the organization need to be black belts, and only 1% of the organization need to be master black belts (reference 9). Individual companies, professional organizations such as the American Society for Quality, and universities such as the University of Miami offer certification programs for green belt, black belt, and master black belt. For more information on certification and other aspects of Six Sigma, see references 9, 10, and 13.

USING STATISTICS   @ Beachcomber Hotel Revisited

In the Using Statistics scenario, you were the manager of the Beachcomber Hotel. After being trained in Six Sigma, you decided to focus on two critical first impressions: Is the room ready when a guest checks in? And, do guests receive their luggage in a reasonable amount of time?

You constructed a p chart on the proportion of rooms not ready at check in. The p chart indicated that the check-in process was in control and that, on average, the proportion of rooms not ready was approximately 0.08 (i.e., 8%). You then constructed $\overline{X}$ and R charts for the amount of time required to deliver luggage. Although there was a considerable amount of variability around the overall average of approximately 9.5 minutes, you determined that the luggage delivery process was also in control.

You have learned that an in control process contains common causes but no special causes. Improvements in the outcomes of in control processes must come from changes in the actual processes. Thus, if you want to reduce the proportion of rooms not ready at check in, and/or lower the mean luggage delivery time, then you will need to change the check-in process and/or the luggage delivery process. From your knowledge of Six Sigma and statistics, you know that during the *Improve* phase of the DMAIC model, you will be able to perform and analyze experiments using different process designs. Hopefully you will discover better process designs which will lead to a higher percentage of rooms being ready on time and/or quicker luggage delivery times. These improvements should ultimately lead to greater guest satisfaction.

SUMMARY

In this chapter you have learned how to use control charts to distinguish between common causes and special causes of variation. For categorical data, you learned how to construct and analyze p charts. For numerically measured variables, you learned how to construct and analyze $\overline{X}$ and R charts. The chapter also discussed managerial approaches used to improve the quality of products and services, including TQM and Six Sigma.

KEY EQUATIONS

Constructing Control Limits

Process mean ± 3 standard deviations

Upper control limit (UCL) = process mean
$\qquad\qquad$ +3 standard deviations

Lower control limit (LCL) = process mean
$\qquad\qquad$ −3 standard deviations $\quad$ **(14.1)**

Control Limits for the p Chart

$$\bar{p} \pm 3\sqrt{\frac{\bar{p}(1-\bar{p})}{\bar{n}}}$$

$$UCL = \bar{p} + 3\sqrt{\frac{\bar{p}(1-\bar{p})}{\bar{n}}}$$

$$LCL = \bar{p} - 3\sqrt{\frac{\bar{p}(1-\bar{p})}{\bar{n}}} \qquad \textbf{(14.2)}$$

Control Limits for the Range

$$\bar{R} \pm 3\bar{R}\frac{d_3}{d_2}$$

$$UCL = \bar{R} + 3\bar{R}\frac{d_3}{d_2}$$

$$LCL = \bar{R} - 3\bar{R}\frac{d_3}{d_2} \qquad \textbf{(14.3)}$$

Calculating Control Limits for the Range

$$UCL = D_4\bar{R} \qquad \textbf{(14.4a)}$$

$$LCL = D_3\bar{R} \qquad \textbf{(14.4b)}$$

Control Limits for the $\bar{X}$ Chart

$$\bar{\bar{X}} \pm 3\frac{\bar{R}}{d_2\sqrt{n}}$$

$$UCL = \bar{\bar{X}} + 3\frac{\bar{R}}{d_2\sqrt{n}} \qquad \textbf{(14.5)}$$

$$LCL = \bar{\bar{X}} - 3\frac{\bar{R}}{d_2\sqrt{n}}$$

Calculating Control Limits for the Mean, Using the A_2 Factor

$$UCL = \bar{\bar{X}} + A_2\bar{R} \qquad \textbf{(14.6a)}$$

$$LCL = \bar{\bar{X}} - A_2\bar{R} \qquad \textbf{(14.6b)}$$

KEY TERMS

CHAPTER REVIEW PROBLEMS

CHECKING YOUR UNDERSTANDING

14.21 What is the difference between common cause variation and special cause variation?

14.22 What should you do to improve a process when special causes of variation are present?

14.23 What should you do to improve a process when only common causes of variation are present?

14.24 What is the difference between attribute control charts and variables control charts?

14.25 Why are $\overline{X}$ and R charts used together?

14.26 What principles did you learn from the red bead experiment?

APPLYING THE CONCEPTS

14.27 A survey sponsored by the American Society for Quality found that master black belts make around $23,000 more a year, on average, than black belts. A partial listing of the survey results concerning annual salaries is given below.

Title	Sample Size	Mean	Standard Deviation
Black belt	194	85,465	18,894
Master black belt	131	108,879	21,946

Source: *Data extracted from H. Lindborg, "Navigate Your Career Path with QP's Annual Salary Survey,"* Quality Progress, *December 2007, pp. 21–50.*

a. Discuss the role of a black belt in a Six Sigma organization.
b. Discuss the role of a master black belt in a Six Sigma organization.
c. Assuming that the population variances are equal, construct and interpret a 95% confidence interval estimate of the difference between the population mean salary of master black belts and black belts. (*Hint:* Use Equation 10.2 on page 319.)

14.28 According to the American Society for Quality, customers in the United States consistently rate service quality lower than product quality (American Society for Quality, *The Quarterly Quality Report*, **www.asq.org**, May 16, 2006). For example, products in the beverage, personal care and cleaning industries, and major appliance sectors all received very high customer satisfaction ratings. At the other extreme, services provided by airlines, banks, and insurance companies all received low customer satisfaction ratings.

a. Why do you think service quality consistently rates lower than product quality?
b. What are the similarities and differences between measuring service quality and product quality?

c. Do Deming's 14 points apply to both products and services?
d. Can Six Sigma be used for both products and services?

14.29 Six Flags Amusement Parks lost $133 million on revenue of $1.09 billion in 2005. To turn things around, Six Flags CEO Mark Shapiro is focusing on big problems (such as cutting long-term debt) and small details (such as cleaner restrooms and grounds). His attention to providing clean parks is part of his overall strategy to get entire families to enjoy their day in the park so much that they want to return (data extracted from L. Petrecca, "Six Flags CEO Waves the Signal Flag for Families," **usatoday.com**, June 13, 2006). Suppose that you have been hired as a summer intern at a large amusement park. Every day, your task is to conduct 200 exit interviews in the parking lot when customers leave. You need to construct questions to address the cleanliness of the park and the customers' intent to return again. When you begin to construct a short questionnaire, you remember the control chart material you learned in a statistics course, and you decide to write questions that will provide you with data to graph on control charts. After collecting data for 30 days, you plan to construct the control charts.

a. Write a question that will allow you to develop a control chart of customers' perceptions of cleanliness of the park.
b. Give examples of common cause variation and special cause variation for the control chart.
c. If the control chart is in control, what does that indicate and what do you do next?
d. If the control chart is out of control, what does that indicate and what do you do next?
e. Repeat (a) through (d), this time addressing the customers' intent to return to the park.
f. After the initial 30 days, assuming that the charts indicate in-control processes or that the root sources of special cause variation have been corrected, explain how the charts can be used on a daily basis to monitor and improve the quality in the park.

14.30 Researchers at Miami University in Oxford, Ohio, investigated the use of p charts to monitor the market share of a product and to document the effectiveness of marketing promotions. Market share is defined as the company's proportion of the total number of products sold in a category. If a p chart based on a company's market share indicates an in-control process, then the company's share in the marketplace is deemed to be stable and consistent over time. In the example given in the article, the RudyBird Diskette Company collected daily sales data from a nationwide retail audit service. The first 30 days of data in the accompanying table (see the file Rudybird) indicate the total number of cases of computer disks sold and the number of RudyBird diskettes sold. The final 7 days of data were taken after RudyBird launched a major in-store promotion. A control chart was used to see if the in-store promotion would result in special cause variation in the marketplace.

Cases Sold Before the Promotion

Day	Total	RudyBird	Day	Total	RudyBird
1	154	35	16	177	56
2	153	43	17	143	43
3	200	44	18	200	69
4	197	56	19	134	38
5	194	54	20	192	47
6	172	38	21	155	45
7	190	43	22	135	36
8	209	62	23	189	55
9	173	53	24	184	44
10	171	39	25	170	47
11	173	44	26	178	48
12	168	37	27	167	42
13	184	45	28	204	71
14	211	58	29	183	64
15	179	35	30	169	43

Cases Sold After the Promotion

Day	Total	RudyBird
31	201	92
32	177	76
33	205	85
34	199	90
35	187	77
36	168	79
37	198	97

Source: *Data extracted from C. T. Crespy, T. C. Krehbiel, and J. M. Stearns, "Integrating Analytic Methods into Marketing Research Education: Statistical Control Charts as an Example,"* Marketing Education Review, *5, Spring 1995, pp. 11–23.*

a. Construct a *p* chart using data from the first 30 days (prior to the promotion) to monitor the market share for RudyBird Diskettes.
b. Is the market share for RudyBird in control before the start of the in-store promotion?
c. On your control chart, extend the control limits generated in (b) and plot the proportions for days 31 through 37. What effect, if any, did the in-store promotion have on RudyBird's market share?

14.31 The manufacturer of Boston and Vermont asphalt shingles constructed control charts and analyzed several quality characteristics. One characteristic of interest is the strength of the sealant on the shingle. During each day of production, three shingles are tested for their sealant strength. (Thus, a subgroup is operationally defined as one day of production, and the sample size for each subgroup is 3.) Separate pieces are cut from the upper and lower portions of a shingle and then reassembled to simulate shingles on a roof. A timed heating process is used to simulate the sealing process. The sealed shingle pieces are pulled apart, and the amount of force (in pounds) required to break the sealant bond is measured and recorded. This variable is called the *sealant strength*. The data file Sealant contains sealant strength measurements on 25 days of production for Boston shingles and 19 days for Vermont shingles.

For the Boston shingles,
a. construct a control chart for the range.
b. construct a control chart for the mean.
c. is the process in control?
d. Repeat (a) through (c), using the 19 production days for Vermont shingles.

14.32 A professional basketball player has embarked on a program to study his ability to shoot foul shots. On each day in which a game is not scheduled, he intends to shoot 100 foul shots. He maintains records over a period of 40 days of practice, with the results stored in the file Foulspc:
a. Construct a *p* chart for the proportion of successful foul shots. Do you think that the player's foul-shooting process is in statistical control? If not, why not?
b. What if you were told that the player used a different method of shooting foul shots for the last 20 days? How might this information change your conclusions in (a)?
c. If you knew the information in (b) prior to doing (a), how might you do the analysis differently?

14.33 The funds-transfer department of a bank is concerned with turnaround time for investigations of funds-transfer payments. A payment may involve the bank as a remitter of funds, a beneficiary of funds, or an intermediary in the payment. An investigation is initiated by a payment inquiry or a query by a party involved in the payment or any department affected by the flow of funds. When a query is received, an investigator reconstructs the transaction trail of the payment and verifies that the information is correct and that the proper payment is transmitted. The investigator then reports the results of the investigation, and the transaction is considered closed. It is important that investigations are closed rapidly, preferably within the same day. The number of new investigations and the number and proportion closed on the same day that the inquiry was made are in the file Fundtran.
a. Construct a control chart for these data.
b. Is the process in a state of statistical control? Explain.
c. Based on the results of (a) and (b), what should management do next to improve the process?

14.34 A branch manager of a brokerage company is concerned with the number of undesirable trades made by her sales staff. A trade is considered undesirable if there is an error on the trade ticket. Trades with errors are canceled and resubmitted. The cost of correcting errors is billed to the brokerage company. The branch manager wants to know whether the proportion of undesirable trades is in a state of statistical control so she can plan the next step in a quality

improvement process. Data were collected for a 30-day period, with the results stored in the file **Trade**.
a. Construct a control chart for these data.
b. Is the process in control? Explain.
c. Based on the results of (a) and (b), what should the manager do next to improve the process?

14.35 As chief operating officer of a local community hospital, you have just returned from a three-day seminar on quality and productivity. It is your intention to implement many of the ideas that you learned at the seminar. You have decided to construct control charts for the upcoming month for the proportion of rework in the laboratory (based on 1,000 daily samples), and time (in hours) between receipt of a specimen at the laboratory and completion of the work (based on a subgroup of 10 specimens per day). The data collected are summarized in the file **Hospadm**. You are to make a presentation to the chief executive officer of the hospital and the board of directors. Prepare a report that summarizes the conclusions drawn from analyzing control charts for these variables. In addition, recommend additional variables to measure and monitor by using control charts.

14.36 For a period of four weeks, record your pulse rate (in beats per minute) just after you get out of bed in the morning and also before you go to sleep at night. Construct and R charts and determine whether your pulse rate is in a state of statistical control. Discuss.

14.37 (Class Project) Use the table of random numbers (Table E.1) to simulate the selection of different-colored balls from an urn, as follows:
1. Start in the row corresponding to the day of the month in which you were born plus the last two digits of the year in which you were born. For example, if you were born October 3, 1986, you would start in row $3 + 86 = 89$. If your total exceeds 100, subtract 100 from the total.
2. Select two-digit random numbers.
3. If you select a random number from 00 to 94, consider the ball to be white; if the random number is from 95 to 99, consider the ball to be red.

Each student is to select 100 such two-digit random numbers and report the number of "red balls" in the sample. Construct a control chart for the proportion of red balls. What conclusions can you draw about the system of selecting red balls? Are all the students part of the system? Is anyone outside the system? If so, what explanation can you give for someone who has too many red balls? If a bonus were paid to the top 10% of the students (the 10% with the fewest red balls), what effect would that have on the rest of the students? Discuss.

THE HARNSWELL SEWING MACHINE COMPANY CASE

PHASE 1

For more than 40 years, the Harnswell Sewing Machine Company has manufactured industrial sewing machines. The company specializes in automated machines called pattern tackers that sew repetitive patterns on such mass-produced products as shoes, garments, and seat belts. Aside from the sales of machines, the company sells machine parts. Because the company's products have a reputation for being superior, Harnswell is able to command a price premium for its product line.

Recently, the operations manager, Natalie York, purchased several books relating to quality at a local bookstore. After reading them, she considered the feasibility of beginning a quality program at the company. At the current time, the company has no formal quality program. Parts are 100% inspected at the time of shipping to a customer or installation in a machine, yet Natalie has always wondered why inventory of certain parts (in particular, the half-inch cam rollers) invariably falls short before a full year lapses, even though 7,000 pieces have been produced for a demand of 5,000 pieces per year.

After a great deal of reflection and with some apprehension, Natalie has decided that she will approach John Harnswell, the owner of the company, about the possibility of beginning a program to improve quality in the company, starting with a trial project in the machine parts area. As she is walking to Mr. Harnswell's office for the meeting, she has second thoughts about whether this is such a good idea. After all, just last month, Mr. Harnswell told her, "Why do you need to go to graduate school for your master's degree in business? That is a waste of your time and will not be of any value to the Harnswell Company. All those professors are just up in their ivory towers and don't know a thing about running a business, like I do."

As she enters his office, Mr. Harnswell, ever courteous to her, invites Natalie to sit down across from him. "Well, what do you have on your mind this morning?" Mr. Harnswell asks her in an inquisitive tone. She begins by starting to talk about the books that she has just completed reading and about how she has some interesting ideas for making production even better than it is now and improving profits. Before she can finish, Mr. Harnswell has started to answer. "Look, everything has been fine since I started this company in 1968. I have built this company up from nothing to one that employs more than 100 people. Why do you want to make waves? Remember, if it ain't broke, don't fix it." With that he ushers her from his office with the admonishment of, "What am I going to do with you if you keep coming up with these ridiculous ideas?"

EXERCISES

HS14.1 Based on what you have read, which of Deming's 14 points of management are most lacking in the Harnswell Sewing Machine Company? Explain.

HS14.2 What changes, if any, do you think that Natalie York might be able to institute in the company? Explain.

DO NOT CONTINUE UNTIL YOU HAVE COMPLETED THE PHASE 1 EXERCISES.

PHASE 2

Natalie slowly walks down the hall after leaving Mr. Harnswell's office, feeling rather downcast. He just won't listen to anyone, she thinks. As she walks, Jim Murante, the shop foreman, comes up beside her. "So," he says, "did you really think that he would listen to you? I've been here more than 25 years. The only way he listens is if he is shown something that worked after it has already been done. Let's see what we can plan together."

Natalie and Jim decide to begin by investigating the production of the cam rollers, which are precision-ground parts. The last part of the production process involves the grinding of the outer diameter. After grinding, the part mates with the cam groove of the particular sewing pattern. The half-inch rollers technically have an engineering specification for the outer diameter of the roller of 0.5075 inch (the specifications are actually metric, but in factory floor jargon, they are referred to as half-inch), plus a tolerable error of 0.0003 inch on the lower side. Thus, the outer diameter is allowed to be between 0.5072 and 0.5075 inch. Anything larger is reclassified into a different and less costly category, and anything smaller is unusable for anything other than scrap.

The grinding of the cam roller is done on a single machine with a single tool setup and no change in the grinding wheel after initial setup. The operation is done by Dave Martin, the head machinist, who has 30 years of experience in the trade and specific experience producing the cam roller part. Because production occurs in batches, Natalie and Jim sample five parts produced from each batch. Table HS14.1 presents data collected over 30 batches (stored in the file Harnswell).

EXERCISE

HS14.3 **a.** Is the process in control? Why?

b. What recommendations do you have for improving the process?

DO NOT CONTINUE UNTIL YOU HAVE COMPLETED THE PHASE 2 EXERCISE.

TABLE HS14.1
Diameter of Cam Rollers (in Inches)

Batch	Cam Roller				
	1	2	3	4	5
1	.5076	.5076	.5075	.5077	.5075
2	.5075	.5077	.5076	.5076	.5075
3	.5075	.5075	.5075	.5075	.5076
4	.5075	.5076	.5074	.5076	.5073
5	.5075	.5074	.5076	.5073	.5076
6	.5076	.5075	.5076	.5075	.5075
7	.5076	.5076	.5076	.5075	.5075
8	.5075	.5076	.5076	.5075	.5074
9	.5074	.5076	.5075	.5075	.5076
10	.5076	.5077	.5075	.5075	.5075
11	.5075	.5075	.5075	.5076	.5075
12	.5075	.5076	.5075	.5077	.5075
13	.5076	.5076	.5073	.5076	.5074
14	.5075	.5076	.5074	.5076	.5075
15	.5075	.5075	.5076	.5074	.5073
16	.5075	.5074	.5076	.5075	.5075
17	.5075	.5074	.5075	.5074	.5072
18	.5075	.5075	.5076	.5075	.5076
19	.5076	.5076	.5075	.5075	.5076
20	.5075	.5074	.5077	.5076	.5074
21	.5075	.5074	.5075	.5075	.5075
22	.5076	.5076	.5075	.5076	.5074
23	.5076	.5076	.5075	.5075	.5076
24	.5075	.5076	.5075	.5076	.5075
25	.5075	.5075	.5075	.5075	.5074
26	.5077	.5076	.5076	.5074	.5075
27	.5075	.5075	.5074	.5076	.5075
28	.5077	.5076	.5075	.5075	.5076
29	.5075	.5075	.5074	.5075	.5075
30	.5076	.5075	.5075	.5076	.5075

PHASE 3

Natalie examines the $\overline{X}$ and R charts developed from the data presented in Table HS14.1. The R chart indicates that the process is in control, but the $\overline{X}$ chart reveals that the mean for batch 17 is outside the LCL. This immediately gives her cause for concern because low values for the roller diameter could mean that parts have to be scrapped. Natalie goes to see Jim Murante, the shop foreman, to try to find out what had happened to batch 17. Jim looks up the production records to determine when this batch was produced. "Aha!" he exclaims. "I think I've got the answer! This batch was produced on that really cold morning we had last month. I've been after Mr. Harnswell for a long time to let us install an automatic thermostat here in the shop so that the place doesn't feel so cold when we get here in the morning. All he ever tells me is that people aren't as tough as they used to be."

Natalie stands there almost in shock. She realizes that what happened is that, rather than standing idle until the environment and the equipment warmed to acceptable temperatures, the machinist opted to manufacture parts that might have to be scrapped. In fact, Natalie recalls that a major problem occurred on that same day, when several other expensive parts had to be scrapped. Natalie says to Jim, "We just have to do something. We can't let this go on now that we know what problems it is potentially causing." Natalie and Jim decide to take enough money out of petty cash to get the thermostat without having to fill out a requisition requiring Mr. Harnswell's signature. They install the thermostat and set the heating control so that the heat turns on a half hour before the shop opens each morning.

EXERCISES

HS14.4 What should Natalie now do concerning the cam roller data? Explain.

HS14.5 Explain how the actions of Natalie and Jim to avoid this particular problem in the future have resulted in quality improvement.

DO NOT CONTINUE UNTIL YOU HAVE COMPLETED THE PHASE 3 EXERCISES.

PHASE 4

Because corrective action was taken to eliminate the special cause of variation, Natalie removes the data for batch 17 from the analysis. The control charts for the remaining days indicate a stable system, with only common causes of variation operating on the system. Then, Natalie and Jim sit down with Dave Martin and several other machinists to try to determine all the possible causes for the existence of oversized and scrapped rollers. Natalie is still troubled by the data. After all, she wants to find out whether the process is giving oversizes (which are downgraded) and undersizes (which are scrapped). She thinks about which tables and charts might be most helpful.

EXERCISE

HS14.6 **a.** Construct a frequency distribution and a stem-and-leaf display of the cam roller diameters. Which one do you prefer?

b. Based on your results in (a), construct all appropriate graphs of the cam roller diameters.

c. Write a report, expressing your conclusions concerning the cam roller diameters. Be sure to discuss the diameters as they relate to the specifications.

DO NOT CONTINUE UNTIL YOU HAVE COMPLETED THE PHASE 4 EXERCISE.

PHASE 5

Natalie notices immediately that the overall mean diameter with batch 17 eliminated is 0.507527, which is higher than the specification value. Thus, the mean diameter of the rollers produced is so high that they will be downgraded in value. In fact, 55 of the 150 rollers sampled (36.67%) are above the specification value. If this percentage is extrapolated to the full year's production, 36.67% of the 7,000 pieces manufactured, or 2,567, could not be sold as half-inch rollers, leaving only 4,433 available for sale. "No wonder we often have shortages that require costly emergency runs," she thinks. She also notes that not one diameter is below the lower specification of 0.5072, so not one of the rollers had to be scrapped.

Natalie realizes that there has to be a reason for all this. Along with Jim Murante, she decides to show the results to Dave Martin, the head machinist. Dave says that the results don't surprise him that much. "You know," he says, "there is only 0.0003 inch in diameter that I'm allowed in variation. If I aim for exactly halfway between 0.5072 and 0.5075, I'm afraid that I'll make a lot of short pieces that will have to be scrapped. I know from way back when I first started here that Mr. Harnswell and everybody else will come down on my head if they start seeing too many of those scraps. I figure that if I aim at 0.5075, the worst thing that will happen will be a bunch of downgrades, but I won't make any pieces that have to be scrapped."

EXERCISES

HS14.7 What approach do you think the machinist should take in terms of the diameter he should aim for? Explain.

HS14.8 What do you think that Natalie should do next? Explain.

MANAGING *THE SPRINGVILLE HERALD*

PHASE 1

An advertising production team is charged with reducing the number and dollar amount of the advertising errors, with initial focus on the ran-in-error category. The team collects data, including the number of ads with errors, on a Monday-to-Saturday basis. Table SH14.1 includes the total number of ads and the number containing errors for a period of one month (see the file **SH14-1**). (Sundays are excluded because a special type of production is used for that day.)

EXERCISES

SH14.1 What is the first thing that the team from the advertising production department should do to reduce the number of errors? Explain.

SH14.2 **a.** Construct the appropriate control chart for these data.

b. Is the process in a state of statistical control? Explain.

c. What should the team recommend as the next step to improve the process?

TABLE SH14.1

Number of Ads with Errors and Daily Number of Display Ads

Day	Number of Ads with Errors	Total Number of Ads	Day	Number of Ads with Errors	Total Number of Ads
1	4	228	14	5	245
2	6	273	15	7	266
3	5	239	16	2	197
4	3	197	17	4	228
5	6	259	18	5	236
6	7	203	19	4	208
7	8	289	20	3	214
8	14	241	21	8	258
9	9	263	22	10	267
10	5	199	23	4	217
11	6	275	24	9	277
12	4	212	25	7	258
13	3	207			

DO NOT CONTINUE UNTIL YOU HAVE COMPLETED THE PHASE 1 EXERCISES.

PHASE 2

The advertising production team examines the p chart developed from the data of Table SH14.1. Using the rules for determining out-of-control points, they observe that day 8 is above the UCL. Upon investigation, they determine that on that day, there was an employee from another work area assigned to the processing of the ads because several employees were out ill. The group brainstorms ways of avoiding the problem in the future and recommends that a team of people from other work areas receive training on the work done by this area. Members of this team can then cover the processing of the ads by rotating in one- or two-hour shifts.

EXERCISES

SH14.3 What should the advertising production team now do concerning the data of Table SH14.1? Explain.

SH14.4 Explain how the actions of the team to avoid this particular problem in the future have resulted in quality improvement.

SH14.5 In addition to the number of ads with errors, what other information concerning errors on a daily basis should the team collect?

DO NOT CONTINUE UNTIL YOU HAVE COMPLETED THE PHASE 2 EXERCISES.

PHASE 3

A print production team also is charged with improving the quality of the *Herald*. The team has chosen the blackness of the print of the newspaper as its first project. Blackness is measured on a device that records the results on a standard scale, where the blacker the spot, the higher the blackness measure. The blackness of the print should be approximately 1.0. The lower and upper specifications for blackness are 0.8 and 1.2, respectively. Five spots on the first newspaper printed each day are randomly selected, and the blackness of each spot is measured. Table SH14.2 presents the results for 25 days (stored in the file `SH14-2`).

EXERCISE

SH14.6 **a.** Construct the appropriate control charts for these data.

   b. Is the process in a state of statistical control? Explain.

   c. What should the team recommend as the next step to improve the process?

TABLE SH14.2

Newsprint Blackness for 25 Consecutive Days

	Spot						Spot				
Day	1	2	3	4	5	Day	1	2	3	4	5
1	0.96	1.01	1.12	1.07	0.97	14	1.03	0.89	1.03	1.12	1.03
2	1.06	1.00	1.02	1.16	0.96	15	0.96	1.12	0.95	0.88	0.99
3	1.00	0.90	0.98	1.18	0.96	16	1.01	0.87	0.99	1.04	1.16
4	0.92	0.89	1.01	1.16	0.90	17	0.98	0.85	0.99	1.04	1.16
5	1.02	1.16	1.03	0.89	1.00	18	1.03	0.82	1.21	0.98	1.08
6	0.88	0.92	1.03	1.16	0.91	19	1.02	0.84	1.15	0.94	1.08
7	1.05	1.13	1.01	0.93	1.03	20	0.90	1.02	1.10	1.04	1.08
8	0.95	0.86	1.14	0.90	0.95	21	0.96	1.05	1.01	0.93	1.01
9	0.99	0.89	1.00	1.15	0.92	22	0.89	1.04	0.97	0.99	0.95
10	0.89	1.18	1.03	0.96	1.04	23	0.96	1.00	0.97	1.04	0.95
11	0.97	1.13	0.95	0.86	1.06	24	1.01	0.98	1.04	1.01	0.92
12	1.00	0.87	1.02	0.98	1.13	25	1.01	1.00	0.92	0.90	1.11
13	0.96	0.79	1.17	0.97	0.95						

REFERENCES

1. Arndt, M., "Quality Isn't Just for Widgets," *Business Week*, July 22, 2002, pp. 72–73.
2. Automotive Industry Action Group (AIAG), *Statistical Process Control Reference Manual* (Chrysler, Ford, and General Motors Quality and Supplier Assessment Staff, 1995).
3. Bothe, D. R., *Measuring Process Capability* (New York: McGraw-Hill, 1997).
4. Cyger, M. "The Last Word-Riding the Bandwagon," *iSixSigma Magazine*, November/December 2006.
5. Davis, R. B., and T. C. Krehbiel, "Shewhart and Zone Control Charts under Linear Trend," *Communications in Statistics: Simulation and Computation*, 2002, 31(1), pp. 91–96.
6. Deming, W. E., *The New Economics for Business, Industry, and Government* (Cambridge, MA: MIT Center for Advanced Engineering Study, 1993).
7. Deming, W. E., *Out of the Crisis* (Cambridge, MA: MIT Center for Advanced Engineering Study, 1986).
8. Gabor, A., *The Man Who Discovered Quality* (New York: Time Books, 1990).
9. Gitlow, H., and D. Levine, *Six Sigma for Green Belts and Champions* (Upper Saddle River, NJ: Financial Times/Prentice Hall, 2005).
10. Gitlow, H., D. Levine, and E. Popovich, *Design for Six Sigma for Green Belts and Champions* (Upper Saddle River, NJ: Financial Times/Prentice Hall, 2006).
11. Hahn, G. J., N. Doganaksoy, and R. Hoerl, "The Evolution of Six Sigma," *Quality Engineering*, 12 (2000): 317–326.
12. Lemak, D. L., N. P. Mero, and R. Reed, " When Quality Works: A Premature Post-Mortem on TQM," *Journal of Business and Management*, 8 (2002): 391–407.
13. Levine, D. M., *Statistics for Six Sigma for Green Belts with Minitab and JMP* (Upper Saddle River, NJ: Financial Times/Prentice Hall, 2006).
14. *Microsoft Excel 2007* (Redmond, WA: Microsoft Corp., 2007).
15. Scherkenbach, W. W., *The Deming Route to Quality and Productivity: Road Maps and Roadblocks* (Washington, DC: CEEP Press, 1987).
16. Shewhart, W. A., *Economic Control of the Quality of Manufactured Product* (New York: Van Nostrand-Reinhard, 1931, reprinted by the American Society for Quality Control, Milwaukee, 1980).
17. Snee, R. D., "Impact of Six Sigma on Quality," *Quality Engineering*, 12 (2000): ix–xiv.
18. Vardeman, S. B., and J. M. Jobe, *Statistical Methods for Quality Assurance: Basics, Measurement, Control, Capability and Improvement* (New York: Springer-Verlag, 2009).
19. Walton, M., *The Deming Management Method* (New York: Perigee Books, 1986).

Appendices

APPENDIX A

Review of Arithmetic, Algebra, and Logarithms

A.1 Rules for Arithmetic Operations

RULE	EXAMPLE
1. $a + b = c$ and $b + a = c$	$2 + 1 = 3$ and $1 + 2 = 3$
2. $a + (b + c) = (a + b) + c$	$5 + (7 + 4) = (5 + 7) + 4 = 16$
3. $a - b = c$ but $b - a \neq c$	$9 - 7 = 2$ but $7 - 9 \neq 2$
4. $(a)(b) = (b)(a)$	$(7)(6) = (6)(7) = 42$
5. $(a)(b + c) = ab + ac$	$(2)(3 + 5) = (2)(3) + (2)(5) = 16$
6. $a \div b \neq b \div a$	$12 \div 3 \neq 3 \div 12$
7. $\dfrac{a + b}{c} = \dfrac{a}{c} + \dfrac{b}{c}$	$\dfrac{7 + 3}{2} = \dfrac{7}{2} + \dfrac{3}{2} = 5$
8. $\dfrac{a}{b + c} \neq \dfrac{a}{b} + \dfrac{a}{c}$	$\dfrac{3}{4 + 5} \neq \dfrac{3}{4} + \dfrac{3}{5}$
9. $\dfrac{1}{a} + \dfrac{1}{b} = \dfrac{b + a}{ab}$	$\dfrac{1}{3} + \dfrac{1}{5} = \dfrac{5 + 3}{(3)(5)} = \dfrac{8}{15}$
10. $\left(\dfrac{a}{b}\right)\left(\dfrac{c}{d}\right) = \left(\dfrac{ac}{bd}\right)$	$\left(\dfrac{2}{3}\right)\left(\dfrac{6}{7}\right) = \left(\dfrac{(2)(6)}{(3)(7)}\right) = \dfrac{12}{21}$
11. $\dfrac{a}{b} \div \dfrac{c}{d} = \dfrac{ad}{bc}$	$\dfrac{5}{8} \div \dfrac{3}{7} = \left(\dfrac{(5)(7)}{(8)(3)}\right) = \dfrac{35}{24}$

A.2 Rules for Algebra: Exponents and Square Roots

RULE	EXAMPLE
1. $(X^a)(X^b) = X^{a+b}$	$(4^2)(4^3) = 4^5$
2. $(X^a)^b = X^{ab}$	$(2^2)^3 = 2^6$
3. $(X^a/X^b) = X^{a-b}$	$\dfrac{3^5}{3^3} = 3^2$
4. $\dfrac{X^a}{X^a} = X^0 = 1$	$\dfrac{3^4}{3^4} = 3^0 = 1$
5. $\sqrt{XY} = \sqrt{X}\sqrt{Y}$	$\sqrt{(25)(4)} = \sqrt{25}\sqrt{4} = 10$
6. $\sqrt{\dfrac{X}{Y}} = \dfrac{\sqrt{X}}{\sqrt{Y}}$	$\sqrt{\dfrac{16}{100}} = \dfrac{\sqrt{16}}{\sqrt{100}} = 0.40$

A.3 Rules for Logarithms

Base 10

Log is the symbol used for base-10 logarithms:

RULE	EXAMPLE
1. $\log(10^a) = a$	$\log(100) = \log(10^2) = 2$
2. If $\log(a) = b$, then $a = 10^b$	If $\log(a) = 2$, then $a = 10^2 = 100$
3. $\log(ab) = \log(a) + \log(b)$	$\log(100) = \log[(10)(10)] = \log(10) + \log(10)$ $= 1 + 1 = 2$
4. $\log(a^b) = (b)\log(a)$	$\log(1{,}000) = \log(10^3) = (3)\log(10) = (3)(1) = 3$
5. $\log(a/b) = \log(a) - \log(b)$	$\log(100) = \log(1{,}000/10)$ $= \log(1{,}000) - \log(10) = 3 - 1 = 2$

EXAMPLE

Take the base-10 logarithm of each side of the following equation:

$$Y = \beta_0 \beta_1^X \varepsilon$$

SOLUTION Apply rules 3 and 4:

$$\log(Y) = \log(\beta_0 \beta_1^X \varepsilon)$$
$$= \log(\beta_0) + \log(\beta_1^X) + \log(\varepsilon)$$
$$= \log(\beta_0) + (X)\log(\beta_1) + \log(\varepsilon)$$

Base e

ln is the symbol used for base e logarithms, commonly referred to as natural logarithms. e is Euler's number, and $e \cong 2.718282$:

RULE	EXAMPLE
1. $\ln(e^a) = a$	$\ln(7.389056) = \ln(e^2) = 2$
2. If $\ln(a) = b$, then $a = e^b$	If $\ln(a) = 2$, then $a = e^2 = 7.389056$
3. $\ln(ab) = \ln(a) + \ln(b)$	$\ln(100) = \ln[(10)(10)]$ $\ln(10) + \ln(10) = 2.302585 + 2.302585 = 4.605170$
4. $\ln(a^b) = (b)\ln(a)$	$\ln(1{,}000) = \ln(10^3) = 3\ln(10) = 3(2.302585) = 6.907755$
5. $\ln(a/b) = \ln(a) - \ln(b)$	$\ln(100) = \ln(1{,}000/10) = \ln(1{,}000) - \ln(10)$ $= 6.907755 - 2.302585 = 4.605170$

EXAMPLE

Take the base e logarithm of each side of the following equation:

$$Y = \beta_0 \beta_1^X \varepsilon$$

SOLUTION Apply rules 3 and 4:

$$\ln(Y) = \ln(\beta_0 \beta_1^X \varepsilon)$$
$$= \ln(\beta_0) + \ln(\beta_1^X) + \ln(\varepsilon)$$
$$= \ln(\beta_0) + (X)\ln(\beta_1) + \ln(\varepsilon)$$

APPENDIX B   Summation Notation and Statistical Symbols

B.1 Summation Notation

The symbol Σ, the Greek capital letter sigma, is used to denote "taking the sum of." Consider a set of n values for variable X. The expression $\sum_{i=1}^{n} X_i$ means that these n values are to be added together. Thus:

$$\sum_{i=1}^{n} X_i = X_1 + X_2 + X_3 + \cdots + X_n$$

The following problem illustrates the use of summation notation. Consider five values of a variable X: $X_1 = 2, X_2 = 0, X_3 = -1, X_4 = 5,$ and $X_5 = 7$. Thus:

$$\sum_{i=1}^{5} X_i = X_1 + X_2 + X_3 + X_4 + X_5 = 2 + 0 + (-1) + 5 + 7 = 13$$

In statistics, the squared values of a variable are often summed. Thus:

$$\sum_{i=1}^{n} X_i^2 = X_1^2 + X_2^2 + X_3^2 + \cdots + X_n^2$$

and, in the example above:

$$\sum_{i=1}^{5} X_i^2 = X_1^2 + X_2^2 + X_3^2 + X_4^2 + X_5^2$$
$$= 2^2 + 0^2 + (-1)^2 + 5^2 + 7^2$$
$$= 4 + 0 + 1 + 25 + 49$$
$$= 79$$

$\sum_{i=1}^{n} X_i^2$, the summation of the squares, is *not* the same as $\left(\sum_{i=1}^{n} X_i \right)^2$, the square of the sum:

$$\sum_{i=1}^{n} X_i^2 \neq \left(\sum_{i=1}^{n} X_i \right)^2$$

In the example given earlier, the summation of squares is equal to 79. This is not equal to the square of the sum, which is $13^2 = 169$.

Another frequently used operation involves the summation of the product. Consider two variables, X and Y, each having n values. Then:

$$\sum_{i=1}^{n} X_i Y_i = X_1 Y_1 + X_2 Y_2 + X_3 Y_3 + \cdots + X_n Y_n$$

Continuing with the previous example, suppose there is a second variable, Y, whose five values are $Y_1 = 1$, $Y_2 = 3$, $Y_3 = -2$, $Y_4 = 4$, and $Y_5 = 3$. Then,

$$\sum_{i=1}^{n} X_i Y_i = X_1 Y_1 + X_2 Y_2 + X_3 Y_3 + X_4 Y_4 + X_5 Y_5$$

$$= (2)(1) + (0)(3) + (-1)(-2) + (5)(4) + (7)(3)$$
$$= 2 + 0 + 2 + 20 + 21$$
$$= 45$$

In computing $\sum_{i=1}^{n} X_i Y_i$, realize that the first value of X is multiplied by the first value of Y, the second value of X is multiplied by the second value of Y, and so on. These products are then summed in order to compute the desired result. However, the summation of products is *not* equal to the product of the individual sums:

$$\sum_{i=1}^{n} X_i Y_i \neq \left(\sum_{i=1}^{n} X_i \right) \left(\sum_{i=1}^{n} Y_i \right)$$

In this example,

$$\sum_{i=1}^{5} X_i = 13$$

and

$$\sum_{i=1}^{5} Y_i = 1 + 3 + (-2) + 4 + 3 = 9$$

so that

$$\left(\sum_{i=1}^{5} X_i \right) \left(\sum_{i=1}^{5} Y_i \right) = (13)(9) = 117$$

However,

$$\sum_{i=1}^{n} X_i X_i = 45$$

The following table summarizes these results:

VALUE	X_i	Y_i	$X_i Y_i$
1	2	1	2
2	0	3	0
3	-1	-2	2
4	5	4	20
5	7	3	21
	$\sum_{i=1}^{5} X_i = 13$	$\sum_{i=1}^{5} Y_i = 9$	$\sum_{i=1}^{5} X_i Y_i = 45$

Rule 1   The summation of the values of two variables is equal to the sum of the values of each summed variable:

$$\sum_{i=1}^{n}(X_i + Y_i) = \sum_{i=1}^{n}X_i + \sum_{i=1}^{n}Y_i$$

Thus,

$$\sum_{i=1}^{5}(X_i + Y_i) = (2 + 1) + (0 + 3) + (-1 + (-2)) + (5 + 4) + (7 + 3)$$

$$= 3 + 3 + (-3) + 9 + 10$$

$$= 22$$

$$\sum_{i=1}^{5}X_i + \sum_{i=1}^{5}Y_i = 13 + 9 = 22$$

Rule 2   The summation of a difference between the values of two variables is equal to the difference between the summed values of the variables:

$$\sum_{i=1}^{n}(X_i - Y_i) = \sum_{i=1}^{n}X_i - \sum_{i=1}^{n}Y_i$$

Thus,

$$\sum_{i=1}^{5}(X_i - Y_i) = (2 - 1) + (0 - 3) + (-1 - (-2)) + (5 - 4) + (7 - 3)$$

$$= 1 + (-3) + 1 + 1 + 4$$

$$= 4$$

$$\sum_{i=1}^{5}X_i - \sum_{i=1}^{5}Y_i = 13 - 9 = 4$$

Rule 3   The sum of a constant times a variable is equal to that constant times the sum of the values of the variable:

$$\sum_{i=1}^{n}cX_i = c\sum_{i=1}^{n}X_i$$

where c is a constant. Thus, if $c = 2$,

$$\sum_{i=1}^{5}cX_i = \sum_{i=1}^{5}2X_i = (2)(2) + (2)(0) + (2)(-1) + (2)(5) + (2)(7)$$

$$= 4 + 0 + (-2) + 10 + 14$$

$$= 26$$

$$c\sum_{i=1}^{5}X_i = 2\sum_{i=1}^{5}X_i = (2)(13) = 26$$

Rule 4   A constant summed n times will be equal to n times the value of the constant.

$$\sum_{i=1}^{n} c = nc$$

where c is a constant. Thus, if the constant $c = 2$ is summed 5 times,

$$\sum_{i=1}^{5} c = 2 + 2 + 2 + 2 + 2 = 10$$

$$nc = (5)(2) = 10$$

EXAMPLE

Suppose there are six values for the variables X and Y, such that $X_1 = 2, X_2 = 1, X_3 = 5,$ $X_4 = -3, X_5 = 1, X_6 = -2,$ and $Y_1 = 4, Y_2 = 0, Y_3 = -1, Y_4 = 2, Y_5 = 7,$ and $Y_6 = -3.$ Compute each of the following:

(a) $\displaystyle\sum_{i=1}^{6} X_i$

(f) $\displaystyle\sum_{i=1}^{6} (X_i + Y_i)$

(b) $\displaystyle\sum_{i=1}^{6} Y_i$

(g) $\displaystyle\sum_{i=1}^{6} (X_i - Y_i)$

(c) $\displaystyle\sum_{i=1}^{6} X_i^2$

(h) $\displaystyle\sum_{i=1}^{6} (X_i - 3Y_i + 2X_i^2)$

(d) $\displaystyle\sum_{i=1}^{6} Y_i^2$

(i) $\displaystyle\sum_{i=1}^{6} (cX_i)$, where $c = -1$

(e) $\displaystyle\sum_{i=1}^{6} X_i Y_i$

(j) $\displaystyle\sum_{i=1}^{6} (X_i - 3Y_i + c)$, where $c = +3$

Answers
   (a) 4   (b) 9   (c) 44   (d) 79   (e) 10   (f) 13   (g) −5   (h) 65   (i) −4   (j) −5

References

1. Bashaw, W. L., *Mathematics for Statistics* (New York: Wiley, 1969).

2. Lanzer, P., *Basic Math: Fractions, Decimals, Percents* (Hicksville, NY: Video Aided Instruction, 2006).

3. Levine, D., *The MBA Primer: Business Statistics* (Cincinnati, OH: Southwestern Publishing, 2000).

4. Levine, D., *Statistics* (Hicksville, NY: Video Aided Instruction, 2006).

5. Shane, H., *Algebra 1* (Hicksville, NY: Video Aided Instruction, 2006).

B.2 Statistical Symbols

$+$ add	$\times$ multiply
$-$ subtract	$\div$ divide
$=$ equal to	$\neq$ not equal to
$\cong$ approximately equal to	
$>$ greater than	$<$ less than
$\geq$ greater than or equal to	$\leq$ less than or equal to

APPENDIX C   Basic Computing Skills

C.1 Introduction

Using Microsoft Excel or Minitab with this book requires certain basic computing skills. If you have ever sent an instant message, surfed the Web, played music or games through a computer, or written word-processed assignments, you probably have already mastered these skills required to use the end-of-chapter appendices. If you already have the basic computing skills that this book requires, this appendix will introduce you to the vocabulary and conventions used in this book to present computer-related operations.

C.2 Mousing Operations

You make extensive use of your mouse (or equivalent pointing device) to move an onscreen mouse pointer as you operate Excel or Minitab. Microsoft Windows expects your mouse to have one mouse button designated as the primary button (this is typically the left button) and another button designated as the secondary button (typically the right button). Throughout the appendices, you will need to distinguish among the following seven mousing verbs that involve moving the mouse and one of these two buttons:

Click, Select, and **Clear** These verbs tell you to move the mouse pointer over the object of the instruction and press the primary button. Click suggests that an action is completed when you press the primary button, as in "click the **OK** button." Select suggests that you will be choosing or highlighting a choice from an onscreen list *or* opening a new onscreen list or submenu. Selecting something is typically followed by clicking something else, as in "select the file name and then click **OK**." Clear is the click operation that clears the checkmark in an onscreen check box (see Figure C.3 on page 537).

Double-click This verb tells you to move the **mouse pointer** over an object and click the primary button twice in rapid succession. You double-click program icons on the Windows Desktop to open programs, and you double-click onscreen objects such as parts of a chart to further edit or format them.

Right-click This verb tells you to move the mouse pointer over an object and click the secondary button. You right-click onscreen objects to display a **shortcut menu** of commands from which you click or select an action.

Drag and **Drag-and-drop** These verbs represent a two-step process. In the first step, you move the mouse pointer over an object and press and hold down the primary button while you move the mouse pointer somewhere else. In the second step, you move the mouse pointer somewhere else and release the primary button. Drag suggests that you are selecting part of a whole; drag-and-drop suggests that you are moving an entire whole. You drag the mouse to select contiguous parts of a worksheet or to move or resize the borders of onscreen windows, but you drag-and-drop a Windows Desktop icon to move it from one part of the screen to another.

C.3 Window Elements

The "windows" in Microsoft Windows are onscreen rectangular frames that divide the screen. When you open a program, Microsoft Windows displays a program window, the typical elements of which are shown in Figures C.1 and C.2 and explained in Table C.1. As you use a program, the program will display **dialog boxes**, specialized windows that contain messages or ask you to make entries and selections. Figure C.3 shows two examples of dialog boxes and the elements commonly found in all dialog boxes and explained in Table C.2.

FIGURE C.1

Microsoft Excel 2003 and Microsoft Excel 2007 Program Windows

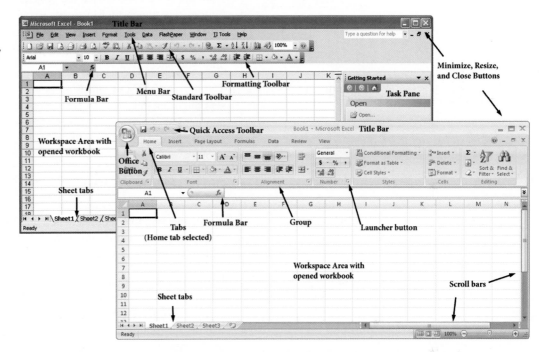

FIGURE C.2

Minitab 15 Program Windows

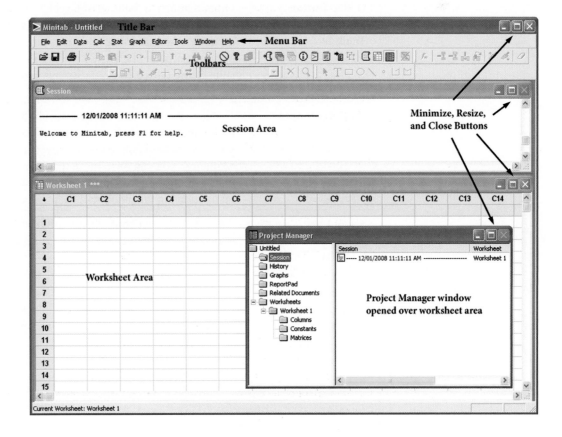

TABLE C.1
Program Window
Elements

Element	Function
Title bar	Displays the name of the program and contains the Minimize, Resize, and Close buttons for the program window. You drag and drop the title bar to reposition a program window on your screen.
Minimize, Resize, and Close buttons	Change the display of the program window. **Minimize** hides the window without closing the program, **Resize** permits you to change the size of the window, and **Close** removes the window from the screen and closes the program. A second set of these buttons that appear in Microsoft Excel perform the three actions for the currently active worksheet. (Similar buttons, obscured in Figure C.2, perform the same functions for the Minitab Session and Worksheet area.)
Menu Bar	The horizontal list of words at the top of the window that represent sets of commands. You select a menu bar word and typically reveal another list of command choices that either lead to some direct action, the display of a dialog box, or the display of another list of choices.
Toolbars	An array of clickable buttons that serve as shortcuts to program commands.
Task Pane	A closable window that lists clickable links that represent shortcuts to menu and toolbar operations (seen only in Excel 2002 and 2003).
Ribbon	Distinctive of Excel 2007, the Ribbon with its **Tabs** and **Tab Groups** performs the combined functions of a menu bar, task pane, and toolbars. Some tab groups contain **Launcher Buttons** that display dialog boxes, task panes, or **galleries**, illustrated sets of choices.
Office Button and Quick Access Toolbar	Other distinctive features of Excel 2007. The **Office Button** displays a menu of commonly issued commands similar to the File menu in other programs and gives you access to many Excel options settings. The **Quick Access Toolbar** (to the immediate right of the Office Button) displays shortcuts to commonly used commands.
Worksheet area	Displays the currently opened workbooks (Excel) or worksheets (Minitab). In Excel, this area also contains **Sheet tabs** on which you can double-click to go to a specific sheet in a workbook. (Although you can open more than one Excel workbook or more than one Minitab worksheet at one time in a worksheet area, no instructions in this book will ever ask you to do so.)
Scroll bars	Allow you to travel horizontally or vertically through a worksheet to reveal parts that cannot otherwise be seen, for example, row 100.

FIGURE C.3
Dialog box elements

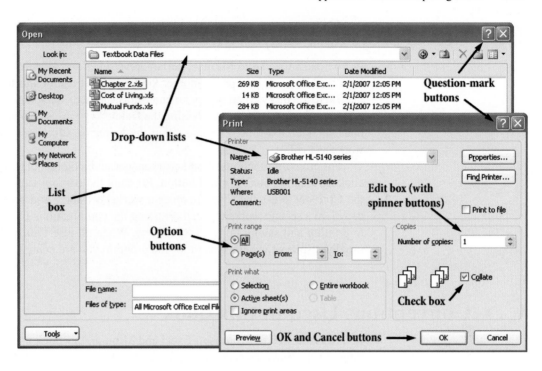

TABLE C.2
Dialog Box Elements

Element	Function
Command buttons	Clickable areas that cause a program to take some action. Many dialog boxes contain an **OK button** that causes a program to take an action using the current entries and selections in the dialog box as well as a **Cancel button** that closes a dialog box and cancels the pending operation associated with the dialog box.
List boxes	Display lists of choices available to you. Should a list exceed the dimensions of a list box, you will see **scroll buttons** or **sliders** (not shown in Figure C.3) that you can click to reveal choices not currently displayed. In Minitab, you will frequently select an item from a list box and then press a command button to perform some action.
Drop-down lists	Display lists of choices when you click over them.
Edit boxes	Areas into which you type entries. some edit boxes contain drop-down lists or **spinner buttons** that you can use to complete the entry. Excel edit boxes for cell ranges typically contain a button that allows you to drag the mouse over a cell range as an alternative to typing the cell range.
Option buttons	Present you with a set of mutually exclusive choices. When you click one option button, all the other option buttons in the set are cleared.
Check boxes	Present you with optional actions that are not mutually exclusive choices. Unlike with option buttons, clicking a check box does not affect the status of other check boxes, and more than one check box can be checked at a time. Clicking a check box that contains a checkmark **clears** the check box as discussed in Section C.2.
Question-mark buttons	Display help messages related to a dialog box. Dialog boxes that do not contain a question-mark button typically contain a command button labeled **Help** that performs this function. (Minitab dialog boxes contain only Help command buttons.)

C.4 Useful Keys and Keystroke Combinations

In Microsoft Excel and Minitab, certain keystrokes and keystroke combinations (one or more keys held down as you press another key) represent useful shortcuts. For data entry, pressing the **Backspace** key when typing an entry erases typed characters to the left of the current position, one character at a time. Pressing the **Delete** key erases characters to the right of the cursor, one character at a time. Pressing either the **Enter** or **Tab** keys finalizes an entry typed into a worksheet cell.

For program functions, the **Esc** key cancels a dialog box or action and is often equivalent to clicking a dialog box's **Cancel** button. Pressing the combination **Ctrl+C** (while holding down the **Ctrl** key, press the **C** key) copies a worksheet entry and pressing **Crtl+V** can paste that copy into a second worksheet cell. Pressing the combinations **Ctrl+P** and **Ctrl+S** are shortcuts to printing and saving things, respectively. When all else fails, pressing **F1** (function key #1) usually displays the help system for the program you are using.

C.5 Conventions Used in this Book

In its instructions for Microsoft Excel and Minitab, this book uses several typographic conventions. In the previous section, you have already been introduced to the convention used for a keystroke combination (e.g., **Ctrl+C**). Throughout this book, the targets of mousing operations are boldfaced, as in "Click **Labels**" or "Click **OK**." For dialog boxes that are divided into subtitled areas or tabs, the book identifies the area or tab as in "click **All** in the **Page range** section" or "in the **Context** tab of the Help dialog box, click the first entry." When object names or labels can vary due to context, the book uses italics as a placeholder for a specific object, as in "Select *variable column*."

To describe a sequence of menu bar or ribbon selections, the book uses an arrow symbol to link selections. For example, when the book says, "**File ➔ New**," first select File and then from the list of choices that appears, select New. ("**File ➔ New**" would be a valid sequence in Excel 97–2003 and in Minitab; the equivalent Excel 2007 sequence would be "**Office Button ➔ New**.") In the PHStat2 appendices, selection sequences are given relative to the PHStat menu, for example, as **PHStat ➔ Descriptive Statistics ➔ Boxplot**. If you use Excel 2007, you will need to click the **Add-Ins** ribbon tab first in order to use these selection sequences.

APPENDIX D · Student CD-ROM Contents

D.1 Student CD-ROM Overview

The Student CD-ROM contains the program and data files that support your learning of statistics with this book. The CD-ROM contains a special menu through which you copy or set up files to your system.

When inserted into a Windows XP or Windows Vista system that has AutoPlay enabled, this special menu will launch automatically. If the special menu does not launch, you can manually launch it by running the **run.exe** file in the root folder of the CD-ROM. If you experience a problem, review the CD readme file (readme.txt), also located in the root folder, for additional information including how to obtain free technical support.

The special menu contains the following clickable choices (subject to change as documented in the CD readme.txt file):

- View CD readme file
- Unzip Data Files
- Unzip Case Files
- Unzip Visual Explorations in Statistics
- Set up PHStat2

- View PHStat2 readme file
- Exit

Clicking **Unzip Data Files** leads to a second menu in which you can choose to copy the data files used in problems and examples as a set of Microsoft Excel workbook (**.xls**) files, a set of Minitab worksheet (**.mtw**) files, or a set of SPSS worksheet (**.sav**) files. When you click **Unzip Excel data files**, you also copy all of the Excel workbooks described and used in the end-of-chapter Excel appendices. To return to the original menu, click the **BACK** link at the bottom of the menu.

Clicking **Unzip Case Files** leads to a second menu in which you can choose to copy the files used in the "Managing the *Springville Herald*" case or the files used in the end-of-chapter Web Cases. To return to the original menu, click the **BACK** link at the bottom of the menu.

Clicking **Unzip Visual Explorations in Statistics** copies the files needed to use the Visual Explorations in Statistics add-in (`Visual Explorations.xla`) in Microsoft Excel. If you plan to use this add-in, review Section E1.8 "Using Add-Ins" that begins on page 19 to make sure your copy of Microsoft Excel is properly configured to allow the use of this add-in.

Clicking **Set up PHStat2** begins the program that sets up PHStat2 version 2.8.1 on your system. You should not click this choice until you have first clicked **View PHStat2 readme file** and have read the technical requirements and operational procedures needed to ensure that PHStat2 gets properly set up on your system.

To repeat, if you experience a problem, review the CD readme file (readme.txt), located in the CD-ROM root folder, for additional information about the CD-ROM as well as instructions for obtaining free technical support.

Section D.2 lists the data files that get copied to your system when you unzip a set of data files.

D.2 Data File Descriptions

The following presents in alphabetical order, a listing of the data files that can be found in the **Excel Data Files, Minitab Data Files** and **SPSS Files** folders. Elsewhere in this book, these file names appear in a special typeface, for example as `Mutual Funds`.

AAAMILEAGE Gasoline mileage from AAA members and combined city-highway driving gasoline mileage according to current government standards (Chapter 10)

ADVERTISE Sales (in thousands of dollars), radio ads (in thousands of dollars), and newspaper ads (in thousands of dollars) for 22 cities (Chapter 13)

ANGLE Subgroup number and angle (Chapter 14)

ANSCOMBE Data sets A, B, C, and D—each with 11 pairs of *X* and *Y* values (Chapter 12)

AUTO Miles per gallon, horsepower, and weight (in pounds) for a sample of 50 car models (Chapter 13)

BANK1 Waiting time (in minutes) spent by a sample of 15 customers at a bank located in a commercial district (Chapters 3, 9, 10)

BANK2 Waiting time (in minutes) spent by a sample of 15 customers at a bank located in a residential area (Chapters 3, 10)

BANKING Banking preference and percentage (Chapter 2)

BANKTIME Waiting times (in minutes) of bank customers (Chapter 14)

BANKYIELD Yield for money market account and yield for five-year CD (Chapters 3, 10)

BB2007 Team, league (0 = American, 1 = National), wins, earned run average, runs scored, hits allowed, walks allowed, saves, errors (Chapters 12 and 13)

BBCOST Team and cost of attending a game (Chapters 2 and 6)

BBREVENUE Team, value (in millions of dollars), and revenue (in millions of dollars) (Chapter 12)

BESTREST State, city, restaurant, hotel, cost (estimated price of dinner, including one drink and tip), and rating (1 to 100, with 1 the top-rated restaurant) (Chapter 3)

BREAKSTW Breaking strength for operators (rows) and machines (columns) (Chapter 10)

BULBS Length of life of 40 lightbulbs from manufacturer A (=1) and 40 lightbulbs from manufacturer B (=2) (Chapters 2, 10)

CANISTER Day and number of nonconforming film canisters (Chapter 14)

CDYIELD Yield of money market account, 6-month CD, 1-year CD, 2.5-year CD, and 5-year CD (Chapter 10)

CEO Company, industry, and total direct compensation of CEOs (Chapters 2, 3)

CHICKEN Sandwich, calories, fat (in grams), saturated fat (in grams), carbohydrates (in grams), and sodium (in milligrams) (Chapters 2, 3, 6, 8)

CIRCULATION Magazine, reported newsstand sales (in thousands), and audited newsstand sales (in thousands) (Chapter 12)

CLOSING Rank, state, and closing costs (Chapter 6)

COFFEE Rating of coffees, by expert and brand (Chapter 10)

COFFEEDRINK Product, calories, and fat in coffee drinks (Chapters 3, 12)

COLA Sales for normal and end-aisle locations (Chapter 10)

COLASPC Day, total number of cans filled, and number of unacceptable cans (over a 22-day period) (Chapter 14)

COLLEGES BASKETBALL School, coach's salary for 2005–2006, expenses for 2004–2005, revenues for 2004–2005 (in millions of dollars), and winning percentage in 2005–2006 (Chapters 2, 3, 12)

COLLEGETUITION State, tuition, and change in tuition (Chapter 3)

CONCRETE1 Compressive strength after two days and seven days (Chapter 10)

COST OF LIVING City, overall cost rating, apartment rent, and costs of a cup of coffee, a hamburger, dry cleaning a men's suit, toothpaste, and movie tickets (Chapters 2, 3)

CRACK Type of crack and crack size (Chapter 10)

DARK CHOCOLATE Cost ($) per ounce of dark chocolate bars (Chapters 2, 3, and 8)

DELIVERY Customer number, number of cases, and delivery time in minutes (Chapter 12)

DIGITALCAMERAS Battery life, camera type, life for subcompact cameras, life for compact cameras (Chapter 10)

DINNER Time to prepare and cook dinner (Chapter 9)

DOMESTICBEER Brand, alcohol percentage, calories, and carbohydrates in U.S. domestic beers (Chapters 2, 3, 6, 13)

DOWMARKETCAP Company, ticker symbol, and market capitalization, in billions of dollars (Chapter 3)

DRILL Time to drill additional 5 feet (in minutes), depth (in feet), and type of hole (dry or wet) (Chapter 13)

DRINK Amount of soft drink filled in a subgroup of 50 consecutive 2-liter bottles (Chapters 2, 9)

ENERGY State and per-capita kilowatt hour use (Chapter 3)

ERRORSPC Number of nonconforming items and number of accounts processed over 39 days (Chapter 14)

ERWAITING Emergency room waiting time (in minutes) at the main facility and at satellite 1, satellite 2, and satellite 3 (Chapter 10)

FIRSTQUARTER Daily closing price of gold, silver, the S&P 500, and the NASDAQ for each trading day in the first quarter of 2008 (Chapter 12)

FORCE Force required to break an insulator (Chapters 2, 3, 8, 9)

FOULSPC Number of foul shots made and number taken over 40 days (Chapter 14)

FUNDTRAN Day, number of new investigations, and number of investigations closed over a 30-day period (Chapter 14)

FURNITURE Days between receipt and resolution of a sample of 50 complaints regarding purchased furniture (Chapters 2, 3, 8, 9)

GASPRICES Week and price per gallon, in cents (Chapter 2)

GCROSLYN Address, appraised value, location, property size (acres), house size, age, number of rooms, number of bathrooms, and number of cars that can be parked in the garage in Glen Cove and Roslyn, New York (Chapter 13)

GLENCOVE Address, appraised value, property size (acres), house size, age, number of rooms, number of bath-rooms, and number of cars that can be parked in the garage in Glen Cove, New York (Chapter 13)

GOLFBALL Distance for designs 1, 2, 3, and 4 (Chapter 10)

GPIGMAT GMAT scores and GPI for 20 students (Chapter 12)

GRADSURVEY Gender, age (as of last birthday), height (in inches), major, current cumulative grade point average, undergraduate area of specialization, undergraduate cumulative grade point average, GMAT score, current employment status, number of different full-time jobs held in the past 10 years, expected salary upon completion of MBA (in thousands of dollars), anticipated salary after 5 years of experience after MBA (in thousands of dollars), satisfaction with student advisement services on campus, and amount spent for books and supplies this semester (Chapters 1, 2, 3, 4, 6, 8, 10, 11)

GRANULE Granule loss in Boston and Vermont shingles (Chapters 3, 8, 9, 10)

HARNSWELL Day and diameter of cam rollers (in inches) for samples of five parts produced in each of 30 batches (Chapter 14)

HOSPADM Day, number of admissions, mean processing time (in hours), range of processing times, and proportion of laboratory rework (over a 30-day period) (Chapter 14)

HOTEL1 Day, number of rooms, number of nonconforming rooms per day over a 28-day period, and proportion of nonconforming items (Chapter 14)

HOTEL2 Day and delivery time for subgroups of five luggage deliveries per day over a 28-day period (Chapter 14)

HOTELS Year and room cost ($) (Chapter 2)

HOUSE1 Selling price (in thousands of dollars), assessed value (in thousands of dollars), type (new = 0, old = 1), and time period of sale for 30 houses (Chapters 12, 13)

HOUSE2 Assessed value (in thousands of dollars), size (in thousands of square feet), and age (in years) for 15 houses (Chapters 12, 13)

HOUSE3 Assessed value (in thousands of dollars), size (in thousands of square feet), and presence of a fireplace for 15 houses (Chapter 13)

INSURANCE Processing time for insurance policies (Chapters 3, 8, 9)

INTAGLIO Surface hardness of untreated and treated steel plates (Chapter 10)

INVOICE Number of invoices processed and amount of time (in hours) for 32 days (Chapter 12)

INVOICES Amount recorded (in dollars) from a sample of 12 sales invoices (Chapter 9)

KEYBOARD DEFECTS Defect and frequency (Chapter 2)

LARGEST BONDS Five-year return of bond funds (Chapter 3)

LUGGAGE   Delivery time, in minutes, for luggage in Wing A and Wing B of a hotel (Chapter 10)

MEASUREMENT   Sample, in-line measurement, and analytical lab measurement (Chapter 10)

MEDREC   Day, number of discharged patients, and number of records not processed for a 30-day period (Chapter 14)

MILEAGE   Mileage of autos calculated by owner, currently reported by the government, and forecasted according to government plans (Chapters 2, 3, 12)

MIXEDCOSTS   Total maintenance costs and patient days (Chapter 12)

MOISTURE   Moisture content of Boston shingles and Vermont shingles (Chapter 9)

MOVIE   Box office gross (in millions) and DVD sales (in thousands) (Chapter 12)

MOVIEPRICES   Movie chain and prices (Chapters 2, 3, 8, 9)

MOVIES   Year and movie attendance (Chapter 2)

MOVING   Labor hours, cubic feet, number of large pieces of furniture, and availability of an elevator (Chapters 12, 13)

MUTUALFUNDS   Category, objective, assets, fees, expense ratio, 2006 return, three-year return, five-year return, and risk (Chapters 2, 3, 4, 6, 8, 10, 11)

MYELOMA   Patient, measurement before transplant, and measurement after transplant (Chapter 10)

NBA2008   Team, number of wins, field goal (shots made) percentage (for team, and opponent) (Chapter 13)

NEIGHBOR   Selling price (in thousands of dollars), number of rooms, and neighborhood location (east = 0, west = 1) for 20 houses (Chapter 13)

NYSE   Day, volume in billions, and value in billions of dollars (Chapter 6)

O RING   Flight number, temperature, and O-ring damage index (Chapter 12)

OMNIPOWER   Bars sold, price (in cents), and promotion expenses (in dollars) (Chapter 13)

ORDER   Time in a restaurant (Chapter 8)

PALLET   Weight of Boston and weight of Vermont shingles (Chapters 2, 8, 9, 10)

PARACHUTE   Tensile strength of parachutes from suppliers 1, 2, 3, and 4 (Chapter 10)

PEN   Gender, ad, and product rating (Chapter 10)

PERFORM   Performance rating before and after motivational training (Chapter 10)

PETFOOD   Shelf space (in feet), weekly sales (in dollars), and aisle location (back = 0, front = 1) (Chapters 12, 13)

PHILLIES   Attendance, temperature, winning percentage, opponent winning percentage, weekend (0 = no, 1 = yes) and promotion (0 = no, 1 = yes) (Chapter 13)

PHONE   Time (in minutes) to clear telephone line problems and location (I and II) for samples of 20 customer problems reported to each of the two office locations (Chapter 10)

PIZZATIME   Time period, delivery time for local restaurant, delivery time for national chain (Chapter 10)

PROPERTYTAXES   State and property taxes per capita (Chapters 2, 6)

PROTEIN   Calories (in grams), protein, percentage of calories from fat, percentage of calories from saturated fat, and cholesterol (in mg) for 25 popular protein foods (Chapter 2)

PUMPKIN   Circumference and weight of pumpkins (Chapter 12)

REDWOOD   Height, diameter, and bark thickness (Chapter 13)

RENT   Monthly rental cost (in dollars) and apartment size (in square footage) for a sample of 25 apartments (Chapter 12)

RESTAURANTS   Location, food rating, decor rating, service rating, summated rating, coded location (0 = urban, 1 = suburban), and price of restaurants (Chapters 2, 10, 12, 13)

RUDYBIRD   Day, total cases sold, and cases of Rudybird sold (Chapter 14)

SAVINGS RATE   Bank, money market rate, one-year CD rate, and five-year CD rate (Chapters 2, 3, 6)

SEALANT   Sample number, sealant strength for Boston shingles, and sealant strength for Vermont shingles (Chapter 14)

SEDANS   Model and miles per gallon (Chapters 3 and 8)

SH2   Day and number of calls received at the help desk (Chapters 2, 3)

SH8   Rate ($) willing to pay for the newspaper (Chapter 8)

SH9   Blackness of newsprint (Chapter 9)

SH10-1   Length of early calls (in seconds), length of late calls (in seconds), and difference (in seconds) (Chapter 10)

SH10-2   Call, presentation plan (structured = 1, semistructured = 2, unstructured = 3), and length of call (in seconds) (Chapter 10)

SH12   Hours per month spent telemarketing and number of new subscriptions per month over a 24-month period (Chapter 12)

SH13   Hours per week spent telemarketing, number of new subscriptions, and type of presentation (Chapter 13)

SH14-1   Day, number of ads with errors, number of ads, and number of errors over a 25-day period (Chapter 14)

SH14-2   Day and newsprint blackness measures for each of five spots made over 25 consecutive weekdays (Chapter 14)

SITE   Store number, square footage (in thousands of square feet), and sales (in millions of dollars) in 14 Sunflowers Apparel stores (Chapter 12)

SPENDING   State and per-capita federal spending ($000) in 2004 (Chapters 2, 3)

SPONGE Day, number of sponges produced, number of nonconforming sponges, proportion of nonconforming sponges (Chapter 14)

SPORTING Sales, age, annual population growth, income, percentage with high school diploma, and percentage with college diploma (Chapter 12)

SPWATER Sample number and amount of magnesium (part per millions) (Chapter 14)

STANDBY Standby hours, staff, remote hours, Dubner hours, and labor hours for 26 weeks (Chapter 13)

STATES State, commuting time, percentage of homes with more than eight rooms, median income, and percentage of housing that costs more than 30% of family income (Chapter 2)

STEEL Error in actual length and specified length (Chapters 2, 6, 8, 9)

STOCKS2008 Date, Week, closing weekly stock price for S&P, IBM, Apple, and GE (Chapters 2, 12)

STUDYTIME Gender and study time (Chapter 10)

SUPERMARKET Day, number of customers, and checkout time (in minutes) (Chapter 12)

SUV Model, miles per gallon (Chapters 3, 8)

TAX Quarterly sales tax receipts (in thousands of dollars) for 50 business establishments (Chapter 3)

TEA3 Sample number and weight of tea bags (Chapter 14)

TEABAGS Weight of tea bags (Chapters 3, 8, 9)

TELESPC Number of orders and number of corrections over 30 days (Chapter 14)

TENSILE Sample number and strength (Chapter 14)

TEXTBOOK Textbook, book store price, and Amazon price (Chapter 10)

THEMEPARKS Name of location and admission price for one-day tickets (Chapter 3)

TIMES Times to get ready (Chapter 3)

TRADE Day, number of undesirable trades, and number of total trades made over a 30-day period (Chapter 14)

TRAINING Assembly time and training program (team-based = 0, individual-based = 1) (Chapter 10)

TRANSMIT Day and number of errors in transmission (Chapter 14)

TRANSPORT Days and patient transport times (in minutes) for samples of four patients per day over a 30-day period (Chapter 14)

TRASHBAGS Weight required to break four brands of trash bags (Chapter 10)

TROUGH Width of trough (Chapters 2, 3, 8, 9)

TUITION2006 School, in-state tuition and fees, and out-of-state tuition and fees (Chapter 3)

TVCHANNELS Year and the number of TV channels received (Chapter 2)

UNDERGRADSURVEY Gender, age (*as of last birthday*), height (*in inches*), class designation, major, graduate school intention, cumulative grade point average, expected starting salary (in thousands of dollars), anticipated salary after five years of experience (in thousands of dollars), current employment status, number of campus club/group/organization/team affiliations, satisfaction with student advisement services on campus, and amount spent on books and supplies this semester (Chapters 1, 2, 3, 4, 6, 8, 10, 11)

UNEMPLOYMENT Year, month, and monthly unemployment rates (Chapter 2)

UTILITY Utility charges for 50 one-bedroom apartments (Chapters 2, 6)

VB Time (in minutes) for nine students to write and run a Visual Basic program (Chapter 10)

WAIT Waiting times and seating times, in minutes (Chapter 6)

WAL-MART Quarter and quarterly revenues (Chapter 2)

WARECOST Distribution cost (in thousands of dollars), sales (in thousands of dollars), and number of orders for 24 months (Chapter 13)

WAREHSE Number of units handled per day and employee number (Chapter 14)

WHOLEFOODS1 Item, price at Whole Foods, and price at Fairway (Chapter 10)

WONDERLIC School, average Wonderlic score of football players trying out for the NFL, and graduation rate (Chapters 2, 3, 12)

YARN Breaking strength, pressure, yarn sample, and side-by-side aspect (nozzle = 1, opposite = 2) (Chapter 10)

E Tables

TABLE E.1
Table of Random Numbers

	Column							
Row	00000 12345	00001 67890	11111 12345	11112 67890	22222 12345	22223 67890	33333 12345	33334 67890
01	49280	88924	35779	00283	81163	07275	89863	02348
02	61870	41657	07468	08612	98083	97349	20775	45091
03	43898	65923	25078	86129	78496	97653	91550	08078
04	62993	93912	30454	84598	56095	20664	12872	64647
05	33850	58555	51438	85507	71865	79488	76783	31708
06	97340	03364	88472	04334	63919	36394	11095	92470
07	70543	29776	10087	10072	55980	64688	68239	20461
08	89382	93809	00796	95945	34101	81277	66090	88872
09	37818	72142	67140	50785	22380	16703	53362	44940
10	60430	22834	14130	96593	23298	56203	92671	15925
11	82975	66158	84731	19436	55790	69229	28661	13675
12	30987	71938	40355	54324	08401	26299	49420	59208
13	55700	24586	93247	32596	11865	63397	44251	43189
14	14756	23997	78643	75912	83832	32768	18928	57070
15	32166	53251	70654	92827	63491	04233	33825	69662
16	23236	73751	31888	81718	06546	83246	47651	04877
17	45794	26926	15130	82455	78305	55058	52551	47182
18	09893	20505	14225	68514	47427	56788	96297	78822
19	54382	74598	91499	14523	68479	27686	46162	83554
20	94750	89923	37089	20048	80336	94598	26940	36858
21	70297	34135	53140	33340	42050	82341	44104	82949
22	85157	47954	32979	26575	57600	40881	12250	73742
23	11100	02340	12860	74697	96644	89439	28707	25815
24	36871	50775	30592	57143	17381	68856	25853	35041
25	23913	48357	63308	16090	51690	54607	72407	55538
26	79348	36085	27973	65157	07456	22255	25626	57054
27	92074	54641	53673	54421	18130	60103	69593	49464
28	06873	21440	75593	41373	49502	17972	82578	16364
29	12478	37622	99659	31065	83613	69889	58869	29571
30	57175	55564	65411	42547	70457	03426	72937	83792
31	91616	11075	80103	07831	59309	13276	26710	73000
32	78025	73539	14621	39044	47450	03197	12787	47709
33	27587	67228	80145	10175	12822	86687	65530	49325
34	16690	20427	04251	64477	73709	73945	92396	68263
35	70183	58065	65489	31833	82093	16747	10386	59293
36	90730	35385	15679	99742	50866	78028	75573	67257
37	10934	93242	13431	24590	02770	48582	00906	58595
38	82462	30166	79613	47416	13389	80268	05085	96666
39	27463	10433	07606	16285	93699	60912	94532	95632
40	02979	52997	09079	92709	90110	47506	53693	49892
41	46888	69929	75233	52507	32097	37594	10067	67327
42	53638	83161	08289	12639	08141	12640	28437	09268
43	82433	61427	17239	89160	19666	08814	37841	12847
44	35766	31672	50082	22795	66948	65581	84393	15890
45	10853	42581	08792	13257	61973	24450	52351	16602
46	20341	27398	72906	63955	17276	10646	74692	48438
47	54458	90542	77563	51839	52901	53355	83281	19177
48	26337	66530	16687	35179	46560	00123	44546	79896
49	34314	23729	85264	05575	96855	23820	11091	79821
50	28603	10708	68933	34189	92166	15181	66628	58599
51	66194	28926	99547	16625	45515	67953	12108	57846
52	78240	43195	24837	32511	70880	22070	52622	61881
53	00833	88000	67299	68215	11274	55624	32991	17436
54	12111	86683	61270	58036	64192	90611	15145	01748
55	47189	99951	05755	03834	43782	90599	40282	51417
56	76396	72486	62423	27618	84184	78922	73561	52818
57	46409	17469	32483	09083	76175	19985	26309	91536

TABLE E.1

Table of Random Numbers (*Continued*)

Row	Column 00000 12345	00001 67890	11111 12345	11112 67890	22222 12345	22223 67890	33333 12345	33334 67890
58	74626	22111	87286	46772	42243	68046	44250	42439
59	34450	81974	93723	49023	58432	67083	36876	93391
60	36327	72135	33005	28701	34710	49359	50693	89311
61	74185	77536	84825	09934	99103	09325	67389	45869
62	12296	41623	62873	37943	25584	09609	63360	47270
63	90822	60280	88925	99610	42772	60561	76873	04117
64	72121	79152	96591	90305	10189	79778	68016	13747
65	95268	41377	25684	08151	61816	58555	54305	86189
66	92603	09091	75884	93424	72586	88903	30061	14457
67	18813	90291	05275	01223	79607	95426	34900	09778
68	38840	26903	28624	67157	51986	42865	14508	49315
69	05959	33836	53758	16562	41081	38012	41230	20528
70	85141	21155	99212	32685	51403	31926	69813	58781
71	75047	59643	31074	38172	03718	32119	69506	67143
72	30752	95260	68032	62871	58781	34143	68790	69766
73	22986	82575	42187	62295	84295	30634	66562	31442
74	99439	86692	90348	66036	48399	73451	26698	39437
75	20389	93029	11881	71685	65452	89047	63669	02656
76	39249	05173	68256	36359	20250	68686	05947	09335
77	96777	33605	29481	20063	09398	01843	35139	61344
78	04860	32918	10798	50492	52655	33359	94713	28393
79	41613	42375	00403	03656	77580	87772	86877	57085
80	17930	00794	53836	53692	67135	98102	61912	11246
81	24649	31845	25736	75231	83808	98917	93829	99430
82	79899	34061	54308	59358	56462	58166	97302	86828
83	76801	49594	81002	30397	52728	15101	72070	33706
84	36239	63636	38140	65731	39788	06872	38971	53363
85	07392	64449	17886	63632	53995	17574	22247	62607
86	67133	04181	33874	98835	67453	59734	76381	63455
87	77759	31504	32832	70861	15152	29733	75371	39174
88	85992	72268	42920	20810	29361	51423	90306	73574
89	79553	75952	54116	65553	47139	60579	09165	85490
90	41101	17336	48951	53674	17880	45260	08575	49321
91	36191	17095	32123	91576	84221	78902	82010	30847
92	62329	63898	23268	74283	26091	68409	69704	82267
93	14751	13151	93115	01437	56945	89661	67680	79790
94	48462	59278	44185	29616	76537	19589	83139	28454
95	29435	88105	59651	44391	74588	55114	80834	85686
96	28340	29285	12965	14821	80425	16602	44653	70467
97	02167	58940	27149	80242	10587	79786	34959	75339
98	17864	00991	39557	54981	23588	81914	37609	13128
99	79675	80605	60059	35862	00254	36546	21545	78179
00	72335	82037	92003	34100	29879	46613	89720	13274

Source: *Data partially extracted from the Rand Corporation,* A Million Random Digits with 100,000 Normal Deviates *(Glencoe, IL, The Free Press, 1955).*

TABLE E.2

The Cumulative Standardized Normal Distribution

Entry represents area under the cumulative standardized
normal distribution from $-\infty$ to Z

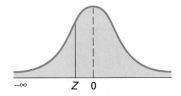

	Cumulative Probabilities									
Z	0.00	0.01	0.02	0.03	0.04	0.05	0.06	0.07	0.08	0.09
−6.0	0.000000001									
−5.5	0.000000019									
−5.0	0.000000287									
−4.5	0.000003398									
−4.0	0.000031671									
−3.9	0.00005	0.00005	0.00004	0.00004	0.00004	0.00004	0.00004	0.00004	0.00003	0.00003
−3.8	0.00007	0.00007	0.00007	0.00006	0.00006	0.00006	0.00006	0.00005	0.00005	0.00005
−3.7	0.00011	0.00010	0.00010	0.00010	0.00009	0.00009	0.00008	0.00008	0.00008	0.00008
−3.6	0.00016	0.00015	0.00015	0.00014	0.00014	0.00013	0.00013	0.00012	0.00012	0.00011
−3.5	0.00023	0.00022	0.00022	0.00021	0.00020	0.00019	0.00019	0.00018	0.00017	0.00017
−3.4	0.00034	0.00032	0.00031	0.00030	0.00029	0.00028	0.00027	0.00026	0.00025	0.00024
−3.3	0.00048	0.00047	0.00045	0.00043	0.00042	0.00040	0.00039	0.00038	0.00036	0.00035
−3.2	0.00069	0.00066	0.00064	0.00062	0.00060	0.00058	0.00056	0.00054	0.00052	0.00050
−3.1	0.00097	0.00094	0.00090	0.00087	0.00084	0.00082	0.00079	0.00076	0.00074	0.00071
−3.0	0.00135	0.00131	0.00126	0.00122	0.00118	0.00114	0.00111	0.00107	0.00103	0.00100
−2.9	0.0019	0.0018	0.0018	0.0017	0.0016	0.0016	0.0015	0.0015	0.0014	0.0014
−2.8	0.0026	0.0025	0.0024	0.0023	0.0023	0.0022	0.0021	0.0021	0.0020	0.0019
−2.7	0.0035	0.0034	0.0033	0.0032	0.0031	0.0030	0.0029	0.0028	0.0027	0.0026
−2.6	0.0047	0.0045	0.0044	0.0043	0.0041	0.0040	0.0039	0.0038	0.0037	0.0036
−2.5	0.0062	0.0060	0.0059	0.0057	0.0055	0.0054	0.0052	0.0051	0.0049	0.0048
−2.4	0.0082	0.0080	0.0078	0.0075	0.0073	0.0071	0.0069	0.0068	0.0066	0.0064
−2.3	0.0107	0.0104	0.0102	0.0099	0.0096	0.0094	0.0091	0.0089	0.0087	0.0084
−2.2	0.0139	0.0136	0.0132	0.0129	0.0125	0.0122	0.0119	0.0116	0.0113	0.0110
−2.1	0.0179	0.0174	0.0170	0.0166	0.0162	0.0158	0.0154	0.0150	0.0146	0.0143
−2.0	0.0228	0.0222	0.0217	0.0212	0.0207	0.0202	0.0197	0.0192	0.0188	0.0183
−1.9	0.0287	0.0281	0.0274	0.0268	0.0262	0.0256	0.0250	0.0244	0.0239	0.0233
−1.8	0.0359	0.0351	0.0344	0.0336	0.0329	0.0322	0.0314	0.0307	0.0301	0.0294
−1.7	0.0446	0.0436	0.0427	0.0418	0.0409	0.0401	0.0392	0.0384	0.0375	0.0367
−1.6	0.0548	0.0537	0.0526	0.0516	0.0505	0.0495	0.0485	0.0475	0.0465	0.0455
−1.5	0.0668	0.0655	0.0643	0.0630	0.0618	0.0606	0.0594	0.0582	0.0571	0.0559
−1.4	0.0808	0.0793	0.0778	0.0764	0.0749	0.0735	0.0721	0.0708	0.0694	0.0681
−1.3	0.0968	0.0951	0.0934	0.0918	0.0901	0.0885	0.0869	0.0853	0.0838	0.0823
−1.2	0.1151	0.1131	0.1112	0.1093	0.1075	0.1056	0.1038	0.1020	0.1003	0.0985
−1.1	0.1357	0.1335	0.1314	0.1292	0.1271	0.1251	0.1230	0.1210	0.1190	0.1170
−1.0	0.1587	0.1562	0.1539	0.1515	0.1492	0.1469	0.1446	0.1423	0.1401	0.1379
−0.9	0.1841	0.1814	0.1788	0.1762	0.1736	0.1711	0.1685	0.1660	0.1635	0.1611
−0.8	0.2119	0.2090	0.2061	0.2033	0.2005	0.1977	0.1949	0.1922	0.1894	0.1867
−0.7	0.2420	0.2388	0.2358	0.2327	0.2296	0.2266	0.2236	0.2206	0.2177	0.2148
−0.6	0.2743	0.2709	0.2676	0.2643	0.2611	0.2578	0.2546	0.2514	0.2482	0.2451
−0.5	0.3085	0.3050	0.3015	0.2981	0.2946	0.2912	0.2877	0.2843	0.2810	0.2776
−0.4	0.3446	0.3409	0.3372	0.3336	0.3300	0.3264	0.3228	0.3192	0.3156	0.3121
−0.3	0.3821	0.3783	0.3745	0.3707	0.3669	0.3632	0.3594	0.3557	0.3520	0.3483
−0.2	0.4207	0.4168	0.4129	0.4090	0.4052	0.4013	0.3974	0.3936	0.3897	0.3859
−0.1	0.4602	0.4562	0.4522	0.4483	0.4443	0.4404	0.4364	0.4325	0.4286	0.4247
−0.0	0.5000	0.4960	0.4920	0.4880	0.4840	0.4801	0.4761	0.4721	0.4681	0.4641

TABLE E.2

The Cumulative Standardized Normal Distribution (*Continued*)

Entry represents area under the cumulative standardized
normal distribution from $-\infty$ to Z

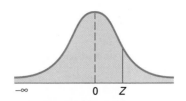

	Cumulative Probabilities									
Z	**0.00**	**0.01**	**0.02**	**0.03**	**0.04**	**0.05**	**0.06**	**0.07**	**0.08**	**0.09**
0.0	0.5000	0.5040	0.5080	0.5120	0.5160	0.5199	0.5239	0.5279	0.5319	0.5359
0.1	0.5398	0.5438	0.5478	0.5517	0.5557	0.5596	0.5636	0.5675	0.5714	0.5753
0.2	0.5793	0.5832	0.5871	0.5910	0.5948	0.5987	0.6026	0.6064	0.6103	0.6141
0.3	0.6179	0.6217	0.6255	0.6293	0.6331	0.6368	0.6406	0.6443	0.6480	0.6517
0.4	0.6554	0.6591	0.6628	0.6664	0.6700	0.6736	0.6772	0.6808	0.6844	0.6879
0.5	0.6915	0.6950	0.6985	0.7019	0.7054	0.7088	0.7123	0.7157	0.7190	0.7224
0.6	0.7257	0.7291	0.7324	0.7357	0.7389	0.7422	0.7454	0.7486	0.7518	0.7549
0.7	0.7580	0.7612	0.7642	0.7673	0.7704	0.7734	0.7764	0.7794	0.7823	0.7852
0.8	0.7881	0.7910	0.7939	0.7967	0.7995	0.8023	0.8051	0.8078	0.8106	0.8133
0.9	0.8159	0.8186	0.8212	0.8238	0.8264	0.8289	0.8315	0.8340	0.8365	0.8389
1.0	0.8413	0.8438	0.8461	0.8485	0.8508	0.8531	0.8554	0.8577	0.8599	0.8621
1.1	0.8643	0.8665	0.8686	0.8708	0.8729	0.8749	0.8770	0.8790	0.8810	0.8830
1.2	0.8849	0.8869	0.8888	0.8907	0.8925	0.8944	0.8962	0.8980	0.8997	0.9015
1.3	0.9032	0.9049	0.9066	0.9082	0.9099	0.9115	0.9131	0.9147	0.9162	0.9177
1.4	0.9192	0.9207	0.9222	0.9236	0.9251	0.9265	0.9279	0.9292	0.9306	0.9319
1.5	0.9332	0.9345	0.9357	0.9370	0.9382	0.9394	0.9406	0.9418	0.9429	0.9441
1.6	0.9452	0.9463	0.9474	0.9484	0.9495	0.9505	0.9515	0.9525	0.9535	0.9545
1.7	0.9554	0.9564	0.9573	0.9582	0.9591	0.9599	0.9608	0.9616	0.9625	0.9633
1.8	0.9641	0.9649	0.9656	0.9664	0.9671	0.9678	0.9686	0.9693	0.9699	0.9706
1.9	0.9713	0.9719	0.9726	0.9732	0.9738	0.9744	0.9750	0.9756	0.9761	0.9767
2.0	0.9772	0.9778	0.9783	0.9788	0.9793	0.9798	0.9803	0.9808	0.9812	0.9817
2.1	0.9821	0.9826	0.9830	0.9834	0.9838	0.9842	0.9846	0.9850	0.9854	0.9857
2.2	0.9861	0.9864	0.9868	0.9871	0.9875	0.9878	0.9881	0.9884	0.9887	0.9890
2.3	0.9893	0.9896	0.9898	0.9901	0.9904	0.9906	0.9909	0.9911	0.9913	0.9916
2.4	0.9918	0.9920	0.9922	0.9925	0.9927	0.9929	0.9931	0.9932	0.9934	0.9936
2.5	0.9938	0.9940	0.9941	0.9943	0.9945	0.9946	0.9948	0.9949	0.9951	0.9952
2.6	0.9953	0.9955	0.9956	0.9957	0.9959	0.9960	0.9961	0.9962	0.9963	0.9964
2.7	0.9965	0.9966	0.9967	0.9968	0.9969	0.9970	0.9971	0.9972	0.9973	0.9974
2.8	0.9974	0.9975	0.9976	0.9977	0.9977	0.9978	0.9979	0.9979	0.9980	0.9981
2.9	0.9981	0.9982	0.9982	0.9983	0.9984	0.9984	0.9985	0.9985	0.9986	0.9986
3.0	0.99865	0.99869	0.99874	0.99878	0.99882	0.99886	0.99889	0.99893	0.99897	0.99900
3.1	0.99903	0.99906	0.99910	0.99913	0.99916	0.99918	0.99921	0.99924	0.99926	0.99929
3.2	0.99931	0.99934	0.99936	0.99938	0.99940	0.99942	0.99944	0.99946	0.99948	0.99950
3.3	0.99952	0.99953	0.99955	0.99957	0.99958	0.99960	0.99961	0.99962	0.99964	0.99965
3.4	0.99966	0.99968	0.99969	0.99970	0.99971	0.99972	0.99973	0.99974	0.99975	0.99976
3.5	0.99977	0.99978	0.99978	0.99979	0.99980	0.99981	0.99981	0.99982	0.99983	0.99983
3.6	0.99984	0.99985	0.99985	0.99986	0.99986	0.99987	0.99987	0.99988	0.99988	0.99989
3.7	0.99989	0.99990	0.99990	0.99990	0.99991	0.99991	0.99992	0.99992	0.99992	0.99992
3.8	0.99993	0.99993	0.99993	0.99994	0.99994	0.99994	0.99994	0.99995	0.99995	0.99995
3.9	0.99995	0.99995	0.99996	0.99996	0.99996	0.99996	0.99996	0.99996	0.99997	0.99997
4.0	0.999968329									
4.5	0.999996602									
5.0	0.999999713									
5.5	0.999999981									
6.0	0.999999999									

TABLE E.3
Critical Values of t

For a particular number of degrees of freedom, entry represents
the critical value of t corresponding to the cumulative probability
$(1 - \alpha)$ and a specified upper-tail area (α).

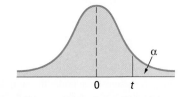

	Cumulative Probabilities					
	0.75	0.90	0.95	0.975	0.99	0.995
	Upper-Tail Areas					
Degrees of Freedom	0.25	0.10	0.05	0.025	0.01	0.005
1	1.0000	3.0777	6.3138	12.7062	31.8207	63.6574
2	0.8165	1.8856	2.9200	4.3027	6.9646	9.9248
3	0.7649	1.6377	2.3534	3.1824	4.5407	5.8409
4	0.7407	1.5332	2.1318	2.7764	3.7469	4.6041
5	0.7267	1.4759	2.0150	2.5706	3.3649	4.0322
6	0.7176	1.4398	1.9432	2.4469	3.1427	3.7074
7	0.7111	1.4149	1.8946	2.3646	2.9980	3.4995
8	0.7064	1.3968	1.8595	2.3060	2.8965	3.3554
9	0.7027	1.3830	1.8331	2.2622	2.8214	3.2498
10	0.6998	1.3722	1.8125	2.2281	2.7638	3.1693
11	0.6974	1.3634	1.7959	2.2010	2.7181	3.1058
12	0.6955	1.3562	1.7823	2.1788	2.6810	3.0545
13	0.6938	1.3502	1.7709	2.1604	2.6503	3.0123
14	0.6924	1.3450	1.7613	2.1448	2.6245	2.9768
15	0.6912	1.3406	1.7531	2.1315	2.6025	2.9467
16	0.6901	1.3368	1.7459	2.1199	2.5835	2.9208
17	0.6892	1.3334	1.7396	2.1098	2.5669	2.8982
18	0.6884	1.3304	1.7341	2.1009	2.5524	2.8784
19	0.6876	1.3277	1.7291	2.0930	2.5395	2.8609
20	0.6870	1.3253	1.7247	2.0860	2.5280	2.8453
21	0.6864	1.3232	1.7207	2.0796	2.5177	2.8314
22	0.6858	1.3212	1.7171	2.0739	2.5083	2.8188
23	0.6853	1.3195	1.7139	2.0687	2.4999	2.8073
24	0.6848	1.3178	1.7109	2.0639	2.4922	2.7969
25	0.6844	1.3163	1.7081	2.0595	2.4851	2.7874
26	0.6840	1.3150	1.7056	2.0555	2.4786	2.7787
27	0.6837	1.3137	1.7033	2.0518	2.4727	2.7707
28	0.6834	1.3125	1.7011	2.0484	2.4671	2.7633
29	0.6830	1.3114	1.6991	2.0452	2.4620	2.7564
30	0.6828	1.3104	1.6973	2.0423	2.4573	2.7500
31	0.6825	1.3095	1.6955	2.0395	2.4528	2.7440
32	0.6822	1.3086	1.6939	2.0369	2.4487	2.7385
33	0.6820	1.3077	1.6924	2.0345	2.4448	2.7333
34	0.6818	1.3070	1.6909	2.0322	2.4411	2.7284
35	0.6816	1.3062	1.6896	2.0301	2.4377	2.7238
36	0.6814	1.3055	1.6883	2.0281	2.4345	2.7195
37	0.6812	1.3049	1.6871	2.0262	2.4314	2.7154
38	0.6810	1.3042	1.6860	2.0244	2.4286	2.7116
39	0.6808	1.3036	1.6849	2.0227	2.4258	2.7079
40	0.6807	1.3031	1.6839	2.0211	2.4233	2.7045
41	0.6805	1.3025	1.6829	2.0195	2.4208	2.7012
42	0.6804	1.3020	1.6820	2.0181	2.4185	2.6981
43	0.6802	1.3016	1.6811	2.0167	2.4163	2.6951
44	0.6801	1.3011	1.6802	2.0154	2.4141	2.6923
45	0.6800	1.3006	1.6794	2.0141	2.4121	2.6896
46	0.6799	1.3002	1.6787	2.0129	2.4102	2.6870
47	0.6797	1.2998	1.6779	2.0117	2.4083	2.6846
48	0.6796	1.2994	1.6772	2.0106	2.4066	2.6822

Degrees of Freedom	Cumulative Probabilities					
	0.75	0.90	0.95	0.975	0.99	0.995
	Upper-Tail Areas					
	0.25	0.10	0.05	0.025	0.01	0.005
49	0.6795	1.2991	1.6766	2.0096	2.4049	2.6800
50	0.6794	1.2987	1.6759	2.0086	2.4033	2.6778
51	0.6793	1.2984	1.6753	2.0076	2.4017	2.6757
52	0.6792	1.2980	1.6747	2.0066	2.4002	2.6737
53	0.6791	1.2977	1.6741	2.0057	2.3988	2.6718
54	0.6791	1.2974	1.6736	2.0049	2.3974	2.6700
55	0.6790	1.2971	1.6730	2.0040	2.3961	2.6682
56	0.6789	1.2969	1.6725	2.0032	2.3948	2.6665
57	0.6788	1.2966	1.6720	2.0025	2.3936	2.6649
58	0.6787	1.2963	1.6716	2.0017	2.3924	2.6633
59	0.6787	1.2961	1.6711	2.0010	2.3912	2.6618
60	0.6786	1.2958	1.6706	2.0003	2.3901	2.6603
61	0.6785	1.2956	1.6702	1.9996	2.3890	2.6589
62	0.6785	1.2954	1.6698	1.9990	2.3880	2.6575
63	0.6784	1.2951	1.6694	1.9983	2.3870	2.6561
64	0.6783	1.2949	1.6690	1.9977	2.3860	2.6549
65	0.6783	1.2947	1.6686	1.9971	2.3851	2.6536
66	0.6782	1.2945	1.6683	1.9966	2.3842	2.6524
67	0.6782	1.2943	1.6679	1.9960	2.3833	2.6512
68	0.6781	1.2941	1.6676	1.9955	2.3824	2.6501
69	0.6781	1.2939	1.6672	1.9949	2.3816	2.6490
70	0.6780	1.2938	1.6669	1.9944	2.3808	2.6479
71	0.6780	1.2936	1.6666	1.9939	2.3800	2.6469
72	0.6779	1.2934	1.6663	1.9935	2.3793	2.6459
73	0.6779	1.2933	1.6660	1.9930	2.3785	2.6449
74	0.6778	1.2931	1.6657	1.9925	2.3778	2.6439
75	0.6778	1.2929	1.6654	1.9921	2.3771	2.6430
76	0.6777	1.2928	1.6652	1.9917	2.3764	2.6421
77	0.6777	1.2926	1.6649	1.9913	2.3758	2.6412
78	0.6776	1.2925	1.6646	1.9908	2.3751	2.6403
79	0.6776	1.2924	1.6644	1.9905	2.3745	2.6395
80	0.6776	1.2922	1.6641	1.9901	2.3739	2.6387
81	0.6775	1.2921	1.6639	1.9897	2.3733	2.6379
82	0.6775	1.2920	1.6636	1.9893	2.3727	2.6371
83	0.6775	1.2918	1.6634	1.9890	2.3721	2.6364
84	0.6774	1.2917	1.6632	1.9886	2.3716	2.6356
85	0.6774	1.2916	1.6630	1.9883	2.3710	2.6349
86	0.6774	1.2915	1.6628	1.9879	2.3705	2.6342
87	0.6773	1.2914	1.6626	1.9876	2.3700	2.6335
88	0.6773	1.2912	1.6624	1.9873	2.3695	2.6329
89	0.6773	1.2911	1.6622	1.9870	2.3690	2.6322
90	0.6772	1.2910	1.6620	1.9867	2.3685	2.6316
91	0.6772	1.2909	1.6618	1.9864	2.3680	2.6309
92	0.6772	1.2908	1.6616	1.9861	2.3676	2.6303
93	0.6771	1.2907	1.6614	1.9858	2.3671	2.6297
94	0.6771	1.2906	1.6612	1.9855	2.3667	2.6291
95	0.6771	1.2905	1.6611	1.9853	2.3662	2.6286
96	0.6771	1.2904	1.6609	1.9850	2.3658	2.6280
97	0.6770	1.2903	1.6607	1.9847	2.3654	2.6275
98	0.6770	1.2902	1.6606	1.9845	2.3650	2.6269
99	0.6770	1.2902	1.6604	1.9842	2.3646	2.6264
100	0.6770	1.2901	1.6602	1.9840	2.3642	2.6259
110	0.6767	1.2893	1.6588	1.9818	2.3607	2.6213
120	0.6765	1.2886	1.6577	1.9799	2.3578	2.6174
∞	0.6745	1.2816	1.6449	1.9600	2.3263	2.5758

TABLE E.4

Critical Values of χ^2

For a particular number of degrees of freedom, entry represents the critical value of χ^2 corresponding to the cumulative probability $(1 - \alpha)$ and a specified upper-tail area (α).

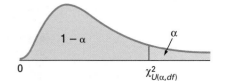

Degrees of Freedom	Cumulative Probabilities											
	0.005	0.01	0.025	0.05	0.10	0.25	0.75	0.90	0.95	0.975	0.99	0.995
	Upper-Tail Areas (α)											
	0.995	0.99	0.975	0.95	0.90	0.75	0.25	0.10	0.05	0.025	0.01	0.005
1			0.001	0.004	0.016	0.102	1.323	2.706	3.841	5.024	6.635	7.879
2	0.010	0.020	0.051	0.103	0.211	0.575	2.773	4.605	5.991	7.378	9.210	10.597
3	0.072	0.115	0.216	0.352	0.584	1.213	4.108	6.251	7.815	9.348	11.345	12.838
4	0.207	0.297	0.484	0.711	1.064	1.923	5.385	7.779	9.488	11.143	13.277	14.860
5	0.412	0.554	0.831	1.145	1.610	2.675	6.626	9.236	11.071	12.833	15.086	16.750
6	0.676	0.872	1.237	1.635	2.204	3.455	7.841	10.645	12.592	14.449	16.812	18.548
7	0.989	1.239	1.690	2.167	2.833	4.255	9.037	12.017	14.067	6.013	18.475	20.278
8	1.344	1.646	2.180	2.733	3.490	5.071	10.219	13.362	15.507	17.535	20.090	21.955
9	1.735	2.088	2.700	3.325	4.168	5.899	11.389	14.684	16.919	19.023	21.666	23.589
10	2.156	2.558	3.247	3.940	4.865	6.737	12.549	15.987	18.307	20.483	23.209	25.188
11	2.603	3.053	3.816	4.575	5.578	7.584	13.701	17.275	19.675	21.920	24.725	26.757
12	3.074	3.571	4.404	5.226	6.304	8.438	14.845	18.549	21.026	23.337	26.217	28.299
13	3.565	4.107	5.009	5.892	7.042	9.299	15.984	19.812	22.362	24.736	27.688	29.819
14	4.075	4.660	5.629	6.571	7.790	10.165	17.117	21.064	23.685	26.119	29.141	31.319
15	4.601	5.229	6.262	7.261	8.547	11.037	18.245	22.307	24.996	27.488	30.578	32.801
16	5.142	5.812	6.908	7.962	9.312	11.912	19.369	23.542	26.296	28.845	32.000	34.267
17	5.697	6.408	7.564	8.672	10.085	12.792	20.489	24.769	27.587	30.191	33.409	35.718
18	6.265	7.015	8.231	9.390	10.865	13.675	21.605	25.989	28.869	31.526	34.805	37.156
19	6.844	7.633	8.907	10.117	11.651	14.562	22.718	27.204	30.144	32.852	36.191	38.582
20	7.434	8.260	9.591	10.851	12.443	15.452	23.828	28.412	31.410	34.170	37.566	39.997
21	8.034	8.897	10.283	11.591	13.240	16.344	24.935	29.615	32.671	35.479	38.932	41.401
22	8.643	9.542	10.982	12.338	14.042	17.240	26.039	30.813	33.924	36.781	40.289	42.796
23	9.260	10.196	11.689	13.091	14.848	18.137	27.141	32.007	35.172	38.076	41.638	44.181
24	9.886	10.856	12.401	13.848	15.659	19.037	28.241	33.196	36.415	39.364	42.980	45.559
25	10.520	11.524	13.120	14.611	16.473	19.939	29.339	34.382	37.652	40.646	44.314	46.928
26	11.160	12.198	13.844	15.379	17.292	20.843	30.435	35.563	38.885	41.923	45.642	48.290
27	11.808	12.879	14.573	16.151	18.114	21.749	31.528	36.741	40.113	43.194	46.963	49.645
28	12.461	13.565	15.308	16.928	18.939	22.657	32.620	37.916	41.337	44.461	48.278	50.993
29	13.121	14.257	16.047	17.708	19.768	23.567	33.711	39.087	42.557	45.722	49.588	52.336
30	13.787	14.954	16.791	18.493	20.599	24.478	34.800	40.256	43.773	46.979	50.892	53.672

For larger values of degrees of freedom (df) the expression $Z = \sqrt{2\chi^2} - \sqrt{2(df) - 1}$ may be used and the resulting upper-tail area can be found from the cumulative standardized normal distribution (Table E.2).

TABLE E.5

Critical Values of F

For a particular combination of numerator and denominator degrees of freedom, entry represents the critical values of F corresponding to the cumulative probability $(1 - \alpha)$ and a specified upper-tail area (α).

α = 0.05

Cumulative Probabilities = 0.95

Upper-Tail Areas = 0.05

Numerator, df_1

Denominator, df_2	1	2	3	4	5	6	7	8	9	10	12	15	20	24	30	40	60	120	∞
1	161.40	199.50	215.70	224.60	230.20	234.00	236.80	238.90	240.50	241.90	243.90	245.90	248.00	249.10	250.10	251.10	252.20	253.30	254.30
2	18.51	19.00	19.16	19.25	19.30	19.33	19.35	19.37	19.38	19.40	19.41	19.43	19.45	19.45	19.46	19.47	19.48	19.49	19.50
3	10.13	9.55	9.28	9.12	9.01	8.94	8.89	8.85	8.81	8.79	8.74	8.70	8.66	8.64	8.62	8.59	8.57	8.55	8.53
4	7.71	6.94	6.59	6.39	6.26	6.16	6.09	6.04	6.00	5.96	5.91	5.86	5.80	5.77	5.75	5.72	5.69	5.66	5.63
5	6.61	5.79	5.41	5.19	5.05	4.95	4.88	4.82	4.77	4.74	4.68	4.62	4.56	4.53	4.50	4.46	4.43	4.40	4.36
6	5.99	5.14	4.76	4.53	4.39	4.28	4.21	4.15	4.10	4.06	4.00	3.94	3.87	3.84	3.81	3.77	3.74	3.70	3.67
7	5.59	4.74	4.35	4.12	3.97	3.87	3.79	3.73	3.68	3.64	3.57	3.51	3.44	3.41	3.38	3.34	3.30	3.27	3.23
8	5.32	4.46	4.07	3.84	3.69	3.58	3.50	3.44	3.39	3.35	3.28	3.22	3.15	3.12	3.08	3.04	3.01	2.97	2.93
9	5.12	4.26	3.86	3.63	3.48	3.37	3.29	3.23	3.18	3.14	3.07	3.01	2.94	2.90	2.86	2.83	2.79	2.75	2.71
10	4.96	4.10	3.71	3.48	3.33	3.22	3.14	3.07	3.02	2.98	2.91	2.85	2.77	2.74	2.70	2.66	2.62	2.58	2.54
11	4.84	3.98	3.59	3.36	3.20	3.09	3.01	2.95	2.90	2.85	2.79	2.72	2.65	2.61	2.57	2.53	2.49	2.45	2.40
12	4.75	3.89	3.49	3.26	3.11	3.00	2.91	2.85	2.80	2.75	2.69	2.62	2.54	2.51	2.47	2.43	2.38	2.34	2.30
13	4.67	3.81	3.41	3.18	3.03	2.92	2.83	2.77	2.71	2.67	2.60	2.53	2.46	2.42	2.38	2.34	2.30	2.25	2.21
14	4.60	3.74	3.34	3.11	2.96	2.85	2.76	2.70	2.65	2.60	2.53	2.46	2.39	2.35	2.31	2.27	2.22	2.18	2.13
15	4.54	3.68	3.29	3.06	2.90	2.79	2.71	2.64	2.59	2.54	2.48	2.40	2.33	2.29	2.25	2.20	2.16	2.11	2.07
16	4.49	3.63	3.24	3.01	2.85	2.74	2.66	2.59	2.54	2.49	2.42	2.35	2.28	2.24	2.19	2.15	2.11	2.06	2.01
17	4.45	3.59	3.20	2.96	2.81	2.70	2.61	2.55	2.49	2.45	2.38	2.31	2.23	2.19	2.15	2.10	2.06	2.01	1.96
18	4.41	3.55	3.16	2.93	2.77	2.66	2.58	2.51	2.46	2.41	2.34	2.27	2.19	2.15	2.11	2.06	2.02	1.97	1.92
19	4.38	3.52	3.13	2.90	2.74	2.63	2.54	2.48	2.42	2.38	2.31	2.23	2.16	2.11	2.07	2.03	1.98	1.93	1.88
20	4.35	3.49	3.10	2.87	2.71	2.60	2.51	2.45	2.39	2.35	2.28	2.20	2.12	2.08	2.04	1.99	1.95	1.90	1.84
21	4.32	3.47	3.07	2.84	2.68	2.57	2.49	2.42	2.37	2.32	2.25	2.18	2.10	2.05	2.01	1.96	1.92	1.87	1.81
22	4.30	3.44	3.05	2.82	2.66	2.55	2.46	2.40	2.34	2.30	2.23	2.15	2.07	2.03	1.98	1.91	1.89	1.84	1.78
23	4.28	3.42	3.03	2.80	2.64	2.53	2.44	2.37	2.32	2.27	2.20	2.13	2.05	2.01	1.96	1.91	1.86	1.81	1.76
24	4.26	3.40	3.01	2.78	2.62	2.51	2.42	2.36	2.30	2.25	2.18	2.11	2.03	1.98	1.94	1.89	1.84	1.79	1.73
25	4.24	3.39	2.99	2.76	2.60	2.49	2.40	2.34	2.28	2.24	2.16	2.09	2.01	1.96	1.92	1.87	1.82	1.77	1.71
26	4.23	3.37	2.98	2.74	2.59	2.47	2.39	2.32	2.27	2.22	2.15	2.07	1.99	1.95	1.90	1.85	1.80	1.75	1.69
27	4.21	3.35	2.96	2.73	2.57	2.46	2.37	2.31	2.25	2.20	2.13	2.06	1.97	1.93	1.88	1.84	1.79	1.73	1.67
28	4.20	3.34	2.95	2.71	2.56	2.45	2.36	2.29	2.24	2.19	2.12	2.04	1.96	1.91	1.87	1.82	1.77	1.71	1.65
29	4.18	3.33	2.93	2.70	2.55	2.43	2.35	2.28	2.22	2.18	2.10	2.03	1.94	1.90	1.85	1.81	1.75	1.70	1.64
30	4.17	3.32	2.92	2.69	2.53	2.42	2.33	2.27	2.21	2.16	2.09	2.01	1.93	1.89	1.84	1.79	1.74	1.68	1.62
40	4.08	3.23	2.84	2.61	2.45	2.34	2.25	2.18	2.12	2.08	2.00	1.92	1.84	1.79	1.74	1.69	1.64	1.58	1.51
60	4.00	3.15	2.76	2.53	2.37	2.25	2.17	2.10	2.04	1.99	1.92	1.84	1.75	1.70	1.65	1.59	1.53	1.47	1.39
120	3.92	3.07	2.68	2.45	2.29	2.17	2.09	2.02	1.96	1.91	1.83	1.75	1.66	1.61	1.55	1.50	1.43	1.35	1.25
∞	3.84	3.00	2.60	2.37	2.21	2.10	2.01	1.94	1.88	1.83	1.75	1.67	1.57	1.52	1.46	1.39	1.32	1.22	1.00

continued

$\alpha = 0.025$

Cumulative Probabilities = 0.975

Upper-Tail Areas = 0.025

Numerator, df_1

Denominator, df_2	1	2	3	4	5	6	7	8	9	10	12	15	20	24	30	40	60	120	∞
1	647.80	799.50	864.20	899.60	921.80	937.10	948.20	956.70	963.30	968.60	976.70	984.90	993.10	997.20	1,001.00	1,006.00	1,010.00	1,014.00	1,018.00
2	38.51	39.00	39.17	39.25	39.30	39.33	39.36	39.39	39.39	39.40	39.41	39.43	39.45	39.46	39.46	39.47	39.48	39.49	39.50
3	17.44	16.04	15.44	15.10	14.88	14.73	14.62	14.54	14.47	14.42	14.34	14.25	14.17	14.12	14.08	14.04	13.99	13.95	13.90
4	12.22	10.65	9.98	9.60	9.36	9.20	9.07	8.98	8.90	8.84	8.75	8.66	8.56	8.51	8.46	8.41	8.36	8.31	8.26
5	10.01	8.43	7.76	7.39	7.15	6.98	6.85	6.76	6.68	6.62	6.52	6.43	6.33	6.28	6.23	6.18	6.12	6.07	6.02
6	8.81	7.26	6.60	6.23	5.99	5.82	5.70	5.60	5.52	5.46	5.37	5.27	5.17	5.12	5.07	5.01	4.96	4.90	4.85
7	8.07	6.54	5.89	5.52	5.29	5.12	4.99	4.90	4.82	4.76	4.67	4.57	4.47	4.42	4.36	4.31	4.25	4.20	4.14
8	7.57	6.06	5.42	5.05	4.82	4.65	4.53	4.43	4.36	4.30	4.20	4.10	4.00	3.95	3.89	3.84	3.78	3.73	3.67
9	7.21	5.71	5.08	4.72	4.48	4.32	4.20	4.10	4.03	3.96	3.87	3.77	3.67	3.61	3.56	3.51	3.45	3.39	3.33
10	6.94	5.46	4.83	4.47	4.24	4.07	3.95	3.85	3.78	3.72	3.62	3.52	3.42	3.37	3.31	3.26	3.20	3.14	3.08
11	6.72	5.26	4.63	4.28	4.04	3.88	3.76	3.66	3.59	3.53	3.43	3.33	3.23	3.17	3.12	3.06	3.00	2.94	2.88
12	6.55	5.10	4.47	4.12	3.89	3.73	3.61	3.51	3.44	3.37	3.28	3.18	3.07	3.02	2.96	2.91	2.85	2.79	2.72
13	6.41	4.97	4.35	4.00	3.77	3.60	3.48	3.39	3.31	3.25	3.15	3.05	2.95	2.89	2.84	2.78	2.72	2.66	2.60
14	6.30	4.86	4.24	3.89	3.66	3.50	3.38	3.29	3.21	3.15	3.05	2.95	2.84	2.79	2.73	2.67	2.61	2.55	2.49
15	6.20	4.77	4.15	3.80	3.58	3.41	3.29	3.20	3.12	3.06	2.96	2.86	2.76	2.70	2.64	2.59	2.52	2.46	2.40
16	6.12	4.69	4.08	3.73	3.50	3.34	3.22	3.12	3.05	2.99	2.89	2.79	2.68	2.63	2.57	2.51	2.45	2.38	2.32
17	6.04	4.62	4.01	3.66	3.44	3.28	3.16	3.06	2.98	2.92	2.82	2.72	2.62	2.56	2.50	2.44	2.38	2.32	2.25
18	5.98	4.56	3.95	3.61	3.38	3.22	3.10	3.01	2.93	2.87	2.77	2.67	2.56	2.50	2.44	2.38	2.32	2.26	2.19
19	5.92	4.51	3.90	3.56	3.33	3.17	3.05	2.96	2.88	2.82	2.72	2.62	2.51	2.45	2.39	2.33	2.27	2.20	2.13
20	5.87	4.46	3.86	3.51	3.29	3.13	3.01	2.91	2.84	2.77	2.68	2.57	2.46	2.41	2.35	2.29	2.22	2.16	2.09
21	5.83	4.42	3.82	3.48	3.25	3.09	2.97	2.87	2.80	2.73	2.64	2.53	2.42	2.37	2.31	2.25	2.18	2.11	2.04
22	5.79	4.38	3.78	3.44	3.22	3.05	2.93	2.84	2.76	2.70	2.60	2.50	2.39	2.33	2.27	2.21	2.14	2.08	2.00
23	5.75	4.35	3.75	3.41	3.18	3.02	2.90	2.81	2.73	2.67	2.57	2.47	2.36	2.30	2.24	2.18	2.11	2.04	1.97
24	5.72	4.32	3.72	3.38	3.15	2.99	2.87	2.78	2.70	2.64	2.54	2.44	2.33	2.27	2.21	2.15	2.08	2.01	1.94
25	5.69	4.29	3.69	3.35	3.13	2.97	2.85	2.75	2.68	2.61	2.51	2.41	2.30	2.24	2.18	2.12	2.05	1.98	1.91
26	5.66	4.27	3.67	3.33	3.10	2.94	2.82	2.73	2.65	2.59	2.49	2.39	2.28	2.22	2.16	2.09	2.03	1.95	1.88
27	5.63	4.24	3.65	3.31	3.08	2.92	2.80	2.71	2.63	2.57	2.47	2.36	2.25	2.19	2.13	2.07	2.00	1.93	1.85
28	5.61	4.22	3.63	3.29	3.06	2.90	2.78	2.69	2.61	2.55	2.45	2.34	2.23	2.17	2.11	2.05	1.98	1.91	1.83
29	5.59	4.20	3.61	3.27	3.04	2.88	2.76	2.67	2.59	2.53	2.43	2.32	2.21	2.15	2.09	2.03	1.96	1.89	1.81
30	5.57	4.18	3.59	3.25	3.03	2.87	2.75	2.65	2.57	2.51	2.41	2.31	2.20	2.14	2.07	2.01	1.94	1.87	1.79
40	5.42	4.05	3.46	3.13	2.90	2.74	2.62	2.53	2.45	2.39	2.29	2.18	2.07	2.01	1.94	1.88	1.80	1.72	1.64
60	5.29	3.93	3.34	3.01	2.79	2.63	2.51	2.41	2.33	2.27	2.17	2.06	1.94	1.88	1.82	1.74	1.67	1.58	1.48
120	5.15	3.80	3.23	2.89	2.67	2.52	2.39	2.30	2.22	2.16	2.05	1.94	1.82	1.76	1.69	1.61	1.53	1.43	1.31
∞	5.02	3.69	3.12	2.79	2.57	2.41	2.29	2.19	2.11	2.05	1.94	1.83	1.71	1.64	1.57	1.48	1.39	1.27	1.00

Cumulative Probabilities = 0.99

Upper-Tail Areas = 0.01

α = 0.01

Denominator, df_2	Numerator, df_1																		
	1	2	3	4	5	6	7	8	9	10	12	15	20	24	30	40	60	120	∞
1	4,052.00	4,999.50	5,403.00	5,625.00	5,764.00	5,859.00	5,928.00	5,982.00	6,022.00	6,056.00	6,106.00	6,157.00	6,209.00	6,235.00	6,261.00	6,287.00	6,313.00	6,339.00	6,366.00
2	98.50	99.00	99.17	99.25	99.30	99.33	99.36	99.37	99.39	99.40	99.42	99.43	44.45	99.46	99.47	99.47	99.48	99.49	99.50
3	34.12	30.82	29.46	28.71	28.24	27.91	27.67	27.49	27.35	27.23	27.05	26.87	26.69	26.60	26.50	26.41	26.32	26.22	26.13
4	21.20	18.00	16.69	15.98	15.52	15.21	14.98	14.80	14.66	14.55	14.37	14.20	14.02	13.93	13.84	13.75	13.65	13.56	13.46
5	16.26	13.27	12.06	11.39	10.97	10.67	10.46	10.29	10.16	10.05	9.89	9.72	9.55	9.47	9.38	9.29	9.20	9.11	9.02
6	13.75	10.92	9.78	9.15	8.75	8.47	8.26	8.10	7.98	7.87	7.72	7.56	7.40	7.31	7.23	7.14	7.06	6.97	6.88
7	12.25	9.55	8.45	7.85	7.46	7.19	6.99	6.84	6.72	6.62	6.47	6.31	6.16	6.07	5.99	5.91	5.82	5.74	5.65
8	11.26	8.65	7.59	7.01	6.63	6.37	6.18	6.03	5.91	5.81	5.67	5.52	5.36	5.28	5.20	5.12	5.03	4.95	4.86
9	10.56	8.02	6.99	6.42	6.06	5.80	5.61	5.47	5.35	5.26	5.11	4.96	4.81	4.73	4.65	4.57	4.48	4.40	4.31
10	10.04	7.56	6.55	5.99	5.64	5.39	5.20	5.06	4.94	4.85	4.71	4.56	4.41	4.33	4.25	4.17	4.08	4.00	3.91
11	9.65	7.21	6.22	5.67	5.32	5.07	4.89	4.74	4.63	4.54	4.40	4.25	4.10	4.02	3.94	3.86	3.78	3.69	3.60
12	9.33	6.93	5.95	5.41	5.06	4.82	4.64	4.50	4.39	4.30	4.16	4.01	3.86	3.78	3.70	3.62	3.54	3.45	3.36
13	9.07	6.70	5.74	5.21	4.86	4.62	4.44	4.30	4.19	4.10	3.96	3.82	3.66	3.59	3.51	3.43	3.34	3.25	3.17
14	8.86	6.51	5.56	5.04	4.69	4.46	4.28	4.14	4.03	3.94	3.80	3.66	3.51	3.43	3.35	3.27	3.18	3.09	3.00
15	8.68	6.36	5.42	4.89	4.56	4.32	4.14	4.00	3.89	3.80	3.67	3.52	3.37	3.29	3.21	3.13	3.05	2.96	2.87
16	8.53	6.23	5.29	4.77	4.44	4.20	4.03	3.89	3.78	3.69	3.55	3.41	3.26	3.18	3.10	3.02	2.93	2.81	2.75
17	8.40	6.11	5.18	4.67	4.34	4.10	3.93	3.79	3.68	3.59	3.46	3.31	3.16	3.08	3.00	2.92	2.83	2.75	2.65
18	8.29	6.01	5.09	4.58	4.25	4.01	3.84	3.71	3.60	3.51	3.37	3.23	3.08	3.00	2.92	2.84	2.75	2.66	2.57
19	8.18	5.93	5.01	4.50	4.17	3.94	3.77	3.63	3.52	3.43	3.30	3.15	3.00	2.92	2.84	2.76	2.67	2.58	2.49
20	8.10	5.85	4.94	4.43	4.10	3.87	3.70	3.56	3.46	3.37	3.23	3.09	2.94	2.86	2.78	2.69	2.61	2.52	2.42
21	8.02	5.78	4.87	4.37	4.04	3.81	3.64	3.51	3.40	3.31	3.17	3.03	2.88	2.80	2.72	2.64	2.55	2.46	2.36
22	7.95	5.72	4.82	4.31	3.99	3.76	3.59	3.45	3.35	3.26	3.12	2.98	2.83	2.75	2.67	2.58	2.50	2.40	2.31
23	7.88	5.66	4.76	4.26	3.94	3.71	3.54	3.41	3.30	3.21	3.07	2.93	2.78	2.70	2.62	2.54	2.45	2.35	2.26
24	7.82	5.61	4.72	4.22	3.90	3.67	3.50	3.36	3.26	3.17	3.03	2.89	2.74	2.66	2.58	2.49	2.40	2.31	2.21
25	7.77	5.57	4.68	4.18	3.85	3.63	3.46	3.32	3.22	3.13	2.99	2.85	2.70	2.62	2.54	2.45	2.36	2.27	2.17
26	7.72	5.53	4.64	4.14	3.82	3.59	3.42	3.29	3.18	3.09	2.96	2.81	2.66	2.58	2.50	2.42	2.33	2.23	2.13
27	7.68	5.49	4.60	4.11	3.78	3.56	3.39	3.26	3.15	3.06	2.93	2.78	2.63	2.55	2.47	2.38	2.29	2.20	2.10
28	7.64	5.45	4.57	4.07	3.75	3.53	3.36	3.23	3.12	3.03	2.90	2.75	2.60	2.52	2.44	2.35	2.26	2.17	2.06
29	7.60	5.42	4.54	4.04	3.73	3.50	3.33	3.20	3.09	3.00	2.87	2.73	2.57	2.49	2.41	2.33	2.23	2.14	2.03
30	7.56	5.39	4.51	4.02	3.70	3.47	3.30	3.17	3.07	2.98	2.84	2.70	2.55	2.47	2.39	2.30	2.21	2.11	2.01
40	7.31	5.18	4.31	3.83	3.51	3.29	3.12	2.99	2.89	2.80	2.66	2.52	2.37	2.29	2.20	2.11	2.02	1.92	1.80
60	7.08	4.98	4.13	3.65	3.34	3.12	2.95	2.82	2.72	2.63	2.50	2.35	2.20	2.12	2.03	1.94	1.84	1.73	1.60
120	6.85	4.79	3.95	3.48	3.17	2.96	2.79	2.66	2.56	2.47	2.34	2.19	2.03	1.95	1.86	1.76	1.66	1.53	1.38
∞	6.63	4.61	3.78	3.32	3.02	2.80	2.64	2.51	2.41	2.32	2.18	2.04	1.88	1.79	1.70	1.59	1.47	1.32	1.00

continued

TABLE E.5

Critical Values of F (Continued)

$\alpha = 0.005$

Cumulative Probabilities = 0.995

Upper-Tail Areas = 0.005

Numerator, df_1

Denominator, df_2	1	2	3	4	5	6	7	8	9	10	12	15	20	24	30	40	60	120	∞
1	16,211.00	20,000.00	21,615.00	22,500.00	23,056.00	23,437.00	23,715.00	23,925.00	24,091.00	24,224.00	24,426.00	24,630.00	24,836.00	24,910.00	25,044.00	25,148.00	25,253.00	25,359.00	25,465.00
2	198.50	199.00	199.20	199.20	199.30	199.30	199.40	199.40	199.40	199.40	199.40	199.40	199.40	199.50	199.50	199.50	199.50	199.50	199.50
3	55.55	49.80	47.47	46.19	45.39	44.84	44.43	44.13	43.88	43.69	43.39	43.08	42.78	42.62	42.47	42.31	42.15	41.99	41.83
4	31.33	26.28	24.26	23.15	22.46	21.97	21.62	21.35	21.14	20.97	20.70	20.44	20.17	20.03	19.89	19.75	19.61	19.47	19.32
5	22.78	18.31	16.53	15.56	14.94	14.51	14.20	13.96	13.77	13.62	13.38	13.15	12.90	12.78	12.66	12.53	12.40	12.27	12.11
6	18.63	14.54	12.92	12.03	11.46	11.07	10.79	10.57	10.39	10.25	10.03	9.81	9.59	9.47	9.36	9.24	9.12	9.00	8.88
7	16.24	12.40	10.88	10.05	9.52	9.16	8.89	8.68	8.51	8.38	8.18	7.97	7.75	7.65	7.53	7.42	7.31	7.19	7.08
8	14.69	11.04	9.60	8.81	8.30	7.95	7.69	7.50	7.34	7.21	7.01	6.81	6.61	6.50	6.40	6.29	6.18	6.06	5.95
9	13.61	10.11	8.72	7.96	7.47	7.13	6.88	6.69	6.54	6.42	6.23	6.03	5.83	5.73	5.62	5.52	5.41	5.30	5.19
10	12.83	9.43	8.08	7.34	6.87	6.54	6.30	6.12	5.97	5.85	5.66	5.47	5.27	5.17	5.07	4.97	4.86	4.75	4.61
11	12.23	8.91	7.60	6.88	6.42	6.10	5.86	5.68	5.54	5.42	5.24	5.05	4.86	4.75	4.65	4.55	4.44	4.34	4.23
12	11.75	8.51	7.23	6.52	6.07	5.76	5.52	5.35	5.20	5.09	4.91	4.72	4.53	4.43	4.33	4.23	4.12	4.01	3.90
13	11.37	8.19	6.93	6.23	5.79	5.48	5.25	5.08	4.94	4.82	4.64	4.46	4.27	4.17	4.07	3.97	3.87	3.76	3.65
14	11.06	7.92	6.68	6.00	5.56	5.26	5.03	4.86	4.72	4.60	4.43	4.25	4.06	3.96	3.86	3.76	3.66	3.55	3.41
15	10.80	7.70	6.48	5.80	5.37	5.07	4.85	4.67	4.54	4.42	4.25	4.07	3.88	3.79	3.69	3.58	3.48	3.37	3.26
16	10.58	7.51	6.30	5.64	5.21	4.91	4.69	4.52	4.38	4.27	4.10	3.92	3.73	3.64	3.54	3.44	3.33	3.22	3.11
17	10.38	7.35	6.16	5.50	5.07	4.78	4.56	4.39	4.25	4.14	3.97	3.79	3.61	3.51	3.41	3.31	3.21	3.10	2.98
18	10.22	7.21	6.03	5.37	4.96	4.66	4.44	4.28	4.14	4.03	3.86	3.68	3.50	3.40	3.30	3.20	3.10	2.99	2.87
19	10.07	7.09	5.92	5.27	4.85	4.56	4.34	4.18	4.04	3.93	3.76	3.59	3.40	3.31	3.21	3.11	3.00	2.89	2.78
20	9.94	6.99	5.82	5.17	4.76	4.47	4.26	4.09	3.96	3.85	3.68	3.50	3.32	3.22	3.12	3.02	2.92	2.81	2.69
21	9.83	6.89	5.73	5.09	4.68	4.39	4.18	4.02	3.88	3.77	3.60	3.43	3.24	3.15	3.05	2.95	2.84	2.73	2.61
22	9.73	6.81	5.65	5.02	4.61	4.32	4.11	3.94	3.81	3.70	3.54	3.36	3.18	3.08	2.98	2.88	2.77	2.66	2.55
23	9.63	6.73	5.58	4.95	4.54	4.26	4.05	3.88	3.75	3.64	3.47	3.30	3.12	3.02	2.92	2.82	2.71	2.60	2.48
24	9.55	6.66	5.52	4.89	4.49	4.20	3.99	3.83	3.69	3.59	3.42	3.25	3.06	2.97	2.87	2.77	2.66	2.55	2.43
25	9.48	6.60	5.46	4.84	4.43	4.15	3.94	3.78	3.64	3.54	3.37	3.20	3.01	2.92	2.82	2.72	2.61	2.50	2.38
26	9.41	6.54	5.41	4.79	4.38	4.10	3.89	3.73	3.60	3.49	3.33	3.15	2.97	2.87	2.77	2.67	2.56	2.45	2.33
27	9.34	6.49	5.36	4.74	4.34	4.06	3.85	3.69	3.56	3.45	3.28	3.11	2.93	2.83	2.73	2.63	2.52	2.41	2.29
28	9.28	6.44	5.32	4.70	4.30	4.02	3.81	3.65	3.52	3.41	3.25	3.07	2.89	2.79	2.69	2.59	2.48	2.37	2.25
29	9.23	6.40	5.28	4.66	4.26	3.98	3.77	3.61	3.48	3.38	3.21	3.04	2.86	2.76	2.66	2.56	2.45	2.33	2.21
30	9.18	6.35	5.24	4.62	4.23	3.95	3.74	3.58	3.45	3.34	3.18	3.01	2.82	2.73	2.63	2.52	2.42	2.30	2.18
40	8.83	6.07	4.98	4.37	3.99	3.71	3.51	3.35	3.22	3.12	2.95	2.78	2.60	2.50	2.40	2.30	2.18	2.06	1.93
60	8.49	5.79	4.73	4.14	3.76	3.49	3.29	3.13	3.01	2.90	2.74	2.57	2.39	2.29	2.19	2.08	1.96	1.83	1.69
120	8.18	5.54	4.50	3.92	3.55	3.28	3.09	2.93	2.81	2.71	2.54	2.37	2.19	2.09	1.98	1.87	1.75	1.61	1.43
∞	7.88	5.30	4.28	3.72	3.35	3.09	2.90	2.74	2.62	2.52	2.36	2.19	2.00	1.90	1.79	1.67	1.53	1.36	1.00

Source: Reprinted from E. S. Pearson and H. O. Hartley, eds., *Biometrika Tables for Statisticians*, 3rd ed., 1966, by permission of the *Biometrika* Trustees.

Table E.6

**TABLE OF BINOMIAL PROBABILITIES
(BEGINS ON THE FOLLOWING PAGE)**

TABLE E.6

Table of Binomial Probabilities

For a given combination of n and π, entry indicates the probability of obtaining a specified value of X. To locate entry, when $\pi \leq .50$ read π across the top heading and both n and X down the left margin; when $\pi \geq .50$ read π across the bottom heading and both n and X up the right margin.

π

n	X	0.01	0.02	0.03	0.04	0.05	0.06	0.07	0.08	0.09	0.10	0.15	0.20	0.25	0.30	0.35	0.40	0.45	0.50	X	n
2	0	0.9801	0.9604	0.9409	0.9216	0.9025	0.8836	0.8649	0.8464	0.8281	0.8100	0.7225	0.6400	0.5625	0.4900	0.4225	0.3600	0.3025	0.2500	2	2
	1	0.0198	0.0392	0.0582	0.0768	0.0950	0.1128	0.1302	0.1472	0.1638	0.1800	0.2550	0.3200	0.3750	0.4200	0.4550	0.4800	0.4950	0.5000	1	
	2	0.0001	0.0004	0.0009	0.0016	0.0025	0.0036	0.0049	0.0064	0.0081	0.0100	0.0225	0.0400	0.0625	0.0900	0.1225	0.1600	0.2025	0.2500	0	
3	0	0.9703	0.9412	0.9127	0.8847	0.8574	0.8306	0.8044	0.7787	0.7536	0.7290	0.6141	0.5120	0.4219	0.3430	0.2746	0.2160	0.1664	0.1250	3	3
	1	0.0294	0.0576	0.0847	0.1106	0.1354	0.1590	0.1816	0.2031	0.2236	0.2430	0.3251	0.3840	0.4219	0.4410	0.4436	0.4320	0.4084	0.3750	2	
	2	0.0003	0.0012	0.0026	0.0046	0.0071	0.0102	0.0137	0.0177	0.0221	0.0270	0.0574	0.0960	0.1406	0.1890	0.2389	0.2880	0.3341	0.3750	1	
	3	0.0000	0.0000	0.0000	0.0001	0.0001	0.0002	0.0003	0.0005	0.0007	0.0010	0.0034	0.0080	0.0156	0.0270	0.0429	0.0640	0.0911	0.1250	0	
4	0	0.9606	0.9224	0.8853	0.8493	0.8145	0.7807	0.7481	0.7164	0.6857	0.6561	0.5220	0.4096	0.3164	0.2401	0.1785	0.1296	0.0915	0.0625	4	4
	1	0.0388	0.0753	0.1095	0.1416	0.1715	0.1993	0.2252	0.2492	0.2713	0.2916	0.3685	0.4096	0.4219	0.4116	0.3845	0.3456	0.2995	0.2500	3	
	2	0.0006	0.0023	0.0051	0.0088	0.0135	0.0191	0.0254	0.0325	0.0402	0.0486	0.0975	0.1536	0.2109	0.2646	0.3105	0.3456	0.3675	0.3750	2	
	3	0.0000	0.0000	0.0001	0.0002	0.0005	0.0008	0.0013	0.0019	0.0027	0.0036	0.0115	0.0256	0.0469	0.0756	0.1115	0.1536	0.2005	0.2500	1	
	4	—	0.0000	0.0000	0.0000	0.0000	0.0000	0.0000	0.0000	0.0001	0.0001	0.0005	0.0016	0.0039	0.0081	0.0150	0.0256	0.0410	0.0625	0	
5	0	0.9510	0.9039	0.8587	0.8154	0.7738	0.7339	0.6957	0.6591	0.6240	0.5905	0.4437	0.3277	0.2373	0.1681	0.1160	0.0778	0.0503	0.0312	5	5
	1	0.0480	0.0922	0.1328	0.1699	0.2036	0.2342	0.2618	0.2866	0.3086	0.3280	0.3915	0.4096	0.3955	0.3601	0.3124	0.2592	0.2059	0.1562	4	
	2	0.0010	0.0038	0.0082	0.0142	0.0214	0.0299	0.0394	0.0498	0.0610	0.0729	0.1382	0.2048	0.2637	0.3087	0.3364	0.3456	0.3369	0.3125	3	
	3	0.0000	0.0001	0.0003	0.0006	0.0011	0.0019	0.0030	0.0043	0.0060	0.0081	0.0244	0.0512	0.0879	0.1323	0.1811	0.2304	0.2757	0.3125	2	
	4	0.0000	0.0000	0.0000	0.0000	0.0000	0.0001	0.0001	0.0002	0.0003	0.0004	0.0022	0.0064	0.0146	0.0283	0.0488	0.0768	0.1128	0.1562	1	
	5	—	0.0000	0.0000	0.0000	0.0000	0.0000	0.0000	0.0000	0.0000	0.0000	0.0001	0.0003	0.0010	0.0024	0.0053	0.0102	0.0185	0.0312	0	
6	0	0.9415	0.8858	0.8330	0.7828	0.7351	0.6899	0.6470	0.6064	0.5679	0.5314	0.3771	0.2621	0.1780	0.1176	0.0754	0.0467	0.0277	0.0156	6	6
	1	0.0571	0.1085	0.1546	0.1957	0.2321	0.2642	0.2922	0.3164	0.3370	0.3543	0.3993	0.3932	0.3560	0.3025	0.2437	0.1866	0.1359	0.0937	5	
	2	0.0014	0.0055	0.0120	0.0204	0.0305	0.0422	0.0550	0.0688	0.0833	0.0984	0.1762	0.2458	0.2966	0.3241	0.3280	0.3110	0.2780	0.2344	4	
	3	0.0000	0.0002	0.0005	0.0011	0.0021	0.0036	0.0055	0.0080	0.0110	0.0146	0.0415	0.0819	0.1318	0.1852	0.2355	0.2765	0.3032	0.3125	3	
	4	0.0000	0.0000	0.0000	0.0000	0.0001	0.0002	0.0003	0.0005	0.0008	0.0012	0.0055	0.0154	0.0330	0.0595	0.0951	0.1372	0.1861	0.2344	2	
	5	—	0.0000	0.0000	0.0000	0.0000	0.0000	0.0000	0.0000	0.0000	0.0001	0.0004	0.0015	0.0044	0.0102	0.0205	0.0369	0.0609	0.0937	1	
	6	—	—	—	0.0000	0.0000	0.0000	0.0000	0.0000	0.0000	0.0000	0.0000	0.0001	0.0002	0.0007	0.0018	0.0041	0.0083	0.0156	0	

n	X	0.50	0.55	0.60	0.65	0.70	0.75	0.80	0.85	0.90	0.91	0.92	0.93	0.94	0.95	0.96	0.97	0.98	0.99
7	0	0.0078	0.0152	0.0280	0.0490	0.0824	0.1335	0.2097	0.3206	0.4783	0.5168	0.5578	0.6017	0.6485	0.6983	0.7514	0.8080	0.8681	0.9321
	1	0.0547	0.0872	0.1306	0.1848	0.2471	0.3115	0.3670	0.3960	0.3720	0.3578	0.3396	0.3170	0.2897	0.2573	0.2192	0.1749	0.1240	0.0659
	2	0.1641	0.2140	0.2613	0.2985	0.3177	0.3115	0.2753	0.2097	0.1240	0.1061	0.0886	0.0716	0.0555	0.0406	0.0274	0.0162	0.0076	0.0020
	3	0.2734	0.2918	0.2903	0.2679	0.2269	0.1730	0.1147	0.0617	0.0230	0.0175	0.0128	0.0090	0.0059	0.0036	0.0019	0.0008	0.0003	0.0000
	4	0.2734	0.2388	0.1935	0.1442	0.0972	0.0577	0.0287	0.0109	0.0026	0.0017	0.0011	0.0007	0.0004	0.0002	0.0001	0.0000	0.0000	—
	5	0.1641	0.1172	0.0774	0.0466	0.0250	0.0115	0.0043	0.0012	0.0002	0.0001	0.0001	0.0000	0.0000	0.0000	0.0000	—	—	—
	6	0.0547	0.0320	0.0172	0.0084	0.0036	0.0013	0.0004	0.0001	0.0000	0.0000	0.0000	—	—	—	—	—	—	—
	7	0.0078	0.0037	0.0016	0.0006	0.0002	0.0001	0.0000	0.0000	0.0000	0.0000	—	—	—	—	—	—	—	—
8	0	0.0039	0.0084	0.0168	0.0319	0.0576	0.1001	0.1678	0.2725	0.4305	0.4703	0.5132	0.5596	0.6096	0.6634	0.7214	0.7837	0.8508	0.9227
	1	0.0312	0.0548	0.0896	0.1373	0.1977	0.2670	0.3355	0.3847	0.3826	0.3721	0.3570	0.3370	0.3113	0.2793	0.2405	0.1939	0.1389	0.0746
	2	0.1094	0.1569	0.2090	0.2587	0.2965	0.3115	0.2936	0.2376	0.1488	0.1288	0.1087	0.0888	0.0695	0.0515	0.0351	0.0210	0.0099	0.0026
	3	0.2187	0.2568	0.2787	0.2786	0.2541	0.2076	0.1468	0.0839	0.0331	0.0255	0.0189	0.0134	0.0089	0.0054	0.0029	0.0013	0.0004	0.0001
	4	0.2734	0.2627	0.2322	0.1875	0.1361	0.0865	0.0459	0.0185	0.0046	0.0031	0.0021	0.0013	0.0007	0.0004	0.0002	0.0001	0.0000	0.0000
	5	0.2187	0.1719	0.1239	0.0808	0.0467	0.0231	0.0092	0.0026	0.0004	0.0002	0.0001	0.0001	0.0000	0.0000	0.0000	0.0000	—	—
	6	0.1094	0.0703	0.0413	0.0217	0.0100	0.0038	0.0011	0.0002	0.0000	0.0000	0.0000	0.0000	—	—	—	—	—	—
	7	0.0312	0.0164	0.0079	0.0033	0.0012	0.0004	0.0001	0.0000	—	—	—	—	—	—	—	—	—	—
	8	0.0039	0.0017	0.0007	0.0002	0.0001	0.0000	0.0000	—	—	—	—	—	—	—	—	—	—	—
9	0	0.0020	0.0046	0.0101	0.0207	0.0404	0.0751	0.1342	0.2316	0.3874	0.4279	0.4722	0.5204	0.5730	0.6302	0.6925	0.7602	0.8337	0.9135
	1	0.0176	0.0339	0.0605	0.1004	0.1556	0.2253	0.3020	0.3679	0.3874	0.3809	0.3695	0.3525	0.3292	0.2985	0.2597	0.2116	0.1531	0.0830
	2	0.0703	0.1110	0.1612	0.2162	0.2668	0.3003	0.3020	0.2597	0.1722	0.1507	0.1285	0.1061	0.0840	0.0629	0.0433	0.0262	0.0125	0.0034
	3	0.1641	0.2119	0.2508	0.2716	0.2668	0.2336	0.1762	0.1069	0.0446	0.0348	0.0261	0.0186	0.0125	0.0077	0.0042	0.0019	0.0006	0.0001
	4	0.2461	0.2600	0.2508	0.2194	0.1715	0.1168	0.0661	0.0283	0.0074	0.0052	0.0034	0.0021	0.0012	0.0006	0.0003	0.0001	0.0000	0.0000
	5	0.2461	0.2128	0.1672	0.1181	0.0735	0.0390	0.0165	0.0050	0.0008	0.0005	0.0003	0.0002	0.0001	0.0000	0.0000	0.0000	—	—
	6	0.1641	0.1160	0.0743	0.0424	0.0210	0.0087	0.0028	0.0006	0.0001	0.0000	0.0000	0.0000	0.0000	—	—	—	—	—
	7	0.0703	0.0407	0.0212	0.0098	0.0039	0.0012	0.0003	0.0000	0.0000	—	—	—	—	—	—	—	—	—
	8	0.0176	0.0083	0.0035	0.0013	0.0004	0.0001	0.0000	—	—	—	—	—	—	—	—	—	—	—
	9	0.0020	0.0008	0.0003	0.0001	0.0000	0.0000	—	—	—	—	—	—	—	—	—	—	—	—
10	0	0.0010	0.0025	0.0060	0.0135	0.0282	0.0563	0.1074	0.1969	0.3487	0.3894	0.4344	0.4840	0.5386	0.5987	0.6648	0.7374	0.8171	0.9044
	1	0.0098	0.0207	0.0403	0.0725	0.1211	0.1877	0.2684	0.3474	0.3874	0.3851	0.3777	0.3643	0.3438	0.3151	0.2770	0.2281	0.1667	0.0914
	2	0.0439	0.0763	0.1209	0.1757	0.2335	0.2816	0.3020	0.2759	0.1937	0.1714	0.1478	0.1234	0.0988	0.0746	0.0519	0.0317	0.0153	0.0042
	3	0.1172	0.1665	0.2150	0.2522	0.2668	0.2503	0.2013	0.1298	0.0574	0.0452	0.0343	0.0248	0.0168	0.0105	0.0058	0.0026	0.0008	0.0001
	4	0.2051	0.2384	0.2508	0.2377	0.2001	0.1460	0.0881	0.0401	0.0112	0.0078	0.0052	0.0033	0.0019	0.0010	0.0004	0.0001	0.0000	0.0000
	5	0.2461	0.2340	0.2007	0.1536	0.1029	0.0584	0.0264	0.0085	0.0015	0.0009	0.0005	0.0003	0.0001	0.0001	0.0000	0.0000	—	—
	6	0.2051	0.1596	0.1115	0.0689	0.0368	0.0162	0.0055	0.0012	0.0001	0.0001	0.0000	0.0000	0.0000	0.0000	—	—	—	—
	7	0.1172	0.0746	0.0425	0.0212	0.0090	0.0031	0.0008	0.0001	0.0000	0.0000	—	—	—	—	—	—	—	—
	8	0.0439	0.0229	0.0106	0.0043	0.0014	0.0004	0.0001	0.0000	—	—	—	—	—	—	—	—	—	—
	9	0.0098	0.0042	0.0016	0.0005	0.0001	0.0000	0.0000	—	—	—	—	—	—	—	—	—	—	—
	10	0.0010	0.0003	0.0001	0.0000	0.0000	—	—	—	—	—	—	—	—	—	—	—	—	—

continued

Table of Binomial Probabilities (Continued)

n	X	0.01	0.02	0.03	0.04	0.05	0.06	0.07	0.08	0.09	0.10	0.15	0.20	0.25	0.30	0.35	0.40	0.45	0.50	X	n
20	0	0.8179	0.6676	0.5438	0.4420	0.3585	0.2901	0.2342	0.1887	0.1516	0.1216	0.0388	0.0115	0.0032	0.0008	0.0002	0.0000	0.0000	—	20	
	1	0.1652	0.2725	0.3364	0.3683	0.3774	0.3703	0.3526	0.3282	0.3000	0.2702	0.1368	0.0576	0.0211	0.0068	0.0020	0.0005	0.0001	0.0000	19	
	2	0.0159	0.0528	0.0988	0.1458	0.1887	0.2246	0.2521	0.2711	0.2818	0.2852	0.2293	0.1369	0.0699	0.0278	0.0100	0.0031	0.0008	0.0002	18	
	3	0.0010	0.0065	0.0183	0.0364	0.0596	0.0860	0.1139	0.1414	0.1672	0.1901	0.2428	0.2054	0.1339	0.0716	0.0323	0.0123	0.0040	0.0011	17	
	4	0.0000	0.0006	0.0024	0.0065	0.0133	0.0233	0.0364	0.0523	0.0703	0.0898	0.1821	0.2182	0.1897	0.1304	0.0738	0.0350	0.0139	0.0046	16	
	5	—	0.0000	0.0002	0.0009	0.0022	0.0048	0.0088	0.0145	0.0222	0.0319	0.1028	0.1746	0.2023	0.1789	0.1272	0.0746	0.0365	0.0148	15	
	6	—	—	0.0000	0.0001	0.0003	0.0008	0.0017	0.0032	0.0055	0.0089	0.0454	0.1091	0.1686	0.1916	0.1712	0.1244	0.0746	0.0370	14	
	7	—	—	—	0.0000	0.0000	0.0001	0.0002	0.0005	0.0011	0.0020	0.0160	0.0545	0.1124	0.1643	0.1844	0.1659	0.1221	0.0739	13	
	8	—	—	—	0.0000	0.0000	0.0000	0.0000	0.0001	0.0002	0.0004	0.0046	0.0222	0.0609	0.1144	0.1614	0.1797	0.1623	0.1201	12	
	9	—	—	—	—	—	—	0.0000	0.0000	0.0000	0.0001	0.0011	0.0074	0.0271	0.0654	0.1158	0.1597	0.1771	0.1602	11	
	10	—	—	—	—	—	—	—	—	—	0.0000	0.0002	0.0020	0.0099	0.0308	0.0686	0.1171	0.1593	0.1762	10	
	11	—	—	—	—	—	—	—	—	—	0.0000	0.0000	0.0005	0.0030	0.0120	0.0336	0.0710	0.1185	0.1602	9	
	12	—	—	—	—	—	—	—	—	—	—	0.0000	0.0001	0.0008	0.0039	0.0136	0.0355	0.0727	0.1201	8	
	13	—	—	—	—	—	—	—	—	—	—	0.0000	0.0000	0.0002	0.0010	0.0045	0.0146	0.0366	0.0739	7	
	14	—	—	—	—	—	—	—	—	—	—	—	0.0000	0.0000	0.0002	0.0012	0.0049	0.0150	0.0370	6	
	15	—	—	—	—	—	—	—	—	—	—	—	—	0.0000	0.0000	0.0003	0.0013	0.0049	0.0148	5	
	16	—	—	—	—	—	—	—	—	—	—	—	—	—	0.0000	0.0000	0.0003	0.0013	0.0046	4	
	17	—	—	—	—	—	—	—	—	—	—	—	—	—	—	—	0.0000	0.0002	0.0011	3	
	18	—	—	—	—	—	—	—	—	—	—	—	—	—	—	—	—	0.0000	0.0002	2	
	19	—	—	—	—	—	—	—	—	—	—	—	—	—	—	—	—	—	0.0000	1	
	20	—	—	—	—	—	—	—	—	—	—	—	—	—	—	—	—	—	—	0	20
n	X	0.99	0.98	0.97	0.96	0.95	0.94	0.93	0.92	0.91	0.90	0.85	0.80	0.75	0.70	0.65	0.60	0.55	0.50	X	n

π

TABLE E.7

Table of Poisson
Probabilities

For a given value of λ, entry
indicates the probability of a
specified value of X.

X	λ									
	0.1	0.2	0.3	0.4	0.5	0.6	0.7	0.8	0.9	1.0
0	0.9048	0.8187	0.7408	0.6703	0.6065	0.5488	0.4966	0.4493	0.4066	0.3679
1	0.0905	0.1637	0.2222	0.2681	0.3033	0.3293	0.3476	0.3595	0.3659	0.3679
2	0.0045	0.0164	0.0333	0.0536	0.0758	0.0988	0.1217	0.1438	0.1647	0.1839
3	0.0002	0.0011	0.0033	0.0072	0.0126	0.0198	0.0284	0.0383	0.0494	0.0613
4	0.0000	0.0001	0.0003	0.0007	0.0016	0.0030	0.0050	0.0077	0.0111	0.0153
5	0.0000	0.0000	0.0000	0.0001	0.0002	0.0004	0.0007	0.0012	0.0020	0.0031
6	0.0000	0.0000	0.0000	0.0000	0.0000	0.0000	0.0001	0.0002	0.0003	0.0005
7	0.0000	0.0000	0.0000	0.0000	0.0000	0.0000	0.0000	0.0000	0.0000	0.0001

X	λ									
	1.1	1.2	1.3	1.4	1.5	1.6	1.7	1.8	1.9	2.0
0	0.3329	0.3012	0.2725	0.2466	0.2231	0.2019	0.1827	0.1653	0.1496	0.1353
1	0.3662	0.3614	0.3543	0.3452	0.3347	0.3230	0.3106	0.2975	0.2842	0.2707
2	0.2014	0.2169	0.2303	0.2417	0.2510	0.2584	0.2640	0.2678	0.2700	0.2707
3	0.0738	0.0867	0.0998	0.1128	0.1255	0.1378	0.1496	0.1607	0.1710	0.1804
4	0.0203	0.0260	0.0324	0.0395	0.0471	0.0551	0.0636	0.0723	0.0812	0.0902
5	0.0045	0.0062	0.0084	0.0111	0.0141	0.0176	0.0216	0.0260	0.0309	0.0361
6	0.0008	0.0012	0.0018	0.0026	0.0035	0.0047	0.0061	0.0078	0.0098	0.0120
7	0.0001	0.0002	0.0003	0.0005	0.0008	0.0011	0.0015	0.0020	0.0027	0.0034
8	0.0000	0.0000	0.0001	0.0001	0.0001	0.0002	0.0003	0.0005	0.0006	0.0009
9	0.0000	0.0000	0.0000	0.0000	0.0000	0.0000	0.0001	0.0001	0.0001	0.0002

X	λ									
	2.1	2.2	2.3	2.4	2.5	2.6	2.7	2.8	2.9	3.0
0	0.1225	0.1108	0.1003	0.0907	0.0821	0.0743	0.0672	0.0608	0.0550	0.0498
1	0.2572	0.2438	0.2306	0.2177	0.2052	0.1931	0.1815	0.1703	0.1596	0.1494
2	0.2700	0.2681	0.2652	0.2613	0.2565	0.2510	0.2450	0.2384	0.2314	0.2240
3	0.1890	0.1966	0.2033	0.2090	0.2138	0.2176	0.2205	0.2225	0.2237	0.2240
4	0.0992	0.1082	0.1169	0.1254	0.1336	0.1414	0.1488	0.1557	0.1622	0.1680
5	0.0417	0.0476	0.0538	0.0602	0.0668	0.0735	0.0804	0.0872	0.0940	0.1008
6	0.0146	0.0174	0.0206	0.0241	0.0278	0.0319	0.0362	0.0407	0.0455	0.0504
7	0.0044	0.0055	0.0068	0.0083	0.0099	0.0118	0.0139	0.0163	0.0188	0.0216
8	0.0011	0.0015	0.0019	0.0025	0.0031	0.0038	0.0047	0.0057	0.0068	0.0081
9	0.0003	0.0004	0.0005	0.0007	0.0009	0.0011	0.0014	0.0018	0.0022	0.0027
10	0.0001	0.0001	0.0001	0.0002	0.0002	0.0003	0.0004	0.0005	0.0006	0.0008
11	0.0000	0.0000	0.0000	0.0000	0.0000	0.0001	0.0001	0.0001	0.0002	0.0002
12	0.0000	0.0000	0.0000	0.0000	0.0000	0.0000	0.0000	0.0000	0.0000	0.0001

X	λ									
	3.1	3.2	3.3	3.4	3.5	3.6	3.7	3.8	3.9	4.0
0	0.0450	0.0408	0.0369	0.0334	0.0302	0.0273	0.0247	0.0224	0.0202	0.0183
1	0.1397	0.1340	0.1217	0.1135	0.1057	0.0984	0.0915	0.0850	0.0789	0.0733
2	0.2165	0.2087	0.2008	0.1929	0.1850	0.1771	0.1692	0.1615	0.1539	0.1465
3	0.2237	0.2226	0.2209	0.2186	0.2158	0.2125	0.2087	0.2046	0.2001	0.1954
4	0.1734	0.1781	0.1823	0.1858	0.1888	0.1912	0.1931	0.1944	0.1951	0.1954
5	0.1075	0.1140	0.1203	0.1264	0.1322	0.1377	0.1429	0.1477	0.1522	0.1563
6	0.0555	0.0608	0.0662	0.0716	0.0771	0.0826	0.0881	0.0936	0.0989	0.1042
7	0.0246	0.0278	0.0312	0.0348	0.0385	0.0425	0.0466	0.0508	0.0551	0.0595
8	0.0095	0.0111	0.0129	0.0148	0.0169	0.0191	0.0215	0.0241	0.0269	0.0298
9	0.0033	0.0040	0.0047	0.0056	0.0066	0.0076	0.0089	0.0102	0.0116	0.0132
10	0.0010	0.0013	0.0016	0.0019	0.0023	0.0028	0.0033	0.0039	0.0045	0.0053
11	0.0003	0.0004	0.0005	0.0006	0.0007	0.0009	0.0011	0.0013	0.0016	0.0019
12	0.0001	0.0001	0.0001	0.0002	0.0002	0.0003	0.0003	0.0004	0.0005	0.0006
13	0.0000	0.0000	0.0000	0.0000	0.0001	0.0001	0.0001	0.0001	0.0002	0.0002
14	0.0000	0.0000	0.0000	0.0000	0.0000	0.0000	0.0000	0.0000	0.0000	0.0001

continued

TABLE E.7

Table of Poisson Probabilities (*Continued*)

					λ					
X	4.1	4.2	4.3	4.4	4.5	4.6	4.7	4.8	4.9	5.0
0	0.0166	0.0150	0.0136	0.0123	0.0111	0.0101	0.0091	0.0082	0.0074	0.0067
1	0.0679	0.0630	0.0583	0.0540	0.0500	0.0462	0.0427	0.0395	0.0365	0.0337
2	0.1393	0.1323	0.1254	0.1188	0.1125	0.1063	0.1005	0.0948	0.0894	0.0842
3	0.1904	0.1852	0.1798	0.1743	0.1687	0.1631	0.1574	0.1517	0.1460	0.1404
4	0.1951	0.1944	0.1933	0.1917	0.1898	0.1875	0.1849	0.1820	0.1789	0.1755
5	0.1600	0.1633	0.1662	0.1687	0.1708	0.1725	0.1738	0.1747	0.1753	0.1755
6	0.1093	0.1143	0.1191	0.1237	0.1281	0.1323	0.1362	0.1398	0.1432	0.1462
7	0.0640	0.0686	0.0732	0.0778	0.0824	0.0869	0.0914	0.0959	0.1002	0.1044
8	0.0328	0.0360	0.0393	0.0428	0.0463	0.0500	0.0537	0.0575	0.0614	0.0653
9	0.0150	0.0168	0.0188	0.0209	0.0232	0.0255	0.0280	0.0307	0.0334	0.0363
10	0.0061	0.0071	0.0081	0.0092	0.0104	0.0118	0.0132	0.0147	0.0164	0.0181
11	0.0023	0.0027	0.0032	0.0037	0.0043	0.0049	0.0056	0.0064	0.0073	0.0082
12	0.0008	0.0009	0.0011	0.0014	0.0016	0.0019	0.0022	0.0026	0.0030	0.0034
13	0.0002	0.0003	0.0004	0.0005	0.0006	0.0007	0.0008	0.0009	0.0011	0.0013
14	0.0001	0.0001	0.0001	0.0001	0.0002	0.0002	0.0003	0.0003	0.0004	0.0005
15	0.0000	0.0000	0.0000	0.0000	0.0001	0.0001	0.0001	0.0001	0.0001	0.0002

					λ					
X	5.1	5.2	5.3	5.4	5.5	5.6	5.7	5.8	5.9	6.0
0	0.0061	0.0055	0.0050	0.0045	0.0041	0.0037	0.0033	0.0030	0.0027	0.0025
1	0.0311	0.0287	0.0265	0.0244	0.0225	0.0207	0.0191	0.0176	0.0162	0.0149
2	0.0793	0.0746	0.0701	0.0659	0.0618	0.0580	0.0544	0.0509	0.0477	0.0446
3	0.1348	0.1293	0.1239	0.1185	0.1133	0.1082	0.1033	0.0985	0.0938	0.0892
4	0.1719	0.1681	0.1641	0.1600	0.1558	0.1515	0.1472	0.1428	0.1383	0.1339
5	0.1753	0.1748	0.1740	0.1728	0.1714	0.1697	0.1678	0.1656	0.1632	0.1606
6	0.1490	0.1515	0.1537	0.1555	0.1571	0.1584	0.1594	0.1601	0.1605	0.1606
7	0.1086	0.1125	0.1163	0.1200	0.1234	0.1267	0.1298	0.1326	0.1353	0.1377
8	0.0692	0.0731	0.0771	0.0810	0.0849	0.0887	0.0925	0.0962	0.0998	0.1033
9	0.0392	0.0423	0.0454	0.0486	0.0519	0.0552	0.0586	0.0620	0.0654	0.0688
10	0.0200	0.0220	0.0241	0.0262	0.0285	0.0309	0.0334	0.0359	0.0386	0.0413
11	0.0093	0.0104	0.0116	0.0129	0.0143	0.0157	0.0173	0.0190	0.0207	0.0225
12	0.0039	0.0045	0.0051	0.0058	0.0065	0.0073	0.0082	0.0092	0.0102	0.0113
13	0.0015	0.0018	0.0021	0.0024	0.0028	0.0032	0.0036	0.0041	0.0046	0.0052
14	0.0006	0.0007	0.0008	0.0009	0.0011	0.0013	0.0015	0.0017	0.0019	0.0022
15	0.0002	0.0002	0.0003	0.0003	0.0004	0.0005	0.0006	0.0007	0.0008	0.0009
16	0.0001	0.0001	0.0001	0.0001	0.0001	0.0002	0.0002	0.0002	0.0003	0.0003
17	0.0000	0.0000	0.0000	0.0000	0.0000	0.0000	0.0001	0.0001	0.0001	0.0001

					λ					
X	6.1	6.2	6.3	6.4	6.5	6.6	6.7	6.8	6.9	7.0
0	0.0022	0.0020	0.0018	0.0017	0.0015	0.0014	0.0012	0.0011	0.0010	0.0009
1	0.0137	0.0126	0.0116	0.0106	0.0098	0.0090	0.0082	0.0076	0.0070	0.0064
2	0.0417	0.0390	0.0364	0.0340	0.0318	0.0296	0.0276	0.0258	0.0240	0.0223
3	0.0848	0.0806	0.0765	0.0726	0.0688	0.0652	0.0617	0.0584	0.0552	0.0521
4	0.1294	0.1249	0.1205	0.1162	0.1118	0.1076	0.1034	0.0992	0.0952	0.0912
5	0.1579	0.1549	0.1519	0.1487	0.1454	0.1420	0.1385	0.1349	0.1314	0.1277
6	0.1605	0.1601	0.1595	0.1586	0.1575	0.1562	0.1546	0.1529	0.1511	0.1490
7	0.1399	0.1418	0.1435	0.1450	0.1462	0.1472	0.1480	0.1486	0.1489	0.1490
8	0.1066	0.1099	0.1130	0.1160	0.1188	0.1215	0.1240	0.1263	0.1284	0.1304
9	0.0723	0.0757	0.0791	0.0825	0.0858	0.0891	0.0923	0.0954	0.0985	0.1014
10	0.0441	0.0469	0.0498	0.0528	0.0558	0.0588	0.0618	0.0649	0.0679	0.0710
11	0.0245	0.0265	0.0285	0.0307	0.0330	0.0353	0.0377	0.0401	0.0426	0.0452
12	0.0124	0.0137	0.0150	0.0164	0.0179	0.0194	0.0210	0.0277	0.0245	0.0264
13	0.0058	0.0065	0.0073	0.0081	0.0089	0.0098	0.0108	0.0119	0.0130	0.0142
14	0.0025	0.0029	0.0033	0.0037	0.0041	0.0046	0.0052	0.0058	0.0064	0.0071

TABLE E.7

Table of Poisson
Probabilities
(*Continued*)

					λ					
X	6.1	6.2	6.3	6.4	6.5	6.6	6.7	6.8	6.9	7.0
15	0.0010	0.0012	0.0014	0.0016	0.0018	0.0020	0.0023	0.0026	0.0029	0.0033
16	0.0004	0.0005	0.0005	0.0006	0.0007	0.0008	0.0010	0.0011	0.0013	0.0014
17	0.0001	0.0002	0.0002	0.0002	0.0003	0.0003	0.0004	0.0004	0.0005	0.0006
18	0.0000	0.0001	0.0001	0.0001	0.0001	0.0001	0.0001	0.0002	0.0002	0.0002
19	0.0000	0.0000	0.0000	0.0000	0.0000	0.0000	0.0000	0.0001	0.0001	0.0001

					λ					
X	7.1	7.2	7.3	7.4	7.5	7.6	7.7	7.8	7.9	8.0
0	0.0008	0.0007	0.0007	0.0006	0.0006	0.0005	0.0005	0.0004	0.0004	0.0003
1	0.0059	0.0054	0.0049	0.0045	0.0041	0.0038	0.0035	0.0032	0.0029	0.0027
2	0.0208	0.0194	0.0180	0.0167	0.0156	0.0145	0.0134	0.0125	0.0116	0.0107
3	0.0492	0.0464	0.0438	0.0413	0.0389	0.0366	0.0345	0.0324	0.0305	0.0286
4	0.0874	0.0836	0.0799	0.0764	0.0729	0.0696	0.0663	0.0632	0.0602	0.0573
5	0.1241	0.1204	0.1167	0.1130	0.1094	0.1057	0.1021	0.0986	0.0951	0.0916
6	0.1468	0.1445	0.1420	0.1394	0.1367	0.1339	0.1311	0.1282	0.1252	0.1221
7	0.1489	0.1486	0.1481	0.1474	0.1465	0.1454	0.1442	0.1428	0.1413	0.1396
8	0.1321	0.1337	0.1351	0.1363	0.1373	0.1382	0.1388	0.1392	0.1395	0.1396
9	0.1042	0.1070	0.1096	0.1121	0.1144	0.1167	0.1187	0.1207	0.1224	0.1241
10	0.0740	0.0770	0.0800	0.0829	0.0858	0.0887	0.0914	0.0941	0.0967	0.0993
11	0.0478	0.0504	0.0531	0.0558	0.0585	0.0613	0.0640	0.0667	0.0695	0.0722
12	0.0283	0.0303	0.0323	0.0344	0.0366	0.0388	0.0411	0.0434	0.0457	0.0481
13	0.0154	0.0168	0.0181	0.0196	0.0211	0.0227	0.0243	0.0260	0.0278	0.0296
14	0.0078	0.0086	0.0095	0.0104	0.0113	0.0123	0.0134	0.0145	0.0157	0.0169
15	0.0037	0.0041	0.0046	0.0051	0.0057	0.0062	0.0069	0.0075	0.0083	0.0090
16	0.0016	0.0019	0.0021	0.0024	0.0026	0.0030	0.0033	0.0037	0.0041	0.0045
17	0.0007	0.0008	0.0009	0.0010	0.0012	0.0013	0.0015	0.0017	0.0019	0.0021
18	0.0003	0.0003	0.0004	0.0004	0.0005	0.0006	0.0006	0.0007	0.0008	0.0009
19	0.0001	0.0001	0.0001	0.0002	0.0002	0.0002	0.0003	0.0003	0.0003	0.0004
20	0.0000	0.0000	0.0001	0.0001	0.0001	0.0001	0.0001	0.0001	0.0001	0.0002
21	0.0000	0.0000	0.0000	0.0000	0.0000	0.0000	0.0000	0.0000	0.0001	0.0001

					λ					
X	8.1	8.2	8.3	8.4	8.5	8.6	8.7	8.8	8.9	9.0
0	0.0003	0.0003	0.0002	0.0002	0.0002	0.0002	0.0002	0.0002	0.0001	0.0001
1	0.0025	0.0023	0.0021	0.0019	0.0017	0.0016	0.0014	0.0013	0.0012	0.0011
2	0.0100	0.0092	0.0086	0.0079	0.0074	0.0068	0.0063	0.0058	0.0054	0.0050
3	0.0269	0.0252	0.0237	0.0222	0.0208	0.0195	0.0183	0.0171	0.0160	0.0150
4	0.0544	0.0517	0.0491	0.0466	0.0443	0.0420	0.0398	0.0377	0.0357	0.0337
5	0.0882	0.0849	0.0816	0.0784	0.0752	0.0722	0.0692	0.0663	0.0635	0.0607
6	0.1191	0.1160	0.1128	0.1097	0.1066	0.1034	0.1003	0.0972	0.0941	0.0911
7	0.1378	0.1358	0.1338	0.1317	0.1294	0.1271	0.1247	0.1222	0.1197	0.1171
8	0.1395	0.1392	0.1388	0.1382	0.1375	0.1366	0.1356	0.1344	0.1332	0.1318
9	0.1256	0.1269	0.1280	0.1290	0.1299	0.1306	0.1311	0.1315	0.1317	0.1318
10	0.1017	0.1040	0.1063	0.1084	0.1104	0.1123	0.1140	0.1157	0.1172	0.1186
11	0.0749	0.0776	0.0802	0.0828	0.0853	0.0878	0.0902	0.0925	0.0948	0.0970
12	0.0505	0.0530	0.0555	0.0579	0.0604	0.0629	0.0654	0.0679	0.0703	0.0728
13	0.0315	0.0334	0.0354	0.0374	0.0395	0.0416	0.0438	0.0459	0.0481	0.0504
14	0.0182	0.0196	0.0210	0.0225	0.0240	0.0256	0.0272	0.0289	0.0306	0.0324
15	0.0098	0.0107	0.0116	0.0126	0.0136	0.0147	0.0158	0.0169	0.0182	0.0194
16	0.0050	0.0055	0.0060	0.0066	0.0072	0.0079	0.0086	0.0093	0.0101	0.0109
17	0.0024	0.0026	0.0029	0.0033	0.0036	0.0040	0.0044	0.0048	0.0053	0.0058
18	0.0011	0.0012	0.0014	0.0015	0.0017	0.0019	0.0021	0.0024	0.0026	0.0029
19	0.0005	0.0005	0.0006	0.0007	0.0008	0.0009	0.0010	0.0011	0.0012	0.0014
20	0.0002	0.0002	0.0002	0.0003	0.0003	0.0004	0.0004	0.0005	0.0005	0.0006
21	0.0001	0.0001	0.0001	0.0001	0.0001	0.0002	0.0002	0.0002	0.0002	0.0003
22	0.0000	0.0000	0.0000	0.0000	0.0001	0.0001	0.0001	0.0001	0.0001	0.0001

continued

TABLE E.7

Table of Poisson
Probabilities
(*Continued*)

					λ					
X	**9.1**	**9.2**	**9.3**	**9.4**	**9.5**	**9.6**	**9.7**	**9.8**	**9.9**	**10**
0	0.0001	0.0001	0.0001	0.0001	0.0001	0.0001	0.0001	0.0001	0.0001	0.0000
1	0.0010	0.0009	0.0009	0.0008	0.0007	0.0007	0.0006	0.0005	0.0005	0.0005
2	0.0046	0.0043	0.0040	0.0037	0.0034	0.0031	0.0029	0.0027	0.0025	0.0023
3	0.0140	0.0131	0.0123	0.0115	0.0107	0.0100	0.0093	0.0087	0.0081	0.0076
4	0.0319	0.0302	0.0285	0.0269	0.0254	0.0240	0.0226	0.0213	0.0201	0.0189
5	0.0581	0.0555	0.0530	0.0506	0.0483	0.0460	0.0439	0.0418	0.0398	0.0378
6	0.0881	0.0851	0.0822	0.0793	0.0764	0.0736	0.0709	0.0682	0.0656	0.0631
7	0.1145	0.1118	0.1091	0.1064	0.1037	0.1010	0.0982	0.0955	0.0928	0.0901
8	0.1302	0.1286	0.1269	0.1251	0.1232	0.1212	0.1191	0.1170	0.1148	0.1126
9	0.1317	0.1315	0.1311	0.1306	0.1300	0.1293	0.1284	0.1274	0.1263	0.1251
10	0.1198	0.1210	0.1219	0.1228	0.1235	0.1241	0.1245	0.1249	0.1250	0.1251
11	0.0991	0.1012	0.1031	0.1049	0.1067	0.1083	0.1098	0.1112	0.1125	0.1137
12	0.0752	0.0776	0.0799	0.0822	0.0844	0.0866	0.0888	0.0908	0.0928	0.0948
13	0.0526	0.0549	0.0572	0.0594	0.0617	0.0640	0.0662	0.0685	0.0707	0.0729
14	0.0342	0.0361	0.0380	0.0399	0.0419	0.0439	0.0459	0.0479	0.0500	0.0521
15	0.0208	0.0221	0.0235	0.0250	0.0265	0.0281	0.0297	0.0313	0.0330	0.0347
16	0.0118	0.0127	0.0137	0.0147	0.0157	0.0168	0.0180	0.0192	0.0204	0.0217
17	0.0063	0.0069	0.0075	0.0081	0.0088	0.0095	0.0103	0.0111	0.0119	0.0128
18	0.0032	0.0035	0.0039	0.0042	0.0046	0.0051	0.0055	0.0060	0.0065	0.0071
19	0.0015	0.0017	0.0019	0.0021	0.0023	0.0026	0.0028	0.0031	0.0034	0.0037
20	0.0007	0.0008	0.0009	0.0010	0.0011	0.0012	0.0014	0.0015	0.0017	0.0019
21	0.0003	0.0003	0.0004	0.0004	0.0005	0.0006	0.0006	0.0007	0.0008	0.0009
22	0.0001	0.0001	0.0002	0.0002	0.0002	0.0002	0.0003	0.0003	0.0004	0.0004
23	0.0000	0.0001	0.0001	0.0001	0.0001	0.0001	0.0001	0.0001	0.0002	0.0002
24	0.0000	0.0000	0.0000	0.0000	0.0000	0.0000	0.0000	0.0001	0.0001	0.0001

X	**λ = 20**	**X**	**λ = 20**	**X**	**λ = 20**	**X**	**λ = 20**
0	0.0000	10	0.0058	20	0.0888	30	0.0083
1	0.0000	11	0.0106	21	0.0846	31	0.0054
2	0.0000	12	0.0176	22	0.0769	32	0.0034
3	0.0000	13	0.0271	23	0.0669	33	0.0020
4	0.0000	14	0.0387	24	0.0557	34	0.0012
5	0.0001	15	0.0516	25	0.0446	35	0.0007
6	0.0002	16	0.0646	26	0.0343	36	0.0004
7	0.0005	17	0.0760	27	0.0254	37	0.0002
8	0.0013	18	0.0844	28	0.0181	38	0.0001
9	0.0029	19	0.0888	29	0.0125	39	0.0001

TABLE E.8

Critical Values of the Studentized Range, Q

Upper 5% Points ($\alpha = 0.05$)

Denominator, df	Numerator, df																		
	2	3	4	5	6	7	8	9	10	11	12	13	14	15	16	17	18	19	20
1	18.00	27.00	32.80	37.10	40.40	43.10	45.40	47.40	49.10	50.60	52.00	53.20	54.30	55.40	56.30	57.20	58.00	58.80	59.60
2	6.09	8.30	9.80	10.90	11.70	12.40	13.00	13.50	14.00	14.40	14.70	15.10	15.40	15.70	15.90	16.10	16.40	16.60	16.80
3	4.50	5.91	6.82	7.50	8.04	8.48	8.85	9.18	9.46	9.72	9.95	10.15	10.35	10.52	10.69	10.84	10.98	11.11	11.24
4	3.93	5.04	5.76	6.29	6.71	7.05	7.35	7.60	7.83	8.03	8.21	8.37	8.52	8.66	8.79	8.91	9.03	9.13	9.23
5	3.64	4.60	5.22	5.67	6.03	6.33	6.58	6.80	6.99	7.17	7.32	7.47	7.60	7.72	7.83	7.93	8.03	8.12	8.21
6	3.46	4.34	4.90	5.31	5.63	5.89	6.12	6.32	6.49	6.65	6.79	6.92	7.03	7.14	7.24	7.34	7.43	7.51	7.59
7	3.34	4.16	4.68	5.06	5.36	5.61	5.82	6.00	6.16	6.30	6.43	6.55	6.66	6.76	6.85	6.94	7.02	7.09	7.17
8	3.26	4.04	4.53	4.89	5.17	5.40	5.60	5.77	5.92	6.05	6.18	6.29	6.39	6.48	6.57	6.65	6.73	6.80	6.87
9	3.20	3.95	4.42	4.76	5.02	5.24	5.43	5.60	5.74	5.87	5.98	6.09	6.19	6.28	6.36	6.44	6.51	6.58	6.64
10	3.15	3.88	4.33	4.65	4.91	5.12	5.30	5.46	5.60	5.72	5.83	5.93	6.03	6.11	6.20	6.27	6.34	6.40	6.47
11	3.11	3.82	4.26	4.57	4.82	5.03	5.20	5.35	5.49	5.61	5.71	5.81	5.90	5.99	6.06	6.14	6.20	6.26	6.33
12	3.08	3.77	4.20	4.51	4.75	4.95	5.12	5.27	5.40	5.51	5.62	5.71	5.80	5.88	5.95	6.03	6.09	6.15	6.21
13	3.06	3.73	4.15	4.45	4.69	4.88	5.05	5.19	5.32	5.43	5.53	5.63	5.71	5.79	5.86	5.93	6.00	6.05	6.11
14	3.03	3.70	4.11	4.41	4.64	4.83	4.99	5.13	5.25	5.36	5.46	5.55	5.64	5.72	5.79	5.85	5.92	5.97	6.03
15	3.01	3.67	4.08	4.37	4.60	4.78	4.94	5.08	5.20	5.31	5.40	5.49	5.58	5.65	5.72	5.79	5.85	5.90	5.96
16	3.00	3.65	4.05	4.33	4.56	4.74	4.90	5.03	5.15	5.26	5.35	5.44	5.52	5.59	5.66	5.72	5.79	5.84	5.90
17	2.98	3.63	4.02	4.30	4.52	4.71	4.86	4.99	5.11	5.21	5.31	5.39	5.47	5.55	5.61	5.68	5.74	5.79	5.84
18	2.97	3.61	4.00	4.28	4.49	4.67	4.82	4.96	5.07	5.17	5.27	5.35	5.43	5.50	5.57	5.63	5.69	5.74	5.79
19	2.96	3.59	3.98	4.25	4.47	4.65	4.79	4.92	5.04	5.14	5.23	5.32	5.39	5.46	5.53	5.59	5.65	5.70	5.75
20	2.95	3.58	3.96	4.23	4.45	4.62	4.77	4.90	5.01	5.11	5.20	5.28	5.36	5.43	5.49	5.55	5.61	5.66	5.71
24	2.92	3.53	3.90	4.17	4.37	4.54	4.68	4.81	4.92	5.01	5.10	5.18	5.25	5.32	5.38	5.44	5.50	5.54	5.59
30	2.89	3.49	3.84	4.10	4.30	4.46	4.60	4.72	4.83	4.92	5.00	5.08	5.15	5.21	5.27	5.33	5.38	5.43	5.48
40	2.86	3.44	3.79	4.04	4.23	4.39	4.52	4.63	4.74	4.82	4.91	4.98	5.05	5.11	5.16	5.22	5.27	5.31	5.36
60	2.83	3.40	3.74	3.98	4.16	4.31	4.44	4.55	4.65	4.73	4.81	4.88	4.94	5.00	5.06	5.11	5.16	5.20	5.24
120	2.80	3.36	3.69	3.92	4.10	4.24	4.36	4.48	4.56	4.64	4.72	4.78	4.84	4.90	4.95	5.00	5.05	5.09	5.13
∞	2.77	3.31	3.63	3.86	4.03	4.17	4.29	4.39	4.47	4.55	4.62	4.68	4.74	4.80	4.85	4.89	4.93	4.97	5.01

continued

TABLE E.8

Critical Values of the Studentized Range, Q (Continued)

Upper 1% Points ($\alpha = 0.01$)

Denominator, df	Numerator, df																		
	2	3	4	5	6	7	8	9	10	11	12	13	14	15	16	17	18	19	20
1	90.00	135.00	164.00	186.00	202.00	216.00	227.00	237.00	246.00	253.00	260.00	266.00	272.00	277.00	282.00	286.00	290.00	294.00	298.00
2	14.00	19.00	22.30	24.70	26.60	28.20	29.50	30.70	31.70	32.60	33.40	34.10	34.80	35.40	36.00	36.50	37.00	37.50	37.90
3	8.26	10.60	12.20	13.30	14.20	15.00	15.60	16.20	16.70	17.10	17.50	17.90	18.20	18.50	18.80	19.10	19.30	19.50	19.80
4	6.51	8.12	9.17	9.96	10.60	11.10	11.50	11.90	12.30	12.60	12.80	13.10	13.30	13.50	13.70	13.90	14.10	14.20	14.40
5	5.70	6.97	7.80	8.42	8.91	9.32	9.67	9.97	10.24	10.48	10.70	10.89	11.08	11.24	11.40	11.55	11.68	11.81	11.93
6	5.24	6.33	7.03	7.56	7.97	8.32	8.61	8.87	9.10	9.30	9.49	9.65	9.81	9.95	10.08	10.21	10.32	10.43	10.54
7	4.95	5.92	6.54	7.01	7.37	7.68	7.94	8.17	8.37	8.55	8.71	8.86	9.00	9.12	9.24	9.35	9.46	9.55	9.65
8	4.74	5.63	6.20	6.63	6.96	7.24	7.47	7.68	7.87	8.03	8.18	8.31	8.44	8.55	8.66	8.76	8.85	8.94	9.03
9	4.60	5.43	5.96	6.35	6.66	6.91	7.13	7.32	7.49	7.65	7.78	7.91	8.03	8.13	8.23	8.32	8.41	8.49	8.57
10	4.48	5.27	5.77	6.14	6.43	6.67	6.87	7.05	7.21	7.36	7.48	7.60	7.71	7.81	7.91	7.99	8.07	8.15	8.22
11	4.39	5.14	5.62	5.97	6.26	6.48	6.67	6.84	6.99	7.13	7.25	7.36	7.46	7.56	7.65	7.73	7.81	7.88	7.95
12	4.32	5.04	5.50	5.84	6.10	6.32	6.51	6.67	6.81	6.94	7.06	7.17	7.26	7.36	7.44	7.52	7.59	7.66	7.73
13	4.26	4.96	5.40	5.73	5.98	6.19	6.37	6.53	6.67	6.79	6.90	7.01	7.10	7.19	7.27	7.34	7.42	7.48	7.55
14	4.21	4.89	5.32	5.63	5.88	6.08	6.26	6.41	6.54	6.66	6.77	6.87	6.96	7.05	7.12	7.20	7.27	7.33	7.39
15	4.17	4.83	5.25	5.56	5.80	5.99	6.16	6.31	6.44	6.55	6.66	6.76	6.84	6.93	7.00	7.07	7.14	7.20	7.26
16	4.13	4.78	5.19	5.49	5.72	5.92	6.08	6.22	6.35	6.46	6.56	6.66	6.74	6.82	6.90	6.97	7.03	7.09	7.15
17	4.10	4.74	5.14	5.43	5.66	5.85	6.01	6.15	6.27	6.38	6.48	6.57	6.66	6.73	6.80	6.87	6.94	7.00	7.05
18	4.07	4.70	5.09	5.38	5.60	5.79	5.94	6.08	6.20	6.31	6.41	6.50	6.58	6.65	6.72	6.79	6.85	6.91	6.96
19	4.05	4.67	5.05	5.33	5.55	5.73	5.89	6.02	6.14	6.25	6.34	6.43	6.51	6.58	6.65	6.72	6.78	6.84	6.89
20	4.02	4.64	5.02	5.29	5.51	5.69	5.84	5.97	6.09	6.19	6.29	6.37	6.45	6.52	6.59	6.65	6.71	6.76	6.82
24	3.96	4.54	4.91	5.17	5.37	5.54	5.69	5.81	5.92	6.02	6.11	6.19	6.26	6.33	6.39	6.45	6.51	6.56	6.61
30	3.89	4.45	4.80	5.05	5.24	5.40	5.54	5.65	5.76	5.85	5.93	6.01	6.08	6.14	6.20	6.26	6.31	6.36	6.41
40	3.82	4.37	4.70	4.93	5.11	5.27	5.39	5.50	5.60	5.69	5.77	5.84	5.90	5.96	6.02	6.07	6.12	6.17	6.21
60	3.76	4.28	4.60	4.82	4.99	5.13	5.25	5.36	5.45	5.53	5.60	5.67	5.73	5.79	5.84	5.89	5.93	5.98	6.02
120	3.70	4.20	4.50	4.71	4.87	5.01	5.12	5.21	5.30	5.38	5.44	5.51	5.56	5.61	5.66	5.71	5.75	5.79	5.83
∞	3.64	4.12	4.40	4.60	4.76	4.88	4.99	5.08	5.16	5.23	5.29	5.35	5.40	5.45	5.49	5.54	5.57	5.61	5.65

Source: Reprinted from E. S. Pearson and H. O. Hartley, eds., Table 29 of *Biometrika Tables for Statisticians, Vol. 1*, 3rd ed., 1966, by permission of the *Biometrika* Trustees, London.

TABLE E.9
Control Chart Factors

Number of Observations in Sample (n)	d_2	d_3	D_3	D_4	A_2
2	1.128	0.853	0	3.267	1.880
3	1.693	0.888	0	2.575	1.023
4	2.059	0.880	0	2.282	0.729
5	2.326	0.864	0	2.114	0.577
6	2.534	0.848	0	2.004	0.483
7	2.704	0.833	0.076	1.924	0.419
8	2.847	0.820	0.136	1.864	0.373
9	2.970	0.808	0.184	1.816	0.337
10	3.078	0.797	0.223	1.777	0.308
11	3.173	0.787	0.256	1.744	0.285
12	3.258	0.778	0.283	1.717	0.266
13	3.336	0.770	0.307	1.693	0.249
14	3.407	0.763	0.328	1.672	0.235
15	3.472	0.756	0.347	1.653	0.223
16	3.532	0.750	0.363	1.637	0.212
17	3.588	0.744	0.378	1.622	0.203
18	3.640	0.739	0.391	1.609	0.194
19	3.689	0.733	0.404	1.596	0.187
20	3.735	0.729	0.415	1.585	0.180
21	3.778	0.724	0.425	1.575	0.173
22	3.819	0.720	0.435	1.565	0.167
23	3.858	0.716	0.443	1.557	0.162
24	3.895	0.712	0.452	1.548	0.157
25	3.931	0.708	0.459	1.541	0.153

Source: *Reprinted from ASTM-STP 15D by kind permission of the American Society for Testing and Materials.*

TABLE E.10

The Standardized Normal Distribution

Entry represents area under the standardized normal
distribution from the mean to Z

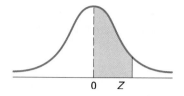

Z	.00	.01	.02	.03	.04	.05	.06	.07	.08	.09
0.0	.0000	.0040	.0080	.0120	.0160	.0199	.0239	.0279	.0319	.0359
0.1	.0398	.0438	.0478	.0517	.0557	.0596	.0636	.0675	.0714	.0753
0.2	.0793	.0832	.0871	.0910	.0948	.0987	.1026	.1064	.1103	.1141
0.3	.1179	.1217	.1255	.1293	.1331	.1368	.1406	.1443	.1480	.1517
0.4	.1554	.1591	.1628	.1664	.1700	.1736	.1772	.1808	.1844	.1879
0.5	.1915	.1950	.1985	.2019	.2054	.2088	.2123	.2157	.2190	.2224
0.6	.2257	.2291	.2324	.2357	.2389	.2422	.2454	.2486	.2518	.2549
0.7	.2580	.2612	.2642	.2673	.2704	.2734	.2764	.2794	.2823	.2852
0.8	.2881	.2910	.2939	.2967	.2995	.3023	.3051	.3078	.3106	.3133
0.9	.3159	.3186	.3212	.3238	.3264	.3289	.3315	.3340	.3365	.3389
1.0	.3413	.3438	.3461	.3485	.3508	.3531	.3554	.3577	.3599	.3621
1.1	.3643	.3665	.3686	.3708	.3729	.3749	.3770	.3790	.3810	.3830
1.2	.3849	.3869	.3888	.3907	.3925	.3944	.3962	.3980	.3997	.4015
1.3	.4032	.4049	.4066	.4082	.4099	.4115	.4131	.4147	.4162	.4177
1.4	.4192	.4207	.4222	.4236	.4251	.4265	.4279	.4292	.4306	.4319
1.5	.4332	.4345	.4357	.4370	.4382	.4394	.4406	.4418	.4429	.4441
1.6	.4452	.4463	.4474	.4484	.4495	.4505	.4515	.4525	.4535	.4545
1.7	.4554	.4564	.4573	.4582	.4591	.4599	.4608	.4616	.4625	.4633
1.8	.4641	.4649	.4656	.4664	.4671	.4678	.4686	.4693	.4699	.4706
1.9	.4713	.4719	.4726	.4732	.4738	.4744	.4750	.4756	.4761	.4767
2.0	.4772	.4778	.4783	.4788	.4793	.4798	.4803	.4808	.4812	.4817
2.1	.4821	.4826	.4830	.4834	.4838	.4842	.4846	.4850	.4854	.4857
2.2	.4861	.4864	.4868	.4871	.4875	.4878	.4881	.4884	.4887	.4890
2.3	.4893	.4896	.4898	.4901	.4904	.4906	.4909	.4911	.4913	.4916
2.4	.4918	.4920	.4922	.4925	.4927	.4929	.4931	.4932	.4934	.4936
2.5	.4938	.4940	.4941	.4943	.4945	.4946	.4948	.4949	.4951	.4952
2.6	.4953	.4955	.4956	.4957	.4959	.4960	.4961	.4962	.4963	.4964
2.7	.4965	.4966	.4967	.4968	.4969	.4970	.4971	.4972	.4973	.4974
2.8	.4974	.4975	.4976	.4977	.4977	.4978	.4979	.4979	.4980	.4981
2.9	.4981	.4982	.4982	.4983	.4984	.4984	.4985	.4985	.4986	.4986
3.0	.49865	.49869	.49874	.49878	.49882	.49886	.49889	.49893	.49897	.49900
3.1	.49903	.49906	.49910	.49913	.49916	.49918	.49921	.49924	.49926	.49929
3.2	.49931	.49934	.49936	.49938	.49940	.49942	.49944	.49946	.49948	.49950
3.3	.49952	.49953	.49955	.49957	.49958	.49960	.49961	.49962	.49964	.49965
3.4	.49966	.49968	.49969	.49970	.49971	.49972	.49973	.49974	.49975	.49976
3.5	.49977	.49978	.49978	.49979	.49980	.49981	.49981	.49982	.49983	.49983
3.6	.49984	.49985	.49985	.49986	.49986	.49987	.49987	.49988	.49988	.49989
3.7	.49989	.49990	.49990	.49990	.49991	.49991	.49992	.49992	.49992	.49992
3.8	.49993	.49993	.49993	.49994	.49994	.49994	.49994	.49995	.49995	.49995
3.9	.49995	.49995	.49996	.49996	.49996	.49996	.49996	.49996	.49997	.49997

Use this appendix to find answers to the most frequently asked questions about using the resources on the Student CD-ROM and using Microsoft Excel and PHStat2.

F.1 About the Student CD-ROM

What does the Student CD-ROM contain?
The Student CD-ROM contains six categories of files that support this book:

1. **Data files.** These files contain the data used in chapter examples or named in problems. They exist as Excel workbook files (in the **.xls** format, compatible with all Excel versions), worksheet (**.mtw**) files and SPSS worksheet **.sav** files. See Appendix D.2 for a complete listing of data files included on the Student CD-ROM.
2. **Case files.** These files, a mix of data and document files as well as facsimiles of Web page files, support both the *Managing the Springville Herald* running case and the various Web Cases.
3. **Excel appendix workbooks.** These files are Microsoft Excel workbooks that contain model solutions for applying Microsoft Excel to various statistical analyses. Most are designed as fill-in-the-data templates that can be reused indefinitely.
4. **Visual Explorations files.** These files support Visual Explorations, the interactive Excel add-in that illustrates selected statistical concepts.
5. **Windows applications.** These files are specific to Microsoft Windows XP or Vista (any version) and include the PHStat2 setup program, and the Adobe Reader setup program, and the Student CD-ROM's own "start" program that simplifies access to the contents of the Student CD-ROM.

Can I use the Student CD-ROM with an Apple Mac running the Mac OS?
Although the Student CD-ROM is marked "For Windows," most Mac users will be able to retrieve and use the first four categories of files listed in the previous answer.

Does the Student CD-ROM contain Microsoft Excel or Minitab?
No, these programs must be acquired separately. Specially priced student-oriented versions of Microsoft Office (containing Excel) are available at many retailers and select retailers, including **mypearsonstore.com**, sell the student version of Minitab.

Can I copy the Excel workbook files to my local hard disk or other storage device?
Yes, you can, and you are encouraged to do so. Windows users can use the CD-ROM's own "start" program to facilitate this task. Some files that you copy may be reported as being a "read-only" file. If you make changes to such files, you will need to save the file under a different name.

Can I buy a replacement Student CD-ROM disk?
No, Student CD-ROM disks are not sold separately. However, a PHStat2 version either identical or similar to the one included on the Student CD-ROM is available for separate purchase.

F.2 About Microsoft Excel

Will I need access to my original Microsoft Office/Excel CDs or DVD?
Yes, if you are using PHStat2 you may need to use the original program disks if the Analysis ToolPak and Analysis ToolPak–VBA (referred to as the "ToolPak" in this book) has not been installed on your system.

What Microsoft Office security settings should I use? How do I change Office security settings?
See Section E1.8, "Using Add-ins" on page 19 for specific answers to these questions. If you plan to use the Prentice Hall PHStat2 Excel add-in, also read the PHStat2 readme file on the Student CD-ROM.

How can I check to see if the ToolPak has been installed in Excel 97–2003?
Open Excel and select **Tools ➔ Add-Ins** and in the Add-Ins dialog box that appears, verify that **Analysis ToolPak** (and **Analysis ToolPak–VBA**, if using PHStat2) is checked in the **Add-Ins available** list. If **Analysis ToolPak** does not appear, you will need to install it separately.

How can I check to see if the ToolPak has been installed in Excel 2007?
Open Excel and click the **Office Button**. In the Office Button pane, click **Excel Options**. In the Excel options dialog box that appears, click **Add-Ins** in the left pane and look for **Analysis ToolPak** (and **Analysis ToolPak–VBA**, if using PHStat2) under **Active Application Add-Ins**. If they do not appear, click **Go** and continue with the instructions for using the Add-Ins dialog box presented in the answer for Excel 97–2003.

How can I install the ToolPak?
Close Microsoft Excel and rerun the Microsoft Office or Microsoft Excel setup program. When the setup program runs, choose the option that allows you to add components.

This option is variously described as the **modify**, **add**, or **custom** option. Then, select install **Analysis ToolPak** (and **Analysis ToolPak–VBA**, if using PHStat2). You may need access to the original Microsoft Office/Excel setup CD-ROMs or DVDs to complete this task.

Do I need to run a setup program to use the Visual Explorations add-in workbook (`Visual Explorations.xla`)?
No, you can copy the files and install the files from the Visual Exporations folder on the Student CD-ROM and use this add-in file as you would use any of the workbook data files. You will need to properly adjust your Microsoft Office security settings (see Section E1.8 on page 19) in order to use this add-in.

In Excel 97–2003, how can I specify the custom settings that you recommend?
First, select **Tools → Customize**. In the Customize dialog box, clear (uncheck) the **Menus show recently used commands first** check box if it is checked and click the **Close** button. Then select **Tools → Options**. In the Options dialog box, click the **Calculation** tab and verify that the **Automatic** option button of the Calculation group has been selected. Click the **Edit** tab and verify that all check boxes except the **Fixed decimal, Provide feedback with Animation**, and **Enable automatic percent entry** have been selected. (Excel 97 does not contain an Automatic percent entry check box.) Click the **General** tab and verify that the **R1C1 reference style** check box is cleared, and, if using Excel 97, check the **Macro virus protection** check box. Enter **3** as the number of **Sheets in new workbook**, select **Arial** from the **Standard font** list, and select **10** from the **Size** drop-down list. Then click **OK** to finish the customization.

In Excel 2007, how can I specify the custom settings that you recommend?
First, click the **Office Button** and then click **Excel Options**. In the Excel Options dialog box, click **Formulas** in the left panel. In the **Formulas** right pane, click **Automatic** under Workbook Calculation and verify that all check boxes are checked except **Enable iterative calculation, R1C1 reference style**, and **Formulas referring to empty cells**. For greater customization, click **Advanced** in the left panel and scroll through the **Advanced options for working with Excel** that appears in the right panel. Click **OK** when finished.

F.3 About PHStat2

What is PHStat2?
PHStat2 is software that makes operating Microsoft Excel as distraction free as possible. As a student studying statistics, you can focus mainly on learning statistics and not worry about having to fully master Excel first. When PHStat2 is combined with the ToolPak add-in supplied with Microsoft Excel, just about all statistical methods taught in an introductory statistics course can be illustrated using Microsoft Excel.

I do not want to use an add-in that will not be available in my business environment. Any comments?
Chapter 1 talks about these issues in detail. To summarize those pages, PHStat2 helps you learn Microsoft Excel, and using PHStat2 will not leave you any less equipped to work with Microsoft Excel in a setting where it is not available.

What do I need to do in order to begin using PHStat2?
You run the PHStat2 setup program (setup.exe) that is included on the Student CD-ROM. To use this program successfully, you must have logged in to Windows using an account that has administrator or software-installing privileges. (Student and faculty accounts to log in to networked computers in academic settings typically do not have this privilege. If you have such an account, ask your network or lab technician for assistance.) If you are using Windows Vista or certain firewall or security-suite programs, you may see messages asking you to permit or allow certain system operations as the PHStat2 setup runs. (If you decline permission, PHStat2 will not be successfully set up.)

What are the technical requirements for setting up and adding PHStat2 to my system?
If your system can run Microsoft Excel, it can also run PHStat2. You need approximately up to 10 MB hard disk free space during the setup process and up to 3 MB hard disk space after PHStat2 is installed. You must also ensure that the Microsoft Excel Analysis ToolPak and Analysis ToolPak–VBA add-ins have been installed. (See related question in Section F.2.)

Are updates to PHStat2 available?
Yes, free minor updates to resolve issues may be available for download from the PHStat2 Web site (**www.prenhall.com/phstat**). When you visit that Web site, note that the Student CD-ROM contains version 2.8 of PHStat2.

How can I identify which version of PHStat2 I have?
Open Microsoft Excel with PHStat2 and select **Help for PHStat** from the PHStat menu. A dialog box will display your current XLA and DLL version numbers. The XLA version number identifies the version of PHStat2 you have. Both of these numbers will initially be 2.8.0 after you set up PHStat2 from the Student CD-ROM.

Where can I get help setting up PHStat2?
First, carefully review the Student CD-ROM PHStat2 readme file. If your problem is unresolved, visit the PHStat2 Web site (**www.prenhall.com/phstat**) for further information. If your problem is still unresolved, contact Pearson Education technical support at **247pearsoned.custhelp.com**.

Where can I find tips for using PHStat2?
While your classmates and instructor can be the best source of tips, you can also visit the online PHStat2 community at **phstatcommunity.org**

F.4 About Minitab

Which versions of Minitab can I use with this book?
You should use Minitab 14 or Minitab 15 when following the instructions in the Minitab appendices. There is a student version of Minitab that can be bundled with the book.

F.5 Additional Information For New Microsoft Excel 2007 Users

I do not see the menu for an add-in workbook that I opened. Where is it?
Unlike earlier versions of Excel that allowed add-ins to add menus to the menu bar, Excel 2007 places all add-in menus under the Add-ins tab. If you click Add-ins, you find the menus of all properly loaded add-ins.

What does "Compatibility Mode" mean?
When you see "Compatibility Mode" in the title bar, Excel 2007 is telling you that you are using a workbook compatible with earlier Excel versions. When you save such a workbook, Excel 2007 will automatically use the .xls file format of earlier versions.

How can I update an older (.xls) workbook to the Excel 2007 .xlsx workbook format?
The simplest way is to open the workbook file and select **Office Button → Convert**. Then save your file (select **Office Button → Save**). You can also open the workbook file and select **Office Button → Save As** and in the Save As dialog box, select **Excel Workbook (*.xlsx)** from the **Save as type** list.

Self-Test Solutions and Answers to Selected Even-Numbered Problems

The following represent worked-out solutions to Self-Test Problems and brief answers to most of the even-numbered problems in the text. For more detailed solutions, including explanations, interpretations, and Excel and Minitab output, see the *Student Solutions Manual*.

CHAPTER 1

1.2 Small, medium, and large sizes represent different categories.

1.4 (a) The number of telephones is a numerical variable that is discrete because the outcome is a count. **(b)** The length of the longest long-distance call is a numerical variable that is continuous because any value within a range of values can occur. **(c)** Whether there is a cell phone in the household is a categorical variable because the answer can be only yes or no. **(d)** Same answer as in (c).

1.6 (a) Categorical. **(b)** Numerical, continuous. **(c)** Numerical, discrete. **(d)** Numerical, discrete.

1.8 (a) Numerical, continuous. **(b)** Numerical, discrete. **(c)** Numerical, continuous. **(d)** Categorical.

1.20 (a) All people living in the United States aged 18 and older. **(b)** A telephone interview of 1,102 respondents. **(c)** The population percentage of people living in the United States aged 18 and older who have made major changes in their shopping and living habits over the last five years to help protect the environment. **(d)** Twenty-eight percent of respondents have made major changes in their shopping and living habits over the last five years to help protect the environment.

1.22 (a) Cat owner households in the United States. **(b)** 1. Categorical. 2. Categorical. 3. Numerical, discrete. 4. Categorical.

1.24 (a) Gender, current major, undergraduate major, current employment status, satisfaction with advisement services. **(b)** Age, height, graduate cumulative grade point average, undergraduate cumulative grade point average, GMAT score, number of full-time jobs, starting salary, salary in five years, amount spent on textbooks and supplies. **(c)** Number of full-time jobs. (GMAT score could also be considered discrete.)

CHAPTER 2

2.4 (b) The Pareto chart is best for portraying these data because it not only sorts the frequencies in descending order, it also provides the cumulative polygon on the same scale. **(c)** You can conclude that friends/family account for the largest percentage of 45%. When other, news media, and online user reviews are added to friends/family, this accounts for 83%.

2.6 (b) 85%. **(d)** The Pareto chart allows you to see which sources account for most of the electricity.

2.8 (b) The bar chart is more suitable if the purpose is to compare the categories. The pie chart is more suitable if the main objective is to investigate the portion of the whole that is in a particular category.

2.10 Stem-and-leaf display of finance scores:

5	34
6	9
7	4
8	0
9	38

$n = 7$

2.12 50 74 74 76 81 89 92.

2.14 (a) Ordered array: Cost(\$) 137, 140, 142, 146, 148, 151, 157, 160, 164, 165, 166, 166, 167, 184, 190, 191, 192, 196, 200, 202, 207, 215, 215, 217, 229, 230, 251, 252, 260, 321
(b) Stem-and-leaf display:

Stem unit: 10

13	7
14	0268
15	17
16	045667
17	
18	4
19	0126
20	027
21	557
22	9
23	0
24	
25	12
26	0
27	
28	
29	
30	
31	
32	1

(c) The stem-and-leaf display provides more information because it not only orders values from the smallest to the largest into stems and leaves, it also conveys information on how the values distribute and cluster over the range of the data.
(d) The costs of attending a baseball game are concentrated around \$160. In addition, the costs appear to spread between \$140 and \$210 with the exception of an outlier at \$321 for Boston.

2.16 (a) Ordered array:

4 5 7 8 16 19 19 20 20 23 24 25 29 29 30 30 30 30 40 56

(b) Stem-and-leaf display for fat; stem, 10 unit:

0	4 5 7 8
1	6 9 9
2	0 0 3 4 5 9 9
3	0 0 0 0
4	0
5	6

(c) The stem-and-leaf display conveys more information than the ordered array because it shows how the values distribute. **(d)** They are concentrated around 29 and 30.

2.18 (a) 10 but less than 20, 20 but less than 30, 30 but less than 40, 40 but less than 50, 50 but less than 60, 60 but less than 70, 70 but less than 80, 80 but less than 90, 90 but less than 100. **(b)** 10. **(c)** 15, 25, 35, 45, 55, 65, 75, 85, 95.

2.20 (a)

Electricity Costs	Frequency	Percentage
$80 up to $99	4	8%
$100 up to $119	7	14
$120 up to $139	9	18
$140 up to $159	13	26
$160 up to $179	9	18
$180 up to $199	5	10
$200 up to $219	3	6

(c)

Electricity Costs	Frequency	Percentage	Cumulative %
$99	4	8.00%	8.00%
$119	7	14.00	22.00
$139	9	18.00	40.00
$159	13	26.00	66.00
$179	9	18.00	84.00
$199	5	10.00	94.00
$219	3	6.00	100.00

(d) The majority of utility charges are clustered between $120 and $180.

2.22 The property taxes per capita appear to be right-skewed with approximately 90% falling between $399 and $1,700, and the remaining 10% falling between $1,700 and $2,100. The center is at about $1,000.

2.24 (a)

Width	Frequency	Percentage
8.310–8.329	3	6.12%
8.330–8.349	2	4.08
8.350–8.369	1	2.04
8.370–8.389	4	8.16
8.390–8.409	5	10.20
8.410–8.429	16	32.65
8.430–8.449	5	10.20
8.450–8.469	5	10.20
8.470–8.489	6	12.24
8.490–8.509	2	4.08

(d) All the troughs will meet the company's requirements of between 8.31 and 8.61 inches wide.

2.26 (a)

Bulb Life (hrs)	Percentage, Mfgr A	Percentage, Mfgr B
650–749	7.5%	0.0%
750–849	12.5	5.0
850–949	50.0	20.0
950–1,049	22.5	40.0
1,050–1,149	7.5	22.5
1,150–1,249	0.0	12.5

(c)

% Less Than	Percentage Less Than, Mfgr A	Percentage Less Than, Mfgr B
750	7.5%	0.0%
850	20.0	5.0
950	70.0	25.0
1,050	92.5	65.0
1,150	100.0	87.5
1,250	100.0	100.0

(d) Manufacturer B produces bulbs with longer lives than Manufacturer A. The cumulative percentage for Manufacturer B shows 65% of its bulbs lasted less than 1,050 hours, contrasted with 70% of Manufacturer A's bulbs, which lasted less than 950 hours. None of Manufacturer A's bulbs lasted more than 1,149 hours, but 12.5% of Manufacturer B's bulbs lasted between 1,150 and 1,249 hours. At the same time, 7.5% of Manufacturer A's bulbs lasted less than 750 hours, whereas all of Manufacturer B's bulbs lasted at least 750 hours.

2.28 (a) Table of frequencies for all student responses:

	STUDENT MAJOR CATEGORIES			
GENDER	A	C	M	Totals
Male	14	9	2	25
Female	6	6	3	15
Totals	20	15	5	40

(b) Table of percentages based on overall student responses:

	STUDENT MAJOR CATEGORIES			
GENDER	A	C	M	Totals
Male	35.0%	22.5%	5.0%	62.5%
Female	15.0	15.0	7.5	37.5
Totals	50.0	37.5	12.5	100.0

(c) Table based on row percentages:

	STUDENT MAJOR CATEGORIES			
GENDER	A	C	M	Totals
Male	56.0%	36.0%	8.0%	100.0%
Female	40.0	40.0	20.0	100.0
Totals	50.0	37.5	12.5	100.0

(d) Table based on column percentages:

	STUDENT MAJOR CATEGORIES			
GENDER	A	C	M	Totals
Male	70.0%	60.0%	40.0%	62.5%
Female	30.0	40.0	60.0	37.5
Totals	100.0	100.0	100.0	100.0

2.30 (a) Table of row percentages:

ENJOY SHOPPING FOR CLOTHING	GENDER		
	Male	**Female**	**Total**
Yes	38%	62%	100%
No	74	26	100
Total	48	52	100

Table of column percentages:

ENJOY SHOPPING FOR CLOTHING	GENDER		
	Male	**Female**	**Total**
Yes	57%	86%	72%
No	43	14	28
Total	100	100	100

Table of total percentages:

ENJOY SHOPPING FOR CLOTHING	GENDER		
	Male	**Female**	**Total**
Yes	27%	45%	72%
No	21	7	28
Total	48	52	100

(b) A higher percentage of females enjoy shopping for clothing.

2.32 (b) The number of MBA and undergraduate students who choose the lowest-cost fund and the second-lowest-cost fund is about the same. More MBA students chose the third-lowest cost fund whereas more undergraduate students chose the highest cost fund.

2.34 (b) Yes, there is a strong positive relationship between X and Y. As X increases, so does Y.

2.36 (b) There is a positive relationship between owner mileage and current government standard mileage.

2.38 (b) There appears to be a positive relationship between the coaches' salary and revenue. **(c)** Yes, this is borne out by the data.

2.40 (b) The unemployment rate was stable at around 4% from January 2000 to around January 2001. Then it trended upward and leveled off at around 6% by December 2001. Around October 2003, it started to trend downward and reached about 4.5% by December 2006 before staying between 4.5% and 5% in 2007.

2.42 (b) There is an obvious upward trend in the average number of TV channels that the U.S. home received from 1985 to 2005. **(c)** With extrapolation, you would predict the average number of TV channels that the U.S. home will receive in 2010 to be around 140.

2.60 (c) The publisher gets the largest portion (64.8%) of the revenue. About half (32.3%) of the revenue received by the publisher covers manufacturing costs. The publisher's marketing and promotion account for the next largest share of the revenue, at 15.4%. Author, bookstore employee salaries and benefits, and publisher administrative costs and taxes each account for around 10% of the revenue, whereas the publisher after-tax profit, bookstore operations, bookstore pretax profit, and freight constitute the "trivial few" allocations of the revenue. Yes, the bookstore gets twice the revenue of the authors.

2.62 (b) The Pareto plot is most appropriate because it not only sorts the frequencies in descending order, it also provides the cumulative polygon on the same scale. **(d)** The Pareto plot is most appropriate because it not only sorts the frequencies in descending order, it also provides the

cumulative polygon on the same scale. **(e)** "Paid search" constitutes the largest category on U.S. online ad spending at 43%. Excluding the generic keyword "sneakers," searches using the keywords "sneaker pimps" and "Jordan sneaker" make up the majority of the searches for sneakers on specific brands.

2.64 (a)

DESSERT ORDERED	GENDER		
	Male	**Female**	**Total**
Yes	71%	29%	100%
No	48	52	100
Total	53	47	100

DESSERT ORDERED	GENDER		
	Male	**Female**	**Total**
Yes	30%	14%	23%
No	70	86	77
Total	100	100	100

DESSERT ORDERED	BEEF ENTRÉE		
	Yes	**No**	**Total**
Yes	52%	48%	100%
No	25	75	100
Total	31	69	100

DESSERT ORDERED	BEEF ENTRÉE		
	Yes	**No**	**Total**
Yes	38%	16%	23%
No	62	84	77
Total	100	100	100

DESSERT ORDERED	BEEF ENTRÉE		
	Yes	**No**	**Total**
Yes	12%	11%	23%
No	19	58	77
Total	31	69	100

(b) If the owner is interested in finding out the percentage of males and females who order dessert or the percentage of those who order a beef entrée and a dessert among all patrons, the table of total percentages is most informative. If the owner is interested in the effect of gender on ordering of dessert or the effect of ordering a beef entrée on the ordering of dessert, the table of column percentages will be most informative. Because dessert is usually ordered after the main entrée, and the owner has no direct control over the gender of patrons, the table of row percentages is not very useful here. **(c)** 30% of the men ordered desserts, compared to 14% of the women; men are more than twice as likely to order desserts as women. Almost 38% of the patrons ordering a beef entrée ordered dessert, compared to 16% of patrons ordering all other entrees. Patrons ordering beef are more than 2.3 times as likely to order dessert as patrons ordering any other entrée.

2.66 (a) 23575R15 accounts for over 80% of the warranty claims. **(b)** 91.82% of the warranty claims are from the ATX model. **(c)** Tread separation accounts for 73.23% of the warranty claims among the ATX model. **(d)** The number of claims is evenly distributed among the three incidents; other/unknown incidents account for almost 40% of the claims, tread separation accounts for about 35% of the claims, and blowout accounts for about 25% of the claims.

2.68 (c) Majority (about 71%) of the beer have percentage alcohol between 4.1% and 5.1% with one beer (O'Doul's) containing only 0.4% alcohol. There are two clusters in the distribution of calories. About 60% of the beer have between 135 and 175 calories and another cluster of 25% has between 95 and 115 calories. The distribution of carbohydrates is slightly right-skewed with carbohydrates for Sam Adams Cream Stout having a value equal to 23.9. There appears to be a positive relationship between percentage alcohol in a beer and its calorie content. There is also an obvious positive relationship between calorie content and carbohydrate content. Percentage alcohol content and calorie content do not appear to be related.

2.70 (c) The distribution of the yields of the money market accounts is right skewed with almost 87% of them having a return of less than 1.2% whereas only about 3% of them have yields higher than 2.0%. The distribution of the yields of one-year CDs is more bell-shaped between 1.2% and 3.8% with only about 15% of them having a yield of less than 1.5%. Only 10% of the five-year CDs have yields that are lower than 2% and about 13% of them have yields higher than 3.5%. There appear to be positive relationships between all pairs of yields with one-year CDs and five-year CDs demonstrating the strongest positive relationship.

2.72 (a)

Frequencies (Boston)

Weight (Boston)	Frequency	Percentage
3,015 but less than 3,050	2	0.54%
3,050 but less than 3,085	44	11.96
3,085 but less than 3,120	122	33.15
3,120 but less than 3,155	131	35.60
3,155 but less than 3,190	58	15.76
3,190 but less than 3,225	7	1.90
3,225 but less than 3,260	3	0.82
3,260 but less than 3,295	1	0.27

(b)

Frequencies (Vermont)

Weight (Vermont)	Frequency	Percentage
3,550 but less than 3,600	4	1.21%
3,600 but less than 3,650	31	9.39
3,650 but less than 3,700	115	34.85
3,700 but less than 3,750	131	39.70
3,750 but less than 3,800	36	10.91
3,800 but less than 3,850	12	3.64
3,850 but less than 3,900	1	0.30

(d) 0.54% of the Boston shingles pallets are underweight, whereas 0.27% are overweight. 1.21% of the Vermont shingles pallets are underweight, whereas 3.94% are overweight.

2.74 (a), (c)

Calories	Frequency	Percentage	Limit	Percentage Less Than
50 but less than 100	3	12%	100	12%
100 but less than 150	3	12	150	24
150 but less than 200	9	36	200	60
200 but less than 250	6	24	250	84
250 but less than 300	3	12	300	96
300 but less than 350	0	0	350	96
350 but less than 400	1	4	400	100

Protein	Frequency	Percentage	Limit	Percentage Less Than
16 but less than 20	1	4%	20	4%
20 but less than 24	5	20	24	24
24 but less than 28	8	32	28	56
28 but less than 32	9	36	32	92
32 but less than 36	2	8	36	100

Calories from Fat	Frequency	Percentage	Limit	Percentage Less Than
0% but less than 10%	3	12%	10	12%
10% but less than 20%	4	16	20	28
20% but less than 30%	2	8	30	36
30% but less than 40%	5	20	40	56
40% but less than 50%	3	12	50	68
50% but less than 60%	5	20	60	88
60% but less than 70%	2	8	70	96
70% but less than 80%	1	4	80	100

Calories from Saturated Fat	Frequency	Percentage	Limit	Percentage Less Than
0% but less than 5%	6	24%	5	24%
5% but less than 10%	2	8	10	32
10% but less than 15%	5	20	15	52
15% but less than 20%	5	20	20	72
20% but less than 25%	5	20	25	92
25% but less than 30%	2	8	30	100

Cholesterol	Frequency	Percentage	Limit	Percentage Less Than
0 but less than 50	2	8%	50	8%
50 but less than 100	17	68	100	76
100 but less than 150	4	16	150	92
150 but less than 200	1	4	200	96
200 but less than 250	0	0	250	96
250 but less than 300	0	0	300	96
300 but less than 350	0	0	350	96
350 but less than 400	0	0	400	96
400 but less than 450	0	0	450	96
450 but less than 500	1	4	500	100

(d) The sampled fresh red meats, poultry, and fish vary from 98 to 397 calories per serving, with the highest concentration between 150 to 200 calories. One protein source, spareribs, with 397 calories, is more than 100 calories above the next highest caloric food. The protein content of the sampled foods varies from 16 to 33 grams, with 68% of the data values falling between 24 and 32 grams. Spareribs and fried liver are both very different from other foods sampled—the former on calories and the latter on cholesterol content.

2.76 (c) Total fat seems to be most closely related to calories because the points in the scatter plot are closer to the imaginary line that passes through the data points.

2.78 (b) There is a downward trend in the amount filled. **(c)** The amount filled in the next bottle will most likely be below 1.894 liter. **(d)** The scatter plot of the amount of soft drink filled against time reveals the trend of the data, whereas a histogram only provides information on the distribution of the data.

CHAPTER 3

3.2 (a) Mean = 7, median = 7, mode = 7. **(b)** Range = 9, S^2 = 10.8, S = 3.286, CV = 46.948%. **(c)** Z scores: 0, −0.913, 0.609, 0, −1.217, 1.522. None of the Z scores are larger than 3.0 or smaller than −3.0. There is no outlier. **(d)** Symmetric because mean = median.

3.4 (a) Mean = 2, median = 7, mode = 7. **(b)** Range = 17, S^2 = 62 S = 7.874, CV = 393.7%. **(d)** Left-skewed because mean < median.

3.6 (a)

	Grade X	Grade Y
Mean	575	575.4
Median	575	575
Standard deviation	6.40	2.07

(b) If quality is measured by central tendency, Grade X tires provide slightly better quality because X's mean and median are both equal to the expected value, 575 mm. If, however, quality is measured by consistency, Grade Y provides better quality because, even though Y's mean is only slightly larger than the mean for Grade X, Y's standard deviation is much smaller. The range in values for Grade Y is 5 mm compared to the range in values for Grade X, which is 16 mm.

(c)

	Grade X	Grade Y, Altered
Mean	575	577.4
Median	575	575
Standard deviation	6.40	6.11

When the fifth Y tire measures 588 mm rather than 578 mm, Y's mean inner diameter becomes 577.4 mm, which is larger than X's mean inner diameter, and Y's standard deviation increases from 2.07 mm to 6.11 mm. In this case, X's tires are providing better quality in terms of the mean inner diameter, with only slightly more variation among the tires than Y's.

3.8 (a) Mean = 36.53, median = 35.6. **(b)** Variance = 19.27, standard deviation = 4.39, range = 12, coefficient of variation = 12.02%. **(c)** The mean is only slightly larger than the median, so the data are only slightly right-skewed. **(d)** The mean cost is $36.53 and the median cost is $35.60. The average scatter of cost around the mean is $4.39. The difference between the highest and the lowest cost is $12.

3.10 (a) Mean = 18.7727, median = 18, mode = 18. **(b)** Variance = 4.0887, standard deviation = 2.0221, range = 7, coefficient of variation = 10.77%. **(c)** Because the mean is larger than the median, the data are right-skewed. **(d)** The distributions of MPG of the sedans is symmetric while the SUVs are skewed to the right. The mean MPG of sedans is 8.15 higher than that of SUVs. The average scatter of the MPG of sedans is higher than that for SUVs. The difference between the highest and the lowest MPG of sedans is also higher than that of SUVs.

3.12 (a) Mean = $0.9257, median = $0.88. **(b)** Variance = 0.1071, standard deviation = $0.3273, range = $0.96, CV = 35.36%. There is no outlier because none of the Z scores has an absolute value that is greater than 3.0. **(c)** The data appear to be skewed to the right because the mean is greater than the median.

3.14 (a) Mean = 46.8, median = 42.5. **(b)** Range = 34, variance = 123.29, standard deviation = 11.10. **(c)** The admission price for one-day tickets is slightly skewed to the right because the mean is slightly greater than the median. **(d)(a)** Mean = 50.8, median = 42.5. **(b)** Range = 69, variance = 382.84, standard deviation = 19.57. **(c)** The admission price for one-day tickets is skewed to the right because the mean is much greater than the median due to the much higher price of the first observation, at $98.

3.16 (a) Mean = 7.11, median = 6.68. **(b)** Variance = 4.336, standard deviation = 2.082, range = 6.67, CV = 29.27%. **(c)** Because the mean is greater than the median, the distribution is right-skewed. **(d)** The mean and median are both greater than 5 minutes. The distribution is right-skewed, meaning that there are some unusually high values. Further, 13 of the 15 bank customers sampled (or 86.7%) had waiting times greater than 5 minutes. So the customer is likely to experience a waiting time in excess of 5 minutes. The manager overstated the bank's service record in responding that the customer would "almost certainly" not wait longer than 5 minutes for service.

3.18 (a) Population mean, μ = 6. **(b)** Population standard deviation, σ = 1.673, population variance, σ^2 = 2.8.

3.20 (a) 68%. **(b)** 95%. **(c)** Not calculable, 75%, 88.89%. **(d)** $\mu − 4\sigma$ to $\mu + 4\sigma$ or −2.8 to 19.2.

3.22 (a) Mean = 12,999.2158, variance = 14,959,700.52, standard deviation = 3,867.7772. **(b)** 64.71%, 98.04%, and 100% of these states have mean per-capita energy consumption within 1, 2, and 3 standard deviations of the mean, respectively. **(c)** This is consistent with 68%, 95%, and 99.7%, according to the empirical rule. **(d)(a)** Mean = 12,857.7402, variance = 14,238,110.67, standard deviation = 3,773.3421. **(b)** 66%, 98%, and 100% of these states have a mean per-capita energy consumption within 1, 2, and 3 standard deviations of the mean, respectively. **(c)** This is consistent with 68%, 95%, and 99.7% according to the empirical rule.

3.24 (a) 4, 9, 5. **(b)** 3, 4, 7, 9, 12. **(c)** The distances between the median and the extremes are close, 4 and 5, but the differences in the tails are different (1 on the left and 3 on the right), so this distribution is slightly right-skewed. **(d)** In 3.2 (d), because mean = median, the distribution is symmetric. The box part of the graph is symmetric, but the tails show right-skewness.

3.26 (a) −6.5, 8, 14.5. **(b)** −8, −6.5, 7, 8, 9. **(c)** The shape is left-skewed. **(d)** This is consistent with the answer in 3.4 (d).

3.28 (a) Q_1 = $0.68 Q_3 = $1.14 Interquartile range = $0.46. **(b)** Five-number summary: 0.55 0.68 0.88 1.14 1.51. **(c)** The distribution is skewed to the right.

3.30 (a) First Quartile = 17, Third Quartile = 20, Interquartile Range = 3. **(b)** Five-number summary: 16 17 18 20 23. **(c)** The MPG of SUVs is right-skewed.

3.32 (a) Commercial district five-number summary: 0.38 3.2 4.5 5.55 6.46. Residential area five-number summary: 3.82 5.64 6.68 8.73 10.49. **(b)** Commercial district: The distribution is skewed to the left. Residential area: The distribution is skewed slightly to the right. **(c)** The central tendency of the waiting times for the bank branch located in the commercial district of a city is lower than that of the branch located in the residential area. There are a few long waiting times for the branch located in the residential area, whereas there are a few exceptionally short waiting times for the branch located in the commercial area.

3.34 U.S. stocks are highly correlated with the German stock market, somewhat correlated with the Brazilian stock market, and not very correlated with the Japanese stock market.

3.36 (a) cov(X, Y) = 591.667. **(b)** r = 0.7196. **(c)** The correlation coefficient is more valuable for expressing the relationship between calories and fat because it does not depend on the units used to measure calories and fat. **(d)** There is a strong positive linear relationship between calories and fat.

3.38 (a) $\text{cov}(X,Y) = 1.2132$. **(b)** $S_X^2 = 0.1944, S_Y^2 = 20.4054$

$$r = \frac{\text{cov}(X,Y)}{S_X S_Y} = \frac{1.2132}{(0.4409)(4.5172)} = 0.6092$$

(c) There is a moderate positive linear relationship between the coaches' salary and revenue.

3.52 (a) Mean $= 43.89$, median $= 45$, 1st quartile $= 18$, 3rd quartile $= 63$. **(b)** Range $= 76$, interquartile range $= 45$, variance $= 639.2564$, standard deviation $= 25.28$, $CV = 57.61\%$. **(c)** The distribution is skewed to the right because there are a few policies that require an exceptionally long period to be approved. **(d)** The mean approval process takes 43.89 days, with 50% of the policies being approved in less than 45 days. 50% of the applications are approved between 18 and 63 days. About 67% of the applications are approved between 18.6 and 69.2 days.

3.54 (a) Mean $= 8.421$, median $= 8.42$, range $= 0.186$, $S = 0.0461$. The mean and median width are both 8.42 inches. The range of the widths is 0.186 inch, and the average scatter around the mean is 0.0461 inch. **(b)** 8.312, 8.404, 8.42, 8.459, 8.498. **(c)** Even though mean $=$ median, the left tail is slightly longer so the distribution is slightly left-skewed. **(d)** All the troughs in this sample meet the specifications.

3.56 (a), (b)

Excel output:

	In-State Tuition/Fees	Out-of-State Tuition/Fees
Mean	6841.8155	17167.71
Median	6340	16340
Mode	7062	14901
Standard Deviation	2212.2215	4274.009
Sample Variance	4893924.034	18267150
Kurtosis	4.29574	−0.33509
Skewness	1.3504	0.5244
Range	14466	20007
Minimum	3094	8965
Maximum	17560	28972
Sum	704707	1768274
Count	103	103
First Quartile	5378	13928
Third Quartile	8143	20134
Interquartile Range	2765	6206
Coefficient of Variation	32.33%	24.90%

(c) Both in-state and out-of-state tuition and fees are right-skewed.

(d) $r = \dfrac{\text{cov}(X,Y)}{S_X S_Y} = 0.4911$.

(e) Both in-state and out-of-state tuition and fees are right-skewed due to the outliers in the right tails. There is a moderate positive linear relationship between in-state and out-of-state tuition and fees. Those schools with high in-state tuition and fees tend to also have high out-of-state tuition and fees.

3.58 (a) Boston: 0.04, 0.17, 0.23, 0.32, 0.98; Vermont: 0.02, 0.13, 0.20, 0.28, 0.83. **(b)** Both distributions are right-skewed. **(c)** Both sets of shingles did quite well in achieving a granule loss of 0.8 gram or less. The Boston shingles had only two data points greater than 0.8 gram. The next highest to these was 0.6 gram. These two data points can be considered outliers. Only 1.176% of the shingles failed the specification. In the Vermont shingles, only one data point answes greater than 0.8 gram. The next highest was 0.58 gram. Thus, only 0.714% of the shingles failed to meet the specification.

3.60 (a) 0.80. **(b)** 0.53. **(c)** 0.92. **(d)** Total fat seems to be most closely related to calories because it has the highest correlation coefficient with calories.

3.62 (a) Mean $= 7.5273$, median $= 7.263$, first quartile $= 6.353$, third quartile $= 8.248$. **(b)** Range $= 7.416$, interquartile range $= 1.895$, variance $= 2.6609$, standard deviation $= 1.6312$, $CV = 21.67\%$. **(c)** The data are skewed to the right. **(d)** The per-capita spending by the 50 states is right-skewed because a few states spend a lot more than the rest.

CHAPTER 4

4.2 (a) Simple events include selecting a red ball. **(b)** Selecting a white ball.

4.4 (a) $60/100 = 3/5 = 0.6$. **(b)** $10/100 = 1/10 = 0.1$. **(c)** $35/100 = 7/20 = 0.35$. **(d)** $9/10 = 0.9$.

4.6 (a) Mutually exclusive, not collectively exhaustive. **(b)** Not mutually exclusive, not collectively exhaustive. **(c)** Mutually exclusive, not collectively exhaustive. **(d)** Mutually exclusive, collectively exhaustive.

4.8 (a) "Makes less than $50,000." **(b)** "Makes less than $50,000 and tax code is unfair." **(c)** The complement of "tax code is fair" is "tax code is unfair." **(d)** "Tax code is fair and makes less than $50,000" is a joint event because it consists of two characteristics.

4.10 (a) "A wafer is good." **(b)** "A wafer is good and no particle was found on the die." **(c)** "Bad wafer." **(d)** A wafer that is a "good wafer" and was produced by a die "with particles" is a joint event because it consists of two characteristics.

4.12 (a) $P(\text{Selected the highest-cost fund}) = (27 + 18)/200 = 0.225$. **(b)** $P(\text{Selected the highest-cost fund and is an undergraduate}) = 27/200 = 0.135$. **(c)** $P(\text{Selected the highest-cost fund or is an undergraduate}) = (45 + 100 - 27)/200 = 0.59$. **(d)** The probability of "selected the highest-cost fund or is an undergraduate" includes the probability of "selected the highest-cost fund," plus the probability of "undergraduate minus the joint probability of highest-cost fund and undergraduate."

4.14 (a) $360/500 = 18/25 = 0.72$. **(b)** $224/500 = 56/125 = 0.448$. **(c)** $396/500 = 99/125 = 0.792$. **(d)** $500/500 = 1.00$.

4.16 (a) $10/30 = 1/3 = 0.33$. **(b)** $20/60 = 1/3 = 0.33$. **(c)** $40/60 = 2/3 = 0.67$. **(d)** Because $P(A/B) = P(A) = 1/3$, events A and B are independent.

4.18 $\frac{1}{2} = 0.5$.

4.20 Because $P(A \text{ and } B) = 0.20$ and $P(A)P(B) = 0.12$, events A and B are not independent.

4.22 (a) $36/116 = 0.3103$. **(b)** $14/334 = 0.0419$. **(c)** $320/334 = 0.9581$. $P(\text{No particles}) = 400/450 = 0.8889$. Because $P(\text{No particles}|\text{Good}) \neq P(\text{No particles})$, "a good wafer" and "a die with no particle" are not independent.

4.24 (a) $P(\text{Selected the highest-cost fund} \mid \text{Is an undergraduate}) = 27/100 = 0.27$. **(b)** $P(\text{Is an undergraduate} \mid \text{Selected the highest-cost fund}) = 27/(27 + 18) = 0.6$. **(c)** The conditional events are reversed. **(d)** Because $P(\text{Selected the highest-cost fund} \mid \text{Is an undergraduate}) = 0.27$ is not equal to $P(\text{Selected the highest-cost fund}) = 0.225$, the two events "student group" and "fund selected" are not independent.

4.26 (a) $0.025/0.6 = 0.0417$. **(b)** $0.015/0.4 = 0.0375$. **(c)** Because $P(\text{Needs warranty repair} \mid \text{Manufacturer based in U.S.}) = 0.0417$ and $P(\text{Needs warranty repair}) = 0.04$, the two events are not independent.

4.28 (a) 0.0045. **(b)** 0.012. **(c)** 0.0059. **(d)** 0.0483.

4.30 0.095.

4.32 (a) 0.736. **(b)** 0.997.

4.34 (a) $P(B'|O) = \dfrac{(0.5)(0.3)}{(0.5)(0.3) + (0.25)(0.7)} = 0.4615.$
(b) $P(O) = 0.175 + 0.15 = 0.325.$

4.36 (a) $P(\text{Huge success} \mid \text{Favorable review}) = 0.099/0.459 = 0.2157;$
$P(\text{Moderate success} \mid \text{Favorable review}) = 0.14/0.459 = 0.3050;$
$P(\text{Break}P(\text{Break even} \mid \text{Favorable review}) = 0.16/0.459 = 0.3486;$
$P(\text{Loser} \mid \text{Favorable review}) = 0.06/0.459 = 0.1307.$ **(b)** $P(\text{Favorable review}) = 0.459.$

4.46 (a)

		Age		
		18–25	**26–40**	**Total**
Goals	Getting Rich	405	310	715
	Other	95	190	285
	Total	500	500	1000

(b) Simple event: "Has a goal of getting rich." Joint event: "Has a goal of getting rich and is between 18–25 years old." **(c)** $P(\text{Has a goal of getting rich}) = 715/1000 = 0.715.$ **(d)** $P(\text{Has a goal of getting rich and is in the 26–40-year-old group}) = 310/1000 = 0.31.$ **(e)** Not independent

4.48 (a) 0.0225. **(b)** 3,937.5 $\cong$ 3,938 can be expected to read the advertisement and place an order. **(c)** 0.03. **(d)** 5,250 can be expected to read the advertisement and place an order.

4.50 (a) 0.4712. **(b)** Because the probability that a fatality involved a rollover, given that the fatality involved an SUV, a van, or a pickup is 0.4712, which is almost twice the probability that a fatality involved a rollover with any vehicle type, at 0.24, SUVs, vans, and pickups are generally more prone to rollover accidents.

CHAPTER 5

5.2 (a) $\mu = 0(0.10) + 1(0.20) + 2(0.45) + 3(0.15) + 4(0.05) + 5(0.05) - 2.0.$

(b) $\sigma = \sqrt{\begin{array}{l}(0 - 2)^2(0.10) + (1 - 2)^2(0.20) + (2 - 2)^2(0.45) \\ + (3 - 2)^2(0.15) + (4 - 2)^2(0.05) + (5 - 2)^2(0.05)\end{array}}$
$= 1.183.$

5.4 (a)

X	$P(X)$
$\$-1$	21/36
$\$+1$	15/36

(b)

X	$P(X)$
$\$-1$	21/36
$\$+1$	15/36

(c)

X	$P(X)$
$\$-1$	30/36
$\$+4$	6/36

(d) $\$-0.167$ for each method of play.

5.6 (a) 2.105769. **(b)** 1.467063.

5.8 (a) 0.5997. **(b)** 0.0016. **(c)** 0.0439. **(d)** 0.4018.

5.10 (a) $P(X = 0) = 0.7351.$ **(b)** If the probabilities of the six events are not all equal, then you would calculate the probability in (a) by multiplying together the probability of no failure in each of the six events.

5.12 Given $\pi = 0.861$ and $n = 3$,

(a) $P(X = 3) = \dfrac{n!}{X!(n - x)!}\pi^X(1 - \pi)^{n-X} = \dfrac{3!}{3!0!}(0.861)^3(0.139)^0 = 0.6383$

(b) $P(X = 0) = \dfrac{n!}{X!(n - x)!}\pi^X(1 - \pi)^{n-X} = \dfrac{3!}{0!0!}(0.861)^0(0.139)^3 = 0.0027$

(c) $P(X \geq 2) = P(X = 2) + P(X = 3)$
$= \dfrac{3!}{2!1!}(0.861)^2(0.139)^1 + \dfrac{3!}{3!0!}(0.861)^3(0.139)^0 = 0.9474$

(d) $E(X) = n\pi = 3(0.861) = 2.583\ \sigma_X = \sqrt{n\pi(1 - \pi)}$
$= \sqrt{3(0.861)(0.139)} = 0.5992.$

5.14 (a) $P(X \leq 5) = .00009919.$ **(b)** $P(X \leq 10) = 0.0719.$
(c) $P(X \leq 15) = 0.8173.$

5.16 (a) 0.2565. **(b)** 0.1396. **(c)** 0.3033. **(d)** 0.0247.

5.18 (a) 0.0337. **(b)** 0.0067. **(c)** 0.9596. **(d)** 0.0404.

5.20 (a) $P(X < 5) = P(X = 0) + P(X = 1) + P(X = 2) + P(X = 3) + P(X = 4)$
$= \dfrac{e^{-6}(6)^0}{0!} + \dfrac{e^{-6}(6)^1}{1!} + \dfrac{e^{-6}(6)^2}{2!} + \dfrac{e^{-6}(6)^3}{3!} + \dfrac{e^{-6}(6)^4}{4!}$
$= 0.002479 + 0.014873 + 0.044618 + 0.089235 + 0.133853$
$= 0.2851.$

(b) $P(X = 5) = \dfrac{e^{-6}(6)^5}{5!} = 0.1606.$

(c) $P(X \geq 5) = 1 - P(X < 5) = 1 - 0.2851 = 0.7149.$

(d) $P(X = 4 \text{ or } X = 5) = P(X = 4) + P(X = 5) = \dfrac{e^{-6}(6)^4}{4!} + \dfrac{e^{-6}(6)^5}{5!}$
$= 0.2945.$

5.22 $\lambda = 7.$ **(a)** $P(X = 0) = 0.0009.$ **(b)** $P(X \geq 1) = 0.9991.$
(c) $P(X \geq 2) = 0.9927.$

5.24 (a) 0.0176. **(b)** 0.9093. **(c)** 0.9220.

5.26 (a) 0.2441. **(b)** 0.8311. **(c)** Because Ford had a lower mean rate of problems per car in 2008 compared to Dodge, the probability of a randomly selected Ford having zero problems and the probability of no more than 2 problems are both higher than their values for Dodge.

5.28 (a) 0.2671. **(b)** 0.8525. **(c)** Because Dodge had a higher mean rate of problems per car in 2008 compared to 2007, the probability of a randomly selected Dodge having zero problems and the probability of no more than 2 problems are both lower in 2008 than their values in 2007.

5.34 (a) 0.74. **(b)** 0.74. **(c)** 0.3898. **(d)** 0.0012. **(e)** The assumption of independence may not be true.

5.36 (a) If $\pi = 0.50$ and $n = 11, P(X \geq 9) = 0.0327.$ **(b)** If $\pi = 0.74$ and $n = 11, P(X \geq 9) = 0.4247.$

5.38 (a) 0.1074. **(b)** 0.2684. **(c)** 0.6242. **(d)** Mean $= 2.0$, standard deviation $= 1.2649.$

5.40 (a) $\mu = n\pi = 2.6.$ **(b)** $\sigma = \sqrt{n\pi(1 - \pi)} = 1.5040.$
(c) $P(X = 0) = 0.0617.$ **(d)** $P(X \leq 2) = 0.5080.$ **(e)** $P(X \geq 3) = 0.4920.$

5.42 (a) If $\pi = 0.50$ and $n = 38, P(X \geq 32) = 0.0001.$ **(b)** If $\pi = 0.70$ and $n = 38, P(X \geq 32) = 0.03595.$ **(c)** If $\pi = 0.90$ and $n = 38, P(X \geq 32) = 0.92005.$ **(d)** Based on the results in (a)–(c), the probability that the Standard & Poor's 500 index will increase if there is an early gain in the first five trading days of the year is very likely to be close to 0.90 because that yields a probability of 92% that at least 32 of the 38 years the Standard & Poor's 500 index will increase the entire year.

5.44 (a) The assumptions needed are (i) the probability that a golfer loses a golf ball in a given interval is constant, (ii) the probability that a golfer loses more than one golf ball approaches 0 as the interval gets smaller, and (iii) the probability that a golfer loses a golf ball is independent from interval to interval. **(b)** 0.0111. **(c)** 0.70293. **(d)** 0.29707.

CHAPTER 6

6.2 (a) 0.9089. **(b)** 0.0911. **(c)** +1.96. **(d)** −1.00 and +1.00.

6.4 (a) 0.1401. **(b)** 0.4168. **(c)** 0.3918. **(d)** +1.00.

6.6 (a) 0.9599. **(b)** 0.0228. **(c)** 43.42. **(d)** 46.64 and 53.36.

6.8 (a) $P(34 < X < 50) = P(-1.33 < Z < 0) = 0.4082$.
(b) $P(X < 30) + P(X > 60) = P(Z < -1.67) + P(Z > 0.83) = 0.0475 + (1.0 - 0.7967) = 0.2508$. **(c)** $P(Z < -0.84) \cong 0.20$,
$Z = -0.84 = \dfrac{X - 50}{12}$. $X = 50 - 0.84(12) = 39.92$ thousand miles, or 39,920 miles. **(d)** The smaller standard deviation makes the Z values larger.

(a) $P(34 < X < 50) = P(-1.60 < Z < 0) = 0.4452$. **(b)**
$P(X < 30) + P(X > 60) = P(Z < -2.00) + P(Z > 1.00) = 0.0228 + (1.0 - 0.8413) = 0.1815$. **(c)** $X = 50 - 0.84(10) = 41.6$ thousand miles, or 41,600 miles.

6.10 (a) 0.9878. **(b)** 0.8185. **(c)** 86.16%. **(d)** Option 1: Because your score of 81% on this exam represents a Z score of 1.00, which is below the minimum Z score of 1.28, you will not earn an A grade on the exam under this grading option. Option 2: Because your score of 68% on this exam represents a Z score of 2.00, which is well above the minimum Z score of 1.28, you will earn an A grade on the exam under this grading option. You should prefer Option 2.

6.12 (a) 0.1189. **(b)** 0.4135. **(c)** 0.0529.

6.14 With 39 values, the smallest of the standard normal quantile values covers an area under the normal curve of 0.025. The corresponding Z value is −1.96. The middle (20th) value has a cumulative area of 0.50 and a corresponding Z value of 0.0. The largest of the standard normal quantile values covers an area under the normal curve of 0.975, and its corresponding Z value is +1.96.

6.16 (a) Mean = 23.2, median = 23.5, range = 52, standard deviation = 12.3868, $6(S_X) = 6(12.3868) = 74.3205$, interquartile range = 14, $1.33(S_X) = 1.33(12.3868) = 16.4744$. The mean is almost equal to the median; the range is smaller than 6 times the standard deviation, and the interquartile range is slightly smaller than 1.33 times the standard deviation. The data appear to be approximately normally distributed but slightly skewed to the right. **(b)** The normal probability plot suggests that the data are skewed to the right.

6.18 (a) Mean = 1040.863, median = 981, range = 1732, $6(S_X) = 2571.2310$, interquartile range = 593, $1.33(S_X) = 569.9562$. There are 62.75%, 78.43%, and 94.12% of the observations that fall within 1, 1.28, and 2 standard deviations of the mean, respectively, as compared to the approximate theoretical 66.67%, 80%, and 95%. Because the mean is slightly larger than the median, the interquartile range is slightly larger than 1.33 times the standard deviation, and the range is much smaller than 6 times the standard deviation, the data appear to deviate slightly from the normal distribution. **(b)** The normal probability plot suggests that the data appear to be slightly right-skewed.

6.20 (a) Interquartile range = 0.0025, $S_X = 0.0017$, range = 0.008, $1.33(S_X) = 0.0023$, $6(S_X) = 0.0102$. Because the interquartile range is close to $1.33(S_X)$ and the range is also close to $6(S_X)$, the data appear to be approximately normally distributed. **(b)** The normal probability

plot suggests that the data appear to be approximately normally distributed.

6.22 (a) Five-number summary: 82 127 148.5 168 213; mean = 147.06, mode = 130, range = 131, interquartile range = 41, standard deviation = 31.69. The mean is very close to the median. The five-number summary suggests that the distribution is approximately symmetrical around the median. The interquartile range is very close to 1.33 times the standard deviation. The range is about $50 below 6 times the standard deviation. In general, the distribution of the data appears to closely resemble a normal distribution. **(b)** The normal probability plot confirms that the data appear to be approximately normally distributed.

6.30 (a) 0.4772. **(b)** 0.9544. **(c)** 0.0456. **(d)** 1.8835. **(e)** 1.8710 and 2.1290.

6.32 (a) 0.2734. **(b)** 0.2038. **(c)** 4.404 ounces. **(d)** 4.188 ounces and 5.212 ounces.

6.34 (a) Waiting time will more closely resemble an exponential distribution. **(b)** Seating time will more closely resemble a normal distribution. **(c)** Both the histogram and normal probability plot suggest that waiting time more closely resembles an exponential distribution. **(d)** Both the histogram and normal probability plot suggest that seating time more closely resembles a normal distribution.

6.36 (a) 0.8413. **(b)** 0.9330. **(c)** 0.9332. **(d)** 0.3347. **(e)** 0.4080 and 1.1920.

6.38 (a) Mean = 3,019.7255, median = 2,972, range = 1174, $6(S_X) = 1,393.4693$, interquartile range = 284, $1.33(S_X) = 308.8857$. There are 70.59%, 86.27%, and 96.08% of the observations that fall within 1, 1.28, and 2 standard deviations of the mean, respectively, as compared to the approximate theoretical 66.67%, 80%, and 95%. Because the mean is slightly larger than the median, the interquartile range is slightly smaller than 1.33 times the standard deviation, and the range is much smaller than 6 times the standard deviation, the data appear to deviate slightly from the normal distribution. The normal probability plot suggests that the data appear to be slightly right-skewed. **(b)** The variable RANK 2006 has a uniform distribution between 1 and 52.

CHAPTER 7

7.2 Sample without replacement: Read from left to right in three-digit sequences and continue unfinished sequences from the end of the row to the beginning of the next row:

Row 05: 338 505 855 551 438 855 077 186 579 488 767 833 170
Rows 05–06: 897
Row 06: 340 033 648 847 204 334 639 193 639 411 095 924
Rows 06–07: 707
Row 07: 054 329 776 100 871 007 255 980 646 886 823 920 461
Row 08: 893 829 380 900 796 959 453 410 181 277 660 908 887
Rows 08–09: 237
Row 09: 818 721 426 714 050 785 223 801 670 353 362 449
Rows 09–10: 406

Note: All sequences above 902 and duplicates are discarded.

7.4 A simple random sample would be less practical for personal interviews because of travel costs (unless interviewees are paid to go to a central interviewing location).

7.6 Here all members of the population are equally likely to be selected, and the sample selection mechanism is based on chance. But selection of two elements is not independent; for example, if A is in the sample, we know that B is also and that C and D are not.

7.8 (a)

Row 16: 2323 6737 5131 8888 1718 0654 6832 4647 6510 4877
Row 17: 4579 4269 2615 1308 2455 7830 5550 5852 5514 7182
Row 18: 0989 3205 0514 2256 8514 4642 7567 8896 2977 8822
Row 19: 5438 2745 9891 4991 4523 6847 9276 8646 1628 3554
Row 20: 9475 0899 2337 0892 0048 8033 6945 9826 9403 6858
Row 21: 7029 7341 3553 1403 3340 4205 0823 4144 1048 2949
Row 22: 8515 7479 5432 9792 6575 5760 0408 8112 2507 3742
Row 23: 1110 0023 4012 8607 4697 9664 4894 3928 7072 5815
Row 24: 3687 1507 7530 5925 7143 1738 1688 5625 8533 5041
Row 25: 2391 3483 5763 3081 6090 5169 0546

Note: All sequences above 5,000 are discarded. There were no repeating sequences.

(b) 089 189 289 389 489 589 689 789 889 989
1089 1189 1289 1389 1489 1589 1689 1789 1889 1989
2089 2189 2289 2389 2489 2589 2689 2789 2889 2989
3089 3189 3289 3389 3489 3589 3689 3789 3889 3989
4089 4189 4289 4389 4489 4589 4689 4789 4889 4989

(c) With the single exception of invoice #0989, the invoices selected in the simple random sample are not the same as those selected in the systematic sample. It would be highly unlikely that a simple random sample would select the same units as a systematic sample.

7.10 Before accepting the results of a survey of college students, you might want to know, for example:

Who funded the survey? Why was it conducted? What was the population from which the sample was selected? What sampling design was used? What mode of response was used: a personal interview, a telephone interview, or a mail survey? Were interviewers trained? Were survey questions field-tested? What questions were asked? Were they clear, accurate, unbiased, and valid? What operational definition of "vast majority" was used? What was the response rate? What was the sample size?

7.12 (a) The four types of survey errors are: coverage error, nonresponse error, sampling error, and measurement error. **(b)** When people who answer the survey tell you what they think you want to hear, rather than what they really believe, it introduces the halo effect, which is a source of measurement error. Also, every survey will have sampling error that reflects the chance differences from sample to sample, based on the probability of particular individuals being selected in the particular sample.

7.14 Before accepting the results of the survey, you might want to know, for example:

Who funded the study? Why was it conducted? What was the population from which the sample was selected? What sampling design was used? What mode of response was used: a personal interview, a telephone interview, or a mail survey? Were interviewers trained? Were survey questions field-tested? What other questions were asked? Were they clear, accurate, unbiased, and valid? What was the response rate? What was the margin of error? What was the sample size? What was the frame being used?

7.16 (a) Virtually zero. **(b)** 0.1587. **(c)** 0.0139. **(d)** 50.195.

7.18 (a) Both means are equal to 6. This property is called unbiasedness. **(c)** The distribution for $n = 3$ has less variability. The larger sample size has resulted in sample means being closer to μ.

7.20 (a) When $n = 2$, the shape of the sampling distribution of $\overline{X}$ should closely resemble the shape of the distribution of the population from which the sample is selected. Because the mean is larger than the median, the distribution of the sales price of new houses is skewed to the right, and so is the sampling distribution of $\overline{X}$. **(b)** If you select samples of $n = 100$, the shape of the sampling distribution of the sample mean will be very close to a normal distribution with a mean of \$296,400 and a standard deviation of \$9,000. **(c)** 0.6554. **(d)** 0.2298.

7.22 (a) $P(\overline{X} > 3) = P(Z > -1.00) = 1.0 - 0.1587 = 0.8413$. **(b)** $P(Z < 1.04) = 0.85; \overline{X} = 3.10 + 1.04(0.1) = 3.204$. **(c)** To be able to use the standardized normal distribution as an approximation for the area under the curve, you must assume that the population is approximately symmetrical. **(d)** $P(Z < 1.04) = 0.85; \overline{X} = 3.10 + 1.04(0.05) = 3.152$.

7.24 (a) 0.30. **(b)** 0.0693.

7.26 (a) $\pi = 0.501, \sigma_P = \sqrt{\dfrac{\pi(1 - \pi)}{n}} = \sqrt{\dfrac{0.501(1 - 0.501)}{100}} = 0.05$
$P(p > 0.55) = P(Z > 0.98) = 1.0 - 0.8365 = 0.1635$.

(b) $\pi = 0.60, \sigma_P = \sqrt{\dfrac{\pi(1 - \pi)}{n}} = \sqrt{\dfrac{0.6(1 - 0.6)}{100}} = 0.04899$
$P(p > 0.55) = P(Z > -1.021) = 1.0 - 0.1539 = 0.8461$.

(c) $\pi = 0.49, \sigma_P = \sqrt{\dfrac{\pi(1 - \pi)}{n}} = \sqrt{\dfrac{0.49(1 - 0.49)}{100}} = 0.05$
$P(p > 0.55) = P(Z > 1.20) = 1.0 - 0.8849 = 0.1151$.
(d) Increasing the sample size by a factor of 4 decreases the standard error by a factor of 2.
(a) $P(p > 0.55) = P(Z > 1.96) = 1.0 - 0.9750 = 0.0250$.
(b) $P(p > 0.55) = P(Z > -2.04) = 1.0 - 0.0207 = 0.9793$.
(c) $P(p > 0.55) = P(Z > 2.40) = 1.0 - 0.9918 = 0.0082$.

7.28 (a) 0.9298. **(b)** 0.8596. **(c)** 0.9865. **(d) (a)** 0.7695. **(b)** 0.5390. **(c)** 0.8656.

7.30 (a) Because $n = 200$, which is quite large, you use the sample proportion to approximate the population proportion and, hence, $\pi = 0.50$.

$$\mu_P = \pi = 0.5, \sigma_P = \sqrt{\dfrac{\pi(1 - \pi)}{n}} = \sqrt{\dfrac{0.46(0.54)}{200}} = 0.0352$$

$P(0.45 < \pi < 0.55) = P(-0.2841 < Z < 2.5568) = 0.6065$.
(b) $P(A < \pi < B) = P(-1.6499 < Z < 1.6449) = 0.90. A = 0.46 - 1.6449(0.0352) = 0.4021. B = 0.46 + 1.6449(0.0352) = 0.5179$. The probability is 90% that the sample percentage will be contained within 5.79% symmetrically around the population percentage.
(c) $P(A < \pi < B) = P(-1.96 < Z + 1.96) = 0.95. A = 0.46 - 1.96(0.0352) = 391. B = 0.50 + 1.96(0.0352) = 0.529$. The probability is 95% that the sample percentage will be contained within 6.9% symmetrically around the population percentage.

7.32 (a) 0.1134. **(b)** 0.0034. **(c)** Increasing the sample size by a factor of 5 decreases the standard error by a factor of $\sqrt{5}$. The sampling distribution of the proportion becomes more concentrated around the true proportion of 0.56 and, hence, the probability in (b) becomes smaller than that in (a).

7.44 (a) 0.4999. **(b)** 0.00009. **(c)** 0. **(d)** 0. **(e)** 0.7518.

7.46 (a) 0.8944. **(b)** 4.617; 4.783. **(c)** 4.641.

7.48 (a) 0.0106. **(b)** 0.7941. **(c)** 0.7650.

7.50 Even though Internet polling is less expensive and faster and offers higher response rates than telephone surveys, it is a self-selection response method. Because respondents who choose to participate in the survey may not represent the view of the public, the data collected may not be appropriate for making inferences about the general population.

7.52 (a) Before accepting the results of this survey, you would like to know (i) how big is the sample size, (ii) what is the purpose of the survey, (iii) what sampling method is being used, (iv) what is the frame being used, (v) what is the response rate, and (vi) how the questions are being phrased. **(b)** The population will be all the AOL users. The frame can be compiled from the list of the AOL subscribers. Because there are two natural strata in the population, adults and teens, a stratified sampling method should be used to better represent the population.

CHAPTER 8

8.2 $114.68 \le \mu \le 135.32$.

8.4 (a) You would compute the mean first because you need the mean to compute the standard deviation. If you had a sample, you would compute the sample mean. If you had the population mean, you would compute the population standard deviation. **(b)** If you have a sample, you are computing the sample standard deviation, not the population standard deviation needed in Equation (8.1). If you have a population and have computed the population mean and population standard deviation, you don't need a confidence interval estimate of the population mean because you already know the mean.

8.6 Equation (8.1) assumes that you know the population standard deviation. Because you are selecting a sample of 100 from the population, you are computing a sample standard deviation, not the population standard deviation.

8.8 (a) 2.2622. **(b)** 3.2498. **(c)** 2.0395. **(d)** 1.9977. **(e)** 1.7531.

8.10 $-0.12 \le \mu \le 11.84, 2.00 \le \mu \le 6.00$. The presence of the outlier increases the sample mean and greatly inflates the sample standard deviation.

8.12 (a) $32 \pm (2.0096)(9)/\sqrt{50}$; $29.44 \le \mu \le 34.56$ **(b)** The quality improvement team can be 95% confident that the population mean turnaround time is between 29.44 hours and 34.56 hours. **(c)** The project was a success because the initial turnaround time of 68 hours does not fall into the interval.

8.14 (a) $31.9267 \le \mu \le 41.1399$. **(b)** You can be 95% confident that the population mean price for two tickets with online service charges, large popcorn, and two medium soft drinks is somewhere between $31.93 and $41.14.

8.16 (a) $17.876 \le \mu \le 19.669$. **(b)** You can be 95% confident that population mean miles per gallon of 2008 SUVs priced under $30,000 is somewhere between 17.876 and 19.669. **(c)** Because the 95% confidence interval for population mean miles per gallon of 2008 SUVs priced under $30,000 does not overlap with that for the population mean miles per gallon of 2008 sedans priced under $20,000, you are 95% confident that the population mean miles per gallon of 2008 SUVs is lower than that of 2008 sedans.

8.18 (a) $31.12 \le \mu \le 54.96$. **(b)** The number of days is approximately normally distributed. **(c)** No, the outliers skew the data. **(d)** Because the sample size is fairly large, at $n = 50$, the use of the t distribution is appropriate.

8.20 (a) $\$0.7367 \le \mu \le \$1.1147$. **(b)** The population distribution needs to be normally distributed. **(c)** Both the normal probability plot and the boxplot show that the distribution for the cost of dark chocolate bars is right skewed.

8.22 $0.19 \le \pi \le 0.31$.

8.24 (a) $p = \dfrac{X}{n} = \dfrac{135}{500} = 0.27$

$$p \pm Z\sqrt{\frac{p(1-p)}{n}} = 0.27 \pm 2.58\sqrt{\frac{0.27(0.73)}{500}} \quad 0.2189 \le \pi \le 0.3211.$$

(b) The manager in charge of promotional programs concerning residential customers can infer that the proportion of households that would purchase an additional telephone line if it were made available at a substantially reduced installation cost is somewhere between 0.22 and 0.32, with 99% confidence.

8.26 (a) $0.2311 \le \pi \le 0.3089$. **(b)** $0.2425 \le \pi \le 0.2975$. **(c)** The larger the sample size, the narrower the confidence interval, holding everything else constant.

8.28 (a) $0.5638 \le \pi \le 0.6362$. **(b)** $0.2272 \le \pi \le 0.2920$.

8.30 $n = 35$.

8.32 $n = 1{,}041$.

8.34 (a) $n = \dfrac{Z^2\sigma^2}{e^2} = \dfrac{(1.96)^2(400)^2}{50^2} = 245.86$

Use $n = 246$.

(b) $n = \dfrac{Z^2\sigma^2}{e^2} = \dfrac{(1.96)^2(400)^2}{25^2} = 983.41$

Use $n = 984$.

8.36 $n = 97$.

8.38 (a) $n = 167$. **(b)** $n = 97$.

8.40 (a) $n = 246$. **(b)** $n = 385$. **(c)** $n = 554$. **(d)** When there is more variability in the population, a larger sample is needed to accurately estimate the mean.

8.42 (a) $p = 0.5498$; $0.5226 \le \pi \le 0.5770$. **(b)** $p = 0.4697$; $0.4424 \le \pi \le 0.4970$. **(c)** $p = 0.2799$; $0.2544 \le \pi \le 0.3045$. **(d) (a)** $n = 2{,}378$. **(b)** $= 2{,}393$. **(c)** $= 1{,}936$.

8.44 (a) If you conduct a follow-up study to estimate the population proportion of individuals who view oil companies favorably, you would use $\pi = 0.15$ in the sample size formula because it provides the most conservative value based on past information on the proportion. **(b)** $n = 545$.

8.50 $940.50 \le \mu \le 1007.50$. Based on the evidence gathered from the sample of 34 stores, the 95% confidence interval for the mean per-store count in all of the franchise's stores is from 940.50 to 1,007.50. With a 95% level of confidence, the franchise can conclude that the mean per-store count in all its stores is somewhere between 940.50 and 1,007.50, which is larger than the original average of 900 mean per-store count before the price reduction. Hence, reducing coffee prices is a good strategy to increase the mean customer count.

8.52 (a) $14.085 \le \mu \le 16.515$. **(b)** $0.530 \le \pi \le 0.820$. **(c)** $n = 25$. **(d)** $n = 784$. **(e)** If a single sample were to be selected for both purposes, the larger of the two sample sizes ($n = 784$) should be used.

8.54 (a) $8.049 \le \mu \le 11.351$. **(b)** $0.284 \le \pi \le 0.676$. **(c)** $n = 35$. **(d)** $n = 121$. **(e)** If a single sample were to be selected for both purposes, the larger of the two sample sizes ($n = 121$) should be used.

8.56 (a) $\$36.66 \le \mu \le \$40.42$. **(b)** $0.2027 \le \pi \le 0.3973$. **(c)** $n = 110$. **(d)** $n = 423$. **(e)** If a single sample were to be selected for both purposes, the larger of the two sample sizes ($n = 423$) should be used.

8.58 (a) $8.41 \le \mu \le 8.43$. **(b)** With 95% confidence, the population mean width of troughs is somewhere between 8.41 and 8.43 inches. **(c)** The assumption is valid as the width of the troughs is approximately normally distributed.

8.60 (a) $0.2425 \leq \mu \leq 0.2856$. **(b)** $0.1975 \leq \mu \leq 0.2385$. **(c)** The amounts of granule loss for both brands are skewed to the right, but the sample sizes are large enough. **(d)** Because the two confidence intervals do not overlap, you can conclude that the mean granule loss of Boston shingles is higher than that of Vermont shingles.

CHAPTER 9

9.2 Because $Z_{STAT} = +2.21 > 1.96$, reject H_0.

9.4 Reject H_0 if $Z_{STAT} < -2.58$ or if $Z_{STAT} > 2.58$.

9.6 p-value $= 0.0456$.

9.8 p-value $= 0.1676$.

9.10 H_0: Defendant is guilty; H_1: Defendant is innocent. A Type I error would be not convicting a guilty person. A Type II error would be convicting an innocent person.

9.12 H_0: $\mu = 20$ minutes. 20 minutes is adequate travel time between classes. H_1: $\mu \neq 20$ minutes. 20 minutes is not adequate travel time between classes.

9.14 H_0: $\mu = 1.00$. The mean amount of paint per one-gallon can is one gallon. H_1: $\mu \neq 1.00$. The mean amount of paint per one-gallon can differs from one gallon.

9.16 $t_{STAT} = 2.00$

9.18 (a) ± 2.1315.

9.20 No, you should not use a t test because the original population is left-skewed and the sample size is not large enough for the t test to be valid.

9.22 (a) $t_{STAT} = (3.57 - 3.70)/0.8/\sqrt{64} = -1.30$; Because $-1.9983 < t_{STAT} = -1.30 < 1.9983$ and the p-value of $0.1984 > 0.05$ There is no evidence that the population mean waiting time is different from 3.7 minutes. **(b)** Since $n = 64$, the central limit theorem should ensure that the sampling distribution of the mean is approximately normal. In general, the t test is appropriate for this sample size except for the case where the population is extremely skewed or bimodal.

9.24 (a) Because $-2.5706 < t_{STAT} = 0.8556 < 2.5706$, do not reject H_0. There is not enough evidence to conclude that the mean price for two tickets, with online service charges, large popcorn, and two medium soft drinks, is different from \$35. **(b)** The p-value is 0.4313. If the population mean is \$35, the probability of observing a sample of six theater chains that will result in a sample mean farther away from the hypothesized value than this sample is 0.4313. **(c)** That the distribution of prices is normally distributed. **(d)** With a small sample size, it is difficult to evaluate the assumption of normality. However, the distribution may be symmetric because the mean and the median are close in value.

9.26 (a) Because $-2.0096 < t_{STAT} = 0.114 < 2.0096$, do not reject H_0. There is no evidence that the mean amount is different from two liters. **(b)** p-value $= 0.9095$. **(c)** and **(d)** Yes, the data appear to have met the normality assumption. **(e)** The amount of fill is decreasing over time. Therefore, the t test is invalid.

9.28 (a) Because $t_{STAT} = -5.9355 < -2.0106$, reject H_0. There is enough evidence to conclude that mean widths of the troughs is different from 8.46 inches. **(b)** That the population distribution is normal. **(c)** Although the distribution of the widths is left-skewed, the large sample size means that the validity of the t test is not seriously affected.

9.30 (a) Because $-2.68 < t_{STAT} = 0.094 < 2.68$, do not reject H_0. **(b)** $5.462 \leq \mu \leq 5.542$. **(c)** The conclusions are the same.

9.32 p-value $= 0.0228$.

9.34 p-value $= 0.0838$.

9.36 p-value $= 0.9162$.

9.38 $t_{STAT} = 2.7638$.

9.40 $t_{STAT} = -2.5280$.

9.42 (a) $t_{STAT} = (2.73 - 2.80)/0.2/\sqrt{25} = -1.75$; Because $t_{STAT} = -1.75 < -1.7109$, reject H_0. **(b)** p-value $= 0.0464 < 0.05$, reject H_0. **(c)** The probability of getting a sample mean of 2.73 feet or less if the population mean is 2.8 feet is 0.0464. **(d)** They are the same.

9.44 (a) H_0: $\mu \leq 5$; H_1: $\mu > 5$. **(b)** A Type I error occurs when you conclude that children take a mean of more than five trips a week to the store when in fact they take a mean of no more than five trips a week to the store. A Type II error occurs when you conclude that children take a mean of no more than five trips a week to the store when in fact they take a mean of more than five trips a week to the store. **(c)** Because $t_{STAT} = 2.9375 > 2.3263$ or the p-value of 0.0021 is less than 0.01, reject H_0. There is enough evidence to conclude the population mean number of trips to the store is greater than five per week. **(d)** The probability that the sample mean is 5.47 trips or more when the null hypothesis is true is 0.0021.

9.46 $p = 0.22$.

9.48 Do not reject H_0.

9.50 (a) $Z_{STAT} = 9.61$, p-value $= 0.0000$. Because $Z_{STAT} = 9.61 > 1.645$ or $0.0000 > 0.05$, reject H_0. There is evidence to show that more than half of readers of online magazines have linked to an advertiser's Web site. **(b)** $Z_{STAT} = 1.20$ p-value $= 0.115$. Because $Z_{STAT} = 1.20 < 1.645$ do not reject H_0. There is insufficient evidence to show that more than half of the readers of online magazines have linked to an advertiser's Web site. **(c)** The sample size had a major effect on being able to reject the null hypothesis. **(d)** You would be very unlikely to reject the null hypothesis with a sample of 20.

9.52 (a) H_0: $\pi = 0.6$; H_1: $\pi \neq 0.6$. Decision rule: If $Z_{STAT} > 1.96$ or $Z_{STAT} < -1.96$, reject H_0.

$$p = \frac{650}{1,000} = 0.65$$

Test statistic:

$$Z_{STAT} = \frac{p - \pi}{\sqrt{\dfrac{\pi(1 - \pi)}{n}}} = \frac{0.65 - 0.60}{\sqrt{\dfrac{0.6(1 - 0.6)}{1,000}}} = 3.2275$$

Because $Z_{STAT} = 3.2275 > 1.96$ or p-value $= 0.0012 < 0.05$, reject H_0 and conclude that there is evidence that the percentage of young job seekers who prefer to look for a job in a place they want to reside is different from 60%.

9.54 (a) H_0: $\pi \leq 0.08$. No more than 8% of students at your school are Omnivores. H_1: $\pi > 0.08$. More than 8% of students at your school are Omnivores. **(b)** $Z_{STAT} = 3.6490$, p-value $= 0.0001316$. Because $Z_{STAT} = 3.6490 > 1.96$ or p-value $= 0.0001316 < 0.05$, reject H_0. There is enough evidence to show that the percentage of Omnivores at your school is greater than 8%.

9.64 (a) Buying a site that is not profitable. **(b)** Not buying a profitable site. **(c)** Type I. **(d)** If the executives adopt a less stringent rejection criterion by buying sites for which the computer model predicts moderate or large profit, the probability of committing a Type I error will increase. Many more of the sites the computer model predicts that will generate moderate profit may end up not being profitable at all. On the other hand, the less stringent rejection criterion will lower the probability of committing a Type II error since more potentially profitable sites will be purchased.

9.66 (a) Because $t_{STAT} = 3.248 > 2.0010$, reject H_0. **(b)** p-value = 0.0019. **(c)** Because $Z_{STAT} = -0.32 > -1.645$, do not reject H_0. **(d)** Because $-2.0010 < t_{STAT} = 0.75 < 2.0010$, do not reject H_0. **(e)** Because $t_{STAT} = -1.61 > -1.645$, do not reject H_0.

9.68 (a) Because $t_{STAT} = -1.69 > -1.7613$, do not reject H_0. **(b)** The data are from a population that is normally distributed. **(c)** and **(d)** With the exception of one extreme point, the data are approximately normally distributed. **(e)** There is insufficient evidence to state that the waiting time is less than five minutes.

9.70 (a) Because $t_{STAT} = -1.47 > -1.6896$, do not reject H_0. **(b)** p-value = 0.0748. If the null hypothesis is true, the probability of obtaining a t_{STAT} of -1.47 or more extreme is 0.0748. **(c)** Because $t_{STAT} = -3.10 < -1.6973$, reject H_0. **(d)** p-value = 0.0021. If the null hypothesis is true, the probability of obtaining a t_{STAT} of -3.10 or more extreme is 0.0021. **(e)** The data in the population are assumed to be normally distributed. **(f)** Both boxplots suggest that the data are skewed slightly to the right, more so for the Boston shingles. However, the very large sample sizes mean that the results of the t test are relatively insensitive to the departure from normality.

9.72 (a) $t_{STAT} = -21.61$, reject H_0. **(b)** p-value = 0.0000. **(c)** $t_{STAT} = -27.19$, reject H_0. **(d)** p-value = 0.0000. **(e)** Because of the large sample sizes, you do not need to be concerned with the normality assumption.

CHAPTER 10

10.2 (a) $t = 3.8959$. **(b)** $df = 21$. **(c)** 2.5177. **(d)** Because $t_{STAT} = 3.8959 > 2.5177$, reject H_0.

10.4 $3.73 \leq \mu_1 - \mu_2 \leq 12.27$.

10.6 Because $t_{STAT} = 2.6762 < 2.9979$ or p-value = 0.0158 > 0.01, do not reject H_0. There is no evidence of a difference in the means of the two populations.

10.8 (a) Because $-1.9706 < t_{STAT} = 0.8904 < 1.9706$ or p-value = 0.3742 > 0.05, do not reject H_0. There is insufficient evidence to conclude that the mean salary of reliability/safety engineers is different from the mean salary of software quality engineers. $-\$2,964.92 \leq \mu_1 - \mu_2 \leq \$7,852.92$. **(c)** The results are the same since the interval includes 0.

10.10 (a) $H_0: \mu_1 = \mu_2$, where Populations: 1 = Males, 2 = Females.
$$H_1: \mu_1 \neq \mu_2$$
Decision rule: $df = 170$. If $t_{STAT} < -1.974$ or $t_{STAT} > 1.974$, reject H_0.
Test statistic:

$$S_p^2 = \frac{(n_1 - 1)(S_1^2) + (n_2 - 1)(S_2^2)}{(n_1 - 1) + (n_2 - 1)}$$

$$= \frac{(99)(13.35^2) + (71)(9.42^2)}{99 + 71} = 140.8489$$

$$t_{STAT} = \frac{(\bar{X}_1 - \bar{X}_2) - (\mu_1 - \mu_2)}{\sqrt{S_p^2\left(\frac{1}{n_1} + \frac{1}{n_2}\right)}}$$

$$= \frac{(40.26 - 36.85) - 0}{\sqrt{140.8489\left(\frac{1}{100} + \frac{1}{72}\right)}} = 1.859$$

Decision: Because $-1.974 < t_{STAT} = 1.859 < 1.974$, do not reject H_0. There is not enough evidence to conclude that the mean computer anxiety experienced by males sand females is different. **(b)** p-value = 0.0648. **(c)** In order to use the pooled-variance t test, you need to assume that the populations are normally distributed with equal variances.

10.12 (a) Because $t_{STAT} = -4.1343 < -2.0484$, reject H_0. **(b)** p-value = 0.0003. **(c)** The original populations of waiting times are approximately normally distributed. **(d)** $-4.2292 \leq \mu_1 - \mu_2 \leq -1.4268$.

10.14 (a) Because $t_{STAT} = 4.10 > 2.024$, reject H_0. There is evidence of a difference in the mean surface hardness between untreated and treated steel plates. **(b)** p-value = 0.0002. The probability that two samples have a mean difference of 9.3634 or more is 0.02% if there is no difference in the mean surface hardness between untreated and treated steel plates. **(c)** You need to assume that the population distribution of hardness of both untreated and treated steel plates is normally distributed. **(d)** $4.7447 \leq \mu_1 - \mu_2 \leq 13.9821$.

10.16 (a) Because $t_{STAT} = -2.1522 < -2.0211$, reject H_0. There is enough evidence to conclude that the mean assembly times, in seconds, are different between employees trained in a computer-assisted, individual-based program and those trained in a team-based program. **(b)** You must assume that each of the two independent populations is normally distributed. **(c)** Because $t_{STAT} = -2.152 < -2.052$ or p-value = 0.041 < 0.05, reject H_0. **(d)** The results in (a) and (c) are the same. **(e)** $-4.52 \leq \mu_1 - \mu_2 \leq -0.14$. You are 95% confident that the difference between the population means of the two training methods is between -4.52 and -0.14.

10.18 $df = 19$.

10.20 (a) $t_{STAT} = (-1.5566)/(1.424)/\sqrt{9} = -3.2772$; Because $t_{STAT} = -3.2772 < -2.306$ or p-value = 0.0112 < 0.05, reject H_0. There is enough evidence of a difference in the mean summated ratings between the two brands. **(b)** You must assume that the distribution of the differences between the two ratings is approximately normal. **(c)** p-value is 0.0112. The probability of obtaining a mean difference in ratings that gives rise to a test statistic that deviates from 0 by 3.2772 or more in either direction is 0.0112 if there is no difference in the mean summated ratings between the two brands. **(d)** $-2.6501 \leq \mu_D \leq -0.4610$. You are 95% confident that the mean difference in summated ratings between brand A and brand B is somewhere between -2.6501 and -0.4610.

10.22 (a) Because $t_{STAT} = 6.7876 > 2.9768$ or p-value = 0.0000 < 0.01, reject H_0. There is evidence to conclude that there is a difference between the mean price of textbooks at the local bookstore and Amazon.com. **(b)** You must assume that the distribution of the differences between the measurements is approximately normal. **(c)** $\$9.27 \leq \mu_D \leq \$23.25$. You are 99% confident that the mean difference between the price of textbooks at the local bookstore and Amazon.com is somewhere between $9.27 and $23.25. **(d)** The results in (a) and (c) are the same. The hypothesized value of 0 for the difference in the price of textbooks between the local bookstore and Amazon.com is outside the 99% confidence interval.

10.24 (a) Because $t_{STAT} = 1.8425 < 1.943$, do not reject H_0. There is not enough evidence to conclude that the mean bone marrow microvessel density is higher before the stem cell transplant than after the stem cell transplant. **(b)** p-value = 0.0575. The probability that the t statistic for the mean difference in density is 1.8425 or more is 5.75% if the mean density is not higher before the stem cell transplant than after the stem cell transplant. **(c)** $-28.26 \leq \mu_D \leq 200.55$. You are 95% confident that the mean difference in bone marrow microvessel density before and after the stem cell transplant is somewhere between -28.26 and 200.55.

10.26 (a) Because $t_{STAT} = -9.3721 < -2.4258$, reject H_0. **(b)** The population of differences in strength is approximately normally distributed. **(c)** $p = 0.000$.

10.28 (a) Because $-2.58 \leq Z_{STAT} = -0.58 \leq 2.58$, do not reject H_0. **(b)** $-0.273 \leq \pi_1 - \pi_2 \leq 0.173$.

10.30 (a) $H_0: \pi_1 \leq \pi_2$. $H_1: \pi_1 > \pi_2$. Populations: 1 = expensive pill, 2 = cheap pill. **(b)** Because $Z_{STAT} = 2.4924 > 1.6449$, or p-value =

$0.0064 < 0.05$ reject H_0. There is sufficient evidence to conclude that the population proportion of people who think the expensive pill works greater than the population proportion of people who think the cheap pill works. **(c)** Yes, the result in (b) makes it appropriate to claim that people think the expensive pill works better.

10.32 (a) H_0: $\pi_1 = \pi_2$. H_1: $\pi_1 \neq \pi_2$. Decision rule: If $|Z_{STAT}| > 1.96$, reject H_0.
Test statistic:

$$\bar{p} = \frac{X_1 + X_2}{n_1 + n_2} = \frac{280 + 320}{505 + 500} = 0.5970$$

$$Z_{STAT} = \frac{(p_1 - p_2) - (\pi_2 - \pi_2)}{\sqrt{\bar{p}(1 - \bar{p})\left(\frac{1}{n_1} + \frac{1}{n_2}\right)}} = \frac{(0.5545 - 0.64) - 0}{\sqrt{0.5970(1 - 0.5970)\left(\frac{1}{505} + \frac{1}{500}\right)}}$$

$$= -2.7644.$$

Decision: Because $Z_{STAT} = -2.7644 < -1.96$, reject H_0. There is sufficient evidence to conclude that there is a difference in the proportion of adults who think the U.S. tax code is unfair between the two income groups. **(b)** p-value $= 0.0057$. The probability of obtaining a difference in proportions that gives rise to a test statistic that deviates from 0 by 2.7644 or more in either direction is 0.0057 if there is no difference in the proportion of adults who think the U.S. tax code is unfair between the two income groups.

10.34 (a) Because $-1.96 < Z_{STAT} = 1.5240 < 1.96$, do not reject H_0. There is insufficient evidence of a difference between undergraduate and MBA students in the proportion who selected the highest-cost fund. **(b)** p-value $= 0.1275$. The probability of obtaining a difference in proportions that gives rise to a test statistic that deviates from 0 by 1.5240 or more in either direction is 0.1275 if there is no difference between undergraduate and MBA students in the proportion who selected the highest-cost fund.

10.36 (a) 2.20. **(b)** 2.57. **(c)** 3.50.

10.38 (a) Population B. $S^2 = 25$. **(b)** 1.5625.

10.40 $df_{numerator} = 24$, $df_{denominator} - 24$.

10.42 Because $F_{STAT} = 1.2109 < 2.27$, do not reject H_0.

10.44 (a) Because $F_{STAT} = 1.2995 < 3.18$, do not reject H_0. **(b)** Because $F_{STAT} = 1.2995 < 2.62$, do not reject H_0.

10.46 (a) H_0: $\sigma_1^2 = \sigma_2^2$. H_1: $\sigma_1^2 \neq \sigma_2^2$.
Decision rule: If $F_{STAT} > 1.556$, reject H_0.

Test statistic: $F_{STAT} = \dfrac{S_1^2}{S_2^2} = \dfrac{(13.35)^2}{(9.42)^2} = 2.008$.

Decision: Because $F_{STAT} = 2.008 > 1.556$, reject H_0. There is enough evidence to conclude that the two population variances are different. **(b)** p-value $= 0.0022$. **(c)** The test assumes that each of the two populations is normally distributed. **(d)** Based on (a) and (b), a separate-variance t test should be used.

10.48 (a) Because $F_{STAT} = 1.0389 < 2.7324$ or p-value $= 0.9789 > 0.05$, do not reject H_0. There is not enough evidence of a difference in the variability of the battery life between the two types of digital cameras. **(b)** p-value $= 0.9789$. The probability of obtaining a sample that yields a test statistic more extreme than 1.0389 is 0.9789 if there is no difference in the two population variances. **(c)** The test assumes that the two populations are both normally distributed. **(d)** Based on (a) and (b), a pooled-variance t test should be used.

10.50 Because $F_{STAT} = 1.2303 < 9.60$, or p-value $= 0.8456 > 0.05$, do not reject H_0. There is not enough evidence of a difference in the variance of the yield between money market accounts and five-year CDs.

10.52 (a) $SSW = 150$. **(b)** $MSA = 15$. **(c)** $MSW = 5$. **(d)** $F_{STAT} = 3$.

10.54 (a) 2. **(b)** 18. **(c)** 20.

10.56 (a) Reject H_0 if $F_{STAT} > 2.95$; otherwise, do not reject H_0. **(b)** Because $F_{STAT} = 4 > 2.95$, reject H_0. **(c)** The table does not have 28 degrees of freedom in the denominator, so use the next larger critical value, $Q_\alpha = 3.90$. **(d)** Critical range $= 6.166$.

10.58 (a) H_0: $\mu_A = \mu_B = \mu_C = \mu_D$ and H_1: At least one mean in different.

$$MSA = \frac{SSA}{c - 1} = \frac{1986.475}{3} = 662.1583.$$

$$MSW = \frac{SSW}{n - c} = \frac{495.5}{36} = 13.76389.$$

$$F_{STAT} = \frac{MSA}{MSW} = \frac{662.1583}{13.76389} = 48.1084.$$

$$F_{0.05,3,36} = 2.8663.$$

Because the p-value is approximately zero and $F_{STAT} = 48.1084 > 2.8663$, reject H_0. There is sufficient evidence of a difference in the mean strength of the four brands of trash bags.

(b) Critical range $= Q_\alpha \sqrt{\dfrac{MSW}{2}\left(\dfrac{1}{n_j} + \dfrac{1}{n_{j'}}\right)} = 3.79\sqrt{\dfrac{13.7639}{2}\left(\dfrac{1}{10} + \dfrac{1}{10}\right)}$

$$= 4.446.$$

From the Tukey-Kramer procedure, there is a difference in mean strength between Kroger and Tuffstuff, Glad and Tuffstuff, and Hefty and Tuffstuff. **(c)** ANOVA output for Levene's test for homogeneity of variance:

$$MSA = \frac{SSA}{c - 1} = \frac{24.075}{3} = 8.025.$$

$$MSW = \frac{SSW}{n - c} = \frac{198.2}{36} = 5.5056.$$

$$F_{STAT} = \frac{MSA}{MSW} = \frac{8.025}{5.5056} = 1.4576.$$

$$F_{0.05,3,36} = 2.8663.$$

Because the p-value $= 0.2423 > 0.05$ and $F_{STAT} = 1.458 < 2.866$, do not reject H_0. There is insufficient evidence to conclude that the variances in strength among the four brands of trash bags are different. **(d)** From the results in (a) and (b), Tuffstuff has the lowest mean strength and should be avoided.

10.60 (a) Because $F_{STAT} = 12.56 > F_{0.05,4,25} = 2.76$, reject H_0. **(b)** Critical range $= 4.67$. Advertisements A and B are different from Advertisements C and D. Advertisement E is only different from Advertisement D. **(c)** Because $F_{STAT} = 1.927 < 2.76$, do not reject H_0. There is no evidence of a significant difference in the variation in the ratings among the five advertisements. **(d)** The advertisements underselling the pen's characteristics had the highest mean ratings, and the advertisements overselling the pen's characteristics had the lowest mean ratings. Therefore, use an advertisement that undersells the pen's characteristics and avoid advertisements that oversell the pen's characteristics.

10.62 (a) Because $F_{STAT} = 53.03 > F_{0.05,3,30} = 2.92$, reject H_0. **(b)** Critical range $= 5.27$ (using 30 degrees of freedom). Designs 3 and 4 are different from Designs 1 and 2. Designs 1 and 2 are different from each other. **(c)** The assumptions are that the samples are randomly and independently selected (or randomly assigned), the original populations of distances are approximately normally distributed, and the variances are equal. **(d)** Because $F_{STAT} = 2.093 < 2.92$, do not reject H_0. There is no evidence of a significant difference in the variation in the distance among the four designs. **(e)** The manager should choose Design 3 or 4.

10.72 (a) $H_0: \sigma_1^2 \geq \sigma_2^2$ and $H_0: \sigma_1^2 < \sigma_2^2$. **(b)** Type I error: Rejecting the null hypothesis that the price variance on the Internet is no lower than the price variance in the brick-and-mortar market when the price variance on the Internet is no lower than the price variance in the brick-and-mortar market. Type II error: Failing to reject the null hypothesis that price variance on the Internet is lower than the price variance in the brick-and-mortar market when the price variance on the Internet is lower than the price variance in the brick-and-mortar market. **(c)** An F test for differences in two variances can be used. **(d)** You need to assume that each of the two populations is normally distributed. **(e) (a)** $H_0: \mu_1 \geq \mu_2$ and $H_1: \mu_1 < \mu_2$. **(b)** Type I error: Rejecting the null hypothesis that the mean price in the electronic market is no lower than the mean price in the physical market when the mean price in the electronic market is no lower than the mean price in the physical market. Type II error: Failing to reject the null hypothesis that the mean price in the electronic market is no lower than the mean price in the physical market when the mean price in the electronic market is lower than the mean price in the physical market. **(c)** A pooled t test or a separate-variance t test for the difference in the means can be used. **(d)** You must assume that the distribution of the prices in the electronic market and in the physical market are approximately normally distributed.

10.74 (a) The researchers can ask the teenagers, after viewing each ad, to rate the dangers of smoking, using a scale from 0 to 10, with 10 representing the most dangerous. **(b)** $H_0: \mu_T \geq \mu_S$ and $H_1: \mu_T < \mu_S$. **(c)** Type I error is the error made by concluding that ads produced by the state are more effective than those produced by Philip Morris even though it is not true. The risk of Type I error here is that teenagers can miss the opportunity from the better ads produced by Philip Morris to recognize the true dangers of smoking and the additional expenses the state will have to incur to produce and run the ads. Type II error is the error made by concluding that ads produced by Philip Morris are no less effective than those produced by the state even though ads produced by the state are more effective. The risk of Type II error here is that more teenagers will miss the opportunity to recognize the true dangers of smoking from the ads produced by the state. **(d)** Because both ads are shown to the same group of teenagers, a paired t test for the mean difference is most appropriate. **(e)** Statistically reliable here means the conclusions drawn from the test are reliable because all the assumptions needed for the test to be valid are fulfilled.

10.76 (a) Because $F_{STAT} = 22.7067 > F_\alpha = 1.6275$, reject H_0. There is enough evidence to conclude that there is a difference between the variances in age of students at the Western school and at the Eastern school. **(b)** Because there is a difference between the variances in the age of students at the Western school and at the Eastern school, schools should take that into account when designing their curriculum to accommodate the larger variance in age of students in the state university in the Western United States. **(c)** It is more appropriate to use a separate-variance t test. **(d)** Because $F_{STAT} = 1.3061 < 1.6275$, do not reject H_0. There is not enough evidence to conclude that there is a difference between the variances in years of spreadsheet usage of students at the Western school and at the Eastern school. **(e)** Using the pooled-variance t test, because $t_{STAT} = -4.6650 < -2.5978$, reject H_0. There is enough evidence of a difference in the mean years of spreadsheet usage of students at the Western school and at the Eastern school.

10.78 (a) Because $t_{STAT} = 3.3282 > 1.8595$, reject H_0. There is enough evidence to conclude that the introductory computer students required more than a mean of 10 minutes to write and run a program in Visual

Basic. **(b)** Because $t_{STAT} = 1.3636 < 1.8595$, do not reject H_0. There is not enough evidence to conclude that the introductory computer students required more than a mean of 10 minutes to write and run a program in Visual Basic. **(c)** Although the mean time necessary to complete the assignment increased from 12 to 16 minutes as a result of the increase in one data value, the standard deviation went from 1.8 to 13.2, which reduced the t value. **(d)** Because $F_{STAT} = 1.2308 < 3.8549$, do not reject H_0. There is not enough evidence to conclude that the population variances are different for the Introduction to Computers students and computer majors. Hence, the pooled-variance t test is a valid test to determine whether computer majors can write a Visual Basic program in less time than introductory students, assuming that the distributions of the time needed to write a Visual Basic program for both the Introduction to Computers students and the computer majors are approximately normally distributed. Because $t_{STAT} = 4.0666 > 1.7341$, reject H_0. There is enough evidence that the mean time is higher for Introduction to Computers students than for computer majors. **(e)** p-value $= 0.000362$. If the true population mean amount of time needed for Introduction to Computer students to write a Visual Basic program is no more than 10 minutes, the probability of observing a sample mean greater than the 12 minutes in the current sample is 0.0362%. Hence, at a 5% level of significance, you can conclude that the population mean amount of time needed for Introduction to Computer students to write a Visual Basic program is more than 10 minutes. As illustrated in part (d), in which there is not enough evidence to conclude that the population variances are different for the Introduction to Computers students and computer majors, the pooled-variance t test performed is a valid test to determine whether computer majors can write a Visual Basic program in less time than introductory students, assuming that the distribution of the time needed to write a Visual Basic program for both the Introduction to Computers students and the computer majors are approximately normally distributed.

10.80 From the boxplot and the summary statistics, both distributions are approximately normally distributed. $F_{STAT} = 1.056 < 1.89$. There is insufficient evidence to conclude that the two population variances are significantly different at the 5% level of significance. $t_{STAT} = -5.084 < -1.99$. At the 5% level of significance, there is sufficient evidence to reject the null hypothesis of no difference in the mean life of the bulbs between the two manufacturers. You can conclude that there is a significant difference in the mean life of the bulbs between the two manufacturers.

10.82 Customer Product Rating Reviews: $-1.96 < Z_{STAT} = -1.6557 < 1.96$ and p-value $= 0.0978 > 0.05$, do not reject H_0. There is not enough evidence that there is a difference between adults and youths in the proportion who use customer product ratings/reviews. For sale listings with seller ratings: $-1.96 < Z_{STAT} = -1.2742 < 1.96$ and p-value $= 0.2026 > 0.05$, do not reject H_0. There is not enough evidence that there is a difference between adults and youths in the proportion who use for sale listings with seller ratings. For sale listings without seller ratings: $-1.96 < Z_{STAT} = -1.0172 < 1.96$ and p-value $= 0.3090 > 0.05$, do not reject H_0. There is not enough evidence that there is a difference between adults and youths in the proportion who use for sale listings without seller ratings. Online classified ads: $-1.96 < Z_{STAT} = -1.3079 < 1.96$ and p-value $= 0.1909 > 0.05$, do not reject H_0. There is not enough evidence that there is a difference between adults and youths in the proportion who use online classified ads. Message-board posts: $Z_{STAT} = -2.0624 < -1.96$ and p-value $= 0.0392 < 0.05$, reject H_0. There is enough evidence that there is a difference between adults and youths in the proportion who use message-board posts. Web blogs: $-1.96 < Z_{STAT} = -1.7397 < 1.96$ and p-value $= 0.0819 > 0.05$, do not reject H_0. There is not enough evidence that there is a difference between adults and youths in the proportion who use Web blogs. Dating site profile/personals: $= -1.96 < Z_{STAT} = -1.4188 < 1.96$ and p-value $= 0.1560 > 0.05$, do not reject H_0. There is not enough evidence that there is a difference between adults and youths in the proportion who use dating site profiles/personals. Peer-generated and peer-referenced information: $Z_{STAT} = -2.7267 < -1.96$ and p-value $= 0.0064 < 0.05$, reject H_0. There is enough evidence that there is a difference between adults and youths in the proportion who use peer-generated and peer-referenced information. Peer-posted event listings: $Z_{STAT} = -3.5878 < -1.96$ and p-value $= 0.0003 < 0.05$, reject H_0. There is enough evidence that there is a difference between adults and youths in the proportion who use peer-posted event listings.

10.84 The normal probability plots suggest that the two populations are not normally distributed. An F test is inappropriate for testing the difference in two variances. The sample variances for Boston and Vermont shingles are 0.0203 and 0.015, respectively. Because $t_{STAT} = 3.015 > 1.967$ or the p-value $= 0.0028 < \alpha = 0.05$, reject H_0. There is sufficient evidence to conclude that there is a difference in the mean granule loss of Boston and Vermont shingles.

10.86 (a) Because $F_{STAT} = 0.075 < F_{0.05,2,15} = 3.68$, do not reject H_0. **(b)** Because $F_{STAT} = 4.09 > F_{0.05,2,15} = 3.68$, reject H_0. **(c)** Critical range $= 1.489$. Breaking strength is significantly different between 30 and 50 psi.

CHAPTER 11

11.2 (a) For $df = 1$ and $\alpha = 0.05$, $\chi^2_\alpha = 3.841$. **(b)** For $df = 1$ and $\alpha = 0.005$, $\chi^2 = 7.879$. **(c)** For $df = 1$ and $\alpha = 0.10$, $\chi^2_\alpha = 2.706$.

11.4 (a) All $f_e = 25$. **(b)** Because $\chi^2_{STAT} = 4.00 > 3.841$, reject H_0.

11.6 (a) Because $\chi^2_{STAT} = 6.212 > 3.841$, reject H_0. There is enough evidence to conclude that there is significant difference between the proportion of people who think the expensive pill works to reduce pain and the proportion of people who think a cheap pill works to reduce pain. **(b)** p-value is 0.0127. The probability of obtaining a test statistic of 6.212 or larger when the null hypothesis is true is 0.0127. **(c)** You should not compare the results in (a) to those of Problem 10.30 (b) because that was a one-tail test.

11.8 (a) $H_0: \pi_1 = \pi_2$. $H_1: \pi_1 \neq \pi_2$.

Observed Frequencies

	Column Variable		
Row Variable	**Less Than $50,000**	**More Than $50,000**	**Total**
Fair	225	180	405
Unfair	280	320	600
Total	505	500	1,005

Expected Frequencies

	Column Variable		
Row Variable	**Less Than $50,000**	**More Than $50,000**	**Total**
Fair	203.5075	201.4925	405
Unfair	301.4925	298.5075	600
Total	505	500	1,005

Level of Significance 0.05 Number of Rows 2 Number of Columns 2 Degrees of Freedom 1 Critical Value 3.841459 Chi-Square Test Statistic $=$ $(225 - 203.5075)^2/203.5075 + (280 - 301.4925)^2/301.4925 +$ $(180 - 201.4925)^2/201.4925 + (320 - 298.5075)^2/298.5075 =$ 7.64198 p-Value 0.005703

Decision: Because $\chi^2_{STAT} = 7.642 > 3.841$, reject H_0. There is enough evidence to conclude that there is a significant difference in the proportion of adults who think the U.S. tax code is unfair between the two

income groups. **(b)** The probability of obtaining a test statistic of 7.642 or larger when the null hypothesis is true is 0.0057. **(c)** The results of (a) and (b) are exactly the same as those of Problem 10.32. The χ^2 in (a) and the Z in Problem 10.32 (a) satisfy the relationship that $\chi^2 = 7.642 = Z^2 = (-2.7644)^2$, and the p-value in Problem 10.32 (b) is exactly the same as the p-value obtained in (b).

11.10 (a) Because $\chi^2_{STAT} = 2.3226 < 3.841$, do not reject H_0. There is not enough evidence to conclude that there is a significant difference between undergraduate and MBA students in the proportion who selected the highest-cost fund. **(b)** p-value $= 0.1275$. The probability of obtaining a test statistic of 2.3226 or larger when the null hypothesis is true is 0.1275. **(c)** The results of (a) and (b) are exactly the same as those of Problem 10.34. The χ^2 in (a) and the Z in Problem 10.34 (a) satisfy the relationship that $\chi^2_{STAT} = 2.3226 = (Z_{STAT})^2 = (1.5240)^2$, and the p-value in Problem 10.34 (b) is exactly the same as the p-value obtained in (b).

11.12 (a) The expected frequencies for the first row are 20, 30, and 40. The expected frequencies for the second row are 30, 45, and 60. **(b)** Because $\chi^2_{STAT} = 12.5 > 5.991$, reject H_0.

11.14 (a) Because the calculated test statistic $\chi^2_{STAT} = 742.3961 > 9.4877$, reject H_0 and conclude that there is a difference in the proportion of people who eat out at least once a week in the various countries. **(b)** p-value is virtually zero. The probability of a test statistic greater than 742.3961 or more is approximately zero if there is no difference in the proportion of people who eat out at least once a week in the various countries.

11.16 (a) $H_0: \pi_1 = \pi_2 = \pi_3$. H_1: At least one proportion differs.

f_0	f_e	$(f_0 - f_e)$	$(f_0 - f_e)^2/f_e$
48	42.667	5.333	0.667
152	157.333	-5.333	0.181
56	42.667	13.333	4.166
144	157.333	-13.333	1.130
24	42.667	-18.667	8.167
176	157.333	18.667	2.215
			16.5253

Decision rule: $df = (c - 1) = (3 - 1) = 2$. If $\chi^2_{STAT} > 5.9915$, reject H_0.

Test statistic: $\chi^2_{STAT} = \displaystyle\sum_{\text{all cells}} \frac{(f_0 - f_e)^2}{f_e} = 16.5253$

Decision: Because $\chi^2_{STAT} = 16.5253 > 5.9915$, reject H_0. There is a significant difference in the age groups with respect to major grocery shopping day. **(b)** p-value $= 0.0003$. The probability that the test statistic is greater than or equal to 16.5253 is 0.03%, if the null hypothesis is true. **(c)** The stores can use this information to target their marketing on the specific groups of shoppers on Saturday and the days other than Saturday.

11.18 (a) Because $\chi^2_{STAT} = 20.3383 > 7.815$, reject H_0. There is evidence of a difference in the percentage working among the groups. **(b)** p-value $= 0.0001$.

11.20 $df = (r - 1)(c - 1) = (3 - 1)(4 - 1) = 6$.

11.22 (b) $\chi^2_{STAT} = 8.3536 < 9.2103$, do not reject H_0 and conclude that there is not enough evidence that men and women feel differently about executive pay. **(c)** $\chi^2_{STAT} = 16.7073 > 9.2103$, reject H_0 and conclude that there is enough evidence that men and women feel differently about executive pay. **(d)** As you can see from the results in (b) and (c), the same proportions will result in a different test statistic and, hence, potentially different decisions.

11.24 (a) H_0: There is no relationship between the commuting time of company employees and the level of stress-related problems observed on the job. H_1: There is a relationship between the commuting time of company employees and the level of stress-related problems observed on the job.

f_0	f_e	$(f_0 - f_e)$	$(f_0 - f_e)^2/f_e$
9	12.1379	−3.1379	0.8112
17	20.1034	−3.1034	0.4791
18	11.7586	6.2414	3.3129
5	5.2414	−0.2414	0.0111
8	8.6810	−0.6810	0.0534
6	5.0776	0.9224	0.1676
18	14.6207	3.3793	0.7811
28	24.2155	3.7845	0.5915
7	14.1638	−7.1638	3.6233
			9.8311

Decision rule: If $\chi^2_{STAT} > 13.277$, reject H_0.

Test statistic: $\chi^2_{STAT} = \sum_{\text{all cells}} \dfrac{(f_0 - f_e)^2}{f_e} = 9.8311$

Decision: Because the $\chi^2_{STAT} = 9.8311 < 13.277$, do not reject H_0. There is not enough evidence to conclude that there is a relationship between the commuting time of company employees and the level of stress-related problems observed on the job.
(b) Because $\chi^2_{STAT} = 9.831 > 9.488$, reject H_0. There is enough evidence at the 0.05 level to conclude that there is a relationship.

11.26 Because $\chi^2_{STAT} = 129.520 > 21.026$, reject H_0. There is a relationship between when the decision is made of what to have for dinner and the type of household.

11.30 (a) Because $\chi^2_{STAT} = 0.412 < 3.841$, do not reject H_0. There is not enough evidence to conclude that there is a relationship between a student's gender and pizzeria selection. **(b)** Because $\chi^2_{STAT} = 2.624 < 3.841$, do not reject H_0. There is not enough evidence to conclude that there is a relationship between a student's gender and pizzeria selection. **(c)** Because $\chi^2_{STAT} = 4.956 < 5.991$, do not reject H_0. There is not enough evidence to conclude that there is a relationship between price and pizzeria selection. **(d)** p-value $= 0.0839$. The probability of a sample that gives a test statistic equal to or greater than 4.956 is 8.39% if the null hypothesis of no relationship between price and pizzeria selection is true.

11.32 (a) Because $\chi^2_{STAT} = 11.895 < 12.592$, do not reject H_0. There is not enough evidence to conclude that there is a relationship between the attitudes of employees toward the use of self-managed work teams and employee job classification. **(b)** Because $\chi^2_{STAT} = 3.294 < 12.592$, do not reject H_0. There is not enough evidence to conclude that there is a relationship between the attitudes of employees toward vacation time without pay and employee job classification.

11.34 (a) Because $\chi^2_{STAT} = 11.635 > 7.815$, reject H_0. There is enough evidence to conclude that there is a relationship between the presence of environmental goals and the type of manufacturing process. **(b)** p-value $= 0.00874$. The probability of obtaining a data set that gives rise to a test statistic of 11.635 or more is 0.00874 if there is no relationship between the presence of environmental goals and the type of manufacturing process. **(c)** Because $\chi^2_{STAT} = 10.94 > 3.841$, reject H_0. There is enough evidence to conclude that there is a difference in improved environmental performance for teams with a specified goal of cutting costs. **(d)** p-value $= 0.000941$. The probability of obtaining a data set that gives rise to a test statistic of 10.94 or more is 0.000941 if there is no difference in improved environmental performance for teams with a

specified goal of cutting costs. **(e)** Because $\chi^2_{STAT} = 0.612 < 3.841$, do not reject H_0. There is not enough evidence to conclude that there is a difference in improved profitability for teams with a specified goal of cutting costs. **(f)** p-value $= 0.4341$. The probability of obtaining a data set that gives rise to a test statistic of 0.612 or more is 0.4341 if there is no difference in improved profitability for teams with a specified goal of cutting costs. **(g)** $\chi^2_{STAT} = 3.454 < 3.841$, do not reject H_0. There is not enough evidence to conclude that there is a difference in improved morale for teams with a specified goal of cutting costs. **(h)** p-value $= 0.063$. The probability of obtaining a data set that gives rise to a test statistic of 3.454 or more is 0.063 if there is no difference in improved morale for teams with a specified goal of cutting costs.

CHAPTER 12

12.2 (a) Yes. **(b)** No. **(c)** No. **(d)** Yes.

12.4 (a) the scatter plot shows a positive linear relationship

(b) For each increase in shelf space of an additional foot, weekly sales are estimated to increase by $7.40. **(c)** $\hat{Y} = 145 + 7.4X = 145 + 7.4(8) = 204.2$, or $204.20.

12.6 (b) $b_0 = -2.37, b_1 = 0.0501$. **(c)** For every cubic foot increase in the amount moved, mean labor hours are estimated to increase by 0.0501. **(d)** 22.67 labor hours.

12.8 (b) $b_0 = -435.065, b_1 = 4.9555$. **(c)** For each additional million-dollar increase in revenue, the mean annual value will increase by an estimated $4.9555 million. Literal interpretation of b_0 is not meaningful because an operating franchise cannot have zero revenue. **(d)** $308,266 million.

12.10 (b) $b_0 = -140.1203, b_1 = 4.3331 \hat{Y} = b_0 + b_1X$.
$\hat{Y} = -140.1203 + 4.3331X$ **(c)** For each increase of one additional million dollars of box office gross, the estimated mean DVDs sold will increase by 4.3331 thousands. **(d)** $\hat{Y} = b_0 + b_1X$. $\hat{Y} = -140.1203 + 4.3331(75) = 184.86285$ thousands.

12.12 $r^2 = 0.90$. 90% of the variation in the dependent variable can be explained by the variation in the independent variable.

12.14 $r^2 = 0.75$. 75% of the variation in the dependent variable can be explained by the variation in the independent variable.

12.16 (a) $r^2 = \dfrac{SSR}{SST} = \dfrac{20,535}{30,025} = 0.684$. 68.4% of the variation in sales can be explained by the variation in shelf space.

(b) $S_{YX} = \sqrt{\dfrac{SSE}{n-2}} = \dfrac{\sqrt{\sum_{i=1}^{n}(Y_i - \hat{Y}_i)^2}}{n-2} = \sqrt{\dfrac{9,490}{10}} = 30.8058.$

(c) Based on (a) and (b), the model should be very useful for predicting sales.

12.18 (a) $r^2 = 0.8892$. 88.92% of the variation in labor hours can be explained by the variation in cubic feet moved. **(b)** $S_{YX} = 5.0314$. **(c)** Based on (a) and (b), the model should be very useful for predicting the labor hours.

12.20 (a) $r^2 = 0.931$. 93.1% of the variation in the value of a baseball franchise can be explained by the variation in its annual revenue. **(b)** $S_{YX} = 56.4059$. **(c)** Based on (a) and (b), the model should be very useful for predicting the value of a baseball franchise.

12.22 (a) $r^2 = 0.7278$. 72.78% of the variation in DVDs sold can be explained by the variation in box office gross. **(b)** $S_{YX} = 47.8668$. The variation of DVDs sold around the prediction line is 47.8668 millions. The typical difference between actual DVDs sold and the predicted DVDs sold using the regression equation is approximately 47.8668 millions. **(c)** Based on (a) and (b), the model is useful for predicting DVDs sold. **(d)** Other variables that might explain the variation in DVDs sold could be the amount spent on advertising, the timing of the release of the DVDs, and the distribution channels of the DVDs.

12.24 A residual analysis of the data indicates a pattern, with sizable clusters of consecutive residuals that are either all positive or all negative. This pattern indicates a violation of the assumption of linearity. A curvilinear model should be investigated.

12.26 There does not appear to be a pattern in the residual plot. The assumptions of regression do not appear to be seriously violated.

12.28 Based on the residual plot, there does not appear to be a curvilinear pattern in the residuals. The assumptions of normality and equal variance do not appear to be seriously violated.

12.30 Based on the residual plot, there appears to be a nonlinear pattern in the residuals. A curvilinear model should be investigated. There is some right-skewness in the residuals and some violation of the equal-variance assumption.

12.32 (a) 3.00. **(b)** ± 2.1199. **(c)** Reject H_0. There is evidence that the fitted linear regression model is useful. **(d)** $1.32 \le \beta_1 \le 7.68$.

12.34 (a) $t_{STAT} = \dfrac{b_1 - \beta_1}{S_{b_1}} = \dfrac{7.4}{1.59} = 4.65 > 2.2281$. Reject H_0. There is evidence that the fitted linear regression model is useful. **(b)** $b_1 \pm t_{\alpha/2} S_{b_1} = 7.4 \pm 2.2281(1.59)$ $3.86 \le \beta_1 \le 10.94$.

12.36 (a) $t_{STAT} = 16.52 > 2.0322$; reject H_0. **(b)** $0.0439 \le \beta_1 \le 0.0562$.

12.38 (a) $t_{STAT} = 19.50 > 2.0484$ or because the p-value is approximately zero, reject H_0 at the 5% level of significance. There is evidence of a linear relationship between annual revenue and franchise value. **(b)** $4.435 \le \beta_1 \le 5.476$.

12.40 (a) $t_{STAT} = 8.65 > 2.0484$ or because the p-value is virtually $0 < 0.05$; reject H_0. **(b)** $3.3072 \le \beta_1 \le 5.3590$.

12.42 (a) (% daily change in UOPIX) $= b_0 + 2.00$ (% daily change in S&P 500 index) **(b)** If the S&P gains 30% in a year, the UOPIX is expected to gain an estimated 60%. **(c)** If the S&P loses 35% in a year, the UOPIX is expected to lose an estimated 70%. **(d)** Risk takers will be attracted to leveraged funds, but risk averse investors will stay away.

12.44 (a) $r = 0.8935$. There appears to be a strong positive linear relationship between the mileage as calculated by owners and by current government standards. **(b)** $t_{STAT} = 5.2639 > 2.3646, p$-value $= 0.0012 < 0.05$. Reject H_0. At the 0.05 level of significance, there is a significant linear relationship between the mileage as calculated by owners and by current government standards.

12.46 (a) $r = 0.5497$. There appears to be a moderate positive linear relationship between the average Wonderlic score of football players trying out for the NFL and the graduation rate for football players at selected schools. **(b)** $t_{STAT} = 3.9485, p$-value $= 0.0004 < 0.05$. Reject H_0. At the 0.05 level of significance, there is a significant linear relationship between the average Wonderlic score of football players trying out for the NFL and the graduation rate for football players at selected schools. **(c)** There is a significant linear relationship between the average Wonderlic score of football players trying out for the NFL and the graduation rate for football players at selected schools, but the positive linear relationship is only moderate.

12.48 (a) $15.95 \le \mu_{Y|X=4} \le 18.05$. **(b)** $14.651 \le Y_{X=4} \le 19.349$.

12.50 (a) $\hat{Y} = 145 + 7.4(8) = 204.2$ $\hat{Y} \pm t_{\alpha/2} S_{YX} \sqrt{h_i}$

$$= 204.2 \pm 2.2281(30.81)\sqrt{0.1373}$$

$$178.76 \le \mu_{Y|X=8} \le 229.64$$

(b) $\hat{Y} \pm t_{\alpha/2} S_{YX} \sqrt{1 + h_i}$

$$= 204.2 \pm 2.2281(30.81)\sqrt{1 + 0.1373}$$

$$131.00 \le Y_{X=8} \le 277.40$$

(c) Part (b) provides a prediction interval for the individual response given a specific value of the independent variable, and part (a) provides an interval estimate for the mean value, given a specific value of the independent variable. Because there is much more variation in predicting an individual value than in estimating a mean value, a prediction interval is wider than a confidence interval estimate.

12.52 (a) $20.799 \le \mu_{Y|X=500} \le 24.542$. **(b)** $12.276 \le Y_{X=500} \le 33.065$. **(c)** You can estimate a mean more precisely than you can predict a single observation.

12.54 (a) $281.1 \le \mu_{Y|X=150} \le 335.5$. **(b)** $189.6 \le Y_{X=150} \le 427.0$. **(c)** Part (b) provides a prediction interval for an individual response given a specific value of X and part (a) provides a confidence interval estimate for the mean value given a specific value of X. Since there is much more variation in predicting an individual value than in estimating a mean, the prediction interval is wider than the confidence interval.

12.64 (a) $b_0 = 24.84, b_1 = 0.14$. **(b)** For each additional case, the predicted mean delivery time is estimated to increase by 0.14 minutes. **(c)** 45.84. **(d)** No, 500 is outside the relevant range of the data used to fit the regression equation. **(e)** $r^2 = 0.972$. **(f)** There is no obvious pattern in the residuals, so the assumptions of regression are met. The model appears to be adequate. **(g)** $t_{STAT} = 24.88 > 2.1009$; reject H_0. **(h)** $44.88 \le \mu_{Y|X=150} \le 46.80$. $41.56 \le Y_{X=150} \le 50.12$.

12.66 (a) $b_0 = -122.3439, b_1 = 1.7817$. **(b)** For each additional thousand dollars in assessed value, the estimated mean selling price of a house increases by $1.7817 thousand. The estimated mean selling price of a house with a 0 assessed value is -122.3439 thousand. However, this interpretation is not meaningful in the current setting because the assessed value cannot be below 0. **(c)** $\hat{Y} = -122.3439 + 1.78171X = -122.3439 + 1.78171(170) = 180.5475$ thousand dollars. **(d)** $r^2 = 0.9256$. So 92.56% of the variation in selling price can be explained by the variation in assessed value. **(e)** Neither the residual plot nor the normal probability plot reveal any potential violation of the linearity, equal variance, and normality assumptions. **(f)** $t_{STAT} = 18.6648 > 2.0484, p$-value is virtually zero. Because p-value < 0.05, reject H_0. There is evidence of a linear relationship between selling price and assessed value. **(g)** $1.5862 \le \beta_1 \le 1.9773$.

12.68 (a) $b_0 = 0.30, b_1 = 0.00487$. **(b)** For each additional point on the GMAT score, the predicted mean GPA is estimated to increase by 0.00487. Since a student receiving a 0 on the GMAT would not be admitted to graduate school, the Y-intercept does not have a practical interpretation. **(c)** 3.222. **(d)** $r^2 = 0.798$. **(e)** There is no obvious pattern in the residuals, so the assumptions of regression are met. The model appears to be adequate. **(f)** $t_{STAT} = 8.43 > 2.1009$; reject H_0. **(g)** $3.144 \le \mu_{Y|X=600} \le 3.301$. $2.886 \le Y_{X=600} \le 3.559$. **(h)** $.00366 \le \beta_1 \le .00608$.

12.70 (a) There is no clear relationship shown on the scatterplot. **(c)** Looking at all 23 flights, when the temperature is lower, there is likely to be some O-ring damage, particularly if the temperature is below 60 degrees. **(d)** 31 degrees is outside the relevant range, so a prediction should not be made. **(e)** Predicted $Y = 18.036 - 0.240X$, where X = temperature and Y = O-ring damage. **(g)** A nonlinear model would be more appropriate. **(h)** The appearance on the residual plot of a nonlinear pattern indicates a nonlinear model would be better. It also appears that the normality assumption is invalid.

12.72 (a) $b_0 = 14.6816$, $b_1 = 0.1135$. **(b)** For each additional percentage increase in graduation rate, the estimated mean average Wonderlic score increases by 0.1135. The estimated mean average Wonderlic score is 14.6816 for a school that has a 0% graduation rate. However, this interpretation is not meaningful in the current setting because graduation rate is very unlikely to be 0% for any school. **(c)** $\hat{Y} = 14.6816 + 0.11347X = 14.6816 + 0.11347(50) = 20.4$. **(d)** $r^2 = 0.3022$. So, 30.22% of the variation in average Wonderlic score can be explained by the variation in graduation rate. **(e)** Neither the residual plot nor the normal probability plot reveal any potential violation of the linearity, equal variance, and normality assumptions. **(f)** $t_{STAT} = 3.9485 > 2.0281$, p-value $= 0.0004$. Because p-value < 0.05, reject H_0. There is evidence of a linear relationship between the average Wonderlic score for football players trying out for the NFL from a school and the graduation rate. **(g)** $19.6 \leq \mu_{Y|X=50} \leq 21.1$. **(h)** $15.9 \leq Y_{X=50} \leq 24.8$.

12.74 (a) $b_0 = -2,629.222$, $b_1 = 82.472$. **(b)** For each additional centimeter in circumference, the mean weight is estimated to increase by 82.472 grams. **(c)** 2,319.08 grams. **(e)** $r^2 = 0.937$. **(f)** There appears to be a nonlinear relationship between circumference and weight. **(g)** p-value is virtually $0 < 0.05$; reject H_0. **(h)** $72.7875 \leq \beta_1 \leq 92.156$.

12.76 (b) $\hat{Y} = 931,626.16 + 21,782.76X$. **(c)** $b_1 = 21,782.76$ means that as the median age of the customer base increases by one year, the latest one-month mean sales total is estimated to increase by $21,782.76. **(d)** $r^2 = 0.0017$. Only 0.17% of the total variation in the franchise's latest one-month sales total can be explained by using the median age of customer base. **(e)** The residuals are very evenly spread out across different range of median age. **(f)** Because $-2.4926 < t_{STAT} = 0.2482 < 2.4926$, do not reject H_0. There is not enough evidence to conclude that there is a linear relationship between the one-month sales total and the median age of the customer base. **(g)** $-156,181.50 \leq \beta_1 \leq 199,747.02$.

12.78 (a) There is a positive linear relationship between total sales and the percentage of customer base with a college diploma. **(b)** $\hat{Y} = 789,847.38 + 35,854.15X$. **(c)** $b_1 = 35,854.15$ means that for each increase of one percent of the customer base having received a college diploma, the latest one-month mean sales total is estimated to increase by $35,854.15. **(d)** $r^2 = 0.1036$. So 10.36% of the total variation in the franchise's latest one-month sales total can be explained by the percentage of the customer base with a college diploma. **(e)** The residuals are evenly spread out around zero. **(f)** Because $t_{STAT} = 2.0392 > 2.0281$, reject H_0. There is enough evidence to conclude that there is a linear relationship between one-month sales total and percentage of customer base with a college diploma. **(g)** $b_1 \pm t_{\alpha/2} S_{b_1} = 35,854.15 \pm 2.0281(17,582.269)$ $195.75 \leq \beta_1 \leq 71,512.60$.

12.80 (a) $b_0 = -39.0137$, $b_1 = 1.3878$. **(b)** For each additional unit increase in summated rating, the mean price per person is estimated to increase by $1.3878. Because no restaurant will receive a summated rating of 0, it is inappropriate to interpret the Y intercept. **(c)** $30.38. **(d)** $r^2 = 0.6586$. So, 65.86% of the variation in price per person can be explained by the variation in the summated rating. **(e)** There is no obvious pattern in the residuals so the assumptions of regression are met. The model appears to be adequate. **(f)** $t_{STAT} = 13.7484$, the p-value is virtually $0 < 0.05$; reject H_0. There is enough evidence to conclude that there is a linear relationship between price per person and summated rating. **(g)** The linear regression model appears to have provided an adequate fit and shown a significant linear relationship between price per person and summated rating. Because 65.86% of the variation in price per

person can be explained by the variation in summated rating, summated rating is moderately useful in predicting the price per person.

12.82 (a) The correlation of IBM and GE is -0.126, IBM and Apple is -0.011, and Apple and GE is -0.141. **(b)** There is a very weak negative linear relationship between the stock price of IBM and GE, almost no linear relationship between the stock price of IBM and Apple, and a very weak positive linear relationship between the stock price of GE and Apple. **(c)** It is not a good idea to have all the stocks in an individual's portfolio be strongly, positively correlated among each other because the portfolio risk can be reduced when a pair of stock prices is negatively related or nearly independent.

CHAPTER 13

13.2 (a) For each one-unit increase in X_1, you estimate that Y will decrease 2 units, holding X_2 constant. For each one-unit increase in X_2, you estimate that Y will increase 7 units, holding X_1 constant. **(b)** The Y-intercept equal to 50 estimates the mean value of Y when both X_1 and X_2 are zero.

13.4 (a) $\hat{Y} = -2.72825 + 0.047114X_1 + 0.011947X_2$. **(b)** For a given number of orders, for each increase of $1,000 in sales, mean distribution cost is estimated to increase by $47.114. For a given amount of sales, for each increase of one order, mean distribution cost is estimated to increase by $11.95. **(c)** The interpretation of b_0 has no practical meaning here because it would represent the estimated distribution cost when there were no sales and no orders. **(d)** $\hat{Y} = -2.72825 + 0.047114(400) + 0.011947(4500) = 69.878$ or $69,878. **(e)** $66,419.93 \leq \mu_{Y|X} \leq 73,337.01$. **(f)** $59,380.61 \leq Y_X \leq 80,376.33$. **(g)** The interval in (e) is narrower because it is estimating the mean value, not an individual value.

13.6 (a) $\hat{Y} = 156.4 + 13.081X_1 + 16.795X_2$. **(b)** For a given amount of newspaper advertising, each increase by $1,000 in radio advertising is estimated to result in a mean increase in sales of $13,081. For a given amount of radio advertising, each increase by $1,000 in newspaper advertising is estimated to result in a mean increase in sales of $16,795. **(c)** When there is no money spent on radio advertising and newspaper advertising, the estimated mean sales is $156,430.44. **(d)** Holding the other independent variable constant, newspaper advertising seems to be more effective because its slope is greater.

13.8 (a) $\hat{Y} = 400.8057 + 456.4485X_1 - 2.4708X_2$, where $X_1 = $ land, $X_2 = $ age. **(b)** For a given age, each increase by one acre in land area is estimated to result in a mean increase in appraised value by $456.45 thousands. For a given acreage, each increase of one year in age is estimated to result in the mean decrease in appraised value by $2.47 thousands. **(c)** The interpretation of b_0 has no practical meaning here because it would represent the estimated appraised value of a new house that has no land area. **(d)** $\hat{Y} = 400.8057 + 456.4485(0.25) - 2.4708(45) = $403.73 thousands. **(e)** $372.7370 \leq \mu_{Y|X} \leq 434.7243$. **(f)** $235.1964 \leq Y_X \leq 572.2649$.

13.10 (a) $MSR = 15$, $MSE = 12$. **(b)** 1.25. **(c)** $F_{STAT} = 1.25 < 4.10$; do not reject H_0. **(d)** 0.20. **(e)** 0.04.

13.12 (a) $F_{STAT} = 97.69 > F_\alpha = 3.89$ with 2 and $15 - 2 - 1 = 12$ degrees of freedom. Reject H_0. There is evidence of a significant linear relationship with at least one of the independent variables. **(b)** The p-value is 0.0001. **(c)** $r^2 = 0.9421$. 94.21% of the variation in the long-term ability to absorb shock can be explained by variation in forefoot absorbing capability and variation in midsole impact. **(d)** $r^2_{adj} = 0.93245$.

13.14 (a) $F_{STAT} = 74.13 > 3.467$; reject H_0. **(b)** p-value $= 0$. **(c)** $r^2 = 0.8759$. 87.59% of the variation in distribution cost can be explained by variation in sales and variation in number of orders. **(d)** $r^2_{adj} = 0.8641$.

13.16 (a) $F_{STAT} = 40.16 > F_\alpha = 3.522$ with 2 and $22 - 2 - 1 = 19$ degrees of freedom. Reject H_0. There is evidence of a significant linear relationship. **(b)** The p-value is less than 0.001. **(c)** $r^2 = 0.8087$. 80.87% of the variation in sales can be explained by variation in radio advertising and variation in newspaper advertising. **(d)** $r^2_{adj} = 0.7886$.

13.18 (a)–(e) Based on a residual analysis, there is no evidence of a violation in the assumptions of regression.

13.20 (a) There appears to be a quadratic relationship in the plot of the residuals against both radio and newspaper advertising. **(b)** Curvilinear terms for both of these explanatory variables should be considered for inclusion in the model.

13.22 (a) The residual analysis reveals no patterns. **(b)** There are no apparent violations in the assumptions.

13.24 (a) Variable X_2 has a larger slope in terms of the t statistic of 3.75 than variable X_1, which has a smaller slope in terms of the t statistic of 3.33. **(b)** $1.46824 \leq \beta_1 \leq 6.53176$. **(c)** For X_1: $t_{STAT} = 4/1.2 = 3.33 > 2.1098$, with 17 degrees of freedom for $\alpha = 0.05$. Reject H_0. There is evidence that X_1 contributes to a model already containing X_2. For X_2: $t_{STAT} = 3/0.8 = 3.75 > 2.1098$, with 17 degrees of freedom for $\alpha = 0.05$. Reject H_0. There is evidence that X_2 contributes to a model already containing X_1. Both X_1 and X_2 should be included in the model.

13.26 (a) 95% confidence interval on β_1: $b_1 \pm S_{b_1}$, $0.0471 \pm 2.0796(0.0203)$, $0.00488 \leq \beta_1 \leq 0.08932$. **(b)** For X_1: $t_{STAT} = b_1/S_{b_1} = 0.0471/0.0203 = 2.32 > 2.0796$. Reject H_0. There is evidence that X_1 contributes to a model already containing X_2. For X_2: $t_{STAT} = b_1/S_{b_1} = 0.01195/0.00225 = 5.31 > 2.0796$. Reject H_0. There is evidence that X_2 contributes to a model already containing X_1. Both X_1 (sales) and X_2 (orders) should be included in the model.

13.28 (a) $9.398 \leq \beta_1 \leq 16.763$. **(b)** For X_1: $t_{STAT} = 7.43 > 2.093$. Reject H_0. There is evidence that X_1 contributes to a model already containing X_2. For X_2: $t_{STAT} = 5.67 > 2.093$. Reject H_0. There is evidence that X_2 contributes to a model already containing X_1. Both X_1 (radio advertising) and X_2 (newspaper advertising) should be included in the model.

13.30 (a) $227.5865 \leq \beta_1 \leq 685.3104$. **(b)** For X_1: $t_{STAT} = 4.0922$ and p-value $= 0.0003$. Because p-value < 0.05, reject H_0. There is evidence that X_1 contributes to a model already containing X_2. For X_2: $t_{STAT} = -3.6295$ and p-value $= 0.0012$. Because p-value < 0.05, reject H_0. There is evidence that X_2 contributes to a model already containing X_1. Both X_1 (land area) and X_2 (age) should be included in the model.

13.32 Because $t_{STAT} = 3.27 > 2.1098$, reject H_0. Variable X_2 makes a significant contribution to the model.

13.34 (a) $\hat{Y} = 243.7371 + 9.2189X_1 + 12.6967X_2$, where $X_1 =$ number of rooms and $X_2 =$ neighborhood (east $= 0$). **(b)** Holding constant the effect of neighborhood, for each additional room, the selling price is estimated to increase by a mean of 9.2189 thousands of dollars, or \$9218.9. For a given number of rooms, a west neighborhood is estimated to increase the mean selling price over an east neighborhood by 12.6967 thousands of dollars, or \$12,696.7. **(c)** $\hat{Y} = 243.7371 + 9.2189(9) + 12.6967(0) = 326.7076$, or \$326,707.6. $\$321,471.44 \leq \mu_{Y|X} \leq \$331,943.71$. $\$309,560.04 \leq Y_X \leq \$343,855.1$. **(d)** Based on a residual analysis, the model appears to be adequate. **(e)** $F_{STAT} = 55.39$, the p-value is virtually 0. Because p-value < 0.05, reject H_0. There is evidence of a significant relationship between selling price and the two independent variables (rooms and neighborhood). **(f)** For X_1: $t_{STAT} = 8.9537$, the p-value is virtually 0. Reject H_0. Number of rooms makes a significant contribution and should be included in the model. For X_2: $t_{STAT} = 3.5913$, p-value $= 0.0023 <$

0.05. Reject H_0. Neighborhood makes a significant contribution and should be included in the model. Based on these results, the regression model with the two independent variables should be used. **(g)** $7.0466 \leq \beta_1 \leq 11.3913$. **(h)** $5.2378 \leq \beta_2 \leq 20.1557$. **(i)** $r^2_{adj} = 0.851$ **(j)** The slope of selling price with number of rooms is the same, regardless of whether the house is located in an east or west neighborhood. **(k)** $\hat{Y} = 253.95 + 8.032X_1 - 5.90X_2 + 2.089X_1X_2$. For X_1X_2, p-value $= 0.330$. Do not reject H_0. There is no evidence that the interaction term makes a contribution to the model. **(l)** The model in (a) should be used.

13.36 (a) Predicted time $= 8.01 + 0.00523$ Depth -2.105 Dry. **(b)** Holding constant the effect of type of drilling, for each foot increase in depth of the hole, the mean drilling time is estimated to increase by 0.0052 minutes. For a given depth, a dry drilling hole is estimated to reduce the mean drilling time over wet drilling by 2.1052 minutes. **(c)** 6.428 minutes, $6.210 \leq \mu_{Y|X} \leq 6.646$, $4.923 \leq Y_X \leq 7.932$. **(d)** The model appears to be adequate. **(e)** $F_{STAT} = 111.11 > 3.09$; reject H_0. **(f)** $t_{STAT} = 5.03 > 1.9847$; reject H_0. $t_{STAT} = -14.03 < -1.9847$; reject H_0. Include both variables. **(g)** $0.0032 \leq \beta_1 \leq 0.0073$. **(h)** $-2.403 \leq \beta_2 \leq -1.808$ **(i)** 69.0%. **(j)** The slope of the additional drilling time with the depth of the hole is the same, regardless of the type of drilling method used. **(k)** The p-value of the interaction term $= 0.462 > 0.05$, so the term is not significant and should not be included in the model. **(l)** The model in part (a) should be used.

13.38 (a) $\hat{Y} = 31.5594 - 0.0296X_1 + 0.0041X_2 + 0.000017159X_1X_2$, where $X_1 =$ sales, $X_2 =$ orders, p-value $= 0.3249 > 0.05$. Do not reject H_0. There is not enough evidence that the interaction term makes a contribution to the model. **(b)** Because there is not enough evidence of any interaction effect between sales and orders, the model in Problem 13.4 should be used.

13.40 (a) The p-value of the interaction term $= 0.002 < 0.5$, so the term is significant and should be included in the model. **(b)** Use the model developed in this problem.

13.42 (a) For X_1X_2, p-value $= 0.2353 > 0.05$. Do not reject H_0. There is not enough evidence that the interaction term makes a contribution to the model. **(b)** Because there is not enough evidence of an interaction effect between total staff present and remote hours, the model in Problem 13.7 should be used.

13.50 (a) $\hat{Y} = -3.9152 + 0.0319X_1 + 4.2228X_2$, where $X_1 =$ number of cubic feet moved and $X_2 =$ number of pieces of large furniture. **(b)** Holding constant the number of pieces of large furniture, for each additional cubic foot moved, the mean labor hours are estimated to increase by 0.0319. Holding constant the amount of cubic feet moved, for each additional piece of large furniture, the mean labor hours are estimated to increase by 4.2228. **(c)** $\hat{Y} = -3.9152 + 0.0319(500) + 4.2228(2) = 20.4926$. **(d)** Based on a residual analysis, the errors appear to be normally distributed. The equal-variance assumption might be violated because the variances appear to be larger around the center region of both independent variables. There might also be violation of the linearity assumption. A model with quadratic terms for both independent variables might be fitted. **(e)** $F_{STAT} = 228.80$, p-value is virtually 0. Because p-value < 0.05, reject H_0. There is evidence of a significant relationship between labor hours and the two independent variables (the amount of cubic feet moved and the number of pieces of large furniture). **(f)** The p-value is virtually 0. The probability of obtaining a test statistic of 228.80 or greater is virtually 0 if there is no significant relationship between labor hours and the two independent variables (the amount of cubic feet moved and the number of pieces of large furniture). **(g)** $r^2 = 0.9327$. 93.27% of the variation in labor hours can be explained by variation in the amount of cubic feet moved and the number of pieces of large furniture. **(h)** $r^2_{adj} = 0.9287$.

(i) For X_1: $t_{STAT} = 6.9339$, the p-value is virtually 0. Reject H_0. The amount of cubic feet moved makes a significant contribution and should be included in the model. For X_2: $t_{STAT} = 4.6192$, the p-value is virtually 0. Reject H_0. The number of pieces of large furniture makes a significant contribution and should be included in the model. Based on these results, the regression model with the two independent variables should be used. **(j)** For X_1: $t_{STAT} = 6.9339$, the p-value is virtually 0. The probability of obtaining a sample that will yield a test statistic farther away than 6.9339 is virtually 0 if the number of cubic feet moved does not make a significant contribution holding the effect of the number of pieces of large furniture constant. For X_2: $t_{STAT} = 4.6192$, the p-value is virtually 0. The probability of obtaining a sample that will yield a test statistic farther away than 4.6192 is virtually 0 if the number of pieces of large furniture does not make a significant contribution holding the effect of the amount of cubic feet moved constant. **(k)** $0.0226 \le \beta_1 \le 0.0413$. You are 95% confident that the mean labor hours will increase by somewhere between 0.0226 and 0.0413 for each additional cubic foot moved, holding constant the number of pieces of large furniture. In Problem 12.36, you are 95% confident that the mean labor hours will increase by somewhere between 0.0439 and 0.0562 for each additional cubic foot moved regardless of the number of pieces of large furniture.

13.52 (a) $\hat{Y} = -120.0483 + 1.7506X_1 + 0.3680X_2$, where X_1 = assessed value and X_2 = time period. **(b)** Holding constant the time period, for each additional thousand dollars of assessed value, the mean selling price is estimated to increase by 1.7507 thousand dollars. Holding constant the assessed value, for each additional month since assessment, the mean selling price is estimated to increase by 0.3680 thousand dollars. **(c)** $\hat{Y} = -120.0483 + 1.7506(170) + 0.3680(12) = 181.9692$ thousand dollars. **(d)** Based on a residual analysis, the model appears to be adequate. **(e)** $F_{STAT} = 223.46$, the p-value is virtually 0. Because p-value < 0.05, reject H_0. There is evidence of a significant relationship between selling price and the two independent variables (assessed value and time period). **(f)** The p-value is virtually 0. The probability of obtaining a test statistic of 223.46 or greater is virtually 0 if there is no significant relationship between selling price and the two independent variables (assessed value and time period). **(g)** $r^2 = 0.9430$. 94.30% of the variation in selling price can be explained by variation in assessed value and time period. **(h)** $r^2_{adj} = 0.9388$. **(i)** For X_1: $t_{STAT} = 20.4137$, the p-value is virtually 0. Reject H_0. The assessed value makes a significant contribution and should be included in the model. For X_2: $t_{STAT} = 2.8734$, p-value $= 0.0078 < 0.05$. Reject H_0. The time period makes a significant contribution and should be included in the model. Based on these results, the regression model with the two independent variables should be used. **(j)** For X_1: $t_{STAT} = 20.4137$, the p-value is virtually 0. The probability of obtaining a sample that will yield a test statistic farther away than 20.4137 is virtually 0 if the assessed value does not make a significant contribution holding time period constant. For X_2: $t_{STAT} = 2.8734$, the p-value is virtually 0. The probability of obtaining a sample that will yield a test statistic farther away than 2.8734 is virtually 0 if the time period does not make a significant contribution holding the effect of the assessed value constant. **(k)** $1.5746 \le \beta_1 \le 1.9266$. You are 95% confident that the mean selling price will increase by an amount somewhere between $1.5746 thousand and $1.9266 thousand for each additional thousand-dollar increase in assessed value, holding constant the time period. In Problem 12.66, you are 95% confident that the mean selling price will increase by an amount somewhere between $1.5862 thousand and $1.9773 thousand for each additional thousand-dollar increase in assessed value regardless of the time period.

13.54 (a) $\hat{Y} = 163.7751 + 10.7252X_1 - 0.2843X_2$, where X_1 = size and X_2 = age. **(b)** Holding age constant, for each additional thousand square feet, the mean assessed value is estimated to increase by $10.7252 thousand. Holding size constant, for each additional year, the mean assessed value is estimated to decrease by $0.2843 thousand.

(c) $\hat{Y} = 163.7751 + 10.7252(1.75) - 0.2843(10) = 179.7017$ thousand dollars. **(d)** Based on a residual analysis, the errors appear to be normally distributed. The equal-variance assumption appears to be valid. There might also be violation of the linearity assumption for age. You may want to include a quadratic term for age in the model. **(e)** $F_{STAT} = 28.58$, p-value $= 0.0000272776$. Because p-value $= 0.0000 < 0.05$, reject H_0. There is evidence of a significant relationship between assessed value and the two independent variables (size and age). **(f)** p-value $= 0.0000272776$. The probability of obtaining an F_{STAT} test statistic of 28.58 or greater is virtually 0 if there is no significant relationship between assessed value and the two independent variables (size and age). **(g)** $r^2 = 0.8265$. 82.65% of the variation in assessed value can be explained by variation in size and age. **(h)** $r^2_{adj} = 0.7976$. **(i)** For X_1: $t_{STAT} = 3.5581$, p-value $= 0.0039 < 0.05$. Reject H_0. The size of a house makes a significant contribution and should be included in the model. For X_2: $t_{STAT} = -3.4002$, p-value $= 0.0053 < 0.05$. Reject H_0. The age of a house makes a significant contribution and should be included in the model. Based on these results, the regression model with the two independent variables should be used. **(j)** For X_1: p-value $= 0.0039$. The probability of obtaining a sample that will yield a test statistic farther away than 3.5581 is 0.0039 if the size of a house does not make a significant contribution holding age constant. For X_2: p-value $= 0.0053$. The probability of obtaining a sample that will yield a test statistic farther away than -3.4002 is 0.0053 if the age of a house does not make a significant contribution, holding the effect of the size constant. **(k)** $4.1572 \le \beta_1 \le 17.2928$. You are 95% confident that the mean assessed value will increase by an amount somewhere between $4.1575 thousand and $17.2928 thousand for each additional thousand-square-foot increase in the size of a house, holding constant the age. In Problem 12.67, you are 95% confident that the mean assessed value will increase by an amount somewhere between $9.4695 thousand and $23.7972 thousand for each additional thousand-square-foot increase in heating area regardless of the age. **(l)** Based on your answers to (a) through (k), the age of a house does have an effect on its assessed value.

13.56 (a) $\hat{Y} = 149.71 - 15.077X_1 - 2.698X_2$, where X_1 = ERA and X_2 = League (American = 0). **(b)** Holding constant the effect of the league, for each additional ERA, the number of wins is estimated to decrease by a mean of 15.077. For a given ERA, a team in the National League is estimated to have a mean of 2.698 fewer wins than a team in the American League. **(c)** 81.86 wins Confidence interval: 77.96 to 85.77 wins Prediction interval: 66.74 to 96.98 wins. **(d)** Based on a residual analysis, there appears to be a no relationship between the residuals and ERA or league. The equal-variance and linearity assumptions appear to be valid. **(e)** $F_{STAT} = 11.03 > 3.35$, p-value is virtually 0. Since p-value < 0.05, reject H_0. There is evidence of a significant relationship between wins and the two independent variables (ERA and league). **(f)** For X_1: $t_{STAT} = -4.66 > 2.0518$, p-value is virtually 0. Reject H_0. ERA makes a significant contribution and should be included in the model. For X_2: $t_{STAT} = -1.03 < 2.0518$, p-value $= 0.312 > 0.05$. Do not reject H_0. The league does not make a significant contribution and should not be included in the model. Based on these results, the regression model with only ERA should be used. **(g)** $r^2_{adj} = 0.6058$ **(h)** The slope of the number of wins with ERA is the same regardless of whether the team belongs to the American or the National League. **(i)** For X_1X_2: the p-value is 0.801. Do not reject H_0. There is no evidence that the interaction term makes a contribution to the model. **(j)** The regression model with only ERA should be used.

13.58 (a) Attendance $= -3,667 + 170.89$ Temperature $- 11.25$ team's winning percentage $+ 22.75$ opponent's winning percentage $+ 1,824$ if the game is a weekend game $+ 9,074$ if the game has a promotion being held. **(b)** $r^2 = 0.386$ 38.6% of the variation in attendance can be explained by variation in temperature, the Phillies winning percentage, the opponent's winning percentage, whether it was a weekend game, and whether a promotion was held. **(c)** Temperature $t_{STAT} = 2.52 >$ 1.993 p-value $= 0.014 < 0.05$, reject H_0. Winning percentage: $-1.993 < t_{STAT} = -0.59 < 1.993$ p-value $= 0.559 > 0.05$, do not reject H_0. Opponent's winning percentage: $-1.993 < t_{STAT} = 1.84 < 1.993$ p-value $= 0.071 > 0.05$, do not reject H_0. Weekend $-1.993 < t_{STAT} = 1.04 < 1.993$, p-value $= 0.30 > 0.05$, do not reject H_0. Promotion: $t_{STAT} = 4.85 > 1.993$ p-value $= 0.000 < 0.05$, reject H_0. Temperature and whether a promotion was held have increased attendance. **(d)** Holding constant the temperature, the Phillies winning percentage, the opponent's winning percentage, and whether the game was played on a weekend, the mean predicted attendance was 9,074 higher when a promotion was held than when a promotion was not held.

CHAPTER 14

14.2 (a) Day 4, Day 3. **(b)** LCL $= 0.0397$, UCL $= 0.2460$. **(c)** No, proportions are within control limits.

14.4 (a) $n = 500, \bar{p} = 761/16{,}000 = 0.0476$

$$\text{UCL} = \bar{p} + 3\sqrt{\frac{\bar{p}(1 - \bar{p})}{n}}$$

$$= 0.0476 + 3\sqrt{\frac{0.0476(1 - 0.0476)}{500}} = 0.0761$$

$$\text{LCL} = \bar{p} - 3\sqrt{\frac{\bar{p}(1 - \bar{p})}{n}}$$

$$= 0.0476 - 3\sqrt{\frac{0.0476(1 - 0.0476)}{500}} = 0.0190$$

(b) Because the individual points are distributed around $\bar{p}$ without any pattern and all the points are within the control limits, the process is in a state of statistical control.

14.6 (a) UCL $= 0.0176$, LCL $= 0.0082$. The proportion of unacceptable cans is below the LCL on Day 4. There is evidence of a pattern over time because the last eight points are all above the mean and most of the earlier points are below the mean. Therefore, this process is out of control.

14.8 (a) UCL $= 0.1431$, LCL $= 0.0752$. Days 9, 26, and 30 are above the UCL. Therefore, this process is out of control; using Minitab with the exact n_i, day 9 is not out-of-control.

14.12 (a) $d_2 = 2.059$. **(b)** $d_3 = 0.880$. **(c)** $D_3 = 0$. **(d)** $D_4 = 2.282$. **(e)** $A_2 = 0.729$.

14.14 (a) $\bar{R} = \dfrac{\sum\limits_{i=1}^{k} R_i}{k} = 3.275, \bar{\bar{X}} = \dfrac{\sum\limits_{i=1}^{k} \bar{X}_i}{k} = 5.9413.$

R chart: UCL $= D_4\bar{R} = 2.282(3.275) = 7.4736$. LCL does not exist. $\bar{X}$ chart: UCL $= \bar{\bar{X}} + A_2\bar{R} = 5.9413 + 0.729(3.275) = 8.3287$. LCL $= \bar{\bar{X}} - A_2\bar{R} = 5.9413 - 0.729(3.275) = 3.5538$. **(b)** The process appears to be in control because there are no points outside the control limits and there is no evidence of a pattern in the range chart, and there are no points outside the control limits and there is no evidence of a pattern in the $\bar{X}$ chart.

14.16 (a) $\bar{R} = 0.8794$, LCL does not exist, UCL $= 2.0068$. **(b)** $\bar{\bar{X}} = 20.1065$, LCL $= 19.4654$, UCL $= 20.7475$. **(c)** The process is in control.

14.18 (a) $\bar{R} = 8.145$, LCL does not exist, UCL $= 18.5869$; $\bar{\bar{X}} = 18.12$, UCL $= 24.0577$, LCL $= 12.1823$. **(b)** There are no sample ranges outside the control limits and there does not appear to be a pattern in the range chart. The mean is above the UCL on Day 15 and below the LCL on Day 16. Therefore, the process is not in control.

14.20 (a) $\bar{R} = 0.3022$, LCL does not exist, UCL $= 0.6389$; $\bar{\bar{X}} = 90.1312$, UCL $= 90.3060$, LCL $= 89.9573$. **(b)** On Days 5 and 6, the sample ranges were above the UCL. The mean chart may be erroneous because the range is out of control. The process is out of control.

14.28 (a) The main reason that service quality is lower than product quality is because the former involves human interaction, which is prone to variation. Also, the most critical aspects of a service are often timeliness and professionalism, and customers can always perceive that the service could be done quicker and with greater professionalism. For products, customers often cannot perceive a better or more ideal product than the one they are getting. For example, a new laptop is better and contains more interesting features than any laptop the owner has ever imagined. **(b)** Both services and products are the results of processes. However, measuring services is often harder because of the dynamic variation due to the human interaction between the service provider and the customer. Product quality is often a straightforward measurement of a static physical characteristic like the amount of sugar in a can of soda. Categorical data are also more common in service quality. **(c)** Yes. **(d)** Yes.

14.30 (a) $\bar{p} = 0.2702$, LCL $= 0.1700$, UCL $= 0.3703$. **(b)** Yes, RudyBird's market share is in control before the in-store promotion. **(c)** All seven days of the in-store promotion are above the UCL. The promotion increased market share.

14.32 (a) $\bar{p} = 0.75175$, LCL $= 0.62215$, UCL $= 0.88135$. Although none of the points are outside the control limits, there is a clear pattern over time, with the last 13 points above the center line. Therefore, this process is not in control. **(b)** Because the increasing trend begins around Day 20, this change in method would be the assignable cause. **(c)** The control chart would have been developed using the first 20 days, and then a different control chart would be used for the final twenty points because they represent a different process.

14.34 (a) $\bar{p} = 0.1198$, LCL $= 0.0205$, UCL $= 0.2191$. **(b)** Day 24 is below the LCL; therefore, the process is out of control; using Minitab with the exact n_i, day 24 is not out-of-control. **(c)** Special causes of variation should be investigated to improve the process. Next, the process should be improved to decrease the proportion of undesirable trades.

Index